Combat Aircraft of the World

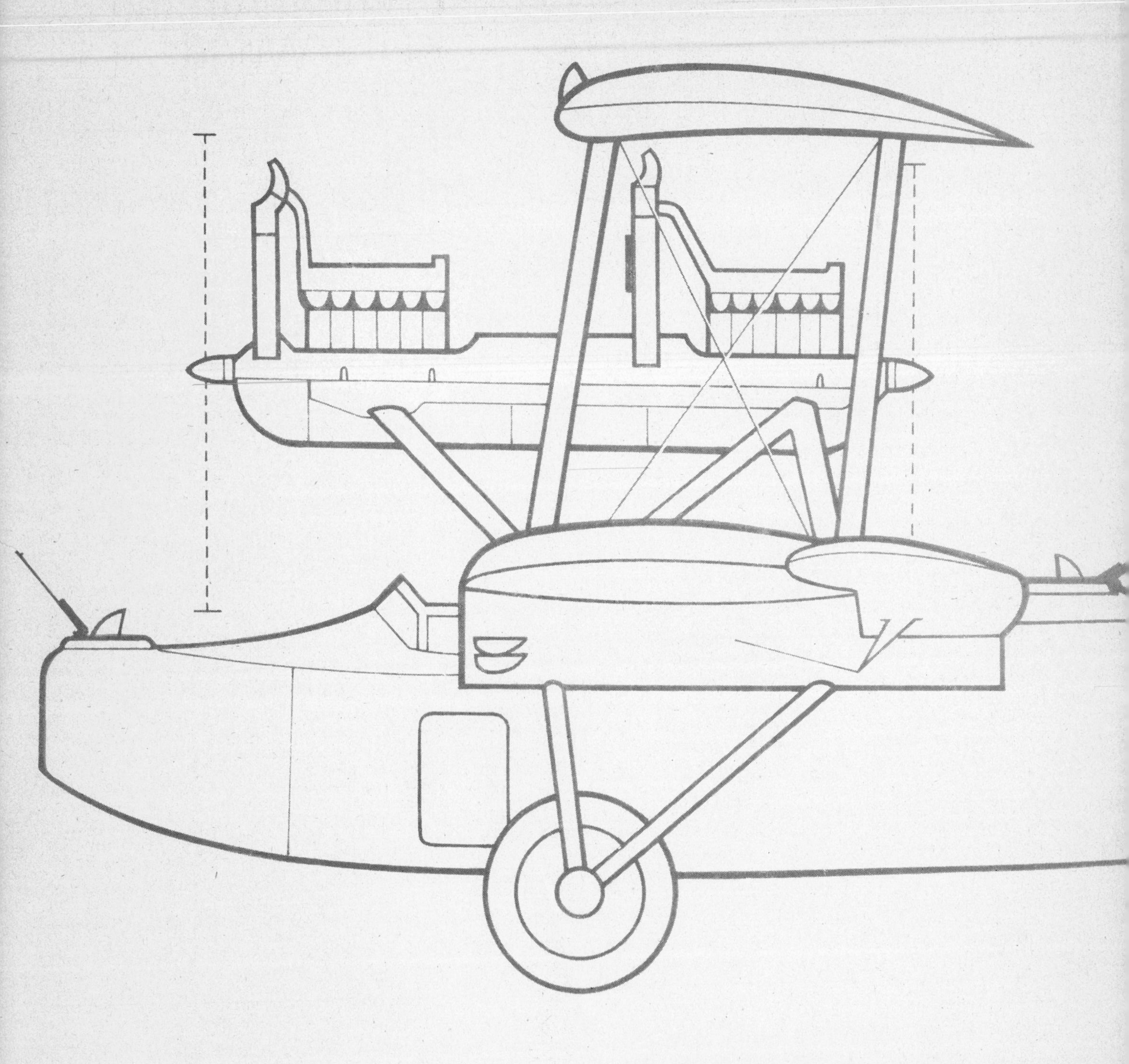

Combat Aircraft of the World

from 1909 to the present

Edited and Compiled
by John W. R. Taylor

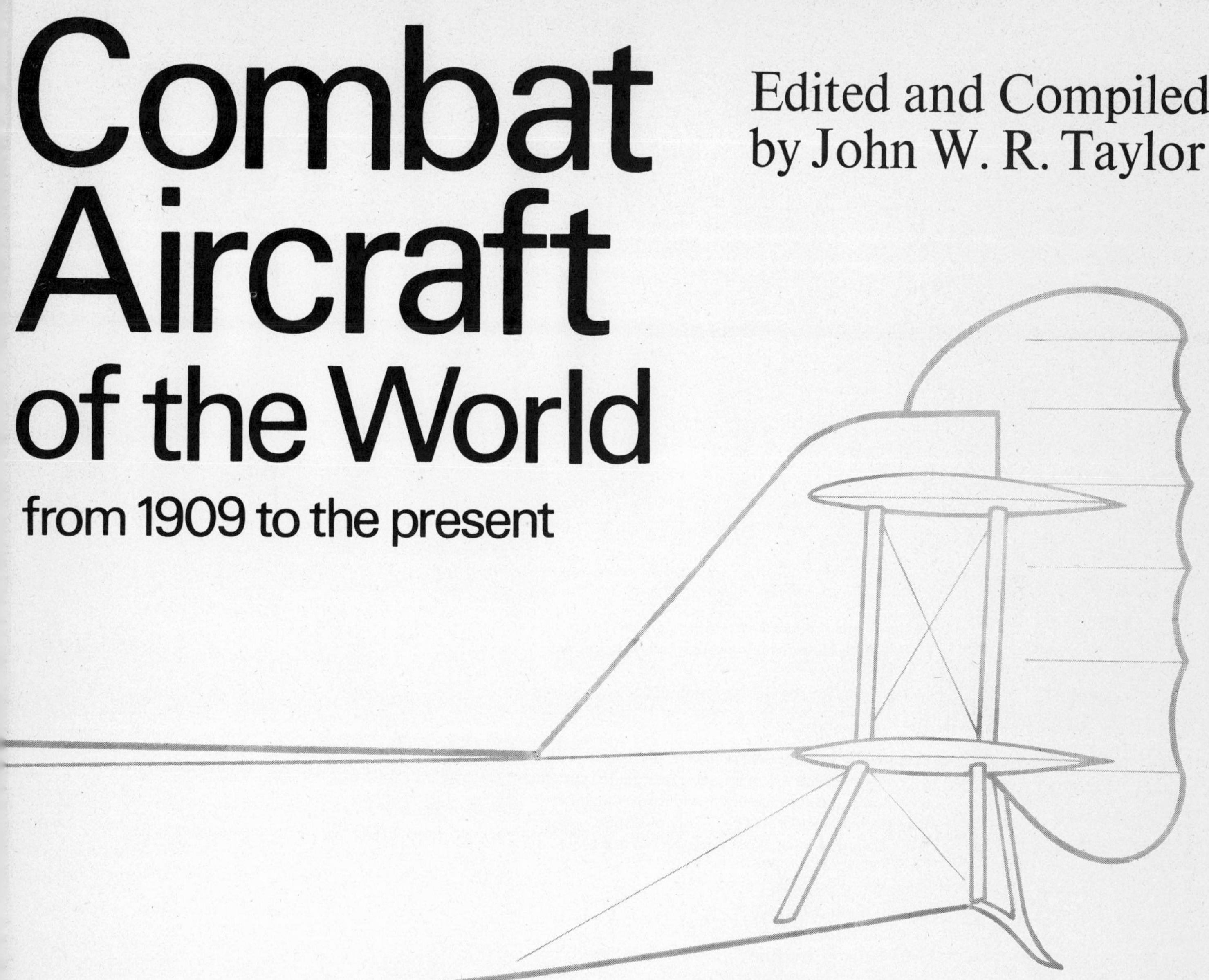

With contributions by:

Jean Alexander
Maurice Allward
J. B. Cynk
W. B. Klepacki
Jean Liron
Kenneth Munson
Václav Němeček
M. B. Passingham
R. J. Ruffle
Gordon Swanborough

A PARAGON BOOK

Designed and produced by George Rainbird Ltd,
Marble Arch House, 44 Edgware Road, London W2

Published by arrangement with G. P. Putnam's Sons

For information address G. P. Putnam's Sons,
200 Madison Avenue, New York, New York 10016

PARAGON BOOKS
are published by
G.P. Putnam's Sons
200 Madison Avenue
New York, New York 10016

First Paragon Books Printing, 1979

ISBN: 0-399-50471-0

Contents

The Arrangement of this Book

The basic division of the contents of COMBAT AIRCRAFT is by country of manufacture, the countries being listed in alphabetical order. Within each country the basic division is by name of manufacturer, again in alphabetical order. The only apparent exceptions are the United Kingdom's Royal Aircraft Factory/Royal Aircraft Establishment, the name of which has never been used as a prefix to the individual designations of its products, so "Factory"-built types such as the B.E.2. and S.E.5 appear in alphabetical order between Pemberton-Billing and Saro with an implied Royal Aircraft Factory prefix; and the Italian manufacturer CRDA Cant, treated alphabetically under the more familiar form "Cant". The products of each manufacturer, finally, are listed in chronological order, the sequence being based normally on the date of the first flight of the prototype, except where arrangement according to makers' designations seemed more practical: e.g. Fiat B.R. types precede Fiat C.R.

In the Addenda on page 635 are details of types that went into production too late to be included in the main text.

Historical Introduction

What is a combat aircraft?

In the widest sense, it could be said that an unarmed assault transport aircraft used to ferry troops to a front-line battle area is a combat vehicle. Troop-carrying helicopters of the kind used so effectively in Vietnam have an even stronger claim to such a classification. Not only do the soldiers they carry often go straight into action; the crews of the helicopters themselves play an active offensive rôle, by firing machine-guns and rockets to keep down the heads of the enemy during disembarkation and deployment of their passengers.

Reconnaissance aircraft, also, might qualify as combat types. The information they provide is used tactically to guide ground forces, air forces and navies in action, so exerting a major and immediate influence on the tide of battle. Many also carry guns, light bombs or other weapons with which to harass "targets of opportunity" and, if necessary, to enable them to fight their way to a target and home again.

However, the primary task of fixed-wing transport aircraft and helicopters is to carry troops, equipment and supplies, just as the primary rôle of the reconnaissance aircraft is to obtain information. This book is concerned with aircraft whose primary duty is to fight, either offensively as bombing, strike or anti-submarine aircraft or defensively as interceptor fighters. The border-line is sometimes poorly-defined. For example, reconnaissance aircraft like the Westland Lysander and training machines like the de Havilland Tiger Moth biplane were pressed hurriedly into service as make-shift ground-attack types in the grim days of mid-1940, when there were all too few real front-line combat aircraft available.

Any choice of types for a book such as this must, therefore, be arbitrary. Even limitations as generous as 375,000 words and 2,000 illustrations demand a well-defined policy of selection, and the basic qualifications laid down for *Combat Aircraft* were that the types to be covered must have been operated primarily as fighter, bomber, strike or anti-submarine aircraft and must have equipped an operational air force unit. This eliminated a vast number of aircraft that were designed for combat use but never progressed beyond the prototype or evaluation stage. However, where these types were of particular significance, they will find a rightful place in this introductory section, which traces the development of the combat aircraft from its earliest beginnings.

It is, perhaps, a regrettable comment on human nature that inventors began considering the warlike potential of aircraft from the first moment that conquest of the air seemed within reach.

By the mid-17th century, the idealists who simply wanted to fly for fun – or for the freedom and sense of achievement that flying would bring – had had their chance and failed. All they had to show for more than 2,000 years of jumping off towers and cliffs, wearing home-made wings, were broken necks, broken limbs and broken hearts. Clearly, man would never leave the ground and fly with the birds until some entirely new "lifting force" was discovered.

As monasteries and the church had been the centres of learning and scientific thought for hundreds of years, it is hardly surprising that monks and priests outnumber the laity in most histories of flying, until well into the second half of the 18th century.

One of the best known of them was a Jesuit priest named Francesco de

Lana-Terzi, who produced the first known design for a lighter-than-air craft in A.D. 1670. It had been realized for some time that if a craft could be made lighter than the weight of air it displaced, it would "float" in the air as a ship floats on water. De Lana believed that he had, therefore, discovered the key to human flight by devising a practical use for the air-pump invented by Otto von Guericke twenty years earlier.

He thought that by using the pump to remove all the air from inside a thin-walled copper sphere, it would be possible to make the sphere lighter than air. After that, it would be necessary only to attach four such spheres to a boat-shaped hull before taking off on the first aerial voyage in history.

Alas it was not as easy as it seemed! If the spheres were made from thin metal, they collapsed when a vacuum was created inside them. If thicker metal was used, the spheres became so heavy that there was no possibility of their being able to lift anything. Far from being abashed by the proven impracticability of his flying boat, de Lana pronounced solemnly that God clearly would not permit such an invention to work, because of the disturbance it would cause to the civil government of men.

In the sixth chapter of his scientific treatise, called the *Prodromo* (as translated by his contemporary, Robert Hooke), he wrote:

> For who sees not that no City can be secure against attack, since our (flying) Ship may at any time be placed directly over it, and descending down may discharge Soldiers; the same would happen to private Houses, and Ships on the Sea: for our Ship descending out of the Air to the Sails of Sea-Ships . . . it may over-set them, kill their men, burn their Ships by artificial Fire-works and Fire-balls. And this they may do not only to Ships but to great Buildings, Castles, Cities, with such security that they which cast these things down from a height out of Gun-shot, cannot on the other side be offended by those from below.

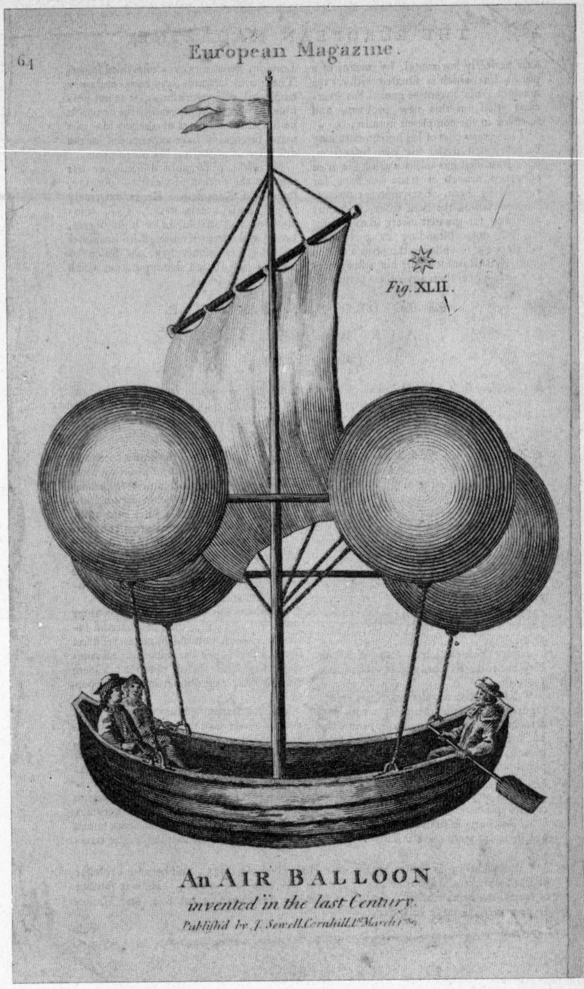

De Lana's "flying boat", 1670.

It would be difficult to imagine a better prophecy of the tactics of airborne assault and bombing that have become familiar in our century. One hundred and thirteen years after it was written, lighter-than-air flying was made entirely practicable by the invention of the balloon, in France.

By the time the French Revolutionary Wars began to gain impetus, there was already a military Company of "Aérostiers" operational and ready to play its part in war. Their first success came at the Battle of Fleurus, in Belgium, on 26 June 1794, when Captain J. M. J. Coutelle remained in the air for several hours. The information he signalled down to General Jourdan's Moselle army contributed greatly to the resounding victory gained by the French, and he repeated his exploits during the subsequent battle on the Ourthe, near Liège.

Despite this, the Aérostiers lasted only five years. The necessity for carting around heavy equipment to produce the hydrogen gas with which the balloons were inflated created problems, especially when armies wanted to move quickly over rough country. And it was not practicable to send up a balloon, tethered to the end of a cable, on any but a relatively calm day.

Sole duty of the Aérostiers had been reconnaissance, their elevated observation platform enabling them to report every movement of the enemy. Later, Napoleon Bonaparte was attracted by the military possibilities of floating whole armies across the English Channel by balloon, so being able to launch a sudden surprise invasion of Southern England. But the wind tended to blow in the wrong direction most of the time, and this emphasized the main drawback of the balloon as a military aircraft.

Once launched in free flight, without any means of propulsion or steering, it was as much a plaything of the wind as is a soap bubble. The idea of flying from A to B and dropping some of de Lana's "artificial Fire-works and Fire-balls" on the enemy *en route* must have occurred to many of the Aérostiers. Unfortunately, a balloon offers only a one-way journey–down-wind–with the result that point B would almost certainly be behind the lines of the enemy on whom one had poured the unpleasant devices. As a balloon would

Observation balloon at the Battle of Fleurus, 1794.

seldom outpace determined cavalry trailing it on the ground, this promised a rather hot reception for the balloonist after landing and probably explains a general lack of enthusiasm for using the balloon as a bomber.

In 1849, the Austrians tried to remedy this shortcoming by launching the first "flying bombs" against Venice. Each consisted of a small hot-air balloon, made of paper and carrying as payload a 30-lb bomb with a time-fuse. Few of these pioneer aerial missiles fell on the city, and those that did caused more panic than actual casualties. Nor were they entirely lacking in hazard to their launch-crews, for on one occasion the wind changed suddenly and the Austrians found that they were being chased by their own bombing aircraft. This may explain why the balloon was restricted to reconnaissance work during the remainder of the 19th century, serving in many major campaigns, including the American Civil War and the Boer War.

Not until the navigable balloon, or airship, was perfected did de Lana's prophecy become fact. The man responsible was a German, Graf Ferdinand von Zeppelin. Because of what his airships achieved in 1914–18, he is remembered mainly as one of the originators of aerial warfare in its least attractive forms; but this is somewhat unfair to one of flying's great pioneers.

When he completed the first of his giant cloth-covered metal-framed Zeppelin airships in 1900, he was already 62 years of age and was every bit as interested in its potential for air travel as in its military capabilities. Indeed, its successors operated the world's first airline services in 1910–14, carrying more than 35,000 passengers in complete safety at a time when aeroplanes were still unreliable contraptions of "stick and string".

However, Germany was ruled by men who were more attracted by the Zeppelin's obvious military applications, and it is interesting to study

Zeppelin LZ-13 *Hansa*, *c.* 1912. This was a passenger-carrying airship, but the military potential of Graf von Zeppelin's designs had already been noticed.

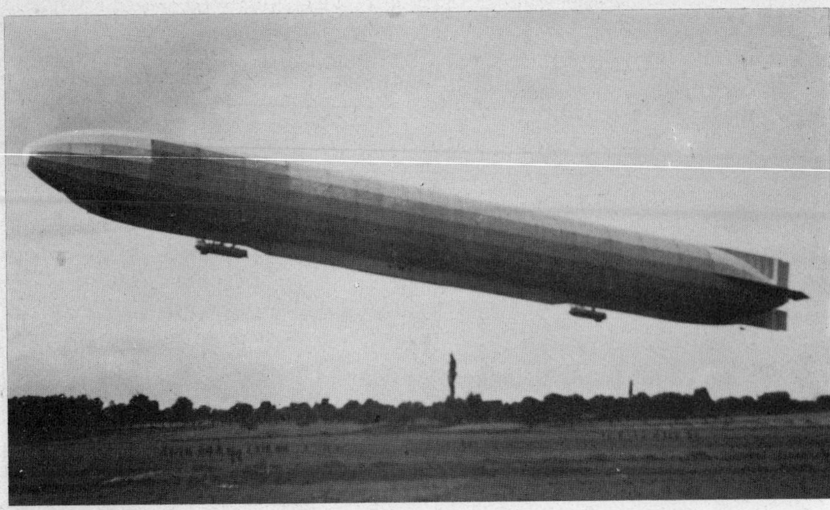

Zeppelin LZ-25 of the 1914–18 War.

briefly how this fact precipitated the evolution of the first real combat aircraft, both lighter-than-air and heavier-than-air.

In 1899, one year before the first Zeppelin was completed and four years before the Wright brothers' first flights in a powered aeroplane, an internationally-agreed Hague Declaration had banned the launching of all forms of projectiles or explosives from balloons or other forms of aerial vessels. This was little more than a formality at the time, and we note a significant change a few years later, when Zeppelins and aeroplanes were flying successfully.

Only 27 of the 44 Powers represented at the 1907 Hague Convention renewed the earlier Declaration, including just four of the nations that were to become involved in the 1914–18 War – Britain, Belgium, Portugal and the United States. A provision in the Declaration absolved even these nations from being bound by the ban if they became involved in war with a non-signatory. So the agreement that attempted to prevent the newly-perfected aircraft from being used to kill was worth little more than the paper on which it was written.

By the outbreak of war, the German army had a comparatively large fleet of six Zeppelins and three smaller airships, to which were added the three airships that had operated the commercial airline service, after they had been fitted with bomb-racks and improved radio. It was believed that these formidable aircraft would be able to play an important rôle in land warfare, but disillusionment came quite early.

Three of the army Zeppelins were lost during their first operational sorties. On 6 August 1914, a mere two days after the war began, Zeppelin Z.6 was holed by shrapnel while attacking Liège and was wrecked when it force-landed in a forest near Cologne. On 23 August, Z.7 was brought down by gunfire during a reconnaissance flight over Alsace. On the same day, Z.8 was shot down and captured by the French.

After this disastrous start, the German High Command never regained its enthusiasm for the airship as an army weapon. A number of bombing raids over England were made subsequently by army airships, but it was the German navy which exploited the potential of the Zeppelin to its fullest extent.

The basic mistake made by the army was in sending airships over heavily-defended battle areas in daylight. No such error was committed by the navy. It had only one Zeppelin on the outbreak of war, following disasters to the L.1 and L.2 in September-October 1913 which had cost the lives of most of the experienced personnel of the naval airship service. Rebirth of the service was entrusted to Kapitän-leutnant Peter Strasser, whose inspired leadership was responsible for much of the Zeppelins' wartime achievement.

What should never be forgotten is that the primary task of the naval Zeppelins was reconnaissance over the North Sea and they performed

Other belligerents also used airships. This close-up of the nacelle of the Italian M.3 shows bombs and gun positions.

it superbly. Whatever successes the German navy had were due in large measure to the constant watch that the airships kept on Allied shipping movements, and each Zeppelin was reckoned to be worth five or six cruisers for this reason alone.

Raids on Britain absorbed only a minor part of the German airships' time and energies, but their effect was by no means negligible. Initially, the Kaiser had sanctioned such raids on the strict understanding that they would be made only against shipyards, arsenals, docks and military establishments generally, and that London would not be attacked. In practice, it was soon found that airship commanders, operating by night, often drifted far off course and had little idea of where their bombs had fallen. This was even more true when the blacking-out of lights on the ground became more general, and there was little point in pretending to spare the capital when the quietest and least warlike East Anglian villages were liable to receive a deluge of bombs in mistake for military targets.

By comparison with aeroplanes of the period, the Zeppelin of 1914–15 was a formidable aircraft. The naval L.3 was basically similar to the pre-war passenger airships, with a length of 490 ft, gas capacity of 795,000 cu ft and three 210-hp engines which gave it a speed of 47 mph and ceiling of 6,000 ft. A typical weapon load comprised five 110-lb high-explosive bombs and twenty 6½-lb incendiary bombs. This may not seem a very devastating destructive capability, but it must be remembered that bombing was a new and unknown terror for the civilian population and the overall effect achieved was out of all proportion to the weight of bombs dropped.

The first airship raid was made by the Zeppelins L.3 and L.4 on the evening of 19 January 1915. The nine bombs dropped by L.3 on Yarmouth killed two people, wounded three others and damaged houses. L.4 first attacked a variety of villages, dropped one bomb near the wireless station at Hunstanton and then delivered its main attack on Kings Lynn, killing two persons, injuring thirteen and damaging a power station and houses. The official German historian recorded that the town "had itself to thank that the airship defended herself by dropping the bombs", as its anti-aircraft guns had been first to open hostilities. In fact, Kings Lynn was undefended and well lighted, as the blackout had not been introduced by then.

L.3 and L.4 did not survive long to enjoy their success. On 16 February they were forced down in Denmark by a gale and, after all but four of the crew had jumped clear, were carried away by the wind and never seen again.

Altogether, 88 Zeppelins were built during the 1914–18 War. They made 51 raids on Britain, during which they dropped 5,806 bombs (totalling 196½ tons), killing 557 people, injuring a further 1,358 and doing an estimated £1,527,585 worth of damage. Quite apart from the effects on the civilian population and hampering of war production, the raids had a very definite military value, by diverting men and equipment from more vital theatres of war. For example, at the end of 1916, Britain's home-based anti-aircraft defences included twelve RFC squadrons, with 2,200 officers and men and 110 aeroplanes, and a large force of anti-aircraft guns and searchlights manned by 12,000 officers and men who would have been very welcome in France.

On the other hand, it was the effectiveness of the home defences that ended the Zeppelins' brief period of success as a bomber. The first victory by a defending fighter at night was achieved on 2 September 1916, when no fewer than twelve naval and four military airships set out to bomb London. One of them was the Schütte-Lanz airship S.L.11, which was shot down in flames by Lieutenant William Leefe Robinson, who was awarded the Victoria Cross for his success.

To reduce the hazard of being caught in searchlight beams and so being illuminated as a target for guns and aircraft, the Germans invented a novel observation device. This consisted of a streamlined car attached to the end of a 2,700-ft steel cable. While the Zeppelin cruised safely above the clouds, an officer could be lowered in the car to a level beneath the clouds, to guide the Zeppelin to its target and direct its bombing by telephone. But even such ideas could not save the airships, which were lost in ever increasing numbers.

The Zeppelins of 1916 were 590 ft long and were powered by four 240-hp engines, which gave them a top speed of 59 mph and ceiling of 10,000 ft. This was not good enough to elude the defences and by November of that year a new series of giant Zeppelins – 640 ft long, with a capacity of nearly two million cu ft and powered by six 240-hp engines – began entering service. They had a top speed of 64 mph and could carry 28 tons of bombs for 4,600 miles (a payload/range never approached by a fixed-wing bomber); but at their ceiling of 12,300 ft these hydrogen-filled giants remained terribly vulnerable to fighter aircraft firing incendiary ammunition and to phosphor shells from anti-aircraft guns.

In addition, the raids on Britain imposed great strain on the airship crews. They were often airborne for anything from 24 to 36 hours in air temperatures that fell as low as 36° below zero in winter. Even if they escaped damage over England, they faced the hazards of storms and gales which caused many losses through forced landings.

In the face of such mounting odds, simultaneously with the growing effectiveness of the bomber aeroplane, the Zeppelin attacks slowly lost their impetus. Eleven airships set out to bomb London on 1 October 1916 but became so scattered that only one person was killed in the capital. The night's work cost Germany the L.31 and its famous commander, Kapitänleutnant Heinrich Mathy, shot down by a B.E.2c of the RFC over Potters Bar. Reluctant to admit defeat, the Germans mounted the last of their 1916 airship raids, with ten Zeppelins, eight weeks later, and lost both L.21 and L.34 in the attempt. It was not the final blow, for on 28 December L.17 and L.24 caught fire in their sheds at Tondern and were destroyed.

Only seven airship raids against Britain were carried out in 1917 and four in 1918. Paris had only two airship raids during the whole war, probably because it could be reached only by battling past the entire Allied air forces in France. It was no coincidence that one of the two Zeppelins which attempted such a raid was destroyed.

The passing of the Zeppelin seemed almost to be symbolized by what happened at Ahlhorn on 5 January 1918. At one moment this great airship base was there in all its glory: within minutes a fire started and all the

Burned-out Zeppelin, shot down over England.

During 1918 the RAF carried out experiments to find a means of protecting highly vulnerable airships from aerial attack. The R.23 was adapted to carry a fighter aircraft for this purpose. A Sopwith Camel was successfully launched from this airship (*above*). The same idea was resurrected 30 years later when the USAF flew successfully the McDonnell Goblin satellite fighter, designed to defend B-36 long-range bombers (*left*).

sheds were blown to pieces by the explosion of Zeppelins L.46, L.47, L.50 and L.58. The end came on 5 August 1918, when five Zeppelins launched a last surprise raid on Britain. In doing so they lost their latest and finest airship, the L.70, and Fregattenkapitän Peter Strasser, who had led the airship force so courageously through its entire period of success and defeat.

Powered by seven 290-hp Maybach engines, the L.70 was 740 ft long and had a range of 7,500 miles – so great that Strasser had even planned to fly it at the head of a formation of three airships across the Atlantic and back, to give New Yorkers their first taste of aerial bombardment. But even though it was able to fly at above 16,000 ft this was no longer high enough to elude Britain's fighter defences and it fell to the D.H.4 of Major E. Cadbury and Captain R. Leckie. With it died the big rigid airship as a weapon of war.

To trace the evolution of its vanquisher, the combat aeroplane, we must go back to the years immediately following the historical first flights of Orville and Wilbur Wright. These two pioneers had no doubts concerning the military potential of the aeroplane. Orville wrote in 1917: "We thought that we were introducing into the world an invention which would make further wars practically impossible." Reflecting sadly on the aerial warfare then being waged in France, he added: "What a dream it was; what a nightmare it has become."

It is easy to understand how Orville Wright made so great a miscalculation. Throughout history, the key to success in war has been to know in advance, or guess correctly, the plans of the enemy. The captive observation balloon contributed to victory in many battles by making it possible to keep track of every movement of opposing armies. The aeroplane, being mobile, fast and high-flying, would clearly extend this capability, by permitting reconnaissance sorties deep into enemy-held territory.

Lest it should seem naive to expect that such operations might prevent war, it is worth remembering that as recently as 1955 President Eisenhower proposed an "open-skies plan", under which the great powers would be permitted to carry out regular air reconnaissance over each other's territory and so ensure that any preparations for war would be observed in good time.

Back in aviation's first decade, few people believed that the aeroplane would be of military value for anything but reconnaissance. This was logical. Engine power was so low that payload was limited to the pilot and, sometimes, one passenger. Attempts to increase power – by techniques such as building a "two-row" version of the famous Gnome rotary engine, by literally mounting two standard engines one behind the other with a common crankshaft – led to unreliability or excessive weight. As a result, even those senior officers who showed an interest in aeroplanes saw them only as a form of airborne light cavalry for scouting.

As America had given birth to the aeroplane in 1903, it is hardly surprising that the US Army was the first combat service to buy one. The $25,000 contract, placed with the Wright brothers in February 1908, called for an aircraft that would carry two persons at a speed of at least 40 mph for 125 miles. An improved Wright biplane was delivered to Fort Meyer, Virginia, in August 1908. Demonstration flights began on 3 September and continued with great success until the 17th of the month when the aircraft crashed, severely injuring Orville Wright and killing his passenger, Lt Thomas E. Selfridge.

A replacement was delivered in June 1909 and, after completion of official tests, became "Aeroplane No. 1, Heavier-than-air Division, United States aerial fleet". But, after this far-sighted, if modest, beginning, America gradually lost its leadership. By 1911, five countries had more certificated pilots than the United States. France had become the world centre for aviation and had 353 pilots, compared with 26 in America of whom only eight were military airmen.

Between 1908 and 1913, France allocated an estimated £5½ million to

The world's first military aircraft – the Wright 1908 military biplane at Fort Meyer.

military and naval aviation. Germany spent a similar sum, Russia some £3 million and even Belgium spent £500,000, compared with £108,000 ($430,000) budgeted for further build-up of the "United States aerial fleet". As a result, when war broke out in Europe in 1914 the US Army had no more than 20 serviceable aircraft. Nor did the prospect of flying these few machines attract many would-be pilots, which is hardly surprising as 12 of the first 48 officers detailed to flying duty had been killed. These and other factors help to explain why no aeroplane of US design took part in the fighting in France during the 1914–18 War, although the British Royal Naval Air Service did use flying-boats designed by the great American pioneer, Glenn Curtiss, for maritime patrol and anti-submarine duties.

Initially, progress had been almost as slow in Britain. At the Army Balloon Factory, Farnborough, S. F. Cody and J. W. Dunne were given financial assistance to develop and build aeroplanes of their own design. Cody's big biplane made the first officially-recognized aeroplane flight in Britain, on 16 October 1908, by covering 1,390 ft at a height of 50-60 ft, and was named "British Army Aeroplane No. 1". Then, in April of the following year, the War Office discovered that it had spent a total of £2,500 on aeroplane experiments up to that time, decided this was too much, and reverted to work on balloons and airships only.

The army ban on heavier-than-air machines lasted until October 1910, when the scope of the Balloon Section of the Royal Engineers was extended "to afford opportunities for aeroplaning". Two months later, the War Office bought for £400 an aeroplane built by a young man named Geoffrey de Havilland and offered him a job as designer and test pilot at Farnborough.

Believing that it would be more economical to build its own aeroplanes than to encourage private enterprise, the War Office renamed the Balloon Factory the Army Aircraft Factory (later Royal Aircraft Factory) and decided to standardize on aircraft types designed and produced there, much to the dismay of the embryo British aircraft industry. Opponents of any form of present-day industrial nationalization point to the consequences as an example of the dire results of putting aircraft production into government hands, but this is somewhat unfair.

The facts are that by the beginning of 1912 the British Government was so alarmed by reports of military aviation progress in Germany and France that it appointed a committee to study the whole question of aircraft supply and operation. It was as a result of the committee's recommendations that the Royal Flying Corps came into being on 13 May 1912, with military and naval wings. This relieved the fears of the aircraft industry, as the naval

Blériot monoplane of the RFC, 1914. The War Office was criticized for its purchase of French aircraft in this period.

The Cody biplane, winner of the 1912 British Military Trials.

wing (which became the independent Royal Naval Air Service on 1 July 1914) preferred the products of the private companies to Farnborough's.

Even the War Office gave token support to free enterprise. It had been criticized for buying French aeroplanes to fill the equipment gap until production at Farnborough built up sufficiently to fulfil all its requirements. So, to prove its impartiality, it organized a series of military trials on Salisbury Plain, in August 1912, to give British companies a chance to prove the superiority of their products in competition with the latest French aircraft.

To the surprise of many people, Cody won the trials convincingly with a new version of his massive bamboo-and-wire biplane, and collected £5,000 in prize money. The key to his success had been the installation of a 120-hp Austro-Daimler engine. Such power gave even Cody's aeroplane a maximum speed of 72.4 mph. As it could stay in the air at a forward speed of only 48.5 mph, this gave it a speed range (difference between maximum and minimum speeds) of 23.9 mph. The best that any other competitor could do in this test, which was rated most important of all, was 18.9 mph.

The results of some of the other tests make amusing reading. In the quick assembly test – which involved removing the aeroplane from a packing case, assembling it and taking off – the winner was an Avro biplane, with a time of 14 min 30 sec. Cody took 1 hr 35 min; but even this did not match the effort required to assemble a Maurice Farman biplane, on which five stalwart mechanics had to struggle and heave for 9½ hours.

Even a cursory glance at the list of tests laid down at the 1912 military trials is sufficient to show that they were aimed at finding the best machine for reconnaissance duties. In this they failed miserably. The Cody biplane was safe in the hands of its tremendously-strong designer, but quite unsuitable for general use. Only two were ordered for the RFC, of which one crashed, killing its specially-trained pilot.

The War Office continued to buy French aeroplanes and to develop its own types at Farnborough. It was well justified in this, for there was unanimous agreement that the best machine seen on Salisbury Plain during the military trials had been the B.E.2, designed by Geoffrey de Havilland and built at Farnborough. Being a government product, it was unable to compete in the trials, but it completed some tests unofficially, beating all the contestants in terms of rate of climb and, more importantly, speed range. Powered by a 70-hp Renault engine, it achieved a top speed of 70 mph and flew under perfect control at only 40 mph, bettering Cody's winning speed range performance by a full 6 mph.

Early production model of the B.E.2, designed by Geoffrey de Havilland.

The B.E.2 was put into production for the RFC at a time when much of the research effort at Farnborough was being devoted to the achievement of inherent stability. It was felt that if an aeroplane could be made so stable in flight that it would remain straight and level with the pilot's hands and feet off the controls, it would be an almost perfect reconnaissance platform. This ideal of inherent stability reached a peak in the B.E.2c version of the de Havilland design, and well over a thousand of these aircraft were delivered to the RFC in the first years of the 1914–18 war.

Their inherent stability, which had appeared so valuable, proved their undoing. When enemy Fokker Monoplane fighters began to carry machine-guns, the stability of the B.E.2cs made them so unmanoeuvrable that they were easy prey and were shot down in huge numbers. In Parliament, Noel Pemberton-Billing, himself a pioneer aircraft designer, went far beyond the usual reference to B.E.2cs as "Fokker Fodder" by saying: "I would suggest that quite a number of our gallant officers in the Royal Flying Corps have been rather murdered than killed." Yet, in retrospect, it must be admitted that the War Office was correct in putting the B.E.2 family into production in an era before military aircraft carried guns, as it was unrivalled for what then appeared to be the sole military aviation duty of reconnaissance. The mistake was in continuing to build and operate this aircraft and its developments long after they had become death-traps in France.

The chain of events which led to the massacre of the B.E.2c can be said to have started in 1910. This was the year in which designers and pilots began to show a practical interest in fitting guns to aeroplanes, and in using them to drop bombs, even though armies and navies thought only in terms of unarmed reconnaissance.

On 30 June 1910, Glenn Curtiss pioneered the technique of bombing by dropping a number of dummy bombs on to a target in the form of a ship. Seven months later, a real bomb was dropped by Lt M. S. Crissy from the open seat of a Wright biplane, piloted by Philip Parmelee. He did this by simply holding the bomb in his hand until over the target area and then letting it go. Realizing that this was, literally, a rather hit-or-miss technique, Lt Riley Scott invented the first bomb-sight. With its help, he won 75,000 francs in a bombing competition staged in France in 1912.

By this time, bombing had progressed beyond the stages of theory and experiment. In Tripolitania, North Africa, the Italo-Turkish War of 1911–12 had seen the first use of aircraft in war, by the Italians. The very first operational sortie, made on a Blériot XI monoplane by Capt Piazza, on 23 October 1911, consisted of a one-hour reconnaissance flight between Tripoli and Azizia. Just over a week later, on 1 November, Sub-Lt Gavotti made the first-ever bombing raid, dropping a single Cipelli heavy grenade on Ain Zara and three more on the oasis of Taguira.

In one way or another, this minor campaign seems to have provided the excuse for trying out most of the aerial warfare tactics conceived up to that time. Propaganda leaflets were dropped instead of bombs for the first time on 10 January 1912, calling on the local Arabs to defect from the Turks and surrender. Capt Piazza made history again on 24 and 25 February, by taking the first reconnaissance photographs of enemy positions. On 19 April, Commandant Sulsi went one better by taking a cine-film of an enemy encampment from the airship P.3.

Whether or not such operations had any effect on the outcome of the war is immaterial. The aeroplane clearly had military uses beyond mere reconnaissance and other air forces were quick to follow the lead of the Italians. When the first Balkan War began in the autumn of 1912, the Bulgarians dropped specially designed bombs on Turkish-held Adrianople. They were not very formidable weapons, consisting of finned canisters of explosive which were aimed by an observer from the rear seat of a Blériot monoplane and dropped over the side by hand; but more effective methods were under development.

One of the first bomber aircraft – a Voisin with both bombs and machine-gun.

Sopwith Cuckoos on board HMS *Furious*, 1918. These were the first aircraft designed specially for torpedo dropping.

Eugene Ely making the first landing on a ship, 1911 (*above right*). Lt C.R. Samson's Short S.27 on board HMS *Hibernia* (*lower right*), ready for the first flight from a moving ship; and (*below*), the take-off.

Soon, it was usual for small bombs to be stowed in a kind of pipe-rack on the side of the fuselage, held in place by a pin which was pulled out over the target by tugging on a string. In Britain, the RNAS began to think in terms of bigger game, and torpedoes were dropped from the air for the first time early in 1914 by Lt (now Air Chief Marshal Sir) Arthur Longmore, from Short and Sopwith seaplanes.

Even the aircraft carrier – destined one day to replace the battleship as the capital ship of the world's navies – was already taking shape. The first flight from a ship had been made by an American pilot named Eugene Ely, on 14 November 1910. Flying a Curtiss biplane, he had taken off from a wooden platform built over the fore-deck of the cruiser *Birmingham* at Hampton Roads, Virginia. There was an anxious moment as the aircraft lost height and almost brushed the water before gaining flying speed, but the flight was successful and Ely followed it with the first landing on a ship, the USS *Pennsylvania*, on 18 January 1911. His Curtiss was dragged to a halt by sandbags attached to each end of ropes stretched across the wooden deck in such a way that they would be picked up by hooks under the aircraft's landing gear – a similar principle to that of the arrester gear fitted to modern carriers.

Almost every major advance in naval aviation since that time was pioneered by the Royal Navy. The first took place in May 1912, when Lt C. R. Samson took off from a platform on HMS *Hibernia* while the vessel was steaming at 10½ knots during a review of the fleet by HM King George V. Although this was the first flight from a moving ship, Samson realized that the forward speed of the ship, into wind, would enable him to take off more easily than on a previous occasion, in January, when he had flown the same Short S.27 biplane from HMS *Africa* when the ship was anchored in Sheerness Harbour.

Despite the success of Samson's experiments, the Navy proceeded cautiously. When war started in August 1914, it took over three cross-Channel steamers, named *Empress*, *Engadine* and *Riviera*, and fitted them out to carry four seaplanes each. However, these were not carriers in the modern sense, as the seaplanes had to be lowered into the water by crane for take-off and were retrieved in the same way after flight. This limited the aircraft's usefulness, as their floats tended to break up if the sea was choppy and several were lost when this happened.

A better technique, first tested on the old cruiser *Hermes* in 1913, was to fly seaplanes off a short deck on wheeled trolleys which fitted under their floats and dropped away as soon as the machines became airborne. By August 1915, even the then high-speed Sopwith Schneider fighter seaplanes were being flown in this way from the 120-ft flight deck of the former Cunard liner *Campania*. It was then only a short step from floats and wheeled trolleys to the use of simpler, faster landplanes.

Fairey IIID seaplane taking off from the carrier HMS *Argus* with the aid of a trolley – this technique was still being used in 1922.

While this development of the sea-going combat aircraft was taking place, the RNAS was showing something of the real potential of air power for the first time, on the continent of Europe. Led by C. R. Samson, now promoted to Wing Cdr, a small force of ten aircraft had been despatched to Belgium on the outbreak of war. Its job, in theory, was to carry out reconnaissance flights over the sea and land, and to engage any Zeppelins or enemy aircraft that might be sighted. This was too tame for Samson, who decided to take the offensive! The fact that he chose Zeppelin sheds as the target for the first-ever strategic bombing raids shows how seriously the RNAS regarded the airship menace.

On 22 September 1914, he despatched four aircraft on the first British air raid into German territory. They did no damage; but on 8 October, Sqn Cdr Spenser Grey dropped some 20-lb bombs on Cologne railway station, while Flt-Lt R. L. G. Marix attacked the Zeppelin sheds at Düsseldorf and had the satisfaction of seeing one of them explode into flames, complete with the new Zeppelin Z.9 inside it.

Both pilots were flying Sopwith Tabloids – small unarmed single-seaters. A few weeks later, on 21 November, a further successful raid was made on the Zeppelin works at Friedrichshafen, this time by three RNAS pilots in equally low-powered Avro 504s.

There could no longer be any doubt of the value of air bombardment, and Capt Murray Sueter, Director of the Air Department of the Admiralty, decided it was time to stop playing with 20-lb bombs. He issued a specification calling for a twin-engined aircraft suitable for extended patrols over the sea. The Handley Page company produced such a promising design that Sueter asked them to think even bigger and build "a bloody paralyser of an aeroplane". The result was the twin-engined O/100, which was destined to become the world's first heavy night bomber.

By the time it flew for the first time, on 18 December 1915, there had been equally important advances in fighter aircraft development.

It is, perhaps, not surprising that bombing aircraft preceded really practical fighters. As already explained, the pre-war emphasis was largely on reconnaissance, and pilots, in general, felt a kind of "brotherhood of the air" that did not disappear entirely in even the grimmest years of the 1914–18 War.

During early reconnaissance flights, German and Allied pilots sometimes waved to each other if they met in the air. The occasional cad took a pot-shot at his opposite number, with a rifle or revolver, and a few aircraft were shot down in this way; but on the whole it was a gentlemanly business. When, however, it became clear that air reconnaissance could sway the course of the ghastly conflict taking place in the mud below – and when bombing was added to reconnaissance – it was appreciated that efforts ought to be made to bring down the enemy aircraft that were becoming more than a mere nuisance. So, the fighter was born, initially as a pure interceptor.

It is not known precisely when the first gun was fitted to an aeroplane. The German pioneer August Euler took out a patent on a machine-gun installation for military aircraft in 1910, and in France a Nieuport two-seater was armed with a machine-gun in the following year. Also in 1911, Major Brooke-Popham of the Air Battalion, Royal Engineers, fitted a gun to a Blériot monoplane, but was promptly told to remove it!

America came near to getting the first armed aeroplanes in 1912. On 2 June that year, at College Park, Maryland, Capt Charles Chandler fired a low-recoil machine-gun, produced by Col Isaac Newton Lewis, from a Wright B biplane piloted by Lt Milling. Impressed by the results, Chandler asked the US Army Ordnance Department for ten more guns with which to continue the experiments. He was told he could not have them, as the Army had decided it did not want the Lewis gun.

Col Lewis himself left for Europe and, in January 1913, formed a company named "Armes Automatiques Lewis" at Liège in Belgium. He soon found a ready market for his weapons, which were lighter than other machine-guns and, instead of the usual ammunition belts, used 47-round detachable drums which were easy to store and handle and protected the bullets from dirt and oil.

Here, then, was a suitable weapon for aerial use; the problem was to find a way of mounting it on a type of aeroplane that would have a good enough performance to catch and shoot down enemy aircraft.

The fastest aeroplanes were usually those with the engine and propeller at the front (i.e., "tractor" types). Unfortunately, if a machine-gun had been mounted in the obvious place – above the fuselage, forward of the cockpit – on such an aircraft, the first casualty in action would probably have been the aircraft's own propeller. As a result, the first real fighting aeroplanes were two-seaters, with "pusher" engines, because such a layout offered a reasonable gun platform with a minimum of problems.

Vickers Ltd initiated a famous series of aircraft of this type with the E.F.B.1 (Experimental Fighting Biplane No. 1), named the Destroyer, which they exhibited at the 1913 Aero Show at Olympia, London. Although similar in general layout to its French contemporaries, such as the Henri Farman and Maurice Farman, it was a much cleaner design. The belt-fed Vickers-Maxim machine-gun mounted in its nose had a field of fire of 60° up and down, and to left and right.

By 1914, the design had been refined into the F.B.5 Gunbus, in which the gunner had a far greater field of fire, following transfer of the weapon (by now a Lewis) to a spigot-mounting above the nose. Although the War Office was still showing only scant interest in anything but reconnaissance aircraft, Vickers were convinced that, with war almost inevitable, the F.B.5 would soon be needed desperately by the British Services; so they decided to build a batch of 50 at their own expense.

After official tests in July 1914, the War Office decided to buy these aircraft, and eventually 109 F.B.5s were delivered to squadrons in France, the first arriving on 5 February 1915. They gave a good account of themselves in action, and earned a particular reputation for sturdiness, as their basic airframe, including the tail-booms, was built of steel tubing. Top speed was only 70 mph; and, at first, their relatively-unproven 100-hp Gnome Monosoupape engines gave so much trouble that one pilot suffered 22 forced landings in 30 flights. Nevertheless, enemy pilots learned to respect these sturdy old "pushers", which helped to establish an air superiority for the RFC until the advent of the Fokker Monoplane in German front-line squadrons.

The Gunbus was by no means the only "fighting aircraft" used in France in the first year of war. RFC pilots, in particular, showed considerable ingenuity in trying to devise a satisfactory method of firing a gun from faster single-seat "tractor" biplanes like the little 93-mph Bristol Scout C.

The most successful idea was to mount the gun at an angle on the side of the fuselage, so that it could be fired outside the propeller arc. Guns fitted in this way included even a breech-loading duck-gun firing chain-shot. There is no reason to believe that its sporting marksman achieved any success; but, on 25 July 1915, Capt Lanoe G. Hawker of No. 6 Squadron forced down three German two-seaters, all armed with machine-guns, during a single evening patrol, although his Bristol Scout was fitted with only a single-shot Martini carbine mounted in this way. The feat earned him a Victoria Cross.

Bearing in mind that the aircraft had to be flown "crabwise" in order to line up the gun on the target, it is remarkable that so many early victories were scored with these angle-mounted weapons. Usual choice of gun was a Lewis machine-gun. An alternative method of firing a Lewis forward from the Bristol Scout was to mount it above the centre-section of the top wing and fire it by pulling on a Bowden cable. This enabled the pilot to point his aircraft directly at the target, as the gun was aligned with a sight mounted in front of the cockpit. The main disadvantage was the difficulty of changing the drums of ammunition in flight.

One of Capt Hawker's colleagues in No. 6 Squadron devised an unconventional form of "armament", consisting of a weight attached to 150 ft of cable with which he hoped to entangle the propeller of any enemy aircraft he encountered over the lines. The official RFC historian described this as being akin to the catching of birds by putting salt on their tails, and it was no more successful. Another pilot suggested trailing from aircraft a bomb fitted with hooks. The idea was to "fish" for the enemy and, having hooked him, explode the bomb electrically by means of a switch in the cockpit.

A more practical alternative to guns was the dart, showered on to the enemy from above. First to be used, by No. 3 Squadron of the RFC in the Autumn of 1914, were steel darts called *flêchettes*, about 5 in long and $\frac{3}{8}$ in in diameter. A canister holding about 250 of these darts was attached to the bottom of the fuselage of each of the squadron's Blériots and Henri Farmans: by pulling a wire, the pilot could open the tin and release the *flêchettes* on enemy horse-lines and troops. However, even on a battlefield, life is sparsely distributed; so, as the darts did no harm unless they scored a direct hit, a whole canister of them was probably less formidable than a small bomb.

Pilots did, in fact, try to bomb enemy aircraft and Zeppelins on many occasions, after climbing above them, and Flt Sub-Lt R. A. J. Warneford of the RNAS was awarded the Victoria Cross for destroying in this way the L.Z.37 – first Zeppelin to fall in aerial combat – on 7 June 1915. The weapons he dropped from his French-built Morane Parasol Type L were six 20-lb bombs. In the hope of repeating this success, the RNAS began equipping its anti-Zeppelin units with explosive darts invented by Engineer Lt Francis

Voisin aircraft with container of *flêchettes*.

Ranken. These Ranken darts were released three at a time from a 24-round container. On release, four vanes spread from the tail of each dart, the idea being that they would grip the envelope of an airship after the head had penetrated it, and so give time for the charge to detonate inside.

Such weapons had only a short life. The steadily increasing speed of air combat offered little hope of consistent success with any weapon but a machine-gun, and the invention of incendiary bullets not only enhanced the superiority of the gun but spelled doom for the Zeppelin, as we have already seen.

The device which eventually made possible the true fighter aircraft was the interrupter gear, or gun synchronizing gear, which enabled bullets to pass between the blades of a spinning propeller. Use of interrupter gear put the Fokker Monoplane so far in advance of any of its contemporaries in 1915 that it almost shot the Allied air forces from the skies over France. Yet, this "secret weapon", far from being new, had been conceived at least a year before the war started.

Its inventor was Franz Schneider, chief designer of the German LVG company, who patented his synchronizing gear on 15 July 1913. Lt Poplavko hit upon a similar idea, in Russia, at about the same time: so did the Edwards brothers in England, but their designs were simply pigeon-holed by the War Office, and forgotten.

Schneider had little more success. He fitted a synchronized gun to the prototype LVG E. VI two-seat monoplane; but this aircraft was lost while on its way to the Front for operational testing in 1915 and no replacement was built.

The only other synchronizing gear known to have been tested up to that time was produced before the war by Raymond Saulnier of the Morane-Saulnier company, in France. This worked fairly well, with the Hotchkiss machine-gun which he had borrowed from the government to carry out tests; but some of the bullets tended to "hang fire". So, to avoid damage to the propeller, Saulnier fitted a steel deflector plate to each blade to kick aside bullets that would otherwise have struck them.

When the war started, Saulnier had to return the gun and further work on his invention had to be suspended.

There were, consequently, no aircraft fitted with interrupter gear in service in the Spring of 1915 and the crew of a German two-seater who saw a Morane-Saulnier Type N single-seat monoplane flying toward them on 1 April that year did not imagine they had much to fear. Too late, they caught sight of the machine-gun mounted above the fuselage, forward of the cockpit. Already, bullets from the gun were tearing into their aircraft, and they did not live to tell their colleagues of this terrifying new development in air combat.

During the fortnight that followed, other German aircraft fell to the mystery Morane. Then, on the 19th, the French aircraft itself was forced down, by engine trouble, behind the German lines. Before its pilot could set fire to it, both he and the aircraft had been captured, and the secret was revealed.

The pilot was none other than Roland Garros, the famous pre-war sporting flyer. The propeller of his Morane was fitted with the steel deflector plates that had been produced for use with Raymond Saulnier's pre-war synchronizing gear. Crude as it was, this revolutionized air combat. For the first time, the fastest types of aircraft – single-seat tractor monoplanes – could be used as fighters in the most effective manner, by sighting and firing a machine-gun straight forward, between the propeller blades. Quite a lot of the rounds fired were kicked aside, harmlessly, by the deflector plates, but sufficient got past to do deadly execution.

The Germans at once ordered Anthony Fokker to copy this idea on his Monoplane. But when he discussed the project with senior members of the staff at his factory, at Schwerin, Heinrich Luebbe and Fritz Heber are

Morane-Saulnier fitted with deflector plates, 1915.

Mass-production 1915 – Fokker monoplanes, the first real fighters.

believed to have suggested that he should resurrect Franz Schneider's interrupter gear instead. Within a few days, they designed, built and installed on a Fokker M.5K Monoplane a mechanism which they called the *Stangensteuerung* (push-rod control). Basically similar to Schneider's system, this consisted of a simple linkage of cams and push-rods between the oil-pump drive of the M.5K's Oberursel rotary engine and the trigger of the gun. It pulled the trigger of a Parabellum machine-gun once during every revolution of the propeller, timing the bullets so that they always passed cleanly between the blades.

Flight trials went well, and by July 1915 eleven German front-line pilots were flying Fokker E.I monoplane fighters fitted with machine-guns and the new interrupter gear. First to achieve a victory in combat was Leut Max Immelmann, who forced down a British aircraft that had been bombing Douai aerodrome on 1 August. He went on to become the leading exponent of the new art of air fighting in the Fokker, claiming another 14 victims and gaining the coveted *Pour le Mérit* decoration, Germany's highest award for courage and skill in war.

The E.I was not particularly fast, with a top speed of around 80 mph; but it was manoeuvrable and its synchronized gun gave it an immense superiority over anything the Allies could put up against it from the summer of 1915 until mid-1916. Immelmann, who became known as the"Eagle of Lille", worked out an attacking manoeuvre that extracted maximum advantage from these qualities. Still called the "Immelmann turn", it consisted of a half-loop and roll off the top, which enabled him to gain height and reverse direction on to the tail of an opponent extremely quickly.

Other famous pilots who gained their early successes on Fokker Monoplanes included Oswald Boelcke and Ernst Udet. They had little to fear at first from the opposition, but it should not be thought that life was entirely carefree for them. Both Immelmann and Boelcke had the experience of shooting off their own propellers when the interrupter gear went haywire, and a repetition of the incident is claimed by the Germans to have caused Immelmann's death on 18 June 1916. They assert that after the propeller had been shot away, the Fokker's engine "ran away" causing the airframe to break up in the air. The RFC believed that the structural failure was really caused by bullets from an F.E.2b fighter flown by Lt G. R. McCubbin and Cpl Waller of No. 25 Squadron.

Immelmann's death symbolized the end of the "Fokker Scourge", but the little fighter had revolutionized the whole concept of aerial warfare during its short reign. In the whole of July 1915, the RFC had recorded only 46 air combats. The same total was reported during a single day in December 1915. The results of the fighting were so disastrous for the Allies that on 14 January 1916, RFC headquarters issued the following order:

> Until the Royal Flying Corps are in possession of a machine as good as or better than the German Fokker it seems that a change in the tactics employed becomes necessary. It is hoped very shortly to obtain a machine which will be able to successfully engage the Fokkers at present in use by the Germans. In the meantime, it must be laid down as a hard and fast rule that a machine proceeding

> on reconnaissance must be escorted by at least three other fighting machines. These machines must fly in close formation and a reconnaissance should not be continued if any of the machines become detached ... From recent experience it seems that the Germans are now employing their aeroplanes in groups of three or four, and these numbers are frequently encountered by our own aeroplanes. Flying in close formation must be practised by all pilots.

Thus the Fokker Monoplane forced the RFC to adopt one of the most drastic changes in the tactics of air warfare – the switch to formation flying. The immediate effect was equivalent to a shrinkage in the strength of the RFC, but even this did not end the massacre, particularly of B.E.2cs. So great was the reputation acquired by the Fokker that when one important reconnaissance flight was planned, on 7 February 1916, the B.E.2c assigned to the task was intended to be escorted by no fewer than twelve other aircraft. In the event, the operation was cancelled.

Most surprising fact of all, perhaps, is that a total of no more than about 425 Fokker Monoplanes were built. Seldom can so much have been achieved by so few. The original E.I gave way quickly to improved versions, and the final E.IV (of which only 45 were built) had a 160-hp Oberursel engine and, usually, two machine-guns. But British and French designers had not been overawed by the Fokkers' apparent invincibility and worked hard to find an antidote.

Still having no reliable synchronizing gear available, the French fitted their little Nieuport Baby tractor biplane with a Lewis gun, mounted above the top wing centre-section and fired by means of a Bowden cable. Although such an armament had its limitations, these were offset by the fact that the Baby was 10 mph faster than both the Fokker E.II and E.III Monoplanes and the best existing fighters in Allied service. It was flown by the French and British air forces and was the type on which Britain's first fighter "ace", Captain Albert Ball, VC, achieved his early successes.

Lack of an interrupter gear caused British designers to retain a pusher biplane configuration for the single-seat D.H.2 and two-seat F.E.2b; but this did not reduce the effectiveness of these types when flown with determination and skill. On 23 May 1916, a report by Sir Henry Rawlinson, commanding the Fourth Army in France, gave a very different picture from the HQ order of 14 January:

> It was about the first week in May that we sent our reconnaissance over Bapaume escorted by the de Havilland machines. Up to that time we had been carefully training our young pilots and it was not till then that Ashmore (Lt-Col E. B. Ashmore, commanding First Wing RFC) thought them sufficiently expert to take on the Fokkers. In carrying out the reconnaissances they were attacked by the Fokkers and rendered a good account of themselves, for they reported that on the first occasion they sent two Fokkers to earth in a damaged condition and on the second they destroyed another which fell in the town of Bapaume and was smashed amongst the houses. All three of these machines fell of course in the enemy's lines so we have no certain information of what actually happened to them. But the fact remains that since this occurrence we have successfully photographed the whole of the enemy's trenches in front of the Fourth Army over a front of more than twenty miles without being once attacked by the Fokkers. This was done on the 15th, 16th, 17th and 18th May and clearly shows that for the moment at any rate we have command of the air by day on the Fourth Army front. I cannot speak too highly of the work of these young pilots, most of whom have recently come out from England, and the de Havilland machine has unquestionably proved itself superior to the Fokker in speed, manoeuvre, climbing and general fighting efficiency.

Good as it was, the D.H.2 – and its factory-built partner, the F.E.2b – represented the limit of usefulness of the pusher biplane layout in fighter design. This was not serious as, by mid-1916, the Allies also had efficient interrupter gears and were able to turn to the more efficient tractor configuration as standard practice.

The first aircraft with interrupter gear delivered to the RFC in France, on 25 March 1916, was a Bristol Scout. The date is significant as Fokker pilots had strict orders not to venture over the Allied lines and it was not until a fortnight later, on 8 April, that an example of the German synchronizing gear fell into Allied hands, following the forced landing of a Fokker Monoplane in the British lines, through engine trouble.

The gear fitted to that first Bristol Scout, and others which followed, was of Vickers design. Its introduction marked the adoption of the Vickers gun, as opposed to the Lewis, as standard forward-firing armament on British fighters. The main reasons were that synchronizing gears could be matched more readily with this gun and, since fire through the propeller called for a fixed gun, mounted on the fuselage, objections to the Vickers on the grounds of weight and unwieldiness disappeared. Pilots were delighted, as the belt-fed Vickers did not involve them in the frequent changes of ammunition drum that had been necessary with the Lewis gun: but the latter was retained as the standard free-mounted weapon for observers and gunners for a further quarter of a century – until the advent of the power-operated gun-turret.

Vickers synchronizing gear was also fitted to the two-seat Sopwith 1½-Strutter, which began to enter service with the RFC in France in May 1916. This aircraft was of the greatest significance, as it began life as a bomber but achieved its primary fame as the pioneer of the completely new class of two-seat fighters.

The RNAS had placed a first order for 1½-Strutters in 1915, to equip the two strategic bombing wings which it intended to base at Coudekerque and Luxeuil in Belgium. Realizing that the aircraft would have to fight its way past defending fighters, the Admiralty decided to supplement the usual gun in the observer's cockpit with a forward-firing gun operated by the pilot.

In January 1916, the Admiralty was offered an interrupter gear that had been designed by Lt-Cdr V. V. Dibovsky of the Imperial Russian Navy and it was this, as developed by F. W. Scarff, a warrant officer gunner on the staff of the Admiralty Air Department, that was fitted to naval 'Strutters. As already noted, the RFC preferred the Vickers gear on the version of the aircraft that it ordered subsequently; but both Services used a Scarff mounting for the rear Lewis gun and, in improved form, this eventually became standard equipment throughout the Allied air forces in the 1914–18 War and in worldwide use for many years afterwards.

RNAS 1½-Strutters began operating with No.5 Wing from Coudekerque in April 1916. No. 3 Wing was to follow, at Luxeuil. However, with the Battle of the Somme about to begin, the RFC found itself so desperately short of aircraft that it appealed to the RNAS for help. At once, the Admiralty handed over large numbers of 1½-Strutters, although it realized that by doing so it would delay for many months its cherished plans for a strategic bombing offensive against Germany.

Having been designed for bombing, the 'Strutter was too stable to offer the high degree of manoeuvrability needed by a pure fighter; nevertheless, it soon made its mark. German pilots seeing the new two-seater for the first time considered it fairly easy game and often attacked from a direction that shielded them from the observer's gun, only to be met by a deadly – and extremely unexpected – hail of fire from the synchronized Vickers.

Almost simultaneously with the 1½-Strutter, the Sopwith Aviation Company developed for the RNAS a tiny single-seat fighting scout which became known as the Pup. This also was adopted by the RFC and did much to establish the reputation of Sopwith (and its successor, the Hawker company) as Britain's greatest manufacturer of fighter aircraft. Although its Le Rhône engine gave only 80 hp, it had a top speed of 111·5 mph and was so manoeuvrable that many pilots still claim that it was the finest flying machine ever built. Certainly, it did superb work in France, and even Germany's ace of aces, Manfred von Richthofen, had to acknowledge that it dominated the sky over the battlefront for many months. In a combat report written on

One experimental divergence from the single-seat biplane fighter with forward-firing armament that had been almost standard since the 1914–18 War was the Westland COW-gun fighter of 1931. The idea was to fly under enemy bombers and destroy them with the large upward-firing gun.

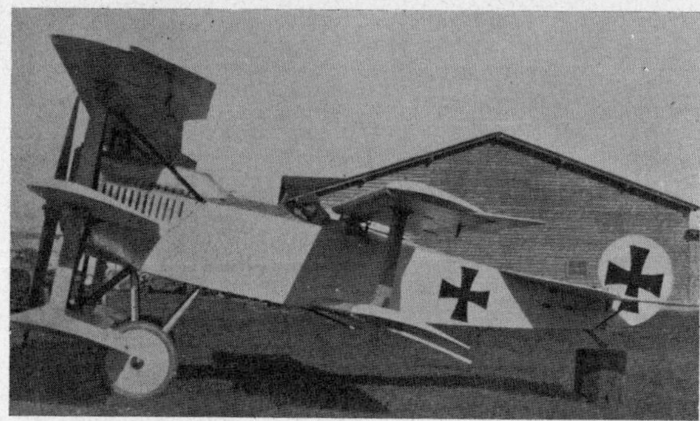

The strange Fokker V.8 multiplane.

135-mph aircraft of 1914, the S.E.4.

4 January 1917, he wrote: "One of the English aeroplanes (Sopwith one-seater) attacked us and we saw immediately that the enemy aeroplane was superior to ours. Only because we were three against one, we detected the enemy's weak points. I managed to get behind him and shoot him down."

Many of his colleagues were less lucky. Indeed, in the weeks preceding the Battle of Arras in early 1917, No. 3 (Naval) Squadron, equipped with Pups, inflicted such heavy losses on the enemy that German pilots avoided combat with them whenever possible. In this period, No. 3 itself suffered no casualties.

The Pup represented what was to be the standard configuration for single-seat fighters for some twenty years – tractor biplane, fixed undercarriage, open cockpit and synchronized, forward-firing armament. Its successors, such as the Sopwith Camel, added a second gun – again establishing the standard that persisted throughout the world into the 1930s. Almost the only other variation was that the Germans continued to prefer their highly-efficient and smoothly-cowled water-cooled in-line engines to the rotaries and radials that were fitted in most Allied types. But, in general, the only basic changes in single-seat fighter design for two decades were to be a gradual improvement in performance, as more powerful engines became available, and a general switch to metal structures in the late 1920s, instead of the wooden construction that was general up to that time.

Briefly, every now and again, there came on the scene something brilliantly unconventional, such as the Sopwith Triplane of 1916. The fuselage was similar to that of a Pup, but the combination of a more powerful engine with the narrow chord and short span made possible by the triplane layout gave the aircraft an exceptional performance, particularly in terms of rate of climb and manoeuvrability. At the same time, the pilot had an almost unrivalled all-round field of view past the narrow wings.

Best proof of the quality of the Sopwith Triplane is given by quoting the record of "B" Flight of No. 10 (Naval) Squadron. Led by Flt Sub-Lt Raymond Collishaw, it was an all-Canadian unit and was known as the "Black Flight", its aircraft being named *Black Death*, *Black Maria*, *Black Prince*, *Black Roger* and *Black Sheep*. Between May and July 1917, it claimed a total of no fewer than 87 enemy aircraft, including 16 which Collishaw shot down in a period of 27 days in June.

Little wonder that the Germans were panicked into building vast numbers of different triplanes in an effort to match the Sopwith success. Of these, only the Fokker Dr. I triplane achieved any great renown, mainly in the hands of von Richthofen.

Some designers tried to go even further, building quadruplanes and multiplanes like the Fokker V.8, which had sets of triplane and biplane wings in tandem. Only the monoplane, which we now know to be the cleanest and best configuration of all, seemed unable to excite any prolonged interest. This was a reflection of the pre-war belief that monoplanes were inherently more difficult to fly and structurally weaker than biplanes. The fallacy was strengthened in England during the Summer of 1912, when five officers and a staff sergeant of the then-tiny RFC were killed in a period of a few weeks in Nieuport, Deperdussin and Bristol monoplanes.

Immediately, the War Office put a ban on monoplanes, and although this was lifted before the outbreak of war the stigma remained. It prevented full use being made of the highly-advanced Bristol M.1C monoplane in 1917, although its introduction on the Western Front might have swung the tide of battle in the Allies' favour during a brief period of German ascendancy.

More difficult to understand is why designers and air forces, in general, failed to take advantage of some of the refinements tested in pre-war days, particularly in respect of streamlining to improve performance. The best fighters of the 1914–18 War were, undoubtedly, the Sopwith Snipe and Fokker D.VII, neither of which was as fast as the experimental S.E.4 biplane built and tested at Farnborough in 1914. This remarkable aeroplane had a plywood-covered fuselage of circular section, single-strut interplane bracing and a huge propeller spinner to reduce drag to a minimum. Innovations included running the aileron control wires through the hollow centre-section support struts, use of a cooling fan for the engine, full-span combined ailerons and camber-changing flaps and even a celluloid transparent cockpit canopy. With a double-row Gnome engine of only 160 hp, it had a top speed of 135 mph and rate of climb of more than 1,600 ft/min, making it the fastest aeroplane in the world at that time.

As already mentioned, the big Gnome proved a troublesome engine and no pilot would fly with the cockpit canopy in place, considering this dangerous; but the only real criticism of the basic design seems to have been that high speed was achieved at the expense of a dangerously high landing speed – 52 mph. In an age when airliners packed with passengers touch down at more than twice that speed, the excuse appears weak.

Increasing the firepower – multiple gun installation on an F.E.2b.

Looking back on the single-seat fighters of the 1914–18 War, one is impressed mainly by the fact that such small, low-powered, and often dainty, little aircraft should have been so very deadly in combat – the Camel alone claiming 1,294 enemy aircraft destroyed. The Pup, fully loaded, weighed a mere 1,225 lb, which is about the same as the weight of the four air-to-air missiles carried by its modern counterpart, the Sea Vixen. Its cost, without instruments and gun, was a mere £1,331, compared with more than £1 million for many modern fighters. In fact, all the Pups ever built (1,770 of them) cost less than one F-111A "swing-wing" fighter of today.

The two-seat fighter formula, pioneered by the 1½-Strutter, reached its 1914–18 War peak in the Bristol Fighter, known affectionately as the "Brisfit". The affection was not immediate, for its career in the RFC began disastrously. Its introduction into service in France was entrusted to No. 48 Squadron, which sent out its first offensive patrol, led by Capt W. Leefe-Robinson, VC, on 5 April 1917. The six "Brisfits" were met by five Albatros D.IIIs led by Manfred von Richthofen. Only two survived the experience and eight more had been lost by 16 April.

Bristol Fighters, April 1918.

A few pilots had the sense to realize that the fault might lie in tactics rather than in the aircraft. It had always been the practice in two-seaters for the pilot to try to bring his aircraft into the best possible position for the rear-gunner to fire on the enemy. Some of the more adventurous pilots decided to take advantage of the "Brisfit's" great structural strength and manoeuvrability by flying it like a single-seater, using the forward-firing Vickers gun as the primary weapon and leaving the gunner to protect the tail. Spectacular successes came at once, as the "Brisfit's" superb 275-hp Rolls-Royce Falcon engine gave it a top speed of 123 mph, despite the penalty of a second crew member, and it could outfly almost anything in the sky. One pilot, Lt A. E. McKeever of No. 11 Squadron, eventually shot down a total of 30 enemy aircraft, almost all of them from a Bristol Fighter.

Mention above of "fighting patrols" reflects the way in which combat tactics evolved as a result of experience on both sides during the "Fokker Scourge". The Fokkers had been allocated to three small, specialized groups, known as *Kampfeinsitzerkommando* (single-seat fighter unit) Nos. 1, 2 and 3, and sometimes hunted in teams. The RFC reacted, as we have seen, by initiating large-scale formation flying.

Special four-gun arrangement on a Bristol Fighter, 1918.

In the summer of 1916, the German air force carried the grouping a stage further by deciding on the formation of 37 special fighting squadrons, known as *Jagdstaffeln* (usually shortened to *Jastas*), by April 1917, each with an establishment of 14 aircraft. Oswald Boelcke was the main instigator of this and was given command of the first *Jasta*, but was killed in a mid-air collision before it became operational.

However, he had done his job well and many of the leaders of other *Jastas* were his pupils, including von Richthofen. When they reached full strength, on schedule, in the spring of 1917, many were already equipped with the new Albatros D.III "vee-strutter". Their primary task was unchanged – to intercept Allied reconnaissance aircraft – and they did this mainly by waiting on their own side of the lines, ready to swoop in overwhelming strength on the unfortunate British and French two-seaters, which were almost as defenceless as in the heyday of the Fokkers.

April 1917 – "Bloody April" – proved to be the blackest month of the war for the RFC, in terms of casualties. The Germans, convinced of the value of operating in large formations, concentrated their fighters into *Jagdgeschwadern* (fighter wings), each made up of four *Jastas*. The idea was to have available a number of large and compact fighter forces which could be switched quickly from one part of the front to another to establish local air superiority wherever required. As many of the aircraft were brightly painted, in the individual insignia of their pilots, the Allies referred to the travelling wings as "Flying Circuses". Best-known was *Jagdgeschwader* No. 1, led by von Richthofen in a blood-red Fokker triplane or Albatros.

Evolution of the fighter-bomber in the 1914–18 War – a Camel being prepared for trench-strafing, 1918.

On 1 May, von Richthofen went on leave. Simultaneously, the RFC's new S.E.5 fighter began to make its presence felt and the Bristol Fighter pilots learned how to operate their new equipment to best effect. A few months later, in July, the first Camels entered service and the French air force started re-equipping with the very fine SPAD S.XIII. Even the huge German "Circuses" then met their match. Dog-fights between scores of fighter aircraft took place above the trenches, as one side launched an attack on enemy reconnaissance or bombing aircraft and were themselves attacked by escorting or patrolling fighters.

Downward-firing guns on a trench-strafing Camel.

This pattern of fighter operations continued until the end of the war; but many secondary tasks were also undertaken by the single-seaters. One of the first and most effective was trench-strafing, in which the lot of the unhappy soldier, locked in a life-and-death struggle in the mud and flame of the battlefield, was made even more unbearable by machine-gun fire and light bombs rained down by fighters that roared a few feet above his head. Armour plating was added to the bellies and around the engines of some of the ground-attack fighters; others were tested with special gun installations, including a Camel with a pair of Lewis guns fixed to fire downward through the floor of the fuselage and a B.E.2c with four Lewis guns mounted above its undercarriage cross-axle for trench-strafing in Mesopotamia. Many upward-firing gun installations were also evolved for anti-Zeppelin operations.

Typical fighter cockpit of the 1914–18 War – the twin synchronized Vickers guns of the Sopwith Dragon.

Although twin synchronized guns became the standard fighter armament, there was no shortage of ideas for alternative installations. Heavy-calibre weapons used in action included 1-pounder Vickers pom-pom guns which were employed for night attacks on ground targets by two F.E.2bs of No. 100 Squadron, RFC, in the spring of 1917, and the French *moteur-canon*. The latter was conceived as early as 1911 by Louis Blériot, who tested on the ground a gun that fired through the hollow propeller-shaft of an aero-engine. If the idea had been considered practical and worthwhile, the tractor monoplane fighter might have emerged much earlier. In the event, it was not until 1917 that the *moteur-canon* was revived by Hispano-Suiza, at the suggestion of the French fighter ace Guynémer.

Hispano-Suiza mounted a 37-mm Puteaux shell-firing gun between the cylinder blocks of their 220-hp geared Vee engine, so that it could be loaded by the pilot with one hand in flight and fired through the hollow propeller shaft. The *moteur-canon* was installed in the specially-designed SPAD XII and 14 fighters which were then used by Guynémer and Fonck to shoot down several enemy aircraft. The low muzzle velocity of the gun, the excessive vibration and the high standard of marksmanship demanded by a single-shot weapon made the *moteur-canon* impractical for general use at that time, but it was to be revived later in improved forms.

An experiment in producing a really mighty gunship – two batteries totalling 28 machine-guns in a Junkers-Larsen JL-12 attack aircraft, 1921.

Another weapon of the future that was tried out briefly was the rocket. In its 1916 form, it consisted of little more than a large firework-type rocket,

Giant bombers of the 1914–18 War. A line-up of Caproni Ca 41s.

on a stick, mounted in sets of four on the interplane struts of a fighter and fired electrically. The main targets were highly inflammable balloons and airships, and several successes were achieved before this primitive weapon was made obsolete by the availability of efficient incendiary ammunition for machine-guns.

It is clear that most of the weapons and ideas used to deadly effect in World War II had their origin in 1914–18, except for devices such as radar and the atomic bomb, which depended on technological progress in other fields. Even searchlights were carried experimentally by some night fighters in an attempt to bring to heel the elusive and hard-hitting night bomber.

The bombing aircraft itself underwent great development as the war progressed, with no one nation having a monopoly in achievement. French Voisin "pushers" began making effective strategic raids by day before the end of 1914, but it was, perhaps, the Italians who led the field in heavy bombing in the early part of the war.

The Caproni company had started to build large aeroplanes in 1913 and quickly standardized on the unique three-engined twin-boom configuration that proved so successful in the Ca 30/33 series of aircraft. They went into action in August 1915, within three months of Italy's declaration of war against Austria and Hungary, and by the spring of 1917 there were no fewer than 14 squadrons of them, as well as two French air force squadrons of Capronis built in France. Up to 1,000 lb of bombs could be carried, and two gun positions enabled the Capronis to put up a strong defensive fire. This did, however, call for considerable heroism and fortitude from the unfortunate rear-gunners, who were expected to – and did–stand on an open platform aft of the top wing during long flights over the Alps in winter.

Another pre-war pioneer of the big bomber was Igor Sikorsky of Russia, whose *Le Grand* biplane, built in 1913, was the world's first four-engined aeroplane. From it he evolved the remarkable series of Il'ya Muromets heavy bombers, more than 70 of which were produced for the Czar's "Squadron of Flying Ships". They made more than 400 raids over East Prussia and lost only one of their number in aerial combat. Even this one destroyed three of its attackers before crashing, and there is little doubt that these large Sikorskys sparked off the Russian predilection for giantism in aircraft that has persisted to the present time.

It is difficult to decide which of the bombers of 1914–18 contributed most to the course of the war. None played a decisive rôle, although they did influence policy and led to moves of tremendous importance for the future. Of no aircraft is this more true than of the German twin-engined bombers (mostly Gothas) which took over the strategic air offensive against Britain after the Zeppelin had been mastered.

The first raid on London by an aeroplane was made on 28 November 1916 by a single LVG C. II, which dropped six 22-lb bombs in the region of

Big bomber, big bomb. A Sikorsky Il'ya Muromets of the 1914–18 War.

Victoria Station without doing much damage. Far more frightening for the civilian population of Britain were the raids made by formations of Gothas from *Bombengeschwader* 3 between 25 May 1917 and May 1918.

The psychological effect of these attacks was far more significant than the number of casualties and the amount of damage they caused. The raids started just as the people of Britain were beginning to feel that their old enemy, the Zeppelin, had been mastered, and morale slumped when the Gothas appeared able to perform their task in daylight with contemptuous ease.

Twenty-one of the bombers took part in the first raid, on 25 May 1917. Because of heavy cloud, they turned back before reaching London, which was their primary objective, and most of the fifty-nine 110-lb and one hundred and four 26-lb bombs they dropped fell on Shorncliffe and Folkestone. Although the Gothas had been over the English mainland for 90 minutes by then, neither place received any warning of the enemy's approach, and 56 of the 95 people killed were women and children caught when bombs fell on a busy shopping centre.

Inevitably, there was a major outcry, as the two Gothas that were lost crashed in the Channel and in Belgium, so that, as far as the British public was concerned, it appeared that the raiders had escaped unscathed.

Even louder voices were raised when 14 Gothas in neat formation circled over London itself, in full view of everyone below, on 13 June and dropped 72 bombs within a radius of one mile of Liverpool Street station and smaller numbers elsewhere. This time, 162 people were killed and 432 injured – more than in any other bombing attack on Britain during the 1914–18 War – and no enemy aircraft was shot down.

This is hardly surprising. The Gothas, powered by two magnificent 260-hp Mercedes engines, could cruise at 15,000 ft. In the absence of an effective early warning system in Britain, they could reach their target, drop their bombs and be on the way home before defending fighters could climb to their height. Lightened of their load, they could make the return trip at even greater altitude. So, although 92 pilots took off in England in an effort to intercept the bombers, most of them never even saw the enemy.

Despite the seriousness of the situation in France, the famous No. 56 Squadron, equipped with the latest S.E.5 fighters, was withdrawn from front-line service and flown to Bekesbourne, near Canterbury, to stiffen the home defence units. No. 66 Squadron with Pups, was transferred to Calais to supplement the aircraft which attempted to cut off the raiders during their return flight. When nothing happened for a fortnight both squadrons rejoined the British Expeditionary Force, on 5 and 6 July. Within hours, the biggest-ever force of Gothas – 22 in all – was over London. Only one was shot down. Two defending fighters were lost.

This was, in fact, the last daylight raid on the capital, although three more attacks were made on other targets in south-eastern England in July and August 1917. They proved costly to the raiders, as Britain's anti-aircraft defences had been completely reorganized after the raids on London, and both the anti-aircraft guns and the fighter pilots took their toll of the Gothas, of which several more were lost in crash landings at their base.

As was to happen in World War II, having been driven from the daylight skies over Britain, the Germans turned to night bombing. Beginning on 2 September, *Bombengeschwader* 3 made 15 night raids in 1917, nine of them against London. This added to the problems of the defences. It had always been considered unsafe to fly single-seat fighters at night, but the pilots of No. 44 Squadron, in Camels, soon proved this to be untrue, and on the night of 28/29 January 1918, two of them achieved the first recorded victory at night in a combat between aeroplanes, by shooting down a Gotha in flames.

By this time, the Germans had begun supplementing these twin-engined bombers with their so-called "Giants" – "R" (*Riesenflugzeug*) biplanes with four, five or six engines, designed mainly by Zeppelin Staaken. Spanning nearly 140 ft and weighing nearly 12 tons fully-loaded, these huge machines usually carried a crew of seven and up to eighteen 220-lb bombs, although occasionally they dropped a single 2,200-pounder – the largest bombs used in the 1914–18 War. Not one "Giant" was lost in action, although they made eleven raids over Britain.

The Gothas were less fortunate and aeroplane raids on Britain ceased completely after the night of 19/20 May 1918, when seven of the 43 aircraft sent to attack Dover and London fell to defending guns and fighters. In August 1918, the German High Command ordered that all bombing of London and Paris was to be stopped "on military and political grounds". By then, it was clear that, good as they were, the Gothas were no match for night-flying Camels, S.E.5as and Bristol Fighters.

Statistically, they had done rather better than the Zeppelins, in that the 52 aeroplane raids on Britain killed 857 persons, injured 2,058, and caused £1,434,526 worth of damage for an expenditure of only 2,772 bombs, totalling about 196 tons in weight. But the effects of their activities went far beyond this.

A combination of official concern over the supply of aircraft to the RFC and RNAS and public disquiet resulting from enemy air attacks led to the complete reorganisation of British military aircraft development and operation in the last two years of the war. The Royal Aircraft Factory at Farnborough was directed to concentrate on research, leaving aircraft design and manufacture to private industry. It did not comply immediately, and its S.E.5a fighter was one of the best Allied aircraft of 1917–18; but it gradually changed its character, becoming in 1918 the now-famous Royal Aircraft Establishment.

Even more significant was the setting up of an Air Ministry, followed on 1 April 1918 by the creation of the world's first major independent air service – the Royal Air Force, into which the RFC and RNAS were merged.

Meanwhile, the aeroplane raids on Britain had prompted the British government to order massive reprisals against the German homeland. The officer entrusted with the task was General Hugh (later Marshal of the Royal Air Force, Viscount) Trenchard, who is remembered today as the virtual creator of the RAF and the architect of modern air power.

He had some of the finest aircraft of the day at his disposal. The old F.E.2b "pusher", one of the vanquishers of the Fokker Monoplane, had found a new lease of life as a night bomber. Geoffrey de Havilland had followed its fighting partner, the D.H.2, with the superb D.H.4 day bomber, which cruised so high and so fast that it could outfly contemporary German fighters. And Handley Page had given Murray Sueter his "bloody paralyser" in the shape of the big twin-engined O/100 and its development, the O/400.

In RNAS service, the D.H.4 and O/100 had made life very uncomfortable for the German Navy on and off the Belgian coast. As early as 25 April 1917, four of the big Handley Pages had caught four enemy destroyers at sea off Ostend and promptly sent one to the bottom. One O/100 was lost to enemy fighters, and shortly afterwards it was decided to use this type only at night. Thereafter, almost every night saw the bombers in action against German-held ports.

One of the Navy's Handley Page squadrons (No. 16), together with No. 55 (D.H.4) and No. 100 (F.E.2b) Squadrons, was allocated to Trenchard's 41st Wing at Ochey, near Nancy. Nine of the big machines accompanied 16 F.E.2bs in a night attack on the Burbach works, near Saarbrücken, on 24/25 October 1917. From then on, a non-stop offensive against German military centres was mounted through the severe winter and the following spring. By 5 June, a total of 142 raids had been made by 41st Wing, which was re-designated VIII Brigade on 1 February and became the nucleus of the famous Independent Force of the RAF on 6 June.

The first independent air force in the world formed solely for a sustained

F.E.2b being bombed up (*top*) and ready for a night raid.

strategic bombing rôle, the new Force was composed of four squadrons of Handley Pages, one of F.E.2bs, one of D.H.4s, two of D.H.9s and one of D.H.9As, plus an escort squadron of Camels to which was allocated the unenviable task of trying to protect the highly-vulnerable D.H.9s in daylight.

On one occasion, on 31 July 1918, twelve D.H.9s of No. 99 Squadron set out, unescorted, to attack Mainz. Three turned back with engine trouble. The others were pounced on by 40 enemy fighters, but battled on to alternative targets at Saarbrücken, losing four of their number before dropping their bombs. Three more fell on the return journey, the two survivors owing their lives to the intervention of two formations of D.H.9s from No. 104 Squadron.

Such was the heroism that produced the cold statistics of 550 tons of bombs dropped by the Independent Force in the five months of its existence, of which 160 tons were dropped by day and 390 tons by night. Was it all worth while? One answer is that, of the total, 220 tons of bombs were dropped on enemy aerodromes, destroying many aircraft. As a result, attacks on Allied aerodromes became negligible, and not a single aeroplane was destroyed by enemy bombing after the formation of the Independent Force.

Handley Page bombers on the ground (*top*) and in flight.

Trenchard never forgot this lesson in strategy, and when he planned the post-war RAF he provided for a long-range strategic bombing force which has remained the heart of British air power to the present day. The achievements of the Independent Force must also have influenced General "Billy" Mitchell, commander of the U.S. Army Air Service, who used Martin MB-2 twin-engined heavy bombers to sink several old German and US battleships at sea in 1921–3. Claiming that this proved the obsolescence of sea power, he crossed swords with senior officers of the army and navy, was court-martialled and suspended from duty.

Twenty years later, after his death, when the truth of his claims was appreciated, he was restored to service with the rank of major general and was awarded the Congressional Medal of Honor.

Trenchard had almost as difficult a time keeping the RAF independent of army and navy control after the end of the 1914–18 War. He succeeded, to the extent that even aircraft carried on board ships of the Royal Navy were manned by RAF crews for some years. Not until 1937 did the Navy regain complete control of what had, since 1924, been known as the Fleet Air Arm, again producing two separate air forces in Britain.

Great strides were made in naval aviation during and after the 1914–18 War, mainly in Britain. The war had caused the RNAS to develop its combat units along two entirely different lines – for maritime patrol and reconnaissance from coastal bases, and for ship-based operation with the fleet at sea (basic functions which remain unchanged to this day, although the coastal work is now performed quite often by "land-based" air forces such as the RAF).

Martin MB-1 bomber, from which was developed the MB-2 used by Billy Mitchell to demonstrate the vulnerability of large warships, 1921–3.

In 1914–18, and for many years afterwards, the coastal duties were entrusted largely to flying-boats and seaplanes, the most effective types being the large twin-engined flying-boats developed at Felixstowe from original Curtiss designs. The F.2As, in particular, were manoeuvrable enough to take on enemy seaplanes in air combat, and had such a good rate of climb and ceiling that one of them succeeded in shooting down the Zeppelin L.62 at a height of 8,000 ft.

More important still, "Large Americas" and F.2As from the RNAS base at Felixstowe inaugurated the technique of methodical "pattern search", initially for anti-submarine duties but equally applicable to other tasks such as air/sea rescue. It involved flying strictly-controlled courses over a patrol area in the North Sea shaped like a giant "Spider Web", 60 miles across. A single flying-boat could search a quarter of the web in five hours, whereas it took a surfaced submarine ten hours to cross the area.

Only five flying-boats were available when the "Spider Web" patrol was

Catapult on ship between the wars. A Hawker Osprey seaplane being launched (*above*).

Ditching trials with a Sopwith Camel during the 1914–18 War (*above left*).

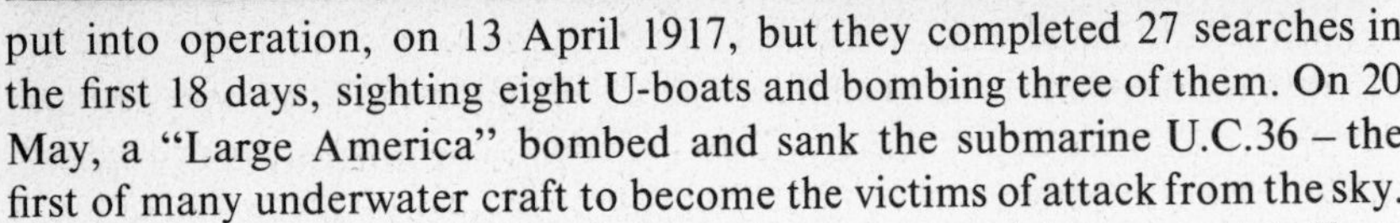

Launching a Parnall Peto reconnaissance seaplane from the M.2. The Peto was designed for stowage in a hangar on the submarine's deck.

put into operation, on 13 April 1917, but they completed 27 searches in the first 18 days, sighting eight U-boats and bombing three of them. On 20 May, a "Large America" bombed and sank the submarine U.C.36 – the first of many underwater craft to become the victims of attack from the sky.

All kinds of ingenious ideas were tried out to extend the range and effectiveness of aircraft at sea. As mentioned earlier, the limitations of carrier-borne seaplanes were overcome early in 1916, when the first landplanes (Sopwith Pups) were put on board primitive carriers like the *Campania* and *Manxman*. The 200-ft deck of these ships was adequate for the Pup when they sailed into wind; but there was no provision for landing-on after flight. Instead, the pilot had to "ditch" in the sea and hope that flotation bags would keep his aircraft afloat until he was picked up.

Although far from ideal, this offered a practical way of taking to sea aircraft fast enough to deal with enemy Zeppelins shadowing the fleet. Unfortunately, there were all too few carriers; so the Navy decided to investigate the possibility of flying Pups from other types of ship. A short (20-ft) wooden platform was installed above the conning tower and forecastle gun of the light cruiser *Yarmouth*, and in June 1917 a Pup was flown successfully from this while the vessel steamed into wind at 20 knots.

Within two months, the value of this innovation was proved dramatically. The *Yarmouth* was helping to provide cover for a mine-laying operation off the Danish coast on 21 August when Zeppelin L.23 began shadowing the British ships. Flt Sub-Lt B. A. Smart clambered into the Pup, made his first-ever take-off from the ship and, having climbed to a greater height than his huge enemy, dived to attack it. Within seconds, L.23 was dropping from the sky, burning so fiercely that very little of her remained to hit the sea.

Soon, flying-off platforms were fitted to many other battleships and cruisers. Nor, after a time, did the ships need to change course in order to launch

Lt S.D. Culley climbs into his lighter-borne Camel before taking off to shoot down Zeppelin L.53.

Sqdn Cdr E.H. Dunning, the first pilot to land on a moving ship, lost his life when his Sopwith Pup went over the side.

Early shipboard landing. A Pup with skid landing gear on HMS *Furious.*

their aircraft, as the platforms were mounted above rotatable turrets that could be turned into wind while the vessel maintained her existing course. Even two-seaters like the 1½-Strutter were launched in this way, providing the fleet with "a view over the horizon" during reconnaissance sorties, and spotting and correcting the aim of naval gunners in action.

"Spotter" planes were carried in this way on large warships right up to World War II, catapults replacing the original turret-platforms as aircraft became heavier, needing a higher launching speed. Experiments were even made in carrying and launching aircraft from submarines; but the cramped accommodation limited the size and usefulness of the aircraft and only the Japanese achieved limited success with their Yokosuka E14Y1 and Aichi M6A1 Seiran floatplanes during World War II. An E14Y1 on a reconnaissance flight was, in fact, the only hostile aeroplane to drop bombs on the United States in that war, although it did no damage.

Another form of "aircraft carrier" was used to extend the range of RNAS flying-boats in 1917–18. It consisted of a lighter, towed behind a destroyer. Fifty-one such lighters were delivered and F.2A flying-boats carried in this way made many useful reconnaissance sorties over areas like the Heligoland Bight, which would otherwise have been beyond their reach.

C. R. Samson, the pioneer naval pilot, volunteered to attempt to fly a Sopwith Camel from one of the lighters. The concept was good, as it offered the possibility of bringing a really high-performance fighter into action against Zeppelins, far beyond the range of shore-based interceptors. Samson nearly lost his life in the first experiment, when the Camel cartwheeled into the sea and was run over by the lighter; but lessons were learned and his courageous leadership was again rewarded on 11 August 1918, when Lt S. D. Culley flew a Camel off a lighter towed by the destroyer *Redoubt* and shot down Zeppelin L.53 at a height of 19,000 ft. It was the last German airship to fall in aerial combat.

Despite the success of such schemes, it was clear by then that the most satisfactory way of taking air power to sea was on board specially designed aircraft carriers. The last real barrier to efficient carrier flying had been overcome on 2 August 1917, when Sqn Cdr E. H. Dunning of the RNAS made the first landing on a moving ship, HMS *Furious.*

Up to that time, pilots had had to ditch their aircraft after each sortie, unless they were close to land. Often this involved both danger to the aircrew and loss of the aircraft, as it was not possible to stop a warship long enough to retrieve a ditched machine in submarine-infested waters. Dunning decided to see if it was feasible to land a Pup on the *Furious*, which had its 228-ft-long flying-off deck *forward* of the funnels and superstructure. On 2 August, he dodged round the superstructure and edged in over the ship until friends on the deck could grab toggles on the little aircraft and tug it down. Realizing that such assistance was not practical for operational use, Dunning repeated the experiment five days later without helpers. A tyre burst as he touched down, the Pup rolled over the side and Dunning was drowned; but his sacrifice gave birth to the true aircraft carrier.

A primitive landing deck installed aft of the funnels and superstructure of the *Furious* represented a first step in the right direction. The Pups and 1½-Strutters based on this ship were fitted with skid landing gear instead of wheels. As they touched down, horns on the skids engaged a series of cables that extended fore-and-aft a few inches above the deck. It was hoped that this would bring the aircraft quickly to a halt. Unfortunately, the midships structure caused such unpredictable air currents over the rear deck that sometimes only one skid engaged the wires, causing the aircraft to tilt over onto a wingtip. On other occasions, the pilots missed the wires and ran on into a "crash barrier" of vertical ropes, which was expensive in terms of broken wings and propellers.

Gradually, however, the aircraft carrier was refined. HMS *Argus* pointed the way to the future by dispensing with all superstructure, to provide a

Modern steam catapult in action. A Hawker Siddeley (Blackburn) Buccaneer preparing for take-off from HMS *Eagle*. Raising the aircraft's nose in this way increases the wing lift and so shortens the take-off run.

completely clear flight deck; and wheeled undercarriages – still with horns – replaced skids in the early 1920s. It was found possible later to build the superstructure to one side of the deck without undue danger, and this became standard. By the beginning of the 1930s, HMS *Courageous* had introduced the now-familiar transverse-wire type of arrester gear (not so very different from that used by Ely in 1911), and carrier-based aircraft exchanged their landing gear horns for modern-style arrester hooks.

Catapults were built into the decks of aircraft carriers from the early 1930s, to assist heavily-loaded aircraft into the air. Even these were not always capable of giving sufficient "urge" to the heavily-laden and high-performance carrier-based aircraft of World War II; so small solid-propellent rocket-motors, known as RATOG (rocket-assisted take-off gear) or JATO (jet-assisted take-off), were produced, which could be attached to the aircraft's fuselage and fired to supplement their built-in engine power, Such devices became unnecessary when the Royal Navy introduced the very powerful steam catapult, used on all modern carriers.

Evolution of the carrier changed completely the character of war at sea. The experiments in torpedo-dropping carried out by the RNAS before the 1914–18 War had their fulfilment on 12 August 1915, when Flt Cdr C. H. K. Edmonds, flying a Short 184 seaplane from the carrier *Ben-my-Chree*, torpedoed and sank a 5,000-ton Turkish ship in the Dardanelles. Impressed by this and later successes, Murray Sueter ordered from Sopwith the first torpedo-bomber designed specifically for operation from the deck of a carrier. Known as the Cuckoo, because it was intended to "lay its eggs in other people's nests", it was just too late to be used in action in the 1914–18 War. However, it proved the practicability of such aircraft, serving with both the British and Japanese Navies. The attacks by Fleet Air Arm Swordfish on Taranto in 1940, and by the Japanese torpedo aircraft on Pearl Harbor in the following year, showed how well the lessons it taught had been learned.

For many years, the performance of carrier-based aircraft was inferior to that of their shore-based counterparts. This was understandable, as ship-borne types needed folding wings to enable them to be stowed in below-deck hangars, arrester gear, catapult attachments, and much other special equip-

Catapult-fighter (Hawker Sea Hurricane Mk IA) used to protect merchant shipping in World War II when insufficient carriers were available. The pilot had to ditch after his sortie, the aircraft being regarded as expendable.

ment that increased both weight and drag. Also, it was felt by the 1930s that a naval pilot had enough to do without having to navigate and find his way back to a base that might have moved many miles since he left it. As a result, even fighters designed for carrier operation were often two-seaters. This changed when wartime necessity compelled the use of navalized versions of single-seat fighters like the British Hurricane and Spitfire, and today naval aircraft lack nothing in terms of overall performance. Indeed, two of the latest combat types operated by the USAF – the McDonnell F-4 Phantom II and LTV A-7 Corsair II – were developed and built originally as carrier-based aircraft.

Looking back, it is clear that almost every basic tactical and strategic application for air power had been tried out, at least experimentally, by the end of the 1914–18 War. Advances since then have been concentrated mainly on refining the weapons, in terms of both aircraft and equipment.

There may seem little similarity between the great Vulcan jet-bomber of today and the Handley Page O/400, its 1918 counterpart; but the rôle allocated to them is the same – that of destroying the enemy's ability and will to wage war. The problems confronting the pilot are also the same – to elude the defences if possible, and to find and destroy the target. If the tools at his disposal give him infinitely more destructive power than any previous military man in history, it is equally true that the weapons against which he has to contend are more deadly.

The combat aeroplane of 1918 was, generally, a biplane of wood and canvas, although some designers, such as Fokker, preferred welded steel-tube fuselages. Metal began to replace wood almost universally in military aircraft in the mid-1920s; but by then far more significant changes were on the way.

Back in December 1915, there had flown in Germany a monoplane designated officially the Junkers J.1. It was better-known at the time as the "Tin Donkey", as the entire airframe was covered with thin sheet iron. The result was such a tremendously strong structure that the wings needed no struts or bracing wires to support them; and this clean cantilever monoplane was the progenitor of a whole generation of Junkers all-metal aircraft, later machines substituting corrugated duralumin sheet for the original iron.

The metal-covered cantilever monoplane might have been accepted generally at a much earlier date if pre-1914 accidents had not made most pilots prefer a sturdily-braced biplane structure. Also, during a war when aircraft were needed in vast numbers, there was good reason to retain simple conventional wood structures that could be built by non-aviation companies, such as furniture manufacturers.

Anthony Fokker commented that the cantilever monoplane would have been adopted much sooner if aircraft designers could have seen the air flowing over their products, as a ship's architect can see the wake passing by a hull in motion. The same is true for other aids to streamlining, such as the smooth, rounded monocoque type of fuselage.

The word monocoque means "single shell" and is applied to a structure such as a fuselage in which the skin bears all the primary stresses, needing no interior supporting structure except, possibly, transverse bulkheads. If longitudinal stiffeners (longerons) are also used, as in most modern aircraft, the result is termed a "semi-monocoque".

Monocoques go back to the early days of flying, and many aircraft of 1914–18 had wooden monocoque or semi-monocoque fuselages, including Germany's Albatros fighters. However, the aeroplane that persuaded designers of the advantages to be gained by combining this form of construction with metal covering was the Silver Streak biplane, conceived by Oswald Short and exhibited at the 1920 Aero Show in London.

Short claimed that, in addition to being more durable, his aluminium construction offered a higher safety factor than wood, weight for weight, and lent itself to rapid production.

The highly specialized design requirements of shipboard aircraft do not always make for beauty of line. The prevalent "squashed grasshopper" look of carrier types when folded for stowage is evident in this World War II flight-deck scene. The aircraft in the foreground is a Fairey Barracuda. The others are, from left to right, a Vought Corsair, a Grumman Avenger and a Grumman Wildcat.

The experimental Sopwith Snark triplane of 1918 (*above*) had a wooden monocoque fuselage. The interior view shows two Vickers guns mounted to each side of the pilot's rudder-bar.

The streamlined Fairey Fox raised the speed of RAF day bombers by nearly 40 per cent (*above*).

The Short Silver Streak which pioneered aluminium monocoque construction (*above left*).

Although it remained only a "one-off" experimental design, the Silver Streak gave birth, in particular, to a new generation of smooth-hulled monocoque flying-boats, of which the first was the Short S.2 of 1924, a re-hulled Felixstowe F.5.

The clean lines of the Silver Streak were marred by the car-type radiator of its 240-hp Siddeley Puma engine. Nevertheless, it offered a thought-provoking contrast with the military aircraft of the early 1920s. Most were left-overs from 1914–18 as, having won the "war to end wars", governments were loath to spend money on new military aircraft. The RAF did succeed in getting a new day bomber, the Fairey Fawn, which was ordered into production in 1923; but it was a wood and fabric biplane and made about as much concession to streamlining as a London omnibus of the period. However, a revolution was on the way.

At that time, the world's aircraft industry was still being run by the handful of enthusiastic pioneers who founded it. Typical was C. R. (later Sir Richard) Fairey. During a visit to the USA, he was so impressed by the cleanly-cowled Curtiss D.12 water-cooled engines fitted to American military-backed racing aircraft that he obtained licence rights in the engine and designed a new day-bomber around it. The result was the Fox.

While carrying the same military load as the Fawn, this aircraft was 12 ft smaller in span, with single-bay instead of two-bay wings. It weighed 30 per cent less and, thanks largely to the streamlining made possible by its closely-cowled D.12 engine, had a top speed of 156·5 mph. The Fox, in fact, raised the speed of RAF day bombers by nearly 40 per cent in one jump.

The next stage, clearly, was for somebody to demonstrate dramatically the possibilities of combining in one design the advantages of metal semi-monocoque construction, monoplane design, and a cleanly-installed in-line engine. This R. J. Mitchell of the Supermarine company did with his series of racing seaplanes that won the coveted Schneider Trophy outright for Britain in 1927, 1929 and 1931, raising the world speed record above 400 mph for the first time in the process.

From these aircraft, Mitchell evolved in due course the famous Spitfire fighter of World War II; but the lead in switching to modern monoplane design for combat aircraft came from America in the early 1930s. First hint of the forthcoming transition was given by the Boeing YB-9, an all-metal twin-engined cantilever monoplane bomber, with a semi-retractable undercarriage and variable-pitch propellers. In terms of maximum speed and climb, it offered a 50 per cent improvement over its lumbering predecessors, the Keystone bombers, without any reduction in bomb-load.

Good as it was, the YB-9 was quickly overshadowed by the Martin B-10B, which represented the greatest single advance in bomber development since the Handley Page O/400. Its speed of 212 mph enabled it to outfly most

The last of the Fairey biplane fighters was the Fantome of 1935. It was perhaps the most beautiful of all biplane fighters, but it came too late to see service – faster monoplane fighters were already going into production.

Supermarine S.6 Schneider Trophy seaplane, forerunner of the Spitfire.

Heinkel He 178, the world's first jet aircraft, which made its maiden flight on 27 August 1939 (*above*).

Gloster/Whittle E.28/39, first British jet aircraft, flown on 15 May 1941 (*right*).

fighters of its day and it introduced refinements such as a retractable undercarriage, enclosed cockpit and internal weapon-bay. It remained only for the British Air Ministry to issue in 1936 the official specifications that led to the four-engined Halifax and Lancaster of World War II – with their power-operated gun-turrets and tremendously heavy bomb-load – to bring the piston-engined heavy bomber to the ultimate peak of its development.

The dive-bomber also attained its maximum effectiveness in World War II. Main proponent of this form of attack throughout the 1920s and 1930s had been the US Navy. The Japanese Navy took note, and the dive-bomber was one of the primary weapons used for the devastating attack on Pearl Harbor that brought America into World War II. This initial success rebounded against the Japanese, whose naval power was smashed subsequently by American carrier-based dive-bombers and torpedo-bombers.

Germany's Luftwaffe also had an early success with its Junkers Ju 87 dive-bombers, which cleared a path through Poland and Western Europe for Hitler's armies in 1939–40. However, the RAF exposed the *Stuka's* shortcomings, and the Ju 87's reign of terror was shortlived.

Over land, the dive-bomber's place was taken largely by the fighter-bomber as World War II progressed. The first major advance in fighter armament had come in 1935, when the Hawker Hurricane introduced the then-unrivalled fire-power of eight machine-guns, mounted in the wings, outside the propeller disc, so that no interrupter gear was needed. By 1940, the Hurricane offered an even-heavier alternative armament of four 20-mm cannon. Later, this one-time interceptor – and, as such, with the Spitfire, victor in the Battle of Britain – began destroying tanks with two 40-mm guns carried under its wings. It also added bombs and air-to-surface rockets to its armament, although the aircraft which proved beyond a shadow of doubt the full capability of the rocket for ground-attack duties were the Russian Ilyushin Il-2 Shturmovik and the RAF's Hawker Typhoon.

Height remained one of the keys to success in action, and America, in particular, supplemented normal engine supercharging with the increased effectiveness of turbo-supercharging on combat types such as the P-47 Thunderbolt fighter and B-17 Fortress bomber. The engine designers, in fact, contributed immensely to rapid aircraft development in World War II and, towards the end of the struggle, introduced into combat service the most significant advance since the first flights of the Wright brothers in 1903 – jet-propulsion.

Sir Frank Whittle was the first to run a jet-engine successfully, in Britain, on 12 April 1937. The German Heinkel He 178 research aircraft was the first jet-propelled aeroplane to fly, on 27 August 1939; but – thanks to the loss of several months while the Messerschmitt Me 262 was converted for fighter-bomber duties, on Hitler's personal orders – the first jet-fighter used in action, on 27 July 1944, was the British Gloster Meteor.

The jet-engine, allied to the results of German wartime research into the advantages of wing sweep-back, revolutionized the design of military aircraft. To take advantage of its tremendous power, wings became not only swept or of delta shape, but of thin section and, sometimes, so strong structurally that they were almost machined from solid metal. Even a variable-geometry "swing-wing" has been adopted for several of the latest aircraft, such as the General Dynamics F-111, to combine the advantages of sweep-back at high speeds with the better low-speed characteristics of a "straight" wing.

Nor are innovations like swing-wings the only changes that have made the modern combat aircraft one of the most complex and costly pieces of engineering in history.

Radar helped the RAF to win the Battle of Britain by allowing a few aircraft to do the work of many. Standing patrols of fighters became unnecessary when the invisible eyes of radar could detect and locate incoming raiders and guide the interceptors into the best position to attack them. By 1942, radar was also giving new accuracy to the RAF's night bombing, by making possible navigational aids of unprecedented accuracy.

And, of course, in 1945 the atomic bomb offered a weapon of such terrifying power that the large bombing formations of World War II became redundant overnight. Today, a single jet-bomber, armed with a nuclear weapon, guided by its own radar, and protected by electronic countermeasures equipment that could play havoc with enemy radar defences, has the destructive power of all the piston-engined bombers ever built. Nor is its range limited any longer, for Britain perfected the technique of air-to-air refuelling from "flying tankers" soon after World War II and this has become a day-to-day routine.

Modern fighters also use flight refuelling, and radar to track down their enemy. Indeed, the pilot of an all-weather interceptor, having taken off, can virtually sit back and let the aircraft find its own way to the target, under the automatic control of radar on the ground and in its nose. The nose radar, working through a fire-control system, will fire the aircraft's weapons automatically at the best moment to ensure a kill, and then turn the aircraft away to avoid the possibility of flying through the debris.

The weapons also have changed, with guided missiles supplementing, but not necessarily replacing, heavy-calibre guns, which remain the most effective armament under some circumstances.

The advent of jet propulsion seemed to promise a rebirth of the flying-boat, as it dispensed with the problem of keeping propellers clear of spray during take-off and landing. The Saunders-Roe SR/A1 (*above*) of 1947 had a top speed of 512 mph and could have made RAF Fighter Command independent of vulnerable runways ashore. However, only three were built.

Massed bombing raid by Boeing B-29 Superfortresses (*below*). Large formations of this sort, typical of World War II, were made virtually obsolete by the atom bomb.

Today the destructive power of World War II formations like that shown on page 38, can be exceeded by a single nuclear-armed jet-bomber, such as the Buccaneer (*above*), shown demonstrating LABS bombing. This technique enables an aircraft to beat a hasty retreat after releasing a nuclear weapon at low level.

BAC Lightning F.Mk 6 fighter refuelling in flight from a Handley Page Victor tanker (*above right*).

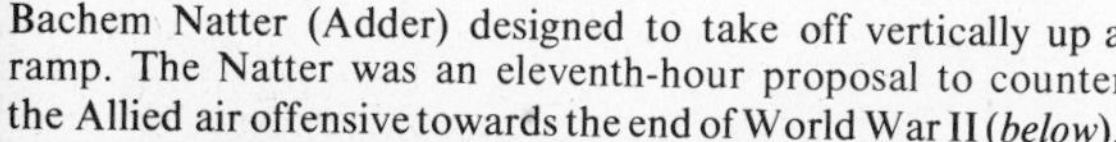

Bachem Natter (Adder) designed to take off vertically up a ramp. The Natter was an eleventh-hour proposal to counter the Allied air offensive towards the end of World War II (*below*).

At one stage, it seemed that the combination of advanced electronics and guided missiles might make the manned combat aircraft redundant; but experience has shown that the human brain is less susceptible to jamming than an electronic control system. Similarly, shells from an "old-fashioned" cannon travel much straighter than certain infra-red homing missiles which may "chase" the sun or reflections from water in preference to the hot exhaust of the enemy aircraft that is their intended target.

In an age of anti-missile missiles, even the once-almighty intercontinental ballistic missile with its nuclear warhead no longer appears to be the complete replacement for bomber aircraft. However, bombers themselves utilize rocket-propelled air-to-surface stand-off missiles which can be launched hundreds of miles from the target, to avoid the need to penetrate the enemy's inner defence rings of missiles, guns and interceptors.

The result of all these technical advances has been the emergence of larger, more complex fighters and smaller, more compact bombers – to the extent that a single basic airframe, such as that of the F-111, sometimes offers the possibility of being adapted for interception, ground attack, bombing and reconnaissance duties – at an incredible price in terms of initial and operating costs.

Paradoxically, such aircraft are too fast, too powerful, too complex and too costly to wage the kind of local, limited wars that seem to be an inescapable part of our modern life. As a result, old piston-engined aircraft like the North American T-28 trainer, and economical, comparatively slow turboprop types like the same manufacturer's OV-10A, have been evolved for what are termed "counter-insurgency" duties.

Even the once-harmless helicopter has come into its own, not only for delivering troops and supplies on the battlefield, but for keeping down the heads of enemy troops with rockets, missiles and guns while doing so. At sea, helicopters have also replaced almost completely the fixed-wing aircraft used formerly for anti-submarine duties. Their ability to hover while "listening" for submerged submarines with their dipping sonar and other devices more than offsets lower performance. And, of course, they can be carried by ships as small as frigates – a development that threatens the eventual extinction of the aircraft carrier.

Vertical take-off and landing (VTOL), as pioneered by the helicopter, was once considered to hold the key to the future for all forms of combat aircraft, by eliminating the need for vulnerable prepared airfields. The Germans were the first to test the possibility in a practical way with their wartime Natter interceptor, which was designed to be shot into the air vertically, up a ramp.

Even more desperate than the German Natter (see page 39) were the Japanese "Kamikaze" aircraft. The type illustrated was specially designed for such suicide attacks. It carried a 2,000-lb warhead just aft of the engine. The landing gear was jettisoned after take-off (*left*).

Among the surprises at the air display put on to celebrate the 50th anniversary of the Soviet Revolution, in July 1967, were two examples of this VTOL fighter (*below left*), attributed to Yakovlev and code-named "Freehand" by NATO. Although far less refined than the British Harrier, these aircraft performed faultless transitions from vertical to horizontal flight and one was shown with underwing rocket pods.

Three different Soviet STOL aircraft, which reflect the traditional Soviet emphasis on tactical close-support, were demonstrated in July 1967. All had vertically-mounted jet-lift engines supplementing normal power plants. This Mikoyan design (NATO code-name "Faithless") is a single-engined, single-seat fighter with a fuselage and tail-unit similar to those of the MiG "swing-wing" fighter unveiled at the same time.

Many other schemes were tested in the 1940s, 1950s and early 1960s; but only one man, Hawker's great chief designer, the late Sir Sydney Camm, has yet succeeded in combining VTOL capability satisfactorily with fighter performance in his superb Harrier reconnaissance and strike aircraft. This interesting machine points the way to the future; but there are still some who feel that the price paid for VTOL in terms of reduced weapon load is not worthwhile, and prefer short take-off and landing (STOL) performance, in the order of 500-yd runs, which impose less of a limitation on payload.

The ideal military aircraft of today is, therefore, a VTOL or STOL type, able to fly at supersonic speed, under virtual automatic control, less than 500 ft above the ground, so that it can sneak in "beneath the radar" of an enemy, carrying nuclear weapons and reconnaissance equipment. Britain had such an aircraft in the TSR.2 tactical strike and reconnaissance aircraft, which flew for the first time on 27 September 1964. As a matter of political expediency it later abandoned further work on the aircraft, in the belief that the cost was too high. One can only wonder whether any price is too high to pay for a type of weapon that has either made a third world war impossible or will one day erase from the map whole nations, and every living thing in them.

Perhaps the most promising tactical combat aircraft yet built, the BAC TSR.2 was developed for the RAF as a Mach 2 strike and reconnaissance bomber able to penetrate virtually any enemy defence system.

Combat Aircraft of the World

Ae.M.B. 1

Ae.M.B. 2

I.Ae.24 Calquin

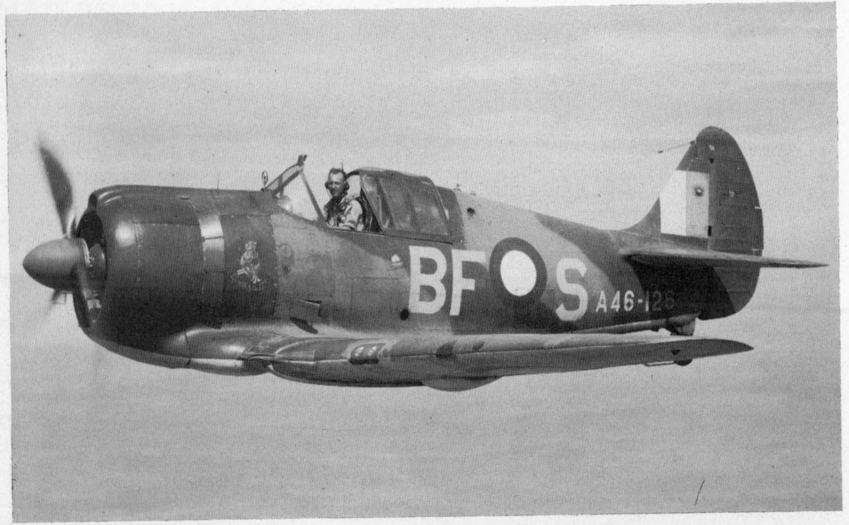

CAC CA-13 Boomerang

Argentine Republic

Ae.M.B.2

Argentina's national aviation industry dates from 10 October 1927, when the Fábrica Militar de Aviones (Military Aircraft Factory) was established at Cordoba. Initially, aircraft of British and French design were built under licence. The first nationally-designed types to enter production were light touring and training monoplanes and a transport for five passengers. They were followed by a prototype light bomber, designated Ae.M.B.1, which flew for the first time on 9 October 1935.

The production version of this bomber retained the 715-hp Wright Cyclone SGR-1820F.3 nine-cylinder radial engine of the prototype but had an extensively modified airframe and was redesignated Ae.M.B.2. It was a conventional cantilever low-wing monoplane with a non-retractable undercarriage, the main legs and wheels being enclosed in large "trouser" fairings.

In its standard form, the Ae.M.B.2 carried 880 lb of bombs and was armed with four machine-guns. A single 7·65-mm Madsen gun was fixed to fire forward through the engine cowling. Two similar guns were mounted in a manually-operated domed turret above the fuselage aft of the flight deck, and an 11·35-mm gun could be fired from a ventral hatch. Operational equipment included a Nistri camera and Telefunken radio.

Fifteen Ae.M.B.2s were built, of which at least one (0-203) had no dorsal turret and was intended for observation duties. Production was completed in 1936.

I.Ae.24 Calquin

The prototype of the I.Ae.24 Calquin (Royal Eagle) two-seat tactical bomber flew for the first time in June 1946. Although developed and built at the Instituto Aerotecnico (formerly Fábrica Militar de Aviones) as an original design, it was clearly based on the wartime de Havilland Mosquito. Construction, as in the British aircraft, was of wood. Externally-apparent differences included a fin and rudder of revised shape and the use of radial engines in place of the Merlin Vee engines of the Mosquito.

It had been intended originally to fit Merlins in the Calquin, but none were available and the 100 production models each had a pair of 1,050-hp Pratt & Whitney R-1830-SC-G Twin Wasp 14-cylinder air-cooled radials. The first aircraft flew on 4 July 1947, and the last was delivered in 1950. Calquins remained in first-line service until about 1960.

Maximum bomb-load was 1,650 lb, carried internally. Four 12·7-mm machine-guns were mounted in the nose, under the bomb-aimer's position, and light attack weapons, including 75-mm air-to-surface rockets, could be carried under the wings. The maximum speed of 273 mph might have been improved by nearly 50 per cent had it been possible to fit Merlin engines.

Australia

CAC Boomerang

When the Japanese attacked Pearl Harbor on 7 December 1941, extending World War II to the Pacific, the Royal Australian Air Force had only two fighter squadrons, equipped with American-built Buffalos. These were in Malaya and there was little hope of obtaining reinforcements from the United Kingdom or United States at that time; so it was decided to develop a stop-gap single-seat fighter in Australia.

A contract for the new aircraft was awarded to Commonwealth Aircraft Corporation, who were then

producing a general-purpose and training aircraft named the Wirraway, developed from the North American NA-33. To ensure early delivery of the fighter, it was designed to incorporate many Wirraway components, including the basic centre-section, tail unit and undercarriage.

Designated CA-12 Boomerang the prototype (A46-1) flew on 29 May 1942, only 14 weeks after its design had been approved. Production began at once and 250 Boomerangs were eventually completed, made up of 105 CA-12s, 95 CA-13s, one CA-14 and 49 CA-19s.

They served mainly in New Guinea, as interceptors, in ground attack and photo-reconnaissance roles in support of Australian Army units, and as target markers for bomber formations. Their performance was limited and they had to rely on their manoeuvrability to keep them out of trouble in combat with Japanese fighters, but this did not prevent their becoming successful and popular with their pilots.

The Boomerang was designed around the 1,200 hp Pratt & Whitney R-1830-S3C4G Twin Wasp 14-cylinder radial, which was the most powerful engine then available in Australia. Construction was conventional, with single-spar stressed-skin wings, welded steel-tube fuselage, retractable main undercarriage and fixed tail-wheel. Armament consisted of two 20-mm Hispano cannon and four 0·303-in Browning machine-guns in the wings.

There were only minor differences between the various models, except in the case of the CA-14. This was taken from the Boomerang production line and fitted with a General Electric turbosupercharger in an attempt to improve performance, particularly at height. Further changes were made, including the addition of sliding gills and an engine-cooling fan. The intercooler air scoop on the port side was deleted, the air being directed instead from the engine bay. In its final form, as the CA-14A, this aircraft also had a new square-cut fin and rudder.

CAC CA-27 Avon-Sabre

When the time came to plan a replacement for the Gloster Meteor fighters of the RAAF in 1950, the Hawker P.1081 – a sweptwing development of the Sea Hawk – seemed the most suitable type available. For various reasons, the North American F-86 Sabre was chosen instead for production under licence in Australia by Commonwealth Aircraft Corporation.

The air fighting in Korea confirmed the superiority of the USAF-operated Sabre over the contemporary Soviet-built MiG-15, but the RAAF had to ensure, for economic reasons, that its new equipment would remain effective until well into the 1960s. The decision was taken therefore to fit a 7,500-lb st Rolls-Royce Avon RA.7 turbojet engine in place of the standard 6,100-lb s t General Electric J-47.

Installation of the Avon was not easy. It required about 25 per cent more airflow than the J-47 and this entailed deepening the nose air intake by 3½ inches. Despite the Avon's higher power, it was some 400 lb lighter than the J-47; consequently, it had to be mounted further aft in the fuselage to maintain the centre of gravity in the correct position and this entailed repositioning the "break" point at which the rear fuselage was removed for engine servicing.

Thus, although 100 sets of F-86F major structural components were ordered from the United States to speed production, CAC eventually had to redesign approximately 60 per cent of the airframe. Fuel capacity was increased, the cockpit layout revised and a considerably heavier armament installed. The original

CAC CA-14 Boomerang

CAC CA-14A Boomerang

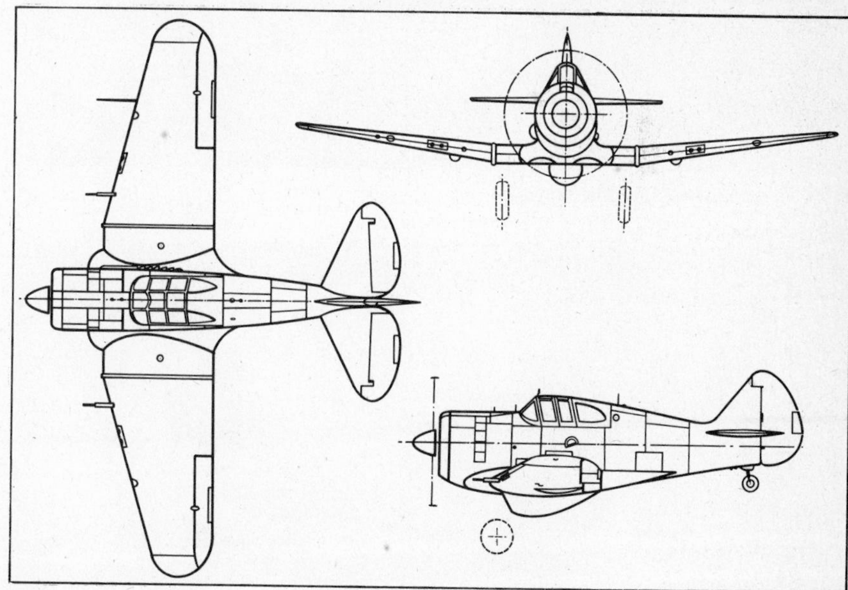

CAC CA-12 Boomerang

TYPE	DIMENSIONS span ft	span in	length ft	length in	height ft	height in	WEIGHT max t-o lb	PERFORMANCE max speed mph	at height ft	service ceiling ft	combat range miles	REMARKS
Ae. M.B.2	56	5¼	35	9¼	9	2¼	7,715	177	6,900	19,700	370	In service until 1945
I. Ae. 24	53	5¾	39	4½	11	4¼	15,875	273	SL	32,800	745	Designed by Brig San Martin
CA-12	36	3	25	6	11	6	7,600	296	7,600	29,000	930	Developed from Wirraway

CAC CA-27 Avon-Sabre Mk 30

CAC CA-27 Avon-Sabre Mk 32

Government Factories/Avro Lincoln B Mk 30

intention was to fit the then standard British armament of four 20-mm cannon, but all Avon-Sabres were delivered with two 30-mm Adens. Thus the Avon-Sabre became by far the most potent member of the Sabre family.

A94-101, the prototype CA-26 Avon-Sabre, flew for the first time on 3 August 1953. It was powered by an imported Rolls-Royce Avon, as was the first production CA-27 Avon-Sabre (A94-901), which followed on 13 July 1954. All subsequent Avon-Sabres had engines built under licence by Commonwealth Aircraft Corporation.

The initial series of 22 production aircraft (A94-901/922) had Avon Mk 20 engines, assembled from imported components, and standard F-86F wings, and were designated Avon-Sabre Mk 30. After service trials, deliveries to No. 3 Squadron began in March 1956.

The wings were fitted with leading-edge slats. These ensured good handling qualities at low speeds, but created considerable drag in high-speed flight. From the summer of 1952, the USAF had begun to modify its F-86Fs in Korea, by replacing the slats with an extended leading-edge. This gave a 7-mph increase in top speed, and improved manoeuvrability at high altitudes. In particular, it removed one of the advantages of the MiG-15, which had proved itself able to make tighter turns than the F-86F.

The next 20 Avon-Sabres (A94-923/942) were, therefore, fitted with this extended leading-edge, which contained additional fuel cells with a total capacity of 70 gallons. They could also carry a drop tank of 100 or 166 gallons capacity under each wing, or bombs totalling 2,000 lb, or sixteen 5-in rockets. These aircraft were designated Mk 31 and the earlier Mk 30 machines were modified to the same standard.

Final version of the Avon-Sabre was the Mk 32, of which 69 were built (A94-943/990 and A94-351/371). These had underwing attachments for either four 100-gallon or two 166- and two 100-gallon drop tanks. The bomb load was unchanged, but twenty-four 3-in rockets could be carried. The armament was further supplemented by Sidewinder air-to-air missiles during 1960. Later production Mk 32 aircraft were equipped to carry these weapons from the start; all earlier Avon-Sabres were modified to have both the Sidewinders and the increased rocket capacity. Another retrospective modification was to equip all aircraft with the Avon Mk 26 engine, which had first been fitted to A94-973.

First Avon-Sabre unit to go into action was No. 3 Squadron which began its transfer to Butterworth in October 1958 for combat operations against terrorists in Malaya. It was joined subsequently by another RAAF Avon-Sabre unit, No. 77 Squadron, and both were still in Malaysia at the beginning of 1967 as part of the British Commonwealth Strategic Reserve in the Far East. Nos. 75 and 76 Avon-Sabre Squadrons remained in Australia. A fifth Squadron, No. 79, was formed in May 1962 to strengthen SEATO forces in Thailand.

Government Factories/Avro Lincoln Mk 30

Although the Australian War Cabinet had planned initially to build the Avro Lancaster bomber for the RAAF in the Government Factories at Fishermen's Bend, Melbourne, it was the more advanced Lincoln that eventually went into production there. Manufacturing drawings began to arrive from England in April 1944. Less than two years later, on 17 March 1946, the first Australian-built Lincoln B Mk 30 made its first flight. The war was over by then, but it was decided to continue the production programme and 73 of the bombers were completed during the next seven years.

The first five were assembled partially from components built in the United Kingdom; later aircraft were manufactured almost entirely in Australia. The first 50 airframes were fitted with Rolls-Royce Merlin 85B engines, but these later gave place to 1,750-hp Merlin 102s built in the Government Engine Factory in New South Wales.

Lincoln-B Mk 30 bombers served with No. 1 Squadron, RAAF, in Malaya for eight years during the operations against Communist guerrillas. During this time, the Squadron dropped 85 per cent of all the bombs released on to the Malayan jungles – a total of 33,000,000 lb.

On its return to Australia, its Lincolns were replaced by Canberras, which already equipped the RAAF's other two bomber squadrons.

This was not the end of the Lincoln's operational life with the RAAF. Some had been rebuilt with a 6-ft-longer nose, housing two extra crew members and specialized equipment to make them suitable for long-range over-water reconnaissance and anti-submarine duties. Redesignated MR.Mk 30, they served with No. 10 (maritime reconnaissance) Squadron until 1962.

Details of the UK-built Avro Lincoln are on p. 315.

Austria

Austrian-Aviatik D.I

This fighter was built in greater numbers than any other Austro-Hungarian single-seater of the 1914–18 War. The company responsible for it, Oesterreichische-Ungarische Flugzeugfabrik Aviatik, was an offshoot of the German Automobil & Aviatik AG. By 1916, the types B.II and B.III two-seat reconnaissance aircraft built by this company had been relegated to training duties; so its chief designer, Julius von Berg, set to work on a replacement known as the Austrian-Aviatik C.I and a single-seat counterpart which became the D.I or "Berg Scout".

Construction was conventional. The D.I had a wooden wing structure with a wire trailing-edge which produced the familiar scalloped plan-form when covered with fabric. Centre-section and interplane struts were of steel tube. Ailerons were fitted only to the upper wing and had considerable wash-out.

The fuselage consisted of a plywood skin over a light wooden framework, with no internal wire bracing. It was unusually deep and the pilot sat high up, with his eyes just below the level of the upper wing. The tail unit was a steel-tube structure, covered with fabric. The undercarriage was carried on simple steel-tube Vees.

Unfortunately, the wings were of such thin section that they sometimes twisted and broke up under normal flying conditions. This was remedied eventually, but most leading Austrian fighter pilots seem to have preferred the contemporary Hansa-Brandenburg D.I "starstrutter" and locally-built Albatros D.III.

Eleven batches of D.Is were built for the Austro-Hungarian Flying Service and it is easy to identify the production series to which a particular machine belonged, thanks to the system of serial numbers used by this Service. Each manufacturer was allocated a code number between 1 and 9, Aviatik's number being 3. This was followed by a number indicating the aircraft type and then, after a stop, by two or three other numbers. Thus, the aircraft illustrated – 38·63 – was the 63rd D.I (type 8) built by Aviatik (code number 3).

D.Is of the 38 series had a 185-hp Austro-Daimler six-cylinder in-line water-cooled engine and were fitted initially with a small radiator on each side of the engine cowling. The need for more efficient cooling led to the introduction of a car-type radiator on later machines, including 38·63. The standard armament at

Government Factories/Avro Lincoln MR.Mk 30

Austrian-Aviatik D.I Series 38

TYPE	DIMENSIONS span ft	in	length ft	in	height ft	in	WEIGHT max t-o lb	PERFORMANCE max speed mph	at height ft	service ceiling ft	combat range miles	REMARKS
Avon-Sabre CA-27 Mk 32	37	1	37	6	14	5	21,000	700	SL	55,000	1,500	Licence F-86F with Avon
GAF Lincoln Mk 30	120	0	84	3	17	10	78,000	310	SL	27,500	2,930	Long-nose version produced only in Australia
Aviatik D.I (185-hp)	26	3	22	7	8	3	1,815	113	SL	20,000	NA	Series 38
Aviatik D.I (200-hp)	26	3	22	7	8	3	1,945	115	SL	20,400	NA	Series 84, 92, 101, 115, 138, 184
Aviatik D.I (225-hp)	26	3	22	7	8	3	1,906	115.5	SL	20,000	NA	Series 284, 338, 384

Austrian-Aviatik D.I Series 138, with Jaray propeller

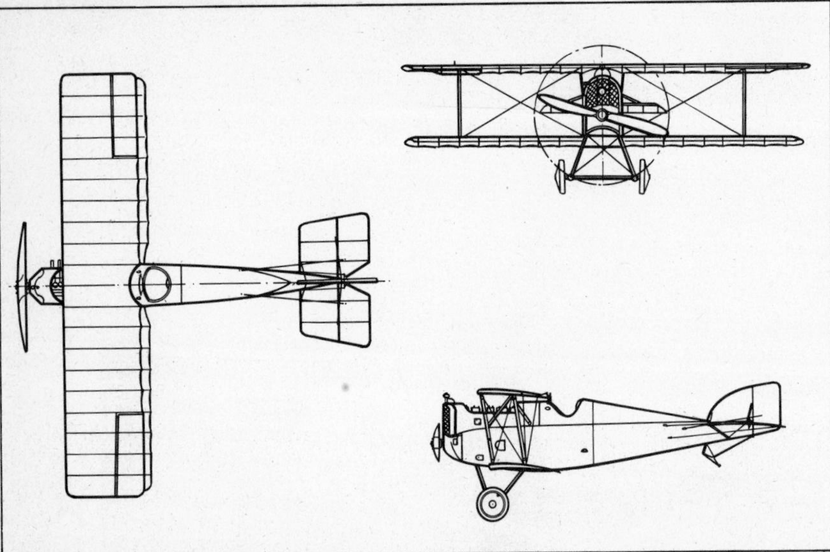

Austrian-Aviatik D.I

Hansa-Brandenburg D.I

this period was a single Schwarzlose machine-gun, mounted forward of the cockpit in such a way that it could be fired above the propeller disc. Later, twin machine-guns, with interrupter gear, became standard.

When the 200-hp Austro-Daimler became available, a second series of D.Is was ordered from Aviatik and these can be identified by serial numbers beginning with "138". Then came the 238 series with 210-hp Austro-Daimler and 338 series with 225-hp Austro-Daimler. The 84 and 184 series were built by Vienna Carriage and Aeroplane Works (WKF) with 200-hp Austro-Daimler, followed by the 284 and 384 series with 225-hp engine. The 92 series was manufactured by Hungarian Engineering Factory, the 101 series by Thöne and Fiala, and the 115 series by Jakob Lohner and Sons, all with 200-hp engines. Most D.Is had two-blade wooden propellers, but a few had Jaray four-bladers with the blades set at 70°/110° to each other.

Some aircraft reverted to side radiators, which improved performance and forward view at the risk of overheating. A final and better solution, on the 338 series, was a box-type radiator mounted on the centre-section leading-edge of the top wing.

Nobody would call any of the D.Is beautiful, but they were surprisingly efficient and could hold their own against most contemporary Italian fighters.

Hansa-Brandenburg D.I

Because of the unique arrangement of its interplane struts, this little aircraft is remembered usually as the "starstrutter". Poor lateral control earned it the grimmer name of "*Sarg*" (coffin) from pilots when it first entered service in the autumn of 1916; but it remained the standard single-seat fighter of the Austro-Hungarian Flying Service until mid-1917 and achieved notable successes in action.

The prototype, known as the KD *Kampfdoppeldecker* (fighter biplane), was designed by Ernst Heinkel and built in Germany by the Hansa und Brandenburgische Flugzeugwerke early in 1916. The owner of this company was an Austrian, Camillo Castiglione, which explains how several Hansa-Brandenburg types, including the KD, came to be licence-built in Austria-Hungary.

Production KDs were given the military designation D.I. They were built by Phönix (Series 28) with a 160-hp Austro-Daimler engine and by Ufag (Series 65) with a 185-hp Austro-Daimler. The design was improved by these companies. In particular, the original tiny triangular fin and inadequate-looking rudder were replaced by a scalloped rudder and a deep top decking on the rear fuselage which ended in a knife-edge at the rear to compensate for lack of a fin. As this still proved inadequate, late production Phönix-built D.Is reintroduced a fixed fin.

Except for the eight-strut interplane bracing "stars", of steel tube with laminated wood fairings, and consequent absence of bracing wires, construction of the D.I was orthodox. The wings were of wood with fabric covering; the fuselage of wood with plywood covering, except for the metal engine cowling. Fore and aft vision from the cockpit was better than it appears in photographs, as the front decking and cowling followed the shape of the pilot's head and the rear decking formed an inverted Vee.

Most production D.Is had their radiator above the top wing, to starboard of the centre-line. However, late production models by Ufag had a car-type radiator and it is probable that these were powered by a Hiero engine as their exhaust stubs discharged to port, whereas earlier D.Is with Austro-Daimler engines had an exhaust manifold on the starboard side of the engine cowling.

Standard armament on all Hansa-Brandenburg D.Is was a single Schwarzlose machine-gun mounted above the upper wing inside a light casing. An obvious disadvantage of this was that the pilot could not reach the gun to clear stoppages in flight.

Phönix D.I, D.II and D.III

By early 1917 it was clear that the Hansa-Brandenburg "starstrutter" had reached the limit of its development and could not take a more powerful engine; so the Phönix company built the prototype of a new single-seat fighter identified by the serial number 20·15. This aircraft differed from late production models of its predecessor mainly in having conventional wooden interplane struts, with wire bracing, and a 200-hp Austro-Daimler engine. The remainder of the airframe consisted largely of "starstrutter" components, with a single Schwarzlose gun and the radiator mounted above the square-tipped upper wing in the usual way.

A second prototype (20·16) followed later in 1917 and introduced several important design changes. In particular, it had wings of greater span, with rounded tips, and a box-type radiator mounted centrally on the leading-edge of the upper wing. From it was evolved the production Phönix D.I, powered by a 200-hp Hiero six-cylinder in-line water-cooled engine and armed with a pair of Schwarzlose guns, synchronized to fire forward through the propeller disc. Three batches of D.Is were built, with serial numbers beginning 128, 228 and 328. Then came three batches of D.IIs (122, 222 and 322 series) which differed only in having balanced elevators.

Both the D.I and D.II were operated extensively by the Austro-Hungarian Flying Service in 1918, proving useful despite a rather poor rate of climb and excessive stability. A few were fitted with cameras for pioneer high-speed single-seat photographic-reconnaissance duties, while a variant, the J series, was flown by land-based naval fighter units.

Just before the Armistice, the naval units began to re-equip with the improved Phönix D.III, with 230-hp Hiero engine and ailerons on both upper and lower wings.

Seventeen of the Series 122 D.IIs were completed as D.IIIs and found their way to the Swedish Army Air Service after the war. They were given the designation J1, indicating that they were the first genuine fighters operated by that service, and were supplemented by ten similar aircraft built in Sweden with 185-hp BMW engines.

Belgium

Avions Fairey Firefly

The story of how Sir Richard Fairey changed the whole pattern of British bomber development, by introducing the licence-built Curtiss D.12 (Fairey Felix) water-cooled Vee engine in the Fox Mk I, is told on page 353. Simultaneously, Fairey built as a private venture a prototype Felix-engined single-seat fighter named the Firefly I, which flew for the first time on 12 November 1925. Its maximum speed of 188 mph was more than 30 mph higher than that of contemporary RAF fighters, but it did not go into production.

Soon afterwards, the RAF began the changeover from wooden to metal construction. So when the Fairey company decided to build an improved Firefly, to take part in an Air Ministry competition for a new interceptor fighter in 1929, it switched to an all-metal structure. The new prototype was designated Firefly IIM (M for metal) and was very different from its predecessor. Its wings were

Phönix D.III (Swedish J1)

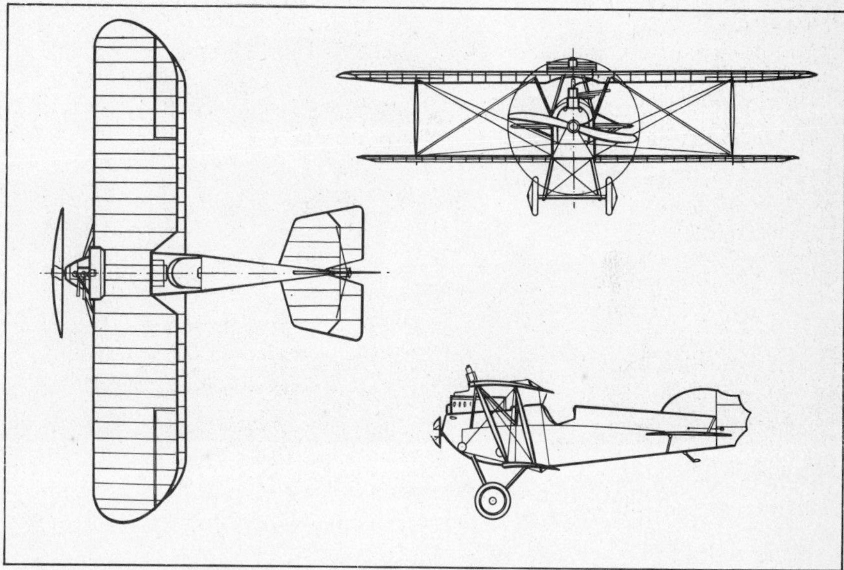
Phönix D.III

Fairey Firefly I prototype

TYPE	DIMENSIONS span ft	span in	length ft	length in	height ft	height in	WEIGHT max t-o lb	PERFORMANCE max speed mph	at height ft	service ceiling ft	combat range miles	REMARKS
Hansa-Brandenburg D.I (160-hp)	27	11	20	10	9	2	2,024	116.5	SL	NA	NA	Series 28
Hansa-Brandenburg D.I (185-hp)	27	11	20	10	9	2	2,046	NA		NA	NA	Series 65
Phönix D.I/D.II	32	2	21	9	9	2	1,771	112.5	SL	NA	NA	D.II with balanced elevators
Phönix D.III	32	2	21	9	9	5	1,831	125	SL	NA	NA	158 built
Avions Fairey Firefly IIM	32	0	24	6	8	8	3,404	223	13,000	NA	NA	First five built in UK

Avions Fairey Firefly IIM

Avions Fairey Firefly IIM

Avions Fairey Fox IIM

Avions Fairey Fox VI

heavily staggered, and as flight testing progressed refinements were made to almost every feature of the design. The interplane struts and undercarriage became less clumsy, the tail fin and rudder more streamlined, and the original interconnected retractable radiator and wing radiators gave way to a fixed underslung radiator. Most important of all, the IIM switched to the new and more powerful (480-hp compared with 430-hp) Rolls-Royce Kestrel IIS supercharged 12-cylinder Vee engine. The result was a highly attractive little fighter with a top speed of 217 mph at 13,000 ft and 193 mph at 26,300 ft.

As a result of the Air Ministry competition, the Hawker Fury was chosen to re-equip RAF fighter squadrons; but the Firefly attracted so much foreign interest that Fairey decided to take part in another contest for single-seat fighters which was then under way in Belgium. Everyone had expected the Czechoslovak Avia to win until the Firefly arrived, in the capable hands of Flight Lieutenant Chris Staniland, after which there was little doubt that the British aircraft was outstanding in terms of speed, climb and manoeuvrability.

To prove that this was no mere reflection of Staniland's brilliant flying, 16 Belgian pilots tested the Firefly. Finally, the Belgian authorities demanded that each of the more promising fighters entered for their competition should be dived at the maximum speed it was capable of attaining (terminal velocity) and pulled out safely under control to demonstrate its strength. Only Staniland felt confident enough to undertake the test, with complete success. His reward was an initial contract for 45 Fireflies for the Belgian Aéronautique Militaire.

A requirement of the contract was that the majority of the work should be done in Belgium. So, only the first five production Firefly IIMs were built in England. The remainder were manufactured by the Société Anonyme Belge Avions Fairey, a company registered on 12 September 1931, with a newly-built factory at Gosselies, near Charleroi. Altogether, 60 Firefly IIMs were delivered from this factory in 1932–33. One experimental model had redesigned wings and tail; the remainder differed little from the prototype and carried the then-standard armament of two Vickers machine-guns, mounted in each side of the fuselage forward of the cockpit.

The pilot still sat in the open at this time, but the interior of the cockpit was heated by hot air from the radiator and *Flight* magazine commented that "a pilot could use his bare hands for writing at 21,000 ft with an outside temperature of $-34°C$." In the official Belgian acceptance tests, a maximum speed of 223 mph was recorded at 13,120 ft and the aircraft climbed to 19,680 ft in 10 min 55 sec.

One further version of the Firefly biplane was built by the parent company in Britain. Designated Mk IIIM (Serial number S1592), it was a single-seat naval fighter built to participate in a competition to re-equip British carrier-based units. Compared with the IIM, it had wings of greater area, a strengthened fuselage for catapulting, more comprehensive equipment, provision for fitting floats, and racks for 20-lb bombs. The trials were won by the Hawker Nimrod and the Firefly IIIM prototype achieved its greatest success as a floatplane "hack" for the RAF pilots who took part in the 1931 Schneider Trophy contest.

Avions Fairey Fox

Details of the development of the Fox I and IA two-seat day bombers are given on page 353. The later all-metal Fox IIM was manufactured under licence by Avions Fairey in Belgium, first deliveries being made to the Belgian Aéronautique Militaire in 1933.

By this time the basic design was nine years old, but constant refinement had maintained the Fox's fighting efficiency and Avions Fairey decided to adapt the airframe to take the 860-hp Hispano-Suiza 12 Ydrs 12-cylinder Vee water-cooled engine. This 80 per cent increase in power, plus the streamlining effect of the newly-introduced cockpit canopy and wheel fairings, increased the maximum speed to well over 220 mph, making the aircraft suitable for fighter-reconnaissance duties. It took off in only 60 yards and could climb to 20,000 ft in 8½ minutes.

A total of 94 were built for the Aéronautique Militaire under the designation Fox VI, with an armament of two machine-guns, mounted in each side of the forward fuselage.

By the time Fox production ended in 1939, a total of 178 had been built by Avions Fairey. This included two examples of a special single-seat fighter development of the Mk VI, known as the Mk VII Mono Fox or Kangourou. The latter name resulted from the marsupial appearance of the aircraft, which had a large ventral radiator well back on the fuselage. It carried two machine-guns in the fuselage and four in the upper wings.

Bulgaria

DAR-10F

The only combat aircraft of Bulgarian design known to have entered squadron service was the DAR-10F bomber of World War II. It was a conventional low-wing monoplane, with two seats in tandem under a long cockpit "glasshouse" and a non-retractable tailwheel-type undercarriage with spatted main wheels. The power plant was an 840/960-hp Fiat A.74 R.C. 38 fourteen-cylinder two-row air-cooled radial engine.

The prototype DAR-10 was designed by Eng. Cwietan Lazerow in 1939 as a multi-purpose military aircraft and was built by the Darjavna Aeroplanna Rabotilnitza at Bojourishte Aerodrome, Sofia. It flew in 1941 and a modified version, designated DAR-10F, was put into production for light bombing and dive-bombing duties with the Bulgarian Air Force. Normal warload comprised one 550-lb and four 110-lb bombs or a single 1,100-lb bomb. In addition, two forward-firing 7·9-mm MG17 machine-guns were mounted in the fuselage, two 20-mm FF cannon in the wings and one 7·9-mm MG 15 machine-gun on a flexible mounting in the rear cockpit.

Hitherto unpublished data for the DAR-10F include an empty equipped weight of 4,475 lb, normal loaded weight of 6,395 lb, economical cruising speed of 227 mph, climb to 9,850 ft in 5-6·7 min and to 16,400 ft in 8·5-11·5 min, and landing speed of 62-68 mph. Other information is given in the table.

Canada

Avro CF-100

The Avro CF-100 – Canada's first jet fighter, the first fighter of any kind designed, built and powered solely by Canadian effort, and the world's first straight-winged combat aircraft to exceed Mach 1 (on 18 December 1952, in a dive) – gave long and useful service to the RCAF, both in Canada and in Europe, and to the Belgian Air Force.

Design of the two-seat CF-100 was begun in October 1946, to a Royal Canadian Air Force specification, and

Avions Fairey Mk VII Mono Fox (Kangourou)

DAR-10F

Avro CF-100 Mk 4

TYPE	DIMENSIONS span ft	span in	length ft	length in	height ft	height in	WEIGHT max t-o lb	PERFORMANCE max speed mph	at height ft	service ceiling ft	combat range miles	REMARKS
Avions Fairey Fox VI	38	0						227	13,000	NA	NA	Built only in Belgium
Avions Fairey Mk VII Mono Fox	38	0	29	8				233	14,000	37,720		Single-seat development of Fox VI
DAR-10F	41	6	32	3	9	9¾	7,540	282	16,400	29,500	870	Only Bulgarian combat design to enter service

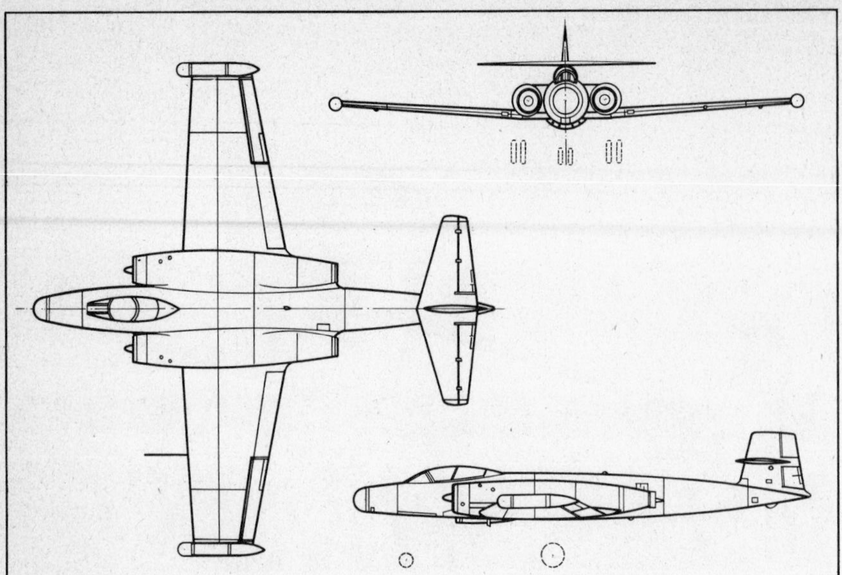
Avro CF-100 Mk 4

Avro CF-100 Mk 5D, modified for ECM duties

Avro CF-100 Mk 5, Belgian Air Force

the first of two Mk 1 prototypes flew for the first time on 19 January 1950, powered by a pair of Rolls-Royce Avon turbojets. The prototypes were followed by ten pre-production Mk 2s, in which the Avons were replaced by two 6,000-lb s t Orenda 2 engines. All of these evaluation aircraft were unarmed, and one Mk 2 was completed as a Mk 2T with dual controls. The first Mk 2 was flown on 20 June 1951, and handed over to the RCAF on 17 October of the same year. On 11 October 1952 came the maiden flight of the first full production model, the CF-100 Mk 3. This was powered by the more efficient Orenda 9 of 6,500 lb s t, and was armed with a battery of eight 0·50-in Colt-Browning machine-guns in a retractable tray in the belly of the aircraft. It entered service first with No. 445 Squadron, RCAF, based at North Bay, Ontario in 1953 as Canada's first all-weather fighter unit. The crew of two sat in tandem on Martin-Baker ejection seats, beneath a long "blister" type canopy.

Of the 70 Mk 3s completed, 50 were converted in later years to Mk 3CT and 3D dual-control trainers. Meanwhile, the tenth Mk 2 had been converted into the prototype for the CF-100 Mk 4, making its first flight in the new configuration on the same day as the first Mk 3. The most noticeable external difference was in the more bulbous contours of the nose, indicating the presence of a newer and more efficient fire-control radar, and in the provision of a pod at each wingtip containing thirty 2·75-in folding-fin air-to-air rockets. The Orenda 9 remained as power plant for the Mk 4A, which entered production during the summer of 1953. An improved model, the Mk 4B, followed it on the assembly line: this was powered by two 7,275-lb s t Orenda 11s and had an all-rocket armament, a ventral pack of 48 2·75-in rockets replacing the Colt-Browning machine-guns of the earlier models. When production of the Mk 4A/4B ended early in 1956, a total of 510 of these versions had been completed.

On 4 November 1956, No. 445 Squadron, now equipped with the Mk 4B, arrived in France to become the first unit in NATO to fly multi-seat all-weather fighters; three further squadrons of Mk 4Bs were added to the Canadian contingent in Europe during 1957, remaining until 1962. By this time, steps had already been taken to evolve a further version of the CF-100 with superior altitude performance. One hundred Mk 5s were produced, converted from standard 4B airframes by the addition of untapered outer wing sections, each some 3½-ft long, and a slight increase in tailplane area, which increased the CF-100's operational ceiling by some 4,000 ft. Larger wingtip pods, each holding 52 air-to-air rockets, were fitted. The first Mk 5 flew on 12 October 1955. In December 1957, delivery began of 53 ex-RCAF Mk 5s to the Belgian Air Force.

Plans were made for the production of a Mk 6 model, which was to have been powered by the Orenda 11R of 8,250 lb s t with re-heat and to have had an armament that included the Sparrow II air-to-air missile; but this project was shelved in the belief that it would be rendered unnecessary by Avro's new fighter design, the CF-105 Arrow – a belief that was shown to be sadly mistaken when the CF-105 programme was cancelled.

Canadair CL-13 Sabre

In 1949 the Canadian government negotiated licence agreements with North American Aviation for the F-86 Sabre jet fighter to be built in Canada for the RCAF; and in August of that year Canadair Ltd were awarded a contract for 100 aircraft of this type.

The first Canadair-built Sabre, corresponding to the USAF's F-86A, was flown at Cartierville on 9 August 1950, and this machine was designated Sabre Mk 1. The second and subsequent aircraft were to F-86E standard, with a General Electric J47-GE-13 turbojet of 5,200-lb s t and "all-flying" tail surfaces, and were redesignated Sabre Mk 2. This model began to be delivered to RCAF fighter squadrons early in 1951, and repeat orders raised to 350 the total number of Mk 2s built. Sixty of these were supplied by Canadair to the US Air Force in 1952, to provide additional support for UN ground forces taking part in the Korean war; and at the end of the same year they also began to deliver a substantial number of Sabre 2s to the Royal Air Force, as an interim type pending the introduction into service of the Hawker Hunter. The Sabres for Britain were flown to the UK by No. 1 Long Range Ferry Unit of RAF Transport Command in December 1952 and were phased into service during the early months of 1953. Apart from one or two Fighter Command squadrons which re-equipped with Sabres, all of these aircraft went to the Second Tactical Air Force in Europe.

By the time that Hunters began to replace them in 1955–6, the RAF had received 400 Sabres. Later machines were to Mk 4 standard, generally similar to the Sabre 2, but with improvements in the cockpit layout and modification to the cabin air-conditioning system. Altogether 438 Mk 4s were built, serving at first only with the British and Canadian air forces; but the RAF Sabres were withdrawn from service by June 1956, and were then passed on to the air arms of Greece, Italy, Turkey and Yugoslavia.

Meanwhile, at Edwards Air Force Base in the United States, a US-built F-86A had been fitted experimentally in 1952 with a 6,000-lb s t Orenda 3 engine. This aircraft – used in May 1953 by Jacqueline Cochran to raise the women's world air speed record – was the Sabre Mk 3, and paved the way for the first Orenda-powered production model, the CL-13A Sabre 5. First flown on 30 July 1953, the Sabre 5 was powered by a 6,355-lb s t Orenda 10 and had a revised wing leading-edge similar to that introduced on the F-86F. Canadair built a total of 370 Sabre 5s, of which 75 were later presented by the Canadian government to the Luftwaffe.

The final Canadian-built model, the CL-13B Sabre 6, had the more powerful Orenda 14 engine of 7,275 lb s t and (apart from early production machines) a leading-edge largely similar to the earlier Sabres. First deliveries of the Sabre 6 were made in November 1954, production continuing until 9 October 1958, when a total of 655 of this model had been built. These went to the Royal Canadian Air Force (390), West Germany (225), South Africa (34) and Colombia (6). The Sabre 6s of West Germany were modified subsequently to carry a pair of Sidewinder air-to-air missiles.

Thus, in a nine-year production run, a total of 1,815 Canadian-built Sabres were completed. There were, in addition, numerous development projects. These included the CL-13C and CL-13J (both involving afterburning power plants); the CL-13D, with an Armstrong Siddeley Snarler auxiliary rocket motor; the CL-13E, to investigate the area rule concept; the CL-13F, a proposed two-seat all-weather fighter variant of the Mk 6; the CL-13G two-seat trainer; and the CL-13H single-seater with all-weather radar.

Canadair CL-28 Argus

In 1952 the Royal Canadian Air Force issued a specification calling for a long-range maritime patrol and anti-submarine aircraft to replace the converted wartime Lancasters and Catalinas that had been responsible for its oversea reconnaissance since the end of World War II. To meet this requirement, Canadair Ltd decided that an acceptable and effective answer could be achieved with an adaptation of the Bristol Britannia commercial airliner. Their proposals were accepted, and a contract for the construction of a prototype was placed in April 1954.

Canadair CL-13 Sabre F. Mk 4, RAF

Canadair CL-13 Sabre 5, Golden Hawks display team

Canadair CL-13B Sabre 6, Luftwaffe

TYPE	DIMENSIONS						WEIGHT	PERFORMANCE				REMARKS
	span ft	*span* in	*length* ft	*length* in	*height* ft	*height* in	*max t-o* lb	*max speed* mph	*at height* ft	*service ceiling* ft	*combat range* miles	
CF-100 Mk 3	52	0	52	3¾	15	6½	34,000	640	10,000	NA	NA	First production version
CF-100 Mk 4B	53	7	54	2	15	6½	35,500	650	10,000	NA	NA	
CF-100 Mk 5	60	10	54	2	15	6½	36,000	650	10,000	54,000	NA	
CL-13 Sabre Mk 4	37	1	37	6	14	7	16,500	670	10,000	53,000	1,250	Similar to F-86E
CL-13B Sabre Mk 6	37	1	37	6	14	7	17,611	710	SL		1,495	Orenda engine

Canadair CL-28 Argus Mk 1

Canadair CL-28 Argus Mk 1

Canadair CL-28 Argus Mk 2

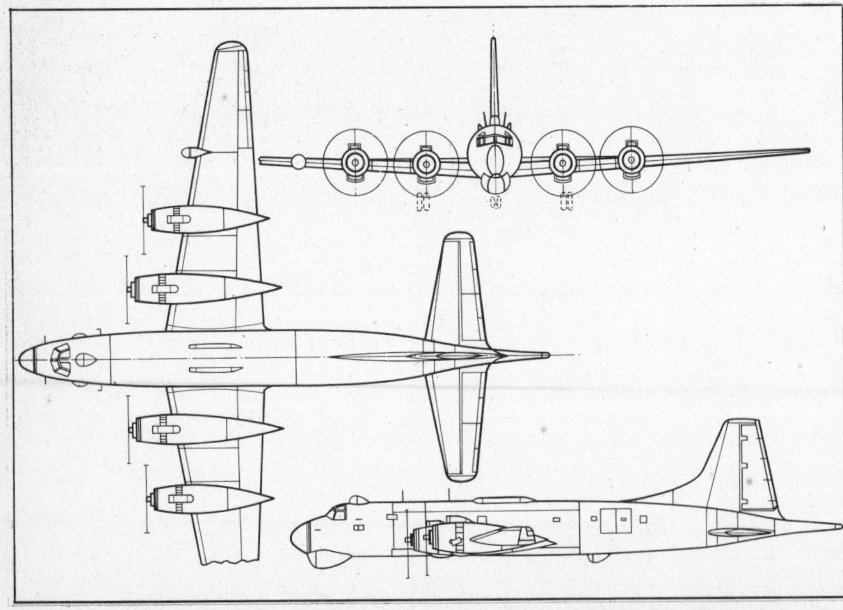
Canadair CL-28 Argus Mk 2

This machine, rolled out on 21 December 1956, was something of a hybrid. The wings, tail surfaces and undercarriage were virtually identical to those of the Britannia; the engines were of American origin; and the fuselage, although similar in appearance to that of the Britannia, had been completely redesigned by Canadair. Instead of the airliner's Proteus turboprops, the CL-28, as the new aircraft was designated, was fitted with four 3,700-hp Wright R-3350 (TC18EA1) 18-cylinder Turbo-Compound radial piston-engines. The new fuselage – unpressurized, by virtue of the CL-28's intended low-level rôle – accommodated a mass of modern equipment for long-range sea patrol, submarine detection and destruction. It also housed a maximum crew of 15, made up of three pilots, three navigators, two flight engineers and seven signallers, who operated on a shift basis during the CL-28's many hours on patrol.

The prototype CL-28 was flown for the first time on 28 March 1957, and a further 12 aircraft were ordered for the RCAF under the designation CP-107 Argus Mk 1; the first of these was delivered in September 1957 and entered service with No. 404 Squadron of Maritime Command in the following May. Production continued with a batch of 20 Argus Mk 2s, the last of which was completed on 13 July 1960. The Argus remains the largest and one of the most comprehensively equipped of anti-submarine aircraft: its equipment includes electronic countermeasures radar, "Julie" echo ranging, sonobuoys and Magnetic Anomaly Detection apparatus in the long tail "sting", and accounts for some 6,000 lb of the all-up weight. Two internal weapons bays, each 18 ft 6 in long, can each accommodate up to 4,000 lb of bombs, mines, depth charges, homing torpedoes or other ordnance; and up to 7,600 lb of similar stores or air-to-underwater guided missiles may be carried externally on underwing pylons. The distinctive "chin" radome houses, in the Argus 1, American APS-20 search radar, and in the smaller radome of the Mk 2 an even more sophisticated radar of British design.

A transport derivative of the Argus, based on the civil CL-44, is also in service with the RCAF as the CC-106 Yukon troop and freight-carrying aircraft. Twelve Yukons were built, with a 12-ft-longer fuselage and an all-up weight of 205,000 lb.

Canadian Vickers Vancouver II

Formation of the Canadian branch of Vickers Ltd in 1923 marked the beginnings of an aircraft manufacturing industry in Canada, and for several years this company was engaged in the manufacture of flying-boats, including the Varuna and Vedette.

The Vancouver resulted from a specification, issued by the Forest Fire Protection Service of the Department of National Defence, for an aircraft to succeed the Varuna on forest fire patrol and general transportation duties. The prototype Vancouver I (two Armstrong Siddeley Lynx IV radials) was well inside the specification, and five production Mk II aircraft were promptly ordered. Modifications, including a change of power plant, delayed the completion of the first Mk II until 1930, although actual construction had occupied less than five months.

The Vancouver II was a metal-hulled biplane flying-boat, powered either by two 300-hp Wright J-6 Whirlwind nine-cylinder radial engines, or by two 240-hp seven-cylinder Lynx IVC radials, mounted midway between the wings and driving two-bladed Standard Steel tractor propellers. After it had given several years of useful service on forestry patrol, aerial survey and general transport duties, the Department of National Defence decided in the mid-1930s that, suitably adapted, the Vancouver would make an acceptable coastal patrol aircraft for the Royal Canadian Air Force. Accordingly, three gun positions were installed, one in the prow and two aft of the wings, in each of which one or two Lewis machine-guns could be installed. Provision was made for a navigator/signaller's compartment, and attachment points for small bombs were added beneath the wings; other modifications included revised tail surfaces.

The military Vancouvers were designated Mk II/SW by the RCAF, the "W" indicating the Whirlwind power plant. Two machines (Nos. 903 and 904) were fitted temporarily with 380-hp Armstrong Siddeley Serval ten-cylinder engines and were then known as the Mk II/SS; but this installation was not a success and after a short period both aircraft had their Whirlwind motors restored.

Plans were evolved during the Vancouver's early career for a Mk III photo-reconnaissance amphibian version, and for a Wasp-powered commercial passenger model, but neither of these projects achieved fruition.

Czechoslovakia

Aero A 11

On 28 October 1918, the Czechoslovak Republic was born, as one result of the 1914–18 War, and its people attained independence after 300 years of Austrian rule.

The greater part of the ancient Austro-Hungarian industry was concentrated in Bohemia and Moravia, in the western part of Czechoslovakia; there was, however, no aircraft industry. During the years 1918–19, three great aeronautical companies came into being, namely Letov, Aero and Avia. Within a few years, they developed into the largest manufacturers and exporters of military and civil aircraft in Central Europe.

The Aero company started production in 1919 by building copies of the Austrian Phönix (Brandenburg), and nearly 100 of these biplanes, designated 276C 1, were built for various duties. Under the direction of the engineer Husník, they soon began development of their own designs.

The Aero A 11 of 1923 was an exceptionally successful two-seat general-purpose machine that replaced the Letov S 1 and S 2 and was the most widely-used reconnaissance and light bombing aircraft in Czechoslovakia during the 1920s. Its speed and manoeuvrability combined to make it a "pilot's aircraft", and its loss was regretted when newer types replaced it.

The A 11 was a development of the A 12 of the same year, although the numerical designations would seem to imply otherwise. The two types were similar, except that the A 11 had a Walter W-IV engine of 240 hp, while the A 12 had a Maybach Mb IVa of 240/260 hp. A great advantage of the basic design was the ease with which different power plants could be installed, ranging from 220 to 500 hp. As a result there were 22 variants, of which 440 examples were produced! They included the A 11 N night-reconnaissance version with W-IV engine; Ab 11 bomber with Breitfeld-Danek Perun II engine of 240 hp, and its Ab 11 N night-bombing variant; A 25 and A 125 day trainers and A 21 night trainer.

The A 29 variant of 1926, of which nine examples were built, was the first Czechoslovak floatplane. It was used for target-towing duties at the Czechoslovak A.A. gunnery range on the Adriatic coast of Yugoslavia. Finland bought a batch of eight of the A 11 HS version in 1927, which was fitted with the French Hispano-Suiza 8 Fb engine of 300 hp. One of the Finnish A 11 HS machines proved the capability of the type in an unusual way when Aero's chief pilot, Novák, made 225 consecutive loops in 44 min 53 sec – a rate of five loops a minute!

Many international FAI records were gained by the A 11 and some remarkable flights were undertaken. They included a 9,321-mile demonstration flight through Europe, part of Asia and Africa by Captain Stanovsky in

Canadian Vickers Vancouver II

Aero Ab 11

Aero Ab 11, ski landing gear

TYPE	DIMENSIONS span ft	in	length ft	in	height ft	in	WEIGHT max t-o lb	PERFORMANCE max speed mph	at height ft	service ceiling ft	combat range miles	REMARKS
CL-28 Argus Mk 2	142	3½	128	9½	36	8½	148,000	315	10,000	NA	4,000	Mk 1 generally similar
Vancouver II	55	0	37	6	15	7	7,600	120	SL	15,000	NA	
Aero A 11	42	0	26	11	10	2	3,264	133	8,200	23,600	466	Walter W-IV 240 hp

Aero A 18

Aero A 30

Aero A 30

Aero A 32

1926, and the achievement of Lt-Col Skála, who flew non-stop around a Prague-Belgrade-Bucharest-Prague circuit in 14 hours.

Aero A 18

In 1923, the Czechoslovak Air Force received a new fighter powered by the high-altitude BMW IIIa engine built by Walter under licence. This was the Aero 18, a small, fast and manoeuvrable interceptor biplane. Its construction was mixed, with wooden wings and a steel-tube fuselage, all fabric-covered.

The twenty A 18s delivered to the Czechoslovak Air Force represented a major combat force at the time. Armament was two synchronized Vickers guns.

In Czechoslovak air history, the A 18 is connected inseparably with the first air races organized in the 1920s by the Aero Club of the Czechoslovak Republic. The absolute winner of the races received a prize given by the President of the Republic.

For the first races in 1923, Aero produced a clipped-wing variant, the A 18 B. The already-short wings of the standard version were reduced to 18ft 7 in, with an area of only 106·4 sq ft. The A 18 B was the winner and was, in fact, unchallenged. The competing Avia BH-7B and Letov S 8, both high-wing monoplanes, crashed during the contest, and the A 18 B was the only machine to complete the course.

The second races, in 1924, were more competitive. Aero entered a new "racer" variant, the A 18 C. Its wings remained small, but it was powered by a high-compression Walter W-IV engine of 300 hp, fitted with evaporative-cooling radiators on the wing and fuselage surfaces. After a close race against the S 8, the A 18 C emerged the winner, at a speed of 162 mph.

Aero A 30

The Aero A 30 long-range reconnaissance aircraft and medium bomber was built to the same requirement and at the same time as the Letov S 16. In all, 79 examples of the A 30 and its variants were built between 1926 and 1933, but they did not attain the same popularity as the S 16.

Basically, the A 30 was an enlarged version of the A 11 design. In 1925, an A 11 LD had been built with a Lorraine-Dietrich engine of 450 hp; but tests soon showed that the airframe was insufficiently strong for such a heavy and powerful engine. So, in 1926, the A 30 was built, characterized by a wide upper wing and narrow lower wing, almost of sesquiplane configuration. It was of mixed construction, with wooden wings and steel-tube fuselage, all fabric-covered.

First impressions of the A 30 were not too favourable, and many refinements had to be made before, in 1927, the type was ready for series production. The first order, for five, came in 1927, followed by contracts for 17 more. The series-built A 30s were powered by the Skoda L engine of 450/500 hp. Armament comprised one fixed Vickers and movable twin Lewis guns; a bomb-load varying between 660 and 1,320 lb could be carried.

One of the A 30s established a world speed record carrying a 1,000-kg payload by averaging 132·7 mph over a 500-km closed circuit in August 1927; but in October of the same year this was beaten by the Letov S 16.

There were several variants, such as the prototype A 130 of 1928, which had a Jupiter VI radial engine, and the series-produced A 230 of 1930 with a Lorraine-Dietrich engine and divided undercarriage. Final variant was the A 330 with a 650/700-hp Praga ESV engine.

Production of the A 30 series ended in 1933.

Aero A 32

The Aero A 32 series were fast and manoeuvrable biplanes, derived from the A 11. The main difference lay in use of the Walter Jupiter IV nine-cylinder radial engine of 420/450 hp.

In 1927, a Jupiter engine had been installed experimentally in an Ab 11 airframe; the National Defence Ministry accepted this modification, under the designation A 11 J, and ordered 31 production models. These embodied further modifications and received the designation Aero A 32.

Prime rôles of the A 32 were close support for the army and light bombing. Armament comprised two fixed Vickers machine-guns and twin movable Lewis guns. Twelve 22-lb anti-personnel bombs were carried on underwing racks.

The Finnish Air Force ordered and received 16 A 32 attack aircraft in 1929. The first of them, designated A 32 IF, was powered by an Isotta Fraschini Asso Caccia 12-cylinder inverted-Vee in-line air-cooled engine of 450/500 hp, but the remaining 15 were powered by French Gnome-Rhône Jupiters of 450 hp and received the factory designation A 32 GR.

In 1930 two new series were laid down. These were the Ap 32 and Apb 32, which were considerably cleaned-up and had a more modern undercarriage of the divided-axle type, with streamline fairings over the rubber shock-absorbers. The Apb 32 remained in production until 1932 and, in all, 116 aircraft of the A 32 family were built.

Aero A 100 and A 101

During the final years of A 30 production, the design team of the Aero company proposed a new variant, the A 430. This was, in fact, an entirely new machine, robust, clean and modern, though still of biplane configuration. To indicate more clearly that it represented a new development, Aero changed the designation to A 100 and offered the project to the National Defence Ministry. In 1933, the Ministry organized a competition for designs within this category of combat aircraft, and it was won by the A 100. As a result, during the following two years, 44 A 100s were built and used by the Air Force.

Like the A 30, the A 100 was of mixed construction, and was powered by an Avia Vr-36 engine of 650/750 hp. Armament comprised two fixed and twin movable Mk 30 machine-guns, and 1,320 lb of bombs could be carried under the fuselage and lower wings.

The A 100 remained a long-range reconnaissance type. For the medium bomber rôle the A 101 was built, similar in general appearance, but powered by a Praga Asso engine of 800 hp, and with a rudder of slightly larger area. Twenty-nine A 101 bombers were produced during 1933–5.

Aero Ab 101s were the last bomber biplanes produced in Czechoslovakia. They entered production immediately after the A 101, in 1936, and 64 were built in the following two years. They were slightly larger than the A 101, and were powered by the CKD-Praga-built HS 12 Ydrs engine of 710/860 hp. Unfortunately, they were cumbersome aircraft and attained only 161 mph, in spite of the more powerful engine, compared with the 167 mph of the original A 100. They were soon replaced by the faster Avia B 71 twin-engined monoplanes.

Aero MB 200

The three-engined Avia-Fokker F IX heavy bombers of the Czechoslovak Air Force were modern at the time of their development, but were considerably behind the times in 1935 when they were still in first-line service.

To accelerate the modernization of the Czechoslovak bomber force, the Ministry of National Defence acquired licence rights from France to build the twin-engined all-metal Marcel Bloch MB 200 BN. 4 high-wing mono-

Aero A 32 GR, Finnish Air Force

Aero A 100

Aero A 101

TYPE	DIMENSIONS						WEIGHT	PERFORMANCE				REMARKS	
	span		length		height		max t-o	max speed	at height	service ceiling	combat range		
	ft	in	ft	in	ft	in	lb	mph	ft	ft	miles		
Aero A 18	24	11	19	4¼	9	6¼	1,900	142	8,200	29,500	249	BMW IIIa	185 hp
Aero A 30	50	2½	32	10	10	9¾	5,974	149	8,200	21,300	621	Skoda L	500 hp
Aero A 32	40	8	26	11	10	2	4,225	140	8,200	18,000	497	Walter Jupiter IV	450 hp
Aero A 100	48	2¾	34	9¼	11	5¾	7,098	167	6,600	21,300	590	Avia Vr-36	650 hp

Aero MB 200

Aero A 304

Aero A 304

plane, appointing the Aero company as manufacturer of the type in Czechoslovakia.

During 1936 and 1937, a total of 124 MB 200 bombers were built by Aero and Avia, the latter serving as a sub-licensee. Powered by two 750-hp Walter K-14 engines, and fitted with neat NACA cowlings instead of the Townend rings of the French originals, the MB 200 attained a speed of 152 mph, but this was still comparatively slow at the time of the first monoplane fighters. Three movable Mk 30 machine-guns were fitted, and up to 3,085 lb of bombs could be carried in and under the fuselage.

Czechoslovak pilots disliked the MB 200s, calling them "flying coffins" because of their tendency to spin after the failure of one engine. After the German occupation, surviving MB 200s were sent to Rumania and Bulgaria.

Aero A 304

Aero A 304 reconnaissance and light bombing aircraft were the most modern types equipping the Czechoslovak Air Force in 1938, and it is interesting to note that they had their origin in a civil prototype, the A 204.

In February 1935, the Czechoslovak State Airlines (CSA) required a small, fast airliner to accommodate eight passengers and a crew of two, for use on the newly-opened Prague-Moscow route. To meet this requirement, the Aero company produced the prototype A 204 airliner, powered by two 360-hp Walter Pollux II.R engines, and it flew for the first time in March 1936. After some delay, CSA refused it, having bought instead four British Airspeed Envoy airliners for the Prague-Moscow route.

Technically, the A 204 was a success and its airframe had the potential for modification and development in many forms. Aero, therefore, produced a number of military variants of the basic A 204 design, including the A 304 light bomber and the A 300 fast medium bomber.

The A 304 three-seat reconnaissance/light bomber was built in 1938 as a small series of 15 machines. These retained the basic features of the A 204 airliner, including fuselage side-windows; but the nose was glazed and a dorsal turret with one movable Mk 30 machine-gun was provided for defence, with another fixed Mk 30 gun mounted in the nose. Up to 660 lb of bombs could be carried. Alternatively, the A 304 could be used for navigation and radio training. Powered by Walter Super Castor engines of 430 hp, it was the first Czechoslovak-designed aircraft to have a retractable undercarriage.

Following the German occupation, ex-Czechoslovak A 304s were handed over to the Bulgarian Air Force, with which they served throughout the war on training duties. Some were also used by the Luftwaffe as personal transports for high-ranking officers.

Back in March 1938, the A 300 fast medium bomber had been test flown, and was to prove the last, and best, aircraft of this category designed in Czechoslovakia. It had two 830-hp Bristol Mercury IX radial engines and was fitted with a slightly-reinforced version of the A 204 wing. The fuselage was new, as was the tail unit, which featured twin fins and rudders. Speed was 292 mph, and a bomb-load of 2,204 lb could be carried.

The A 300 was developed too late to be of use to the Czechoslovak Air Force, and the Germans used the prototype for test purposes at the Focke-Wulf plant in Bremen, where it finally ended on the scrap-heap.

Avia BH-3

The BH-3 monoplane was the first Czechoslovak fighter to go into series production. It was a design of the Avia company, founded in 1919 and established in what had been a small sugar factory in the eastern suburbs of Prague. Two young engineers named P. Benes and M. Hajn were its designers, hence the BH designation.

In 1920, Avia produced a small sporting two-seat low-wing monoplane with an Austro-Daimler engine of 30/35 hp, which was later replaced by a Gnome Omega rotary engine of 48 hp. It was an exceptionally clean aircraft, with a thick wing, supported on each side by a pair of struts. Success with this BH-1 prototype encouraged the designers to take part in a contest initiated in 1921 by the Czechoslovak National Defence Ministry. The specification called for a single-seat fighter powered by a BMW IIIa engine, armed with two machine-guns, and with a speed of at least 130 mph.

Avia entered the BH-3 low-wing monoplane fighter, the wings of which were supported by a Vee-strut on each side of the fuselage. Its speed of 133 mph was higher than that required by the specification, and this, combined with excellent manoeuvrability and rate of climb, encouraged the National Defence Ministry to order a batch of ten production machines. These were used by the Air Force under the military designation B 3 (all Avia-built aircraft were given a B designation).

Five of the series-produced BH-3s had BMW IIIa engines of 185 hp; the remaining five had Walter W-IV engines of 220 hp, and the speed of this version proved to be 140 mph. All ten machines were of wooden construction, covered partially with plywood, the rest of the structure being fabric-covered.

Characteristic of the modest beginnings of the Avia company is the fact that space available in the old sugar factory was too small for the series production of ten BH-3s. To overcome the problem, Avia hired some restaurant rooms in the neighbourhood and built the machines there.

With the BH-3, Avia began its career as the greatest producer of fighters for the Czechoslovak Air Force.

Avia BH-21

In 1922 the Czechoslovak National Defence Ministry announced a requirement for a fighter aircraft to be powered by the new eight-cylinder in-line HS 8 Fb engine, built by Skoda under licence from Hispano-Suiza. Aero, Letov and Avia each submitted prototypes for the competition. Avia, having more adequate accommodation by this time, developed no fewer than five prototypes utilizing the HS 8 Fb engine. These were the BH-6, -8 and -17 biplanes, BH-7A high-wing monoplane and BH-19 low-wing monoplane.

The Ministry chose the BH-17 biplane and ordered a small batch in 1924. These fighters were very manoeuvrable, but had a number of shortcomings, including limited view from the cockpit and insufficiently rigid I-section interplane struts. When the Ministry ordered a second batch in the autumn of 1924, the designers decided to change the configuration of the BH-17, and within three months the first BH-21 fighter had been completed.

This machine (military designation B 21) was the best fighter serving in Czechoslovakia during the 1920s. It was fast, with a high rate of climb, and of robust construction, and about 120 were built. In July 1925, it won a fighter competition initiated by the Belgian Air Force, and 50 aircraft were built under licence by SABCA in Belgium.

One BH-21 was modified to compete in air races, being provided with a new clipped wing, which reduced the area from 234·6 sq ft to 146·4 sq ft. A modified Skoda HS 8 Fb engine of 400 hp was installed, driving a Reed-Levasseur propeller. This machine, designated BH-21 R, won the 1925 national air races at an average speed of 186·7 mph.

The series-produced BH-21 fighters, powered by normal HS 8 Fb engines of 300 hp, and armed with two fixed Vickers machine-guns, had a top speed of 149·5 mph.

Parallel with production of the BH-21 fighter, Avia built some 30 BH-22s – a lighter version with a different wing arrangement, which had no armament but was fitted

Avia BH-3

Avia BH-21, ski landing gear

TYPE	DIMENSIONS						WEIGHT	PERFORMANCE				REMARKS	
	span		*length*		*height*		*max t-o*	*max speed*	*at height*	*service ceiling*	*combat range*		
	ft	*in*	*ft*	*in*	*ft*	*in*	*lb*	*mph*	*ft*	*ft*	*miles*		
Aero MB 200	73	8	51	10	12	10½	15,762	152	6,600	19,700	621	2 × Walter K-14 I	750 hp
Aero A 304	63	0	43	3¾	11	2	9,600	201	6,600	20,700	745	2 × Walter Super Castor	430 hp
Avia BH-3	33	7¼	22	11¾	9	2	2,260	133	6,600	25,600	310	BMW IIIa	185 hp
Avia BH-21	29	2½	22	7¾	8	10¼	2,369	149.5	SL	25,300	341	Skoda HS 8 Fb	300 hp

Avia BH-33, Polish-built

Avia BH-33 L

Avia BH-33 L

Avia F IX

with a camera-gun. Power plant was the Hispano Suiza 8 Aa engine of only 180 hp. The B 22, as the type was designated by the Air Force, was extremely manoeuvrable and gave valuable service in the training rôle.

Avia BH-33

In 1929, the designers Benes and Hajn left the Avia company and founded the Aeroplane Division of CKD-Praga. Their last design for Avia was the BH-33 fighter.

This aircraft, produced in 1926, was a development of the BH-21 J, fitted experimentally with a 420/480-hp Jupiter radial engine. The first BH-33 was completed in 1927, its Jupiter VI giving it a speed of 171·5 mph and an initial rate of climb of 2,165 ft/min. The fuselage sides were flat, as in earlier BH types, but the BH-33 was the first Avia machine to have a fin, the slab-sided fuselage of the earlier machines having provided sufficient directional stability without a fin. In 1928, Poland acquired licence rights for the type and built it in the PWS works.

In the following year, the BH-33 was redesigned to BH-33 E standard, a steel-tube fuselage structure being used for the first time in Avia history. The upper wing was redesigned, and a divided-axle type of undercarriage was fitted. A Jupiter VI or VII engine was installed, and on export versions helmet-type cylinder cowlings were fitted.

A very impressive demonstration in Paris, on the occasion of the 1929 *Salon*, resulted in export orders. BH-33 Es were bought by the USSR and Yugoslavia, the latter country building the BH-33 L under licence in the Ikarus factory at Zemun. The Czechoslovak Air Force also used the BH-33 E under the designation B 33.

Final version of the BH-33 was the BH-33 L, powered by a 12-cylinder Skoda L engine of 450/525 hp. Under the designation Ba 33, it served as the standard fighter of the Czechoslovak Air Force at the beginning of the 1930s. Armament consisted of two Mk 28 machine-guns, which were Vickers guns modified to take the standard 7·92-mm ammunition of the Czechoslovak Armed Forces.

Avia F IX

The experience and financial resources of the Czechoslovak aircraft industry were inadequate to permit development of heavy bombers during the first ten or twelve years of its existence. The number of machines of this type required by the Czechoslovak Air Force was too small to cover development costs, and export potential was low. Only a single twin-engined bomber prototype appeared, in 1924, in the shape of the A 24 biplane with Maybach Mb.IVa engines, and this was not successful.

In 1929, Avia acquired licence rights from Fokker to build the F VII/3m three-engined commercial monoplane, and manufactured it in series. Avia offered a bomber variant, the F VIIb, but the Air Force required a heavier machine. This resulted in Avia acquiring licence rights for the Fokker F IX, and it produced 12 bomber aircraft of that type in 1932, each powered by three Walter Jupiter engines of 450 hp.

Avia F IXs were of mixed construction, with all-wood wings, steel-tube fuselage structure and overall fabric covering. The company experimented with the armament of the type, with the result that almost every one of the 12 F IXs that were built showed variations. Twin Mk 28, and later Mk 30, machine-guns were mounted in a dorsal position in front of, or behind, the wing (the front position caused turbulence over the wing and fuselage and affected tail unit effectiveness). Another gun was positioned in a step in the under-fuselage; but some of the F IXs had no step and therefore had a retractable cylindrical belly turret. Other guns were installed at fuselage side-windows, and in the floor of the bomb-aimer's cockpit, behind the central engine. Bomb-load of the F IX was between 1,763 and 3,306 lb. Avia developed its own export variant, the F 39, and two of these machines were delivered to Yugoslavia, each powered by three Gnome-Rhône Jupiter engines of 560 hp. Yugoslavia also acquired licence rights.

Three examples of the F IX D civil airliner were built, one in a de-luxe form for VIP transport. The

State airline, CSA, used two F IX Ds, one continuing in service until the German occupation in 1939. The F IX Ds were powered by three Walter Pegasus II radial engines of 550 hp, and could accomodate 17 passengers.

Avia B 534

The Avia B 534 biplane was the most widely-used fighter of the Czechoslovak Air Force and was standard equipment at the time of the Munich crisis, in the autumn of 1938. In all 445 were built, enabling the Air Force to present a fairly strong defence against the German fighter squadrons.

The B 534 was the work of Avia's new designer, F. Novotny, who had replaced Benes and Hajn in 1930. His first design for Avia, which had appeared in 1931, was the B 34 fighter. This was a development of the Ba 33 type, powered by an Avia Vr-36 engine of 650/850 hp, and had an all-steel airframe structure, with some detachable duralumin skin panels, the remainder being covered in fabric.

During 1932, the B 34 airframe was used to test various engines, and of the projected B 134 to B 534 variants only two were completed. The B 234 of 1932 was powered by a 600-hp Avia R 29 radial engine, but this proved unreliable and the type did not fly. During the winter of 1932/33, the B 234 airframe was redesigned to take the Hispano-Suiza HS 12 Ybrs in-line engine. After some aerodynamic refinements, the new type received the designation B 534, and flew for the first time in August 1933.

The National Defence Ministry ordered a large series, powered by the improved HS 12 Ydrs engine of 760/860 hp, which was manufactured by Avia under licence. The first series-built B 534s had open cockpits and very clean lines, and could attain a speed of 233 mph.

Armament comprised four Mk 30 machine-guns, mounted two in the fuselage sides and two in the lower wing; but the wing guns were later repositioned in the fuselage sides, as the wings had suffered from severe vibration when the guns were fired. The machine-guns mounted in the fuselage sides were given characteristic "bubble" fairings.

The final batch of series-built machines had enclosed cockpits and wheel spats and were aerodynamically cleaner, which enabled them to attain a speed of 249 mph. Thirty-five B 534s were produced under the designation Bk 534, these being adapted to accommodate a motor-cannon by removing the fuselage fuel tank and making provision to house fuel in the centre-section of the upper-wing. A Hispano-Suiza No. 404 cannon was tested, but it was decided later to fit the Swiss Oerlikon FFS 20-mm cannon, in addition to two machine-guns on the fuselage sides. However, for financial reasons the Oerlikon FFS could not be purchased in sufficient quantity, which resulted in a third Mk 30 machine-gun being mounted on the HS 12 Ycrs engine, firing through the propeller hub.

The Avia B 534 was the finest fighter biplane in Continental Europe, and during the Zürich Air Meeting in 1937 came second in all important contests, close behind the new Messerschmitt Bf 109. In the three-aircraft team race, the Bf 109s finished first, with a speed of 230·15 mph, the B 534s coming second, at 223·75 mph.

In March 1939, after the division of Czechoslovakia and the German occupation of Bohemia and Moravia, many B 534s were taken over by the so-called Slovak

Avia B 534

Avia B 534

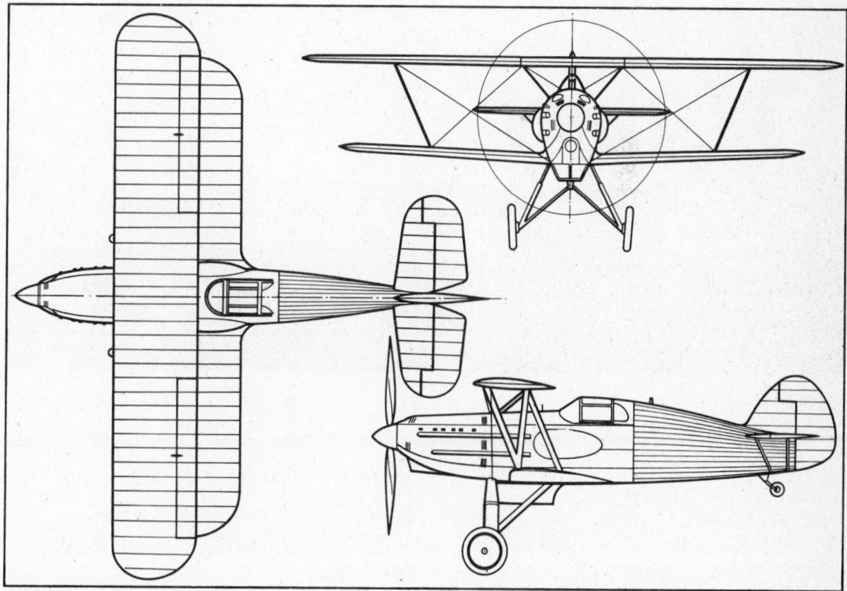

Avia B 534

TYPE	DIMENSIONS span ft	span in	length ft	length in	height ft	height in	WEIGHT max t-o lb	PERFORMANCE max speed mph	at height ft	service ceiling ft	combat range miles	REMARKS	
Avia BH-33L	31	2	23	7½	10	2	3,588	184	6,600	28,500	280	Skoda L	500 hp
Avia F IX	89	0½	63	6¾	15	8¾	20,194	130	SL	14,800	621	3 × Walter Jupiter	450 hp
Avia B 534	30	10	26	7	10	2	4,364	249	13,100	34,800	373	Avia HS 12 Ydrs	860 hp

Avia B 71

Avia B 71, Luftwaffe

Avia B 35.2

Avia B 35.2

State Air Arm, the remainder being used by the Luftwaffe for target and transport-glider towing. Three were diverted for experiments on board the German aircraft carrier *Graf Zeppelin*, which was never completed.

The Slovak Air Arm continued to use these machines against the Soviet Air Force, but many Slovak fighter pilots landed behind Soviet lines and joined Czechoslovak units of the Red Air Force. In Slovakia, three B 534s survived to fight against the Germans during the revolt in 1944.

Avia B 71

In May 1935, when Hitler's Germany was building up its military force and proclaiming its expansionist plans against neighbour states, the Czechoslovak Republic signed a military aid pact with the Soviet Union. Soviet and Czechoslovak delegations made exchange visits to airfields and factories, leading to the interchange of ideas and experience.

This resulted in the Czechoslovak Air Force appreciating that its A 100/101 bombers were outdated; but it was impossible to replace them with high-speed monoplane aircraft at short notice. The fast and rugged Soviet ANT-40 medium bomber (which had the military designation SB-2) was, therefore, chosen as a suitable replacement for the Czechoslovak biplanes.

During 1937–8, 54 ANT-40s were collected from the USSR, Czech pilots flying them back to their home bases. The Czechs thus received one of the most modern medium bomber types then available in Europe, which was designated B 71 by the Air Force.

Together with this batch of 54 Soviet-built B 71s, the Avia company had acquired a licence to build the type. In the spring of 1938, production began, supplemented shortly afterwards by parallel production in the Aero works, this company having been co-opted as a sub-licensee. Avia went on to build 66 of these machines and Aero built 45, but none of these was completed before the German occupation on 15 March 1939.

Powered by two Avia-built Hispano-Suiza 12 Ydrs engines of 760/860 hp, the B 71 attained a speed of 267 mph, which was faster than the contemporary B 534 fighter. It carried 1,322 lb of bombs internally, and was armed with three movable Mk 30 machine-guns, mounted in nose, dorsal and ventral positions.

The B 71s were popular with Czechoslovak pilots, who nicknamed the type *Katiushka.*

Avia soon began development work on these machines, and a tunnel radiator was designed to replace the frontal radiator of the original Soviet version. Fitted to a test machine, the new radiators boosted the speed to 276·5 mph, but German occupation brought an end to this development work.

The production series of B 71s was completed during the German occupation; some were used for training purposes in the Luftwaffe, others going to Bulgaria. The Luftwaffe also used this machine for target-towing, a winch for the target cable being installed under the rear gunner's cabin. To compensate for the weight of the winch and cable drum, a concrete block was mounted in the fuselage nose.

Avia B 35 and B 135

During the tense days of mobilization of the Czechoslovak Army at the time of the Munich crisis, in September 1938, the first flight took place of a prototype low-wing monoplane fighter, the Avia B 35.1. This was Czechoslovakia's best pre-war fighter aircraft; unfortunately, it came too late to be of help at the time of the national disaster.

Ing. Novotny's B 35 fighter was of mixed construction. The fuselage and tailplane were all-steel structures, covered partially by detachable duralumin panels and elsewhere with fabric. The clean elliptical wings were of all-wood construction, covered with plywood faced with aluminium sheet on the outer surface. The undercarriage was fixed but well streamlined.

Power plant was an Avia HS 12 Ycrs engine of 760/860 hp, although the project had been designed around a new engine, the 1,000-hp Avia 12Y-1000 C. The prototype was armed initially with two Mk 30 machine-guns, an Oerlikon FFS 20-mm cannon being added later.

The first prototype, the B 35.1, attained a speed of 307·5 mph; the B 35.2, which followed in January 1939, was similar. The B 35.3, tested during the first days of the German occupation, had an Olaer retractable undercarriage, and it had a speed of 332·4 mph.

In the summer of 1939 a new prototype, the B 135, was shown at the Brussels Aeronautical Exhibition. The Bulgarian Air Force ordered 12, and also acquired licence rights to build the type. During 1940, all 12 B 135s were delivered to Bulgaria, but in 1941 all work on Avia's own designs ceased.

The B 135 was almost identical to the B 35.3. The wing had a straight leading-edge for ease of production, and the undercarriage retraction mechanism was of Avia's own design.

In Bulgaria, the B 135s achieved some success in operation against USAAF bombers attacking Rumanian oilfields, but eventually all but one were destroyed. This last machine was still serviceable during the first post-war months, but was soon scrapped.

Avia S 199

After World War II, the Czechoslovak Republic was again free and began to form a new Air Force. In the early days, it had to make use of any available aircraft, chiefly ex-German types found in the country after liberation by the Red Army. These were refurbished by the aircraft industry, before being used in conjunction with types that had been flown by Czechoslovak units of the RAF and the Red Air Force.

This resulted in some strange designations: the Spitfire LF Mk IX became the S 89 (S = stíhac = fighter); some examples of the Fw 190A became S 90s; the Me 262A became the S 92; the designation S 95 was given to the Lavochkin La-5FN and S 97 to the La-7 fighter; the Messerschmitt Bf 109G-6 became the S 99 as a fighter and C 10 as a trainer (C = *cvicny* = training); whilst the C 110 was the two-seat equivalent of the Bf 109G-14.

The Bf 109 was to be seen in large numbers on German airfields in Czechoslovakia, and on many scrap-heaps in various stages of disrepair. With the diligence of ants, Avia engineers concentrated all the available Bf 109s together, and from them reconstructed 500 serviceable airframes, after manufacturing all missing components.

Only twenty of the reconstructed Bf 109 fighters could be powered by the original DB 605A engine of 1,475 hp, these serving as S 99s. As there were no more Daimler-Benz engines to be had, Czechoslovak engineers adapted the airframe for the only engine available in large numbers – the 1,350 hp Jumo 211F. This had powered the Ju 88 bomber, and had low rpm and a large torque moment. Modified VS-11 three-blade propellers, with large paddle blades, were fitted to these engines.

The new fighter, with Jumo 211F, received the designation S 199. A two-seat variant became the CS 199, or C 210 when flying without armament.

Armament of the S 199 consisted of two MG 131 machine-guns, mounted on the engine, and two MG 151/20 cannon under the wings. Use of the Jumo 211F engine, combined with the VS-11 paddle-bladed propeller, resulted in some unpleasant characteristics, particularly a tendency to turn over the left wing during take-off run at full throttle. The S 199s, disliked by their pilots, who nicknamed them *mezek* (mule), were used until the first MiG-15s were received in the early 1950s.

Avia B 135

Avia S 199

Avia S 199

TYPE	DIMENSIONS						WEIGHT	PERFORMANCE				REMARKS	
	span		*length*		*height*		*max t-o*	*max speed*	*at height*	*service ceiling*	*combat range*		
	ft	*in*	*ft*	*in*	*ft*	*in*	*lb*	*mph*	*ft*	*ft*	*miles*		
Avia B 71	66	8½	40	3	13	5½	13,227	267	9,800	29,500	621	2 × Avia HS 12 Ydrs	860 hp
Avia B 135	33	7½	27	10½	9	6¼	5,427	332	9,800	27,900	341	Avia HS 12 Ycrs	860 hp
Avia S 199	32	6½	29	2½	8	6½	7,716	360	11,500	31,200	528	Jumo 211F	1,350 hp

Letov S 1

Letov S 16

Letov S 16

Letov S 20

Letov S 1 and S 2

The Letov company stemmed out of the Military Air Arsenal in November 1918. Its designer was the engineer Alois Smolík, a former assistant of the leading Austrian aerodynamicist, von Mises. The Arsenal began by repairing ex-Austrian aircraft, but in the winter of 1919–20 produced the first machine of its own design. This was the Smolík S 1, a robust biplane for reconnaissance and light bombing duties. The fuselage was of plywood monocoque construction, the rest of the structure being of wood with fabric covering.

In all, 90 examples of the S 1 and its derivatives were produced. The first were of the SH 1 type, the letter H indicating that they were powered by a Hiero L engine of 230 hp. The SM 1 had a 260-hp Maybach Mb.IVa, the S 2 being similarly powered. All the S 1 and S 2 machines were armed with three machine-guns, and could carry up to 265 lb of bombs.

The service life of the S 1 and S 2 was rather uneventful; but they have great significance in Czechoslovak air history, being the first military types originated by that country. One Letov S 2 is preserved in its original form in the Technical Museum at Prague.

Letov S 16

The Letov S 16 long-range reconnaissance aircraft and medium bomber was a typical product of the late 1920s and early 1930s, its slender wings being a familiar sight on airfields of the time.

The prototype, after only a few initial test flights, was exhibited at the Paris *Salon* of 1926. The airframe was entirely of metal, fabric-covered, and the power plant comprised a Lorraine-Dietrich 12-cylinder engine of 450 hp, built under licence by the Skoda works and CKD-Praga. Armament consisted of a fixed Vickers machine-gun and twin Lewis guns on a movable mounting. Bomb-load could vary between 660 and 1,320 lb.

A production series of 22 Letov S 16s were built in 1927 for Latvia. These machines, designated S 16 Ls, had Hispano-Suiza 50 engines of 450 hp. Jezek, chief pilot of the Letov company, established a world speed record with an S 16 L by attaining a speed of 143.4 mph over a 100-km closed circuit, with a 1,000-kg payload. Another export order was for 16 S 16 Ts, which went to Turkey in 1929. First orders for the Czechoslovak Air Force had been placed in 1928. In all, 115 S 16s of all marks were produced and delivered to this Air Force, the majority of them having Lorraine-Dietrich engines.

A remarkable performance by an S 16 was the Prague-Tokyo flight of Lt-Col Skála and his mechanic Taufer, during August and September of 1927. They reached Tokyo, but on the return flight they crashed near Chita, in Siberia, fortunately without loss of life.

S 16s were capable of easy modification for the installation of other power plants within the 450-800-hp class. Thus, the S 116 had a Skoda L in-line engine of 500 hp; the S 216 a Walter Jupiter VI; the S 316 a Hispano-Suiza 12 N of 450/600 hp; and the S 416 a Breitfeld-Danek BD-500 of 500 hp. The most powerful variant was the S 516, with an Isotta Fraschini Asso of 800 hp.

The S 616 had an Avia Vr-36 of 600 hp; the S 716 a Skoda L with Farman reduction gear; the S 816 a 550 hp Praga ESV in-line engine; and, finally, the S 916 had a Lorraine-Dietrich with Farman reduction gear. The S 516 captured world speed records in 1930, by carrying a 500-kg payload over 100-, 500- and 1,000-km closed circuits, at 172·5, 171·7 and 171·05 mph.

There was also a twin-float variant, the S 16 J, built for Yugoslavia in 1929. Its all-duralumin floats were constructed on the principles developed by Dornier in Germany.

Letov S 20

Development of the Skoda HS 8 Fb engine, which had powered the Avia BH-21, led to the design and series production of 95 S 20 biplanes by the Letov company.

The S 20 was, in its original form, a tubby and ugly machine, its bulky fuselage being literally stuck between the two wings, leaving no free space and limiting the pilot's view. The first production machines also had the bulky fuselage, but this was soon replaced by a redesigned slim fuselage and the resulting machines received the designation S 20 M (M = modified). They were good and reliable fighter biplanes, although not as popular as the Avia BH-21s. Twenty were built for the Lithuanian Air Arm as S 20 Ls.

All S 20s were of mixed construction, with wooden wings, steel-tube fuselage and fabric covering. Armament consisted of two Vickers machine-guns.

As in the case of the Avia BH-21, there was a training version of the S 20, originally designated SA 20, but later changed to S 21. This was a lightweight variant, without guns, and powered by an HS 8 Aa engine of 180 hp: a total of 25 examples of the type were built.

Letov S 328 and S 528

In the second half of the 1930s, all the reconnaissance and light bombing biplanes of the A 11 family were replaced by a series of Letov S 328 biplanes. These aircraft served in Czechoslovak Air Force squadrons until 1939.

The S 328 biplane originated in 1933, when the Finnish Air Force ordered a robust general-purpose aircraft, similar to the Letov S 228 supplied to the Estonian Air Force. During 1933, Letov completed the first prototype for Finland, as the S 328 F. It had a Bristol Pegasus II.M-2 engine of 560/580 hp, and was armed with two fixed Mk 30 machine-guns in the upper wing and twin movable Mk 30 guns on a retractable mounting in the observer's cockpit.

The Finnish contract did not materialize. However, because the political situation in Europe suffered violent changes after Hitler's *coup d'etat*, the Czechoslovak National Defence Ministry ordered 445 aircraft of the S 328 type. In addition, 13 two-seat night-fighters, designated S 328 N, were produced, each with four fixed and two movable machine-guns. There were also four S 328 V seaplanes, the floats for which were supplied by Short Brothers of Britain. They replaced the A 29 floatplanes that had been used on the A.A. gunnery range in Yugoslavia.

Other engine installations produced the S 428 prototype, with an Avia Vr-36 12-cylinder in-line engine of 650 hp and four fixed guns; and the S 528, with Gnome-Rhône Mistral Major of 800 hp. Only six examples of this latter type were built, for use by the National Security Air Arm. In external appearance, the S 528 differed from the S 328 only in having a large NACA engine cowling instead of the latter's Townend ring.

After the German occupation of Czechoslovakia, all S 328s were confiscated and used partly by the Luftwaffe for training purposes and partly by the Slovak Air Force and Bulgarian Air Arm.

Some Slovak S 328s were used in the war against Russia; but many of their crews landed behind the Soviet lines and entered service with Czechoslovak Army units in the USSR. Three S 328s remained in serviceable condition and, in the summer of 1944, when Slovakia rose against the occupying Germans, were used in the initial fighting.

Letov S 328

Letov S 328 V

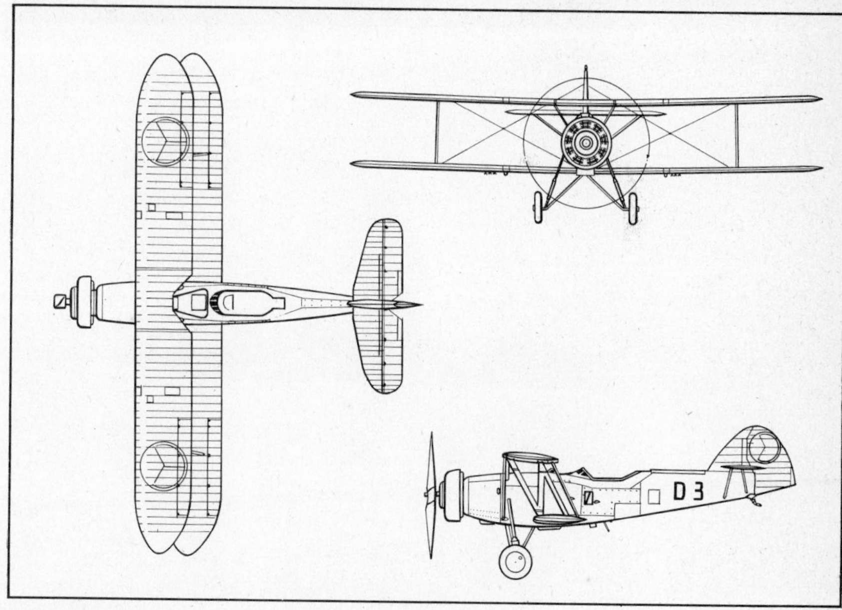

Letov S 328

TYPE	DIMENSIONS span ft	span in	length ft	length in	height ft	height in	WEIGHT max t-o lb	PERFORMANCE max speed mph	at height ft	service ceiling ft	combat range miles	REMARKS	
Letov S 1	43	5	27	3¼	10	6	3,031	120	6,600	19,700	445	Hiero L	230 hp
Letov S 16	50	2½	33	5¾	11	2	5,026	146	8,200	23,000	621	Lorraine-Dietrich	450 hp
Letov S 20	31	9¾	24	3¼	9	10	2,309	159	8,200	23,600	328	Skoda HS 8 Fb	300 hp
Letov S 328	44	11¼	34	1½	11	2	5,820	174	9,800	23,600	435	Walter Pegasus II.M-2	560 hp

Hawker Dankok

Hawker Dankok

Helwan HA-300, Orpheus engine

Helwan HA-300, Orpheus engine

Denmark

Hawker Dankok (Danecock)

In the early 1920s, Hawker Aircraft Ltd produced a dumpy little two-bay biplane fighter named the Woodcock I, powered by a single Armstrong Siddeley Jaguar engine. Flight tests with this aircraft were not entirely satisfactory, revealing an inefficient rudder design and a tendency to wing flutter, and a modified version appeared subsequently as the Woodcock II, with single-bay wings and a Bristol Jupiter IV power plant.

The Mk II largely eliminated the problems of the original model, though the new engine was itself not completely trouble-free. However, with further engine modification and additional refinement of the tail surfaces, the Woodcock was finally accepted by the RAF at the end of 1924.

During the following year, the Danish government expressed interest in the design and a Woodcock was loaned to them for evaluation. As a result of all this, Hawkers were asked to supply three machines to Woodcock II standard but powered by 385-hp Jaguar IV 14-cylinder radial engines, and incorporating minor alterations to the wing spars and a slight lengthening of the fuselage. Simultaneously, negotiations were opened for limited construction of the type under licence in Denmark.

Delivery of the Hawker-built machines was made in February 1926, and construction of 12 similar Dankoks (or Danecocks) was undertaken at Orlogsværftet (the Royal Danish Naval Dockyard) in 1927–8. The Dankoks – single-seaters with one 7·7-mm Madsen machine-gun ahead of the cockpit on either side – equipped one Army Air Service squadron and one Naval Air Service unit (No. 2 Luftflotille, Ringsted) and remained in operational service until 1937. A small number were still in existence in Denmark during World War II, until, with other vintage aircraft, they were destroyed by sabotage in 1943 to prevent them falling into German hands. However, one Dankok survived and is today an exhibit in Copenhagen Museum.

Egypt

Helwan HA-300

The first jet fighter to be built in Egypt traces its origins back to the late 1950s, when a team of engineers under Professor Willy Messerschmitt designed, at the Hispano Aviación works at Seville, a small lightweight delta-winged fighter for the Spanish Air Force. Designated HA-300, it was to be powered by a single Bristol Siddeley Orpheus turbojet of 6,740 lb s t, and a full-scale glider model had been tested in Spain before, in 1960, the Hispano company dropped the project. It was taken over in its entirety by the United Arab Republic, and further extensive development produced the present-day HA-300 at the Helwan Aircraft Works near Cairo.

A mid-wing monoplane of all-metal construction, the HA-300 has a small delta wing and a low-set all-moving tailplane. The first of two single-seat prototypes, flown on 7 March 1964, was powered by a 4,850-lb s t Orpheus 703 turbojet, with which its performance was probably in the vicinity of Mach 1.

The definitive version, which in mid-1967 had still not materialized, will require an afterburning engine of much greater power in order to reach its intended speed of around Mach 2, and Egyptian development of the E-300 engine, based on the Orpheus, was instigated under the direction of Dr Ferdinand Brandner. The E-300, probably developing about 7,050 lb s t

(9,920 lb with re-heat), is first being flight tested in a Hindustan HF-24 aircraft and is being considered also for the Mk II version of this Indian fighter.

Armament of the HA-300 is likely to comprise two or more cannon and two air-to-air missiles, possibly of the Russian "Atoll" type.

Finland

IVL A-22

The proven value of airpower in the later stages of the 1914–18 War led to the establishment of many new aircraft manufacturing plants in the years immediately afterwards, and in the spring of 1921 the Finnish government set up its own State Factory, the Industria Valtion Lentokonetehdas, at Sveaborg, near Helsinki.

One of the IVL's first commitments was to undertake production of the Hansa-Brandenburg W.33 seaplane, for which a licence was obtained in 1922. In Finnish Air Force service this aircraft was designated A-22, and differed from the original German model in being powered by a 300-hp Fiat six-cylinder water-cooled vertical engine. The first IVL-built machine was flown in November 1922 and series production began early in the following year.

Of mixed construction, the A-22 made considerable use of home-produced plywood for its skin covering and was mounted on a pair of long, single-step wooden floats. A feature of the design was the large rectangular rudder, extending beneath the lower line of the fuselage, with the tailplane mounted T-fashion on top. A single movable machine-gun was installed on a gun-ring in the rear cockpit. Performance, including a climb to 3,000 m (9,840 ft) in 22 minutes, was quite good for the period, and the A-22 was a standard reconnaissance and light day-bomber for many years.

Most of the 122 aircraft built were seaplanes, being assigned to the naval air bases at Sortavala, Turkinsaari and Viipuri, and to the training school at Santahamina; some examples were, however, completed with ski undercarriage for winter operations.

IVL Kotka

Finland's State Aircraft Factory evolved several types of its own design during the 1920s, but only a small number of these reached production status for the Finnish Air Force. Among them was the Kotka, a sturdy little two-bay biplane for maritime reconnaissance and day bombing.

The prototype, powered by a Bristol Jupiter radial engine, appeared in the mid-1920s. Like other machines produced in this period by the smaller aircraft manufacturing nations, the Kotka was designed to meet the particular needs of its country of origin, with costs kept to a minimum by the use of materials readily available within the country. Thus, the basic design was for a seaplane but, in common with most aircraft destined to serve in the Finnish climate, the twin, single-step floats could be exchanged for a wheel or ski landing gear.

The Kotka was a typical biplane of the period, of

IVL A-22

IVL Kotka

TYPE	DIMENSIONS span ft	span in	length ft	length in	height ft	height in	WEIGHT max t-o lb	PERFORMANCE max speed mph	at height ft	service ceiling ft	combat range miles	REMARKS
Hawker Dankok	32	7	26	1¼	10	1	3,045	145	SL	22,800	2½ hr approx	
Helwan HA-300	19	4	40	8	10	4	12,000					Weight estimated
IVL A-22	52	0	36	5	11	0	4,630	106				
IVL Kotka												No data available

IVL Myrsky II

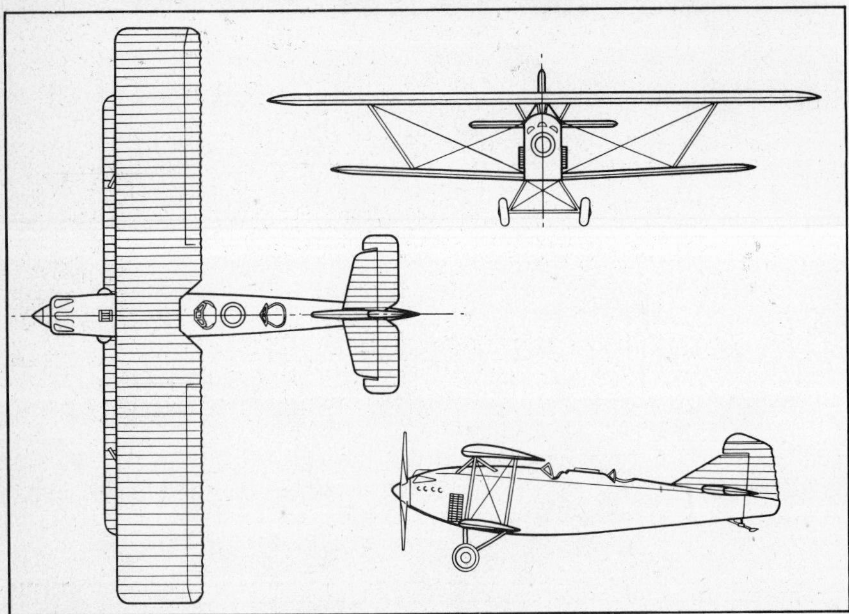
Amiot 122 BP 3

Amiot 122

Amiot 143

steel-tube and plywood construction, with a wide-track undercarriage. Both the pilot's and the observer's cockpits were roomy, the latter having a rotating ring on which was mounted a single machine-gun for defence. Small bombs could be suspended beneath the lower mainplane. Production aircraft were powered by a 575-hp Wright R-1820-E Cyclone nine-cylinder, air-cooled radial engine.

The Kotka entered service with the Finnish Air Force before the end of the first post-war decade, and remained in use by first-line squadrons for several years on a variety of duties.

IVL Myrsky (Storm)

Only one combat aircraft of Finnish design achieved production status during the World War II period, and the single-seat fighter concerned, the Myrsky, could hardly be termed a success. Designed by Dr E. Wegelius of the Finnish State Aircraft Factory, it made its appearance in prototype form in 1942, bearing the serial MY-1. A second prototype and two production Myrsky Is were added to the test programme, but several latent defects soon became apparent – weakness in the undercarriage and wing joints being the most serious – and all of the first four machines were ultimately lost in crashes. Despite this, the Finnish government decided to persevere with the Myrsky, and after extensive modification of the original design, the Myrsky II entered production at Tampere in 1944.

Power unit of the Myrsky II was the Swedish SFA-built version of the Pratt & Whitney R-1830-SC3-G Twin Wasp 14-cylinder radial engine; however, its 1,065 hp gave the fighter no more than the modest speed, for the time, of 329 mph.

The Myrsky II, of which 47 were completed (serials MY-5 to -51), was too late for combat against the Russian forces, but aided the latter, mostly in the close-support rôle, in driving the Germans from Finnish territory during the later stages of the war. Its armament comprised four 12·7-mm Browning machine-guns, located in the upper half of the engine cowling.

The factory at Tampere had ten machines of an improved model, the Myrsky III, under construction at the end of the war, but completion of these was halted by the Allied Control Commission.

France

Amiot 122 BP 3

Abandoning the Renault engine which had powered the Amiot 120 and 120S, the Société d'Emboutissage et de Constructions Mécaniques (SECM) produced in 1928 a 3-seat bomber-escort aircraft designated 122 BP 3 (BP 3 = Bombardment Protection, 3-seater). Powered by a geared Lorraine engine of 650 hp, this aircraft combined the handling qualities of a light single-engined machine with a load-carrying capacity equivalent to that of the twin-engined aircraft serving with the French Air Force at that time.

During the years 1928 and 1929 the prototype, registered F-AIUQ, was demonstrated in Rumania, Turkey, Greece and Serbia by the company's pilot, Pollon, accompanied by a mechanic named Vigroux. From it was evolved the production version with increased wing span, a first batch of 50 being constructed in 1929. The last aircraft of a second production series of 30 aircraft was delivered during 1934.

Nicknamed *La grosse Julie* (Fat Julie), the Amiot 122 BP 3 served with the 11th Air Regiment at Metz. Five were sold to Brazil in 1931; others would have gone to Poland, under an agreement concluded between that country and M. Amiot, had the crossing of the North Atlantic by the Polish crew of Idzikowski and Kubala been successful.

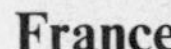

Fusilage, wings and tail unit of the 122 were of fabric-covered light alloy construction. Armament comprised five machine-guns; bomb load could vary from 880 to 1,760 lb.

In 1932, three Amiot 122s were adapted as flying test-beds for new prototype engines which, although more powerful than the Lorraine 18Kd, were of the same broad-arrow layout. The three machines were re-designated Amiot 124, 125 and 126 and were fitted respectively with a Hispano 18 Sb of 1,000 hp, a Renault 18 Jbr of 900 hp and a Lorraine 18 Gad Orion of 900 hp.

Since two-seat biplanes were beginning to be outdated by that time, no production order was received for any of these.

Amiot 143

In 1928, a plan was formulated for the production of a class of day and night bombers to be known as Multi-place de Combat. In 1930, the twin-engined Blériot 137M, Breguet 410M, SPCA 30M and Amiot 140M were produced to meet this specification: but in October 1933 the French Ministry of Aviation replaced the original plan with a new one called "Programme for Multi-seaters B.C.R." – the letters B.C.R. signifying Bombardment, Pursuit and Reconnaissance respectively.

An order for 40 Amiot 140 Ms was placed in November 1933, after intensive trials of the prototype. This was followed by an order for an improved model, designated Amiot 143, with Gnome-Rhône engines. Finally, in 1935, further orders for the Amiot 143 were received, bringing the total production of this type to 153. Only a single example of the Amiot 142 – similar except for having Hispano engines – was produced.

The prototype Amiot 143 M, powered by two Gnome-Rhône 14Krsd engines of 740 hp, made its first flight in August 1934. The first production machine, with Gnome-Rhône 14Kirs/Kjrs of 870 hp, flew in April 1935, and deliveries to the French Air Force began in July of the same year.

In December 1936, to replace a cancelled order for the Amiot 144, a final order for 25 Amiot 143s was placed under the new "Five-Year Plan". These aircraft were delivered from December 1937 and were designated 143 BN4 for the night version and 143 B5 for the day model. The single Amiot 142 was used for test purposes and was finally converted into Amiot 143 No. 75, with Gnome-Rhône engines, for service with the French Air Force.

The Amiot 143 was used by the 14th Independent Group and by the 21st, 22nd, 34th, 35th, and 38th Bomber Squadrons, each squadron consisting of two groups of 15 aircraft. It was capable of carrying a bomb-load of 1,984 lb and was armed with four machine-guns, so disposed that they could defend the aircraft against attack from any direction. In this respect, the all-metal Amiot 143 foreshadowed the B-17 Fortress of World War II.

At the outbreak of war in 1939, five bomber groups (including II/35, I and II/34 and II/38) still retained Amiot 143s, with a total of 60 machines. These were used for leaflet raids over Germany until 10 May 1940, after which they undertook bombing missions over enemy territory, dropping a total of 528 tons of bombs.

The action for which the Amiot 143s are best remembered was the daylight attack on bridges at Sedan, by 13 aircraft of the 34th and 38th Squadrons.

In November 1942, German forces in France pressed into service 11 Amiot 143s which they used for a variety of duties.

Amiot 143

Amiot 143

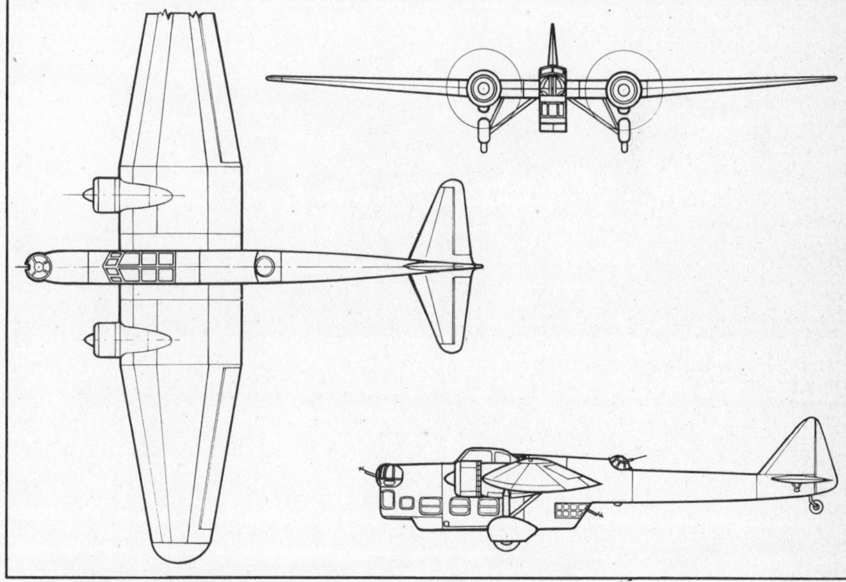

Amiot 143

TYPE	DIMENSIONS span ft	span in	length ft	length in	height ft	height in	WEIGHT max t-o lb	PERFORMANCE max speed mph	at height ft	service ceiling ft	combat range miles	REMARKS	
IVL Myrsky II	36	1	27	4¾	9	10	7,080	329		29,500	310		
Amiot 122 BP 3	70	6½	45	0¼	16	10¾	9,259	127		20,300	621	LO 18 Kd	650 hp
Amiot 143	80	2¼	58	10¾	16	9¾	22,023	190	13,000	31,200	807	2 × GR 14 Kirs/Kjrs	870 hp

Amiot 351 prototype

Amiot 353 prototype

Amiot 354, Vichy French mailplane

Blanchard Brd 1

Amiot 350 series

SECM produced in 1934 a multi-seat bomber with retractable undercarriage, which was provisionally designated E6/E7. On completion, it was considered better suited for the rôle of long-range mail carrier and was redesignated the Amiot 341. Before being flown, however, it was redesigned as a military aircraft and redesignated Amiot 340.

The fuselage, of circular cross-section, was metal-covered; the wings were of stressed-skin metal construction, and only the rudders were fabric-covered. Early tests showed that the 340 had an excellent performance, and the French Air Ministry placed an initial production order for it. Before long, however, it was redesigned as a four-seater to meet an official requirement and was redesignated Amiot 350. One hundred of the revised aircraft were ordered, the original contract for the Amiot 340 being cancelled.

Progressive development of the basic 350 led to a number of variants. Of these, the types produced in quantity were the Amiot 351 with two Gnome-Rhône 14N 38/39 engines and twin fins, the 353 with two Rolls-Royce Merlin III engines and twin fins, and the 354 with two Gnome-Rhône 14N 48/49 engines and a single fin. The remaining models 350, 352, 355, 356 and 357 were prototypes or projects only.

On the declaration of war, orders for the Amiot 351/354 series totalled 285 aircraft, all of which were to be delivered by 1 April 1940 at the latest. But the first Amiot 351 did not fly until January 1940 and only 86 aircraft had been delivered to bomber squadrons by the end of the French campaign. Armament comprised either three machine-guns or two machine-guns and one cannon, according to the series, with a bomb-load of between 1,760 and 2,645 lb.

Four bomber groups (I/21, II/21, I/34 and II/34), making up No. 9 Group, received Amiot 351/353/354s in 1940, but were unable to utilize any of the aircraft for bombing missions, since they either arrived without armament, or were sabotaged or otherwise destroyed.

In 1942, when the Germans crossed the demarcation line that split France in two, they seized four Amiot 351/354s. One of these was converted by *Luftflotte* III into a transport aircraft, while Amiot 354 No. 11 was made into a VIP transport for Admiral Darlan.

Blanchard Brd 1

The first squadron of the French Marine Air Service in the HB3 category (3-seat bomber flying-boats) was formed in 1923, equipped with Blanchard flying-boats of the Brd 1 type. The HB2 category, represented by the Schreck FBA 19, did not enter service. The Brd 1 was a two-seat aircraft with a hull of beech and mahogany construction. Its two 260-hp Hispano-Suiza engines, or Gnome-Rhône Jupiters, were carried above the hull on tubular-steel mountings, the tubes forming a kind of cage of pentagonal cross-section. The upper wing was of slightly greater span than the lower, and was in two parts, with almost full-span ailerons. An amphibious version, with folding wings, was projected but not built.

The prototype Brd 1 was built in the workshops of the Société des Avions Blériot, and flew from the Seine in 1922. In April 1924, Lieutenant de Vaisseau Pelletier d'Oisy used it to capture several world altitude records with payloads varying from 550 to 3,300 lb. For these attempts the Brd 1 was provided with an enclosed cockpit and carried no armament.

Fourteen Brd 1s equipped the 5R1 Squadron which was based at St-Raphaël in 1923, and then at Berre at the end of 1926. Their armament consisted of four machine-guns, mounted in two cockpits, in the nose and amidships; and four bombs of either 110 or 220 lb could be carried. The service career of the type was somewhat short-lived, as it displayed rather poor stability in flight.

Blériot 127

In 1925, the Société Blériot Aéronautique of Suresnes, near Paris, produced a four-seat escort fighter, powered by two Lorraine engines of 400 hp, which they designated Type 117. Too advanced in an age of "stick and string" two-seaters, this aircraft aroused little interest and remained only a prototype. Not until 1928 was the formula of the monoplane of thick wing section, with machine-gun positions in the engine nacelles, revived with the Blériot 127M.

The prototype 127 was a large monoplane, with two 500-hp unsupercharged Hispano 12Gb engines. The thickness of the wing section was such that it was possible to pass from the fuselage to the engine nacelles in flight. The cockpit for pilot and navigator was situated in front of the wing. Twin main wheels, directly below the engines, supported the aircraft on the ground. Machine-guns were mounted in the rear of the engine nacelles to permit a completely free field of fire to the rear.

Built entirely of wood, with fabric covering, the prototype attained a speed of 138 mph at 6,500 ft and could climb to 13,000 ft in 12 min 21 sec, with a service ceiling of 26,575 ft.

The standard production model was the Blériot 127/2. Beginning in 1929, 42 of these machines were built for the French Air Force and equipped, in particular, the 11th Aviation Regiment at Metz. The 127/2 differed from the prototype in having Hispano engines of 550 hp and lateral radiators. Later examples also introduced tubular-steel engine mountings and Blériot sprung wheels. One other variant, designated 127/3, was built; this was the 127M prototype with a turret mounted in the front of the fuselage.

In service the 127/2 was armed with one or two machine-guns in front of and two behind the trailing-edge of the wing; its bomb-load varied between 1,100 and 2,200 lb. Unfortunately, adaptation of the Blériot 127/2 to its military rôle brought an increase in all-up weight, to the detriment of performance. Even more serious was that the increased weight led to deformation of the wings in flight, necessitating its quick withdrawal from service.

In 1930, an all-metal version with a cantilever wing made its appearance, but only two aircraft of this type were built, under the designation Blériot 137.

Bloch 131

It was in 1933 at Courbevoie – a suburb of Paris – in a factory used previously for the manufacture of car bodies, that the engineer Marcel Bloch installed some offices and a workshop that were to play an important part in the history of the French aircraft industry.

After producing a few tourist and light transport aircraft, and a small series of ambulance machines, the company built its first fighter aircraft. Designed to meet the requirements of the B.C.R. (Bombardment-Pursuit-Reconnaissance) specification, the Bloch 130 (named *Guynemer*) flew for the first time on 29 June 1934. Its development problems took a long time to cure, but eventually 40 of the type were ordered. When the improved type 131 was evolved, the orders for the 130 were transferred to the new design, before it had flown.

On 16 August 1936, the prototype Bloch 131 made its first flight, during the course of which it became evident that extensive modifications were required. The second prototype, which flew on 8 May 1937, had increased wing

Blériot 127/2

Bloch 131

Bloch 131, second prototype

TYPE	DIMENSIONS span ft	span in	length ft	length in	height ft	height in	WEIGHT max t-o lb	PERFORMANCE max speed mph	at height ft	service ceiling ft	combat range miles	REMARKS	
Amiot 351	74	11	47	6¾	13	2	24,251	301		32,800	1,550	2 × GR 14N 38/39	950 hp
Amiot 353	74	11	47	6¾	13	2	24,251	301		32,800	1,550	2 × RR Merlin III	990 hp
Amiot 354	74	11	47	6¾	13	2	24,251	301		32,800	1,550	2 × GR 14N 48/49	1.060 hp
Blanchard Brd1	62	4	43	6¾	16	5	8,664	104	SL	11,500		2 × HS 8 Fd	260 hp
Blériot 127/2	76	1	48	2	11	2½	10,950	124	6,500	22,500	500	2 × HS 12Hb	550 hp
Bloch 131	66	3	58	6	13	1½	18,796	217	13,000	24,500	930	2 × GR 14 N10/11	870 hp

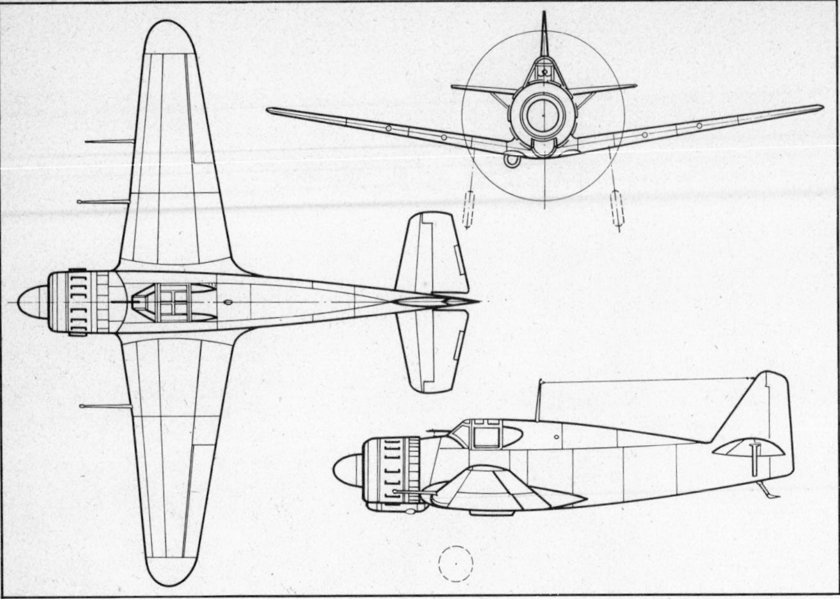

Bloch 151

Bloch 152

Bloch 155 (second aircraft from left) and 152s

and tail areas, a dihedral tailplane and an entirely new fuselage. It was an all-metal low-wing monoplane powered by two Gnome-Rhône engines and carrying a crew of four. Armament comprised three machine-guns and 1,760 lb of bombs could be carried.

The standard model, intended to replace the wooden Potez 540, went into production at the end of 1937 in the SNCASO factories at Courbevoie and Chateauroux. (Nationalization of the French aircraft industry had amalgamated the Bloch and Blériot companies under the title of Société Nationale de Constructions Aéronautiques du Sud-Ouest – SNCASO).

The first production Bloch 131 RB4 (four-seat reconnaissance bomber) was delivered in June 1938. A total of 181 had been ordered, but only 121 were built, for this aircraft, which had been ordered as a fast day bomber with an anticipated speed of 239 mph at 13,000 ft, had to be demoted to reconnaissance duties because of its mediocre performance. Thus in September 1939, those in service equipped only reconnaissance units.

Even this restricted use did not save the Bloch 131 from heavy losses, and it had to be replaced in the reconnaissance squadrons by the faster Potez 63/11. By 10 May 1940, only group I/61, stationed in North Africa was still operating this type.

When German troops overran France, 21 Bloch 131s were captured by them, but were scrapped. The Bloch 132, 133 and 134 variants were built only as prototypes.

Bloch 151, 152 and 155

An all-metal low-wing monoplane fighter, designated Bloch 150, with retractable undercarriage, was built to meet the requirements of a specification issued in 1934 by the French Air Ministry. The company's pilot, Curvale, attempted to get it off the ground for its first flight on 17 July 1936, but it was too heavy and could not be coaxed into the air. With a new Gnome-Rhône engine and different wing, a second attempt was made on 8 August 1936, with no greater success.

The prototype finally made its first flight in October 1937, at Villacoublay, after its weight had been reduced and larger wings fitted. An order for 25 production models followed, subject to slight modifications, and these were to be built at the Chateauroux factory of SNCASO. Unfortunately, the design detail of the 150 did not lend itself to mass production, and it was redesigned as the Bloch 151, which first flew in August 1938.

Existing orders for the Bloch 150 were transferred to the 151, which had an armament of four 7.5-mm machine-guns. It was anticipated that by December 1938, an average of 180 of these machines would be coming off the production lines each month, utilizing components made in five SNCASO factories. In the event, production difficulties resulted in only 85 of the fighters being available when World War II broke out.

In parallel production was the Bloch 152, which differed from the 151 in having a more powerful engine and redesigned fin. The prototype 152 had flown at the end of 1938; it entered production in 1939 and 614 were produced during the war. Armament comprised either two cannon and two machine-guns or four machine-guns.

On 3 September 1939, not one of the 120 Bloch 151s and 152s in service was fit for action: 95 were without propellers, the remainder without gun-sights. By 30 November 1939, the Armée de l'Air had received 358 of these aircraft, but 157 were still without propellers and, moreover, required important modifications to the engine cooling system.

By 20 June 1940, a total of 593 Bloch 151s and 152s had been delivered, of which 12 equipped the French Navy Squadron AC3, while nine 151s had been transferred to Greece. They equipped eight of the 22 pursuit groups of the Armée de l'Air at the time of the German attack on 10 May 1940, as follows: GC I/1, II/1, II/10, III/10, I/8, II/8, II/9, and III/9. After the Armistice, a number of the surviving aircraft were used by the Vichy government; 173 were captured by the Germans, who transferred 20 to Rumania.

A third production version, the Bloch 155 – a development of the 152 with a 1,180-hp Gnome-Rhône 14 N 49 which gave it increased performance – flew for the first time on 3 December 1939, followed by the first production 155 (No. 701) on 3 April 1940.

Early production 155s had the same armament as the 151/152, but this was later supplemented by two extra machine-guns, and armour protection was provided for the pilot. The 15 or so examples produced at Chateauroux were used by Vichy and later seized by the Germans.

Bloch 175

The Bloch 175 light bomber was a development of the Bloch 174, which had been switched to a reconnaissance rôle because of its limited bomb load. It was a three-seat all-metal monoplane, with retractable undercarriage, and carried an armament of five machine-guns and up to 3,416 lb of bombs. It was powered by two Gnome-Rhône 14N 48/49 engines.

Only 21 MB 175s had been produced, in the Bordeaux factory of SNCASO, by the time of the Armistice, and none of these was used in action. A further 200 air-frames were almost completed at that time, and components for a further batch of 200 had been produced.

After the Armistice, the Germans tested the MB 175 and, satisfied with its performance, authorized SNCASO to complete the 200 machines on the assembly lines with the reservation that they were not to be armed. In the event, only a further 56 MB 175s were completed, between October 1940 and June 1941. By order of the occupying forces they were sent to Germany, where three were tested later with DB 601 and DB 605 engines.

Other MB 175s were almost ready for delivery when the Germans decided to use the Gnome-Rhône engines, propellers and engine cowlings from these aircraft for their Messerschmitt 323s. The airframes were stripped of their engines, which were replaced by Hispano 12 Y31s, leading to a change of designation to Bloch 177 (the Bloch 176 prototype had been powered by two Pratt & Whitney SC 3G/SC 4G).

In November 1942, all production of the MB 175 ceased; but this was not the end of the story. In the immediate post-war years the French Navy was short of torpedo-carrying aircraft, and placed an order for 80 Bloch 175s to fill the gap. These derived from a version designed in 1941, known as the 175A, and were built in two forms, as the Bloch 175T (T = Torpedo) with Gnome-Rhône 14N 54/55 or N 68/69 engines, and as the Bloch SO 175T with Gnome-Rhône 14N 48/49s. Armament of the MB 175T comprised four machine-guns and a torpedo, or three 550-lb anti-submarine weapons. The SO 175T had a more rounded nose, lengthened to include a radome, and was armed with three cannon and rockets.

The first MB 175T flew on 15 May 1946, and this version equipped Flotille 6F at Agadir until 1953.

Bloch 200

In 1932, the French Air Ministry issued specification BN 5, for a five-seat night bomber, and six companies produced a total of eight different designs to meet the specification. These comprised the Lioré et Olivier 300

Bloch 174

Bloch 175, Luftwaffe

Bloch 175T

TYPE	DIMENSIONS						WEIGHT	PERFORMANCE				REMARKS	
	span		length		height		max t-o	max speed	at height	service ceiling	combat range		
	ft	in	ft	in	ft	in	lb	mph	ft	ft	miles		
Bloch 151	34	6¾	29	8½	13	0	5,667	298	13,000	32,800	398	GR 14N 35	920 hp
Bloch 152	34	6¾	29	8½	13	0	5,842	323	13,000	32,800	373	GR 14N 25	1,080 hp
Bloch 155	34	6¾	29	9¼	13	0	6,262	348	18,000	33,500	652	GR 14N 49	1,180 hp
Bloch 175	58	10¾	41	5½	11	9¾	18,739	323		33,800	1,243	2 × GR 14N 48/49	1,180 hp
Bloch 175T	58	10¾	41	5½	11	9¾	18,739	323		33,800	2,050	2 × GR 14N 54/55	1,120 hp
Bloch 175T (SO)	58	10¾	40	9¼	11	9¾	18,739	335		33,800	2,050	2 × GR 14N 48/49	1,180 hp
Bloch 200	73	8	52	6	12	10¼	16,049	143		26,300	620	2 × GR 14 Kirs/Kjrs	870 hp

Bloch MB 200 without nose and dorsal turrets

Bloch MB 200

Bloch MB 210

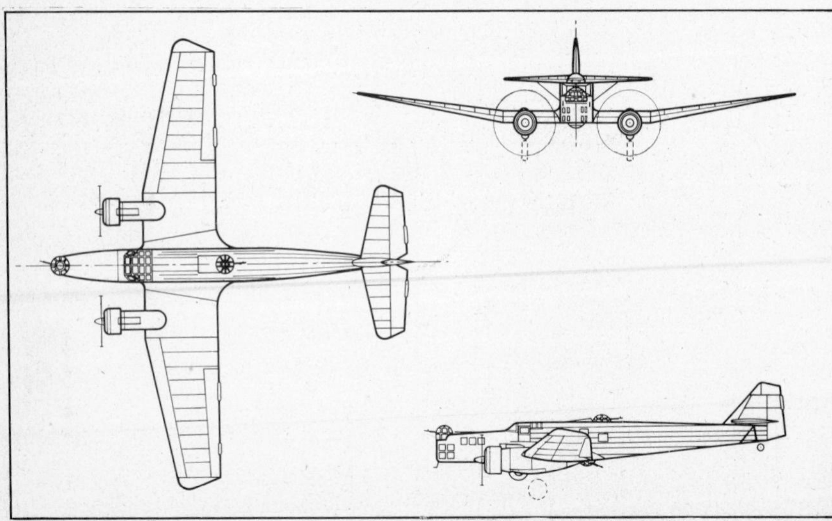
Bloch MB 210

and 301, Farman 220 and 221, Potez 41, Sté Aéronautique Bordelaise (SAB) AB 20, Couzinet 90 and Bloch 200.

The designation of the programme was modified later to BN 4, to cover production of the Farman 221 and Bloch 200. A contract for three prototypes of the type 200 BN 4 was awarded to the Bloch company, and the first of these, built at Courbevoie, flew in July 1933. An initial order for 25 production aircraft was placed on 1 January 1934, and by the end of the year the first of these had entered service.

Under an agreement between the Bloch and Potez companies, 25 aircraft a month were produced by Potez in its Méaulte plant and by Hanriot at Bourges from January 1935. By the end of that year, 12 bomber squadrons had been equipped with the type, and 10 more had been ordered for the naval base at Bizerte. A single machine was also delivered to Czechoslovakia in May 1935. Altogether, 208 MB 200s were delivered to the French Air Force. Others were built under licence in Czechoslovakia with the designation Aero MB 200.

The MB 200 was a cantilever high-wing monoplane of all-metal construction, powered by two Gnome-Rhône 14 Krsd engines in prototype form, and by two 14 Kirs/Kjrs in the production version. Armament comprised three machine-guns, and 3,300-5,500 lb of bombs could be carried. Fuel capacity was 304 gallons.

Unfortunately, the aircraft's maximum speed proved to be some 31 mph lower than anticipated, which meant that with a top speed of only 143 mph, it had a far from satisfactory performance. In September 1938, a total of 320 MB 200s and 210s (see below) were in service. Just one year later, 65 remained operational with six bomber groups and were already considered outdated. By the start of the German offensive, not a single machine of the type remained in squadron service.

There were three variants of the type: the MB 201 powered by two Hispano engines, the MB 202 with four Gnome-Rhône engines and the MB 203 with two Renault (later Clerget diesel) engines, all of which appeared in prototype form only. In addition, in 1939, MB 200 No. 83 was converted into a ministerial VIP transport aircraft and given the registration F-APFG.

Bloch 210

The MB 210, developed from the MB 200, flew for the first time at the end of November 1934. It was a low-wing monoplane of all-metal construction, with retractable undercarriage, and was powered by two Gnome-Rhône engines of 760 hp each.

Following nationalization of 80 per cent of the French aircraft industry, production increases of 35-40 per cent were anticipated for 1937. Instead, there was a considerable drop, and only 370 military aircraft were produced in 1937, among them a few dozen MB 210s.

In 1935, the prototype MB 210 had been converted into a seaplane and sent first to Berre and later to St-Raphaël where it was used for various tests, with the serial number SR-24. The standard version, built in the SNCASO factories at Courbevoie and Bordeaux, began to equip night bomber units of the French Air Force in 1937. It differed from the prototype in having increased power (two Gnome-Rhône 14 Kirs/Kjrs of 870 hp, with Ratier propellers), an upswept fin and engine nacelles reinforced by external ribs. Armament comprised three machine-guns, and bomb load varied from 2,116 to 4,340 lb. SNCASO also developed an experimental version of the MB 210 BN5 with a wooden wing, intended to conserve duralumin in wartime.

A total of 253 MB 210s were delivered to the Air Force, and a further 45 were produced for other customers, 35 of these going to the Republican forces in Spain during the Civil War, and 10 to Rumania.

Pending deliveries of the Lioré 451 and Amiot 350 bombers, production of the MB 210 continued and in September 1939 a total of 155 aircraft of this type were in service, in 13 bomber groups. On 10 May 1940, Bomber Groups I/23, II/23, I/21, II/21, I/11, II/11, I/19, II/19 and II/61 still flew MB 210s, with a maximum speed of 186 mph, matched against Luftwaffe bombers which could attain a maximum speed of 279 mph with comparable bomb load and cruising range. The 210 was robust, but its lack of power and poor controllability at low speeds made it unpopular with aircrew.

MB 210 No. 6, registered F-APOT, was used in 1937 by the ministerial squadron stationed at Villacoublay, while another served as a flying test-bed for the Messier-Renollaud variable-pitch propeller. No. 87 flew on 31 December 1937 powered by two Renault L2 Fas engines of 860 hp, and in 1940, at Lyons, a further machine of this type was tested with two Bristol Hercules I engines of British manufacture.

When German forces occupied the free zone of France, they seized 37 Bloch 210s, which they assigned to equip Bulgarian bomber units.

Developments were the Bloch 211, powered by Hispano engines, and the Bloch 212, with Hispano radial engines, which flew in September 1935 and October 1936 respectively, but remained only prototypes.

Breguet-Michelin

In 1915, Louis Breguet built a prototype biplane bomber designated BU3, with a 200-hp Canton-Unné engine. Of fabric-covered metal construction, this aircraft had a tricycle undercarriage, with a single wheel on each unit, and was of "pusher" layout, with the cockpit in front of the wings and the propeller behind them. This arrangement had been specified by the French Chief of Staff, to simplify identification of the BU3 by anti-aircraft batteries, since German bombers of that period were all of tractor configuration.

On 20 August 1914, soon after the outbreak of war, the industrialists Edouard and André Michelin made an approach to the Ministry of War, offering their entire productive capacity for the construction of aircraft. On 11 November they contracted to build 100 Breguet aircraft under licence; early in 1915, therefore, the Breguet BU3 went into production, by Michelin, under the designation BUM or BM. The first "Michelin" squadron was formed at Avord, followed by BM 118, BM 120, BM 121 and other squadrons.

In mid-1915, the Minister of War initiated a competition for what he called "powerful aeroplanes", capable of destroying the enemy's munition factories. The specification called for a speed of 78 mph at 6,500 ft and range of 370 miles with a bomb load of 660 lb.

The competition proved to be a walkover for Louis Breguet's new SN 3 bomber, since his sole rival was the Schmitt Sch VI B2, which was eliminated by its tractor configuration. The SN 3, known also as the Type V and BUC, differed from the BUM by having sesquiplane wings, three main landing wheels and streamlined bomb-racks. It went into production at the beginning of 1916 and was produced also by the Michelin factory at Clermont-Ferrand, as was the Breguet VI development, with Canton-Unné DF 9 engine and smaller radiators.

These aircraft were neither fast nor manoeuvrable enough for use as day bombers, and had to be relegated to night missions. Later, with a single 37-mm forward-firing cannon as defensive armament, they were employed on reconnaissance duties.

The generally-similar BM V aroused the interest of the British government, who arranged for the Grahame-White company to produce it at Hendon, in 1917, powered by a 250-hp Rolls-Royce engine. Only ten were built, as GW 19s, as performance fell below expectation.

Meanwhile, in France, the Renault-powered BMs were having trouble, particularly from engine fires during take-off. This led to many of them being re-engined with

Breguet-Michelin II

Breguet-Michelin IV

Breguet-Michelin V

TYPE	DIMENSIONS						WEIGHT	PERFORMANCE				REMARKS	
	span ft	span in	length ft	length in	height ft	height in	max t-o lb	max speed mph	at height ft	service ceiling ft	combat range miles		
Bloch 210	74	10	62	0	15	9	21,055	186	13,000	29,500	683	2 x GR 14 Kirs/Kjrs	870 hp
BM II (BUM)	61	8	32	5	12	9½	4,662	78			248	CU DF9	200 hp
BM V (BUC)	57	8	26	0¾	12	6½	4,739	86	SL		435	RE 8 Gd	220 hp

Breguet 14 A2

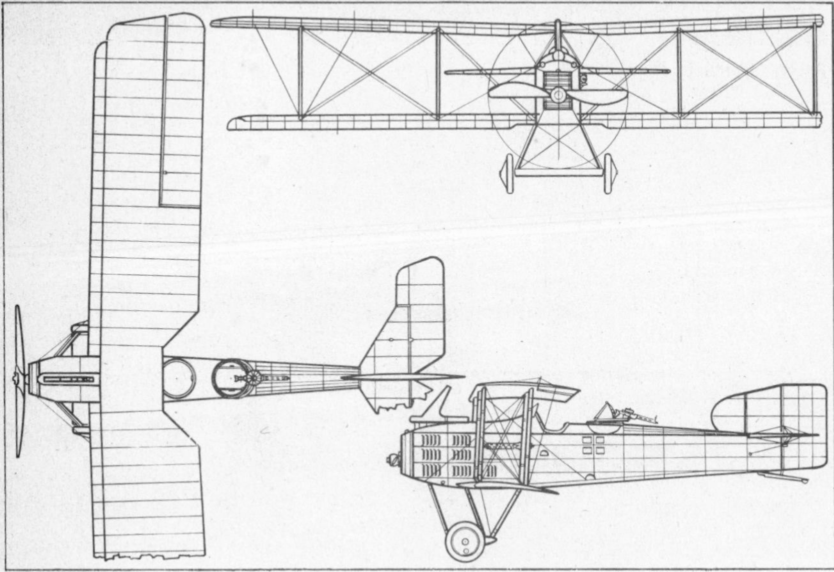
Breguet 14 A2

Breguet 16 BN2

Breguet 19 A2, Renault engine

Canton-Unnés, until modifications to the Renault brought it back into service.

By 11 November 1918, the Michelin factories had built 1,884 Breguet aircraft of all types, and had also produced 8,600 bomb-racks and 342,000 bombs.

Breguet 14 B2 and 16 B2

Of the 17 different versions of the Breguet 14, three were utilized as bombers. These were the 14 B2 two-seat day bomber, 14 BN2 two-seat night bomber and 14 B1 single-seat bomber. The latter was intended for raids on Berlin and was, in fact, a converted B2, additional petrol being carried in place of the observer/gunner.

The prototype Breguet 14 flew for the first time on 21 November 1916, under the designation Breguet AV, these letters indicating that the aircraft, contrary to the stipulations of the Chief of Staff, was of tractor configuration. Designed by Vuillierme, it had progressed from drawing board to prototype in only six months and was a remarkable machine, some three years ahead of contemporary design. It was built largely of light alloy and had automatic flaps on the lower wings. With a normal load of 32 bombs, each weighing 22 lb, the AV could reach an altitude of 16,400 ft in 39 minutes. Its maximum speed exceeded 112 mph and its range was 435 miles. It was powered by a 300-hp Renault 12 Fe engine, cooled by a frontally-mounted radiator.

Constructed from 1917 onwards by Breguet, SECM, Renault, Bellanger and Hanriot, Schmitt, Darracq and Michelin, the AV entered service with observation squadrons at the end of that year, under the designation 14 A2, and with bombardment squadrons as the 14 B2.

Among the bombardment squadrons equipped with these aircraft were BR 66, BR 107, BR 117 and BR 129. Units belonging to the First Air Division built up a formidable reputation as a striking force in 1918, when entire squadrons made daily raids on enemy targets, the most famous squadron being that led by Sqdn Ldr Vuillemin. In March 1918, the American Expeditionary Forces in France also received 47 Breguet 14 B2s, and by the end of the war the bomber versions of this design had dropped more than 1,900 tons of bombs.

Orders for the 14 A2 and 14 B2 reached such proportions in 1918 that the Breguet factory at Villacoublay had to be enlarged to enable it to deliver four machines a day. Production did not end until 1926, by which time a total of over 8,000 had been built, of which 5,500 were A2 or B2 versions.

After the war, 40 Breguet 14 B2s were sold to Poland, 20 to Rumania and 20, on floats, to Finland. Spain bought 40 and also built 14 B2s under licence, fitting them with Liberty engines. In Japan, Nakajima also built this aircraft under licence, powered by a Rolls-Royce Eagle engine, under the designation Nakajima B6.

The 14 B2 remained in service with the French Air Force until 1930. It made a number of important flights, one of the best known being a long-distance flight led by Sqdn Ldr Vuillemin which, between 3 November 1922 and 8 January 1923, involved crossing the Mediterranean and the Sahara Desert, before returning to Paris via Morocco and Spain.

In parallel production and service from the end of 1917 was the Breguet 16 B2, a larger version of the 14 B2. Its wings were of increased span, with three bays instead of two, and with ailerons instead of automatic flaps on the lower wings. The improved performance of this model permitted 1,322 lb of bombs to be carried at a speed of 99 mph at 13,000 ft.

The prototype retained the fin of the 14 B2, but production aircraft, which remained in service in France and Czechoslovakia until 1927, had a fin of more modern appearance.

Breguet 19

The prototype of this two-seat biplane made its first public appearance at the seventh Paris Air Show in 1921. Designed as a successor to the Breguet 14, it was to enjoy even greater success, being built in several versions with many different power plants, ranging from

375 to 800 hp. It was of robust fabric-covered metal construction, easily maintained, and remained in service for more than 15 years.

Apart from the tail unit, there was little similarity to the Breguet 14. The sesquiplane wings had only a single interplane strut each side, and the fuselage was of circular cross-section. A Renault engine was fitted at the time of the first flight, in May 1922, but was later replaced by a Lorraine Vee-type engine of 375 hp, and then by a 450-hp engine of the same make. With the latter, the prototype attained a maximum speed of 142 mph at sea-level, which was a good performance by contemporary standards.

By making several successful long-distance flights, the Breguet 19 attracted the interest of foreign air forces and was ordered in both landplane and seaplane versions. Series production began in 1925 and soon reached an output of four aircraft per day. By the end of 1926, Breguet had built 1,100 A2s (reconnaissance) and B2s (bombers) for the French, Polish, Serbian, Argentinian, Belgian, Greek, Bolivian, Chinese and Persian Air Forces. In addition, licence production was undertaken in Belgium, Japan, Yugoslavia, Greece and Spain. As late as 1 January 1936, 116 Breguet 19 A2s and B2s were still serving with the French Air Force. Some of the foreign-built machines were still in service in 1940!

Variants of the basic type included the 19 *ter* (F-AIXP), with increased wing area and 600-hp Hispano engine; the 197, which was bought by Greece, Turkey and Yugoslavia; and the 198 (F-ALPN) which was sold to Yugoslavia. Last of the series was the model 199 of 1934, which had an 860-hp engine and attained 174 mph.

A special Breguet 19, named *Question Mark*, was used by Costes and Bellonte for the first successful east-west crossing of the North Atlantic.

Breguet Bizerte

In the early 1930s, Breguet obtained a manufacturing licence for the Calcutta flying-boat from the British firm of Short Brothers. A military version of the Calcutta served in small numbers with the French Navy and from it was developed the Br 521 Bizerte which operated with five long-range bomber-reconnaissance squadrons (E1, E2, E3, E5 and E9) during the period 1935–40.

The prototype Bizerte flew for the first time in September 1933 and production machines began to appear in 1935. The second production model differed considerably from the prototype and first production machine. The long glazed cockpit canopy was extended to the bow, and the open gun position, previously located in the nose, was deleted. Blister gun positions were installed on each side of the hull just forward of the leading-edge of the lower wing. The original single midship gunner's cockpit was replaced by two gun mountings, firing to the port and starboard, housed under sliding hatches. The defensive armament of five 7·5-mm Darne machine-guns was completed by a mounting on a cockpit in the extreme tail. An offensive load of four 165-lb bombs was carried on under-wing racks.

Production in small quantities continued into 1940, a total of more than 30 Bizertes being completed. The standard model was powered by three Gnome-Rhône 14 Kirs radial engines, each delivering 900 hp. Examples captured by the Germans were utilized for air/sea rescue, operating from former French seaplane stations. One was recaptured by the French in 1944, still serviceable.

Breguet 19, Spanish-built

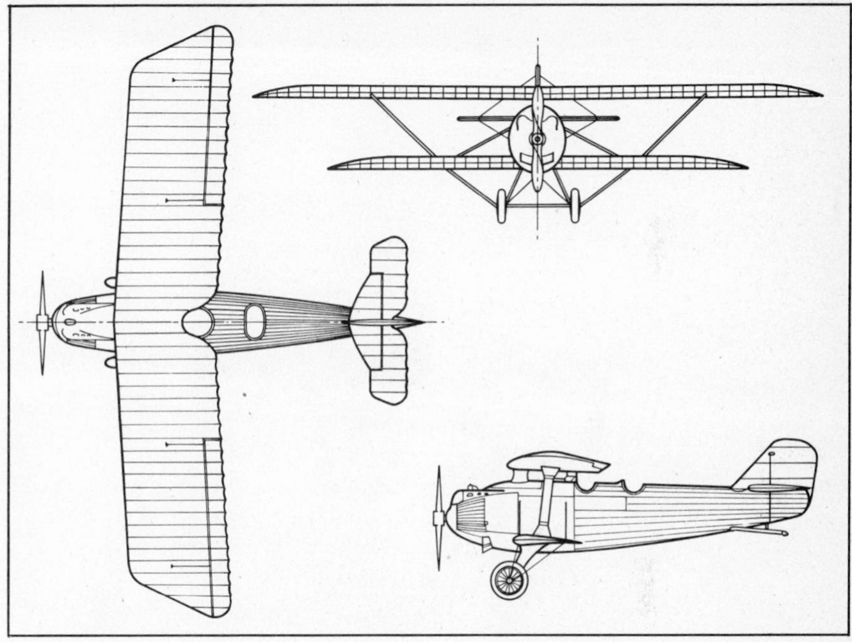

Breguet 19

Breguet Br 521 Bizerte prototype

TYPE	DIMENSIONS span ft	span in	length ft	length in	height ft	height in	WEIGHT max t-o lb	PERFORMANCE max speed mph	at height ft	service ceiling ft	combat range miles	REMARKS	
Br 14 B2	48	11½	29	1¼	10	9¾	4,144	112	SL	18,000	435	RE 12 Fe	300 hp
Br 16 B2	55	7½	31	3¾	10	10¾	4,850	99	SL	15,100	497	RE 12 Fe	300 hp
Br 19 B2	48	8	31	2½	10	11½	4,850	141		22,000	497	LO, HS or RE	450 hp
Br 521 Bizerte	115	4	67	2¼	24	6½	36,600	151	3,200	19,700	1,305	3 × GR 14 Kirs 1	900 hp

Breguet 690 prototype

Breguet 691

Breguet 693

Breguet 690 series

In 1934 the French Chief of Air Staff initiated a programme calling for a three-seat twin-engined fighte (Class C 3), and the Potez 630, Romano 110, Loire Nieuport 20 and Hanriot 220 were produced to meet thi requirement. Breguet departed intentionally from th official specification, by constructing a heavier aircraf which they considered would be suitable for more varie rôles.

This aircraft, known as the Breguet 690, was designe in 1935 by Georges Ricard and completed in May 1937 but since Breguet had not joined the nationalize industry, it no longer enjoyed any priorities, with th result that the prototype had to wait a whole year fo its Hispano engines and did not make its first fligh until 23 March 1938.

The 690 was very different from the rectangular winged biplanes built previously by Breguet, being clean-looking cantilever monoplane of all-metal cons truction. During early trials it achieved a maximun speed of 295 mph, making it as fast as the Dewoitine 52 single-seat fighter and faster than the Morane 406, th latest single-seat fighter then in French service.

The first version to enter production in 1938 wa equipped as a two-seat light assault bomber, with th new designation of Breguet 691. Seventy of this versio were built with Ratier propellers and 28 with Hispan propellers manufactured under licence from Hamilton

The Hispano engines which powered the 691s wer not entirely satisfactory, and were replaced with Gnome Rhône 14 M4/M5s in the Breguet 693, of which 120 wer constructed from 1940. With alternative 800-hp Pratt & Whitney R-1830 SIE 3G engines, the aircraft becam the Breguet 695, and 50 of this version were built. Fina production variant was the 696, which was the 693 a built by SNAC at Bourges and by Farman at Billancourt All versions were armed with one Hispano cannon an four machine-guns, and could carry eight 110-lb bombs

The Breguet 692 remained a project only, but severa other versions appeared in prototype form. For example the 694 was ordered by Belgium and Sweden, but th course of events prevented its production; the 694-01 only aircraft of the type, flew on 20 January 1940 and wa eventually delivered to the French Navy on 1 June. Th 697 was a two-seat fighter with larger nacelles to hous 1,180-hp Gnome-Rhône 14 N 48/49 engines, drivin Ratier propellers. On 13 June 1940, this prototype wa set on fire deliberately at Landes-de-Bussac, since was impossible to transport it elsewhere.

The 698 was a two-seat dive-bomber, intended fo the Navy, and was to be equipped with dive-brakes. On hundred were ordered, but neither it nor the 699, a bombe version of the 695, was ever constructed.

Last of the series, and what would have been the fastest with an estimated speed of 372 mph, was designate Breguet 700. Two prototypes were ordered, one with single fin and the other with twin fins, but neither wa completed.

By 3 September 1939, 21 Breguet 691s had bee delivered to the French Air Force; but engine trouble and undercarriage weakness resulted in these aircraf like the Potez 633s, being used only for instructiona duties with assault groups.

Of the 224 Breguet 693s and 50 695s which were buil the Air Force accepted only 106 and 33 respectively because of lack of equipment. On 10 May 1940 thes were disposed as follows: 45 with bomber groups GB I/54, II/54, II/35, I/51 and II/51, 12 in reserve, 22 a test and training centres, 19 awaiting equipment and 1 damaged.

Breguet 693s of GBA I/54 and II/54 distinguished them selves on 17 May 1940, by low-level attacks on Germa trenches in Belgium.

After the collapse of France, the Italians took pos session of many 693s which were put into service by thei own attack groups. Their German allies also capture 25, but these were found to be in such poor conditio that they were not considered worthy of repair and wer destroyed after their engines had been removed t power Henschel 129 aircraft.

Breguet 1050 Alizé

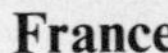

Development of the Alizé can be traced back to 3 August 1951, when Breguet flew for the first time the prototype of a two-seat naval strike aircraft known as the Br 960 Vultur. At first glance, the Vultur looked a fairly conventional single-engined low-wing monoplane; but, in addition to the Armstrong Siddeley Mamba turboprop in its nose, it had a French-built Rolls-Royce Nene turbojet inside its rear fuselage. The idea was to use only the Mamba in normal cruising flight, to ensure a lengthy endurance, and to switch on the Nene when extra power was needed for take-off, climb and combat.

Only two prototypes of the Vultur were completed. With no prospect of a production order for the strike version, Breguet decided to adapt the design to meet French Navy requirements for a carrier-based anti-submarine aircraft. A high top speed was no longer essential, so the Nene engine was removed to make way for a retractable radar scanner for submarine detection. The Mamba was replaced by a more powerful Rolls-Royce Dart turboprop, and the cockpit was redesigned to accommodate a second radar operator, to the rear of the side-by-side seats for the pilot and forward radar operator.

The main armament, consisting now of one torpedo or three 353-lb depth charges, was transferred to a fuselage weapon-bay, with racks under the inner wings for two more 353-lb or 385-lb depth charges and attachments under the outer wings for six 5-in rockets or two Nord SS.11 air-to-surface missiles. This left little space for sonobuoys, but Breguet solved the problem by designing two nacelles which could be mounted on the wing leading-edges to house the sonobuoys and the main undercarriage units when retracted.

By this time little of the original design remained and Breguet gave the designation Br 1050 to the anti-submarine project. Impressed by its military potential and compact size, the French Navy awarded Breguet a contract for two prototypes and three pre-production aircraft.

To speed development of the Br 1050, it was decided to flight test some of its aerodynamic features on the second prototype Vultur. The Nene engine of this aircraft was removed and a retractable radome was installed in the rear fuselage. The flight deck was modified to accommodate a third crew member, and nacelles similar in shape to the sonobuoy/undercarriage housings of the Br 1050 were built on to the wing leading-edges. In its new form, as the Br 965, this aircraft flew for the first time on 26 March 1955.

It was followed on 26 October 1956 by the first prototype of the Br 1050, which was given the name Alizé (Trade-wind). The second prototype and the pre-production machines introduced a number of detail refinements. In particular, the original jet-pipe from the 1,975-shp Dart RDa7 Mk 21 turboprop, which ran down under the leading edge of the wing, was replaced by a shorter and more efficient horizontal jet-pipe.

A further 70 Alizés were produced for the French Navy, for operation on both light and fleet type aircraft carriers. Deliveries began on 20 May 1959, and were completed in 1961. In addition, there was an order from the Indian Navy, which purchased 17. The first of these was handed over officially on 7 January 1961, and they were used to equip its No. 310 Squadron, based on the aircraft carrier *Vikrant*.

Breguet 1050 Alizé, wings folded

Breguet 1050 Alizé, with Nord air-to-surface missiles

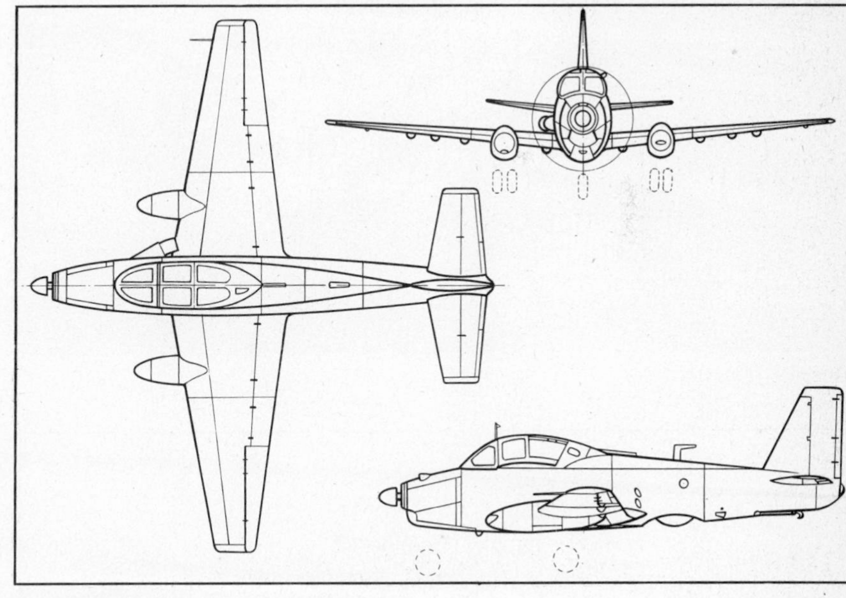

Breguet 1050 Alizé

TYPE	DIMENSIONS						WEIGHT	PERFORMANCE				REMARKS	
	span ft	span in	length ft	length in	height ft	height in	max t-o lb	max speed mph	at height ft	service ceiling ft	combat range miles		
Br 691	50	4¾	32	2	13	1½	11,023	301	13,000	27,900	810	2 × HS 14 AB10/11	640 hp
Br 693	50	4¾	33	7	10	3¾	10,582	317	13,000	27,900	870	2 × GR 14 M4/5	680 hp
Br 695	50	4¾	33	7	10	3¾	11,905	350	13,000	29,500	932	2 × PW R-1830	800 hp
Br 696	50	4¾	33	7	10	3¾	11,023	329		27,900	994	2 × GR 14 M4/5	680 hp
Br 1050 Alizé	51	2	44	10½	15	9	18,099	273		26,000	1,240	RR Dart R.Da.21	2,100 eshp

Breguet 1150 Atlantic, radar lowered, weapon-bay open

Breguet 1150 Atlantic

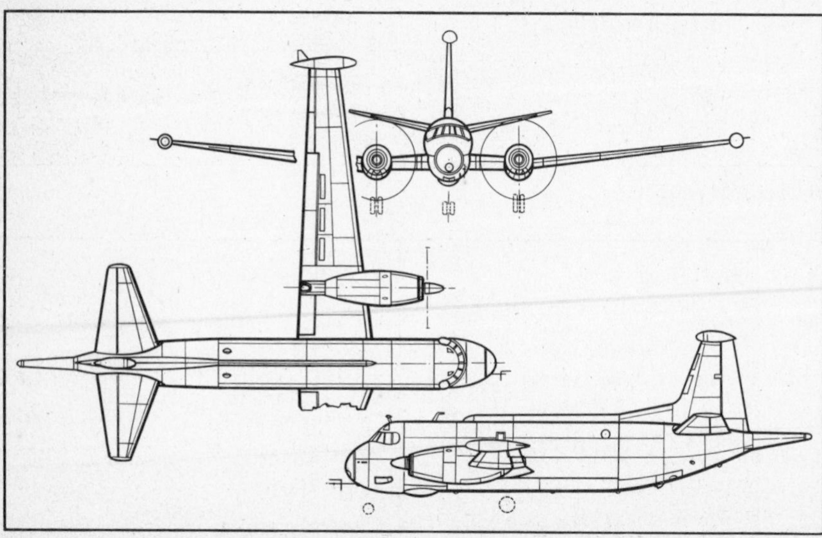
Breguet 1150 Atlantic

Breguet 1150 Atlantic

Requirements for a new maritime patrol aircraft to replace the Lockheed P-2 Neptune were drawn up in 1958, under the auspices of the NATO Armaments Committee. After evaluation of the 25 design studies submitted by manufacturers in several countries, the Breguet 1150 was chosen for development, under the name "Atlantic", and two prototypes were ordered in December 1959. This set in motion one of the most amazing production programmes in aviation history.

The governments of France, Belgium, the Netherlands, West Germany and the USA assumed joint responsibility for supervision and financing of the aircraft's development. In consequence, it was decided that the design and manufacture of the Atlantic should be divided among the aircraft industries of the four European partners, under the leadership of the Breguet company.

Before long, Dornier in Germany were busy on the detail design and construction of the rear fuselage and tail unit. Fokker in the Netherlands were given similar responsibility for the centre wing and engine nacelles and the Belgian ABAP group, consisting of the Avions Fairey, SABCA and FN companies, were awarded contracts for various airframe components. French companies involved in the programme were Sud-Aviation for the outer wings, Hispano for the undercarriage and Breguet for the main fuselage and final assembly.

The 6,105-hp Rolls-Royce Tyne turboprop engines for the prototypes were ordered from the UK, but similar power plants for production Atlantics are being built under licence in France by Hispano, assisted by Rolls-Royce and the Belgian FN and German MAN companies.

When all the parts of the first prototype were collected at the Breguet works, they went together without any problems and the aircraft flew on 21 October 1961, less than two years after it was ordered. The second prototype flew on 23 February 1962, and is being followed by an initial production series of 40 Atlantics for the French Navy and 20 for Germany.

The Atlantic has a "figure-eight" fuselage, with a pressurized upper deck for the 12-man crew, seven of whom work in a central operations room, and a 30-ft-long weapons bay in the unpressurized lower portion. The accommodation is designed to provide a high standard of comfort during patrols that might last as long as 18 hours, and includes a rest room and kitchen.

A vast range of electronic equipment is fitted, including a retractable search radar installation under the forward fuselage, an MAD (magnetic anomaly detection) "tail-sting", and an electronic countermeasures pod at the tip of the tail-fin. All types of anti-shipping and anti-submarine weapons can be carried, including homing torpedoes, air-to-surface missiles with both nuclear and high-explosive warheads, depth charges, rockets and the full range of NATO standard bombs.

CAMS 33 B

Under the technical management of Maurice Hurel, Chantiers Aéro-Maritimes de la Seine (CAMS) specialized in the production of flying-boats and flying-boat hulls. On 5 September 1923, it entered a twin-engined commercial aircraft which it designated 33 C No.2 (F-AHDB) in a long-distance race over the Mediterranean. By flying for 18 hours with only a single stop for refuelling, this aircraft came second in the contest.

In the same year a military version of the 33 C was produced, under the designation CAMS 33 B. Intended for maritime bombing duties as well as for reconnaissance, it was a biplane of wooden construction, manned by a crew of three, and powered by two 275-hp Hispano-Suiza 8 Fg engines arranged in tandem.

Two prototypes, registered F-ESFA and F-ESFB, flew respectively in April 1923 and at the end of the same year were sent for official trials at the St-Raphael base. This resulted in a contract for 12 for the French Navy. These aircraft equipped squadron 1 R 1 at Cherbourg.

In 1926 Yugoslavia also bought a small number of similar machines. Each was armed with four machine-guns and carried a modest bomb load.

CAMS 55

The CAMS 55 was derived from the CAMS 51 R-3, which in turn was the military version of the 51 C. In 1928 four prototypes of the CAMS 55 were produced, two being of the 55 J type, with Jupiter engines, and two of the 55 H type with Hispano engines. They were very similar to the CAMS 33 B in general appearance, but were larger and had considerably more powerful engines. Each carried a crew of four and normal armament of four machine-guns and two 165-lb bombs.

Subsequently, three versions, all of wooden construction with folding wings went into production, as follows: CAMS 55/1, with two 600-hp Hispano 12 Lbr engines, 43 built, beginning in 1929. CAMS 55/2, with two 480-hp Gnome-Rhône 9 Akx engines, 29 built, beginning in 1930. CAMS 55/10, with two 500-hp Gnome-Rhône 9 Kbr engines, 32 built, beginning in 1934. This last version could climb to 8,200 ft in 28 min, had a ceiling of 11,150 ft and a range of between 795 and 1,165 miles. It was equipped with SIF 404 radio.

The first squadron to receive CAMS 55s, in 1930, was 3 E 1, followed by 4 E 1, 1 E 1, 3 E 2, and 3 E 3. When the CAMS 55 was replaced by the Breguet Bizerte, the remaining machines were transferred to squadrons 1 S 1, 2 S 1, 3 S 4, 4 S 1 and 8 S 5 for reconnaissance duties. Squadron 1 BS succeeded 4 S 1 on 1 July 1940; the CAMS 55/10s which equipped it until 30 August 1940 made 464 wartime sorties, totalling 1,566 flying hours, during this period. After the collapse of France, all the CAMS 55s still in service were destroyed, except for two used by the Free French Forces until 15 January 1941.

Several other versions of the CAMS 55 were projected, with various engines, but only two of these flew, in prototype form. First of them was the 55/3, with an all-metal hull and Hispano 12 Lbr engines. Bought by the French Navy for 1,275,000 francs, it was destroyed accidentally on 4 January 1932. The other prototype was the 55/6, with Jupiter 9 Akx engines driving three-bladed propellers, an all-metal hull and stepped floats. It was assigned to the CEPA at St-Raphaël and was used by Squadron 3 E 3 for various trials.

Caudron C 23

At the end of the 1914–18 War there appeared, simultaneously with the Farman F 60, the first Caudron bomber which could compete with the twin-engined Handley Page O/400. This was the C 23, powered by two 260-hp Salmson 9 Z engines. Constructed entirely of wood, it was a large four-bay biplane, and belonged to the BN 2 category of two-seat night bombers. Defensive armament comprised a forward-firing machine-gun and it carried three large bombs under the lower wing centre-section. The wide-track undercarriage had twin wheels on each main unit.

Fifty-four C 23s were built to equip night bomber squadrons of the French Air Force. Their withdrawal from first-line use in February 1920 was due mainly to a shortage of pilots able to fly aircraft of this size.

Caudron C 714

Among the most interesting aircraft built to compete in races for the Coupe Deutsch de la Meurthe in 1933–5 were the small Caudron monoplanes designed by Marcel

CAMS 33 B prototype

CAMS 55/2

Caudron C 23

TYPE	DIMENSIONS span ft	span in	length ft	length in	height ft	height in	WEIGHT max t-o lb	PERFORMANCE max speed mph	at height ft	service ceiling ft	combat range miles	REMARKS	
Br 1150 Atlantic	119	1	104	2	37	2	95,900	382		33,000	4,150	2 × RR Tyne R. Ty20.Mk 21	6,105 eshp
CAMS 33 B	57	9½	43	5	16	0	8,820	109	SL	16,400	510	2 × HS 8 Fg	275 hp
CAMS 55/10	66	11	49	2½	18	4½	14,400	134	SL	11,150	810	2 × GR 9 Kbr	500 hp
Caudron C 23	80	0	42	4	9	10	5,885	84	SL			2 × SA 9 Z	260 hp
Caudron C 714	29	5	27	11¾	9	5	3,826	302	13,000	32,800	560	RE 12 RO 3	450 hp

Caudron C 714, Finnish Air Force

Dassault MD 450 Ouragan

Dassault MD 450 Ouragan, Israeli Air Force

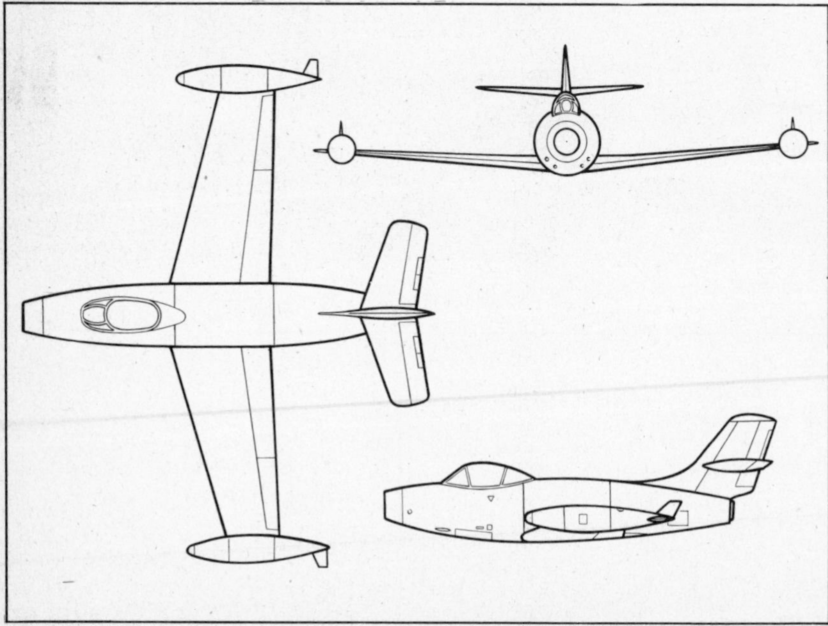
Dassault MD 450 Ouragan

Riffard. To take advantage of experience gained with them, he designed a lightweight fighter, designated C 710, which flew for the first time on 18 July 1936, powered by a 450-hp Renault engine. It was followed in December 1937 by the C 713 Cyclone, which introduced a retractable undercarriage, and then by the C 714 with a wing of improved profile, a 450-hp Renault 621 type 12 RO-3 engine, and armament of four machine-guns, mounted in pairs in fairings under each wing.

Raymond Delmotte, chief pilot of the Caudron-Renault company, made the first flight in the C 714 in September 1938. Following satisfactory trials of the aircraft at the CEMA test centre at Villacoublay, an initial order for 100 machines was placed in November 1938 under Plan V. A second order, for a similar quantity, followed in early 1939, but shortly afterwards both contracts were cancelled by the Government, as the French Air Force had decided that the aircraft's rate of climb was not good enough by contemporary standards. In other respects, the C 714 was comparable with fighters then in service, although it had only half their weight and engine power. Furthermore, it could be built in about 5,000 man-hours, mainly of wood.

There was consolation in the fact that 80 C 714s were to be built for Finland. Indeed, an article of Plan V provided for the export of 100 C 714 fighters, of which 80 were intended for Finland and 20 for Yugoslavia. But by 3 September 1939, when war broke out in France, and 30 November 1939, when Russo-Finnish hostilities began, not a single C 714 had been completed. In February 1940 a contract was signed with Finland for the supply of 175 aircraft, comprising 30 Morane-Saulnier 406s, 50 Koolhoven 58s, 25 Hanriot H 232/2s and 70 of the original 80 C 714s. The balance of ten went to the French Air Force for evaluation as fighter trainers.

When the fighting in Finland came to a temporary halt on 12 March 1940, only six C 714s had been delivered and these had not seen operational service as their high landing speed did not permit their use on the short runways then available in Finland.

It is impossible to know the exact number of C 714s produced. All that is certain is that on 1 February 1940 the French Air Force had accepted five and that four months later the number accepted had risen to 56.

At the beginning of 1940, France had proposed sending a squadron of C 714s to Finland to help that country in its fight against the Russian invaders. These aircraft were to be additional to those purchased by Finland. The squadron became known as the "Warsaw Group" since it was composed mainly of Polish pilots who, before taking over their C 714s, trained on Morane 406s and Bloch 152s, painted in Polish colours. This plan was abandoned and, when the Germans invaded Belgium on 10 May, the French government retained the "Warsaw Group" (as GCI/145) for home defence.

Dassault MD 450 Ouragan

Founded during the early 1930s, the Société des Avions Marcel Bloch was one of the leading French aviation companies until, in 1937, it became the SNCASO, of which Marcel Bloch was made managing director. On his return from German deportation in 1945, Bloch changed his name to Marcel Dassault and set up the Société des Avions Marcel Dassault which is now the most important private French aircraft company.

In September 1947 the French Air Force was equipped mainly with obsolete aircraft. While awaiting modern fighter aircraft of French manufacture, the Chief of Air Staff decided to buy DH Vampires from Great Britain and to have a light fighter built around a Rolls-Royce Nene engine and armed with four 20-mm cannon.

To meet this "specification", Dassault initiated the MD 450 Ouragan project and in December 1947 detail design was initiated at St-Cloud by the engineers Deplant, Cabriére and Rouault. Construction began on 7 April 1948, some two months before an official order for three prototypes was received, and on 28 February 1949 the prototype MD 450 made its first flight.

The Ouragan was a single-seat, low-wing monoplane of all-metal construction, powered by a Rolls-Royce

Nene manufactured under licence by Hispano, the engine being mounted within the circular-section fuselage with a frontal air intake. It had a pressurized cockpit and a Messier retractable tricycle undercarriage. Armament consisted of four 20-mm cannon in the nose and provision was made to carry 16 rockets or two 1,000-lb bombs under the wings.

Following completion of the prototypes and 12 pre-series machines, the first of 350 production Ouragans for the French Air Force flew in 1951. The Indian Air Force received 104 Ouragans (known as *Toofanis*) in 1953–4, and in 1955 the Israeli Air Force was supplied with 12 production-line aircraft and at least 42 more from surplus French stock.

Several Ouragans were used for test purposes. For example, MD 450-9 was used to develop rocket packs for the later Mystère IVAs and IVBs; MD 450-11, later re-designated MD 450-30L, was tested on 21 January 1952 with lateral air intakes and two 30-mm cannon. Several other aircraft were used for experiments with braking parachutes and twin-wheeled main undercarriage units.

Dassault Mystère I to IV

Two years after the Ouragan had been designed, work began on the MD 452, and this aircraft made its first flight on 23 February 1951. Outwardly it was very similar to the MD 450 but its wings were swept at an angle of 30 degrees. Known as the Mystère, nine prototypes (Nos. 01-09) were constructed between 1951 and 1953, of which three were Mystère Is, two Mystère IIAs and four Mystère IIBs, followed by 11 pre-production Mystère IICs (Nos. 10 to 20).

The first prototype Mystère was powered, like the Ouragan, by a Rolls-Royce Nene; the other eight each had a Hispano-built Rolls-Royce Tay. From aircraft No. 10, the Tay was superseded in turn by the French SNECMA Atar 101 turbojet.

On 28 October 1952, the Mystère II was the first French aircraft to exceed Mach 1, piloted by an American staff officer named Davies then serving in France.

From 1954, 180 Mystère IICs were produced, made up of 156 for the French Air Force and 24 intended for Israel, although the latter were not delivered. The IIC had a ceiling of 59,000 ft and a range of 745 miles.

Next to appear in the Mystère series was the Mystère IV (originally named the Super Mystère) which made its first flight on 28 September 1952. With a longer fuselage but smaller span, it was powered by a Hispano-built Rolls-Royce Tay. The prototype was followed by nine pre-production aircraft, known as Mystère IVAs, and 483 production models were then built, of which 225 were for France, 67 for India and 50 for Israel. In 1956 the Mystère IVA saw service during the Suez Operation and nine of these aircraft equipped the aerobatic team known as the *Patrouille de France*, like the Ouragan before them.

Also built in small numbers, the Mystère IVB had an afterburning turbojet. The first IVB flew on 16 December 1953, followed by two more prototypes and 16 pre-production aircraft, each fitted with radar equipment in the modified front fuselage, which foreshadowed the nose of the Super Mystère B2. It was a Mystère IVB which, on 24 February 1954, became the first aircraft in France to exceed the speed of sound in level flight.

The Mystère IVC, the IVD, IVM, 20N, 26 and 28 remained as projects only, but the IVN, a prototype two-

Dassault Mystère II, fifth prototype

Dassault Mystère IVA

Dassault Mystère IVB

TYPE	DIMENSIONS						WEIGHT	PERFORMANCE				REMARKS	
	span		length		height		max t-o	max speed	at height	service ceiling	combat range		
	ft	in	ft	in	ft	in	lb	mph	ft	ft	miles		
MD 450 Ouragan	43	2	35	2¾	13	7	14,990	585	SL			HS 104B	5,070 lb s t
MD 450 Ouragan	43	2	35	2¾	13	7	13,602	585	SL			HS 105A	5,100 lb s t
MD 452 Mystère IIC	42	9¾	38	6¼	13	11¾	16,441	658	SL			SNECMA Atar 101D3	6,600 lb s t
MD 454 Mystère IVA	36	5¾	42	2	14	5	15,983	683	SL	45,000	820	HS 250A	6,280 lb s t
MD 454 Mystère IVA	36	5¾	42	2	14	5	20,050	695	SL	45,000	820	HS 350	7,710 lb s t

Dassault Super Mystère B-2

Dassault Super Mystère B-2, with Sidewinders

Dassault Etendard IV prototype

Dassault Etendard IV-M

seat all-weather fighter, flew on 19 July 1954. Equipped with radar in a conical nose radome, it had a chin air intake and could carry a total of 128 rockets.

Dassault Super Mystère B-2

Final development of the Mystère series of single-seat fighters, the Super Mystère introduced a thinner and more sharply-swept wing, with "sawtooth" leading-edge, a flatter nose to improve the pilot's field of view, and other refinements.

The prototype Super Mystère B-1 flew for the first time on 2 March 1955, powered by a Rolls-Royce Avon RA.7R turbojet with afterburner, and exceeded Mach 1 on its fourth test flight. A switch to the 9,700-lb s t SNECMA Atar 101G afterburning turbojet was made on the five pre-production and 180 production Super Mystère B-2s. The first production machine flew on 26 February 1957 and the last was delivered in 1959. Twenty were supplied to Israel: these remained in service in the mid-sixties, as did at least two wings of Super Mystères of the French Air Force.

Standard armament of the Super Mystère B-2 comprises two 30-mm cannon and a fuselage pack of 55 air-to-air rockets. Two underwing attachments can each carry a pack of 19 air-to-air rockets or a 1,100-lb bomb. French Air Force machines are equipped to carry a Sidewinder air-to-air missile under each wing.

One aircraft was fitted experimentally with an Atar 9 turbojet, giving 13,250 lb s t with afterburning, and designated Super Mystère B-4. It first flew in February 1958 and had a rate of climb of nearly 30,000 ft/min.

Dassault Etendard IV

In the mid-fifties, most NATO air forces were attracted by the idea of a lightweight, comparatively low-cost single-seat tactical support fighter, and Dassault undertook the development of three widely-differing variants of a design which it called the Etendard.

First to fly, on 23 July 1956, was the Etendard II, of which three prototypes had been ordered by the French Air Force. In general layout, it followed closely the earlier Mystère series, with a 45° swept wing; but it was smaller and was powered by two Turboméca Gabizo turbojets of only 2,420 lb s t each. The engines were mounted side-by-side in the rear fuselage and were supplied with air through lateral intakes. This made it possible for the pilot to be seated well forward, in a pointed nose that ensured a superb field of view during ground attack missions. For such work, the fixed armament of two 30-mm cannon could be supplemented by 990 lb of bombs and rockets under the wings.

The Etendard II did not progress beyond the prototype stage. Neither did the Etendard VI, with a single 4,850-lb s t Orpheus turbojet, which was Dassault's entry in the NATO design contest won by the Fiat G91. NATO was sufficiently impressed by the VI to order three prototypes, of which the first flew on 15 March 1957: but it was the French Navy that, most of all, appreciated the possibilities of the Etendard.

Dassault had felt that both of the officially-backed versions of the Etendard were underpowered and, at their own expense, built a version known as the Etendard IV. This aircraft flew for the first time on 24 July 1956, powered by an 8,155-lb s t SNECMA Atar 101E.4 turbojet, and was re-engined subsequently with a 9,700-lb s t Atar 8. It showed such promise that the Navy awarded Dassault a contract for a prototype and six pre-production models of a shipboard version, to be known as the Etendard IV-M.

The prototype IV-M flew on 21 May 1958, and in due course proved to be Europe's first truly supersonic carrier-based fighter, with a speed of Mach 1·14 in a dive and Mach 1·02 (677 mph) in level flight at 36,000 ft. With a top speed of Mach 0·9 (685 mph) at sea level and rate of climb of nearly 20,000 ft/min, it was clearly suitable for both low-level attack and high-altitude interception. This was just what the French Navy needed, and the Etendard was ordered into production to equip the new carriers *Clémenceau* and *Foch*.

Sixty-nine standard Etendard IV-M fighters were

ordered, with Atar 8 turbojet and fixed armament of two 30-mm cannon. Four underwing attachments provide for an external load of up to 3,000 lb of bombs, rockets, Sidewinder or Nord 5103 air-to-air missiles or two 132-gallon external fuel tanks. An Aida radar unit in the nose is used to locate sea or air targets.

At the same time, 21 Etendard IV-Ps were ordered, with cameras in a redesigned nose and belly pack for all-weather photographic-reconnaissance missions by day and night. These aircraft can also be operated as flight refuelling tankers, carrying a "buddy pack" hose-reel unit under their fuselage. All Etendards are equipped to refuel in flight, the IV-Ps having a nose-probe and the IV-Ms a retractable probe forward of the windscreen.

The final pre-production model of the Etendard was equipped as a prototype of the IV-P and flew for the first time on 19 November 1960. The third pre-production machine was an experimental variant, with an 11,200-lb s t Rolls-Royce Avon 51 turbojet and a flap-blowing system that would have enabled it to operate from the shorter catapults of light fleet carriers had there been a requirement for this. It was designated Etendard IV-B.

Deliveries of the Etendard IV-M to the French Navy began on 18 January 1962 and were completed in 1964.

Dassault Mirage III and 5

Like the Etendard IV, the Mirage single-seat fighter had its origin in the French Air Force lightweight fighter programme of the mid-1950s.

The prototype Mirage I, which flew for the first time on 25 June 1955, was powered by two Dassault-built Armstrong Siddeley Viper turbojets, giving only 2,200 lb s t each, with afterburning. However, it had provision for a 3,300-lb s t SEPR liquid-propellent rocket engine under its rear fuselage, for added thrust during take-off, climb and combat, and began flight tests with the rocket in operation on 17 December 1956.

Again, as in the case of the Etendard, it was decided that a switch to the greater power of a single SNECMA Atar turbojet, in place of the two Vipers, at the cost of increased size and weight, would produce a far superior fighter. The result was the Mirage III, which flew on 17 November 1956. In prototype form, this version had a 9,900-lb s t Atar 101G.2 turbojet and a jettisonable under-fuselage SEPR rocket engine. On 30 January 1957 it exceeded Mach 1·5 (1,000 mph) in level flight at 36,000 ft on the power of the turbojet alone. Later, with the rocket fitted, it attained Mach 1·9 (1,255 mph). The design was capable of even higher performance when developed, and the French Air Force ordered ten improved pre-production models under the designation Mirage III-A.

To take full advantage of the increased power of the Atar 9B turbojet (13,225 lb s t with afterburning) that was available for the Mirage III-A, Dassault redesigned the wing to have a thickness/chord ratio of only 3·5 per cent, instead of the former 5 per cent. The first III-A flew on 12 May 1958, and five months later exceeded Mach 2 on turbojet power alone. With its 3,700-lb s t SEPR 841 auxiliary rocket also in operation, it achieved Mach 2·2 (1,450 mph) at 50,000 ft and climbed to 82,000 ft. No less important, it combined this

Dassault Etendard IV-P

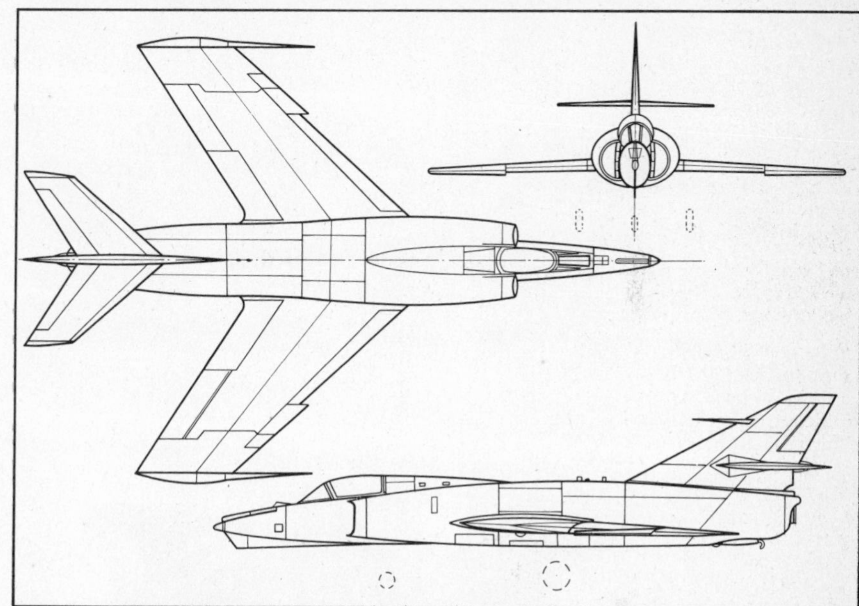
Dassault Etendard IV-M

Dassault Mirage III-B

TYPE	DIMENSIONS						WEIGHT	PERFORMANCE				REMARKS	
	span ft	span in	length ft	length in	height ft	height in	max t-o lb	max speed mph	at height ft	service ceiling ft	combat range miles		
Super Mystère B-2	34	6¼	46	1	14	11	22,050	743	38,000	55,750	730	SNECMA Atar 101G1	9,700 lb s t
Etendard IV-M	31	5¾	47	0¾	13	7½	22,046	677	36,000	49,200	1,000	SNECMA Atar 8	9,700 lb s t
Etendard IV-P	31	5¾	47	0¾	13	7½	23,809	677	36,000	49,200	1,000	SNECMA Atar 8	9,700 lb s t
Mirage III-C	26	11¾	48	5¼	13	11½	26,015	1,430	36,000	65,600	745	SNECMA Atar 9B + SEPR 841	13,225 + 3,700 lb s t
Mirage III-E	26	11¾	49	3½	13	11½	27,115	1,430	36,000	65,600	745	SNECMA Atar 9C + SEPR 841	14,110 + 3,700 lb s t
Mirage III-R	26	11¾	50	10¼	13	11½	27,115	1,430	36,000	65,600	745	SNECMA Atar 9C + SEPR 841	

Dassault Mirage III-C

Dassault Mirage III-E

Dassault Mirage 5

Dassault Mirage IV prototype

performance with an ability to take off and land in less than 2,500 ft on grass fields. The French Air Force had no hesitation in ordering this type into large-scale production.

Designated Mirage III-C, the first production model flew on 9 October 1960, and this version became operational with the *Cigogne* Group of the French Air Force at Dijon late in the following year. Its normal armament for high-altitude interception comprises a Matra R.530 air-to-air missile with semi-active radar homing head, carried under the fuselage and used in conjunction with nose-mounted CSF Cyrano I fire-control radar. It can, however, carry also two 30-mm cannon and two Sidewinder infra-red air-to-air missiles; while for ground attack it can supplement the cannon with two 1,000-lb bombs or a Nord A.S.30 air-to-surface missile under its fuselage, and two 1,000-lb bombs, launchers for up to 72 rockets or long-range fuel tanks under its wings.

Long before the first series of 100 Mirage III-Cs had been completed, at a rate of ten a month, orders for a further 340 were being negotiated by the French Air Force. Many of these are, in fact, Mirage III-Es, for long-range intruder duties, with a 14,110-lb s t Atar 9C turbojet, 3,700-lb s t SEPR 844 auxiliary rocket engine, Cyrano II fire-control radar and navigation computer, with Marconi Doppler radar for blind low-level navigation, and a one-foot-longer fuselage, placing the pilot further forward of the air intakes.

The first Mirage III-E flew on 5 April 1961. In parallel production for the French Air Force is the Mirage III-R, with reconnaissance cameras in a modified nose, a self-contained navigation system and the same ground attack armament as the III-C. Twenty late models, designated III-RD, have an improved navigation system and automatic cameras.

Flown for the first time in mid-1967, the Mirage 5 is basically similar to the III-E, but is equipped only for daylight operation, with 110 gallons of additional fuel and heavier weapon load made possible by deletion of the III-E's all-weather electronic systems. Most of the first production series of 60 Mirage 5s were ordered by Israel.

To facilitate conversion training on to the Mirage, Dassault flew a prototype of the Mirage III-B, with two seats in tandem in a two-foot-longer fuselage, on 21 October 1959. Addition of the second seat, with dual controls, has virtually no effect on performance, and the III-B can carry the same ground attack armament as the III-C, enabling it to serve in a dual trainer/fighter rôle if required. The first of 26 for the French Air Force flew on 19 July 1962.

By then, the qualities of the Mirage III had earned it important oversea contracts, in countries that were traditionally customers for British or American fighters. The Royal Australian Air Force began by ordering 30 of a version of the III-E designated III-O, and eventually increased the number to 100. Except for the first few aircraft, these are being manufactured in Australia at the Government Aircraft Factories, assisted by Commonwealth Aircraft Corporation.

Switzerland is building under licence 36 similar aircraft, with the designation Mirage III-S. The main difference in this version is that the usual Cyrano radar is replaced by a Hughes TARAN electronic system, to control a primary armament of HM-55 Falcon air-to-air missiles. In addition, the Swiss Air Force has two two-seat III-BSs and is building 17 reconnaissance III-RSs.

Other oversea customers include South Africa, which has 16 Mirage III-CZ and 8 III-EZ fighters and 3 III-BZ trainers, and Israel, which has received 72 Mirage III-CJs with changed electronic equipment.

At one stage, it seemed likely that Australia might prefer a British engine to the Atar, so Dassault flew a Mirage with a Rolls-Royce RB.146 afterburning turbojet on 13 February 1961 and announced that this version could also be fitted with Ferranti Airpass radar. The prototype carried the designation III-O, but should not be confused with the Australian production III-O which has an Atar and Cyrano radar.

Other experimental versions include the Mirage III-T, which served as a flying test-bed for the 19,840-lb s t

SNECMA TF-106 turbofan engine, the Balzac jet-lift research aircraft, and two Mirage III-V prototype VTOL fighters.

Dassault Mirage IV

When the French Air Force made known its need for a high-speed strategic bomber to carry the newly-developed French atomic bomb, Dassault produced the Mirage IV by simply scaling up the basic design of the Mirage III.

Features inherited from the fighter include 60° delta wings, elevon control surfaces, an area-ruled fuselage and lateral engine air intakes, each with a half-cone centre-body. Power is provided by two afterburning SNECMA Atar 9 turbojets, mounted side-by-side in the rear fuselage. To give the bomber an adequate range, even the tail fin is sealed, like the wings, to form an integral fuel tank. In addition, two 550-gallon external tanks can be carried under the wings.

The Mirage IV is manned by a crew of two in tandem, and has a large CSF radar in a circular radome under its centre fuselage to assist navigation and target location. Immediately aft of this radome, the fuselage is recessed to accommodate the free-fall nuclear weapon.

The first prototype Mirage IV flew on 17 June 1959, powered by two 13,225-lb s t Atar 9Bs. By its fourteenth test flight it had reached a speed of Mach 1·9 (1,250 mph). This was raised above Mach 2 by the three pre-production aircraft which followed, with slightly larger overall dimensions and more power. The first and second pre-production machines had 14,110-lb s t Atar 9Cs; the third had 14.770-lb s t Atar 9Ks.

Sixty-two Mirage IV-As were ordered for the French *force de frappe*, for delivery in 1963–6. Almost indistinguishable from the third pre-production aircraft, they have 14,990-lb s t Atar 9Ds, or 9Ks, and have a normal operational radius of more than 1,000 miles, with a proportion of the flight at Mach 1·7 at high altitude. Such a range is short by strategic bomber standards, but can be extended by flight refuelling. Furthermore, France is closer to many potential targets than either Britain or the United States and its bomber force does not need such a long range as those of the RAF and USAF.

Dewoitine D 1

The first aircraft produced by this Toulouse firm was the D 1 monoplane fighter designed by Emile Dewoitine. Flown for the first time on 18 November 1921, it marked the beginning of a remarkable series of parasol-wing monoplanes of simple light metal construction, for Dewoitine aircraft up to the D 500 were, almost without exception, built of duralumin with fabric-covered wings.

The D 1 was demonstrated in Japan in 1923 by the company's pilot, Georges Barbot. His successor, Marcel Doret, gave demonstration flights in Yugoslavia on 23 February 1924 and in Czechoslovakia two months later, on 19 April. Seventy-nine D 1s were ordered subsequently by Yugoslavia; two were purchased by Switzerland and a single machine by Japan. In addition, the Italian Ansaldo company built 126 under licence, with the designation AC 1, while France equipped naval escadrilles 4 C 1, 7 C 1 and 7 C 3 with a total of 29 D 1s.

Powered by an in-line Hispano-Suiza engine of 300 hp the D 1 reached a top speed of 156 mph, climbed to 16,400 ft in 15 minutes 6 seconds, had a ceiling of 27,900 ft and landed at 50 mph. On 23 December 1924, Marcel Doret captured three World speed records (with and without load) in a D 1, at a speed of 144·84 mph.

When the Dewoitine company went into liquidation for the first time in 1928, Doret bought a D 1 (No. 111)

Dassault Mirage IV-A

Dassault Mirage IV-A, pre-production model

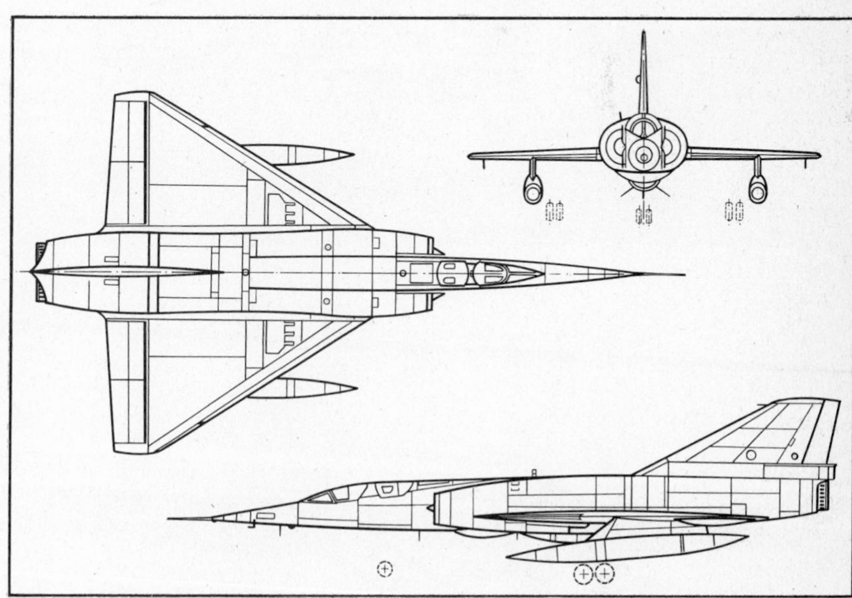

Dassault Mirage IV-A

TYPE	DIMENSIONS span ft	span in	length ft	length in	height ft	height in	WEIGHT max t-o lb	PERFORMANCE max speed mph	at height ft	service ceiling ft	combat range miles	REMARKS	
Mirage IV-A	38	10½	77	1	18	6½	69,665	1,450	36,000	65,600		2 × SNECMA Atar 9K	**14,990 lb s t**
D 1	36	11	24	3¾	9	0¼	2,751	156		27,900	435	HS 8 Fb	300 hp

Dewoitine D 1, Swiss Air Force

Dewoitine D 9, Swiss Air Force

Dewoitine D 19 prototype

Dewoitine D 21 prototype

for his own use. This aircraft was re-designated D 1*ter* and registered F-AHAZ. With armament removed and red diagonal bands painted on the wings, it became Doret's first aerobatic aircraft and was the centre of attraction at many shows in the period up to 1933.

Dewoitine D 9

The Dewoitine D 9, a smaller development of the D 1, made its appearance in 1924, powered by a 420-hp Jupiter radial engine. Armament comprised two machine-guns mounted on the fuselage decking and two in the leading-edge of the wing, firing outside the propeller disc.

Two prototypes of the D 9 were built and were followed by 147 production models built by Ansaldo in Italy for the Regia Aeronautica and designated AC 3. Eight others were built by Dewoitine for Yugoslavia and two for Belgium. In 1928 Switzerland assembled three, with military serials 876, 877 and 878, from components purchased in France.

The Swiss aircraft constructor Alfred Compte, gaining inspiration from the Dewoitine series, developed and built the AC 1, which bore a striking resemblance to the Dewoitine D 9. Despite all this interest abroad, the French authorities purchased only the prototype.

Dewoitine D 21

Before the birth of the successful Dewoitine D 21 in 1927 came the D 12 prototype, an enlarged version of the D 9 with a Lorraine engine and frontal radiator, and, in 1925, the D 19 with a 450-hp Hispano-Suiza. Demonstrated in Switzerland by Doret in August 1925, the D 19 sufficiently impressed the Swiss for three machines to be built experimentally at the EKW State Workshops.

It was the D 21, however, which was the next Dewoitine type built in quantity. Its lines were generally similar to those of the D 1, but its in-line Hispano engine was capable of delivering 575 hp for take-off. The width of this engine set the designer a problem with regard to the frontal radiator and considerable care was given to its installation. The armament of four 7·5-mm machine-guns was disposed in the same way as on the D 9.

Argentina built 58 D 21s in 1929, some of which were afterwards ceded to Paraguay by the Argentine authorities. Switzerland received one D 21 from France and 25 were produced at the Czechoslovak Skoda works, equipped with licence-built Hispanos.

Dewoitine D 27

In 1928 Emile Dewoitine, having received no French production orders since those for the D 1, took up residence in Switzerland. Thus, the next in his series of fighter aircraft, the D 27, with Hispano engine of 500/600 hp, was built at the Swiss Federal Workshops at Thun, near Berne. Unrivalled at the time of its appearance, this aircraft was ordered in considerable numbers for Swiss Military Aviation, sixty-six going into service from 1930 onwards, bearing military serials 200-265. There was also a D 26 version with 250-hp Wright radial engine, which remained in service into the 1960s, latterly as a glider tug. Between 1929 and 1933 a total of 85 D 27s were constructed in Switzerland, while Rumania also produced the version with a 500-hp Hispano engine.

Like its predecessors, the D 27 had a metal wing of distinctive planform. The fuselage was of circular section, constructed wholly in dural, with fuel in a belly tank which could be jettisoned. Speed range was 56 to 194 mph. The name of Dewoitine was kept alive in France from 1930 onwards by a series of prototypes and variants (the D 271 to D 274) and, more especially, by the flying of Marcel Doret, who had adopted the D 272 in place of his old D 1*ter*. Painted red and silver, and registered F-AJTE, this aircraft was a regular performer at air displays right up to the outbreak of World War II.

Dewoitine D 37 series

In order to achieve a substantial advance over the D 27, Emile Dewoitine evolved in 1931 the D 53 with a more powerful engine and strengthened wing structure. It was developed concurrently with the D 500, a low-wing monoplane with liquid-cooled engine, which is described separately. French Air Force technical authorities favoured liquid-cooled engines at the time, but Dewoitine decided to design the initial version of the D 53 around an air-cooled engine, under the designation D 531. Tests soon showed the makers that major increases in performance would be achieved only with an entirely new aircraft.

The former Société des Avions Dewoitine, known since its founder's return to France as the Société Aéronautique Française, had established close links with another well-known aircraft manufacturer, Les Etablissements Lioré et Olivier. This latter company was now entrusted with the work of transforming the D 531 into a new aircraft – the D 37 – a task which was undertaken in the LeO factory at Argenteuil.

The maiden flight of the D 37, scheduled originally for late 1931, did not take place until August 1932. The private-venture prototype was powered by a Gnome-Rhône 14 Kbrs engine, driving a four-bladed wooden propeller, but the D 371 which followed was modified in accordance with Plan I of the French General Air Staff. It had to wait a long time for its intended power plant – the Gnome 14 Kds – and, as a result, did not fly until September 1934. Twenty-eight production D 371s were ordered, but only 18 of these were built, appearing in 1935. The prototype was converted subsequently into an experimental aircraft for use in testing new parachutes.

The wings of the production version had a pronounced dihedral and were manufactured by the motor car body builder, Kellner. Armament comprised either two cannon in the wings or two wing-mounted machine-guns and two more in the fuselage.

The D 371s saw service with Groupe de Chasse II/4 of the Armée de l'Air, and then with the 574th Escadrille Régionale in Tunisia. Lithuania ordered 20 of the type, but these were never delivered. Instead, some of the Armée de l'Air D 371s and some of those built originally for Lithuania were modified into D 372s and despatched to Spain on the instructions of the French Government, to fight on the Spanish Republican side.

The French Navy, anxious to replace its ancient Wibault 74 fighters in Escadrilles 7 C 1 and 7 C 2, ordered 40 D 373s on 5 November 1934. These were carrier versions of the D 371 with a deck-landing hook. The first of them was not delivered until 23 March 1936, after undergoing structural strengthening at the LeO factory and having flaps fitted.

A variant was the type D 376, which differed from the D 373 only in having folding wings.

On 28 December 1937, Escadrille 7 C 1 had ten D 373s and D 376s on its strength, while Escadrille 7 C 3 at Hyère had a similar number available. Unfortunately, these aircraft had to be withdrawn from service shortly after the outbreak of World War II, because of a tendency of their Gnome-Rhône 14 Kfs engines to lose their crankshafts in flight.

In January 1940, naval squadrons AC 1 and AC 2, then operating the D 373s and D 376s, received as replacements 20 Potez 631s, formerly the equipment of Armée de l'Air Groupe II/8.

Dewoitine D 27, Swiss-built

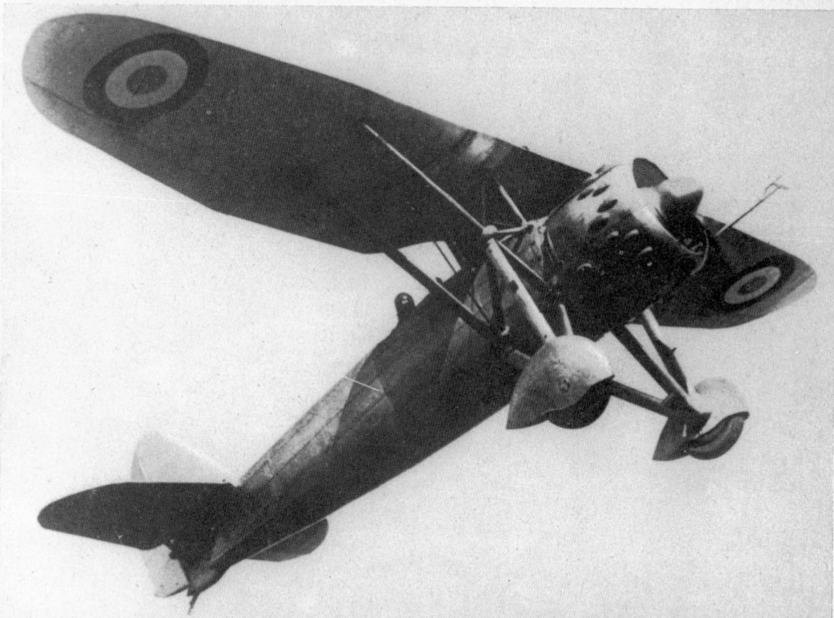
Dewoitine D 371 prototype

Dewoitine D 373 prototype

TYPE	DIMENSIONS						WEIGHT	PERFORMANCE				REMARKS	
	span ft	span in	length ft	length in	height ft	height in	max t-o lb	max speed mph	at height ft	service ceiling ft	combat range miles		
D 9	35	7¼	22	7½	9	2¾	3,152	162		27,900	466	GR 9 Ac	420 hp
D 19	35	7½	21	8	9	6¼	2,866	143		27,900	466	HS 12 Hb	450 hp
D 21	42	0	25	11¾	10	10¾	3,482	166		29,500	466	HS 12 Gb	575 hp
D 27	32	2	21	4	9	2	3,047	194		30,200	372	HS 12 Mc	600 hp
D 371	36	10	24	5	10	6	3,703	230		36,100	466	GR 14 Kes	800 hp
D 372	36	10	24	5	10	6	4,034	249		36,100	466	GR 14 Kfs	930 hp
D 373/376	36	10	24	5	11	2¾	4,342	249		32,800	435	GR 14 Kfs	930 hp

Dewoitine D 500 prototype

Dewoitine D 500

Dewoitine D 510

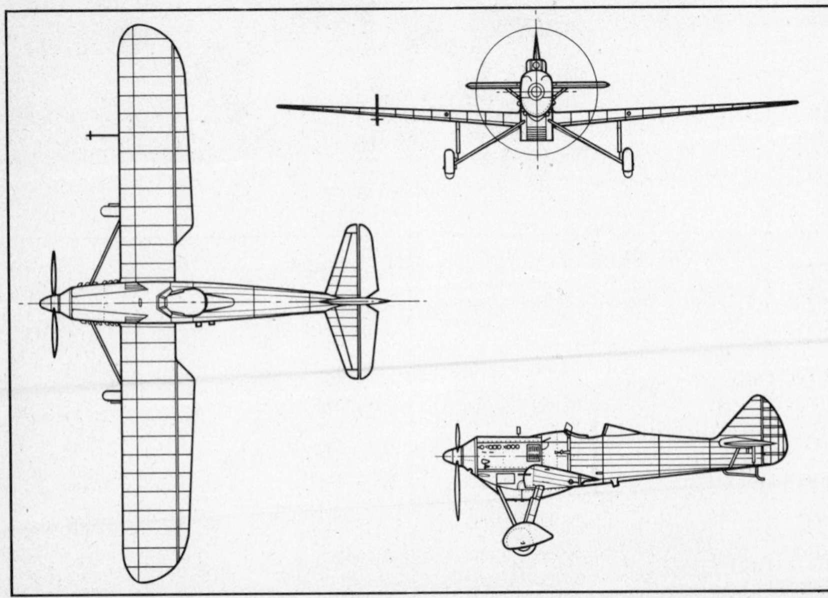
Dewoitine D 510

Dewoitine D 500 series

The Dewoitine D 500 was designed to meet requirements laid down in the French General Air Staff programme of 1930. This sought a replacement for the Nieuport 62s and 622s then in service with fighter elements of the Armée de l'Air, as the performance of the Nieuports was clearly inadequate for contemporary operational needs.

Purchased for 870,000 francs by the French Government and bearing the civil registration F-AKCK, the prototype D 500 flew for the first time on 19 June 1932, with Doret at the controls. Construction was all-metal, including the skin covering, and the D 500 had a single-spar wing. On 23 November 1933, an order for 57 was placed. In addition, three more prototypes made their appearance – D 500 No. 47, intended as the definitive aircraft for series production; D 500 No. 56, to flight test the Hispano-Suiza 12 Y; and the D 503 with single-strut main undercarriage units and frontal radiator.

Of the initial order for 57 aircraft, 12 were D 501s, identical with the D 500 except for the installation of the famous *moteur canon*, mounted above the crankcase and firing through the propeller boss. A further prototype, designated D 510 No. 48 (F-AODZ) was built at Toulouse as a demonstrator for the benefit of foreign missions visiting France.

D 500 No. 1, first aircraft of the production series, was due for delivery in August 1934; but, following an accident to the prototype aircraft No. 47, the wings of all machines then under construction had to be strengthened. By 1 July 1935, a total of 35 D 500s and nine D 501s had been accepted by the official Centre de Réception des Avions de Série (CRAS). Meanwhile, 50 additional D 500s (numbered from 62 to 113) had been ordered from Lioré et Olivier under Plan I. Of these, No. 68 was a D 510 with more powerful Hispano-Suiza 12 Ycrs engine and No. 112 was converted into a D 501. The remaining 48 D 500s covered by this order were each fitted with two Darne guns in the wings, in addition to the two machine-guns mounted over the engine which had formed the armament of the first 45 aircraft.

Thirty-six D 510s were ordered by Turkey towards the end of 1934. Designated D 510T, they were armed with Colt machine-guns and had underwing bomb racks. Only nine were accepted: the Turkish authorities refused the rest, saying that delivery dates had not been met.

In January 1935, a further 140 D 501s were ordered by the French government, 30 of them being intended for the Navy. Chatellerault (MAC) machine-guns were to be fitted to the aircraft in place of Darnes. In May of the same year, 32 D 510s were ordered from Lioré et Olivier. In summer 1936, Lithuania took delivery of seven D 501s, some of which found their way to Republican Spain.

Thus, by 10 December 1936, the French Air Force had received 240 Dewoitine D 500s and D 501s; while the first D 510 had been accepted in September of that year. Several foreign powers displayed great interest in this last version, particularly because of its *moteur canon*. In 1936 the Soviet and the British authorities each bought a single machine for evaluation, while the Hedjaz obtained two (which were afterwards sold to Republican Spain). Thirty-four D 510s were purchased by China and Japan bought two. At the end of October 1936, a French order for 30 D 510s was received and at the beginning of 1937 came the final purchase of 50 more for France.

Of a total of 359 fighter aircraft in French service on 15 June 1938, there were 59 D 500s and 104 D 501s in the 2nd, 3rd, 4th and 5th Escadres de Chasse. In addition 67 D 510s served on that date with the 1st and 8th Escadres de Chasse and the 3rd Autonomous Group in Tunisia. However, when war came in September 1939, only three complete groups (GC I/1, II/1 and I/8) still retained their D 510s, with a few dozen other D 500s, D 501s and D 510s in various Escadrilles Régionales.

By 10 May 1940, only two fighter groups (GC III/4 and III/5) – both of which had been withdrawn to the safety of North Africa – still had D 500s and D 510s on their strength. The last heard of the type was when the Germans seized two D 510s which they discovered during the occupation of southern France in 1942.

Dewoitine D 520

On 2 October 1938, the ever-youthful Marcel Doret, chief test pilot of the Société Nationale de Constructions Aéronautiques du Midi (successor to the Dewoitine concern after the French Nationalization Law), took up a new Dewoitine fighter, the D 520-01. A few weeks later, on 27 November, the aircraft was severely damaged in a belly landing which resulted from the pilot's forgetting to lower the retractable undercarriage!

The D 520 was a refined development of the D 510, with a Messier undercarriage and a Hispano 12 Y 21 (later Y 29) engine of 860 hp. It had been designed around an engine of 1,300 hp, in order to achieve speeds in the region of 370 mph. In the event, neither the prototype D 520s nor the production aircraft had such a power plant, since no reliable engine of this power became available. The intended performance was, therefore, never achieved.

SNCAM received an initial order for 200 D 520S ("S" = Series) fighters on 17 April 1939. Less than two months later, on 5 June, a further 400 were ordered. All these were to have the Hispano-Suiza 12 Y 31, the engine fitted to the Morane 406, already in series production.

Output of the D 520S was intended to reach an average of 50 machines a month in the first half of 1940. This was thought possible by reason of the care taken by its designers to cater for the needs of rapid large-scale production – a factor that had been given scarcely any consideration by most of the other nationalized aircraft concerns. Unfortunately, between April and November 1939, the French Air Force technical authorities insisted on a large number of modifications. Many of these were doubtless justified, but they delayed the introduction into service of the production fighters. Even so, 100 D 520S aircraft left the factories in May 1940 – too late to alter the outcome of the Battle of France.

The second prototype D 520 had flown on 28 January 1939. It differed from the first prototype in having larger vertical tail surfaces, an enclosed cockpit with a sliding hood, a Hispano 12 Y 29 engine (later replaced by a 12 Y 31), a ventral radiator instead of wing radiators, and armament. The "No. 1" painted on its rudder gave the intentionally false impression, for propaganda purposes, that the first production machine was now flying. The third prototype, which flew on 15 March 1939, was similar to the second except that a tail-wheel replaced the former tail skid.

The Hispano-Suiza 12 Y 45 engine was the production version of the 12 Y 29, with a Szydlowski supercharger, and was intended to replace the 12 Y 31 in the production D 520 as soon as possible. When it became clear that the 12 Y 45 would not be available, SNCAM designed a version of the D 520 to utilize the Rolls-Royce Merlin III, which had already been ordered, together with the Merlin X, for the Amiot 353 and 356 bombers. It was impossible to instal a Hispano cannon in this British power plant; so the Merlin-powered version, designated D 521, was laid out to have four wing-mounted machine-guns.

Only one D 521 was produced and flown, in May 1940. Tests showed it to have only a marginally better performance than that of the D 520S; so this version was abandoned and all the other Merlin engines delivered to France were used in Amiot bombers.

On 2 November 1939, D 520S No. 1, the first true production aircraft, flew with a Hispano-Suiza 12 Y 45 engine. Aircraft No. 2 took off for the first time on 3 December. After initial problems with the propeller, the

Dewoitine D 520

Dewoitine D 520

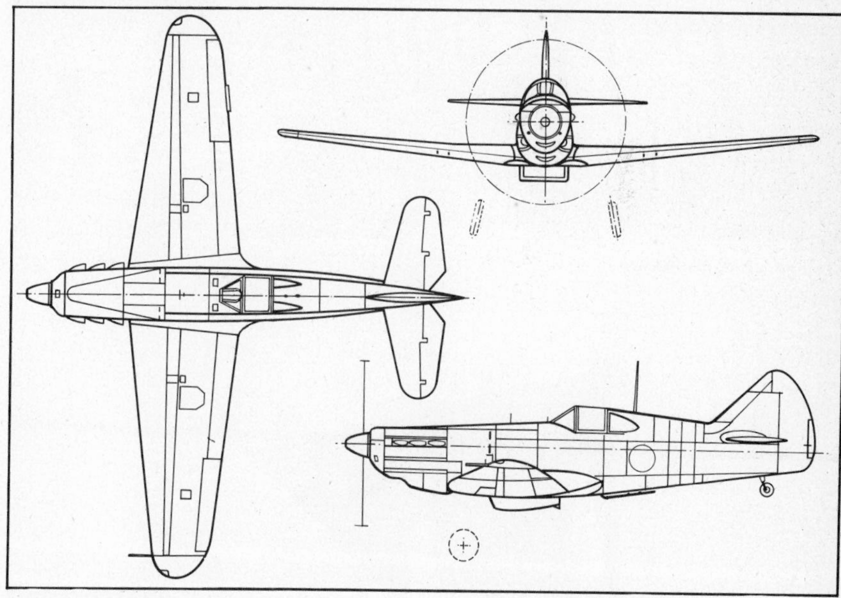
Dewoitine D 520

TYPE	DIMENSIONS						WEIGHT	PERFORMANCE				REMARKS	
	span		length		height		max t-o	max speed	at height	service ceiling	combat range		
	ft	in	ft	in	ft	in	lb	mph	ft	ft	miles		
D 500	39	8	25	3½	8	10½	3,792	224		35,400	530	HS 12 Xbrs-1	690 hp
D 501	39	8	25	1¼	8	10½	4,193	224		35,400	530	HS 12 Xcrs	690 hp
D 510	39	8	26	0¾	8	10½	4,234	250	16,000	34,500	435	HS 12 Ycrs	860 hp
D 520S	33	5¾	28	8¾	11	3	5,900	342	19,700	34,500	777	HS 12 Y 45	910 hp

Dewoitine D 520

Farman F 50

Farman FF 60 prototype

Farman F 60

engine cooling system and supercharger had been cleared up, eight D 520S fighters were taken on charge by the Armée de l'Air by 1 February 1940. The total rose to 31 by 1 March, and to 312 by 20 June 1940. In addition, 44 aircraft went to naval squadrons from 1 June onwards. Between 10 May and 25 June 1940, Groupes de Chasse I/3, II/3, III/3, II/6, III/6, II/7 and III/7, equipped with the D 520S, claimed a total of 147 enemy aircraft destroyed; 108 of these victories were officially confirmed.

About 430 D 520S fighters were completed before the Armistice, of which 403 were taken on charge by the French services. Of these, the first 349 had an electrically-operated Ratier propeller; the remainder had to have a Chauvière propeller, with mechanically-operated pitch change, due to shortage of the Ratier type.

In 1941 the Vichy Government decided to adopt the D 520 as its standard fighter. The Franco-German Armistice Commission authorized the production of 180 additional D 520s by the SNCASE, which by then had absorbed the SNCAM, to equip nine Vichy fighter units. Thus, 740 D 520S fighters were built in all.

When the Germans invaded the southern zone of France in November 1942, they confiscated 411 D 520Ss, of which 242 had been built prior to the Armistice and 169 dated from 1941 onwards. About 50 of these machines were used to train pilots of the Luftwaffe's JG 103 and JG 105 fighter units; a further 242 were handed over to Bulgaria and Rumania. The Italians also made use of 60 D 520s to equip their 13°, 22°, 24° and 167° Gruppi.

After August 1944, when the liberation of France began, Groupe de Chasse I/8 reformed with 30 D 520S fighters left behind in good condition by the enemy. Commanded by Marcel Doret, and with their German insignia painted out, these aircraft helped to eliminate the last traces of Nazi resistance in France.

Farman F 50

During the 1914-18 War, Maurice Farman 11 and Farman 40 reconnaissance aircraft were used at times for bombing missions, but these aircraft cannot really be classed as bombers. They carried only small bombs which the observer could drop on enemy concentrations. The first bomb-racks appeared in 1915, from which time the total weight of bombs carried by single-engined aircraft increased rapidly from about 130 to 440 lb.

It was not until 1918 that the first true Farman bomber appeared. This was the large two-seat F 50 B 2 biplane, the general lines of which recalled the twin-engined Gotha. It was powered by two Lorraine engines of 265 hp, mounted on the lower wing, one each side of the fuselage, between the Vee interplane struts. Few were produced, though there were some F 50s in squadrons F 114 and F 119. Of all-wooden construction with fabric covering, they had a wing area of 1,022 sq ft.

The gunner/bomb-aimer was accommodated in the nose of the fuselage, the pilot's cockpit being to the rear of this position and just in front of the wings. Eight 165-lb bombs were carried under the fuselage, between the legs of the wide-track undercarriage, each of which carried a pair of main wheels.

In March 1918, two F 50s were handed over to the American Expeditionary Forces in France; but at the end of the war those F 50s still in service were soon dropped by the bomber squadrons. Two were sold to the French Navy, which modified them to serve as torpedo-carriers, and one version, known as the F 50 P, went to Japan. Three more had their armament removed and, with six seats in the fuselage and a glazed canopy, served as type 50 T, for public transport trials.

One of these F 50s was still in service with the Compagnie des Grands Express Aériens in 1922.

Farman F 60 series

The Farman 60, first type to be named Goliath, appeared originally under the designation FF 60 (Frères Farman) in the closing stages of the 1914–18 War. It was a large two-seat night bomber powered by two 260-hp Salmson radial engines, mounted on the lower wing. The pilot sat in an open cockpit, but the second crew member had a

glazed cockpit canopy. This aircraft, and the derivatives which followed, was immensely successful and in the civil version was to become the keystone of French commercial fleets for some ten years.

After a few examples of the F 60 had been sold to Belgium and Japan, and while the French Navy was becoming interested in a seaplane version, there appeared in 1923 the F 60 M, powered by two 310-hp Renault 12 Fcy engines; about 20 of this three-seat night bomber version equipped the 21st Air Regiment based at Nancy. In 1925, 24 F 60s, powered by 380-hp Jupiter engines, took part in the Rif campaign in Morocco, serving with squadrons 5 B 2, 6 B 1, and 6 B 2 of l'Aviation Maritime. Equipped with alternative wheel or float undercarriages, the marine version carried either bombs or a torpedo.

The year 1925 also saw the appearance of the F 65, similar to the F 60 M but with different engines. There followed in 1927 the F 63 BN 4, with Jupiter engines, which equipped the 22nd Air Regiment at Chartres, and a final version, the F 68 three-seat night bomber, of which 32 examples were built for Poland.

To investigate the maximum potential of the basic design, the Farman company produced in 1923 a Super Goliath, designated F 140, powered by four engines of Farman manufacture, mounted in tandem pairs on the lower wing. Capable of carrying a very large load, this aircraft made its first flight in April 1924, and on 12 and 16 November 1925 captured 12 world records for endurance and altitude with loads of four and six tons.

The Super Goliath could climb to 3,000 m (9,850 ft) in 17 minutes and 5,000 m (16,400 ft) in 41 min 10 sec.

Six were ordered for experiments concerned with the carriage of heavy loads over long ranges, but this version did not enter squadron service.

Farman F 160 to 168

In 1928, a new range of twin-engined Farman biplanes succeeded the Goliaths of the F 60 family.

Designated F 160 to F 168, they were developments of the same basic design, with strengthened wings and more powerful engines. The military versions were as follows:

Type	*Engines*	*hp*	*Class*	*Year*	*Remarks*
F 160	Farman	500	BN 4	1928	Bomb load 3,300 lb
F 161	Farman	500	BN 3	1928	Bomb load 2,200 lb
F 162	Salmson	500	Torp 4	1928	Seaplane version
F 165	Salmson	260	BN 2	1928	Later fitted with 2 Jupiters Used at Naval seaplane school
F 166	Jupiter	380	Torp 4	1928	Dual control, side-by-side
F 167	Jupiter	380	Torp 4	1928	As 166, with folding wings
F 168	Jupiter	480	Torp 4	1928	Dual control in tandem

This last version, the F 168, had been ordered originally by the Air Force as a night bomber. It suffered at first from tail unit vibration. Consequently when it was handed over to the Navy the rear fuselage was reinforced, after which it was operated satisfactorily as a seaplane, with wooden floats.

The Aéronautique Maritime used Farman F 168s for many years in squadrons 1 B 1, 3 B 2, 4 B 1, 4 B 2 and 4 B 3, until they were replaced by Liorés. Squadron GB II/25 of the Air Force still had a number of F 168s in service in 1936.

Farman F 168

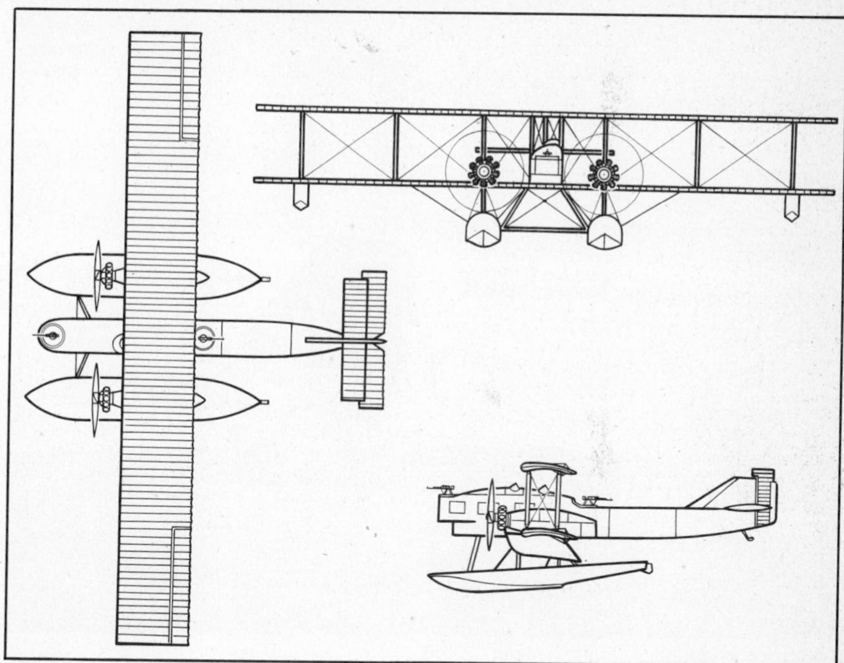

Farman F 168

TYPE	DIMENSIONS						WEIGHT	PERFORMANCE				REMARKS	
	span		*length*		*height*		*max t-o*	*max speed*	*at height*	*service ceiling*	*combat range*		
	ft	*in*	*ft*	*in*	*ft*	*in*	*lb*	*mph*	*ft*	*ft*	*miles*		
F 50	75	1	39	5¾	10	9¾	6,869	93		13,100	217	2 × LO 8 Bd	265 hp
F 60	86	11¼	47	6¾	17	4½	12,786	90		18,000	341	2 × GR 9 Aa	380 hp
F 140	114	9¾	65	7½	23	11½	25,573	107		21,300	745	4 × FA 12 We	500 hp
F 168	86	1½	49	10½	20	4½	14,991	102		13,100	621	2 × GR 9 Akx	480 hp

Farman F 221 prototype

Farman F 222 prototype

Farman F 2233

Gourdou-Leseurre Type A

Farman F 221 series

In 1931 the Farman company designed the F 210, a large monoplane bomber powered by four 350-hp Hispano J 12 engines. A derivative of the type, the F 211, flew in October 1931, but was intended only as a stop-gap, pending production of the F 220 and F 221 called for by the Chief of Air Staff under a programme for aircraft in the BN 5 (five-seat night bomber) category. This programme was changed later to one for seven-seat BN 7s.

The F 220 and F 221 differed only in power plant, that of the former being water-cooled, whereas the F 221 had air-cooled engines. They were of all-metal construction, with a high rectangular wing which spanned 118 ft and a fuselage more than 70 ft long. At an all-up weight varying between 15 and 18 tons, maximum speed was 185 mph.

Flight trials of the F 220 showed that it had little to offer as a heavy night bomber in its original form; so the prototype was first converted into a variant designated F 220A and then, after further modification, into the F 220B. In 1935 the French Government loaned this aircraft to Air France, who used it under the name of *Le Centaure* (F-ANLG) for their air mail service over the South Atlantic.

The F 221 (BN 7 category) went into production in 1934, under the government's Plan I. With the F 222, described later, it was destined to form the backbone of the French heavy bomber force for some years. Meanwhile, during its trials, piloted by Lucine Coupet, the company's chief test pilot, it captured an international altitude record with payload, by attaining 22,965 ft.

In 1935, the prototype F 221 was converted into a military transport, able to carry 20 fully-armed troops. An initial order for 12 F 221s followed, and these were built on new assembly lines in the Farman factory at Boulogne-Billancourt, which cost the company more than eight million francs.

When this production line got under way, the 221 was joined by the F 222, which differed by having more powerful Gnome-Rhône engines and an undercarriage which retracted into the engine nacelles. The prototype F 222 flew for the first time in June 1935, and a batch of 12 of these aircraft was built in 1936. In the following year, a number of F 221s were equipped with a retractable undercarriage and Gnome-Rhône 14 Kdrs engines, after which they were re-designated F 222s.

A variant of the F 222, designated F 222/2, appeared in October 1937, with a streamlined nose section and outer wings with pronounced dihedral. Twelve of these aircraft served with the 15th bomber squadron, based at Reims-Courcy, and on 10 May 1940 squadrons GB I/15 and II/15, equipped with F 221s and F 222s, were sent to reinforce the Northern Air Operations Zone.

Back in 1937 the Société Nationale de Constructions Aéronautiques du Centre, which had taken over Farman and Hanriot, had produced a final variant of the F 220. This aircraft, designated F 223, had a wing of smaller span than that of the F 222, with full-span flaps and a redesigned tail unit with twin fins. Four supercharged Hispano radial engines of 1,100 hp, in NACA cowlings, powered the aircraft, and a cannon was fitted for defence against attack from behind. The payload of this version was seven tons.

It was decided after a time to change the power plant of the F 223s, as their original Hispano engines proved unreliable. They were replaced with Hispano 12 Y 50/51 engines, which were well proven, and the eight machines thus converted were designated F 2233s. The remaining two were modified after the collapse of France and, with reduced fuel capacity, were designated F 2232s. Registered F-BAFM and F-BAHM, they were used by Air France for cargo transport between Brazzaville and Cairo in 1941–2.

Gourdou-Leseurre B 3

Gourdou and Leseurre, engineers of the "Aéronautique", built in 1918 two prototype fighter aircraft known successively as the types A and B.

The B had a parasol wing of rectangular planform, made up of two steel and duralumin spars and wooden

ribs, with fabric covering. A large number of struts braced the wings to the fuselage, which was built as a lattice-girder box with duralumin longerons, again covered with fabric. Power plant was the 180-hp Vee Hispano.

The B was followed by the Gourdou-Leseurre B 2, (GL 21) which took part in the 1919 race for the Coupe Deutsch de la Meurthe. When fitted with a more powerful radial, in 1934, this machine was redesignated B 6.

To meet the requirements of a competition for advanced training aircraft, announced in 1923, the Gourdou-Leseurre company developed the B 3 (GL 22) – a derivative of both the B 2 and the Navy ET type, with a reinforced undercarriage. Fifty were built, with Hispano 8Ac engine and an armament of two machine-guns firing through the propeller disc, for service as low-cost fighters in various foreign countries. In 1924, B 3s were exported to Finland, Estonia and Czechoslovakia, and the type was licence-built by the Yugoslav company ZMAJ.

Because of its low structure weight and good handling qualities, the B 3 was fully aerobatic and soon earned a reputation as an excellent and dependable aircraft. One B 3, registered OK-AZD, was still in use as a sporting aircraft at a Czechoslovak aero club as late as 1934.

Hanriot HD 1

In 1915, René Hanriot drew up the specification for a small single-seat fighter, which was designed subsequently by Engineer Dupont. Known as the HD 1, this aircraft, which made its first flight at Villacoublay in December 1916, was light, very manoeuvrable and offered excellent visibility due to careful positioning of the interplane struts. It was powered by a 120-hp Le Rhône 9 Jb (or 9 Jby) rotary engine, driving a Ratmanoff propeller of 8 ft diameter.

The HD 1 was a sesquiplane, with 7° of dihedral on the upper wing only. Wing spars were of duralumin and the ribs of wood, the whole being covered with fabric. The fuselage was of fabric-covered wooden construction, and the undercarriage was of duralumin and steel.

When demonstrated to the French authorities, the HD 1 failed to arouse any interest. However, Italy adopted the machine for its fighter groups at the end of 1916, and later arranged to have it constructed under licence by Nieuport-Macchi of Varese. It was in an HD 1 that the Italian ace, Scaroni, achieved most of his combat victories. In the autumn of 1917, the Belgian Air Force also received 79 HD 1s which equipped the 1st and 9th Belgian squadrons and became the "war horses" of such pilots as Willy Coppens, Jean Olieslagers and André Demeulmeester. One of them can still be seen today in the Musée Royal de l'Armée in Brussels. A few also saw service with the American coastal air-sea forces in France. Several Swiss squadrons flew HD 1s.

The HD 1 could climb easily to 20,000 ft, attaining a height of 13,000 ft in 15 minutes; but this was achieved at the expense of its armament, which consisted of only a single machine-gun firing through the propeller disc. To combine similar performance with greater fire-power, Hanriot built a more powerful version – actually the 301st HD 1 – which could carry two machine-guns. Powered by a 160-hp Gnome engine and distinguished by an enlarged fin, this aircraft flew in 1917, but was soon

Gourdou-Leseurre B 3, Finnish Air Force

Hanriot HD 1

Hanriot HD 1 No. 301

TYPE	DIMENSIONS						WEIGHT	PERFORMANCE				REMARKS	
	span ft	span in	length ft	length in	height ft	height in	max t-o lb	max speed mph	at height ft	service ceiling ft	combat range miles		
F 221	118	1½	70	8¾	17	2¼	39,242	185		19,700	745	4 × GR 14 Kbrs	800 hp
F 222	118	1½	70	8¾	17	2¼	41,226	199		19,700	745	4 × GR 14 Kdrs	860 hp
F 222/2	118	1½	70	4½	17	0¼	41,226	202		27,900	932	4 × GR 14 Kdrs	860 hp
F 223	110	2¾	72	2	16	8¾	39,683	261	13,000	26,300	1,490	4 × HS 14 Aa08/09	1,100 hp
F 2233	110	2¾	72	2	16	8¾	39,815	264		26,300	1,490	4 × HS 12 Y50/51	1,100 hp
Gourdou-Leseurre B 3	29	7¾	21	3¾	7	9¼	1,984	143		24,600	300	HS 8 Ac	180 hp
HD 1	28	1½	19	5¾	8	6	1,532	112	SL	20,000	217	RO 9 Jb	120 hp

Hanriot HD 1, Macchi-built

Hanriot HD 1

Hanriot HD 3

abandoned, since the engine had not been fully developed and proved unreliable.

Another version was armed with a cannon firing through the propeller boss; but early tests showed this to be unsatisfactory, as vibration of the rotary engine made it impossible to aim the gun accurately.

In 1922, the Hanriot company fitted out HD 1 No. 513 (F-AFFX) as a sports and aerobatic aircraft for its chief pilot, Haegelen. Another HD 1 was rebuilt in 1929 for the same pilot; this machine (F-AJFL) was powered by an 80-hp Le Rhône engine and had rounded wingtips.

In 1917, an HD 1 had been fitted with floats instead of wheels and, as the HD 2, had been tested on the Seine. In the autumn of the same year, the marine base of St-Pol, near Dunkirk, received a number of production HD 2s to oppose German seaplanes over the North Sea; this model later interested both the USA and Japan.

A landplane version of the HD 2, designated HD 2 C, was the first French aircraft to take off from the deck of a warship. On 26 October 1918, Georges Guierre, a naval pilot, made a successful take-off from a wooden platform, 33 ft in length, which had been built on the superstructure of the battleship *Paris*. Two years later, on 26 October 1920, an HD 2 C was landed for the first time on the temporary deck of the *Béarn*, which was then being converted from battleship to aircraft carrier at Toulon.

Hanriot HD 3

The Hanriot HD 3, a two-seat biplane derived from the HD 1, flew for the first time in June 1917. Powered by a 260-hp engine, this aircraft was able to carry heavier armament than its predecessor, consisting of a machine-gun in the rear cockpit and two 7·5-mm guns firing through the propeller disc.

Although designed as a two-seat fighter, the HD 3 could also be used in a reconnaissance rôle, the rear machine-gun then being replaced by a camera. Its high performance well suited it for this duty, since it could attain 130 mph at sea level, and needed take-off and landing runs of only 160 ft and 230 ft respectively.

Like the HD 1 it had staggered wings, with the total wing area increased from 198·2 sq ft to 242·1 sq ft. Though relatively heavy, it retained aerobatic capability.

The HD 3 had hardly entered service with squadron HD 174 and the 2nd Air Regiment at Strasbourg when the Armistice was signed. It continued in use and on 26 October 1920, shortly after the landing on the future aircraft carrier *Béarn* by the HD 2 C, the same pilot, accompanied by a lieutenant from the warship *Levèque*, made a second successful landing with the two-seat HD 3.

HD 3 No. 2000, fitted with floats, was tested on the Seine as a prototype for the HD 4 which did not, however, enter production. A prototype night-fighter, designated HD 3*bis*, was also built, with a thicker wing section and trim-tabs on the ailerons.

Latécoère 28/9

The Société Industrielle d'Aviation Pierre Latécoère (SIDAL) developed this three-seat bomber from the Latécoère 28/3 in which Jean Mermoz made his famous first air mail crossing of the South Atlantic, and from the Latécoère 28/0 and 28/1 transports used by Compagnie Générale Aéropostale. Three were ordered, in 1931, for the Venezuelan Air Force. This was logical, as the Linea Aeropostal Venezolana was already operating two ex-Aéropostale Latécoère 28/1s and three 28/6s.

The 28/9 was a braced high-wing monoplane of composite construction. The wing had two duralumin spars and wooden ribs; the fuselage was of metal construction with metal covering, except at the rear which, like the wings and tail unit, was fabric-covered. The wide-track undercarriage consisted of two independent main units incorporating Messier shock-absorbers. Power plant was a 650-hp Hispano 12 Nb engine, driving either a Levasseur Mt 199 metal propeller or a Ratier Bb 745 wooden propeller. Armament comprised one forward-firing machine-gun and another in a gun position above the rear fuselage, with a number of small bombs housed vertically inside the fuselage.

Latécoère 290

At the end of 1930, SIDAL built at its Toulouse factory two prototype torpedo seaplanes known as the Latécoère 290 and 440. Similar to the type 28 in overall lines and general construction, they differed from each other in that the 290 had an enclosed cabin for the crew. Both made their first flights in landplane form in 1931, their metal floats being fitted when they were sent to the CEPA at St-Raphaël for official tests. A second 290 and another 440 followed the first prototypes in 1932. All four aircraft were bought by the French Navy, and the Latécoère 290 was chosen for series production, as it satisfied all official requirements and was the cheaper to produce. The last of 40 production machines was delivered in July 1934. They served with the first French torpedo squadrons, 1 T 1 and 4 T 1 (later known as the T 2 and T 1 respectively). When the more modern Latécoère 298 entered service in 1938, the 290s were relegated to coastal surveillance duties with squadron 1 S 2.

The Latécoère 290 was armed with three machine-guns, one firing forward through the propeller disc, the other two being mounted in a rear turret. A torpedo or two 330-lb bombs could be carried beneath the fuselage. Maximum speed was 130 mph at sea level when carrying full load, or 137 mph without torpedo or bombs. The 290 could climb to 6,560 ft in 12 minutes. Landing speed was 63 mph.

There were eight known variants. Three of which were produced as prototypes, the remainder being projects only:

Type		*Power plant*	*Remarks*
291.	Project only	Hispano 18 Sbr	As 290, with 1,000-hp engine
292.	Project only	Hispano 18 Sbr	
292/2.	Project only	Hispano 18 Sbr	As 291, but with low wing
293.	Prototype	Gnome 14 Kcrs	800-hp radial-engined conversion
294.	Prototype	Gnome 14 Kdrs	Used by squadron T 1
295.	Project only	Hispano 18 Sbr	As 293, with 1,000-hp engine
296.	Prototype	Hispano 12 Ydrs-1	As 294, with 890-hp Vee engine
297.	Project only	Hispano 12 Ybrs	As above, with 650-hp engine

Latécoère 298

Of completely different design to the earlier Latécoère seaplanes, the 298 was an all-metal low-wing monoplane, only the control surfaces being fabric-covered. The wing had slotted ailerons and flaps, the fuselage was of oval section, streamlined floats were fitted, and the torpedo was carried in an enclosed bay.

Designed during 1935, as a replacement for the 290, the prototype 298 made its first flight on 8 May 1936. It was sent to St-Raphaël on 25 September 1936 and, after demonstration by SIDAL test pilots Crespy and Gonord, was taken over by Hébert, the chief Naval pilot. It was to remain at St-Raphaël until 25 October 1939, being used for testing equipment – in particular the Alkan automatic pilot. It was also used for training pilots for the production version of the seaplane.

Both prototype and production aircraft were powered by the 880-hp Hispano 12 Ycrs-1, but without the *moteur canon*, since there was not room to accommodate this weapon. Armament consisted of two wing-mounted

Latécoère 28/6 transport

Latécoère 290

Latécoère 298 B

TYPE	DIMENSIONS						WEIGHT	PERFORMANCE				REMARKS	
	span		*length*		*height*		*max t-o*	*max speed*	*at height*	*service ceiling*	*combat range*		
	ft	*in*	*ft*	*in*	*ft*	*in*	*lb*	*mph*	*ft*	*ft*	*miles*		
HD 3	29	7	23	8¾	9	10¼	2,506	130	SL	18,700	310	SA 9 Z	260 hp
Latécoère 28/9	63	2	42	11½	11	9	8,315	149		13,100	500	HS 12 Nb	650 hp
Latécoère 290	63	2	44	9	10	11½	10,249	130	SL	15,000	435	HS 12 Nbr	650 hp
Latécoère 298 D	50	10¼	41	2½	16	10	10,096	180	6,600	19,700	1,367	HS 12 Ycrs-1	880 hp

Latécoère 298 F

Latham 42

Latham 47-02; lost with Amundsen aboard

machine-guns and a third machine-gun in the rear cockpit, and one torpedo or two 550-lb bombs could be carried.

A first batch of 36 Latécoère 298s was ordered in 1937, made up of 24 type 298 As and 12 type 298 Bs; in addition 12 more "Bs" were ordered later. The 298 A (the letters A, B, C, etc. were not used in designations on the tail of seaplanes after the 298) was similar to the prototype, except for having a more-rounded cockpit canopy. The 298 B had folding wings for ship-board stowage and was fitted with dual controls. When it was used for reconnaissance, a fuel tank could be fitted in the torpedo bay, extending the range to over 930 miles.

The 298 C remained a project only. The 298 D which followed was similar to the "A", but equipped with dual controls. Shortage of Ratier variable-pitch metal propellers resulted in the installation of fixed-pitch wooden propellers after the 6th machine. About 95 were built.

At the beginning of 1940, type 298 D No. 80 was converted into a 298 E. This was a reconnaissance version, with a range of 1,240 miles, in which the torpedo bay was replaced by a glazed observation bay. Unfortunately, this became drenched in salt spray during take-off and landing, making the window opaque and useless for observation purposes. The 298 E, therefore, remained a prototype only, ending its career in June 1940 at Arzew (North Africa) with squadron T2.

At the outbreak of war, Latécoère 298s were distributed among squadrons T 1, T 2, T 3, T 4, HB 1, HB 2, 1 S 1, and 3 S 6 of the Aéronautique Maritime. They flew side-by-side with aircraft of the French Air Force in an attempt to arrest the German advance on the Somme in May 1940.

In 1942, the Germans authorized the manufacture of 30 Latécoère 298 Fs, a version of the 298 D without dual controls. But after the total occupation of France, in November of that year, only squadrons 1 T, 2 T, 3 T, 4 T, 5 T, 6 T and 4 S possessed 298s, the number of these machines gradually diminishing through lack of spares. So, by the end of 1943, only squadrons 2 S and 3 S still flew the type. Sole post-war 298 squadron was No. 53 S, and the type disappeared from service in 1951.

Two examples of a landplane version, designated Latécoère 299, were produced in September 1939, the -01 being destroyed at Cherbourg and the -02 at Bayonne. A final derivative, the experimental 299 A, with two Hispano 12 Y 31 engines arranged in tandem, driving co-axial contra-rotating propellers, was constructed at Toulouse in 1940. Unfortunately, it was destroyed by fire during a bombing attack on the aerodrome at Lyon-Bron a few days after its first taxying trials and never flew.

Latham 42

The old-established aviation company of Avions Latham, whose first engineer had been M. Levavasseur, produced in 1924 a three-seat flying-boat patrol bomber in the same HB 3 category as the CAMS 33 B, 5I-R-3 and Lioré et Olivier H 135. Known as the Latham 42, this aircraft was of all-wooden construction, its biplane wings having a total area of 1,344 sq ft. It was powered by two Lorraine 12 Da engines of 370 hp, mounted on struts between the wings. Armament comprised four machine-guns, two in the nose cockpit and two in a second gun-position in the rear fuselage. Two 165-lb bombs, or four smaller bombs, could be mounted beneath the lower wing.

The prototype, registered C 17, was flown in 1924 by the company's test pilot, Alphonse Duhamel, and was joined at St-Raphaël in 1925 by a second prototype. France ordered 18 of these machines, and a number were built also for Poland. The standard version introduced modified wing floats, and the original Lorraine engines were replaced by Gnome-Rhône Jupiters of 380 hp. This latter change was necessitated by the unreliability of the Lorraine engines.

The Latham 42 equipped 4 R 1 squadron, based at Berre in 1925, until replaced by the Latham 47.

Latham 47

The Latham 47 was not strictly a bomber, being designed rather for long-range naval reconnaissance; but since it was able to carry a bomb load it merits inclusion. Two prototypes were produced at Caudebec in 1928, the -01 being powered by two Farman 12 We engines, driving Levasseur four-blade metal propellers, while the -02 had Renault 12 Jb engines.

Of all-wooden construction, the Latham 47 was a biplane flying-boat in which the pilot was accommodated under a glazed canopy, with the two machine-gunners in open cockpits. During the latter half of 1929 the production version, designated 47 R3B4 (three-seat reconnaissance, four-seat bomber) entered service with 1 R 1 Squadron at Cherbourg and 5 E 1 (formerly 4 R 1) Squadron at Berre. The production flying-boats differed from the prototypes in having a bomb-aiming position in the front of the hull and were powered by Hispano-Suiza 12 Lbs of 600 hp, mounted in tandem between the wings. They were withdrawn from service in 1930.

A civil version, designated Latham 47 P, appeared in 1929. This was designed for use on the Mediterranean air mail service and accommodated a crew of three. The prototype was destroyed by heavy seas during trials, but the second machine, registered F-AJKO, was used by Compagnie Aéropostale.

Both prototypes of the military Latham 47 came to a tragic end; the -01 was destroyed by fire when its petrol tank exploded on the Seine; the -02 was lost attempting to rescue the crew of the airship *Italia* in the Arctic.

A routine message had been received from the *Italia* on 23 May 1928. After that nearly three weeks passed before her crew were able to signal that they were in difficulties on the pack ice in the far north. Once the airship's position was known, on 11 June, a major world-wide effort was mounted to save her crew, which included General Nobile. Although lacking any experience of polar flying, France offered the Latham 47 to assist in the search, it being the only machine available with adequate cruising range. Piloted by Capitaine de Corvette Guildaud, and carrying the great Norwegian explorer Roald Amundsen, the machine left Cherbourg on 18 June and flew to Bergen in Norway. There, a radiator muff of balloon fabric was fitted, this being the only modification that could be made quickly to enable the aircraft to operate in low polar temperatures.

Nothing more was heard of the 47-02 after it left Norway until, almost three months later, a wing float was washed up on the shores of the Arctic Ocean. This disaster proved to be the final blow for Jean Latham, and he sold his business to the Amiot company in 1929.

LeO 7

Fernand Lioré and Henri Olivier established an aircraft factory at Levallois-Berret in March 1912. It was used by a number of pioneers for experimental work and, in particular, was the birthplace of the first Morane-Saulnier aircraft. By the outbreak of war, the factory was turning out some ten aircraft a month, but within a short time this figure was tripled. From 1916, the Sopwith 1½-Strutter, which had been adopted by France for observation duties, was built by Lioré et Olivier, and other French manufacturers, and received the company designation 1 SOL. From it was developed the LeO 4.

In 1919 there appeared the prototype of an armoured twin-engined aircraft, powered by two 170-hp Le Rhône 9R engines. Designated LeO 5, it went into production for the infantry support rôle, and was followed by a three-engined flying-boat designated LeO H 6.

In 1922 the LeO 7/2 went into production. This was a

Latham 47-02

LeO 7/2

LeO 7/3, Aviation Maritime

TYPE	DIMENSIONS span ft	span in	length ft	length in	height ft	height in	WEIGHT max t-o lb	PERFORMANCE max speed mph	at height ft	service ceiling ft	combat range miles	REMARKS	
Latham 42	73	10	50	10	17	8½	11,815	98	SL			2 × GR Jupiter	380 hp
Latham 47 R3B4	82	8	53	1¾	18	0½	15,180	112	SL		1,240	2 × HS 12 Lb	600 hp
LeO 7/2	61	0	38	0¾	13	2¼	6,614	126		23,000		2 × HS 8 Fb	300 hp
LeO 7/3	65	7¼	38	0¾	15	2½		118		16,400		2 × HS 8 Fb	300 hp

LeO 20

LeO 20

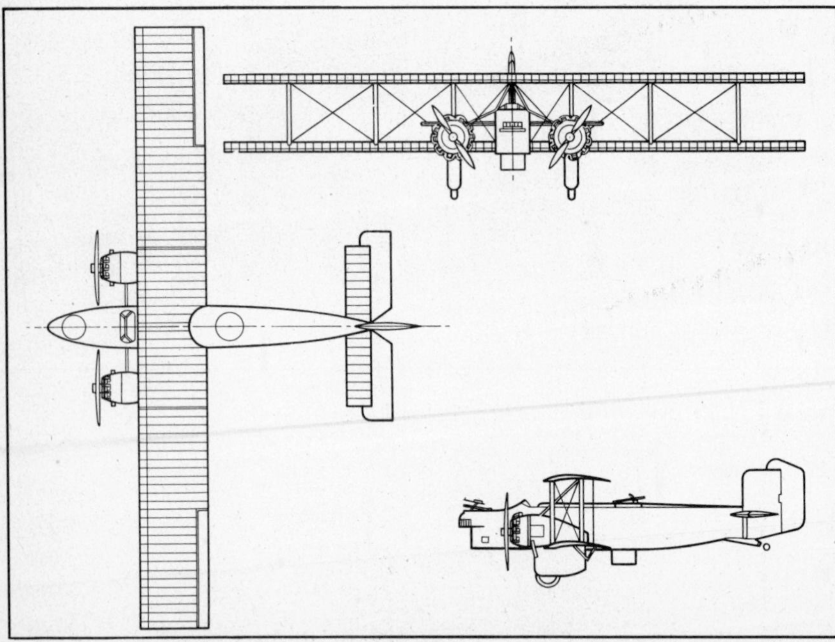
LeO 20

three-seat twin-engined bomber biplane, powered by two 300-hp Hispano engines, each mounted in a nacelle which also contained the fuel and oil tanks. A gunner/observer was accommodated in the nose of the fuselage. Immediately behind him were two armoured positions, the forward cockpit being occupied by the pilot, with a machine-gunner to his rear. The aircraft was supported on the ground by spatted wheels, mounted directly beneath the engine nacelles, the two wheels being connected by an auxiliary lifting surface.

The LeO 7/2 could attain a speed of 106 mph at 16,400 ft. Twenty were built for squadron service on an experimental basis. They were followed by a larger, marine version, the LeO 7/3, of which 12 were built. They were intended to serve as three-seat torpedo-bombers and were, in effect, amphibians, each main wheel and the tail skid being encased in small floats to permit emergency landing and take-off from the sea. This version was not a success, however, and was soon scrapped.

LeO 12

First exhibited at the Salon de l'Aéronautique in 1924, the LeO 12 was a twin-engined two-seat night bomber in the same category as the Amiot SECM 120. It was of fabric-covered duralumin construction, and had narrow-chord biplane wings of equal span, without sweepback or dihedral. The square-section fuselage was mounted on the lower wing, as were the two 400-hp Lorraine engines. Directly beneath the engines were the main landing wheels, encased in large streamlined "pantalons".

One month after the first flight, in June 1924, an official demonstration of the machine took place. Carrying a 3,525-lb load, the LeO 12 climbed to 2,000 m (6,560 ft) in 9 min 18 sec, and attained a speed of 118 mph at a height of 7,500 ft. With a load of 3,970 lb, it climbed to 18,000 ft in one hour, and also demonstrated that it could perform well on the power of one engine. Four more prototypes were built and these aircraft, like the LeO 7/2, were taken into squadron service on an experimental basis.

There followed a civil version, designated LeO 121, with accommodation for 12 passengers. Another variant, designated LeO 122, appeared in 1926. This was a twin-engined bomber, differing from the LeO 12 in its power plant, which consisted of two Jupiter engines. It served as the prototype for the LeO 20.

Final development was the LeO 123, an experimental three-seater produced in 1933 and purchased by the French Government for use at the CEMA at Villacoublay. Registered F-AKDO, it had the first enclosed cockpit seen in France, and was used both for the surveying of air routes and for research in instrument flying.

LeO 20

A direct development of the LeO 122, the three-seat LeO 20 was a rival of the Farman Goliath, and equipped French night bomber squadrons for many years. It was of similar construction to the LeO 12, with slightly larger overall dimensions than the LeO 122 which had been its prototype. Its armament comprised five machine-guns, one of which was mounted in a streamlined fairing which retracted into the fuselage. With a bomb load of 1,100 lb, it could climb to 2,000 m (6,560 ft) in 7 min 16 sec and to 4,000 m (13,125 ft) in 25 min 13 sec.

The French Air Force took delivery of 320 Leo 20s and, following demonstration flights by the civil-registered F-AIFI, Brazil and Rumania ordered two and seven examples respectively.

Unfortunately, the maximum speed of the LeO 20 was below 125 mph, which led to withdrawal of the type from squadron service in 1937. A few machines, redesignated LeO 201, were converted for the training of airborne troops and were based at Istres and Avignon-Pujaut.

From 1929 onwards, several LeO 20s were used for research and development work. For example, one aircraft was equipped with a 37-mm cannon; in June 1932 another was tested with a sesquiplane wing configuration and in November 1933 a LeO 20, re-engined with supercharged Gnome-Rhône 9 Asbs, attained 130 mph.

LeO 206

Seeking to develop still further the successful LeO 20, Lioré et Olivier first designed the LeO 202, powered by two Salmson 9 Abc engines. Realizing the advantages of extra power, they decided to investigate the possibility of adapting the basic airframe to take four engines, mounted in tandem pairs on the lower wing. First aircraft of the new formula to appear, in March 1931, was the LeO 203 prototype, with four 350-hp Gnome-Rhône 7 Kb engines, 4½° of sweepback and a spatted undercarriage. A naval version, the LeO H 204, also flew in 1931 and was tested at St-Raphaël, but remained a prototype only. It was followed in the same year by the LeO 205, which was generally similar except for having four Renault 9 Ca radial engines; these failed to give their planned performance and this variant, too, was abandoned.

In 1932, 40 examples of the LeO 206 were ordered. The first of these flew in 1933, and series production of the type started later that year. Powered by four supercharged Gnome-Rhône engines, the LeO 206 was generally similar to the 203, but introduced a long ventral fairing, with a gun position at the rear, and a tail-wheel. It could climb to 3,000 m (9,850 ft) in 15 min, and had a speed of 146 mph at that height. With 323 gallons of fuel and a ton of bombs, maximum range was over 1,200 miles at an operational height of 13,000 ft. Robust construction and the ability to maintain height on two engines helped to keep the 206 in service until 1939, when a total of 25 aircraft still equipped two bomber groups based in North Africa.

Three examples of a variant, designated LeO 207, were also built. These were simply 206s with Gnome-Rhône Titan-Major radial engines. Final version was the LeO 208 of 1934, powered by two Gnome-Rhône 14 Krsd radial engines, with reduction gear and supercharger. This machine utilized the basic fuselage of a 206, but introduced new wings, of which the upper had only half the chord of the lower, I-type interplane struts and a retractable undercarriage. It proved very fast for its category, but was scrapped in 1936 when the superiority of the monoplane became generally accepted.

LeO 25 series

November 1928 saw the debut of the Lioré et Olivier 25 BN 4, an enlarged version of the LeO 20, with two 500-hp Hispano 12 Hb Vee-type engines. Its range was considered insufficient for night bombing, so it was converted into an amphibian coastal bomber, with two Hispano 12 MBR engines, under the designation LeO 252. Meanwhile, three LeO 253s (export versions of the LeO 25) had been sold to Brazil. A lightened, reduced-power version, the LeO 251, remained a project only.

The French Navy was anxious to replace the Farman 168s which it had used as torpedo-bombers since 1928, and tested the next version, the LeO H 254, at Berre in 1932. Two were built and, when more advanced versions of the 250 series became available, were used as training seaplanes alongside the Farman Goliaths.

Powered by Hispano 12 X engines with superchargers, the LeO 255 flew in 1933. Bourdin, chief pilot of the company's amphibian division, established several altitude records with this machine, which was used later by the Harbour Squadron at St-Raphaël base, under the designation SR-21. It preceded the H 256, of which four

LeO 203 prototype

LeO H 252

LeO H 257

TYPE	DIMENSIONS						WEIGHT	PERFORMANCE				REMARKS	
	span		length		height		max t-o	max speed	at height	service ceiling	combat range		
	ft	in	ft	in	ft	in	lb	mph	ft	ft	miles		
LeO 12	70	6¼	39	4½	15	5	10,141	118	7,500	19,700	372	2 × LO 12 Db	400 hp
LeO 20	72	0	45	3¾	13	11¾	12,037	123		18,900	620	2 × GR 9 Ady	420 hp
LeO 206	80	6¼	48	5½	19	7½	18,628	146	10,000	25,000	1,240	4 × GR 7 Kds	350 hp
LeO 257bis	83	8	57	6¾	22	3¾	20,679	155	11,500	26,300	932	2 × GR 14 Kirs/Kjrs	870 hp
LeO 258	83	8	57	6¾	22	3¾	20,679	149	SL	18,100	745	2 × HS 12 Nbr	650 hp

LeO 257*bis*

LeO 45 prototype

LeO 451 prototype

LeO 451

examples were built and which was distinguished from the normal "25" series by having increased wing span. The LeO H 257, which followed, was tested at St-Raphaël in April 1933, and was the first operational prototype to have a glazed cockpit canopy to protect the pilot.

These seaplanes, and those which were to follow, accommodated a crew of four, but had six "action stations", linked by a corridor. They were all large-capacity twin-engined machines, which could be utilized in a bomber, reconnaissance or torpedo rôle. Twenty-six LeO 258s, with Hispano 12 Nbr engines, were built during and after 1935; and 60 LeO 257*bis*, powered by Gnome-Rhône 14 Kirs/Kjrs engines, were produced during and after 1937.

The 257*bis* differed from the 257 by having a strengthened fuselage, more powerful engines driving contra-rotating propellers, a different nose turret and a retractable ladder. The 258 differed from the 256 by having no forward turret and a modified rear fuselage. The propellers of this version rotated in the same direction and the ladder was fixed.

This family of aircraft was completed by the projected LeO H 258*bis*, a standard 258 with Hispano 12 Y engines and a single example of the H 259, last of the "25" series. This had reduced drag and improved handling qualities compared with the 257*bis* and 258, but was turned down by the French Navy, who regarded air-cooled engines as more reliable than the 259's Hispano 12 Ys.

The LeO H 257*bis* and H 258 were put progressively into squadron service, equipping squadrons 1 B 1 (later B 2, then 5 S), 3 B 1 (later B 1, then 16 S), 3 B 2 (later B 3), 2 S 4, 3 S 4, 4 B 1, 4 B 2, 4 B 3, 4 S 2 and E 7. The 11/25 Bombardment Group of the French Air Force also used the LeO 257*bis* in a landplane version, with a wheeled undercarriage. On 15 August 1940, a total of 45 LeO H 257*bis* and 7 LeO 258s still remained on active service.

LeO 451

The Lioré et Olivier 451 was an excellent bomber, but appeared too late to be of value in World War II. It was a four-seater, and was designed to utilize engines of 1,600 hp each. Unfortunately, it had to be fitted with engines of only 1,000 hp, in the absence of more powerful engines of proven reliability. Furthermore, the desire to use the same propellers for both the Amiot 350 and LeO 451 led to a compromise detrimental to both aircraft. Those fitted to the 451 limited maximum engine speed to 2,100 rpm, instead of the designed normal speed of 2,400 rpm.

Of all-metal construction, the LeO 451 was a cantilever low-wing monoplane with 6° of dihedral. It had an elliptical-section fuselage, the nose of which was glazed. The tailplane carried twin end-plate fins, and the engines were faired in cowlings with controllable gills.

Despite the bomber's lack of power, its performance was excellent, with a speed of 306 mph at 4,000 m (13,125 ft) – which altitude it attained in 10 min – and 311 mph at 18,000 ft. Normal cruising speed was 252 mph; range varied from 1,040 miles at 292 mph to 1,800 at 230 mph.

The course of events did not allow sufficient time for full development of the ancillary equipment, with the result that the electrical, pneumatic and hydraulic systems were too complicated and unreliable, the armament installation was unsatisfactory, and control at low speed was poor. Armament comprised one fixed forward-firing machine-gun, a Hispano cannon in a defensive position above the rear fuselage and a rearward-facing machine-gun on a retractable mounting beneath the fuselage. Up to 3,085 lb of bombs could be carried.

The LeO 45-01 prototype flew for the first time on 16 January 1937, powered by two 1,200-hp Hispano 14 Aa 08/09 engines in Chanard cowlings, with oil coolers mounted in the leading-edge of the wing. Piloted by Jean Doumerc, chief pilot of SNCASE (into which company Lioré et Olivier had been incorporated in 1937), it attained an officially-recorded level speed of 310 mph, and 388 mph in a dive. Unfortunately, this version quickly proved unsuitable for service use, as its engines failed after 18 flying hours, or less. The problem was serious: six failures of both engines and one failure of a single engine were suffered in 1937.

It was decided, therefore, that production LeO 45 aircraft, two of which had been ordered in May 1937, 20 in November 1937, 20 in May 1938 and 100 in June of the same year (by September 1939 total orders were to reach 484) were to be fitted with Gnome-Rhônes.

The prototype of this re-engined version, designated LeO 451, flew on 21 October 1938, and was in fact the original 45-01 with two Gnome-Rhône 14 N 20/21 engines in Mercier cowlings. The first production machines, on which the tail fins were further modified, flew on 24 March 1939. This was the date on which the first phase of Plan V should have been completed, yet only one LeO had been delivered by then to the French Air Force.

The low rate of production was due largely to the fact that, despite the participation of 33 sub-contractors, the delivery of vital equipment such as gun turrets, windscreens and radio-compasses fell far behind schedule. In addition, the manufacture of this aircraft demanded no fewer than 80,000 man-hours – a time which was reduced later to 51,000 man-hours.

On 3 September 1939, out of the total of 390 bombers in the French Air Force, the only modern aircraft were five LeO 451s which had been taken off the strength of the Experimental Squadron at Reims and transferred to the 31st Bomber Squadron. The number two LeO 451 had flown on 28 April 1939, and the Air Force received a total of 10 aircraft by 3 September 1939, 55 by 1 January 1940, 192 by 1 May 1940 and 360 by 20 June 1940 (of which 180 were operational). The II/12 Group took delivery of its first two 451s on 16 October 1939, and by 10 May 1940 had only 13 of these aircraft. At the same date, GB I/23 was still equipped with the Bloch 210. Thus on 10 May 1940, only the following groups had been equipped with the LeO 451: I/12, II/12, II/23, I/31, II/31, I/11, II/11, and I/25.

A total of 450 LeO 451s were built before May 1940 and 150 during the German occupation of France. The latter were used by the Vichy Government and by the French Navy (type 451M), with Squadrons 6 B and 7 B in Syria. After 1942, a total of 94 aircraft were captured by the Germans who removed the armament and used them as transports for the Luftwaffe (type 451T).

Although series production had been concentrated exclusively on the 451, with Gnome-Rhône 14 N 20/21 engines, four new versions had been designed in 1939-40, comprising the LeO 452 with two Gnome-Rhône 14N 38 engines, the LeO 453 with Pratt & Whitney R-1830 engines, the LeO 454 with Bristol Hercules engines, and a LeO 458 with two 1,600-hp Wright R-2600 engines. Before completion, these machines were dismantled and the components dispersed throughout France to avoid detection by the Armistice Commission. Another variant, the LeO 455, with Gnome-Rhône 14 R engines, had flown on 3 December 1939, but was destroyed during a bombing attack on Marignane airfield.

After the liberation of France, those LeO aircraft which had survived were converted and used by SNCASE for various rôles – under the designation 451 E2 for experimental purposes and designation 453 for air-sea rescue and long-range communications – and by the National Geographic Institute, under the designation 455 PH, for topographical surveys.

Letord 3, 4, 5 and 7

The E. Letord company, founded in 1908 for the manufacture of balloons and airships, had available at the beginning of the 1914-18 War two important factories, at Meudon, near Paris, and at Lyon-Villeurbane.

At the end of 1916, Colonel Dorand, head of the engines department of the French Service Technique,

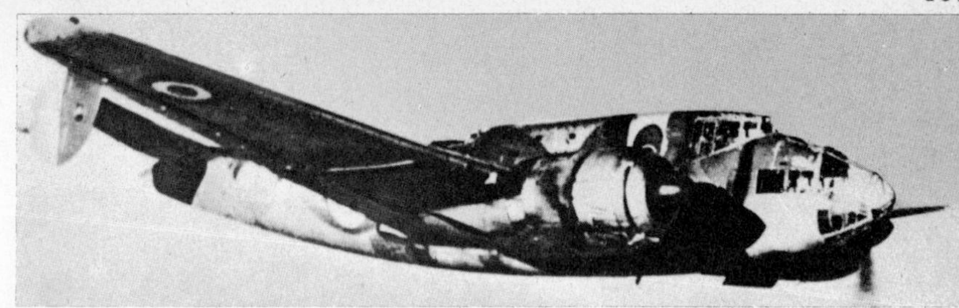

LeO 451

LeO 451T, USAAF markings

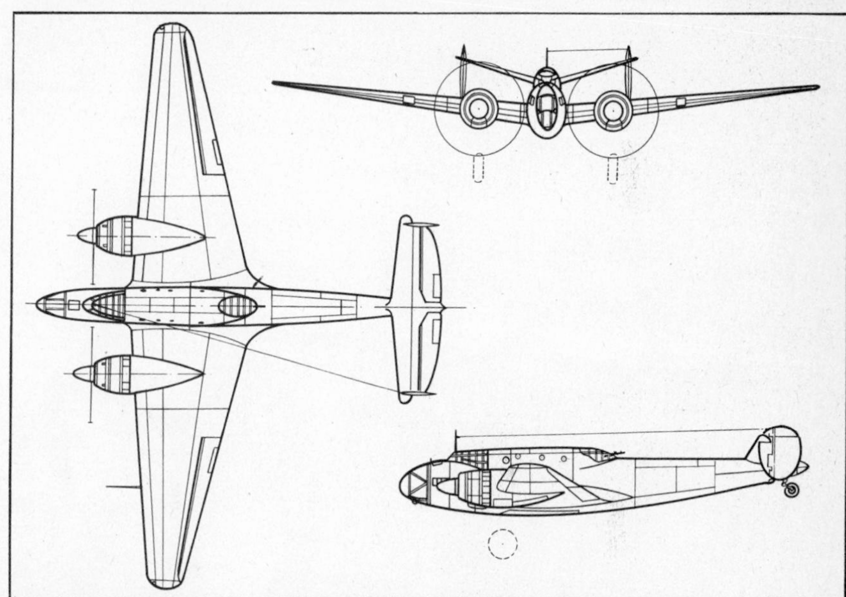

LeO 451

Letord 5

TYPE	DIMENSIONS						WEIGHT	PERFORMANCE				REMARKS	
	span		length		height		max t-o	max speed	at height	service ceiling	combat range		
	ft	in	ft	in	ft	in	lb	mph	ft	ft	miles		
LeO 451	73	10¾	56	4	14	9¼	26,014	311	18,000	27,000	1,040	2 × GR 14 N20/21	1,000 hp
Letord 3	55	9½	36	3	11	5¾	5,291	93				2 × HS 8 Ba	200 hp

Letord 7

Letord 9

Levasseur PL 2 AT 2, second prototype

Levasseur PL 2 AT 2

designed several twin-engined three-seat aircraft for reconnaissance, fighter and night bombing rôles. These machines were all similar in general outline, with the back-staggered wings which were a characteristic of aircraft designed by Dorand, and were built in small numbers by the Letord company between 1917 and the end of the war.

The Letord 1, 2 and 4 were intended for reconnaissance missions, the Letord 6 for fighter and escort duties, and the Letord 3, 5, 7 and 9 for night bombing. Some Letord 4s were converted into bombers at the time of the 1917 offensive and, after the end of the war, into early air mail transports.

The Letord 3, which flew in 1917, had two 200-hp Hispano 8 Ba engines and was built in two versions, designated Let 3 B3 and Let 3 CA 3. It was a three-bay biplane and had a nose-wheel to prevent the aircraft from nosing-over in the event of a bad landing. This was considered essential to safeguard the gunner, who was accommodated in a cockpit in the nose.

The Letord 5 was of sesquiplane configuration, and had only the four-wheel main undercarriage common to all Letord aircraft, without a nose-wheel. It was powered by two 220-hp Lorraine 8 Fb engines, which were cooled by radiators placed above them. A total of 51 of this model were built, each armed with two machine-guns and carrying a bomb load of up to 440 lb.

The prototype of the Letord 7 (No. 297) flew in 1918. It had the same wing arrangement as the Letord 3, but the wing area was increased to give an additional 107 sq ft of lifting surface. Two 275-hp Lorraine engines were mounted on the lower wing, and primary armament consisted of a cannon mounted in the front of the fuselage. No nose-wheel was fitted.

The last of the series, the Letord 9, arrived on the eve of the Armistice. It was in the same class as the big Handley Page bombers, with a span of 85 ft and total wing area of 1,076 sq ft. The power plant consisted of two Liberty XII engines, each developing 400 hp, and the aircraft was distinguished by its biplane tail surfaces.

Too late to be of any use in the war, the Letord 9 remained merely a prototype, since the Farman 60 had been selected as standard post-war equipment for the night bomber squadrons.

Levasseur PL 2

Best remembered today for its seaplanes, the Société Pierre Levasseur began by obtaining a licence to build carrier-based torpedo-bombers designed by the Blackburn Company of England. These aircraft inspired the French company to produce a design of its own and, in 1921, the Levasseur PL 2 AT 1 was built in Paris, under the supervision of a Blackburn engineer. It was a large wooden biplane, with folding wings of 49 ft span, and was intended to be powered by a Renault engine of 580 hp. This power plant had not completed its bench-tests by the time the airframe was ready; so, in order not to delay flight trials, a 480-hp Renault engine was installed. Military load comprised a 1,477-lb naval torpedo, slung between the undercarriage legs.

In November 1922, this PL 2 prototype completed its acceptance tests at Villacoublay, still with the 480-hp engine installed. At an all-up weight of 7,419 lb, it attained a speed of 108 mph at sea level, and landed at 47 mph. It could climb to 11,500 ft in 40 minutes and had a speed of 97 mph at that height. To suit it for operation over water, it was fitted with a jettisonable undercarriage and flotation gear, consisting of watertight air-bags, which could be inflated immediately by CO_2 bottles if the pilot had to "ditch" at sea.

This first machine was followed by a second prototype, with a four-blade propeller and lateral radiators for the water-cooled engine; and in 1923 nine production PL 2s were ordered – sufficient to equip a single carrier-based squadron. These aircraft differed from the prototypes in that they were two-seaters, with the originally intended Renault engine of 580 hp.

The PL 2s did not enter service with No. 7 B 2 Squadron, based on the aircraft carrier *Béarn*, until June 1926, as it took five years to convert the old battleship into an aircraft carrier. Then, the Renault engine which powered the PL 2s proved unreliable; so, in 1928, they were demoted for use by the training section of the *Béarn*, based at Hyères-Palyvestre.

Levasseur PL 7

In 1926, the Société Levasseur designed a torpedo aircraft for shipboard service, to replace the PL 2. This new machine, designated PL 7, was derived from the coastal-reconnaissance PL 4. It was a two-seat sesquiplane, with a span of 59 ft, powered by a 550-hp Farman engine. The fuselage was watertight and the landing gear, which could be jettisoned, was of wide track to permit the carriage and launching of a torpedo.

After interim experiments with a Renault engine in place of the Farman, a 600-hp Hispano engine was chosen as the definitive power plant of the PL 7. At the same time, the number of interplane struts was reduced from eight to four. Thus modified, the prototype made its first flight in 1928, during which it attained a height of nearly 10,000 ft in 21 minutes. This was sufficiently impressive for the French Navy to order 15 production aircraft.

To discover the optimum configuration, the Navy requested Levasseur to build nine PL 7s with the 59-ft span of the prototype, one with a span of 56 ft 7¼ in and the remaining five with a span of 54 ft 1½ in. Not until 11 March 1931 was it finally decided to standardize on the smallest span; the other ten PL 7s were then modified by "pruning" the wing-tips. Thus, the standard PL 7s, of which 39 were built, all had square tips on the upper wing. Defensive armament consisted of two machine-guns firing rearward; a torpedo, or equivalent weight of bombs, could be carried for attack.

These aircraft equipped No. 7 B 1 Squadron on board the carrier *Béarn*, but were grounded in June 1931 after two machines broke up in flight. With strengthened wing attachments and a three-blade propeller to reduce engine vibration, they re-entered service in 1932. Although heavy and of mediocre performance, they remained in service until 1939, since no other torpedo-carrying aircraft was ordered to replace them.

Levasseur PL 14

This was simply a twin-float seaplane version of the PL 7, retaining the original 59-ft-span folding wings and watertight fuselage. It was a two/three-seat aircraft and was employed in three rôles: as a bomber with a 900-lb bomb-load; as a torpedo aircraft with a 1,477-lb torpedo; and for long-range reconnaissance duties, with extra fuel instead of armament.

The PL 14 was of similar construction to previous Levasseur aircraft. In the "T2" (two-seat torpedo) version, it had a maximum speed of 102 mph, could climb to 3,000 m (9,840 ft) in 35 minutes and had a ceiling of 10,650 ft. It could take off in 30 seconds and had a cruising range of 400 miles.

The prototype PL 14 made its first flight late in 1929, powered by a 650-hp Hispano 12 Nb engine. During its trials at St-Raphaël it was joined by a second prototype and, in 1931, 28 of these aircraft were ordered to equip No. 7 B 2 Squadron on board the aircraft carrier *Commandant Teste*.

The first production PL 14s, received at Orly at the beginning of 1932, differed from the prototypes in having

Levasseur PL 7 T2 B2b

Levasseur PL 14 prototype

Levasseur PL 14 T2 B2b

TYPE	DIMENSIONS span ft	span in	length ft	length in	height ft	height in	WEIGHT max t-o lb	PERFORMANCE max speed mph	at height ft	service ceiling ft	combat range miles	REMARKS	
Letord 5	59	3	36	7¾	12	1¾	5,390	99				2 × LO 8 Fb	220 hp
Letord 7	62	4	37	2¾	10	2	6,304	89				2 × LO	275 hp
PL 2	49	8½	36	0¾	13	3¼	8,052	112		13,800	435	RE 12 Ma	580 hp
PL 7	54	1½	38	3¾	15	11½	8,708	106		9,400	400	HS 12 Lbr	600 hp
PL 14	59	0¾	42	2	16	1	9,369	102		10,650	400	HS 12 Nb	650 hp

Levasseur PL 15 T2 B2b prototype

Levasseur PL 15 T2 B2b

Levy GL 40 HB 2

a modified tail unit. From 28 September 1932, all those in service were fitted with a three-blade propeller and, following the accidents with the PL 7, were considerably strengthened.

Despite these modifications, intensive operation of the PL 14s led to distortion of the engine mountings, and the type was taken out of service in July 1933. After stringent new tests at St-Raphaël, it was decided that the PL 14s could continue in service only in landplane form. Accordingly, four PL 14s were allocated for operation from the carrier *Béarn* in 1936; but in the following year all machines of this type were withdrawn from service.

Levasseur PL 15

The PL 15 T2 B2b seaplane was, in effect, a PL 14 without a watertight fuselage and was fitted from the start with a three-blade propeller driven through a reduction gear. The prototype made its first flight in landplane form at Villacoublay in October 1932, and then in seaplane form at Les Mureaux, where the Levasseur company had a hangar.

Like the PL 14, it could be used for various rôles, and was equipped with radio manufactured by Radio-Industrie. It was of wooden construction, except for the duralumin wing spars. The floats also could be of either wood or metal construction.

The first production PL 15 was accepted at Les Mureaux in March 1933. In the following year, No. 7 B 2 Squadron, stationed on board the *Commandant Teste*, received 16 PL 15s, to replace its obsolete PL 14s. They remained in service until the end of 1938, when 7 B 2 Squadron was redesignated HB 1 and re-equipped with Latécoère 298 monoplanes. The remaining five PL 15s were used for a time as conversion trainers, but when war was declared they were taken over by the newly-formed 3 S 6 Squadron. One of them distinguished itself on 30 October 1939 when, on patrol near Lorient, it became the first French seaplane to sink a German submarine. On 20 August 1940, No. 3 S 6 Squadron was disbanded and the remaining PL 15s passed out of service.

Levy GL 40

The banker, Léon-Georges Levy, formed a company in 1915 to build aircraft for the Aviation Maritime. Two chief petty officers from that service, named Le Penn and Blanchard, who had been aeronautical engineers in civilian life, became the design team of the new company. Their first product was the Georges Levy 40 HB 2, a two-seat single-engined seaplane of pusher biplane configuration, armed with a machine-gun and able to carry a bomb-load of 550 lb. Pilot and observer/gunner were accommodated in the front of the fuselage, which was of wooden construction. The power plant was a 300-hp Renault 12 Fe engine, of the kind which was later to equip the famous Breguet 14.

The first flight of the GL 40 took place in November 1917, and it immediately demonstrated a first-class rate of climb, being able to reach an altitude of 3,300 ft in 9 minutes and 6,550 ft in 22 minutes. The estimated cruising duration of 6 hours proved, in fact, to be only four hours which restricted the radius of action to 125 miles. Nevertheless, an initial order for 100 machines was placed, and these aircraft were quickly distributed between all the seaplane bases in France, Algeria, Tunisia, Morocco, Senegal and Greece. Finland also bought two GL 40s and Belgium acquired six for use in the Congo.

At the end of the war, there were still a fair number of these aircraft in service. Three were modified as high-speed seaplanes and flew to Palermo in 1919; three others took part in a race meeting at Monaco in 1920.

In 1919, two GL 40s were equipped with additional fuel tanks and, piloted by Lieutenant-Commander Lefranc and Sub-Lieutenant Montrelay, took off from St-Raphaël on 29 November 1919, bound for Dakar, with the intention of establishing an air route to the French Colonies. Because of the extra fuel load they could only fly very slowly, and an engine failure forced Montrelay to land on the sea off Morocco. Lefranc continued alone, arriving in Dakar on 25 January 1920 and so establishing the first air link with this great port of French West Africa. Unfortunately, he made a bad landing, broke a leg, and was unable to continue his flight to the Upper Niger as intended.

In 1922, the last GL 40 aircraft in service were used in a research programme concerned with large reconnaissance aircraft, at the Centre de Cherbourg.

Loire-Nieuport 41

As early as 1930 the Aéronautique Navale Francaise had carried out dive-bombing experiments with the old Levasseur PL 7; but the High Command of the Army had failed to agree that cooperation between the Services on air matters was likely to be of value. Even the Air Council, responsible for the re-equipment programme, had shown only mild interest in dive-bombers, to the extent that barely 50 out of 876 bombers ordered under Plan V were dive-bombers. The only really interested party had been the Navy, who had sought aircraft of this type to equip their one and only aircraft carrier.

In 1931, a Gourdou-Leseurre had been tested at St-Raphaël, and on 12 March 1935 the prototype Nieuport 140 made its first flight, followed by the 140-02 in February of the following year. At the same time Gourdou were testing their models 432 and 521. Unfortunately, serious accidents were to delay the production of these aircraft.

Eventually, the single-seat Loire-Nieuport 40 passed the required test programme, which resulted in an order for 120 improved LN 41s, with a strengthened and more slender fuselage. Of these, 70 were intended for the Navy and 50 for the Air Force: in fact, the Air Force cancelled their order, and the Navy contract was reduced.

This explains, to a large extent, why the Navy had to be called in to help the Army break up advancing German columns during the invasion of France in 1940. Led by Capitaine de Corvette Corfmat, Naval Squadrons AB 1, AB 2, AB 3, and AB 4, flying 24 Vought 156Fs and an equal number of LN 41s, attacked the German units and the locks and bridges of the Meuse where German tanks were filtering through. Squadrons AB 2 (Commandant Lorenzi) and AB 4 (Commandant Lainé), which had been formed with LN 41s only a few days earlier, suffered heavy losses, their crews sacrificing themselves in heroic attacks for which they had received no training whatsoever.

The Loire-Nieuport 40, which was the prototype for the L 41, was the third version of the Nieuport Model 140. It was powered by a Hispano 12 Xcrs engine of 690 hp, driving a three-blade Chauvière propeller. It had folding wings, arrester gear, and a rudder which split to operate as a dive-brake. Tested at St-Raphaël by an SNCAC pilot named Hubert, the prototype reached a speed of 199 mph at sea level and 236 mph at 13,000 ft, to which it could climb in 10 minutes. Its maximum speed in a dive, with undercarriage retracted, was 296 mph. This performance was almost equal to that of the German Ju 87.

The series production model appeared in 1940 in two versions, with differing armament. The L 401 had an Hispano-Suiza 404 cannon, two 7·5-mm MAC machine-guns, mounted in the wings, and an Alkan Type II bomb-sight. The LN 411 had three MAC machine-guns and a Gallus bomb-sight. Both versions carried a single 496-lb bomb, or one 330-lb bomb, or nine 33-lb bombs or ten 22-lb bombs.

The Air Force's LN 411 had non-folding wings, no arrester hook, lighter undercarriage and reduced fuel capacity, which permitted the carriage of a heavier bomb-load. Construction of both versions was all-metal, except for the rudder of the Army version which was fabric-

Levy GL 40 HB 2

Loire-Nieuport 40, first prototype

Loire-Nieuport 40, first prototype

TYPE	DIMENSIONS						WEIGHT	PERFORMANCE				REMARKS	
	span		length		height		max t-o	max speed	at height	service ceiling	combat range		
	ft	in	ft	in	ft	in	lb	mph	ft	ft	miles		
PL 15	59	0¾	42	2	16	8¾	9,259	124	SL	14,800	932	HS 12 Nbr	650 hp
GL 40	60	8½	40	8¼	12	7½	5,400	88		11,500	270	RE 12 Fe	300 hp
LN 41	45	11	32	0¼	11	5¾	6,223	162		31,200	745	HS 12 Xcrs	690 hp

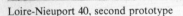

Loire-Nieuport 40, second prototype

Loire 46

Loire 46

covered. The radio set carried was a Sadir 514.

The split-rudder dive-brake of the LN 40 was not retained on the LN 41, which relied for its braking on the undercarriage legs being lowered, large shields being placed upon each leg to increase drag. Unfortunately, the LN 41, with an all-up weight of nearly three tons, was under-powered with an engine of only 690 hp; and its cruising speed of 149 mph was far too slow for this type of machine.

In total, 7 LN 40s were built, of which 6 became LN 401s, followed by 42 more LN 401s. A single LN 402 was built.

In 1942 the Germans captured 12 LN 411s in southern France, but as these were unserviceable and there were no spares available for them, they were destroyed.

A developed version, with a straight wing and Hispano 12 Ycrs engine of 860 hp, had been projected, but this appeared too late to be of any use, only one example being built by SNCAC as the LN 42.

Loire 46

After being associated with the Gourdou-Leseurre company, the Ateliers et Chantiers de la Loire amalgamated, in 1933, with Nieuport-Delage. The latter company, however, retained a separate design office.

To meet the French requirement for fighter aircraft, as specified in 1930, Loire produced in 1932 their type 43 C1, powered by a Hispano 12X engine. This was purchased by the Government for 870,000 francs, and was flown for the first time on 14 January 1933. Unfortunately, it was destroyed during this first flight when the pilot succumbed to a stroke whilst flying at an altitude of nearly 30,000 ft. From the type 43 was developed the Loire 45, with a Gnome-Rhône radial engine, which flew for the first time on 20 February 1933.

The 1930 programme stressed the need for good all-round visibility, and the majority of the aircraft produced to meet its requirements were given a gull-wing configuration, in an effort to improve forward vision for the pilot. The results were disastrous. All four of the aircraft designed and built with this wing layout – the Mureaux 170, Gourdou-Leseurre 480 (later 482), Dewoitine 560 and Loire 43 (later 45) – were found to have wings which blocked the pilot's vision through 180°, and visibility was virtually nil during combat and climb. Tests conducted by the CEMA at Villacoublay proved conclusively that a better choice would have been a swept-forward wing.

Meanwhile, Loire had persevered with development of the type 45, replacing the original Gnome-Rhône Kds engine with a Kes and modifying the tail fin. Experience gained with this machine enabled Engineer Asselot to develop it still further, by embodying a new fuselage and a wing of the type recommended by the CEMA. The resulting aircraft, known as the Loire 46, was included in an order for 60 machines given under Plan I, with varying numbers of Dewoitine 371s, 500s and 501s and Spad 501s making up the balance.

The prototype Loire 46, which flew for the first time on 1 September 1934, was powered by an 880-hp Gnome-Rhône engine, driving a three-blade Ratier propeller; armament comprised two cannon mounted in the wing. During early tests, a 930-hp Gnome-Rhône 14 Kfs engine was substituted for the Kes; a three-blade Gnome-Rhône propeller was fitted and the NACA engine cowling was enlarged and cleaned up. The final change was in the armament, the two cannon being replaced by four wing-mounted machine-guns.

The production version of the Loire 46, which appeared in 1936, was manufactured in the SNCAO factories and began to enter service in November 1936 with the four squadrons comprising the 6th Fighter Wing, based at Chartres. One machine, designated Loire-Nieuport 46, was exhibited at the Paris Air Show at the end of that year.

The Loire 46 was of all-metal construction, with Warren girder members in both the fuselage and wing structures. It had a ceiling of 36,500 ft, and could climb to 4,500 m (14,760 ft) in 6 min 12 sec. Unfortunately, the wide-track undercarriage proved insufficiently strong, and was responsible for a number of accidents during landing. In addition, carburation troubles limited the endurance of the Loire 46 to one-and-a-half hours, and in July 1938 it was withdrawn from service. On the declaration of war, those still remaining were sent to the training base at Cazaux for firing practice.

It is interesting to record that in 1937 twenty Loire 46s were sent by rail to Republican Spain under the guise of agricultural machinery, the French Government not wishing to be involved openly in Spain's internal troubles. It was in this manner, therefore, that the Loire 46 fought alongside other French types in the Spanish Civil War.

Loire 210

Utilizing the fuselage of a Loire 46, the Loire-Nieuport company produced in 1936 a low-wing fighter seaplane with a central float, designated Loire 210. It was intended for catapult-launching from ships of the line, and was designed to the same 1934 specification as the Potez 453, Romano 90 and Bernard H 110. A special requirement was a stalling speed of less than 62 mph.

Piloted by Lefèvre, the Loire 210 first flew at St-Nazaire on 21 March 1935. It was not until 1937, however, that 20 production machines of this type were ordered, and manufacture began towards the end of that year at the SNCAO factory (formerly the Nieuport works) at Issy-les-Moulineaux. The first production machine flew on 18 November 1938.

When the Loire 210 entered service with Squadrons HC 1 and HC 2 in 1939, it was the first seaplane fighter of French design to become operational since 1918. Unfortunately, the wing construction was unsatisfactory; a number of machines lost a wing in flight and the remainder were soon withdrawn from service. They were placed in storage at St-Mandrier and were not used during the war.

The fuselage of the Loire 210 was of all-metal construction; the wings, fitted with split flaps, had a metal structure with fabric covering, and were designed to fold for shipboard stowage. The large central float, with six watertight compartments, was attached to the fuselage by three vertical struts, with further bracing struts supporting the wing. Small wing floats maintained stability when the seaplane was on the water.

Armament comprised four machine-guns mounted in the wings, and the Hispano engine was faired by a NACA cowling, which was of a different shape to that used on the prototype.

Maximum speed of the Loire 210 was 195 mph at an altitude of 9,200 ft; its cruising speed was 124 mph and it could climb to 3,000 m (9,850 ft) in 5 min 19 sec.

Loire-Gourdou-Leseurre 32

In 1923, the French Air Force initiated a design study programme aimed at providing new aircraft to replace the out-of-date left-overs from the 1914–18 War. Two years later, the Gourdou-Leseurre company amalgamated with Chantiers de la Loire and the new company participated in the fighter aircraft competition of 1926, which stemmed from these studies. Their design, the Loire-Gourdou-Leseurre 32 C 1, was successful, and they received a first order for 25 aircraft, followed later by other contracts.

The prototype of the LGL 32 had flown in 1925 and was exhibited at the Salon de l'Aéronautique in the following year. It was then redesignated LGL 32 HY and fitted with two wooden floats instead of wheels. On 28 March 1927, piloted by Demougeot, it captured the world altitude record for seaplanes, by climbing to a height of 30,478 ft.

During 1927, LGL 32 C 1s, armed with two machine-guns firing through the propeller disc, began to equip

Loire 46

Loire 210 prototype

Loire 210 prototype

TYPE	DIMENSIONS						WEIGHT	PERFORMANCE				REMARKS	
	span		*length*		*height*		*max t-o*	*max speed*	*at height*	*service ceiling*	*combat range*		
	ft	*in*	*ft*	*in*	*ft*	*in*	*lb*	*mph*	*ft*	*ft*	*miles*		
Loire 46	38	8½	25	2½	13	8½	4,375	254		36,500	535	GR 14 Kfs	930 hp
Loire 210	38	8	31	2¾	12	5	4,629	195	9,800	27,800	466	HS 9 Vbs	720 hp
LGL 32	40	0¼	24	9¼	9	8	3,356	155		31,800	310	GR 9 Ac Jupiter	420 hp

Loire-Gourdou-Leseurre 32

Morane-Saulnier Type N

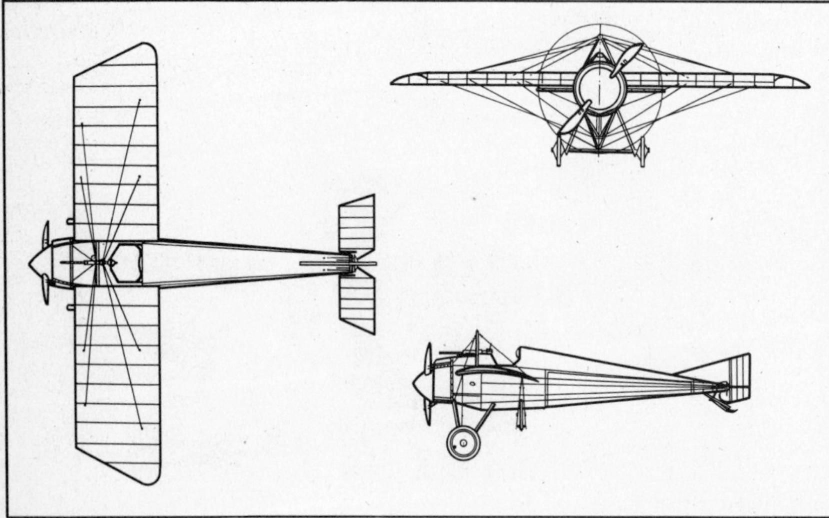
Morane-Saulnier Type N

French fighter squadrons. Together with Nieuport-Delage 62s and 622s and some Wibault 72s, they constituted the whole of the French fighting force until 1934. Of the 350 machines ordered, however, only 70 remained in service on 15 December 1932. Three years later, on 1 January 1936, the Air Force still had 135 LGL 32s in service, but these had been converted into training aircraft with modified undercarriages.

Rumania bought a total of 50 of these aircraft in 1928, after an LGL 32 won a competition organised by the Rumanian Air Force.

LGL 32s had an excellent rate of climb, thanks to their 420-hp Jupiter engine, and could reach a height of 3,000 m (9,850 ft) in 7 minutes 20 seconds. The LGL 32 was somewhat reminiscent of the GL B 3, because of its high wing configuration, but the design had been cleaned up by reducing the number of bracing struts and the result was a stable, controllable aircraft, which became a firm favourite with pilots of the fighter groups.

Pierre Lemoigne, a well-known sporting pilot, used LGL No. 5 (F-AJVH) from 1926 to 1937 for aerobatic performances at aviation shows. Other versions of the 32, such as types 322, 323, 324, 33, 34 and 35, were produced only as prototypes or in small series.

In 1937, twelve years after the flight of the first LGL 32, the Gourdou-Leseurre company (G-L had by then separated from Chantiers de la Loire) put this design back into production at the request of a private company. Eleven aircraft were built, No. 462 (F-APYG) being of particular interest as it was later converted into a dive-bomber, known as the type GL 633, with a wide-track undercarriage. Together with eight other GL 32s, this aircraft was sold to Spain during the Civil War, and nothing further is known of their history.

Morane-Saulnier – 1914–18 period

The first Morane-Saulnier monoplane to enter squadron service in 1914, was the type H (Military Type I). This aircraft, sometimes known as the "14-mètre", from the area of its wing (14 sq m), was a simple development of the Type I which, piloted by Roland Garros, had made the first crossing of the Mediterranean in 1913. When fitted with wings of 16 sq m, the Type H was known as Military Type XII.

A total of 25 examples of the two versions of the type H were delivered to the first French fighter squadrons, and one was supplied to the Royal Flying Corps for test purposes.

The type L and LA parasol monoplanes were used primarily for reconnaissance, but at least one – a type L flown by Lt R. A. J. Warneford of the RNAS, achieved combat success when bombs dropped from it destroyed the Zeppelin LZ 37 over Belgium in June 1915.

In 1914, the type N (Military Type V) appeared, powered by the 80-hp Le Rhône 9 C rotary engine. Built entirely of wood, with fabric covering, the M-S N climbed to an altitude of 2,000 m (6,560 ft) in 6min 45 sec, to 3,000 m (9,840 ft) in 12 min, and had a ceiling of 4,000 m (13,125 ft). It was very manoeuvrable, but the pilot had poor downward visibility, because the wing was immediately beneath his cockpit.

Early in 1914, M. Saulnier had considered the possibility of synchronizing a machine-gun with the engine of the type N, so that the bullets from a fixed forward-firing gun could pass between the propeller blades without causing damage. To this end, he mounted a Hotchkiss cavalry machine-gun on one aircraft. As might have been anticipated, both this gun and the St-Etienne machine-gun, which was also fitted experimentally, had a rate of fire which synchronized with the engine only at one predetermined engine speed. In order to fire without hitting the blades, therefore, it was imperative to maintain a constant engine speed, which made such an armament installation impracticable for combat purposes. With no alternative system available, the scheme was abandoned.

In the absence of synchronized guns, the company's pilot Roland Garros, who had witnessed the experiments, fitted to each propeller blade of his aircraft a steel deflector plate at the point where the bullets would make contact. He thus gave his Morane N a primitive form of forward-firing armament and achieved several successes in action until engine failure led to a forced landing and capture.

The Morane-Saulnier N was used in France by MS 23 and MS 38 Squadrons, amongst others, and the "aces" Garros and Gilbert – who nicknamed this type the "Avenger" – flew these machines, of which a total of 49 were built. Great Britain allocated a few to its No. 1, 3, 4 and 60 Squadrons, each of these machines being powered by a 110-hp Le Rhône 9 Ja rotary engine and armed with a forward-firing Vickers machine-gun. They had, in addition, large cone-shaped propeller spinners which earned them the nickname of "Bullet Scouts".

In 1916 an improved, more powerful and larger version of the Type N was produced. This was the M-S AC (Military Type XXIII), of monocoque construction with rigid bracing struts beneath the wings, replacing the flexible wire bracing of the earlier Moranes. As the mechanism of its Vickers machine-gun resembled that of the Maxim and Parabellum, Morane-Saulnier were able to synchronize it with the 120-hp Le Rhône engine by which this version was powered. Thirty-one type ACs were built, one of which was fitted experimentally with two machine-guns, mounted side-by-side and firing through the propeller disc.

There were two versions of the Morane-Saulnier A1 which followed: a fighter (Military Type XXVII) and a trainer (Military Type XXX). The former was powered by a 160-hp Le Rhône engine and had a wing area of 140 sq ft and empty weight of 980 lb. It was of all-wooden construction – save for a steel undercarriage – and fabric covered. The tapered parasol wing was supported by several steel struts extending from the bottom of the circular-section fuselage. Armament comprised a fixed forward-firing machine-gun. Three of this version were supplied to Belgium.

The Type XXX was powered by either a 120-hp Le Rhône or 130-hp Clerget engine. In 1918, 51 aircraft of this type were sold to the USA, and Japan and Spain later received a number of these aircraft. A total of 1,210 Morane-Saulnier A1s were built, including both fighters and trainers.

In France, after the war, Nungesser used one (with the registration F-NUNG) for aerobatic demonstrations. Fronval, chief pilot of the Morane company, also flew an A1 (registration F-ABAO) when, on 26 May 1920, he completed 1,111 consecutive loops.

Morane-Saulnier 225

In 1932 came the first flight of the prototype M-S 225, developed from the M-S 121 of 1927 and the M-S 224; and 74 machines of this type were produced in the following year. The French Air Force received 55 of these during the first six months of 1933, for use until the fighter aircraft called for under the "1930 Programme" entered service. Twelve were delivered to the Navy, for use by Squadron 3 C 1 at Hyères, and seven were sold to China in September 1933.

The Armée de l'Air used the M-S 225 to equip Squadron No. 7, based at Dijon. When they were superseded by the "1930 Programme" fighters, nine of them were transferred to the *Patrouille de Dijon*, a crack aerobatic team under the command of Capitaine Weiser.

The M-S 225 was a parasol monoplane, with the wings swept back at 13°. Wing spars were of duralumin and ribs of wood, the whole being fabric-covered, as was the fuselage, which had a duralumin structure. Streamlined

Morane-Saulnier AC Type XXIII

Morane-Saulnier M-S 225

TYPE	DIMENSIONS						WEIGHT	PERFORMANCE				REMARKS	
	span		*length*		*height*		*max t-o*	*max speed*	*at height*	*service ceiling*	*combat range*		
	ft	*in*	*ft*	*in*	*ft*	*in*	*lb*	*mph*	*ft*	*ft*	*miles*		
M-S XII	33	7¼	21	5¾				87				RO 9 C	80 hp
M-S N (Type V)	27	4¾	22	4¾	7	4½	1,610	102		13,125	174	RO 9 C	80 hp
M-S XXIII	32	2	22	3¼	7	6½						RO 9 Jb	120 hp
M-S XXVII	28	0¾	18	7¾	7	10½	1,430	134				RO 9 R	170 hp
M-S 225	34	7¾	23	9¼	10	9½	3,460	207	13,125	34,500	590	GR 9 Kbrs	500 hp

Morane M-S 225

Morane-Saulnier M-S 405 prototype

Morane-Saulnier M-S 406

struts braced the wing to the fuselage, and the wide-track divided undercarriage had Messier shock-absorbers.

Powered by a 500-hp Gnome-Rhône 9 Kbrs supercharged engine, driving a two-blade propeller, the M-S 225 could fly at 207 mph at 13,125 ft and 174 mph at sea level. It could climb to 9,000 m (29,500 ft) in 24 min 30 sec and was an inherently-stable aircraft, of robust construction and easy to maintain. Armament comprised two Vickers guns firing through the propeller disc.

There were five derivatives of the M-S 225: the M-S 226, three examples of which were produced at the end of 1933 for carrier-borne duties, with arrester gear and tail-wheel; the M-S 226*bis*, which was a 226 with folding wings; and three experimental prototypes, the M-S 227, 275 and 278.

Morane-Saulnier 406

Most famous French fighter aircraft of World War II was the Morane-Saulnier 406, of which 1,081 examples were produced – a very considerable number compared with the totals of other aircraft issued to the Air Force.

The M-S 405, prototype of the 406, was the first French fighter aircraft to exceed 250 mph in level flight and, like the 406, was a low-wing monoplane, fitted with flaps, a retractable undercarriage and an enclosed cockpit for the pilot. The structure was entirely of metal, covered in "Plymax" (plywood and aluminium), except for the rear fuselage which was fabric-covered. Armament consisted of a Hispano 9 cannon, firing through the propeller-boss, and two machine-guns mounted in the wings.

Although its 850-hp Hispano 12 Y-31 engine gave the M-S 405 a maximum speed of 304 mph at height, this was inadequate by comparison with contemporary German fighters. Moreover, when the 405 entered service the sliding cockpit canopy had to be strengthened, and no rear armour was provided for the pilot at first.

After being built in great secrecy, the prototype M-S 405 had flown for the first time on 8 August 1935, powered by a Hispano 12 Ygrs "cannon" engine, driving a Chauvière propeller. It was bought by the State and, with the registration F-AKHZ, was exhibited at the Paris Air Show in 1936 and Brussels Show in 1937. Unfortunately, it was destroyed on 8 December 1937, while being flown by a Lithuanian pilot at Villacoublay.

The M-S 405-02 second prototype, powered by a different Hispano engine, driving a Levasseur propeller, flew for the first time in late 1936. In the following year, a Hamilton three-blade propeller was installed and this aircraft, too, crashed on 29 July 1937, causing the death of its test pilot, Raoul Ribière.

On 1 March 1937, Morane-Saulnier received a first contract for 16 M-S 405s, altered subsequently to 15 M-S 405s and one M-S 406. It was followed on 5 April by an order for an additional 50 M-S 405s, later amended to 50 M-S 406s. Final production figures totalled 17 M-S 405s (including the two prototypes) and 1,081 M-S 406s. The last order, received in 1939, was for eight aircraft (Nos. 1087-1094), to be paid for by private funds.

In October 1938 arrangements were completed for the mass production of these aircraft, with SNCAC responsible for the mainplanes, SNCAM for the tail unit and SNCASO (the prime contractor) for the fuselage, final assembly and flight testing. The parent company retained only a small manufacturing interest in the machine.

The first production M-S 405 flew for the first time on 3 February 1938 and seven of the first batch of 15 were reserved for special purposes, including the following:

Nos. 3 and 10. Used as mock-ups.

No. 4. Became the prototype of the M-S 406 and, powered by a Hispano 12 Y 31 engine, first flew on 20 May 1938.

No. 12. This aircraft, powered by a Hispano 12 Y 45 engine, had a wing structure of reduced weight, which became standard on all subsequent aircraft. It flew on 24 January 1939, under the company designation M-S 411.

No. 13. Produced in November 1939 as the M-S 408, this was a night-fighter version equipped with four landing lights. It was built to meet a Swiss requirement, and formed the prototype of the Swiss model D 3800. A licence for the manufacture of the M-S 405 had been acquired by Switzerland in July 1938.

No. 14. Produced in November 1938 under the designation M-S 407LP (LP = *lance-parachute*) for the air dropping of supplies. Two more M-S 407LPs, with Hispano 12 Y 51 engine, were produced in 1939. During the campaign in France, No. 14 was converted into a standard M-S 406.

In 1938 it was proposed to flight test a Clerget 14 F2 diesel engine in an M-S 405, but this failed to materialize, as did the projected M-S 409, a 406 with a frontal radiator mounted beneath the engine cowling.

The first production M-S 406, registered N2-66, first flew on 29 January 1939, after being exhibited at the 1938 Paris Air Show. In addition to the 405/406s delivered to the French Air Force, and those transferred to the French Navy in June 1940, a total of 267 M-S 406s were planned for export. They included 12 for China, which were recalled by France while in transit to Haiphong and used later by Squadron II/595 at Tonkin; 30 for Finland, used by No. 28 Squadron of the Finnish Air Force; 30 for Turkey; 160 for Poland, of which 50 were completed but not delivered because of the early collapse of Polish resistance; 13 for Lithuania, delivery of which was prevented by the declaration of war; 2 for Switzerland, which were delivered during 1938–39 under the designation D 3800 and later redesignated D 3801 after installation of a different engine; and 20 for Yugoslavia, which were ordered in April 1940 but were completed too late to be delivered.

The French Air Force, which had placed orders for a total of 1,069 M-S 405/406s by March 1938, received 27 of these aircraft by 1 April 1939, 572 by 3 September 1939, 892 by 1 December 1939, and 1,080 by 20 June 1940. Thus, despite a fairly rapid increase in production from May 1939, by the time France entered World War II the Air Force had received little more than half of the 955 machines that had been programmed for that date. Inadequate production of the Hispano 12 Y engine contributed to this situation, despite the fact that the Skoda company in Czechoslovakia was delivering 25 of these engines to France each month (built under licence) and that the Swiss company Saurer was also supplying this type of power plant. The situation was considered so serious that proposals were made to purchase 200 M 100 engines (Hispano 12 Ys built under licence) from Russia in May 1939. By October 1939 the position had become even more critical, and an attempt was made to exchange 50 M-S 406s for 150 Hispano-Suiza 12 Y 51s of Swiss manufacture, but the transaction did not materialize.

The M-S 406 equipped the following French fighter groups: III/1, I/2, II/2, III/2, II/3, III/3, III/4, III/5, I/6, II/6, III/6, I/7, II/7, III/7, I/9, II/9, I/10, II/595 and II/596 as well as the EC 565, GAM 550 and the training "Groupe Varsovie", which was later to become Squadron C 714 and finally GC I/145.

In 1942, after the collapse of France and occupation of the entire country, 46 M-S 406s were captured by the German forces and 36 of these were handed over to the Croatian Air Force. Twenty others, captured by the occupying troops at Châteauroux, were given to Finland. Equipped with Russian Klimov M 105 P engines, these were named by the Finns *MorköMorane* (Super Morane).

In December 1940, M-S 406 No. 1005 was equipped with auxiliary fuel tanks beneath the wings, giving it a range of 932 miles. When the Vichy Government sent a number of 406s to Syria to fight against British forces, they were all equipped with such tanks.

One other major variant, which flew in May 1940 under the designation M-S 410, was the M-S 406 No. 1028, powered by a Hispano 12 Y 31 engine and fitted with a strengthened wing housing four machine-guns. A second machine, M-S 406 No. 1040, was similarly converted,

Morane-Saulnier M-S 406

Morane-Saulnier M-S 406 (Swiss D-3800)

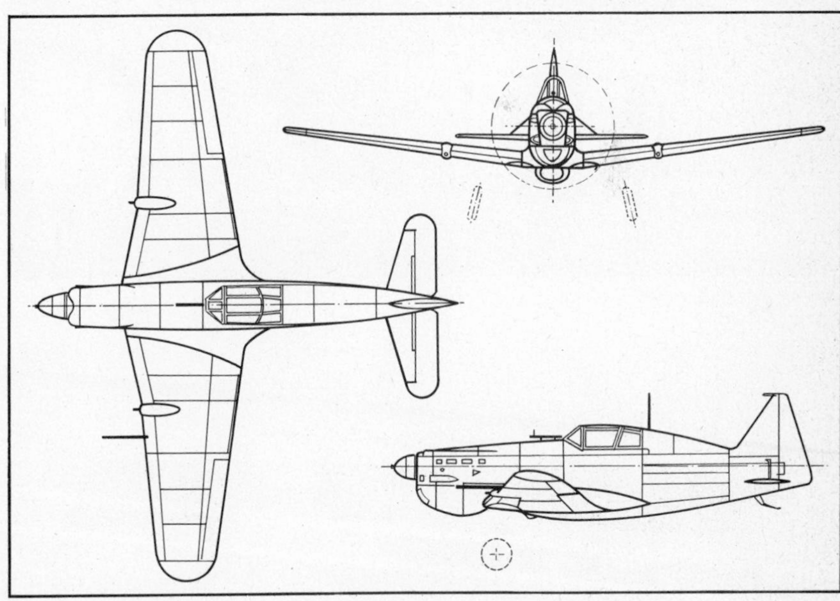
Morane-Saulnier M-S 406

TYPE	DIMENSIONS						WEIGHT	PERFORMANCE				REMARKS	
	span		*length*		*height*		*max t-o*	*max speed*	*at height*	*service ceiling*	*combat range*		
	ft	*in*	*ft*	*in*	*ft*	*in*	*lb*	*mph*	*ft*	*ft*	*miles*		
M-S 405	35	1¼	26	9¾	8	10¼	5,511	304		36,100	560	HS 12 Y-31	850 hp
M-S 406	35	1¼	26	9¾	10	7¾	5,445	305	16,400	32,300	497	HS 12 Y-31	850 hp

Morane-Saulnier M-S 406, Finnish Air Force

Morane-Saulnier M-S 733 A Alcyon, Cambodian Air Force

ANF Les Mureaux 113

Nieuport X C1

and after extensive testing it was decided to modify 500 M-S 406s to M-S 410 standard. The SNCAC factory at Bourges was made responsible for the conversion, but due to the rapidly-deteriorating position in France in the early months of 1940, only 74 aircraft had been modified to M-S 410 standard by 25 June 1940.

Morane-Saulnier 733 A Alcyon

This aircraft merits mention in the "A" version (A = Army), although it was, in fact, a training aircraft adapted for ground attack duties.

French forces fighting the rebels in Algeria soon discovered that fast and heavy fighter aircraft were useless to seek out and attack small groups of the enemy well hidden on the hillsides. There was an urgent requirement for a well-armed, fairly slow and manoeuvrable machine for these duties. Recalling the Potez 25, used successfully for "colonial policing" duties before the war, French military planners drew up a specification which resulted in development of the Potez 75 and Morane 1500, amongst others, especially designed for these duties. Lack of funds for series production of these types compelled the Army to have a number of Air Force training aircraft converted for the ground support rôle.

The sire of the M-S 733 A Alcyon was the M-S 730, first flown in 1949 with a Mathis G8R engine of 220 hp. In the following year it was re-engined with a Salmson AS 10C and redesignated M-S 731. Then followed the M-S 732, differing from the 730/731 in having a retractable undercarriage, and this flew for the first time on 13 February 1951. Two were built and sold to Belgium.

The prototype M-S 733 flew for the first time on 23 June 1952, powered by a Potez 6 D-01 engine. A series of 200 were built from 1955 onward, each with a Potez 6D-30A engine. Of these, 145 entered service with the French Air Force, St-Yan Flying School, Army Co-operation units and the Air France pilots' training school; 40 were sold to the Aéronavale and 15 to Cambodia.

The few M-S 733s which were converted into 733 As were each armed with four rockets, mounted beneath the wings, and carried two machine-guns. After intensive service in Algeria, a number were bought by Morocco for aerial policing duties; the rest were converted into standard M-S 733 training aircraft.

ANF Les Mureaux 113 series

Les Ateliers de Constructions du Nord de la France et des Mureaux, which had been established before the 1914–18 War by M. Pélabon, began to produce from 1930, under the direction of the engineer André Brunet, a series of long-range reconnaissance aircraft, which at times were used in the fighter and light bomber rôle.

First of these was the ANF 110, an all-metal monoplane with a braced parasol wing. It was powered by a Hispano-Suiza engine, and it was with this power plant that French aircraft engineers first encountered the problem of detonation, which they remedied temporarily by obtaining 100-octane aviation fuel from America. The supercharged Hispano 12 Y engine of the ANF 110 enabled it to attain heights in excess of 33,000 ft.

There followed the ANF 113, another reconnaissance version ordered under Plan I. With special modifications, including the installation of landing lights, this became the ANF 114, for use as a night fighter. In September 1933 four ANF 114s – two of them converted 113s and two 114 prototypes built in 1932 – were tested and entered squadron service, together with 52 ANF 113s produced during the following year. This version could climb to 8,000 m (26,246 ft) in 16 min 20 sec, at which height it attained a speed of 203 mph and was capable of normal aerobatic manoeuvres. In 1938, the 18 ANF 113s in service were used solely as two-seat fighters: twelve in No. 1 and six with No. 4 Squadron.

The ANF 117 R2, which first appeared in 1935, was another reconnaissance aircraft, generally similar to the ANF 113 except for its strengthened wing spars and doubled engine power. Out of the 114 aircraft of this type that were produced, 12 (Nos. 115 to 126) were specially equipped with racks for four 110-lb bombs beneath the wings, two machine-guns in the nose and two more in a rear turret, under the designation ANF 117 R2 B2. From May 1937 a number of these machines were allocated to No. 54 Squadron, to develop low-level bombing techniques, and were joined in March 1938 by several ANF 115 R2 B2s.

These latter aircraft differed from the 117 in having a frontally-mounted radiator and a cannon firing through the propeller boss. A production order for 119 ANF 115s had been placed under Plans I, II, V and Quinquennial, and 22 of these (Nos. 94, 98 and 101 to 120) were used in the R2 B2 version. In addition to the forward-firing cannon, they mounted two MAC machine-guns in the rear turret and could carry 440-660 lb of bombs. In service use, the cannon caused a number of problems and was replaced in 1939 by either one MAC machine-gun in the wing or two mounted inside the engine cowling.

At the outbreak of World War II a total of 145 Les Mureaux were in service with the French Air Force.

Nieuport X C1

The race for the Gordon-Bennett Trophy was to have taken place in 1914, as in previous years, and M. Delage designed the Nieuport X to take part in this event. Regulations for that year demanded a very low minimum speed. With this in mind, and in order to achieve as wide a speed range as possible, Delage designed a small biplane, the lower wing of which had variable incidence so that it could be used as an aerodynamic brake. This was achieved by pivoting the small lower wing around its single spar. Its relationship with the upper wing was maintained by Vee-shaped struts in place of the traditional parallel struts, the base of the Vee being hinged to permit movement of the lower wing.

The outbreak of the 1914–18 War led to cancellation of the Gordon-Bennett meeting; but since the design of the Nieuport X was very advanced for the time, Delage decided to adapt it for military observation duties under the designation Nieuport X AV or X AR, according to whether the machine-gun was in front of or behind the pilot. In the military versions the lower wing was fixed.

Because of the extreme shortage of fighter aircraft, the Nieuport X was soon adapted for the single-seat fighter rôle, joining squadrons at the front in 1915.

Like all Nieuport sesquiplanes produced before 1918, the Nieuport X was of all-wooden construction with fabric covering. The lower wing, with its single spar, was of narrow rectangular shape, without sweepback; while the top wing had considerable sweepback, and had a Hotchkiss machine-gun mounted above the centre-section, from where it fired clear of the propeller disc. An 80-hp Le Rhône or Anzani engine gave the Nieuport X a maximum speed of 87 mph.

When the more powerful Nieuport XVI appeared in 1916, the Nieuport X C1s were removed from squadron service and used as training aircraft powered by a Clerget 7Z engine. The two-seat training version was designated Nieuport 83.

Nieuport XI and XVI

This aircraft, nicknamed "Baby" because of its small dimensions, had a total wing area of 140 sq ft, the upper wing having exactly twice the area of the lower one. It was always referred to as a sesquiplane by

Nieuport 11000 (Macchi-built Nieuport XI)

Nieuport 11000 (Macchi-built Nieuport XI)

Nieuport XI

TYPE	DIMENSIONS						WEIGHT	PERFORMANCE				REMARKS	
	span		length		height		max t-o	max speed	at height	service ceiling	combat range		
	ft	in	ft	in	ft	in	lb	mph	ft	ft	miles		
M-S 733 A	37	0½	30	7¾	11	4¼	3,736	160	SL	15,700	560	PO 6 D-30	240 hp
Mureaux 114 CN2	50	6	32	11½	12	5½	5,687	194		34,100	570	HS 12 Ybrs	650 hp
Mureaux 115 R2 B2	50	6	32	7¾	11	9	5,643	211		34,100	930	HS 12 Ycrs	860 hp
Mureaux 117 R2 B2	50	6	32	11½	11	9	6,359	217		29,500	930	HS 12 Ycrs	860 hp
Nieuport X C1	25	11	22	11½	8	11	1,235	87		13,800	155	RO 9 C	80 hp

Nieuport XVII, Belgian Air Force

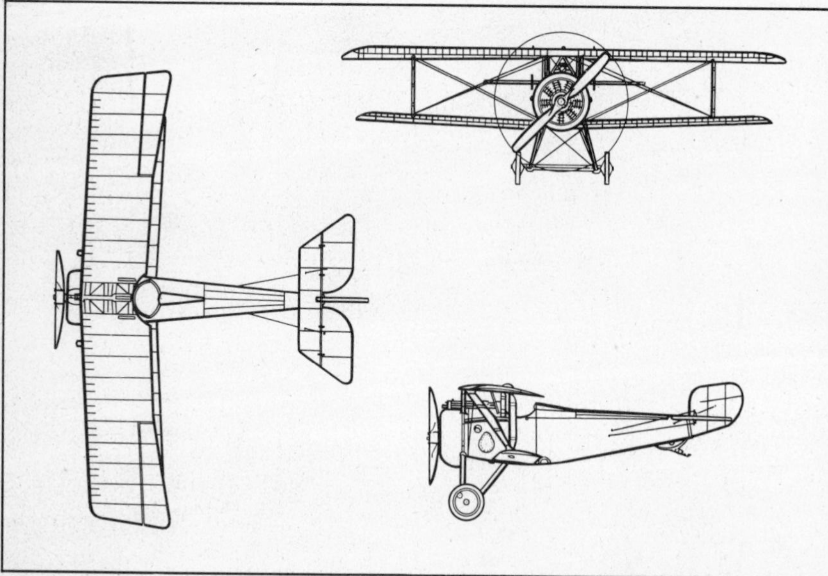
Nieuport XVII

Nieuport XXI

M. Delage, who hoped by this simple ruse to placate both sides in the monoplane-versus-biplane controversy.

The Nieuport XI had an 80-hp Le Rhône rotary engine, driving a Levasseur propeller, and was armed with a single Lewis gun mounted on the upper wing. Its good rate of climb and manoeuvrability helped to make it popular with its pilots and it was used by several aces, including Capitaine Tricornot De Rose, who pioneered French fighter tactics in 1915–16.

The Royal Flying Corps had a number of these machines and Belgium equipped its 5th Squadron with the type. In Italy, Macchi produced 450 under licence, as the Nieuport 110 or 11000; Holland purchased five and built another 20 under licence. Even Germany had a single machine, built by the Trompenburg company.

Following the success of the Sopwith and Fokker triplanes, an experimental triplane version was produced in 1917, designated XI C. However, its performance was unsatisfactory and the project was abandoned.

A derivative of the Nieuport XI, known as the Nieuport XVI, was produced in 1916, with a more-rounded front fuselage, a head-rest for the pilot and an engine of 120 hp. In France, it was the first machine to endear itself to the great ace Guynemer, acquiring his personal nickname of *Vieux Charles*. Belgium used the XVI to equip two of its fighter squadrons and the RFC also had some. The standard armament could be exchanged for eight Le Prieur rockets, mounted on the interplane struts, for attacking German balloons and airships.

Nieuport XVI No. 9761 is displayed today in perfect condition in the Musée de l'Air at Chalais-Meudon.

Nieuport XVII, XXI and 23

The Nieuport XVII was basically a Nieuport XI with larger wings, the total wing area of this version being 161·5 sq ft. Like the Nieuport XVI, it was powered by a Le Rhône 9 Jb rotary engine of 120 hp, and its empty weight was only 760 lb. Armament comprised a single Vickers machine-gun mounted on top of the front fuselage, with synchronizing gear permitting it to fire through the propeller disc. Twin machine-guns were fitted experimentally, one being mounted on the engine cowling and the other above the wing, but this lowered both climbing speed and ceiling and was soon abandoned.

French squadrons equipped with the Nieuport XVII included No. 3, the famous Escadrille des Cigognes, and Nos. N 38, N 55, N 65 and N 103. Nungesser used a Nieuport XVII, No. 880, and Navarre and Dorme also flew this type. Fighter squadrons of the Royal Flying Corps, Belgium and Russia were equipped with XVIIs, of which 20 were also supplied to Holland and two to Finland, while 150 were built by Macchi in Italy. In September 1917 the American Expeditionary Force received 75, and among the American-manned squadrons which flew this type was No. 124, known as the Escadrille Lafayette. After the war a few were purchased by Switzerland.

With the Le Rhône engine replaced by a Clerget 9B, the XVII was designated XVII*bis*. Only external difference was a modified cowling which completely covered the rotary engine. This version was used in the French, Rumanian and Dutch Air Forces; Nungesser of France flew No. 1895, later converted into a Nieuport 23.

One machine of this type went to the United States in October 1918, for comparative tests against similar types then being produced by America's own aircraft industry. Another Nieuport XVII*bis* went to Great Britain where it was converted into an experimental triplane with the serial number A6686.

A further variant of the Nieuport XVII, powered by an 80-hp Le Rhône engine and having enlarged ailerons, giving more positive lateral stability, was known as the Nieuport XXI. This machine could climb to 500 m (1,640 ft) in 2 min, 1,000 m (3,280 ft) in 4 min, 2,000 m (6,560 ft) in 8 min 45 sec, and 4,000 m (13,125 ft) in 25 min 40 sec. Armament comprised a single machine-gun mounted in the engine cowling or eight rockets carried on the interplane struts.

A number of these aircraft were supplied to Russia; and America bought 181 Nieuport XXIs in September 1917 and another 17 in January 1918, these being equipped with 110-hp Le Rhône 9 J engines.

After the war several Nieuport XXIs, classed as war surplus, were used as sporting aircraft and flown at air meetings to thrill the crowds with mock dog-fights reminiscent of those fought high over the Western Front.

The Nieuport 23 was another variant of the XVII, with the machine-gun mounted in the right-hand side of the engine cowling which, as on the XVII*bis*, entirely covered the engine.

The Air Forces of France, Italy, Belgium and Great Britain used this model, an example of which can still be seen in the Musée Royal de l'Armée in Brussels. America also received 47 in January 1918, with a further two following in September of the same year. The machines supplied to the Americans had more powerful engines than those fitted to the standard models.

Nieuport 24

The prototype Nieuport 24, which first flew in 1916, was none other than Nungesser's XVII*bis*. This machine had earlier been converted into the Nieuport 23, and was to be modified yet again when, with a different tailplane and tail-skid of the type fitted to the Nieuport 27, it was to be designated Nieuport 25.

The Nieuport 24 was the first production "Baby" to have a fixed fin in front of the rudder and a fuselage of circular section, although these features had already been tried out on the experimental Nieuport XVIII. Its armament consisted of two machine-guns mounted in the engine cowling.

The United States acquired 121 of this version in November 1917. Others were supplied to Belgium and Italy, and several were built in Japan under licence in 1919 by the Nakajima company as KO 3s.

In 1917 there appeared a variation of the Nieuport 24, utilizing the tail unit of the Nieuport XVII and having rectangular wing-tips. Armed with two machine-guns, this variant was known as the Nieuport 24*bis*. It equipped French squadrons, as well as the American Expeditionary Force, which acquired 140 Nieuport 24*bis*.

One machine of this type acquired a dubious fame when, in 1919, it was retrieved from a scrapyard and put in flying condition by a pilot named Godefroy. Contravening both military and civil regulations, he then used it to fly under the Arc de Triomphe in Paris.

Nieuport 27

The Nieuport 27 was basically similar to the Nieuport 24, differing in its tail-skid and undercarriage. It was also the last Nieuport fighter to have Vee-shaped interplane struts. Armament comprised a single machine-gun which was mounted in the engine cowling.

This version was built in France by both Nieuport and the Société Savary. It was used by the air forces of Sweden and Great Britain (which purchased 523 Nieuports of all types); and 287 examples of the Nieuport 27 were bought by the United States in November 1917. This type was also built under licence in Italy by the Macchi company.

Nieuport XVII

Nieuport 24

Nieuport 27

TYPE	DIMENSIONS span ft	span in	length ft	length in	height ft	height in	WEIGHT max t-o lb	PERFORMANCE max speed mph	at height ft	service ceiling ft	combat range miles	REMARKS	
Nieuport XI	24	9¼	19	0¾	8	0¾	1,058	96	SL	13,800	155	RO 9 C	80 hp
Nieuport XVI	24	5¾	19	0½	7	10½	1,135	102	6,500	16,400	186	RO 9 Jb	120 hp
Nieuport XVII	26	9¾	19	7	7	7½	1,179	109	6,500	17,400	186	RO 9 Jb	120 hp
Nieuport XVII*bis*	26	9¾	19	8½	8	6¼	1,252	112		18,400	186	CL 9 B	130 hp
Nieuport XXI	26	9¾	19	9	8	0½	1,181	99		14,800	150	RO 9 C	80 hp
Nieuport 23	26	9¾	19	7	7	11¼	1,179	93		14,800	150	RO 9 C	80 hp
Nieuport 24	26	11	19	0½	8	0½	1,207	110		17,700	155	RO 9 Jb	120 hp
Nieuport 24*bis*	26	11	19	0½	8	0½	1,225	109		17,700	155	RO 9 Jb	120 hp

Nieuport 28, first prototype

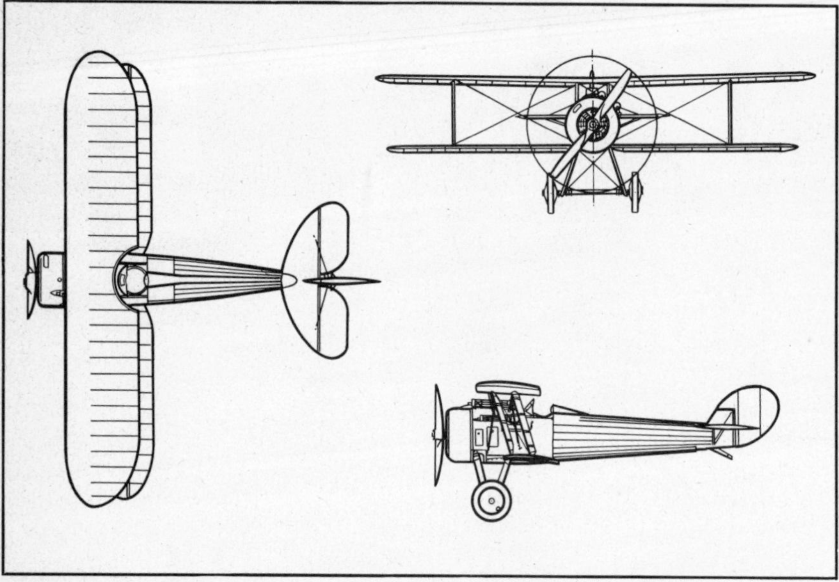

Nieuport 28

Nieuport 29 C1

Nieuport 28

Four prototypes of the Nieuport 28 were built, powered by Gnome 9 R engines and designated Nieuport 28 G. Unlike Nos. 03 and 04, the first two prototypes had no dihedral in the upper wing. Maiden flight of the Nieuport 28-01 took place on 14 June 1917.

Production versions of the 28 were powered by a Le Rhône 9 N engine of 170 hp, and large-scale manufacture provided machines for France, the United States (297 aircraft, delivered from March 1918), Greece and Switzerland. The circular-section fuselage was of monocoque construction and the uncambered biplane wings were linked by parallel interplane struts. Two Vickers machine-guns were mounted in the engine cowling.

Experimental versions of the Nieuport 28 were produced with different power plants, including the Hispano 8 Fb, Lorraine 8 Bb and the large rotary Clerget 11 Eb. Another version was built with only two interplane struts, and this machine was powered by a Gnome engine of 180 hp. Finally, Nieuport 28 No. 6125 had the centre-section of the upper wing modified, the depth of the ribs being reduced to improve forward vision.

The Nieuport 28 climbed to 1,000 m (3,280 ft) in 2 min, 3,000 m (9,840 ft) in 7 min 25 sec, and 5,000 m (16,400 ft) in 16 min 30 sec. It entered service just prior to the Armistice and was used mainly by American squadrons in France including Nos. 27, 95, and 103.

In 1920, four civil Nieuport 28s were used during a French postal strike to fly mail between Paris and London. The final version, produced in 1921, was the civil three-seat Nieuport 28*bis*, but this failed to achieve popularity.

Nieuport 29

Produced too late to see service in the 1914–18 War, the Nieuport 29 became a standard post-war fighter type in the air forces of several countries. A single-engined biplane, it had ailerons on both upper and lower wings, a true monocoque fuselage and a Vee engine, and was armed with two machine-guns mounted in the engine cowling. Total wing area was 289 sq ft, and it had a maximum speed of 146 mph at sea level, no mean performance for those days. It could climb to 2,000 m (6,560 ft) in 4 min 37 sec, 4,000 m (13,125 ft) in 10 min 59 sec, and 6,500 m (21,325 ft) in 25 min 1 sec.

One Nieuport 29 was fitted with two wooden floats, as the Nieuport 29 SHV (high-speed seaplane), to compete in the 1919 Schneider Trophy race.

In 1921, the design was modified considerably and fitted with wings of increased span, with ailerons on the lower wing only. This new version was designated Nieuport-Delage (ND) 29 C1. It appeared at the Paris Air Show of 1922 and was soon in service with French fighter squadrons, remaining operational until 1928. During the Rif risings in Morocco, a number of ND 29s were converted to serve as fighter-bombers, carrying anti-personnel bombs as well as machine-guns.

Twenty ND 29s, produced by the Nieuport and Levasseur company, were sold to Spain; others went to Sweden, where they were designated J2. They were also built in Italy and Japan; in Belgium SABCA built 108 for the Belgian Air Force.

A 29*bis* prototype was demonstrated in Spain and about 100 ND 29 fighter-trainers, powered by a Hispano engine of only 180 hp, were built for France and Belgium. Some special models (ND 29 V, 29 V*bis* and 29 SHV) with reduced wing area and boosted engines, competed in contests for the Schneider Trophy and Coupe Deutsch de la Meurthe. Another variant, originally designated ND 29 G, with a radial engine, was produced soon after the war as the ND 32 RH for service on board carriers.

Final version was the ND 40, powered by a supercharged engine to make it suitable for operation as a high-altitude fighter. It was not ordered by the French Air Force, but was later fitted with wings of increased span, as the ND 40 R, for an attempt on the world height record. In it, Sadi-Lecointe raised the record to 36,565 ft on 30 October 1923. Shortly afterwards, with the original wheel undercarriage replaced by floats, he captured the seaplane height record.

Nieuport-Delage 42

The ND 42, which appeared in 1924, was designed as a high-altitude fighter. The prototype was a parasol monoplane, with a total wing area of 286·7 sq ft, the wings being braced by streamlined duralumin struts, running from the rear of the undercarriage, behind the wheel on each side. Between the wheels was a small lifting surface, which faired in the axle.

The design was based on experience gained with the ND 42 S, a high-performance machine which competed for the Beaumont Cup in 1923, 1924 and 1925.

A two-seat sesquiplane version, designated ND 42 C2, also appeared in 1924, with a machine-gun mounted on the observer's cockpit for rear defence.

By the time the single-seat ND 42 took part in the French Air Force fighter competition of 1925, it too had become a sesquiplane, powered by a 500-hp Hispano 12 Hb engine. It proved to be the fastest of all the competing types, with a top speed of 165 mph at sea level, and an initial batch of 25 was ordered. As the ND 42 C1, this version was armed with one machine-gun in the engine cowling and two others mounted in the wings to fire clear of the propeller. It had a speed of 140 mph at 7,500 m (24,600 ft), which it attained in 32 min 36 sec.

Fuselage construction was similar to that of the Nieuport 29, while the fabric-covered wing was of mixed wood and duralumin construction. The fuel tanks, which had a total capacity of 75 gallons, could be jettisoned in an emergency. The Hispano engine drove a two-bladed wooden Ratier propeller, with a pointed spinner, although tests had been made with a Nieuport-Astra (Duhamel licence) steel propeller.

Between 29 August and 16 October 1924, the test pilot Fernand Lasne captured 16 world speed and distance records, with and without payload, in an ND 42 (F-AHDQ) which had been fitted with special tanks to increase the fuel capacity. Another ND 42 was sold to the Spanish *infante*, Don Alfonso de Orléans, who used it for aerobatic displays. A seaplane version, designated ND 42 H, was also produced, with duralumin floats of special design to prevent sea water from fouling the propeller during take-off, but was not successful.

Experimental variants included the ND 44, basically similar to the standard model except for its Lorraine 12 Ew engine and frontal radiator; the ND 46 (F-AIGN), which was powered by a supercharged Hispano 12 Gb W engine; and the ND 47 (F-AIII), with slight modifications and the same power plant as the standard ND 42.

There was also the ND 48, a smaller and lighter version built to meet the requirements of the "Jockey" programme, which limited engine power to 400 hp. This had only two machine-guns and smaller fuel capacity, and was abandoned as a combat aircraft when the programme was dropped. The prototype was later fitted with a Lorraine engine of 300 hp and, as the ND 481, was used by Lasne and Paulhan for aerobatic displays.

Nieuport-Delage 52

A development of the ND 42 appeared in 1928, designated ND 52, and was readily distinguishable from the earlier models by its all-metal fuselage, and the installation of Lamblin radiators in the lower wing.

This aircraft was demonstrated in Spain in competition

Nieuport-Delage 29 C1

Nieuport-Delage ND 52, Hispano-built

TYPE	DIMENSIONS span ft	span in	length ft	length in	height ft	height in	WEIGHT max t-o lb	PERFORMANCE max speed mph	at height ft	service ceiling ft	combat range miles	REMARKS	
Nieuport 27	26	10	18	6	7	11¼	1,289	110		17,700	155	RO 9 Jb	120 hp
Nieuport 28	27	4¾	21	3¼	7	0¾	1,378	133		23,000	248	RO 9 N	170 hp
Nieuport 29	32	1¼	21	9¾	8	4¾	2,535	147		26,200	360	HS 8 Fb	300 hp
ND 29	32	10	21	8	7	10½	2,623	143		26,200	372	HS 8 Fb	300 hp
ND 42	39	4½	24	7¼	9	10	3,986	165		26,900	528	HS 12 Hb	500 hp
ND 52	39	4½	24	7¼	9	10	4,005	150		26,900	310	HS 12 Hb	500 hp

Nieuport-Delage ND 62

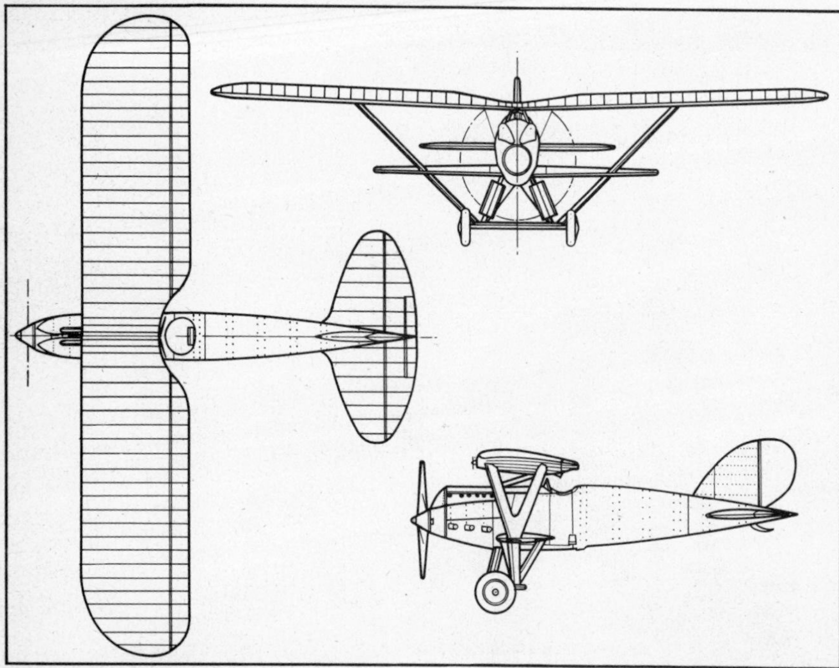
Nieuport-Delage ND 622

Nieuport-Delage ND 622

with the Dewoitine 27. The ND 52 proved to be the faster and Spain acquired a licence to build the type. Altogether 125 were built by Hispano-Suiza, sole difference between the French and Spanish models being the substitution of a Corominas-built radiator.

In the early days of the Spanish Civil War, 36 ND 52s were still in service, distributed among four fighter groups. At a later date, 29 remained in service with the Government forces, while seven had been captured by the Nationalists: this resulted in aerial combat between like aircraft, the only difference being in their insignia.

With a maximum speed of 158 mph at 23,000 ft, the ND 52 could climb to 5,000 m (16,400 ft) in 13 min 22 sec, and to 7,000 m (22,965 ft) in 25 min 16 sec. Armament comprised two 7·7-mm Vickers machine-guns.

Nieuport – Delage 62 and derivatives

The 725 Nieuport-Delage 62, 622 and 629 aircraft used by the French Air force were, with the Loire-Gourdou-Leseurre 32 and Wibault 72, the backbone of the French fighter forces until the advent of the Dewoitine 500.

Developed from the ND 42, the basic ND 62 was a sesquiplane, retaining the between-leg lifting surface of the ND 42. It could climb to 1,000 m (3,280 ft) in 2 min 12 sec and to 6,000 m (19,685 ft) in 18 min 16 sec.

The ND 62 was followed by the ND 622 and 629, and ND 72, which were of metal construction, with fabric covering; and finally the ND 82, the last of the sesquiplanes. This was of all-metal construction and could climb to 6,000 m (19,685 ft) in 13 min 57 sec, compared with the 18 min 16 sec required by the ND 622. Ceiling of the ND 82 was 31,000 ft, but it did not enter production.

At the outbreak of war there were still some ND 622s and 629s in the regional squadrons and in May 1940 Squadrons GC III/4 and III/5 had to use ND 629s.

Details of the ND 62 series follow. HS and LO indicate Hispano-Suiza and Lorraine engines respectively.

Type	*Engine*	*hp*	*Year*	*No. Built*
62	HS 12Mb	500	1928	345
ND 42 with larger tailplane, wooden propeller, ailerons of reduced span, increased chord.				
62	HS 12Hb	500	1928	1
Ex ND 42 No. 5 (F-AHDQ). Special version for records, logged 118 flying hours.				
62	HS 12Hb	500	1928	1
Ex ND 62 No. 62, for testing metal fuselage (F-AIRS).				
62	HS 12Lb	600	1928	2
F-AIPO (Ex ND 62 No. 50) and F-AIPQ (Ex ND 62 No. 61) for testing more powerful engine. F-AIPQ became ND 72 after 49½ flying hours.				
621	HS 12Hb	500	1929	3
Seaplane versions for Schneider Trophy training. Later re-fitted with wheels.				
622	HS 12Md	500	1931	330
ND 62 with metal propeller-Ratier or Levasseur. Farman supercharger. Ailerons along entire trailing-edge. 226 ND 622s still in service 15 Dec. 1932.				
623	LO 12Fd	600	1931	1
For speed record attempt, with payload.				
624	HS 12Md	500	1931	1
Monoplane version of ND 62.				
625	HS 12Md	500	1932	1
ND 622 converted for supply-dropping by parachute.				
626	LO 12Hdr	500	1933	12
ND 622s with different engine for Peru.				
628	Hi 12Mc	500	1932	2
ND 622 with increased wing area. Taken into French Air Force.				

Type	Engine	hp	Year	No. Built
629	HS 12Mdsh	500	1932	50

ND 622 with Messier oleo undercarriage, Szydlowski supercharger.

Type	Engine	hp	Year	No. Built
72	HS 12Hb	500	1929	4

ND 62 with fabric-covered metal fuselage. 3 for Belgium.

Type	Engine	hp	Year	No. Built
72	LO 12Fa	600	1931	1

Ex ND 62 F-AIPQ, converted to monoplane. Scrapped in 1933 after 48 flying hours.

Type	Engine	hp	Year	No. Built
82	LO 12Ha	500	1931	1

All-metal. Square wing-tips. Re-shaped tail fin.

Type	Engine	hp	Year	No. Built
82	LO 12Ha	500	1931	1

Above model converted to monoplane. Sold to Spain.

Potez 540 series

The aeronautical engineers Henry Potez, Marcel Bloch and Louis Coroller joined forces in 1917 to found the Société d'Etudes Aéronautiques (SEA), with a view to producing a two-seat observation aircraft to replace the Sopwith 1½-Strutters in service with French reconnaissance squadrons. In due course they designed and constructed the SEA 1, at Suresnes, near Paris; but the 200-hp Clerget engine chosen to power this aircraft proved unreliable and prevented the type from going into production. Its successor, the SEA 4, with a 370-hp Lorraine, was more successful, and 115 were built.

Between the two wars, Henry Potez was the leading designer of French reconnaissance aircraft, producing no fewer than 5,500 machines in this category, comprising Potez XVs, 25s and 39s – a total which does not include the type 63/II. The Potez company also produced multi-seat fighter-bombers, the first being the Potez 540.

Out of 82 military prototypes – the subject of 53 official contracts in the period 1928–33 – involving a total expenditure of 119 million francs, only 10 were adopted by the French Air Ministry and ordered into quantity production under Plan I. Particularly important among the chosen types were the Amiot 140 and Potez 540, more than 200 of the latter being ordered.

In 1933, the Air Ministry had cancelled their day and night multi-seat fighter-bomber programme, replacing it with one for BCR aircraft, which meant that machines built to this requirement had to be able to perform the triple rôle of bomber, fighter and reconnaissance aircraft. This scheme (Plan I) was adopted in June 1934.

Following a private conversation between General Denain (Minister for Air) and M. Potez, the prototype Potez 540 was ordered. Henry Potez had anticipated the Air Ministry's requirements and work on this machine had started on 25 August 1933. As a result, the prototype was able to make its first appearance on 14 November of the same year, and official tests were completed by 5 May 1934. On 25 November 1934, the first production model was delivered to the Air Force.

The prototype had appeared with twin fins and rudders and had been powered by two Hispano 12 Xbrs engines; the production models had a single fin and two Hispano 12 Xirs/12 Xjrs engines, driving propellers which turned in opposite directions. The Potez 540 was a high-wing monoplane with pronounced dihedral. The large fuselage was extensively glazed and accommodated a crew of five. The undercarriage retracted into the engine nacelles.

Nieuport-Delage ND 622

Potez 540

Potez 540, with insignia of all French units which used the type

TYPE	DIMENSIONS span ft	span in	length ft	length in	height ft	height in	WEIGHT max t-o lb	PERFORMANCE max speed mph	at height ft	service ceiling ft	combat range miles	REMARKS	
ND 62	39	4½	24	7¼	9	10	4,076	150		26,900	310	HS 12 Mb	500 hp
ND 622	39	4½	25	0¾	9	10	4,144	168		26,900	310	HS 12 Md	500 hp
ND 629	39	4½	26	4½	10	2	4,144	186		29,000	310	HS 12 Mdsh	500 hp
Potez 540	72	6	53	2½	12	9	13,025	193	13,000	32,800	775	2 × HS 12 Xirs/Xjrs	690 hp
Potez 542	72	6	53	2½	12	9	12,785	217	13,000	32,800	745	2 × LO 12 Hfrs/Hgrs	780 hp

Potez 541 prototype

Potez 630, second prototype

Potez 630, Swiss Air Force

Potez 63-II

Construction was fairly typical of the period, the wings being of metal with fabric covering, the fuselage entirely of wood. Armament comprised a machine-gun in a nose turret and two rear machine-guns, of which the lower was housed in a retractable fairing. It could carry ten 110-lb bombs, or four of 500 lb, over a range of 620 miles. Handling qualities were excellent and it could climb to 4,000 m (13,125 ft) in 10 min 36 sec and to 6,000 m (19,685 ft) in 18 min.

Take-off could be effected "hands off", a fact which was discovered accidentally when a Potez 540 left the ground safely although the pilot had forgotten to release the control column lock – a device used to prevent control surfaces from being moved by the wind when the aircraft is parked on the ground.

The Air Force received 94 Potez 540s. Four went to the National Geographical Service and 49 were supplied to Spain; ten were used by the Ministerial Squadron based at Villacoublay, and one by the French Navy.

Because of its low speed of 192 mph, the Potez 540 was not used on operational service during World War II, being reserved for transport and liaison duties. Five were captured by the Germans in 1942 and offered to Italy; it is not known whether they were accepted.

A prototype Potez 541 flew for the first time in August 1934, powered by two Gnome-Rhône K 14 radial engines. The 12 production aircraft which followed from September 1935 were designated Potez 543, and were intended for Rumania. However, four were retained and supplied to Spain during 1936–7.

A variant, designated Potez 542, had the usual Hispano engines replaced by Lorraine Pétrel engines. Twenty of this model entered service with the St-Jean d'Angely Radio School, and 39 went to the Air Force, serving alongside Potez 540s. Several Potez 542s were sent to overseas squadrons in Indo-China. When, at the outbreak of war, replacement engines were in short supply, the 860-hp Hispano 12 Ybrs was installed in the 542s, the extra power considerably improving performance.

Final version, which appeared early in 1936, was the Potez 544 (serial number 4133), powered by two Hispano Ybrs engines, intended for air mail service.

Potez 630 series

In October 1934, the French Air Minister initiated a programme to develop a new twin-engined three-seat day and night fighter. Among the prototypes built under this programme were the Hanriot 220, Loire-Nieuport 20, Romano 110, Breguet 690 and Potez 630.

The first design study for the Potez 630 was based on the use of two flat Potez 12 D engines of 450 hp, which were to be mounted within the wings. As these engines were not ready in time, the two prototypes were built with Hispano 14 Hbs engines. Construction of the 630-01 started in April 1935 and it first flew exactly one year later.

It was of all-metal construction, except for the control surfaces, which were fabric-covered. The wing centre-section was integral with the fuselage; the tailplane carried two angular fins and rudders, which were replaced by others of circular shape in August 1936. In this form the Potez 630 could climb to 4,000 m (13,125 ft) in 9 min and could attain 280 mph in horizontal flight and 485 mph in a dive.

The first of a production series of 80 Potez 630s, all with Hispano engines, flew in February 1938. In parallel production were 210 Potez 631s, the first of which flew in March 1937 and differed mainly in having enlarged fins and Gnome-Rhône 14 Mars engines. The combined production of both types amounted to 25 by September 1938, when each aircraft required 7,500 man-hours to produce. Unfortunately, when the war started one year later, all the 630s were grounded, due to serious trouble with the engines, the cylinder heads of which were failing after as little as ten hours' use.

Delivery of 630/631s to French Air Force squadrons had started at the end of 1938 and reached its peak in May 1940. In this month, SNCAN, which had absorbed Potez and Les Mureaux in 1936, pushed production to 121 aircraft – a rate which exceeded the formation of units and trained crews to man them.

Standard armament for Potez 630/631 fighters was two nose-mounted Hispano 9 or 404 cannon, plus one MAC machine-gun for rear defence, although shortage of cannon necessitated arming early machines with four machine-guns. In February 1940, it was decided to increase the fire-power by supplementing the two cannon with six machine-guns mounted under the wings.

At the time of the German attack, seven squadrons equipped with Potez 631s were based in the north of France – ECMJ I/16, ECN I/13, ECN II/13, ECN III/13, ECN IV/13, GAM 550 and GC I/7 – with one other squadron, ECN V/13, based at Lyons. Of the total of 290 Potez 630/631s on the strength of the Air Force, 60 had been robbed of their propellers to keep other Potez aircraft serviceable. Useless to the French, they were captured by the Germans, who had only to fit propellers to render them airworthy.

There were several other operators of these aircraft. In February 1938 two Potez 630s had been ordered by Switzerland, and in October of the same year the French Government leased two (F-ARIR and F-AREY) to the Air-Bleu air mail service, one of which was the original prototype re-engined with Hispano Ab 02/03s.

During the war 12 Potez 631s were despatched to Finland but failed to reach their destination. Group II/8 transferred 18 to the French Navy, whose AC 1 and AC 2 Squadrons were under strength due to a shortage of Dewoitine D 376s. Another two, registered F-AREL and F-ARQV, were used by the French Government for various duties.

The total of 1,250 aircraft produced included the following variants:

Potez 632. Experimental dive-bomber version for the Navy, armed with two cannon mounted under the fuselage.

Potez 633. A ground-attack version ordered for the Air Force in 1938. Initial order for 125 aircraft was later reduced to 35. Because of the limitations of their Hispano engines, the initial production machines were redesignated Potez 634 and used for training. In 1940, GBA I/51 and II/51 were the only groups equipped with Potez 633s. Nineteen were used for various test purposes; 8 were exported to China, none of which reached its destination; 24 went to Greece and 4 to Rumania in July 1938, followed by an additional batch of 25 for Rumania in March 1940. Finally, Japan acquired a licence for this version to be produced by Mitsubishi.

Potez 636. This was the 633 as produced under licence by Avia in Czechoslovakia.

Potez 637 and 639. Reconnaissance versions, with a ventral observation position. The first of 17 Potez 637s was produced on 1 October 1938, followed by a single 639 in 1939.

Potez 63/II. This was a three-seat reconnaissance version of the 630, with a glazed nose. The first of 748 production models flew on 10 July 1939, and 717 were on the strength of the French Air Force in June 1940. In 1942, 134 were captured in Vichy France by the Germans.

Three other experimental prototypes flew with 63-series designations, as follows:

63/12. First flown in February 1939, with two Pratt & Whitney engines.

63/13. Completed in 1940. This was a dive-bomber, and was equipped with dive-brakes and reversible-pitch propellers.

63/16. Completed in 1940. A torpedo-bomber with extended wing-tips.

Potez 63-II

Potez 633, Rumanian Air Force

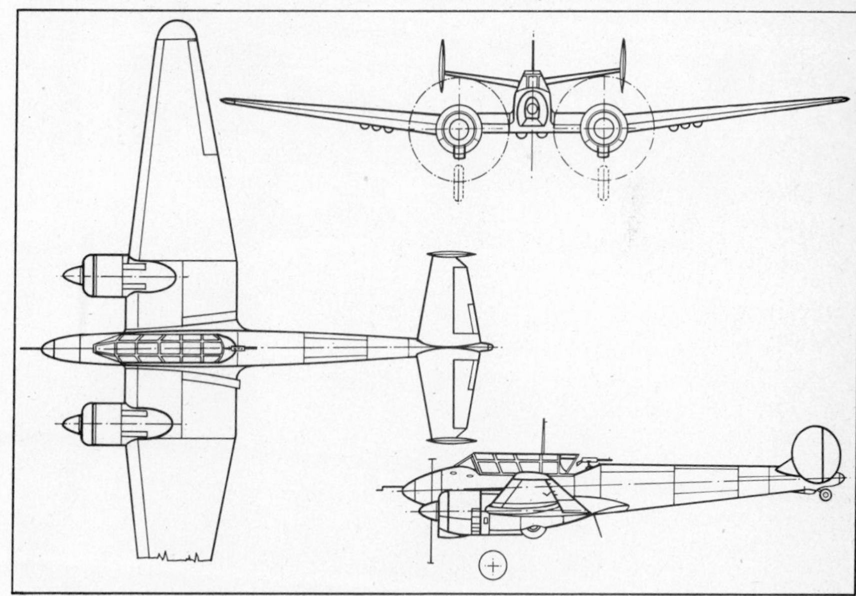

Potez 631

TYPE	DIMENSIONS span ft	in	length ft	in	height ft	in	WEIGHT max t-o lb	PERFORMANCE max speed mph	at height ft	service ceiling ft	combat range miles	REMARKS	
Potez 543	72	6	53	2½	12	9	12,765	217	13,000	32,800	745	2 × GR 14 Kds	700 hp
Potez 630	52	6	36	4	11	9¾	8,025	280	13,000	32,800	760	2 × HS 14 Ab 10/11	640 hp
Potez 631	52	6	36	4	11	9¾	8,232	276	13,000	32,800	620	2 × GR 14 M3/M4	670 hp
Potez 633	52	6	36	4	11	9¾	9,040	273	13,000	26,250	810	2 × GR 14 M3/M4	670 hp

Potez (Air Fouga) Magister, Israeli Air Force

Potez (Air Fouga) Magister, Finnish Air Force

SIPA S 111A

SIPA S 121

Potez (Air Fouga) Magister

Originating as the Fouga CM.170, the first of three prototype Magisters was flown on 23 July 1952 and was the world's first jet basic trainer. It has since become the most widely-used one as well, the Armée de l'Air having received 10 pre-production and 387 production Magisters and Super Magisters, while the Aéronavale received 32 "hooked" equivalents known as the CM.175 Zéphyr. Further large quantities were supplied to, and built in, Finland and Germany, and other Magister trainers were bought by Austria and Belgium. The standard Magister power plant comprises two 880 lb s t Turboméca Marboré IIA turbojets.

Smaller numbers have also been delivered of an armed version of the Magister, which has two 7.5-mm or 7.62-mm nose-mounted machine-guns and underwing points for two 110-lb bombs, two AS.11 wire-guided anti-tank missiles, or two Matra launchers for batteries of 37-mm or 68-mm rockets. Four Magisters of this type have been supplied to Cambodia, six to the Congolese Republic, and eight to Morocco. Prime user of the armed Magister, however, is the Israeli Defence Force/Air Force, which bought four from France in 1965 and has since received a further 36 built locally by Israel Aircraft Industries. Israeli Magisters, in company with the IDF/AF's Ouragan fighter-bombers and Mirage III-CJ fighters, played a major part in establishing Israeli air supremacy at the start of the "six days' war" against neighbouring Arab states early in June 1967.

SIPA S 10 to 1100

The Société Industrielle pour l'Aéronautique (SIPA) was formed in 1938 to supplement the immense efforts being made at that time by the French aircraft industry to re-equip the Air Force. With factories at Asnières, Neuilly and Nantes, it began by producing components for aircraft built by SNCAN, SNCASE, SNCASO, SNCAO and Morane-Saulnier. On the eve of World War II, SIPA also held the contract for the main wing assemblies for the Amiot 350; but the ink had barely dried before the contract was cancelled.

In 1941 the Couzinet de Levallois-Perret factory, on the island of La Grande Jatte in the Seine, was taken over by the German occupying forces. In it they installed SIPA, who built Arado 196s and 199s under German supervision, and it was not until April 1949 that René Couzinet, designer of the famous *Arc-en-Ciel* long-range aircraft, was able to regain possession.

SIPA's own factory at Neuilly, which had been closed at the time of the occupation, was also reopened on the orders of General Udet. In it, the Germans installed a group of engineers who had formerly represented General Motors, with the task of producing Arado 199s and prototypes of the Arado 296 and 396 training aircraft.

Not until the autumn of 1944 was SIPA free of enemy control. It restarted by taking over the design of the Arado 296/396, which it designated S 10, and the prototype made its first flight on 29 December 1944. In 1949, SIPA moved to its present factory at Suresnes.

Twenty-eight examples of the all-wooden S 10 were produced, followed by 50 S 11s in which construction was changed to mixed wood and metal. A batch of 54 S 111s was then built, of which four were prototypes, the remaining 50 being converted S 11s.

An all-metal version of the S 11 came next, of which 52 were built as S 12s. This family of training aircraft was then completed for the Air Force by a lightweight development of the S 12, known as the S 121, of which 58 were built.

In 1955, thirty SIPA 111s were modified to carry light bombs and rockets, and were also fitted with metal wing-tips and increased fuel capacity. Redesignated S 111As, they were used in Algeria. A 580-hp SNECMA S 12-SO2-3H engine (an Argus As 411 built by Renault) gave them 199 mph at sea level and 224 mph at 8,000 ft.

In 1956, a small number of S 121s were modified in the same way, becoming S 121As. They carried the same armament as the original S 111As or, alternatively, two machine-guns.

The prototype SIPA S 1100, a twin-engined aircraft designed especially for oversea "policing" duties, flew on 24 April 1958, but was destroyed in an accident on 2 July 1958. A second prototype was completed but, as in the case of the similar Sud/Dassault 117, no series production followed.

SNCAC NC 900

When the French aircraft industry was nationalized in 1936, the Farman and Hanriot companies were combined as the Société Nationale de Constructions Aéronautiques du Centre, sometimes known as Aero-centre, with factories at Billancourt, Fourchambault and Bourges. The most important military aircraft produced by the SNCAC before the events of 1940 were the four-engined Farman F 223 and its variants (see page 92).

Immediately prior to the war, the French Government began utilizing natural quarries and caves for the concealed and underground accommodation of factories producing war materials. Thus the quarries at Cravant were equipped to produce the LeO 451 bomber, with a planned production of 200 aircraft per month by the end of 1940. The French collapse prevented the plan from materializing; but after the retreat of the German occupying forces, this underground factory was used by SNCAC for manufacture of the Focke-Wulf 190A-5 and A-8, under the designation NC 900. The first of these machines flew on 16 March 1945, and a total of 64 were built. Forty went to the French Air Force, to equip Squadron GC III/5, and several of these were transferred to the Argentine, after only limited use. The remaining 24 were operated by the Navy at Cazaux until 1947.

Unfortunately, the BMW 801D/2 engines which powered the NC 900s proved unreliable, despite the fact that they had been completely stripped and rebuilt by the Société des Aéroplanes Gabriel Voisin in their factory at Issy-les-Moulineaux.

A full description of the NC 900 is not given here, as it was generally similar to the German-built Fw 190A-5. The sixty-second production machine survives and is displayed in the Musée de l'Air in Paris.

SNCASE Vampire and Mistral

Nationalization of the French aircraft industry united the companies of Lioré et Olivier, Romano and SPCA on 21 December 1936, under the title Société Nationale de Constructions Aéronautiques du Sud-Est (SNCASE). This company absorbed the SNCA du Midi, formerly Dewoitine, in 1941 and was itself merged with SNCASO in 1956 to form the world-famous organization known today as Sud-Aviation.

A decade earlier, after the liberation of France, it had been clear that her aircraft industry would need time to reorganize before it could meet the urgent needs of the French Air Force for new equipment. So, in 1948, SNCASE obtained from the British de Havilland company a licence to build the Vampire Mk 5 jet fighter. The first flight of a French-built FB. 5 Vampire took place in January 1950.

In accordance with French official policy, SNCASE set out to utilize as much French equipment as possible in the licence-built Vampires. In particular it proposed to substitute a Rolls-Royce Nene engine of 5,000-lb s t built in France by Hispano-Suiza, for the Vampire's usual DH Goblin III of 3,000-lb s t as soon as possible during the production run.

SNCAC NC 900

SNCASE Vampire FB.5

SNCASE Mistral

TYPE	DIMENSIONS						WEIGHT	PERFORMANCE				REMARKS	
	span		*length*		*height*		*max t-o*	*max speed*	*at height*	*service ceiling*	*combat range*		
	ft	*in*	*ft*	*in*	*ft*	*in*	*lb*	*mph*	*ft*	*ft*	*miles*		
Potez CM 170 Magister	39	10	33	0	9	2	7,055	440		36,000	735	Armed version. Span over tip-tanks	
S 111A	36	0¾	30	6¾	8	0	4,563	224	8,000	27,300	435	SNECMA S 12-SO2-3H	580 hp
S 121A	36	0¾	30	6¾	8	0	6,326	224	8,000	26,300	620	SNECMA S 12-SO2-D	580 hp

SNCASE Mistral Mk 53, fourth prototype

SNCASE Mistral Mk 535

SNCASE Aquilon Mk 20

SNCASE Aquilon Mk 202, wings folded

De Havilland and Rolls-Royce assisted SNCASE with the design modifications made necessary by the change of power plant, including the addition of cooling-air intakes, nicknamed "elephant's ears", above the engine bay. The first of the re-engined fighters, designated Vampire FB.51, flew on 21 December 1950, and within two years a total of 183 FB.5s and FB.51s had been supplied to the Air Force – the first jet aircraft flown by this service. They were formidable aircraft for their time, each being armed with four 20-mm cannon and eight rockets, and able to carry two 500-lb or 1,000-lb bombs, or two jettisonable fuel tanks; but low performance of the air intakes prevented the FB.51 from attaining the speed which had been expected following installation of the more powerful Nene engine.

The research department of SNCASE worked in conjunction with de Havilland, Rolls-Royce and Boulton Paul to overcome the problem, and this resulted in production of a new variant known as the Mk 53 Mistral. The major part of the equipment of this aircraft was of French origin, including an ejection seat built by SNCASO, replacing the former fixed seat.

With its re-designed air intakes, the Mistral was 47 mph faster than the Vampire FB.51 at low altitude and had a 65 per cent better rate of climb. A total of 528 gallons of kerosene, in internal and under-wing tanks, gave it an equivalent range to the Vampire, although fuel consumption of the Nene was considerably higher than that of the Goblin. Armament remained the same as that of the FB.51, and the general configuration was similar to that of the Vampire, including a pressurized cockpit for the pilot.

The prototype Mistral flew for the first time on 2 April 1951, followed by several other prototypes, one of which (the fourth aircraft built) was fitted with wing fences. The first production machine flew at the end of 1951, and two versions were built in series – the Mk 532 and 535, of which the latter was the only one fitted from the start with an ejection seat, although the Mk 532s were given such seats retrospectively later. Altogether, 247 Mistral Mk 532/535s were produced by SNCASE. Even when they were superseded by the series of Dassault fighters in the interception rôle, they continued to give good service as fighter-bombers and interceptor training aircraft for many years.

SNCASE Aquilon

Wishing to improve the potential of the Vampire, de Havilland produced a new version in which the wing was slightly swept. This was the DH 112 Venom, from which was developed the two-seat DH 112 Venom night fighter and, later, the carrier-borne Sea Venom. As the French Navy had an urgent requirement for such an aircraft, SNCASE acquired a licence to build it in France.

The aircraft ultimately produced by SNCASE was sufficiently different from the British version to justify its new name of Aquilon. Modifications included the replacement of fixed seats by SNCASO ejection seats and the installation of a Ghost 48/1 jet engine, built under licence by Fiat in Italy.

The prototype Aquilon 20 made its maiden flight on 31 October 1952, and was followed by four pre-production and 25 Mk 20 production aircraft. These machines were intended for operation from land bases and were fitted with a Vampire-type undercarriage and standard upward-opening cockpit canopy.

Meanwhile the second prototype had flown in 1953 as the Aquilon 201, with modified tail fins. From this was developed the Aquilon 202, of which 25 were built, the first flying on 24 March 1954. The Mk 202 had a sliding cockpit canopy and a special undercarriage for deck landing. Its armament comprised four cannon and eight rockets and it was fitted with a radar gun-sight. The next production version, the Aquilon 203, of which 40 were built, was a single-seat version with fire-control radar inside a dielectric nose-cone, and could be armed with the Nord 5103 air-to-air missile.

Final production version, appearing in 1956, was the Aquilon 204 trainer, of which 19 were built. These together with the 202s and 203s, were used by the Navy in Flottilles 11 F, 16 F, 17 F, 2 S, 10 S, 54 S and 59 S, until replaced by the Etendard IV-M and the American F-8E Crusader.

SO 4050 Vautour

At the end of 1936, when the French aircraft industry was nationalized, the Société Nationale de Constructions Aéronautiques du Sud-Ouest (SNCASO) was formed by combining the Société des Avions Marcel Bloch and Blériot-Aéronautique; five years later it absorbed SNCAO. During the German occupation it was compelled to manufacture components for Heinkel He 111 bombers and Focke-Wulf Fw 189 reconnaissance aircraft in its nine factories at Courbevoie, Châteauroux, Deols, Bordeaux-Bègles, Bordeaux-Bacalan, Bordeaux-Mérignac, Rochefort-Bouguenais, St-Nazaire and Suresnes.

In March 1951, SNCASO flew an experimental jet bomber known as the SO 4000, and then began design work on a twin-jet transonic bomber, the SO 4050, which they named Vautour (Vulture). In 1953, this was ordered into production for the French Air Force in three forms, as a single-seat ground-attack aircraft, two-seat bomber and two-seat all-weather fighter.

Of all-metal construction, the Vautour has a swept wing of 484·3 sq ft, with large camber-changing flaps. Air-brakes are fitted on each side of the rear fuselage. It has two twin-wheel main undercarriage units in tandem, retracting into the fuselage, and a small retractable balancer wheel extending from each engine nacelle.

The first SO 4050, which was the prototype of the all-weather fighter version, made its first flight at Melun-Villaroche airfield on 16 October 1952, powered by two 5,510-lb s t SNECMA Atar 101B turbojets. It can be identified in its original form by the number "001" painted on its nose and the letter "U" on the rear fuselage. During the following year it underwent various modifications including the addition of a dorsal spine, extending from the cockpit to the tail fin. The Atar 101B engines were replaced by 6,175-lb s t Atar 101Ds and radar was installed in the nose. So modified, the Vautour was demonstrated at the Paris Air Show in June 1953.

The second prototype had two Atar 101C engines, and appeared in the form of the single-seat ground-attack version. It made its first flight on 4 December 1953, and differed externally from the all-weather fighter version in having only a single cockpit and "solid" nose.

The prototype of the two-seat bomber version, the SO 4050-003, powered by two 8,157-lb s t Armstrong Siddeley Sapphire 6 engines, flew on 5 December 1954 and differed externally from the ground-attack version in having a glazed nose for the bomb-aimer. It was followed by six pre-production aircraft, of which SO 4050-04 was a two-seat bomber, 05 and 07 single-seat ground-attack aircraft, and 06, 08 and 09 all-weather fighters.

The ninth aircraft differed from the others in having Rolls-Royce Avon RA 28 Mk 21 engines installed experimentally.

At the beginning of 1956, strategic units of the French Air Force began to re-equip with production Vautours, powered by 7,715-lb s t Atar 101E-3 turbojets. An order was received for 140 of the all-weather fighter version, designated SO 4050 Vautour II N, but in 1958 this was

SNCASO Vautour II A, Israeli Air Force

SNCASO Vautour II B

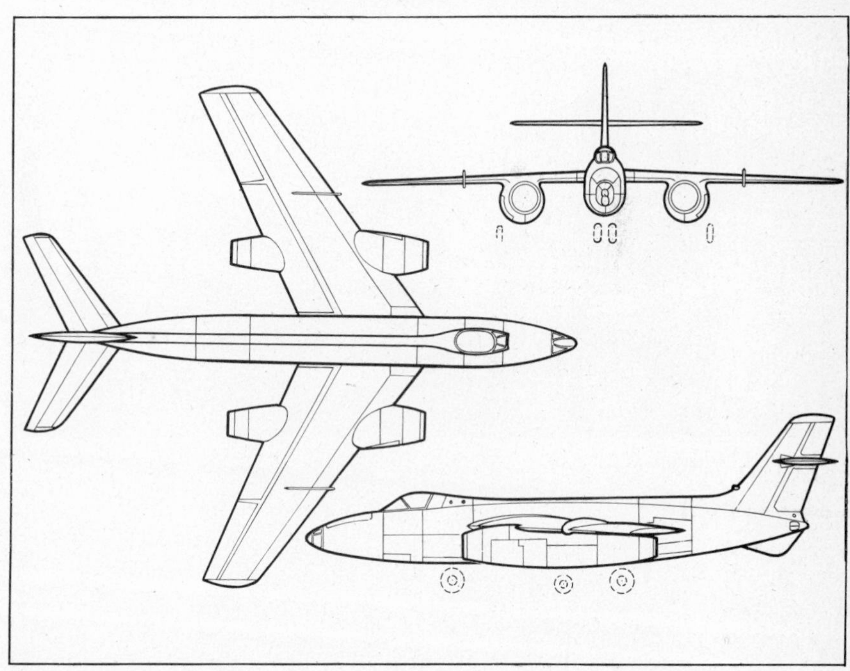

SNCASO Vautour II B

TYPE	DIMENSIONS						WEIGHT	PERFORMANCE				REMARKS	
	span ft	span in	length ft	length in	height ft	height in	max t-o lb	max speed mph	at height ft	service ceiling ft	combat range miles		
Vautour II N	49	6¾	51	11¾	16	2½	45,635	685	SL	50,000	2,485	2 × SNECMA Atar 101E-3	7,720 lb s t
Vautour II A	49	6¾	51	0¾	16	2½	45,635	685	SL	50,000	2,485	2 × SNECMA Atar 101E-3	7,720 lb s t
Vautour II B	49	6¾	51	11¾	16	2½	45,635	685	SL	50,000	2,485	2 × SNECMA Atar 101E-3	7,720 lb s t

SO 4050 Vautour II N, missiles under wings, guns uncovered, rocket packs extended

SPAD A 4, (Imperial) Russian Air Force

SPAD VII, British-built for RFC

SPAD VII

reduced to 70. Numbered 301 to 370, these machines are each armed with four DEFA 30-mm cannon, plus rocket pods or air-to-air missiles on four underwing attachments, and 112 rockets in an internal weapon bay. Alternatively, all versions of the Vautour can carry two external fuel tanks with a total capacity of 550 gallons, on the underwing attachments.

The SO 4050 Vautour II A, the ground-attack version, had been the subject of an order for 300 aircraft. In fact, only 30 were completed, (numbered 1 to 30), of which 25 were supplied to Israel in 1960. Armament is similar to that of the II N.

A total of 40 of the bomber version, designated SO 4050 Vautour II B, were produced (numbered 601 to 640) and some of these were sold to Israel in 1960. The SO 4050 II B is able to carry up to 5,300 lb of bombs in an internal weapon bay, plus further bombs, rockets or missiles on underwing attachments. No cannon are fitted.

A development of the II B appeared in 1958, under the designation Vautour II BR. The prototype of this variant was distinguished externally from the standard bomber by having a nose radome and flight refuelling probe.

SPAD A 4

Formed in 1910, the Société des Productions Armand Deperdussin was renamed the Société Anonyme Pour L'Aviation et ses Dérivés in 1915, thus retaining the abbreviation SPAD. It produced some of the finest fighter aircraft of the 1914–18 War, under the design leadership of Louis Béchereau until 1918 and then under André Herbemont. In 1921, SPAD was taken over by the Blériot company, after which its aircraft were known as Blériot SPAD designs.

More than 2,000 SPADs of various types were produced at the Suresnes factory during the 1914–18 War. Between the end of the war and nationalization in 1936, this factory produced a further 700 SPADs, 50 Breguet 14s and 200 Potez 25s, not including Blériot aircraft built there.

The first SPAD aircraft to be produced had, like the British BE 9, a pusher engine, with the propeller rotating more or less in the middle of the fuselage. The observer was accommodated in the nose, with the pilot behind the propeller. This arrangement was not popular with the aircrews because of the close proximity of the propeller, and the aircraft was little used by the French. However, several prototypes with this layout were built, including the SPAD A 1 with a Le Rhône 9 C engine, the SPAD A 2, with a Le Rhône 9 J, the SPAD A 3 dual-control version of the A 2, the SPAD A 5, produced for the Military Competition of 1916 and powered by a Renault 8 Fg engine, the SPAD "D" Bomber, with a 250-hp Panhard engine, and the SPAD "G" with a Clerget 9 B engine.

In addition, the SPAD A 4 first flew in February 1916, as a development of the A 1, and 12 machines of this type were sold to Russia.

SPAD VII

Towards the end of 1915 the SPAD V tractor biplane was produced, becoming, in effect, the prototype of the SPAD VII which flew for the first time in April 1916. Construction of the VII was conventional, with a fabric-covered wooden structure. Powered by a Hispano-Suiza Vee engine, driving a Bloch or Galia propeller, the prototype attained a speed of 122 mph at sea level and 112 mph at 6,500 ft. It could climb to 3,000 m (9,840 ft) in 15 min and to 6,000 m (19,685 ft) in an hour. Armament was a single Vickers 7·65-mm machine-gun.

Delivery of production machines, with a 150-hp supercharged Hispano 8 Aa engine, began on 2 September 1916, and these aircraft progressively replaced the Nieuport "Baby" in squadron service. By 30 October 1916, a total of 25 SPAD VIIs (Numbers S 112 to S 136) were in service, and by 1 August 1917 a total of 495 had been built.

The second production version, which was built

also by Blériot and Sommer, was powered by a 180-hp Hispano 8 Ac engine and had wings of about 8-in greater span. It remained in production until the more powerful and better armed SPAD XIII was available, a total of around 6,000 being built.

France equipped, amongst others, her S 3, S 8, S 12, S 23 and S 124 Squadrons with SPAD VIIs. The Royal Flying Corps used half of the 200 SPAD VIIs built in Britain (Serial Nos. A 8794-8893) to equip Nos. 19, 23, 30, 63 and 72 Squadrons, the other half going to the Royal Navy. The Italians received 214 machines from the second French production series, which went to her 71, 72, 75, 77 and 91 Squadriglia; while 15 others (SP 1 to SP 15) equipped the Belgian Vth Squadron. The United States also received 189 SPAD VIIs in December 1917, which were operated by their 124, 150 and 151 to 155 Squadrons.

Considerable numbers went overseas, to Peru, Portugal, Brazil, Greece, Rumania, Siam (Thailand), Yugoslavia and Russia, this last country equipping a number of machines with two Le Prieur rockets.

In 1917 two experimental SPAD VIIs were built, with increased wing span and, initially, a 200-hp Hispano 8 B engine. One was tested later with a Renault 12 D engine; the other became the SPAD XII with cannon armament.

About 100 SPAD VIIs were used by the École Blériot at Buc, and by other French companies, until 1928. Of this total, about 36 had been rebuilt from war stocks, and all were powered by a Hispano 8 AB engine. In addition, to meet requirements for new training and advanced training aircraft in 1923, two derivatives of the SPAD VII were built: the SPAD 72 single-seater with conventional wing layout, and the SPAD 62 two-seater with dual controls and staggered wings.

SPAD XII

In January 1917, at the request of Captain Guynemer, a SPAD VII was modified to carry a 37-mm cannon, mounted in the Vee of the engine cylinders and firing through the propeller disc, in addition to the usual Vickers machine-gun. Designated SPAD XII, this version also had a greater wing span.

The prototype (S 382) flew for the first time on 5 July 1917. In it Guynemer achieved four victories, while René Fonck, who had machine No. S 445, achieved 11 victories. One SPAD XII was sold to America in July 1918, and the British Royal Naval Air Service had several XIIs, fitted with floats.

First production models were powered by a 200-hp Hispano 8 Bc engine; but later aircraft had the 220-hp Hispano 8 Bec. A total of 300 were built by Blériot, Levasseur and Janoir – a figure which, compared with other types, was very small. One reason was that the cordite fumes produced each time the cannon fired tended to overcome the pilot.

SPAD XIII

From the end of May 1917 this new model began to replace the SPAD VIIs still in service with fighter squadrons. When it became available in quantity, additional squadrons were formed, and total production of the SPAD XIII eventually reached 8,440. At the Armistice, orders for a further 10,000 machines, including 6,000 for America, were cancelled.

The SPAD XIII differed from the VII in having

SPAD XII

SPAD XIII

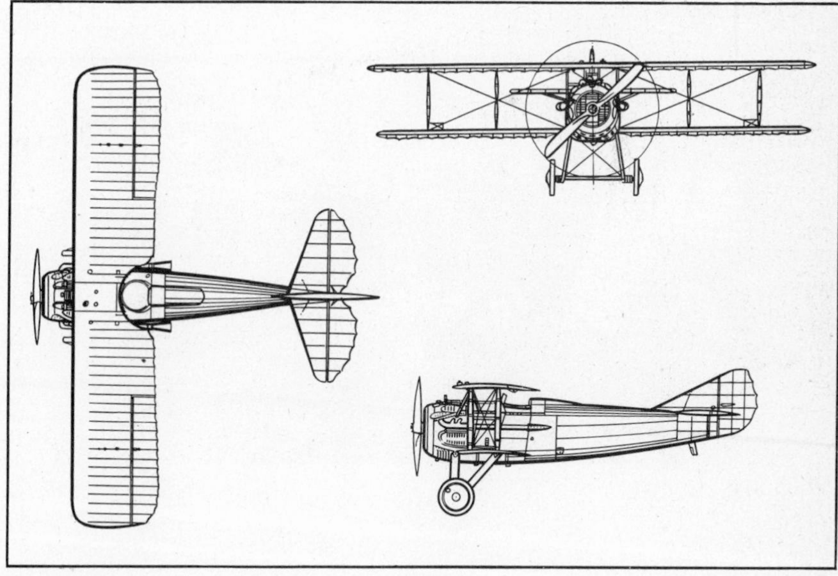
SPAD XIII

TYPE	DIMENSIONS span ft	span in	length ft	length in	height ft	height in	WEIGHT max t-o lb	PERFORMANCE max speed mph	at height ft	service ceiling ft	combat range miles	REMARKS	
SPAD A 4	31	3¾	23	11½	8	6½	1,565	93		15,800	155	RO 9 C	80 hp
SPAD VII	25	7¾	20	2½	6	11½	1,664	122	6,500	18,400	185	HS 8 Ac	180 hp
SPAD XII	26	10¼	20	9	7	8½	1,840	131		19,400	185	HS 8 Bec	220 hp
SPAD XIII	26	6	20	4¼	7	8½	1,862	139	6,500	21,800	185	HS 8 Be	220 hp

SPAD XIII

SPAD XIII, second series

SPAD XIV

increased power and range. The wings had more rounded tips; the chord of the ailerons was increased towards the tips; and the tail surfaces were enlarged. Armament was increased to two 7·65-mm Vickers machine-guns.

The prototype (S 392) made its first flight at Dorme on 4 April 1917 and proved able to climb to 1,000 m (3,280 ft) in 2 min 16 sec, to 4,000 m (13,125 ft) in 12 min 29 sec, and to 6,000 m (19,685 ft) in 36 min 2 sec. Maximum speed at sea level was over 138 mph.

The first production model was powered by a 200-hp Hispano 8 B engine; but the second series of SPAD XIIIs, produced from the end of 1917, had the supercharged Hispano 8 Be of 220 hp. The wing-tips of the second series were slightly less rounded.

Altogether, 81 French squadrons flew SPAD XIIIs, which also equipped Squadrons 19 and 23 of the British Royal Flying Corps and Squadrons 77 and 91 of the Italian air forces. Belgium had 37 (numbered S 1 to S 37), and America received 893 from March 1918 onward.

Built by Blériot, Levasseur, De Marcay, Kellner and Bernard, the SPAD XIII was exported after the war to Japan, Czechoslovakia and Poland (40 machines). In 1921, Belgium acquired sufficient to equip its Nos. 3, 4 and 10 fighter groups.

One SPAD XIII (S 706) was tested at Buc with a Rateau supercharger, which enabled its Hispano 9 Be engine to retain full power at much higher altitudes.

SPAD XIV

In 1916 the SPAD company flew a twin-float seaplane variant of the VII, powered by a 180-hp engine, under the designation SPAD X. The production version, built at the Levasseur works, was known as the SPAD XIV and made its first flight, from the Seine, on 15 November 1917.

Powered by a 200-hp Hispano 8 Bc "cannon" engine, the XIV had a SPAD XII fuselage and wings (with the total area increased to 282 sq ft) and Tellier floats. Armament consisted of the *moteur canon* and one machine-gun.

Forty were built for the Forces Aériennes de Mer, based on the English Channel. One of the survivors was flown at Monaco after the war by the famous French pilot Sadi-Lecointe, who was training at the time for the Schneider Trophy contest to take place at Bournemouth on 11 September 1919.

A variant of the XIV, which flew on 5 November 1918, was the SPAD XXIV, a wheeled version designed for carrier use; but only a prototype was built.

SPAD XVII

This modernized and strengthened version of the SPAD XIII was designed by Béchereau's successor, Herbemont. It was intended for both fighter and photo-reconnaissance duties, and was therefore equipped with a machine-gun and two cameras. A 300-hp Hispano engine gave it a maximum speed of 149 mph.

Twenty SPAD XVIIs were produced, some of them going to the famous *Cigognes* escadrille. A variant, designated SPAD XXI, was projected in 1918, with modified wings and armament. It was not built; so the same designation was given later to the racing seaplane produced for the Schneider Trophy contest of 1919. A variant of the XVII which did fly, at Villacoublay, at the end of the war, was the SPAD XXII, identified by its swept upper wing and two-bay layout.

SPAD XX

The prototype SPAD XVIII C2 was built in April 1918, but did not fly. It was a two-seat biplane fighter, with swept upper wing, single interplane struts, and ailerons on the lower wings only. The fuselage was of monocoque construction and it was powered by a 300-hp Hispano 8 Fbc engine, with *moteur canon*. The production version appeared at the end of 1918, as the SPAD XX, with two forward-firing Vickers machine-guns and a Lewis in the rear cockpit, but no *moteur canon*.

One hundred were built for France, and a licence to manufacture the type was sold to Japan; but there was little demand for such a machine now that the war had ended and most of those built were modified for other jobs. One was flown by Sadi-Lecointe in the 1919 race for the Coupe Deutsch. Others worthy of note were the SPAD XX*bis*, produced in 1920 as a two-seat fighter prototype (No. 828) with very large fin; the SPAD XX*bis* 5, of which two were built to compete in the Gordon-Bennett Cup race, the first one making its maiden flight on 22 October 1920; and the SPAD XX*bis* 6, first flown on 6 October 1920. This was the aircraft Bernard de Romanet used to raise the world speed record to 192·01 mph on 4 November 1920.

Final variants of the SPAD XX were the long-range SPAD 28 and 28*bis*, the first of which flew for the first time on 26 September 1919, and the SPAD 71, which began basically as a XX with four ailerons, but was shown in Spain in February 1923 in monoplane form.

SPAD 61

The SPAD 61 single-seat fighter utilized the same wings as the SPAD 81, but was better armed and had a more powerful engine. It was a straight-wing biplane, with single interplane struts and ailerons on both the upper and lower wings. The wooden monocoque fuselage was built up of three diagonally-crossed layers of tulip-wood veneer, the fin and lower wing being integral with the fuselage. The spatted undercarriage housed sprung, articulated axles to carry the main wheels.

To enhance still further its clean lines, the prototype SPAD 61/1 had a Vincent André retractable honeycomb radiator. When tested, it climbed to 26,250 ft, at which height it had a maximum speed of 130 mph.

The following table lists the 11 different versions of the SPAD 61:

(Abbreviations: LO = Lorraine, HS = Hispano-Suiza)

Type	*Engine*	*hp*	*First flight*	*No. built*
61/1	LO 12Ew	450	6 Nov. 1923	1
Metal structure, fabric-covered				
61*bis*	LO 12Eb	450	1927	1
Ex 61/2 No. 6. Sports version (F-AIKU). Scrapped in 1931.				
61/2	LO 12Ew	450	1925	350
Series-built 61/1. 250 for Poland, 100 for Rumania. Wooden structure, 2 machine-guns. F-AHDG, F-AHDN & F-AIRN for testing by Blériot.				
61/3	LO 12Ew	450	9 May 1925	1
61/2 with metal structure, for 1925 fighter competition. Four Darne machine-guns; increased fuel tankage.				
61/4	LO 12Ee	480	6 Jun. 1925	1
As above, but higher-revving engine, for 1925 fighter competition. Frontal radiator.				
61/5	HS 12Gb	500	13 May 1925	3
As above with W-engine. On 5 April 1926, piloted by Polish Capt. Stachon, climbed to 6,000m (19,685 ft) in 14 min 38 sec.				
61/6	LO 12Eb	450	31 Mar. 1925	2
Flying test-bed for Lorraine 12 Eb. Flown in 1925 Michelin Cup race by Pelletier d'Oisy and in 1927 by Challe (F-ESAU). Wing area reduced to 225 sq ft.				

SPAD XX prototype

SPAD 61/4

TYPE	DIMENSIONS						WEIGHT	PERFORMANCE				REMARKS	
	span		*length*		*height*		*max t-o*	*max speed*	*at height*	*service ceiling*	*combat range*		
	ft	*in*	*ft*	*in*	*ft*	*in*	*lb*	*mph*	*ft*	*ft*	*miles*		
SPAD XIV	32	1¾	24	3	13	5½	2,425	127		16,400	155	HS 8 Bc	200 hp
SPAD XVII	26	6	20	7¾	7	10¼	1,984	149		18,000	185	HS 8 F	300 hp
SPAD XX	31	10¼	23	11½	9	1¾	2,888	143		25,800	250	HS 8 Fb	300 hp
SPAD 61/2	31	6	22	3	9	1¾	3,623	174	SL	29,500	375	LO 12 Ew	450 hp

SPAD 81

SPAD 510

Tellier T.3

Type	Engine	hp	First flight	No. built
61/7	LO 12Eb	450	1926	1
61/6 with increased wing area, and supercharger.				
61/8	HS 12Hb	500	9 Sept. 1927	1
Ex 61/5 No. 2 with Vee engine.				
61/9	LO 7Ma	240	27 Apr. 1929	1
Ex 61/6 with radial engine. For Michelin Cup 1929, piloted by Challe (F-AJCR). Scrapped in 1933.				
61ses	LO 12Eb	450	1 May 1926	1
Sesquiplane version of 61/2, ordered by Poland.				

SPAD 81

The SPAD 81 was designed to meet the latest requirements of the official specification for fighters in the 300-hp category – a class that was to disappear in favour of 400/500-hp aircraft in 1926. It first flew in prototype form in March 1923, powered by a 300-hp Hispano-Suiza 8 Fb engine. In the following year, a production batch of 80 SPAD 81s were built and entered service with the French Air Force. They were biplanes of mixed metal and wood construction, the production version differing from the prototype in having normal centre-section struts instead of a central support structure, and a fin of improved design.

In 1924, its designer, Herbemont, produced a variant designated SPAD 81*bis*, with a wing span of 26 ft 10¾ in and a total wing area of only 226 sq ft, compared with the 323 sq ft of the 81. This was intended for high-speed sporting competitions, but was abandoned in favour of the SPAD 61/6 which offered superior performance.

A final version of the SPAD 81 appeared in 1925, powered experimentally by a 500-hp Hispano 12Mb.

SPAD 510

Last of a series of nine prototypes bearing the designation S.91, the SPAD 510 was built to meet the requirements of the 1930 fighter programme, and became the last biplane fighter to serve with the French Air Force.

Heart of the design was the duralumin and steel centre-fuselage, the dimensions of which were based on the minimum space required to accommodate the pilot and armament without loss of comfort and efficiency. To this central structure were attached the engine mounting and fabric-covered metal wings, the upper of which was swept. The rear fuselage was a duralumin monocoque, constructed with Béchereau hollow moulds.

Power plant of the prototype, and the initial batch of production machines, was the 690-hp Hispano 12 Xbrs.

The prototype SPAD 510 (F-AKGW) made its first flight at Buc on 6 January 1933, piloted by Massotte. During early tests, the original two-bladed Ratier metal propeller was replaced by a wooden propeller of the type that was to equip the production aircraft, and the frontal radiator was modified. In this form, the prototype climbed to 3,000 m (9,840 ft) in 3 min 33 sec, and to 5,000 m (16,400 ft) in 5 min 30 sec. Maximum speed attainable in a dive was 373 mph.

In his flight report, the official test pilot had commented that the aircraft had been put *voluntarily* into a flat spin. The report as received by the Air Ministry omitted the word "voluntarily", with the result that the 510 was not accepted for first-line use until it had completed service tests with a squadron at Reims.

Under Plan I a total of 60 SPAD 510s were ordered, production beginning in 1936. The first 58 were powered by the 690-hp Hispano 12 Xbrs engine and armed with four machine-guns, two in the wing and two in the engine cowling. Nos. 59 and 60 had a *moteur canon* Hispano 12 Xcrs, armament then comprising one cannon and two wing-mounted machine-guns.

When the first production aircraft were received at Villacoublay, the Blériot-SPAD company was requested to improve the longitudinal stability. Herbemont solved the problem by increasing the length of the rear fuselage, and 510s began entering service with Squadrons II/7, I/3 and II/3 in July 1937.

Although they were pleasant machines to handle, landing was tricky due to a far from robust undercarriage. Furthermore, at steep angles of climb, the engine suffered from fuel starvation. As a result, the SPAD 510s were taken out of front-line service on 12 August 1937 and transferred to regional squadrons. Twenty-seven were sold to Spain.

In 1939, together with Nieuport-Delage 622s and 629s and Dewoitine 501s, a number of SPAD 510s were still in service with regional squadrons, including ER 591 based at Villacoublay. Even as late as May 1940, the type was still operational with GC III/4 and III/5 in North Africa and with ER 571 at Sidi-Ahmed in Tunisia.

Projected developments of the SPAD 510 were the 510J2, an "inverted sesquiplane" with a Gnome-Rhône 9 Kers engine; the 510J3 with a 14 Ksd engine; the 511 with a Lorraine 12 Hars engine; and the SPAD 610 with sesquiplane wings and twin floats.

Tellier T.3

In the early months of the 1914–18 War, the French Navy desperately needed more seaplanes, and a young engineer named Alphonse Tellier received the sum of 25,000 francs from the Défense Nationale to finance design of a suitable machine. The hull of his prototype was built by Voisin at Issy-les-Moulineaux and the complete aircraft, designated Tellier T.2, was ready for test by June 1916. It was destroyed during an early flight, but thanks to the generosity of Emile Dubonnet a second machine was produced in a few months, powered by a 200-hp Hispano engine.

After satisfactory tests of the second prototype in February 1917, Tellier received an initial order for ten production models, and these were built by Alcyon under the designation T.3. A total of 96 T.3s were built eventually, including 47 by Nieuport.

The T.3 was a two-seat biplane bomber, powered by a 200-hp Hispano 8 Ba engine. A machine-gun was mounted on the nose and two or four light bombs could be carried. At an all-up weight of 3,860 lb, the T.3 took off in 30 sec and climbed to 1,000 m (3,280 ft) in 6 min 30 sec, and to 2,000 m (6,560 ft) in 15 min 30 sec, at which height it had a speed of 81 mph.

Tellier was so impressed by early experiments in firing a cannon from an aircraft that he designed a variant of the T.3 armed with a cannon. This was designated T.C.6 and, armed with a 47-mm cannon, was supplied to the French Navy. A total of 110 were ordered, but only 55 were delivered.

The Tellier T.4, which followed in December 1918, introduced folding wings and was powered by a Sunbeam engine of 350 hp. Later came the T.5, a twin-engined machine with metal wings and a wooden hull.

Voisin III

Of the 24 French squadrons in existence at the beginning of the 1914–18 War, four were equipped with Voisin type L "pusher" biplanes. Powered by an engine of only 80 hp, these machines were used mainly for artillery observation; but thoughts soon turned to the possibility of using aircraft in an offensive rôle. The Voisins were the most suitable aircraft available for the job, although the Type L could carry no more than about 130 lb of small bombs, which were simply placed on the floor

Voisin III

TYPE	DIMENSIONS span ft	span in	length ft	length in	height ft	height in	WEIGHT max t-o lb	PERFORMANCE max speed mph	at height ft	service ceiling ft	combat range miles	REMARKS	
SPAD 81	31	6	21	0	9	1¾	2,821	143		26,200	310	HS 8 Fb	300 hp
SPAD 510	29	0	23	3¾	9	10¼	3,703	236		34,400	500	HS 12 Xbrs	690 hp
Tellier T.3	51	2	38	10	11	2	3,860	90	SL		435	HS 8 Ba	200 hp
Voisin LA/LAS - III	52	4½	31	6¾	12	6	3,020	69	SL	9,800	124	CU M9	120 hp

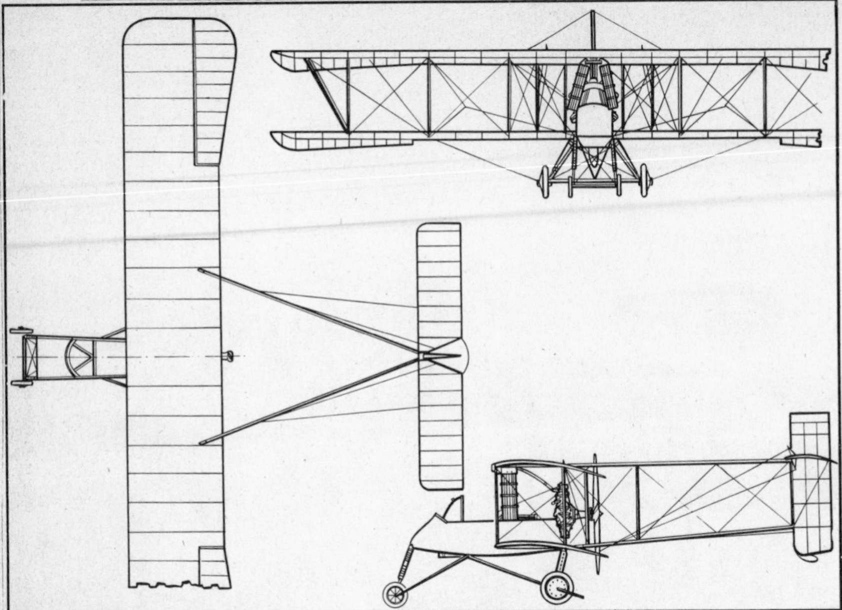
Voisin III LA

Voisin III, Italian Air Force

Voisin IV LBS

Voisin V

of the cockpit until the time came for the observer to drop them over the side of the aircraft!

Not until 1915 were bombing operations effectively organized and the first operational units brought into being. By May 1915, France had four groups, each of four squadrons, for bombing missions, and on 27 May eighteen Voisins, led by Commandant De Goys, bombed the factories of the Badische Anilinine Gesellschaft at Ludwigshaven. Night-bombing operations did not develop until the spring of 1917.

The succession of Voisin aircraft flown by the French Squadrons VB 101, 102 and 114, amongst others, were equipped as either fighters or bombers. They were all large biplanes, with pusher engines and a cruciform tail unit, linked to the wings by metal struts. Construction was a mixture of steel and wood, with fabric covering, and a four-wheel undercarriage was standard.

Like most French aircraft of the 1914–18 War, the Voisins were given two designations. That used by the constructor consisted normally of one or more letters; the other was bestowed by the War Ministry in order to avoid confusion between types that might have the same contractors' designation, and to standardize type references. Ministerial orders to this effect were issued on 20 April 1917, and were retrospective for all aircraft in service, however old. Few of the official designations were widely used, since service personnel preferred the company designations or well-deserved nicknames.

The prototype of the Voisin III – company designation LA – first flew in February 1914, and was powered by a 120-hp Canton-Unné water-cooled engine. It was immediately purchased by the Navy, who converted it into a seaplane by fitting three floats. Large-scale production of the standard landplane version began in April 1915, the series-built aircraft having an increased wing area.

There were two versions of the Voisin III: the LA and the LAS. The latter had the engine raised about 6 in (the letter S of the designation signifying *surélevé* = raised), and the interplane struts at the wing-tips were vertical and not inclined like those on the LA. There was also a type III D2 (LAS) two-seat, dual-control trainer without armament.

A total of 2,162 Voisin IIIs were produced in the Voisin, REP, Nieuport and Breguet factories, of which 800 went to French and Belgian units, 1,200 to Russia (where this aircraft was also produced under licence), 50 to the Royal Flying Corps and 112 to Italy.

The distinction of shooting down the first enemy aircraft of the war went to a Voisin III, number V.89, flown by Frantz and Quénault on 5 October 1914.

Voisin IV

This variant of the Voisin III differed in the shape of its fuselage, which was rectangular, and in having staggered wings. As in the case of the III, there were two versions: the LB bomber and the LBS fighter with raised engine and one 37-mm Hotchkiss cannon.

The first LB flew in March 1915, followed by the first LBS (V 503) at the end of the same year. There was also a Voisin IV D2, for dual-control training.

Of the 200 Voisin IVs which were built, two went to Great Britain for evaluation.

Voisin V

The Voisin V was a variant of the LAS bomber, powered by a 150-hp Canton-Unné engine. Other changes included a cut-out in the upper wing and strengthening of the undercarriage legs.

A total of 350 Voisin Vs were built, the last being numbered V 1480. They first appeared at the end of 1915, and were usually known as "150-hp Voisins"

Voisin VIII

The Voisin VII was restricted to reconnaissance duties as its engine was not sufficiently powerful to permit the carriage of a practical bomb load. It was the first of a new family of Voisins with long-span wings, and introduced streamlined fuel tanks mounted between the wings. The Voisin VIII was derived from the VII and appeared in two forms, designated LAP and LBP.

The first LBP (V 1655) appeared at the front in August 1916. It was a two-seat fighter, armed initially with a centrally mounted 47-mm Hotchkiss cannon, which was superseded by a 37-mm gun mounted on the right of the front cockpit.

The first LAP (V 1700) was produced in the early part of 1917, and was intended for night bombing missions, with a bomb load of 400 lb. Like the LBP, it was powered by a converted lorry engine, the 220-hp in-line Peugeot 8 Aa, which was best-known for its negative qualities! Maximum speed worked out at only 82 mph at sea level and 74 mph at 6,500 ft, to which height the aircraft could climb in 25 minutes.

A total of 1,123 Voisin VIIIs were built – all for the French Air Force, with the exception of 8 supplied to America in April 1918. In August of that year, 145 were still in service, with Squadrons 51 LAP and 33 LBP at the front, 10 LAP and 26 LBP in the Réserve Générale, and 20 LAP and 5 LBP at training centres.

The French Navy had 20 Voisin VIIIs, based at Dunkirk; but these were seldom used because of the unreliability of their engines and were finally destroyed on the ground in a German bombing raid.

The Voisin IX, of which a small batch was built for reconnaissance duties, was a lightened version of the VII.

Voisin X

The Voisin X (company designation LAR) was basically a Voisin VIII with a different power plant, the only change in the airframe consisting of a modified rudder. The engine chosen for it was the 300-hp Renault, driving a propeller of increased diameter. This gave the X a much better performance than that of the VIII, and 900 were built, the first machine being numbered V 2600.

The first Voisin Xs appeared at the front in January 1918, and were painted all black. They were armed with a 37-mm Hotchkiss cannon and could carry 660 lb of bombs.

Two were supplied to America in July 1918.

Voisin XI

Last of the Voisin "chicken-coops" was the XI (company designation E 94), which first appeared in July 1918. A total of 20 were built, of which 10 had a 350-hp Panhard 12-cylinder engine, and the others a Fiat engine of 280 hp. The Panhard-engined version had balanced ailerons which extended beyond the ends of the wings.

The Fiat engine had a habit of catching fire in flight and this led to a number of fatal accidents, as French aircrews of that time were not equipped with parachutes. Several crews were placed under arrest for refusing to fly this version before it was taken out of service.

Wibault 7 series

Michael Wibault produced his first fighter aircraft in 1917. It appeared at the same time as the Nieuport 29,

Voisin X

Voisin X

Voisin XI, 280-hp Fiat engine

TYPE	DIMENSIONS span ft	span in	length ft	length in	height ft	height in	WEIGHT max t-o lb	PERFORMANCE max speed mph	at height ft	service ceiling ft	combat range miles	REMARKS	
Voisin LB/LBS - IV	52	4½	33	8¾	12	6	3,064	74	SL	9,800	300	CU M9	120 hp
Voisin LAS V	52	4½	31	6¾	12	6	3,240	74		11,500	155	CU P9	150 hp
Voisin LBP VIII	58	9¾	35	11	12	11¾	4,100	82	SL	11,800	200	PE 8 Aa	220 hp
Voisin LAP VIII	58	9¾	33	11½	12	11¾	4,100	82	SL	11,800	200	PE 8 Aa	220 hp
Voisin LAR X	58	9¾	33	11½	12	11¾	4,850	84		11,800	310	RE 12 Fe	300 hp
Voisin E94 XI	59	3¾	33	7¼	12	11¾	4,519	78		11,800	218	PA 12 Cb	350 hp
Voisin XI	58	9¾	35	11	12	11¾		81		11,800	310	FI A 12bis	280 hp

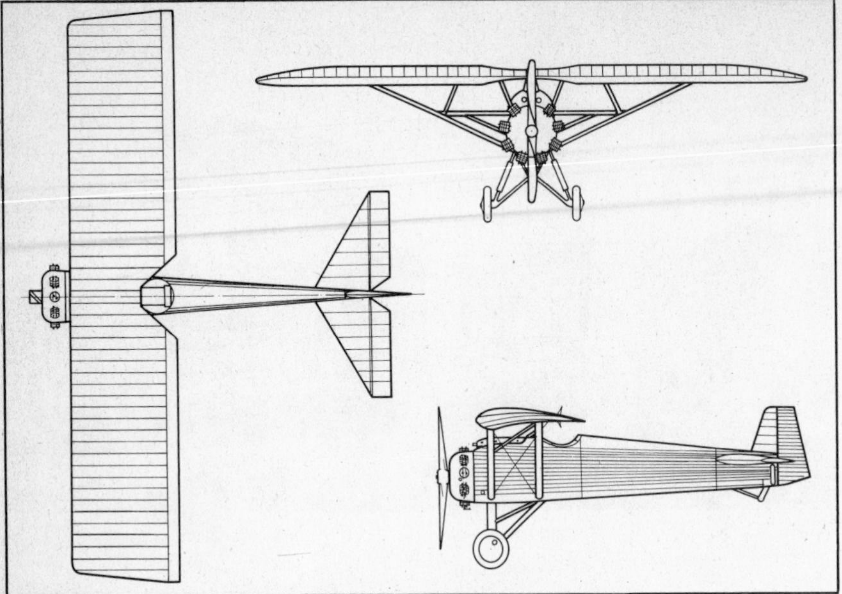
Wibault 7

Wibault 72

A.E.G. G.II

which was chosen for production, and remained a prototype only.

After the war, Wibault became more adventurous in his designs. In 1921 he abandoned the use of thin wooden wings in favour of metal structures of thicker section; and in 1923 he changed from biplane to monoplane configuration, producing the Wibault 3.C1. The engine powering this machine was fitted with a Rateau turbo-supercharger which enabled it to climb to a height of more than 10,000 m (32,800 ft).

The final stage of Wibault's work involved the substitution of metal for fabric covering. The resulting aircraft, known as the Wibault 7, was entered for the French fighter aircraft competition of 1925 and, as a result of its outstanding qualities – in particular its rate of climb – a small batch was ordered for evaluation.

The prototype Wibault 7, powered by a Gnome-Rhône Jupiter 9 Ae engine, had flown for the first time in 1924. It was followed by a second machine with a Jupiter 9 Ac, driving a Chauvière 2624 wooden propeller. At an all-up weight of 3,185 lb, this version climbed to 2,000 m (6,560 ft) in 5 min 14 sec, to 4,000 m (13,125 ft) in 10 min 56 sec, and to 8,000 m (25,250 ft) in 48 min at Villacoublay on 3 and 8 August 1925. Maximum speed at 13,000 ft was 145 mph.

A third prototype Wibault 7, named *Rafale*, was bought by Jullerot in 1927 and took part in a number of speed trials under the civil registration F-AIHX.

The production models entered service in 1926 with the 32nd Régiment d'Aviation at Dijon, who used them in the rôle of high-altitude fighters. They were followed later the same year by the Wibault 72, a strengthened and improved version with an oleo-pneumatic undercarriage and an armament of two Vickers machine-guns in the engine cowling and two Darne machine-guns in the wing. Sixty of this version were built.

On 15 December 1932, 45 Wibault 72s were still in squadron service at Dijon (Group I/7, 2nd Squadron; Group II/6, 3rd Squadron), and the Air Force still had 12 of these aircraft on 1 January 1936. This long service life was due largely to the very strong construction of the Wibault 72, which was demonstrated convincingly when two of these machines were involved in a mid-air collision. Despite severe damage to the wings of both aircraft, they made fairly normal landings.

A number of standard Wibault 7s or 72s were sold to Brazil and Bolivia. In addition, the following variants were produced:

Wibault 71. A prototype powered by a Hispano 12 Mb Vee engine.

Wibault 73. Second prototype 7, re-engined with a Lorraine 12 Eb W engine. This version was designed for Brazil and Paraguay. A licence to build it was acquired by Poland, and 50 were produced by P.Z.L.

Wibault 74 and 75. Naval versions, with arrester gear, used on the French aircraft carrier *Béarn* until 1934.

The Vickers company in Great Britain acquired manufacturing rights for the Wibault 7, and built 25 for Chile in 1925, under the designation Vickers 121.

Germany

A.E.G. G.IV

The G (for *Grossflugzeug*) series of bombers produced by the Allgemeine Elektrizitäts Gesellschaft of Henningsdorf during the 1914–18 War began early in 1915 with the G.1 (originally K.1), a twin-engined, three-seat general-purpose biplane powered by a pair of 100-hp Mercedes D.I engines. Built in only small numbers, it was followed during the summer of that year by the G.II, which was slightly larger, with additional power provided by Benz engines of 150 hp each. The G.II was also built in only small numbers, some having a single vertical tail surface and others a triple tail unit. The G.II could carry a bomb load of 440 lb.

In December 1915, limited production of the G.III began, this being still larger than the G.II and powered by 220-hp Mercedes D.IV geared eight-cylinder engines, driving four-blade opposite-rotating propellers. With a maximum weight of 6,633 lb, the G.III had a 660-lb bomb load and carried two machine-guns for defence.

The major production model in the A.E.G. series was the G.IV, which began to appear in combat in the latter part of 1916. Powered by two 260-hp Mercedes D.IVa six-cylinder, water-cooled inline engines, the G.IV had a fuselage of welded steel-tube construction, with mixed wood and fabric covering. Two Parabellum machine-guns – one each in the front and rear cockpits – were provided for defence, but the bomb load was still modest at 770 lb, and the G.IV's range did not compare with that of contemporary German bombers, so the type was employed primarily on short-range tactical missions or photographic reconnaissance.

A three-bay experimental version of the G.IV with a greater wing span, the G.IVb, was built, and another project tested was the G.IVk (*Kanone*), fitted with a 20-mm Becker cannon in the nose. As the war came to an end, the ultimate aircraft in this series, the G.V, was beginning to appear. Similarly powered to the G.IV, this had a biplane tail unit and a much-improved bomb load of 1,320 lb. Altogether 542 aircraft in the G series were built by A.E.G. during the 1914–18 War, of which the G.IV was by far the most important.

Albatros C.III

The Albatros series of powerful two-seat general-purpose biplanes began with the C.I in 1915. This was put into production by various constructors during the 1914–18 War, and was followed by the slightly improved C.Ia.

The next model – in a line destined to continue through to the end of hostilities – was to become the most widely produced of the entire Albatros C series. This was the C.III, which was more compact than the C.I, although basically similar except for a remodelled tail unit. This tended more towards the rounded "fishtail" look that was to become almost a trademark of Albatros machines during the later years of the war, and made the C.III much more responsive on the controls than its predecessors. The fuselage of the C.III was a square-sided, round-topped affair with plywood covering; the wings were of two-spar construction and fabric-covered, with a box-type radiator mounted on the centre leading-edge of the upper wing. The two-bay wings were of unequal span, and the landing gear comprised a conventional "Vee" main chassis with a wooden skid beneath the tail.

The sturdy construction of the C.III enabled it to absorb a considerable degree of combat punishment when it entered service during the winter of 1916–17. Early examples were armed with a single Parabellum gun only, on a Schneider ring mounting in the observer's cockpit; but, later, a fixed forward-firing Spandau was added on the starboard side of the upper decking for the pilot. Since the science of gun synchronization was comparatively undeveloped at this time, the propeller of the Albatros was prone to suffer from the effects of firing this latter gun.

A.E.G. G.III (nearer aircraft) and G.I

A.E.G. G.IV, captured aircraft, Allied markings

Albatros C.III

TYPE	DIMENSIONS						WEIGHT	PERFORMANCE				REMARKS	
	span		length		height		max t-o	max speed	at height	service ceiling	combat range		
	ft	in	ft	in	ft	in	lb	mph	ft	ft	miles		
Wibault 72	36	0¾	24	9¼	9	8¾	3,350	156		27,900	373	GR 9 Ac Jupiter	420 hp
Wibault 74/75	36	0¾	24	11¼	9	8¾	3,416	137		26,900	373	GR 9 Ady Jupiter	480 hp
A.E.G. G.I	52	6	28	4½			3,199	78	SL				
A.E.G. G.II	53	1⅞	29	10⅜			5,434	87	SL				
A.E.G. G.III	60	6	30	2¼			6,633	99	SL	13,100	435		
A.E.G. G.IV	60	2⅜	32	3¾	12	9⅝	8,003	103	SL	13,120	4-5 hr		
Albatros C.III	38	4¼	26	3	10	2	2,983	87½	SL	11,100	4 hr	Benz-engined model:	10 ft 0¾ in height

Albatros C.III

Albatros D.I., Mercedes D.III engine

Albatros D.II

Albatros D.III prototype

The C.IIIs were employed generally either on reconnaissance missions or, with a small (200-lb) bomb load, for artillery co-operation missions. The bombs were housed in a vertical drum-shaped container built into the fuselage between the two cockpits. As with most of the Albatros C series of aircraft, manufacture of the C.III was sub-contracted to a number of German manufacturing firms, including the Ostdeutsche Albatros Werke, Deutsche Flugzeugwerke AG, Hanseatische Flugzeugwerke, Link-Hofmann Werke, Luft-Verkehrs Gesellschaft, and the Siemens-Schuckert Werke. The prototype had been powered by a 150-hp Benz III engine, but the standard installation in the majority of production C.IIIs was the Mercedes D.III of 160 hp. Early production aircraft featured a "rhino horn" exhaust, although many other styles were seen on later machines.

With an eight-cylinder Mercedes D.IV engine, giving 220 hp, the C.III was further developed into the C.V. This aircraft was redesigned, with increased-span wings and a roomier fuselage. It proved to be heavier on the controls than its predecessors, and soon after the C.V's appearance in service the unreliability of its power plant caused manufacture of the Mercedes D.IV, and thereby that of the C.V, to be curtailed.

The C.IV had been a purely experimental model, as was the C.VI; and the C.VII was produced, with a 200-hp Benz engine, only as a stop-gap until the arrival of the C.X, which entered service in 1917 with a 260-hp Mercedes D.IVa engine.

Final aircraft in the Albatros C series was the C.XII of late 1917, a much improved model built around the Mercedes D.IVa and bearing a marked external resemblance to the single-seat scouts produced by the Albatros Werke.

Albatros D.I and D.II

Possessing a particularly good rate of climb, the Albatros D.I and D.II were flown in combat by many of the famous German aces of the 1914–18 War, including Boelcke, Richthofen and Prinz Friedrich Karl of Prussia. The D.I was introduced into service in the autumn of 1916, the D.II following it during the winter, and a total of 214 of the two types were in use at the peak of their career in January 1917. Pleasant to fly, the Albatroses were more than a match for the B.E.2cs, D.H.2s and French Nieuports against which they were operated.

The D.I was introduced as a replacement for the Fokker Monoplane and Halberstadt single-seaters. It was based on a racing biplane built by the Albatros Werke in 1914 and had the comparative novelty of a semi-monocoque fuselage construction, both the framework and the covering panels being of wood. This terminated in a characteristic Albatros "fishtail" tail unit, with a small underfin which supported the wooden tailskid. The main landing gear was a conventional Vee type steel-tube arrangement. The single-bay sesquiplane wings were of normal, wooden box-spar construction, and were fabric-covered. Either a 150-hp Benz Bz III or 160-hp Mercedes D.III engine could be fitted, neatly installed in a streamlined cowling, with the radiators set "ear" fashion on each side of the engine decking, and a bulbous propeller spinner. A pair of forward-firing Spandau guns were fitted.

By modifying the centre-section struts, in order to reduce the gap between the fuselage and the upper wing, the all-round visibility from the cockpit was substantially improved, and thus was born the D.II. All D.II's were powered by the Mercedes D.III, the radiator arrangement being cleaned up on the later production aircraft.

Production of the D.II was undertaken by LVG at Koeslin, as well as by the parent company, and a further 20 were built at Wiener-Neustadt for the Austro-Hungarian forces by the Oesterreichische Flugzeugfabrik AG. These aircraft were powered by 185-hp Austro-Daimler engines. Both the D.I and D.II continued in production after the end of the war, under the designations L. 15 and L. 17 respectively.

Albatros D.III

The D.III began to appear in German air force units during the early part of 1917. Some of the first to be delivered were assigned to Jagdstaffel 11, commanded by Germany's "Red Knight of the Air", Baron Manfred von Richthofen, and thereafter the numbers in squadron service increased steadily. Units in Macedonia and Palestine received the D.III, as well as squadrons in the West, and the type was built in Austria by Oeffag.

Dipl-Ing Robert Thelen, of the Albatros Werke, had begun to evolve the D.III as a potential successor to the D.I and D.II while the first two types were still in production. It combined experience gained from the earlier Albatros machines with some features of the French Nieuport scouts, captured examples of which had been examined by the Germans.

The D.III was powered by the Mercedes D.IIIa six-cylinder, water-cooled in-line engine – an uprated version of the D.III giving 170 hp by virtue of an increased compression ratio. The profile of the single-bay wings was somewhat revised from that of the D.II, having Vee struts and no forward stagger; construction was of the typical box-spar all-wood formula, fabric covered with a scalloped trailing-edge. The remainder of the D.III's airframe was composed of standard D.II components, although a few of the final production machines were built with the more rounded rudder of the later D.V fighter, which began to appear alongside them in the summer of 1917. Armament consisted of two fixed, synchronized Spandau guns.

At the peak of their service life, in November 1917, almost 450 Albatros D.IIIs were in operational use. During the beginning of their career they were particularly severe on the British B.E.2cs; but as time progressed they encountered stiffer opposition from the Sopwith Triplane and Camel, the S.E.5a and the SPAD VII. After the 1914–18 War, the D.III continued in production for a time under the designation L.20.

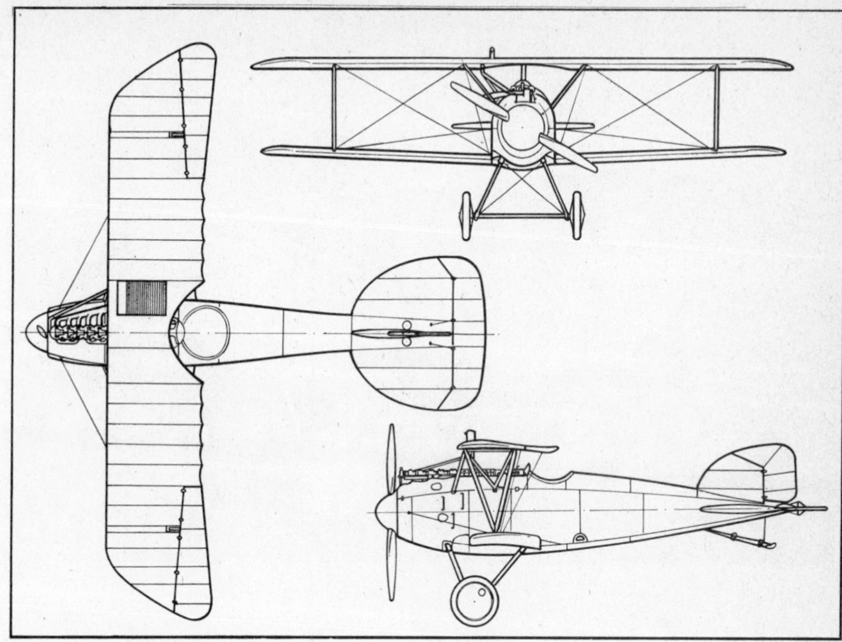

Albatros D.III

Albatros D.V, built by OAW

Albatros D.V and D.Va

The Albatros D.V and D.Va did not show a sufficient increase in performance over the earlier Albatros single-seat fighters to regain the superiority of the air which was gradually being wrested from them by the Allied air forces. Nevertheless, both versions were ordered in fairly substantial quantities, and remained in production by Albatros Werke at Johannisthal and by the Ostdeutsche Albatros Werke at Schneidermühl until the early part of 1918.

With an almost elliptical fuselage section, a larger propeller spinner, revised ailerons and a rudder of new design (except for the prototype), the D.V entered service during the summer months of 1917 and was joined, and then replaced, by the D.Va. At the peak of their career, in May 1918, over a thousand D.V/Vas were in front-line service, some on the Western front, others in Italy and Palestine. The gap between the fuselage and upper wing was reduced, compared with the D.III, in an attempt to improve pilot visibility, and both models were built with a headrest behind the

TYPE	DIMENSIONS						WEIGHT	PERFORMANCE				REMARKS
	span		length		height		max t-o	max speed	at height	service ceiling	combat range	
	ft	in	ft	in	ft	in	lb	mph	ft	ft	miles	
Albatros C.V	41	11¼	29	4⅜	14	9¼	2,387	106	SL	16,400	3¼ hr	
Albatros C.VII	41	11¼	28	6½	11	9¾	3,410	106	SL	16,400	3⅓ hr	
Albatros C.X	47	1½	30	0¼	11	1⅞	3,669	109	SL	16,400	3½ hr	
Albatros C. XII	47	1⅞	29	0⅜	10	7⅞	3,616	109	SL	16,400	3¼ hr	
Albatros D.I	27	10¾	24	3⅛	9	6⅜	1,976	109	SL	17,000	1½ hr	
Albatros D.II	27	10¾	24	3⅛	8	8	1,958	109	SL	17,000	1½ hr	
Albatros D.III	29	8¼	24	0⅝	9	9¼	1,953	109	3,280	18,000	2 hr	
Albatros D.V./D.Va	29	8¼	24	0⅝	9	4½	2,066	116	3,280	20,500	2 hr	

Albatros D.Va

Albatros W.4

Arado Ar 68E

cockpit, although this latter feature was often removed from machines on active service. Otherwise, the two models were quite similar, and had the same engine. However, a further increase in the compression ratio of the D.IIIa Mercedes provided 180 hp for the D.V.

The German authorities became too complacent about their earlier superiority in the air, with the result that when they began to encounter the more efficient Allied machines of the later war years, they had not done enough to ensure the development of fighters which would retain that superiority for them. The later Albatros machines certainly failed in this respect. The D.V and D.Va were reported as "elegant, but weakly constructed", and several were lost through structural failure in the air, especially during diving manoeuvres. The final indication of the decline of the Albatros fighter came in February 1918, when the factory was ordered to build the Fokker D.VII under licence. A few D.Vs were, however, built after the war's end, and these were designated L.24.

Albatros W.4

During the summer of 1916 the German Admiralty, anxious to curb the attacks upon its naval air stations along the Flanders coast, issued a specification for a single-seat "station defence seaplane" to patrol the North Sea coastline and ward off Allied air attacks. The shortest cut to producing such an aircraft was to adapt the design of an existing scout, and this course was followed by a number of German aircraft manufacturers.

The aircraft thus produced by the Albatros Werke was a development of the Albatros D.I and was designated W.4. Although based on the D.I's wooden-framed, semi-monocoque fuselage, the W.4 was altogether larger. The tail assembly was modified by removing the underfin of the D.I, compensating for this by increasing the area of the main fin and enlarging the tailplane. The rudder was horn-balanced and fabric-covered. The engine, a 160-hp Mercedes D.III in-line, driving a two-bladed propeller, was installed in a neatly streamlined cowling with a large spinner. The wings, made of wood and fabric, were of considerably greater span than those of the D.I, with a larger gap between the fuselage and upper wing than appeared on the landplane.

Twin-float landing gear was fitted to the W.4, floats of various patterns being tried out. Generally these were single-step units, of square section and very utilitarian in their design and appearance. Yet, despite the lack of any attempt to streamline this gear, the W.4 possessed a good edge in speed over most of the attacking Allied aircraft with which it came into contact, except for the later British flying-boats. Most of the W.4s in service – and 118 were delivered to the German Naval Air Service between September 1916 and December 1917 – were employed on patrol missions over the north-west coast of Europe, although some were also reported in action in the Aegean Sea area. They were eventually replaced by the two-seat Hansa-Brandenburg W.12.

Arado Ar 68

When Hitler formed the new German Luftwaffe in 1933, the two standard single-seat fighters chosen to equip his air force were the Heinkel He 51 and the Arado Ar 68. The latter was a single-bay biplane of tubular steel and wooden construction, having forward-staggered wings with "N" type interplane bracing struts, an open cockpit and a fixed, spatted main undercarriage.

Three prototypes were laid down, the Ar 68V1 appearing in 1933, powered by a single 660-hp BMW VI in-line engine. The second and third machines, bearing the civil registrations D-IVUS and D-IBAS respectively, differed in having the 610-hp Junkers Jumo 210B liquid-cooled engine installed, and this power plant was selected for the first major production version, the Ar 68E, which entered Luftwaffe squadron service in 1935. Normal armament of the Ar 68 consisted of two 7.9-mm MG 15 machine-guns, mounted in the upper engine decking and firing through the propeller disc. Attachments for six 112-lb bombs could be fitted beneath the lower wings.

Subsequent production centred mainly on the Ar 68F, which was powered by the 675-hp BMW VI motor, and the Ar 68G, in which the power of this engine was raised to 750 hp. A prototype only (D-ISIX) of the Ar 68H appeared, with a BMW 132 radial engine, enclosed cockpit and armament increased to four MG 15 guns. By the outbreak of World War II, the Ar 68 was left far behind in performance by later German fighters, and continued in use for a time only as a fighter trainer, except for a few pressed into temporary service on night defence.

A development of the Ar 68 which appeared in 1937 was the Ar 197, modified for shipboard employment on the aircraft carrier *Graf Zeppelin.* Three prototypes were completed, the Ar 197V1 (D-ITSE) with a Jumo 210C powerplant and the V2 (D-IVLE) and V3 with the 815-hp BMW 132J. Although performance was well up to expectations during the ensuing trials at Travemünde, no production order was placed and further development of this model was abandoned.

Arado Ar 196

The origins of the Ar 196 twin-float reconnaissance-bomber can be traced back to the Ar 95 biplane which was first flown (prototype D-OLUO) in 1936. Design of the Ar 95 had begun in the preceding year as a general-purpose torpedo-bomber-reconnaissance type capable of operating with either a land or a float undercarriage. Six Ar 95s were assigned to the Condor Legion in Spain for evaluation in the late summer of 1938; and export models were produced for Chile in 1939 (Ar 95L land-planes) and Turkey (Ar 95W floatplanes). Some of the Turkish machines were held back for training duties with the Luftwaffe when war broke out, but the German air force did not order the type.

Arado Flugzeugwerke had begun work on a progressive development of the Ar 95 in 1937, with a new monoplane low wing. Of welded steel-tube fuselage construction, with the tandem cockpit placed further forward, the new machine, designated Ar 196, bore an obvious family likeness to its predecessor and was developed as a potential replacement for the ageing He 60 seaplane. Four prototypes were flown in 1938, of which the Ar 196V1 (D-IEHK) and V2 (D-IHQI) were both fitted with twin floats, the second machine having a slightly larger fin and rudder than the first. From these was derived the first production model, the Ar 196A-1, of which manufacture began at Warnemünde towards the end of 1938. Twenty-six of this model were built before being supplanted in late 1940 by the A-3 series, which ran to 198 machines. Later Ar 196A sub-types were built in numbers by the French SNCA factories and by Fokker in Holland, total production of all A-series models amounting to 493.

Standard armament for the A-1, which began to replace the He 60s in service from August 1939, comprised two 7.9-mm MG 17 machine-guns, one in the rear cockpit and one in the starboard side of the forward fuselage, while two 110-lb bombs could be slung on underwing racks. The Ar 196A-3 had twin MG 17s in the rear cockpit and a 20-mm MG FF cannon mounted in each leading-edge.

The Ar 196A made its first operational appearance in the *Graf Spee* action off Montevideo harbour in December 1939, and the type was supplied to such major warships as the *Bismarck, Scharnhorst, Gneisenau, Prinz Eugen, Admiral Scheer* and *Lützow.* It was used widely over practically every sea area of the European theatre of operations, including the Bay of Biscay, English Channel, Baltic, Mediterranean and Adriatic.

The Ar 196V3 (D-ILRE) and V4 (D-OVMB) differed

Arado Ar 196A-3

Arado Ar 196A-3

Arado Ar 196A-3

TYPE	DIMENSIONS span ft	span in	length ft	length in	height ft	height in	WEIGHT max t-o lb	PERFORMANCE max speed mph	at height ft	service ceiling ft	combat range miles	REMARKS
Albatros W.4	31	2	27	10¾	11	11¾	2,359	100	3,280	9,840	3 hr	
Ar 68G	36	0	31	2	10	10	4,400	192	13,120	24,278	341	
Ar 196A-3	40	10½	36	1	14	5	8,200	193	13,120	23,000	670	

Arado Ar 234V10 Blitz, second prototype for the B series

Arado Ar 234B-1/b Blitz

Arado Ar 234V13 Blitz, prototype for the four-engined C series

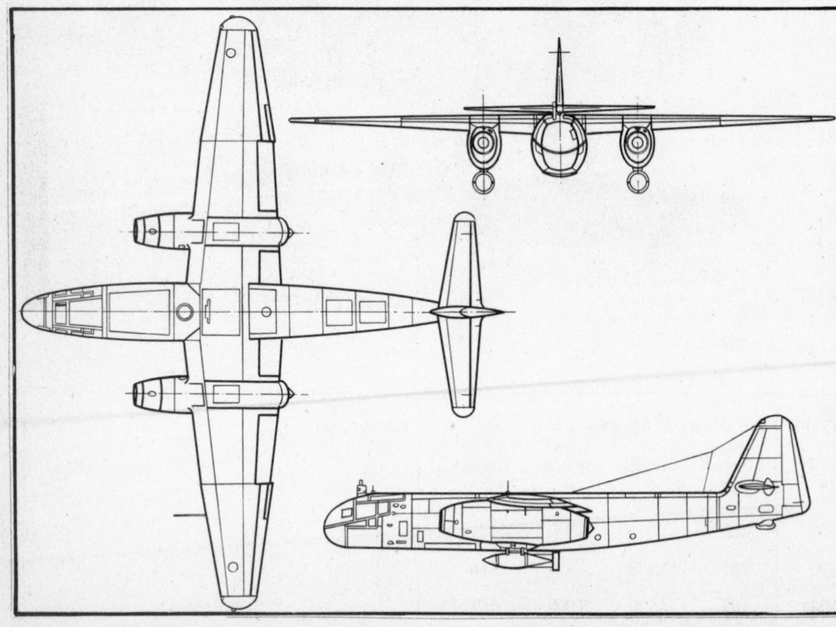
Arado Ar 234B Blitz

from the first two prototypes in having a single large central float and small outboard stabilizing floats, and were intended to pave the way for an Ar 196B production series which was, in the event, abandoned. The V4 was the first Ar 196 to have guns fitted. Power unit for the prototypes was the 880-hp BMW 132Dc nine-cylinder air-cooled radial, but this was replaced in production aircraft by the 970-hp BMW 132K.

Arado Ar 234 Blitz (Lightning)

Like many other early designs for jet-propelled aircraft, the Arado Ar 234 Blitz was a handsome machine with extremely clean lines. It was the subject of extensive development throughout almost the whole of World War II, more than 30 *Versuchs* (experimental) machines being completed, some with two and some with four engines. But although it can claim the distinction of being the world's first operational jet bomber, comparatively few examples acquired actual combat status.

The Blitz was a shoulder-wing monoplane of metal construction, with an extensively glazed cabin in the extreme forward fuselage. Design work began at the end of 1940, and construction of the first prototypes was started early in the following year. Development delays with the intended power plant, the 1,850-lb s t Junkers Jumo 004A, deferred the first flight of the Ar 234V1 until 15 June 1943, by which time eight prototypes were ready to receive their power installations. The Ar 234V3 was equipped with a pressurized cabin, ejection seat and rocket-assisted take-off gear; and in the Ar 234V5 the BMW 003A of 1,980 lb s t was installed as an alternative power plant. It was intended originally that the first production series, the Ar 234A, should use a jettisonable wheeled trolley when taking off, and utilize skids beneath the centre fuselage and engine nacelles for landing. In the event, trials with this gear on the prototypes proved troublesome and the A series was abandoned.

Prototype for the Ar 234B series, which was the first to go into production, was the Ar 234V9. This had two 1,980-lb s t Junkers Jumo 004B axial-flow turbojet engines and a conventional retractable tricycle undercarriage, housed entirely in the fuselage. It was flown in March 1944 and was followed closely by a small pre-production batch of Ar 234B-0s built at Alt Loennewitz. The B-0 was an unarmed photo-reconnaissance model of which deliveries began in June 1944. The first full production contract was awarded to the generally similar Ar 234B-1. Only a few of these were completed, becoming operational in autumn 1944, before giving way to the Ar 234B-2 bomber and dive-bomber, which entered service with Kampfgeschwader 76 at the end of the same year. Armament of this model comprised two 20-mm MG 151 cannon in the lower rear fuselage and a 3,300-lb bomb capacity.

The Blitz was one of a small number of selected types awarded a high production priority by the RLM at this time; but due to accidents in training, by pilots unaccustomed to the different techniques required in handling jet aircraft, and other causes, only a small percentage of the 210 Ar 234B series became operational.

The Ar 234C-3, the next production model, was a multi-purpose machine powered by BMW 003A-1 turbojets. In addition to the standard pair of rearward-firing MG 151s, this aircraft could carry a twin 20-mm ventral gun pack for the night fighter rôle, a battery of anti-personnel bombs for ground attack, or larger bombs for dive-bombing missions. However, only 19 C-3s were completed, and none became operational during World War II. When the war in Europe ended, further C variants were being developed and 10 more prototypes for the proposed Ar 234D series were under construction. The Blitz was an excellent aircraft, with a fine performance; but it arrived too late to make any difference to the final outcome of the war.

Arado Ar 240

Arado Flugzeugwerke was only one of the companies which endeavoured to produce a *Zerstörer* (destroyer) aircraft for the German Luftwaffe at the end of the 1930s. The Arado Ar 240, like one of its competitors, the Me

210, got off to a rather bad start, from which, unlike the Messerschmitt design, it did not recover until the war in Europe was nearly over. During the six years of its development, numerous prototypes and small evaluation batches were completed, with considerable engine and armament permutations, and only these experimental models became truly operational.

Design of the Ar 240 was begun in 1939 and the Ar 240V1 flew in June 1940 powered by two 1,175-hp DB601A engines. This machine, although itself unarmed, was a prototype for the two-seat heavy fighter version of the design, as were the next two prototypes, which differed principally in their gun and bomb installations. Tests with the first two machines revealed serious tendencies towards instability and generally bad landing characteristics, with the result that the V3 incorporated extensive design changes to the forward fuselage and tail cone. Remotely controlled dorsal and ventral barbettes, housing twin MG 81 machine-guns, appeared for the first time on the Ar 240V4, which also introduced 1,750-hp DB603A motors. This fourth aircraft, with provision for four 550-lb or 1,100-lb bombs, was a prototype for a dive-bomber variant.

First pre-production version was a reconnaissance model, the Ar 240A-0, with 1,440-hp BMW 801J radial engines and six machine-guns – four MG 81s and two MG 17s. Two unarmed variants of this model were designated Ar 240A-0/U1 and Ar 240A-0/U2. The second pre-production series was broadly similar, except for a further engine change, this time to 1,475-hp DB605As.

When the European war came to an end, evaluation of the Arado Ar 240C sub-series was under way, embracing the C-1 heavy fighter (four MG 151 cannon), the C-2 night fighter (six MG 151), the C-3 light bomber (two MG 151 and a 4,000-lb bomb load) and the C-4 reconnaissance model, all powered by 1,900-hp DB603Gs. Other projects included the Ar 240D (engine change), Ar 240E high-altitude bomber (DB603Gs, greater span and bomb load), and Ar 240F, a heavy fighter derivative of the E.

Four prototypes of the Ar 440, a potential successor to the Ar 240, were also tested, but no production orders had been placed before VE-day.

Aviatik C.I/C.III

Upon the outbreak of the 1914–18 War, the Automobil und Aviatik AG transferred its works from Mühlhausen, in Alsace, to a less vulnerable site at Freiburg-im-Breisgau, where it became responsible initially for the design and production of the B series of two-seat unarmed reconnaissance aircraft for the Kaiser's air force. The B.I was powered by a 100-hp Mercedes and the B.II by a 120-hp engine of similar manufacture.

The Aviatik C.I, which appeared for the first time in 1915, followed a broadly similar design pattern to its forebears, being an unequal-span two-bay biplane with a box-girder fuselage, covered with aluminium panels on the forward section and fabric at the rear. The wing framework was wooden, with fabric covering. The fixed undercarriage was of conventional Vee type and the aircraft was powered by a single Mercedes D.III six-cylinder water-cooled in-line engine of 160 hp.

The pilot sat in the rear cockpit, with an observer in the front seat, ahead of which a single Parabellum machine-gun could be mounted on a rail on either the port or starboard side of the upper engine decking. This arrangement of crew seating was contrary to the current trend in two-seat aircraft of the period, considerably restricting both the observer's field of view for re-

Arado Ar 240V3

Arado Ar 240V3

Aviatik C.I, early model with side radiators

TYPE	DIMENSIONS						WEIGHT	PERFORMANCE				REMARKS
	span		length		height		max t-o	max speed	at height	service ceiling	combat range	
	ft	in	ft	in	ft	in	lb	mph	ft	ft	miles	
Ar 234B-2	46	3⅜	41	5½	14	1¼	20,613	461	19,685	37,730	967	
Ar 240C-0	54	5½	43	9½	12	11½	23,258	419	19,680	34,450	1,162	
Aviatik C.I	41	0¼	26	0	9	8⅛	2,732	89	SL	11,480	3 hr	

Aviatik C.III

Blohm und Voss Bv 138C-1

Blohm und Voss Bv 138

Blohm und Voss Bv 138MS

connaissance missions and his field of fire when in combat; consequently, on later production aircraft, designated C.Ia, the crew positions were transposed and a Schneider ring mounting was provided for the gun in the rear cockpit. The C.I/C.Ia was put into quantity production by both the parent firm and the Hannoversche Waggonfabrik during 1915.

With only minor modifications, apart from the adoption of a 200-hp Benz engine, the C.II made a brief appearance in small numbers during 1915; but the next major production model was the C.III of 1916.

The object of the C.III was to achieve an increase in performance over the C.I which would keep the Aviatik aircraft abreast of contemporary machines coming into service; but, in fact, it was only a slightly more "polished" version of the C.I, retaining the same 160-hp power plant. The engine cowling was more streamlined. So, when fitted with a propeller spinner and revised exhaust manifolds, the forward section of the fuselage was considerably cleaner. The view forward from the cockpit was improved, and the C.III's performance was enhanced to the extent of an additional 11 mph or so on maximum speed. The C.III had a somewhat greater loaded weight than the C.I, partly as a result of the addition of a second Parabellum gun. Like its predecessors, the C.III originally had the back-to-front crew arrangement, which was revised on later aircraft. Machines of this type formed part of the initial equipment of the first *Kampfgeschwader* (bombing groups), as well as being employed on reconnaissance and escort duties.

Blohm und Voss Bv 138

The Bv 138 long-range patrol flying-boat first made its appearance in 1935 as the Ha 138, this designation indicating that it was a product of the Hamburger Flugzeugbau, the aircraft division of the famous Blohm und Voss shipbuilding concern. Three prototypes were ordered and the Ha 138V1 (registered D-ARAK) made its first flight on 15 July 1937, powered by three 600-hp Junkers Jumo 205C engines. The similarly-powered Ha 138V2 (D-AMOR), incorporating revisions to the hull design, followed on 6 November of the same year. By the time the third machine (D-ADJE) was ready for flight in 1938, the "Ha" designations had been dropped from Blohm und Voss aircraft, and it was known as the Bv 138A-01. First of half-a-dozen pre-production machines, it incorporated extensive changes from the original design. In particular, the hull was much larger, the tail booms were re-designed, and the original gull-type wing centre-section was replaced by a horizontal section.

In this form, a batch of 25 Bv 138A-1s entered production late in 1939. Each carried a crew of five and was armed with three 7·9-mm MG 15 machine-guns, in the nose, lower rear of the hull and dorsal positions. An offensive load of four 330-lb depth charges or six 110-lb bombs was permissible, but the full load was rarely carried; indeed, the first two Bv 138A-1s off the production line were assigned to a Luftwaffe unit in Norway as 10-passenger transports, and the A-1 was not considered to be a particularly successful model. First operational use of the "Flying Shoe", as it was nicknamed, came in France in October 1940, and thereafter the Bv 138 in its successive models was employed extensively by the German Navy on convoy patrol in Russian Arctic waters, from bases in Norway, and in collaboration with U-boat packs on anti-shipping raids over the North Atlantic and Mediterranean.

Second production model was the Bv 138B-1, which began to replace the unsatisfactory A-1s in the last months of 1940. The open gun position in the nose was replaced by a turret-mounted MG 151 20-mm cannon, and a similar gun also replaced the MG 15 in the tail position. The 21 B-1s built were each powered by three 880-hp Junkers Jumo 205D 12-cylinder diesel engines, as was the Bv 138C-1, the chief production version, which appeared in the spring of 1941. During the ensuing two years, 227 Bv 138C-1s were completed, differing from the B-1s principally in the adoption of a 13-mm MG 131 gun for the upper turret and in the employment of more efficient propellers for the Jumo engines.

The Bv 138 eventually proved rugged and adaptable, despite some early vicissitudes and production delays, and was capable of withstanding considerable punishment. A few Bv 138B-0s were converted to Bv 138MS for minesweeping duties, and a considerable number were adapted for catapult launching.

Dornier Do C, D and T

The above designations covered but three members of a sizeable family of civil/military aircraft produced in the late 1920s, about which much of the surviving information is so conflicting as to be highly suspect. Development began in 1920 with the Dornier C.III, a high-wing transport with a crew of two and seating for six passengers. The C.III was powered by a 185-hp BMW IIIa engine and was known in commercial service as the Komet I. Somewhat larger numbers were built of the Komet II, an improved model with a 250-hp BMW IV engine, revised cockpit arrangement and other detail refinements. On 7 December 1924 came the first flight of the Komet III (alias Do.B), which had a 360-hp Rolls-Royce engine. A similarly-powered parasol-wing development, the Do C, was produced as a training aircraft. A twin-float counterpart to the C was the Do D, a variant of which was built in 1927 as a torpedo-bomber with a 600-hp BMW VI.

Meanwhile, in 1925, two other versions of the Komet III had appeared – an ambulance version known as the Do T and a passenger version with a 460-hp BMW VI which received the name Merkur. The Merkur served, *inter alia*, with Deutsche Luft Hansa and the Russo-German airline Deruluft, and Komets II and III with the Ukrainian operator Ukrvozduchput; and a small quantity of Do Cs were in service around 1930 as light bombers with the newly-formed Fuerza Aérea de Chile. As regards production details of the various models, there are as many accounts as there are "authorities" on the subject. However, the civil Komet/Merkur series, and probably the Do T ambulance, were presumably "legitimate" enough to have been built in Germany; while the suggestion that the para-military variants were built at Dornier-Altenrhein in Switzerland seems as likely as most.

Dornier Do 11, Do 13 and Do 23

Although, until the emergence of the Do 17 in the middle 1930s, the Dornier company had been concerned primarily with the evolution of waterborne aircraft, one design – and its derivatives – did serve with the first medium bomber squadrons of the infant Luftwaffe. This type had its origins in the Do F, built at Dornier's Altenrhein factory in Switzerland in the latter part of the 1920s. Ostensibly a mail and freight transport, the Do F was impressed by the Luftwaffe, upon its formation in 1933, as a makeshift bomber. An early "luxury" was a retractable undercarriage, abandoned on later models.

It was not long before a specifically military development appeared in the form of the Do 11, the prototype of which had a slightly reduced wing span and was flown for the first time on 7 May 1932.

The Do 11 was a twin-engined, high-wing monoplane

Dornier Do D

Dornier Do 11

Dornier Do 13A

TYPE	DIMENSIONS span ft	span in	length ft	length in	height ft	height in	WEIGHT max t-o lb	PERFORMANCE max speed mph	at height ft	service ceiling ft	combat range miles	REMARKS
Aviatik C.III	38	5⅝	26	6⅛	9	8⅛	2,948	100	SL	14,760	3 hr	
Bv 138B-1	88	7	65	3½	21	7⅞	31,724	180		13,780	2,410 max	
Bv 138C-1	88	7	65	3½	21	7⅞	31,967	177		16,400	2,670 max	
Do C	64	3½	40	9⅓	11	4¼	8,598	121		22,965	870 max	
Merkur L	64	3½	41	0			7,936	124		17,060		
Do 11	91	10⅓	61	1⅞	17	8½	18,111	161	7,220	13,120	596	

Dornier Do 13C

Dornier Do 23

Dornier Do 17V1

Dornier Do 17K, export model

Dornier Do 17E-1

with a rectangular-section, all-metal fuselage having a glazed observation section in the nose. The crew consisted of a pilot, wireless operator and two gunners, the latter sharing between them three single 7·9-mm MG 15 machine-guns – one each in dorsal and ventral positions and the third on a ring mounting in the extreme nose. Maximum bomb capacity was 2,200 lb. Two-blade wooden propellers were driven by the 650-hp Siemens Jupiter nine-cylinder air-cooled engines.

The Do 11 was further developed into the Do 13, modifications including the abolition of the nose glazing, armament installations and small auxiliary horizontal stabilizers fitted underneath the tailplane of the earlier machine. Initially, the Do 13 used the same powerplant as the Do 11, but alterations to the wing trailing-edge lifting surfaces gave it improved landing characteristics. Later, with the Jupiter engines replaced by a pair of 750-hp twelve-cylinder liquid-cooled BMW VIUs driving four-blade propellers, and with the guns, bombing equipment and auxiliary stabilizers restored, the type was redesignated Do 13C, and was ordered into series production for the Luftwaffe by the RLM as the Dornier Do 23.

Production of the Do 23 ended in 1935, after more than 100 of these bombers had been completed, to make way for the Dornier Do 17.

The Do 23 was obsolete by the outbreak of World War II, but a small number continued in service during the early war years, equipped with a large de-gaussing ring for clearing British mines from areas around the north German coastline.

Dornier Do 17 and Do 215

One of the star performers entered for the International Military Aircraft Competition held at Zurich in July 1937 was the French Dewoitine D.510, then considered to be the best single-seat fighter being produced anywhere in Europe. The reaction can, therefore, be imagined when this agile little machine was outstripped in performance by a twin-engined medium *bomber* produced by the Dornier Werke GmbH of Friedrichshafen.

It was established subsequently that the machine which exhibited this remarkable performance was not a standard production model, but a specially-stripped prototype with boosted engines; nevertheless, the standard models of this bomber, the Dornier Do 17, were outstanding for their time and were destined for a long and valuable career with Luftwaffe units both before and during World War II.

The exceptionally clean and slender lines of the Do 17V1 prototype, which made its maiden flight in the autumn of 1934, rapidly earned it the nicknames of "Eversharp" and "Flying Pencil". Powered by a pair of 660-hp BMW VI twelve-cylinder liquid-cooled engines, the type was originally evolved as a six-passenger, high-speed mailplane for Deutsche Luft Hansa's European route network. Three prototypes were completed for Deutsche Luft Hansa, all with a single fin and rudder assembly; but their extreme slimness was to prove their undoing as commercial transports, as the narrow fuselage called for undue agility on the part of a passenger before he could reach his seat in the cabin. For a while the design languished, until the Reichsluftfahrtministerium, seeking a new medium bomber for the Luftwaffe, decided to evaluate the Do 17 as a possible contender for the job. Further prototypes were ordered by the RLM, the first of which, the Do 17V4, set the future design pattern by appearing with twin fins. Otherwise it was generally similar to the original machines, apart from a decrease of approximately two feet in overall length. The fuselage was of all-metal construction, and the two-spar shoulder wings were of metal, with metal and fabric covering. A rearward-retracting main undercarriage and retractable tailwheel were fitted, and a crew of three was carried. Except for 770-hp Hispano-Suiza 12Y engines in the fifth machine, the second trio of prototypes were all generally similar, and on the seventh airframe a defensive armament was installed for the first time.

Towards the end of 1936 the first production line

for the Do 17 was laid down. This was for the Do 17E-1, powered by two 750-hp BMW VI radial engines, which carried up to 1,760 lb of bombs and was defended by two or three 7·9-mm MG 15 machine-guns. (Later on, during World War II, this armament was increased to five machine-guns.) The Do 17F-1 was placed in production at the same time as a photo-reconnaissance counterpart to the E-series. Both models were in service with Luftwaffe squadrons by the summer of 1937, and during the following year they were included among the types selected to equip the Condor Legion squadrons participating in the Spanish Civil War.

Meanwhile, the performance of the Do 17V8 at Zurich had caused considerable foreign interest, the outcome of which was an order for the type by the Yugoslav government. This export model was designated Do 17K, and at the request of the Yugoslav authorities was powered by 986-hp Gnome-Rhône 14N fourteen-cylinder radial engines, conferring upon it an improved range and maximum speed. Bomb-load was 2,200 lb, and defensive armament was increased to four machine-guns and one 20-mm cannon. Do 17Ks were supplied from Germany and were also built under license by the Yugoslav State Aircraft Factory; at the time Germany invaded Yugoslavia in April 1941 about 70 were still in service. Those which survived the campaign were allocated by Germany to the Croatian air force after the occupation of Yugoslavia.

By the end of the 1930s, contemporary fighter performance had overhauled that of the early Do 17s, and an attempt was made to counteract this by fitting supercharged engines. Installation of the 900-hp Bramo 323A led, via the Do 17L (which did not go into production) to the Do 17M series, which otherwise were largely similar to the Do 17E-1. To replace the Do 17F-1, the Do 17P was developed in parallel for photo-reconnaissance duties, with 865-hp BMW 132N nine-cylinder radial engines.

Next to be evolved were two experimental series, the Do 17R and Do 17S. The former were powered by Daimler-Benz engines; the latter series was evolved primarily to improve the armament installation over that of earlier models. Between them, these two versions led first to the Do 17U, a five-seat pathfinder model with DB 600A engines, which was produced in only small numbers, and subsequently to the Do 17Z. The latter, with Bramo 323A or 1,000-hp Bramo 323Ps and a crew of four or five, embodied a more bulbous and angular forward section, with extensive glazing, first seen on the Do 17S. The Z-1 and Z-2 were bombers, the Z-3 a reconnaissance version and the Z-4 a dual-control trainer, while the Z-5 was equipped for rescue missions; over 500 of the Z series were built.

Two Do 17Z-0s, for some reason given fresh designations as the Do 215V1 and V2, were produced as demonstration models in the hope of attracting further foreign orders for the bomber. The Do 215V1 had Bramo engines, while the V2 had Gnome-Rhône 14N radials; but orders for the Do 215A-1 received from Sweden and Yugoslavia in mid-1939 specified the DB 601A inverted Vee engine as power plant. Before these aircraft could be delivered, they were taken over by the Luftwaffe, with slight modifications, for its own use. They were followed into production by the generally similar Do 215B-1 reconnaissance-bomber. Subsequent models were the B-3, two of which were supplied to Russia in 1939/40, the B-4 (similar to the B-1 except in the type of cameras

Dornier Do 17MV1, prototype with DB 600A engines

Dornier Do 17Z-1

Dornier Do 215B-1

TYPE	DIMENSIONS span ft	span in	length ft	length in	height ft	height in	WEIGHT max t-o lb	PERFORMANCE max speed mph	at height ft	service ceiling ft	combat range miles	REMARKS
Do 23	83	11⅞	61	8⅛	17	8½	20,282	161	3,940	13,780	839	
Do 17E-1	59	0⅔	53	3¾	15	1	15,520	220	13,120	18,050	990	
Do 17Z-2	59	0⅔	51	10	15	1	19,481	263	16,400	26,740	745	
Do 215A-1	59	0⅔	51	10	15	1	19,599	292	16,400	31,170	965	

Dornier Do 217V4, third Jumo-powered prototype

Dornier Do 217E

Dornier Do 217J-2

Dornier Do 217K-2

Dornier Do 217N-2, radar aerials removed

installed), and the B-5. This last, which served with Nachtjagdgeschwader 2 during 1940, was a night fighter/intruder conversion of the earlier B series bombers, with a "solid" fuselage nose housing a 20-mm MG FF cannon and four 7·9-mm MG 17 machine-guns. Total production of the Do 215B series amounted to just over 100 machines before giving way to the "Flying Pencil's" final development, the Dornier Do 217.

Dornier Do 217

Continuing the pattern of development set by its predecessors, the Dornier Do 17 and Do 215, the Do 217 proved itself a versatile and valuable bomber in Luftwaffe service for most of World War II. It, too, appeared with both in-line and radial engines, remaining in production until the end of 1943 and in operational service right up to the end of hostilities in Europe.

The Do 217V1 prototype, which was flown for the first time in August 1938, was very similar to the Do 215B, although the design had been further developed in order to accommodate a greater variety of offensive loads for a wider range of missions. These ranged from normal bombing operations to dive bombing, torpedo bombing, minelaying, reconnaissance and anti-shipping strikes.

A substantial number of prototype aircraft were completed: the first retained the power plant of the Do 215B, the second and third machines changing to Junkers Jumo 211A 12-cylinder inverted Vee engines of 950 hp; the seventh had a radial power plant (1,550-hp BMW 139s), as did the eighth and ninth (1,600-hp BMW 801As). All the first six prototypes, and some early production Do 217E-2s, featured a novel four-part air-brake, opening umbrella-fashion when in operation and forming an elongated tail-cone when retracted. This proved troublesome to operate, however, and was discarded on later models.

After a small evaluation batch of Do 217A-0s had been placed in service during 1940, the first major production series, the Do 217E, got under way in the following year. With a crew of four, the Do 217E-1 was powered by two 18-cylinder BMW 801A two-row air-cooled radial engines and was armed with one 15-mm MG 151 and one 7·9-mm MG 15 in the nose, two MG 15s in the dorsal turret and a further two firing laterally from the rear windows of the crew cabin. An internal bomb-load of 5,550 lb, plus two externally-slung 550-lb bombs, could be carried by the E-1. Various permutations of bomb-load and defensive armament were used in the otherwise similar Do 217E-2 and E-3. The E-4 was powered by BMW 801C radials, and the E-5 was a specially-developed version with additional radio equipment for launching and guiding the Henschel Hs 293 glider bomb, one of which could be suspended under each outer wing.

During 1942, in an attempt to combat the serious shortage of specialist night fighters, 157 examples of the E-2 series were converted for this kind of operation. They became the Do 217J series, with four 20-mm MG FF cannon and four MG 17s in a "solid" nose and a ventrally-mounted MG 131 of 13-mm calibre. With a variety of small bombs in an E-2 bomb-bay, the type became the J-1 intruder; while the J-2 night fighter had Lichtenstein airborne interception radar and no bomb-bay. A number of J series aircraft were supplied to the Italian Air Force in 1943.

With an even deeper and more bulbous glazed nose than the original E series, the next bomber/anti-shipping variant to be developed was the Do 217K. Again radial-powered, with the 1,700-hp BMW 801D, this series operated with various combinations of armament and offensive weapons. The K-2 and K-3 both featured a much-extended wing of 81 ft $4\frac{1}{3}$ in span, under which could be carried armour-piercing bombs or (K-3 only) Hs 293 glider bombs for attacking shipping.

A further change of power plant – to the 1,750-hp DB 603A in-line – produced the Do 217M series, of which the M-11 also had the capacity for carrying Hs 293s or armour-piercing weapons. A number of M series bombers were converted in 1943 to Do 217Ns to replace the earlier J series night fighters, and were equipped with Lichtenstein radar installations.

The final version of this aircraft to be built was the Do 217P, a high-altitude reconnaissance bomber with an 80 ft 4½ in wing span and DB 603A engines. Only six were completed – three prototypes and three production Do 217P-1s – but all save the first machine were put into operational service.

Total production of the Do 217 amounted to 1,730 aircraft, of which all but 364 were built as bombers. Projects included the Do 217W (sometimes known as the Do 216), a twin-float torpedo-bomber version which was never completed, and the extensively developed Do 317, which reached the prototype stage only.

Dornier Do 18

The Dornier Do 18 first appeared in 1934 as a transatlantic mail-carrying flying-boat, developed from the earlier Wal, for the German airline Deutsche Luft Hansa. Five Do 18Es were delivered to DLH, all basically similar and each powered by two 540-hp Junkers Jumo 205 diesel engines. The first three of these, all bearing *Versuchs* numbers, were the V1 (D-AHIS *Monsun*), V2 (D-AANE *Zephir*) and V3 (D-ABYM *Aeolus*), the first of which made its maiden flight on 15 March 1935.

A sixth and much modified machine, D-ANHR, was given the designation Do 18F and was used extensively for record attempts.

In 1938 the first maritime reconnaissance model, the Do 18D, began to enter Luftwaffe service. Preceded by a pre-production batch of Do 18D-0s, a small number of D-1s and D-2s were constructed by Weserflugzeugbau, with Jumo 205C engines of 600 hp, and carrying a crew of four. Open gun positions, in the bow and aft of the cockpit, each mounted a 7·9-mm machine-gun, and four 110-lb bombs could be carried on underwing racks. In 1939, the D series was superseded by the Do 18G-1, a more powerful and more heavily armed model. A power-operated dorsal turret, mounting a 20-mm MG 151 cannon, replaced the former mid-upper machine-gun, and the bow position, although still not enclosed, mounted a 13-mm MG 131. Two 880-hp six-cylinder Jumo 205D engines provided the power. The Do 18H was an unarmed, dual-control counterpart of the Do 18G.

Production of the Do 18 came to an end in 1940 after just over 100 of all versions had been built, 71 of these being G or H models; but in the same year the service life of several Do 18Gs was extended by their conversion into Do 18N-1 air/sea rescue aircraft.

Dornier Do 22

This three-seat torpedo-bomber and reconnaissance aircraft was developed in 1934 by the Dornier Werke's subsidiary at Altenrhein in Switzerland, where two prototypes were completed. The Do 22 was an all-metal, fabric-covered parasol monoplane, with a slightly swept mainplane and externally-braced horizontal tail surfaces; the first appeared as the Do 22/See seaplane, with two long, single-step floats.

No orders for the Do 22/See were placed by the Luftwaffe, but it was built in small numbers at Friedrichshafen for export to Latvia (Do 22 Kl), Greece (Do 22 Kg) and Yugoslavia (Do 22 Kj). The first production

Dornier Do 217P V1

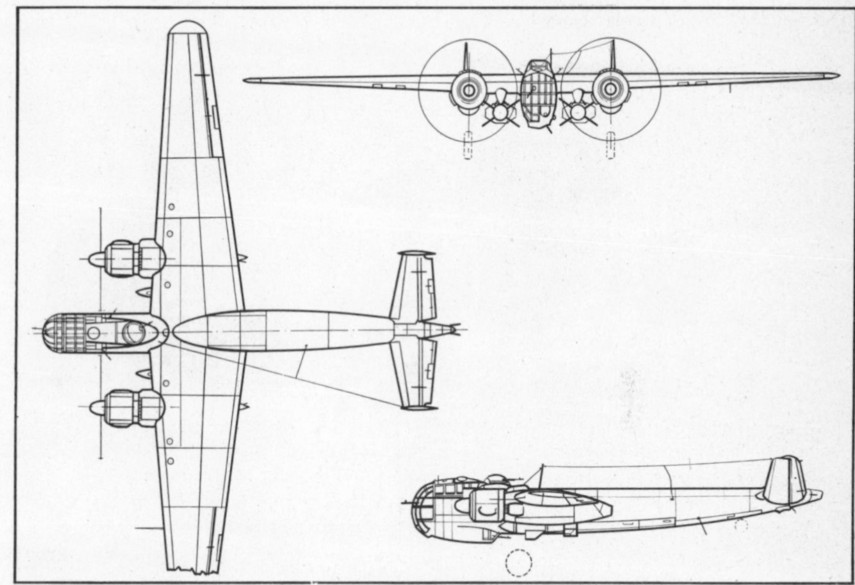

Dornier Do 217K

Dornier Do 18D

TYPE	DIMENSIONS						WEIGHT	PERFORMANCE				REMARKS
	span ft	span in	length ft	length in	height ft	height in	max t-o lb	max speed mph	at height ft	service ceiling ft	combat range miles	
Do 217E-1	62	4	60	10⅓	16	3⅔	33,730	326	18,500	29,850	1,500	
Do 217M-1	62	4	55	9¼	16	3⅔	36,817	348	18,700	24,000	1,550	
Do 217N-1	62	4	58	9	16	3⅔	30,203	311	19,685	27,560	1,550	
Do 217P-1	80	4½	58	10½	16	3⅔	35,200	388	46,000	53,000	1,500	
Do 18G-1	77	9	63	7	17	5½	23,800	165	6,560	13,800	2,175	Maximum range

Dornier Do 22Kj, Yugoslav Navy

Dornier Do 22/Land

Dornier Do 24V1

Dornier Do 24K, Royal Netherlands East Indies Naval Air Service

Do 22/See flew on 15 July 1938, and was followed on 10 March 1939 by the Do 22/Land (a landplane model registered D-OXWD), which was basically similar except for the fitting of a wheel undercarriage. Both models were powered by a single 860-hp Hispano-Suiza 12 Ybrs twelve-cylinder liquid-cooled engine, driving a three-blade metal propeller, and were armed with one 7·9-mm machine-gun firing through the propeller boss, two more on a Scarff-type mounting in the observer's cockpit, and a fourth in the underside of the fuselage. A single torpedo, or its equivalent weight in bombs, could be slung under the fuselage centre-section.

The Do 22 had the unusual distinction of fighting on both sides during World War II. Of the 12 Do 22 Kjs delivered to the Royal Yugoslavian Naval Air Service, four escaped to Egypt in April 1941 to serve with the Allied forces in the Mediterranean; while four Do 22Kgs were captured by the invading Axis forces and sold to the Finnish Air Force in 1942.

Dornier Do 24

Similar in general configuration to the earlier Do 18, the Dornier Do 24 three-engined maritime patrol flying-boat was designed in the late 1930s to a requirement issued by the Royal Netherlands East Indies Naval Air Service (MLD). The Do 24V1 and V2, powered by 600-hp Junkers Jumo 205C diesel engines, were later allocated to a Luftwaffe transport squadron and took part in the 1940 airborne invasion of Norway; but the first machine to fly was in fact the third prototype, the Do 24V3. This aircraft, which differed in having three 890-hp. Wright Cyclone R-1820-F52 radial engines, made its maiden flight on 3 July 1937, and was delivered to Holland later that year.

The Weserflugzeugbau delivered 11 Do 24K-1s to the MLD between 1938 and 1939; and a licence was obtained for production in Holland of the Do 24K-2 by the Aviolanda and de Schelde companies. The first Dutch-built machines reached the MLD early in 1939, and by the time of the German invasion in May 1940, 26 had joined the original 11 in service in the Far East (serial numbers X-1 to X-37). Within a month of the outbreak of war in the Pacific, nearly all of these aircraft had been lost through enemy action, but five succeeded in escaping to Australia and served with the RAAF until the summer of 1945.

The Do 24Ks still on the assembly lines in Holland were completed by order of the occupying forces and assigned to the Luftwaffe, which gave them the designation Do 24N-1. They also authorized continued development of the type, and further variants were the maritime Do 24T-1 and transport Do 24T-2 with 1,000-hp Bramo Fafnir 323R-2 nine-cylinder radial engines. Carrying a five- or six-man crew, the Do 24T-1 was armed with a 7·9-mm MG 15 machine-gun in the bow, another in the tail, and a 20-mm MG 151 cannon (later a 30-mm MK103) in a dorsal turret; underwing racks provided for the carriage of up to twelve 110-lb bombs.

Altogether, the Dutch factories produced 170 Do 24s for the Luftwaffe, and a further 48 Do 24Ts were completed in French factories. Some of these were supplied to the Luftwaffe; the remainder (completed after the liberation), and a further 20 put in hand before VE-day, served with French Aéronavale squadrons in the transport and air/sea rescue rôles until 1953. The surviving aircraft were then sold to the Spanish Air Force, joining 12 Do 24T-3s purchased by Spain in 1944, and continued to serve under the designation HR-5 until the early 1960s. One Luftwaffe Do 24T-1, which force-landed in Sweden in 1944, was appropriated by the Flygvapnet with the transport designation Tp 24; this machine, having originally been based in what became the Soviet Zone of Germany after the war, was handed over to Russia in 1951 under the terms of the German surrender agreement.

Dornier Do 335 Pfeil (Arrow)

A concept attracting several of today's aircraft designers, called centre-line thrust, derives from an idea patented in 1937 by Dr Claude Dornier. Tried out in a small experimental monoplane, the Gö 9, in 1940, the principle was then applied to a fighter project designated Do 231. Although it was not taken up at the time by the RLM, Dornier was able in 1942 to revise this design as the Do 335, and the prototype of this single-seat fighter-bomber flew for the first time in the autumn of 1943. It was powered by two 1,800-hp DB 603E liquid-cooled inverted Vee engines, one mounted conventionally, with an annular cowling ring, in the nose, and the other installed just aft of the cockpit with an extension shaft to a pusher propeller behind the cruciform tail unit.

A long-stroke nosewheel landing gear, and a pilot ejection seat, were other interesting features of this advanced aircraft.

Dornier received from the RLM an initial contract for 38 aircraft; made up of 14 *Versuchs* machines, ten pre-production Do 335A-0s, 11 production Do 335A-1s and three Do 335A-10 or A-12 two-seat trainers. The A-0s joined the extensive test programme in the autumn of 1944. They were armed with twin 15-mm MG 151 guns in the upper cowling of the forward engine and a 30-mm MK 103 cannon, firing through the propeller hub, and a pair of 550-lb bombs could be stowed internally. The A-1 production model was basically similar except for its DB 603G engines of 1,900 hp each; and the A-4 was a photo-reconnaissance counterpart. By the end of the war in Europe only a few A-1s and A-10 trainers, of the score or so built, had reached Luftwaffe squadrons, and the type was not met in combat.

Other Do 335 projects included the V10 (1,750-hp DB 603A-1s and airborne interception radar); and the Do 335B series with heavier armament (three MK 103s and two 20-mm MG 151s) and DB 603E engines. The latter series included the B-4 (60 ft 4½ in span for high-altitude interception), B-6 (two-seat night fighter), B-7 (as -6 with different engine) and B-8 (as -7, but with the -4 wing).

The Do 335V4 became a prototype for the proposed Do 435 two-seat night fighter, and the Do 635 was a projected "twin" version for long-range reconnaissance, consisting of two standard Do 335s joined together by a new wing centre-section.

Focke-Wulf Fw 189 Uhu (Owl)

In 1936, to meet an RLM specification for a two-seat light-bomber/ground-attack aircraft, the design team of the Focke-Wulf Flugzeugbau GmbH, under the technical direction of Kurt Tank, evolved an unorthodox twin-boom design to which the designation Fw 189 was allocated. The first prototype of this machine, the Fw 189V1 (bearing the civil registration D-OPVN), made its maiden flight early in 1938. Power was provided by a 450-hp Argus As 410 twelve-cylinder air-cooled inverted Vee engine in each of the slender booms, and the crew of two were seated in an extremely short and slim nacelle, mounted over the wing centre-section and projecting fore and aft. The tail-booms, each bearing its own fin and rudder, were spanned by a single tailplane.

The Fw 189V1 was unarmed; but the second machine, D-OVHD – a three-seater which featured the much larger and extensively glazed crew nacelle that was to characterize production aircraft – was provided with a single 7·9-mm MG 15 machine-gun, two MG 17s of similar calibre, and external bomb racks.

The Fw 189V3 was the prototype for a reconnaissance variant.

Dornier Do 335 Pfeil

Dornier Do 335A two-seat trainer, captured aircraft, RAF markings

Focke-Wulf Fw 189 Uhu

TYPE	DIMENSIONS						WEIGHT	PERFORMANCE				REMARKS
	span		*length*		*height*		*max t-o*	*max speed*	*at height*	*service ceiling*	*combat range*	
	ft	*in*	*ft*	*in*	*ft*	*in*	*lb*	*mph*	*ft*	*ft*	*miles*	
Do 22	53	2	43	0	15	10	8,800	217	13,120	30,176	1,430 max	Data for seaplane: landplane differed in dimensions only.
Do 24T	88	6⅞	72	2⅛	18	10⅓	40,565	211	6,560	19,360	2,950 max	
Do 335A-1	45	3⅓	45	5¼	16	4¾	25,800	413	26,200	37,400	1,280	

Focke-Wulf Fw 189A Uhu

Focke-Wulf Fw 190A-4/R6, with 21-cm rocket-tubes

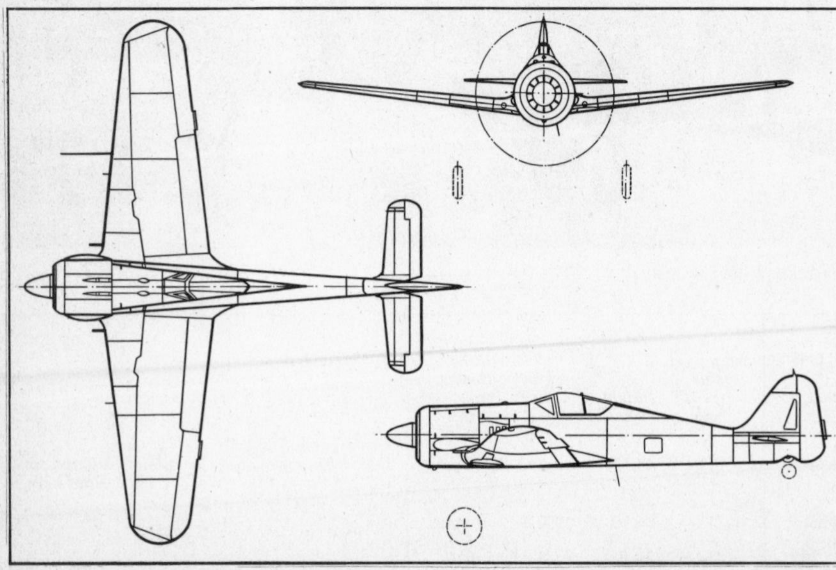
Focke-Wulf Fw 190A-3

The Uhu, as the Fw 189 was dubbed by the Luftwaffe, entered production in 1939, six pre-production Fw 189A-0s (for evaluation) being followed by the first full production series, designated Fw 189A-1. Production aircraft were basically similar to the first prototype, but with the more spacious nacelle of the later machines (which offered an uninterrupted view in almost every direction), and an additional MG 15 gun. External racks allowed for the carriage of four 110-lb bombs. Subsequent production models were the Fw 189A-2, with different armament, and Fw 189A-3, equipped for communications and ambulance duties but otherwise similar to the A-1.

The first Fw 189A-1s began to reach Luftwaffe units at the end of 1940, and the type was employed extensively on the Russian front. Its duties consisted initially of short-range reconnaissance, army co-operation and close support; but with the gradual improvement in performance of opposing fighters (for whom the "Owl" was more of a "sitting duck") it was progressively withdrawn to less vulnerable duties such as liaison and casualty evacuation. Construction of the Uhu naturally took second place to the Fw 190 interceptor, but by the time its production ended early in 1944, 846 examples (excluding prototypes) had been completed.

Focke-Wulf Fw 190

Any aircraft which remains in production for nearly six years, during which time more than 20,000 examples of it are built, must clearly be classed as outstanding. Very few aircraft in the history of aviation have achieved a production record of this magnitude, and the Focke-Wulf Fw 190 interceptor of World War II is by no means the least among this select company.

The most eminent of many first-class designs to emerge under the technical direction of Dipl-Ing Kurt Tank of the Focke-Wulf Flugzeugbau, the Fw 190 not only exhibited considerable technical achievement in its design but proved itself a versatile and highly efficient aircraft in service, from the end of 1940 until the conclusion of hostilities in Europe. It was fast and manoeuvrable; its performance was good at both high and low altitudes; it possessed good handling characteristics and was also a first-class gun and bomb platform.

An RLM specification for a single-seat fighter, issued in the autumn of 1937, had produced two proposals from Focke-Wulf, one drawn up around the DB601 engine and the other around the BMW 139 radial. The latter design was selected by the RLM in the following summer, after which prototype construction began. The Fw 190V1, registered D-OPZE, was flown for the first time on 1 June 1939, powered by a BMW 139 engine of 1,550 hp, in a very neat installation of minimum diameter and having a large rounded spinner with a central duct conveying air to a cooling fan for the engine. The second prototype, flown in October 1939, dispensed with the ducted spinner and was used principally for armament trials, being equipped with two MG 131 and two MG 17 guns. By this time, however, the BMW 139 had been dropped from the RLM's schedule of production engines, and in subsequent machines the BMW 801, a larger and heavier power plant offering slightly more power (1,600 hp), was substituted. The early prototypes, and the first seven of 18 pre-production Fw 190A-0s ordered in 1940, had a 31 ft 2 in wing span, but an increase to 34 ft 5½ in became standard on production machines. Other modifications from the earlier models included re-siting of the cockpit further aft on the fuselage and a revision of the armament to four 7·9-mm MG 17s.

One hundred Fw 190A-1s were ordered, deliveries taking place from late 1940 to the spring of 1941. They were followed by the A-2, in which 20-mm MG FF cannon replaced two of the MG 17 machine-guns, and then by the A-3. Armament was increased to six guns in the Fw 190A-3, by adding two 20-mm MG 151s, and a power plant change was made to the 1,700-hp BMW 801Dg. Production of the Fw 190A series was now mounting steadily, and the type began to be used on low-altitude hit-and-run missions over southern England.

Several new Fw 190A sub-types emerged in 1942. Among these were the A-4, utilizing a BMW 801 D-2 fourteen-cylinder air-cooled engine, giving 2,100 hp with the aid of MW50 power boost; the A-4/U8 fighter-bomber with reduced fixed armament, but carrying a 1,100-lb bomb-load and auxiliary fuel tanks; the A-4/Trop with full fixed armament and a 550-lb bomb; and a rocket-firing version, designated the A-4/R6.

Nearly 2,000 Fw 190s had been built by the end of 1942, by which time they were being despatched in ever-increasing numbers to the Western Desert and Russian front. A number were employed on night interception duties over Europe early in 1943, but in general this theatre took third place behind Russia and the Mediterranean area in Fw 190 deliveries.

Production moved on with the Fw 190A-5 series, most of which went to European-based *Nacht-Jagdgeschwaderen* or to fighter-bomber and close support units The A-6 and A-7 represented further attempts to improve the Fw 190's firepower; the A-8s were mostly fighter-bombers, with some as all-weather fighters or dual-control trainers; and the A series finally came to an end with the A-9 (BMW 801F engine) and the A-10 (BMW 801T) which were fighter-bombers.

Ten prototypes of the Fw 190B were completed, this and the Fw 190C being re-worked to take the super-charged DB 603 engine; but both of these models were abandoned in favour of the Fw 190D. This version arose from trials with a few *Versuchs* (experimental) machines fitted with the 1,776-hp Junkers Jumo 213A-1 engine. The Jumo engine, which offered 2,240 hp with MW50 boost, was liquid-cooled by an annular radiator duct which gave the installation the appearance of a radial engine.

The first Fw 190D-0 and D-1 aircraft, with this engine, were delivered to evaluation units in the spring and summer of 1943. Their larger cowling was counter-balanced by a corresponding increase in the length of the rear fuselage, and the fin area was also increased on the D-1. Sub-type numbers D-2 to D-8 were not allocated, the first major production version being the D-9 which entered service with Jagdgeschwader 3 in the interceptor rôle. Ground attack versions were developed from this: the D-11 being a stop-gap model with two 30-mm MK 108 wing-mounted cannon, followed by the D-12 and D-13.

These last two were powered by the 2,060-hp Jumo 213F and had, respectively, a single MK 108 or MK 103 cannon firing through the propeller boss, in addition to the standard armament.

There was no Fw 190E, the next model on the assembly line being the Fw 190G fighter-bomber. With fewer guns, machines in the G series could carry a single 3,970-lb bomb or several smaller weapons of equivalent total weight. The BMW 801D-2 was restored as power plant for the Fw 190G, and also for the final production model, the Fw 190F, which had a modified cockpit hood and increased armour protection for the pilot. The sub-types in the F series were usually armed with two MG 17s and two MG 151s; external load could be a single 3,086-lb armour-piercing bomb, various small bombs of up to 1,100 lb, or 24 rocket projectiles.

When production of the Fw 190 finally ended in favour of the Ta 152, a total (excluding prototypes) of 20,051 examples had been completed, of which 6,634 were for the fighter-bomber rôle.

Focke-Wulf Fw 190A-5/U3 Trop

Focke-Wulf Fw 190D-9

Focke-Wulf Fw 190/Junkers Ju 88 Mistel composite aircraft

TYPE	DIMENSIONS						WEIGHT	PERFORMANCE				REMARKS
	span		*length*		*height*		*max t-o*	*max speed*	*at height*	*service ceiling*	*combat range*	
	ft	*in*	*ft*	*in*	*ft*	*in*	*lb*	*mph*	*ft*	*ft*	*miles*	
Fw 189A-1	60	5	39	4	10	2	8,700	221	8,530	27,550	430	
Fw 190A-2	34	5½	28	10½			7,716	389	18,000			
Fw 190A-8	34	5½	29	0	13	0	10,800	408	20,600	37,400	500	
Fw 190D-9	34	5½	33	5¼	11	0¼	10,670	426	21,653	32,810	520	
Fw 190F-3	34	5½	29	0	13	0	10,850	394	18,000	34,780	500	

Focke-Wulf Fw 200C Condor

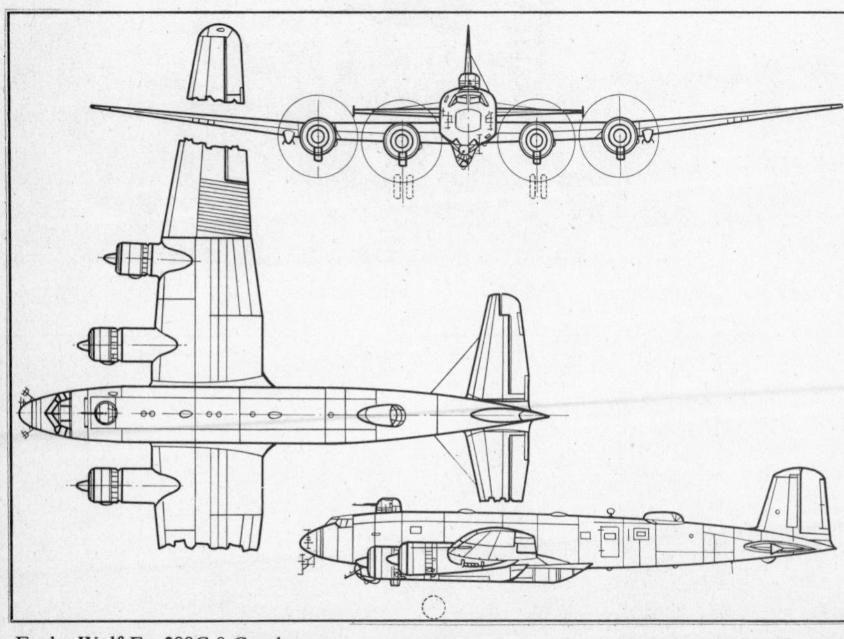

Focke-Wulf Fw 200C-8 Condor

Focke-Wulf Fw 200 Condor

Considering that it was only a stop-gap conversion to the rôle which it carried out during World War II, and that only a relatively small number were built, the Focke-Wulf Condor established a remarkable reputation as a long-range anti-shipping aircraft. Over the North Atlantic and the waters off north-eastern Europe the marauding Fw 200, operating alone or in partnership with the German U-boat fleet, was responsible for the destruction of vast quantities of Allied merchant shipping. Not until the middle war years, with the advent of long-range coastal types such as the Beaufighter and Liberator, and the sea-going conversions of the Hurricane, did the Condor's success begin to wane, after which it was diverted to the rôle for which it was designed.

It was in the spring of 1936 that Kurt Tank began the design of a 26-passenger commercial transport for Deutsche Luft Hansa, and the Focke-Wulf Fw 200V1 (D-ACON *Brandenburg*) made its maiden flight in July 1937 under the power of four 720-hp BMW 132G-1 nine-cylinder air-cooled radial engines. This and the second machine (D-AERE *Saarland*) undertook a series of long-distance demonstration flights from Berlin to points such as Cairo and New York. Altogether, DLH received seven. The RLM acquired two prototypes for evaluation, which subsequently became personal transports for Hitler and his staff; two Fw 200As were delivered to DDL, the Danish airline, and two Fw 200Bs to a Brazilian operator.

The first suggestion of the Condor's potential as a maritime reconnaissance aircraft came from the Japanese, although the five Fw 200s which they ordered (but which were never delivered owing to the outbreak of war in Europe) would have been employed in the transport rôle. It was as a result of this Japanese interest that the major production series, the Fw 200C, was adapted for ocean patrol and bombing duties. With a considerably strengthened airframe, the Fw 200C was powered by 830-hp BMW 132H-1 radials; but despite the RLM's request for adaptation of the type for maritime reconnaissance, the first production Fw 200Cs (and some earlier machines) were more urgently called into service as transports during the German invasion of Norway.

The Fw 200C-1, which entered production at Cottbus in 1940, had a normal crew of five. Its all-metal fuselage was of semi-monocoque construction, and the two-spar low wing was metal and fabric-covered. Armament consisted of two 7·9-mm MG 15 guns on the upper fuselage, with a third MG 15 and a 20-mm MG FF cannon in the offset ventral "gondola". This gondola also contained the bomb-aiming position and stowage for a 550-lb bomb; further bombs of similar size could be carried beneath the outer nacelles and wing panels.

Kampfgeschwader 40 was the first Luftwaffe unit to receive the C-1, towards the end of 1940. With slightly revised outer nacelles and other minor modifications, the C-2 followed in 1941; but both of these models were prone to structural failure and were succeeded by the further strengthened C-3 in the summer of 1941. Powered by 1,200-hp Bramo 323R-2 radials, the Fw 200C-3 carried a crew of six, a greater variety of bombs (4,620 lb maximum) and, according to sub-type, differing defensive armament.

Major Fw 200C production centred on the C-4, which carried advanced radar and radio equipment (reducing its performance somewhat), and the series came to an end with the C-6 (the C-3 modified to take an Hs 293 glider bomb beneath each outboard engine nacelle) and the C-8 (built from the outset for the same purpose). By 1943, the reconnaissance part of the Condor's duties had been taken over by the Ju 290, the Fw 200 (in company with the He 177) concentrating upon actual attack once a target had been pinpointed. When Condor production finally ended early in 1944, a total of 278, including prototypes, had been completed.

Focke-Wulf Ta 152

Towards the end of World War II the Focke-Wulf design office, under the technical direction of Kurt Tank, evolved two designs, the Ta 152 and Ta 153, as potential successors to the Fw 190 interceptor. The Ta 153 differed extensively from the Fw 190 in having a wing of increased span, a new fuselage and tail unit and modified internal equipment, the whole powered by a DB 603 liquid-cooled engine.

Many of its features were test flown successfully on Fw 190 airframes, but the RLM preferred the alternative project.

Except for the provision of hydraulically-operated flaps and landing gear, the Ta 152A-0 and A-1 differed little from the Fw 190D-9, and these models served as the prototypes for the new fighter. The Ta 152B was generally similar, save for the installation of a 1,750-hp Jumo 213E-1 engine, in which was mounted a 30-mm MK 108 cannon, and production of this model was initiated at the end of August 1944. Comparatively few had been completed at the Sorau factory, however, before this series was abandoned in favour of the Ta 152C, which was destined to become the only operational model.

The Ta 152C-1, designed for medium-altitude interception duties, was powered by a DB 603LA twelve-cylinder liquid-cooled engine of the inverted Vee type, installed in a cowling of "radial" appearance and giving 2,300 hp with MW50 power boost. The engine-mounted MK 108 cannon was retained, the remaining armament comprising four 20-mm MG 151 guns. The Ta 152C-3 was generally similar, except that the DB 603L (2,100 hp with MW50) was employed, while an MK 103 cannon of 30-mm calibre replaced the MK 108. Only enough C series machines had been completed to equip one or two Luftwaffe units before production at the Sorau factory was terminated by the advancing Russian forces.

However, the Cottbus factory was able to produce a few examples of the Ta 152E, a reconnaissance-fighter variant with a Jumo 213E power plant. The RLM had ordered no fewer than 630 Ta 152Es, but this model also failed to reach operational status.

The only other version to enter production was the Ta 152H, of which four were completed by the war's end. Powered by a Jumo 213E, giving 1,880 hp (2,250 hp with MW50 boost), the Ta 152H was designed for the high-altitude rôle, with a much-extended wing of higher aspect ratio, and a pressurized cockpit. Armament comprised one MK 108 cannon and two MG 151s.

Projects in hand by VE-day included the Ta 152S (two-seat conversion trainer); a low-altitude fighter development; and another derivative powered by a BMW 801 radial engine. Like many other excellent German designs, the Ta 152 suffered from a confused domestic officialdom on the one hand and increasing Allied air attack on the other, which combined to hold it back from front-line service until it was too late to make any effective contribution to the war.

Focke-Wulf Ta 154

The Focke-Wulf Ta 154 was a twin-engined, shoulder-wing monoplane of wooden construction, with a high top speed. It was unofficially dubbed "Moskito" by the Germans; but any similarity between the Ta 154 and its famous British namesake ended with the name. Although eulogized by German propagandists as a formidable new addition to the Luftwaffe's armoury, it was, in fact, one of their aircraft industry's least

Focke-Wulf Ta 152H-1

Focke-Wulf Ta 152H-1

Focke-Wulf Ta 154

TYPE	DIMENSIONS						WEIGHT	PERFORMANCE				REMARKS
	span		*length*		*height*		*max t-o*	*max speed*	*at height*	*service ceiling*	*combat range*	
	ft	*in*	*ft*	*in*	*ft*	*in*	*lb*	*mph*	*ft*	*ft*	*miles*	
Fw 200C-3	107	9½	76	11½	20	8	50,045	224	15,750	19,000	2,210	
Ta 152C-3	36	1	35	5½	13	0	12,125	439	37,000	40,350		Speed increased to 443 mph at 44,300 ft with GM 1 boost.
Ta 152H-1	47	6¾	35	5½	13	0	11,508	431	35,000	48,560	745	Speed increased to 472 mph at 41,000 ft with GM 1 boost.

Focke-Wulf Ta 154A-1

Fokker E.I

Fokker E.III

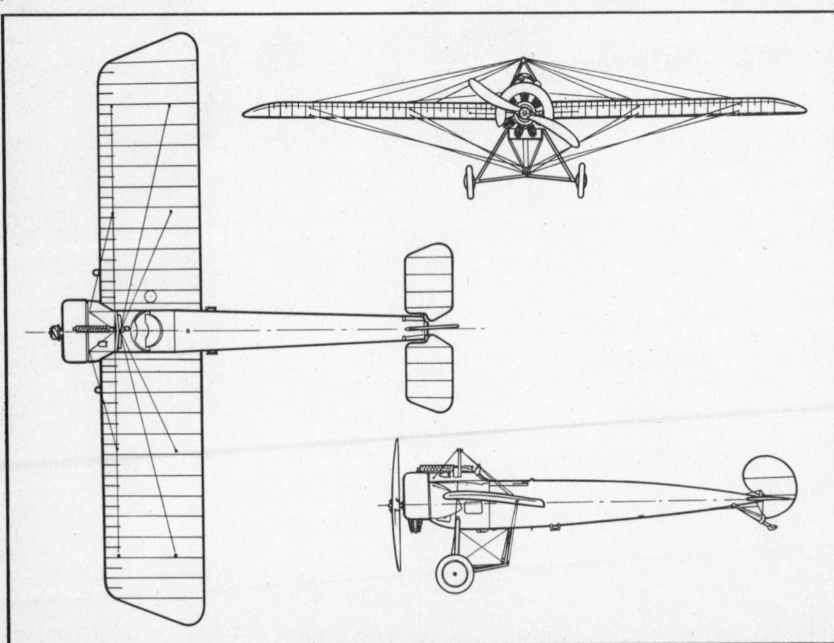

Fokker E.III

successful enterprises during the World War II period.

The design of the Ta 154 was completed in less than ten months from the issue of an RLM specification calling for a specialist night fighter capable of rapid development and using non-strategic materials, primarily wood, in its construction. The Focke-Wulf team, under Kurt Tank's direction, produced plans for both single- and two-seat machines to meet this requirement, development finally being authorized of the latter version only.

Powered by two 1,500-hp Junkers Jumo 211 liquid-cooled engines, the Ta 154V1 was flown for the first time on 7 July 1943, and the similarly-powered second machine notched up a level speed of 435 mph during flight trials. Flight testing revealed the need for additional strengthening of the forward fuselage, to absorb the loads produced when firing the two 30-mm MK 108 and two 20-mm MH 151 guns with which the "Moskito" was armed. Lichtenstein C-1 airborne interception radar was installed in the Ta 154V3, which was flown in November 1943 and was powered with 1,776-hp Jumo 213A engines. After completion of a further four prototypes, eight pre-production Ta 154A-0s made a brief appearance with Luftwaffe evaluation units in the summer of 1944, before most of them were withdrawn to become the lower components of Mistel composite aircraft, carrying Fw 190s as their directors.

Meanwhile, the Posen factory had tooled up for production of the Ta 154A-1, but crashes of some of the early machines curtailed production after fewer than a dozen had been completed of the 250 ordered at the end of 1943. Work was also suspended on the proposed Ta 154C and Ta 254 developments.

Fokker E.I to E.IV

The Fokker series of E-type fighters (E for *Eindecker*, or monoplane) reached the peak of their operational career in about the middle of the 1914-18 War. None was produced in enormous quantities, but they gave an excellent account of themselves from the autumn of 1915 to the spring of the following year – the period of the so called "Fokker Scourge" – causing particular havoc among B.E.2c units of the Royal Flying Corps.

Key to the E series' success lay in the fact that they were the first manoeuvrable single-seaters to employ an effectively-synchronized forward-firing gun. This resulted from Anthony Fokker's study of the crude gun installation on the captured Morane scout of the French ace, Roland Garros. His staff developed a synchronizing gear in preference to copying this and, having persuaded the German authorities of its reliability, Fokker obtained permission to evolve a fighter design in which the gear could be incorporated.

This design, the M.5K, was demonstrated by Fokker himself to the German authorities. With a seven-cylinder Oberursel U.O rotary engine of only 80 hp, it was under-powered for a fighter. Nevertheless, 68 were built, before being superseded by the E.II (100-hp Oberursel U.I), a refined and structurally stronger machine which entered service in September 1915. This gave way to the further-developed E.III after about 50 examples had been completed.

The E.III was the major production E type, delivery papers indicating that 260 were built. Power plant remained the same as in the E.II and, like its predecessors, the E.III was a mid-wing monoplane with a steel-tube fuselage and wooden box-spar wings, the whole being covered with a mixture of metal, wood and fabric. Lateral control was effected by warping the wings.

Many famous German pilots flew the E.III, among them Boelcke and Immelmann. Indeed, it was on a machine of this type that the celebrated Immelmann Turn was first evolved. When first introduced, the E series achieved considerable success against opposing pilots who did not expect to be attacked with forward-firing armament, but later their chief employment was on escort and similar duties. A single Parabellum gun was fitted initially, but later the Spandau was installed as standard armament.

About 45 examples of the final version, the E.IV, were also produced. This was basically an enlarged

E.III, with twin guns and a 160-hp U.III 14-cylinder rotary. However, it was not a great success: the power plant proved none too reliable and, being heavier, it was less manoeuvrable than the earlier machines of the series.

Fokker Dr.I

The original designation of this single-seat fighting scout was F.I; but after the first three production aircraft had been completed in the summer of 1917, this was changed to Dr.I, signifying *Dreidecker*, or triplane. It was the success achieved by Britain's Sopwith Triplane, demonstrating the great advantage in manoeuvrability conferred by having three instead of two mainplanes, that spurred the German authorities to instruct their own manufacturers to design and build fighters to a similar formula.

The prototype of the Dr.I, designed by Reinhold Platz of the Fokker Flugzeug-Werke GmbH, had a trio of short-span, cantilever wings – thick in section, with neither interplane struts nor external bracing wires. Flight tests showed that undesirable vibration was produced by the unsupported wings, and lightweight interplane struts were added to the second machine to overcome this tendency. A braced tailplane of more conventional and simple shape was also introduced. The Dr.I's fuselage was of typical box girder construction, both it and the tail assembly consisting of a welded steel-tube framework, covered with a mixture of wood and fabric. The landing gear comprised a typical Vee type main chassis and a steel-tipped wooden tail-skid.

Normally, the Dr.I was powered either by a 110-hp Le Rhône nine-cylinder rotary engine or by the Oberursel URII, which was a copy of the French power plant. Other engines which were installed experimentally included the Oberursel UR.III of 145 hp, the 160-hp. Goebel III and the 160-hp Siemens-Halske Sh-3. The armament, typical of the period, consisted of a pair of Spandau machine-guns in front of the cockpit.

The Fokker Dr.I entered squadron service in August 1917, but combat experience revealed that the wing structure was slightly suspect and the type was withdrawn from operations in October until the closing weeks of the year. After that, it continued to serve into the summer of 1918, numbering among its famous pilots Werner Voss and Manfred von Richthofen, the latter finally meeting his death while flying a machine of this type on 21 April 1918. The Dr.I was not, perhaps, as fast as contemporary fighters; but in addition to its excellent agility it possessed a useful rate of climb and was quite a successful operational type. Wartime production came to an end in May 1918 after 320 Dr. Is had been completed, but a rebuilt and modified version known as the S.P.5 made its appearance after hostilities were over.

Fokker D.I and D.IV

Appearing for the first time in the summer of 1916, the Fokker D.I single-seat fighting scout was evolved as a potential successor to the Fokker E series of monoplanes. It was a two-bay, equal-span biplane, powered by a 120-hp Mercedes D.II six-cylinder in-line engine and armed with a single Spandau machine-gun. Its fuselage was a welded steel-tube box-girder

Fokker Dr.I

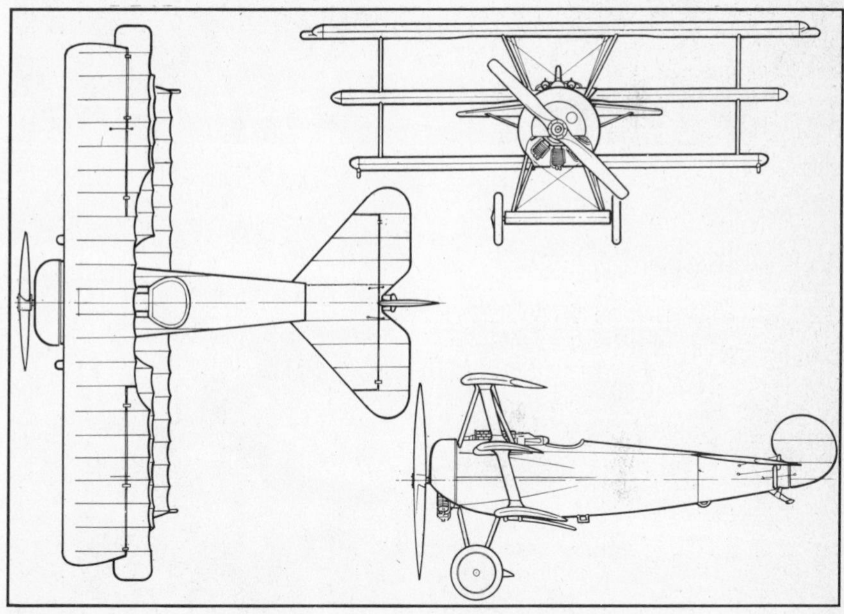

Fokker Dr.I

TYPE	DIMENSIONS						WEIGHT	PERFORMANCE				REMARKS
	span		length		height		max t-o	max speed	at height	service ceiling	combat range	
	ft	in	ft	in	ft	in	lb	mph	ft	ft	miles	
Ta 154A-1	52	6	41	3	11	9¾	19,842	399	26,240	35,800	855	
Fokker E.I	28	0	22	2	9	6	1,239	82		10,000		
Fokker E.II	32	8	23	2	7	10	1,340	86.8		12,000		
Fokker E.III	31	2¾	23	11⅓	9	1¾	1,400	83	6,500	11,500	2¾ hr	
Fokker Dr.I	23	7⅜	18	11⅛	9	8⅛	1,289	103	13,120	20,000	1½ hr	

Fokker D.IV

Fokker D.II

Fokker D.III

Fokker D.V

and wing-warping was employed for lateral control. The landing gear consisted of a conventional Vee main chassis and a wooden tail-skid.

The D.I was introduced into service on the Western front and for a short time acquitted itself reasonably well; but it was not adequately powered for a single-seat fighter and was soon transferred to less exacting theatres of operations. A few were also diverted to the Austro-Hungarian forces.

Production of the D.I ended after completion of only 25 aircraft, in favour of the D.IV, a slightly modified and enlarged model with a 160-hp Mercedes D.III engine and provision for a second Spandau. This, however, was no great improvement over the earlier machine, and only 33 D.IVs were built.

Fokker D.II, D.III and D.V

Based on a generally similar airframe to that of the D.I, though somewhat shorter in wing span and longer in the fuselage, the D.II appeared at the beginning of 1916. The fuselage was a box-girder steel-tube framework with a rounded decking above the engine where the single Spandau gun was mounted. An aluminium horseshoe cowling enveloped the 100-hp Oberursel U.I nine-cylinder rotary engine, and the D.II's fuselage terminated in a typical Fokker comma-shaped rudder. The equal-span, two-bay wings were built around two box-spars and fabric covered, with lateral control by wing-warping. The undercarriage was of characteristic Fokker pattern, although the main units were somewhat more forward-raked than on other designs.

The D.II entered service in the spring of 1916 as a replacement for the E series on escort and defence duties. The Fokker Flugzeug-Werke produced a combined total of 291 examples of this and a developed model, the D.III, which had a 160-hp Oberursel U.III two-row rotary engine and carried two Spandau machine-guns forward of the pilot's cockpit. To match the greater power and weight of this engine, the fuselage was strengthened and was mated with a wing of similar type and size to that of the Fokker D.I. However, the U.III engine proved somewhat troublesome in the field, resulting in a curtailing of the D.III's operational life; and when this fighter's performance was overtaken by those of the Albatros and Halberstadt scouts, it became relegated to fighter trainer duties. Some were sold to the Dutch government, and other D.IIIs (and D.Is) were assigned to Austro-Hungary, where they were also built under licence.

This line of development ended with the Fokker D.V, which reverted to the U.I power plant. A cleaner engine installation, in a fully circular cowling with a propeller spinner, characterized the D.V, and a much-improved general appearance included a modified wing planform with mild sweepback; 216 of this model were built, but they were limited mainly to the training rôle.

Fokker D.VI

Two D.VI prototypes were entered by the Fokker Flugzeug-Werke in a competition for D class single-seat fighting scouts, held at Adlershof in January 1918; one powered by a 145-hp Oberursel UR.III engine, and the other by a 160-hp Siemens-Halske Sh-3. Neither of these engines was viewed with great favour at the time by the German authorities; nevertheless, the aircraft's basic design was considered to be promising. Subject to the installation of the proven Oberursel UR.II nine-cylinder rotary of 110 hp, therefore, a small production order for the type was placed in the spring.

It is probable that this order was primarily an insurance against failure of the later D.VII design, and production of both types proceeded in parallel from April 1918 until closure of the D.VI line in the following August, after 59 examples had been completed. Thereafter, production concentrated on the D.VII, which by then had proved highly successful. Seven D.VIs were supplied to Austro-Hungary (where local alternatives were substituted for the normal twin-Spandau armament), but relatively few of the remaining machines of this type became operational, most of them ending up as combat trainers.

The D.VI was something of a mixture. Its wings were modified and scaled down from those of the D.VII, while the fuselage and tail unit were developed from those of the Dr.I triplane. The fuselage was a normal steel-tube box, and was ply- and fabric-covered, as were the box-spar cantilever wings. The two mainplanes were unequal in span, and were supported by N interplane struts without any external wire bracing.

The D.VI was, like most of Anthony Fokker's products, extremely manoeuvrable, and had, in particular, a first-class low-altitude performance.

Fokker D.VII

The aircraft which was to become the scourge of the skies in the closing months of the 1914-18 War, and one of the great, if not immortal, warplanes of all time, had its origins in a machine called the V.11, designed by Fokker's Reinhold Platz in 1917. This aircraft was designed in an extremely short space of time as an entry for the military competition for D class (single-seat) fighting scouts held at Adlershof in January 1918. The V.11 was completed a bare two months before the date of the competition and made only one short trial hop before entering. It won hands down from the other competitors and was ordered into immediate production in quantity in the expectation that here at last was the fighter that Germany needed to regain its former supremacy from the British S.E.5as and French SPAD VIIs. Four hundred examples, under the designation D.VII, were ordered from the parent company, where they followed the Fokker Triplane on the assembly lines, and others from the Albatros factories at Johannisthal and Schneidermühl.

The fuselage of the D.VII was a box-girder structure of welded and braced steel-tube, covered with metal panels forward and ply and fabric at the rear. The single-bay wings were wooden two box-spar units, with N-type interplane struts and no external wire bracing. In fact, the wings were really of cantilever construction, the struts being added only as a concession to those who could not accept that the airframe was sturdy enough to do without them. A typical Fokker feature was the enclosing of the main undercarriage axle in a fairing of aerofoil section.

The Fokker D.VII was a beautiful machine to fly: it had good control and an excellent all-round performance, although it was highly sensitive at low speeds. D.VIIs began to reach the Western Front in April 1918, and by the end of the war the Fokker Flugzeug Werke had delivered 366 examples of the type. A small series of the C.I, a two-seat development, had also been completed by the time the war was over but did not become operational. Alternative power units were the 160-hp Mercedes D.III and 185-hp BMW III, both six-cylinder water-cooled engines. Armament comprised two fixed Spandau guns, mounted on top of the engine decking and synchronized to fire through the propeller disc.

As befits a superb aircraft, the Fokker D.VII was

Fokker D.VI

Fokker D.VII, 185-hp BMW III engine

TYPE	DIMENSIONS						WEIGHT	PERFORMANCE				REMARKS
	span		length		height		max t-o	max speed	at height	service ceiling	combat range	
	ft	in	ft	in	ft	in	lb	mph	ft	ft	miles	
Fokker D.I	29	8⅜	18	8½	7	4⅝	1,476	94		13,120	1½ hr	
Fokker D.IV	31	10	20	8	8	0½	1,850	100		16,400	1½ hr	
Fokker D.II	28	8½	21	0	8	2⅞	1,267	94	SL	13,120	1½ hr	
Fokker D.III	29	8⅜	20	8	7	4⅝	1,562	100		15,500	1½ hr	
Fokker D.V	29	0½	19	10¼	7	6½	1,245	106		13,120	1½ hr	
Fokker D.VI	25	1¼	20	5⅜	8	4⅜	1,285	122	3,280	19,685	1½ hr	

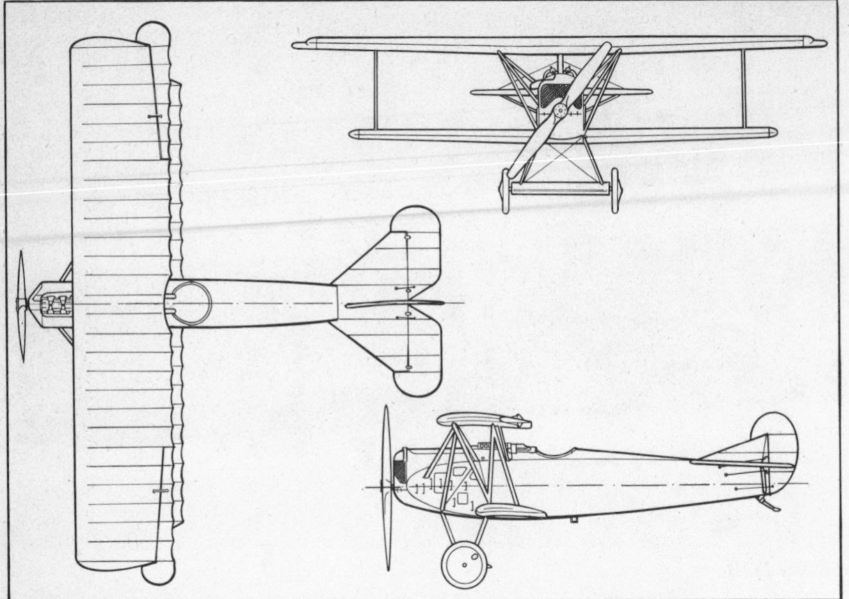

Fokker D.VII

Fokker D.VII, Royal Netherlands Air Force

Fokker E.V (D.VIII)

Friedrichshafen G.III, captured aircraft

destined to continue to give good service after the end of the 1914–18 War, and for this Anthony Fokker himself was primarily responsible. Article IV of the Armistice Agreement, discussing the items to be handed over to the Allies, had specified "especially all machines of the D.VII type" – the only time a specific aircraft type has ever figured in such a document; but Fokker was determined to get round this proviso. Accordingly, he began to hide airframes, engines and any D.VII or part of a D.VII that he could lay his hands on, in barns, cellars and other hiding places in and around the town of Schwein, near the Fokker factory. Altogether, he managed to smuggle over the border into Holland something like 120 more or less complete D.VIIs as well as smaller numbers of some other Fokker types and various tools and items of equipment. From this beginning he was able to establish, in time, the Dutch Fokker factories, which are so famous today. There, in those early days, he continued manufacture of the D.VII after the 1914–18 War, for service with the Royal Netherlands Air Force and in the Dutch East Indies, until the end of the 1920s. Ex-wartime D.VIIs were supplied during this period to the air forces of Belgium and Switzerland.

Fokker D.VIII

After some experimental flying by a Fokker D.VII biplane with its lower mainplane removed, Fokker's chief designer, Reinhold Platz, produced the prototype of a parasol-wing monoplane powered by a 110-hp Oberursel UR II rotary engine. With some modifications, this machine was entered for a single-seat fighter competition held in May 1918. It exhibited such great agility and diving ability, as well as first-class take-off and climbing performance, that an immediate production order for the type was placed under the designation E.V, and the first half-dozen off the assembly lines were rushed to the front for evaluation under combat conditions.

The E.V's steel box-girder fuselage resembled that of the Dr.I triplane, with a typically Fokker tail unit, having a smaller fin but larger rudder than the D.VII. Twin Spandau machine-guns were mounted on top of the engine decking to fire forward through the propeller disc, and all-round visibility from the cockpit was excellent. Twin box-spars formed the basis of the tapered cantilever wings, and the usual Fokker aerofoil fairing appeared round the undercarriage axle.

As further E.Vs joined the early machines in service, the wing structure was found to be suspect under stress. Wing failures, added to troubles with the engine lubrication, caused production and operation of the type to be suspended after about 60 E.Vs had been completed. Both troubles were satisfactorily overcome, and production was resumed, under the new designation D.VIII.

Intended ultimately to replace the D.VII biplane, to which it was superior in many respects, the D.VIII equipped air force and naval *Jagdgeschwadern* during the latter part of 1918, but by this time the war was almost at an end and the type barely became operational. Experiments included the fitting of 140-hp Oberursel, 160-hp Goebel and 160-hp Siemens-Halske engines, but did not progress beyond the prototype stage.

Friedrichshafen G.III

During the 1914–18 War, the Flugzeugbau Friedrichshafen GmbH was noted primarily for its construction of naval seaplanes; but in 1914 chief engineer Theodor Kober produced a twin-engined, three-bay landplane bomber ultimately to be known as the G.I. This machine, with two 150-hp Benz Bz III pusher engines and a biplane tail unit, did not enter production, but led in the following year to the G.II, which was built in small numbers, mainly under licence by the Daimler Motoren-Werke.

The G.II was a two-bay biplane, spanning 66 ft 7⅜ in and powered by two 200-hp Bz IV motors, which remained in service from late 1916 until the end of 1917. With a defensive armament of one Parabellum machine-gun in the nose and another in a dorsal position, its all-up weight of 6,934 lb included a bomb-load of some 1,000 lb.

Chief external difference from the G.I lay in the single fin and rudder assembly of the G.II.

The G.III, which was the main production model of the Friedrichshafen G series, was a progressive development of the G.II. Like the G.I, it was a three-bay biplane, and was altogether larger and more powerful than its predecessors. The 260-hp Mercedes D.IVa six-cylinder liquid-cooled in-line engines, mounted on Vee bearer struts between the mainplanes, drove two-bladed pusher propellers, and the G.III carried a crew of three – pilot, gunner and bomb-aimer/second gunner. The central fuselage and wing centre-section were an integral unit, housing crew, fuel, engines and the internal bomb-load. The square-section fuselage had a steel-tube frame, and was wood-covered at nose and tail, with fabric over the remainder. It terminated in a single, large triangular fin and an extremely broad-chord tailplane.

The inner wing panels were built around steel-tube spars, with reduced chord to clear the propellers; while the slightly-swept outer wings had wooden box-spars, the whole being covered with mixed wood and fabric. The G.III's landing gear was a rather clumsy-looking affair: there were twin main wheels beneath each engine nacelle and the usual steel-shod wooden tail-skid, but a fifth main wheel was mounted under the nose as a precaution against overturning in the event of a bad landing. Two or three Parabellum guns could be carried, in the extreme front fuselage and at the rear of the crew positions.

The G.III's bomb-load varied, but was usually in the region of 2,200 lb; small bombs could be stowed internally, those of larger calibre being suspended beneath the centre fuselage or engine nacelles.

A modified version of the G.III, produced later, was the G.IIIa, which differed in reverting to a biplane tail unit with twin vertical surfaces. Both models were extensively licence-built, in addition to production by the parent company. The Daimler Motoren-Werke built 245 G.III/IIIas and a further 93 were completed by the Hanseatische Flugzeug-Werke. In 1918 they were joined by a small quantity of the G.IV, a further development with a shorter nose and no front cockpit, a modification which reduced the overall length by some three feet.

Wing span was reduced by a similar amount, and the Mercedes engines drove tractor propellers.

Gotha G.II to G.V

In company with the Friedrichshafen biplanes, the twin-engined bombers emanating from the Gothaer Waggonfabrik AG formed the mainstay of German *Bombengeschwadern* during the 1914–18 War. In addition to the parent company, other concerns engaged in their construction were the Luft Verkehrs Gesellschaft and the Siemens-Schuckert Werke.

Most of the LVG-built machines were delivered to Austria, where they were fitted with engines of local design and manufacture.

First of the series was the G.II, a three-bay design with twin 220-hp Benz pusher engines, which appeared early in 1916. With a ply- and fabric-covered fuselage of typical wooden box-girder construction, the G.II had a single fin and rudder, and sweptback wings,

Friedrichshafen G.IIIa, Daimler-built, captured aircraft

Gotha G.III

Gotha G.V

TYPE	DIMENSIONS span ft	span in	length ft	length in	height ft	height in	WEIGHT max t-o lb	PERFORMANCE max speed mph	at height ft	service ceiling ft	combat range miles	REMARKS
Fokker D.VII	29	2⅓	22	9¾	9	0¼	1,984	117	3,280	19,685	1½ hr	Figures for Mercedes version; BMW performances slightly better.
Fokker D.VIII	27	6¾	19	2¾	9	3	1,238	115	SL	20,670	1½ hr	
Friedrichshafen G.III	77	11	42	1⅞	12	0	8,686	88	3,280	14,800	5 hr	

Gotha G.V

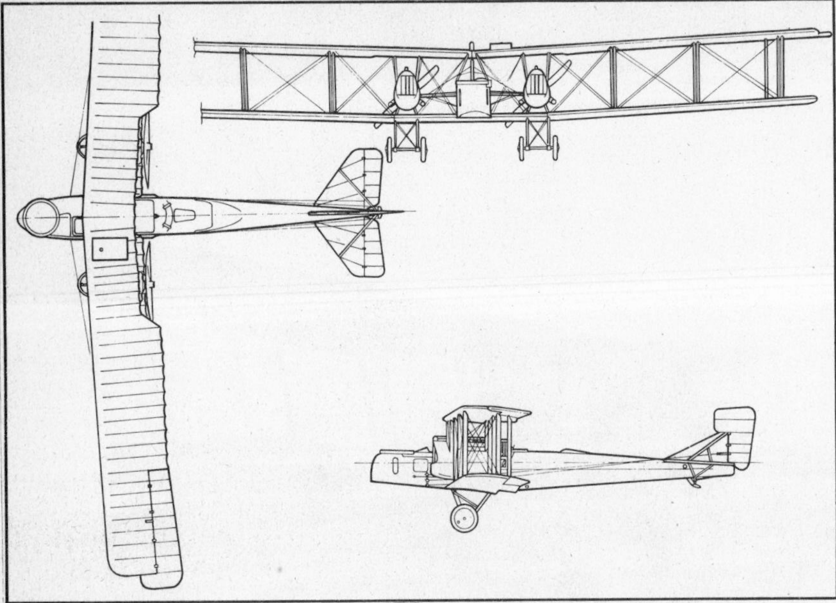
Gotha G.V

Halberstadt CL.II

Halberstadt CL.IV

also of fabric-covered wooden construction. It was armed with two Parabellum machine-guns on ring mountings, one in the nose and the other at the rear of the crew positions.

Only a small quantity of G.IIs were built, and the same was true of the G.III, which underwent a change of power plant to the 260-hp Mercedes D.IVa in-line engine. A novel feature of the G.III – retained and improved on the later G models – was a tunnel through the centre of the fuselage by means of which the operator of the dorsal gun could train his weapon downward to fire rearward *beneath* the tail.

The principal Gotha G types were the G.IV and G.V, still powered by the Mercedes D.IVa. They were three-bay machines with unequal-span wings, of two-spar construction and having their inner trailing-edges cut back to clear the pusher propellers. There were twin main wheels beneath each nacelle, and on later machines these were preceded by pairs of raised wheels designed to eliminate the Gothas' tendency of nosing-over on landing.

The G.IV made its appearance in service during the autumn of 1916, taking over the long-range bombing programme from the Zeppelin airships of earlier years. Its bombs – up to 1,000 lb in total – were carried on external racks. In June 1917, German heavy bomber units began daylight attacks on London with Gothas, which created such damage and alarm that fighters were withdrawn hurriedly from France to defend the British capital. The fighters then in service were, however, too slow in climbing to the Gotha's operational altitude to catch them, and it was not until the advent of more efficient interceptors, such as the Sopwith Camel, that the German bombers were made to pay the price for their attacks. They then switched to night bombing until the spring of 1918, when their attrition rate – including many lost through landing accidents on returning from their missions – became too high to be acceptable to the German authorities.

Halberstadt CL.II/CL.IV

To the Halberstädter Flugzeugwerke fell the distinction of putting into German air force service the first aircraft designed to the new CL category of small, lightweight, modestly-powered two-seaters for fighter escort duties. This was the Halberstadt CL.II, which was in service by the summer of 1917, design of the type having been initiated at the beginning of that year.

With a single 160-hp Mercedes D.III six-cylinder water-cooled in-line engine, the CL.II was an equal-span, single-bay biplane of wooden construction, the fuselage being plywood-covered and the forward-staggered wings fabric-covered. The pilot and observer shared a communal cockpit, the latter operating a single Parabellum gun from a raised ring for rearward defence. One or two Spandau guns could be installed in the forward fuselage.

Initially, the CL.IIs were employed as escorts to reconnaissance types, but they were quickly brought into use also as close support aircraft, with considerable success. They figured in attacks on the Somme bridges in September 1917 and made their mark in attacks on trenches at the Battle of Cambrai on 30 November of the same year.

Four or five 22-lb bombs, or a quantity of grenades could be carried for this ground-attack rôle.

The CL.II, which was built by the Bayerische Flugzeug-Werke AG as well as by the parent concern, was a good-looking little aircraft which, although of light construction, proved robust and pleasant to handle in action. The forward and upward view from the cockpit was particularly good.

With a 185-hp BMW engine in a slightly more streamlined nose, the type became the CL.IIa, but the next major production model was the CL.IV. This reverted to the original Mercedes engine, but had a number of significant differences from its predecessors. The wings were repositioned on a somewhat shorter fuselage, the tailplane was raised and elongated, the fin and rudder outline re-designed and the propeller spinner removed. The C.IV was sub-contracted to the LFG (Roland) concern, to supplement production by the parent company.

Halberstadt D.II/D.III

The series of D class single-seat fighting scouts produced by the Halberstädter Flugzeugwerke during the 1914-18 War were not notable from a numerical viewpoint – probably no more than 100 were built altogether – but they were strong and manoeuvrable little machines which had a reasonably successful, if brief, service life.

First of the series was the D.I, which appeared late in 1915, powered by a 100-hp Mercedes D.I engine, and was in service by the following February. It was an attractive two-bay machine, with a box-girder fuselage and mixed fabric and wood covering. Extensive use was made of steel tubing in its design, in the ailerons and interplane struts, the Vee-type under-carriage chassis and parts of the tail assembly.

A modified version with a 120-hp six-cylinder Argus As II engine was designated D.Ia; and with the 120-hp Mercedes D.II six-cylinder water-cooled engine it became the D.II. The next model, the D.III, reverted to the Argus As II power plant but was otherwise generally similar; while the D.IV, examples of which were exported to Turkey, utilized the 150-hp Benz III.

A number of D.IIs and D.IIIs were constructed under licence by the Hannoversche Waggonfabrik AG at Hanover-Linden.

In the ultimate Halberstadt D type, the D.V of 1917, the engine cowling was considerably cleaned up and a spinner was fitted over the propeller boss. Armament of all models consisted normally of a single Spandau machine-gun, mounted to one side of the upper front fuselage and synchronized to fire between the two blades of the propeller; but occasionally a second gun was fitted.

The Halberstadt D class scouts had a fairly brief operational life on the Western Front, being obsolescent within about a year of entering service. They were then transferred to less demanding theatres of the war, such as Palestine and Macedonia.

Hannover CL.IIIa

Following the outbreak of the 1914-18 War, the German government prevailed upon a number of engineering concerns to adapt themselves to aircraft construction; among these was the Hannoversche Waggonfabrik AG, whose prior activities had been concerned with the manufacture of railway rolling stock.

"Hawa", as the company was sometimes called, set up the necessary plant at Hanover-Linden, and there, in 1915-16, they made their debut into the aviation field by manufacturing Aviatik C.I, Rumpler C.Ia and Halberstadt D.II scouts under licence. However, in 1917, in response to a Flugmeisterei specification for a two-seat fighter/ground-attack type in the new CL category, Hannover began work upon a design of its own conception.

The numeral I having been allocated already to the licence types it had been building, the new Hannover design was given the designation CL.II. It was a compact single-bay biplane of mixed wood

Halberstadt D.II

Halberstadt D.III

Hannover CL.II

TYPE	DIMENSIONS						WEIGHT	PERFORMANCE				REMARKS
	span		length		height		max t-o	max speed	at height	service ceiling	combat range	
	ft	in	ft	in	ft	in	lb	mph	ft	ft	miles	
Gotha G.III	77	10	38	8¼	12	8	7,022	92	13,120			
Gotha G.IV and G.V	77	9¼	40	6¼	12	11½	8,763	87	SL	21,320	522	Max weight of G.V. = 8,745 lb
Halberstadt CL.II	35	4	23	11⅜	9	0¼	2,498	103	16,400	16,730	3 hr	
Halberstadt CL.IV	35	2⅞	21	5½	8	9⅛	2,350	103		13,500	3–3½ hr	
Halberstadt D.II/D.III	28	10½	23	11½	8	9⅛	1,609	90	SL	13,000	1½ hr	

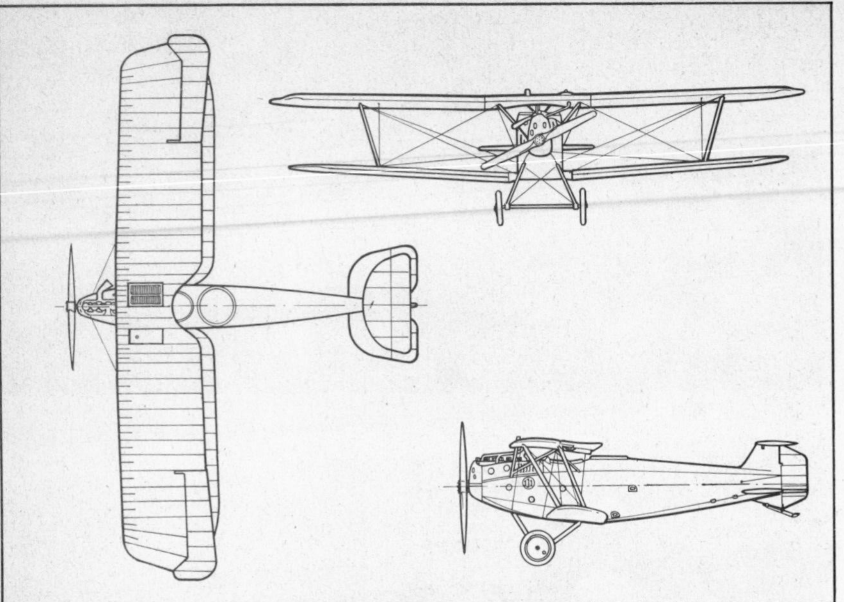

Hannover CL.IIIa

Hansa-Brandenburg KDW

Hansa-Brandenburg W.12, fitted experimentally with 195-hp Benz Bz IIIb engine

and metal construction, with fabric covering, and a conventional Vee main undercarriage with a wooden tail-skid. Power was provided by the engine specified in the official requirement, the 180-hp Argus As III six-cylinder water-cooled in-line, with a two-bladed propeller. The CL.II entered service with the German air force in December 1917, and a total of 439 machines of this type were completed, proving themselves capable in combat and able to withstand a remarkable amount of punishment.

The CL.II was followed into production by a slightly modified version, the CL.III, which had a 160-hp Mercedes D.III engine. As this power plant was required more urgently to keep pace with single-seat fighter production, only 80 CL.IIIs were built. Their place on the production line was taken by the CL.IIIa, which retained the structural and equipment improvements of the CL.III but reverted to the As III power unit of the CL.II. Production of the CL.IIIa totalled 537, of which a quantity were sub-contracted to the Luftfahrzeug Gesellschaft (Roland), whose designation for this type was CL.IIa.

The Hannover CL series had two features which impressed themselves – in different ways – upon their opponents. One was their biplane tail unit, unique among single-engined aircraft of the period; the other was their small size. Many Allied pilots mistook them initially for single-seaters, until they got to close quarters, when they were swiftly disillusioned by a burst of fire from the observer's Parabellum gun in the rear cockpit. This was made the more lethal by the wide arc of fire which the smaller span of the tail unit made possible. A second machine-gun, a Spandau, was fixed in the forward part of the fuselage for use by the pilot.

The Hannover CL fighters were used extensively in combat during the summer and autumn of 1918, and before the end of the 1914-18 War further models, most of them experimental, made their appearance. The CL.IIIb was a test-bed for the 190-hp N.A.G. engine; the CL.IIIc was a development with two-bay wings of increased span. The CL.IV, which appeared early in 1918 powered by a 245-hp Maybach Mb IV engine, did not enter production; but about 50 examples of the CL.V are believed to have been completed, although they were not used operationally. The CL.V was given a much-improved performance by its 185-hp BMW IIIa engine, and existed in two versions, one with the biplane-like tail unit of the earlier types and the other with a more conventional tail assembly.

Hansa-Brandenburg KDW

For coastal patrol and local defence of the German seaplane stations on the north-west European and Mediterranean coasts, a small number of seagoing single-seat fighters were evolved during the 1914-18 War; among these was the KDW (*Kampfdoppeldecker, Wasser* = fighting biplane seaplane). A product of the Hansa und Brandenburgische Flugzeug-Werke GmbH, of Brandenburg/Havel, the KDW was a modification of the D.I landplane fighter produced by this company for Austria and designed by Ernst Heinkel.

Main differences compared with the D.I were a slight increase in wing span and replacement of the wheeled undercarriage by a twin-float landing gear. The single-step floats were mounted on cross-braced N-shaped struts and the first three KDWs built (in the summer of 1916) were powered by the 150-hp Benz Bz III six-cylinder in-line engine. The fuselage was of all-wood construction while the equal-span wings had a wooden two-spar framework, with fabric covering and "star" pattern interplane struts.

A further 55 KDWs were completed in batches of 10, 10, 15 and 20. The first ten of these had a 160-hp Mercedes engine as standard, whilst the remainder were powered by the Maybach Mb III liquid-cooled engine of the same power. A single Spandau machine-gun armed all but the last 20 aircraft, on which a second Spandau was installed. Later production models had a small stabilizing fin atop the rear fuselage.

Production of the KDW ended in February 1918, by

which time it was obsolete and was beginning to be replaced by types such as the same company's W.12.

Hansa-Brandenburg W.12 and W.19

When it began to arrive for service in the summer of 1917, the Hansa-Brandenburg W.12 was a very welcome addition to the defences of German seaplane stations on the Flanders coast. Previous station defence types had been hasty adaptations of landplane fighters, with consequently poorer performance due to the additional weight of large and often cumbersome floats for waterborne operations. Also, the interim types had usually been single-seaters and thus vulnerable from the rear.

The W.12 was designed from the outset to accommodate an additional crew member, whose rear cockpit was equipped with a Parabellum machine-gun; one or two forward-firing Spandau guns were mounted ahead of the front cockpit for use by the pilot. After tests with the prototype W.12 at Warnemünde in January 1917, which revealed the necessity for slight modification of the wings, the type was ordered into series production.

Structurally, the W.12 had a ply-covered wooden fuselage and single-bay, unequal-span wings with interplane struts free of any additional wire bracing. The fuselage was swept up towards the high-mounted tailplane, thus affording the observer an excellent view and freedom to fire his gun in both fore and aft directions. The twin single-step floats, also wooden, were of square section and mounted on heavy struts. Power for the W.12 – another Ernst Heinkel design – was provided by the 150-hp Benz Bz III engine or, as an alternative, the 160-hp Mercedes D.III.

Although somewhat large and heavy for a two-seater, the W.12 was an excellent design, with fine manoeuvrability and a good turn of speed. It proved very successful against raiding British flying-boats and one, flown by Oberleutnant Christiansen, was responsible for shooting down the British airship C.27 in December 1917. The W.12 remained in series production, with only minor modifications, from February 1917 until mid-summer 1918, 146 being built.

A larger and heavier development of the W.12 was the Hansa-Brandenburg W.19, which was basically a scaled-up version of the earlier machine intended for the maritime reconnaissance rôle over a greater radius than its predecessor. W.19's clashed often with British sea patrol aircraft, and frequently worked in conjunction with W.12s, the former reconnoitring a target and the latter making the "kill". Installation of the 260-hp Maybach Mb IV water-cooled engine in the W.19 kept its performance roughly the same as that of its stablemate, and the same armament was carried by both types.

Of a total of 55 W.19s delivered, one was fitted experimentally with a 20-mm Becker cannon, but no production of such a version was undertaken. In addition one example was completed of the W.27, a development with a 195-hp Bz IIIb Vee engine, followed by three W.32s, which were virtually W.27s with a 160-hp Mercedes.

Hansa-Brandenburg W.29 and W.33

Excellent though the W.12 was, as the war moved into its final phase in Europe in 1918 it was clear that a successor would be necessary if the Germans were to maintain the superiority of performance conferred

Hansa-Brandenburg W.19

Hansa-Brandenburg W.29, Benz Bz III engine

Hansa-Brandenburg W.29

TYPE	DIMENSIONS span ft	span in	length ft	length in	height ft	height in	WEIGHT max t-o lb	PERFORMANCE max speed mph	at height ft	service ceiling ft	combat range miles	REMARKS
Hannover CL.II	39	4	25	5	9	2	2,442	103	2,000	24,600		
Hannover CL.IIIa	38	4¾	24	10½	9	2¼	2,381	103	1,970	24,600	3 hr	
Hansa-Brandenburg KDW	30	4¼	26	3	10	11⅞	2,293	106	SL	13,120	2½ hr	
Hansa-Brandenburg W.12	36	9	31	7⅞	10	10	3,230	100	SL	16,400	3½ hr	
Hansa-Brandenburg W.19	45	3⅜	34	11⅜	13	5½	4,411	94			5 hr	

Hansa-Brandenburg W.33

Heinkel He 51

Heinkel He 51B floatplane

by the earlier design; to this end, Ernst Heinkel evolved the Hansa-Brandenburg W.29. He reasoned that the best way to achieve the necessary performance was to opt for a monoplane design, and the W.29 consisted, basically, of the fuselage and engine installation of the W.12 allied to a completely new single mainplane.

The engine exhaust manifolds of the Bz III engine were slightly modified and the shape of the tailplane revised; but otherwise the W.29's fuselage remained the same upswept affair with its rudder curling below, and the twin-float gear was identical to that of the W.12. The wing, however, was a wide-chord structure of much greater span, with an area almost as great as the two wings of the W.12. Thick in section, narrowing at the roots and towards the blunt, rounded tips, it was constructed on the twin wood-spar principle, with fabric covering. Armament consisted of one or two forward-firing Spandaus and a rear-firing Parabellum gun, those aircraft with the single Spandau also carrying radio equipment.

Although their career was necessarily brief, the W.29s were well received by German coastal patrol units and were used successfully against Allied aircraft and shipping in the North Sea and English Channel areas. They entered service in April 1918, and by the Armistice 78 had been delivered, of which the last four had the uprated Bz IIIa engine of 185 hp. The Danish air force employed a version of the W.29 after the cessation of hostilities.

Twenty-six examples were also delivered of the W.33, an enlarged and more highly powered version of the W.29, with a 245-hp Maybach Mb IV motor. Span of the W.33 was 52 ft 0 in, and maximum loaded weight increased to 4,510 lb; so performance remained much the same as that of the W.29. Like the earlier W.12, one W.33 underwent trials with cannon armament, but this version was not pursued. The W.33 was built under licence in Finland after the war as the A-22, and by the Norwegian Naval Aircraft Factory in the early 1920s.

Heinkel He 51

The lineage of Ernst Heinkel AG's He 51 may be traced through a series of earlier small, streamlined biplanes: the He 37, He 38, He 43 and He 49. The He 49a, which was, in effect, the prototype for the later machine, was flown for the first time in November 1932. Powered by a single BMW VI twelve-cylinder engine developing 660 hp, it was followed by the He 49b which, with its original wheeled landing gear replaced by a twin-float undercarriage, was later to be used as the prototype for the He 51B floatplane fighter.

The He 49a was adopted by the German Air Ministry as the He 51, which was destined to become the first standard single-seat fighter of the newly-created but still clandestine Luftwaffe; and deliveries began with ten pre-production He 51A-0s during 1933. Between July 1934 and January 1936, 75 He 51A-ls were completed for the Luftwaffe, licence production being undertaken by the Ago, Arado, Erla and Fieseler companies. In the first production models the BMW engine was uprated to 750 hp, and a fixed armament of two forward-firing 7·9-mm machine-guns was installed.

The He 51 was an exceptionally clean-looking, well-streamlined single-bay biplane of mixed construction, with wings of unequal span and a neat, fixed undercarriage. Its operational debut came in November 1936, when three dozen machines of this type were despatched with the Condor Legion to the Civil War in Spain. They proved to be somewhat inferior in performance to other fighter types involved in the conflict, but their sturdy construction and good low-level flying ability made them suitable for close support duties, in which rôle they enjoyed a reasonable degree of success.

By this time the A-l series had been succeeded on the production lines by the He 51B-0 and B-1, twelve of each of these versions being completed. The B models were of floatplane configuration and, together with 38 He 51B-2s were supplied to the German naval air arm. The final production model was the He 51C-l landplane, of which 51 were delivered to the Luftwaffe and a further 28 to the Condor Legion.

Although obsolete as a fighter, the He 51 was still in squadron service on the outbreak of World War II and continued to find useful employment on training duties until some four years later.

Heinkel He 59

Like its stablemate the He 51, which it actually preceded although bearing a later German Air Ministry designation, the He 59 was designed to operate on either a land or float undercarriage. It differed in function, being intended primarily for the torpedo-bomber/reconnaissance rôle. Two prototypes were completed, the first flight being made in September 1931 by D-2215, which was a landplane. The floatplane prototype, D-2214, made its maiden flight four months later.

The He 59 was a solid-looking two-seat equal-span biplane with two 660-hp BMW VI liquid-cooled engines and twin single-step floats. Production began in the spring of 1932 with an evaluation batch of 14 He 59A floatplanes. The series He 59B differed only in internal equipment, and the first armed version, the He 59B-1, carried a 7·9-mm ring-mounted machine-gun in the extreme nose of the fuselage. A crew of four was accommodated in the He 59B-2, the additional members handling further 7·9-mm guns in dorsal and ventral installations, and this model received a substantial production order, a number also being completed by the Arado Flugzeugwerke.

Subsequent production models included the He 59B-3 (for long-range reconnaissance, with extra fuel in lieu of one of the defensive guns); the He 59C-l (another reconnaissance model, with a rounded, "solid" nose and no bomb-aiming facilities); the He 59C-2 (for air/sea rescue, carrying six dinghies, additional radio equipment, and no guns); the He 59D general aircrew trainer; the He 59E-1 torpedo trainer; the He 59E-2 photographic reconnaissance model; and the He 59N, a conversion of the He 59D for specialized navigation training duties. Many other examples were utilized as flying test-beds.

When the He 59 made its combat debut with the Condor Legion in Spain in the latter part of 1936, it was put into operation mainly as a night bomber, though some examples, armed with a 20-mm MG FF cannon, were employed in attacks on shipping. The type remained in service until the middle of World War II, on the less belligerent if equally important tasks of minelaying, convoy shadowing and coastal reconnaissance, as well as in the training rôle.

Heinkel He 70

Evolved originally as a four-passenger high-speed mailplane with a crew of two, the prototype He 70a flew for the first time on 1 December 1932, powered by a single 637-hp BMW VI liquid-cooled engine. After it had captured a number of international speed records in its class during the early part of 1933, the type was adopted and placed in service by Deutsche Luft Hansa on domestic express routes.

The He 70 was offered to the Luftwaffe, but was not adopted by the German air force. Thus, the only military models to see service were the He 70C and He 70F. Adapted to light bombing missions via an He 70E prototype (D-UBYL) and carrying a single 7·9mm MG 15 machine-gun for defence, the He 70F was supplied to the Spanish insurgent forces during the latter

Heinkel He 59B-3, equipped for air/sea rescue

Heinkel He 59N

Heinkel He 70, Spanish Air Force.

TYPE	DIMENSIONS span ft	span in	length ft	length in	height ft	height in	WEIGHT max t-o lb	PERFORMANCE max speed mph	at height ft	service ceiling ft	combat range miles	REMARKS
Hansa-Brandenburg W.29	44	3½	30	8½	9	10⅛	3,243	109	SL		4 hr	
Hansa-Brandenburg W.33	52	0	36	4	11	1	4,510	108				Performance with 260-hp Mercedes
He 51A-1	36	1	27	6¾	10	6	4,180	205	SL	25,356	242	
He 59	77	9	57	1	23	3½	19,842	137	SL	11,480	1,087 max	Data for floatplane

Heinkel He 170A

Heinkel He 111B-1

Heinkel He 111B

Heinkel He 111H, captured aircraft, RAF markings

part of 1930. It was an elegant monoplane of mixed construction, with a semi-elliptical low wing and tail surfaces which foreshadowed shapes that were later to become familiar on the He 111 bomber.

Developed versions included the He 170A, of which 20 were delivered to Hungary for reconnaissance duties, powered by a 910-hp Gnome-Rhône 14 radial engine; and the He 270, with a 1,175-hp Daimler-Benz DB 601A liquid-cooled engine. The He 270 had a maximum level speed of 286 mph, but was not adopted for service.

Heinkel He 111

The Heinkel He 111's production life spanned nine years, and the type has been in first-line service somewhere in the world from the beginning of 1937 to the late 1960s – a record matched by comparatively few designs in the history of aviation.

It was early in 1934 that Walter and Siegfried Günther of the Ernst Heinkel AG began work on the design of an all-metal low wing, twin-engined monoplane, and the first prototype, the He 111V1, emerged at the end of that year as an uncommonly clean-looking and efficient aircraft. With two 660-hp BMW VI liquid-cooled engines, it flew for the first time early in 1935, fitted out as a bomber prototype with a 2,200-lb internal load and armament of three 7·9-mm machine-guns, in nose, dorsal and ventral positions. Three more prototypes followed, of which the V2 (D-ALIX) and V4 were completed as commercial transports accommodating ten persons and a cargo of mail. Some efforts were made to interest Deutsche Luft Hansa, the state airline, in the He 111 as a commercial venture, and when the aircraft's existence was made public, officially, in January 1936 the German authorities tried to convince all and sundry that the He 111 was a purely civil type, although its true purpose was more than obvious.

The He 111V3 served as prototype for the initial military version, the He 111A-O, which entered production during the summer of 1935 and was being delivered to the test centre at Rechlin for evaluation by late 1936. Although inheriting the graceful lines of its single-engined predecessor, the He 70, and despite generally good handling characteristics, it was found that the BMW engines provided insufficient power for the He 111 to realize its desired performance and the similarly-powered He 111A-1s already completed were rejected by the Luftwaffe. The DB 600A engine was therefore chosen for the He 111B-0 and B-1, deliveries of which began at the end of 1936, and these models were succeeded in turn by the He 111B-2 (DB 600C and He 111D-1 (DB 600G).

Along with many other Luftwaffe types, the He 111B-2 was assigned to the Condor Legion in Spain at the beginning of 1937. It met with considerable success acquiring a reputation of superiority over the opposition that was to prove, ultimately, something of a mixed blessing. In particular, the speed of the He 111 was such that, in Spain, it could outrun the opposing fighter and thus carry out unescorted raids with impunity. Continuation of these tactics in the face of the Spitfire and Hurricanes of 1940 had very different results, and before long the He 111 was diverted to night attacks.

Meanwhile, Heinkel had evolved a further civil model the He 111G, which featured a new, straight-tapered wing in lieu of the more familiar semi-elliptical pattern. No customers were forthcoming; so production of th bomber models continued with the He 111E. In order to preserve supplies of DB 600 engines for the fighte programme, the power plant of the He 111E was changed to two Jumo 211A engines of 1,050 hp each. The sam power plant, plus the straight-tapered wing of the H 111G, were featured in the next bomber variant, the H 111F, and both E and F models were used during th Spanish conflict. A total of 75 He 111s served in Spair and at the end of the war the 58 survivors became a par of the Spanish Air Force.

By the outbreak of World War II, production of th He 111 had almost reached the thousand mark, most c these being of the B, D, E or F models. A new variar had recently begun to enter service, however, in the form of the He 111P. This had a completely re-designed nose, with a continuous-curve contour (i.e. having no cockpit "step"). Extensively glazed, this new nose incorporated the offset-to-starboard ball turret, a characteristic of all subsequent He 111s.

The He 111P was powered by two 1,050-hp DB 601As; armament comprised three MG 15 machine-guns and it could carry a maximum bomb-load of 4,410 lb, made up of small bombs of up to 550-lb in size. Due partly to the need, once again, to reserve Daimler-Benz engines for fighter production, a comparatively small number of He 111Ps were built. The next, last, and most widespread version of the design now appeared – the He 111H.

Except for having Jumo 211A engines instead of DB601As, the early He 111Hs were generally similar to the P series. The total number of H series machines built, before production ended in 1944, was in excess of 5,200, and covered a wide range of sub-types. Following their rough treatment by British fighters during the Battle of Britain, defensive armament was progressively strengthened, the number of crew being increased to five or six members accordingly. Two 7·9-mm beam guns were added on the He 111H-2; some H-3s were fitted with a 20-mm MG FF cannon in the nose; the H-10 carried one MG FF, one MG 17 and one MG 131 or two MG 81s; the H-20 carried three MG 131s and four MG 81s. Successive models of the Jumo 211 engine powered most of the H series, although the H-20 and H-21 differed in having the 1,776-hp Jumo 213A or 1,750-hp Jumo 213E.

The He 111H series came in for a wide range of duties in various combat theatres, in addition to their medium bombing rôle, and carried a large variety of weapons and equipment. The He 111H-6 became a first-rate torpedo bomber, carrying two of these weapons and entering operational service in the spring of 1942; the H-12 was modified to carry Henschel Hs 293 glider bombs, and other H variants acted as air-launch platforms for the FZG-76 (or V.1) flying-bomb. Some H types were fitted with huge fenders to push aside or cut the cables of barrage balloons. More remarkable still was the He 111Z Zwilling (Twin), a "marriage" of two H-6s, joined by a new centre section carrying a fifth Jumo engine and piloted from the port fuselage, which was evolved in 1941-2 as a tug for the enormous Me 321 Gigant trooping glider. The final H model to be built for the Luftwaffe was the H-23, an assault transport accommodating eight paratroops.

The career of the He 111 did not come to an end with the cessation of hostilities in Europe, for in 1941 the Spanish government acquired a licence to build the He 111H-16 at the CASA plant at Tablada. Subsequent production of the type was undertaken as the CASA C.2111, powered by Jumo 211F engines, and as the C.2111-B (bomber) and -D (reconnaissance) when powered with Rolls-Royce Merlins. Some of the CASA-built Heinkels continue to serve with the Spanish air force to this day, and are more fully described in the Spanish section of the book.

Heinkel He 112

Evolved in the middle 1930s as a competitor to the Messerschmitt Bf 109, the He 112 was not destined to become anything like as famous as its great con-

Heinkel He 111P

Heinkel He 111H-6 torpedo bomber

TYPE	DIMENSIONS						WEIGHT	PERFORMANCE				REMARKS
	span		length		height			max	at	service	combat	
	ft	in	ft	in	ft	in	max t-o lb	speed mph	height ft	ceiling ft	range miles	
He 70	48	6⅔	38	4⅔	10	2	7,282	222		19,680	500	
He 111E-1	74	1¾	56	7⅛	12	9½	23,370	267	13,120	22,950		
He 111P-1	74	1¾	54	5½	13	9	24,692	264	12,300	24,100	1,120 max	
He 111H-6	74	1¾	54	5½	13	9	27,400	258	16,400	25,500	760	
He 111Z	115	6	54	5½	13	9	63,050	270	19,290	31,500	1,490	

Heinkel He 112B-0

Heinkel He 115A-2, Swedish Air Force

Heinkel He 115B-1

Heinkel He 115B-1

temporary. Spurned by a government whose pilots liked it, bought by a government whose pilots hated it, and by another government whose pilots used it only as a trainer, the He 112 single-seat fighter was one of Ernst Heinkel's great disappointments and little more than 50 production examples were completed.

D-IADO, the prototype He 112VI, was powered by a British engine, the 695-hp Rolls-Royce Kestrel, with which it made its maiden flight in the summer of 1935. Thirty He 112B-0s, with 680-hp Junkers Jumo 210E twelve-cylinder liquid-cooled engines, were built for evaluation, but the type was rejected by the Luftwaffe despite favourable test reports. Seventeen B-0s had a brief spell of operations in Spain during 1938, 15 of them surviving to continue with the Spanish air force after the Civil War; and 12 of the others were sold to the Imperial Japanese Navy. The only He 112s used operationally during World War II were 24 B series built for the Rumanian air force, which had a brief spell of action during 1941. The He 112 was reasonably armed, with two 20-mm MG FF cannon and twin 7·9-mm MG 17 guns, and in the fighter-bomber rôle could carry six 22-lb anti-personnel bombs on external racks.

Heinkel He 115

The twin-engined, twin-float He 115 was one of the leading maritime aircraft of World War II, being employed on a variety of missions ranging from torpedo-bombing, minelaying and long-range oversea reconnaissance to agent dropping in enemy territory. It was an all-metal mid-wing monoplane with single-step metal floats, of basically similar configuration to the Fokker T. VIII-W, but larger overall. For its size, it handled extremely well and possessed a creditable performance.

The He 115V1 prototype (D-AEHF) was powered by two 830-hp BMW 132K nine-cylinder radial engines. After early flight trials, it was extensively modified and streamlined for an attack on international seaplane speed records, eight of which it succeeded in capturing on 20 March 1938. First machine to have the extensively glazed nose of the definitive production version was the He 115V3 (D-ABZV), and the 1937 evaluation batch of ten He 115A-0s were followed in 1938 by 34 He 115A-1s, in which the total window area was increased still further by the introduction of a long "greenhouse" canopy housing two of the three crew members. Powered by BMW 132K engines, now uprated to 960 hp, the He 115A-0s carried a single 7.9-mm machine-gun in the extreme nose; an additional MG 15 was fitted in the A-1 model.

The A-2 was an export counterpart of the A-1 which was purchased by Norway (six) and Sweden (ten). The A-3 was the Luftwaffe's first large-scale service model, but this was quickly supplanted in production in 1939 by the He 115B series, with increased fuel capacity for a greater range. Ten B-0s and 52 B-1/B-2s were built, with provision for carrying five 550-lb bombs, or two such bombs and a 1,760-lb torpedo or 2,028-lb sea mine.

The He 115C series entered production in 1940 and service in 1941, comprising the C-0 (with an MG 151 cannon added, and some with two MG 17s as well), the C-1 and C-2 (generally similar except for the reinforced floats of the latter), the C-3 (embodying minelaying capabilities) and the C-4 torpedo-bomber armed with only a single MG 15 gun.

One He 115A-1 was converted to He 115D standard, with a cannon, five machine-guns and 1,600-hp BMW 801C radial engines, and this solitary example was employed operationally although no series production of the variant was undertaken.

After a temporary suspension of production, the final models, the He 115E-0 and E-1, appeared in 1943–4; 141 of the E type were built, which brought total He 115 production to somewhere in the region of 400 aircraft.

In Luftwaffe service, the He 115 adhered largely to the tasks for which it was designed, and which it performed with no small measure of success. The agent-smuggling adventures referred to above were, in fact, carried out on behalf of the United Kingdom by one of the two Norwegian He 115A-2s which escaped to Britain during the occupation of Norway in 1940.

Heinkel He 162 Salamander

Known, for morale-boosting purposes, as the Volksjäger, or People's Fighter, the He 162 Salamander may not have been among the world's greatest single-seat fighters – far from it, in fact; but it was certainly one of the most quickly conceived warplanes of any era. In only 15 days from the issue of the RLM specification, on 8 September 1944, the Ernst Heinkel AG completed a wooden mock-up for examination; five days later a large production order was issued, and the He 162V1 made its maiden flight on 6 December – which was less than ten weeks from commencement of the design.

The He 162 was not unattractive in layout: a shoulder-wing monoplane with turndown tips, carrying a single 1,760-lb s t BMW 003 turbojet in a pod along the fuselage top. To avoid the jet blast, a dihedral tailplane was fitted, with rectangular endplate fins and rudders. The single-seat cockpit was mounted well forward on the snub nose and the whole machine rested on a short-legged nose-wheel-type undercarriage, all members of which retracted into the fuselage. Construction was largely of duralumin and wood.

Although several other jet- or jet-and-rocket-powered developments of the Salamander were under consideration at the end of World War II, only the He 162A series were actually operational, the first of them entering service with Jagdgeschwader 84 in March 1945. The pre-production He 162A-0, and the He 162A-1 and A-2s, were all basically similar apart from certain items of internal equipment, and all were armed with twin 20-mm MG 151 cannon installed in the underside of the forward fuselage, one either side of the nose-wheel door. In the He 162A-3 these guns were replaced by two 30-mm MK 108 cannon.

Under Hitler's "panic" fighter production programme, in the closing stages of the war in Europe, manufacture of the He 162 was undertaken by several factories and substantial numbers were in a partly-assembled state at the German surrender; but only 116 A-series machines were actually completed.

Because of the Salamander's unpleasant flying characteristics, very few of these aircraft were encountered in combat.

Heinkel He 177 Greif (Griffin)

The He 177 was the only long-range strategic bomber put into production by Germany during World War II, and if the career of this unfortunate aircraft is any guide it is little wonder that no others were considered seriously. Hamstrung by official indecision and political bickering as to its future, the design faults which manifested themselves at the beginning of the Greif's evolution were never eliminated, and the aircraft was forced into service in a thoroughly unsatisfactory and undeveloped state.

As a design, the He 177 was a rugged, angular machine of conventional metal construction, with a mid-mounted wing and single fin and rudder assembly. Its most distinctive feature was the use of two

Heinkel He 162A-2 Salamander

Heinkel He 162A-2 Salamander

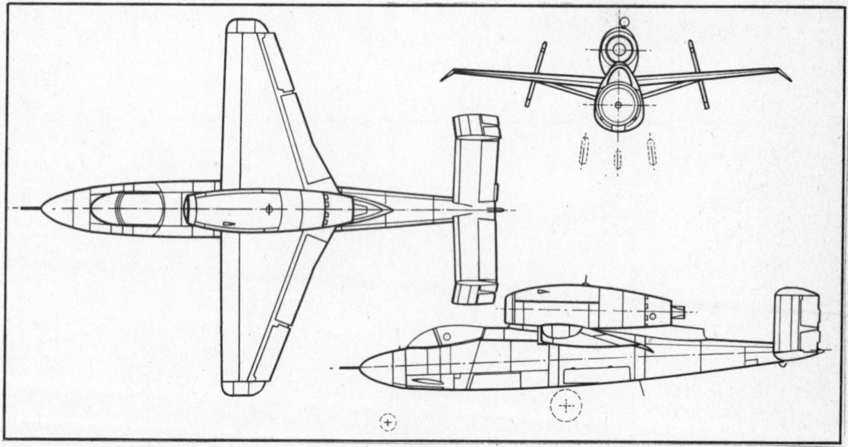

Heinkel He 162A-2 Salamander

TYPE	DIMENSIONS span ft	span in	length ft	length in	height ft	height in	WEIGHT max t-o lb	PERFORMANCE max speed mph	at height ft	service ceiling ft	combat range miles	REMARKS
He 112B	29	10¼	30	6	12	7½	4,960	317	13,120	27,890	683	
He 115B-1	73	1	56	9	21	7¾	22,928	203	11,150	17,060	1,300	
He 162 A	23	7¾	29	8½	8	4⅜	5,940	522	19,700	39,500	410	

Heinkel He 177A-5, captured aircraft, RAF markings

Heinkel He 177A-02, second pre-production aircraft

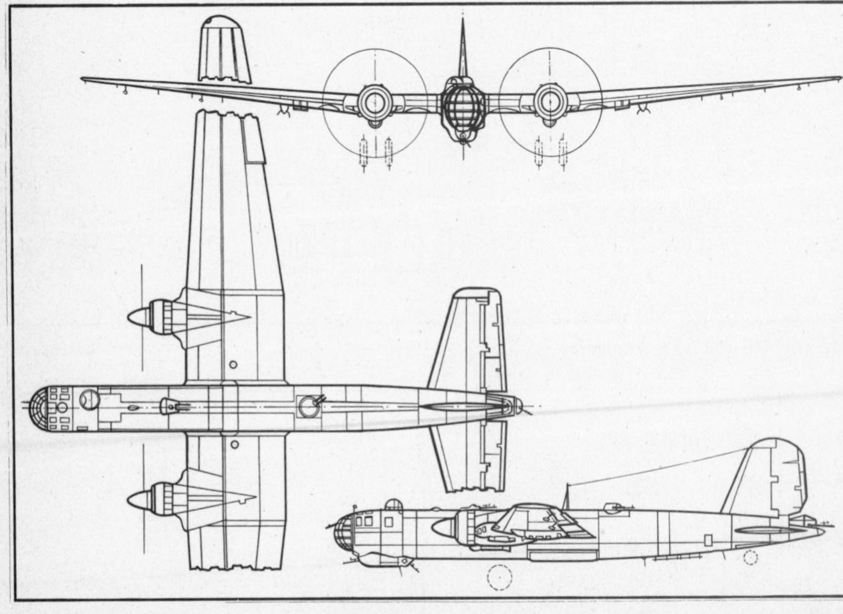

Heinkel He 177A-5

pairs of coupled engines, each pair driving a single propeller – a feature sound enough in principle, but destined to provide the He 177's biggest headache during its entire service life.

The RLM specification to which the machine was designed was issued in 1938, calling for a dual-purpose heavy bomber and anti-shipping aircraft. Attempts to keep down the loaded weight to the required 59,000 lb were persistently frustrated, not least by the RLM's request that this 100-foot-span, 20-ton warplane should be structurally strong enough for dive-bombing! The original design thus got heavier, needing a stronger (and therefore heavier) undercarriage, and by the time the prototype He 177V1 was ready for its maiden flight on 19 November 1939, it was little short of miraculous that the all-up weight had been kept within the bounds of the original specification.

The first flight was cut short, on account of rapidly overheating engines – a foretaste of the future, when engine fires were to cause the loss of several prototype and production He 177s.

After completion of numerous prototypes, 35 pre-production He 177A-0s were built jointly by Heinkel and Arado. The all-up weight had by now increased to 66,140 lb, including a 5,290-lb bomb-load. One MG FF cannon, two MG 131s and two MG 81s were installed for defence and the aircraft was normally manned by a crew of five.

Arado completed 130 He 177A-1s by mid-1943. The early machines of this batch were officially assigned for further testing; the remainder proved so troublesome on their brief operational debut that they, too, were withdrawn and used for testing or training purposes. Meanwhile, Heinkel had put the He 177A-3 into production with a lengthened fuselage and the engine nacelles placed somewhat further out on the wing. The A-3 entered service in early 1943. Several sub-types of this version and the later A-5 were built, and were used extensively on the Russian front – for transport and ground-attack duties as well as in the bombing rôle. This produced some interesting armament variations, including the fitting of 50-mm or 75-mm cannon for ground attack. The A-3/R7 was adapted to carry the Hs 293 glider bomb. Power plant on all versions of the He 177 comprised two 2,950-hp Daimler-Benz 610 (coupled DB 605A) 24-cylinder liquid-cooled engines.

Apart from production of a handful of He 177A-6s, the further career of the Greif was concentrated around developing the aircraft with four normal, separate engines to avoid the persistent fire troubles of the coupled power plant.

First of the new models was the He 177A-4, development of which was assigned to the German-controlled Farman factory in France under the new designation He 274A.

Only one prototype was completed and this was still awaiting its first flight when the Germans had to evacuate Paris.

A converted A-3 airframe became the four-engined He 277, development of which was continued by Heinkel under the spurious designation "He 177B" to overcome the RLM's official disinterest in the re-engining programme. With four 1,750-hp DB 603As, this was flown late in 1943, followed by a second, similar prototype and a third with a twin tail assembly. A small production batch was built, but these were not put into service.

All in all, the He 177 can be rated as one of the German aircraft industry's greatest failures of the 1939–45 war; but if the RLM planners had seen fit to allow the manufacturers to resolve the aircraft's shortcomings before forcing it into service prematurely, its story might have been very different.

Heinkel He 219 Uhu (Owl)

When Ernst Heinkel AG first put forward their proposals for a multi-purpose *Zerstörer* (destroyer) aircraft in August 1940, the RLM, still believing that the war would be finished in Germany's favour within a matter of months, were not particularly interested. By the end of the following year, however, their beliefs had changed, and they authorized the company to begin detailed design work in January 1942. On 15 November of that year the first prototype of the He 219, as the project was now designated, made its first flight, powered by two 1,750-hp DB 603A liquid-cooled inverted Vee engines. It was transferred in the following month to Peenemünde for trials of its armament, which comprised a single 13-mm MG 131 gun in the rear cockpit and a ventral fuselage tray housing a pair of 20-mm MG 151 cannon.

The initial order was for 100 He 219s, but by the time tooling-up began at various factories throughout Germany, in April 1943, this original contract had been increased threefold.

By July 1943 about 20 pre-production He 219A-0s were ready for evaluation, although many more prototype aircraft were yet to appear for future models. Series production began with 40 He 219A-2s (the A-1 having been abandoned). The A-2, with the same engine as the first prototype, carried a crew of two and an armament of two dorsal MK 108 30-mm cannon, two MG 151s in the ventral tray and a further two installed in the wing roots. The He 219A-3 and A-4 were proposals for a three-seat bomber and a high-altitude reconnaissance bomber respectively and were not adopted; so production continued with the A-5, A-6 and A-7 models. Most of these were powered by variants of the DB 603 engine, although the A-7/R5 and A-7/R6 had Jumo 213E and Jumo 222 engines respectively. The A-5 accommodated a third crew member and had an increased fuel capacity.

Numerous variations of armament were installed in these A sub-types.

The entire A series amounted to 268 aircraft. Together with about 20 prototype or pre-production machines, they were the only He 219s to go into squadron service with Luftwaffe units, apart from a handful of two-seat He 219B-2s, developed from the A-6. When the war in Europe ended, prototype airframes of the C-1 night fighter and C-2 fighter-bomber (three 1,100-lb bombs) were awaiting delivery of their Jumo 222 engines. A crew of four was to have been carried in the C series, the fourth member manning a tail turret housing four MG 131 guns.

Henschel Hs 123

It was appropriate that the first flight of the Hs 123V1 prototype, on 8 May 1935, should have been in the hands of General Ernst Udet, for it was largely as the result of this officer's recommendations that the dive-bomber, as a type, was evolved for use by the Luftwaffe. The Hs 123, in early prototype form, was a single-seat, single-bay biplane with an oval-section metal fuselage and fixed, faired undercarriage. Power was provided by a single 650-hp BMW 132A radial engine (a licence-built version of the Pratt & Whitney Hornet) in a smooth cowling, and the first machine carried no armament. The Hs 123V2, bearing the civil registration D-ILUA, had a smaller, fluted cowling and was also unarmed. However, two 7·9-mm MG 17 machine-guns, and underwing racks for one 550-lb or four 110-lb bombs, were fitted to the Hs 123V3 (D-IKOU) and Hs 123V4 (D-IZXY). The latter machine also had strengthened wings, to combat weaknesses revealed in diving tests by its predecessors.

A small pre-production batch of Hs 123A-0s was completed in 1936 for service evaluation, and was followed by the first major production version, the slightly

Heinkel He 219A-7 Uhu, captured aircraft, RAF markings

Heinkel He 219 Uhu, captured aircraft, USAAF markings

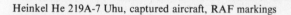

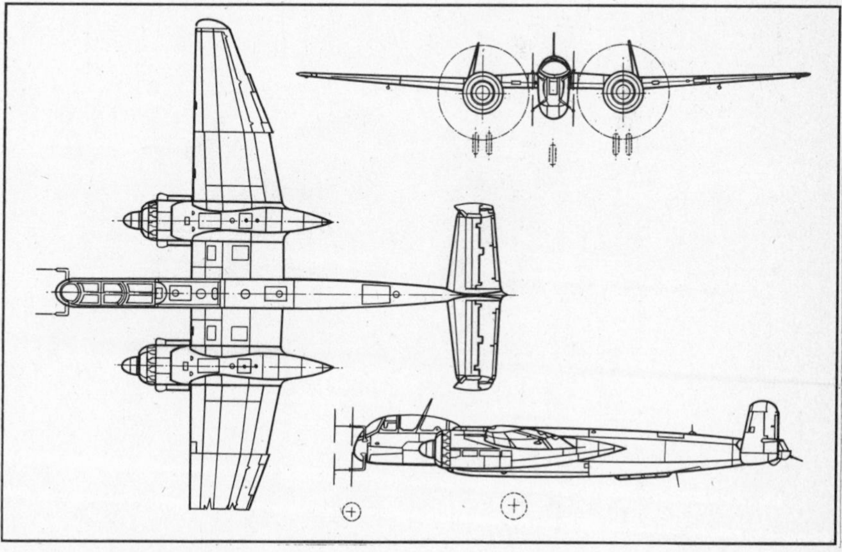

Heinkel He 219A-5/R1 Uhu

TYPE	DIMENSIONS						WEIGHT	PERFORMANCE				REMARKS
	span ft	span in	length ft	length in	height ft	height in	max t-o lb	max speed mph	at height ft	service ceiling ft	combat range miles	
He 177A-1	103	0¼	67	6¼	21	10½	66,139	317	19,685	22,966	746	Max range 3,480 miles
He 177A-5	103	1¾	66	11⅛	20	11⅞	68,343	303	21,650	26,250	3,417 max	
He 219A-7	60	8⅓	50	11¾	13	5½	33,730	416	22,965	41,660	1,243	

Henschel Hs 123V2

Henschel Hs 123A-1

Henschel Hs 129

Henschel Hs 129B

modified Hs 123A-1. These aircraft were all powered by the 870-hp BMW 132Dc nine-cylinder radial engine, driving a two-bladed propeller. The first Hs 123s entered Luftwaffe service at the beginning of 1937, and in the spring of that year five were despatched to Spain for testing under battle conditions by the Condor Legion.

By 1939, the Hs 123 – Germany's last operational biplane – was obsolete by world standards, but in Poland, France and the early stages of the Russian campaign, against limited opposing air strength, it continued to be used with some success, mainly in the ground-attack rôle.

The Hs 123A-1 was the only model to achieve series production, although two further prototypes were evolved later. The Hs 123V5, with a 960-hp BMW 132K engine and three-bladed propeller, was intended to lead to an Hs 123B production model; likewise, the Hs 123V6 (D-IHDI), with a similar power plant, sliding cockpit hood and four MG 17 guns, was to have been the progenitor of the Hs 123C.

However, the era of the biplane was at an end, and no further production was undertaken. The Hs 123 ended its career on second-line duties, such as supply dropping and glider towing.

Henschel Hs 129

The combat reports of the Luftwaffe units which took part in the Civil War in Spain clearly indicated the need for a specialized close support and ground-attack aircraft, and in 1938 the RLM issued a detailed requirement for such a type, calling for a well-armoured single-seat machine built around a pair of Argus As 410 air-cooled engines. To this specification, Dipl-Ing F. Nicolaus of the Henschel Flugzeugwerke AG produced the Hs 129, a low-wing monoplane with a fuselage of triangular cross-section, protected by extensive armour plate in the forward section as well as an armoured glass windscreen on the pilot's cabin.

Three prototypes were constructed, the Hs 129V1 making its maiden flight during the early part of 1939, powered by two 495-hp As 410A-ls. The prototypes were followed by a small pre-production batch of Hs 129A-0s in 1940, which were sent to a Luftwaffe test squadron for evaluation. The test pilots' reports were sufficiently damning to prevent any production order from materializing, though it is notable that these early machines were not too unsatisfactory to be passed on to the Rumanian Air Force, which used them for a time on the Russian front.

To eliminate the shortcomings found in the Hs 129A-0, Nicolaus's team came up with a fresh design, which they dubbed project P.76, based on a substantially more powerful engine installation. However, the RLM refused to accept the P.76 on the grounds that existing production jigs were not utilized and that different engines from those chosen were more readily available, at much less expense. The recent fall of France had put at their disposal substantial quantities of French power plants, and they directed that the original Hs 129 design be adapted to take the 690-hp Gnome-Rhône 14M fourteen-cylinder radial engine.

With this power plant, cockpit and other internal modifications, and more up-to-date guns, the type re-emerged in 1941 as the Hs 129B. Seven pre-production Hs 129B-0s were delivered for evaluation in that year, and the type entered series production that autumn, as the Hs 129B-1. The first machines became operational with Luftwaffe units during the Crimean fighting of 1942, and further quantities were drafted to units in North Africa. In both theatres, their chief success was in the anti-tank rôle.

A number of sub-variants of the B-1 series appeared, with armament changes. Standard armament, as fitted to the B-1/R1, comprised two 20-mm MG 151 cannon and two 7·9-mm MG 17 machine-guns, with provision for carrying two 110-lb bombs or two containers each holding 48 anti-personnel weapons. Without the bombs, and with a 30-mm MK 101 cannon added to the fixed armament, the type became the B-1/R2. The B-1/R3 had the standard guns plus a ventral tray carrying four more

MG 17 guns; the B-1/R4 carried standard armament and a more widely varied ordnance load of one 550-lb or four 110-lb bombs, or 96 anti-personnel weapons in a single container; and the B-1/R5 had the standard guns, with fewer rounds per gun in order to accommodate an aerial reconnaissance camera.

The success of the B-1/R2 as an anti-tank aircraft led to the evolution of a B-2 sub-series equipped with guns only. The standard equipment of the B-2/R1 was similar to that of the B-1/R1 except for the substitution of 13-mm MG 131 machine-guns for the MG 17s of the earlier machine. To this armament the B-2/R2 added a 30-mm MK 103 cannon; while the B-2/R3 dispensed with the MG 131s in favour of two further MG 151s and a 37-mm BK 3·7. The final version, the B-2/R4, mounted a 75-mm BK 7.5 cannon in an enormous jettisonable housing under the centre fuselage, with the muzzle projecting nearly eight feet ahead of the nose of the aircraft. The considerably greater weapon load carried by this version reduced its maximum speed to only 199 mph at sea level.

Production of Hs 129s came to an end in the summer of 1944, by which time a total of 841 of the type had been constructed.

Junkers D.I and CL.I

In October 1917 there first appeared a small, single-seat low-wing Junkers monoplane bearing the manufacturer's designation J.7. This machine, powered by a 160-hp Mercedes engine, neatly installed in a well-streamlined nose with a small, round spinner, was entered for the D class fighter trials held during June 1918. Fast and manoeuvrable, it featured the now-familiar Junkers method of metal construction, with corrugated metal skin panels, and was ordered into production for the German air force in modified form, under the designation D.I.

The production fighter was basically similar to the prototype, although some two feet longer and powered by a 185-hp BMW engine; armament consisted of a pair of fixed, forward-firing Spandau guns ahead of the cockpit. Because of lack of experience with the aircraft's then-unconventional metal construction, only 41 D.Is were completed and delivered to the Front before the Armistice in November 1918.

However, a number of D.Is served after the war with anti-Bolshevik partisan forces in several of the Baltic countries.

A two-seat development of the D.I, the Junkers CL.I, also entered production during the latter half of 1918, as a replacement for the obsolescent Halberstadt CL types. Prototype for the CL.I was the Junkers J.10, and a change of power plant from the D.I brought the 180-hp Mercedes D.IIIa liquid-cooled engine into use in place of the earlier machine's BMW engine. The second crew member was provided with a ring-mounted Parabellum gun in the rear cockpit.

By the end of the war, 47 CL.Is had been completed. Some of these served in Estonia, Finland and Lithuania after the 1914–18 War, alongside the D.Is. Three examples of a seaplane version, known as the CLS.I (Junkers J.11), were also delivered to the German Navy during 1918. Intended for fighter-reconnaissance duties, they differed from the CL.I in having two single-step floats, a fixed fin forward of the rudder and a 200-hp Benz engine, which increased the loaded weight to 3,124 lb. No production order was placed for the CLS.I.

Henschel Hs 129B-2/R4, armed with 75-mm cannon

Junkers D.I

Junkers CL.I

TYPE	DIMENSIONS						WEIGHT	PERFORMANCE				REMARKS
	span		length		height		max t-o	max speed	at height	service ceiling	combat range	
	ft	in	ft	in	ft	in	lb	mph	ft	ft	miles	
Hs 123A-1	34	5⅓	27	4	10	6⅓	4,652	214	4,000	29,530	530	
Hs 129B-1	46	7	31	11⅞	10	8	11,265	253	12,467	29,530	547	
Junkers D.I	29	6⅜	23	9⅜	7	4½	1,841	116	SL	19,680	1½ hr	
Junkers CL.I	39	6⅜	25	11	7	8½	2,326	105	SL	19,680	2 hr	

Junkers J.I

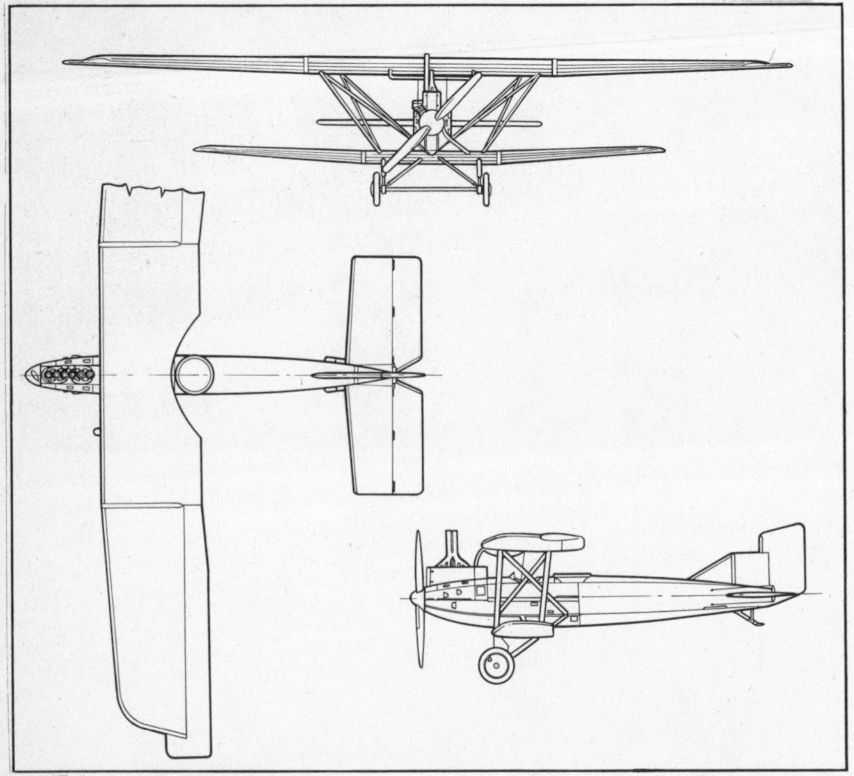

Junkers J.I

Junkers W.34, Finnish Air Force

Junkers J.I

When the J.I, designed jointly by Dr Hugo Junkers and Professor Madelung of the Junkers Flugzeug-Werke AG at Dessau, first entered service in the late spring and early summer of 1917, it rapidly acquired the nickname *Möbelwagen* (furniture van). Paradoxically, this was a tribute to its large and extremely sturdy appearance, which was the result of extensive pioneer work by Junkers over the preceding two years in the development of aircraft of all-metal construction.

To capitalize on this pioneering, the Flugmeisterei had requested Junkers to design an armoured two-seat biplane for close support duties. The prototype J.I (or J.4, to give it the manufacturers' designation) was completed in the early part of 1917, as an unequal-span design with two cantilever wings of very thick section. Built around the 200-hp Benz Bz IV six-cylinder in-line engine, it was large for a single-engined type, the upper mainplane spanning over 50 ft. This wing was carried well clear of the fuselage top decking on support struts running from the lower wing and the bottom of the fuselage. The lower wing was similar in planform, but with considerably shorter span and only about one-third the area of the top plane.

The J.I's hexagonal-section fuselage was covered extensively with steel skin armour (only the rear parts being fabric-covered), and terminated in a distinctive fin and rudder and a near-rectangular tailplane. Although the neatly-spinnered two-blade propeller was of generous dimensions, the J.I utilized an uncommonly short-legged landing gear. A ring-mounted Parabellum machine-gun was installed in the observer's cockpit, while the pilot had two forward-firing Spandau guns.

Junker's Dessau factory completed in all 227 J.I aircraft. These were employed primarily on low-level observation and close support duties over the front-line trenches, some late production machines carrying a cine-camera for photographic reconnaissance. As its rugged appearance suggested, the J.I was a tough aircraft which could withstand a considerable amount of damage in combat, but its very sturdiness made it somewhat heavy on the controls and necessitated plenty of ground for take-off and landing. Nevertheless, had the war been prolonged, this type might well have figured with increasing frequency in combat reports.

Junkers W.33, W.34 and K.43

The W.34 ("W" for *Werkflugzeug*, or general-purpose aircraft), with its stablemate the W.33, first appeared in 1926. Both were derivatives of the world's first all-metal transport aeroplane, the six-seat Junkers F.13 of 1919, and were basically similar save for their power plants.

The W.33 (one 310-hp Junkers L-5) and the W.34 (assorted engines, but chiefly the BMW 132, the Bramo 322 and various models of the BMW Hornet) were built in substantial numbers, for military and civil use within Germany and also for export. They were employed in places as far afield as Greece, Canada, Japan and South America, were built under licence in Sweden by AB Flygindustri at Limhamn, and appeared in versions with wheel, ski and float landing gear.

Between 1934 and 1937, a small number of W.34s served in an interim capacity with Luftwaffe squadrons in the light bomber rôle; but the military careers of both types were spent mainly on second-line duties such as instrument flight training, meteorological observation, communications, ambulance, coastal patrol and mine detection. A small number were still in service in the early days of World War II, when they supplemented Junkers Ju 52/3ms as light transports.

The designation K.43 ("K" for *Kampfflugzeug* – warplane – followed by a reversal of the digits in the W.34 designation) was applied to a reconnaissance-bomber development, with dimensional and other data generally similar to the W.34. Sufficient K.43s were supplied to the Finnish Air Force to equip one floatplane squadron based at Viipuri. These were supplied originally with Bristol Jupiter power plants, but were subsequently re-engined with the 600-hp Pratt & Whitney Hornet. One light machine-gun was installed behind the cockpit and a second in a dorsal mounting aft of the cabin. The air force of Colombia also operated a few K.43s, as well as W.33s and W.34s, as transports.

Junkers R.02 and K.53

The origins of these two related types begin with the A.20, a so-called "postal aircraft" evolved by the Junkers Flugzeug-Werke in the early 1920s. The A.20 was a two-seat, low-wing monoplane with a BMW IIIa engine, and was built in modest numbers by Junkers' Moscow-Fili plant under the designation R.02 ("02" being the digits of "A.20" in reverse, and the prefix letter signifying *Razvedchik*=reconnaissance). At least 25 R.02s are known to have been in service with the Red Air Force in 1925, and the Russian service designation Yu-20 may have applied to them. Some Fili-built machines may also have been supplied to the Turkish Air Force, and it is possible that Junkers' Turkish factory at Kayseri built a small quantity.

A development of the A.20, the A.35, became by a similar change of designation the K.53, and differed from its predecessor chiefly in having a 310-hp Junkers L-5 water-cooled engine, two forward-firing machine-guns fixed in the engine decking, and two movable guns on a ring mounting in the second cockpit. The K.53 had an internal fuel capacity of 66 gallons, and a choice of wheel, float or ski landing gear. A small number were built in Sweden in 1926–7 as R.53s, but no record appears to survive of the overall production total or of their military career.

Junkers R.42

Most German "civil" aircraft of the middle and late 1920s were designed with some pretensions to military usage, and the Junkers G.24 was no exception. This three-engined passenger transport was certainly operated by several central European airlines; but at the Dessau plant, then the centre for design, construction and testing of all Junkers prototypes, it was developed in modified form as the K.30 and offered both for civil use and as a medium bomber. The commercial version was purchased in small numbers; but the military model underwent further revision before it, too, entered limited production by AB Flygindustri in Sweden and by Junkers' subsidiary plant at Kayseri in Turkey.

This model, following the customary practice of "hiding" its origins by reversing the numerals of the civil model, was designated R.42 and was powered by three 310-hp Junkers L-5 engines. The K.30 had essayed a redesigned vertical tail unit, but the original G.24 shape was restored on the R.42. No internal bomb-bay was provided, the R.42's modest weapon load being suspended under the wings. One or two machine-guns – probably Madsens – were carried on a dorsal ring mounting, with an additional gun in a retractable installation in the belly. A small batch of R.42 bombers was supplied to the Fuerza Aérea de Chile about 1930.

Junkers Ju 52/3m

Famous for more than two decades as "Iron Annie" of the Luftwaffe and as a post-war hack transport (a few examples are still flying today), the Junkers Ju 52/3m

Junkers K.43, Finnish Air Force

Junkers K.53, Swedish-built

Junkers R.42, Swedish-built

TYPE	DIMENSIONS						WEIGHT	PERFORMANCE				REMARKS
	span		length		height		max t-o	max speed	at height	service ceiling	combat range	
	ft	in	ft	in	ft	in	lb	mph	ft	ft	miles	
Junkers J.I	52	6	29	10⅜	11	1⅝	4,795	97	SL		192	
Junkers W.34	58	2¾	36	1			5,952	102		20,340		
Junkers K.53	52	3½	26	11¼	11	5¾	3,527	129		19,680		
Junkers R.42												No data available

Junkers Ju 52/3m

Junkers Ju 86D-1

Junkers Ju 86P-1

Junkers Ju 87A-0

was an ugly, angular machine with a distinctly porcine appearance, attributable largely to its bulky fuselage and the triple-engined configuration.

Its origins lay in the Ju 52 of the latter 1920s, which was a single-engined machine and was retrospectively dubbed Ju 52/1m to distinguish it from its tri-motor development. First envisaged in 1928, the prototype Ju 52/1m flew on 13 October 1930, powered by an 800-hp Junkers L.88 twelve-cylinder liquid-cooled engine. Production aircraft of this type switched to the 750-hp Jumo 4 six-cylinder engine, giving a maximum speed of 128 mph at sea level, with an all-up weight of 16,740 lb.

Because of the success of the Ju 52/3m, which was flown some 18 months later, comparatively few Ju 52/1ms were built. The three-engined version (575-hp BMW 132A radial engines, which entered production in 1934), soon proved extremely popular as a commercial transport with Deutsche Lufthansa and foreign operators, particularly in South America. A number of the DLH machines were Ju 52/3mWs, similar to the land transports but equipped for waterborne operations, with two single-step metal floats replacing the normal wheeled undercarriage.

With the emergence of the new Luftwaffe in the early 1930s, the Ju 52/3m was adapted for service as an interim bomber. It made its operational debut during the Civil War in Spain, but with the arrival in service of true bomber designs, such as the Ju 86 and He 111, the Ju 52/3m reverted to the task for which it had originally been designed.

The bomber version, known as the Ju 52/3m g3e, was armed with two 7·9-mm MG 15 guns; 450 of this model were built. Its sturdy construction (typical Junkers corrugated metal skinning) made for reliability and efficiency in operation, and in the military transport rôle the Ju 52/3m gave the Luftwaffe many years of faithful service. During World War II it figured in every major German invasion campaign. Whether in Norway, Greece, Libya, Crete, Belgium or the Netherlands, the Ju 52/3m was always there, dropping paratroops, delivering supplies and performing a multitude of other duties in support of the German Wehrmacht. Wheel, ski or float landing gear all came alike to this ubiquitous aircraft, and the Dutch Fokker Factory, under German control, was forced to construct float gear for the conversion of landplanes to the Ju 52/3mW configuration.

Total production of the Ju 52/3m amounted to 4,845 machines between 1934 and 1944. These included the g4e, g5e, g6e and g7e, of which the last named could accommodate 16-18 soldiers or, as an ambulance, 12 stretchers and their patients. Most production aircraft were powered by 830-hp BMW 132T nine-cylinder air-cooled radial engines.

Junkers Ju 86

A contemporary of the Heinkel He 111, the Ju 86 first appeared in 1934 in answer to a Deutsche Lufthansa requirement for a fast twin-engined airliner capable of seating ten passengers. It was designed by Dipl-Ing Zindel of the Junkers Flugzeug und Motorenwerke and was, like the He 111, equally capable of doubling as a bomber.

The first two models to appear were the Ju 86A (12 built), powered by two 600-hp Junkers Jumo 205 six-cylinder diesel engines, and the Ju 86B which had nine-cylinder BMW 132Dcs of 845 hp. Both of these models were commercial airliners, South African Airways purchasing 18 of the latter version with American Hornet engines. The first bomber version was the Ju 86D, which was produced for the Luftwaffe in two forms: the Ju 86D-1, which was a military counterpart of the Ju 86A, and the D-2, which corresponded to the B version. Armament of the D series consisted of three 7·9-mm MG 15 machine-guns and an internal bomb-load of 2,200 lb. An export version was the Ju 86K, 40 of which were sold to the Swedish government and which was also built under licence by SAAB for the Flygvapnet. Known in Swedish service as the B-3, this version was powered by SFA-built Bristol Mercury XXIV engines of 980 hp.

The Ju 86D's brief blooding in the Spanish Civil War

soon revealed that its performance was inadequate against contemporary opposition, and attempts were made to improve this. Following production of a small number of Ju 86Gs (intended as bombers but quickly relegated to aircrew training duties), the first such attempt was the Ju 86P. The greater power of two 880-hp Jumo 207A-1 engines, coupled with an improved wing some 10 ft greater in span, enabled the Ju 86P to operate at safer altitudes than its predecessors, and at somewhat higher speeds. Bomb-load (made up of four 550-lb or sixteen 110-lb bombs) remained the same, but the armament was reduced to a single defensive 7·9-mm MG 17 machine-gun.

The Ju 86P series was succeeded by the Ju 86R (built in R-1, R-2 and R-3 models), with 950-hp Jumo 207B-3s and an even greater wingspan, now some 30 ft more than that of the original design. The Ju 86's speed remained too poor for a modern bomber, but with the excellent ceiling made possible by its progressively lengthened wings it was admirably suited to the reconnaissance rôle, and it was on such duties that the type was employed during the late 1930s and the early years of World War II. Two projected developments were the Ju 186 (four Jumo 208s of 950 hp) and the Ju 286 with six Jumo 208s, but neither of these entered production.

Junkers Ju 87

The dive-bomber was very much in vogue in German military circles during the later 1930s and the early months of World War II; and while the Luftwaffe retained air supremacy in its various theatres of operations it was undoubtedly an effective and terrifying weapon. Thus the Ju 87, personification of all the *Sturzkampfflugzeuge* or "Stukas" before and since, screamed and blasted its way across the virtually defenceless frontiers of Poland, France, Belgium and Holland to no small purpose.

The origins of the Ju 87 can be traced back to the K.47 design evolved by Junkers' Swedish department as early as 1928; but design of the Ju 87 proper began in 1934, the Ju 87V1 prototype making its maiden flight towards the end of the following year. Powered by a 640-hp Rolls-Royce Kestrel V in-line engine and featuring twin end-plate fins and rudders, it was lost in a crash shortly afterwards; but flight trials continued with the single-tailed V2 and V3 (D-UKYQ), to such effect that the Ju 87 emerged winner of a dive-bomber competition held at Rechlin in 1936. By the late autumn of that year, the V4 had flown, and completion of ten pre-production Ju 87A-0s was well advanced. Deliveries to the Luftwaffe of the first production model, the Ju 87A-1, began in the spring of 1937.

Of all-metal construction, with an oval-section fuselage mounting a "greenhouse" canopy for the crew of two, and a two-spar inverted gull wing with a fixed and heavily "trousered" undercarriage, the Ju 87 was an awe-inspiring aircraft of decidedly ugly appearance. Its bomb-load consisted of one 550-lb or 1,100-lb bomb, and a defensive armament of one MG 15 and one MG 17 gun was installed. The Ju 87A-2 was essentially similar to the A-1. Three A-1s joined the Condor Legion in Spain at the end of 1937, for evaluation under genuine battle conditions, but comparatively few A series machines were completed.

The Ju 87B-1 appeared in the summer of 1938, with a

Junkers Ju 87B-1

Junkers Ju 87G-1, armed with two 37-mm cannon

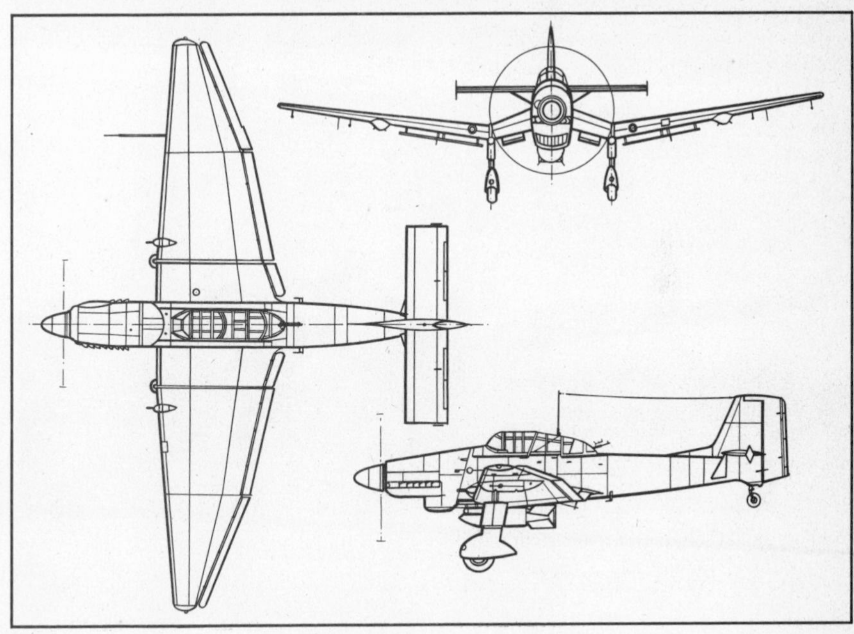

Junkers Ju 87D-3

TYPE	DIMENSIONS span ft	span in	length ft	length in	height ft	height in	WEIGHT max t-o lb	PERFORMANCE max speed mph	at height ft	service ceiling ft	combat range miles	REMARKS
Ju 52/3m	95	10	62	0	14	10	24,200	165	3,000	16,580	800	Performance data for BMW 132T-powered models
Ju 86E-1	73	9¾	57	9	15	5	18,078	202	9,840	22,310	1,243	
Ju 86P-1	83	11⅞	54	0	15	5	22,928	224	19,685	39,370	621	
Ju 86R-2	104	11⅞	54	0	15	5	25,419	261	29,530	49,210	975	
Ju 87A-1	45	3⅓	35	5⅛	12	9½	7,495	199	12,000	22,965	620 max	600-hp Jumo 210Ca engine

Junkers Ju 88A-1

Junkers Ju 88A-15

Junkers Ju 88C-6b, with Lichtenstein radar

Junkers Ju 88G-1, with improved Lichtenstein radar and Ju 188 fin and rudder

1,100-hp Jumo 211D engine, redesigned cockpit canopy and undercarriage fairings, and a larger fin and rudder. The Ju 87B-2 had a few additional minor refinements and most of the 335 Ju 87s in front-line service at the outbreak of World War II were of the B type. After their initial, unopposed campaigns of terror in the first few months of the war they received a somewhat sharp rebuff when they tried similar tactics over southern England during the Battle of Britain, and suffered heavy losses.

The Ju 87B was supplied in substantial numbers to units of the Regia Aeronautica, and also to the Bulgarian, Hungarian and Rumanian air forces. A variant of the B-1, with additional fuel tankage giving a range of 875 miles, was known as the Ju 87R-1 (R for *Reichweit* = range). This version was used primarily for attacks on shipping. It was also intended to use the Ju 87 from the carrier *Graf Zeppelin*; but when it became clear that this vessel would not be completed the few B series machines that had been converted for shipboard operation were restored to their original standard.

The next and largest production series was the Ju 87D, which first appeared in 1940. Utilizing the 1,400-hp Jumo 211J – which gave it more than twice the engine power of the Ju 87V1 – the D series could carry up to 3,960 lb of bombs, and had an additional pair of 7·9-mm MG 81s for defence, plus additional armour protection for the crew. Several D sub-types were produced, among them the D-3 ground attack model with a six-MG 81 or twin-MG FF pack beneath each wing, and the D-5 with wing span extended by some 5 ft. The D-5 and D-7 were developed for night attack missions.

Many D series aircraft were employed with success on the Russian front, where the Ju 87G-1 also gave a good account of itself. This was a specialized "tank-buster", with a 37-mm cannon beneath each wing.

Of the other Ju 87 variants, the Ju 87F was not produced; the Ju 87H was a two-seat trainer model; and the proposed Ju 187 replacement was abandoned. A total of 4,881 Ju 87s of all versions were completed during the war period; together with pre-war production, this brought the overall figure to well over 5,000 aircraft.

Junkers Ju 88

The de Havilland Mosquito has a deservedly good reputation for versatility and longevity, but the Ju 88, although less pleasing from an aesthetic point of view, outstripped the British warplane in the variety of duties performed and was produced in more than double the numbers, lending itself to considerable improvement and adaptation during its operational career. It was just coming into service when the War in Europe began, and was still in production when hostilities ended five and a half years later.

The RLM specification which led to the Ju 88 was issued early in 1935, calling for a fast, twin-engined medium bomber. Competing designs were the Focke-Wulf Fw 57 and Messerschmitt Bf 162, but the development contract went to the Junkers project and the Ju 88V1 made its first flight on 21 December 1936, powered by two 900-hp Daimler-Benz DB600 liquid-cooled engines. The Ju 88V2 which appeared in April 1937 was basically similar, but a redesigned cockpit enclosure and twin 950-hp Junkers Jumo 211A engines were introduced on the Ju 88V4, which followed some five months later. A fourth crew member was allowed for in the Ju 88V4, which brought additional design changes such as a much-glazed nose section made up of numerous flat rectangular panels, and a lengthened fuselage, with correspondingly increased gross weight.

Typical practice of the time was followed by modifying and streamlining the Ju 88V5 for various speed record attempts in 1939; but it was the V4 which set the pattern for the first service models. Both the ten pre-production Ju 88A-0s and the first Ju 88A-1s (1,200-hp Jumo 211B) were put into operation with Luftwaffe squadrons. They arrived in service in time to make their debut in attacks over the United Kingdom in September 1939. The Ju 88A-1's normal bomb load of 3,968 lb (5,510 lb maximum) was reasonable, but its armament of three (later four)

7·9-mm MG 15 machine-guns proved inadequate, and steps were taken to augment this in subsequent models. The latter extended (with the exception of A-9, A-10, A-11 and A-15) up to the A-17 torpedo-bomber, including versions built for such varied rôles as medium and dive-bombing, long-range reconnaissance, shipping attack, and conversion training.

Perhaps the most significant advance was represented by the Ju 88A-4, the first to incorporate experience gained during the Battle of Britain. This version was given a longer-span wing, increased armour protection, better defensive armament (two MG 131s and two MG 81s, or one MG 131 and four MG 81s), a greater bomb-load (6,614 lb) and the increased power (on later aircraft) of the 1,410-hp Jumo 211J. Twenty of this model were also supplied to the Finnish government and others to the Regia Aeronautica.

Before deliveries of the A series began, there appeared on the drawing boards in 1939 the Ju 88B. The prototype of this version was flown early in 1940, followed by the normal pre-production quantity of Ju 88B-0s. No further production of the Ju 88B as such was undertaken, however, as this version was developed instead into the Ju 188 (page 180).

In parallel with the Ju 88A bomber series, development had been progressing on the Ju 88C heavy fighter. With its excellent turn of speed and robust construction, the Ju 88 was a "natural" for the *Zerstörer* (destroyer) role, and was put into major production as the Ju 88C-2 (the C-1 version being abandoned).

The C-2 was a straightforward adaptation of the A-1, mounting one 20-mm MG FF cannon and three MG 17 machine-guns in a "solid" nose, plus a single MG 15 aft of the cockpit for rearward defence. First unit to receive the Ju 88C-2 was Nachtjagdgeschwader 1, which put the type in service before the end of 1940. Next major fighter model was the Ju 88C-6, the C-3 being experimental and the C-4 and C-5 being produced in only small numbers. With Jumo 211J engines and the enlarged wing of the A-4 bomber, the Ju 88C-6 had two further MG FFs in the nose, and the rearward-firing gun was increased to MG 131 calibre: it operated as both a day (C-6a) and night (C-6b) fighter. Final C model was the C-7, also in separate day and night configurations.

Further adaptation of the Ju 88A-4 gave rise, in 1940, to the Ju 88D-1, D-2 and D-3, over 1,800 examples of which were completed for strategic reconnaissance duties. The designation Ju 88E applied to the B-0 aircraft which eventually became the Ju 188 prototype and, there being no Ju 88F, the next model in alphabetical sequence was the Ju 88G.

This model emerged during the summer of 1944 and, with improved Lichtenstein radar, was a more sophisticated night fighter than the earlier C variants employed for this rôle. Principal production versions – which had enlarged and more square tail surfaces, similar to those of the Ju 188 – were the Ju 88G-1 (BMW 801D), G-6 (BMW 801G or Jumo 213A) and G-7 (Jumo 213E-1). Another heavy fighter was the Ju 88H-2 (the H-1 being for photographic reconnaissance), but relatively few H series were built. Final fighter series was the Ju 88R, produced in R-1 day fighter and R-2 night fighter versions. Altogether, somewhere in the region of 6,000 of the various fighter models had been completed by the end of World War II.

Junkers Ju 88G-7c, captured aircraft, RAF markings

Junkers Ju 88P-2

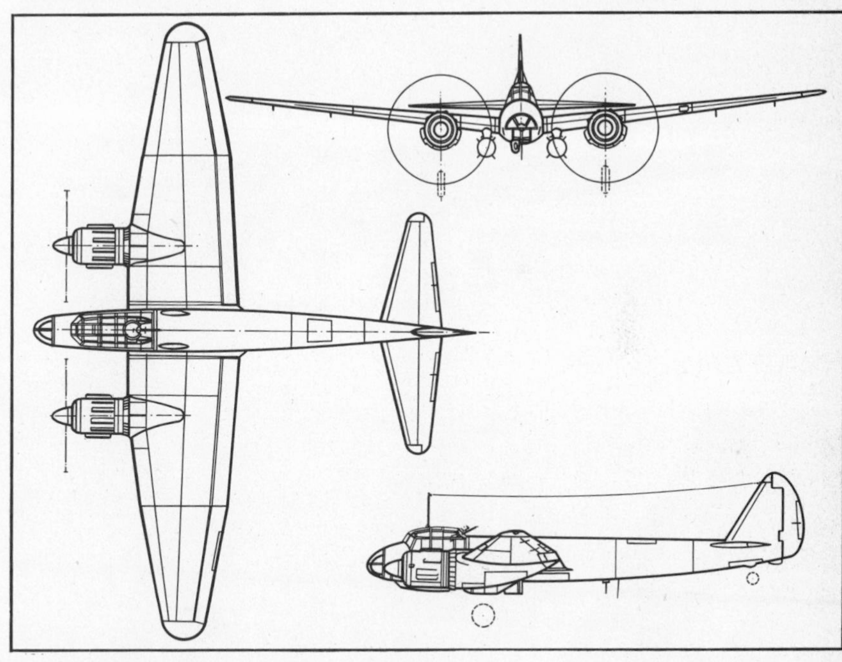

Junkers Ju 88S-1

TYPE	DIMENSIONS span ft	span in	length ft	length in	height ft	height in	WEIGHT max t-o lb	PERFORMANCE max speed mph	at height ft	service ceiling ft	combat range miles	REMARKS
Ju 87B-1	45	3⅓	36	5	12	9½	9,370	232	13,500	26,575	370	
Ju 87D-1	45	3⅓	37	8¾	12	9⅛	14,500	255	13,500	23,950	620	
Ju 88A-1	59	10¾	47	1⅓	15	9	27,500	286	18,045	30,675	1,553	
Ju 88A-4	65	10½	47	1⅓	15	9	26,724	293	17,390	27,020	1,695	
Ju 88C-6	65	10½	47	1⅓	16	7½	26,125	311	19,685	32,480	2,131 max	
Ju 88G-7	65	10½	54	1½	15	11	32,350	389	29,800	28,800	1,380	Performance with MW 50 power boost

Junkers Ju 88S-1

Junkers Ju 188F-1

Junkers Ju 388K-1

Junkers Ju 290V-8

Meanwhile, the potential of the Ju 88 as a bomber had not been neglected. After a limited number of Ju 88P-1 and P-2 ground attack aircraft had been built, mainly for anti-tank operations on the Russian front, with one 75-mm or two 37-mm cannon respectively, the next – and last – bomber model to appear was the Ju 88S. It had a very much smaller, smoother and completely rounded glazed nose, and carried a more modest bomb-load (1,760 lb) than its predecessors; but with 1,700-hp BMW 801Gs in the S-1 sub-type, and 1,810-hp BMW 801TJs in the S-2, the new bomber offered a much improved performance. Both versions were comparatively lightly armed, as was the S-3, which resembled the S-1 except in the use of 1,750-hp Jumo 213E-1s as its power plant. Counterparts of the S-1 and S-3 for photographic missions were designated Ju 88T-1 and T-3 respectively.

Including fighter models, total production of the Ju 88 amounted to approximately 15,000 machines. During the course of this redoubtable aircraft's career it performed the duties of day and night fighter, day and night bomber, dive-bomber, torpedo-bomber, shipping attack aircraft, photographic reconnaissance aircraft, minelayer, close support aircraft, VIP transport and operational trainer, with considerable distinction. One other function completes the record – its rather ignominious use as a pilotless missile when, as the explosive-laden lower component of Mistel composite weapons, guided by an Fw 190 or Bf 109 "pilot" aircraft, it was used in an attempt to stem Allied landings and advances in the last year of the war. Mainly converted A-4s or G-1s were used for this task.

Junkers Ju 188 and Ju 388

Excellent and adaptable though the Ju 88 was, the time inevitably came when a successor was required, and this appeared in the form of the Ju 188. Its evolution began as early as 1940, the design being developed from the Ju 88V27 via a converted Ju 88B-0, which was redesignated Ju 88E. Featuring a much revised, enlarged and considerably more glazed forward section, and pointed-tipped wings of greater span, the first Ju 188 variants to enter production were the Ju 188E and Ju 188F. Built in E-0 and E-1 (bomber) and F-1 and F-2 (reconnaissance) models, 120 were delivered during 1942.

All four types were powered by 1,700-hp BMW 801G-2 radial engines; but as soon as the power plant originally intended for the Ju 188 – the 1,776-hp Junkers Jumo 213A – became available, it was possible to place the Ju 188A-1 and A-2 on the production lines, together with the torpedo-bomber A-3. Reconnaissance counterparts of the A bombers were the Ju 188D-1 and D-2.

Several further variants were either produced or proposed, including the Ju 188G bomber, the Ju 188H-2, M-1, M-2 and T photo-reconnaissance models, the Ju 188R night fighter and the Ju 188S high-altitude bomber. Total production of all models was about 1,000.

Development of the design continued with the Ju 388, which began to appear in 1943 and was based on the pressurized, high-altitude S and T models of the Ju 188. First and only model to go into service in any numbers was the photographic Ju 388L, 89 machines of this type being completed. Carrying a crew of three and a trio of aerial cameras, the Ju 388L was armed with three (later four) MG 131 guns. The Ju 388J Störtebeker night fighter was given priority treatment by the RLM, but only three had been completed by VE-day. Likewise, the Ju 388K bomber had been delivered in only small numbers by the end of World War II and was too late to see operational service.

Final stage in the development of this design was the Ju 488, which was still under construction at the end of the war. With a lengthened fuselage and four BMW 801TJ engines on a revised wing, this was to have been used for high-altitude bombing and reconnaissance.

Junkers Ju 290

The Ju 290 maritime patrol and reconnaissance bomber of World War II owed its origins to the pre-war Ju 90 commercial transport. The 40-seat Ju 90V1 (registered D-AALU) had made its first flight on 28 August 1937. After three more prototypes had flown, a small batch of Ju 90Bs were produced, most of which were delivered to the Luftwaffe. The remainder joined the prototypes in the test programme, but this did not go well and extensive redesign was decided upon.

The Ju 90V7 (sometimes known as the Ju 90S) thus became the prototype for the new Ju 290, revision of the original design being supervised during 1940 by Dipl-Ing Zindel of the Junkers Flugzeug und Motorenwerke. It was hoped that the 290 would develop into a replacement for the Fw 200 Condor, but it proved only moderately successful in this rôle.

Somewhat underpowered for a heavy bomber, with four 1,600-hp BMW 801A radials, the Ju 290A-0 was produced in only small numbers. The Ju 290A-1 was a transport model, followed in 1943 by the A-2 and A-3 (long-range reconnaissance), the A-5 (U-boat co-operation), A-7 and A-8 (Hs 293 carrier).

A much more heavily armed bomber model, which appeared in 1944, was the Ju 290B, carrying a 9,900-lb bomb-load, eight MG 131s and four MG 151s in a strengthened fuselage. The Ju 290C reconnaissance transport was similar except for a BMW 801E power plant (4 × 2,000-hp) and the MG 151s only. No production was undertaken of the Ju 290D, a proposed long-range bomber, or of the Ju 290E night bomber, based on the C.

Two prototypes and a few production examples of the Ju 390 appeared, from 1943. This was a long-range reconnaissance bomber, powered by six BMW 801Es. The Ju 390B was even more heavily armed than the Ju 290B, having eight MG 131s and six MG 151s, but it saw very little combat service.

LVG C.II

The C.II was the progeny of Franz Schneider, the Swiss-born chief designer of the Luft-Verkehrs Gesellschaft mbH of Johannisthal, and first appeared at the end of 1915. It had been preceded earlier in the same year by the C.I, which was basically a strengthened adaptation of the company's B.I, with a 150-hp Benz Bz III in-line engine. The C.I was evolved at fairly short notice in order to fill a requirement for an armed two-seat reconnaissance aircraft in the newly established C class, and was, in fact, the first German operational two-seater to carry an observer with a movable rearward-firing gun.

As the C.I was an adaptation, only limited production of the type was undertaken, soon giving way to the C.II. Combined production of the C.I and C.II was probably in the region of 250 aircraft. Apart from modifications necessary for the installation of the 160-hp Mercedes D.III six-cylinder in-line engine, the C.II resembled closely the company's earlier B.II and was put into widespread use on armed reconnaissance and light bombing duties, for which it could carry a number of small (22-lb) bombs. It was a C.II which was credited, in November 1916, with making the first daylight aeroplane raid of the war on London. Of basically wooden construction, with plywood and fabric covering, the C.II originally carried only the single Parabellum gun in the rear cockpit, but a forward-firing Spandau gun was added to some later production models.

Two developed versions of the C.II which did not achieve production status were the C.III (in which the

Junkers Ju 290A-3

Junkers Ju 290A-3

LVG C.II

TYPE	DIMENSIONS						WEIGHT	PERFORMANCE				REMARKS
	span		length		height		max t-o	max speed	at height	service ceiling	combat range	
	ft	in	ft	in	ft	in	lb	mph	ft	ft	miles	
Ju 88S-3	65	10½	48	8¼	15	9	24,375	371	20,340	30,180	1,240	
Ju 188E-1	72	2	49	0⅞	16	0⅞	32,000	315	19,685	31,000	1,550	
Ju 388K-1	72	2	49	0½	16	0⅞	31,400	378	38,000	42,200	1,100	
Ju 290A-8	138	0	92	6	22	4⅞	88,000	280	18,000	19,700	3,785	
LVG C.II	42	2	26	7	9	7¼	3,091	81	SL		4 hr	

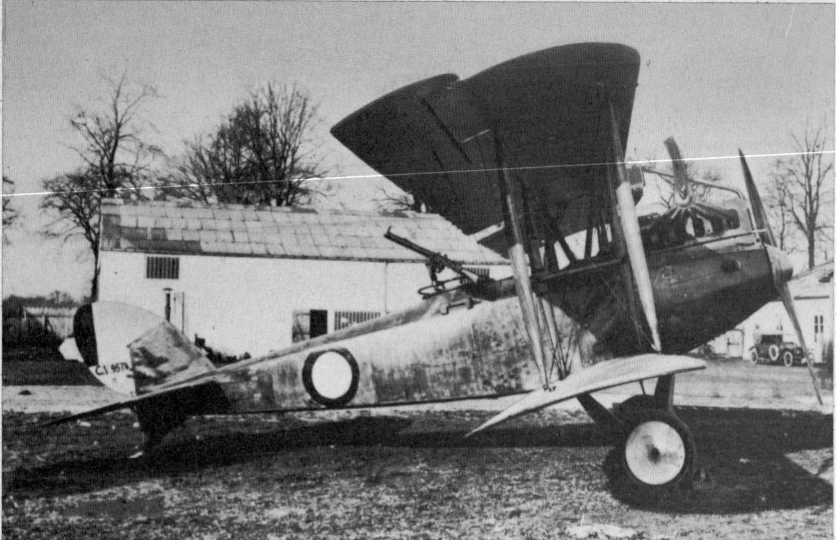
LVG C.V, captured aircraft, Allied markings

Messerschmitt Bf 109B

Messerschmitt Bf 109E-3

positions of the two crew members were reversed) and the C.IV, a somewhat larger machine with a 220-hp Mercedes D.IV engine, driving a larger-diameter propeller. Ultimately the C.Is and C.IIs in service gave way to the later and much improved C.V.

LVG C.V and C.VI

Luft-Verkehrs Gesellschaft's C.V biplane was a considerable improvement over the general-purpose C.II, from the viewpoints of both structural soundness and combat performance, and, like its predecessors, it was used widely on light bombing, artillery observation and armed reconnaissance missions. It was one of the biggest two-seaters produced by Germany during the 1914–18 War, which helped to make it a rugged and steady platform for fighting or bombing. The worst feature of the design was the rather poor view from the pilot's cockpit, due to the absence of any stagger on the two-bay wings; but there was ample power from the 220-hp Benz Bz IV six-cylinder water-cooled engine, neatly installed in a metal cowling. The remainder of the fuselage was ply-covered, terminating in a somewhat Albatros-like tail. The C.V was armed with a Spandau gun forward and a Parabellum in the observer's cockpit. It was in widespread use by the autumn of 1917, and acquitted itself well in combat.

It was followed into service in 1918 by substantial quantities of the C.VI. This was a slightly smaller and lighter model, with the same engine and armament as the C.V, but with a slight stagger to the wings to afford better pilot visibility. Final version was the C.VIII, with an uprated Benz Bz IV engine, offering 240 hp, and slightly greater endurance; but only one C.VIII was completed.

Messerschmitt Bf 109

It is unlikely that any discussion of what was, qualitatively, the greatest single-seat fighter in aviation history will ever be resolved to universal satisfaction; but there can be no doubt whatever that the fighter produced in the greatest quantity was the Messerschmitt Bf 109. For 25 years this aircraft was under construction somewhere in the world, serving the Luftwaffe for eight years and equipping the air arms of nearly a dozen other nations, with some examples still in use in the mid-1960s. Estimates of total production put the figure in the region of 35,000 machines, and over the period 1936 to 1945 production of the Bf 109 accounted for nearly two-thirds of Germany's entire output of single-seat fighters.

It was in 1933 that the RLM placed a development contract with the Bayerische Flugzeugwerke AG, and the resultant project was designed around Germany's most powerful aero-engine of the time, the 610-hp Junkers Jumo 210A. An engine of this type was not, however, available in time for the first flight of the prototype Bf 109V1 (D-IABI), which took place in September 1935 with a Rolls-Royce Kestrel V installed. By the time the Jumo 210A-powered second prototype (D-IUDE) flew in January 1936, the company had been rewarded with an order for ten machines for evaluation. The twin-MG 17 armament of the V3 (intended as the prototype of the Bf 109A series) was considered insufficient, and was accordingly increased in the V4 and the B series prototype, the Bf 109V7.

By the middle of 1937 the first Luftwaffe unit to receive the new fighter, Jagdgeschwader 2, was replacing its obsolete He 51 biplanes with the Bf 109B-1, powered by a 635-hp Jumo 210D engine and armed with either three MG 17s or two MG 17s and an MG FF cannon, the third gun firing through the hollow propeller shaft. During the previous year the Bf 109 had made a brief public debut in connection with the Olympic Games in Berlin, but now, in order to strengthen German prestige abroad, a team of these aircraft was sent to the International Flying Meeting at Zurich, where they scored many victories. The year was crowned for the Bf 109 when, on 11 November, the Bf 109V13, with a specially-boosted DB 601, set a landplane speed record: 379·38 mph.

Inevitably, the type gravitated to the Civil War in Spain, two dozen B-2s being sent initially to equip

Jagdgruppe 88 of the Condor Legion in 1937, followed by more of the same model shortly afterwards. Despite considerable success in combat, the armament of the B series was still poor, and the number of MG 17s was increased to four in the C-0 and C-1 and five in the C-3. Fighters of the Bf 109C series were despatched to Spain in 1938. In this year the company was renamed Messerschmitt AG, and orders for the Bf 109 were now such that five other manufacturers – Ago, Arado, Erla, Fieseler and WNF – were brought into the programme.

Installation of the DB 600A in converted B-2 airframes produced the Bf 109D-0, followed by the D-1, of which small numbers were exported to Hungary and Switzerland. On the outbreak of World War II there were 235 D series aircraft in Luftwaffe service, but these were already being replaced in increasing numbers by the Bf 109E. Powered by the 1,100-hp DB 601A, the E-0 had first appeared at the end of 1938, and the E-1 was produced both as a fighter (with four MG 17s) and as a fighter-bomber (with one 550-lb or four 110-lb bombs). Later E-1s substituted MG FF cannon for the two wing-mounted machine-guns, and 15 machines of this type were delivered to Spain.

Against all types of opposing fighter throughout Poland, Czechoslovakia, France, Belgium, Holland and southern England, with the exception of the Spitfire (which it greatly outnumbered), the Bf 109E proved itself superior in both performance and manoeuvrability. The production rate continued to mount steadily, to such an extent that Germany could afford to export considerable numbers of the Bf 109E-3 which appeared at the end of 1939. This model was supplied to Bulgaria (19), Hungary (40), Japan (2), Rumania (69), Russia (5), Slovakia (16), Switzerland (80) and Yugoslavia (73), and was also the major version used by the Luftwaffe in the Battle of Britain. The Swiss Dornier-Werke at Altenrhein later acquired a licence to build the Bf 109E, but for various reasons succeeded in completing only eight machines in 1941–3.

The Fieseler-Werke began in July 1940 to convert ten E-3s to Bf 109T (*Träger* = carrier) for proposed operation from the aircraft carrier *Graf Zeppelin*, but these were restored to E-3 standard in November 1941. Various other E models, up to the E-9, appeared with minor variations, some as fighters and others for reconnaissance duties.

Meanwhile, Messerschmitt AG had been developing a DB 601E-powered version which, in definitive form as the Bf 109F, was generally considered to be the finest mark of this versatile fighter. At last, it gave the Luftwaffe an aircraft which could outmanoeuvre the Spitfire V. Powered by either the 1,200-hp DB 601N or the 1,300-hp DB 601E, the Bf 109F series represented a considerable advance over earlier series in terms of both performance and cleanliness of line. The whole fuselage was cleaner aerodynamically, culminating in a more rounded rudder, an unbraced tailplane and retractable tail-wheel. The wings, of slightly increased span, were rounded off at the tips, and performance of the Bf 109F at all altitudes was considerably better than that of its predecessors.

Several Messerschmitt 109Fs were utilized as test-bed aircraft, the items tested including Jumo 213 and BMW 801 engines, a "butterfly" tail unit, and nosewheel landing gear similar to that fitted later on the Me 262. An interesting variant, although it was never flown,

Messerschmitt Bf 109D, Swiss Air Force

Messerschmitt Bf 109 two-seater

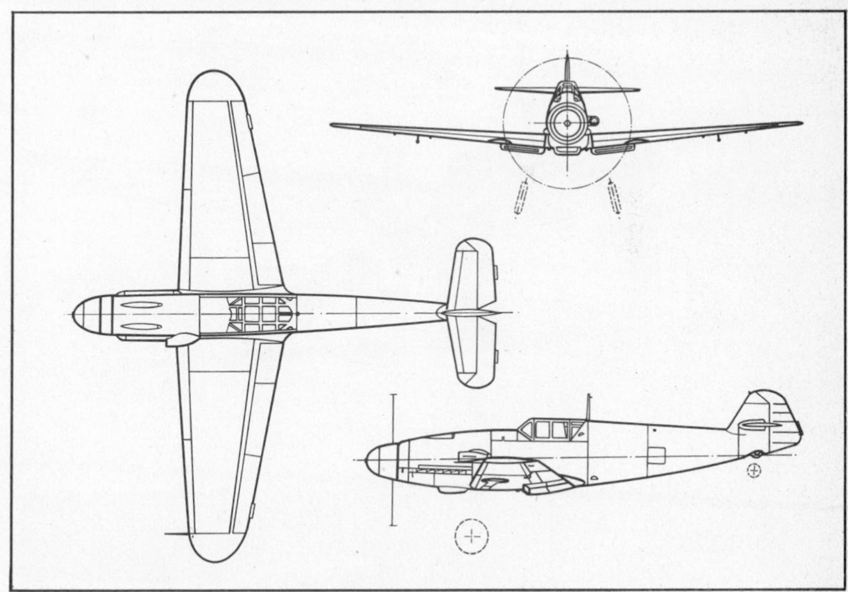
Messerschmitt Bf 109F

TYPE	DIMENSIONS span ft	span in	length ft	length in	height ft	height in	WEIGHT max t-o lb	PERFORMANCE max speed mph	at height ft	service ceiling ft	combat range miles	REMARKS
LVG C.V	44	8½	26	5¾	10	6	3,372	103	6,560	16,500	3½ hr approx	
LVG C.VI	42	7¾	24	5¼	9	2¼	2,888	106	SL	21,320	3½ hr	
Bf 109B-1							4,850	292	13,120	26,575		
Bf 109E-1	32	4½	28	4	7	5½	5,523	354	12,300	36,000	412	
Bf 109F-3	36	6½	29	0½	8	6	6,054	390	22,000	37,000	440	

Messerschmitt Bf 109G-10

Messerschmitt Bf 110B

Messerschmitt Bf 110C

was the Bf 109Z, in which two Bf 109F-1s were "married" by a new, common wing centre-section and tailplane, with a pilot in the port fuselage only.

By the end of the summer of 1942 the Bf 109F had been supplanted, both in production and service, by the last major production model, the Bf 109G. Made heavier and less manoeuvrable by their DB 605 engines and additional equipment, the "Gustavs", as the G series were nicknamed, were less successful than their predecessors. They were, however, widely used in Russia and the Middle East as well as in Europe, and Bf 109 production showed no sign of decreasing. Quite the reverse, in fact: from the middle of 1943, when output averaged 725 aircraft a month, the figure increased to no fewer than 1,605 a month by September 1944, despite wider and wider dispersal of production facilities to avoid the depredations of Allied bombing attacks.

Over 14,000 Bf 109s were completed in 1944 alone. The Bf 109G series covered a variety of models, with DB 605A or DB 605D power plants, for fighter, fighter-bomber and reconnaissance duties. Many G-6 aircraft, equipped with homing radar, were employed on night fighter duties in 1943. Like the E-3, the G models were also widely exported, customers including Bulgaria (145), Finland (162), Hungary (59), Japan (2), Rumania (70), Slovakia (15), Spain (25) and Switzerland (12).

Final wartime models to be used operationally by Germany were the Bf 109H and Bf 109K. Only a small number of the extended-span H-0/H-1 were completed, as development priority for a high-altitude fighter was then being accorded to the Focke-Wulf Ta 152. A few Bf 109Ks, basically refined versions of the G series, entered service early in 1945, but did not see much combat; and the projected Bf 109L (Jumo 213E) and Bf 109S did not achieve production status.

However, the 109's production and service record did not finish with the end of the war in Europe. Having retained the Civil War survivors and acquired a further batch of Bf 109E-1s in 1942, Spain subsequently negotiated a licence to build the Bf 109G-2 in the Hispano plant at Seville. Designated HA-1109-J1L, the first Spanish-built production 109 was flown on 2 March 1945. Variants were built as HA-1109 and HA-1112, together with two-seat conversion trainers designated HA-1110 and HA-1111. These are further described in the Spanish section.

The other nation which perpetuated 109 production was Czechoslovakia. Co-opted in 1944 to build the Bf 109G-14 at the Avia factory near Prague, the Czechoslovak government were, surprisingly, left with intact production machinery when the Germans evacuated their country. Putting the type into production for their own post-war air force, as the S-99, they soon found themselves short of the necessary DB 605A engines, and all subsequent machines (designated S-199) were powered instead by the 1,350-hp Jumo 211F; but performance of the Jumo-engined machines was generally considered inferior to the original Bf 109G-14. A small batch of S-199s was sold in 1948 to the Israel Defence Force, and nearly all Czechoslovak fighter units were equipped with them for many years. In gradually reducing numbers they served until 1952 – when replaced by Russian jet fighters – and for some five years more a number remained in service in the training rôle.

Messerschmitt Bf 110

Willy Messerschmitt's second warplane design, and his first to embody a twin-engine configuration, the Bf 110, was evolved at the Bayerische Flugzeugwerke AG to meet an RLM specification issued early in 1934 for a long-range escort fighter and *Zerstörer* (destroyer) type. The design was drawn up around the new Daimler-Benz DB 600 liquid-cooled engine, then being developed, and three prototypes were completed with this power plant. The Bf 110V1 made its first flight on 12 May 1936, and the V2 and V3 had both flown by the end of the year.

In January 1937 the Bf 110V2 was sent to the Luftwaffe evaluation centre at Rechlin for service trials, and was received with somewhat mixed feelings. It had an excellent turn of speed – 316 mph had been achieved by the V1 on its maiden flight – but it was heavy to fly and its manoeuvrability left much to be desired. Nevertheless, Rechlin recommended that four Bf 110A-0 pre-production aircraft be ordered, each armed with four 7·9-mm MG 17 machine-guns in the nose and a fifth MG 17 in the rear cockpit. Supplies of the DB 600 engine still being at a premium, the A-0 machines were fitted instead with 610-hp Jumo 210Bs, but these were sadly inadequate for a machine of the Bf 110's calibre and had a serious effect on performance. Two further pre-production machines, designated Bf 110B-0, were completed in the spring of 1938, and with 690-hp DB 600As these served as evaluation aircraft for the B-1 initial production series.

Unfortunately from the Luftwaffe's point of view, the Spanish Civil War ended before the Bf 110B-1s were ready for service, and it was decided, accordingly, to use these machines, too, for evaluation purposes. Thus the first series to go into operational service was the Bf 110C, which took advantage of the increased power of the 1,100-hp DB 601A twelve-cylinder inverted Vee engine, and introduced certain aerodynamic refinements, including clipped wingtips (to improve manoeuvrability) and a modified enclosure for the crew of two. It began to enter service in 1939, and over 500 aircraft of this series were in use by the end of that year. The fighter versions were generally similar to each other, save for minor variations in equipment and armament. Other C models were produced as fighter-bombers, with two 550-lb or 1,100-lb bombs slung externally, or as reconnaissance types with their armament proportionally reduced to accommodate aerial cameras.

In the German invasion of Poland, the Bf 110 was employed largely in the ground-attack rôle, and it was not until 1940, when it first encountered serious fighter opposition in the Battle of Britain, that its shortcomings as a fighter became evident. Such were the losses among Bf 110s escorting German bombers against targets in the United Kingdom that, before the type was prudently withdrawn from such missions, it was necessary to send single-engined Bf 109s with the formations to protect the escorts! After their withdrawal from escort duties, some early Bf 110Cs were converted for glider towing; but production was continued and later C variants were fitted with DB 601N engines of 1,200 hp.

An attempt was made, with the ensuing Bf 110D model, to improve the aircraft's range by means of auxiliary fuel tanks. The D-0 and D-1 were produced as fighters, the D-2 and D-3 as fighter-bombers; but by the middle of 1941 most of the C and D series machines had been transferred from the European theatre of operations to Russia or the Middle East. Production now began to wane, in anticipation of the Bf 110's replacement by the later Me 210; but the year saw the appearance of the DB 601N-powered Bf 110E in fighter and reconnaissance versions and, with a greater variety of ordnance (up to 4,410 lb), as a fighter-bomber. The early Bf 110F models (with the exception of the F-2 which had provision for underwing rocket projectiles) followed closely those of the E series except in power plant, now changed again to the 1,300-hp DB 601F. The Bf 110F-4, however, carried two 30-mm MK 108 cannon and a third crew member, and was built from the outset for night fighting.

By the end of 1942, it was clear that the Me 210 was unlikely to be an acceptable successor, so production of the Bf 110 was stepped up again with the introduction of the G series. The initial G models followed the pattern of earlier series until the G-4 night fighter

Messerschmitt Bf 110C-5

Messerschmitt Bf 110G-4/R7, captured aircraft, RAF markings

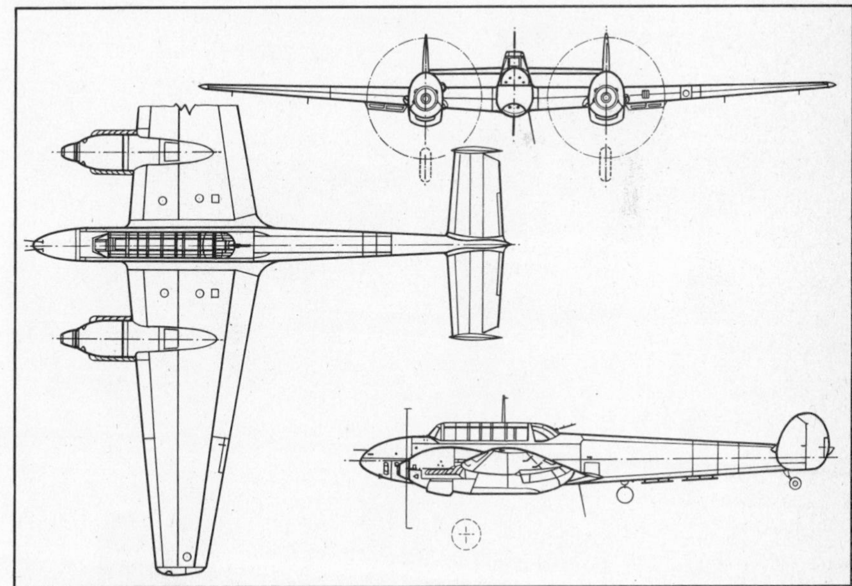

Messerschmitt Bf 110C-4

TYPE	DIMENSIONS span ft	span in	length ft	length in	height ft	height in	WEIGHT max t-o lb	PERFORMANCE max speed mph	at height ft	service ceiling ft	combat range miles	REMARKS
Bf 109G-6	32	6½	29	8	8	6	7,500	387	22,970	38,500	450	
Bf 109K-4	32	6½	29	4	8	6	7,438	452	19,685	41,000	365	
Bf 110C-4	53	4⅞	39	8½	11	6	15,300	349	22,965	32,000	565	

Messerschmitt Me 163B Komet

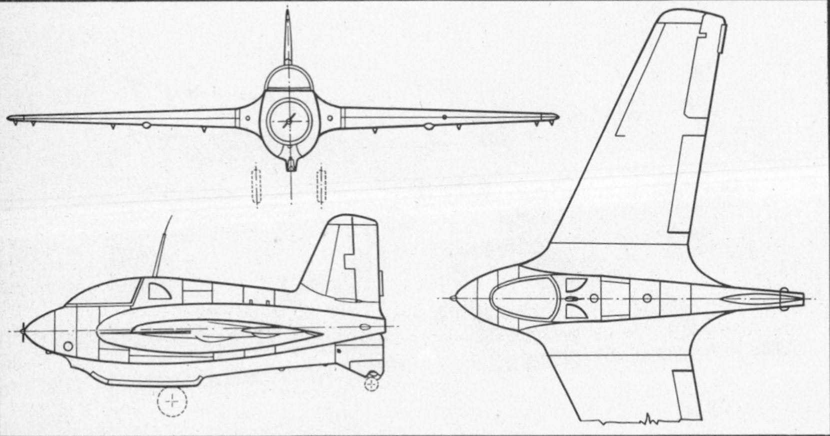
Messerschmitt Me 163B-1 Komet

Messerschmitt Me 210V13

Messerschmitt Me 410 Hornisse

emerged. This carried an armament of two or four 20-mm MG 151 cannon and four MG 17 machine-guns and, like the rest of the G series, was powered by 1,475-hp DB 605B engines. The G-4/R3, with a fourth crew member and built-in Lichtenstein SN-2 airborne interception radar, was the first night fighter variant designed to include such equipment. Produced alongside the G series was the Bf 110H, generally similar save for heavier armament.

Peak production of the Bf 110 was achieved in 1943 and 1944, the last few dozen machines being delivered to the Luftwaffe during the early part of 1945. Total production of all Bf 110 variants, excluding prototypes, amounted to approximately 6,150 machines.

Messerschmitt Me 163 Komet (Comet)

Like so many other ingenious German designs of World War II, the Messerschmitt Me 163 reached combat units too late and in too small numbers to affect the ultimate course of the war. Nevertheless, in the nine months or so that it was operational, it achieved no small measure of success in its primary rôle of bomber interceptor. But for a clash of personalities between its designer, Professor Alexander Lippisch, and its manufacturer, Professor Willy Messerschmitt, coupled with delays in the delivery of its power plants during the middle years of the war, its story might well have been very different.

Based on the Lippisch-designed DFS 194 test-bed of 1938 (a project transferred, with its staff, to Messerschmitt AG for further development), the Me 163V1 and V2 prototypes were flown in the spring of 1941 as unpowered gliders. The V1 was removed to Peenemünde that summer for installation of a 1,650 lb s t Walter HWK R.II rocket motor, using T-Stoff (hydrogen peroxide and water) propellent, with which engine it made its first powered flight in August. When speeds in excess of 620 mph were recorded during trials the RLM needed little prompting to order the type's development as a fighter, and this was put in hand at the end of the year. Ten unpowered Me 163As were, meanwhile, completed as conversion trainers.

The Me 163V3, prototype for the B-0 and B-1 production series of 70 aircraft, was ready in May 1942, but had to wait more than a year for its new power plant, the 3,750-lb s t HWK 509A, which ran on T-Stoff and C-Stoff (a mixture of methyl alcohol and hydrazine hydrate). By this time more than half of the original production batch had also been built and were awaiting engines. When this order was completed, subsequent Me 163s were built by the Hans Klemm Flugzeugbau, total production amounting to between 350 and 370 aircraft.

The first *Staffeln* to equip with the Me 163B received their fighters in late June and early July 1944, and the Komet's operational debut was made against a formation of raiding B-17s on 16 August. The Komet carried a fixed armament of two 30-mm MK 108 cannon in the wing roots; provision was also made for 24 unguided rockets beneath the wings or four rockets within the wings, firing upwards at right angles to the line of flight. The rocket fighter's success against Allied bombers was due largely to the element of surprise and its unexpected speed, but its all-up weight – nearly a ton more than originally planned – demanded auxiliary booster rockets to get it off the ground, while landings – especially if any of the highly inflammable fuel remained in the tank – were fraught with danger. All too often, Komets did come literally to a comet-like end, with fatal results for the pilot.

The developed Me 163C (4,410-lb s t HWK 509C), pressurized and refined aerodynamically, had reached only the pre-production stage when the war ended, and of the Me 263 derivative (originally Me 163D) only a prototype had been tested.

Messerschmitt Me 210 and Me 410 Hornisse (Hornet)

Although they were far from being among the Messerschmitt AG's better warplane designs, both the Me 210 and the Me 410 were employed in substantial numbers during World War II. The company received RLM approval in 1937 to proceed with their Me 210 project as a potential successor to the Bf 110, and the twin-finned Me 210V1 prototype (registered D-AABF) made its first flight on 2 September 1939. It proved very unstable in the air, and an attempt was made to remedy this in the second prototype by substituting a single fin and rudder of greater area. Even this did not fully correct the Me 210's short-comings, but by this time the RLM had already committed itself to a large production order for 1,000 of the type.

The pre-production Me 210A-0s were followed by the Me 210A-1 and A-2, which entered Luftwaffe service early in 1941 for heavy fighter and fighter-bomber duties respectively. As production continued, various modifications were made to the design, including a lengthening of the rear fuselage, but the accident rate among serving Me 210s remained high.

There were three main models, each powered by two 1,395-hp Daimler-Benz DB 601F 12-cylinder in-line engines: the A-1, A-2 and B-1. Armament of the A-1 and A-2 consisted of two 20-mm MG 151 cannon, two remotely-controlled 'midships MG 131 guns of 13-mm calibre, and two 7·9-mm MG 17s. The A-2 had external racks for two bombs of 550 lb, 1,100 lb or 2,200 lb; and the B-1 dispensed with the MG 17 guns to make room for two photo-reconnaissance cameras. Production of the Me 210 was halted by the RLM in April 1942, but later resumed for a short period, 352 aircraft of this type finally being completed.

In looking for a replacement for the Me 210, the RLM discarded the proposed Me 310, a pressurized development which would have utilized the 1,750-hp DB 603A engine, in favour of a more straightforward derivative with the same power plant, the Me 410. Dubbed Hornisse, the Me 410 was in production from the end of 1942 until 1944, during which time 1,121 were completed, including 108 built under licence for the Luftwaffe in Hungary. It was built in A-1, A-2, A-3, B-1, B-2 and B-3 basic models and several sub-types, and was employed on heavy fighter, bomber destroyer and photographic reconnaissance duties with varying installations of armament and/or cameras. The A-1/U4, for example, was equipped solely with a 50-mm BK 5 cannon, while the B-2/U1 had no fewer than six MG 151s and two MG 131s. Special bulged housings in the bomb-bay of the A-3 and B-3 contained three aerial cameras.

Messerschmitt Me 262

The Me 262, first jet-propelled fighter to go into squadron service anywhere in the world, took six years to achieve this distinction; and even then, little more than 200 of the 1,433 that were completed were employed operationally. Delays in the development of satisfactory turbojet engines, damage to production lines by Allied air attack and, not least, the refusal of Adolf Hitler to be guided by his advisers as to the aircraft's most suitable rôle, all contributed to this situation.

The RLM first asked Messerschmitt AG in 1938 to design an aircraft around the new turbojet engines then being developed by BMW and Junkers. After approving a mock-up of the twin-engined design, three prototypes were ordered in the spring of 1940. The airframes of these were ready long before their engines, with the result that when the Me 262V1 first flew, on 4 April 1941,

Messerschmitt Me 410 Hornisse

Messerschmitt Me 262A-1

Messerschmitt Me 262B-1a/U1

TYPE	DIMENSIONS						WEIGHT	PERFORMANCE				REMARKS
	span		*length*		*height*		*max t-o*	*max speed*	*at height*	*service ceiling*	*combat range*	
	ft	*in*	*ft*	*in*	*ft*	*in*	*lb*	*mph*	*ft*	*ft*	*miles*	
Bf 110G-4	53	4⅞	41	6¾	13	1¼	21,800	342	22,900	26,000	1,305 max	
Me 163B-1	30	7	18	8	9	0	9,500	596	30,000	39,500	2½ min after climb	
Me 210A	53	7¼	40	3	14	0½	25,150	385		22,965	1,491 max	
Me 410A	53	7¾	40	11⅓	14	0½	23,500	388	21,980	32,800	1,450 max	
Me 262A-1	40	11½	34	9½	12	7	14,101	540	19,685	37,565	652	

Messerschmitt Me 262B-1a/U1

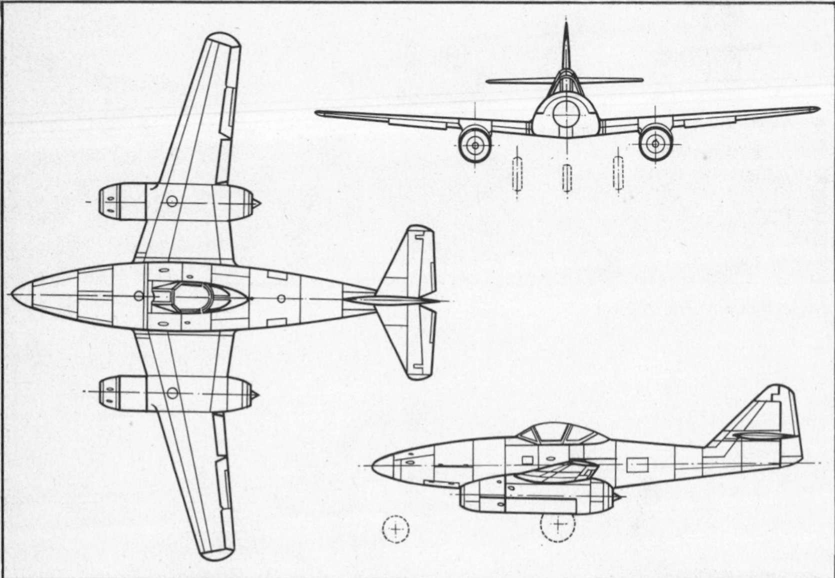
Messerschmitt Me 262A-1b

Pfalz E.I

Pfalz E.V

it did so under the power of a single Jumo 210 piston-engine. On 25 November that year it was flown with two BMW 003 turbojets, supplemented by the Jumo 210. The first all-jet flight was made on 18 July 1942, by the Me 262V3 powered by two 1,850-lb s t Jumo 004s, the BMW engines having proved unsatisfactory. Several further prototypes were completed, for trials of armament and equipment installations, by which time the pre-production Me 262A-0s were also flying. These, like all prototypes from the fifth machine onwards, were fitted with a nose-wheel undercarriage.

Priority production was ordered by the RLM, but was delayed by extensive devastation of Messerschmitt's Regensburg factory by Allied bombers. As a result, deliveries began much later than the planned date of May 1944, and the type did not enter full service until late that year. Two major versions became operational, the first of these being the Me 262A-1a Schwalbe (Swallow) interceptor. Basic armament of the A-1a series comprised four 30-mm MK 108 cannon, mounted in the nose, though several sub-types were built with differing installations, including rocket projectiles. Hitler's insistence that the fighter be turned into a bomber resulted, after further delays, in the Me 262A-2a Sturmvogel (Stormbird), with racks for two 550-lb bombs beneath the fuselage. The Me 262A-3 and A-5 were ground-attack and fighter-reconnaissance variants.

A small number of Me 262Bs were completed as tandem-seat conversion trainers, a development which led to the investigation of a two-seat night fighter development, but the latter never became operational. Further proposals included the rocket-assisted Me 262C-1a and C-3, and the Me 262D and E with further variations in armament, all of which were still under active consideration when Germany capitulated.

Pfalz E.I, E.II and E.IV

The Pfalz Flugzeug-Werke GmbH, established in July 1913 at Speyer-am-Rhein, was independent of the German Flugmeisterei, being financed directly by the Bavarian government, which wished to decide for itself the types of aircraft with which its forces should be equipped. For the first year or two of its existence, the Pfalz company occupied itself in building foreign types under licence, but in 1915 it was able to produce the first of its own designs.

Designated E.I, this machine was, in effect, a modification of the Morane-Saulnier Type H monoplane (which was one of Pfalz's licence types), adapted to take an 80-hp Oberursel U.0 nine-cylinder rotary engine. The E.I was originally unarmed, being used solely for scouting; but with the addition of a synchronized Spandau, mounted centrally in front of the pilot, it was placed in production as a single-seat fighter, some 60 examples being built.

The E.I had a box-section fuselage of wood, covered with plywood panels forward and fabric aft, the rotary engine being cowled "horseshoe" fashion. The two-spar shoulder wings were also fabric-covered, as was the small rudder. Wingtips were sharply raked back, and the wing-warping control wires extended to about two-thirds span above and beneath each wing.

The other Pfalz monoplane put into major production was the E.II, which was virtually the same as the E.I save for the substitution of a higher-powered Oberursel rotary, the 100-hp U.I. The two types were used as defensive and escort fighters by Bavarian units on the Western Front and ultimately – as better biplane fighters came into service – for training duties.

A strengthened version, the E.IV (the E.III was an entirely different design) employed the U.III 14-cylinder two-row rotary engine of 160 hp enclosed in a fully circular cowling, and it was fitted with a second Spandau gun; but owing to the unreliability of this engine – which in any case did not confer the expected increase in performance – only 24 E.IVs were built. Final model was the E.V, an adaptation of the E.II with a 100-hp Mercedes D.I engine.

Twenty were ordered, but these were delivered too late for operational service.

Pfalz D.III and D.IIIa

This first D class single-seat fighter produced by the Pfalz Flugzeug-Werke appeared during the summer of 1917. Since the ending of production of its E type monoplanes some twelve months earlier, the company had been engaged on licence manufacture of LFG/Roland D.I and D.III fighters, and much of the experience thus acquired was applied to the new aircraft.

The D.III's closely-cowled and spinnered 160-hp Mercedes D.III in-line engine was installed in a semi-monocoque streamlined fuselage of wooden construction, terminating with a small fin and large, curving rudder. The undercarriage was a clean-looking conventional Vee type, with a wooden tail-skid beneath the fuselage sternpost, and the parallel-chord single-bay wings were raked back sharply at the tips. The wings were slightly staggered, with a trailing-edge cut-out in the upper plane to give the pilot a fairly good view in most directions. Armament consisted of twin Spandau machine-guns, mounted originally beneath the engine decking but later re-sited on top of the cowling.

When it entered service with German *Jagdstaffeln* in September 1917, the Pfalz was reasonably fast, though perhaps less satisfactory in climb and general manoeuvrability than the Albatros and Fokker scouts alongside which it fought. It was, however, pleasant to fly, and its strong construction made it an excellent weapon for "balloon busting" and other duties for which good diving characteristics were desirable.

The D.III was joined in 1918 by the D.IIIa, which had more rounded wingtips, a tailplane of semi-circular plan and the increased power of the 180-hp Mercedes D.IIIa engine. Approximately 600 D.III/D.IIIas were built altogether, and well over half of these were still in front-line service in November 1918.

Pfalz D.XII

Upon its entry into service in the early autumn of 1918, the Pfalz D.XII received initially a somewhat cool reception from its pilots. This was due mainly to extensive German propaganda extolling the Fokker D.VII, which caused disappointment and even resentment among units which received the Pfalz machine instead. Nevertheless, once the pilots had become acquainted with their new mount, they found that it not only compared favourably with the Fokker machine but was even better in some respects. Certainly it acquitted itself well against British Camels and S.E.5as in the closing months of the war.

Based on the unsuccessful D.XI, which was itself a derivative of the earlier D.III, the Pfalz D.XII made its first appearance in June 1918 at the fighter trials at Adlershof. Both BMW- and Mercedes-powered examples were evaluated, but it was the latter version which was preferred and ordered into production. The 160-hp Mercedes D.IIIa engine, with frontal radiator, was cleanly installed in a semi-monocoque wooden fuselage terminating in a steel-and-fabric vertical fin and wooden rudder. The parallel-chord two-bay wings, of unequal span, were of generally similar construction to those on the D.III, and their N interplane struts, coupled with the M pattern struts bracing them to the fuselage, gave the D.XII a robustness which stood it in good stead during diving manoeuvres. Two fixed, synchronized forward-firing Spandau guns were mounted on top of the engine decking, ahead of the cockpit.

Pfalz D.III

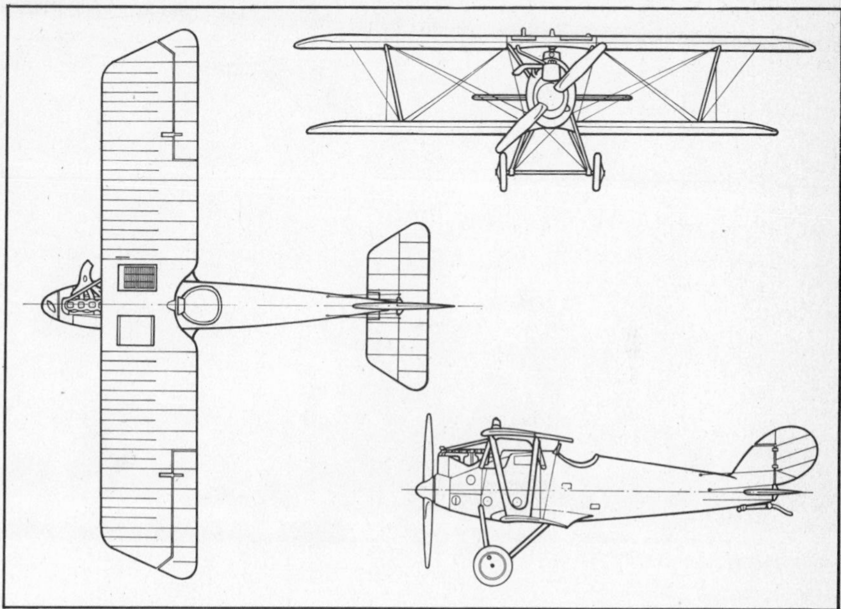
Pfalz D.III

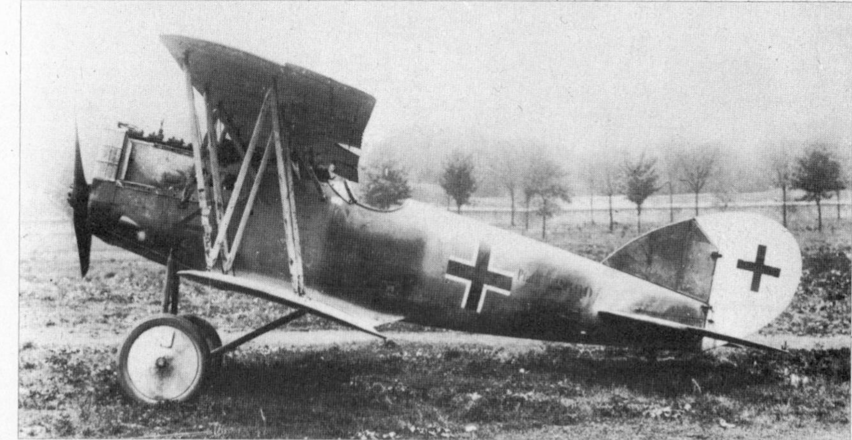
Pfalz D.XII

TYPE	DIMENSIONS						WEIGHT	PERFORMANCE				REMARKS
	span		length		height		max t-o	max speed	at height	service ceiling	combat range	
	ft	in	ft	in	ft	in	lb	mph	ft	ft	miles	
Pfalz E.I	30	4⅝	20	8	8	4⅜	1,177	90½	SL		2 hr	Endurance approximate
Pfalz E.II	33	5⅝	21	2	8	4⅜	1,364	94	SL		2 hr	Endurance approximate
Pfalz E.IV	33	5⅝	21	7⅞	8	4⅜	1,526	100	SL		1 hr	
Pfalz D.III/D.IIIa	30	10⅛	22	9¾	8	9⅛	2,056	102	10,000	17,060	2½ hr	Endurance approximate

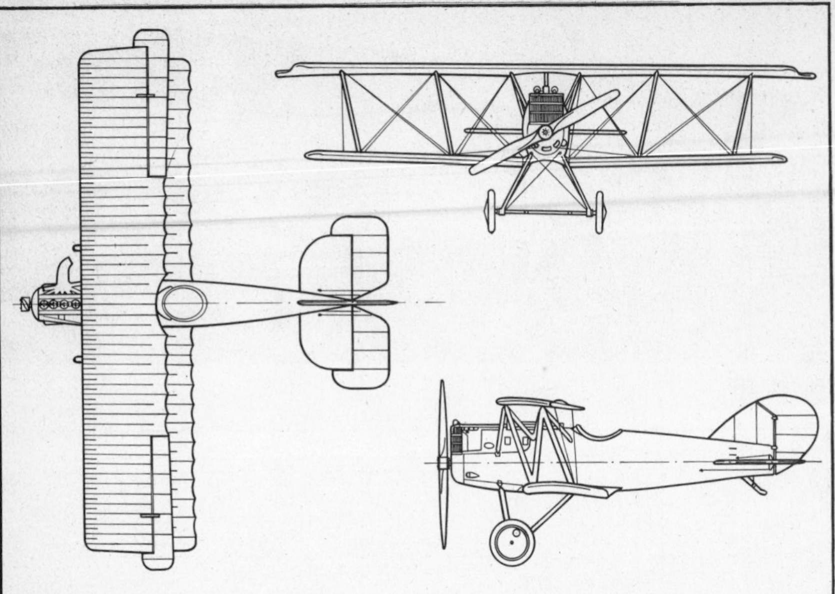

Pfalz D.XII

Roland C.II

Roland D.I

Roland D.IIa

In view of the priority given to the Fokker D.VII – and the proximity of the Armistice – it is unlikely that more than about 200 D.XIIs were completed, though nc precise figures are available; but both types were employed as replacements for the Albatros D.Va and the Pfalz D.III, in particular, during the final months of the 1914–18 War. Two further developments of the D.XII were the D.XIV, with the 200-hp Benz Bz 14ü and enlarged fin area, and the D.XV, powered alternatively by the 180-hp Mercedes D.IIIa or the 185-hp BMW IIIa. The latter was officially tested at the beginning of November 1918 and a substantial order was placed, but no production models are believed to have beer completed.

Roland C.II

The name "Roland" was adopted by the Luftfahrzeug Gesellschaft shortly before the outbreak of the 1914–18 War, to avoid any possible confusion between its formal title of LFG and the more widely-known LVG concern. Until 1915, LFG/Roland had concentrated on the construction of airships, Wright biplanes and Albatros scouts but in that year the company evolved an original product of its own – a dumpy little machine which, although not destined for great achievements, was nevertheless to have considerable effect upon the subsequent trend o German aircraft design.

The Roland C.II, as this design was known, was cleaner aerodynamically than many of its contemporaries, despite its nickname of *Walfisch* (Whale). Considerable reduction in drag was achieved by keeping interplane bracing to a minimum, and a good field of view in all directions (except downward) was obtained by the use of cut-outs in the upper and lower wing roots.

Some 250 to 300 C.IIs were built, primarily for reconnaissance, some of them under licence by the Linke-Hofmann Werke AG of Breslau, and the type began to enter operational service during the early part of 1916. Although possessed of a sturdy body, the durability of the C.II's wings left something to be desired. This restricted its manoeuvrability and resulted in rather limited use of the type as a combat fighter. However, the C.II did have quite a useful radius of action, and many were, accordingly, employed as fighter escorts to their reconnaissance brethren, remaining in service until about a year before the Armistice. The C.II's standard power plant was a 160-hp Mercedes water-cooled engine; the armament comprised a hand-operated Parabellum machine-gun in the rear cockpit and, on later models, a forward-firing Spandau which was operated by the pilot. The C.IIa was similar but had modified and reinforced wingtips.

Roland D.I and D.II

Once the basic soundness of the design of his two-seater C.II had been proved, Dipl-Ing Tantzen of the LFG Roland company decided to develop a single-seat fighter along similar lines. The result was the Roland D.I, a slightly smaller and slimmer machine than its progenitor but with a marked family likeness to it. Again, the fishlike body outline gave rise to an appropriate nickname, in this case *Haifisch* (Shark).

The D.I was followed quickly by a further developed version, the D.II, the two prototypes making their maiden flights in July 1916 and October 1916 respectively. Each was powered by a single 160-hp Mercedes water-cooled in-line engine, and a further variant was also evolved, the D.IIa, which utilized a 180-hp Argus in place of the Mercedes power plant. All were armed with a pair of synchronized Spandau guns, one on either side of the engine in the upper decking.

Towards the end of 1916 the D.I was put into production by the parent company and also by the Pfalz Flugzeugwerke; and by early 1917 both the D.I and D.II were in operational service. They had, however, some limitations in the fighter rôle. Apart from being rather heavy machines to fly, the view ahead of and below the pilot was considerably poorer than from the C.II, and the various improvizations which were made in attemp

to alleviate these shortcomings were not entirely successful. This, coupled with the more conspicuous achievements being made concurrently by the latest models of the Albatros fighter, contrived to have the Roland machines relegated to the Eastern Front and other less vital theatres of operations. No unit appears to have been equipped exclusively with D.Is or D.IIs, and as the Rolands were lost in operations or through other causes they were usually replaced by Albatros or other fighters.

Some 300 D.I/D.II/D.IIas were built, a substantial number of them by Pfalz.

A small batch of about 25 of a later variant, the D.III, also saw limited service during the 1914–18 War, but most examples of this model were allocated to non-operational duties.

Roland D.VI

In design and performance capabilities, the Roland series of aircraft produced during the 1914–18 War tended to be overshadowed by their more illustrious contemporaries, such as the Albatros and Fokker scouts. They were nevertheless produced in fairly substantial numbers; and the prototype of the D.VI single-seat fighter, designed as an entrant for the Adlershof fighter trials in January 1918, was in fact the thousandth machine of LFG/Roland origin to be built.

The winner of the Adlershof competition was the Fokker D.VII; but as an insurance against possible production failures with the Fokker, a small number of Roland D.VIas and D.VIbs were ordered. These served operationally with the German Navy as well as the German Air Force, during the latter months of the War.

The D.VI was altogether better looking than its forebears, a fact attested by the absence of a "fishy" sobriquet such as had been applied to the C.II and D.II. It also embodied an interesting new method of fuselage construction, based on the "clinker" system of overlapping longitudinal wood strips used in small boat building – a method which may have been something of a mixed blessing. Had its construction been more orthodox it might have been ordered in more substantial quantities, for pilots spoke of the D.VI as a good machine to fly; its manoeuvrability was first-rate and the view from the cockpit was a vast improvement over that of earlier Roland designs.

The *Klinkerrumpf* construction system was first tried out in the experimental Roland D.IV, a triplane fighter which appeared in the summer of 1917; it was dropped on the D.V which followed, in favour of a return to the semi-monocoque wooden construction employed on the earlier Roland types, but made its reappearance in the D.VI.

The first production version was the D.VIa, with either a 160-hp or 180-hp Mercedes engine, and differing from the prototype in having horn-balanced ailerons and a smaller gap between the fuselage and the upper wing. Two synchronized Spandau guns were mounted on the upper decking of the fuselage just forward of the cockpit. Owing to uncertainty about sustained deliveries of the Mercedes engine, a third model, the D.VIb, was produced, powered by a 200-hp Benz and having further refinements to the ailerons and tail flying control surfaces. One example of this model was taken to the United States for testing after the Armistice.

Roland D.IIa

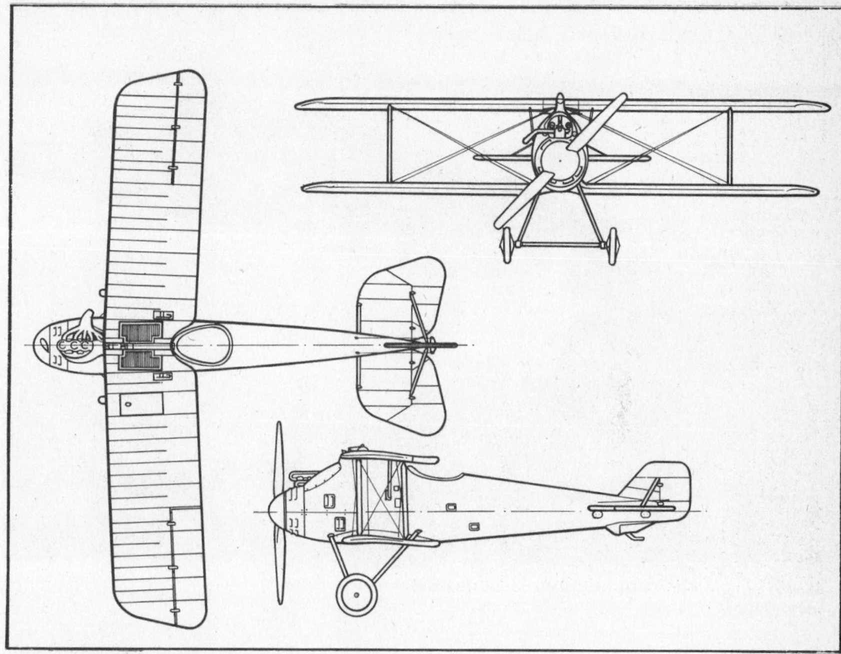

Roland D.II

Roland D.VIb, captured aircraft, in USA

TYPE	DIMENSIONS						WEIGHT	PERFORMANCE				REMARKS
	span		length		height		max t-o	max speed	at height	service ceiling	combat range	
	ft	in	ft	in	ft	in	lb	mph	ft	ft	miles	
Pfalz D.XII	29	6⅜	20	10	8	10¼	1,978	106	9,840	18,500	2½ hr	
Roland C.II	33	10¾	24	8⅛	9	5¾	2,886	103	SL	13,120	4–5 hr	
Roland D.II	29	4	22	8⅞	10	2⅜	1,753	105	SL	16,400	2 hr	
Roland D.VIb	30	10⅛	20	8¾	9	2¼	1,896	114	6,560	19,000	2 hr	

Rumpler C.I, captured aircraft, Allied markings

Rumpler C.IV, captured aircraft, Allied markings

Rumpler 6B-1

Siemens-Schuckert D.I

Rumpler C.I, C.IV and C.VII

Widely used on all fronts during the 1914–18 War, the Rumpler C.I two-seat armed reconnaissance aircraft first appeared early in 1915, and was joined shortly afterwards by the C.Ia. Together they served on the Western Front, then later in Palestine, Macedonia and adjacent theatres, and ended their days as operational trainers – though a few were still on front-line duties as late as February 1918.

The C.I, powered by a 160-hp Mercedes D.III engine, driving a two-blade propeller, was an attractive machine with the typical box-girder construction of the period. Plywood and fabric covered the round-topped fuselage structure of wood strips and steel tube. The semi-circular radiator was neatly installed under the leading-edge of the upper wing centre-section. Both of the two-bay, unstaggered wings were mildly swept back, with backward-raking tips, and were braced by four interplane struts on each side. Initially, only a single Parabellum gun was fitted, on a Schneider ring-mounting in the observer's cockpit; but later a forward-firing Spandau was mounted on the port side of the engine decking.

The C.Ia was identical save for the use of a 180-hp Argus As III liquid-cooled engine. Both could undertake "nuisance" raids, carrying up to 220 lb of small bombs.

In addition to those constructed by the Rumpler Flugzeug-Werke at Johannisthal, the C.I and C.Ia were built under licence by Germania Flugzeug-Werke, Märkische Flugzeug-Werke, Hannoversche Waggonfabrik and Albert Rinne Flugzeug-Werke. Total production figures are not known, but at the peak of their career in October 1916 there were 250 in service.

At about this time there also appeared the much-improved Rumpler C.IV (some 75 examples of the much-modified C.III, with 220-hp Benz engine, had gone into service in February 1917, but were withdrawn only two months later). Of generally similar construction to the C.I, but considerably more refined aerodynamically, the C.IV was a truly excellent aeroplane. Much greater power was forthcoming from the 260-hp Mercedes D.IVa engine, installed in a very clean and streamlined cowling, with a pointed spinner. Over the Western Front, and in Italy and Palestine, the C.IV was used primarily for long-range armed photographic reconnaissance, there being a trap in the floor of the observer's cockpit through which the camera could be operated. The sweptback wings had a slight backward stagger and the near-triangular tailplane of the C.I gave way to a more rounded, almost semi-circular one on the C.IV. Over short ranges, the C.IV could indulge in tactical missions, carrying four 55-lb bombs on external racks beneath the lower wing, but its *forte* was high-altitude work, where its climb to, and performance at, heights above 15,000 ft gave it an undoubted advantage over contemporary Allied fighters. It was built under licence by the Pfalz company and the Bayerische Rumpler-Werke.

An even better development of the C.IV, which emerged towards the end of 1917, was the Rumpler C.VII. The Maybach Mb IV engine of this model had a higher compression ratio which gave it improved all-round performance. Externally, except for the smaller exhaust manifolds and absence of a propeller spinner, there was little difference between the C.IV and the C.VII, but the latter was slightly smaller overall. Two versions were produced: the standard C.VII for long-range reconnaissance, armed with a Spandau forward and a Parabellum gun in the rear cockpit; and the C.VII *Rubild* (= Rumpler photographic) which, with the Spandau and other non-essential equipment replaced by special cameras, could undertake high-altitude reconnaissance from a ceiling of almost 24,000 ft. This was an outstanding performance for an aircraft of the period, and necessitated items such as oxygen supplies and heated flying suits for the crew.

Rumpler 6B

One of a trio of landplane adaptations for seaplane defence duties – the others being the Albatros W.4 and

Hansa-Brandenburg KDW – the Rumpler 6B was basically a modified version of the Rumpler C.I described above, and was similarly powered. It was converted to single-seat operation by removing the rear Parabellum gun and fairing-over the observer's cockpit. Slight forward stagger was given to the wings, and the rudder area was increased, to offset the two-step floats which replaced the land undercarriage of the C.I.

Serving at Zeebrugge and Ostend, and in the Black Sea area, the Rumpler 6B existed in two versions – the 6B-1 and the 6B-2, differing mainly in that the 6B-2 sported a rounded tailplane similar to that of the C.IV landplane. Deliveries began in July 1916, 38 6B-1s and 50 6B-2s being supplied before production ended in January 1918.

Siemens-Schuckert D.I

The Siemens-Schuckert Werke, after dabbling in airship construction and an aeroplane or two of its own design in the early years of powered flight, faded from the aeronautical scene temporarily in 1911, but was recalled to its former activity in 1914. It was for a time allocated work in connection with the *Riesenflugzeug* types, after which 20 examples of its own E-I were completed. A development of this type, the E-II, crashed during tests and the SSW's next assignment – along with a number of other German aircraft constructors – was to come up with a copy of the highly successful French Nieuport Scout.

The Siemens-Schuckert copy, which bore a closer resemblance to the French machine than any of the others, was based principally on the Nieuport 17 but was powered by the nine-cylinder Siemens-Halske Sh-1 geared rotary engine offering 110 hp. The fuselage was of box-girder construction, part-metal and part-fabric covered with a single-seat open cockpit and a single Spandau machine-gun synchronized to fire through the arc of the two-bladed propeller. Designated D.I, it was a single-bay biplane with unequal-span wings; landing gear consisted of two main wheels on a conventional Vee chassis and a tail-skid beneath the rear fuselage.

The D.I was placed in production following successful evaluation tests, 150 being ordered on 25 November 1916; but the delivery rate was slow owing to delays in the supply of the Siemens-Halske engines, which were not really developed sufficiently for operational use. By the time the aircraft was ready for issue to units, the balance of air supremacy had changed and their presence was less urgently required. A follow-on order for 100 more D.Is, which had been placed on 21 March 1917, was therefore cancelled. Nevertheless, a considerable number were assigned to the Russian Front, and a few to the Western Front, although many others were relegated to instructional duties. Later production D.Is were fitted with large streamlined spinners over the propeller hub and some had an extra Spandau gun added. Developed versions, the D.Ia (one built) and D.Ib (two built) were not given contracts, and production of the type ceased in July 1917 after the completion of 95 aircraft.

Siemens-Schuckert D.III and D.IV

After its experience with the D.I, which was little more than a copy of a French fighter, the Siemens-Schuckert design team under Dipl-Ing Harald Wolff began work on an entirely new project of its own conception, and three

Siemens-Schuckert D.III prototype

Siemens-Schuckert D.III

Siemens-Schuckert D.IV

TYPE	DIMENSIONS						WEIGHT	PERFORMANCE				REMARKS
	span		length		height			max speed	at height	service ceiling	combat range	
	ft	in	ft	in	ft	in	max t-o lb	mph	ft	ft	miles	
Rumpler C.I and C.Ia	39	10⅜	25	9	10	0½	2,932	95	SL	16,570	4 hr	
Rumpler C.IV	41	6½	27	7	10	8	3,373	107	1,640		3½–4 hr	
Rumpler C.VII	41	2⅛	26	10⅞	11	1⅜	3,267	109	3,280	23,944	3½ hr	
Rumpler 6B-1	39	6⅜	30	10⅛	11	9¾	2,513	95	SL	16,400	4 hr	
Siemens-Schuckert D.I	24	7⅜	19	8¼	8	9	1,485	97	6,500		2⅓ hr	

Siemens-Schuckert D.IV

Zeppelin Staaken V.G.O. I

Zeppelin Staaken R.VI

Zeppelin Staaken R.XVI

prototypes of this machine, designated D.II, D.IIa and D.IIb, were completed early in 1917. These prototypes were intended, in addition, to act as flying test-beds for an improved version of the D.I's power plant, the 160-hp Siemens-Halske Sh-3 eleven-cylinder geared rotary. Flight tests were generally satisfactory and three more aircraft were commissioned, with the proviso that an increase in performance should be achieved. The three new machines were eventually designated D.III, and an order was placed at the end of 1917 for a pre-production run of 20 aircraft of this type.

The D.III was a compact and sturdy single-seat, single-bay biplane fighter, of mostly wooden construction, armed with two forward-firing Spandau guns. On test, it exhibited an excellent turn of speed and a very high rate of climb. The first aircraft began to be delivered in January 1918, differing from the prototype in employing a four-blade propeller of smaller diameter, which allowed the undercarriage legs to be shortened slightly. A further 30 D.IIIs were ordered in February 1918, and these began to arrive at the Front some two months later, most of them being allocated to Jagdgeschwader 2. Initial reaction to the D.III was highly encouraging, as pilots found it easy to handle, with an excellent performance; but again, as with the D.I, the engine became a source of trouble. After about ten hours' flying, the pistons began to seize, and it was soon necessary to withdraw the D.IIIs from service.

The aircraft were returned to the factory, where the improved Sh-3a engine, offering up to 240 hp, was installed. With this and a few minor airframe changes, the D.IIIs began to resume operations in July 1918, though they were now employed principally on home defence duties. By this time, a further order for 30 D.IIIs had been placed, but although all 80 were delivered, only about 50 were engaged on combat duties.

Concurrently with the original D.III pre-production order, the company had received a contract for three examples each of two developments, the D.IV and D.V; in the event, the D.IV was sufficiently successful for the D.V, which was basically similar, to be dropped.

The Siemens-Schuckert D.IV followed broadly the design of its predecessors, with the same power plant as the D.III, although the upper wing was smaller in area than that of the earlier type. An interesting feature of the D.IV was that the two port wings were each approximately four inches longer than the starboard ones, in order to counteract the left-hand torque of the rotary engine. Flight trials were extremely promising, and the type was ordered into immediate production in March 1918. Of a total of 280 ordered, 119 were actually delivered before the end of the 1914–18 War; but, as with the D.III, only about 50 became truly operational before the Armistice. Reception of the D.IV was highly enthusiastic, some pilots rating it superior to any other fighter at the Front at the end of the war.

Under construction at the end of the war were three prototypes of the D.VI, a parasol monoplane development of the D.IV. Two of these were completed after the Armistice, and attained 137 mph and 26,250 ft during trials

Zeppelin Staaken R "Giants"

Work on the original German Zeppelin "Giant" bombers was begun by the triumvirate of Baumann, Hirth and Klein on an airfield site provided by the Gothaer Waggonfabrik, known as the Versuchsbau Gotha-Os (East Gotha Experimental Works), and the initials of this concern appeared in the designations of the early machines. In the summer of 1916, the company moved its equipment to Staaken, changing its name first to Flugzeugwerft Staaken and finally to Zeppelin Werke Staaken. The "Giants" produced at these various places were a remarkable series of aircraft, apart from their great size; and although most of them appeared as only single examples or in very small numbers, all were used operationally on either the Eastern or Western Front.

The first of the leviathans to appear was the V.G.O.I, a tri-motor design powered by 240-hp Maybach engines, which flew for the first time on 11 April 1915. Klein was later killed in a crash at Staaken involving this machine

In October 1915, it was followed by the generally similar V.G.O.II, but three engines were found to provide insufficient power for these nine-ton machines and the third aircraft, the V.G.O.III, had twice this number. They were different engines – 160-hp Mercedes D.IIIs – two mounted in tandem in each of the port and starboard nacelles driving pusher propellers, and the other pair side-by-side in the nose, driving a single tractor propeller.

It was with the fourth machine of the line that the "R" designations (for *Riesenflugzeug* = giant aeroplane) were introduced, although the second and third machines were retrospectively redesignated R.II and R.III. The R.IV of 1917 was basically similar to the R.III, except that the four nacelle engines were Benz motors of 220 hp apiece. Armament, which had been increased in successive machines, consisted of six or seven machine-guns in the R.IV. This was reduced to five in the R.V, which appeared in September 1917 with five of the original Maybach engines – a tandem pair in each nacelle, with tractor propellers, and a single one in the nose. One machine-gun was mounted in a wooden fairing above the centre leading-edge of the upper wing.

So far, one machine of each type had been built, and the only "R" type to be produced in any quantity was the R.VI, which had four Maybach or 260-hp Mercedes D.IVa water-cooled in-line engines, paired in tandem. Only one was built by Zeppelin Staaken, but seven more were completed by the Luftfahrzeugbau Schütte-Lanz, six by the Automobil und Aviatik AG, and four by the Ostdeutsche Albatros-Werke GmbH. The nose cockpit of the R.VI mounted a Parabellum machine-gun and release mechanism for the eighteen 220-lb bombs that could be carried internally. Two similar guns were located in a dorsal position and a fourth one ventrally. The usual crew was seven. Landing gear consisted of 18 wheels – eight under each engine nacelle and two beneath the nose. Some R.VIs were used in raids over France and the United Kingdom. The one seaplane model built was destroyed during trials.

Development of the "R" series continued with the R.VII (one only), very similar to the R.IV, and the R.XIV (three built), R.XIVa (one built), R.XV (three built) and R.XVI (one built). Five Maybach engines powered the R.XIV, R.XIVa and R.XV, while the R.XVI had one 220-hp and one 550-hp Benz coupled in each engine nacelle. The final "Giant" type was another seaplane version, of which three are known to have been built, incorporating features of the R.VI, R.XIV and R.XV.

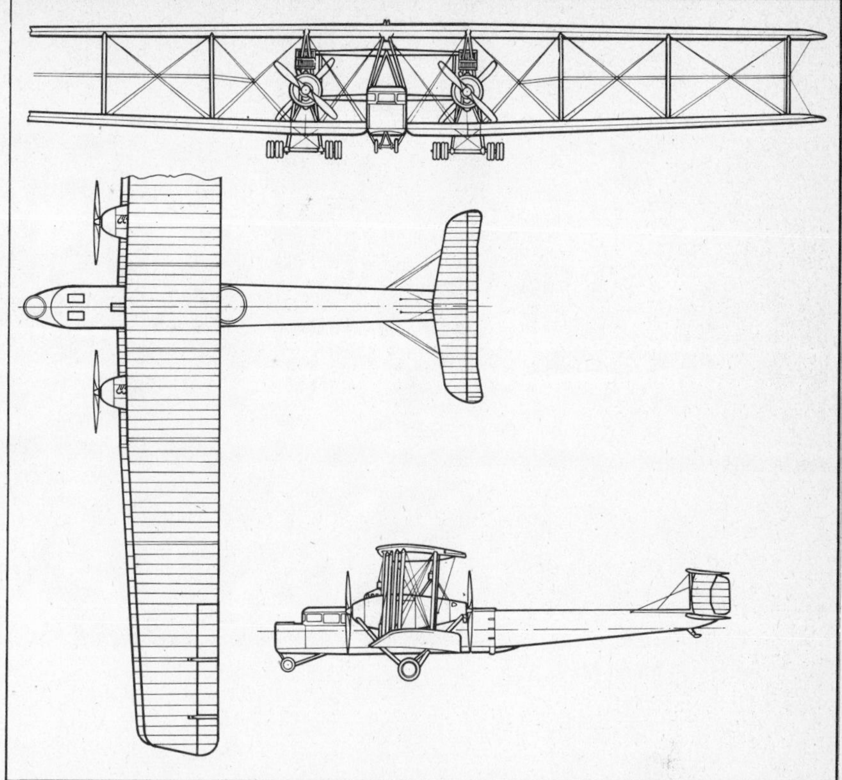

Zeppelin Staaken R.VI

India

Hindustan HF-24 Marut (Wind Spirit)

A slim, swept-wing all-metal monoplane, the HF-24 Marut is India's first home-designed jet fighter. It was evolved to meet an Indian Air Force specification for a replacement for its Hunters, Mystères and Ouragans, and design work began in 1956 under a German-Indian team headed by Dr Kurt Tank, formerly of Focke-Wulf. After flight tests with a full-size wooden glider in 1959, the first of two HF-24 prototypes (BR-462) was flown on 17 June 1961 powered by two 4,850-lb s t Bristol Siddeley Orpheus 703 turbojets, mounted side-by-side in the area-ruled fuselage. The second machine

Hindustan HF-24 Marut Mk I

TYPE	DIMENSIONS						WEIGHT	PERFORMANCE				REMARKS
	span		length		height		max t-o	max speed	at height	service ceiling	combat range	
	ft	in	ft	in	ft	in	lb	mph	ft	ft	miles	
Siemens-Schuckert D.III	27	7⅞	18	8½	9	2¼	1,598	112	SL	26,580	2 hr	
Siemens-Schuckert D.IV	27	4¾	18	8½	8	11	1,620	118		26,240	2 hr	
Zeppelin-Staaken R.VI	138	5⅝	72	6¼	20	8	25,265	81	SL	12,460	7-10 hr	

Hindustan HF-24 Marut Mk I

Ansaldo A-1 Balilla

Ansaldo A.300/4

(BR-463) followed four months later and was joined by BD-828, the first production Mk I, in March 1963.

Development having been abandoned of the Orpheus BOr.12, which, giving 8,170 lb s t with afterburning, was to have powered production Maruts, the Hindustan company has experienced difficulty in finding a suitable alternative. Thus, in early production aircraft at least, the Orpheus 703 is used in conjunction with a locally-developed afterburner, and the first such installation was made in BD-829, which is serving as the Mk 1A prototype.

Initial production of HF-24s, now in hand, comprises a total of 60 aircraft, made up of Mk Is (without afterburners) and Mk IAs with re-heated Orpheus 703s.

The Marut is armed with four 30-mm Aden cannon and has provision for four Russian "Atoll" infra-red homing missiles, Matra rocket pods or 1,000-lb bombs on external attachments beneath the wings. The Mks I and IA will serve as interceptors, while the Mk IB will be a tandem two-seat strike and reconnaissance variant.

When the HAL afterburner is fully developed, these early versions of the Marut will have a maximum speed of around 790 mph (Mach 1·2) at 36,000 ft. The definitive version, however, will be the Mk II with a Mach 2 performance, provided that the power plant problem reaches a satisfactory solution. This may be achieved by use of the Egyptian E-300 turbojet, derived from the Orpheus and already tested in an HF-24.

Italy

Ansaldo A-1 Balilla (Hunter)

Until the summer of 1917 the fighter units of the Aeronautica del Regio Esercito were in the main equipped with French single-seaters of Hanriot, Nieuport or SPAD manufacture. Then, in an attempt to provide Italian pilots with a mount of indigenous design, the Società Ansaldo evolved the A-1 Balilla, a small single-bay biplane powered by a 220-hp SPA 6A engine. The view from the cockpit was quite good, and twin Vickers machine-guns were mounted on top of the engine decking to fire between the blades of the two-bladed propeller. The Balilla's constant-chord wings, of wood and fabric construction, were blunt-tipped with a semi-hexagonal cut-out in the upper wing trailing-edge. Its ply-covered wooden fuselage terminated in a tri-angular fin and rudder and a braced "wing-nut" tailplane.

In November 1917, the A-1 was evaluated at Turin by senior Italian air force pilots who, although they appreciated the aircraft's top speed of nearly 140 mph, felt unable to recommend the type for large-scale production due to its extremely poor manoeuvrability. It was, in fact, inferior in overall characteristics to the foreign fighters already serving with the air force. With suggested modifications, the marginally improved Balilla was placed in production, but only 150 were built. These were employed mainly for home defence.

Seventy-five Balillas were bought for the Polish air force, of which the first 20 reached Poland in June 1920, at a critical stage of the Russo-Polish War. The Balillas went into action immediately, some with the famous Kościuszko Squadron, and played some part in checking the enemy offensive. The remaining 55 machines arrived after the war, in 1921, and a further 50 Balillas were licence-built in Poland by Plage & Laśkiewicz Works, Lublin, in 1921–3. They played an important part in Polish fighter defence until 1925.

Ansaldo A.300/4

Between the end of the 1914–1918 War and the time of its absorption by the Fiat group of companies, the Società Ansaldo developed the A.300, which first flew in prototype form in 1919. This aircraft was taken on an extended sales promotion tour across Europe by pilots Brezzi and Stoppani, before being modified into the two-seat A.300/2, which appeared in 1920. A small batch of this developed version was built, followed by approximately 90 three-seat A. 300/3s, which were used for reconnaissance duties by the Italian air force. The A.300/3 was powered by a single 300-hp Fiat A.12*bis*.

The most successful model was the A.300/4, the prototype of which was flown for the first time in 1922. Chosen under the reconstruction programme of the Italian forces, which culminated in the formation of the Regia Aeronautica as Italy's first independent air arm on 23 March 1923, the Ansaldo A.300/4 was put into widespread service as an armed general-purpose machine: reconnaissance and light offensive missions could be undertaken, and the type was also employed by training establishments later in its career. Some 700 were built, serving in Corfu, Libya and elsewhere.

Almost identical to the A.300/3, the A.300/4 was powered by an improved model of the A.12*bis* engine with a new-style radiator. Its constant-chord equi-span wings were of orthodox two-bay configuration, with a semi-circular cut-out in the upper plane which helped to ensure quite a good view from the pilot's cockpit. A conventional fixed undercarriage was fitted to the wood-and-metal fuselage. Two fixed machine-guns were mounted in the upper engine decking, with a third, movable gun in the rear cockpit.

Subsequent versions included the Lorraine-powered A.300/5, which remained a prototype; the proposed civil A.300C and T; the A.300/6, which followed the A.300/4 into service; and the A.400 prototype.

Ansaldo S.V.A.5 Primo (First)

This slender, elegant biplane design by Ing Verduzio of the Società Ansaldo made its first appearance during the summer of 1917, following flight evaluation of earlier S.V.A. (Savoia Verduzio Ansaldo) designs numbered 1 to 4. Intended for single-seat fighter duties, the S.V.A.5 was of mixed construction. The fuselage was mainly plywood-covered, and carried roughly triangular tail surfaces, with scalloped trailing-edges. The wings were of unequal span, braced with Warren-girder struts and with dihedral on the lower planes only.

The first S.V.A.5s were delivered to operational training units for evaluation in the autumn of 1917, and the type subsequently achieved considerable success as a fighter, 1,248 S.V.As being completed. Armament consisted of a pair of synchronized Vickers guns, mounted above the cowling of the 220-hp SPA 6A engine. A further 50, generally similar, machines were equipped with twin-float landing gear for naval use and designated Idro-S.V.A. (*Idro* = water).

In service, the S.V.A.5 demonstrated an impressive turn of speed and the ability to carry heavy loads. As a result, at the recommendation of units such as No. 87 Squadriglia, the type was adapted early in 1918 to carry a second crew member and additional fuel for long-range strategic reconnaissance missions. Many fine flights were made by the two-seaters during the 1914–18 War, to such points as Innsbruck and Friedrichshafen, but the most notable came after the war, in 1920, when one of these machines flew from Rome to Tokyo (over 11,000 miles) in 109 hours' flying time. The two-seater was designated S.V.A.9 and was unarmed, with the observer occupying the front cockpit. It was not built in such large quantities as the fighter version.

Final development of the series was the generally similar S.V.A.10, in which a movable gun was installed in the rear cockpit, and which could be powered alternatively by the 250-hp Isotta-Fraschini Semi-Asso.

Ansaldo A.300/4

Ansaldo S.V.A.5 Primo

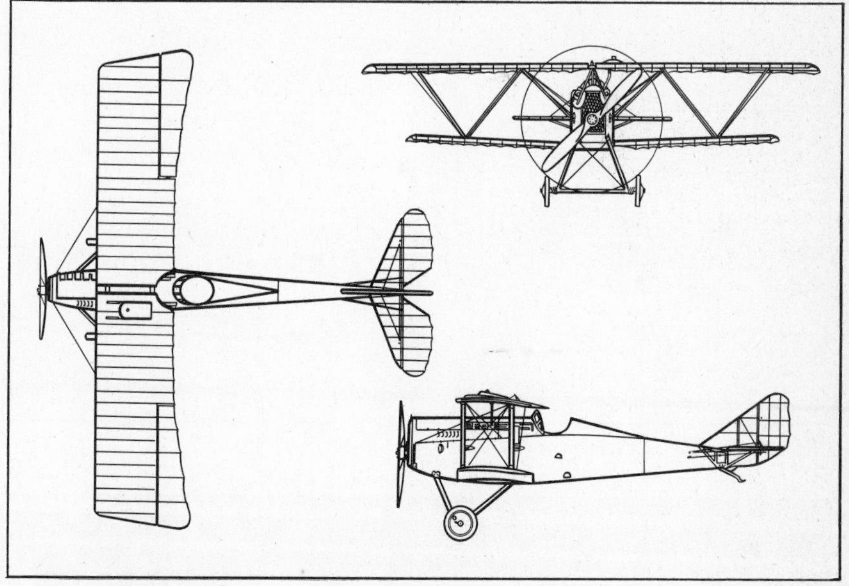

Ansaldo S.V.A.5 Primo

TYPE	DIMENSIONS						WEIGHT	PERFORMANCE				REMARKS
	span		*length*		*height*		*max t-o*	*max speed*	*at height*	*service ceiling*	*combat range*	
	ft	*in*	*ft*	*in*	*ft*	*in*	*lb*	*mph*	*ft*	*ft*	*miles*	
Ansaldo A-1	25	2⅓	22	5¼	8	3⅔	1,951	137	SL	16,400	1½ hr	
Ansaldo A-300/4	36	10½	28	8½	9	9	3,748	124		21,320	3½ hr	
Ansaldo S.V.A.5	29	10¼	26	6⅞	10	6	2,315	143	SL	19,680	4 hr	Data for single-seat fighter model

Breda Ba 27, Chinese Air Force

Breda Ba 65, single-seat version

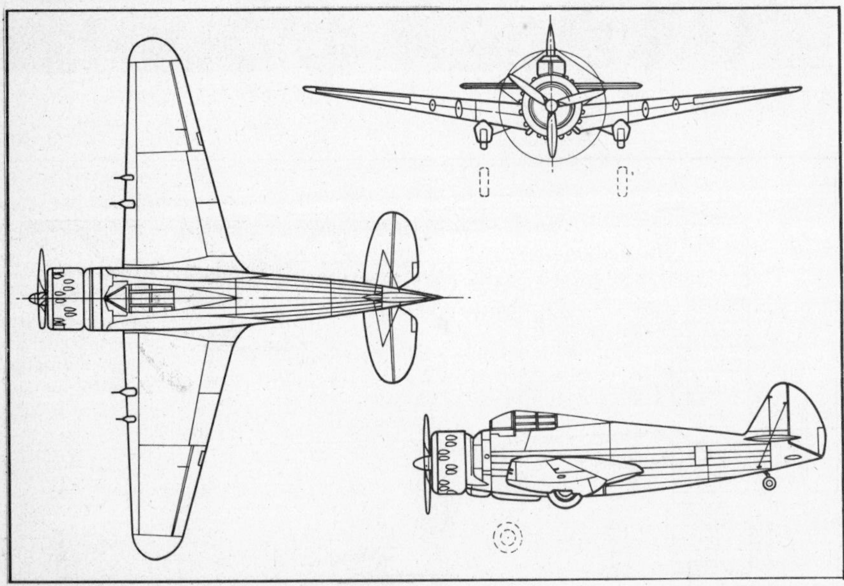
Breda Ba 65, single-seat version

Breda Ba 65*bis*

Breda Ba 27

The Ba 27, produced in 1935 by the Società Italiana Ernesto Breda of Milan, was a small single-seat fighter monoplane of mixed wood and metal construction which bore a strong resemblance to the Boeing P-26 fighter, produced in the United States during the 1930s. No production order for the Ba 27 came from the Regia Aeronautica but, following the visit of an Italian Air Mission to China in 1935, a contract for a small quantity was placed by the Chiang Kai-Shek government.

These eventually equipped one Chinese air force squadron which was based in the Shanghai-Nanking district at the outbreak of the Sino-Japanese war in July 1937; but their operational career was not extensive. The Ba 27 was powered by the Alfa Romeo Mercurius IV nine-cylinder, air-cooled radial engine, and carried two 7·7-mm Breda-SAFAT machine-guns.

Breda Ba 65

Although it made its first appearance in 1935, the Breda Ba 65 was a development of the Ba 64 monoplane of a year or two earlier. It was an all-metal low-wing monoplane with retractable undercarriage and an extensively-braced tailplane, and was designed for attack bomber and close support duties, carrying a single 2,000-lb bomb, two 800-lb bombs or 160 small anti-personnel weapons. Fixed armament consisted of one 7·7-mm and one 12·7-mm machine-gun in each wing.

First customer for the Ba 65 was the Royal Iraqi Air Force, which ordered a small number in 1937. These were delivered to Iraq during the following year, and equipped No. 5 Squadron of the RIAF. The type was also exported in modest numbers to the air forces of Hungary, Paraguay and Portugal, and a substantial order was received from the Regia Aeronautica.

The Ba 65 saw its first operational service with the Aviazione Legionaria during the Spanish Civil War, but because of early development troubles was used at first only for reconnaissance missions. It was produced in both single- and two-seat versions, each of which could be powered by either the 1,000-hp Fiat A.80 RC 41 or the 900-hp Isotta-Fraschini K-14 (licence-built version of the Gnome-Rhône K-14) radial engine. Armament of the two-seater was augmented by a further 7·7-mm gun in a movable turret in the observer's cockpit.

A small number of a later version, the Ba 65*bis*, were completed with a 12·7-mm gun in a hydraulically-operated Breda L-type turret.

Breda Ba 88 Lince (Lynx)

In the mid-1930s, the Italian Air Ministry decided that a replacement was urgently required for the ageing Caproni A.P.1 and Ba 65 attack aircraft then in service. To meet this requirement, the Breda company designed and built a twin-engined, mid-wing medium attack bomber with a single fin and rudder, the Ba 88.

The Lince, as the Ba 88 was to become known, first appeared in 1937, and in December of that year the prototype made news by setting up official speed records over 100 km and 1,000 km with a 1,000-kg payload. It was powered by a pair of 900-hp Gnome-Rhône K-14 radial engines, built under licence in Italy by Isotta-Fraschini, and could carry externally several variations of bomb-load up to a maximum of 2,200 lb. Armament consisted of three Breda-SAFAT 12·7-mm machine-guns in the "solid" nose and a single 7·7-mm gun in a Breda Type L powered dorsal turret.

During its acceptance trials, the Lince exhibited a number of dubious tendencies, including a poor degree of controllability, especially during take-off. Moreover, its rate of climb was low and its maximum speed left something to be desired. Nevertheless, Mussolini was convinced that the Ba 88 was a potential world-beater; so it was ordered into production for the Regia Aeronautica with certain modifications.

Chief among these were the substitution of more powerful 1,000-hp Piaggio P.XI RC 40 radial engines for the Isotta-Fraschinis originally fitted, and replacement of the single-tail assembly by a dual empennage in an attempt to improve stability. In this form, the Ba 88 was put into production in 1938, by both the parent company and IMAM (Meridionali).

When Italy entered World War II, Ba 88s equipped the 7th Gruppo Autonomo Combattimento in Libya and the 19th Gruppo in Corsica, but they were still seriously underpowered and were far from successful. Production terminated in 1941 after 105 had been completed, and only a small number remained in service after the Italian capitulation in 1943.

Between 1941 and 1943, the Agusta plant at Cascina Costa produced three examples of a modified version, the Ba 88M, as potential dive-bombers. With an increased wing span of 58 ft 0¾ in, two 840-hp Fiat A.74 RC 38 engines, a fourth 12·7-mm gun in the nose and a further-modified tail unit, the Ba 88M was a heavier machine, with a loaded weight of 15,260 lb. It could muster a maximum speed of only 239 mph, and further development of the type was abandoned.

CRDA Cant Z.501 Gabbiano (Seagull)

The CRDA Cant Z.501 was one of a series of waterborne aircraft designed by Ing. Zappata, and appeared in prototype form in 1934. It was a large, parasol-winged monoplane flying-boat of mainly wooden construction, with a two-step hull and twin stabilizing floats descending from the wing bracing. The single engine was a 900-hp, 12-cylinder, liquid-cooled Isotta-Fraschini Asso XI Rc 15.

The Z.501, which was used as a light reconnaissance bomber, had a crew of four or five, was armed with two or three 7·7-mm Breda-SAFAT machine-guns, and carried up to 1,404 lb of bombs externally. Just over 200 Gabbiani were in service with maritime reconnaissance squadrons when Italy entered World War II in 1940. The type continued to operate until the Armistice in September 1943, latterly on rescue and coastal patrol duties. A few served with the post-war Italian Air Force until as late as 1950.

CRDA Cant Z.506B Airone (Heron)

The Cantieri Riuniti dell'Adriatico was founded in 1923, as a subsidiary of the well-known Italian firm of shipbuilders, and soon established a reputation for the design of water-borne aircraft. One of these was the Z.506A commercial floatplane, the Z of the designation indicating that it was designed by Filippo Zappata.

In 1936 this aircraft, which followed the Italian industry's partiality for the tri-motor configuration, was adapted by Zappata for the military rôle of reconnaissance-bomber, with a crew of five. The Z.506B Airone, as the military version was known, was a mid-wing monoplane of wooden construction, with two long, single-step floats. It handled well, and its pleasing lines differed little from those of the civil model except for the Breda M.1 dorsal turret, mounting two 12·7-mm Breda-SAFAT machine-guns, and a long ventral gondola housing the bomb-aimer, bomb-bay and, at the rear, a 7·7-mm Breda-SAFAT machine-gun for rearward defence. Up to 2,200 lb of bombs of various sizes, or a single 1,764-lb torpedo, could be carried in the bomb-bay, and power was provided by three 750-hp Alfa Romeo 126 RC 34 nine-cylinder air-cooled radial engines, driving three-bladed propellers.

After individual Z.506Bs had acquired 16 international class records for speed, distance and payload-to-altitude

Breda Ba 88 Lince

CRDA Cant Z.501

CRDA Cant Z.501

TYPE	DIMENSIONS						WEIGHT	PERFORMANCE				REMARKS
	span		*length*		*height*		*max t-o*	*max speed*	*at height*	*service ceiling*	*combat range*	
	ft	*in*	*ft*	*in*	*ft*	*in*	*lb*	*mph*	*ft*	*ft*	*miles*	
Ba 27	31	1	24	11	11	2	3,938	236		29,520		
Ba 65	39	8⅜	31	6	10	6	5,512 (6,504)	267 (225)		27,230 (25,920)	342	Figures in parenthesis relate to 2-seat model
Ba 88	51	2⅛	35	4⅞	9	10⅛	14,881	304	13,120	26,250	1,019	
Cant Z.501	73	9⅞	46	10⅞	14	6	15,542	171	8,200	22,965	1,490 max	

CRDA Cant Z.506B Airone

CRDA Cant Z.506B Airone

CRDA Cant Z.1007*bis* Alcione, single-fin version

CRDA Cant Z.1007*bis* Alcione, twin-fin version

during 1937, the type participated briefly with the Aviazione Legionaria in the Spanish Civil War towards the end of the following year. The Airone had entered production in 1937, and 32 examples of the Series I were soon followed by further series. The Polish government placed an order for 30 in 1938, but only one of these had been delivered before the German invasion and the remainder were taken on charge by the Italian Navy.

When Italy entered World War II she had nearly 100 Airones in service, and by then the type was being licence-built by Piaggio as well as by the parent company.

Most important of the subsequent models was the Series XII, in which the bomb-load was increased to 2,645 lb. An improved dorsal turret, bearing a single 12·7-mm Scotti machine-gun, was also installed, together with two extra, laterally-mounted, 7·7-mm guns, and various modifications were made to internal equipment.

During the early part of the war, the Z.506B was employed widely on bombing or torpedo-bombing missions, against targets in France and in the Mediterranean theatre; but after the Italian campaign in Greece it was switched increasingly to maritime reconnaissance, convoy escort and anti-submarine duties. A number of Airones were converted to Z.506S (for *soccorso* = help) as air/sea rescue machines, being used on these duties by both the Regia Aeronautica and the Luftwaffe. After the Italian armistice a small number survived to fight with the co-belligerent air force on the side of the Allies, and the Z.506 continued to serve with the post-war Aviazione Militare until 1959, in unarmed form, on rescue and transport duties.

CRDA Cant Z.1007*bis* Alcione (Kingfisher)

This stylish mid-wing monoplane saw extensive service with the Italian air force during World War II, being second in importance to only the S.M.79 Sparviero as a medium bomber. It was one of two projects evolved in the mid-1930s by Ing Filippo Zappata of the CRDA, as the first landplane designs produced since the company's formation a decade or so earlier. Both designs were based on the 840-hp Isotta-Fraschini Asso IX RC 35 inverted "Vee" engine, the Z.1007 being a tri-motor and the Z.1011 a twin-engined machine.

Of the two, the Regia Aeronautica preferred the Z.1011, and ordered five prototypes for evaluation. It transpired, however, that two Assos – then the highest-powered aero-engines available in Italy – were inadequate to give the Z.1011 a reasonable combat performance, and the Z.1007 was, therefore, the design finally accepted.

The first Alcione prototype flew towards the end of 1937, followed by others in the ensuing 18 months; and in 1939 the type entered quantity production. Armed with four 7·7-mm machine-guns, the initial production Z.1007s retained the Asso power plant in annular cowlings, which gave them a radial-engined appearance. Before long, however, it became possible to instal the more powerful 1,000-hp Piaggio P.XI*bis* RC 40 air-cooled radial engine, in which form the aircraft became known as the Z.1007*bis*, with considerably improved performance over its predecessor.

Production facilities were extended by enlisting the factories of IMAM (Meridionali) and Piaggio.

In addition to having more powerful engines, the Z.1007*bis* differed from the initial production model in having a 33-in greater wing span, 8 ft longer fuselage and a more robust undercarriage to cater for an increased all-up weight. It was capable of carrying – although it very rarely did – up to 4,410 lb of bombs in an internal bomb-bay; armament was improved by substituting 12·7-mm guns for two of the original 7·7-mm weapons. Unusually, the Alcione retained wooden construction throughout, and was produced in both single- and twin-tailed versions.

Italian units which employed the Z.1007*bis* included the 172nd Squadriglia da Ricognizione Strategica, with whom, from bases in Sicily, Sardinia and the Aegean theatre, it ranged the length and breadth of the Mediterranean on both bombing and torpedo attack missions, carrying a pair of 1,000-lb torpedoes in the latter rôle. The Z.1007*bis* also saw service, for most of the war, in other combat areas from North Africa to Russia; and it says much for Zappata's wooden design that it stood up well to the rigours of such contrasting climates.

Late in 1942, a third version, the Z.1007*ter*, entered service with the Regia Aeronautica. In an attempt to improve still further the Alcione's performance, it was designed to utilize the 1,175-hp Piaggio P.XIX radial engine and to operate with a reduced bomb-load. Another development, the Z.1015, was evolved simultaneously with 1,500-hp Piaggio P.XII RC 35s. These models had a maximum speed of 310 mph and 348 mph respectively, but neither was produced in large numbers owing to the greater promise shown by the Z.1018, described below.

CRDA Cant Z.1018 Leone (Lion)

Zappata began the design of a successor to his Z.1007 in 1938, and forsook the familiar but outmoded wooden construction in favour of an all-metal airframe – although one prototype had a wooden fuselage. As in the Z.1007, both single and dual tail assemblies were considered, but all production models had a single fin and rudder.

First prototype of the Z.1018, as the type was designated, made its maiden flight in 1940, powered by a pair of Piaggio P.VII RC 45 radial engines, driving four-bladed propellers. A variety of alternative power plants were studied on subsequent prototypes, including a Fiat licence-built version of the German DB605A in-line. Eventually two alternative power plants were chosen for production aircraft – the 1,320-hp Piaggio P.XII RC 35 and the 1,350-hp Alfa Romeo Tornado – both 18-cylinder two-row air-cooled radials of proven performance.

Handsome by any standards, the Z.1018 Leone was accepted immediately by the Regia Aeronautica, and orders were placed for 300 aircraft, with production to be shared by CRDA and IMAM (Meridionali). The first of these entered squadron service at the beginning of 1943, but comparatively few had attained operational status by the time of Italy's surrender, and these were employed only in the Mediterranean theatre. The Leone's offensive load consisted usually of six 550-lb bombs stowed internally, and it was armed with three 12·7-mm machine-guns – one in the starboard wing leading-edge and one each in dorsal and ventral positions – with a single 7·7-mm gun on each side amidships for beam defence.

Such was the potential of the Z.1018 that two fighter variants were proposed, each with seven 20-mm MG 151 cannon in the nose and three 12·7-mm machine-guns. It was expected that these versions would achieve speeds of up to 385 mph but further development was halted in 1943. They were intended as "heavy" day and night fighters, the latter equipped with German Lichtenstein SN-2 airborne interception radar.

Caproni A.P.1

Designed by Ing Pallavicino of the former Cantieri Aeronautica Bergamaschi, the Caproni A.P.1 appeared in 1934 as one of the first Italian aircraft intended specifically for the close-support rôle. It was a cantilever low-wing monoplane of mixed construction, with a braced tail unit and a sturdy wing of thick section, well able to withstand the stresses of diving into action.

The prototype was a single-seat aircraft, armed only with two forward-firing 7·7-mm machine-guns and with a heavily "trousered" fixed undercarriage. The "trousering" was simplified considerably on production A.P.1s, which were two-seaters with an observer's cockpit behind that of the pilot and an additional machine-gun for rearward

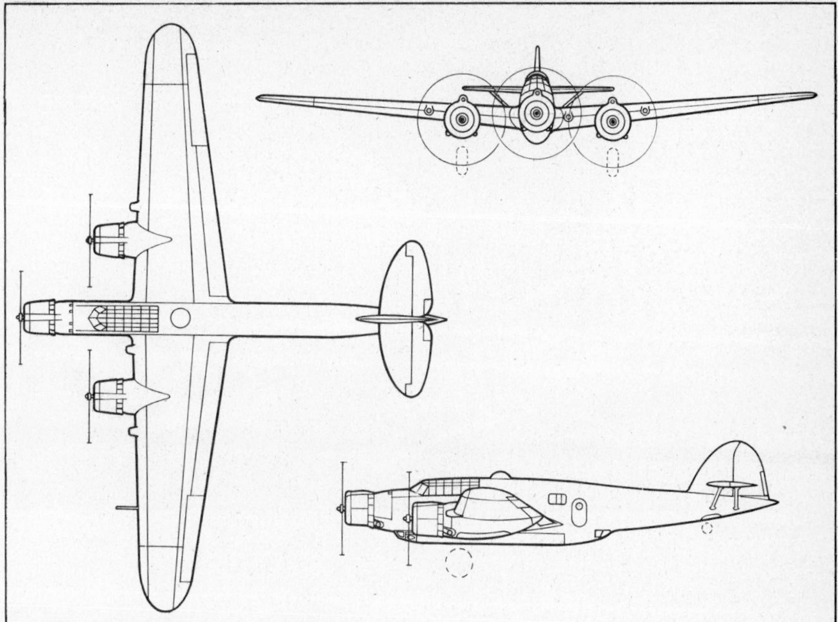

CRDA Cant Z.1007*bis* Alcione

CRDA Cant Z.1018 Leone

Caproni A.P.1

TYPE	DIMENSIONS						WEIGHT	PERFORMANCE				REMARKS
	span		*length*		*height*		*max t-o*	*max speed*	*at height*	*service ceiling*	*combat range*	
	ft	*in*	*ft*	*in*	*ft*	*in*	*lb*	*mph*	*ft*	*ft*	*miles*	
Cant Z.506B	86	11⅓	63	1⅔	24	5½	28,008	217	13,120	26,250	1,243	
Cant Z.1007*bis* Ser.XII	81	4	61	0¼	17	1½	29,211	280	15,000	24,600	1,243	
Cant Z.1018	73	9¾	57	9	19	11½	26,455	323		23,785	700	

Caproni Ca 33

Caproni Ca 36

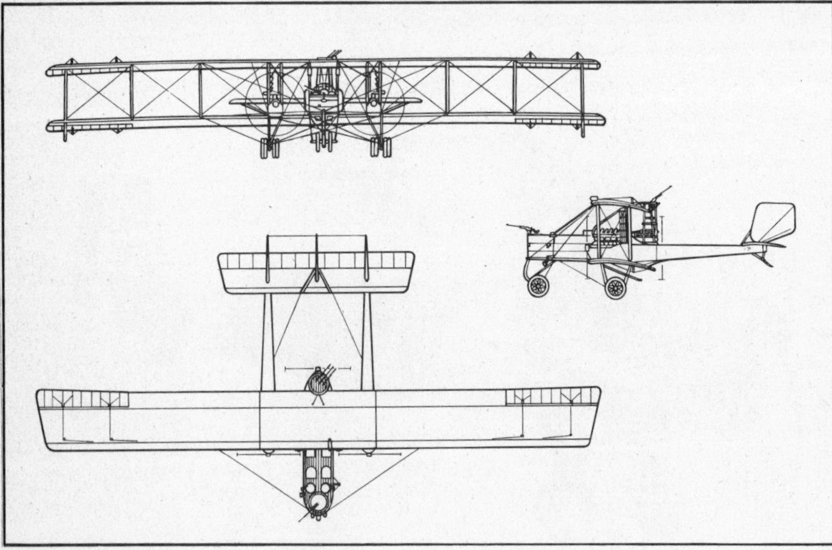
Caproni Ca 36M

Caproni Ca 42

defence. Both cockpits were open. Power was supplied by a single 895-hp Piaggio C.35 radial engine.

The A.P.1 was not built in great numbers, equipping only one Stormo d'Assalto based at Ciampino, near the Italian capital, and did not see combat service. Small numbers were exported to South America, the standard version going to San Salvador and a seaplane adaptation, the A.P.1 Idro, to Paraguay. Two experimental models, which remained only prototypes, were fitted respectively with a retractable undercarriage and with ski landing gear.

Caproni Ca 32 and Ca 33

As the course of the 1914–18 War unfolded, several nations were to embark upon the design and construction of large, multi-engined aircraft; but Italy, like Russia, had evolved such a type before the war started. This was the Caproni Ca 30 which appeared in 1913. It was powered by three Gnome rotary engines, with one engine mounted as a "pusher" in a central nacelle and the other two driving tractor propellers in twin fuselage booms through a differential transmission gear. This indirect drive arrangement was abandoned on the Ca 31, which made its first flight at the end of 1914, the outer pair of engines being relocated at the front of the booms. The Ca 31 could be powered either by three Gnomes or by two Gnomes in the outer positions and a 90-hp Curtiss in the centre nacelle.

First version to go into production for the Italian Army Air Service was the Ca 32, in which the power plant was uprated to a trio of 100-hp Fiat A.10 liquid-cooled engines. Three were delivered in August 1915, a further 28 by the end of that year, and 133 more during 1916. Stable and pleasant to handle, the Ca 32 possessed an excellent range and a useful payload, attributes which enabled it to lay the foundations of a strategic bomber arm in Italy's air force; it also equipped her first night bomber squadron.

A development of the Ca 32 with three 150-hp Isotta-Fraschini V4B engines was the Ca 33, which followed it into production towards the end of 1916. Of wood-and-fabric construction, with three-bay equal-span wings, the Ca 33 had a multi-wheel landing gear which enabled it to operate from rough terrain. The two pilots sat side-by-side in the centre fuselage, with a nose gunner operating a single Revelli machine-gun from the front cockpit and a fourth crew member at the rear with one, two or sometimes three similar guns.

Altogether, 269 Ca 33s were built in Italy in 1916–18, serving with units of the Italian army at home, the French army and (as a torpedo-bomber) with the Italian navy. The type was also built under licence in France as the C.E.P. (Caproni-Esnault-Pelterie), and remained in service until the end of the 1914–18 War.

Various other versions were evaluated, including the Ca 34, Ca 35 (tandem seats for the pilots), Ca 36 (detachable wings to facilitate stowage or transportation), Ca 37 (single-engined two-seater for ground-attack) and Ca 39 (seaplane). A post-war proposal was for a commercial model designated Ca 57.

In 1923,the Ca 36 was put into production in improved form as the Ca 36M, with uprated V4Bs of 190 hp, to equip the re-formed Italian air force. It continued in service for the next four years, during the initial stages of Mussolini's campaigns to "restore Italy's lost colonies".

Caproni Ca 40 to Ca 43

Pursuing the multi-engined concept first established in the Ca 30 series of bombers, the Società di Aviazione Ing Caproni brought out in the middle of the 1914–18 War an aircraft that was even larger than the earlier type. With the company designation Ca 40, this was a huge triplane with equal-span wings measuring almost 100 ft from tip to tip, and was built on the twin-boom-and-centre-nacelle pattern.

Inevitably, with such a wing span, the Ca 40 was liberally provided with interplane struts and wire bracing, but the crew nacelle was of the more streamlined oval section first introduced on the Ca 35. It was first tested at Pensuti in 1916, powered by three 200-hp Isotta-Fraschini engines. The crew consisted of two pilots side-by-side in the middle of the nacelle, with gunners to front and rear.

Three Ca 40s were delivered in 1917, before being followed into limited production by the Ca 41. Among refinements introduced by the latter were higher-powered engines, a more pointed nacelle (in which the pilots were seated in tandem) and a less complicated landing gear, from which the nose-wheels of the Ca 40 were omitted.

Principal production model, however, was the Ca 42, in which 270-hp Fiat, Isotta-Fraschini or American Liberty engines could be installed. The Ca 42 reverted to side-by-side pilot seating and carried up to 3,910 lb of small bombs in an external container mounted in the middle of the bottom plane. A front gunner operated two machine-guns in the extreme nose, while third and fourth guns were located in the two engine booms, just aft of the wing trailing-edge, to fire rearwards.

During 1918, 35 Ca 41s and Ca 42s were delivered to units of both the Italian army and navy, and six were flown by the British RNAS. A further development, which saw service in small numbers, was the Ca 43, a seaplane torpedo-bomber. In service, the Ca 40 to Ca 43 (these were the manufacturer's designations) were referred to by the overall type designation Ca 4.

Two military developments which were not used in service were the Ca 51 and Ca 52. These were basically similar (the Ca 52 being a proposed export model of the 51), with a biplane tail assembly which incorporated a mounting for a machine-gun. Post-war commercial aviation derivatives included the 12/17-passenger Ca 48, based on the Ca 42, which was used briefly on the Milan-London route; and the Ca 58 and Ca 59 – further developments of the Ca 48, with enlarged nacelles.

Caproni Ca 44 to Ca 47

The Caproni Ca 4 series of heavy bombers proved themselves in service to be rugged, reliable machines with a fine range and useful payload; but these very qualities tended to make them slow and vulnerable to fighter and anti-aircraft defences. In 1917, therefore, Caproni produced the first of a new series of aircraft – designated Ca 5 in official circles – which attempted to alleviate these shortcomings. Known by the company designation Ca 44, the new aircraft was about three-quarters the size and weight of the Ca 4 series and was much improved aerodynamically, with biplane instead of triplane configuration. It was powered by uprated Fiat engines, each developing 300hp.

The Ca 44 was developed into the Ca 45, similar except for a rather more pointed crew nacelle, and this model was built in some numbers by the French manufacturer Robert Esnault-Pelterie. However, as with the Ca 4s, the third design in the series became the major production version. Receiving the company designation Ca 46, this was generally similar to the Ca 45 except in power plant, for which alternative installations of 250-hp Isotta-Fraschini V4Bs, 300-hp Fiat A.12*bis* or 400-hp Libertys were possible. Italian production for the Ca 46, amounting to 255 machines, was shared between the plants of Bastianelli, Breda, Caproni, Miani-Silvestri and Savigliano; the type was also constructed by Bessaneau and Esnault-Pelterie in France and by Fisher Body and Standard in the United States.

In parallel with its lower all-up weight and reduced bomb load of 1,188 lb, the Ca 46 also had a shorter range than its predecessors, but in other respects performance showed a marked increase and the type was widely used by day and night bomber units in 1918, as a replacement

Caproni Ca 46

Caproni Ca 46, American-built

TYPE	DIMENSIONS span ft	span in	length ft	length in	height ft	height in	WEIGHT max t-o lb	PERFORMANCE max speed mph	at height ft	service ceiling ft	combat range miles	REMARKS
A.P.1	39	4½	28	6⅛			4,916	221		24,600	683	
Ca 32	72	10	35	9⅛	12	1⅔	6,252	81	SL		340	
Ca 33	72	10	35	9⅛	12	1⅔	7,302	94	SL	13,450	280	
Ca 42	98	1⅛	49	6½	20	8	16,535	87	SL	9,840	7 hr	
Ca 43	98	1⅛	49	6½	21	11¾	16,314	81				

Caproni Ca 73

Caproni Ca 73

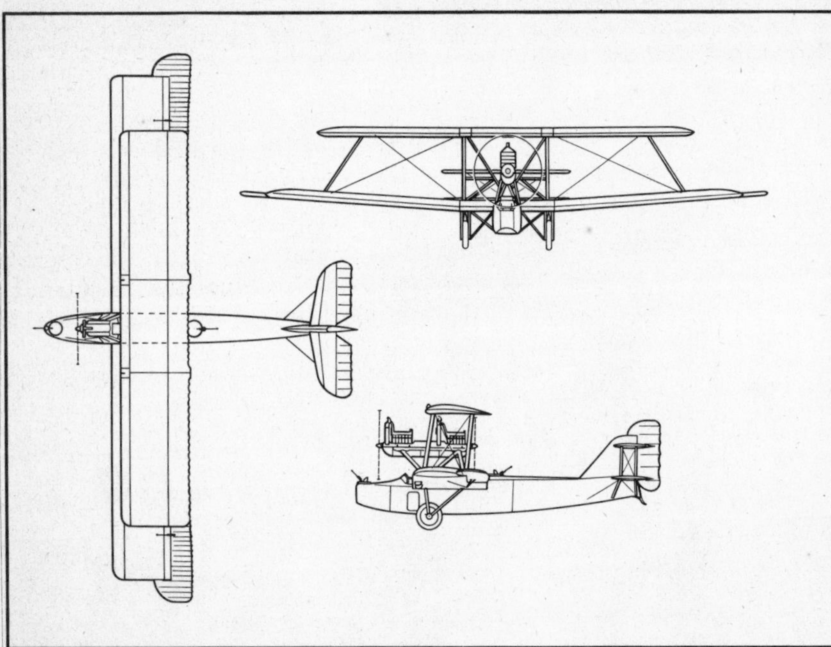

Caproni Ca 73

Caproni Ca 101

for the Ca 3s. A small batch of Ca 47 seaplanes were also produced for Italian naval air squadrons. These were conversions from landplane models, ten such conversions being made by Piaggio and others by Bastianelli. An ambulance version of the Ca 46 was designated Ca 50.

After the end of the 1914–18 War, some Ca 46s were converted to commercial standard by Breda as Caproni Ca 57s (alias Breda M-1s) to seat ten passengers, and a scheduled service between Milan and Rome was inaugurated on 29 January 1919 with aircraft of this type.

Caproni Ca 73 series

With the formation of the Regia Aeronautica in March 1923, it was decided to continue the policy, inaugurated during the 1914–1918 War, of maintaining a strategic bomber force as an integral part of Italy's new autonomous air arm. Inevitably, since they had pioneered the long-range multi-engined bomber during the war, the Società di Ing Caproni were selected to design and produce the new machines that were required. Thus, in 1925, there emanated from the design team led by Caproni's Ing Verduzio a new medium-sized twin-engined biplane bomber which was given the factory designation Ca 73.

Evolved from the Ca 66, which had been evaluated at the first post-war competition for bomber aircraft held in Italy, the Ca 73 was of unusual configuration in that it was an inverted sesquiplane – that is, the upper wing was much shorter in span than the lower one. The lower wing was attached to the top decking of the boat-like fuselage, with the upper mainplane carried well clear of the fuselage, with a minimum of struts and external wire bracing. The power "egg" consisted of two 400-hp Lorraine engines mounted in tandem in a single nacelle between the mainplanes, one driving a tractor propellor and the other a pusher propeller. A biplane tail, with single fin and rudder, was fitted; and the twin-wheel main undercarriage was made up of two separate "Vees".

The Ca 73 was ordered for service in substantial numbers and appeared subsequently in a variety of models. Standard basic armament consisted of one machine-gun in the extreme nose, another in a dorsal installation to the rear of the wing trailing-edge and a third in a ventral position. Bomb-load was normally carried externally, on the sides of the fuselage beneath the bottom wing.

Second model to appear was the Ca 73*bis* of 1926, which differed in having 440-hp Lorraine engines; this was followed by the Ca 73*ter*, powered by 490-hp Isotta-Fraschini Asso engines and later redesignated Ca 82. A modified version of the latter, the Ca 82Co, was also produced in small numbers as a colonial transport.

The Ca 82 – in which the bombs were carried on attachment points beneath the lower wing – eventually supplanted the earlier Ca 73s in service and was itself followed by the Ca 88 and Ca 89 (formerly Ca 73*quater*). The Ca 89 introduced a windscreen for the pilot's cabin, glazed nose panels to improve the bomb-aiming facilities, a turret housing for the dorsal machine-gun and a retractable ventral gun installation.

Side-by-side with light bombers produced by Fiat, the Caproni "heavies" formed the mainstay of the Regia Aeronautica's Aviazione da Bombardamento for over eight years; even then the basic design was perpetuated for a further year or two by the Ca 74, which saw extensive service in the Italian campaigns ın North Africa during the first half of the 1930s. Several examples of the Ca 73 series were, in addition to their bombing duties, employed as paratroop transports, others for ambulance work.

Caproni Ca 101

Derived from the earlier Ca 97, the Ca 101 became in turn the basis for a number of designs, notably the Ca 111 and Ca 133. It was a three-engined high-wing monoplane bomber, which entered service with the Stormi da Bombardamento shortly before the Italian campaign against Ethiopia. In this campaign, it was employed to considerable effect in support of the invading army, both on attack missions and in maintaining supplies.

A civil model of the Ca 101 existed, in which various alternative power plants were fitted; but the normal installation in the military version consisted of three 235-hp Alfa Romeo D.2 engines, driving two-blade metal propellers. The square-section fuselage had a robust steel-tube basic structure, and a feature of the Ca 101 was the thickness of the wing, which combined great strength with considerable lifting power. The bomb-load could be carried either internally, in special containers, or externally beneath the fuselage. Defensive armament consisted of machine-guns in dorsal and ventral positions and, on occasion, two additional machine-guns amidships.

After the conclusion of Italian campaigning in East Africa, the Ca 101 was phased out of service; but one further modification worthy of mention was the Ca 102, which was similar but of twin-engined configuration. One Ca 102 at least was fitted with pairs of twin motors, each pair mounted in tandem, and saw service with the 62nd Sperimentale Bombardieri Pesanti (Experimental Heavy Bomber Squadron).

Caproni Ca 111

The Ca 111 was another aircraft which embodied much of the design of the Ca 101. It retained an essentially similar wing and rear fuselage yet, despite its great size, was powered by only a single 950-hp Isotta-Fraschini Asso 750 RC engine.

The Ca 111 was intended primarily for reconnaissance duties and appeared in both landplane and twin-float versions, the latter being designated Ca 111*bis* Idro. It was used widely during the Italian campaign in Ethiopia, where its load-carrying ability and all-round good performance enabled it to give excellent support to the armies in the field. Later, in World War II, it was used with similar success against partisan groups in Yugoslavia, and one Ca 111 was still in service with the Regia Aeronautica when Marshal Badoglio surrendered to the Allies on 8 September 1943. Like the earlier Ca 101, the Ca 111 was armed with dorsal, ventral and lateral machine-guns, and could carry a modest bomb-load either internally or externally.

Caproni Ca 133

Following quickly on the heels of the Ca 101 and Ca 111, the Ca 133 also became a standard medium-bomber/supply transport type with the Regia Aeronautica during the campaign in Ethiopia. A number of squadrons of Ca 133s were retained in that country after the occupation, and when Italy entered World War II in 1940 she still had on strength 14 Squadriglie da Bombardamento Terrestre stationed at various points in East Africa.

The Ca 133 continued to give excellent service throughout the war, despite its age, and was used to particular effect for transporting paratroops during Italy's invasion of Albania. Many other Ca 133s put in valuable work as trainers, and the aircraft's plodding but tractable nature often led to its being nicknamed *Caprona* (she-goat) or *Vacca* (cow). After the Italian surrender, a number continued to serve in Northern Italy with the Aviazione della RSI, and at least one flew with the co-belligerent Italian air force on the side of the Allies.

Although it followed the same basic layout as its predecessors, the Ca 133 had a wing of greater span and reverted to the tri-motor configuration of the Ca 101. The engines were 450-hp Piaggio P.VII C.14 air-cooled radials, driving two-bladed metal propellers. Two bomb-

Caproni Ca 102, four-engined version

Caproni Ca 111

Caproni Ca 133

TYPE	DIMENSIONS						WEIGHT	PERFORMANCE				REMARKS
	span		length		height		max t-o	max speed	at height	service ceiling	combat range	
	ft	in	ft	in	ft	in	lb	mph	ft	ft	miles	
Ca 46	76	9¼	41	4⅞	14	5¼	11,685	94	SL	14,760	4 hr	Data for A.12*bis*-engined model
Ca 73	82	0¼	49	6½	18	4½	11,023	109		15,092	404	
Ca 82	82	0¼	49	6½	18	4½	12,566	121		16,896	683	
Ca 101	64	6¾	47	1¾	12	9		129		20,013	1,243	
Ca 111	64	6¾	50	2⅓	12	7½	11,795	185		21,982	1,243	

Caproni Ca 135

Caproni Ca 135*bis*, Hungarian Air Force

Caproni Ca 135*bis*

Caproni Ca 310, Royal Norwegian Air Force

bays were provided within the fuselage, and the Ca 133 could carry an additional load externally. Defensive armament consisted of two 7·7-mm machine-guns in a movable dorsal turret, another gun beneath the fuselage and one on each side, firing laterally fore and aft. Some war-weary bombers were converted subsequently to Ca 133S (for *sanitaria* = ambulance) and were used mostly in the Libyan theatre. Others, converted to Ca 133T (for *trasporto* = transport) appeared on the Russian front.

There were two further derivatives of the Ca 133. The first, which existed only in prototype form, was the Ca 142, with a retractable undercarriage. The other was the civil Ca 148, several of which were impressed for military transport service during World War II.

Caproni Ca 135

The Ca 135 was but one of a number of modern designs which began to take shape on the Caproni drawing boards after the company acquired the services of Ing Cesare Pallavicino from Breda. Designed in the middle of 1934 to an official requirement for a twin-engined medium bomber, the prototype made its maiden flight on 1 April 1935, powered by 800-hp Isotta-Fraschini Asso XI RC 40 12-cylinder liquid-cooled engines.

A mid-wing monoplane, with a twin tail assembly, the Ca 135 prototype was of mixed construction and was unarmed. Flight testing continued into 1936, when the Regia Aeronautica ordered an evaluation batch of 14 of the *Tipo Spagna* (Spanish Type), with a view to using them in the Spanish Civil War, and the Peruvian government ordered six of the *Tipo Peru* with 815-hp Asso XI RC 45 engines. These production Ca 135s could carry from two to twelve bombs internally, up to a total of 3,520 lb; defensive armament comprised three Breda turrets in nose, dorsal and ventral positions, each mounting one 12·7-mm or two 7·7-mm machine-guns.

Eventually, 32 Ca 135s were delivered to the Peruvian Air Force, with uprated Asso XI RC 40s of 900 hp. The Regia Aeronautica, however, was not satisfied that the aircraft was adequately powered. Tests were carried out with a slightly modified version, powered by 1,000-hp Fiat A.80 RC 41 radials, but these engines proved unreliable and the Ca 135s were relegated to secondary duties. Later, airframe modification and the installation of 1,000-hp Piaggio P.XI RC 40 radials resulted in a much improved performance, but by this time better designs were available from other Italian manufacturers and the type was not adopted for first-line service in its own country. However, Caproni succeeded in selling a substantial number of the Piaggio-powered model to the Hungarian government during 1939–40; these were used by units of the Hungarian Air Force attached to Luftflotte IV during the opening months of the invasion of Russia in World War II.

Caproni Ca 309 to Ca 314

Ing Cesare Pallavicino, of the former Cantieri Aeronautici Bergamaschi (absorbed by Caproni in 1931 as the Compania Aeronautica Bergamasca), designed in 1936 two prototype aircraft designed for policing and general duties in Italian overseas territories. The basic difference between the Ca 309 Ghibli (Desert Wind) and Ca 310 Libbecio (South-west Wind) lay in the latter's retractable undercarriage and 450-hp Piaggio P.VII C.16 radials.

The Ca 309 was powered by 185-hp Alfa Romeo 115 air-cooled inverted "Vee" engines and was produced in several small series, which served chiefly in North Africa as light reconnaissance-bombers and six-passenger transport aircraft. The Series VI, with a nose-mounted 20-mm cannon, could be used also for close support.

The Ca 310 offered a much improved performance, by virtue of its more powerful engines and cleaner aerodynamic form, yet, curiously, was not adopted for service by the Regia Aeronautica. It was, however, used widely elsewhere, by the Nationalist forces in Spain, and by the air arms of Croatia, Hungary, Norway and Yugoslavia. Armament consisted of one dorsal and two forward-firing 7·7-mm machine-guns, and a bomb-load of 880 lb could be carried. An experimental twin-float model, the

Ca 310 Idro, was not proceeded with; but another modified version, originally designated Ca 310*bis*, became the prototype for the Ca 311.

Apart from a further change in power plant, to 500-hp Piaggio P.VII C. 35 engines, the Ca 311 differed mainly from its predecessor in having a larger and more extensively glazed nose section with no "step" to the crew canopy, although a later model, the Ca 311M, reverted to a "stepped" windscreen. With a crew of three and similar armament and bomb-load to the Ca 310, the Ca 311 entered production for the Regia Aeronautica as a light bomber, but was not built in great numbers.

Further development produced the Ca 312, in which the major change was the substitution of yet more powerful engines, in the shape of 700-hp Piaggio P.XVI RC 35 radials. This model, like its immediate predecessor, appeared with both "stepped" (Ca 312M) and "unstepped" windscreens. Two 7·7-mm guns were mounted in a dorsal turret, and a third in the port wing leading-edge. It was not built in great quantity. Some were exported to Norway, but most of the Italian machines in service were employed on communications or training duties. The Ca 312*bis* was a twin-float seaplane variant, and the Ca 312IS an experimental twin-float torpedo-bomber.

With yet another engine change, the Ca 311 became the Ca 313, powered by two Isotta-Fraschini Delta RC 35s. The prototype appeared early in 1940, and the Ca 313 entered quantity production soon afterwards, for both the Regia Aeronautica and the Swedish government, who placed an order for 90. It was much more heavily armed than its progenitors, with three 12·7-mm and two 7·7-mm machine-guns, and bomb-load was also increased, to 1,100 lb. Engine troubles plagued the Swedish Ca 313s, resulting in extensive losses, but those in Italian service performed well, equipping several groups in Russia.

In mid-1941 the Ca 313 was superseded on the production lines by the final type in this long-lived series, the Ca 314. Two factories, at Castellamare and Taliedo, combined to produce some 500 of this version to Italian orders, but their production rate was so slow that an additional order, from the Luftwaffe, for 1,000 machines was never fulfilled.

Basically similar to the Ca 313, the Ca 314 served largely with Italian naval units as the Ca 314RA (*Ricognizione Aerosilurante*) on reconnaissance and torpedo-bombing, convoy protection and general naval support missions. Another model, the Ca 314C (*Combattimento*), was employed on giving close support to land forces, with two additional 12·7-mm guns mounted beneath the wings. Combined production of the Ca 313 and Ca 314 totalled approximately 1,000 aircraft.

Caproni-Vizzola F.5

Ing Fabrizi of the Caproni-Vizzola SA at Vizzola Ticino, Varese, produced two designs in 1938 for low-wing, single-seat fighters. The first of these was designated F.4 and was powered by an 890-hp Isotta-Fraschini Asso 121 RC 40 liquid-cooled in-line engine. It was of mixed wood and metal construction, with a retractable undercarriage, and carried a fixed armament of two 12·7-mm machine-

Caproni Ca 313

Caproni Ca 314

Caproni-Vizzola F.5 prototype

TYPE	DIMENSIONS						WEIGHT	PERFORMANCE				REMARKS
	span		*length*		*height*		*max t-o*	*max speed*	*at height*	*service ceiling*	*combat range*	
	ft	*in*	*ft*	*in*	*ft*	*in*	*lb*	*mph*	*ft*	*ft*	*miles*	
Ca 133	69	8¼	50	4¾	13	1½	14,471	174		18,045	839	
Ca 135	61	8	47	2	11	2	21,050	273	15,750	21,300	745	Data for Piaggio-engined model
Ca 309	53	1¾	43	7⅔	10	8¾	6,067	155		13,940	930 max	
Ca 310	53	1¾	40	0⅓	11	6½	10,252	227		22,965	1,025	
Ca 311	53	1¾	38	6¼	11	11¾	10,714	227	13,120	19,685	1,210	
Ca 312	53	1¾	40	0⅓	11	5¾	11,464	267		26,247	965	
Ca 313	52	10⅔	38	8½	13	3	13,007	271	16,400	23,950	745	
Ca 314	54	7½	38	8½	12	1⅔	13,580	259	16,400	23,950	745	

Fiat B.R.1

Fiat B.R.2

Fiat B.R.3

Fiat B.R.20 Cicogna

guns mounted in the wing-roots. The Asso engine was not a particularly happy choice, however, and was replaced by a German DB601A, which delayed the first flight of the one and only F.4 until 1940.

Meanwhile the prototype of the second design, the F.5, had made its maiden flight in 1939. Structurally, it was identical to the F.4 except for the power plant, for which the Fiat A.74 RC 38 fourteen-cylinder radial engine of 840 hp was chosen. Construction of a pre-production series of 14 F.5s began in 1940, with slightly increased fin and rudder area, a revised cockpit canopy and other modifications. They were operational for a short time in the night defence of Rome.

In 1941, an F.5 airframe was adapted to take a 1,475-hp DB605A, becoming the prototype F.6; and in 1942 the F.6MZ was flown with a 1,175-hp Isotta-Fraschini Zeta RC 42. Plans to manufacture a pre-production batch of F.6MZs were abandoned after September 1943.

Fiat B.R.1., B.R.2 and B.R.3

During the closing stages of the 1914–18 War, Ing Celestino Rosatelli of Fiat was busy on the design of his first bomber, known as the B.R. (*Bombardamento Rosatelli*). The prototype made its maiden flight in 1919. Five years later, when a few B.R's were in service, Rosatelli produced an improved model which he called the B.R.1, with a 700-hp Fiat A-14 engine. This aircraft introduced a number of novel features, including the "W" pattern interplane bracing that was to become almost a trademark of this designer.

The B.R.1 was an unequal-span biplane which accommodated a crew of two in tandem cockpits. A dorsal gun was fitted for defence, and there was a rotating cylinder arrangement in the lower fuselage for carrying and launching bombs. The B.R.1's suitability as a torpedo-bomber was also investigated; but it was not an entirely successful aircraft and its main claim to fame was that on 23 December 1924 it set up an altitude record of 18,097 ft carrying a 1,500-kg payload.

The B.R.2 made its appearance in 1925, as a progressive development of the B.R.1 with the more powerful 1,090-hp Fiat A-25 engine. Its basic configuration was similar to that of its predecessor, but performance was improved considerably despite a higher loaded weight, and later production machines incorporated Handley Page slotted wings to improve take-off and landing. During 1925, a *squadriglia* of B.R.2s made an extensive demonstration tour of major cities in Europe.

The B.R. series reached its culmination in the B.R.3, which was flown for the first time in 1930 and was ordered into production shortly afterwards, more than 100 being completed eventually. The "3" retained the A-25 power plant in an airframe of improved strength and cleanness of line, and remained a standard Italian bomber type for several years. Armament consisted of a fixed 7·5-mm machine-gun in a nose mounting, with a second, movable, 7·5-mm gun in the observer/gunner's cockpit. For reconnaissance missions an aerial camera could also be fitted. Towards the end of its career, the B.R.3 was phased out of first-line service, but continued to do good work at bombing schools as an instructional aircraft up to the outbreak of World War II.

A final development in the series was the B.R.4, but no orders for this were forthcoming and it did not progress beyond the prototype stage.

Fiat B.R.20 Cicogna (Stork)

By the middle of the 1930s, Italy, like Germany, had re-established itself as a major air power, and Mussolini's Regia Aeronautica was numerically an important force, even if the quality of its equipment was not always a match for that of other air arms. In the autumn of 1935, Italy's invasion of Ethiopia gave the Regia Aeronautica a taste of genuine battle conditions, and with the outbreak of the Civil War in Spain in the following year Italian military aid was accorded to General Franco's insurgent forces.

It was in 1936 also that Fiat evolved the B.R.20 (the B.R. indicating *Bombardamento Rosatelli*), in an attempt

to give Italy's air force a fast, well armed, light bomber that was rugged yet simply constructed and easily serviced. So, when the Italian airborne participation in the Spanish war was established in the form of the Aviazione Legionaria, the Fiat B.R.20 formed part of the 35th Gruppo Autonomo Bombardamento Veloce of this force. It was also constructed for export and a grand total of approximately 350 were eventually built for the Regia Aeronautica and the air forces of Japan (75), Spain and Venezuela.

The first version of the B.R.20 was powered by two 1,000-hp Fiat A.80 RC 41 radial engines driving three-bladed propellers, and was armed with four 7·7-mm Breda-SAFAT machine-guns in nose, dorsal and ventral installations, with 500 rounds per gun. Maximum bomb-load was 3,528 lb.

The second military version was the B.R. 20M, which also appeared in 1939. It featured a revised nose and cabin for the crew of five, with much enhanced visibility, and the defensive armament was improved by substituting a 12·7-mm machine-gun for one of the 7·7-mm guns of the earlier model. These and other refinements were the result of the operational experience gained with the B.R. 20 in Spain and in the Italian invasion of Albania which took place in the spring of 1939. More than 200 B.R. 20Ms were eventually produced, and a number of B.R. 20s were modified to B.R. 20M standard.

When Italy entered World War II in 1940, the Regia Aeronautica had 219 B.R.20/20Ms, of which 172 were in operational condition. In October 1940, two Groups, with 38 and 37 of these bombers respectively, formed a component of the Corpo Aereo Italiano operating from Melsbroeck and Chievres in Belgium against targets in the United Kingdom. Owing to poor support offered by the current generation of Italian fighters, daylight attacks were soon called off in favour of sporadic night attacks; but after about three months of operations the entire force was recalled in January 1941 and sent to support the Italian invasion of Greece, where their presence was more urgently required.

Most of the B.R.20's subsequent wartime employment was in the vicinity of Malta, Yugoslavia, Greece and Libya, and included raids against Resistance units in the Balkans. In 1942, however, after the Italian Air Force had assigned a number of units to support the Luftwaffe on the Russian front, the contingent was reinforced by Cant Z.1007*bis* and B.R.20 bombers. Even so, the Italian force took a considerable hammering at Soviet hands, and what was left of it was recalled to the home front in 1943.

Meanwhile, in 1941, Fiat had evolved a third bomber version, the B.R.20*bis*, which had improved flying control surfaces and more powerful (1,250-hp) Fiat A.82 RC 42 radial engines. The number of guns was further increased, to five, by the addition of a 12·7-mm machine-gun in a blister on each side of the fuselage amidships. Allied air raids and the early Italian Armistice prevented this model from being constructed in very large numbers.

As the continued attention given to its defensive armament indicates, the B.R.20 was vulnerable to fighter attack, and its attrition rate was high, with the result that towards the end of the war it was employed for reconnaissance rather than bombing operations. When Italy surrendered to the Allies in 1943, only 81 B.R.20s remained in service – of which 59 were serviceable – out of nearly 600 built.

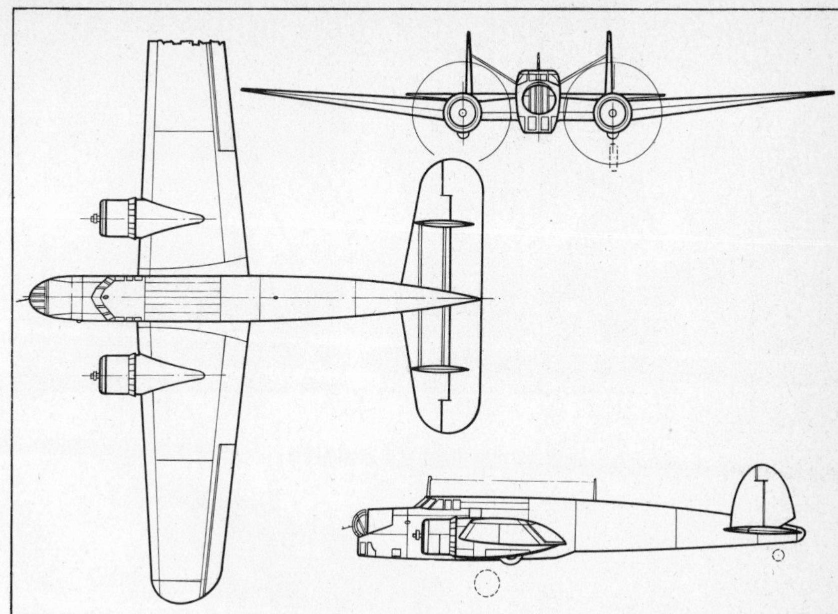

Fiat B.R.20 Cicogna

Fiat B.R.20M Cicogna

Fiat B.R.20*bis* Cicogna

TYPE	DIMENSIONS						WEIGHT	PERFORMANCE				REMARKS
	span		*length*		*height*		*max t-o*	*max speed*	*at height*	*service ceiling*	*combat range*	
	ft	*in*	*ft*	*in*	*ft*	*in*	*lb*	*mph*	*ft*	*ft*	*miles*	
Caproni-Vizzola F.5	37	0⅞	25	11¾	9	10⅛	5,004	317	9,840	31,170	478	
B.R. 1	56	9	34	4¼	12	10	8,642	149		18,040	404	
B.R. 2	56	9	34	11⅔	12	10	9,251	149		20,500	621	
B.R. 3	56	9	34	7⅓	12	10	9,590	143		20.505	466	
B.R. 20M	70	8¾	54	8⅔	15	7	22,267	273½		26,246	1,710 max	

Fiat C.R.1

Fiat C.R.20

Fiat C.R.20-I floatplane

Fiat C.R.30

Fiat C.R.1

First nationally-designed fighter to go into standard service in Italy after the 1914–18 War was the Fiat C.R.1. Development of this aircraft began with the construction of a C.R. (*Caccia Rosatelli*) prototype at the Fiat works in 1923. This machine was powered by a 300-hp Hispano engine, driving a two-bladed wooden propeller. After satisfactory conclusion of its flight trials, the type was ordered into production in slightly modified form in 1924, as the C.R.1., with the more powerful Isotta-Fraschini Asso (Ace) air-cooled engine, and just over 100 C.R.1s were eventually completed.

The C.R.1 was a distinctive design, in that the lower mainplane had considerably greater span than the upper one. Both wings were of wooden construction and were extensively braced to support the greater weight of the lower wing. The fuselage was of triangulated metal tube construction, with a braced tailplane, and the undercarriage was also of a conventional fixed type. The pilot sat in an open cockpit, protected from the elements by only a shallow windshield, and had twin synchronized 7·7-mm machine-guns in the forward fuselage.

The C.R.1 was delivered to units of the 1st Stormo Caccia, based in the Italian homeland, and eventually found its way to the aerobatic squadrons where it performed with considerable brilliance.

It remained in service for several years, until replaced by the more modern and efficient C.R.20.

Fiat C.R.20

In 1926, the first of Ing Rosatelli's C.R.20 series of classic fighter biplanes was flown, and it was not long before this type was put into series production, to become a standard fighter with the Regia Aeronautica for several years, in a variety of models. A further claim to distinction by the C.R.20 lay in the fact that it was chosen as the initial equipment of the Pattuglie Acrobatiche, the official aerobatic team of the Italian air force at displays and exhibitions in Italy and abroad.

The C.R.20 saw a certain amount of combat, first in the closing stages of the troubles in Libya, and later during the Italian occupation of Ethiopia, despite the gradual emergence of more modern types in squadron service.

Towards the end of its career as a fighter it became relegated to training duties; but well before this, in 1927, a two-seat dual-control version, the C.R.20B, was produced specifically for training. In the following year, the second combat model of the C.R.20 appeared: the C.R.20-I seaplane, which was produced in modest numbers to equip the Squadriglie da Caccia Marittima and the Scuola Alta Velocità di Desenzano. The C.R.20-I was followed into production and service by the C.R.20*bis*, basically similar to the earlier models but with improved accommodation for the pilot, internal equipment and landing gear.

All these versions of the C.R.20 were fitted with the same power plant – the 400-hp Fiat A.20 – but the installation of an uprated 425-hp engine in the C.R.20 AQ (*alta quota* = high altitude) conferred a better all-round performance, including a much-improved rate of climb. The final version, produced by Fiat's CMASA plant at Marina di Pisa, was the C.R.20 Asso (Ace), so called from the installation of the 450-hp Isotta-Fraschini engine of that name. This engine was particularly appreciated by members of the Pattuglie, who found it gave an extra "edge" to their performance.

Structurally, all versions of the C.R.20 were basically similar – with a fabric-covered metal fuselage, unequal-span wings characterized by Rosatelli's typical use of "W" pattern interplane struts, and a braced tailplane and fixed landing gear. Armament in all models consisted of two synchronized Vickers machine-guns.

Fiat C.R.30

The Fiat C.R.30 of 1932 continued the Rosatelli line of small fighter biplanes that were the mainstay of the Regia Aeronautica's fighter squadrons in the 1930s. In the year of its debut, it notched up successes in the

"Dal Molin" speed trials, and a two-seat model was entered for the international Coppa Bibescu competition in the following year. Like its stablemates of earlier and later years, the C.R.30 was chosen to equip the Pattuglie Acrobatiche aerobatic squadron, with which it distinguished itself in displays in many European capitals.

While retaining the basic features of the earlier C.R.20, the C.R.30 was an unequal-span biplane of mixed construction. The wings had the characteristic "W" interplane bracing and the fuselage, which was more compact and much more refined aerodynamically, was also more robustly built. A conventional fixed undercarriage was fitted and the tail assembly was of completely new design. Both the single-seat and two-seat versions had open cockpits.

The C.R.30 was quickly ordered into production, and deliveries were made to both home-based units and to the 2nd Stormo of the Regia Aeronautica based in Libya. In addition to its primary rôles of interceptor and bomber escort, the C.R. 30 could be fitted with an aerial camera for photographic reconnaissance missions. Power was provided by a single 600-hp Fiat A.30 liquid-cooled engine, driving a two-blade metal propeller, and armament consisted of a pair of machine-guns of 7·7-mm or 12·7-mm calibre, just ahead of the pilot's cockpit.

Although superseded by both the C.R.32 and the C.R.42 Falco before the outbreak of World War II, one or two examples of the C.R.30 were still to be found in service in minor rôles at the end of hostilities.

Fiat C.R.32

The 1930s saw the appearance of several biplane fighters of outstanding quality, and by no means the least of these was Fiat's attractive little C.R.32. A progressive development of the C.R.30, by Celestino Rosatelli, the prototype C.R.32 flew for the first time in 1933. It was of sesquiplane configuration, with Warren style interplane bracing, and was built of steel and light alloy, with fabric covering. The tailplane was braced by single struts above and below, and the main landing wheels were heavily "spatted".

Between its appearance and the outbreak of World War II, the Fiat C.R.32 became a favourite mount of the Pattuglie aerobatic display teams, for it was a highly agile little aircraft, sturdy and easy to fly. Its first blooding under combat conditions came in the Spanish Civil War. In August 1936, C.R.32s were despatched to Spain to form *La Cucaracha* squadron, a unit which grew until the C.R.32 became the mainstay of the fighter forces on Franco's side.

By the time war broke out in Europe in September 1939 and production was terminated, a total of 1,212 C.R.32s had been constructed in four major versions. When Italy entered the war a year later, the C.R.32 and its successor, the C.R.42, still constituted about two-thirds of the country's single-seat fighter strength, about 400 of the total being C.R.32s. Substantial quantities were built for export to China, Hungary, Paraguay and Venezuela, and the type was built under licence in Spain as the Hispano-Suiza HA-132-L Chirri.

The initial C.R.32 production model, of which over 350 were completed, was powered by a single 600-hp Fiat A.30 RA*bis* liquid-cooled in-line engine and carried a fixed armament of two 12·7-mm Breda-SAFAT machine-guns. It was supplanted on the production

Fiat C.R.32, Spanish Nationalist Air Force

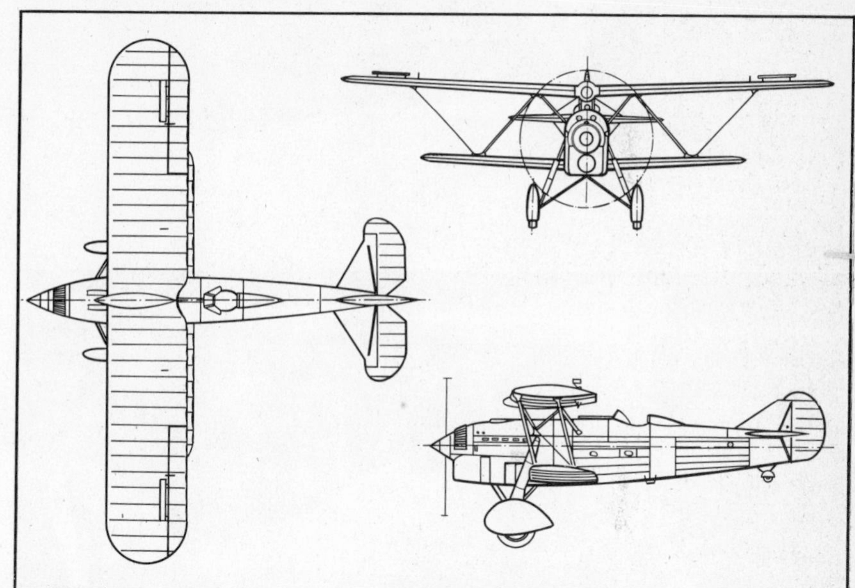

Fiat C.R.32

TYPE	DIMENSIONS						WEIGHT	PERFORMANCE				REMARKS
	span		length		height		max t-o	max speed	at height	service ceiling	combat range	
	ft	in	ft	in	ft	in	lb	mph	ft	ft	miles	
C.R. 1	29	4⅓	20	5⅔	7	10½	2,546	168		24,440	404	
C.R. 20	32	1⅞	21	11¾	9	0¼	2,998	171		24,610	466	
C.R. 20-I	32	1⅞	21	11¾	9	7¾	3,064	158		20,010	466	
C.R. 20 "Asso"	32	1⅞	21	11¾	9	0¼	3,278	155		16,404	310	
C.R. 30	34	5⅓	25	8¼	8	7½	4,178	217		28,545	528	

Fiat C.R.32*bis*

Fiat C.R.32*quater*

Fiat C.R.42 Falco prototype

Fiat C.R.42, Belgian Air Force

lines by the C.R.32*bis*, which had two additional guns, of 7·7-mm calibre, mounted in the wings and provision to carry two 110-lb or a single 220-lb bomb. This model also ran to over 300 machines before giving way in turn to the C.R.32*ter* of 1936, about 100 of which were completed, with minor alterations to the undercarriage and other changes. The major production version, however, was the C.R.32*quater*, which reverted to the original twin 12·7-mm armament.

The C.R.32 was outclassed as a fighter long before Italy's entry into World War II; but what it lacked in speed and firepower it more than made up in versatility, and it was used quite widely during the early war years, chiefly in Greece and East Africa, as a night fighter and close-support aircraft.

Fiat C.R.42 Falco (Falcon)

Ing Celestino Rosatelli enjoyed such success with the series of small, fast and manoeuvrable biplane fighters which emanated from his design office throughout the 1930s that it is, perhaps, understandable that he should have wished to prolong the series with one more design, even at the end of that decade when every other major air power was adopting the monoplane.

Accordingly, he developed his C.R.41 fighter design of 1936 (which had not gone into production) into the C.R.42, a rugged, compact little machine with unequal-span wings of light alloy and steel, with fabric covering and Warren-type interplane struts. The fuselage was of welded steel-tube construction, metal covered in the forward part, with fabric panels at the rear; the undercarriage comprised a heavily "trousered" and "spatted" main landing gear and a retractable tail-wheel on the prototype, but this latter feature was to be omitted from production C.R.42s. Power plant for the C.R.42 was the 840-hp Fiat A.74 RC 38 air-cooled radial engine, as against the 900-hp Gnome-Rhône K-14 of the C.R.41.

The prototype C.R.42 made its maiden flight during the early part of 1939, and despite the tendencies in other countries to veer away from the biplane – especially for combat rôles – the Ministero dell'Aeronautica decided to order the type into production for the Regia Aeronautica. Nor were they the only customers: the Belgian air force ordered 34 in September 1939, which were delivered during the following year; a number were exported to Hungary at the end of 1939, and the Swedish Flygvapnet took delivery of a further 72 in 1940.

The C.R.42 Falcos in Italian air force service were employed on a variety of different missions. They acted as escorts to bomber squadrons in the Mediterranean area, as fighter-bombers in the Western Desert and as night fighters at home, in addition to their prescribed rôle; and a force of 50 Falcos formed part of the Corpo Aereo Italiano operating from the Brussels area during the closing months of 1940. In a surprising assortment of guises the Fiat C.R.42 was developed and experimented with for a number of years, production finally terminating in 1942 after 1,784 had been completed.

One of the principal changes made in successive versions of the Falco was a steady improvement of its firepower. Early production C.R.42s mounted one 12·7-mm and one 7·7-mm gun, but the C.R.42*bis* which succeeded them on the production line had two guns of the larger calibre. In the C.R.42*ter*, this was increased to four 12·7-mm guns, the additional two being installed in fairings underneath the lower mainplane. A ground-attack variant, evolved for close-support duties during the North African fighting, was the C.R.42AS, with provision for carrying a 220-lb bomb beneath each lower wing. In its night fighter form the Falco was designated C.R.42N. As more modern fighters began to enter squadron service with the Regia Aeronautica, a number of Falcos were also modified into two-seat trainers.

Two interesting experimental versions of the Falco are worth mention. The first of these was conceived in 1939, when it was felt that a replacement would soon be required for the Meridionali Ro 44 floatplane fighter. Known as the I.C.R. 42 (the "I" signifying *Idrovolante* = seaplane), it was evolved by the Costruzioni Meccaniche Aeronautica SA at Marina di Pisa and consisted of a

C.R.42 airframe fitted with two large single-step floats. The I.C.R.42 was flown in 1940, but Italian policy towards seaplane fighters had altered in the meantime and no orders were forthcoming.

A final attempt to keep the Falco abreast of its contemporaries was made in 1941, when a single example of the C.R.42B was built and tested, with a 1,010-hp Daimler-Benz DB601A in-line engine. The German power plant gave the C.R.42B the very creditable speed, for a biplane, of 323 mph; but by this time even the Italians were forced to admit that the biplane era was over, and the project was not pursued.

Fiat C.R.25

Fiat produced the C.R.25 in 1938 to participate in a design competition, sponsored by the Italian Air Ministry, for a twin-engined fighter and general combat aircraft, with the main emphasis on range, speed and armament. It was a three-seat low-wing monoplane of clean lines, which answered the first two requirements well enough, but was not adequately armed, even after improvement.

Two prototypes flew during 1939, each powered by a pair of 840-hp Fiat A.74 RC 38 radial engines and armed initially with four 7·7-mm machine-guns in the forward fuselage and a dorsal turret containing a single 12·7-mm gun. Provision was made for up to 661 lb of bombs in an internal weapons-bay and a further 220-lb bomb or fuel tank could be suspended inboard of each nacelle.

A small pre-production batch of ten C.R.25s was put in hand in 1939, and these began to enter service with the 173rd Squadriglia of the Regia Aeronautica in Sicily during 1941, under the designation C.R.25*bis*. They were employed chiefly on maritime reconnaissance duties in the Mediterranean. But even after replacement of the four 7·7-mm guns with two of 12·7-mm calibre their armament was unequal to their task; so they were utilized instead as light transports.

No further production of the C.R.25*bis* was undertaken, and the projected C.R.25*quater* of 1940, with improved equipment and higher gross weight, was abandoned before completion.

Fiat R.S.14

A product of Fiat's Costruzione Meccaniche Aeronautiche SA (CMASA) plant at Marina di Pisa, the R.S. 14 was designed by Ing Stiavelli. It was a handsome twin-engined, low-wing, all-metal monoplane with dual controls and side-by-side seating for the pilots. Full crew complement was four or five men. Two prototypes, designated R.S.14A, were built and flown for the first time during 1938. Flight trials were so satisfactory that the Ricognizione Marittima immediately placed a production order for the type with only minor modifications, under the designation R.S.14B.

Two long single-step floats, mounted on struts directly beneath the engine nacelles, and a generously glazed nose revealed the R.S.14's primary rôle of maritime reconnaissance. That this rôle was far from being a passive one was demonstrated by the E-type Lanciana dorsal turret, mounting a single 12·7-mm Scotti machine-gun, and by emplacements for 7·7-mm Breda-SAFAT guns in the fuselage sides. A long pannier under the fuselage could accommodate two 350-lb depth charges, or four 220-lb, six 110-lb, or six 88-lb bombs.

Thus armed, the R.S.14 began to be delivered to Italian service units in 1941, and operated in the Sardinian, Aegean and other Mediterranean theatres

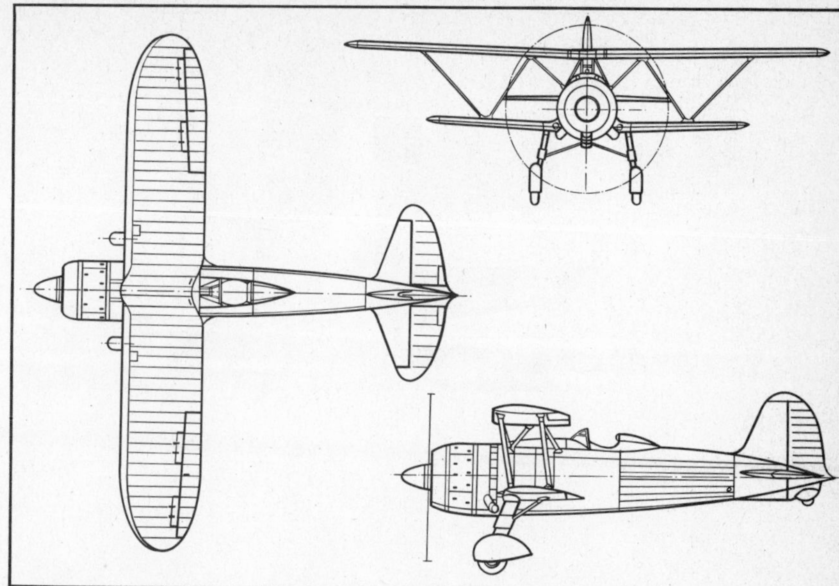

Fiat C.R.42

Fiat C.R.25

Fiat R.S.14

TYPE	DIMENSIONS span ft	span in	length ft	length in	height ft	height in	WEIGHT max t-o lb	PERFORMANCE max speed mph	at height ft	service ceiling ft	combat range miles	REMARKS
C.R. 32	31	2	24	5⅜	7	9	4,111	233	9,840	29,530	466	
C.R. 42	31	9⅞	27	1¼	10	11⅞	5,060	267	17,485	34,450	481	
C.R. 25	52	6	44	5⅞	11	1⅞	13,625	304½		31,496	1,305	

Fiat R.S.14

Fiat G.50 Freccia

Fiat G.50*ter* Freccia

Fiat G.55 Centauro

during World War II. Its duties included maritime patrol and reconnaissance and convoy escort, and it even performed as a defensive fighter on occasion. A further version, differing only in omission of the ventral weapons tray, was the R.S.14C, used for air/sea rescue operations. Power plant for all versions was a pair of 840-hp Fiat A.74 RC 38 air-cooled radial engines.

In addition to the prototype, a total of 150 R.S.14s were built by Fiat-CMASA. By September 1943, only a handful of these remained in service; but a few continued to serve on both sides until the war in Europe ended.

Fiat G.50 Freccia (Arrow)

In the mid-1930s, the Italian Air Ministry issued a specification for an all-metal, single-seat fighter monoplane, and one of the half-dozen designs submitted in response to this requirement was the Fiat G.50. Under the direction of Ing Giuseppe Gabrielli, construction of the first prototype began in 1936. This machine made its maiden flight on 26 February 1937, powered by an 840-hp Fiat A.74 RC 38 engine, and successful flight trials were rewarded by an initial order for 45, which entered production in 1938.

The Fiat G.50 received its first taste of combat in the closing months of the Spanish Civil War, when a dozen of the production machines joined the Aviazione Legionaria supporting Franco's forces. On the strength of their showing in this conflict a further production order was placed for 200, this time without the sliding cockpit canopies which pilots in Spain had found troublesome. Mass production was delegated to the CMASA works.

In 1939 the G.50 began to enter service with the Regia Aeronautica, replacing the obsolete C.R.32 biplane fighters; and by the time Italy entered World War II in 1940, more than 100 were in service. They were employed on a variety of duties including interception, ground attack, convoy and bomber escort, in Belgium (with the Corpo Aereo Italiano), Greece, the Balkans, as well as in the Mediterranean and North African theatres.

The Finnish Air Force ordered 35 G.50s and, after some delay, these were delivered, performing admirable service from 1940 to 1944 under severe conditions.

September 1940 saw the maiden flight of an improved model, the G.50*bis*, which featured a redesigned fuselage with better all-round visibility from the cockpit, armour protection for the pilot and self-sealing fuel tanks. It became the most widely produced version, a total of 450 being manufactured by CMASA and the Aeronautica d'Italia in Turin, of which a small batch were supplied to the Croatian Air Force. Armament of the G.50*bis* remained the same as for the G.50, and consisted of twin 12·7-mm Breda-SAFAT machine-guns mounted in the upper engine decking.

There were several other variants of the basic model. The G.50B was a tandem-seat unarmed trainer, similarly powered to the versions already described, of which more than 100 were built by Fiat-CMASA between 1940 and 1943. Only one G.50*bis*-A was produced, in 1942; this was a two-seat fighter-bomber, with an additional pair of 12·7-mm guns in wings of increased span and with provision for carrying two 350-lb bombs. The G.50*ter* was another experimental model, with a 1,000-hp A.76 RC 40S engine in an airframe of slightly larger dimensions. The top speed of this model reached 329 mph, but further development was abandoned in favour of the G.50V, which showed even greater promise. This last-named variant, with a 1,000-hp Daimler-Benz DB601A in-line engine, achieved a maximum speed of 360 mph, and led to development of the G.55 Centauro, described below.

Fiat G.55 Centauro (Centaur)

Excellent results achieved from the experimental installation of a German DB 601A engine in the Fiat G.50V airframe led the Fiat design team, under Ing Gabrielli, to pursue further the idea of an in-line-powered development of the G.50. Before their efforts crystallized into the G.55 Centauro, two intervening projects were examined. These were the G.51, which was to have had the Fiat-built A.75 RC 53 engine, and the G.52, with a Daimler-Benz DB60IN. Both were abandoned in favour of the even

more promising G.55 which, with a 1,475-hp DB605A engine, made its first flight on 30 April 1942.

The G.55 was accepted immediately by the Italian Air Ministry and entered production towards the end of 1942. Deliveries began early in the following year, but few had reached Regia Aeronautica squadrons by the time of the Badoglio surrender in September 1943, and none had become operational. However, the construction centres for the Centauro were in that part of Italy unaffected by the capitulation, and production was able to continue. So, by the time the Allied occupation of Italy was complete, 105 G.55s had been built for the Aviazione della Repubblica Sociale Italiana.

These aircraft were of two basic types, differing only in armament. The G.55/0 was equipped with four Breda-SAFAT 12·7-mm machine-guns and one 20-mm Mauser MG 151 cannon; while the G.55/I, which superseded it fairly early in its production life, had two 12·7-mm guns and three 20-mm cannon.

Two further variants, which did not attain production status, were the G,55/II, formidably armed with five 20-mm cannon, and the G.55S (for *Scorta* = escort), a modified version intended to carry a 2,176-lb torpedo under the centre fuselage. Neither of these types flew until 1944 and no further development was undertaken.

After the end of hostilities in Europe, production of the G.55 continued for some years in the form of the single-seat G.55A fighter and armament trainer and the dual-control G.55B advanced trainer. Some of these were supplied to the Italian Air Force, but the majority were produced for export, about 50 being supplied to Argentina and more than 40 to Egypt and Syria.

Fiat G.91

In the spring of 1954 the NATO Advisory Group for Aeronautical Research and Development issued a specification for a lightweight tactical strike fighter which, it was intended, would become standard equipment with the air forces of the Organization's member countries. It called for a compact, rugged aircraft, easy to maintain and able to operate from existing airfields with modest runways, or from grass strips, yet with the ability to carry a wide range of conventional or small nuclear weapons at near-sonic speed.

With one exception, the designs submitted for this competition came from the leading aircraft designers of France, a nation fast re-establishing itself among the leading aviation powers in Europe. Yet it was the exception, the Fiat G.91, which received development and production contracts after a stiff evaluation contest.

Designed by a team under Ing Giuseppe Gabrielli, the prototype did not have a successful first flight on 9 August 1956, as trouble was experienced with the tail control surfaces and test pilot Riccardo Bignamini had to eject for safety. Nevertheless, orders had already been placed "off the drawing board" for three prototypes and a pre-production batch of 27 G.91s, and less than one year later a second prototype was in the air, powered by a 4,850-lb s t Bristol Orpheus 801 turbojet in place of the original 4,050-lb s t Orpheus.

A number of other changes were made in the second machine, including modifications to the horizontal tail surfaces, cockpit and internal equipment. Not surprisingly, perhaps, it bore a marked superficial resemblance to the F-86K Sabre fighter which Fiat had been building under licence in Italy for a number of years, and was reported as being a particularly pleasing machine to fly.

Fiat G.55S Centauro

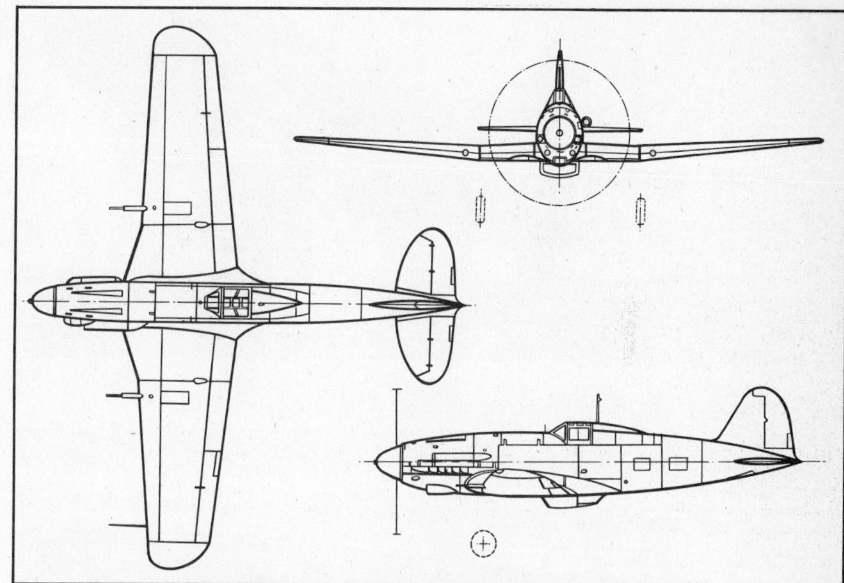

Fiat G.55 Centauro

Fiat G.91

TYPE	DIMENSIONS span ft	span in	length ft	length in	height ft	height in	WEIGHT max t-o lb	PERFORMANCE max speed mph	at height ft	service ceiling ft	combat range miles	REMARKS
R.S. 14	64	1¼	46	3	12	9⅓	17,637	242	13,120	16,400	1,553 max	
G. 50	36	0⅔	25	7	9	8⅛	5,966	293	16,400	32,480	620	
G. 55	38	10½	30	8⅞	10	3¼	8,179	385	22,966	42,650	1,025 max	

Fiat G.91R/4

Fiat G.91Y

IMAM Ro 37

IMAM Ro 37*bis*

Apart from the G.91N, a special version built for the evaluation of navigation aids, the G.91 was produced in two basic versions, the single-seat G.91R reconnaissance-fighter and the two-seat G.91T. The Italian air force placed successive orders amounting to a total of 98 G.91R/1s, 1As and 1Bs, and 76 G.91T/1s, and these began to enter service in the summer of 1959. The largest, and only other customer – as the G.91 did not become the universal NATO weapon that it was originally intended to be – was the German Federal Republic. Successive orders for Fiat-built machines totalled 50 G.91R/3s and 44/G.91T/3s and the first of these was delivered in September 1960. In addition, 50 G.91R/4s ordered by America were diverted to Germany, and 294 G.91R/3s were built in Germany under licence. The forward fuselage and tail assemblies of these aircraft were built by Messerschmitt and the wings by Heinkel, while Dornier handled construction of the centre-fuselage units, as well as final assembly and flight testing.

Basically, these two versions of the G.91 differ only in minor details and internal equipment. The power plant for each is the 5,000-lb s t Bristol Siddeley Orpheus 803 turbojet, the installation of which is so engineered that the entire rear fuselage can be detached for ease of maintenance. The single cockpit of the G.19R is replaced in the G.91T by two seats in tandem, with the rear crew member's seat a few inches higher than that of his companion. The G.91T can operate either as a trainer or as a tactical fighter.

It is in armament and weapon load that the widest variations are found. The Italian G.91R/1s carry four 0·50-in Colt-Browning machine-guns, whereas the German G.91R/3s have a pair of French-designed 30-mm DEFA cannon. All versions except the G.91T/1 have four underwing pylons, on which typical loads of two 500-lb high-explosive or napalm bombs, Nord 5103 air-to-air guided missiles, pods of small folding-fin unguided rocket projectiles or small nuclear weapons can be carried. The G.91T/1 has only two underwing pylons.

A tactical development, the G.91Y, flew for the first time on 27 December 1966. Two prototypes and 20 pre-production aircraft are being completed; these are powered by two 4,080 lb s t afterburning J85-GE-13s side-by-side in the rear fuselage.

IMAM Ro 37

This two-seat biplane was designed by the former Romeo company, which was taken over by the Breda group in 1936 and given the lengthy new title of Società Anonima Industrie Meccaniche e Aeronautica Meridionale. The prototype made its maiden flight in 1934, and the Ro 37's operational debut came during the campaigns in Ethiopia. Its layout afforded excellent visibility from both the pilot's and observer's cockpits, and it was armed with one or two 7·7mm machine-guns in the forward fuselage and an additional gun of similar calibre in the rear cockpit. It was powered by a single 550-hp Fiat A.30 RA*bis* liquid-cooled in-line engine. Provision could be made, in the close-support rôle, for small bombs to be carried beneath the lower wing or fuselage. The Ro 37 had some success in this rôle during the Spanish Civil War, as well as being a standard reconnaissance type with the Squadriglie da Osservazione Aerea.

The original Ro 37 was followed into production by the generally similar Ro 37*bis*, in which the in-line engine was replaced by a 560-hp Piaggio P.IX air-cooled radial. A substantial number of these aircraft, mostly of the Ro 37*bis* model, were in service with the Regia Aeronautica when Italy entered World War II in June 1940, and saw widespread service on practically every front on a variety of duties. In the East African theatre they were pressed into use, despite their age, as stop-gap interceptors; others were employed on anti-partisan missions in the Balkan area.

IMAM Ro 43 and Ro 44

During the mid-1930s, it was decided to develop the Ro 37*bis* with a view to providing the Italian Navy with a small floatplane for spotting and coastal station defence duties. To this end two designs were evolved in parallel, designated Ro 43 and Ro 44, the latter flying for the first time in 1936. Each was powered by a single 670-hp Piaggio P.XR nine-cylinder radial, the Ro 43 being a two-seat reconnaissance aircraft and the Ro 44 a single-seat fighter.

A single-step main central float was fitted, with smaller stabilizing floats near the tips of the lower mainplane. The wings could be folded back for ease of stowage.

The Ro 43 was operated normally from on board ship, up to three being carried by some of the larger Italian warships; whilst the Ro 44 was employed mainly from coastal bases. Armament of the former type consisted of two 7·7-mm Breda-SAFAT machine-guns, to which two guns of 12·7-mm calibre were added in the Ro 44.

One hundred and five Ro 43s and about thirty Ro 44s were in service at the time of Italy's entry into World War II, although their subsequent employment was not extensive. Activities of the land-based machines were confined largely to the Aegean area, and only a few of each remained in service at the Italian Armistice.

IMAM Ro 57

The Ro 57 was first proposed, some twelve months before Italy's entry into World War II, to meet a requirement for a twin-engined, single-seat interceptor fighter, and was designed by a team under the leadership of Ing Giovanni Galasso. It was a clean-looking, low-wing monoplane of mixed construction, with an all-metal fuselage and wooden wings, on which were mounted centrally two 840-hp Fiat A.74 RC 38 fourteen-cylinder air-cooled radial engines. A single, rounded fin and rudder assembly was fitted, together with a braced tail-plane and a retractable undercarriage; and the aircraft was armed with twin 12·7-mm Breda-SAFAT machine-guns in a "solid" nose.

The Ro 57 was built in fairly small numbers and, following its introduction into squadron service in 1942, was generally considered to be both underpowered and insufficiently manoeuvrable to hold its own as an interceptor. When switched to fighter-bomber and dive-bomber duties, it was somewhat more successful, and this led to the development of the Ro 57*bis* in which dive-brakes were fitted as standard. The Ro 57*bis* was equipped with under-fuselage racks for bombs of up to 1,100 lb in weight and had two 20-mm cannon added to its nose armament. It entered service at the beginning of 1943 but, again, was built only in small numbers. Little more than a dozen Ro 57s were operational at the Italian surrender.

Macchi M.5

Società Anonima Nieuport-Macchi entered the aviation field in 1912 to construct Nieuport designs under licence at Varese. While they were manufacturing the French Hanriot HD-1 early in 1915, there came into their hands an Austro-Hungarian Lohner flying-boat. On instructions from the Italian government, they produced copies of this machine designated L.1 and L.2, followed in 1913 by the M.3, used widely by Italian naval units for reconnaissance and general-purpose missions. An aircraft of this type set up an international altitude

IMAM Ro 44

IMAM Ro 57

Macchi M.5

TYPE	DIMENSIONS span ft	span in	length ft	length in	height ft	height in	WEIGHT max t-o lb	PERFORMANCE max speed mph	at height ft	service ceiling ft	combat range miles	REMARKS
G. 91R	28	2½	34	2½	13	1	11,365	675	5,000	43,000	390	
G. 91T	28	2½	38	4	13	9	11,794	675	5,000	43,000	390	
Ro 37	36	4¼	28	3⅓	9	8½	5,280	202		21,980	1,025 max	
Ro 37*bis*	36	4¼	28	1	10	4	5,346	199		23,622	932 max	
Ro 44	37	11⅝	31	10½	11	6⅛	4,898	193	8,200	21,650	298	
Ro 57	41	0	28	10½	9	6⅛	11,000	311	16,400	25,590	745	

Macchi M.7

Macchi M.8

Macchi C.200 Saetta prototype

Macchi C.200 Saetta

record for its class of 17,716·5 ft over Lake Varese and, shortly after this, designers Calzavara and Felice Buzio developed the design further into the M.5.

This was a small single-seat biplane flying-boat fighter, armed with two Fiat machine-guns and powered by a single 160-hp Isotta-Fraschini V4B engine, driving a two-blade pusher propeller. It was ordered into production in 1917 and was delivered to several Squadriglie della Marina, a total of 240 machines of this type eventually being completed. The M.5 handled well, being quite manoeuvrable, with a good rate of climb and comparatively high level speed. It was employed principally in the Adriatic.

Despite the emergence later of improved models, the M.5 continued to give service for several years after the 1914–18 War, some later examples having the increased power of a 250-hp Isotta-Fraschini V6 engine.

Macchi M.7 and M.8

Next in the line of flying-boat fighters which emanated from the SA Nieuport-Macchi during the 1914–18 War was the M.6, a development of the M.5. This type was not adopted for service use, but development continued and the next model, the M.7. was ordered into production for units of the Italian navy. Slightly smaller than its predecessors, it was powered by a single 250-hp Isotta-Fraschini V6B and, having a simplified structure, offered a considerable increase in overall performance.

The M.7 was not in service in time to see much combat, only three of the 17 aircraft completed by the end of the 1914–18 War actually becoming operational. However, it continued in service after the cessation of hostilities, and several successive versions appeared, with engines of gradually increasing power – culminating in the M.7*ter* B which had a Lorraine engine of 475 hp. In August 1921, an M.7*bis* won the Schneider Trophy contest at an average speed of 110.9 mph, and the type was not finally phased out of Italian naval service until 1928.

A progressive development of the M.7 was the Macchi M.8, which first appeared at the end of 1917. Armed with a single movable gun in the prow, it was substantially larger than the M.7, but had only the power of a 160-hp Isotta-Fraschini V4B engine. Photographic and radio equipment was generally installed, and four small bombs or mines could be carried externally.

By the end of the 1914–18 War, 57 M.8s had been completed and were being used primarily for coastal patrol and anti-shipping missions; after the war they graduated to training establishments. A further derivative was the larger M.9, of which 30 were built with 300-hp Fiat A.12*bis* engines. Some of these were converted post-war into M.9*bis* four-passenger transports.

Macchi C.200 Saetta (Lightning)

Evolved under the re-equipment programme which followed the conclusion of Italy's campaigns in East Africa, the C.200 Saetta was the first single-seat fighter designed by Aeronautica Macchi's brilliant engineer, Dr Mario Castoldi. It was backed by experience gained in the evolution of the famous Macchi racing seaplanes of the 1920s and 1930s, and was of neat design, though marred by the necessity of using a bulky radial engine.

The prototype C.200, with an 850-hp Fiat A.74 RC 38 air-cooled radial, made its maiden flight on 24 December 1937, and won an official fighter competition in the following year. An initial production series of 99 was ordered. These had an enclosed cockpit and were armed with two 12.7-mm Breda-SAFAT machine-guns in the upper engine decking. Production machines were powered by an uprated 14-cylinder model of the Fiat A.74 engine developing 870 hp, and deliveries began in October 1939. A total of 156 were in squadron service when Italy entered World War II in June 1940.

The Saetta made its operational debut over Malta serving subsequently in Greece, Russia and Yugoslavia. Later production aircraft switched to an open cockpit which their pilots preferred; and despite their lack of power – to counteract which they were extremely lightly armoured – they were exceptionally manoeuvrable and could absorb a considerable amount of punishment

The Saetta fought in all theatres where Italian forces were engaged, and production was shared between the parent company and the Breda and SAI-Ambrosini concerns.

Despite the emergence of the superior C.202, described below, the C.200 remained in production until the end of World War II, somewhere in the region of 1,000 being built. After the arrival in service of more advanced interceptors, the Saetta was employed primarily as a bomber escort or fighter-bomber. In the latter category, two 110-, 220- or 350-lb bombs, or eight smaller ones, could be carried beneath the wings. For escort duties, these were replaceable by auxiliary fuel tanks. Some C.200s were converted into two-seat trainers.

Late in 1938, the Macchi C.201 appeared, an attempt to improve upon the Saetta's performance by modifying the fuselage and installing a 1,000-hp Fiat A.76 RC 40 radial engine. In the event, development of this engine was abandoned. The C.201 was flight tested using a standard Saetta engine, but the project was then dropped in favour of the in-line powered C.202.

Macchi C.202 Folgore (Thunderbolt)

The first opportunity afforded to Aeronautica Macchi to realize fully the performance potential in Castoldi's C.200 Saetta came early in 1940, when the company acquired from Germany a specimen of the Daimler-Benz DB601A-1 liquid-cooled in-line engine. This was installed in a C.200 airframe, and the resulting combination was flown for the first time on 10 August 1940. Such was the improvement in overall performance, not to mention aerodynamic cleanliness, that it was decided to put the new model into immediate production under the designation C.202. Named Folgore, the new fighters were, to begin with, powered by DB601 engines imported from Germany; but a manufacturing licence for the engine was soon acquired and it was constructed in Italy as the Alfa Romeo RA. 1000 RC41 Monsone (Monsoon), giving 1175 hp for take-off.

The C.202 was produced alongside the C.200, by the same team of manufacturers, and began to enter service with the Regia Aeronautica in the summer of 1941. Initially, it retained the same armament as its predecessor, but later machines had a further pair of 7·7-mm guns installed in the wings, and one production batch had twin 20-mm MG 151 cannon installed in underwing pods. Although vastly superior to the C.200 in performance, the C.202 was still not entirely a match for opposing Allied fighters, and tended to be employed more as a bomber interceptor or fighter-bomber, with similar provision for small bombs or auxiliary fuel tanks to be carried beneath each wing.

Among the theatres in which the Folgore saw action were Malta, Libya (from November 1941) and Russia (from September 1942). Between 1941 and 1943 a total of approximately 1,500 were built, of which 392 were completed by Aeronautica Macchi.

Macchi C.205V Veltro (Greyhound)

The prototype C.205 was a standard C.202 airframe converted to take a 1,475-hp DB605A engine, in which form it was flown for the first time on 19 April 1942. Fast, highly manoeuvrable and a "pilot's aeroplane" through and through, the C.205V Veltro, as the service model was known, at last gave the Regia Aeronautica a fighter that could compete on equal terms with the best contemporary

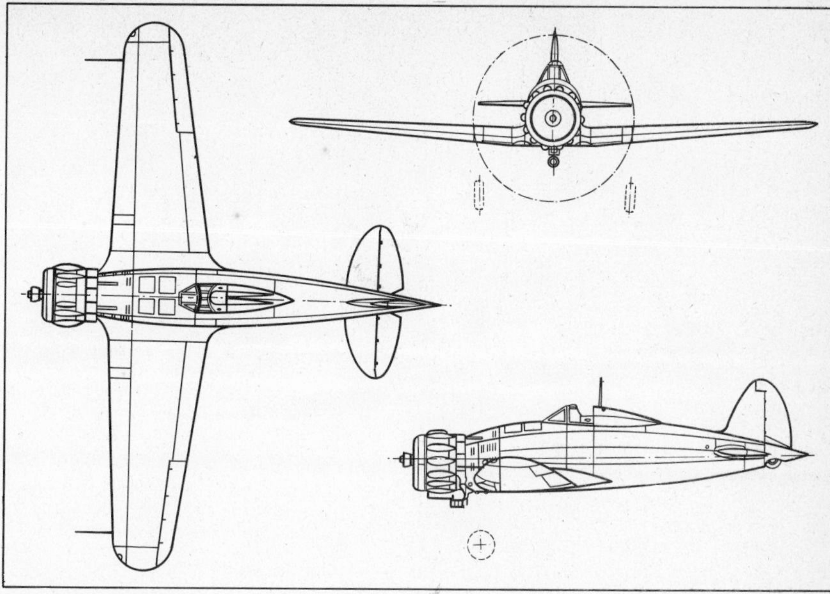

Macchi C.200 Saetta

Macchi C.202 Folgore

Macchi C.202 Folgore, 20-mm cannon fitted under the wings

TYPE	DIMENSIONS span ft	span in	length ft	length in	height ft	height in	WEIGHT max t-o lb	PERFORMANCE max speed mph	at height ft	service ceiling ft	combat range miles	REMARKS
M.5	39	0½	26	5⅓	10	4¼	2,138	118	SL	15,100	373	
M.7	32	7¾	26	6⅞	9	8⅞	2,381	130	SL	21,325	435	
M.8	52	5⅞	32	8½	10	11⅛	3,153	104	SL	16,076	280	
C.200	34	8½	26	10⅜	11	6	5,715	312	14,750	29,200	354	
C.202	34	8½	29	0½	9	11½	6,636	370	16,400	37,730	475	

Macchi C.205V Veltro prototype

Macchi C.205V Veltro

Macchi M.B.326G

Piaggio P.108B

Allied fighters. Unfortunately for the Italian air force, however, the Veltro did not enter service until early in 1943, and made its first operational sortie only a month before Marshal Badoglio surrendered to the Allies.

The prototype and early production C.205Vs were each armed with two 12·7-mm and two 7·7-mm Breda-SAFAT machine-guns, though on later aircraft the smaller-calibre guns were replaced by a pair of wing-mounted MG 151 cannon. As a fighter-bomber, the Veltro could carry similar bomb-loads to the C.200 and C.202. Production aircraft were powered by the DB605 engine, built under licence as the Fiat RA.1050 RC 58 Tifone (Typhoon).

At the time of the Italian surrender the Regia Aeronautica had 66 Veltros on charge, but about half of these were unserviceable. Six served with the Allies, the remainder with the Aviazione della RSI, and limited production continued after the capitulation, until a total of 262 had been completed.

Prototypes were also flown of the C.205N Orione (Orion). With a new wing of 36 ft 10⅞ in span, these were intended as high-altitude interceptors, the N-1 and N-2 differing only in armament (four 12·7-mm and one 20-mm, and two 12·7-mm and three 20-mm guns respectively). Also under development were the C.206 and C.207, with wings further extended to 40 ft 9 in span.

Macchi M.B.326

One of the world's leading basic jet trainers, the Macchi M.B.326 was flown for the first time on 10 December 1957 with a 1,750 lb s t Bristol Siddeley Viper 8 turbojet. The second prototype, and all production M.B.326s to date, have Piaggio-built 2,500 lb s t Viper 11 engines. The handling characteristics necessary in such an aircraft suit it well for the light attack rôle, and in addition to large numbers of trainers for the Italian Air Force and the RAAF, armed versions are now in service with three other air forces.

In mid-1965, eight M.B.326Bs were supplied to Tunisia and seven M.B.326Fs to Ghana. Just over a year later, Macchi began supplying a similar version to the South African Air Force, by whom it is known as the Impala. South Africa plans to have 300 Impalas; the first batches were assembled from Italian-built components, but eventually some 80 per cent of each aircraft will be built in South Africa by Atlas Aircraft Corporation.

Attack versions of the M.B.326 have two fuselage-mounted 7·7-mm guns and six underwing pylons on which can be carried four 100-lb bombs, four napalm containers, twelve 5-in HVAR rockets, two 0·50-in machine-gun pods, two AS.11 or AS.20 air-to-surface missiles or two jettisonable tanks with extra fuel. Early in 1967 the prototype was flown of the M.B.326G, a developed trainer/counter-insurgency version with a 3,410 lb s t Viper 20 engine.

Piaggio P.108B

The P.108, produced by the Società Anonima Piaggio & Cia, was Italy's largest aircraft and only heavy bomber of World War II and proved fairly successful, although only a comparatively modest number were built. Designed by Ing Giovanni Casiraghi, and based on experience gained with the four-motor P.50-II of 1938, the P.108 was projected in four models: the P.108A (for *Artiglieri*), P.108B (*Bombardiere*), P.108C (*Civile*) and P.108T (*Trasporto*).

The first of these to be ordered into production, and the only one to see widespread service, was the P.108B. An evaluation batch of 12 was ordered in 1939, the year of the prototype's first flight, and the first of a grand total of 163 production P.108Bs made their operational debut with the 274th Squadriglia Bombardieri a Grande Raggio (Long-Range Bomber Squadron) over Gibraltar in 1942. They were employed subsequently on bombing missions over the Mediterranean, and in the North African and Russian theatres of operations, and it was in an aircraft of this type that Bruno Mussolini, son of the Italian dictator, met his death.

The P.108B was an all-metal, low-wing monoplane powered by four 1,500-hp Piaggio P.XII RC 35 air-cooled radial engines, driving three-blade metal propellers, and carried a crew of seven. A maximum bomb-load of 7,716 lb

or three 18-in torpedoes, could be carried internally; and the bomber was equipped with eight 12·7-mm Breda-SAFAT machine-guns. Single guns were installed in nose and ventral turrets, and in staggered sideways-firing barbettes amidships. The remaining four guns were installed in pairs in the rear upper portion of the cowling of each of the outboard engine nacelles, and were fired remotely from the bomber's fuselage.

To permit German factories to concentrate on the manufacture of fighters and bombers, the Luftwaffe asked the Italian government to undertake series production of the P.108T military trooper and freighter, but this model did not progress beyond the completion of a prototype. However, the prototype P.108C had made its maiden flight just after Italy's entry into World War II, followed by 15 production examples; these were impressed as troop transports, and a number of P.108Bs were also converted for similar employment by the Luftwaffe.

An interesting development appeared in the spring of 1943, when the prototype P.108 airframe was converted into the P.108A anti-shipping aircraft by installing a 102-mm cannon in the nose. After firing tests at the Italian Navy range at Viareggio, this aircraft was returned to the factory to have a computer gunsight installed. While it was there the capitulation of Italy was announced, the aircraft was captured by the Germans and further development was stopped. Marshal Badoglio's surrender to the Allies similarly prevented fuller development of the P.108M (for *Modificato*), which had one 20-mm and four 7·7-mm guns in place of the single-gun nose turret, and of the proposed P.133 with uprated engines and greater bomb-load.

Pomilio PC, PD and PE

The Fabbrica Aeroplani Ing. O. Pomilio was established in Turin during 1916, and in March of the following year the first of a series of two-seater armed reconnaissance biplanes began to enter service with the Italian air force.

This was the Pomilio PC, a trim little two-bay aircraft with a single 260-hp Fiat A.12 engine, and it was followed by first the PD and later the PE, all utilizing the same power plant and a basically similar airframe. The wings were of equal span, and both they and the rudder had the scalloped trailing edge that was characteristic of the period; the main landing gear was of the conventional Vee-type, with a tail skid under the rear fuselage. The fuselage itself was a slab-sided affair of box-girder construction, having the upper decking rounded over and the cockpits close behind one another, with a Revelli gun in the observer's position and a second gun atop the upper mainplane in order to fire outside the arc of the two-blade airscrew.

The PC was fast enough to outrun the fighters in service at the time of its introduction, but was prone to a rather alarming degree of instability, with the result that the PD incorporated modifications designed to overcome this fault: the addition of a small underfin beneath the rear fuselage and revision of the engine cowling and radiator arrangement. These modifications were taken a stage further in the PE (300-hp A.12*bis*), in which the entire tail assembly was redesigned, emerging with extra upper fin area and an enlarged tailplane. On later production aircraft, armament was improved by giving the pilot a synchronized gun and the observer a Scarff mounting with one or two Lewis guns, and the final Pomilio machines exhibited a marked general improvement over the earlier models. During 1917, the Pomilio factories turned out 545 of the PC or PD type aircraft, and a further

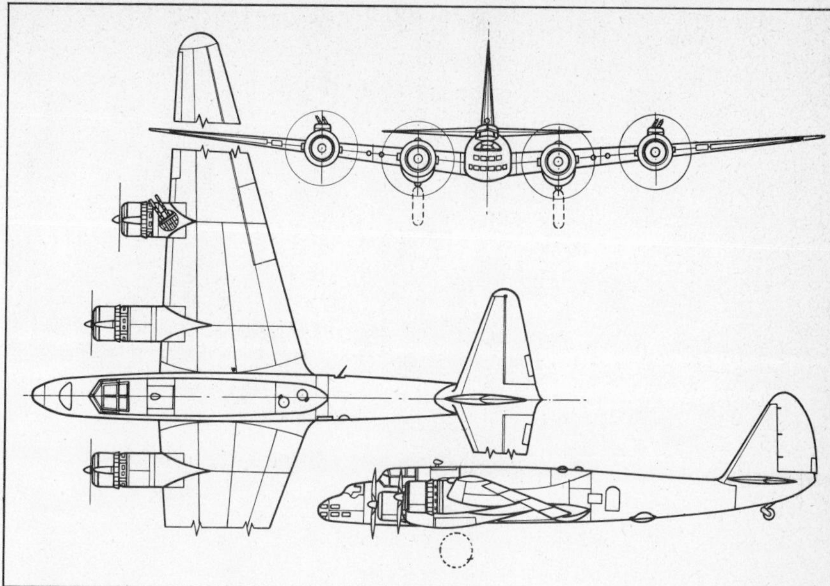

Piaggio P.108B

Piaggio P. 108A, Luftwaffe, with 102-mm nose cannon

Pomilio PD

TYPE	DIMENSIONS span ft	span in	length ft	length in	height ft	height in	WEIGHT max t-o lb	PERFORMANCE max speed mph	at height ft	service ceiling ft	combat range miles	REMARKS
C. 205V	34	8½	29	0½	9	11½	7,514	399	23,620	36,090	646	
MB 326B	34	8	34	11¼	12	2½	10,000	392	20,000	36,000	580 max	Armed version. Service ceiling approx.
P. 108B	104	11⅞	73	1½	19	8¼	65,885	267	13,780	19,685	2,190	

Reggiane Re 2000 Falco I

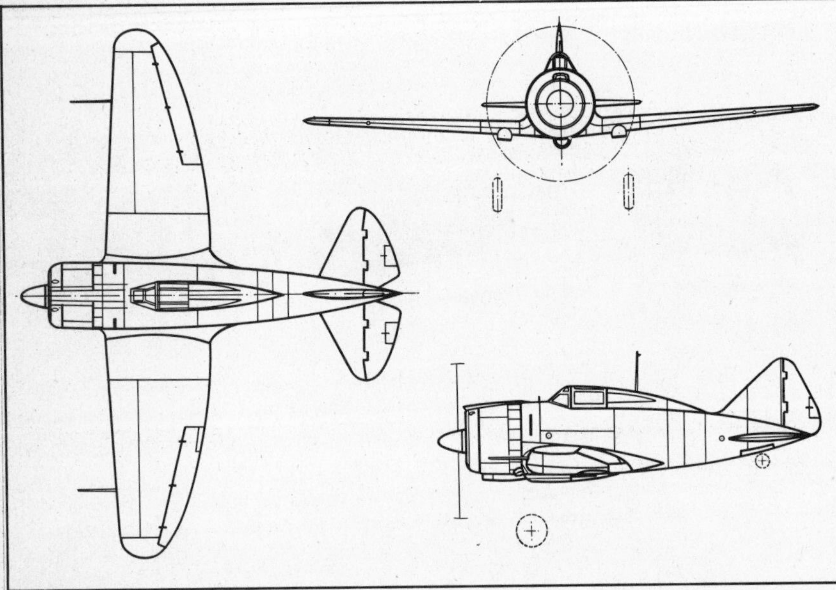

Reggiane Re 2000 Falco I

Reggiane Re 2001 Falco II

1,071 PDs or PEs in 1918. A final type was evolved, designated PY, but only seven of these were completed in 1918, and in this year the Pomilio brothers sold out to the Ansaldo concern.

Reggiane Re 2000 Falco I (Falcon)

A subsidiary of the Caproni group, the Reggiane SA, produced during the latter 1930s a line of small, compact single-seat fighters. They were well designed and possessed quite good performance, but tended to be overshadowed by products of the more prominent Italian manufacturers and hence did not see widespread service during World War II.

The first of the line, the Re 2000 Falco, was evolved by designers Alessio and Longhi in 1937, and clearly owed much to the contemporary American Seversky P-35 fighter, having a short stubby fuselage, semi-elliptical wing planform and a "wing-nut" shaped tail assembly. The prototype was flown in the following year, and handled extremely well during its evaluation trials. It could out-manoeuvre both the Macchi C.200 and Messerschmitt Bf 109, against which it was flown for comparison; but, due to its rather less robust construction, the Regia Aeronautica decided against placing a production order. However, a small number did enter service with Italian naval squadrons, 12 *Serie II* and later 24 *Serie III* aircraft being delivered.

Both models were powered by the 1,025-hp Piaggio P.XI*bis* RC 40 fourteen-cylinder air-cooled radial engine (as compared with the 986-hp P.XI RC 40 of the *Serie I* prototype), and carried two 12·7-mm Breda-SAFAT machine-guns in the upper engine cowling. The *Serie II* machines, strengthened for catapulting, were utilized for shipboard trials during 1942; whereas the *Serie III*, which had a revised cockpit canopy and internal refinements, were used from naval bases in Sicily either on naval escort duties or in the fighter-bomber rôle with a 440-lb bomb slung beneath the fuselage.

In the meantime, the Falco had achieved some success as an export item – indeed, most of the 170 Re 2000s which were completed were accounted for by foreign orders. The Swedish government ordered 60 in 1940 to equip Flygvapnet fighter squadrons, and these served from 1941 to 1945 under the Swedish Air Force designation J 20. The other prime user of the type was Hungary, whose first Re 2000s began to arrive in 1940. Named Hejja, these saw service on the Russian front. Production of the Falco was also undertaken by Hungarian factories, with a licence-built Wright Cyclone engine of 1,000 hp as the power plant, but only a comparatively small number were delivered.

Reggiane Re 2001 Falco II (Falcon)

Development of the Re 2000 series of aircraft followed, in essence, the same line of evolution as that which produced the successors to the Macchi C.200. In 1940, with a view to securing the improvement in aerodynamic qualities and all-round performance which would ensue from the installation of an in-line engine, the Re 2000 was adapted to take the German DB601A-1. Following successful trials, the type was ordered into production as the Re 2001.

Only the first few production machines received German-built engines, since supplies were limited and the Macchi C.202 had prior claim to those which were available. The majority of the Re 2001s were, therefore, equipped with the Italian-built version of the DB601, the 1,175-hp Alfa Romeo RA.1000 RC 41 Monsone (Monsoon).

Only 252 Re 2001s were completed, in various sub-series. The *Serie I* and *IV* had two 12.7-mm Breda-SAFAT machine-guns in the upper cowling. In the *Serie II* and *III* these were augmented by two wing-mounted 7·7-mm guns, and in the major production model, the Re 2001CN, by two 20-mm MG 151 cannon in underwing fairings. In addition, the *Serie IV* model could operate as a fighter-bomber, with a single 1,410-lb bomb beneath the fuselage; or, with an auxiliary fuel tank in place of the bomb, as a naval escort-fighter.

The first Squadriglia to receive the Re 2001 *Serie I* made its operational debut with the type over Malta in May 1942. Other models followed it into service later in the year, with the Re 2001CN–used mainly as a defensive night fighter in the northern part of its homeland–entering service in 1943. After the Armistice in September 1943, the latter model continued to serve for a time with the Aviazione della RSI.

A number of experimental models of the Re 2001 were evolved. These included a tandem-seat conversion trainer; a test-bed for the 840-hp Isotta-Fraschini Delta engine; a torpedo-fighter conversion (Re 2001G); and an anti-tank model (Re 2001H). At the time of the Armistice, two further Re 2001s were being prepared for catapult trials on board converted merchant carriers.

Reggiane Re 2002 Ariete (Ram)

A progressive development of the late-series Re 2000, via the Re 2001, the Re 2002 Ariete was evolved specifically for the fighter-bomber rôle and entered service with the Regia Aeronautica during 1942.

It represented a return to a radial-engine configuration, being powered by a 1,175-hp Piaggio P.XIX RC 45 fourteen-cylinder air-cooled engine, and featured a slightly lengthened and more robustly constructed fuselage with a revised cockpit canopy. Armament of the Ariete comprised two 12·7-mm Breda-SAFAT machine-guns in the top of the engine cowling, with a single 7·7-mm gun mounted in each wing. For assault rôles, the Re 2002 could carry a useful load of up to 1,430-lb of bombs, and trials were also carried out with a single torpedo slung beneath the centre fuselage.

Only 40–50 Re 2002s were built, these serving with Nos. 5 and 50 Stormi d'Assalto and participating in the defence of Sicily during the Allied landings. Withdrawn progressively to less forward bases as the Allies advanced into Italy, a few Re 2002s survived the Armistice to fight with the Aviazione della RSI.

Developments of the Re 2002 included the Re 2002*bis*, with revised undercarriage retraction which was later adopted in the Re 2005; the Re 2003, of which only two prototypes were completed as two-seat reconnaissance-bombers with a P.XI*bis* RC 40 engine; and the uncompleted Re 2004, which was to have had a more powerful 24-cylinder radial engine.

Reggiane Re 2005 Sagittario (Archer)

The Reggiane Re 2005 Sagittario shared with the Macchi C.205V Veltro the distinction of being one of the best single-seat fighters produced by the Italian aircraft industry during World War II; but, like its compatriot, it arrived on the operational scene too late to have any material effect on the result of the war. Of 48 Sagittarios delivered to the Regia Aeronautica, most were used in the defence of Sicily or the major Italian cities during the Allied advances through the country.

Flown in prototype form in September 1942, the Re 2005 bore a certain external resemblance to its progenitors, although it embodied a considerable amount of new design internally. It retained the excellent handling characteristics of the earlier Reggiane fighters, allied to the vastly superior performance bestowed by the 1,475-hp DB605A liquid-cooled in-line engine.

Production Re 2005s utilized the Fiat-built version of

Reggiane Re 2002 Ariete

Reggiane Re 2005 Sagittario

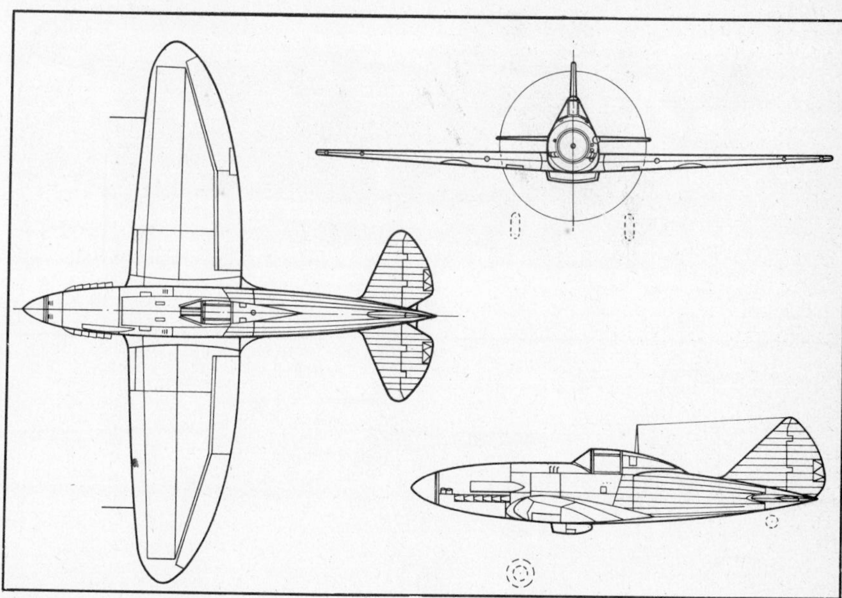

Reggiane Re 2005 Sagittario

TYPE	DIMENSIONS span ft	span in	length ft	length in	height ft	height in	WEIGHT max t-o lb	PERFORMANCE max speed mph	at height ft	service ceiling ft	combat range miles	REMARKS
Pomilio PD	38	8½	29	4	11	0	3,477	114	SL	16,400	3 hr	
Pomilio PE	38	8½	29	4	11	0	3,388	120	SL	16,400	3½ hr	
Re 2000	36	1	26	2½	10	6	5,722	329	16,400	36,745	522	Data for Serie I
Re 2001	36	1	26	10¾	10	2¾	7,231	337	16,400	39,200	466	Data for Serie III
Re 2002	36	1	26	9½	10	4	7,143	329	18,045	34,450	684	

Savoia-Marchetti S.M.72

Savoia-Marchetti S.M.79-I prototype

Savoia-Marchetti S.M. 79-II

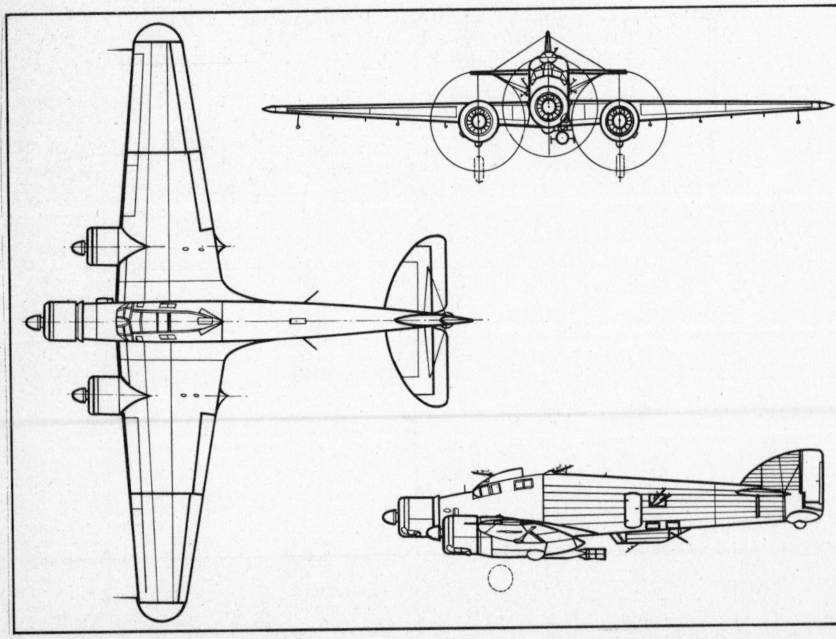

Savoia-Marchetti S.M. 79-II

this engine, the RA.1050 RC 58 Tifone (Typhoon), deliveries to squadrons beginning in the early part of 1943. Preparations made for a production line of 300 Sagittarios were thwarted by the surrender in September 1943; but several of the aircraft that did reach combat units continued to serve with the Aviazione della RSI, participating in the defence of Bucharest and, finally, of Berlin. Normal armament consisted of three 20-mm MG 151 cannon and two 12·7-mm Breda-SAFAT machine-guns. When utilized as a fighter-bomber, the Re 2005 could carry up to 1,390 lb of bombs.

An interesting project being examined when Italy capitulated was the Re 2005R (for *Reazione* = reaction), in which an auxiliary compressor would have added a component of thrust to the power of the piston-engine to boost the maximum speed to more than 450 mph.

Savoia-Marchetti S.M. 72

In 1935 an Italian Air Mission, under General Silvo Scaroni of the Regia Aeronautica, arrived in China to assist in the build-up of the air arm belonging to the Central (Nanking) Government of General Chiang Kai-Shek. A flying school was set up, and before long Scaroni had sent home orders for a variety of Italian aircraft.

One such aircraft was the S.M. 72, a three-engined bomber developed by Savoia-Marchetti from the S.M. 71 eight-passenger airliner of the early 1930s. Of mixed wood and metal construction, it had a high, cantilever wooden wing and a fixed undercarriage with mainwheel "spats". Power was provided by three 550-hp Bristol Pegasus II radials, each driving a two-bladed duralumin propeller of Savoia-Marchetti design.

The prototype S.M. 72, bearing the civil registration I-ABMO, had flown in 1934, but had not obtained a production order from the Regia Aeronautica. It was flown out to China as a demonstration aircraft, and after evaluation by Chinese pilots a limited order was placed for 20 aircraft, to be built by Savoia at Sesto Calende

Savoia-Marchetti S.M. 79 Sparviero (Hawk)

Designed by Alessandro Marchetti, the S.M. 79 first made its appearance at the end of 1934 as the prototype (registered I-MAGO) of an eight-passenger commercial airliner. Although this object was ultimately achieved in the form of the S.M. 83 of 1937, it was as a bomber fo the Regia Aeronautica that the S.M. 79 truly made it mark. Before its front-line career ended, a decade or sc later, some 1,200 examples had been built, and the S.M 79 had established a reputation as one of the best land based bomber aircraft of World War II.

The first prototype of the S.M. 79, after changing it original trio of 610-hp Piaggio Stella radial engines fo 750-hp Alfa Romeo 125 RC 35s, established severa speed-with-payload records during 1935, and added t these in 1936 after a further power plant change to th 780-hp Alfa Romeo 126 RC 34. Following completion o the second prototype as a military bomber, it was wit the last-named type of engine that the aircraft entere quantity production as the S.M. 79-I Sparviero.

The sleek lines of the original civil design were some what marred in the bomber version by the addition of dorsal hump – in which were housed two 12·7-mm Breda SAFAT machine-guns – and a ventral gondola for th Sparviero's bombardier, who was also provided with 12·7-mm gun. One laterally-firing 7·7-mm gun amidship completed the defensive armament, and the internal loa comprised twelve 220-lb, five 550-lb, or two 1,100- bombs. A crew of five was normally carried.

Considerable successes were achieved by the 8th an 111th Stormi Bombardamento Veloce (High Spee Bomber Groups) in Spain with the S.M. 79-I, and in 193 the Yugoslav government placed an order for 45.

Meanwhile, encouraged by the evaluation of the S.M 81B for torpedo-carrying, it was decided to test th Sparviero in a similar capacity. Trials began in Novemb 1937, at first with a single torpedo, mounted externall and later with a pair of these weapons. The trials we highly successful, and a new model, the S.M. 79-I entered quantity production in October 1939 to equip the Squadriglie Aerosiluranti (Torpedo Bomber Squadron). The S.M. 79-IIs, except for one batch with 1,030-hp Fiat A.80 RC 41 engines, were powered by 1,000-hp Piaggio P.XI RC 40 radials and were equipped to carry two 450-mm torpedoes beneath the centre fuselage. The Macchi and Reggiane companies were brought into the Sparviero production programme, and when Italy entered World War II there were 594 S.M. 79s of both models in service.

As with the S.M. 81, a twin-engined model of the S.M. 79 was also produced, and enjoyed some success as an export item. Known as the S.M. 79B, it had the bombardier transferred to an extensively-glazed nose section, so eliminating the ventral gondola, and first appeared in prototype form in 1936. It was demonstrated in no fewer than a dozen countries, and was ordered by three of them, with four different types of power plant. Three S.M. 79Bs with 950-hp Alfa Romeo 128 RC 18s were delivered to Brazil; four with 1,030-hp Fiat A.80 RC 41s to Iraq in 1937; and 24 with 950-hp Gnome-Rhône 14Ns to Rumania. The Rumanian government subsequently purchased another two dozen and began licence production of the type at the I.A.R. factories near Bucharest, with 1,220-hp Junkers Jumo 211D in-line engines.

The S.M. 79-IIs in service with the Regia Aeronautica during World War II were active on almost every front. They operated throughout the Mediterranean area, in North Africa and over the Balkan countries, their duties ranging from torpedo attack to conventional bombing, reconnaissance and close-support missions. When Marshal Badoglio surrendered to the Allies, some three dozen Sparvieros remained to fight with the co-belligerent air force, while the Aviazione della RSI availed itself of small numbers of the improved S.M. 79-III, a cleaned-up model with a forward-firing 20-mm cannon and with the ventral gondola removed. Towards the end of the war, the Sparviero was also pressed into use as a transport, and in this or the training rôle a number served until 1952 with the re-formed Italian Air Force.

Savoia-Marchetti S.M. 81 Pipistrello (Bat)

The Savoia-Marchetti S.M. 81 followed the current vogue in Italy for the tri-motor configuration. It appeared for the first time in 1935, as a military development of the S.M. 73 commercial airliner, and was designed by Ing Alessandro Marchetti. The S.M. 81 was also well defended, having two machine-guns in a turret atop the fuselage just aft of the crew cabin, a further pair in a retractable ventral turret to the rear of the bomb-bay, and one each side amidships for beam defence. An internal bomb-load of up to 2,205 lb was permissible.

The S.M. 81 was ordered into quantity production for the Regia Aeronautica and entered squadron service shortly before the Italian invasion of Ethiopia on 3 October 1935. It was employed widely during that campaign in a variety of rôles, varying from low-level bombing to reconnaissance and supply transport. Twelve S.M. 81s became, a few years later, the first Italian aircraft to be sent to the aid of General Franco in the Spanish Civil War, and further machines of this type joined them as part of the Aviazione Legionaria.

When Italy entered World War II in June 1940, she had approximately 100 S.M. 81 bombers in service, most

Savoia-Marchetti S.M. 79-III

Savoia-Marchetti S.M. 79B

Savoia-Marchetti S.M. 81 Pipistrello, Piaggio P.X engines

TYPE	DIMENSIONS span ft	span in	length ft	length in	height ft	height in	WEIGHT max t-o lb	PERFORMANCE max speed mph	at height ft	service ceiling ft	combat range miles	REMARKS
Re 2005	36	1	28	7¾	10	4	7,848	390	22,800	40,000	677	
S.M. 72	98	4⅞	63	11	18	0½	28,160	184	13,120	21,600	1,060	
S.M. 79-I	69	6⅝	51	10	14	1¾	23,100	267	13,120	21,325	1,180	
S.M. 79-II	69	6⅝	53	1¾	13	5½	24,912	270	12,000	22,965	1,243	
S.M. 79B	69	6⅝	52	9	13	5	22,450	255	15,100	23,300	995	

Savoia-Marchetti S.M. 81 Pipistrello, Piaggio P.VII engines

Savoia-Marchetti S.M. 84

Savoia-Marchetti S.M. 85

of them scattered among overseas units in Albania, Libya and Italian East Africa. They operated in Greece, North Africa, the Mediterranean theatre and Russia throughout the war, although towards the end they had to be relegated to less hazardous duties such as supply dropping, paratroop transportation and training. In the early days of the war some successes were also achieved in anti-shipping missions in the Mediterranean, but the age and slow speed of the S.M.81s made them vulnerable to fighter attack and these aircraft were soon diverted to night operations, notably in North Africa and Palestine.

A variety of successively more powerful radial engines was fitted to the S.M. 81 throughout its career, including the 580-hp Alfa Romeo 125, the 680-hp Piaggio P.IX, the 700-hp Piaggio P.X, the 900-hp Alfa Romeo 126 and the 1,000-hp Gnome-Rhône K-14. When the Italian surrender came in September 1943, S.M. 81s still served in small numbers on both sides; and a few of those which remained with the co-belligerent air force continued to fly for a time with the post-war Italian Air Force.

A few examples were built of the S.M. 81B (for *Bimotore*), a version with twin in-line engines and a redesigned, heavily glazed nose. These were used for test purposes, and at least one was modified for torpedo-dropping trials.

Savoia-Marchetti S.M. 84

A progressive development of the S.M. 79 Sparviero, the Savoia-Marchetti S.M. 84 offered an increase in performance over its predecessor and was a cleaner machine aerodynamically. The hump-backed gun emplacement gave way to a single, shallow dorsal turret, mounting two 12·7-mm machine-guns; the ventral bomb-aiming position was reduced to little more than a blister fairing, above which were further 12·7-mm guns in open positions on each side of the fuselage; and a cantilever tailplane supported a twin fin and rudder assembly. The S.M. 84's offensive load could consist of up to 4,410 lb of bombs, or two externally-slung torpedoes, and power was supplied by three 1,000-hp Piaggio P.XI*bis* radial engines.

Among the first units with which the S.M. 84 entered service in 1941 was the 35th Stormo Aerosiluranti, which employed the type on torpedo-bombing missions in the Mediterranean. It was also used on bombing attacks in the Aegean, in Sardinia, and with the 43rd Stormo Bombardamento during the Allied invasion of Sicily.

Generally speaking, Italian bomber crews had grown so attached to the S.M. 79 that they viewed its replacement with some resentment; but this was in no way a reflection on the capabilities of the later aircraft, which performed ably the tasks allotted to it. The S.M. 84 was not produced in anything like the numbers of the S.M 79, but several of these aircraft which survived the war were stripped of their combat equipment and flew with post-war transport units until 1948.

Savoia-Marchetti S.M. 85

The S.M. 85 possessed inadequate power and mediocre flying qualities, and was not one of the Italian aircraft industry's great successes of World War II. Although designed as a single-seat dive-bomber, it was quite large and was unusual in being of twin-motor configuration, with 500-hp Piaggio P.VII RC 35 radial engines.

The S.M. 85 was a shoulder-wing monoplane of mainly wooden construction, with the cockpit set well forward on the nose, and was flown for the first time in 1938. Dive-brakes were incorporated on the inboard wing trailing-edges, and there was a glass panel in the cockpit floor through which the offensive load of one 550-lb or 1,100-lb bomb could be aimed. One or two 12·7-mm Breda-SAFAT machine-guns could be mounted in the nose for ground-attack missions.

In the event, the S.M. 85 served with only one Regia Aeronautica unit, this being No. 96 Gruppo Bombardamento a Tuffo, based on the island of Pantelleria. The machines that equipped this unit were 32 pre-production S.M. 85s, the only series aircraft of this type to be built. Reports indicate that some ended their days being used for suicide missions. They did not remain long in service, the unit subsequently re-equipping with the Ju 87.

One prototype was completed of the S.M. 86, a developed model with cleaner lines and Isotta-Fraschini Delta engines.

S.I.A. 7B and 9B

The S.I.A. 7B1 was an armed two-seater designed by Savoia and Verduzio and constructed by the Fiat subsidiary Società Italiana Aviazione. It appeared for the first time in 1917 and was a clean-looking, equal-span, two-bay biplane, of wood construction throughout, with fabric panels covering the wings. Powered by a single 250-hp Fiat A-12 engine, with a car-type radiator, it was both speedy and agile, with an excellent rate of climb; and its performance capabilities were well demonstrated by outstanding altitude and distance flights carried out soon after its first appearance.

A total of 501 7B1s were eventually completed, each armed with two Revelli machine-guns, one above the upper wing for use by the pilot, and another on a movable mounting in the observer's cockpit. Nineteen were purchased by the USA early in 1918 for training.

The first 7B1s began to arrive at the front in November 1917, but did not achieve the success expected of them due to structural weakness in the wings. Several instances occurred of wings collapsing under stress in the air.

They were followed in May 1918 by the 7B2, of which 72 were built. This represented an attempt to overcome the earlier version's structural shortcomings, and also utilized the more powerful A-12*bis* engine of 300 hp. However the trouble persisted and in the summer of 1918 all aircraft of the 7B type were withdrawn from service.

Meanwhile, in February 1918, there had appeared in service the S.I.A.9B, a much enlarged and heavier development of the 7B, powered by a 700-hp Fiat A-14 engine. Deterred by the failure of the 7B, the Italian Army refused to accept the 9B, but 62 were completed and used by three squadrons of the Italian Navy.

S.I.A.I. S.8

This neat, compact two-seat single-engined flying-boat was evolved in 1917 by the Società Italiana Aeroplani Idrovolanti, primarily for reconnaissance and anti-submarine patrol duties. Designed by Ing Confienti, it had equal-span, two-bay wings, between which was mounted a single 170-hp Isotta-Fraschini V4B engine, driving a two-bladed wooden pusher propeller. The single-step hull accommodated a pilot and observer, in separate side-by-side cockpits, the observer operating a pair of machine-guns. Small stabilizing floats were affixed to the lower mainplane, about 3 ft from each wingtip, and a single fin and rudder were carried on the upswept rear fuselage.

A substantial production order for the S.8 was placed by the Italian Navy, and 172 aircraft of this type had been delivered by the end of the 1914–18 War. Some had a 120-hp Colombo F.150 engine, and at least one S.8 was fitted experimentally with a 200-hp Hispano-Suiza 44; but the Isotta-Fraschini remained the standard unit.

A development of the S.8, the S.I.A.I. S.9 with a 300-hp Fiat A-12*bis* engine, appeared during 1918. This type, however, was not adopted for service, the Italian Navy expressing a preference for the Macchi M.9 instead.

S.I.A.7B

S.I.A.9B prototype

S.I.A.I. S.8

TYPE	DIMENSIONS						WEIGHT	PERFORMANCE				REMARKS
	span		length		height		max t-o	max speed	at height	service ceiling	combat range	
	ft	in	ft	in	ft	in	lb	mph	ft	ft	miles	
S.M.81	78	8¾	58	4¾	14	7⅛	23,000	211	13,120	22,965	932	Performance with Piaggio PX engines
S.M.84	69	6⅝	58	4¾	14	9	29,650	266	16,400	21,600	1,137	
S.M.85	45	11⅛	34	5⅓	10	9⅞	9,237	228	13,820	19,190	515	
S.I.A. 7B2	43	8½	29	8⅔	9	10	2,425	124	SL	22,965	315	
S.I.A. 9B	50	10¼	31	9⅞	12	3	4,189	127	SL	18,040	373	
S.I.A.I. S. 8	41	10¾	31	11⅞	11	1⅞	3,142	88	SL	16,400	4¼ hr	

Aichi D1A1

Aichi D1A2

Aichi D3A

Japan

Aichi D1A

In 1933 the Imperial Japanese Navy, still to a large extent lacking experience in the operation of carrier-borne aircraft, realized that the designing of such types by the country's own infant industry would be no simple task. Consequently, when inviting the Aichi and Nakajima companies to compete for its 8-*Shi* requirement for a shipboard dive bomber during that year, it granted the former manufacturer permission to enter an aircraft that was not in fact a completely original design.

As might have been expected, therefore, the Aichi design proved to be the superior machine, particularly from the viewpoints of stability and of control during the dive. Designated D1A1, it was a medium-sized, two-seat two-bay biplane, which owed much in its conception to the German single-seat Heinkel He 50. Power was provided by a single Nakajima Kotobuki 2-I air-cooled radial engine, enclosed by a Townend ring and developing 580 hp for take-off. There were two 7·7-mm machine-guns ahead of the front cockpit, and a third movable gun in the observer's position.

The D1A1 exhibited a satisfactory degree of manoeuvrability, and at the end of 1933 it was placed in production for the JNAF as the Type 94 shipboard dive-bomber Model 1, the first Japanese military aircraft to be produced specifically for this rôle and able to carry a 682-lb bomb-load. During the next three years a total of 162 D1A1s were completed as Type 94, first deliveries being made early in 1934 to a JNAF squadron on board the carrier *Ryujo*. They remained in Navy service, alongside the later DIA2s, until the arrival of the Type 99.

To meet the JNAF's 9-*Shi* (1934) requirements for a new carrier-based bomber, Aichi Kokuki decided to improve still further upon the He 50-inspired D1A1 which was then beginning to enter service. While preserving the basic configuration, the new model, the D1A2, introduced improvements in the wing structure and to the main landing gear, the wheels of which were encased in oval-pattern "spat" fairings. The structure was also strengthened, to allow an increased maximum bomb-load of 880 lb and to accept a more powerful engine. The latter took the form of a neatly-cowled Nakajima Hikari 3 air-cooled radial, of either 610 or 730 hp, which raised the top speed of the D1A2 nearly 20 mph above that of its predecessor, although the combat radius was somewhat reduced. Defensive armament was the same.

The prototype D1A2 was flown for the first time in October 1936, and its adoption by the JNAF was immediate, 428 being built as Type 96 carrier-based bombers. Some of them created an international incident when they dive-bombed the US gunboat *Panay* in the Yangtse.

In the D1A1 and D1A2 Aichi provided the JNAF's last carrier-based biplane bombers. A small number of D1A2s, relegated to non-combatant duties, survived into the early days of World War II, when they were given the Allied code name "Susie".

Aichi D3A

In 1936 the Imperial Japanese Navy invited the Aichi, Mitsubishi and Nakajima companies to tender for its 11-*Shi* requirement for a new carrier-based dive-bomber to succeed the Type 96 D1A2. Mitsubishi, after completing a mock-up of their design, withdrew from the competition to concentrate their efforts on the A5M1 fighter and B5M1 attack aircraft. After comparison of the other two entrants, the Navy awarded a development contract for the Aichi design.

Both the Army and the Navy had, unbeknown to one another, a "secret" agreement with the Ernst Heinkel AG, and the Aichi design in particular showed a strong similarity to Heinkel aircraft of the period – especially the He 118, one of which had been purchased by the IJN in connection with the 11-*Shi* project.

The Aichi machine, ordered into production for the JNAF in December 1937, became the first Japanese low-wing dive-bomber of all-metal construction. For stowage on board IJN carriers, the outer section of each wing, for about 6 ft from the tip, folded upward.

The initial model, designated Type 99 carrier-based dive-bomber, or D3A1 Model 11, was a sturdily-built machine, well suited to its design rôle. Despite its modest performance and fixed undercarriage, it was nimble enough to undertake combat manoeuvres if need be, after delivering its quota of bombs. A single 550-lb bomb, on a centre cradle which swung forward and downward to clear the propeller, could be augmented by two bombs of up to 132 lb weight on underwing shackles. With two fixed 7·7mm guns firing forward and a third on a movable mounting in the rear cockpit, the D3A1 was no mean opponent, and was a standard JNAF type at the outset of the Pacific war. Indeed, bombers of this type (later code-named "Val" by the Allies) formed the first wave of attack on Pearl Harbor in December 1941. In April 1942, Aichi D3A1s sank the British carrier *Hermes* and the cruisers *Cornwall* and *Dorsetshire*.

The D3A1 remained in production until August 1942, 478 being completed with 1,075-hp Mitsubishi Kinsei 44 radial engines. It was then superseded by the Model 22, or D3A2, with minor airframe improvements and a 1,300-hp Kinsei 54 engine. The D3A2 remained in production until January 1944, by which time Aichi had completed 816 of this model.

Throughout the first half of the war in the Far East, both D3A1s and D3A2s were active in most theatres, from carrier and shore bases. They took part in the battle of Santa Cruz in October 1942; but in the campaigns at Midway and in the Solomons the Navy suffered heavy losses of experienced pilots and bombing accuracy fell off rapidly. A single-seat conversion of the D3A2 was used later in the suicide attack rôle, and a number were also converted to D3A2-K trainers.

Aichi H9A1

More than two dozen amphibians of the H9A1 type were in JNAF service, from mid-1942 until the end of the war; yet their existence remained undetected until six months before VJ-day, when one was spotted in Ibusuki harbour, near Kagoshima. Hence this was one of the few Japanese service aircraft not allotted a code-name.

Known officially as the Type 2 Model 11 training flying-boat, the prototype of the H9A1 flew for the first time in 1940. Its original purpose was to provide instruction for potential crews of the H8K patrol bomber flying-boat then being developed by Kawanishi. Accommodation was provided for three pupils, in addition to the normal five-man crew. Twin 710-hp Nakajima Kotobuki 3 radial engines were underslung from a sturdy parasol wing, braced to the hull by heavy "N" struts.

During 1942–43, the parent company's Eitoku factory completed 27 H9A1s, and a further four were built in the following year by Nippon Hikoki K.K. Initially, the H9A1 fulfilled its training rôle only; but in the latter stages of World War II it was pressed into service as an anti-submarine patrol aircraft, in which capacity it could carry two 550-lb bombs or depth charges on racks beneath the wings. A light defensive armament was installed, consisting of one 7·7-mm machine-gun in the bow and one in the mid-upper position.

Aichi D3A1

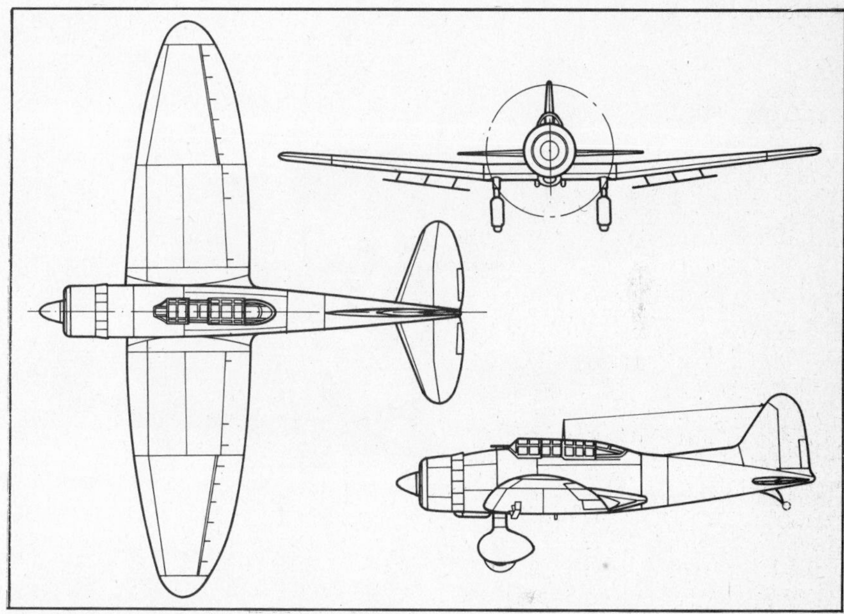

Aichi D3A2

Aichi H9A1

TYPE	DIMENSIONS						WEIGHT	PERFORMANCE				REMARKS
	span		*length*		*height*		*max t-o*	*max speed*	*at height*	*service ceiling*	*combat range*	
	ft	*in*	*ft*	*in*	*ft*	*in*	*lb*	*mph*	*ft*	*ft*	*miles*	
Aichi D1A1								174			659	
Aichi D1A2								193			575	Model 11
Aichi D3A1	47	1½	33	5⅓	10	11⅞	8,047	242	7,612	31,200	1,131	
Aichi D3A2	47	1½	33	6¾	10	11⅞	9,088	266	18,537	35,695	969	
Aichi H9A1	78	8⅞	55	7⅓	17	2¾	16,689	202	9,810	22,250	1,300 approx	

Aichi E16A1 Zuiun

Aichi E16A1 Zuiun

Aichi B7A1 Ryusei

Aichi B7A1 Ryusei

Aichi E16A1 Zuiun (Auspicious Cloud)

A little over a year before the attack on Pearl Harbor, the JNAF issued a specification for a new reconnaissance seaplane, able to operate also as a dive-bomber, to succeed the Aichi E13A ("Jake"). Aichi Kokuki K.K. began to design the new aircraft in October 1940, and the first of three prototypes was flown for the first time in May 1942, having as its power plant a 1,300-hp Mitsubishi Kinsei 51 radial engine. The E16A was mounted on two large, single-step floats each attached to the fuselage by a pair of wide struts, with a narrow cross-brace forming an "N". Dive-brakes were incorporated in the two front struts.

Modifications were necessary to flaps, floats and fuselage, to overcome instability problems; the dive-brakes in particular caused buffeting until the use of perforated brakes cleared up the trouble. Finally, in August 1943, the JNAF ordered the E16A1 into production as the Zuiun Model 11A. Power plant of production machines was the 14-cylinder air-cooled Mitsubishi Kinsei 54 radial, which offered 1,300 hp for take-off, and the armament was increased in calibre to make the E16A1 the heaviest-armed reconnaissance seaplane put into service by the Japanese forces. Two wing-mounted 20-mm cannon were fitted, together with a single 12·7-mm gun on a movable mounting in the observer's cockpit; whereas all three had been 7·7-mm calibre on the prototypes.

When the E16A1 ("Paul" in the Allied coding system) first entered service, Navy reconnaissance pilots were reluctant to accept it as being superior to the earlier "Jake" with which they were familiar; hence it was used more widely in its dive-bomber rôle, with one 550-lb or two 132-lb bombs. It appeared first in the Philippines area, but was to be found later in the Okinawa theatre as one of the many types employed by the Japanese for suicide attacks. Production of the E16A1 amounted to 253 machines, 194 from the parent company and 59 built (from late 1944) by Nippon Hikoki K.K. At the time of the Japanese surrender, a Model 12, or E16A2, version with a Kinsei 62 power plant was under evaluation.

Aichi B7A1 Ryusei (Shooting Star)

Last Japanese carrier-borne attack aircraft to go into production in World War II, the Aichi B7A1 (code name "Grace") arrived in service only after Japan had lost all her carriers to Allied attack, and those aircraft which did operate, from shore stations, were engaged sometimes in suicide raids. These and other factors restricted what might otherwise have been a useful, if not spectacular, career, for the Ryusei was a nimble aircraft, with good performance and handling qualities.

With the project designation X-16, it was evolved to a 16-*Shi* (1941) specification for a successor to the Yokosuka D4Y and Nakajima B6N, and the first prototype made its maiden flight in May 1942. Large for a single-engined type, the two-seat Ryusei was of mid wing layout, with an inverted gull wing designed to reduce the length of the main undercarriage legs. A 2,200-lb torpedo could be carried beneath the centre fuselage, or a 1,764-lb bomb-load accommodated within the bomb-bay; on test flights the aircraft achieved 35[illegible] mph, which was 11 mph above that called for by the specification. It carried two forward-firing 20-mm cannon and one rear-firing 13·2-mm machine-gun.

All of the prototypes, and the early production B7A1s had a 1,825-hp Nakajima Homare 11 radial engine; subsequent service aircraft used the Homare 12, with the same take-off power but a better performance at altitude. However, neither version of this troublesome engine was entirely satisfactory. The Homare was mechanically unreliable and difficult to service, and it was due largely to these power plant problems that the Ryusei did not enter production until April 1944.

One B7A1 airframe was re-engined, as the B7A2 with a 2,000-hp Homare 39; and in January 1945 development was initiated of a Ryusei-Kai prototype for the B7A3, to utilize the more reliable Mitsubishi Kinsei of 2,200 hp. But in May 1945 a severe earthquake devastated the Tokai district, putting an end not only to these

two projects but to any further production of the B7A1. At this time Aichi had completed 89 aircraft and the Ohmura Naval Air Arsenal about ten more. The Ryusei was met in limited numbers, in conventional and Kamikaze attacks, off the Japanese mainland in 1944–5.

Aichi M6A Seiran (Mountain Haze)

A class of 18 large, ultra-long-range submarines, known as the I-400 class, was projected by the Imperial Japanese Navy prior to Japan's entry into World War II, and it was intended that each of these should carry two (later three) attack bombers of a new design, in a special hold within the hull. Among missions envisaged for this combined weapons system was to put out of action the Panama canal, the US supply route to the south-west Pacific.

Design of the flying half of the combination was entrusted to Aichi Kokuki K.K., in June 1942, and the work proceeded with great secrecy, in close collaboration with the IJN. At first it had been planned that the M6A1 seaplane bomber should be expendable and would have no undercarriage, being launched from a catapult on board the submarine and ditched near the ship on return from a mission, so that the pilot could be picked up; but this idea was abandoned. Thus, the first of eight M6A1 prototypes (all powered by the 1,400-hp Aichi Atsuta 21 liquid-cooled engine) was completed in November 1943, and was a two-seat, all-metal, low-wing monoplane mounted on a pair of large, single-step jettisonable floats. Wings, tailplane and the tip of the fin and rudder all folded for stowage inside the submarine.

In addition to the prototypes, 20 production aircraft were built in 1944–5, some of these being M6A1-K conversion trainers with a squared-off fin and rudder and land undercarriage; the latter were known as Nanzans (Southern Mountain), a name originally reserved for the undercarriage-less operational model. All production M6As were powered by the 12-cylinder water-cooled Atsuta 32 engine, with the same take-off rating as the Atsuta 21, but offering greater power at altitude. The operational Seirans could carry a 1,765-lb torpedo or an equivalent weight of bombs, and mounted one 12·7-mm defensive gun in the rear of the two-man cockpit.

In the event, although thoroughly and extensively rehearsed, the Panama raid never took place. Development difficulties with the I-400 submarines (only three were completed) led to some of the smaller I-13 class being modified to carry a pair of M6As, and a total of ten Seirans eventually entered active service with the 1st Submarine Flotilla of the IJN early in 1945. This Flotilla was despatched southward for its first operation, but was ordered back before reaching the target area when the war ended.

Hiro G2H1

Late in 1932 the Hiro Navy Air Arsenal embarked upon the design of a twin-engined medium bomber to meet a JNAF requirement for a land-based attack aircraft. It revealed considerable Junkers influence in its layout and construction. Development trials with the completed prototype, which flew for the first time in March 1933, revealed a number of serious faults, including some weakness of the basic structure and a tendency to wing flutter. Difficulties with the 825-hp Hiro Type 94 water-cooled Vee engines contributed to the delay.

Production of the G2H1 was eventually embarked

Aichi M6A Seiran

Aichi M6A1-K Nanzan

Hiro G2H1

TYPE	DIMENSIONS						WEIGHT	PERFORMANCE				REMARKS
	span		length		height		max t-o	max speed	at height	service ceiling	combat range	
	ft	in	ft	in	ft	in	lb	mph	ft	ft	miles	
Aichi E16A1	42	0	35	6¾	15	6⅔	9,326	277	18,307	33,727	599	Model 11
Aichi B7A1	47	3	37	8⅓	13	4¼	14,330	337	20,341	29,364	1,150 max	Model 11
Aichi M6A1	40	2⅔	34	10⅞	15	0⅓	10,426	292	13,120	31,627	712	
Hiro G2H1							24,251	152			1,790	

Kawanishi H6K2

Kawanishi H6K5

Kawanishi H6K4, Indonesian Air Force

upon in 1935, as the Navy Type 95, but was suspended after the completion of only eight machines, two of which were built by Mitsubishi, with 900-hp engines. The majority of these were delivered for squadron use, and took part in a few raids on the Chinese mainland during the Sino-Japanese war; after a comparatively short career, most of them were destroyed by a fire which broke out at their base on Cheju Island in the Korea Strait. The G2H1 carried a seven-man crew, a normal bomb-load of 3,527 lb and a maximum of 4,409 lb.

A long-range reconnaissance monoplane, based on the G2H1, was evolved by Mitsubishi in 1934, and both types had a direct influence on the successful G3M bomber.

Kawanishi H6K

With a maximum range, in its later versions, of some 4,000 miles and the ability to remain airborne for well over 24 hours, the Kawanishi H6K maritime patrol flying-boat was one of the most efficient aircraft used by the Japanese air forces in the late 1930s.

By the end of 1936, three out of the five prototypes ordered had been test-flown, the first in July. Each was powered initially by four 840-hp Nakajima Hikari 2 radial engines, centrally mounted on the broad parasol wing, and the armament included a dorsal gun turret. Three prototypes were re-engined subsequently with Mitsubishi Kinsei 43 radials of 1,000 hp, and were put into JNAF squadron service in January 1938 as Type 97 flying-boats; the fifth aircraft became the first of ten Model 11s (H6K2), also with Kinsei 43s. The H6K3 was a military and civil transport version.

The JNAF machines were later re-designated H6K2-L, and production included a batch of 18 supplied to Japan Air Lines as 16-passenger airliners.

The early models of the H6K flew on operational missions during the Sino-Japanese conflict; but by the outbreak of World War II (when the flying-boat received the Allied code name of "Mavis") the principal version in service, and the one subsequently built in the greatest numbers, was the H6K4 or Model 22. Up to August 1941 this model had, like its predecessors, been powered by Kinsei 43 engines; but after this date the more powerful Kinsei 46 of 1,070 hp was installed. The power-operated dorsal turret was replaced by an open gun position mounting a single 7·7-mm gun, just ahead of which were two beam blisters each containing a further 7·7-mm gun for lateral defence. A fourth 7·7-mm was installed in the open prow cockpit, and the tail turret mounted a single 20-mm cannon. The H6K4's offensive load could comprise two 1,765-lb bombs or torpedoes, or twelve 132-lb bombs. A number of transport H6K4-Ls were also in service at this time.

By the summer of 1942 it was becoming increasingly evident that the defensive armament and slow speed of the H6K were inadequate, and it had to be taken off daylight operations. An attempt was made to prolong its active life by evolving a new version designated Model 23 or H6K5, with 1,300-hp Kinsei 53 engines. This went into production in August 1942; but only a comparatively small number were built before, in 1943, production of the H6K was phased out in favour of the much superior H8K. By the end of that year the H6K had virtually disappeared from service. A total of 217 H6Ks of all models, including 36 transports, were built by Kawanishi.

Kawanishi H8K

When the prototype H8K1 made its first appearance at the end of 1940, its performance on test gave little indication of the first-class combat aircraft it was eventually to become. Its narrow hull made it extremely unstable on the water, and during take-off and landing it was liable to "porpoise" at the slightest opportunity.

The H8K had been designed by Dr Kikuhara to an exacting specification, drawn up by the JNAF in 1938, for a Type 97 (H6K) replacement with a speed of some 300 mph and range of 4,500 km (2,800 miles). The major service version, the H8K2, had a maximum range of nearly 4,500 *miles*, and fell short of the required speed

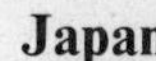

by only 10 mph, despite an all-up weight some four tons higher than specification.

Incorporation of a second step in the planing surface, and a deepening of the hull by about 2 ft, coupled with some adjustments to the wing flaps, eliminated the stability problems, and second and third prototypes were completed with these changes. Each was powered by four 1,530-hp Mitsubishi Kasei 11 air-cooled radial engines, mounted centrally on the slim, high-set cantilever wing, and was equipped with the heavy defensive armament of five 20mm cannon (in nose, tail and dorsal positions) and three 7·7-mm machine-guns. Armour protection for the ten-man crew was of a high order. One prototype was fitted with retractable wing-tip floats.

The H8K1 entered production for the JNAF as the Type 2 Model 11 flying-boat for maritime patrol, bombing and reconnaissance duties. Kawanishi's Kohnan factory, near Kobe, built 17 of this model. They made their first raid in March 1942, when three H8K1s, flying from the Marshall Islands and refuelling at a submarine rendezvous 650 miles east of Hawaii, attacked Oahu Island in Hawaii – only to have their intentions thwarted by dense cloud which obscured the target. Thereafter the H8K – code-named "Emily" by the Allies – ranged all over the Pacific theatre, its endurance on a single mission being anything up to 24 hours.

By far the most numerous version in service was the Model 12 or H8K2, over 100 of which were built. The H8K2 carried one more 7·7-mm gun, heavier armour protection and search radar, while the substitution of Kasei 22 radials of 1,850 hp increased the maximum speed from 250 to 290 mph. Offensive load comprised eight 550-lb bombs or two 1,765-lb torpedoes.

Thirty-six additional Model 12s, with only a single 20-mm gun and one 13-mm gun for defence, were built in 1943 as 64-seat troop transports (plus crew of nine), under the designation H8K2-L, and were named Sei-ku (Clear Sky) by the Japanese. Two examples were also completed of an H8K3 variant, with retracting wing-tip floats. These were redesignated H8K4 when re-engined later with Kasei 25b engines.

Last, largest and best Japanese flying-boat, the H8K remained in production until 1945; and had it not been for the necessity for Japan to concentrate on building defensive fighters it would doubtless have been built in greater numbers than the total of 167 reached by VJ-day. Postwar evaluation of the type in the United States confirmed that it was superior to US, British, German and Italian flying-boats in service during World War II, both hydrodynamically and in terms of performance.

Kawanishi N1K1 Kyofu (Mighty Wind)

With Japan's sights set on conquest of the innumerable islands of the south-west Pacific, an obvious requirement for the naval air service was a fighter, independent of land bases, which could secure and maintain local air supremacy during the landing of occupying forces. The JNAF issued a specification in September 1940, entrusting the design to the Kawanishi Kokuki K.K. at Naruo.

The warplane which emerged after 18 months' work, and which was to become the most potent floatplane fighter of its day, was a heavy, single-seat, mid-wing monoplane of all-metal construction, mounted on a long single-step float, with smaller stabilizing floats near the wing-tips. (An earlier proposal for retractable floats was discarded, to save weight and simplify maintenance).

Kawanishi H8K1, original hull

Kawanishi H8K2

Kawanishi H8K2-L, transport version

TYPE	DIMENSIONS						WEIGHT	PERFORMANCE				REMARKS
	span		length		height		max t-o	max speed	at height	service ceiling	combat range	
	ft	in	ft	in	ft	in	lb	mph	ft	ft	miles	
Kawanishi H6K2	131	2⅞	84	1	20	6⅞	35,274	206	6,890	24,934	2,566	Model 11
Kawanishi H6K4	131	2⅞	84	1	20	6⅞	50,706	211	13,120	31,529	3,728 max	Model 22
Kawanishi H8K1	124	8	92	3½	30	0¼	68,343	269	16,404		2,933	Model 11
Kawanishi H8K2	124	8	92	3½	30	0¼	71,650	282	16,404	28,773	4,474 max	Model 12

Kawanishi N1K1 Kyofu

Kawanishi N1K1 Kyofu

Kawanishi N1K1-J Shiden

Kawanishi N1K1-J Shiden, captured aircraft, US markings

The bulky power plant was the 14-cylinder, two-row Mitsubishi Kasei 14 radial, fitted with counter-rotating propellers to offset the torque expected from such a large engine. The advantages conferred by these were, however, marginal and production machines changed to a single three-bladed propeller.

By early 1943 eight prototypes had been built. The first of them had flown on 1 August 1942, and had been joined by the second machine in October. In December 1942, the JNAF officially accepted the fighter as the N1K1 Model 11, ordering it into immediate production at the Kawanishi factories at Naruo and Himeji. The Kyofu (which was given the code-name "Rex" by the Allies) entered service in the early summer of 1943, supplanting the Nakajima-built A6M2-N ("Rufe") which had fulfilled its rôle in the interim.

"Rex" served at Balikpapan on the east coast of Borneo, and in the latter stages of World War II was engaged in defence of the Japanese homeland, with the Ohtsu Naval Air Corps, from bases on Lake Biwa, Shiga Prefecture. A comparatively small number (97) of Kyofus were built, production ceasing in March 1944 in favour of a landplane development – also a first-class fighter – the N1K1-J Shiden. Most of the service N1K1s were powered by the 1,460-hp Mitsubishi Kasei 13 two-row radial engine, though the Kasei 15 was fitted in later machines. All were armed with two 20-mm Type 99 wing cannon and two 7·7-mm Type 97 machine-guns in the engine cowling. Before development was switched to the Shiden, an N1K2 version with a 1,900-hp Kasei 23 had been under consideration.

Kawanishi N1K1-J and N1K2-J Shiden (Violet Lightning)

Unique among combat landplanes of World War II in being evolved from an original floatplane design, the Kawanishi Shiden was one of the finest fighter aircraft flown in the Pacific theatre. The fact that it achieved this reputation despite being hurried into production, before a full test programme had eliminated the development snags of both engine and airframe, underlines the excellence of the original design by Dr Kikuhara.

Work on the evolution of a land-based interceptor from the N1K1 Kyofu began on 15 April 1942, four months before the floatplane prototype flew at Naruo. The basic airframe was retained in the first model, the N1K1-J, which was test-flown on 24 July 1943, and it was clear immediately that the Shiden would prove extremely fast and manoeuvrable. Nonetheless, there were difficulties to overcome. The powerful 1,990-hp Nakajima Homare 21 radial engine necessitated a large-diameter four-blade propeller, and this, coupled with retention of the Kyofu's mid-wing layout, involved the use of an unusually long-legged main landing gear, with attendant problems of retraction.

The Homare 21 had been pressed into production without an adequate development period, and series production of the Shiden Model 11 also began, in August 1943, before all the prototype machines had been completed or fully tested. Consequently, the rate of production was interrupted constantly by modifications found necessary as the result of prototype testing.

A second production line for the N1K1-J was opened at Kawanishi's Himeji factory in December 1943. Meanwhile, at the time the N1K1-J was first entering production at Naruo, Kawanishi had embarked on a major redesign of the fighter, under the designation Shiden-Kai, or N1K2-J Model 21. Their main aim, to simplify the design to speed production, they achieved by reducing the total number of airframe parts by about one-third.

A major change was the adoption of a low-wing configuration (thereby dealing successfully with the undercarriage retraction problem). Other outwardly visible changes included a completely new fin and rudder outline, and a slightly longer fuselage with aerodynamic improvements to the engine cowling and better visibility for the pilot. The 18-cylinder Homare 21 was retained.

The first NlK2-J was flown on 3 April 1944, and again by the time all the prototypes had been completed, in mid-1944, the type was already in production at Naruo for the JNAF. Output continued to be hampered by the necessity of incorporating modifications on the production line, by the effects of US bombing on the supplies of equipment and, in particular, by the shortcomings of the Homare 21 engine. Nevertheless, at the end of World War II, construction and further development of the Shiden were still being continued.

The Naruo factory completed 8 prototype and 535 production N1K1-Js, and 8 prototype and 354 production N1K2-Js. Himeji built 468 N1K1-Js and, in March-August 1945, 44 N1K2-Js. In addition, further N1K2-Js were completed by Aichi (1), Mitsubishi (9) and Showa (2), and by the Hiro (1) and Omura (10) Naval Air Arsenals, bringing the grand total to 1,440 aircraft.

Variants produced or projected included a few dual-control conversion trainers (N1K2-K); the proposed N1K3-J and N1K3-A (Models 31 and 41) with heavier armament; three N1K4-J (Model 32) with 2,000-hp Homare 23 engines; the similar N1K4-A (Model 43) – not built; and the prototype N1K5-J (2,200-hp Mitsubishi Ha-43-II), which was destroyed at Himeji in a B-29 raid. Some N1K1-Js were tested, successfully, with a booster rocket beneath the rear fuselage, but the technique was not adopted on operational aircraft.

Variations in armament were made, as follows:

N1K1-J: two 20-mm guns within the wings, two 20-mm underwing, two 7·7-mm in the front cowling;

N1K1-Ja: as above but without the 7·7-mm guns;

N1K1-Jb: four 20-mm, all within the wings. (This model, which had a squared-off fin and rudder, also carried six small rocket bombs beneath the fuselage);

N1K2-J: four 20-mm Type 99 guns within the wings, with increased ammunition. (This model also operated with two 550-lb bombs underwing).

In service from the early spring of 1944, the Shiden ("George" to the Allied powers) was prominent in many Pacific theatres, notably on Honshu, Japan, in the Philippines and around Formosa, in the rôle of an area defence fighter. At Okinawa it served both in this rôle and as a suicide aircraft; indeed, a special Kamikaze model was mooted at one time.

Kawanishi P1Y2-S Kyokko (Aurora)

As a result of their experience with the Nakajima Homare radial engine in the P1Y1 Ginga bomber, when Kawanishi were asked to evolve a night fighter variant of this aircraft, they decided to utilize a more reliable power plant and also to simplify the airframe by extensive re-design. They proposed two new models – a bomber (P1Y2) and a night fighter (P1Y2-S); but in view of the urgent need for improved defence of industrial targets in Japan, the JNAF decided to concentrate on the fighter. The prototype was flown in June 1944; yet none of the 96 production aircraft reached squadrons, still being with the trials unit on VJ-day. Only a few interim conversions of existing Ginga bombers, designated P1Y1-S, were met in service.

The P1Y2-S Kyokko was powered by two 1,850-hp Mitsubishi Kasei 25 air-cooled radial engines. It carried rudimentary AI radar and an armament of one movable 20-mm cannon in the rear of the cabin, with two more fixed 20-mm guns amidships, firing forward and upward. The P1Y1-Ss, without radar, sometimes had a hand-operated turret mounting two 20-mm guns behind the crew cabin. A further variant, the P1Y3-S with 1,990-hp Homares, remained a project only.

Kawanishi N1K2-J Shiden

Kawanishi N1K2-J Shiden

Kawanishi P1Y2-S Kyokko, captured aircraft, US markings

TYPE	DIMENSIONS						WEIGHT	PERFORMANCE				REMARKS
	span		length		height		max t-o	max speed	at height	service ceiling	combat range	
	ft	in	ft	in	ft	in	lb	mph	ft	ft	miles	
Kawanishi N1K1	39	4½	34	9	15	8⅛	8,184	299	18,700	34,645	1,050 max	Model 11
Kawanishi N1K1-J	39	3¼	29	1⅞	13	3¾	9,526	362	19,357	39,698	989	Model 11
Kawanishi N1K2-J	39	3¼	30	8⅛	12	11⅞	10,714	369	18,373	35,400	1,069	Model 21
Kawanishi P1Y2-S	65	7⅓	49	2½	14	1¼	29,762	325	17,720	31,365		Model 11

Kawasaki Type 88

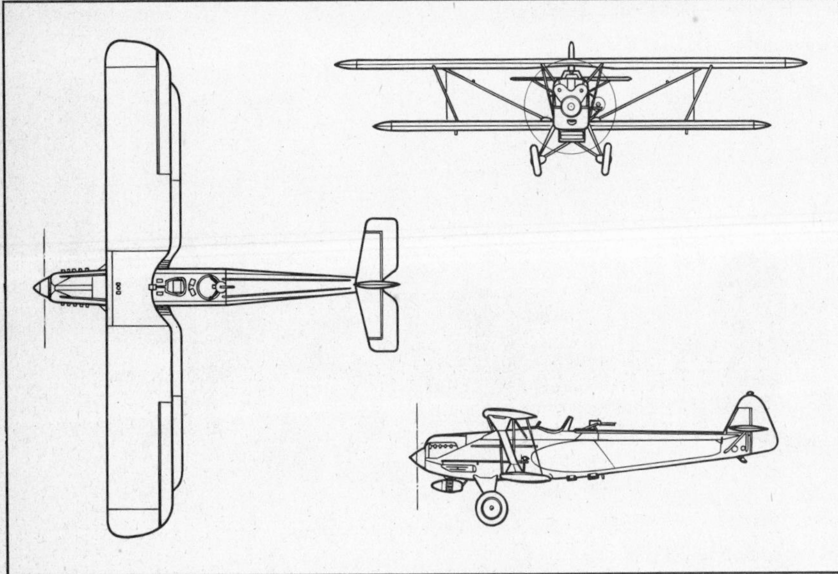
Kawasaki Type 88

Kawasaki Type 92

Kawasaki Ki-3

Kawasaki Type 88

The Kawasaki Type 88 Army biplane was designed to a March 1925 specification for a two-seat reconnaissance aircraft, by Dr Richard Vogt, who was chief designer of the Kawasaki Kokuki Kogyo K.K. from 1923 until 1933.

Known as the A-2 biplane, the prototype was completed in February 1927. On test, it achieved a level speed of 149 mph and climbed to 16,400 ft in 20 minutes. In August 1927, it was officially accepted by the Army, and received the designation Type 88-I when placed in production in the following February. The power plant, of German origin, was a Kawasaki licence-built version of the 500-hp BMW VI 12-cylinder inverted "Vee".

This model was followed by the Type 88-II, in which the basic design was adapted to perform as a light bomber, carrying a 550-lb load. It was similarly powered, but had a much cleaner engine installation. Two forward-firing and one rear-firing 7·7-mm guns were installed. The bomber version was built by Kawasaki and Tachikawa Army Arsenal (520 and 187 respectively) and, with the reconnaissance model, gave more than a decade of service to the JAAF, including operations in Tsinan and Manchuria and during the Shanghai incident.

Kawasaki Type 92

Designed by Dr Richard Vogt, and bearing the manufacturer's designation A-5, this small single-seat biplane fighter project was eliminated by the Japanese Army at an early stage in the 5-*Shi* fighter competition. Nevertheless, confident of the merits of their design, Kawasaki Kokuki Kogyo decided to press ahead with construction of a prototype as a private venture. This machine was completed in the autumn of 1930, and was subsequently flown in comparative tests with the Nakajima Type 91.

Incorporating the latest western design trends and techniques, the Kawasaki fighter's capabilities (including climb to 16,400 ft in 8 minutes) were good by any contemporary standards, and it proved far superior in almost every respect to the parasol-winged Nakajima machine. Faced with these results, the JAAF could no longer justify its earlier rejection of the design, and after further evaluation of five pre-production machines the aircraft was ordered for the Japanese Army in 1932 as the Type 92 Model 1 – Kawasaki's first production fighter.

With huge exhaust fairings above, and a prominent chin-type oil cooler beneath the engine, the Type 92 was a distinctive machine. The engine was a Kawasaki licence-built version of the water-cooled BMW VI, developing 500 hp and driving a two-bladed propeller. Immediately ahead of the open cockpit were twin 7·7-mm machine-guns, firing over the top of the engine decking.

Kawasaki built 180 Model 1 fighters before switching to the Model 2, which had the engine uprated to 600 hp.

Kawasaki Ki-3

Last biplane bomber produced for the Japanese Army by Kawasaki Kokuki Kogyo K.K., the Ki-3 was a two-seater with underwing racks for ten bombs of up to 110 lb in weight. Its defensive armament consisted of one fixed 7·7-mm machine-gun, firing forward, and a similar gun on a rotatable mounting in the second cockpit.

The prototype of the Ki-3 was flown in March 1933 and, after undergoing service acceptance trials, was placed in production for the JAAF later that year as the Type 93 light bomber. Although bearing an obvious family likeness to the Type 92 fighter, it was an altogether larger machine, of very robust construction. The power plant, of German origin, was the BMW IX 12-cylinder liquid-cooled "Vee" engine, developing 800 hp and driving a two-bladed propeller.

Most of the 243 completed were built by Kawasaki but some came from the Tachikawa Army Air Arsenal.

Kawasaki Ki-10

To meet the 1934 Army fighter specification, Kawasaki and Nakajima each evolved a low-wing monoplane design, designated respectively the Ki-5 and Ki-11

Kawasaki, however, decided in favour of the more conservative Ki-10 single-seat biplane.

Designed by Dr Takeo Doi, the Ki-10 followed closely the lines of Vogt's earlier Type 92 fighter, though incorporating many refinements and a higher-powered engine. It was a single-bay biplane of unequal span and with a somewhat narrower fuselage than its predecessor; and was powered by an 800-hp Ha-9 water-cooled Vee engine. A novel feature, which saved weight and simplified manufacture, was that the lower wing and forward fuselage formed a single integral unit; the entire aft section of the fuselage was detachable. Two fixed, forward-firing 7·7-mm guns were mounted in the top of the engine decking.

Kawasaki's decision to adhere to the biplane paid dividends, for when the prototype (completed in March 1935) was flown in competition with the Nakajima Ki-11, the JAAF decided in favour of the more traditional machine – although the Ki-10 became, in fact, its last biplane fighter. Nakajima were instructed to contribute to the Ki-10 construction programme.

Altogether the parent company completed 364 aircraft, under the designation Type 95 fighter Model 1 (Ki-10-I), while a further 280 Model 2s (Ki-10-II) were built by Nakajima. The two models were basically similar, the Ki-10-II having slightly greater wing area to increase manoeuvrability. Fighters of both models were busy during the Sino-Japanese incident, against Russian-built I-15s and I-16s, and 75 trainer versions were produced in 1939, by converting the single-seaters to take a second cockpit with dual controls. A small number still in service as trainers at the outbreak of the Pacific war were allotted the code-name "Perry".

Kawasaki Ki-32

Designed by Dr Isamu Imachi, one of several Japanese designers who came to the fore in the Kawasaki company after the return to Germany of Dr Richard Vogt, the Ki-32 light bomber monoplane followed earlier Kawasaki practice in utilizing a liquid-cooled in-line engine at a time when most Japanese manufacturers favoured the air-cooled radial. A wooden mock-up of the design was completed in June 1936, to be followed in March 1937 by the first of eight prototype Ki-32s.

The Ki-32 had a low mid-wing, a fixed undercarriage with streamlined main wheel fairings, and accommodated a crew of two beneath a long "greenhouse" type enclosure.

The prototypes were each powered by an 850-hp Ha-9-IIB Vee engine. Problems were encountered with the water cooling system of this engine, but subsequent use of glycol instead of water eliminated the trouble and in July 1938 the Ki-32 was placed in production as the Type 98 Army light bomber. It remained in production until the spring of 1940, by which time a further 846 aircraft had been completed.

The Ki-32 saw most of its combat service in the war with China. It was employed as a light bomber and on ground-attack and reconnaissance missions in support of Army formations, being especially prominent in the areas around Wuchang and Hankow. Small anti-personnel bombs, up to a maximum of 992 lb, or a single 550-lb bomb could be carried beneath the fuselage; defensive armament comprised a single rearward-firing 7·7-mm machine-gun in the rear cockpit, with one or two further 7·7-mm guns in the forward fuselage.

Kawasaki Ki-10

Kawasaki Ki-10

Kawasaki Ki-32

TYPE	DIMENSIONS span ft	span in	length ft	length in	height ft	height in	WEIGHT max t-o lb	PERFORMANCE max speed mph	at height ft	service ceiling ft	combat range miles	REMARKS
Kawasaki Army 88	49	2½	42	0			6,283	138		20,341	6 hr	
Kawasaki Army 92	31	2	23	7¾	10	4⅓	3,726	199		31,168	373	Model 1
Kawasaki Ki-3	42	7⅞	32	9⅔	9	10⅛	6,834	162	1,000	22,966		Model 1
Kawasaki Ki-10-I	33	0	26	2½	9	10	4,000	246	13,120	32,808	621	Model 1
Kawasaki Ki-32	49	2½	37	10	9	6⅛	7,496	261	13,120	24,600	840	Model 11

Kawasaki Ki-45-Kai-C Toryu

Kawasaki Ki-45-Kai-C Toryu

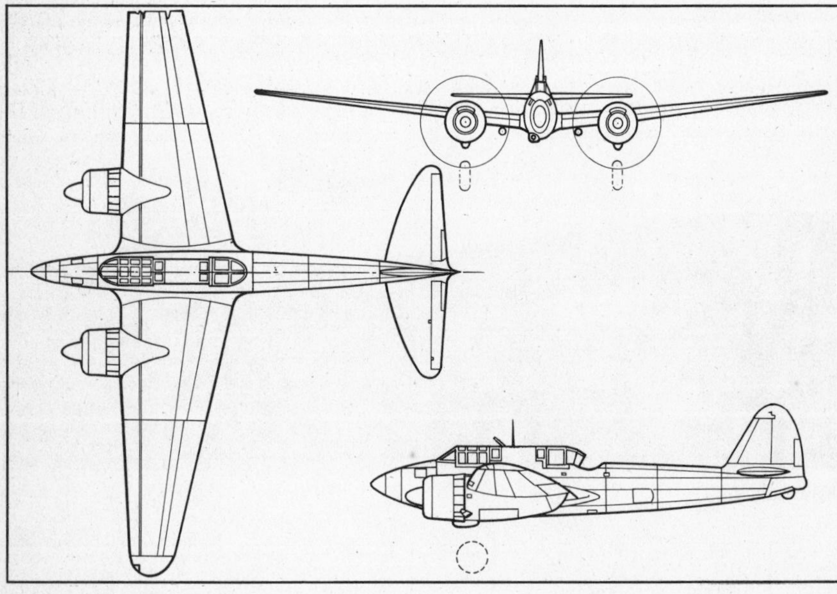

Kawasaki Ki-45-Kai-C Toryu

Under operational conditions another engine weakness – a tendency to crankshaft failure – manifested itself, thus limiting the effectiveness of the type as a combat weapon. Nevertheless, the Ki-32 was still in service with the JAAF at the outbreak of the Pacific war, its last operation of any consequence being in support of the attack and capture of Hong Kong, shortly after the raid on Pearl Harbor. Thereafter, the type (code-named "Mary" by the Allies) was used largely as a trainer and for other duties of a second-line nature.

Kawasaki Ki-45 Toryu (Dragon Killer)

The Allied code-name "Nick" identified a World War II combat aircraft of clean, conventional lines and no mean ability – one which was called upon by the JAAF to perform a variety of different rôles throughout the war.

"Nick", or the Ki-45, had its origins in an earlier Kawasaki design, the Ki-38, which was evolved to meet an Army requirement issued in March 1937 for a two-seat, twin-engined long-range escort fighter; but so extensive were the modifications demanded by the JAAF before acceptance that the second mock-up, completed in December, was allocated an entirely new designation.

Six prototypes were built initially, the first of them being ready in January 1939; but the evaluation programme ran into many setbacks. Most serious was the performance of the Nakajima Ha-20B. This engine never did achieve its designed output, and in July 1940 the Ki-45 flight test programme was resumed with three of the prototype aircraft re-engined with 1,000-hp Mitsubishi Ha-25s. Damage sustained on the first flight delayed progress for another month; but eventually all the prototypes were converted to Mitsubishi Kasei power and, in slightly modified and enlarged form, the type entered production at Kawasaki's Gifu factory in September 1941. Its JAAF designation was now Ki-45-Kai Toryu, or Type 2 heavy fighter.

In place of the rounded form of the early machines, the production Toryu featured a more pointed nose, in the forepart of which were mounted a pair of 12·7-mm machine-guns. Below and behind these, on the starboard side of the lower front fuselage, was a 20-mm cannon; and a flexible, rearward-firing 7·92-mm gun was installed in the observer's cockpit.

A second Kawasaki plant, at Akashi, joined in the building programme in August 1942, by which time the 1,080-hp Mitsubishi Ha-102 engine had been adopted as standard power plant for the fighter, improving both its performance and its reliability in service. With Ha-102s and the original armament, it was designated Ki-45-Kai-A; the 'Kai-B carried (at first, though other variations were to follow) one 12·7-mm and one 37-mm gun in the front fuselage; while the 'Kai-C and 'Kai-D were similar except for internal equipment changes.

A typical armament of the 'Kai-C models, indicative of the Ki-45's adoption by then for night fighting duties, was a single 37-mm gun forward, twin fixed 20-mm guns amidships, firing forward and upward, and (on some aircraft) a small searchlight in the extreme nose. Yet another variation was the installation in some Toryus of a 50-mm or 75-mm gun for shipping attack missions, while others could carry a pair of 550-lb bombs underwing.

A total of 1,698 Ki-45-Kai models were built by the two Kawasaki assembly plants, including 11 prototypes.

The Ki-45 entered JAAF service early in 1942, being particularly active in and around the southern battle areas during the first half of the Pacific war, where its long range made it an ideal escort and patrol aircraft between the widely scattered island groups. It was used against shipping in both conventional and suicide attacks. Indeed, a suicide assault on US shipping off the New Guinea coast on 27 May 1944, by four Ki-45s, was the first use of this form of warfare by Japanese Army aircraft during World War II. Toryus were also encountered in mainland engagements over Burma, Indo-China and Manchuria. From about mid-1944, when B-29 raids began on Japan, Ki-45s were among the more successful types hurriedly called to night defence duties, and scored several successes against the high-flying US bombers, particularly over Tokyo and Osaka.

In August 1942, Kawasaki began work on a projected Ki-45-II development, powered by 1,500-hp Mitsubishi Ha-112-II engines. In December, acting on JAAF instructions, they began converting this to a single-seat fighter designated Ki-96, completing three prototypes. The first of these, flown in September 1943, revealed a good turn of speed (375 mph) and was similarly armed to the Ki-45-Kai-C. Shortly after this, however, the JAAF discarded the single-seat project and several Ki-96 components were used later in Ki-102 prototypes.

Kawasaki Ki-48

Kawasaki Kokuki Kogyo K.K. ventured into the light bomber field with the Ki-48, designed to a 1937 requirement of the Japanese Army Air Force. It was a twin-engined, mid-wing monoplane of conventional, if not especially attractive, appearance, the first of nine prototypes making its maiden flight in July 1939. There followed four months of flight testing, resulting in a number of modifications to the design, before the aircraft entered production for the JAAF in November, as the Type 99 Model 1 light bomber.

The changes included a strengthening of the rear fuselage (which was narrowed by the steps for dorsal and ventral gun positions) and raising of the low-set tailplane to a position level with the top line of the fuselage. The aircraft's manoeuvrability and general stability still left something to be desired; but series construction of the Ki-48-I was initiated despite these shortcomings and a dozen aircraft were completed by the end of 1939.

The Ki-48-I, powered by two 1,000-hp Nakajima Ha-25 fourteen-cylinder radial engines, carried a crew of four or five and could accommodate up to 792 lb of bombs (six 110-lb or twenty-four 33-lb) in the deep internal bay. Armament varied between the Ki-48-Ia and Ki-48-Ib, there being a single 7·7-mm gun in both the nose and ventral stations and one or two in the dorsal position.

Kawasaki built a total of 569 Ki-48-Is, which were delivered to JAAF units from July 1940 onwards and assigned to bases in China for their first operational duties. Shortly after the outbreak of war in the Pacific, in February 1942, Kawasaki flew the first of three prototypes of the Ki-48-II, or Model 2, with an increased bomb-load (1,765 lb), more armour protection for crew and fuel tanks, and 1,130-hp Nakajima He-115 radials.

The Ki-48-IIa and -IIb were level- and dive-bombers respectively, similarly armed to the previous series. The -IIbs had a dorsal fin extension to provide greater directional stability in a dive, and air-brakes under each wing. On the Ki-48-IIc, a single 12·7-mm gun was substituted in the dorsal position.

From 1942 until October 1944, Kawasaki completed 1,408 Model 2 bombers, bringing the grand total, including prototypes, to 1,997 aircraft.

During World War II, in which it was allotted the code-name "Lily", the Ki-48 was encountered in most combat areas in South-East Asia and the Pacific, notably in Burma, New Guinea (from where it had sufficient range to bomb Port Darwin, Australia) and the Marshall Islands. Slow and with a modest bomb-load, it was no major thorn in the Allied side. Many were transferred to night operations, others were used for suicide attacks.

A few Ki-48-IIs had interesting jobs as test-bed aircraft: one machine air-tested, in a pod under the belly, the Ne-0 jet engine, and four others were adapted in 1944 as carriers for the Kawasaki-designed I-Go-lb guided missile. The Ki-81 multi-seat heavy fighter development did not progress beyond the project stage.

Kawasaki Ki-48

Kawasaki Ki-48-1a

TYPE	DIMENSIONS						WEIGHT	PERFORMANCE				REMARKS
	span		*length*		*height*			*max speed*	*at height*	*service ceiling*	*combat range*	
	ft	*in*	*ft*	*in*	*ft*	*in*	*max t-o lb*	*mph*	*ft*	*ft*	*miles*	
Kawasaki Ki-45-Kai-C	49	3⅓	36	1	12	1⅝	12,125	336	19,685	32,808	746	
Kawasaki Ki-48-I	57	3¾	41	4	12	5½	13,338	298	11,483	31,168	1,491	Model 1
Kawasaki Ki-48-II	57	3¾	41	10	12	5½	14,881	314	18,373	32,808	1,491	Model 2

Kawasaki Ki-61-I Hien

Kawasaki Ki-61 Hien, Chinese Air Force

Kawasaki Ki-61-Ic Hien. Chinese Air Force

Kawasaki Ki-61 Hien (Flying Swallow)

Although widely believed at one time to be a licence-built version of the Messerschmitt Bf 109, the Ki-61 in fact owed nothing whatever to the German aircraft, although its design was based on the DB601A engine, for which Kawasaki had secured manufacturing rights in 1937.

To the JAAF's February 1940 specification, Dr Takeo Doi of Kawasaki produced two designs, the heavy Ki-60 fighter and the lightweight Ki-61. The Ki-60 performed well on test, but after the completion of three prototypes (the first was flown in March 1941) was discarded in favour of the more conventional Ki-61, whose performance was even better. The first of twelve basically similar prototypes of the latter design flew in December 1941, and the Ki-61 was extensively tested throughout the first half of 1942, including comparative tests with a Bf 109E and a captured Curtiss P-40E, in which the Japanese fighter proved superior to both. It was powered by the 1,100-hp Ha-40 liquid-cooled engine, a light-weight development by Japanese engineers of the DB601A.

Designated Type 3 fighter by the Army, the Hien entered production for the JAAF at Kawasaki's Gifu works in 1942, a total of 34 Ki-61-Is being delivered between August and the end of December. The initial series, somewhat under-armed with two fuselage 7·7-mm and two wing-mounted 12·7-mm guns, was followed hurriedly by the Ki-61-Ia (two 7·7-mm guns and two wing-mounted 20-mm Mausers); the Ki-61-Ib (four 12·7-mm); the Ki-61-Ic (two nose 12·7-mm and two 20-mm Ho-5s in the wings); and the Ki-61-Id (two 12·7-mm and two 30-mm in the wings.) Total production of the various Model 1s amounted to 2,654 machines.

The Hien (or "Tony" in the Pacific coding system) made its combat debut in the New Guinea theatre in April 1943, appearing subsequently as both an interceptor and convoy protector in the Rabaul area, in the defence of Manila and in the battle of Leyte Island. By the end of hostilities, it had been encountered in virtually every theatre of the Pacific war, and at one stage formed a major part of Japan's home defence fighter force.

The Hien was not without maintenance troubles in the field, chiefly on account of the rather unreliable Ha-40 engine. As early as September 1942, Kawasaki had made a move to remedy this with the evolution of the Ki-61-II, based on the upcoming Ha-140 in-line, which was to offer 1,450 hp. With a lengthened fuselage, 10 per cent more wing area and a modified cockpit hood, the first Model II was finished in August 1943; but due to teething troubles with the new engine and certain airframe weaknesses only a further seven were completed by January 1944.

In the following month the Ki-61-IIa appeared, retaining the Ha-140 power plant, but reverting to the original wing form. It incorporated the necessary structural strengthening and had an armament similar to the Model Ic. The Ki-61-IIb was similar, except in having four guns of 20-mm calibre; and 30 Model IIa/IIbs were built before production began to slow down, as the output of engines was not keeping pace with that of airframes. A further 374 airframes were completed, but only 99 of them received engines and between 30 and 40 of those were destroyed by air attack before they could be delivered to the JAAF.

It was this shortage of engines for the Hien airframes that led to the highly successful Ki-100 improvization, described separately; and the success of the Ki-100 obviated further development of the proposed Ki-61-III, which would have had an all-round-vision cockpit hood among other refinements.

Although the Hien was never popular with pilots, because of its unreliable engine, its fine performance at high altitude made it one of the most effective interceptors employed against the B-29 Superfortress. However, many Hien pilots achieved their "kills" by the use of *Tai-Atari* (Suicide Crash) methods, ramming their targets, rather than by using their guns.

Kawasaki Ki-100

Improvization is not popular among those whose task is to produce high-performance combat aircraft; and few would have envied the Kawasaki engineers the problem set them by the JAAF in November 1944, of allying a heavy radial engine, some 4-ft in diameter, with a slim fighter airframe, only $2\frac{1}{2}$-ft wide. Yet the resultant aircraft, as Allied bomber crews and their escorts learned to their cost in March 1945, turned out to be the best fighter used by the Japanese Army during the whole period of the Pacific war, superior even to the Nakajima Ki-84 Hayate.

The situation arose when Japan, desperately short of fighters for home defence, found itself with 275 Ki-61-II Hien airframes, vainly awaiting delivery of their Kawasaki Ha-140 in-line engines. It was decided to attempt to make them airworthy by installing 1,500-hp Mitsubishi Ha-112-II fourteen-cylinder radials – excellent engines, but hardly built to blend with the Hien's slender contours. Nevertheless, the Kawasaki design team got down to the problem, putting the outcome of their studies into effect on three trial airframes, the first of which flew on 1 February 1945. The results were a revelation to all concerned. The new machine, designated Ki-100-Ia or Type 5 fighter, surpassed the Ki-61 in speed, climb and general manoeuvrability, and had the further advantage of being easier to service in the field.

By the end of May, Kawasaki's factories at Gifu and Ichinomiya had successfully converted most of the powerless Ki-61s, and in June the plant at Gifu began production of the improved Ki-100-Ib, with a rear-vision cockpit canopy and other detail refinements. Eventually, 99 of this version were built from scratch for the JAAF, but air raids on the factory then put paid to further output of the fighter.

From March 1945 the Ki-100 (which was not allocated a wartime code-name) began to appear as a bomber interceptor in the areas around Chofu, Yokkaichi and Kyushu. Its ceiling was good enough to enable it to reach the high-flying B-29s and it proved itself equal or superior to contemporary US fighters. Armament consisted of two 20-mm and two 12·7-mm guns, the former in the wings and the latter in the upper cowling of the engine. The Ki-100 was also capable of carrying a pair of underwing 550-lb bombs, though little, if any, use was made of this facility.

In March 1945, following the encouraging results achieved with the early Ki-100-Is, development was started of a Ki-100-II model with a boosted and turbo-supercharged version of the Mitsubishi Ha-112-IIru engine, for better performance at B-29 altitudes. It was planned to begin series production of this model in September; but by VJ-day only three prototypes had been flown. They demonstrated that, despite a higher all-up weight, the new model had a 30-mph higher speed than its predecessor at 30,000 ft.

Kawasaki Ki-102

As a step in the continued development of the Ki-45 fighter, the Japanese Army decided in August 1943 that the single-seat derivative of the Ki-45-II, known as the Ki-96, should be modified into a two-seat attack aircraft. The project was given the JAAF designation Ki-102. Three prototypes were ordered, and the first of these made its maiden flight in March 1944, followed by a pre-production batch of 20 before series production of the type, as the Ki-102B anti-shipping attack aircraft, began in October.

The Ki-102B was impressively armed, with a 57-mm cannon (with 150 shells and a firing rate of 80 rpm) and

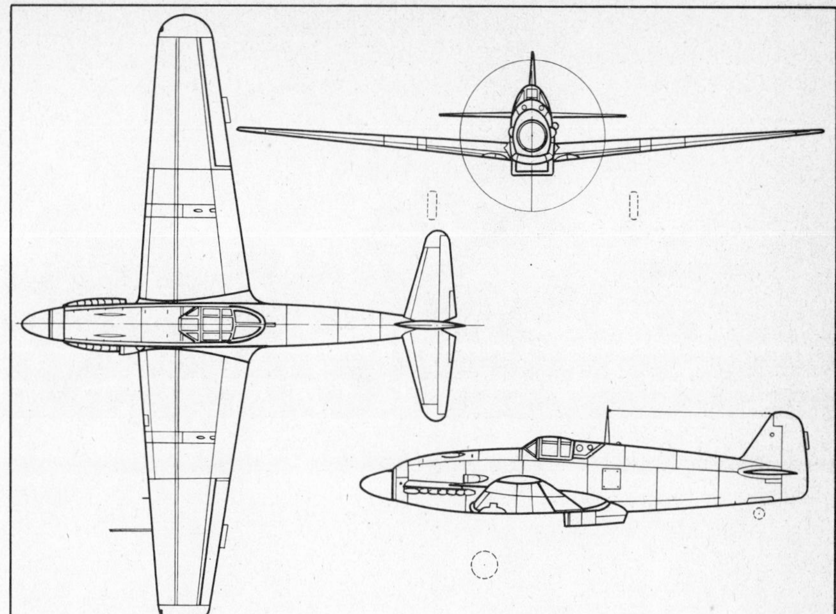

Kawasaki Ki-61 Hien

Kawasaki Ki-100-Ib

Kawasaki Ki-96, third prototype

TYPE	DIMENSIONS						WEIGHT	PERFORMANCE				REMARKS
	span		length		height		max t-o	max speed	at height	service ceiling	combat range	
	ft	in	ft	in	ft	in	lb	mph	ft	ft	miles	
Kawasaki Ki–61–Ia	39	4½	29	4	12	1⅝	7,650	348	16,404	32,808	1,118 max	Model 1A
Kawasaki Ki–61–IIa	39	4½	30	0⅝	12	1⅝	8,433	379	19,685	36,089	994	Model 2A
Kawasaki Ki–100–Ia	39	4½	28	11¼	12	3⅝	7,705	367	19,685	37,729	1,243	Model 1A

Kawasaki Ki-102B

Kawasaki Ki-102

Kawasaki P-2J

Kawasaki P-2J

two 20-mm cannon concentrated in the nose, and a 12·7-mm machine-gun in the rear cockpit firing obliquely upward to the rear. Underwing attachment points could carry two 550-lb bombs.

Before the aircraft (code-named "Randy" by the Allies) entered service, one of the pre-production Ki-102Bs on a test flight from Tachikawa ran into a B-29 formation, and with a single shot from its heavy cannon demolished an engine of one of the bombers. This was doubly encouraging, for by now the JAAF had decided to develop a high-altitude interceptor version of the Ki-102, and six of the pre-production machines were modified to this end, the first flying in June 1944.

Chief outward differences lay in the abbreviated blister-shaped canopy (hence eliminating the rear-firing 12·7-mm gun), revision of the fin and rudder to more rounded contours, and the fitting of turbo-superchargers to the 1,500-hp Mitsubishi Ha-112-IIru radial engines. Designated Ki-102A, the high-altitude fighter variant ran into difficulties with its power plant and, although given priority status in November 1944, only 15 production aircraft reached the JAAF before VJ-day.

Main production continued to centre on the Ki-102B, which entered service about the turn of the year to supplement the Ki-45, J1N1-S and P1Y1-S extempore defensive fighters that were trying to cope with mounting US bombing attacks against the Japanese homeland. At this stage, consideration was given to developing the design as a night fighter, and two Ki-102C aircraft were completed with this in view. They were based on the Ki-102B, but differed in having a greater length and wing span, crude AI radar, and twin fixed 20-mm cannon amidships, firing forward and upward. Further production proved impossible, owing to the severe damage to Japanese aircraft factories caused by the very raiders the Ki-102C was intended to forestall. Total Ki-102 production, including prototypes, amounted to 218 aircraft.

One other variant appeared before VJ-day: the Ki-108. This represented a further attempt to evolve a high-altitude interceptor from the basic design, and two Ki-102Bs were rebuilt as Ki-108 prototypes in the late summer of 1944. Their specially designed pressure cabins proved satisfactory but, inevitably, the Ki-108 was attended by the same supercharger troubles that beset the Ki-102A. Although two further prototypes were tested in the spring and early summer of 1945 – Ki-108-Kais, based on the larger Ki-102C – no decision had been taken to build the type in quantity by the time of the Japanese surrender.

Kawasaki P-2J

In October 1960, Kawasaki began work on a modernized development of the Lockheed P2V-7 Neptune to provide the JMSDF with a modern anti-submarine patrol aircraft in the late 1960s and early 1970s. The project, developed by Kawasaki in co-operation with the JMSDF, bore the company designation GK-210A, and a prototype was completed at Kawasaki's Gifu factory in the early summer of 1966. This aircraft, a converted P-2H (formerly P2V-7) airframe, was flown for the first time on 21 July 1966. Known originally as the P2V-Kai (= modified), it was later redesignated P-2J to conform to current US practice.

The P-2J differs from the P-2H principally in power plant and internal equipment, flight performance of the two models being virtually the same. Two Japanese-built General Electric T64-IHI-10 turboprops, each developing 2,850 shp and driving a three-blade Hamilton Standard propeller, constitute the P-2J's main power plant, auxiliary power being provided by two 3,085 lb s t J3-IHI-7C turbojets in underwing pods.

Other external differences compared with the original P-2H include a 4 ft 2 in longer front fuselage, to offset which the rudder area is increased. The enlarged fuselage houses an additional crew member, a crew rest room, increased fuel and a range of ASW equipment comparable to that carried by the P-3 Orion. This includes APS-80 search radar, Julie echo-ranging and Jezebel long-range sonobuoy equipment, and a magnetic anomaly detector. Despite these changes, the gross weight of the P-2J is some 8,000 lb lighter than that of the P-2H.

The prototype P-2J (serial 4637) was delivered to the JMSDF for service trials on 14 November 1966, and current plans call for delivery of the first six production aircraft during the 1969 fiscal year, followed by 12 each in FY 1970 and FY 1971, and a further 24 after this.

Kyushu Q1W Tokai (Eastern Sea)

In an effort to reduce the depredations by Allied submarines near the Japanese homeland in the latter half of World War II, the JNAF issued a specification for a modest, simply designed coastal patrol aircraft, able to locate and dispose of these boats. One result was the Kyushu (formerly Watanabe) Q1W1.

With a crew of three clustered in a bulbous and heavily-glazed nose, the Q1W, known to the Allies as "Lorna", could carry two 550-lb bombs or depth charges under the wings and was capable of dive attacks on its target, using its large slotted flaps as air-brakes. Its low speed was quite adequate for low-level visual searching, and if attacked the Q1W could protect itself with one 20-mm and one 7·7mm gun.

There were two variants, the Q1W1 with primitive search radar and the Q1W2 with magnetic detection gear. The Kyushu company built a total of 153 of these models but they did not reach JNAF squadrons until 1945, and spent only the last few months of the war patrolling Japanese territorial waters and the Korean Strait. Each was powered by two 610-hp Hitachi Tempu 31 radials.

A wooden variant was planned as an operational trainer for the Ginga attack bomber, but not built.

Mitsubishi 1MF and 2MR

It was in February 1921 that the Mitsubishi Internal Combustion Engine Manufacturing Co invited Herbert Smith of Sopwith, together with seven engineers, to its Nagoya plant to initiate the design of a shipboard fighter. Prior to this, the JNAF had used the Gloster Sparrowhawk, flown from special platforms over the gun turrets of battleships like the *Yamashiro*; but now its first carrier, the *Hosho*, was under construction.

The single-seat prototype fighter, completed in October 1921, proved a complete success at the official trials held in November. It was ordered into production, with the JNAF designation Type 10 shipboard fighter (1MF1), the "Type 10" indicating the tenth year (1921) of the reign of the Emperor Taisho. The *Hosho* was launched in November 1921, and at the end of February 1923 the first take-off and landing were made by the 1MF1, with Mitsubishi's British test pilot, Captain Jordan, at the controls. For his achievement Jordan was awarded a 10,000-yen prize by the company. A few days later, at the beginning of March, 1st Lieutenant Shun-Ichi Kira of the IJN, flying a 1MF1, became the first Japanese airman to perform a similar feat.

Squadron delivery began later in 1923, and the Type 10 fighter remained in service for the next six years. Indeed, production continued until December 1928, by which time 128 aircraft had been built. These included a number of variants: those with a honeycomb radiator were designated Type 10-1, and those with a Lamblin radiator Type 10-2. The 1MF1A had increased wing area; the 1MF2 an enlarged tailplane; the 1MF3 a Lamblin

Kyushu Q1W1 Tokai

Kyushu Q1W1 Tokai

Mitsubishi 1MF1

TYPE	DIMENSIONS						WEIGHT	PERFORMANCE				REMARKS
	span		length		height		max t-o	max speed	at height	service ceiling	combat range	
	ft	in	ft	in	ft	in	lb	mph	ft	ft	miles	
Kawasaki Ki–102A	51	1	37	6¾	12	1⅝	15,763	360	32,808	42,650	1,243	
Kawasaki Ki–102B	51	1	37	6¾	12	1⅝	16,094	360	19,685	32,808	1,243	
Kawasaki P–2J	103	10	95	10	29	4	71,800 approx	NA	NA	NA	NA	
Kyushu Q1W1	52	6	39	8	13	6⅛	11,755	200	4,396	14,731	814	Model 11
Mitsubishi 1MF1	30	6	21	11¾	9	6⅛	2,513	140	6,562	22,966	2½ hrs. max	

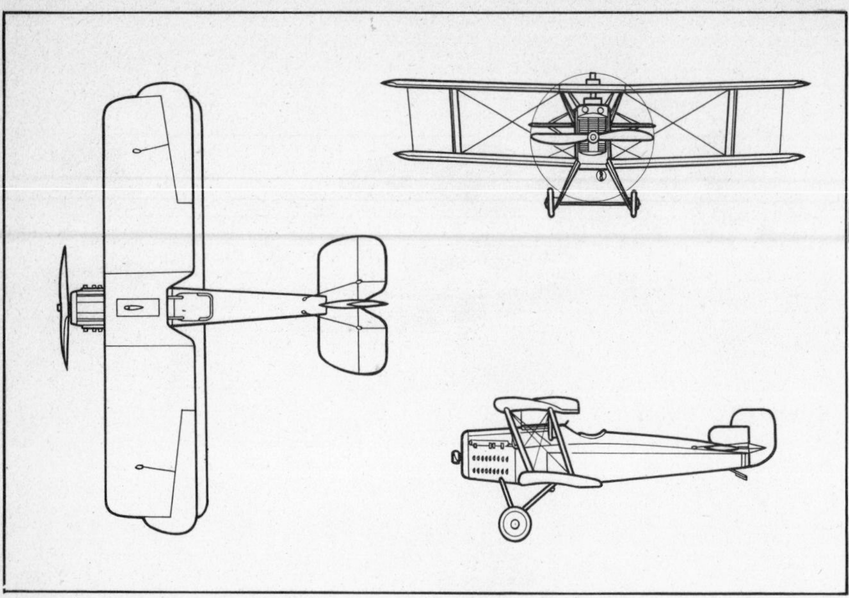
Mitsubishi 1MF1

Mitsubishi 1MT1N

Mitsubishi B1M

radiator; the 1MF4 had a cockpit sited further forward; the 1MF5A was a fighter trainer, with increased wing area, and was equipped with a torpedo-shaped float and jettisonable landing gear for emergency ditching. Power plant of the 1MF series was a 300-hp Hispano-Suiza engine; armament comprised two forward-firing 7·7-mm machine-guns mounted in the upper front fuselage.

The Type 10 carrier-based reconnaissance aircraft, also designed by Herbert Smith, was a two-seater based on the 1MF series and designated 2MR1/3. A total of 159 aircraft of this type were built during 1922–30.

Mitsubishi 1MT

One of three Navy Type 10 shipboard aircraft designed by Herbert Smith and manufactured by Mitsubishi for the Japanese Navy (the other two were the 1MF fighter and 2MR reconnaissance aircraft), the 1MT1 was the only triplane ever adopted by the Japanese air services; it was also the first nationally-built torpedo-bomber flown by the JNAF. Heavily strutted, it was a single-seater with a wide-track main undercarriage designed to give ample clearance to the torpedo when launched.

The prototype was completed at Nagoya in August 1922, and was flown for the first time by a British pilot, Captain Jordan. In November of the same year this machine, the 1MT1N, which was powered by a Napier Lion engine of 450 hp, and the second prototype (1MT1L), with a 370-hp Lorraine, underwent comparative trials at the JNAF test centre at Kasumigaura. The Napier-powered model was selected for production; but only 20 were built. Each carried an 18-in (1,765-lb) torpedo, but had no other armament.

Mitsubishi B1M

The Navy Type 13 shipboard attack aircraft (B1M1/3), or Mitsubishi 2MT1/2MT3, was the last product of Herbert Smith's design team at Mitsubishi for the JNAF. It was the first Japanese aircraft which could be operated in naval torpedo attack, bombing and reconnaissance rôles. Design, performance and serviceability were excellent, and the B1M series remained in service as the mainstay of the Japanese carrier force until 1938.

The first prototype of the 2MT1 (B1M1) was completed in January 1923 and was adopted as the Navy Type 13 (13th year of Emperor Taisho) in that year, as a replacement for the Type 10 torpedo-bomber (1MT1). Between 1924 and 1933 a total of 442 were built, including 197 B1M1s (2MT1/3 or Type 13-1), 115 B1M2s (2MT4/5 or Type 13-2) and 128 B1M3s (2MT2 or Type 13-3); the Hiro Naval Arsenal manufactured 40 of the last type. A land-based variant, designated 2MB1, was adopted by the Army as the Type 87 light bomber in 1927.

The major variants differed chiefly in power plant, the B1M1 having a 450-hp Napier Lion, while the B1M2 and M3 were equipped with Mitsubishi-built Hispano-Suiza engines of the same power. Bomb-load consisted of one 18-in (1,765-lb) torpedo or 1,070 lb of bombs. Armament of the B1M1 comprised two 7·7-mm machine-guns on a swivel mounting; that of the B1M3 consisted of two fixed forward-firing 7·7-mm guns and two more on a swivel mounting. The B1M1 and B1M2 were two-seat aircraft; the B1M3 had three seats.

The B1M was the first Japanese military aircraft to see aerial combat when, on 22 February 1932, three B1M3s, escorted by three Type 13-2 fighters, jointly shot down a Boeing P-12 fighter piloted by American Robert Short. This fight took place over Soochow, near Shanghai.

The prototype 2MT4 Ohtori (Phoenix) was one of three types evaluated by the JNAF in 1925 for reconnaissance floatplane duties; but all three were rejected. The 2MT5 Tora (Tiger), or Type 13-2 Model 2, was more successful, 115 being built by 1929 as reconnaissance-bombers.

Mitsubishi 2MB1

First home-produced light bomber of the Japanese Army Air Force, the Mitsubishi 2MB1 (designed by Dr Matsubara) was entered for a design contest held in 1925 for an experimental light bomber based on an Army specification. Other contestants included a Kawasaki two-seater designed by Dr Richard Vogt and his team (which was withdrawn), and the Mitsubishi 2MB2 Washi (Eagle) sesquiplane designed by Dr Baumann.

The 2MB1, which was essentially a land-based version of Mitsubishi's Type 13 (B1M) shipboard attack aircraft, won the competition, despite the ambitious design of the other machines. The prototype was completed in March 1926 and differed from the Type 13 in the following ways: a Hispano-Suiza engine of 450 hp, driving a metal propeller, replaced the 450-hp Napier engine with wooden propeller; a honeycomb radiator was mounted in front of the engine; wing-folding mechanism was discarded; dihedral was eliminated from the upper wing; seating was reduced from three to two; dual controls were provided; and fuel tankage was increased from 83·8 gallons to 132 gallons.

The 2MB1 entered production and service in 1927 as the Army Type 87 light bomber ("Type 87" here indicating the Japanese calendar year 2587, or 1927 AD); by 1929 a total of 48 had been built. They saw action in the initial stages of the Manchurian fighting, armed with one 7·7-mm machine-gun in the fuselage, and three more on swivel mountings – two in a dorsal and one in a ventral position. A bomb-load of 1,100 lb could be carried.

One machine, specially equipped with an additional 176-gallon belly tank and a 22-gallon fuselage tank, flew non-stop from Kagoshima to Taipei, a distance of 881 miles.

Mitsubishi Ki-20

In 1928 Mitsubishi acquired licence rights to build the K-51, a bomber development of the Junkers G-38 civil transport. Manufacture of this machine, which had a far larger wing area than any so far built in Japan, was conducted in strict secrecy, under Army instructions.

Mitsubishi sent staff engineers to the Junkers plant late in 1928, and again in the spring of 1930, to study the basic design and to arrange for supply of the necessary jigs, tools, materials and machinery to start manufacture. Junkers engineers were also invited to Mitsubishi to collaborate in developing the Japanese version.

Essentially similar to the K-51, but with two dorsal gun positions at the trailing-edge of the wing and a different power plant, the first Ki-20 was completed in 1931, its maiden flight being carried out secretly at Kagamigahara Army airfield. The second and third machines were built in 1932, the fourth in 1933, and the fifth and sixth in 1934. The first two were assembled from materials purchased from Germany; the third included only a proportion of imported components; the remaining machines were of all-Japanese manufacture. The engines of the first four Ki-20s, lost in the gigantic wing, were Junkers L. 88s, each of 800 hp; the last two aircraft were powered by Junkers Jumo-4 diesel engines of 720 hp. At a later date these engines were interchanged and the type was also used as a test-bed for the Kawasaki Ha-9 engine.

Adopted by the Army in 1932 as the Type 92 heavy bomber, the Ki-20 had a wing span 3 ft greater, and a wing area double that of the Boeing B-29 Superfortress of ten years later. In its day it was the world's second largest military aircraft. But by the time the test programme was completed it was apparent that "The Monster", as the Ki-20 became known, was unsuitable for operational service, which dashed the Army's hopes of a long-range strategic bomber capable of attacking the Philippines, from Taiwan, and Siberia.

Mitsubishi 2MB1

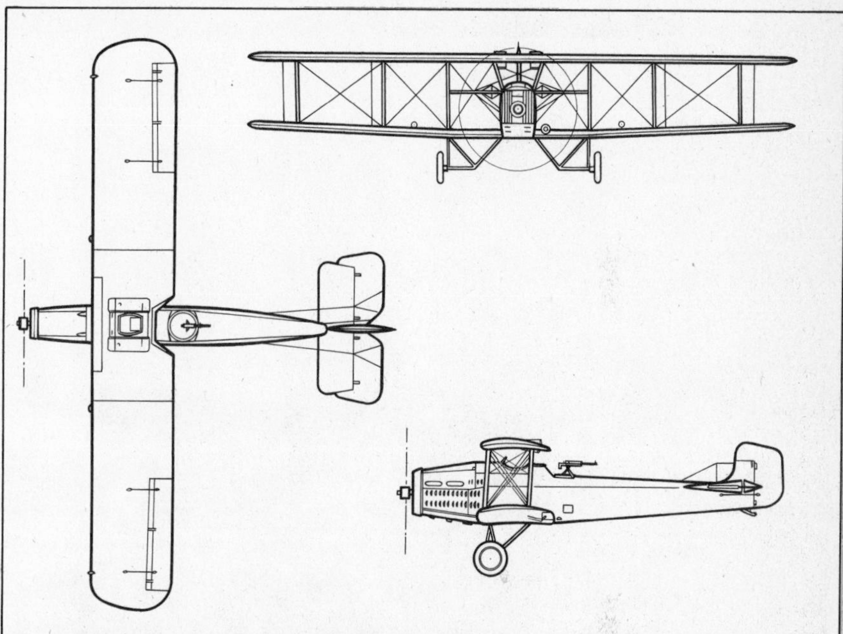

Mitsubishi 2MB1

Mitsubishi Ki-20

TYPE	DIMENSIONS						WEIGHT	PERFORMANCE				REMARKS
	span		length		height		max t-o	max speed	at height	service ceiling	combat range	
	ft	in	ft	in	ft	in	lb	mph	ft	ft	miles	
Mitsubishi 1MT1	42	6	32	1	14	7½	5,512	127	10,007	19,685	2⅓ hrs. max	
Mitsubishi B1M1	48	5½	32	0⅝	NA		5,946	130	NA	NA	2½ hrs.	Model 1
Mitsubishi 2MB1	48	7	32	10	NA		7,278	115	NA	14,000	3hrs. max	
Mitsubishi Ki–20	144	4¼	76	1⅓	22	11½	50,400 approx	124	NA	NA	1,864	

Mitsubishi B2M1

Mitsubishi Ki-2-1

Mitsubishi Ki-2-2

The Ki-20 carried a crew of ten and was armed with one 20-mm cannon and eight 7·7-mm machine-guns, mounted in six barbettes. Standard bomb-load was 4,400 lb, with a maximum load of 11,000 lb. In squadron service great difficulty was experienced in maintaining the engines, and although the giant bombers were flown in both Japan and Manchuria, they were never used in action.

Existence of the Ki-20 was revealed to the public when three of them joined the formation fly-past for the great military review held in Tokyo in January 1940.

Mitsubishi B2M

In February 1928 the Imperial Japanese Navy issued a specification for a replacement for the B1M (Type 13 shipboard attack aircraft) which, though popular, was of wooden construction. Four manufacturers were asked to take part in the contest – Aichi, Kawanishi, Nakajima and Mitsubishi. To ensure success, Mitsubishi assigned the preliminary design to three British design teams, namely, Blackburn (3MR4, with 600-hp Mitsubishi Hispano-Suiza engine), Handley Page (3MR5, with 650-hp Mitsubishi Hispano-Suiza) and a team headed by Herbert Smith (3MR3, with 650-hp Armstrong Siddeley Leopard). In the event, only the Blackburn design was submitted to the JNAF, and this was adopted in 1928.

The prototype was built by Blackburn, and delivered to Japan in February 1930. G. E. Petty, Blackburn's chief engineer, also arrived in Japan to supervise the manufacture of further examples. There were teething troubles with the second and third machines, but the fourth, incorporating various modifications, finally achieved the required performance.

In March 1932, the three-seat B2M1 was adopted as the Navy Type 89-1, and entered production. (The designation system based on the Japanese calendar replaced the former practice used by the Navy and continued unchanged from 1929 until the end of World War II. The Army had adopted the same system from Type 87 in 1927).

The B2M1 was the first naval attack aircraft with an all-metal basic structure, but suffered from poor serviceability. In 1934 a major modification resulted in the B2M2 (Type 89-2), and a total of 204 B2M1/2s were built between 1930 and 1935. They remained in service longer than anticipated, with the result that a small number of these aircraft saw action during the "Shanghai Incident", together with some B1M1s. Their bomb or torpedo capacity was similar to that of the B1M, and they were armed with two 7·7-mm machine-guns.

Mitsubishi Ki-2

In January 1932, a Junkers K-37 bomber was donated to the Japanese Army and, as the Aikoku (Patriot) No. 1, saw active service in Manchuria. It was clearly superior to the Mitsubishi Type 87 (2MB1) and Kawasaki Type 88 light bombers, then in front-line service. So, in September 1932, the JAAF ordered Mitsubishi to produce a prototype bomber based on the K-37.

The specification called for a bomber able to carry from 660 to 1,100 lb of bombs; and fuel sufficient for a 4½-hour flight, cruising at 149 mph at 10,000 ft. Performance requirements were a maximum endurance of 6 hours with no bomb-load; an operational altitude of 6,500 to 10,000 ft; a service ceiling of 23,000 ft; a maximum speed of 161 mph; an all-up weight not exceeding 9,475 lb; and accommodation for a crew of three. Adequate manoeuvrability to permit vertical turns was required, and the power plant specified was two Nakajima-built air-cooled radial engines of 450 hp.

With the Ki-20 "super-bomber" and Ki-1 heavy bomber behind them, Mitsubishi had the experience to design and manufacture a bomber of the Junkers all-metal type, and recommended that the prototype should have an oval-shaped nose barbette, an oleo-strut undercarriage – with an eye to a future retractable landing gear – and two of the new Mitsubishi A-4 engines; but in November 1932 the Army declined these proposals.

The first Ki-2, conforming to the original specification,

was completed in May 1933, two months ahead of schedule, and when tested at Kagamigahara proved to have a top speed of 156 mph at 10,000 ft, and remarkable handling characteristics. Unfortunately one engine developed trouble and when the pilot attempted an emergency landing the aircraft stalled and the rear fuselage was damaged. In order to provide a maximum field of fire for the dorsal guns, as requested by the Army, the rear fuselage had been made very slender in this first prototype. Following the accident, the second machine had a rear fuselage similar to that of the Junkers K-37, and this version was adopted in 1933 as the Army Type 93 twin-engined light bomber.

A total of 113 Ki-2-1s were built up to 1936, after which production switched to a developed version, the Ki-2-2. This differed from the earlier machine in having Type 95 air-cooled radial engines of 550 hp; a retractable undercarriage; an enclosed cabin for the pilot and gunner; an oval-section nose barbette; an internal bomb-bay for twenty 33-lb bombs; and other detail refinements. The Ki-2-2 was faster than the Ki-2-1 by 19 mph, and was in production from 1937 to 1938, a total of 61 being built.

Ki-2 bombers were used widely in the initial stages of the Sino-Japanese conflict, mainly in Manchuria and North China. Some were used later for training bomber crews, and a few survived until the outbreak of World War II, when they were given the Allied code name "Louise".

Mitsubishi A5M

The Mitsubishi A5M single-seat Navy fighter marked a notable step forward in Japanese aeronautical design, as it was the JNAF's first monoplane fighter and the first Japanese warplane in service to have full-scale landing flaps. The IJN requirement of 1934, to which it was designed, called for a land-based fighter to replace the ancient Type 90 and 95 biplanes then in Navy service. Jiro Horikoshi (responsible a year or two later for the Zero) decided to design a low-wing monoplane, of all-metal construction and employing, for the first time in Japan, a flush-riveted finish. The main undercarriage was to be of fixed cantilever design. One potential drawback to this layout was that the low wing might result in a rather poor downward view; to mitigate this, the first prototype had an inverted gull wing of semi-elliptical planform.

On its maiden flight from Kagamigahara airfield on 4 February 1935, the first A5M topped 270 mph, and within days had attained 279 mph – 61 mph higher than the speed demanded by the original specification. This was achieved on the power of a single 550-hp Nakajima Kotobuki 5, a bulky radial based on the Bristol Jupiter built under licence by Nakajima in preceding years.

Despite these encouraging results, the gull wing was not entirely satisfactory and the engine reduction gear also gave a certain amount of trouble. Hence, the second prototype appeared with a more conventional straight-tapered wing and was powered by a 560-hp Kotobuki 3 engine. An identical machine was evaluated by the Army Air Force as the Ki-18, but failed to gain any orders.

Performance of the Kotobuki 3 still left much to be desired, and various other possible alternatives, among them the Nakajima Hikari 1, were tried before the 585-hp Kotobuki 2-Kai-1 engine was chosen to power the production fighter. By now it had been decided to operate this from aircraft carriers, and it was as the A5M1, or Type 96 Model 11 carrier-based fighter, that it entered production.

Mitsubishi A5M4

Mitsubishi A5M2a

TYPE	DIMENSIONS span ft	span in	length ft	length in	height ft	height in	WEIGHT max t-o lb	PERFORMANCE max speed mph	at height ft	service ceiling ft	combat range miles	REMARKS
Mitsubishi B2M1	49	11	33	8	12	2	7,940	132	NA	14,304	1,104 max.	Model 1
Mitsubishi Ki-2-I	65	5⅞	41	4	15	2¼	10,031	140	NA	22,966	559 max.	Model 1
Mitsubishi A5M2a	35	6	25	7	10	6	3,545	265	10,000	14,026	460	Model 21

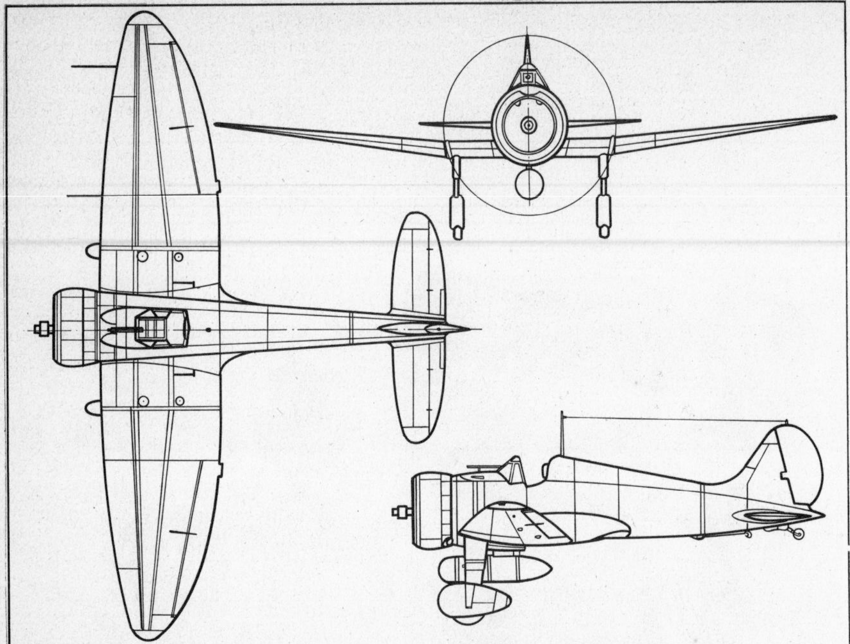

Mitsubishi A5M4

Mitsubishi G3M2

Mitsubishi G3M3

Comparatively few A5M1s were built before, from the 37th machine, they were replaced on the assembly line by the Model 21, or A5M2a. One of the two major combat versions, this featured "wash-out" at the wingtips, a slightly larger fin, and the extra power of the 610-hp Kotobuki 2-Kai-3 engine.

These were the models introduced into the Sino-Japanese conflict when, in September 1937, they embarked for Shanghai as part of the 2nd Combined Air Flotilla. The A5Ms carried out their first combat mission on 18 September, and their subsequent performance more than vindicated those who had supported the monoplane as the "new look" for fighter design. On 2 December the A5Ms had a field day, destroying no fewer than ten Russian I-16Bs in an engagement over Nanking. They flew at first from their parent carriers, but later also from captured airfields on the Chinese mainland. One pilot, Flt-Lt Kashimura, lost two-thirds of his port wing in air combat, but was able to return to base, proving the durability of the aircraft in a startling manner!

Reports that some Navy pilots were frightened by the much higher speed of their new machines were probably exaggerated; but they certainly took a dislike to the enclosed cockpit of the next service variant, the A5M2b or Model 22. They had always been accustomed to open cockpits and, in any case, the field of vision for the pilot was already limited, without being further reduced by the installation of a hood. Hence the A5M2b (which had a 610-hp Kotobuki 3 and provision for two 66-lb underwing bombs) was withdrawn after a rather short service life.

Japanese interest in the Dewoitine D.510 led to the experimental installation of a 610-hp Hispano-Suiza 12Xcrs *moteur-canon* in-line engine in an A5M airframe, for comparative purposes; this version was designated A5M3a, Model 23. Competitive trials left the Japanese convinced that their own fighter was better, and its production continued in 1938 in the form of the A5M4 Models 24 and 34 (710-hp Kotobuki 41). A number of A5M4-Ks were also built as conversion trainers. The standard armament of all A5M fighters was two 7·7-mm machine-guns, mounted side-by-side over the engine immediately in front of the pilot's windscreen.

At the time of Pearl Harbor, A5M4s were the principal models still in service, though somewhat dated by the arrival of the A6M Zero. Nevertheless they were employed, in diminishing numbers, for the first six months or so of the Pacific war, being encountered in the Aleutians and other island groups, and allotted the Allied code-name "Claude". After this they were transferred to non-combat duties, some being utilized inside Japan as Zero transition trainers. Total A5M production reached nearly a thousand machines: about 200 were built by the Kyushu Aircraft Company and the Sasebo Naval Air Arsenal; the balance of 782 by the parent company.

Mitsubishi G3M

The Navy 9-*shi* (1934) competition for new equipment for the JNAF marked a big step forward for Japanese aviation, putting the weapons of its aerial services and the products of its aviation industry on a par with any in the western world. One of the new aircraft was the G3M Type 96 land-based attack bomber, which reflected much Junkers influence and the results of experience gained with the Hiro G2H1 bomber and its derivative, the Mitsubishi 8-*Shi* reconnaissance aircraft flown in April 1934.

Designed under the direction of Prof Kiro Honjo, the Ka-15, as the new bomber was designated temporarily, was an ugly yet streamlined mid-wing cantilever monoplane with twin fins and rudders, flush-riveted skin and a retractable undercarriage.

The first of 21 Ka-15s, flown in July 1935, had two 600-hp Hiro Type 91 water-cooled in-line engines, with which it achieved a level speed of 236 mph and a range in "clean" condition of 3,780 miles. Three more prototypes had Hiro engines, but others switched to 825-hp Kinsei 2 radials and early production G3M1s (Type 96 Model 11s), up to the twenty-first machine, were also powered by the latter engines. Subsequent aircraft (G3M1cs) had the Kinsei 3 of 840-hp, and this model also introduced a transparent bombing station in the nose. The circular-section fuselage housed a bomb-bay for a load of up to 1,765 lb, or a torpedo of similar weight could be slung externally.

Fifty-five G3M1 bombers were completed. Their original armament included a retractable ventral turret for two 7·7-mm guns; but severe buffeting of the turret when extended led to its replacement by a pair of waist blisters, with a single 7·7-mm machine-gun in each. Some G3M1s were also fitted with a "turtle-back" dorsal turret mounting two further guns of the same calibre.

The second, and major, version of the Type 96 was the G3M2, nearly 700 of which were built. About half of these (Model 21s) were powered by Kinsei 41 or 42 engines and the remainder (Model 22s) by 1,000-hp Kinsei 45s. The dorsal turret mounted a single 20-mm cannon.

The final bomber model was the G3M3, generally similar to the previous series but powered by 1,300-hp Mitsubishi Kasei 51 radials. About 360 G3M3s were built, bringing total production of the Type 96 bomber to 1,103 aircraft by early 1942. Many of these were built by Nakajima and some by the Hiro Navy Air Arsenal.

Only about a quarter of this total, mostly G3M2s and G3M3s, were in service at the time of Pearl Harbor when, with about 120 G4M1s, they formed the core of the Japanese long-range naval striking force. They had made their debut in the Sino-Japanese campaign, making world headlines with their trans-oceanic raids on Hankow and Nanking in August 1937 from bases in Kyushu and Formosa. The false assumption during the China war that the G3M could dispense with a fighter escort resulted in heavy losses. Additional fighter protection was urgently summoned from Japan, but in 1940 two G3Ms found themselves acting as escorts to China of the first two squadrons of A6M2 Zero fighters! The G3M airframe was very robust, and many pilots struggled back to their bases in severely crippled aircraft.

In World War II the G3M (code name "Nell") soon made headlines with the attack on HMS *Prince of Wales* and *Repulse* three days after Pearl Harbor, and was used subsequently in most Pacific theatres, throughout the war. A few improvized conversions into G3M2-L transports were made and used as paratroop transports during the invasion of Celebes island. More thorough conversions for this rôle, carried out by the Yokosuka Arsenal, produced the ten-seat L3Y1 (from G3M1d) and the L3Y2 (G3M2d), armed only with a single 7·7-mm gun.

Mitsubishi F1M

The Mitsubishi F1M, designed by Eitaro Sano, deserved more credit than it received. For an aircraft intended simply to provide spotting cover for Japanese warships, it had a remarkably varied career, serving throughout the war in the Far East from both ship and shore stations, in practically every theatre and in such widely-assorted rôles as area defence fighter, light bomber, anti-submarine aircraft, convoy escort and coastal patrol aircraft, as well as its basic function of reconnaissance.

The F1M (known by the Pacific code-name "Pete") had its origins as far back as September 1934, when the Japanese Navy called for a shipboard observation float-plane to succeed the Nakajima E8N ("Dave"). Mitsubishi's design for a compact, two-seat, single-bay biplane was selected, against competing entries from the Aichi and Kawanishi companies (F1A1 and F1K1 respectively), and work began on four prototypes (designated F1M1), the first of which was flown at Nagoya in June 1936.

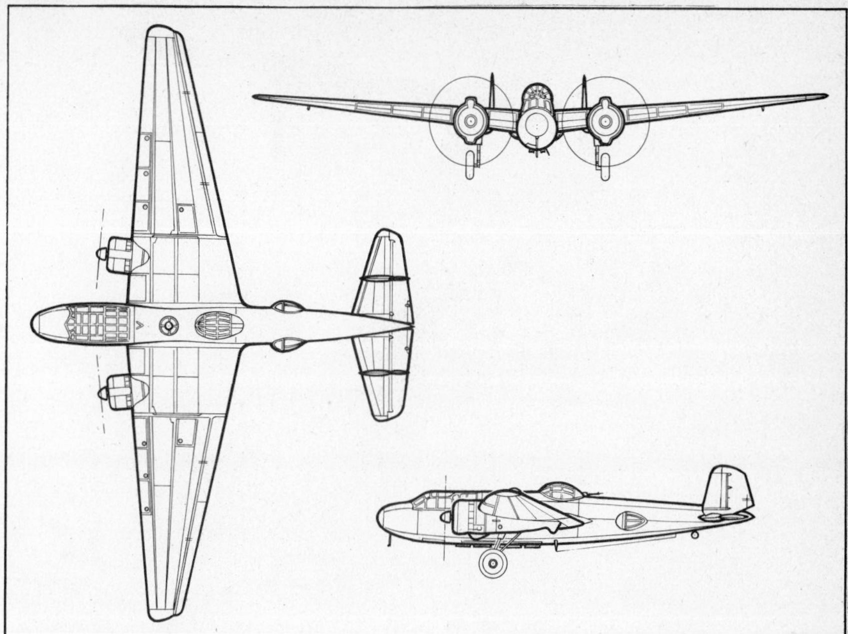

Mitsubishi G3M2

Mitsubishi F1M2

TYPE	DIMENSIONS span ft	span in	length ft	length in	height ft	height in	WEIGHT max t-o lb	PERFORMANCE max speed mph	at height ft	service ceiling ft	combat range miles	REMARKS
Mitsubishi A5M4	36	1	24	9½	10	6	3,763	273	9,840	32,150	746 max	Model 24
Mitsubishi G3M1	82	0¼	NA		NA		16,870	234	10,039	29,889	NA	Model 11
Mitsubishi G3M2	82	0¼	53	11⅝	11	11¾	22,707	236	13,714	29,889	2,902	Model 21
Mitsubishi G3M3	82	0¼	53	11⅝	11	11¾	22,707	258	19,357	33,727	3,828 max	Model 23

Mitsubishi F1M2

Mitsubishi Ki-30

Mitsubishi Ki-21-I

Mitsubishi Ki-21-II

Powered by a single 820-hp Nakajima Hikari 1 (Splendour) radial engine, the F1M1s revealed serious stability troubles during the early flight programme, and a prolonged series of modifications had to be undertaken before the JNAF would accept the type for service. These included a complete revision of the wing planform, from semi-elliptical to straight taper. The dihedral angle was increased; the fin and rudder area virtually doubled; the main and wing-tip floats were enlarged; and, in August 1938, the 875-hp Mitsubishi Zuisei 13 (Holy Star) 14-cylinder, air-cooled radial replaced the Hikari.

The effect of these modifications was to make the F1M a highly manoeuvrable warplane, with an excellent rate of climb (5 min 4 sec to 3,000 m); and in October 1939 the JNAF ordered it into production as the Type 0 Model 11 observation floatplane, or F1M2.

Last front-line biplane to serve with the Japanese Navy, the F1M2 entered service in 1941. It was lightly armed, with two fixed 7·7-mm machine-guns in the engine cowling and a third on a movable mounting in the rear cockpit. As a defensive fighter, the F1M2 was used in the battle of the Solomon Islands and at Attu in the Aleutians, achieving a number of successes; other actions in which the type was encountered included the battle of the Coral Sea (in which many were lost), and campaigns in the Philippines, New Guinea and the Marshall Islands. Attempts to equip the F1M2 with a single 550-lb bomb were unsuccessful, but "Pete" was seen frequently with a pair of 132-lb bombs suspended beneath the lower mainplane. It remained in production until March 1944, Mitsubishi building 524 F1M2s and the Sasebo Navy Arsenal completing about 180.

Mitsubishi Ki-30

The Mitsubishi Ki-30 was a contemporary of the Kawasaki Ki-32, both of these aircraft, together with the Ki-21 heavy bomber and Ki-27 fighter, being ordered as a result of the decision taken in 1935 to re-equip the JAAF with up-to-date combat types.

The general layout of the two light bombers followed a broadly similar pattern, save that the Mitsubishi design favoured the more traditional radial engine and was a true mid-wing monoplane. It was superior to the Ki-32, and among many design features novel for their time were an internal bomb-bay and wing flaps. It was powered by a 950-hp Ha-5 Zuisei 14-cylinder two-row radial engine with a variable-pitch propeller (another "new" feature), and despite its size was quite agile.

Like the Ki-32, the Ki-30 carried a crew of two under a long "greenhouse" canopy. One fixed 7·7-mm machine-gun fired forward, while the observer operated a similar gun on a movable mounting in the rear cockpit. The bomb-load was rather less than that of the Ki-32, but adequate: three 220-lb, six 110-lb or twenty 33-lb bombs.

The Ki-30 (first flown in February 1937) made its debut in the Sino-Japanese war, and was still in JAAF service during the early stages of World War II in the Pacific; though after the Philippines campaign of 1942 it was seen little on front-line duties. Production, as the Type 97 light bomber, began in 1938 and ran until 1941, Mitsubishi building 636 at its Nagoya factory and a further 68 being completed by the Tachikawa Army Air Arsenal. The code name "Ann" was given to the Ki-30 by the Allies.

Mitsubishi Ki-21

The Japanese Army's heavy bomber specification issued in February 1936 was an exacting one. It called for a four-seater, with a five-hour endurance, 1,650-lb bomb-load and top speed of 250 mph at 10,000 ft. Mitsubishi's Ki-21 design won the competition from the Nakajima Ki-19, and the first of five prototypes was completed in November 1936. Performance, with two 850-hp Kinsei Ha-6 radials, was well above specification, but the field of fire from the guns was poor. This was remedied on later prototypes and, subject to use of the 850-hp Nakajima Ha-5-Kai engine, the aircraft was adopted by the JAAF as the Ki-21-Ia, or Type 97 heavy bomber.

The Type 97 entered service later in 1937, serving almost throughout the "Chinese Incident". Its production was assigned also to Nakajima, who delivered their first Ki-21s in August 1938. Combat experience gained in China led to several modifications being made. These included an enlarged bomb-bay, wing flaps of greater area, increased armour protection for the crew and an increase in defensive armament from three to five or six 7·7-mm guns, including a remotely-controlled tail gun. With these improvements, the type became known as the Ki-21-Ib or Model 1B, which outnumbered the Model 1A in service during the China war.

In November 1939, Mitsubishi began development of the Model 2A, or Ki-21-IIa, which had a wider-span tailplane and 1,490-hp Ha-101 engines.

By the time of Pearl Harbor, the various versions of the Ki-21 were standard front-line bombers with the JAAF, taking part in operations in Burma (where they were severely handled by British Hurricanes), Hong Kong, India, Malaya, the Netherlands East Indies and the Philippines. The Allies gave them the code-name "Sally"; but the name "Gwen" was applied temporarily to the last production variant, the Ki-21-IIb, until it was recognized as a version of "Sally". The IIb had been produced because, although use of the Ha-101 engine vastly improved the bomber's performance, it was still inadequately armed; in the Model 2B the rear cockpit "glasshouse" was eliminated to make room for a dorsal turret mounting a 12·7-mm machine-gun.

With the arrival in service of the Model 2B, many of the earlier Ki-21-I series of bombers became relegated to training duties, or were converted into military or civil (M.C.21) transports. Bomb-load of the Ki-21-IIb was 2,200 lb. However, as the war progressed the range and bomb capacity of the aircraft could not match up to increasing demands and after 1943 it began to be replaced by more modern types. Production terminated in September 1944 with 2,064 Ki-21s built, 351 of these by Nakajima (up to February 1941). A projected Ki-21-III was discarded in favour of the Ki-67 Hiryu. Near the end of World War II, nine Ki-21s were prepared at Kyushu as assault transports, for landing demolition troops on Okinawa; but only one of these reached its target.

Mitsubishi B5M1

The Mitsubishi B5M1 was a contender for the same JNAF specification, for a carrier-based attack aircraft, that produced the Nakajima B5N1. Both companies decided to reject a biplane layout in favour of a low-wing, all-metal monoplane; but any resemblance between the two types ended there. The Mitsubishi machine had wings of a semi-elliptical planform, which were fitted with slotted flaps and folded manually for stowage on board ship; the main wheels of its fixed landing gear were shrouded by enormous "spats", comparable with those of the British Lysander A neat cowling encased the 1,000-hp Kinsei 43 radial engine, and the three-man crew was accommodated beneath a long "greenhouse" canopy. A large-area fin and rudder helped to give the fuselage of the B5M1 a strong external resemblance to the Douglas DB-8.

The Mitsubishi machine's capabilities were almost identical with those of the B5N1 – indeed, its take-off performance was better, and it could carry the same load of one 1,765-lb torpedo or an equivalent weight of bombs. A single 7·7-mm gun was situated in the rear cockpit.

Mitsubishi Ki-21-IIb

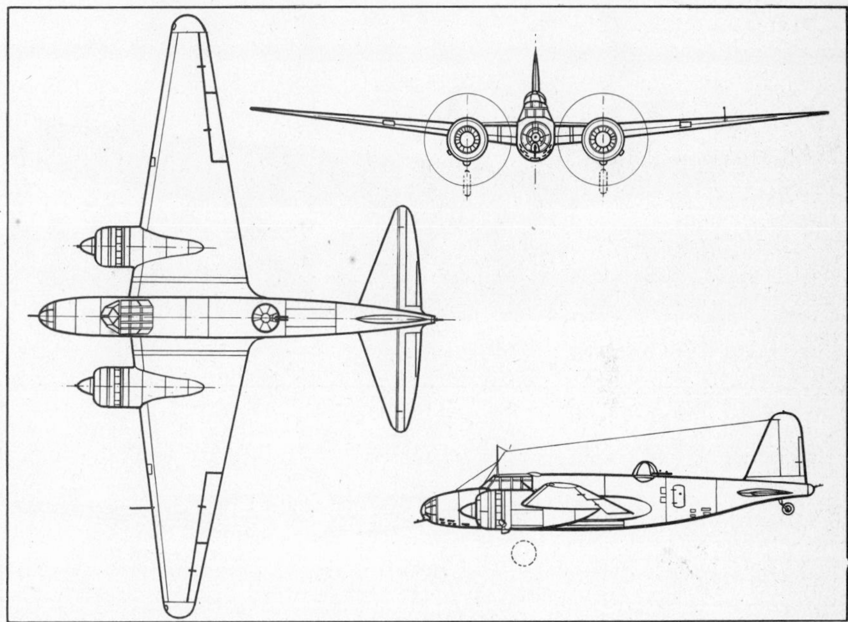

Mitsubishi Ki-21-IIb

Mitsubishi B5M1

TYPE	DIMENSIONS						WEIGHT	PERFORMANCE				REMARKS
	span ft	span in	length ft	length in	height ft	height in	max t-o lb	max speed mph	at height ft	service ceiling ft	combat range miles	
Mitsubishi F1M2	36	1	31	2	13	1½	6,296	230	9,843	30,971	276	Model 11
Mitsubishi Ki-30	47	8⅞	33	11	11	11¾	7,324	263	13,120	28,117	1,056	Model 1
Mitsubishi Ki-21-Ia	73	9⅞	52	6	14	3¼	16,517	269	13,120	28,215	1,678	Model 1A
Mitsubishi Ki-21-IIa	73	9⅞	52	6	15	11	NA	251	13,120	32,808	NA	Model 2A
Mitsubishi Ki-21-IIb	73	9⅞	52	6	15	11	21,407	297	13,120	32,808	1,350	Model 2B
Mitsubishi B5M1	50	2⅓	33	9½	14	2	8,819	235	8,038	27,100	1,460	Model 2

Mitsubishi A6M3 Model 22 Zero-Sen

Mitsubishi A6M3 Model 32 Zero-Sen

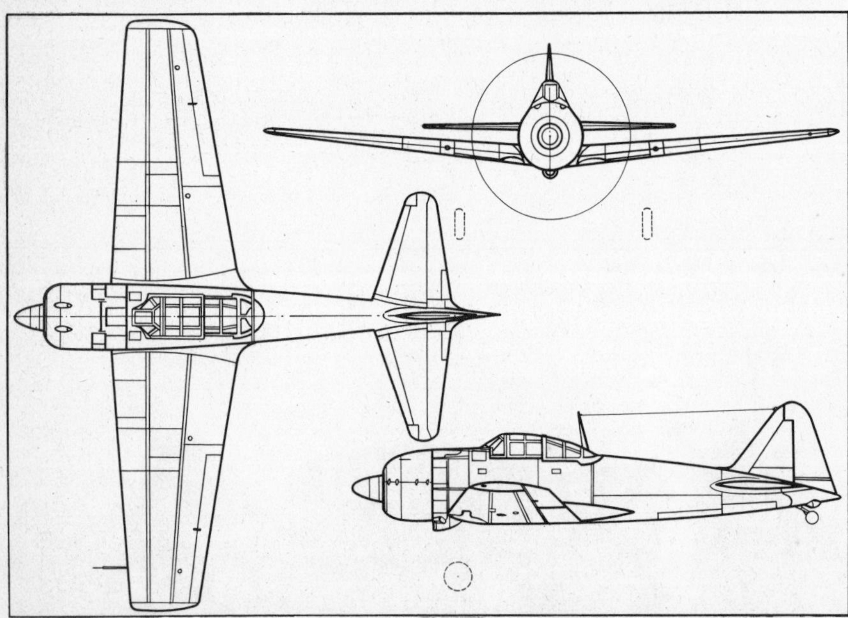
Mitsubishi A6M3 Model 32 Zero-Sen

Mitsubishi A6M5 Model 52 Zero-Sen

The Nakajima design was preferred by the JNAF; but as it incorporated so many advanced features the Navy decided to guard against possible failure by ordering a quantity of B5M1s as well. Thus, the B5M1 entered production in 1937 as the Type 97 Model 2 (the Nakajima machine being the Model 1), and a total of 125 were built by the parent company before the Navy decided to end B5M production in order to leave Mitsubishi free to concentrate on the G3M and A5M. They saw service as attack aircraft during the Sino-Japanese war and were also employed, then and later, on coastal patrol missions.

Mitsubishi A6M Zero-Sen

Notwithstanding the exacting terms of the 12-*Shi* (1937) Navy specification for a new carrier-based fighter, it is doubtful if either the JNAF or the Mitsubishi Jukogyo K.K. could have foreseen the prolonged production and service career of this most famous of all Japanese warplanes, which stemmed from it.

When the Navy requirements were issued in October 1937, calling for a fast (310 mph), light, manoeuvrable fighter with a twin-cannon, twin-machine-gun armament, they were exacting enough to cause the withdrawal of Nakajima from the competition. Under chief designer Jiro Horikoshi, the Mitsubishi company accepted the challenge and produced a clean, light and highly-agile low-wing monoplane prototype – the A6M1.

Two A6M1s were built, each with a 780-hp Zuisei 13 two-row radial engine, two 7·7-mm fuselage-mounted machine-guns and two 20-mm wing cannon. The first of these was flown by Katsuzo Shima on 1 April 1939. With an engine change to the 925-hp Nakajima Sakae 12, the fighter went into production as the Type 0 carrier-based fighter, or A6M2 Model 11, in 1940. Prior to official acceptance by the JNAF at the end of July, fifteen A6M2s were despatched to the Chinese front for evaluation under operational conditions, and here the Zero-Sen (Zero (Type 0) Fighter) swept all opposition before it, such was its superiority over all the opposing types.

After 64 Model 11 Zeros had been built, the A6M2 Model 21 followed them on the production line at Nagoya from November 1940, and was also built in substantial numbers in Nakajima's Koizumi factory. The Model 21 featured folding wingtips and (except for the first 62 aircraft) mass-balanced ailerons, which improved the fighter's manoeuvrability. It was this version of the Zero which was the principal service model at the time of Pearl Harbor, although six months previously the A6M3 Model 32 had made its first appearance. Similar at first to the A6M2, except for its 1,300-hp Sakae 21 engine, with two-speed supercharger, the A6M3 failed to meet its performance requirements; so the wings were "clipped", by the simple expedient of removing the foldable tip portions. This reduced the fighter's agility in the air and the full-size wing, in non-folding form, was replaced to produce the A6M3 Model 22. The Zero was code-named "Zeke" by the Allied powers, and the Model 32, until it was recognized as another Zero variant, was first dubbed "Hap" and, later, "Hamp".

Until this time, the Zero-Sen had been equal or superior to any opposing Allied fighter; but in the air battles for Guadalcanal early in 1943 it began to be apparent that both quality and quantity needed augmenting if this lead was to be maintained. This gave rise to the Model 52 (A6M5), which retained the Sakae 21 engine, but utilized a shorter-span wing – effectively, that of the Model 32, but with the square tips rounded off.

The first A6M5 appeared in August 1943, and this model quickly went into intensive production. Sub-variants included the A6M5a (Model 52A) with strengthened wings and additional machine-gun ammunition, built from March 1944; the A6M5b (Model 52B) with increased armament and armour protection; and the A6M5c (Model 52C), even more heavily armoured and with two 13-mm and two 20-mm wing guns, plus a third 13-mm gun in the fuselage.

The A6M5c was hastily put into production in the summer of 1944 to compensate for non-availability of Mitsubishi's new carrier fighter, the A7M1 Reppu; but its higher gross weight penalized performance to an unacceptable degree and only a comparatively modest total was completed. The A6M6c (Model 53C), with Sakae 31, methanol-injection, bullet-proof fuel tanks and underwing racks for four rocket projectiles, was built solely by Nakajima, except for the prototype. Severe damage to the Sakae engine production lines gave rise to the A6M8c (Model 54C), with a 1,500-hp Kinsei 62 and only the four wing guns.

Although almost every available Japanese Army and Navy type was pressed into suicide attacks in the final year of World War II, the Zero-Sen was by far the most widely used, being responsible for over half of the JNAF Kamikaze attacks. Very many Zeros, of all marks, were adapted to this fatalistic pursuit, with a pair of 132-lb, 220-lb or 550-lb bombs or a single one of 1,100-lb. Range was frequently augmented by auxiliary underwing fuel tanks. In 1945 a specialized Kamikaze version appeared, the A6M7, or Model 63.

Two-seat conversion trainer variants were produced in 1942 and 1944. These were respectively the A6M2-K Zero-Rensen built by Hitachi (272) and Sasebo Naval Air Arsenal (236); and the A6M5-K, a very few of which were completed by Hitachi and the Omura Navy Arsenal.

The Zero-Sen, in all its variants, was built in far greater numbers than any other Japanese combat type. Of the grand total of 10,937, the lion's share was completed by Nakajima, who built 6,217 landplane models and 327 examples of the A6M2-N floatplane (described separately). Mitsubishi's own total of 3,879 was made up as follows: 2 A6M1; 64 A6M2 Model 11; 740 A6M2 Model 21; 343 A6M3 Model 32; 560 A6M3 Model 22; 747 A6M5 Model 52; 1 A6M5-K; 391 A6M5a; 470 A6M5b; 93 A6M5c; 1 A6M6c; 465 A6M7; and 2 A6M8c.

Mitsubishi G4M

The G4M, which the Allies called "Betty", was a large and bulky aircraft; and if Mitsubishi officials had had their way it would probably have been larger. Certainly it would have had four engines instead of two. However, the Japanese Navy insisted that its 12-*Shi* (1937) requirement for a bomber, with a 1,765-lb weapon load and a range of nearly 3,000 miles, be met by a twin-engined design, and a team under Kiro Honjo set to work to satisfy the requirement early in 1938. The "range-at-all-costs" concept could be met only by cramming 1,100 gallons of fuel into the wings – and then only by sacrificing any kind of armour protection for the crew or fuel tanks.

Pilot Katsuzo Shima flew the first G4M1 prototype in October 1939 but then, despite Mitsubishi's protests, development was channelled temporarily in a different direction. The Yokosuka Flight Test Air Corps, backed by the Navy, suggested that the company should turn the design into a bomber escort with a crew of ten and a heavier armament. Only after 30 such machines (designated G6M1) had been built and service tested, demonstrating a performance well below the minimum required, was the escort idea discarded. The 30 redundant aircraft were relegated at first to the training rôle (as G6M1-Ks) and later became G6M1-L2 troop transports.

Meanwhile, a second G4M1 had flown in December 1940, followed by 13 more by the end of March 1941; and in April the JNAF officially adopted the G4M1 as the Type 1 land-based attack-bomber Model 11. This version had one 20-mm cannon in the tail, single flexible 7·7-mm guns in nose, dorsal and ventral positions, and two 1,530-hp Mitsubishi Kasei 11 two-row radial engines. Its first operational missions were against targets in south-east China before the outbreak of the Pacific war.

Mitsubishi A6M2 Zero-Sen, with long-barrelled wing cannon; RAF markings

Mitsubishi G4M1

Mitsubishi G4M1

TYPE	DIMENSIONS span ft	span in	length ft	length in	height ft	height in	WEIGHT max t-o lb	PERFORMANCE max speed mph	at height ft	service ceiling ft	combat range miles	REMARKS
Mitsubishi A6M2	39	4½	29	9	11	5¾	5,313	316	16,570	33,790	1,165 max	Model 21
Mitsubishi A6M5	36	1	29	9	9	2	6,047	346	19,685	35,100	975	Model 52
Mitsubishi A6M6c	36	1	29	9	9	2	6,047	346	19,685	35,100	875	Model 53c

Mitsubishi G4M2

Mitsubishi G4M2, captured aircraft, RAF markings

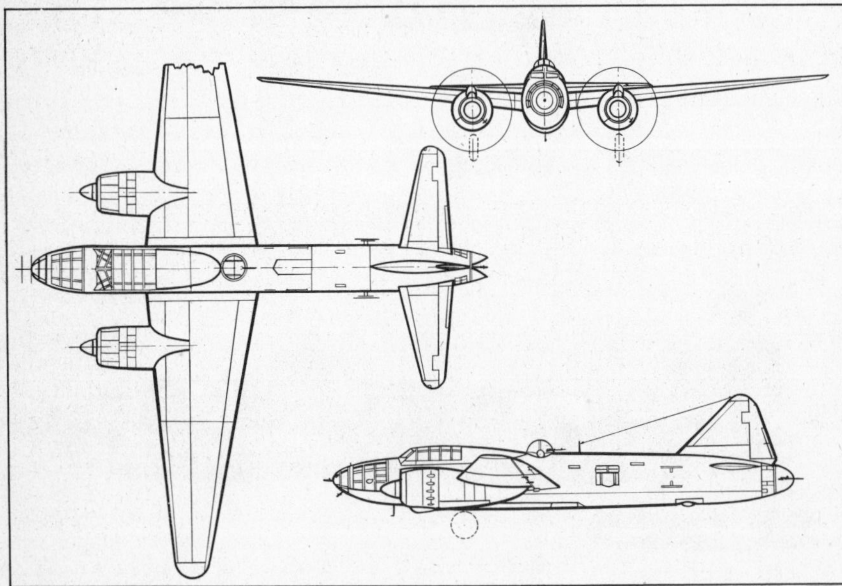
Mitsubishi G4M2

Mitsubishi Ki-51

By the time of Pearl Harbor the JNAF had 120 G4M1s in service, and three days afterwards (10 December 1941) aircraft of this type, with G3Ms, were responsible for sinking the British battleships *Prince of Wales* and *Repulse*. These early successes were, however, short-lived, and once the initial surprise of the Japanese attacks had passed the G4M1 proved to be more vulnerable than most Japanese aircraft. Combustible in the extreme, thanks to the unprotected fuel tanks, it soon became known to US pilots as the "one shot lighter" and by even less complimentary epithets to its own crews.

In the battle for the Solomon Islands (August 1942) the G4M1s took a particularly heavy beating, and three months later work was started at Nagoya on an improved version, the G4M2 (Model 22). There was a change to 1,850-hp Kasei 21s with methanol injection, more extensive glazing in the nose, an increased arc of fire for the tail gun, and an electrically-operated dorsal turret with one 7·7-mm gun. All this led to a better performance, but still no fuel-tank protection was given; in fact the amount of fuel carried in the integral wing tanks was increased by a further 330 gallons. The G4M2 was the most extensively built series, appearing in five forms: the G4M2 (Model 24) with bulged bomb doors and Kasei 25s; the G4M2b (Model 25) with Kasei 27s; the G4M2c (Model 26) with armament increased to two 20-mm and four 7·7-mm guns; the G4M2d (flying test-bed for the Ne-20 turbojet); and the G4M2e (Model 24-J) with four 20-mm and one 7·7-mm guns. This last version was the one adapted later to carry the Ohka suicide aircraft.

"Betty" served widely throughout the Pacific war; but losses continued to mount and, finally, the JNAF were forced to admit the need to protect both crew and fuel tanks. Thus, towards the end of 1943, Mitsubishi began to evolve two further developments of the bomber. One of these, given the new title G7M1 Taizan (after a famous mountain in China), was to a new 16-*Shi* (1941) requirement; but its development was discarded in favour of the G4M3 with only a 968-gallon fuel load, in fully-protected tanks in a much-redesigned wing. Sixty of this version were built as the G4M3a (Model 34) and G4M3b (Model 36). The G4M3d (Model 37) and G4M4 were projects, still incomplete when Japan surrendered.

The total number of G4Ms built came to 2,479 aircraft, many of these being converted to 20-seat troop transports before the war's end.

Mitsubishi Ki-51

Experience with the Mitsubishi Ki-30 light bomber during the hostilities in China prompted one of the JAAF's leading pilots, Captain Yuzo Fujita, to suggest adapting the design to provide the Army with a robust yet manoeuvrable *guntei* (tactical reconnaissance/ground-support) aircraft, and early in 1939 work began on modifying the Ki-30 to meet these requirements.

The result was the Ki-51, an aircraft of smaller overall size and weight, but with much the same performance as its predecessor. It was of sturdy construction, capable of dive-bombing if required and – as was proved later – of withstanding considerable punishment. The Ki-51 also differed from the Ki-30 in having the internal bomb-bay eliminated; a low wing position and thereby a shorter undercarriage; a much shorter cabin for the two-man crew; and a 940-hp Ha-26-II air-cooled radial.

In June 1939 this much-modified design entered production in two basic versions: the Ki-51a for reconnaissance rôles, and the Ki-51b for ground attack. The latter model was armed with two 12·7-mm and two 7·7-mm wing-mounted machine-guns, a movable 7·7-mm gun in the rear cockpit, and underwing racks for up to ten 44-lb bombs.

The Ki-51a made its operational debut over China early in 1940, and both versions proved extremely agile in service, with excellent short-field performance. They could, and often did, out-manoeuvre enemy fighters.

Production of the Ki-51 was extensive, though prolonged and of low priority. It was still in production at the end of World War II, by which time Mitsubishi and the Tachikawa Army Air Arsenal had built 1,472.

Known to the Allies as "Sonia", the Ki-51 was used

in many Pacific theatres, and was one of the types accepted for the suicide rôle in 1944–5. A proposed development, the Ki-71, was undertaken in 1941 by the Mansyu Hikoki Company. This would have had a much-refined airframe, a retractable undercarriage, two 20-mm wing cannon, increased bomb-load and a 1,300-hp Ha-112 radial engine; but only three prototypes were built.

Mitsubishi J2M Raiden (Thunderbolt)

After the success of the Zero fighter, Horikoshi's next design for the JNAF was something of an anti-climax. It took four and a half years to get into service, was plagued by constructional and power plant difficulties and – of the 3,600 it was planned to build – only about 500 (what should have been one month's peak output) were finally completed, 476 of them by the parent company. Yet the US Tactical Air Intelligence Unit, testing the type after World War II, wrote of its "splendid climbing performance" and "fine controllability", and rated it one of the best enemy fighters put up against the B-29. It was, incidentally, the first Japanese Navy aircraft built specially for interception, a function hitherto regarded strictly as an Army province.

Mitsubishi were first approached in October 1938 to design a land-based interceptor for the JNAF and submitted their design, for a bulky but aerodynamically clean aircraft, in April 1940. The first of three J2M1 prototypes was completed by February 1942 and flew on 20 March; it was powered by a 1,430-hp Kasei 13 radial engine, with an extended shaft and large spinner, and had a low-line cockpit canopy to help reduce overall drag. Trials showed that speed, climb and manoeuvrability (despite the Fowler-type flaps) were below specification, the undercarriage retraction was unreliable, the engine far from satisfactory and cockpit visibility, especially on landing, extremely poor. A deeper cockpit hood, internal improvements, and an 1,820-hp Kasei 23a engine were therefore introduced from the fourth machine. This, the J2M2 (Model 11), was finally accepted for production in October 1942, and Mitsubishi went on to build 155 of this model, with two 7·9-mm machine-guns in the front engine cowling and two 20-mm wing cannon.

Despite continued engine troubles and several unexplained break-ups in the air during test flights, the J2M2 entered service with the 381st Air Corps in December 1943. At the end of 1943 it was succeeded in production by the J2M3 and J2M3a (Models 21 and 21a), the most widely used versions, which had four wing cannon. In addition to the 281 Models 21/21a built by Mitsubishi, small batches were built by Koza Naval Air Arsenal.

One J2M3a was converted into a J2M6a (Model 31a) in June 1944 by further deepening the canopy. A month before this, the first Model 33 (J2M5) was completed, with a wing armament of two 20-mm cannon only. It was this version of the Raiden which drew post-war praise and was, thanks to the far more satisfactory 1,820-hp Kasei 26a engine, one of the best high-altitude interceptors encountered by Allied bombers in the final year of the war. But the Kasei 26a was in short supply, and this, with increasing destruction of Japanese factories, prevented more than 35 J2M5s being built at Suzuka.

There were reports of some Raidens with an unusual addition to their firepower, in the shape of a fixed

Mitsubishi Ki-51

Mitsubishi J2M1 Raiden

Mitsubishi J2M3 Raiden, captured aircraft, RAF markings

TYPE	DIMENSIONS span ft	span in	length ft	length in	height ft	height in	WEIGHT max t-o lb	PERFORMANCE max speed mph	at height ft	service ceiling ft	combat range miles	REMARKS
Mitsubishi G4M1	81	7⅞	65	6¼	16	1	26,645	265	13,780	30,250	3,132	Model 11
Mitsubishi G4M2	81	7⅞	64	4⅞	13	5⅞	33,069	271	15,092	29,364	3,486	Model 22
Mitsubishi G4M3	81	7⅞	64	4⅞	13	5⅞	33,069	283	16,404	29,626	2,262	Model 34
Mitsubishi Ki-51b	39	8⅓	30	2⅝	8	11½	6,437	263	9,843	27,133	659	
Mitsubishi J2M3	35	5¼	31	9⅞	12	6	8,699	380	19,685	37,799	656	Model 21
Mitsubishi J2M5	35	5¼	32	7¾	12	11⅛	NA	382	21,604	37,729	348	Model 33

Mitsubishi Ki-67 Hiryu

Mitsubishi Ki-67-Ib Hiryu

Mitsubishi Ki-67-Ib Hiryu

Mitsubishi Ki-109

cannon, mounted behind the cockpit on the port side to fire upwards at 30 degrees into Allied formations.

The J2M4 (Model 32) was an experimental version: two were built to examine the possibilities of fitting engine turbo-superchargers, but the project was discarded. The designations J2M7 and J2M7a (Models 23 and 23a) covered a proposal to re-engine some J2M3s and J2M3as with the Kasei 26a, but no conversions were made.

Although first met in the Marianas in September 1944, the Raiden (code-name "Jack") was used almost exclusively in the defence of the Japanese homeland.

Mitsubishi Ki-67 Hiryu (Flying Dragon)

Although it did not enter service until less than a year before the end of World War II, the Ki-67 was conceived well before Pearl Harbor, to a JAAF specification issued in February 1941. The terms of this indicated the need for a marked improvement over existing Army bombers, and this the Ki-67 achieved handsomely, being considerably less vulnerable to attack than the Ki-21 and Ki-49 while possessing a much superior performance.

The design staff at Nagoya, led by Dr Hisanojo Ozawa, began work late in 1941 and the first prototype was flown at Kagamigahara at the beginning of 1943. Considerable emphasis was placed on protection for the crew and fuel tanks, and despite its size and weight the bomber handled well, with first-class manoeuvrability. Fifteen had been completed by the end of the year.

The Ki-67 carried a crew of six to eight men, a 1,765-lb internal bomb-load and a defensive armament of one 20-mm and four 12·7-mm guns. Power came from two 1,900-hp Mitsubishi Ha-104 eighteen-cylinder radials.

Accepted by the JAAF, the Hiryu was ordered into production early in 1944 as the Type 4 heavy bomber, the initial version being the Ki-67-Ia or Model 1A. The first Hiryu squadrons began to form during the summer, and Allied forces (who dubbed it "Peggy") first encountered the type in the Battle of the Philippine Sea – where, although flown by Army crews, it was operating under JNAF direction as a torpedo-bomber, with the Naval name Yasukuni. After a fairly short production run, the Ki-67-Ia gave way to the Ki-67-Ib, the chief difference being the replacement of the former's flush-mounted waist guns by "blister" enclosures.

Considering the difficulties under which the Japanese industry laboured in the final year of the war, the completion of 727 Hiryu bombers by VJ-day was a creditable achievement. Of these, the parent company built 606, others being contributed by Kawasaki (91), Nippon Hikoki (29) and the Army Air Arsenal (1). Ki-67s were much in evidence in raids on Iwo Jima, the Marianas Islands and Okinawa, from their bases on Kyushu.

A number of experimental versions of the Hiryu made their appearance, some of them testing alternative engine installations to pave the way for the Ki-67-II (two 2,500-hp Ha-214s); but the latter project was still incomplete at the end of the war. Another proposed use of the Ki-67 which did not materialize was as a tug for the Ku-7 Manazura (Crane) tank-carrying glider.

Other projects led to the Ki-109 heavy fighter (described separately), and ten were converted into "mother-planes" for the I-Go-1A radio-controlled missile. Several Ki-67-Ibs were also converted by Tachikawa Army Air Arsenal into three-seat suicide bombers, with a 1,765-lb warload and a long rod protruding from the nose to trigger off the explosive on impact. This version was supplied to both Army and Navy units, some aircraft being fitted to carry a further 1,765 lb of explosive externally.

Mitsubishi Ki-109

So marked was the advance in performance of the Ki-67 Hiryu over earlier Army bombers that, in the summer of 1942, the JAAF ordered a long-range escort fighter variant, designated Ki-69. The need to concentrate on Hiryu output caused development of the escort version to be suspended shortly afterwards; but in 1943 it was revived as the basis for the Ki-112 specification for a multi-seat "heavy" fighter. This project, in turn, was discarded; but in January 1944, in daily expectation of

B-29 raids on the Japanese homeland, the concept was again revived in an urgent attempt to find an interceptor with good high-altitude performance and fire-power.

Two Ki-67-1b bombers were assigned to the Tachikawa Army Air Arsenal to be converted for this rôle. The modification consisted basically of adapting the design to mount a 75-mm Type 88 heavy cannon, with 15 rounds of ammunition, in the nose. Firing trials were satisfactory, and it was planned to produce the type as the Ki-109, achieving the necessary altitude performance by installing turbo-supercharged Mitsubishi Ha-104ru engines. In the event, however, Mitsubishi failed to deliver any of these engines, and all aircraft completed from mid-1944 onward were powered by unsupercharged Ha-104s of 1,900 hp – preventing them attaining the height necessary to do the job for which they were built.

All Ki-109s carried a crew of four; the first two aircraft were converted Ki-67 bombers, retaining the latters' mid-upper, waist and tail gun installations. The 20 production Ki-109s utilized wings, engines and tail units of the Hiryu, allied to a much revised fuselage in which the only other armament beside the heavy cannon was a single 12·7-mm gun in the tail-cone.

Mitsubishi Ki-46-III-Kai

Considering that the Japanese authorities had ample time to anticipate the eventual concentration of US air attacks on their home territory, the number of hasty improvizations of existing aircraft that had to be rushed through to combat the menace, when it came, was surprisingly high. One such was the adaptation, by the Army Aerotechnical Research Institute, of Mitsubishi's outstanding Type 100 Army reconnaissance aircraft, the Ki-46-III, known to the Allies as "Dinah".

The Ki-46-III, powered by two 1,500-hp Mitsubishi Ha-112-II 14-cylinder radials, was one of the few Japanese warplanes serving in the summer of 1944 which had the proven ability to operate at the B-29's level. Even with the weight penalty of a 37-mm Ho-203 cannon (mounted between the front and rear cabins to fire forward and upward at a 30-degree angle), and two 20-mm Ho-5s in the nose, the Ki-46-III-Kai could still reach 356 mph at 29,000 ft.

A considerable number of these conversions were carried out between October 1944 and March 1945, and were used mainly for night interception duties, as the structure was not sturdy enough for day fighting. Subsequently Mitsubishi took over further development of the type, evaluating a Ki-46-IIIb for the ground-attack rôle (without the dorsal gun) and preparing designs for a Ki-46-IIIc, with revised nose armament; but neither project achieved fruition by the end of the war.

Nakajima A1N

Two years after the introduction into service of the Gloster Sparrowhawk, as a Navy carrier fighter, Nakajima Hikoki acquired the licence to manufacture in Japan another fighter from the same stable, the Gloster Gambet. This was built as a Sparrowhawk replacement, with the designation Navy Type 3 (A1N1) carrier-based fighter.

A squat, angular biplane, with a close similarity to the Gamecock fighter in production for the RAF, the A1N1 made extensive use in its construction of duralumin alloy – then a fairly recent discovery and one which offered wide scope to aircraft designers because of its

Mitsubishi Ki-46-III-Kai

Nakajima A1N1

TYPE	DIMENSIONS						WEIGHT	PERFORMANCE				REMARKS
	span		length		height		max t-o	max speed	at height	service ceiling	combat range	
	ft	in	ft	in	ft	in	lb	mph	ft	ft	miles	
Mitsubishi Ki-67-ib	73	9⅞	61	4¼	18	4½	30,346	334	19,980	31,070	1,740	
Mitsubishi Ki-109b	73	9⅞	58	10¾	19	0⅓	23,810	342	19,980	NA	1,367	
Mitsubishi Ki-46-III-Kai	48	2¾	37	7⅞	12	5½	13,730	391	19,685	34,200	1,245	
Nakajima A1N1	31	9⅞	21	3⅞	10	10	2,205	136	9,840	23,000	3¼ hrs	

Nakajima A2N

Nakajima Type 91

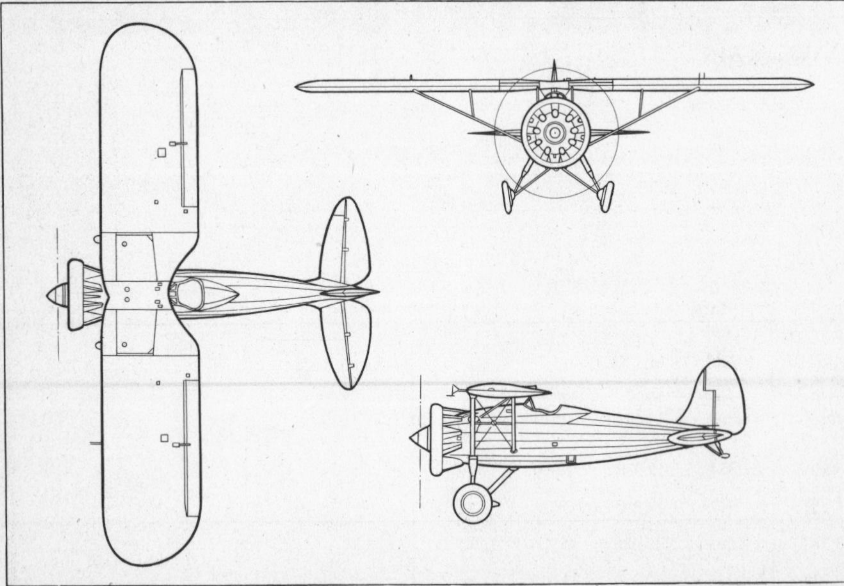
Nakajima Type 91

combination of lightness and great structural strength. Two versions were built, the early A1N1 having a Bristol Jupiter VI nine-cylinder air-cooled radial engine. The later A1N2, with a similar engine uprated to 450 hp, also introduced a sliding canopy over the cockpit. Two Vickers 7·7-mm machine-guns were installed, recessed in shallow troughs on each side of the forward fuselage. An under-fuselage rack, forward of the deck arrester hook, enabled the A1N to carry four 20-lb bombs for ground-support missions.

Nakajima A2N

This extremely agile and highly popular little aircraft was a standard Japanese Navy fighter during the first half of the 1930s. It was conceived as a replacement for the Type 3 (A1N1/2), and first flew in prototype form in 1930, entering production later that year as the Type 90 carrier-based fighter. A single-seat, single-bay biplane, with curved-taper wings and angular tail surfaces, it was powered by a 450-hp Nakajima-built version of the Bristol Jupiter VI, with a wide Townend cowling ring.

The Type 90 was built in two forms, production totalling 100 machines. The A2N1 was the standard single-seat fighter with a landplane undercarriage; the A2N2 was a strengthened version with dihedral on the upper wings. Each was armed with two forward-firing guns, installed ahead of the cockpit.

Popular with pilots and ground crews alike, the Type 90 was a first-class dog-fighter and, although obsolescent, was considered superior in this respect to its successor, the A4N1. Among the campaigns in which it served was the so-called Shanghai Incident of 1932, during which 24 A2Ns were embarked in the aircraft carrier *Kaga*.

Nakajima Type 91

The Type 91 fighter was among the first home-designed types to go into service as replacements for the foreign machines which, until then, had formed the front-line equipment of the Japanese air forces. Distinctive in appearance, it was evolved to an Army specification issued in 1927, to which both the Mitsubishi and Nakajima companies submitted design proposals. Unfortunately, Mitsubishi's Hayabusa crashed and was abandoned, leaving only the Nakajima fighter, which was a single-seat, parasol-wing monoplane, with a cantilever tailplane, an unusual feature among combat aircraft of this period. At first, the JAAF rejected the design on the grounds of structural weakness, and evaluated the Curtiss P-1C as a possible substitute. However, although the American fighter showed a high degree of agility in the air, its performance generally was not up to the standard required by the Japanese Army. So, the Army authorities decided after all in favour of a modified version of the Nakajima fighter, ordering it into production in 1931. First deliveries were made that December, replacing the Koshiki Type 4, a licence-built version of the Nieuport 29C-1, also produced by Nakajima.

By March 1934, when production of the Type 91 ceased, a total of 320 of these rugged little fighters had been completed by the parent company, and they became one of the principal standard fighter types of the JAAF. Production aircraft were powered by the Nakajima licence-built version of the Bristol Jupiter VII nine-cylinder radial, encased in a large Townend ring and developing 500 hp for take-off. Armament, characteristic of the period, comprised a pair of fixed, forward-firing 7·7-mm machine-guns in front of the cockpit; and the Type 91 could climb to 3,000 m (9,840 ft) in four minutes.

A modified version of the Type 91, with reduced wing span, modified armament and a change of power plant, was submitted for the Japanese Navy's 7-*Shi* carrier fighter competition, but was not adopted.

Nakajima A4N1

In 1934, Nakajima Hikoki K.K was called upon to produce a new carrier-based fighter for the Japanese Navy and decided to develop further the established and highly popular Type 90 (A2N). Basic changes included

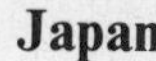

the introduction of a higher-powered engine – the 770-hp Nakajima Hikari 1 radial, encircled by a broad Townend ring – a slimmer fuselage and a cockpit windscreen for the pilot. The forward-staggered, unequal-span wings were braced by "N" struts on each side.

Although very manoeuvrable and faster than the Type 90, the new machine, the A4N1, was received with only lukewarm enthusiasm by Navy pilots, who still rated the earlier machine its superior in a dog-fight. In extensive flight tests with the Mitsubishi A5M monoplane fighter the A4N1 performed well, and since service pilots were still unconvinced by the merits of monoplane fighters, both types received production orders.

As Type 95 carrier-based fighters, a total of 300 A4N1s were built, seeing their first combat service in the Sino-Japanese campaign, in 1937, when a squadron was embarked in the carrier *Hosho*. In China, it was found that the A4N1's rather limited range was a handicap, and the aircraft was adapted to carry an auxiliary fuel tank beneath the lower wing centre-section. The tank, however, was badly designed, and in action many pilots preferred to jettison it in order to preserve the manoeuvrability of their machine against enemy fighters.

Production A4N1s were all armed with two forward-firing 7·7-mm machine-guns, although tests were carried out with a projected armament of 20-mm cannon. They were the last carrier-based biplane fighters to serve with the Japanese Navy.

Nakajima Ki-27

A contemporary of the Navy's Mitsubishi A5M1, to which it bore a broad superficial resemblance, the Nakajima Ki-27 was evaluated in company with the Ki-18 (a duplicate of the second prototype A5M1) and the Kawasaki Ki-28. All three designs were contenders for the Army's 1935 requirement for a new single-seat fighter, the Ki-28 proving the fastest in level and climbing flight. The Japanese, however, believed that lightness and extreme manoeuvrability were the chief requisites of a fighter, and so the Nakajima design was clearly the choice.

The Ki-27, of which three prototypes were ordered, thus became the first low-wing monoplane to serve with the Japanese Army Air Force, and its first enclosed-cockpit fighter, making its maiden flight on 15 October 1936. All three prototypes were powered by the 650-hp Nakajima Ha-1a nine-cylinder radial engine, and were identical except for their wings, which were of progressively greater area. The largest was adopted as standard, and a further batch of ten pre-production Ki-27s was built for evaluation before, in the summer of 1937, the fighter went into series production as the Type 97 Model A, or Ki-27a.

The Nakajima Ha-1b engine of 710 hp was adopted for service aircraft, which were armed with a pair of 7·7-mm machine-guns in the forward part of the fuselage.

Deliveries of the Ki-27a to JAAF units in Manchuria began in 1938. They replaced the obsolete Kawasaki Ki-10, and made their combat debut against the Red Air Force in the vicinity of Nomonhan in the north-west. By the spring of 1939 five of the Army's seven fighter wings in Manchuria were equipped with Ki-27as, which scored notable successes against Russian I-15 fighters. The faster I-16s proved more of a match for them; nevertheless, they accounted for a considerable proportion of the 1,252 Russian aircraft which the JAAF claimed as destroyed during the conflict, against the loss of about 100 Ki-27s. They also served with units of the Manchurian Air Force.

Nakajima A4N1

Nakajima Ki-27

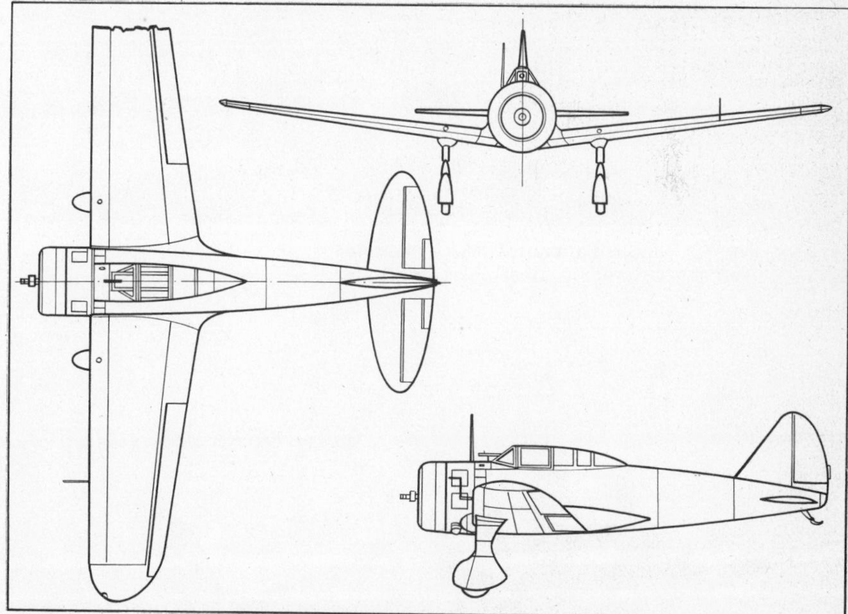

Nakajima Ki-27

TYPE	DIMENSIONS span ft	span in	length ft	length in	height ft	height in	WEIGHT max t-o lb	PERFORMANCE max speed mph	at height ft	service ceiling ft	combat range miles	REMARKS
Nakajima A2N1	30	10	21	7	10	6	2,866	201	6,562	32,152	404	
Nakajima Type 91	36	1	22	11	9	10	3,308	187	6,562	29,528	373	
Nakajima A4N1	32	8	NA		NA		NA	219	9,840	NA	NA	

Nakajima B5N1

Nakajima B5N2, captured aircraft, USAAF markings

Nakajima B5N2

In 1939 the Ki-27a was supplanted in production by the Model B (Ki-27b), similar to its predecessor save for a modified cockpit hood and detail refinements.

A total of 3,386 Ki-27s was built – 2,079 by the parent company and 1,307 by Tachikawa Aircraft Co and the Mansyu Hikoki Seizo K.K. (Manchurian Aircraft Co). The type was still in widespread service, although obsolescent, at the time of Pearl Harbor, after which it was allotted the code-name "Nate" by the Allies.

During the first six months of the Pacific war the Ki-27 was encountered in the mainland areas of Burma, China and Malaya, and in the island theatres of the Philippines and the Netherlands East Indies. In mid-1942, a number of Ki-27s were converted into Type 2 two-seat advanced trainers, with the Army designation Ki-79 and powered by a 450-hp radial engine. By this time the new Ki-43 Hayabusa (whose readiness had curtailed development of a proposed Ki-27-Kai in 1940 after the completion of only three machines) was beginning to enter service; but many JAAF pilots tried to hang on to their ageing Ki-27s, for which they had built up a respectful admiration.

Nakajima B5N

Japan's entry into World War II took the Western powers by surprise in more ways than one. Hitherto, world opinion was apt to dismiss Japanese aircraft designers as scarcely more than competent copyists of western ideas and techniques. After Pearl Harbor, however, pending a fuller appreciation of the true picture of Japanese aviation, few would have denied Japan's supremacy in at least one category of warplane – the carrier-based torpedo-bomber. To complete the irony, in the type that was the mainstay of the Pearl Harbor attack – a five-year-old design, though still superior to its US or British counterparts in service – Japanese engineers *had* made use of American design techniques!

This aircraft, dubbed "Kate" by the Allies later in the war, was the Nakajima B5N, a low-wing monoplane with a two/three-man crew, which had been evolved to meet a JNAF specification of 1935. Two companies, Mitsubishi and Nakajima, were invited to compete for the contract, and although the latter's B5N1 was chosen a small order for the less-radical Mitsubishi B5M1 was placed as an insurance – unnecessary, as it proved – against failure of the Nakajima design.

The prototype B5N1, which flew in January 1937, was a clean-cut, all-metal low-wing monoplane, incorporating (for the first time in a Japanese shipboard bomber) a hydraulically-retracting main undercarriage. In this, as in other features, such as the Fowler-type flaps, mechanically-folding wings, integral fuel tanks, and the NACA cowling and Hamilton Standard propeller for its 770-hp Hikari 3 nine-cylinder engine, the B5N1 showed a considerable leaning towards contemporary US design trends. On subsequent test flights the B5N1 prototypes attained 230 mph – 23 mph above that called for by the Navy – and a combat range of 685 miles.

As the Type 97 Model 1 carrier-based attack aircraft the B5N1 Model 11 entered production late in 1937. It went into service during the Sino-Japanese conflict as a light bomber, in which rôle it could carry two 550-lb bombs or up to six 132-lb bombs on underwing racks and mounted a single rearward-firing 7·7-mm machine gun for defence. To save weight and simplify construction, service B5N1s adopted manual wing folding, and slotted flaps replaced the Fowler variety. Later production B5N1s, known as the Model 12, switched to the 985-hp Sakae 11 engine.

In December 1939 there appeared the prototype of a further-improved version, the Type 97 Model 3 (Mitsubishi's B5M1 having been the Type 97 Model 2), or B5N2 Model 23. Powered by a 14-cylinder 1,115-hp Sakae 21, the B5N2 was intended specifically for the torpedo-bomber rôle, with a single 18-in (1,765-lb) torpedo slung beneath the centre fuselage, although this could be replaced by an equivalent load of bombs. Defensive armament was increased to two fixed forward-firing 7·7-mm guns and one or two 7·7-mm guns in the rear crew station on a movable mounting.

With the arrival of the B5N2 in service during 1940

some B5N1s were converted into B5N1-K trainers; but bombers of both types took part in offensive operations against the US fleet at Pearl Harbor. One hundred and three bomb-carrying B5N1s were accompanied by forty B5N2 torpedo aircraft from the *Soryu* and other carriers, and at least half of the latter's weapons found their mark. Among the capital ships struck were the battleships *Arizona* and *Oklahoma*.

In subsequent actions, particularly at Midway, Nakajima B5Ns were largely or totally responsible for sinking the carriers *Yorktown*, *Lexington*, *Wasp* and *Hornet*. "Kates" appeared on front-line operations as late as the Marianas campaign of June 1944; but for more than a year before this they had been obsolescent and in this campaign they were, for the first time, accompanied by Nakajima's newer and faster torpedo-bomber, the B6N Tenzan. More than 1,200 B5N1s and B5N2s were built, a proportion of them by Aichi Kokuki K.K.

Nakajima Ki-43 Hayabusa (Peregrine Falcon)

In 1938, when it needed a replacement for the Ki-27, the Japanese Army issued a requirement for a new fighter, laying emphasis on manoeuvrability as the prime consideration. Nakajima's design team, headed by Dr Hideo Itokawa, submitted drawings for a single-engined monoplane with obvious Ki-27 ancestry, but of much more slender and delicate appearance. They were asked to complete three prototypes of this aircraft, the Ki-43, and the first of these flew in January 1939. But, although trials revealed a good speed (323 mph) and range, it was heavy on the controls and its manoeuvrability left much to be desired.

Over the next few months, major design alterations were undertaken, and when the first of ten pre-production Ki-43s appeared in November 1939 a vast improvement was evident. Increased wing area and the use of "combat flaps", coupled with a reduction in overall weight, had improved the fighter's handling qualities out of all recognition, and JAAF lost no time in ordering its production. The Ki-43 (given the Allied code-name "Oscar") was to remain in production and service throughout the war in the Far East, during which time it was, numerically at least, the leading JAAF type. On paper, the Ki-43 was even superior to the A6M2 Zero, but comparative trials held in January 1941 showed the Navy fighter to be the better all-round fighting machine.

In March 1941 Nakajima put the Ki-43-I into production at its Ohta factory as the Type 1 Model 1 Army fighter. Though its flying qualities were now established, a weakness in firepower was evident, and this was remedied in successive versions. The initial production model (the Ki-43-Ia) had only two 7·7-mm machine-guns, mounted in the upper engine cowling. On the Ki-43-Ib this was increased to one 12·7-mm and one 7·7-mm; and on the Ki-43-Ic, the major variant in the Model 1 series, to two 12·7-mm guns. The entire Ki-43-I series (716 were built) was powered by the 975-hp Sakae Ha-25 radial.

About 40 Hayabusas were in JAAF service at the time of Pearl Harbor, and their general operational capabilities and handling qualities quickly made them popular with their pilots. Combat experience revealed, however, a need for greater engine power and more pilot protection in the form of armour plating and self-sealing fuel tanks. Thus emerged the Ki-43-II embodying these improvements, five prototypes first being built before

Nakajima Ki-43-IIa Hayabusa

Nakajima Ki-43-II Hayabusa

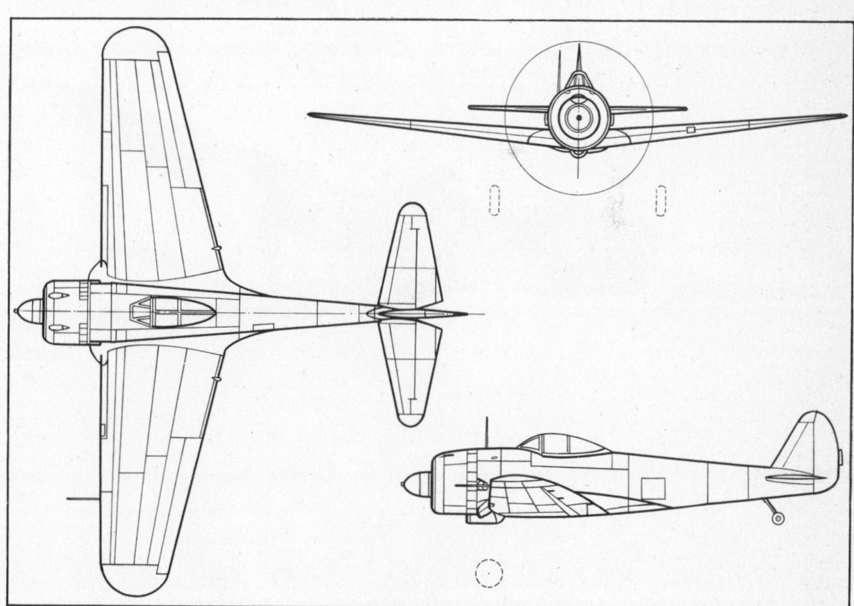

Nakajima Ki-43-IIa Hayabusa

TYPE	DIMENSIONS span ft	span in	length ft	length in	height ft	height in	WEIGHT max t-o lb	PERFORMANCE max speed mph	at height ft	service ceiling ft	combat range miles	REMARKS
Nakajima Ki-27b	37	0⅞	24	8½	9	2¼	3,638	286	11,483	NA	389	
Nakajima B5N1	50	11	33	11	12	1¾	8,047	217	8,333	24,280	684	Model 1
Nakajima B5N2	50	11	33	9½	12	1¾	9,039	235	11,810	25,065	609	Model 3
Nakajima Ki-43-Ia	37	6⅓	28	11¾	10	8¾	5,695	308	13,120	38,500	745	Model 1 A

Nakajima Ki-43-IIa Hayabusa

Nakajima Ki-49-II Donryu

Nakajima Ki-49-II Donryu

Nakajima Ki-49-II Donryu

the Ki-43-IIa entered production in the early spring of 1942. Twin 12·7-mm armament remained standard; but the wings, of slightly smaller span, now had racks for a pair of 550-lb bombs and the new model was powered by the 1,105-hp Sakae Ha-115 radial engine.

The Tachikawa Army Arsenal built 49 of this model, followed from May 1943 by more extensive construction by Tachikawa Hikoki K.K., before production of the Ki-43-IIa was phased out in November 1943. Its place had already been taken, in production and service, by the Ki-43-IIb, a generally similar model except for its clipped wings which made the Hayabusa's manoeuvrability equal to that of any opposing Allied fighter. Only in firepower was the Ki-43 still deficient.

Introduction of the Ki-43-IIIa, built jointly by Nakajima and Tachikawa Hikoki from December 1944, improved the fighter's performance still further by utilizing the Mitsubishi Kasei (Ha-112) radial of 1,250 hp. Finally, in a belated attempt to put the Hayabusa on equal terms with its opponents, came the Ki-43-IIIb, developed by Tachikawa, with two 20-mm cannon; but only two prototypes had been completed by VJ-day.

The total number of Hayabusa fighters built, including 3,200 by the parent company, was 5,751. This elegant warplane performed in virtually every theatre of the Pacific war, both as an interceptor and as long-range escort to convoys and bomber formations. It was encountered in Bengal, Burma, China, Java, Malaya, New Guinea and Sumatra; in large numbers at the battle of Leyte Island in the Philippines; and in defence of the Kurile Islands to the north of Japan. It was one of the types hastily adapted for suicide missions towards the end of the war, and in the final stages several of these fighters (mostly Ki-43-IIIas) took part in the attempted defence of Tokyo and other major cities in the Japanese homeland. Six squadrons of the JAAF were still equipped with Ki-43-IIIs at the end of the war.

Nakajima Ki-49 Donryu (Dragon Swallower)

The main criticisms levelled by JAAF crews at the Mitsubishi Ki-21 bomber concerned its slow speed and poor defensive armament; the Ki-49, intended as the Ki-21's replacement, placed so much emphasis on higher speed, more powerful engines and, in the later models, heavy armament that it was castigated in its turn for having a poor range and inadequate bomb-load.

The JAAF specification to which the Ki-49 was designed was issued late in 1938, and the first prototype flew in the following August; this was powered by two 1,160-hp Nakajima Ha-5B radial engines, as was the second machine. It was both stable and manoeuvrable, and could carry a maximum internal bomb-load of 2,200 lb over short ranges; but it was quite lightly armed (one 20-mm cannon and two 7·92-mm machine-guns), its operational ceiling was well below that required, and it was only some 20 mph faster than the Ki-21.

Subsequent prototypes, and the Ki-49-I which entered series production in the late spring of 1940 as the Type 100 heavy bomber, improved peformance somewhat by utilizing the 1,250-hp Ha-41 radial. However, both the power and the defensive capability of this model were still inadequate and it was superseded, during 1942, by the Ki-49-II. This was built in two models, the Ki-49-IIa increasing the number of 7·92-mm guns by three and the Ki-49-IIb replacing all five by 12·7-mm guns. Each was powered by 1,450-hp Nakajima Ha-109-II radials.

Series production of the Donryu amounted to 129 Ki-49-Is, 679 Ki-49-IIs (including 50 in 1943–4 by Tachikawa Hikoki K.K.), and a small number of Ki-49-IIs built by Mansyu Hikoki Seizo at Harbin. The Ki-49-III, six of which were built by Nakajima with 2,500-hp Ha-117 two-row radial engines, did not progress any further, and Ki-49 production came to an end in December 1944.

The Donryu (code-name "Helen") made its debut on 19 February 1942, when a force of Ki-49-I bombers flew from New Guinea to attack Port Darwin in Australia. The type appeared subsequently in Burma and India and with the arrival in service of the Ki-49-II from September 1942, was encountered in China, the Netherlands East

Indies, Formosa and the Philippines. In the battle for Leyte Island, the Donryus suffered particularly heavy losses, and thereafter many were converted for use as suicide aircraft. Others undertook coastal patrol and mine-detection duties. The last JAAF flight of the war was made by an aircraft of this type, when a Ki-49 conveyed Lieutenant-General Torashiro Kawabe, the Emperor Hirohito's special envoy, to Okinawa to sign the Japanese surrender agreement on 19/20 August 1945.

Considering the Ki-49's shortcomings as a bomber, it is surprising that two fighter developments were proposed at one stage. Three prototypes were built of the Ki-58 escort version, based on the Ki-49-IIa, with no fewer than five 20-mm and three 12·7-mm guns; and two Ki-49-IIIs were converted as Ki-80 formation leaders; but neither of these ventures was pursued further.

The Donryu was originally so-called by the manufacturer, after the famous Shinto shrine in Ohta; "Dragon Swallower" is only a colloquial translation.

Nakajima Ki-44 Shoki (Demon)

A contemporary of the Ki-43, Nakajima's Shoki fighter was intended for an entirely different purpose – defence of potential targets within the Japanese homeland. For this rôle a much shorter range was acceptable, and the prime qualities called for by the JAAF in their 1938 specification were high speed, ample firepower and, even more essential, a rapid rate of climb to altitude.

Nakajima began their design in the latter part of the year and the JAAF subsequently ordered no fewer than 10 prototypes. The first of these was flown in August 1940, and some of the aircraft from this batch were temporarily in combat service at the outset of the Pacific war. The terms of the Army requirement were well met, the first aircraft being armed with two 12·7-mm and two 7·7-mm machine-guns and able to climb to 16,400 ft (5,000 m) in under 4½ minutes. In comparative test flights with a Messerschmitt Bf 109 at Kagamigahara airfield, the Ki-44 Shoki gave a good account of itself.

On the other hand the Shoki was bulkier and heavier than any single-seaters that Army pilots had encountered before, and with its high wing loading and fast take-off and landing speeds it needed to be handled by an experienced pilot. This led to an initial dislike of the fighter when it first entered service; but as pilots became accustomed to the different handling techniques required they came to accept the Ki-44 as an effective warplane.

Delivery of the Ki-44 fighters to JAAF units began in the summer of 1942, and six production models were eventually built, to a total of 1,233 aircraft. The various models differed principally in engine and armament, though the Ki-44-II series also featured a strengthened main undercarriage, retractable tail-wheel, modified cockpit canopy and other minor refinements.

First production version (40 built) was the Ki-44-Ia, or Type 2 Army fighter, Model 1a. This was armed as above and powered by the 1,260-hp Nakajima Ha-41 radial engine. All subsequent production machines had the 1,450-hp Nakajima Ha-109 14-cylinder radial. The Ki-44-Ib and -Ic, which entered service in 1943, had four 12.7-mm guns; the Ki-44-IIb (production version of the -IIa) was similarly armed; the Ki-44-IIc, which performed particularly well against US Liberator bombers, had two 12·7-mm and two 40-mm cannon; and the Ki-44-III, a model of reduced all-up weight, was armed with two 12·7-mm and two 20-mm guns.

Nakajima Ki-44 Shoki

Nakajima Ki-44 Shoki

Nakajima Ki-44 Shoki

TYPE	DIMENSIONS						WEIGHT	PERFORMANCE				REMARKS
	span		length		height		max t-o	max speed	at height	service ceiling	combat range	
	ft	in	ft	in	ft	in	lb	mph	ft	ft	miles	
Nakajima Ki-43-IIB	35	6¾	29	3⅛	10	8¾	5,825	320	19,685	36,794	1,006	Model 2B
Nakajima Ki-49-II	66	7¼	53	1¾	13	11⅓	23,545	304	16,404	26,772	1,491	Model 2
Nakajima Ki-44-IA	31	0	28	8½	10	8	5,622	360	12,140	NA	575	Model 1A
Nakajima Ki-44-IIc	31	0	28	8½	10	8	6,107	376	17,060	36,745	539	Model 2 C

Nakajima Ki-44-II Shoki

Nakajima J1N1-C Gekko

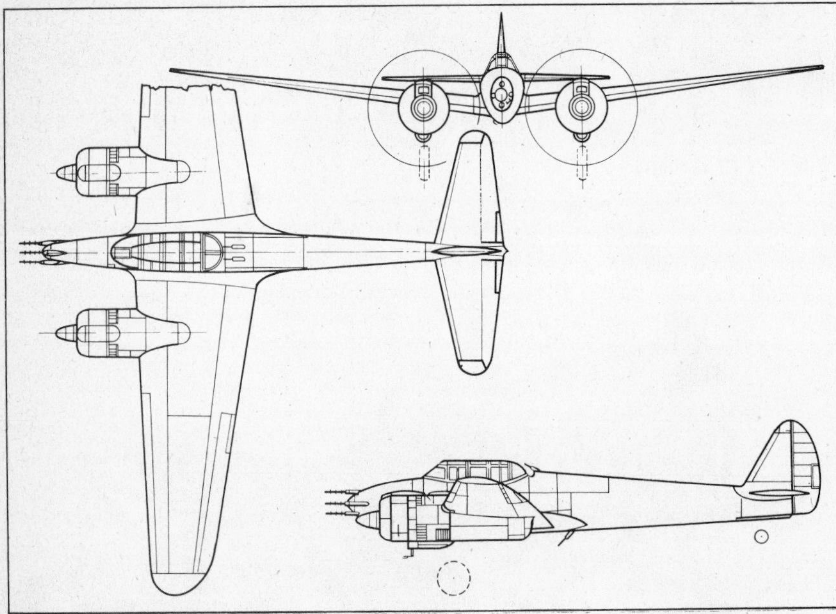

Nakajima J1N1-S Gekko

Nakajima A6M2-N

Comparatively few of the last-named version of this aircraft were completed.

Code named "Tojo" by the western powers, the Ki-44 was not used widely outside Japanese home territory, though some were encountered in Burma and others in New Guinea, in 1944. In the summer of that year nearly all Shokis on JAAF strength were deployed in the defence of Kyushu Island, Japan, and the key cities of Kobe, Kyoto, Osaka and Tokyo on Honshu Island, against American B-29 attacks from the Chinese mainland.

Nakajima J1N1-S Gekko (Moonlight)

An elegant, all-metal low-wing monoplane, the Nakajima J1N was intended at the outset to be a twin-engined, multi-seat escort fighter and attack aircraft with a range of up to 2,485 miles (4,000 km) and a top speed of 320 mph. Both Nakajima and Mitsubishi prepared designs to the JNAF specification, issued in June 1938, but the latter company was allowed to withdraw its entry shortly afterwards, due to a shortage of design staff.

Nakajima's prototype, designed by K. Nakamura, was flown for the first time in May 1941 and, although it performed reasonably well, was difficult to handle and on the whole too large to indulge in fighter-type manoeuvres. Difficulty was also experienced with the mechanism of the two rear gun barbettes, each mounting twin 7·7-mm guns, which were remotely controlled from the navigator's seat. The remaining armament, which functioned satisfactorily, was concentrated in the nose and consisted of one 20-mm cannon and two further 7·7-mm guns.

Although the J1N did not measure up to expectations for the escort fighter rôle, the JNAF were sufficiently enthusiastic about its general capabilities to adopt it as a reconnaissance type.

With the rear guns removed, and equipped with two 1,130-hp Nakajima Sakae 21 fourteen-cylinder radial engines, the aircraft was adopted in July 1942 by the JNAF as the three-seat Type 2 Model 11 J1N1-C for land-based reconnaissance. First deliveries were made to units in the Solomon Islands towards the end of the year and it was from their service in this theatre that their later combat rôle originated.

In March 1943, at the request of the commander of the 251st Air Corps in Rabaul, Navy authorities agreed to the modification of two J1N1-Cs to have two pairs of 20-mm cannon, to the rear of the cockpit, with one pair firing obliquely forward and upward at 30 degrees and the other pair forward and downward at the same angle. On their return to Rabaul in May, they were welcome (anti-aircraft artillery then being the only defence against raiding B-17s and B-24s), and soon proved the new gun installations to be effective for night fighting.

From this experiment derived the principal service version, the two-seat J1N1-S Gekko Model 11, which was placed in immediate production. The nose guns were eliminated from this model, and the fuselage top line aft of the cockpit was straightened and made cleaner aerodynamically. As a temporary measure, some J1N1-Cs were modified as J1N1-Fs, with a conventional hand-operated dorsal turret mounting a single 20-mm cannon.

Nakajima built a total of 477 J1Ns of all versions, including prototypes. The Allied code name "Irving" was applied to both the J1N1-C and the J1N1-S. Later Gekkos, equipped with rudimentary AI radar, served within Japan on night interception duties against the B-29, but lacked the speed or ceiling to be successful.

Some J1N aircraft were employed in the attack rôle, with two 550-lb and two 66-lb bombs under their wings. Another project, which proved abortive, was for a torpedo-carrying variant.

Nakajima A6M2-N

As an interim type, pending introduction of the Kawanishi Kyofu floatplane fighter, the Japanese Navy ordered in the early winter of 1940 an adaptation of the A6M2 Zero fighter under the designation A6M2-N or Type 2. The task was allocated to Nakajima Hikoki K.K., at Koizumi, as this company had had more experience of seaplane construction than Mitsubishi; in fact, the float

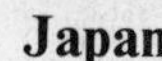

gear developed for the A6M2-N was based largely on that fitted to Nakajima's own Type 95 (E8N) observation aircraft. It consisted of a large, single-step centre float, and two comparatively large stabilizing floats carried on single struts at about two-thirds span. A narrow stabilizing strake was added beneath the fin and rudder, and the rudder itself was also increased in area.

Construction of the first machine was begun in February 1941, and it was completed in December; by the end of 1942 Nakajima had produced 107 A6M2-Ns and a further 220 were built before production ceased in September 1943.

In service from 1942, the A6M2-N ("Rufe" to the Allies) served in both northern and southern Pacific theatres, from the Aleutian Islands (based on Kiska Island) to the Solomons. In the event, it operated more in a defensive than a belligerent rôle, and a number of A6M2-Ns were based at Paramushiru, in the Kiril Islands north of Hokkaido, and at Lake Biwa on Honshu, in an attempt to counter US bomber attacks in that area.

"Rufe" was well armed, with two wing-mounted Type 99 20-mm cannon and two 7·7-mm Type 87 machine-guns in the top front of the engine cowling; it could also (although it rarely did) carry a pair of 66- or 132-lb bombs on underwing racks. However, its combat performance was well below that of its contemporaries on both sides, and by mid-1943, when the Kyofu began to arrive in JNAF service, it was already beginning to be transferred to training and other second-line duties.

Nakajima B6N Tenzan

The Tenzan (named after a mountain in China) maintained the degree of advancement over Allied torpedo-bombers set by its predecessor, the B5N "Kate". A contemporary of the Grumman TBF and the Fairey Barracuda, it was in most respects superior to both. Between April and June 1945, JNAF Tenzans mounted a substantial torpedo and Kamikaze campaign against Allied shipping massed in the Okinawa area, and there is little doubt that if Japan had still possessed a carrier fleet and sufficient skilled pilots in the final year of the Pacific war, this efficient aircraft would have inflicted even greater damage on Allied sea power.

First flown in prototype form in March 1942, the B6N1 exhibited a remarkable slimness and cleanliness of line, a distinctive feature being the forward-raked rudder. The oil cooler of its 14-cylinder 1,870-hp Nakajima Mamori II radial engine, on the underside of the cowling, was offset to port so as to clear the fuselage centre-line for launching a 1,765-lb torpedo. A ventral, rearward-firing 7·7-mm machine-gun, operated by the second crew member, could be extended after releasing the torpedo to discourage retaliatory anti-aircraft fire from the ship just attacked. Like its predecessor, the B6N1 also carried a dorsal 7·7-mm gun to protect it from rear attack.

In service, the bulky Mamori engine produced more than its fair share of operating problems, being subject to excessive vibration and overheating. The B6N1 (Model 11) was consequently withdrawn from production (though not from service) and its place was taken by the Model 12, or B6N2. Most of the 1,268 Tenzans built at Nakajima's Handa and Koizumi factories were of the latter version. Power plant for the B6N2 was the proven Mitsubishi Kasei 25, with a four-blade Hamilton constant-speed propeller. This engine developed only

Nakajima B6N1 Tenzan

Nakajima B6N2 Tenzan

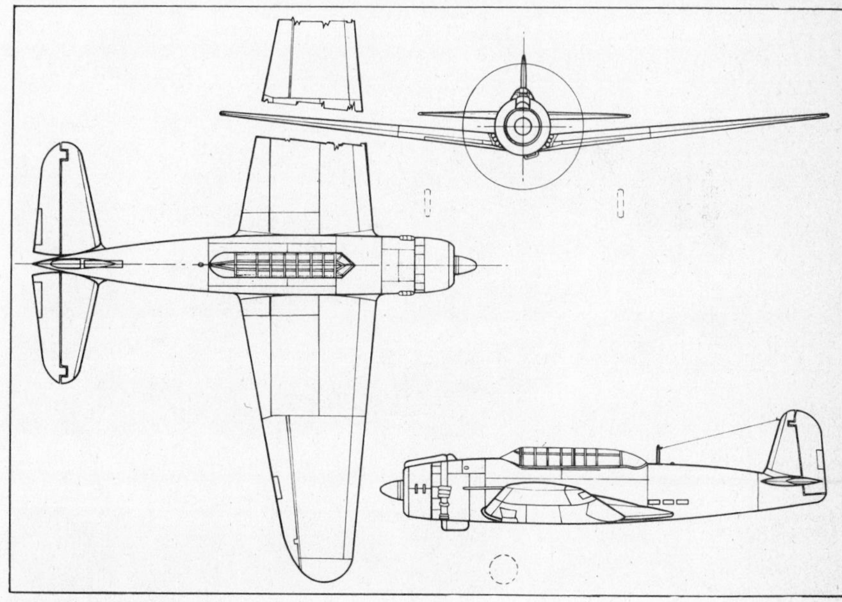

Nakajima B6N2 Tenzan

TYPE	DIMENSIONS						WEIGHT	PERFORMANCE				REMARKS
	span		*length*		*height*		*max t-o*	*max speed*	*at height*	*service ceiling*	*combat range*	
	ft	*in*	*ft*	*in*	*ft*	*in*	*lb*	*mph*	*ft*	*ft*	*miles*	
Nakajima J1N1-S	55	8½	39	11½	14	11½	16,594	315	16,404	30,578	1,584	Model 11
Nakajima A6M2-N	39	4½	33	2¾	14	1¼	5,423	270	14,110	32,000	1,108 max	Model 11
Nakajima B6N1	48	10¼	35	7½	12	1⅔	12,456	289	15,748	28,379	907	Model 11
Nakajima B6N2	48	10¼	35	7½	12	5⅐	12,456	299	16,076	29,659	1,084	Model 12

Nakajima Ki-84-Ia Hayate

Nakajima Ki-84-Ia Hayate

Nakajima Ki-84-Ia Hayate

Nakajima Ki-84-Ia Hayate, captured aircraft, US markings

1,850 hp for take-off, but the slight power loss was more than offset by its lighter weight and ease of maintenance, and the B6N2's performance showed a marked improvement over the B6N1. A further 7·7-mm gun was added in one wing, in order to provide some forward defence.

The Tenzan (code-name "Jill") was first encountered in December 1943, when a US task force attacking the Marshall Islands was raided by a formation of B6N1s. The first combat engagement with B6N2s occurred in the Marianas six months later, and Tenzans took part in other operations at Truk Island in the Carolines, Bougainville Island in the Solomons and at Iwo Jima. Allied naval forces off Kyushu in March 1945 also came under night attack from radar-equipped aircraft of this type. From ship or shore station, the Tenzan was effective both as a torpedo-bomber and (with six 220-lb bombs) in the close support rôle. In "clean" condition, it had the speed to act also as a reconnaissance aircraft.

Nakajima Ki-84 Hayate (Gale)

With a hint of Ki-44 ancestry in its neat but conventional contours, the Ki-84 was an entirely new design, embarked upon by a Nakajima team under T. Koyama in April 1942 as a second-generation single-seat fighter to follow the Hayabusa, Shoki and Hien into JAAF service. Reflecting Japanese realization that "manoeuvrability at all costs" was no longer the essence of modern fighter design, it laid greater emphasis on such factors as armour protection for the pilot, self-sealing fuel tanks and more sturdy construction. Had its career not been hampered by continual difficulties with the Homare two-row radial engine which powered it, the Hayate would doubtless have made a greater impact on the air war in the Pacific; even so, its general performance was good, with the capability of performing half-an-hour's combat duty at ranges up to 375 miles from base; and it could hold its own against US Hellcat, Mustang and Thunderbolt fighters at heights up to 30,000 ft.

The prototype Ki-84 flew for the first time in March 1943, and immediately displayed a better performance than either the Ki-43 or Ki-44, with a greater range than the latter. Mass production was quickly ordered, beginning in August at Nakajima's Ohta factory with the Ki-84-Ia, or Type 4 Army fighter Model 1a. Other plants which joined in the production programme were the Nakajima works at Utsunomiya and (from early 1945) the Mansyu Hikoki Seizo works at Harbin. The first Hayates began to join Japanese squadrons in April 1944, and five months later were met in action when, from bases near Hangkow on the Chinese mainland, they were despatched against attacking formations of the US 14th Air Force.

There were three models in the Ki-84-I series, all powered by the 1,900-hp Nakajima Homare Ha-45 Model 11 eighteen-cylinder radial air-cooled engine and differing chiefly in the armament installed. The Ki-84-Ia had two 20-mm wing cannon and twin 12·7-mm guns in the upper engine cowling. In the Ki-84-Ib, all four guns were of 20-mm calibre, and in the Ki-84-Ic the wing cannon were raised to 30-mm calibre.

Throughout its service career, which saw it employed as day and night fighter, dive-bomber and ground-support aircraft (with two underwing bombs of up to 550-lb weight), the Hayate ("Frank" in the Pacific coding system) was beset by difficulties arising from the insufficiently-developed Homare power plant. A tendency for fuel and hydraulic pressures to drop without warning at high altitude limited its capacity to perform efficiently upwards of 30,000 ft, and the situation was further aggravated by a shortage of fitters and engineers.

Another shortcoming was the Hayate's rather weak main landing gear, which led to numerous attempts to evolve a lighter-weight version of the fighter while at the same time improving all-round performance. Ironically, most of the results proved to be heavier than the original model. Such experiments included the all-wood Ki-106 (redesigned by Tachikawa at Tomakomai, and three built by the Ohji Paper Company at Ebetsu, one of which was test flown against a captured Mustang); the mainly-steel Ki-113 (one built in 1945 by Nakajima at Ohta); and the mixed wood/metal Ki-84-II, later discarded. Projects incomplete at the end of World War II included the Ki-84R (2,000-hp supercharged Ha-45), the Ki-84N and Ki-84P (2,500-hp Ha-219 and increased wing area), and the Ki-84-III (2,000-hp turbo-supercharged Ha-45ru). Perhaps the most promising variant was the Mansyu-developed Ki-114. With Mitsubishi Ha-112-II engine, increased length and larger tail surfaces, this aircraft achieved a weight saving of nearly 10 per cent over the Ki-84-Ia and brief testing of the prototype before VJ-day held considerable promise.

Thus the Ki-84-I series remained the only Hayates to see combat. Nakajima production of the three service models amounted to 2,686 at Ohta (peak rate being 518 a month, during 1944) and 727 at Utsunomiya, with a further 100 by Mansyu Hikoki bringing the grand total to 3,513 aircraft. The Hayates' first big action was in the battle of Leyte, in which at least six squadrons took part; they were encountered subsequently in most theatres of war in the Far East. At Okinawa they appeared in the ground-attack rôle, and several were employed in the day and night defence of Tokyo.

Nakajima C6N Saiun (Colourful Cloud)

A 17-*Shi* (1942) design by Yasuo Fukuda, the Nakajima C6N Saiun ("Myrt" in the Allied coding system) was another excellent warplane whose entry into service in World War II was delayed by the troublesome Homare engine. In the early stages of design, twin 1,000-hp radial engines in tandem were contemplated, but with the Homare then promising around 2,000 hp as a single, compact unit, a more orthodox layout was followed.

The Saiun's slim lines and forward-leaning rudder bore a close family resemblance to the B6N ("Jill") torpedo-bomber, and a crew of three was housed beneath a similar, long, glazed canopy. A Nakajima Type K laminar-flow aerofoil was adopted, with integral wing tanks holding 300 gallons of fuel; and the 18-cylinder Homare 21 two-row radial gave 1,990 hp for take-off.

In an attempt to speed development, 23 prototype aircraft were ordered, several of these appearing in 1943 under the designation 17-*Shi*. Production of the C6N Model 11 began a year later, deliveries beginning in August, but well before this several of the prototypes had been assigned to service units as part of the test programme, and it was one of these that reconnoitred the US task force massing in June 1944 for the attack on the Marianas Islands. Similar Saiun patrols, this time from a carrier base, picked up the US force preparing to attack Saipan.

Primarily a carrier-based reconnaissance type, the Saiun's speed and altitude performance enabled it to out-run and out-climb most Allied fighters in 1944, and it carried normally only a single rearward-firing 7·92-mm gun for defensive purposes. However, several were converted for night fighter duties in defence of Japan; these were designated C6N1-S, and carried a two-man crew and two fixed 20-mm cannon in the rear fuselage, firing obliquely forward and upward. Others were adapted as C6N1-B Model 21 torpedo-bombers; and two prototypes were completed of the C6N2 (Model 22) with a 2,000-hp Homare 24 engine.

The final development, which remained a project only, was the C6N3 Saiun-Kai, for which the Hitachi 92 engine with exhaust turbine was intended. The original C6N1 was still in production at the end of World War II, when Nakajima's Handa and Koizumi factories had built 498.

But for Japan's lack of aircraft carriers in the final year of the war, more would undoubtedly have been seen of this excellent aircraft.

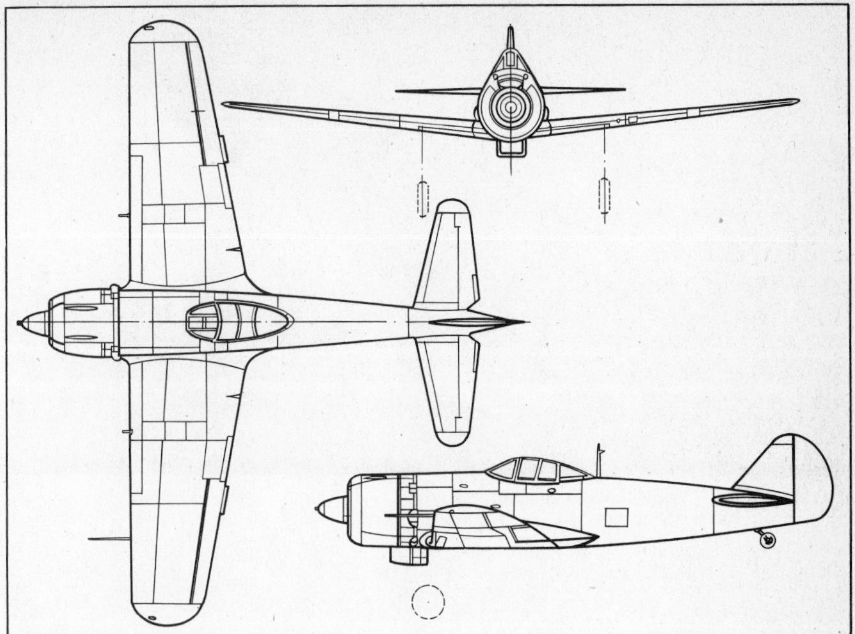

Nakajima Ki-84-Ia Hayate

Nakajima C6N1 Saiun

Nakajima C6N1 Saiun

TYPE	DIMENSIONS						WEIGHT	PERFORMANCE				REMARKS
	span ft	span in	length ft	length in	height ft	height in	max t-o lb	max speed mph	at height ft	service ceiling ft	combat range miles	
Nakajima Ki-84-I	36	10½	32	6½	11	1½	8,267	388	19,685	34,450	1,025	Model 1
Nakajima C6N1	41	0⅛	36	1	12	11⅞	11,627	378	19,685	35,236	1,914	Model 11

Tachikawa Ki-77, long-range record aircraft

Tachikawa Ki-74

Toyo FD-25A Defender

Toyo FD-25B Defender

Tachikawa Ki-74

Code-named "Patsy" by the Allied powers, the Ki-74 was the only pressurized, long-range strategic bomber produced in Japan in World War II. It originated early in 1939 as a reconnaissance project, only to be shelved a year later in favour of the Ki-77, an aircraft sponsored by the *Asahi* newspaper group for a non-stop goodwill flight from Tokyo to New York to celebrate the 2600th anniversary of the accession of the first emperor. Two Ki-77s were built, one of which set an unofficial world distance record of 10,271 miles in July 1944.

The Ki-74 project was revived after the attack on Pearl Harbor, and was developed as a long-range bomber, to more stringent Army requirements. Tachikawa completed their further design work by the autumn of 1942 but, because of prolonged development of the pressurization system, it was May 1944 before the first prototype made its maiden flight. In addition to the circular-section pressurized fuselage, it introduced several other advanced features, including laminar-flow wings, bullet-proof integral fuel tanks and a remotely-controlled defensive gun of 12·7-mm calibre in the tail-cone.

Sixteen Ki-74-Is were built for service evaluation, the first two being powered by 2,200-hp Mitsubishi Ha-211ru radial engines and the remainder by 1,900-hp Mitsubishi Ha-104ru radials. A maximum internal bomb-load of 2,200 lb could be carried in the ventral gondola.

In the summer of 1945, these bombers were being worked up in readiness for an attack on Saipan, but the war ended before the raid could be carried out. A mock-up of the improved Ki-74-II bomber was completed in 1944, but neither this nor a proposed transport development achieved fruition.

Toyo FD-25 Defender

The Defender, an American design, owed its inspiration to former Lockheed design engineer John Thorp, who sold his idea for a small, low-cost ground-support aircraft to the Fletcher brothers in 1950, soon after the outbreak of the Korean War. Three demonstration aircraft were built in the USA, the first being a single-seat FD-25B (flown on 14 April 1951) and the second a tandem two-seat FD-25A with a slightly longer fuselage.

Thorp's idea was that such an aircraft, costing less than 10 per cent as much as a complex jet fighter, was also far more suited to the type of combat operations encountered in south-east Asian territories and was capable of carrying an equally lethal load.

The Defender, weighing only 1¼ tons fully laden, had a pair of wing-mounted 0·30-in machine-guns and under-wing racks for two 33-gal napalm tanks, two 250-lb H.E. or fragmentation bombs; up to forty 2·75-in folding-fin air rockets; four 5-in heavy rockets; or twenty 80-mm Oerlikon rockets. It was received enthusiastically at numerous demonstrations to field units throughout the USA, but no official support was gained and the US forces lost what today would have been a useful COIN type.

In 1952, the Toyo Koku K.K. in Tokyo realized the aircraft's possibilities and acquired a manufacturing licence for the Defender with the aim of selling it to several south-east Asian air forces. The first Toyo-built Defender (an FD-25B) was flown in March 1953, but in August 1954 the company became bankrupt and production ceased. About half-a-dozen FD-25Bs had then been sold to the Cambodian air force, and two FD-25Bs and an FD-25A to North Vietnam. A number of completed but unsold aircraft were stored on Fujisawa airfield, and three of them were bought by a Tokyo aeronautical engineering college early in 1961 for study purposes. All models of the Defender were powered by a six-cylinder, 225-hp Continental E-225-8 air-cooled engine.

Yokosuka B3Y1

One of the Japanese aircraft industry's less successful products for the Navy, the B3Y1 was designed by the Yokosuka Naval Air Arsenal as a potential replacement for the ageing Mitsubishi Type 13 (B1M1) attack-bomber and appeared in prototype form in 1932. It was a bulky three-seat biplane, with forward-staggered two-bay wings and an uncommonly sturdy main undercarriage. The fuselage was long and slender, with prominent cylinder-block fairings over the engine cowling.

A 500-hp V-12 liquid-cooled engine powered the prototype, but this was changed in production aircraft for the 750-hp Type 91 liquid-cooled Vee, an Aichi-built version of the French Lorraine. A bomb-load of up to 1,765 lb could be suspended on underwing racks, or a 1,765-lb torpedo or auxiliary fuel tank installed beneath the centre fuselage.

At the end of 1932, the B3Y1 went into series production for the Japanese Navy, and was designated the Type 92 carrier-based attack aircraft. It was strongly built, and had a good combat range, but was cumbersome in the extreme and difficult to handle in the confined spaces on board contemporary carriers. Navy pilots were outspoken in their criticism of its shortcomings. Only 130 production aircraft were built (by Aichi) and the aircraft participated only briefly in the Sino-Japanese war. Finally, it was withdrawn from service and its place taken, temporarily at any rate, by the same B1M1s it had been intended to succeed.

Yokosuka B4Y1

The B4Y1 was a large, two-bay, single-engined biplane with a strong superficial likeness to the British Westland biplanes of the mid-1930s. It sprang from a 9-*Shi* (1934) requirement for a three-seat torpedo-bomber, to which specification Nakajima designed and built two B4N1 prototypes. The first of these was powered by a 710-hp Nakajima Hikari air-cooled radial and the second by a similar engine developing 830 hp. The fluted cowlings of the engines were distinctive, as was the uncommonly long tail-wheel leg, presumably to give easier access for bombing-up.

By 1936, the Nakajima company was heavily committed to products of greater priority, including the B5N monoplane torpedo-bomber and Ki-27 Army fighter, and the entire B4N project was handed over to the Yokosuka Naval Air Arsenal for completion. Two hundred B4Y1 bombers were built (as Type 96 carrier-based attack aircraft), powered by various models of the Hikari engine, ranging from 710 to 750 and 840 hp.

Extensive use of duralumin was made in the B4Y1's construction, keeping all-up weight to a minimum while conferring great structural rigidity. For defensive purposes, a single 7.7-mm machine-gun was carried on a movable mounting in the rear cockpit.

A small number of these bombers, relegated to the training rôle, were still in service on the outbreak of World War II and were given the code-name "Jean".

Yokosuka D4Y Suisei (Comet)

Japan's Suisei of World War II represented a major change in the contemporary approach to designing dive-bombers, which had generally been large and relatively slow-flying aircraft. For this it had to thank the demanding requirements of the Japanese Navy, issued in 1937, for a carrier-based two-seater capable of flying at least 920 miles (maximum 1,380 miles) with a 550-lb bomb-load and with a minimum top speed of 320 mph – as fast as the current A6M2 Zero fighter. This pointed to a comparatively small airframe, and the Yokosuka Naval Air Arsenal based its proposal on the use of a liquid-cooled in-line engine – a new departure for Japanese naval

Yokosuka B3Y1

Yokosuka B4Y1

Yokosuka D4Y1 Suisei

TYPE	DIMENSIONS span ft	span in	length ft	length in	height ft	height in	WEIGHT max t-o lb	PERFORMANCE max speed mph	at height ft	service ceiling ft	combat range miles	REMARKS
Tachikawa Ki-74	88	7	57	10⅞	16	8¾	44,092	360	27,887	39,370	4,350	
Toyo FD-25B	30	0	20	11	6	3	2,500	187	SL	16,500	630	
Yokosuka B3Y1	NA		NA		NA		NA	130	NA	NA	4½ hrs.	Model 1
Yokosuka B4Y1	49	2½	33	3½			7,937	173	NA	NA	978	Model 1

Yokosuka D4Y2 Suisei

Yokosuka D4Y2 Suisei

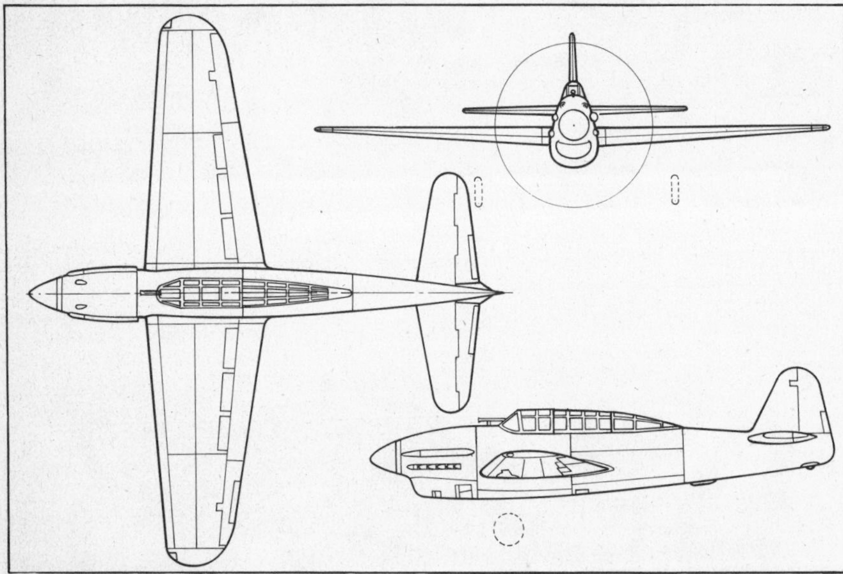
Yokosuka D4Y2 Suisei

Yokosuka D4Y3 Suisei

aircraft designers. The last Navy aircraft with an in-line engine had been the Aichi Type 92 of 1932.

The first prototype was powered by an imported Daimler-Benz DB600G engine of 960 hp, with which it made its first flight in November 1940. It was accepted by the JNAF and entered series production in the following year as the D4Y1 Model 11, or Type 2 carrier-based dive-bomber. Manufacture was handled for the Navy by Aichi Kokuki K.K., service aircraft being powered by a single 1,200-hp Aichi Atsuta 21 12-cylinder inverted Vee engine. In addition to one internally-stowed 550-lb bomb, the D4Y1 could carry a 66-lb bomb beneath each wing, and had a defensive armament of two fixed 7·7-mm guns forward and a flexible 7·92-mm gun in the rear cockpit.

Early service aircraft revealed a number of structural weaknesses and when the Suisei ("Judy" in the Pacific coding system) made its operational debut, flying from the carrier *Soryu* during the battle of Midway late in 1942, it was as a reconnaissance aircraft, designated D4Y1-C (or Type 2 carrier-based reconnaissance). The second production version, the D4Y2 (Model 12) introduced a strengthened airframe and a 1,400-hp Atsuta 32 engine, and this did begin its career as a dive-bomber; but by September 1944, the date of its first major action against a US task force off Truk Island in the Marianas, most aircraft of this mark had also been relegated to reconnaissance, as D4Y2-Cs.

Although the structural deficiencies had been minimized, the Suisei's rather complex construction posed a number of maintenance problems under operational conditions. In particular, there were difficulties with the undercarriage retraction mechanism, and deliveries of the Atsuta engine were not keeping pace with airframe construction. Thus, an important change was made in the next version, the D4Y3 (Model 33), by installing a radial engine, the 1,560-hp Mitsubishi Kinsei 62. The loss of performance brought about by the heavier, bulkier engine was considered acceptable as the price for virtual elimination of the other difficulties.

By this time, owing to heavy Japanese losses in the Pacific, the Suisei was compelled to operate from shore bases as much as from aircraft carriers. For the final battle in the Philippines, a special suicide version was evolved: this was the D4Y4, or Model 43, a single-seat conversion of the D4Y3 packed with 1,765 lb of high-explosive and fitted with two or three small assisted take-off rockets, which was built in small numbers.

A total of 2,319 Suiseis of all versions was completed, 500 of these by the Hiro Naval Air Arsenal and the remainder by Aichi Kokuki. The final version – another emergency conversion – saw the aircraft in the night fighter rôle, defending Japanese home territory in 1945. For this, a number of D4Y2s were converted (as D4Y2-S) to have one or two 20-mm cannon fixed obliquely behind the rear cockpit to fire forward and upward at a 30° angle.

Yokosuka P1Y1 Ginga (Milky Way)

This handsome twin-engined naval bomber had its origins in a 15-*Shi* (1940) requirement for a land-based aircraft capable of performing both level and dive-bombing missions. In practice it became also a torpedo-bomber and a night fighter (as the Kawanishi-developed P1Y1-S Kyokko); while the Ginga-Kai was intended to become a mother-plane for the Model 22 Ohka piloted flying bomb.

After three years of intensive work, the first of several prototypes (designated Y-20 by Yokosuka) made its maiden flight early in 1943. Its 1,820-hp Homare 11 engines gave it a speed of 347 mph at 19,300 ft, and in "clean" condition it had a combat range of 3,100 miles. Extendable air-brakes were fitted beneath the wing for use when dive-bombing.

Before final acceptance, the JNAF dictated modifications designed to simplify the Ginga's rather complex construction; these included the use of a simpler form of skin riveting, flat instead of curved perspex panels in the crew stations, a fixed instead of retracting tail-wheel, and additional armour protection for the crew.

In August 1943 production began of the P1Y1 Model 11, construction and assembly of the Ginga having been assigned to the Nakajima factories at Koizumi and

Fukushima. In the ensuing two years Nakajima completed 906 Ginga bombers, bringing total production of the P1Y types (with the P1Y1-S Kyokko) to 1,002 machines.

Code-named "Frances" by the Allies, the Ginga began to be delivered to JNAF units in the spring of 1944. It was pleasant to handle, nimble for its size and probably capable of considerable development; but it was prevented from realizing its full potential by shortage of skilled assembly workers, skilled pilots and supplies of the proper grade of fuel; and by the problematical Homare engine, installed at the Navy's insistence.

Usual armament of the P1Y1 comprised one 20-mm nose cannon and a single 12·7-mm dorsal machine-gun, though some aircraft were fitted with a dorsal turret mounting two 12·7- or 20-mm guns. Typical weapon loads included two 550-lb bombs internally, with further, smaller bombs beneath the wings; a single 1,870- or 1,765-lb torpedo beneath the centre fuselage; or two 1,100-lb bombs inboard of the engine nacelles.

Gingas were not used extensively in the Pacific island campaigns, but were active from land bases in Japan, particularly from Kyushu; and they sank at least one US carrier. Several were employed in the suicide rôle at Okinawa. Also, during 1945, one Ginga was used to flight-test the Ne-20 turbojet engine.

Yokosuka MXY-7 Ohka (Cherry Blossom)

Epitomizing the desperate measures resorted to by Japanese forces in the later stages of World War II, the Ohka piloted bomb was a product of the Imperial Japanese Navy, with whom the Kamikaze concept originated in 1944, although there had been earlier instances of both Army and Navy pilots crashing already-doomed aircraft into the nearest feasible Allied target.

In August 1944 the Naval Air Research and Development Centre opened a *Marudai* project to evolve a specialist machine for the suicide rôle, able to carry a high-explosive warhead of up to 2,645 lb weight. Previously, most *Kamikaze* attacks had been made with Zeros, whose destructive effect was limited.

The outcome of these studies was the MXY-7 Ohka (together with the unpowered MXY-7 trainer), evolved by the Yokosuka Naval Air Arsenal and built under priority programmes in a number of Japanese factories. The first model – and the only one employed operationally – was the Model 11, carrying 2,645 lb of explosive, powered by a three-barrelled Type 4 Model 20 solid-propellent rocket motor of 1,765 lb s t and air-launched from a specially adapted G4M2e "Betty" mother-plane. Altogether 755 Model 11s were built. They were followed by about 50 slightly smaller Model 22s, with a 1,320-lb warhead and powered by a TSU-11 jet-engine, the compressor of which was driven by a 110-hp Hatsukaze piston-engine to produce 440 lb of thrust. The Model 22 was to have been carried by the P1Y1 Ginga bomber, but test machines failed repeatedly, through being underpowered, and this version never reached service.

An April 1945 proposal, the Model 33, was to have had a 1,765-lb warhead and a 1,047-lb s t Ne-20 turbojet (based on the German BMW 003) and to have been carried by the G8N1 Renzan bomber; but it was still incomplete at VJ-day. The projected Models 43A and 43B (the former with folding wings), for launching from submarine-based

Yokosuka P1Y1 Ginga

Yokosuka P1Y1 Ginga

Yokosuka MXY-7 Ohka, training version

TYPE	DIMENSIONS						WEIGHT	PERFORMANCE				REMARKS
	span		length		height		max t-o	max speed	at height	service ceiling	combat range	
	ft	in	ft	in	ft	in	lb	mph	ft	ft	miles	
Yokosuka D4Y1-C	37	8¾	33	6⅜	10	9½		339	15,580	32,350	1,110	Model 11
Yokosuka D4Y2	37	8¾	33	6⅜	10	9½	9,596	360	17,225	35,170	750	Model 12
Yokosuka D4Y3	37	8¾	33	6⅜	10	9½	10,267	350	19,360	34,450	944	Model 33
Yokosuka P1Y1	65	7⅓	49	2½	14	1¼	29,762	345	19,357	33,530	2,728	Model 11
Yokosuka MXY-7	16	4⅞	19	10½	NA		4,718	535	NA	NA	55	Model II: speed of up to 620 mph in dive

Yokosuka MXY-7 Ohka

Fokker D.XI

Fokker D.XI (PW-7)

Fokker D.XIII

and land-based catapults respectively did not progress beyond the study stage.

Unbeknown at the time to the US forces, they deferred their initial encounter with the Ohka when, in November 1944, they sank the giant carrier *Shinano*, en route to the Philippines on her maiden voyage with a cargo of 50 of the piloted bombs. Thus, the first combat appearance of the Model 11 was made on 21 March 1945, when 16 Ohka-carrying G4M2es, escorted by 30 Zeros, made for a US task force some 300 miles off Kyushu; but the Japanese formation ran into a defensive force of more than 50 Hellcats, lost every Ohka-carrying bomber and half of the Zero escort without launching a single weapon. Later, some 300 Ohkas were assigned to the Okinawa theatre, but records suggest that only about a quarter of this total were launched at Allied targets. Many of them scored direct hits and had at least a temporary effect on Allied morale, despite the derisive name *Baka* (Japanese for "fool") bestowed on them by the US Navy.

The Ohka can scarcely be counted a success as a warplane. From March to August 1945, most suicide attacks continued to be carried out with conventional aircraft, and more than half of the JNAF's remaining pilots resorted (or were ordered) to this form of warfare.

Netherlands

Fokker D.XI

Following the end of the 1914–18 War, Anthony Fokker established a new aircraft factory in his native Holland and set about the task of securing orders for fighters developed from the outstanding D.VII of 1918. Among the first of the new designs was the D.IX, a larger machine than the D.VII, with a 300-hp Hispano engine and redesigned tail unit. The one and only D.IX attracted interest (including that of the US Army Air Corps, which evaluated it under the designation PW-6) but no customers. However, it formed the basis of the later D.XI, which was more successful.

A single-bay, unequal-span biplane, the D.XI single-seat fighter was also powered by the 300-hp Hispano liquid-cooled engine. Armament consisted of two forward-firing machine-guns mounted in front of the cockpit.

The D.XI appeared in 1923, making its first flight on 5 May. The Dutch air forces did not order it, but a contract for 125 came from the Soviet Union, where German pilots were training clandestinely, against the day when the Luftwaffe would be reborn. Three other D.XIs were supplied to the US Army Air Corps. Re-engined with the 440-hp Curtiss D-12 and with modified undercarriage, they were tested as PW-7s; but no further examples were ordered. The remaining machines of the total of 177 built by Fokker were supplied in small numbers to Argentina, Rumania, Spain and Switzerland.

Fokker D.XIII

A further development in the family of fighters stemming from the Fokker D.VII, via the D.IX and D.XI, was the D.XII of 1924. First flown on 21 August that year, it was powered by a 385-hp Curtiss V-1150 liquid-cooled engine and had fabric-covered wings in place of the plywood wings of its predecessors. Like them, however, it failed to penetrate the American market at which it had been aimed and was built only in prototype form.

The design was taken a stage further with the evolution in the same year of the D.XIII single-seat fighter. Powered by a 450-hp Napier Lion 12-cylinder liquid-cooled engine, this aircraft flew for the first time on 12 September 1924, and set up four world speed records with 550-lb and 1,100-lb payloads in the following year. Its normal armament consisted of twin machine-guns mounted over the engine.

Like the D.XI before it, the D.XIII assisted indirectly in the renaissance of German air power, for the 50 production machines that were built were ordered by Russia on behalf of Germany, which was prohibited by international treaty from training with military weapons.

Fokker DC.I

The designation DC.I (D = fighter, C = reconnaissance) was applied by the NV Vliegtuigen Fokker to a short-span variant of the Fokker C.IV. The latter aircraft, which appeared first in 1922, was basically a reconnaissance type and was evolved as a successor to the C.I. It was a sturdy two-seat biplane, of typical Fokker construction and configuration, with a somewhat roomier fuselage than its predecessor, and was used quite widely by both the LVA (Dutch Air Force) and several foreign air forces. Its chief feature was the ability to utilize wings of varying spans, which could be interchanged between machines according to the mission each was required to perform. Basically, however, the long-span models (the C.IVB, C.IVC and seaplane C.IV-W) were used for reconnaissance, while the shorter-span wings were employed on the C.IVA and DC.I fighters.

Powered by a 450-hp Napier Lion liquid-cooled engine, the DC.I was armed with two light machine-guns in the front upper engine decking, fired by the pilot, and two additional guns on a flexible mounting in the observer's cockpit at the rear. Production of the DC.I was small: apart from the prototype (H-NABZ), only ten production examples were built; these were assigned to the Army Air Service in the Netherlands East Indies in the late autumn of 1925.

Fokker C.V-C, -D and -E

The C.V was perhaps the most successful military aircraft ever built by the Fokker company. It saw service with the air forces of nearly a dozen countries and enjoyed a career which spanned almost the entire period between World Wars I and II. Not only was it a delight to fly; the ease with which servicing – including the replacement of complete wings or engines – could be carried out made it as popular with ground staffs as it was with the men who flew it. The interchange of wings of varying span, and the variety of engines of from 350 hp to 730 hp which were fitted to the different models, were a feature of the C.V. So few machines needed to be returned for attention during their lives that for a number of years there was an acute shortage of work at the Fokker factory.

The C.V. was of mixed construction, having a welded steel-tube fuselage structure and wooden wings. The original C.V-A and C.V-B had angular, untapered wings with protruding ailerons, and this planform was retained by the C.V-C which first appeared in 1923. Recipients of the C.V-C during the middle 1920s included the Marine Luchtvaartdienst (Dutch Naval Air Service) and one combat group of the Bolivian Cuerpo de Aviación. Ten examples of the C.V-W, a floatplane adaptation for advanced training duties, were also built for the MLD; but these were later converted back to C.V-C standard.

In its normal rôle of light bomber and reconnaissance aircraft, the C.V-C was armed with two light machine-guns, one firing forward from in front of the cockpit and one carried on a ring mounting in the rear cockpit. The usual power plant was the 450-hp Hispano-Suiza, although a few MLD machines were flown with the 400-hp Lorraine-Dietrich. The C.V-C was employed by the MLD both at home and in the East Indies.

Fokker DC.I

Fokker C.V-C, Royal Netherlands Navy

Fokker C.V-D, Kestrel engine

TYPE	DIMENSIONS span ft	in	length ft	in	height ft	in	WEIGHT max t-o lb	PERFORMANCE max speed mph	at height ft	service ceiling ft	combat range miles	REMARKS
Fokker D.XI	38	0	22	11	9	6	2,755	140	NA	NA	NA	
Fokker D.XIII	36	1	25	11	9	6	3,637	160	NA	24,600	373	
Fokker DC.I	37	6	30	0	11	2	4,026	148	NA	NA	NA	
Fokker C.V-C	47	10	30	10	12	3	5,368	146	NA	NA	NA	

Fokker C.V-E, Pegasus engine, Royal Norwegian Air Force

Fokker C.V-E, Swiss Air Force

Fokker D.XVI, Jaguar engine

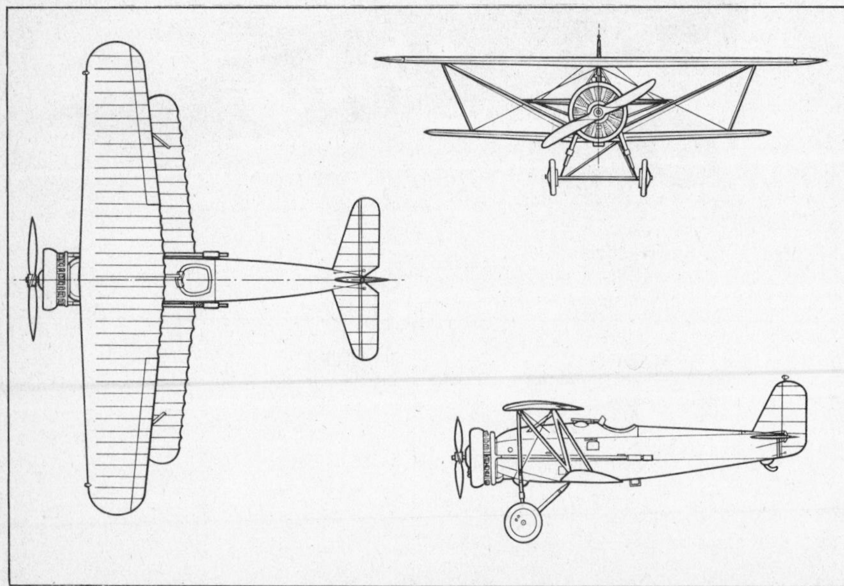
Fokker D.XVI

The principal production versions were, however, the C.V-D and C.V-E, on which a new wing planform was introduced – tapered and altogether cleaner aerodynamically than that of the earlier versions. The C.V-D, with a short-span wing, was basically a fighter or army co-operation type; whereas the long-span C.V-E was used for reconnaissance and light bombing duties. Standard power plant of the LVA (Dutch Air Force) C.V-Ds was the 450-hp Hispano-Suiza, although 26 aircraft (sometimes known as C.VIs) had a 350-hp Hispano-Suiza and some of the ground-support machines had the 450-hp Armstrong Siddeley Jaguar. Other engines installed experimentally included the Rolls-Royce Kestrel and Bristol Jupiter. Well over 100 C.V-Ds served with the LVA, the fighter versions having two guns forward and two aft. The type began to be replaced in 1936, but when Holland was invaded in 1940 there were still no fewer than 28 of these veteran aircraft in service.

The C.V-D and -E enjoyed considerable success outside the Netherlands, particularly in Scandinavia. The Danish government acquired a number of Dutch-built machines in 1924 and, after testing a 730-hp Pegasus radial engine in a C.V-E in 1933, built a further 23 similarly-powered machines at Kløvermarken for the Army Air Corps. Norway's Hærens Flyfabrikk (Army Aircraft Factory) acquired a licence for the C.V-E and the Flyvåpnet still had a few in service in 1940. Dutch-built C.V-Es were also supplied to Sweden, being joined later by 39 licence-built aircraft; the Flygvapnet C.V-Es, designated S 6, were powered by Pegasus engines.

It was a Swedish C.V-E ski-plane which rescued General Umberto Nobile in June 1928 after his airship, the *Italia*, had failed to reach the North Pole. Finland was another Fokker customer for the C.V-Es in the mid-1930s; and both Finnish and Swedish C.V-Es were still in service at the outbreak of World War II. Large numbers were built in Italy, from 1927, as the Meridionali Ro.1 (420-hp Bristol Jupiter) and Ro.1 *bis* (550-hp Piaggio-built Jupiter VIII); and after delivery of three to the Swiss Fliegertruppe in 1931 a further 50 were built (serial numbers 302-5, 311-59) by EKW at Thun and Dornier at Altenrhein in 1932–36, as replacements for obsolete Haefelis. The Swiss-produced C-35 (see page 304) was directly evolved from the Fokker design.

Fokker D.XVI and D.XVII

By 1929, having rejected both the Fokker D.XI and D.XIII, the Luchtvaartafdeling was badly in need of a modern fighter to succeed the early post-war D.VIIs which had been in service for nearly a decade. To meet this requirement, the Fokker company produced the D.XVI, a development of the D.XII design via the projected (but not built) D.XV and D.XVa of 1928. A lightweight, very manoeuvrable single-seater of sesquiplane layout, the prototype D.XVI was flown for the first time in 1929, powered by a 450-hp uncowled Armstrong Siddeley Jaguar radial air-cooled engine. Fifteen aircraft of this type, their engines fitted with Townend rings, were ordered for the LVA and entered service with the serial numbers 275-289. Later, D.XVI No. 277 was re-engined with a Bristol Mercury for one of Holland's leading aerobatic pilots, Lieutenant Sandbergh.

D.XVIs were also built for China (1), Hungary (4) and Italy (1). The Chinese D.XVI, delivered in late 1929 or early 1930, became the personal aircraft of the military governor of Manchuria, Marshal Chang Hsueh-Liang. The Hungarian machines differed from the others in having Bristol Jupiter radial engines in place of the usual Jaguars. Armament in all cases consisted of twin 7·5-mm machine-guns, mounted over the engine cowling.

A second prototype D.XVII (F-32) was fitted with a Curtiss Conqueror V-1570 12-cylinder liquid-cooled engine and flew in this form in 1931. The object was to produce a D.VII replacement suitable for the Netherlands East Indies Army Air Service, but no orders were placed and in 1932 F-32 was the subject of further modifications, to re-emerge as the prototype for the D.XVII.

By this time the NEI Army, whose requirements would have been met by the new machine, had insufficient funds to purchase it. However, it was evaluated by the LVA, with a resultant order for 11 aircraft of this type. Slightly larger and heavier than their predecessor, the D.XVIIs began to enter service with LVA fighter squadrons in 1933. Most of them were fitted with 595-hp Rolls-Royce Kestrel IIS engines, though their known power plants included the 690-hp Hispano-Suiza 12Xbrs and the 790-hp Lorraine Petrel. Armament was as on the D.XVI.

On 18 January 1935, a D.XVII set up a new Dutch national altitude record by flying to 33,399 ft.

Although built in only limited numbers, the D.XVII – the last biplane fighter to come from the Fokker stable – was highly popular with its pilots. Six were still in service at the Texel flying school when Holland was overrun in May 1940, although they apparently undertook no combat duty in the "five-day war" which followed.

An improved version, the D.XVIIB, was on the Fokker drawing boards at the beginning of 1936. This would have had an enclosed cockpit and a Hispano-Suiza 12Y *moteur-canon* engine; but the project was abandoned in favour of the D.XXI monoplane.

Fokker C.X

Evolved as a successor to the famous C.V, the prototype C.X was flown for the first time in 1934. It was a sturdy, single-bay unequal-span biplane of mixed construction, with a fixed undercarriage, and carried a crew of two in open cockpits. Power was supplied by a 650-hp Rolls-Royce Kestrel V liquid-cooled engine, the coolant radiator of which projected prominently beneath the fuselage between the main landing gear struts. Designed for reconnaissance and light ground-attack work, the C.X was fitted with underwing racks for two 385-lb or four 220-lb bombs, and was armed with two forward-firing 7·9 mm machine-guns in the top of the engine cowling and a third, movable gun in the observer's cockpit.

Although it was not to achieve either the production or the service record of its predecessor, work began in 1935 on the construction of 10 C.X's for the Netherlands East Indies Army Air Service, and deliveries of these began in 1937. A further order was placed in 1937, this time for 20 aircraft for the LVA at home; the last 15 of these were fitted with closed-in cockpits, and a tail-wheel replaced the skid of earlier machines. The Kestrel remained the standard power plant for C.Xs in Dutch service, although experimental installations are known to have been made, among them the 925-hp Hispano-Suiza 12Ycrs *moteur-canon* engine.

Fokker also built four C.Xs for Finland, these being fitted, at the Finns' request, with 835-hp Bristol Pegasus XXI radial engines, which conferred a slightly enhanced performance. A manufacturing licence was negotiated and the Valtion Lentokonetehdas (State Aircraft Factory) built 30 Pegasus-powered C.Xs in 1938. In 1942 a further five, presumably replacement aircraft, were completed in Finland.

When Holland was invaded in May 1940, ten serviceable C.Xs were still operating with the LVA, and were pressed into action during the "five-day war" for reconnaissance and ground strafing duties.

Fokker F.VII-3m/M and F.IX/M

The Fokker F.VII series of airliners were a byword in the years between the two World Wars, and are assured of

Fokker D.XVII

Fokker C.X

Fokker C.X, Finnish Air Force

TYPE	DIMENSIONS						WEIGHT	PERFORMANCE				REMARKS
	span		length		height		max t-o	max speed	at height	service ceiling	combat range	
	ft	in	ft	in	ft	in	lb	mph	ft	ft	miles	
Fokker C.V-D	41	$0\frac{1}{8}$	31	$3\frac{1}{8}$	10	$9\frac{7}{8}$	4,222	158	NA	22,965	NA	Short span wing
Fokker C.V-E	50	$2\frac{1}{3}$	30	$4\frac{1}{8}$	11	$0\frac{1}{8}$	4,894	143	13,120	20,340	NA	Long span wing
Fokker D.XVI	30	10	23	8	8	10	3,086	205	NA	31,980	560	
Fokker D.XVII	31	6	23	$7\frac{1}{2}$	9	$10\frac{1}{8}$	3,262	208	NA	28,710	528	Performance with Kestrel
Fokker C.X	39	4	30	2	10	10	4,960	199	10,000	27,230	516	Dutch-built with Kestrel
Fokker C.X	39	4	30	2	10	10	5,500	212	10,000	27,400	520	Finnish-built with Pegasus

Fokker F.VIIA-3m/M

Fokker F.VIIB-3m/M

Fokker D.XXI

their place in commercial aviation history. Stemming from the original single-engined F.VII, designed by W. Rethel (later to become chief designer to the Arado Flugzeugwerke in Germany), the trimotor development was inspired by Anthony Fokker and engineered by Reinhold Platz in the middle 1920s, becoming one of the most successful transport aircraft ever built.

The military version was rather less successful. The F.VIIA-3m/M, powered by three 200-hp Armstrong Siddeley Lynx radial engines, was evaluated by the LVA in various rôles, including those of bomber (load 2,200 lb), torpedo-carrier (one 2,200 lb torpedo slung externally) and air ambulance (accommodation for six stretcher cases). Ten were ordered, three of these being used in Holland for night flying and bombing training or general transport duties, while the remaining seven were assigned to the Netherlands East Indies Army Air Service as bomber-transports. Some of these were F.VIIB-3m/Ms, an improved model with increased wing span and 300-hp Wright Whirlwind radial engines.

In the bomber rôle, the F.VII-3m/M carried a single dorsal machine-gun, with another located in the belly and firing downwards through the fuselage floor.

Apart from a few which served with the Spanish Air Force, the only other military F.VIIB-3ms were a small batch of bombers built under licence by the Plage and Laskievicz factory in Poland: these became relegated to transport duties in 1936 and were still in service when the Germans invaded Poland three years later. The F.VII-3m/M was evaluated in Great Britain and (as the C-2) by the United States, but this did not result in any military production orders or licence manufacture.

An enlarged development of the F.VII-3m was the F.IX, Fokker's largest trimotor design. This was not so successful as an airliner, but a licence was acquired by the Avia company in Prague, who built it as the F-39 with 635-hp Walter Pegasus radials, as an air-liner for CSA, and as a four-man bomber for the Czechoslovak and Yugoslav air forces.

Fokker D.XXI

The design of the D.XXI, by E. Schatzki of the Fokker company, was undertaken in 1936 to meet a specification issued by the Royal Netherlands East Indies Army for a single-seat fighter. The outcome was a tough, sturdy little aircraft of conventional appearance – a low-wing monoplane of mixed construction with a fixed, "spatted" undercarriage. The prototype (FD-322) was flown at Welschap on 27 March 1936, by which time official Dutch re-equipment plans favoured the bomber rather than the fighter, hence no immediate contract was received. In the early summer of 1937, however, a further change of outlook led to an order for 36 D.XXIs for the LVA, to be powered by the 830-hp Bristol Mercury VII or VIII nine-cylinder air-cooled radial engine in place of the 645-hp Mercury VI-S of the prototype. These aircraft (serialled 211-246) entered service in 1938-9, and the prototype was subsequently brought up to the same standard and placed in service as No. 247. In September 1938, aircraft No. 217 reached a height of 34,060 ft, to set a new Dutch national altitude record.

Dutch pilots found the D.XXI an easy machine to fly, combining the properties of a stable gun platform with a high degree of manoeuvrability. Standard armament comprised two 7·9-mm FN-Browning machine-guns, installed in the upper engine cowling, and a second pair in the wings outboard of the propeller disc.

When the Germans invaded Holland on 10 May 1940, there were 29 serviceable D.XXIs on strength, made up of eleven with the 1st Fighter Group at De Kooy, ten with the 2nd Fighter Group at Schiphol and eight with the 5th Fighter Group at Ypenburg. Although handicapped by their comparatively low speed, the D.XXIs gave a good account of themselves until, after three days, the survivors were grounded for lack of ammunition.

This was not the extent of the Fokker D.XXI's participation in World War II. In 1937 the Finnish government had placed an order for the type, and seven aircraft (FR-76 to -82) were delivered from Holland. The Valtion Lentokonetehdas (Finnish State Aircraft Factory) at Tampere acquired a manufacturing licence, and delivered a further 38 Mercury VIII-powered machines (FR-83 to -120) in 1938, to the 2nd Air Regiment. Finnish production of the D.XXI was then suspended until 1941, by which time the Mercury engines were required more urgently for the Blenheim bombers also being built under licence. The VL, therefore, redesigned the D.XXI airframe to accept the 825-hp Pratt & Whitney Twin Wasp Junior SB4G engine, 80 of which it had purchased from the USA in 1940. Principal outward changes were the placing of all four guns in the wings, and a revised fin and rudder of greater area, resulting in a higher all-up weight and some reduction in performance.

Fifty Wasp-powered D.XXIs were delivered during 1941. Finnish production of the D.XXI concluded with an additional five machines in 1944. These fighters fought with distinction in the "winter war" against Russia (November 1939 – March 1940) and in the later campaigns which began in the spring of 1941, frequently being employed with ski landing gear. Towards the end of the D.XXI's Finnish service, when it was relegated largely to the reconnaissance rôle, the V.L. carried out further modifications which resulted in improved rearward visibility from the cockpit.

Two other customers who acquired licences for the D.XXI were Spain and Denmark. The Spanish Republican government aircraft factory at Carmoli, however, fell into Nationalist hands before any of the completed machines could be flown, and there is no evidence that they took any active part in the conflict. Two D.XXIs were purchased from Holland by the Danish government in 1937, and ten aircraft were built subsequently by Orlogsværftet (the Danish Naval Dockyard) at Kløvermarken in 1939–40. The Danish machines differed in having the Mercury VI-S engine and a 20-mm Madsen cannon in a blister fairing beneath each wing, in addition to the wing-mounted machine-guns; they were in service with the 2nd Eskadrille at the time of the German invasion.

Experimental D.XXIs evolved by Fokker before the war included one with a completely re-designed wing; and engine test-beds for the Rolls-Royce Kestrel V and Hispano-Suiza 12Y in-line engines. Projects 150, 151 and 152, all with retractable undercarriage, were for versions with 1,375-hp Hercules, 1,050-hp Merlin and 1,090-hp DB 600H engines respectively; and a version of the D.XXI with retractable undercarriage was also examined by the V.L. in Finland.

Fokker T.IV

To meet a requirement of the Marine Luchtvaartdienst (Naval Air Service, or MLD), the Fokker company began in 1926 the design of a twin-engined seaplane for torpedo-bomber and reconnaissance duties. Designated T.IV, the prototype (T-1) flew for the first time on 7 June 1927. A shoulder-wing monoplane of mixed wood and metal construction, with open cockpits, the T.IV was mounted on twin floats and was powered by two 450-hp Lorraine-Dietrich "W" liquid-cooled Vee engines. A further eleven machines (T-2 to T-12) were ordered in 1927, mainly for the use of the Royal Netherlands East Indies Navy, and later that year three were delivered to the Aviação Maritima of Portugal.

Eight years later, despite its age, the design was revived,

Fokker D.XXI prototype

Fokker D.XXI, Finnish Air Force

Fokker T.IV

TYPE	DIMENSIONS span ft	span in	length ft	length in	height ft	height in	WEIGHT max t-o lb	PERFORMANCE max speed mph	at height ft	service ceiling ft	combat range miles	REMARKS
Fokker F.VIIA-3m/M	63	4	47	10	12	10	9,020	115	NA	15,584	634 max	
Fokker F.IX (Avia F-39)	88	7	60	8	15	11	19,836	132	NA	NA		
Fokker D.XXI	36	1	26	10¾	9	8	4,519	286	14,500	36,090	590	Dutch-built with Mercury
Fokker D.XXI	36	1	26	3	9	2¼	4,820	272	9,000	32,000	560	Finnish-built with Twin Wasp
Fokker T.IVa	85	11½	57	8⅞	19	8¼	15,873	161	2,625	19,360	970	

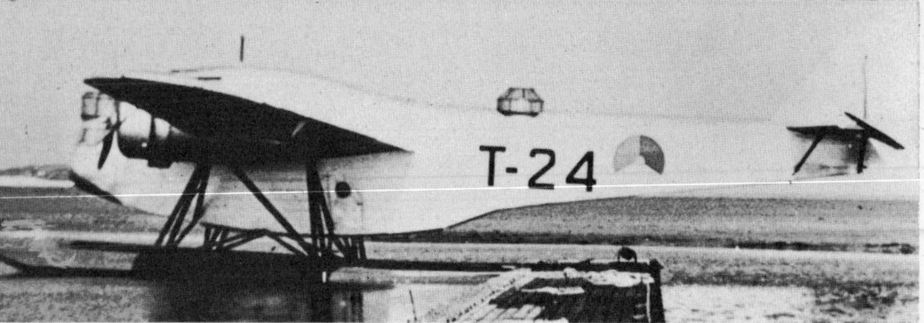

Fokker T.IVa

Fokker T.V

Fokker T.V

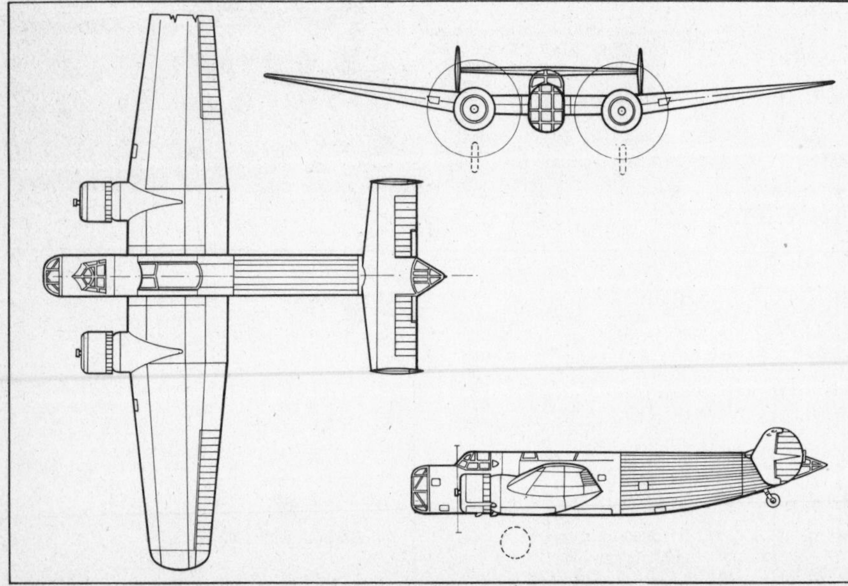
Fokker T.V

and the Dutch government ordered a second batch of 12 aircraft (T-13 to T-24), considerably modified and strengthened to accommodate more powerful Wright Cyclone SR-1820-F2 nine-cylinder radial engines, developing 768-hp each for take-off. The new model, designated T-IVa, was armed with three 7·9-mm FN-Browning machine-guns for defence, one each in nose, dorsal and ventral emplacements, and could carry four 440-lb or eighteen 110-lb bombs internally or a single torpedo slung beneath the centre fuselage. The surviving Dutch T.IVs were also brought up to T.IVa standard in 1936, and the type was still giving reliable service in the Netherlands East Indies at the time of the Japanese invasion, its duties including coastal and sea reconnaissance, and air/sea rescue. Some of the later production T.IVas had enclosed gun positions in the bow and upper rear fuselage. Although far from being an appealing design visually, the T.IV proved an eminently seaworthy and capable machine throughout more than a decade.

Fokker T.V

The LVA requirement to which the T.V was designed called for a three-seat, long-range fighter-bomber; but the resultant design, with its thick broad wings and portly, slab-sided fuselage, was patently incapable of indulging in fighter-type manoeuvres and, consequently, the design was developed instead as a medium bomber. There was no prototype as such, the first T.V to take the air, on 16 October 1937, being the first of a batch of 16 ordered by the Dutch government in 1937. Of mixed wood and metal construction, the T.V was a mid-wing monoplane with a retractable undercarriage and twin fins and rudders, powered by two 925-hp Bristol Pegasus XXVI air-cooled radial engines; it accommodated a crew of five. Twin 7·9-mm machine-guns were mounted in the nose, with single 7·9-mm guns in dorsal, ventral, lateral and tail positions. A maximum internal bomb load of 2,200 lb could be carried.

The T.Vs formed the equipment of the LVA's one and only bomber squadron – Bomva 1, of the 1st Air Regiment, to which deliveries were begun in 1938. In service they were found to be far from docile to handle, and their stability left much to be desired. When Germany invaded the Netherlands on 10 May 1940, only 12 of the original 16 remained on strength and three of these were unserviceable. In all fairness, however, the remaining T.Vs put up a gallant performance. They destroyed nearly 30 German aircraft massed on the airfield at Wallhaven, and made valuable attacks upon vital bridges over the Meuse and other nearby waterways. All nine were finally destroyed, two by their compatriots' ground fire.

The T.V was obsolescent by World War II standards, and a replacement design was under consideration before the outbreak of hostilities. This was the T.IX, of much slimmer appearance, with a wing of 81 ft 6 in span and 1,375-hp Bristol Hercules engines; but only the prototype of this bomber was completed.

Fokker T.VIII-W

The Fokker T.VIII-W was one of that small band of aircraft which, through force of circumstance, found itself fighting both for and against the Axis powers in World War II. Evolved in 1937 to an MLD specification for a successor to the T.IVa torpedo-bomber/reconnaissance floatplane, the first T.VIII-W to fly (R-1), in 1938, was one of an initial batch of five aircraft ordered by the MLD. Six of a subsequent order for 14 had also been delivered by 10 May 1940, the Dutch aircraft all being three-seaters, powered by two 450-hp Wright Whirlwind R-975-E-3 nine-cylinder radial engines and having an armament of three 7·9-mm FN-Browning machine-guns. A torpedo or up to 1,300 lb of bombs could be carried.

The aircraft thus far ordered were designated T.VIII-W/G, to distinguish them from the later T.VIII-W/Ms with all-metal rear fuselages. After the Germans had occupied the Netherlands, the twelve T.VIII-W/Ms on Fokker's assembly line, together with the remaining eight T.VIII-W/Ms, were completed and put into service by the Luftwaffe on reconnaissance, anti-shipping and air/sea rescue duties over the North Sea and Mediterranean. Five other T.VIII-Ws also found their way into Luftwaffe service. These were of an enlarged model (span 65 ft 7⅓in, length 48 ft 7¾in), powered by 890-hp Bristol Mercury XI radial engines, which was under construction to a Finnish contract placed at the beginning of 1939. They were to have had interchangeable wheel, float or ski gear, and one was completed as a T.VIII-L landplane; the remaining four were designated T.VIII-W/C.

Meanwhile, the serving Dutch T.VIII-W/Gs had been ordered to evacuate to France on 14 May 1940. For a few days they carried out anti-submarine patrols from Cherbourg along the French Channel coast; then, on 22 May they left France for the United Kingdom. Eight machines (R-1/3/6/7/8/9/10/11) arrived safely, and were impressed into RAF service (with British serials AV958 – 965), to become No. 320 Squadron of Coastal Command, based at Pembroke Dock. From then until September 1940, when the six surviving machines were grounded through lack of spares, they carried out extensive convoy patrol duties over the North Sea, often meeting their Luftwaffe counterparts, abroad on similar missions.

Fokker G.I

When it first appeared on public view, at the 1936 Salon de l'Aéronautique, the prototype Fokker G.I was swiftly dubbed *Le Faucheur* ("The Grim Reaper"), a tribute to its potential for carrying no fewer than nine machine-guns – eight of them concentrated in the nose – in its design rôle as a bomber-interceptor. The G.I was evolved by Fokker as a private venture, and the first machine (registered X-2) made its first flight from Welschap airfield, near Eindhoven, on 16 March 1937. A mid-wing monoplane of mixed construction, it embodied a central two-seat crew nacelle and twin 750-hp Hispano Suiza radial engines in nacelles which were extended in the form of narrow booms to support the tail assembly.

On 21 October 1937, the Dutch government ordered 36 of a somewhat modified production version – a three-seater designated G.IA and powered by 830-hp Bristol Mercury VIII nine-cylinder air-cooled radial engines. A slightly smaller two-seat model, the G.IB with 750-hp Pratt & Whitney Twin Wasp Junior SB4G fourteen-cylinder engines, was offered for export. The prototype G.I was flown by visiting pilots from Denmark, Finland and Turkey, but the first firm overseas response came from Spain, which ordered 12 in 1937. A further 18 were ordered later by Sweden, with the stipulation that they should be fitted with Swedish-built Bofors machine-guns; in 1939, licence production was planned by Denmark.

Deliveries of the G.IAs (serial numbered 301 – 336) to the LVA commenced in 1938, these being made to the 1st Air Regiment's 3rd and 4th Fighter Groups at Waalhaven and Bergen respectively. Experiments were conducted with aircraft No. 304, which had a large perspex observation station, nicknamed the "bathtub", below the centre nacelle; and with another G.IA equipped with hydraulic dive-brakes to evaluate the aircraft's capability as a dive-bomber. Neither of these ideas was adopted generally, although the G.IA was able in the normal course of duty to carry an internal bomb-load of 880 lb for attack missions. Standard armament of the G.IA consisted of eight 7·9-mm Browning machine-guns in the nose and a ninth in the rear of the crew nacelle.

At the outbreak of World War II, the G.IA was by far the most effective military aircraft available in Holland,

Fokker T.VIII-W

Fokker G.IB

Fokker G.IA three-seater

TYPE	DIMENSIONS						WEIGHT	PERFORMANCE				REMARKS
	span		length		height		max t-o	max speed	at height	service ceiling	combat range	
	ft	in	ft	in	ft	in	lb	mph	ft	ft	miles	
Fokker T.V	68	10	52	6	16	5	15,950	259	10,000	25,260	1,012	
Fokker T.VIII-W/C	65	7⅓	48	7¾	17	8½	15,432	222	NA	19,030	1,056	
Fokker T.VIII-W/G	59	0⅔	42	7¾	16	4¾	11,030	177	NA	22,300	1,305	
Fokker G.IA	56	3¼	37	8¾	11	1¾	10,560	295	13,990	30,500	945	
Fokker G.IB	54	1½	33	9½	11	1¾	10,520	268	13,120	28,535	913	

Fokker G.I, reconnaissance version

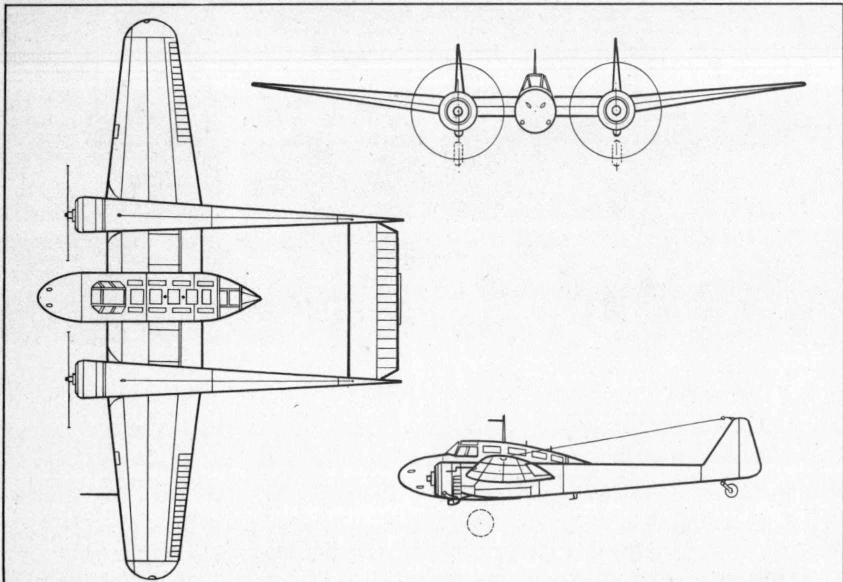

Fokker G.IA

Koolhoven F.K.31, Finnish Air Force

and when German forces invaded the country on 10 May 1940 the LVA had 23 of these machines operational – 12 at Bergen and 11 at Waalhaven. Several were destroyed before they could get into the air, but the remainder acquitted themselves well, although all but one were lost by the final day. (In this last machine two senior Fokker pilots escaped, a year later, to England).

There were also at Schiphol the 12 G.IBs (337-348, of which 341 was the prototype, X-2, rebuilt) ordered by the Spanish government, their export having been forbidden by the Dutch authorities. All were airworthy, but no armament had been installed. Hastily, the Fokker workers stripped enough machine-guns from other damaged Fokker aircraft to fit three of the G.IBs with four guns apiece, and these aircraft too were thrown into the vain attempt to stem the German invasion. (The G.IB was to have had two 23-mm Madsen cannon and two 7·9-mm Brownings in the nose, with a third Browning in the tail-cone.) The remaining nine, and other G.IBs under construction, were completed by mid-1941 and taken over by the Luftwaffe for use as trainers.

Koolhoven F.K.31

Although overshadowed by his contemporary, Anthony Fokker, Frederik Koolhoven was a talented aircraft designer whose later products revealed a great deal of ingenuity. During the 1914–18 War, he acquired valuable experience in the British aircraft industry, working in turn for Armstrong Whitworth and the British Aerial Transport Company. After the war, he was engaged by the NV Nationale Vliegtuigindustrie, for whom in the early 1920s he designed the two-seat F.K.31.

The F.K.31 was evolved to perform the duties of pursuit, interception and army observation, and carried an observer/gunner in addition to the pilot. There were two fixed machine-guns firing forward, and a second pair on a rotating ring mounting in the rear cockpit. The reconnaissance model carried a fifth, downward-firing gun. The Dutch-built F.K.31s were powered by a 400-hp Bristol Jupiter radial engine; a small quantity completed in France by Louis de Monge had Jupiters built under licence by Gnome-Rhône.

The F.K.31 entered production in 1924–5 but, although a highly manoeuvrable aircraft and easy to service, its performance was somewhat below the LVA's requirements and many were assigned to the Netherlands East Indies Army Air Service, with which they remained in use until about 1930. When the NVI company was dissolved in 1926, production of the F.K.31 had already ceased.

Koolhoven F.K. 58

In 1938, the NV Koolhoven Vliegtuigen at Rotterdam acquired the services of one of Fokker's leading technicians, designer E. Schatzki, and his first task for his new employer was the design of a compact single-seat fighter, the F.K. 58. Two prototypes of this aircraft were built, the first (PH-ATO) flying on 22 September 1938 and the second (PH-AVA) about five months later. Each was powered by a single 1,080-hp Hispano Suiza 14A 14-cylinder two-row radial.

No immediate contract from the Dutch government was forthcoming, but a demonstration of PH-ATO at the Centre d'Essais en Vol at Villacoublay in October 1938 was sufficient to secure an order for 50 aircraft from the French authorities one month later. These were to be either Hispano-powered F.K.58s, or F.K.58As with the French-built Gnome-Rhône 14N/16 engine, also of 1,080 hp. Both were to have four 7·5-mm FN-Browning machine-guns, two each in underwing fairings just outboard of the main wheel housings.

As part of its last-minute re-equipment programme, the Dutch government placed an order for 36 F.K. 58s in March 1939, specifying the Bristol Taurus as power plant; but none of these aircraft had reached the LVA by the time of the German invasion in 1940. The two prototypes were lost at Waalhaven in January and May 1940.

Deliveries of the first F.K. 58s to the Armée de l'Air had begun on 17 June 1939, and by the middle of September the Koolhoven factory had delivered seven F.K. 58s and eleven F.K. 58As. To make room for the Dutch order, the French F.K. 58A contract was shared with the Belgian SABCA company, which had ten airframes almost complete before Belgium was invaded, although the French engines to power them were still awaited.

No further Dutch-built fighters reached France, and thus the original 18 were the only F.K. 58s to see combat service. Employed by the Patrouilles de Protection defending Caen, Clermont-Ferrand, Cognac, La Rochelle and Salon, they must have been among the most cosmopolitan opposition encountered by the Luftwaffe – for in addition to Dutch airframes, French engines and Belgian armament, many of them were flown by escaped Polish pilots!

Norway

Marinens Flyvebåtfabrikk M.F.9

Unlike neighbouring Sweden, Norway has never had a flourishing aircraft industry, and extremely few designs of national origin have been developed. Of these, the Norwegian Navy's M.F.9 of the 1920s was the one and only fighter aircraft.

It was the initiative of a single naval officer, Lieutenant Hans Dons, which gave the Norwegian Navy its first aircraft (a Rumpler Taube monoplane) in 1912, but not until four years later did the Norwegian government establish a Naval Air Force (Marinens Flyvevæsen) and authorize the setting up of the Naval Flying-boat Factory (Marinens Flyvebåtfabrikk) at Horten.

The M.F.9 appeared in 1925, as a single-bay biplane fighter (with the lower wing of greater span than the upper), mounted on a pair of long, square-section floats. It was equipped with two forward-firing machine-guns, mounted one each side of the upper engine decking, just ahead of the single open cockpit, and was powered initially by a 300-hp Hispano-Suiza eight-cylinder water-cooled Vee engine. In operation, the M.F.9 proved unpopular with Norwegian naval pilots, due to a marked tendency to spin at the smallest provocation; and of the score or so built, one or two are believed to have been fitted with Bristol Jupiter engines, presumably in an attempt to cure this fault. The move was evidently unsuccessful, and after some five years' service the M.F.9 was withdrawn from squadron use.

Poland

L.W.S.4 and L.W.S.6 Żubr

In marked contrast to other quantity-produced combat aircraft of Polish design, the L.W.S. Żubr twin-engined bomber monoplane was a complete failure. A strange mixture of various structural methods, the Żubr never achieved acceptable standards, in spite of a lengthy and strenuous development process and exorbitant cost per production unit, which was some 10 per cent higher than that of the P 37 Łos.

The study for the aircraft which eventually emerged

Koolhoven F.K.58

Koolhoven F.K.58

Marinens Flyvebåtfabrikk M.F.9

TYPE	DIMENSIONS span ft	span in	length ft	length in	height ft	height in	WEIGHT max t-o lb	PERFORMANCE max speed mph	at height ft	service ceiling ft	combat range miles	REMARKS
Koolhoven F.K.31							3,874	146	8,200	NA	NA	
Koolhoven F.K.58	36	1	28	6½	9	10	5,610	313	14,760	34,110	466	
Marinens Flyvebåtfabrikk M.F.9	34	3½	25	6	10	2¾	2,712	NA	NA	NA	NA	

L.W.S. 4 Żubr

L.W.S. 6 Żubr

P.W.S. 10

P.W.S. 10

as the Zubr bomber was initiated early in 1933 by Zbysław Ciołkosz. Evolved around two Pratt & Whitney Wasp radial engines and designated P.Z.L.30, the original project was for a passenger transport, intended for the P.L.L. "Lot" airline's international network as replacement for the Polish-built Fokker F.VII/3ms. However, as "Lot" did not show the slightest interest in the design and ordered Douglas DC-2 airliners, it was decided to complete the P.Z.L.30 prototype, then already under construction, as a combat proficiency trainer and bomber. It flew for the first time in March 1936, powered by two 406-hp Wasp Junior engines, and formed the basis for the production model P.Z.L. 30A Żubr.

The prototype was a high-wing cantilever monoplane of mixed construction. Its wing was an all-wood structure, covered with plywood, and was attached directly to the top of the fuselage. The rectangular fuselage, with the pilot's cockpit offset to port, consisted of a metal-covered forward portion of duralumin and a fabric-covered steel-tube rear section. The tail unit was also a steel-tube structure, covered with fabric, and the undercarriage retracted inward, with the wheels fairing into the fuselage sides. Armament comprised twin machine-guns in nose and dorsal turrets, and a single ventral gun. A bomb-load of 2,200 lb was carried in the fuselage.

During I.T.L. airworthiness and service trials, the Wasp-powered P.Z.L.30/I gained a good reputation. Although performance was rather poor, pilots were enthusiastic about the aircraft's flying characteristics. The spacious fuselage appealed particularly to aircrew.

Influenced by these favourable reports, and by the predictions of some experts that the P.37 Łoś was too radical in design to make a practical service machine, the Aviation Department instructed Ciolkosz to re-engine the P.Z.L. 30/I with 680-hp P.Z.L. Pegasus VIII radials, to boost performance and to bring it up to full operational standards. The Pegasus-powered bomber, originally designated P.Z.L.30B, was then to be manufactured in quantity as the L.W.S.4, at the newly formed L.W.S. (Lublinian Aeroplane Manufacturing Co). Ciolkosz, appointed to the post of L.W.S.'s Technical Director, had transferred there all his contemporary projects to ensure work for the new factory. The Polish Air Force placed an initial order for 16 L.W.S.4s, and Rumania began negotiations for delivery of 24 similar machines.

Early in 1936, the P.Z.L.30/I was transferred to L.W.S. and hastily re-equipped with Pegasus VIIIs. To gain time, modifications were kept to the absolute minimum, and in spite of the 60 per cent increase in power the basic structure was not strengthened appreciably. During subsequent flight tests in 1937, the plywood skin on the wings began to split; but these warning signals were ignored except for gluing in pieces of thicker plywood. In early September 1937, the prototype, with the Rumanian acceptance mission on board, disintegrated in mid-air, killing the entire crew. Rumania at once withdrew its order and work on the 16 L.W.S.4 bombers for the Polish Air Force was halted.

Prolonged investigations revealed serious weaknesses in the wing structure and a considerable disparity between the theoretical and actual strength of the glue. These shortcomings were eventually overcome and work on the production aircraft was resumed. The first substantially modified L.W.S.4, with a new undercarriage which retracted into the engine nacelles, flew before the end of 1937, but its empty weight was higher than planned. A twin-float development, the L.W.S.5 seaplane, had been offered to the Polish Navy, which needed a heavy patrol bomber; but because of the high empty weight the machine could lift hardly any offensive load and was not acceptable to the Naval Department.

The basic structure was further modified, and the second L.W.S.-built Żubr began tests in the spring of 1938, fitted with a twin tail assembly, this variant being designated the L.W.S.6. This feature was not standard on the remaining 14 production L.W.S.4 bombers, delivered a year later to the IIIrd (Training) Wing. These also were too heavy, and several were completed with the undercarriage locked permanently in the "down" position because of persistent troubles with the electric motors which were too weak to raise the undercarriage.

Development of the aircraft was still continuing when World War II broke out. In the summer of 1939, L.W.S. was developing a new wing of welded chrome-molybdenum steel-tube construction, to replace the wooden wing and restore confidence in the design.

During the September campaign, except for a few transport and liaison sorties, most of the Żubrs stood idle, as they were not fit for combat. Several were destroyed on air fields, but some fell almost intact into German hands, and, according to German reports, were used subsequently by the Luftwaffe as trainers.

P.W.S.10

Following formation of the para-military government in Poland in May 1926, the aviation industry was encouraged to evolve indigenous combat aircraft as successors to the licence-produced types then equipping the Lotnictwo Wojskowe (Military Aviation). Development contracts were placed with Plage & Laśkiewicz's Lublin factory for the R.VIII biplane bomber and with P.W.S. (Podlasian Aeroplane Manufacturing Co) for the P.W.S.1 two-seat fighter-reconnaissance monoplane; but in the event only a small batch of six R.VIIIs was built, in addition to prototypes. These equipped a short-lived experimental squadron before being converted later to seaplane configuration for use by the Polish Naval Wing.

The P.W.S.1 did not progress beyond the prototype stage, and the first P.W.S. design to be ordered in quantity, as standard equipment for first-line units, was the P.W.S.10 fighter monoplane.

The P.W.S.10 was conceived in 1927 by A. Grzedzielski and A. Bobek (who later changed his name to Zdaniewski), when the Lotnictwo Wojskowe expressed the need for a single-seat fighter. The original project, which bore strong resemblance to the Samolot Sp.1 fighter-trainer, built in prototype form in 1925–6, had a 450-hp Lorraine "W"-type water-cooled engine and utilized the Polish Bobek No. 3 thick aerofoil section, tested at Göttingen (as Gö 647) in October 1927. At the time, the newly-formed P.Z.L. (National Aviation Establishments) were busy developing the revolutionary P.1 all-metal fighter and, consequently, further work on the less advanced P.W.S.10 was deferred.

Towards the end of 1928, the P.W.S.10 design study was extensively revised, the original basic wing being matched with a redesigned fuselage and new tail surfaces. A prototype contract for the improved design was placed in 1929, as an insurance against possible failure of the P.Z.L. fighter. The first prototype, powered by the Polish-built 450-hp Skoda-Lorraine "W"-type engine (which was also the standard power plant in subsequent production models) was completed in March 1930 and flew for the first time in May. By the end of 1930 it had completed successfully rigid airworthiness tests at the ITBL (Institute for Aviation Technical Research) and its service trials. As development of the P.Z.L. fighter had, meanwhile, been prolonged by an official request to adapt the design for a radial engine, production contracts were placed with P.W.S. for a total of 65 P.W.S.10 fighters as a stop-gap measure.

From a constructional viewpoint, the P.W.S.10 was a typical high-wing braced monoplane of the period. The wing was a one-piece two-spar wooden structure, covered with plywood and fabric. The fuselage and tail unit were welded steel-tube assemblies, covered mainly with fabric, except for the metal-covered forward fuselage. Armament comprised two forward-firing machine-guns, mounted above the side banks of cylinders.

The first production P.W.S.10s began to leave the assembly line towards the end of 1931 and deliveries

P.W.S. 10

TYPE	DIMENSIONS						WEIGHT	PERFORMANCE				REMARKS
	span		length		height		max t-o	max speed	at height	service ceiling	combat range	
	ft	in	ft	in	ft	in	lb	mph	ft	ft	miles	
L.W.S.4 Zubr	60	8½	50	6¼	11	6	16,690	236	14,750	26,250	775	
P.W.S.10	36	1	24	7	8	10	3,306	150	NA	20,100	324	

P.Z.L. P.7/I, first prototype

P.Z.L. P.7a

P.Z.L. P.7a

began early in 1932. Fighter squadrons of the 3rd and 4th Air Regiments were the first to become operational, but the service career of the fighter was rather brief. During 1933, combat squadrons were re-equipped with P.7s and most P.W.S.10s were transferred first to advanced fighter training units, and then to the Aviation Training Centre at Deblin.

In 1936, fifteen specially-overhauled P.W.S.10 fighters were sold to the Spanish Nationalists and took part in the Spanish Civil War. This transaction was surrounded by the greatest secrecy and was revealed only in more recent years. A substantial number of the remaining P.W.S.10s continued to be used in Poland for fighter and aerobatic training until the outbreak of World War II, and several were taken over by the Germans.

P.Z.L. P.7.

In 1927, the P.Z.L. (National Aviation Establishments) were founded in Warsaw to undertake development and production of indigenous aircraft and to specialize in all-metal structures. An ambitious programme of aircraft design was initiated and work began on five basic types: The P.1 fighter, the Ł.2 liaison aircraft, the P.Z.L.3 heavy bomber (which never materialized), the P.Z.L.4 transport, and the P.Z.L.5 tourer-trainer. Development of the fighter was entrusted to Zygmunt Puławski, a young graduate of the Warsaw Technical University who created a monoplane that was to place Poland in the forefront of international fighter development.

Puławski selected for his fighter a high-wing monoplane configuration and, to give the best possible all-round visibility for the pilot, conceived a wing of unique layout, which became known as the Puławski wing. This consisted of a gull-type structure, which tapered sharply in chord and thickness towards the roots, and with very thin sloping inboard panels which lined up with cylinder banks for the Vee engine. The new Polish Bartel BM 37/IIa aerofoil section, chosen for the wing, contributed to the fighter's later success.

The undercarriage was of the "scissor" type, in which each leg acted by means of an extension lever upon an oleo-pneumatic shock absorber mounted on the opposite side, inside the fuselage. This offered aerodynamic advantages and protected the shock-absorbers from dust and low temperatures. All-metal structure with metal covering was employed throughout.

The first P.1/I prototype flew in September 1929; the second, improved, P.1/II prototype flew early in 1930 and achieved a notable success at the International Fighter Contest in Bucharest. Both were powered by 600-hp Hispano-Suiza Vee-type engines.

At this time it was still uncertain what types of engines were to be manufactured in Poland; but as negotiations with Bristol were progressing well, Puławski was instructed to produce a radial-engined development of the P.1. This led to construction of the P.6, powered by a low-altitude Jupiter VI, and the high-altitude Jupiter VII-powered P.7, each of which had an entirely new oval section fuselage of all-metal stressed-skin construction married to the P.1's wing, tail assembly and undercarriage.

The first of two P.6 prototypes, which flew in August 1930, was generally acclaimed as the most outstanding exhibit at the 1930 Paris Salon, and created a highly favourable impression in the USA during the 1931 National Air Races at Cleveland. The first P.7/I prototype followed in October 1930. Its Jupiter VII engine was enclosed in a neat helmeted cowling which, although excellent from the aerodynamic viewpoint, left much to be desired so far as ease of manufacture was concerned. Thus the P.7/II appeared with less elaborate cylinder fairings combined with a narrow-chord Townend ring.

The P.6 and P.7 prototypes were subjected to extensive programmes of experimental and development flying and the P.7 was chosen eventually as the fighter best suited to the requirements of the Lotnictwo Wojskowe. By the autumn of 1931, the P.7/II had completed the final round of flight trials and was declared ready for service.

In the meantime, an initial order for ten P.7a fighters had been placed with P.Z.L. and this was subsequently increased to a total of 150 machines. The production

P.7a featured a slimmer rear fuselage, with a short headrest fairing, a new PZL-developed Townend ring and other refinements. It was powered by the Polish-built 485-hp Skoda Jupiter F.VII radial engine and was armed with two Vickers machine-guns in the fuselage sides. Deliveries began towards the end of 1932, and the initial batch of 30 P.7as was completed before the spring of 1933. The first squadron to be fully re-equipped with the fighter was the famous Eskadra Kosciuszkowska.

During fighter exercises at Warsaw in September 1933, all participating operational fighter elements of the 1st, 2nd, 3rd and 4th Air Regiments flew P.7as. In the following month, 28 machines (7 from each Air Regiment) flew in formation to Rumania on an official visit; and by the end of 1933, the Lotnictwo Wojskowe had become the first air force in the world to re-equip its entire first-line fighter force with all-metal monoplanes. On the outbreak of World War II, well over 100 P.7a fighters were still in existence. Most of them had been relegated to training duties; but 30 were still on the operational strength of Nos. 123, 151 and 162 Squadrons. They took part in air combat and flew several ground strafing sorties; but, due to their by-now slow speed and weak firepower, did not achieve any notable success.

P.Z.L. P.11.

After the P.Z.L. P.7 fighter had entered service, Pulawski began studies for more powerful derivatives of the basic design. To offset the partial restriction of visibility arising from use of a radial engine, he proposed a machine with a lowered engine and raised pilot's seat. After Pulawski's untimely death in an air accident in March 1931, these ideas were developed further by his successor, W. Jakimiuk. The direct development of the P.7, designated P.11, was stressed to take engines of up to 700 hp, and a smaller-diameter Mercury engine was envisaged as a standard power plant.

The first P.11/I prototype, powered by a Gnome-Rhône Jupiter IX radial, flew in August 1931. It had a fuselage of simplified construction, and the method of covering the structure with sheet metal, which at first presented great difficulties, was considerably improved.

The P.11/II, with a fuselage exactly similar to that of the production P.7a, flew for the first time in December 1931, powered by a Mercury IVa engine, enclosed in a new long-chord cowling ring This machine was placed second in the single-seat fighter class at the 1932 Zurich Meeting and the third prototype, the P.11/III, which was generally similar to the second, performed well a month later at the 1932 National Air Races at Cleveland. The P.11/II was used for exhaustive comparative trials, flying with Mercury IVa and Gnome-Rhône K.9 Mistral radials, driving a variety of propellers, and achieved its best speed of 215 mph with a K.9 engine and Chauvière propeller. The Mistral-powered P.11/II was shown at the 1932 Paris Salon.

Thirty production P.11as were ordered. Apart from some minor modifications and introduction of an exhaust collector ring, they were generally similar to the P.11/II, and, powered by the 497/517-hp Polish-built Mercury IV S.2 radial and armed with two guns, were delivered in 1934. The P.11a order was not increased, as the more advanced P.11c version was then under development. But, in the meantime, the Rumanian government had expressed great interest in the fighter and had ordered 50 machines, designated P.11b, which differed from the P.11a in having the 595-hp I.A.R. (Rumanian-built) Gnome-Rhône K.9 engine in place of the usual Mercury.

By the end of 1934, the substantially improved P.11c became the major production model, 175 aircraft of this

P.Z.L. P.7a, No.111 Squadron, 1st Air Regiment

P.Z.L. P.11a

P.Z.L. P.11c

TYPE	DIMENSIONS span ft	span in	length ft	length in	height ft	height in	WEIGHT max t-o lb	PERFORMANCE max speed mph	at height ft	service ceiling ft	combat range miles	REMARKS
P.Z.L. P.7a	33	10	23	6	9	0	3,047	203	16,400	32,800	435	
P.Z.L. P.11c	35	2	24	9	9	4	3,960	242	18,000	36,100	435	

P.Z.L. P.11c

P.Z.L. P.11c

P.Z.L. P.24/II, second prototype

P.Z.L. P. 24/III, third prototype

type being ordered by the Lotnictwo Wojskowe. Although the new machine retained the same factory number (P.11), it had, in fact, far less in common with the P.11a than the P.11a had with the P.7a. Its forward fuselage was extensively redesigned, the engine was lowered, and the pilot's seat was raised considerably. The inboard wing sections were modified, their dihedral angle was increased, and provision was made for the installation of two 7·7-mm guns in the wings to supplement the fuselage-mounted pair. New vertical tail surfaces were also fitted.

Early production P.11cs were fitted with the Polish Skoda-built Mercury V S.2, but the main production model had the 645-hp P.Z.L.-built Mercury VI S.2. Two 27-lb fragmentation bombs could be carried under the wings, and provision was made for R/T equipment, although this was not fitted to all aircraft.

The Gnome-Rhône K.9-powered P.11c, fitted with four guns and low-pressure tyres, represented the prototype for the proposed export model which was offered to foreign air forces with various equipment and armament. Rumania decided to acquire manufacturing rights for this model which, after modification to meet that nation's requirements, received the designation P.11f. Production began towards the end of 1935 but, due to the limited potentialities of the I.A.R. factory, progressed rather slowly and averaged only about 40 aircraft a year.

By the end of 1936, deliveries of the P.11c to Polish fighter squadrons were completed, all but three squadrons (flying P.7s) then being equipped with this model. At the outbreak of war, Nos. 121, 122, 131, 132, 141, 142, 152, and 161 Squadrons of the Armies' Air Force, and Nos. 111, 112, 113, and 114 Squadrons of the Pursuit Brigade defending Warsaw, flew the P.11c. In September 1939 these obsolete fighters, operating without the advantage of an early warning system, lacking replacements, spares and fuel, and often deployed by army commands in unsuitable rôles, managed to harass the German forces for 17 days, shooting down 126 Luftwaffe aircraft and strafing the advancing Wehrmacht. Altogether, 114 of them were lost in the unequal combat. Rumanian P.11s were also used operationally during the Russo-German conflict.

In 1939 it had been decided to give the then-obsolete P.11 a new lease of life, and the design was restressed to take the 840-hp P.Z.L. Mercury VIIIa power plant intended originally for installation in the P.50 Jastrzab, a more advanced low-wing monoplane fighter which failed to come up to expectations. Production of the new and more powerful four-gun P.11, named Kobuz, began at the P.W.S. factory in July 1939, a month before the P.Z.L.-built prototype took the air. Deliveries were planned for early summer 1940, but events overtook the programme.

P.Z.L. P.24

Ultimate development of a long line of Pulawski fighters, the P.24 was evolved by W. Jakimiuk. It was virtually a more powerful edition of the P.11, stressed to take radial engines of up to 1,000 hp; but as such power plants were not manufactured in Poland, and the design did not offer any major advantage over the P.11c, it was decided to produce it for export only.

The P.24 and P.11c were developed almost in parallel and incorporated several common improvements, such as redesign of the forward fuselage combined with lowering of the engine and raising of the pilot's cockpit, an aerodynamically cleaner rear fuselage and revised inboard wing sections. The first prototype, the P.24/I, was fitted with a 760-hp Gnome-Rhône 14 Kds double-row radial engine, driving a two-blade propeller with the hub enclosed in a spinner, and began tests in May 1933. The second, generally cleaned-up prototype, the P.24/II – often referred to as the Super P.24 – was powered by the 760-hp Gnome-Rhône 14 Kds engine, driving a three-blade propeller, and had provision for two 20-mm Oerlikon FF cannon in fairings on the wing struts.

In June 1934, this aircraft established an F.A.I.-recognized international speed record, achieving 257·2 mph in level flight, and thus became officially the fastest radial-powered fighter in the world. When shown at the 1934 Paris Salon, with two cannon in the wing strut fairings and two guns on top of the fuselage, it created great interest not only by reason of its performance, but as the world's first twin-cannon interceptor. It was offered for export with various combinations of armament.

In 1935, Turkey awarded P.Z.L. an order for 40 P.24 aircraft, made up of 14 P.24as, armed with two cannon in the wing strut fairings and two wing-mounted guns, and 26 P.24cs armed with four guns in the wings. Turkey also acquired a licence to manufacture the P.24a and ordered raw materials and semi-prepared parts for 20 more machines.

The production model was completed in the second half of 1935 and was shown later at the 1936 Paris Salon. It differed from the prototypes in having a tail unit identical with that of the P.11c and a new enclosed cockpit. The Turkish P.24s were powered by 930-hp Gnome-Rhône Kfs radials, deliveries of the P.Z.L.-built machines taking place in the latter half of 1936.

At the end of October 1936, Ing W. Gibałka, chief of the P.Z.L. technical mission, arrived in Turkey to organize production of the P.24a at the Tayyara Fabrikasi Kayseri. In spite of primitive working conditions, the first Turkish-built P.24a – first all-metal aircraft to be produced in Turkey – took the air on 29 May 1937, with Lt Irfam of the Turkish Air Force at the controls. By September of that year, five fighters had been completed and production continued at the rate of four aircraft per month. The Kayseri-built P.24a was usually armed with two guns, carried in the wing strut fairings, which were interchangeable with Oerlikon cannon, and with two machine-guns in the wings outboard of the struts. About 50 were completed before production ceased at the end of 1939. Many Turkish P.24s were, in later years, re-engined with Pratt & Whitney Twin Wasp engines, and some were still flying in the early 1960s.

Bulgaria ordered in 1936, fourteen P.24b fighters, which differed from the P.24c in equipment fitted. They were delivered at the beginning of 1938 and were followed by 20 P.24cs and then 26 P.24fs (see below).

The next production variant, the P.24e, was developed to meet a Rumanian requirement. Powered by the I.A.R.-built 930-hp 14 Kmc/36 radial engine, and armed with two Oerlikon cannon in the wing strut fairings, two wing-mounted machine-guns, and four racks for 25-lb bombs, it was very similar to the P.24c. Six P.Z.L.-built P.24es and manufacturing rights for the type were acquired by the Rumanian Government. This version followed the P.11f on the I.A.R. production lines and a total of about 120 machines of both types were completed between 1935 and the autumn of 1939, when production ended.

In the last months of 1939, the Rumanian-developed I.A.R. 80, which was in fact a low-wing derivative of the P.24e, with a new wing and redesigned forward fuselage, entered production under the supervision of former members of the P.Z.L. staff who had found their way to Rumania in the closing stages of the September campaign. P.24e fighters were used operationally from 1941 on the Russian front and were also encountered on a few occasions by US bombers during raids on Rumania.

The ultimate developments of the P.24 series were the twin-cannon and twin-gun P.24f and four-gun P.24g. Both were powered by the smaller-diameter 970-hp Gnome-Rhône 14 N7 engine, enclosed in a new low-drag P.Z.L. cowling ring, and except for armament were identical. Thirty P.24fs and six P.24gs were ordered from P.Z.L. by Greece, and were delivered towards the end of 1938. Together with nine Bloch 151 fighters, they constituted the entire fighter strength of the Royal Hellenic Air Force and achieved notable successes against the Regia Aeronautica and Luftwaffe.

On 1 November 1940, a Greek P.24 of No. 21 Squadron shot down the first enemy aircraft destroyed during the Greco-Italian war. During the next two days, P.24 fighters

P.Z.L. P.24c

P.Z.L. P.24g

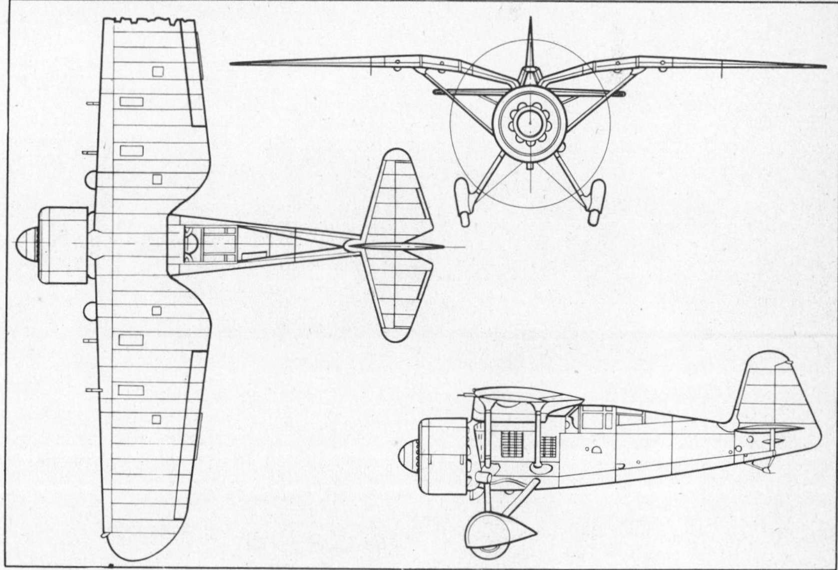

P.Z.L. P.24f

TYPE	DIMENSIONS						WEIGHT	PERFORMANCE				REMARKS
	span		length		height		max t-o	max speed	at height	service ceiling	combat range	
	ft	in	ft	in	ft	in	lb	mph	ft	ft	miles	
P.Z.L. P.24f	35	2	24	7	8	10	4,232	267	13,900	34,450	497	

P.Z.L. P.23A Karaś A

P.Z.L. P.23A Karaś A

P.Z.L. P.23A Karaś A, first production models

P.Z.L. P.23A Karaś A, Rumanian Air Force

destroyed a number of Italian raiders attacking Salonica, and in the following months P.24s of all four Greek fighter squadrons achieved scores of air victories in defensive battles and while escorting Greek bombers.

Bulgaria ordered 26 P.24f fighters, and deliveries of these continued uninterrupted until the outbreak of war, one of the last machines of this batch being destroyed at P.Z.L.'s Airframe Plant No. 1, at Warsaw-Okecie, during September 1939.

An improved version of the P.24 was ordered into quantity production for the Lotnictwo Wojskowe in the summer of 1939.

P.Z.L. P.23 and P.43 Karaś

The P.23 Karaś was unique among single-engined bomber-reconnaissance aircraft of the late 1930s, in that it constituted the major offensive equipment of a large air force.

The design, evolved in 1931–2 by a P.Z.L. team headed by Stanisław Prauss, was based on the abandoned P.Z.L. 13 high-speed passenger transport. Construction of a static test airframe and flying prototype began in the autumn of 1932, and the structural tests were completed a year later. Modifications to the prototype P.23/I, which was powered by a 570/590-hp Bristol Pegasus IIM$_2$, delayed the date of the first flight until August 1934.

The second, extensively modified machine (the P.23/II) flew early the following year. This aircraft featured a new low-drag P.Z.L. cowling ring, and, to improve the pilot's visibility, its engine was lowered, giving the Karaś its characteristic humped nose. The bomb-bay was deleted from the fuselage, the entire bomb-load being carried externally under the wing centre-section. Crew accommodation was rearranged and the wing was modified and provided with more effective flaps and ailerons.

The P.23/II crashed during its trials. It was followed by the P.23/III, which had a raised pilot's seat, higher canopy and redesigned windscreen. Various modifications were introduced to this machine, until it reached the standard of the production Karaś. It was shown at the Stockholm Aviation Exhibition in May 1936 and, six months later, at the 1936 Paris Salon.

In 1935, production orders for 40 Karaś As and 210 Karaś Bs were placed with P.Z.L. by the Lotnictwo Wojskowe, powered by Polish-built 580-hp P.Z.L. Pegasus II and 680-hp P.Z.L. Pegasus VIII radial engines respectively. The first production Karaś A flew in June 1936 and deliveries began towards the end of that year. The programme was delayed by unreliability of the Pegasus II engine, as a result of which all Karaś As were relegated to the operational training rôle and had their ceiling restricted to 3,000 m (9,840 ft). The major production variant, the Pegasus VIII-powered Karaś B, entered service towards the middle of 1937, replacing Polish-built Potez 25B.2 biplanes, and eventually equipped 14 first-line squadrons.

From the structural viewpoint, the all-metal cantilever monoplane Karaś was an advanced aircraft for the period. Its wing construction represented one of the earliest examples of a metal sandwich structure in aviation engineering. The armament consisted of one fixed forward-firing machine-gun and single swivelling guns on P.Z.L.-type hydraulic mountings in dorsal and ventral positions. Maximum bomb-load was 1,543 lb, typical loads including six 220-lb bombs, eight 110-lb bombs or forty-eight 27·5-lb bombs. The crew of three comprised pilot, observer-bombardier, and gunner.

One of the production P.23Bs was fitted experimentally with a retractable ventral gondola and twin fin and rudder assembly, which were to be incorporated in the successor to the Karaś, the P.46 Sum. This machine, designated P.42, was later reconverted to Karaś B standard.

In 1936 the Karaś was ordered by the Bulgarian Air Force, with a 930-hp Gnome-Rhône 14 Kfs radial, as the P.43A. Its armament was increased by the addition of a second forward-firing gun, and the crew accommodation was improved. Bomb-load remained the same as for the P.23B. No prototype was built. Twelve P.43As were delivered to Bulgaria late in 1937, and orders were then placed for a further 42 aircraft, these being of the P.43B type, with 980-hp Gnome-Rhône 14 N. 1 radial engine

Deliveries of the P.43B continued until the outbreak of war, by which time more than 30 had reached Bulgaria.

Twelve first-line squadrons of the Polish Air Force flew the Karaś B in September 1939. Seven of these were attached to various land armies, and five, together with four P.37 Łoś squadrons, equipped the independent Bomber Brigade. Karaś units carried out the bulk of the armed reconnaissance and bomber work, achieving notable successes against German armour concentrations, but they suffered heavily from the German defences. During the campaign, five P.43Bs, awaiting delivery to Bulgaria, were taken over by the Polish Air Force and used by No. 41 Squadron as replacement aircraft. Only a few P.23Bs survived until mid-September; these, together with Karaś As, were evacuated to Rumania, and were later impressed by the Rumanian Air Force and used operationally on the Russian Front.

Quantity production of the Karaś' successor, the much superior P.46 Sum, which flew for the first time in October 1938, was getting under way in the summer of 1939, but the outbreak of war put an end to this work.

P.Z.L. P.37 Łoś

The P.37 Łoś twin-engined all-metal stressed-skin bomber monoplane was one of the most formidable products of the Polish aircraft industry. An extremely compact design, combining an exceptional degree of aerodynamic efficiency with advanced thoughts on structural design, the Łoś could carry a bigger bomb-load than its foreign counterparts of the period, yet was the smallest and one of the fastest aircraft of its kind.

The P.37 story goes back to the year 1934, when the Lotnictwo Wojskowe began to show a firm interest in a multi-engined bomber to replace the Polish-built Fokker F.VII/3ms, 36 of which constituted the entire Polish bomber force. Most outstanding among the proposals for such an aircraft was the project evolved by Jerzy Dabrowski. Designated P.37, the study was submitted in July 1934, and in the following October P.Z.L. was authorized to proceed with detail design and development work.

In August 1935, first metal was cut on the prototype airframes and assembly of the first flying prototype, the P.37/I, was completed in April 1936. At about this time, however, static tests conducted at the I.T.L. with the non-flying airframe revealed weaknesses in the wing structure; so the flight trials of the P.37/I were postponed until the necessary modifications had been carried out. In the last days of June 1936, the P.37/I flew for the first time, powered by two 873-hp Bristol Pegasus XIIB radial engines, driving Hamilton three-blade metal variable-pitch propellers. P.Z.L.-built Pegasus XIIB engines were specified for the initial production model, the P.37A Łoś A, the order for which was increased from 10 to 30 aircraft after the successful flight of the prototype.

The second prototype, the P.37/II, incorporated several modifications dictated by the trials with the first machine. It was fitted with more powerful 918-hp Pegasus XX engines, as specified for the major production variant the Łoś B, a twin fin and rudder tail assembly and a revolutionary new undercarriage consisting of cantilever oleo-pneumatic legs, each carrying two independently suspended wheels. During 1937 and 1938 the P.38/II was used extensively for development flying, with various radial engines. These included the 970-hp Gnome-Rhône 14 N.1 and 1,050-hp 14 N.20/21, as well as 1,020-hp Renault 14T and 1,000-hp Fiat A.80 RC41 engines for the

P.Z.L. P.43A, Karaś, modified air intake

P.Z.L. P.37 Łoś, first prototype

P.Z.L. P.37 Łoś

TYPE	DIMENSIONS span ft	span in	length ft	length in	height ft	height in	WEIGHT max t-o lb	PERFORMANCE max speed mph	at height ft	service ceiling ft	combat range miles	REMARKS
P.Z.L. P.23B Karaś B	45	9	31	9	11	6	6,918–7,774	198	11,975	24,000	410–932	
P.Z.L. P.43B Karaś Export	45	9	32	10	11	6	6,800–7,755	227	13,100	27,900	870	
P.Z.L. P.37B Łoś B	58	10	42	5	16	8	18,739–19,577	273	12,150	19,700	932–1,615	

P.Z.L. P.37 Łoś

P.Z.L. P.37B Łoś B

P.Z.L. P.37 Łoś

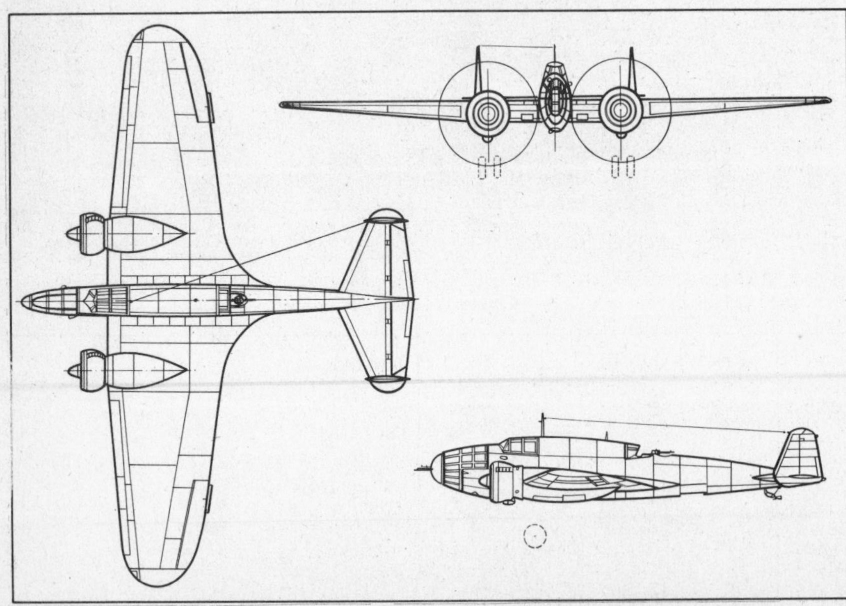

P.Z.L. P.37B Łoś B

proposed Łoś C and D export variants respectively. Speeds in excess of 310 mph were recorded by the lightly-loaded P.37/II with 1,050-hp Gnome-Rhône engines.

The third production Łoś A airframe, also fitted with twin fins and rudders, was specially equipped and finished to serve as the demonstration model, appearing first in May-June 1938 at the Belgrade Exhibition, and later in the same year at the 1938 Paris Salon. This machine created enormous international interest, and in the summer of 1939 orders were received from Bulgaria for delivery of 15 P.37C bombers, from Yugoslavia for 20 P.37Cs, from Rumania for 30 P.37Ds, and from Turkey, which ordered 10 P.37Ds, semi-prepared parts for 15 more, and manufacturing rights in the aircraft. All of these bombers were to be delivered during 1940. In addition, exploratory negotiations were in progress with Denmark, Estonia and Finland.

In the spring of 1938, the first production Łoś A bombers were delivered to the Polish Air Force. Nine of the initial batch of 10 (the demonstration model was the exception) had a single fin and rudder assembly, as used on the P.37/I, while the remaining 20 P.37As were fitted with a twin tail assembly, similar to that of the P.37/II. All the Łoś As were subsequently equipped with dual controls and used by the IIIrd Dyon, a training unit, for conversion training. Deliveries of the Pagasus XX-powered Łoś B began towards the end of 1938. By the following spring Nos. 211, 212, 216 and 217 Squadrons, with nine bombers each, reached operational status and were incorporated in the Bomber Brigade. The Łoś Bs were armed with three machine-guns, one in the nose and one each in dorsal and ventral positions, and could carry internally up to 5,685 lb of bombs, the disposable load being the same as the aircraft's empty weight!

In 1939, it was decided to limit the bomber force in favour of the increased production of fighters, and the original orders, calling for a total of 180 Łoś aircraft, were cut back to 130. About 100 machines (A and B variants) were completed by September 1939; but only the 36 Łoś Bs of the Bomber Brigade were fully equipped for operational duties. These bombers played the major part in attacks on German armour concentrations and inflicted heavy casualties on the advancing enemy, but their effort could not be sustained.

Only about ten additional Łoś bombers could be fitted out in time to be used as replacement aircraft. Most of the Łoś As and a number of Łoś Bs, well over 40 machines in all, flew to Rumania in mid-September, and were later taken over by the Rumanian Air Force for operational use against Russia throughout the war. One or two of these were still going strong in the late 1950s, serving as target tugs.

The prototype of the P.49 Miś, a much more heavily armed development of the Łoś, with 1,300/1,500-hp radials, was well advanced at the outbreak of war.

Rumania

Fabrica de Avione S.E.T. XV

From the time of its foundation at Bucharest in 192 until the mid-1930s, the Fabrica de Avione S.E.T. pro duced a string of biplane designs, most of them for trainin or general duties. However, in the early 1930s the compan undertook limited production for the Rumanian Air Forc of the S.E.T. XV, a small single-seat fighter biplane

Powered by a nine-cylinder Gnome-Rhône 9-Krs air-cooled radial engine, supercharged to develop 500 h at operating altitude, the S.E.T. XV was designed by En Grigore Zamfirescu, construction being a mixture c welded steel tube, plywood and fabric. The unequal-spa wings were supported by single "N" struts on eithe side, and the main landing gear was of the divided-Ve pattern with streamlined fairings encasing the wheels Twin machine-guns were installed ahead of the enclose cockpit to fire between the blades of the two-blad propeller, and the S.E.T. XV possessed quite a good performance for its time. Its maximum speed was 211 mph at 13,000 ft, and climb to 6,000 m (19,680 ft) was accomplished in 11¼ minutes. However, only a relatively small number were built, the Rumanian Air Force fighter strength at this time being composed predominantly of the I.A.R.-built P.11 of Polish origin.

I.A.R. 37, 38 and 39

During 1938, to replace the ancient Potez 25 and 27 and Breguet 19B-2 bomber-reconnaissance aircraft which had served with Rumanian Air Force squadrons since the middle 1920s, production began at Bucharest of a small number of single-engined aircraft of national design. They were evolved by the Regia Autonoma Industria Aeronautica Romana (formerly the privately-owned Società Anonima I.A.R.), and the first to appear was the I.A.R. 37 three-seat bomber.

A single-bay biplane with unequal-span wings, the I.A.R. 37 was powered by an 870-hp I.A.R. licence-built version of the Gnome-Rhône 14K fourteen-cylinder, air-cooled radial engine. It was mainly of wood and fabric construction, and had single-leg cantilever main undercarriage members with streamlined "spats" over the wheels. Excellent visibility was afforded to the crew, both from the long "glasshouse" cockpit enclosure and via a large rectangular glazed panel let into each side of the centre fuselage. Beneath this canopy sat the pilot, in the front seat, with the observer/bombardier/gunner immediately to his rear (operating a machine-gun which fired downward through the floor), and the third crew member beneath the hinged rear portion of the canopy, wielding a second, movable gun for rearward defence. The I.A.R. 37's normal bomb-load was 883 lb, but up to 1,325 lb could be carried over short distances. The similar I.A.R. 39 is illustrated.

The I.A.R. 38 was essentially the same aircraft, used purely for reconnaissance with the crew reduced to two.

I.A.R. 80 and 81

At the outbreak of World War II, the home defence squadrons of the Rumanian Air Force were equipped with an extremely varied assortment of aircraft, all of them outdated and of virtually no consequence as an effective fighter force. With the German occupation of the country, Luftwaffe Bf 109s were brought in to help protect the oil fields, which were of tremendous importance to the German war effort, and the Regia Autonoma I.A.R. began production of a new, nationally-designed fighter with very clean lines and a performance comparable with many of its foreign contemporaries.

The design of this machine, the I.A.R. 80, had been initiated at the beginning of 1938, under Eng Grossu-Viziru, with the object of making use of as many components as possible of the Polish P.24e fighter then being built under licence in Rumania; and the first prototype had flown by the end of the year. A true resemblance to the P.24e would have been hard to detect, for although the I.A.R. 80 used the rear fuselage and tail assembly of the Polish fighter, it had an entirely new forward fuselage, in which were a single open cockpit and a neatly installed 940-hp I.A.R.-built version of the Gnome-Rhône 14K radial engine; while the high, braced gull wing and fixed, "spatted" main undercarriage of the Polish fighter had given way to a cantilever low wing accommodating inward-retracting main wheel units.

The first examples of the initial production model, the I.A.R. 80A, did not begin to come off the assembly

Fabrica de Avione S.E.T. XV

I.A.R. 39

I.A.R. 80

TYPE	DIMENSIONS span ft	in	length ft	in	height ft	in	WEIGHT max t-o lb	PERFORMANCE max speed mph	at height ft	service ceiling ft	combat range miles	REMARKS
S.E.T. XV	30	10	22	11½	9	10	3,410	211	13,120	30,800		
I.A.R. 37	40	2	31	2	NA		7,640	208	12,150	26,240		Performance for bomber
I.A.R. 80A	32	10	26	9½	11	10	5,480	343	22,965	34,500	590 max	

I.A.R. 81C

CASA C-2111

CASA C-2111

Hispano HA-1112-K1L

lines until some three years later, and were delivered to Rumanian Air Force squadrons at the beginning of 1942. During this time various improvements had been made to the original design, chief among these being the provision of an enclosed cockpit for the pilot and the substitution of a more powerful Gnome-Rhône radial engine, the 1,025-hp, fourteen-cylinder air-cooled I.A.R. 14K115. Armament of the I.A.R. 80A comprised four 7·7-mm machine-guns in the wings outboard of the propeller arc, and a 20-mm Oerlikon cannon in each wing root.

The I.A.R. 80A was soon joined by the 80B, identical save for more up-to-date radio equipment, and the 80C, in which the Oerlikon cannon were replaced by German MG 151s of the same calibre. Final production model was the I.A.R. 80D, in which additional armour protection was coupled with the facility to carry two 110-lb or 220-lb bombs beneath the wings. About 120 I.A.R. 80s of these four models were completed, and besides being employed on home defence duties some also served alongside units of the Luftwaffe in the German invasion of Russia.

Production ended early in 1943 in favour of the Messerschmitt Bf 109G, but not before a small number of I.A.R. 81 fighter-bombers had been built by the company. Basically a modification of the I.A.R. 80D, the I.A.R. 81A, B and C differed in internal equipment and the degree of armour protection. All had an under-fuselage attachment point for a 440-lb bomb. Smaller bombs or rocket projectiles could be carried underwing.

After Rumania's deliverance from the invaders, the Air Force was reorganized by its Soviet liberators, but both the I.A.R. 80 and 81 continued in squadron service until the Soviet government began to re-equip the force with Russian-designed aircraft in 1949.

Spain

CASA C-2111

Seventy-five Heinkel He 111 bombers were sent to Spain by the Luftwaffe to take part in the Civil War, and were flown by Spanish as well as German pilots. At the end of hostilities, 58 of these still remained, a mixture of B-2, D-1, E-1 and F-1 models, and were assigned to the 14th Regiment of the Spanish Air Force at Logrono and the 15th Regiment at Zaragoza.

The Spanish crews' reports of the bomber's qualities were such that, in 1941, endeavours were made to obtain a manufacturing licence for the He 111H-3; in the event, however, it was the He 111H-16 which was selected to be built at the new Tablada plant, near Seville, of the Construcciones Aeronauticas SA, as the CASA C-2111. The German power plant of the H-16 was the 1,340-hp Jumo 211F-2 inverted Vee engine, and it was with this installation that construction began of an order for 200 of these five-man bombers for the Spanish Air Force.

The first machine did not fly until 1945, and by the time that 130 had been completed, supplies of the German engines had run out. The first 130 included C-2111A bombers, C-2111C reconnaissance-bombers (with cameras in the starboard half of the bomb-bay) and C-2111F dual-control operational trainers. An internal load of 2,200 lb could be carried by the bomber variants, which had a defensive armament of one 12·7-mm Breda-SAFAT machine-gun in the nose blister and two 7·92-mm MG 15 guns, one in the rear of the crew cabin and the other in the ventral gondola. The Spanish Air Force designation for all Jumo-powered machines was B.2H.

When supplies of the Jumo engines ceased, consideration was given to utilizing instead the French Hispano-Suiza HS-12Z-17; but a decision was finally made in favour of a British power plant, the Rolls-Royce Merlin. The Spanish government ordered 173 examples of the Merlin 500-20, and with these began both the conversion of a number of Jumo-engined machines and the completion of further aircraft.

The Merlin-powered bombers received the manufacturer's designation C-2111B, and were followed by the C-2111D reconnaissance-bomber, with 1,610-hp Merlin 500-29 twelve-cylinder, liquid-cooled Vee engines. The Merlin version was known to the Spanish Air Force as the B.2I. There were also 15 conversions of bomber aircraft (some Jumo-, some Merlin-powered) into C.2111E nine-passenger troop transports with the military designation T.8. Although production of the C-2111 ceased many years ago, it was still serving with a few units at the time of writing, mainly for aircrew training.

Hispano HA-1109 series

The Messerschmitt Bf 109 was no stranger to Spanish skies, the country having seen the Bf 109B-2s and Bf 109Cs of the Condor Legion during the Civil War and having ordered the Bf 109E-1 for itself a few years afterwards. From this experience the Spanish government decided in 1942 to negotiate a licence with Messerschmitt AG to build the Bf 109G-2 at the Hispano-Aviación works at Seville. The licence was granted early in the following year and, to get things moving, 25 machines were to be sent by Germany to give the Spanish industry assembly experience, and its pilots flying experience of the type.

Although the airframes arrived, delivery of the engines was prevented by Allied air attack, and it became necessary for Hispano technicians to adapt the aircraft to accommodate a home-designed Hispano-Suiza engine instead. The first of these adaptations was flown on 2 March 1945, and this model was designated HA-1109-J1L. Performance was not fully up to expectations and the -J1L was retained in service for little more than a year, being withdrawn from use in July 1947.

A more satisfactory version emerged with the appearance of the HA-1109-K1L, utilizing the French Hispano-Suiza HS-12Z-89 engine of 1,300 hp. The first -K1L flew in May 1951, and up to 1954 about 200 fighter-bombers of this type were built for the Spanish Air Force; they were armed with a pair of wing-mounted machine-guns and underwing racks for four 80-mm Oerlikon air-to-ground rocket projectiles. The -K1L was a cleaner aircraft aerodynamically than the original Bf 109G and, according to the Spanish pilots who flew it, was also appreciably easier to handle.

In 1953 there appeared a further development of the fighter-bomber version. Designated HA-1109-M1L and named Buchón (Pigeon), this model was built in substantial quantities for the Spanish Air Force, its principal difference from the -K1L being the installation of a new power plant, the 1,400-hp Rolls-Royce Merlin 500-45, driving a four-blade Rotol propeller. The final fighter-bomber model was the HA-1112, generally similar to the HA-1109-K1L-M1L except that it carried twice the latter's quota of Oerlikon rockets, while the wing machine-guns were replaced by 20-mm Hispano HS-404 cannon. With the completion of HA-1112-M1L deliveries, production of the Spanish variants came to an end late in 1956.

During the HA-1109's operational career, three tandem-seat, dual-control versions were also evolved for operational training. Counterparts to the various fighter-bombers, as their designations imply, these were the Hispano-powered HA-1110-K1L and HA-1111-K1L (the latter having auxiliary wingtip fuel tanks), and the HA-1110-M1L with Merlin engine.

Hispano HA-1110-K1L

Hispano HA-1112-M1L

TYPE	DIMENSIONS						WEIGHT	PERFORMANCE				REMARKS
	span		*length*		*height*		*max t-o*	*max speed*	*at height*	*service ceiling*	*combat range*	
	ft	*in*	*ft*	*in*	*ft*	*in*	*lb*	*mph*	*ft*	*ft*	*miles*	
CASA C-2111A	74	3	54	6	13	9	30,865	253	16,400	21,980	1,103 max	
CASA C-2111D	74	3	54	6	13	9	30,865	260	14,764	27,890	1,553 max	
Hispano HA-1109-J1L	32	6½	29	5	8	6⅓	6,058	394	13,780	NA	435	
Hispano HA-1109-K1L	32	6½	29	6⅜	8	6⅓	6,349	404	20,669	32,800	460	
Hispano HA-1109-M1L	32	6½	29	10½	8	6⅓	7,011	419	13,120	33,450	476	

F.F.V.S. J22A

F.F.V.S. J22B

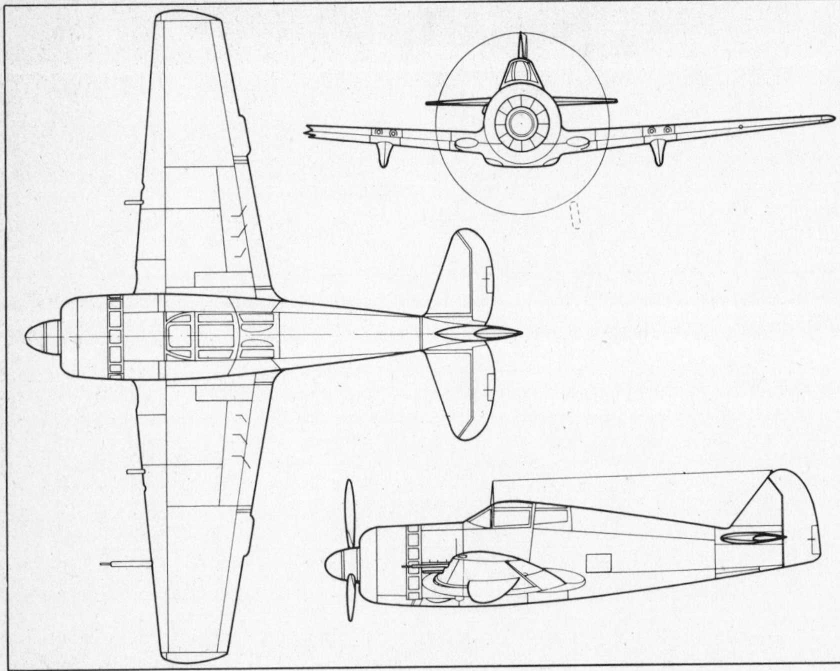

F.F.V.S. J22A

Junkers Ju 86K

Sweden

F.F.V.S. J22

Part of the price paid by Sweden for the retention of her neutrality, when almost all the other European nations were involved, willingly or otherwise, in World War II, was that it left her air force in a weakened position. Because of the war, orders placed abroad for combat aircraft either could not be fulfilled at all or could be placed only for types of aircraft no better than those which the Flygvapnet already had in service.

The SAAB company was already fully committed to the production of bomber and reconnaissance aircraft. Thus it was that, in the autumn of 1940, the Royal Swedish Air Board set up a team with Major-General Nils Söderberg at its head and Bo Lundberg as chief designer, to produce a single-seat fighter with a good, modern performance.

Design work on the project began on 1 January 1941. Light metals being in short supply, the design made extensive use of wood and steel in its construction, and utilized as its power plant the 1,065-hp Pratt & Whitney R-1830 Twin Wasp radial engine. The Twin Wasp, which was then being built in Sweden – without the luxury of a production licence – was the only engine readily available whieh was capable of conferring the required performance.

On 1 September 1942, the prototype of the new fighter made a successful maiden flight; but some six months before this, on 21 March, the design had shown sufficient promise for an initial quantity of 60 to be ordered "off the drawing board". About 500 companies of all sizes, mostly unconnected with the Swedish aircraft industry, were given the task of building components for the fighter, which received the official Flygvapnet designation J22.

Assembly of the J22 – which in external appearance was reminiscent of the Focke-Wulf Fw 190 – was undertaken by the Flygförvaltningens Verkstad, or F.F.V.S., at Bromma, near Stockholm, and the first production J22 was rolled out on 1 September 1943. The initial production model, the J22A, had a fixed armament of two 13·2-mm M/39A and two 7·9-mm M/22F machine-guns in the wings. The J22B differed only in that all four guns were M/39As.

The first deliveries of J22As were made to F9 at Gothenburg on 23 November 1943. By the end of the following year, 75 J22s were in squadron service, replacing such assorted earlier types as the Fiat C.R.42*bis*, Reggiane Re 2000, Republic EP-106 and Gloster Gladiator. A total of 198 production models were ultimately completed, all by the F.F.V.S. except the final 18, which were assembled in the Flygvapnet Workshops at Arboga. Some J22s remained in service until 1952, although most units had by then re-equipped with the SAAB-21R jet fighter.

Junkers Ju 86K

On 30 June 1936, the Swedish Government ordered, fron the Junkers Flugzeug und Motorenwerke at Dessau, a Junkers Ju 86K medium bomber for evaluation. Thi was the export model of the Ju 86D then in productio for the Luftwaffe, carrying a crew of four and an interna load of eight 275-lb bombs. Armament consisted o three 7·9-mm MG 15 machine-guns, one in the nose, on in a semi-enclosed dorsal emplacement and the third i a retractable ventral turret aft of the bomb-bay.

An order was next placed for the supply of 40 airframe from Dessau, the intention being to power these wit engines already being manufactured in Sweden, in plac of the standard Jumo 205C diesels. Deliveries began i March 1937 and were completed (except for the loss o one machine which crashed during its delivery fligh by September 1938.

The Ju 86s entered service with the Flygvapnet fror 1937 and were of three basic models: the B3 (Ju 86K- with two 885-hp Pratt & Whitney S1E-G Hornet radia engines; the B3A (Ju 86K-4) with 830-hp SFA-built Bristo

Mercury IIIs; and the B3B (Ju 86K-5), which had 980-hp SFA-built Mercury XXIVs. It was intended that a further 40 aircraft should be constructed under licence by SAAB at Trollhättan, but in the event the Swedish company completed only 16; these were Mercury XXIV-powered versions of the Ju 86K-13, which were built between November 1939 and January 1941 and went into service as the B3C. SAAB also undertook the conversion of a number of B3As into B3C-2s by the substitution of Mercury XXIVs in place of the original power plant.

The installation of 905-hp Mercury XIXs gave rise to the designation B3D for the final service version. In addition to the 55 B3 bombers in service (serial Nos. 118-175), the former mailplane SE-BAE of AB Aerotransport, a Ju 86Z-7, was taken over for service as a transport aircraft, with the serial number 911 and the Flygvapnet designation Tp 9.

The Ju 86 equipped Flygflottiljer 1 (the prime user), 7, 8, 11, 14, 17 and 21 during a long career with the Swedish Air Force. During World War II it served both as a bomber and as a reconnaissance aircraft. In 1944, twelve B3Bs and B3C-2s were adapted to carry mines while in service with F17, and another dozen B3Ds were converted for the carriage of a 450-mm torpedo. During May 1940, one of Fl's B3s made a forced landing in Germany; both it and its crew were interned for a time, but were later exchanged for an He 111 and its crew which had suffered a similar fate while flying over Sweden.

Towards the end of their military career, which lasted until 1958, many B3s were modified for use as 12-passenger transports, and a number of these subsequently found their way to the Swedish civil register. One B3 is preserved in the Air Force Museum, based with F3 at Malmen.

SAAB-17

Towards the end of 1937 the Svenska Aeroplan Aktiebolaget embarked upon a design study for a new two-seat reconnaissance monoplane to which they originally gave the project number L10. An order was received in November 1938 for the completion of two prototypes, and SAAB acquired the services of some 40 technicians from the United States to provide knowledge of the techniques involved in building all-metal aircraft. After about a year, however, the Swedish manufacturer's own staff had acquired sufficient experience to take over and complete the design.

On 18 May 1940, the first prototype of the SAAB-17, as the aircraft was now called, made its maiden flight at Linköping. Bearing the serial number 17001, it was revealed as a well-proportioned machine with a long cockpit "glasshouse", a mid-mounted wing, and a single 980-hp Bristol Mercury XXIV nine-cylinder radial engine.

In general configuration, the SAAB-17 was not unlike the American Curtiss Helldiver. In fact, the company suggested to the Flygvapnet that the aircraft might well prove suitable for the dive-bomber rôle, a category in which several other air forces were showing an interest at the time. Approval was given for this possibility to be studied, and subsequent evaluation indicated that SAAB's suggestion had been a sound one. The aircraft's main landing gear, which retracted into prominent fore-and-aft "knuckle" fairings on the underside of the wings, served as excellent dive-brakes, and the fuselage was roomy enough to accommodate bombs of a modest size. Heavier bombs could be suspended externally under

SAAB-17 (B17)

SAAB-17 (B17)

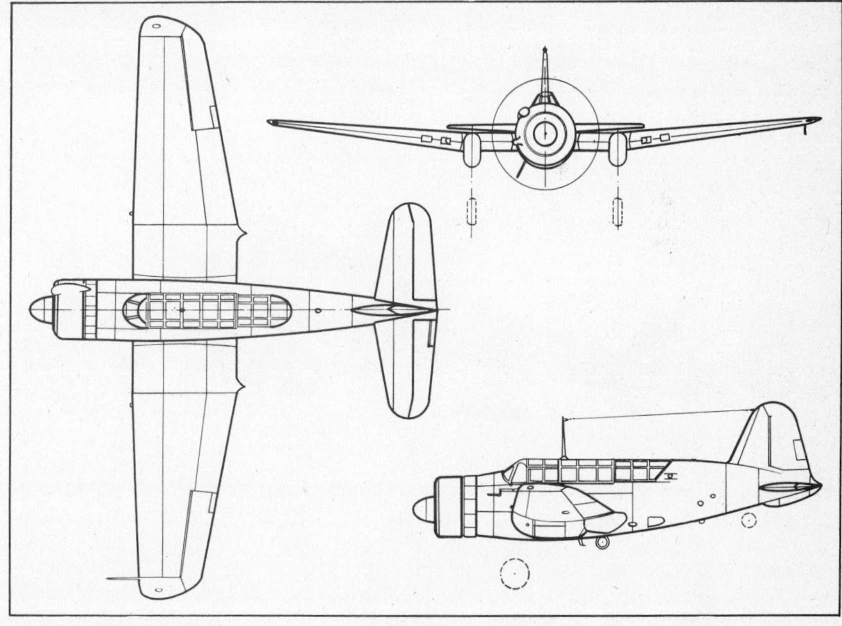
SAAB-17 (B17)

TYPE	DIMENSIONS span ft	in	length ft	in	height ft	in	WEIGHT max t-o lb	PERFORMANCE max speed mph	at height ft	service ceiling ft	combat range miles	REMARKS
F.F.V.S. J22	32	9½	25	7	9	2	6,300	358	11,500	30,000	780 max	
Ju 86K (B3C)	73	9	59	0	15	8	18,040	232	13,120	23,000	1,500	
SAAB-17 (B17C)	45	1	32	10	14	1	8,520	270	NA	NA	NA	
SAAB-17 (S17BS)	45	1	32	10	15	10	8,430	215	NA	NA	NA	

SAAB-17 (B17), ski landing gear

SAAB-18A (B18A)

SAAB-18A (S18A)

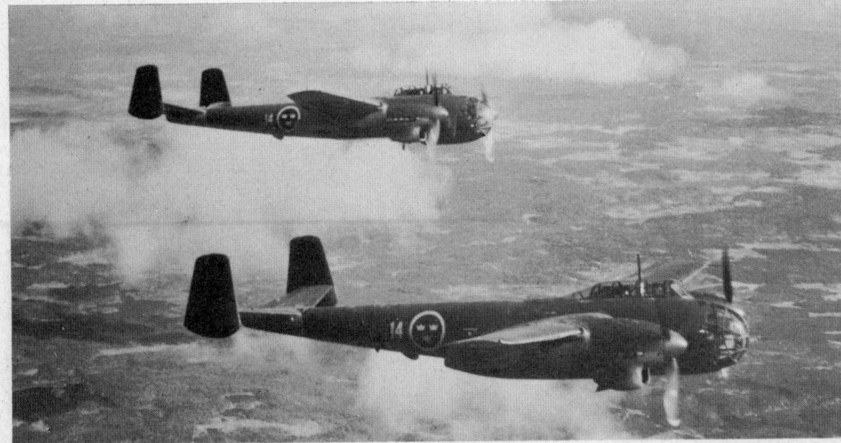
SAAB-18B (B18B)

the fuselage, on a rack which swung them down clear of the propeller for launching during a dive. Provision could also be made for further bombs to be suspended under the wings.

The type was produced for the Swedish Air Force in three basic versions, each with a different power plant. The SAAB-17A had a 1,065-hp Swedish-built Pratt & Whitney R-1830-SC3G Twin Wasp radial; the SAAB-17B, like the first prototype, had the Bristol Mercury XXIV (also built in Sweden); and the SAAB-17C was powered by a 1,020-hp Piaggio P.XI*bis* RC 40D radial engine. Between December 1940 and September 1942, four production contracts were placed, for 88, 86, 88 and 60 machines respectively. Breakdown of these, with their Flygvapnet designations, was as follows: 132 B17A dive-bombers, 114 B17B bombers and S17B reconnaissance aircraft (the latter including 38 S17BS floatplanes built at Trollhättan), and 77 B17C bombers. (The discrepancy of one in these overall totals is due to the fact that the first machine to fly was actually the first production SAAB-17B; the second was to -17A standard.)

The SAAB-17 proved to be an excellent aircraft in service, its career with the Flygvapnet lasting from 1941 to 1948. It was also adaptable, for in addition to a special twin-float model, many landplanes were converted to a ski undercarriage for operation in snow-covered regions. A typical armament – that of the B17C – comprised two 13·2-mm and one 7·9-mm machine-guns, and this model could carry up to 1,500 lb of bombs. Towards the end of World War II a Danish Air Force squadron was formed in Sweden with nine B17Cs, though it saw no actual combat operation. After the war, 60 SAAB-17s were sold to the Ethiopian Air Force, deliveries beginning in 1947. Some were still in service 20 years later.

SAAB-18

Like its single-engined predecessor, described above, the L 11 or SAAB-18 also began its life as a projected reconnaissance aircraft. Two prototypes were ordered for the Flygvapnet in November 1939 and February 1940, but the first of these was not to fly until some two and a half years later. During this time, air force tactical requirements had undergone a change of mind and the original design also underwent several modifications. The tricycle undercarriage layout first envisaged was replaced by the (then) more conventional tailwheel type, and the projected circular fins and rudders materialized in considerably more angular form.

When the first prototype SAAB-18A finally did take to the air on 19 June 1942, powered by two 1,065-hp Swedish-built Twin Wasp R-1830-SC3G radial engines, it was seen to bear no small resemblance to the Dornier Do 215. One notable difference was that the crew cabin was offset towards the port side, to improve the pilot's view downward. A crew of three was carried – pilot, navigator/gunner and bomb-aimer – for by now the primary rôles envisaged for the SAAB-18 were those of light day-bomber and dive-bomber.

Despite the fact that, with the Twin Wasps, the aircraft was somewhat underpowered, production of an initial batch of 60 was put in hand in July 1942; these began to enter Flygvapnet service from June 1944, as the B18A bomber and the S18A for reconnaissance. The S18A carried, in place of bombs, aerial cameras and (on later production machines) radar equipment beneath the nose.

By this time, there was available in Sweden a liquid-cooled engine offering a substantial power increase over the Twin Wasp. This was the 1,475-hp Daimler-Benz DB605B, which was being built under licence for the SAAB-21 fighter, and it was decided to adopt this power plant for the next production model, the SAAB-18B. The first DB605B-powered B18B was flown on 10 June 1944, and 120 of this model were built, entering service early in 1946. Improvements incorporated into the B18B in service included SAAB-designed ejection seats for the "upstairs" crew members and provision for twelve 10-cm, eight 14·5-cm or two 18-cm air-to-air rockets, in addition to the fixed armament of two 13·2-mm and one 7·9-mm machine-guns. Normal internal bomb-load was 3,300 lb.

On 7 July 1945, the final production model of the

SAAB-18 made its first flight. This was the T18B, developed from a B18B originally as a torpedo-bomber, but produced ultimately as an attack aircraft. For this rôle it carried a two-man crew, and was armed with twin 20-mm cannon, with a 57-mm Bofors gun in an extended housing beneath the nose. Production ended late in 1948 with the completion of the 62nd T18B, bringing the total number of SAAB-18s built to 242. They served with the Flygvapnet until the mid-1950s, the T18B finally being withdrawn from service in 1956.

SAAB-21A

In March 1941, feeling the need for new equipment to replace the motley collection of US and Italian fighters which were then in service with the Flygvapnet, the Royal Swedish Air Board issued a specification calling for a new fighter with considerably improved performance and greatly increased fire-power. Within two weeks, the SAAB team under Frid Wänström had devised and presented to the Board proposals for a remarkable and radical new aircraft, employing a twin-tail-boom layout and a pusher engine configuration. It was planned originally to use the American Twin Wasp radial engine, but the liquid-cooled DB605 was adopted instead.

The design was accepted and three prototypes of the new fighter, now designated J21, were ordered. The first of these flew on 30 July 1943 – not without incident, for a brake fault very nearly caused a crash during take-off. A nose-wheel landing gear had been chosen as the most suitable arrangement, with the main wheels retracting into the tail-booms. View from the high-mounted cockpit was excellent, and because of the association of high-speed performance with a pusher layout the pilot was provided with an ejection seat. (The SAAB company had made a prolonged study of escape problems connected with high-speed aircraft, and the J21 was one of the world's first production types to have such a device.)

The development problems associated with such an unorthodox design, although of a comparatively minor nature, delayed the delivery of production J21s until the latter part of 1945, when the first aircraft entered service with F9 Wing at Gothenburg. Imported DB605B power plants, developing 1,475-hp for take-off, were installed in the first few production machines, but before long these gave way to the Svenska Flygmotor-built version.

The J21A-1 was well armed, having a 20-mm Hispano cannon and two 13·2-mm Brownings clustered in the nacelle nose; 54 of this model were completed. They were followed by 124 similarly-armed J21A-2 fighters, some of which were later adapted for attack duties. The final model, the B21A-3 (A21A in the attack rôle), had wingtip auxiliary fuel tanks, underwing racks for bombs or rocket projectiles, and provision for a ventral gun pack containing a further eight 13·2-mm guns.

Production of the J21A ended at SAAB's Trollhättan factory in 1948 with the completion of 120 A-3s, bringing total production to 299 machines, including prototypes. Plans existed in 1945 for a SAAB-21B, with a pressurized cockpit and a 2,000-hp Rolls-Royce Griffon engine, but these were shelved for a more attractive proposition – the conversion of the J21 to jet propulsion.

SAAB-21R

The SAAB-21 was remarkable in many ways. It was the Swedish company's first fighter design; it was the first fighter to be built in that country with a liquid-cooled

SAAB-21A (J21A-1)

SAAB-21A (J21A-1)

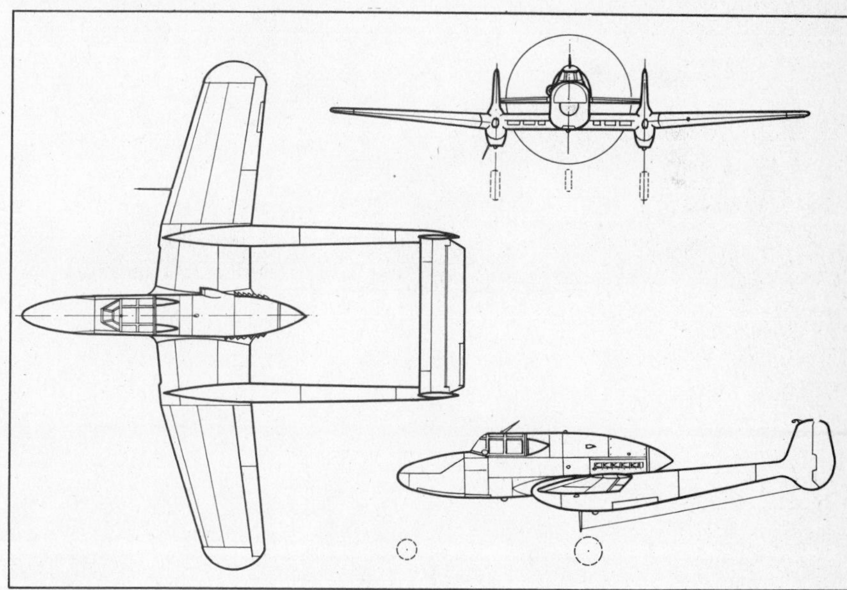

SAAB-21A

TYPE	DIMENSIONS span ft	span in	length ft	length in	height ft	height in	WEIGHT max t-o lb	PERFORMANCE max speed mph	at height ft	service ceiling ft	combat range miles	REMARKS
SAAB-18 (B18A)	55	11	43	2	14	6	17,960	289	NA	26,200	1,370 max	
SAAB-18 (B18B)	55	11	43	2	14	6	19,390	357	NA	32,100	1,620 max	
SAAB-21A (J21A-2)	38	0¾	34	3	13	1½	9,110	398	NA	36,000	NA	

SAAB-21R (J21R)

SAAB-29 (J29A)

SAAB-29 (S29C)

engine, and the last piston-engined warplane to be built there at all; it was one of the first types in the world to be fitted with an ejection seat, and was the only twin-boom, pusher-engined fighter to go into quantity production during World War II. But above all it was unique in being produced in both piston- and turbine-engined forms.

Conversion of the SAAB-21A to take a de Havilland Goblin turbojet was intended to be a straightforward and comparatively inexpensive means for Sweden to acquire its first jet fighter; but the problems encountered proved to be greater than had been anticipated. Four SAAB-21A airframes were allocated as prototypes for the new SAAB-21R. The rear portions of the centre nacelles were widened to accommodate the turbojet engines, and the position of the tailplane was raised to clear the jet blast. Without the need to provide ground clearance for a propeller, it was also possible to shorten the undercarriage legs.

After various experiments had resulted in further modification to the landing gear, re-location of the air intakes and strengthening of wing and tail units, the first SAAB-21R prototype flew at Norrköping on 10 March 1947. Further development problems delayed delivery of production J21Rs until February 1949, the type finally entering service with Skånska Flygflottilj (F10) at the beginning of the following year. The original Flygvapnet order for 120 aircraft had meantime been cut to half this figure (in favour of the later SAAB-29), and after a fairly brief period with F10 the aircraft were modified for the ground-attack rôle, re-designated A21R and transferred to F7 (Skaraborgs Flygflottilj). These aircraft were powered by either a 3,000-lb s t Goblin 2 engine (SAAB-21RA) or a 3,300-lb s t Swedish-built Goblin 3 (SAAB-21RB), 30 of each model being built.

Despite the lengthy gestation period and early teething troubles, the SAAB-21R became extremely popular with the men who flew it, and was an exceptionally good weapons platform. In the fighter rôle it was armed with a 20-mm Bofors cannon and four 13·2-mm Bofors machine-guns, which could be augmented by a further eight guns mounted in a pack under the central nacelle. Ten 10-cm or five 18-cm Bofors rocket projectiles, or ten 8-cm British anti-tank rockets, could be carried by the A21R.

SAAB-29

Under project number R 1001, the SAAB-29 in its original design configuration was a straight-winged aircraft with the tail assembly carried on a high, narrow tail-boom. SAAB intended to power it with a 3,100-lb s t de Havilland Goblin turbojet, but availability of the more powerful Ghost meant that a much better performance could be achieved, and SAAB decided to redesign the aircraft as a sweptwing fighter.

A scaled-down wing, with 25-degree leading-edge sweep was flight-tested on a Safir aircraft (SAAB-201) and arrangements were made for licence production of the Ghost engine by Svenska Flygmotor AB. The first prototype of the SAAB-29, with a 4,400-lb s t Ghost, made its first flight on 1 September 1948, and three further test aircraft were completed subsequently.

In April 1951, the SAAB-29 became the first swept-wing jet fighter to enter production in Western Europe. Later that year, the first J29A fighters began to enter service with F13 at Norrköping. Although no official name was given to the J29, it soon attracted an unofficial one, and was widely referred to as *Tunnan* (the Barrel).

Early in 1953 the SAAB-29A was replaced on the assembly lines by a new model with increased tankage, the SAAB-29B. It was first flown on 11 March 1953, and was built in both J29B fighter and A29B attack models.

Following the established Swedish practice of meeting its reconnaissance requirements by the adaptation of front-line combat types, the next version to go into series production was the S29C, first flown on 3 June 1953 and in service by the end of that year. Improved navigational equipment was a feature of the S29C, in which up to six aerial cameras could be installed for photographic missions. In 1955, a new 1,000-km closed-circuit speed record was set up by a pair of S29Cs; and this version, together with J29Bs of F22 Volunteer Air

Component, did valuable work with the United Nations peace force in the Congo from 1961 to 1963.

Only a few examples were built of the SAAB-29D, these being primarily an evaluation batch to test a new reheat installation of Swedish design, although they were assigned subsequently to squadron duties as J29Ds. The first of them was flown in March 1954.

An important modification appeared in the next model, the SAAB-29E. On this version, flown for the first time on 3 December 1953, the wing was redesigned to incorporate a "saw-tooth" leading-edge, improving the aircraft's performance in the transonic speed range. During the production life of the J29E, the afterburner tested on the D model was introduced as a standard feature, and all S29Cs were converted retrospectively to have the E-type wing.

The fifth and final production model, which incorporated all the improvements of earlier variants, was the J29F which flew for the first time on 20 March 1954. It was powered by a 4,750-lb s t (6,170-lb s t with reheat) SFA-built RM 2B (licence D.H. Ghost) turbojet and deliveries to Flygvapnet squadrons began late in 1954, an attack model (A29F) being produced concurrently. Normal J29F armament comprised four 20-mm cannon, and in the attack rôle the A29F was able to carry also twenty-four 75-mm Bofors air-to-air rockets, or up to 1,100 lb of bombs, napalm tanks or other underwing weapons.

Production of the SAAB-29F came to an end in April 1956, but the task of converting 308 29Bs and Es to F standard kept the company's workshops busy for a further three years. During the five years that the SAAB-29 remained in production a total of 661 were completed. In June 1961, 15 ex-Flygvapnet J29Fs were supplied to the Austrian government, followed by a further 15 in 1962. These were still in service in 1968.

SAAB-32 Lansen (Lance)

When the SAAB Lansen entered Flygvapnet service towards the end of 1955, it gave the Swedish Air Force one of the most effective and versatile multi-purpose aircraft to appear in Western Europe since the end of World War II. The first stage in the Lansen story was SAAB's project R119 for an all-weather attack aircraft to be powered by two de Havilland Ghosts; but this proposal was abandoned in October 1948 for the less complex and expensive P1150, designed around a turbojet of Swedish origin, the STAL Dovern.

On 20 December 1948, SAAB received the go-ahead for the new venture, and decided, because of development delays with the Swedish engine, to utilize instead the Rolls-Royce Avon Series 100. The wing of the new aircraft, with a 35-degree sweepback and Fowler-type trailing-edge flaps, was flight-tested on a modified Safir trainer (redesignated SAAB-202), and after completion of these and other necessary preliminaries the first of four SAAB-32 prototypes was flown for the first time on 3 November 1952. Bearing the serial number 32001, this prototype was powered by a single 7,500-lb s t Avon RA.7 engine, and revealed itself as a handsome two-seat low-wing monoplane of all-metal construction.

In 1953 the Lansen entered quantity production and, incidentally, became during this year the first Swedish aircraft to exceed Mach 1, in a shallow dive on 25 October. The first model to be built was the A32A attack version, armed with four 20-mm cannon and with underwing

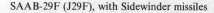

SAAB-29F (J29F), with Sidewinder missiles

SAAB-29F, Austrian Air Force

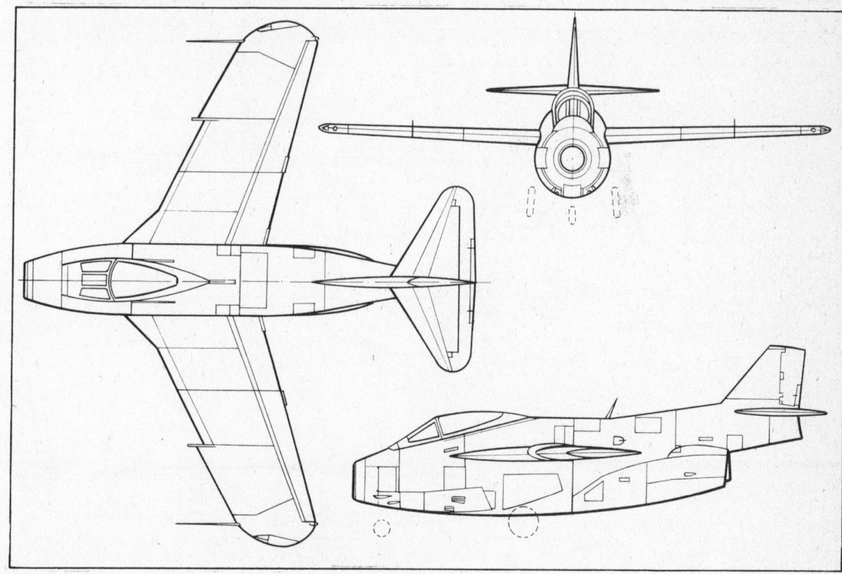

SAAB-29F

TYPE	DIMENSIONS						WEIGHT	PERFORMANCE				REMARKS
	span		length		height		max t-o	max speed	at height	service ceiling	combat range	
	ft	in	ft	in	ft	in	lb	mph	ft	ft	miles	
SAAB-21RB (J21RB)	37	4	34	3	9	8	11,000	497	26,250	39,370	447	
SAAB-29 (J29F)	36	1	33	2½	12	3½	17,637	658	5,000	50,850	1,678 max	
SAAB-32A (A32A)	42	7¾	48	0¾	15	7	28,660	700	SL	49,200	2,000 max	
SAAB-32B (J32B)	42	7¾	47	6¾	15	3	29,800	710	SL	52,500	2,000 max	

SAAB-32B (J32B) Lansen

SAAB-32C (S32C) Lansen

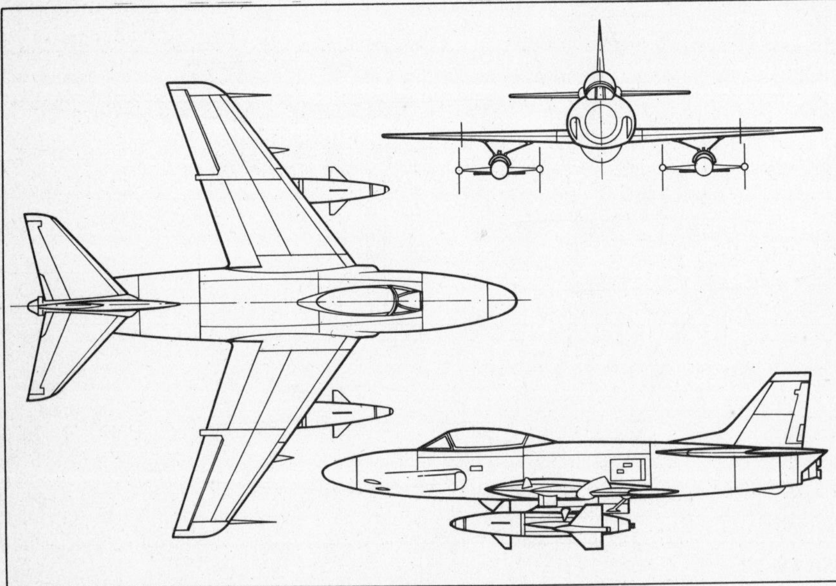
SAAB-32A (A32A) Lansen, with Rb 04 missiles

SAAB-35A (J35A) Draken

attachment points for loads such as four 550-lb or two 1,100-lb bombs; twelve 18-cm or twenty-four 13·5-cm or 15-cm air-to-air rockets; or two Rb 04 air-to-surface anti-shipping missiles. Power unit of the production A32A was the 8,050-lb s t (9,920 lb with reheat) Avon RA.7R, built under licence by SFA as the RM5.

The first A32As were delivered to F17 in December 1955, subsequently equipping a total of twelve squadrons with the Flygvapnet's four attack wings – F6, F7, F14 and F17 – by the end of 1957. The Lansen quickly proved itself popular with pilots and ground crews alike. Its straightforward layout meant easy maintenance, it was a pleasant aircraft to fly, and an extremely stable gun and missile platform. Performance was such that Lansens could reach a land or coastal target anywhere in Sweden within an hour from a centrally located base.

On 7 January 1957, the first example was flown of the SAAB-32B, produced for the Flygvapnet as the J32B night and all-weather fighter. A more powerful engine, the RM.6A (SFA-built Avon Series 200), gave 11,250 lb s t dry and 15,190 lb s t with reheat, and necessitated some enlargement of the air intakes. Fixed armament was raised to 30-mm calibre (Aden cannon), integrated with the SAAB S6 all-weather fire control system; the external ordnance could include four rocket pods (each containing nineteen 75-mm or eighteen 13.5-cm unguided rockets), or four Rb 324 Sidewinder air-to-air homing missiles. Deliveries of the J32B began in July 1958, first to F12 and then to F1 and one squadron of F21 – seven squadrons in all.

Inevitably, a photographic reconnaissance model made its appearance in the Lansen programme, with several alternative installations of cameras for aerial photographic work. The first S32C, flown on 26 March 1957, was based on the J32B and built in parallel with it. Production took place in 1958 and the first half of 1959, F11 being among the formations to receive this model. Production of the Lansen came to an end on 2 May 1960, with delivery of the last J32B. In all, about 450 Lansens were built.

SAAB-35 Draken (Dragon)

In 1949, at a time when the world's only successful supersonic aircraft was the American Bell X-1 and the delta wing was still a new idea, the Swedish Air Force issued the most demanding specification it had yet devised. This called for an interceptor with high supersonic speed; a fast climb to high altitude, combined with great manoeuvrability at all heights; the ability to carry a wide variety of ordnance loads related to a modern radar and fire control system; and good short-field take-off and landing characteristics.

SAAB's project R1250, begun in August 1949 under Chief Designer Erik Bratt, set out to satisfy these demands in a typically bold fashion. To meet the joint requirements of manoeuvrability and good STOL performance, a wing of "double delta" configuration was chosen. This was conceived as an inner, very low aspect ratio delta with 80-degree sweep on the leading-edge, which would give minimal drag at supersonic speeds, and a broader, outer delta with 57 degrees of sweep to provide stability in the subsonic speed range. The principle was first tried out on the SAAB-210, a small-scale research aircraft powered by an 1,100-lb s t Armstrong Siddeley Adder turbojet, which first flew on 21 January 1952.

Meanwhile, work had already begun on design of the full-size fighter, and after completing a wooden mock-up in 1952, SAAB received an order in August 1953 to build three prototype SAAB-35s and three pre-production SAAB-35As.

The first prototype (unarmed and serial numbered appropriately, 35-1) made its first flight on 25 October 1955, the second and third machines following in January and March 1956 respectively. All three had British built Avon engines with Rolls-Royce afterburners, and the third aircraft carried armament. A production order followed within six months for the J35A, in which the SFA-built RM6B (Avon 200) of 11,000 lb s t (15,200 lb with reheat) was installed.

The J35A was armed with twin 30-mm cannon, and had underwing or fuselage attachment points for Rb 32-

(Sidewinder) air-to-air missiles, pods of nineteen 75-mm Bofors rockets or twelve 13·5-cm rockets, up to 2,200 lb of ordinary bombs, or auxiliary fuel tanks. An initial batch of 65 J35As was built, the first of these entering service with F13 at the end of 1959.

The Draken was well liked by its pilots, who appreciated particularly its easy handling, high rate of roll and tight turning radius. Although all Draken models have a tricycle undercarriage, the J35As were later modified to have, in addition, small retractable twin tail-wheels, a feature first introduced on the J35B; this enabled the aircraft to land in a tail-down attitude, using the broad-chord wings as braking surfaces. By deploying its tail parachute as well the Draken can land in something like 650 yards.

The J35B, first flown on 29 November 1959, followed the A model into production at the end of 1961 and introduced a number of refinements. These included the new SAAB S7 collision-course radar (first air-tested in a Draken nose-cone mounted on an A32A airframe), an improved cockpit canopy, and a slightly longer fuselage. Power plant and armament remained the same.

Among the wings to receive the J35B were F16 and F18. Concurrent with the mounting production of the J35B, a dual-control conversion trainer was evolved by giving a number of J35As an entirely new front fuselage with tandem seating and twin ejection seats, that of the instructor being set slightly higher than the pupil's. The trainer, designated Sk 35C, was first flown on 30 December 1959.

The next major step in the Draken's development was to increase the engine power. Thus, with the J35D, the power plant was changed to the Series 300 Avon, built in Sweden by Svenska Flygmotor as the RM6C and developing 13,220 lb st dry (17,635 lb using its SFA afterburner). Other changes included the SAAB FH5 autopilot and greater internal fuel capacity, and the climb rate improved to approximately 50,000 ft/min. The J35D was first flown on 27 December 1960, entered series production in the autumn of 1962, and began to join Flygvapnet squadrons in the following year.

Also in 1963, on 27 June, a photographic-reconnaissance model of the J35D, the S35E, made its first flight, and this version too was ordered in substantial numbers. S35Es began to replace the ageing S29Cs in squadron service at the end of 1964.

Latest Flygrapnet production model of the Draken is the J35F, which is being built in greater numbers than any earlier version. Two converted Ds acted as prototypes, being flown early in 1961, and the J35F differs from its predecessors chiefly in having an improved model of the S7 fire control system, providing for the carriage of two or four Rb 327 (radar-guided) or Rb 328 (infra-red) Falcon air-to-air missiles.

Two other variants of the Draken remain to be recorded. In 1960, two years after the Swiss government had evaluated a J35A, SAAB produced a single SAAB-35H (for "Helvetia") with Ferranti Airpass II radar, in the hope of selling the type to the Swiss Air Force. This version was abandoned when the Swiss indicated their preference for the French Mirage III.

In a further effort to sell the Draken abroad, details of the advanced SAAB-35X (for export) were announced in mid-1967. By raising the maximum loaded weight of the aircraft to 35,270 lb, SAAB have been able to offer increased internal fuel tankage, for longer range, and an increased external weapon load of 9,000 lb, primarily for ground-attack duties. Forty of this version were ordered in 1968, as the SAAB-35XD, by the Royal Danish Air Force, plus six SAAB-35XT trainers.

SAAB-35D (J35D) Draken, with Sidewinder missiles

SAAB-35F (J35F) Draken, with Falcon missiles

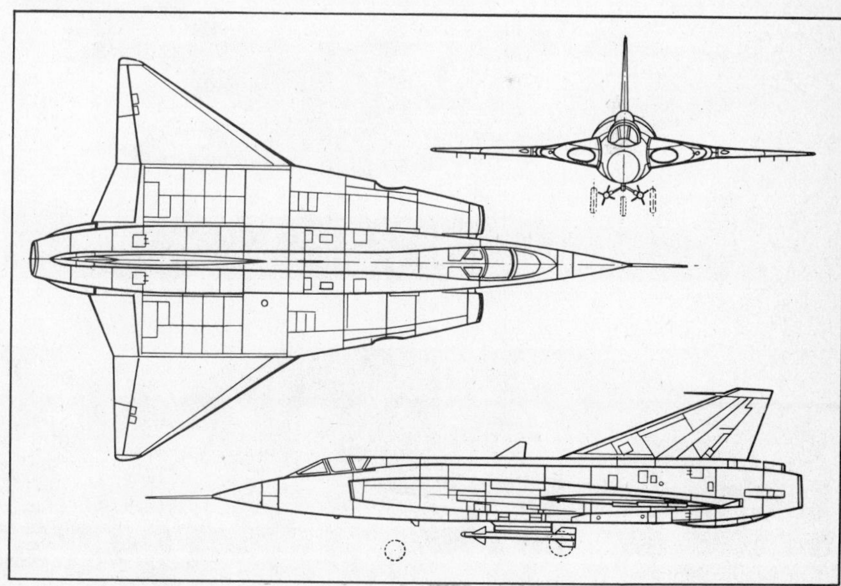
SAAB-35A (J35A) Draken

TYPE	DIMENSIONS						WEIGHT	PERFORMANCE				REMARKS
	span ft	*span* in	*length* ft	*length* in	*height* ft	*height* in	*max t-o* lb	*max speed* mph	*at height* ft	*service ceiling* ft	*combat range* miles	
SAAB-35 (J35B)	30	10	51	10	12	9½	21,900	1,188	36,000	+60,000		
SAAB-35 (S35E)	30	10	52	0	12	9½	26,000	1,320	40,000	+55,000		
SAAB-35 (J35F)	30	10	51	10	12	9½	27,050	1,320	40,000	70,000		

SAAB-37 (AJ37) Viggen, first prototype

SAAB-37 (AJ37) Viggen, first prototype, with Rb 04 missiles

SAAB-105 (Sk 60C)

Svenska J6A Jaktfalk

SAAB-37 Viggen (Thunderbolt)

The Viggen, outcome of some ten years' hard work by the SAAB design team under Erik Bratt, represents the biggest and costliest engineering project ever undertaken in Sweden. It is an impressive warplane by any standards and, having been tailored to operate from Sweden's 500-metre trunk-road airstrips, has better STOL capabilities than any comparable aircraft now flying.

Detailed design of the Viggen began in mid-1962, and a full-scale mock-up was completed in 1965. Constructional methods remain straightforward, but the Viggen's unusual canard configuration – chosen to give it its STOL ability – combines advanced aerodynamic thinking with an excellent launching platform for a variety of weapons.

The first of six single-seat Viggen prototypes was flown by Erik Dahlström on 8 February 1967; the seventh will be a two-seat prototype for the Sk37 trainer version. Three combat versions of the Viggen have been proposed: the AJ37, due to enter service in mid-1971 to replace the Lansen in the attack rôle; the JA37 interceptor, to replace the Draken in the mid-1970s; and the S37 reconnaissance model. As their designations indicate, the AJ37 and JA37 have secondary capabilities for interception and attack respectively.

Primary armament of the AJ37 will be twin 30-mm cannon pods on two of the five external strong-points, supplemented by Rb 04 or Rb 05 air-to-surface missiles; the JA37 will carry Rb 27 or Rb 28 (Falcon) air-to-air weapons. Power plant for all variants is the RM8, an afterburning turbofan developed by Svenska Flygmotor AB from the civil Pratt & Whitney JT8D-22 and currently (mid-1968) developing approximately 26,450 lb s t. The Viggen's computerized navigation and fire-control systems are integrated with Sweden's STRIL 60 ground defence network.

An initial order for 83 AJ37s and 17 Sk37 trainers was supplemented by one for a further 75 Viggens in the spring of 1968.

SAAB-105

Designed by SAAB as a private venture to fulfil a variety of military and civil rôles, the SAAB-105 may be regarded as a jet successor to the piston-engined SAAB-91 Safir. The first design studies were begun in 1959, but progress was held up to some extent by the search for a suitably small yet reasonably powerful engine. The choice eventually fell on the little Turbomeca Aubisque turbofan of 1,640 lb s t, and when the first of the two SAAB-105 prototypes was flown on 29 June 1963 it was also the first time that the Aubisque had flown in an aircraft.

The Flygvapnet has ordered 150 SAAB-105s, some of which are advanced trainers and some ground-attack aircraft. The first production machine, an Sk 60A trainer, flew on 27 August 1965, and deliveries began in the following spring. The attack version, formerly called the A 60, is now known as the Sk 60B, and has six underwing attachment points for a variety of loads. These can include two 30-mm cannon pods, two SAAB-305A air-to-surface missiles, launchers for twelve 13.5-cm rockets or other ordnance up to a total load of 1,764 lb. The Sk 60C is a dual-rôle reconnaissance/attack version carrying a tape recorder and a camera in the nose. On 29 April 1967 the first example was flown of the SAAB-105XT, which has more powerful 2,850-lb s t General Electric J85 turbojet engines and has been ordered by the Austrian Air Force (20 SAAB-105XOs).

Svenska J6 Jaktfalk (Gerfalcon)

In 1929 the Svenska Aero Aktiebolaget of Lidingö produced, as a private venture, the prototype of a small single-seat fighter. Powered by a 500-hp Armstrong Siddeley Jaguar radial engine, it was a neat, if dumpy, single-bay biplane with a fixed, "spatted" undercarriage. The prototype was purchased by the Flygvapnet in January 1930, for evaluation, and given the air force designation J5. Its attributes warranted an order for two further prototypes, designated J6, to be powered by 500-hp Bristol Jupiter VIIFs.

During the first half of 1930, the Swedish machines were evaluated in competitive trials with Bristol Bulldogs from England, resulting in an order for five more Jaktfalkar in June of that year. After delivery of these machines the Svenska Aero concern, which had run into financial difficulties, was wound up and its effects were taken over by AB Svenska Järnvägsverkstäderna. The latter company completed three further Jaktfalkar towards the end of 1931 (Jupiter-powered J6As) and seven Jaguar-powered J6Bs in 1934, bringing total production to 18 aircraft.

Although built in only small numbers, the J6 was a first-class fighter for its time and gave long and satisfactory service with the Flygvapnet, the last example not being retired until 1941. At least one Jaktfalk found its way to Finland, where it was used on fighter trainer duties in the early stages of World War II.

Thulin Type K

Sweden's "flying doctor", Dr Enoch Thulin, was a leading pioneer of aviation in that country, and in six years he probably did more than any other man to lay firm foundations for a Swedish aircraft manufacturing industry.

The first tangible results of his efforts came in 1913 when, in collaboration with a fellow enthusiast, Oskar Ask, he formed the Aeroplanvarvet i Skåne company (AVIS) to build two modified examples of a Blériot design. A year later, Thulin assumed full control of the AVIS company, re-naming it AB Enoch Thulins Aeroplanfabrik (AETA). The new company continued production of the AVIS-Blériot, under the designation Thulin Type A, and completed another 23 machines of this type. Two were supplied to the Swedish Army, but the remainder were used as training aircraft at a flying school run by Dr Thulin.

The activities of AETA continued with a variety of other products, among them licence-built versions of the Morane Parasol and a number of experimental projects of the company's own design. Among the most interesting in the latter category was the Type H of 1917, the world's first tri-motor floatplane; this aircraft was subsequently given a wheel undercarriage and, for a time, seemed likely to earn a production order from the Swedish Army. Another Thulin design, of which ten were delivered to the Army, was the type FA two-seat reconnaissance aircraft, and a small number of reconnaissance floatplanes were also built for the Swedish Navy.

It was in 1917 that Thulin produced his first fighter design – a single-seat monoplane of mixed construction that bore clear evidence of AETA's Blériot/Morane associations in its neat lines. It was a stocky little machine, with a fully-covered fuselage, oval tail surfaces and constant-chord shoulder wings employing the wing-warping principle for lateral control. Power was provided by a single 90-hp Thulin A (licence-built Gnome) rotary engine, driving a two-blade propeller encased in a large flat spinner. Between 1917 and 1919, AETA completed 18 Type K fighters, but succeeded in selling only two of these to the Swedish Army. Another was sold to a private customer, and 12 of the remaining 15, shortly after the 1914–18 War, to the Royal Netherlands Naval Air Service, with which they served for several years.

When Dr Thulin died in a flying accident in 1919, his company had completed a total of 100 aircraft of no fewer than 14 different types, and more than 700 aero-engines of six types (of Gnome, Le Rhône and Benz origin).

Svenska J6B Jaktfalk

Thulin Type K

Thulin Type K, ski landing gear

TYPE	DIMENSIONS span ft	span in	length ft	length in	height ft	height in	WEIGHT max t-o lb	PERFORMANCE max speed mph	at height ft	service ceiling ft	combat range miles	REMARKS
SAAB-37	34	9⅓	53	5¾	18	4½	35,275	1,320	39,370	+60.000	NA	Data for first prototype
SAAB-105 (Sk 60C)	31	2	34	5	8	10	9,920	475	20,000	39,400	1,106 max	
SAAB-105XT	31	2	34	5	8	10	14,330	605	SL	45,000	1,380	
Svenska J6B	29	8	23	5	11	4	3,240	193	14,760	30,500	342	
Thulin Type K	29	6¼	21	7⅞	8	4⅜	1,151	93	SL	18,000	NA	

D-3801 (Morane-Saulnier M-S 406)

D-3802

E.K.W. C-35

Switzerland

D-3800, D-3801 and D-3802

Continuing its drive to acquire more modern aircraft for the Schweizerische Flugwaffe, in 1938 the Swiss government purchased two Morane-Saulnier M-S 405 single-seat fighters from France, gave them the Swiss Air Force serials J-1 and J-2 and, after satisfying itself that the aircraft met its requirements, took out a licence to manufacture the definitive version, the M-S 406, which was already being built for the Armée de l'Air.

Production of the M-S 406, under the Swiss designation D-3800, was undertaken by the Swiss Dornier-Werke AG at Altenrhein, and began in 1939. The D-3800 differed slightly from the French-built model in having an 860-hp Hispano-Suiza 12Y-31 engine, built under licence by the Saurer/SLM concern, and a non-retracting radiator. A total of 82 D-3800s (J3 – J84) were built before being supplanted on the assembly lines, in 1940, by the D-3801, which was essentially an M-S 406C-1 with a 1,000-hp Hispano 12Y-51 engine. Armament of both models comprised one 20-mm cannon in the engine Vee and two wing-mounted 7·7-mm machine-guns; two 110-lb bombs could be carried underwing. Dornier's Altenrhein factory turned out 207 D-3801s (J91 – J297) between 1940 and 1944, the largest quantity of a single aircraft type that had been built in Switzerland up to that time.

The first D-3800s began to reach Flugwaffe squadrons in the early part of 1940; by the end of that year seven squadrons had D-3800s or D-3801s and the build-up continued steadily throughout the next two years. Both the D-3800 and the D-3801 remained in service for several years, being diverted to close-support duties and ultimately to the training rôle after the arrival of de Havilland Vampires in 1946.

Meanwhile, in France, Morane-Saulnier had produced a new type called the M-S 450 as a potential replacement for the M-S 406. It secured no home orders, but continued to develop the design into the M-S 540. From drawings of this latter machine supplied in 1943, Dornier-Altenrhein built the D-3802 prototype, powered by a 1,250-hp Hispano 12Y-52 engine, which offered a much higher performance than that of the earlier Dornier-built fighters. The D-3802 flew for the first time on 29 September 1944; a second prototype, the D-3802A, followed, and ten of a contract for 100 D-3802As were completed before the order was curtailed. The wing machine-guns of the D-3801 were replaced in the D-3802A by two 20-mm FFK-HS cannon.

A further model made its appearance in 1947, when Dornier produced the one-off D-3803. Developed from the D-3802A, this had a 1,500-hp 12Y-53 engine and featured a cut-down rear fuselage with a new cockpit hood affording all-round vision. It could carry up to 880 lb of bombs underwing, had a service ceiling of 39,370 ft and the very creditable maximum speed of 422 mph at 23,300 feet. However, by the time it appeared the jet-fighter had become established, and no production orders were forthcoming.

E.K.W. C-35

When, in 1934, the Swiss government issued a specification for a single-engined, two-seat reconnaissance/close support aircraft to replace the Fokker C.V-E, the Eidgenössische Konstruktions Werkstätte evolved two entirely distinct designs, the C-35 and C-36. The former was a biplane which unmistakably owed much to the aircraft it was intended to replace; while the C-36 was of much more modern conception, being a very clean-looking, low-wing, all-metal monoplane. Perhaps because it felt that the small Swiss industry was not yet ready to embark upon a modern project, the Federal government chose the C-35 for its immediate needs and the first of the two prototype C-35s (serial numbers 101 and 102) was flown in 1936.

A production order ensued for 80 C-35s, and first deliveries from the factory at Thun began to reach Swiss Army Air Corps squadrons towards the end of 1937. The C-35 was powered by one of the more interesting aero-engines of the inter-war period, the so-called *moteur-canon* Hispano-Suiza 12Ycrs, which developed 860 hp for take-off and mounted a 20-mm cannon between the Vee cylinder banks. Further armament consisted of one 7·5-mm machine-gun in each lower main plane, firing outside the area swept by the three-bladed propeller, and a third gun of like calibre on a flexible mounting in the rear cockpit. Provision was made for racks beneath the lower wings to carry small bombs. Both cockpits were enclosed.

On the limited power available from its engine, the C-35 had quite a reasonable performance, and could climb to 16,400 ft in 8½ minutes. When World War II broke out, 78 of the original 80 production aircraft were still in service, equipping six AAC squadrons; and in 1942 a further eight C-35s were completed from spares, bringing the total constructed (including prototypes) up to 90 aircraft.

E.F.W. C-3603 and C-3604

As the threat of war in Europe appeared ever more likely to materialize, the Swiss Federal Government revived, in 1938, the C-36 design evolved a few years previously by the E.K.W. (now the Eidgenössische Flugzeug-Werke), with a view to providing the Swiss Air Force with more modern ground-attack equipment. The original single-tailed C-3600 project remained a design only, but two prototypes with twin tail assemblies were ordered. These differed in power plant only, the C-3601 having an 860-hp Hispano-Suiza 12Ycrs engine, and the C-3602 a 1,000-hp Hispano 12Y-51. Both machines had a non-retracting undercarriage, and the two-man crew were accommodated in tandem seats beneath an extended cockpit canopy. The C-3601 (serial number C-1) made its maiden flight in the spring of 1939, the C-3602 (C-2) following on 30 November of the same year.

A thorough test programme on these two machines was followed by an order for 160 production aircraft under the designation C-3603. The first flew at Emmen in 1941, differing from the prototype machines in having a fully-retracting main undercarriage and a Saurer/SLM licence-built version of the 12Y-51 engine. Like the C-35, the C-3603 had an engine-mounted Oerlikon cannon firing through the propeller boss, in addition to two wing-mounted 7·5-mm machine-guns and two further 7·5-mm guns in the after end of the cockpit providing defence to the rear. Underwing racks were provided for four 110-lb or 220-lb bombs.

Deliveries of the C-3603, as replacements for the now-obsolete C-35s, began to be made to units of the Schweizerische Flugwaffe during 1942. A more powerful model made its appearance with the first flight, on 21 August 1944, of the C-3604, and an order was placed for 100 machines of this type. The C-3604 had a total of three Hispano cannon in addition to the wing and rear-cockpit machine-guns, and a considerably better performance stemmed from the use of the 1,250-hp Hispano 12Y-52 liquid-cooled Vee engine. As things turned out, however, the advent of jet-engined fighters caused the Swiss government to curtail its order for the C-3604, and production of the type ceased after only 13 had been completed.

E.F.W. C-3603

E.F.W. C-3603

E.F.W. C-3604

TYPE	DIMENSIONS span ft	span in	length ft	length in	height ft	height in	WEIGHT max t-o lb	PERFORMANCE max speed mph	at height ft	service ceiling ft	combat range miles	REMARKS
D-3801	34	9¾	26	9¼	9	3¾	6,005	325	13,950	35,400	NA	
D-3802A	35	3¼	30	6	10	11½	8,014	391	21,325	NA		
E.K.W. C-35	42	7½	30	4	NA		NA	211	13,120	32,800	NA	
E.F.W. C-3603	45	1	33	6¾	11	0	7,600	295	NA	NA	NA	
E.F.W. C-3604	45	1	33	7½	11	0	9,480	348	14,760	32,800	NA	

Haefeli DH-5

A.D. Flying-Boat, first prototype

A.D. Flying-Boat, 200-hp Hispano-Suiza

Haefeli DH-5 and DH-5A

Haefeli, a pioneer of Swiss military aviation, had been co-designer of the German Ago C.II, and his first venture in his own country, the DH-1, was essentially a copy of this pusher-engined observation type. Six DH-1s were built at Thun in 1916 by the Eidgenössische Konstruktions Werkstätte, but they were not very favourably received by pilots of the Fliegertruppe when they entered service. An equally small number were built of the tractor-engined DH-2 biplane, but an improved model with a shortened fuselage entered production in 1917 as the DH-3 two-seat reconnaissance-bomber. One hundred and ten of these two-bay unequal-span biplanes were ultimately completed, the initial batch being powered by the 120-hp Argus-SLM engine and the second batch, which were built in 1926, by the 150-hp Saurer-Hispano. They were serial-numbered 501-599 and 501-510, and the machines of the second series had a maximum speed of 90 mph.

Haefeli's DH-4 fighter design of mid-1918 did not go into production, but in 1919 there appeared the DH-5; this was both a development of, and a replacement for, the earlier DH-3. Described as "safe, if unspectacular", the DH-5 was powered by a 180-hp Argus-SLM liquid-cooled engine, and was ordered into quantity production, deliveries beginning in 1922. Slightly smaller than its predecessor, the DH-5 had good altitude capability and one set a national height record of 23,786 ft on 12 September 1919. The DH-5 was armed with two forward-firing machine-guns in front of the cockpit and a third on a flexible mounting in the observer's cockpit. Sixty were built, and were given the serial numbers 402-461 in service. The DH-5A, which appeared in 1928, was an improved model with a steel-tube fuselage and a more powerful SLM engine developing 220 hp, which raised the maximum speed to 116 mph. Twenty-two DH-5As were completed by the E.K.W.

United Kingdom

A.D. Flying-Boat

Designed by the Air Department of the Admiralty and built by Pemberton-Billing Ltd (later Supermarine), the A.D. flying-boat was a two-seat patrol aircraft powered by a Hispano-Suiza engine of either 150 or 200 hp. The two-bay wings were designed to fold forward for stowage on board ship; another unusual feature was that the lower half of the gap between each pair of centre-section interplane struts was enclosed with fabric.

The lower tailplane of the biplane tail unit, being mounted directly on top of the hull, became awash when the aircraft was taxying and was constructed as a watertight plywood structure. The upper tailplane had an inverted aerofoil section and was installed with a slight negative angle of incidence in the belief that this would help to keep the aircraft level after an engine failure.

The hull, designed by Lt Linton Hope, was a sturdy wooden monocoque, with an unusually smooth surface finish. Unfortunately, it tended to porpoise badly and much effort had to be devoted to curing this.

Armament of the A.D. flying-boat consisted of a single Lewis machine-gun mounted on the front cockpit, and a small bomb-load could be carried under the wings. Wheels could be fitted to the hull, enabling the aircraft to take off from the decks of aircraft carriers; after take-off the wheels were jettisoned. Two prototypes and 27 production machines were built in 1917–18, but did not distinguish themselves in service.

Alcock Scout

The Alcock Scout was a "one-off" aircraft, and only earns its place in this book because it was armed and served with a front-line squadron.

It was designed by Fl Lt J. W. Alcock, the fuselage,

undercarriage and bottom wing coming from a crashed Sopwith Triplane; the upper wing belonged originally to a Sopwith Pup. This unusual parentage resulted in the aircraft's being nicknamed the "Sopwith Mouse". Quite short interplane struts were fitted, so that the top wing, almost level with the pilot, interfered little with his view. Originally a 100-hp Gnome Monosoupape engine was fitted, but this was replaced by a 110-hp Clerget.

Armament consisted of two fixed Vickers guns synchronized to fire between the propeller blades.

Alcock – famous later for his pioneer Atlantic flight – was a prisoner-of-war when his aircraft flew for the first time and the news of the event was sent to him in the following message: "Your baby was taken for an airing, but is still having trouble with teeth. She has been fitted with new clothing. Now a great improvement in health."

The Scout served with No. 2 Wing of the RNAS and operated from Mudros in the Aegean.

Armstrong Whitworth F.K.3.

This aircraft was designed to be a structurally-simpler version of the inherently-stable B.E.2c produced by the Royal Aircraft Factory, but equal to it in performance. The prototype, powered by a 90-hp RAF 1a engine, appeared in 1915 and bore a recognizable resemblance to the Factory aircraft.

On production machines further departures from the B.E.2c were made. The most important change was the merging of the two separate cockpits, with the pilot in the front and the gunner at the rear, where he was able to use the single Lewis machine-gun more effectively. The undercarriage incorporated a central skid and was sprung by oleo shock-absorbers based, it is said, upon the recoil mechanism of the French 75-mm field gun.

As a combat type the F.K.3 was no more effective than the ill-fated B.E.2c upon which it was based, and it was sent to serve on fronts of secondary importance in the Middle East. There it was used for reconnaissance, artillery co-operation and bombing. As a bomber it could carry up to 112 lb of bombs on external racks.

In Britain the F.K.3 was used extensively for training, a duty for which its pleasant flying qualities, due to its built-in stability, made it eminently suitable. In common with its contemporaries it had a nickname – the "Little Ack" – distinguishing it from the later and larger F.K.8 or "Big Ack."

Armstrong Whitworth F.K.8

Developed from the smaller F.K.3 of 1915, the F.K.8 was a two-seat tractor biplane reconnaissance aircraft. It was known generally as the "Big Ack", to distinguish if from the F.K.3 "Little Ack."

The prototype F.K.8 flew in May 1916, and was powered by a 120-hp Beardmore engine enclosed in an unusually angular cowling. This incorporated a bold name-plate, consisting of the capital letters A and W, and long radiator blocks on each side of the fuselage extended upward to join just above the top wing. Other distinctive features of the F.K.8 were the inverted Vee-struts supporting the upper wing above the fuselage, so that the top wing was without a centre-section, and the undercarriage. This was sprung by oleo units attached

Alcock Scout

Armstrong Whitworth F.K.3, in initial form

Armstrong Whitworth F.K.8, Beardmore engine, early cowling

TYPE	DIMENSIONS span ft	in	length ft	in	height ft	in	WEIGHT max t-o lb	PERFORMANCE max speed mph	at height ft	service ceiling ft	combat range miles	REMARKS
Haefeli DH-5	37	10	24	11	10	2	2,720	108	NA	21,000	NA	
A. D. Flying-Boat	50	4	30	7	13	1	3,327	91	2,000	7,500	NA	150-hp Hispano-Suiza
A. D. Flying-Boat	50	4	30	7	13	1	3,567	100	2,000	11,000	NA	200-hp Hispano-Suiza
Alcock Scout	NA		NA		NA		NA	NA	NA	NA	NA	
F.K.3	40	1	29	0	11	11	2,056	87	SL	12,000	NA	90-hp RAF la
F.K.3	40	1	29	0	11	11	2,010	88	6,500	13,000	NA	105-hp RAF lb

Armstrong Whitworth F.K.8, Beardmore engine, early cowling

Armstrong Whitworth F.K.8, Beardmore engine, improved cowling

Armstrong Whitworth F.K.8, Beardmore engine, late production model

Armstrong Whitworth F.K.10, 130-hp Clerget engine

to each side of the fuselage, yet still incorporated a rather old-fashioned and cumbersome central skid. Dual controls were fitted, so that, if the pilot were incapacitated, the observer in the rear cockpit could control the elevators and rudder – the latter by means of handgrips located on the rudder control cables where they passed through the cockpit – but not the ailerons. The tailplane was adjustable in flight.

Armament consisted of one fixed Vickers machine-gun, synchronized to fire through the propeller disc, and one Lewis machine-gun on a Scarff ring-mounting in the rear cockpit. An assortment of small bombs could be carried.

On production F.K.8s the engine cowling was cleaned up, and a 160-hp Beardmore engine, with smaller, improved radiators, was fitted to the final production version. These aircraft also had simpler undercarriages.

The F.K.8 was used by the RFC on several fronts, proving itself an efficient combat type, and one able to engage the opposing German single-seat scouts on equal terms. On one occasion, 2nd Lt Alan A. McLeod of No. 2 Squadron and his observer, Lt A. W. Hammond, were returning from a bombing raid behind the Western Front in their F.K.8, when they were attacked by a Fokker Dr. 1. Hammond shot this down with his Lewis gun, but seven more Fokkers then began to attack the F.K.8. McLeod destroyed one of these, and was then wounded. Hammond shot down two more in a "dog-fight", during which he was wounded six times, and the aircraft was badly damaged. The petrol tank was hit and flames engulfed the cockpit, forcing McLeod, badly wounded, out on to the wing. From that position he controlled the F.K.8 by one hand on the burning control stick, side-slipping to keep the flames away from his body, until the machine crash landed between the Allied and German trench positions. Both airmen were rescued and recovered. McLeod, only 18 years old, was awarded the Victoria Cross for his gallantry.

A second Victoria Cross was gained in an F.K.8 by Captain F. M. F. West. After a low-level bombing attack on enemy artillery concentrations, the F.K.8 was attacked by six enemy aircraft. On opening fire, their first burst almost severed West's left leg. Pulling the now useless limb from the rudder bar, West was then hit in the other leg. Nearly fainting from the loss of blood and pain, West managed to fly the F.K.8 home, while his observer fought off further attacks.

Armstrong Whitworth F.K.10

One of four quadruplanes produced by Britain during the 1914–18 War, the F.K.10 was a two-seat fighter-reconnaissance aircraft.

The main reason for adopting this unusual layout was to provide the crew with the best possible view and to obtain maximum manoeuvrability. To these ends, the four wings were of narrow chord and short span, with four ailerons each side. They were of equal span and braced by wires and single interplane struts which projected slightly below the bottom wing, the ends carrying small skids. The bottom wing was in one piece, passing slightly below the underside of the fuselage. The undercarriage was unconventional in that the wheels were mounted at the end of a single strut which was wire-braced fore, aft and sideways. Another unorthodox feature for a British aircraft was that no fixed tailplane was fitted, but only a balanced elevator.

The first aim was achieved, for the pilot, positioned in front of the wings, had an excellent unobstructed view forward and upward. The enormous drag of the wings, however, resulted in a relatively poor performance, and there was a tendency for the wings to flutter. Longitudinal control was also unsatisfactory.

The prototype was fitted with a 110-hp Clerget engine, but production machines normally had the 130-hp Clerget, although one, at least, was fitted with a 110-hp Le Rhône.

Armament consisted of one fixed Vickers machine-gun, mounted on top of the fuselage in front of the pilot and synchronized to fire through the propeller disc, and a single Lewis machine-gun mounted on a rocking post in the rear cockpit. F.K.10s built for the RNAS had a Scarff mounting-ring for the observer's gun.

Because of the aircraft's poor performance, only about ten were built; these were flown by the RFC at Gosport and by the RNAS at Manston.

Armstrong Whitworth Siskin III

Superseding the Sopwith Snipe, the Siskin single-seat fighter was, with its contemporary the Gloster Grebe, one of the first types selected for re-equipment of the RAF after the 1914–18 War.

The prototype of the Siskin III was the Siddeley Siskin. This was of conventional wood and fabric construction, and was powered by a 340-hp ABC Dragonfly engine. From it were developed the Siskin II two-seat trainer and fighter, both of which had conventional parallel interplane struts.

From these aircraft, in turn, was developed the Siskin III single-seat high-performance fighter, constructed partly of steel. It was a distinctive biplane of the sesquiplane type; that is, the lower wing had only one-third the area of the upper wing. The steel-framed, fabric-covered top wing was constructed in two pieces, joined at the centre and supported by four splayed-out struts from the fuselage, and a splayed-out Vee-strut at each outer end. Ailerons were fitted to the upper wing only.

The steel-tube fuselage was constructed in two units, connected immediately aft of the cockpit. The undercarriage was of the cross-axle type, and incorporated oleo struts in the main members.

Armament consisted of two fixed, forward-firing Vickers machine-guns, mounted on top of the fuselage in front of the pilot, and synchronized to fire between the propeller blades.

The standard power plant on production aircraft was the 325-hp Armstrong Siddeley Jaguar III engine.

A total of about 70 Siskins were built, the first squadron to be equipped with the type, No. 41, being formed in 1924. Some Siskins were also produced as two-seaters, with dual-control, for training purposes.

In October, 1925, an improved version, designated Siskin IIIA, flew for the first time. The major change was the fitting of the more powerful 420–450-hp supercharged Armstrong Siddeley Jaguar IV, which increased the maximum speed by over 20 mph. Externally, Siskin IIIAs can be distinguished from the earlier versions by the absence of a small dorsal fin beneath the tail and the marked reduction in dihedral on the upper wing. Siskin IIIAs could carry four 20-lb fragmentation bombs on racks beneath the wings.

The Siskin IIIA entered service in 1927 with Squadrons No. 1 and 56, replacing the long-serving Sopwith Snipe and Gloster Grebe. Eventually 11 squadrons were equipped with the type. When production ceased in 1931, over 350 Siskin IIIAs had been built.

Armstrong Whitworth Atlas

The Atlas was a two-seat, single-engined army co-operation aircraft, and was the first type designed specifically for these duties to enter service with the RAF.

Powered by a 450-hp Armstrong Siddeley Jaguar air-cooled radial engine, the prototype flew for the first time on 10 May 1925. It had single-bay, staggered wings of unequal span and chord. Of fabric-covered metal

Armstrong Whitworth Siskin IIIA

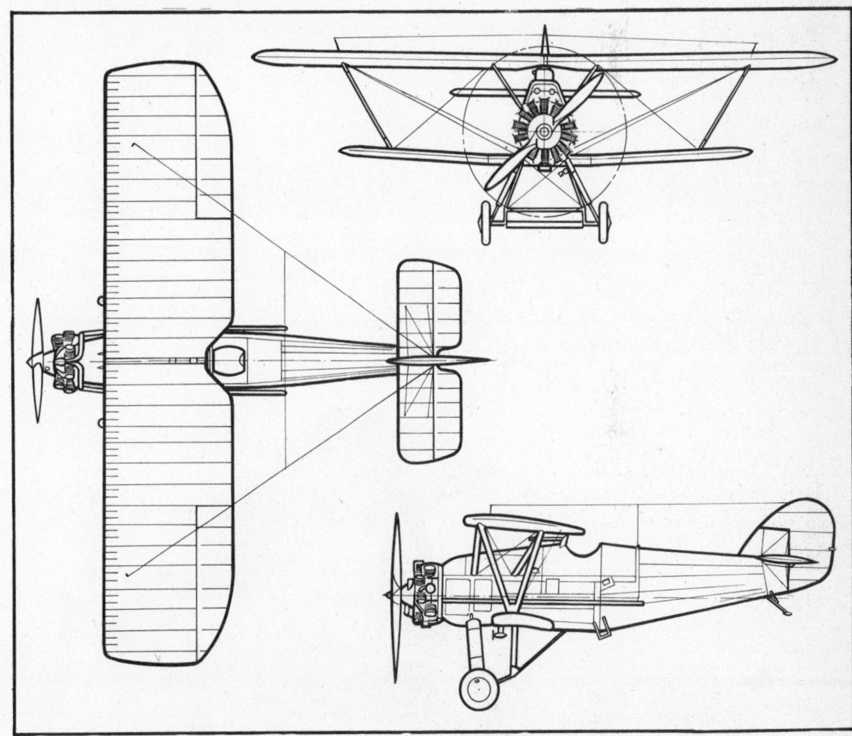
Armstrong Whitworth Siskin III

TYPE	DIMENSIONS span ft	span in	length ft	length in	height ft	height in	WEIGHT max t-o lb	PERFORMANCE max speed mph	at height ft	service ceiling ft	combat range miles	REMARKS
F.K.8	43	6	30	11	10	11	2,447	83	8,000	12,000	NA	120-hp Beardmore
F.K.8	43	6	31	0	11	0	2,811	98	SL	13,000	NA	160-hp Beardmore
F.K.10	27	10	22	3	11	6	2,019	84	6,500	10,000	NA	Endurance 2¼ hours
Siskin III	33	1	23	0	9	9	2,735	134	6,500	20,500	NA	
Siskin IIIA	33	2	25	4	10	2	3,012	156	SL	27,000	NA	
Siskin IIIA	33	2	25	4	10	2	3,180	186	15,000	32,700	NA	Supercharged Jaguar Major

Armstrong Whitworth Atlas

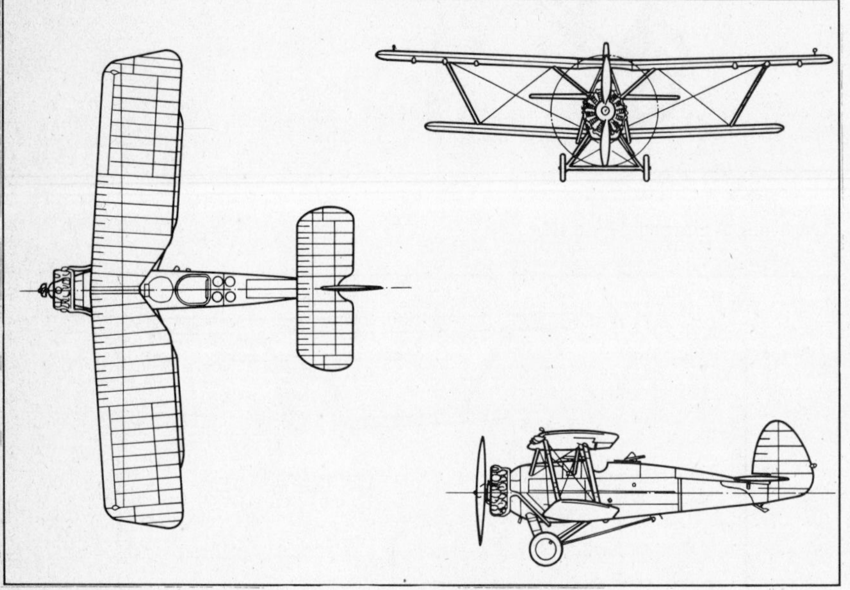

Armstrong Whitworth Atlas

Armstrong Whitworth A.W.16

Armstrong Whitworth Whitley Mk I

construction, the upper wing was built in two sections, and was supported at the centre by a W-strut assembly and at each end by a single pair of splayed-out interplane struts. Handley Page slots were fitted to the top wing.

The fuselage was basically a braced, steel-tube box girder, faired to an oval section and covered with fabric. The horizontal stabilizer was adjustable. The undercarriage was of the cross-axle Vee-type, the front members incorporating oleo struts with a very long travel.

Armament consisted of one fixed, forward-firing Vickers machine-gun, mounted on top of the fuselage in front of the pilot and synchronized to fire between the propeller blades, and one Lewis machine-gun in the rear cockpit mounted on a Scarff ring-mounting. Four 112-lb bombs could be carried under the wings; a prone bombing position, with bomb-aiming equipment, was provided.

Special army co-operation equipment included radio transmitting and receiving sets, cameras and a message pick-up gear, consisting of a retractable hook pivoted on the undercarriage spreader bar.

Production machines were built to Air Ministry Specification 33/26, and the Atlas went into service with No. 26 Squadron in 1927. It was powered by a variety of Jaguar or Jaguar-Major engines, which could be supercharged, or unsupercharged, and which could have a Townend ring fitted. The propeller could be geared or ungeared.

In service the Atlas proved rugged and reliable. In addition to its army co-operation work in Britain, it was used for communication duties in the Middle East. A small number were fitted with twin floats for seaplane duties, and a dual-control version, produced to Air Ministry Specification 8/31, was a standard advanced trainer with Flying Training Schools from 1931 to 1935.

The Atlas remained in production until 1933, by which time a total of 449 had been built.

Armstrong Whitworth A.W.16

The A.W.16 was a high-performance single-seat biplane fighter, three of which were sold to China in 1932. The cockpit was specially roomy and was designed to give the best possible view forward and downward.

During its design and construction, great care was taken to reduce drag-producing projections to the minimum, and the A.W.16 was one of the cleanest aeroplanes produced up to that time. Powered by a 510-hp Armstrong Siddeley Panther, it was considered the fastest radial-engined fighter in the world with a maximum speed of over 200 mph. It was equipped with oxygen, Sutton harness, an electrical system for heating and night flying lighting, two-way radio and a fire extinguisher.

The slow-running propeller made the A.W. 16 particularly quiet, and it was docile at low speeds and while landing, in spite of its high top speed. Armament consisted of two fixed Vickers machine-guns, synchronized to fire between the propeller blades, and racks for light fragmentation bombs were fitted under the wings.

Armstrong Whitworth Whitley

A twin-engined, long-range night bomber with a crew of five, the Whitley was one of the mainstays of Bomber Command in the early months of World War II. It was designed to Air Ministry Specification B.3/34, and was chosen to re-equip the heavy bomber squadrons of the RAF. The prototype first flew in March 1936, and Mk I production aircraft, powered by two 795-hp Armstrong Siddeley Tiger IX air-cooled radials, went into service in 1937 with No. 10 Squadron, superseding Heyfords.

The Whitley was a mid-wing monoplane of all-metal, stressed-skin construction. The wing was constructed in three sections and was built around a single box-spar, consisting of two vertically-corrugated walls connected by sheeting corrugated spanwise, which formed the top and bottom of the box. The Frise-type ailerons had a metal structure and were fabric-covered; hydraulically operated split-flaps extended from the ailerons to the fuselage.

The fuselage was a metal monocoque structure, stiffened by frames and stringers, and incorporated girder-frames to take the wing spar, tailplane and tail-wheel loads. A maximum bomb load of 7,000 lb was carried internally in the fuselage below the floor, and in the wings, the apertures being closed by spring-loaded doors.

A retractable undercarriage was fitted, the wheels, carried between two hydraulic shock-absorbers, being raised forward into the engine nacelles by hydraulic jacks.

On early Whitleys the wings had no dihedral, but this was introduced towards the end of the production run of 34 Mk Is. They were followed by 46 Mk IIs, fitted with a two-stage supercharger, the first RAF aircraft to be so equipped. In turn, these were followed by 80 Mk IIIs, powered by 920-hp Tiger VIII engines, and incorporating a ventral "dustbin" turret aft of the wing.

Mk IV aircraft were powered by two Rolls-Royce Merlin liquid-cooled in-line engines, and had a Nash and Thompson powered turret, mounting four Browning 0·303-in machine-guns, in the tail. The Whitley was the first bomber to carry this heavy armament which later became a standard feature of RAF heavy bombers. Forty Mk IVs were built, in two variants, basic Mk IVs having two 1,030-hp Merlin IV engines and Mk IVAs having two 1,145-hp Merlin Xs.

The major production variant and best-known version, the Mk V, was also powered by Merlin X engines, but had a lengthened fuselage and redesigned fins with straight leading-edge instead of the curved units on earlier machines. A total of 1,476 Mk Vs was built.

The last variant, the Mk VII, was specially produced for reconnaissance and anti-submarine duties with Coastal Command. Known as the Whitley GR VII, it was fitted with ASV radar, had a crew of six and carried additional fuel. One hundred and forty-six Mk. VIIs were built; additionally some Mk Vs were converted to VII standard.

During the first night of the war, Whitleys dropped six million leaflets on Germany, and on 19 March 1940, accompanied by Hampdens, they made the first bombing raid on German soil in World War II. Whitleys were also the first British bombers to attack Italy. Bomber Whitleys were withdrawn from first-line service in the spring of 1942, and the reconnaissance version followed towards the end of that year. However, Whitleys continued in use for paratroop dropping and glider-towing duties.

Avro 504

The Avro 504 is best remembered as the aircraft with which the whole foundation of modern flying training was laid; but it was designed originally for front-line reconnaissance duties and first made headlines as a bomber. The date was 21 November 1914. Three 504s, each carrying four 20-lb bombs, attacked the German Zeppelin sheds at Friedrichshafen, on Lake Constance. A Zeppelin was seriously damaged and a gasworks destroyed, for the loss of one 504.

Other bombing raids followed, including one on a German submarine depot near Antwerp in which two U-boats were destroyed. Such missions, by pilots of the Royal Naval Air Service, did much to persuade Britain's early air force leaders of the value of strategic bombing.

Avro 504Cs (RNAS) and Ks (RFC/RAF), converted into single-seaters, also served as home defence anti-

Armstrong Whitworth Whitley Mk V

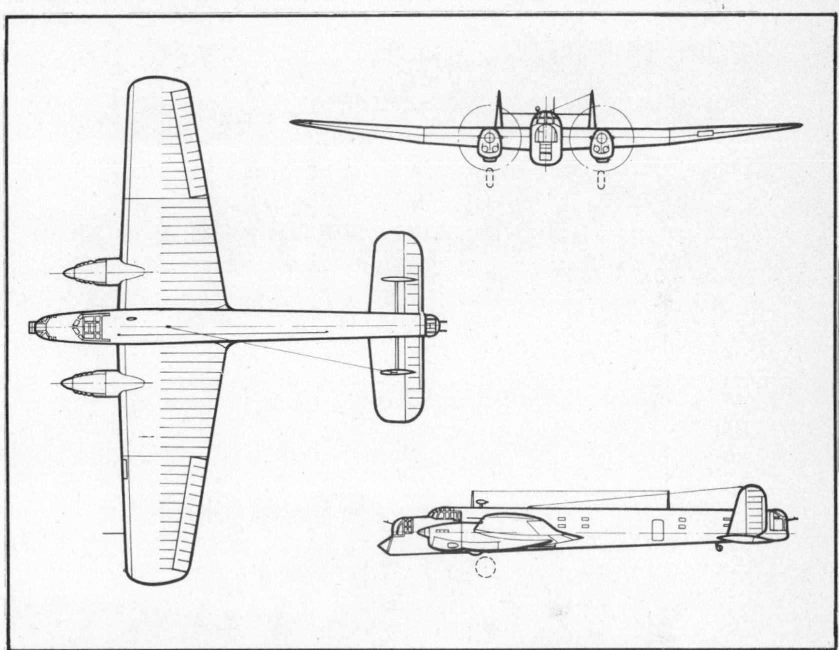
Armstrong Whitworth Whitley Mk V

Armstrong Whitworth Whitley Mk VII

TYPE	DIMENSIONS span ft	in	length ft	in	height ft	in	WEIGHT max t-o lb	PERFORMANCE max speed mph	at height ft	service ceiling ft	combat range miles	REMARKS
Atlas	39	6	28	6	10	6	4,020	142	SL	16,800	NA	Jaguar IVC
Atlas seaplane	39	6	NA		NA		4,500	142	SL	14,500	NA	Geared Jaguar
A.W.16	33	0	25	0	11	6	3,600	203	NA	31,000	NA	
Whitley MK I	84	0	69	3	15	0	21,660	192	7,000	19,000	1,250	
Whitley Mk II	84	0	69	3	15	0	22,991	215	15,000	22,000	1,315	
Whitley Mk III	84	0	69	3	15	0	24,000	215	15,000	22,000	1,315	
Whitley Mk IV	84	0	69	3	15	0	NA	NA	NA	NA	NA	
Whitley Mk V	84	0	70	6	15	0	28,000	222	17,000	17,600	1,650*	*With 3,000-lb bomb load
Whitley Mk VII	84	0	70	6	15	0	NA	NA	NA	NA	NA	

Avro 504, machine used in Friedrichshafen raid, November 1914

Avro Aldershot Mk III

Avro Aldershot Mk III, No. 99 Squadron

Avro Anson Mk I

Zeppelin fighters. Initially, the idea was to climb above the enemy airships and drop bombs on to their inflammable hulls; later, the 504s often had a machine-gun above the top wing or in front of the cockpit, fixed to fire forward and upward. Squadrons of 504 fighters remained operational until the Armistice; but the majority of the 8,340 built during the 1914–18 War, and afterwards, went to training units, serving until 1932–3 and becoming among the most popular trainers ever built.

Construction of the 504 was conventional, with a wire-braced wooden fuselage and wooden wings, all fabric-covered. The prototype had inversely-tapered ailerons which, although separate surfaces, were secured at their inner ends, the outer ends being warped by means of cables. Production machines, however, were fitted with normal hinged ailerons and had a much-improved engine cowling.

During its long life, the Avro 504 had a variety of power plants. Most of those that saw combat service were powered by an 80-hp Gnome rotary engine; but the 504K had a 100-hp Gnome Monosoupape, 110-hp Le Rhône or 130-hp Clerget.

Avro Aldershot

Designed to meet Air Ministry Specification 2/20, the Aldershot was one of the first new types of bomber to be designed for the RAF after the 1914–18 War. It had two-bay biplane wings of equal span, and was of composite wood and metal construction.

Powered by a 650-hp Rolls-Royce Condor III engine, it was unusually big and heavy for a single-engined machine, and its maximum bomb-load of 2,000 lb was equal to that of some of its twin-engined contemporaries. A split undercarriage was fitted, the bracing of which was arranged to leave a clear gap under the fuselage. The tailplane was mounted above the fuselage, level with the top of the fin. A sturdy ladder, fixed permanently to the port side of the fuselage, facilitated entry to the open cockpits.

A crew of three was carried. Armament consisted of one Lewis gun on a Scarff mounting in the rear cockpit.

Two prototypes were built in 1922, and the Aldershot entered service with the specially-revived No. 99 Squadron in 1924. Its service life was short, for it was replaced after only two years when the Air Staff finally decided against the idea of a single-engined heavy bomber.

A few ambulance versions of the same design, known as Andovers, were supplied to the RAF; these had a completely new fuselage. The original prototype was used to test the 1,000-hp Napier Cub engine, for which purpose a four-wheeled undercarriage was fitted; and the Aldershot was also used to flight-test the Beardmore Typhoon engine.

Avro Anson

A general-reconnaissance aircraft with a crew of three, the Avro 652A Anson Mk I was a military development of the Avro 652 six-passenger commercial transport, two of which were used by Imperial Airways. Over 10,000 Ansons were built and the type was used widely by the RAF and many other air forces. In 1956 they completed 20 years' service with the RAF, equalling the longevity record of their famous ancestor, the Avro 504 biplane, and a handful were still being used by the RAF in 1968.

It was in May 1934 that the Air Ministry requested Avro to look into the design of a twin-engined landplane for coastal reconnaissance duties. The prototype flew for the first time on 24 March 1935. Major differences from its civil counterpart were the installation of Armstrong Siddeley Cheetah VI engines instead of Cheetah Vs, the introduction of military equipment, including a manually-operated Armstrong Whitworth gun-turret, and square cabin windows instead of the 652's oval type.

Anson Mk Is went into service in 1936 with No. 48 Squadron. The standard power plant initially was the 350-hp Armstrong Siddeley Cheetah IX; but other variants of this engine, and different engines, were installed in later versions.

The Anson Mk I had a one-piece cantilever monoplane wing, built around two wooden box-spars, with spruce ribs and plywood covering. The wing was let into the fuselage so that its undersurface was flush with the bottom of the fuselage. Narrow-chord Frise-type balanced ailerons were fitted.

The fuselage was a rectangular welded steel-tube structure, covered with fabric. The fin, also of welded steel-tube construction, fabric-covered, was built integrally with the fuselage. A bomb-aimer's panel was fitted in the nose.

The undercarriage was retractable by means of a hand-crank, being stowed in the engine nacelles. The Anson was, in fact, the first RAF aircraft to have a retractable undercarriage, which was still a comparative novelty at the time. Oleo-pneumatic shock-absorbers were fitted.

Standard armament consisted of one fixed 0·303-in machine-gun, mounted on the port side of the fuselage and firing forward, and another in the dorsal turret; but Ansons of No. 500 Squadron carried experimentally two additional guns firing through the side windows, and the CO's machine had a single hand-operated 20-mm cannon in the bottom of the fuselage. A maximum of 360 lb of bombs could be carried – 200 lb internally and the remainder on racks under the wings.

When war started in 1939, Ansons equipped 12 squadrons of Coastal Command; and although they were becoming obsolescent, and were being superseded by Hudsons, they did good work in the early days. On one occasion, in June 1940, three Ansons were attacked by a formation of nine Bf 109s and succeeded in shooting down two and damaging another of the enemy fighters.

After their withdrawal from first-line service, Ansons were used for training and light transport duties, for which the type was produced in thousands.

Later variants introduced numerous refinements, including hydraulic operation of the undercarriage and flaps, a redesigned fuselage with increased headroom and oval windows and all-metal wings.

Ansons served with many air forces, including those of Australia, Canada, Egypt, Finland, Greece, Ireland, South Africa and Southern Rhodesia, as well as the US Army Air Corps. In Britain, the type was in continuous production for 17 years, reaching a peak output of 130 a month in 1943–4. A total of 8,138 were built, before production ended in 1952. Another 2,882 were built in Canada.

Avro Manchester

The Manchester was a medium-heavy bomber, designed to Air Ministry Specification P.13/36 which stipulated the use of two of the new and unorthodox 1,760-hp Rolls-Royce Vulture 24-cylinder "X" engines. It was a cantilever monoplane, of all-metal, stressed-skin construction, and carried a crew of seven.

The wing comprised an untapered centre-section, mounting the engines, and two symmetrically-tapered outer wings, with split flaps fitted inboard of the ailerons. The fuselage was of oval section and was made in five portions. The cockpit incorporated a heating system and the cavernous bomb-bay, extending nearly half the length of the fuselage, was big enough to accommodate what aircrews referred to as "slum-clearing" bombs. The main undercarriage units retracted rearward into the engine nacelles.

Armament consisted of eight 0·303-in machine-guns, of which two were mounted in a power-operated turret

Avro Anson Mk I

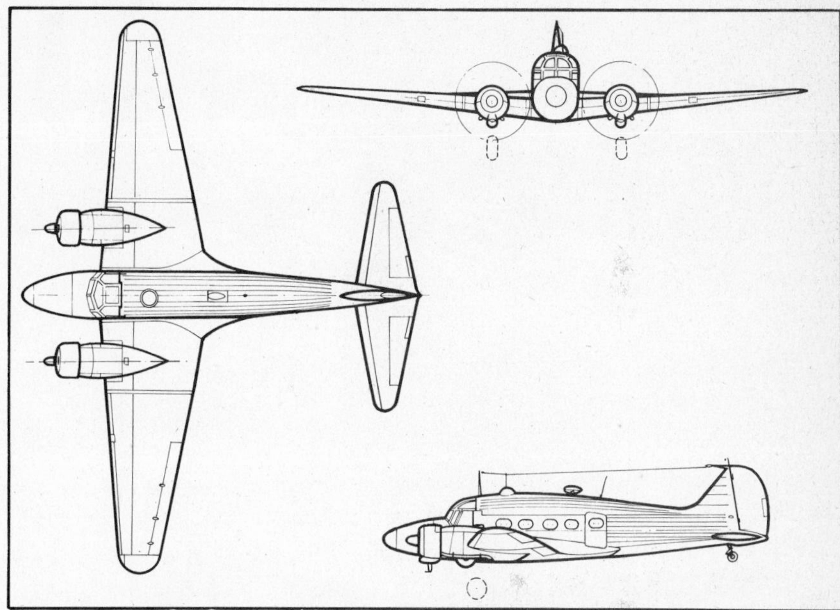
Avro Anson Mk 21 trainer

Avro Manchester Mk IA

TYPE	DIMENSIONS span ft	span in	length ft	length in	height ft	height in	WEIGHT max t-o lb	PERFORMANCE max speed mph	at height ft	service ceiling ft	combat range miles	REMARKS
Avro 504A	36	0	29	5	10	5	1,574	62	6,500	NA	250	
Aldershot	68	0	45	0	15	3	10,950	110	SL	11,500	652	
Anson Mk I	56	6	42	3	13	1	8,000	188	7,000	16,000	660	
Manchester	90	1	70	0	19	6	50,000	265	17,000	19,200	1,630*	*With 8,100-lb bomb load.

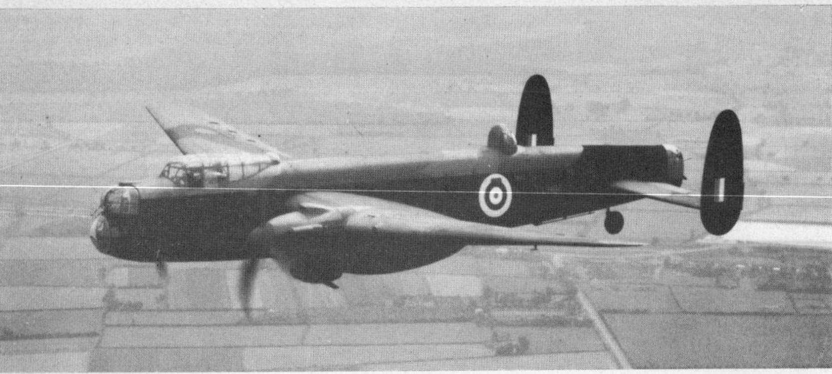

Avro Manchester Mk IA

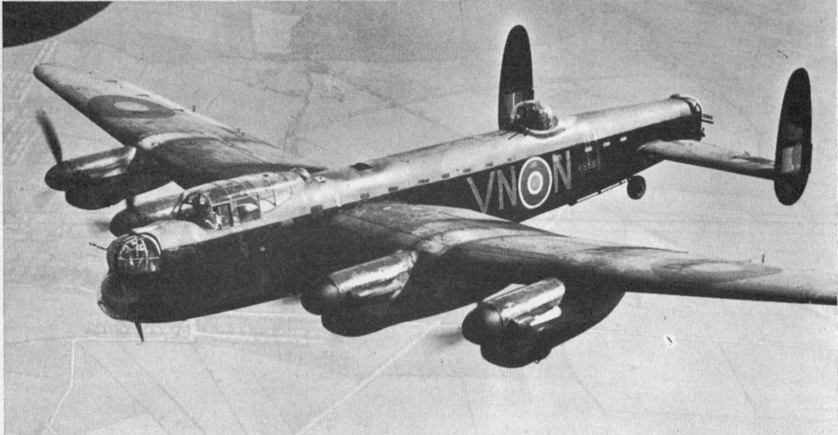

Avro Lancaster Mk I

Avro Lancaster Mk I, equipped for "dam-busting" operation

Avro Lancaster Mk II

in the nose, two in a dorsal turret and four in a turret in the tail. The maximum bomb-load was 10,350 lb.

The Manchester went into service in November 1940, with No. 207 Squadron, and soon became very unpopular with its crews owing to the troubles experienced with the insufficiently-developed Vulture engines. These not only fell short of their designed power but proved unreliable, and operational sorties were marred by frequent engine failures. The bomber could, however, maintain height on one engine. One Manchester, with an engine knocked out by gunfire and other extensive damage, flew 600 miles from Berlin to its base in England.

Initial production machines had triple fins and rudders; on later aircraft, known as Mk IAs, the centre fin was deleted and the size of the remaining two fins and rudders was increased.

About 200 Manchesters were built, serving with eleven squadrons before the type was withdrawn from service in June 1942.

Avro Lancaster

The Lancaster was a four-engined heavy bomber which formed the backbone of Bomber Command's offensive against Germany during the period 1943 to 1945. It was the most famous and most successful heavy night bomber used in Europe in World War II, delivering 608,612 tons of bombs in 156,000 sorties.

The Avro Type 683 Lancaster was a direct development of the ill-fated Type 679 Manchester twin-engined bomber. The prototype, a modified Manchester airframe powered by four 1,145-hp Rolls-Royce Merlin X engines, instead of two Vultures, was in fact known initially as the Manchester III.

Of all-metal stressed-skin construction, the wing was made in five sections, comprising a parallel-chord centre-section manufactured integrally with the fuselage, two tapering outer wings and two wing-tips. The leading-edge and trailing-edge sections were built as separate units. Split trailing-edge flaps were fitted between the ailerons and fuselage.

The oval-section fuselage was of semi-monocoque construction and was made in five main portions. Pairs of extruded longerons, positioned half-way down the sides, formed the backbone of the three middle sections; beams between these longerons supported the floor and formed the roof of the massive bomb-bay, which extended over half the length of the fuselage. As much equipment, cable and piping as possible was installed in the wing and fuselage sub-assemblies before final assembly, to speed up the latter process.

Each main undercarriage unit consisted of a large single wheel supported between a pair of oleo-pneumatic shock-absorber struts, and retracted rearward into the end of the inner engine nacelle.

Lancaster Mk Is went into service early in 1942, with No. 44 Squadron. This version was powered by 1, 280-hp Merlin XX engines, and was armed with ten 0.303-in Browning machine-guns, disposed two each in nose, dorsal and ventral turrets, and four in a turret in the extreme tail, all turrets being of Nash and Thompson design and hydraulically operated. The maximum bomb-load was 14,000 lb, made up of a wide variety of high-explosive and incendiary weapons.

In service, the care taken during the design stages regarding servicing problems paid dividends, for the Lancaster was appreciably easier to maintain in the field than its contemporaries.

By mid-1943 the generally good all-round performance of the new bomber was firmly established, and was reflected in statistics showing the number of Lancasters lost per tonnage of bombs dropped. These revealed that one Lancaster was lost for every 132 tons delivered, compared with only 56 tons for each Halifax lost and 41 tons for each Stirling.

One of the features which made the Lancaster so versatile was its cavernous bomb-bay. Designed initially to accommodate bombs of up to 4,000-lb in weight, this was, on the Lancaster Mk I (Special), modified progressively to take 8,000-lb bombs (first used against Essen), then 12,000-lb bombs (first used against the Dortmund-

Ems Canal) and finally the massive 22,000-lb "Earthquake" or Grand Slam bombs (first used against Bielefeld Viaduct). Lancasters were also chosen to drop the specially-developed Wallis "spinning-drum" bombs, used in the famous attack by 617 Squadron on the Mohne and Eder dams on 17 May 1943. When carrying a 22,000-lb bomb, the dorsal turret was deleted.

Another sub-variant of the Mk I was the Mk I (FE), intended for use in the Far East against Japan.

The Lancaster Mk II was powered by four 1,650-hp Bristol Hercules VI radial engines, and some examples of this version had bulged bomb-bays. The Lancaster Mk III was essentially similar to the Mk I, but was powered by four Packard-built Merlin 28, 38 or 224 engines. The Mark numbers IV and V were allotted to improved variants which materialized ultimately as the Lincoln Mk I and II. The Lancaster Mk VI was a special variant carrying jamming devices for electronic countermeasures duties. It was powered by Merlin 87 engines, driving four-bladed propellers, and had the nose and dorsal turrets deleted.

The Mk VII was the final production version, on which the normal Nash and Thompson dorsal turret was replaced by a Martin turret mounted nearer the wing.

After the war the Lancaster was used by Coastal Command for maritime reconnaissance duties and for air-sea rescue work. In the latter rôle, the ASR Mk III carried an airborne lifeboat which could be dropped by parachute. Some Lancaster Is were also equipped with cameras for photographic reconnaissance and survey duties. Designated PR I, these surveyed over 1,000,000 square miles of Central Africa.

Lancasters were retired from first-line service with the RAF in 1954, but Canada continued to use PR Lancasters until April 1964 – 23 years after the prototype first flew.

Lancaster production in Britain totalled 6,944 aircraft, including 3,444 Mk Is, 300 Mk IIs, 3,020 Mk IIIs and 180 Mk VIIs. In addition, 422, designated Mk X, were built in Canada.

Avro Lincoln

Last of the Royal Air Force's piston-engined heavy bombers, the Avro Type 694 Lincoln was the mainstay of Bomber Command in the immediate post-war years. Designed to Specification B.14/43, to succeed the Lancaster, it was developed from the latter; the Lincoln Mks 1 and 2 were, in fact, known originally as the Lancaster Mks IV and V respectively.

Of all-metal stressed-skin construction, the Lincoln followed closely the well-proven Lancaster formula, the major design changes being wings of increased span, a lengthened fuselage and the installation of 1,750-hp Rolls-Royce Merlin 85 engines.

The Lincoln was able to carry 14,000 lb of bombs, and its standard defensive armament consisted of six 0.50-in machine-guns in pairs in nose, dorsal and tail turrets. Some aircraft were produced with twin 20-mm cannon in a dorsal turret and a single 0.50-in ventral machine-gun. Towards the end of their service life, most Lincolns had their dorsal turrets removed. A crew of seven was carried.

Three operational variants were produced. The B Mk 1 was powered by Merlin 85s, and the B Mk 2 by Merlin

Avro Lancaster Mk III

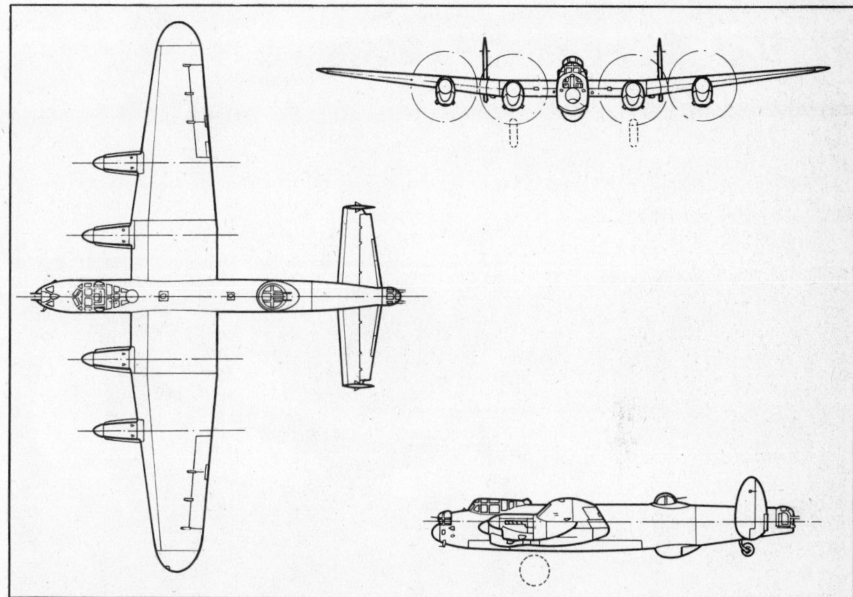
Avro Lancaster Mk 1

Avro Lincoln B Mk 2

TYPE	DIMENSIONS span ft	span in	length ft	length in	height ft	height in	WEIGHT max t-o lb	PERFORMANCE max speed mph	at height ft	service ceiling ft	combat range miles	REMARKS
Lancaster Mk I	102	0	69	6	20	0	63,000	281	18,500	23,500	2,695	
Lancaster Mk II	102	0	69	6	20	0	65,000	NA	NA	NA	NA	
Lancaster Mk III	102	0	69	6	20	0	70,000	287	11,500	24,500	1,660*	*With 14,000-lb bomb load.
Lancaster Mk VI	102	0	NA		NA		NA	NA	NA	NA	NA	
Lancaster Mk VII	102	0	NA		NA		NA	NA	NA	NA	NA	
Lincoln Mk I	120	0	78	3	17	3	75,000	319	18,500	30,500	1,470	

Avro Shackleton MR Mk 1

Avro Shackleton MR Mk 2

Avro Shackleton MR Mk 3, Phase 3 aircraft with Viper auxiliary turbojets

Avro (Hawker Siddeley) Vulcan B Mk 1

66, 68A or 300 engines. Lincoln B Mk 4s were Mk 2s converted to take Merlin 85s.

Lincolns saw service in operations against terrorists in Malaya and against the Mau-Mau in Kenya.

A number of Lincolns were supplied to Argentina. A total of 73 were built in Australia for the RAAF.

Avro Shackleton

The Avro Type 696 Shackleton is a long-range maritime reconnaissance and anti-submarine patrol bomber which was designed to replace Lend-Lease Liberators and Fortresses, and the Lancasters and Sunderlands used by Coastal Command immediately after the war. It was evolved from the Lincoln III, a 1945 project for an anti-submarine version of the bomber. Of all-metal stressed-skin construction, it combined the bomber's wings, tailplane and undercarriage with a redesigned fuselage, to accommodate search radar and other specialized equipment needed for the new rôle, and to provide room for adequate crew facilities during protracted flights.

A feature of the fuselage is the cavernous bomb-bay, extending for half its length and well able to accommodate bulky stores such as depth charges, sonobuoys and bombs up to the heaviest calibre. All variants are powered by four 2,450-hp Rolls-Royce Griffon 57 engines, driving contra-rotating propellers.

The first of three prototypes flew on 9 March 1949 and Shacketon MR Mk 1s went into service in 1951, armed with a pair of 20-mm cannon in a Bristol B.17 dorsal turret, and with a chin-type radome under the nose. A total of 77 of this variant were built.

The MR Mk 2 is a cleaner and more powerfully armed version of the Mk 1, with an additional pair of 20-mm cannon in the nose and a new type of semi-retractable radome under the fuselage aft of the bomb-bay. The rear fuselage is faired off with a transparent cone, for use as a gunner's sighting position, and the single fixed tail-wheel of the Mk 1 is replaced by twin retractable wheels. About sixty Mk 2s were built.

The Shackleton MR Mk 3, which went into service in 1957, represented a major improvement. Changes included the introduction of a nosewheel-type undercarriage, wing-tip fuel tanks, and a new clear-view cockpit canopy, and the deletion of the dorsal turret. To improve crew comfort a sound-proofed wardroom was also introduced. In the mid-sixties, these aircraft were being modernized and improved by the addition of a Bristol Siddeley Viper turbojet in the rear of each outboard nacelle. About 30 MR Mk 3s were built, eight of which were supplied to the South African Air Force.

Avro (Hawker Siddeley) Vulcan

Second of Britain's V-class four-jet bombers to go into service, the Avro Type 698 Vulcan has a delta-wing configuration. This layout, adopted for the first time on a large bomber, was chosen because it offered the best combination of good load-carrying capabilities, high speed at high altitudes and long range.

The massive wing is a two-spar, stressed-skin structure, and combines vast internal stowage, for the engines, fuel and military equipment, with minimum drag. The leading-edge has a basic sweepback of 50°, but compound sweep on the outer half of each wing gives a 20 per cent increase in chord at about the three-quarter span position. The thickness-to-chord ratio at the centre-section to outer-wing joint is about 10 per cent, the chord at this point being 46 ft. Each wing carries two ailerons and two elevators at the trailing-edge, and rotating-flap air-brakes are incorporated in each centre-section near the leading-edge.

The fuselage is a circular-section, semi-monocoque structure, with a large dielectric panel under the nose. A conventional fin and rudder are fitted; there is no tailplane. The undercarriage is of the retractable tricycle type, actuated hydraulically. Each main unit consists of an eight-wheel bogie. Wheel brakes are supplemented by a large ribbon-type parachute.

Vulcan B Mk 1s entered service in August 1956, first with No. 230 Operational Conversion Unit, and then with No. 83 Squadron in the middle of 1957. Early versions were powered by four 11,000-lb s t Bristol Siddeley Olympus Mk 101 turbojets; later machines had the 12,000-lb s t Olympus Mk 102 and the 13,500-lb s t Olympus Mk 104.

These aircraft were followed by the B Mk 2, with a wing of increased span, incorporating elevon controls, and powered by 17,000-lb s t Olympus Mk 201 or 20,000-lb s t Mk 301 turbojets. Like the B Mk 1, these bombers carry no defensive armament, but very effective anti-radar jamming equipment is housed in an enlarged tail-cone. Similar equipment can be fitted in the earlier version, aircraft so modified being designated B Mk 1As.

The Vulcan B Mk 2 can carry the nuclear-armed Blue Steel stand-off weapon, which can be programmed to make either high or low altitude run-ins to the target. Each version can carry twenty-one 1,000-lb HE bombs.

To extend the period of the aircraft's effectiveness as a deterrent weapon, in the face of the growing efficiency of anti-aircraft missile systems, Vulcans have been modified so that approach to the target can be made at a low level, below radar screens. When so adapted the aircraft are camouflaged on the upper surface and carry specialized equipment permitting accurate navigation at low altitudes.

BAC Lightning

Designed to Specification ER.103, issued by the Ministry of Supply in 1947, the Lightning is a single-seat, twin-engined all-weather fighter, and was the first fully supersonic aircraft to go into service with the RAF. It can exceed the speed of sound in level flight without reheat, and can accelerate from Mach 1 to Mach 2 in less than 3½ minutes.

The Lightning is a cantilever mid-wing monoplane, each wing having a 60° sweepback on the leading-edge and a thickness-to-chord ratio of about 5 per cent. Of all-metal construction, the wings are five-spar structures with thick skinning, and are joined on the centre-line. The powered ailerons extend across the wingtips at right-angles to the airflow. Other unusual features include the use of notches in the wing leading-edge instead of fences, sealing of the large plain trailing-edge flaps to permit their use as integral fuel tanks, and outward retraction of the main undercarriage legs.

The fuselage is a semi-monocoque structure, with air-brakes on each side immediately in front of the fin. The two engines are installed one above the other, with the lower engine positioned well forward of the upper one. A bulged fairing under the fuselage is used as an external fuel tank. The tailplane is of the all-moving type and is positioned low down on the fuselage.

Twenty pre-production and some early production Lightnings were designated F Mk 1 and were each powered by two Rolls-Royce Avon 210(RA 24R) turbojet engines with variable-area nozzles, developing 14,430 lb s t with reheat. Without reheat, these fighters could take off, cruise economically and land on one engine. They first went into service in 1960 with No. 74 Squadron and eventually equipped also Nos. 56 and 111. Later models, designated F Mk 1A, had provision for flight refuelling and other changes.

Armament for the Mk 1/1A consisted of two 30-mm

Avro (Hawker Siddeley) Vulcan B Mk 2, with Blue Steel missile

Lightning F Mk 1A, No. 56 Squadron

TYPE	DIMENSIONS span ft	in	length ft	in	height ft	in	WEIGHT max t-o lb	PERFORMANCE max speed mph	at height ft	service ceiling ft	combat range miles	REMARKS
Shackleton MR Mk 1	120	0	77	6	16	9	NA	NA	NA	NA	NA	
Shackleton MR Mk 2	120	0	87	3	16	9	86,000	NA	NA	NA	NA	
Shackleton MR Mk 3	119	10	92	6	23	4	100,000	302	12,000	19,200	4,215	
Vulcan B Mk 1	99	0	97	1	26	1	NA	NA	NA	NA	NA	
Vulcan B Mk 2	111	0	99	11	27	2	NA	NA	NA	NA	NA	
Lightning F Mk 1A	34	10	55	3	19	7	NA	1,400	NA	60,000+	NA	

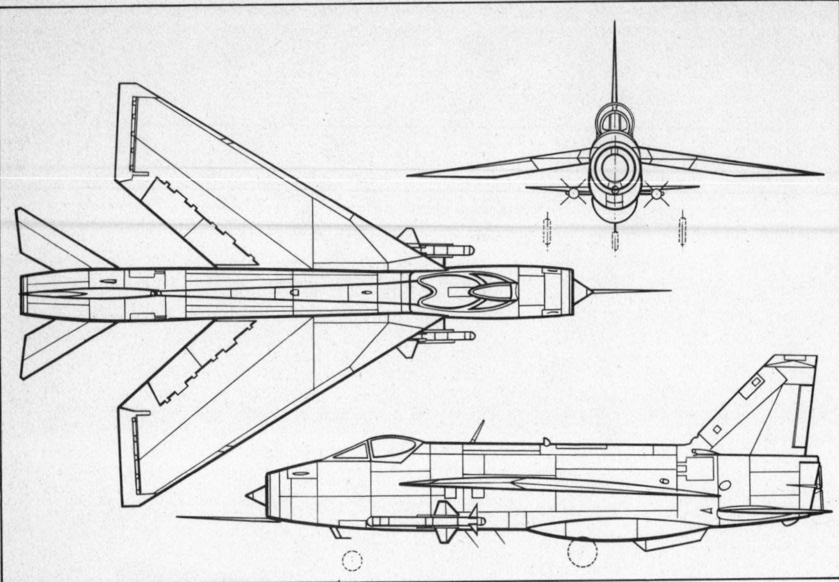
BAC Lightning F Mk 3

BAC Lightning F Mk 3, No. 111 Squadron

BAC Lightning F Mk 6, No. 74 Squadron, with overwing ferry tanks

BAC Lightning, ground-attack version, rocket packs extended

Aden Mk 4 cannon mounted in the fuselage, and two Hawker Siddeley Firestreak missiles mounted on pylons projecting from the fuselage. Provision was made for forty-eight 2-in rockets in retractable packs in each side of the fuselage nose, or Aden guns or camera packs in place of guns. The centre-body in the air intake contained Ferranti Airpass Mk 1 interception and fire control radar.

The F Mk 1A was followed by the F Mk 2, an interim version incorporating some of the changes, such as a liquid oxygen breathing system and a steerable nose-wheel, intended for the F Mk 3. The latter variant is powered by Avon 300 series engines, each developing 16,360 lb s t with reheat, has improved range, speed and ceiling, and can be armed with the more advanced Hawker Siddeley Red Top air-to-air missile. No guns are fitted. For ferrying, two jettisonable auxiliary fuel tanks are carried, rather surprisingly, on top of the wings.

Lightning F Mk 2 fighters were delivered to Nos. 19 and 92 Squadrons and six were supplied to Saudi Arabia in 1966. Mk 3s entered service with No. 74 Squadron in 1964 and were supplied subsequently to Nos. 23, 56 and 111. They were followed in 1965 by the fully-developed F Mk 6, with decreased sweepback on the outer wings, which also have cambered leading-edges, and an enlarged belly fuel tank. First Squadron to be equipped with the Mk 3, in late 1965, was No. 5. The Lightning F Mk 53 for Saudi Arabia and Kuwait is similar to the Mk 6, but carries 30-mm cannon in the front of the belly tank and also has underwing racks for rockets or bombs.

There are also several side-by-side two-seat training versions of the Lightning, with full combat capability.

BAT Bantam

First aircraft produced by the British Aerial Transport Company, the Bantam was a small single-seat fighter incorporating several features which at that time were unconventional for a British design.

Most noteworthy was the fuselage which, instead of being a fabric-covered braced box-girder, was of wooden monocoque construction, with the fin built integrally with it. The top wing was attached directly to the fuselage and the pilot sat with his head protruding through a circular hole in the centre-section. The undercarriage was of the divided-axle type, with coil-spring shock-absorbers, and extended the complete width of the lower centre-section.

Bearing the BAT type number F.K.22, the prototype had the new 170-hp ABC Wasp seven-cylinder air-cooled radial engine and was flight-tested in 1918.

Production Bantams were much smaller and differed from the prototype to such an extent that BAT allotted to them the new type number F.K.23, although the official designation of Bantam Mk I was retained.

Armament consisted of two fixed forward-firing Vickers machine-guns, mounted low down in the fuselage and synchronized to fire between the propeller blades.

During trials the Bantam proved to be fast and manoeuvrable, but with disastrous spinning characteristics. The spin began at a normal rate, but accelerated rapidly until a remarkable rate of autorotation was reached, and recovery could be effected only by very heavy control movement. This was caused by the extreme rearward position of the centre of gravity, and the combination of zero stagger and small gap of the wings.

Five Bantam Mk Is were built, embodying modifications to ease the spinning problem. The airframe of the original F.K.22 prototype was fitted subsequently with a 100-hp Gnome Monosoupape rotary engine and is referred to officially as the Bantam Mk II.

Beardmore W.B.III

The Beardmore W.B.III was a development of the Sopwith Pup produced specifically for operation from ships. To facilitate stowage, the wings were made to fold and the undercarriage could be drawn upward ("folded") into the fuselage to reduce the overall height.

The prototype, bearing the constructor's type number W.B.III, was a converted Pup. To enable the wings to fold, they were repositioned without any stagger and with the dihedral reduced; in addition the centre-section was redesigned to incorporate four full-length interplane struts. Ailerons were fitted to both upper and lower wings, and were operated by a system of rods on early W.B.IIIs; a conventional wire cable-control system was installed subsequently. The upper and lower ailerons were interconnected by struts. The undercarriage could be jettisoned to render ditching in the sea less hazardous, and flotation gear was fitted.

The standard engine was the 80-hp Le Rhône, but an 80-hp Clerget was fitted to some aircraft.

Armament comprised a single forward-firing Lewis machine-gun, mounted above the centre-section and inclined slightly upward to clear the propeller blades.

Production models were designated S.B.3D and S.B.3F, the "D" indicating aircraft with a "Dropping" or jettisonable undercarriage, and the "F" indicating those with a "Folding" undercarriage only.

About 50 W.B.IIIs were built. They operated, without distinguishing themselves, from the aircraft carriers *Furious*, *Nairana* and *Pegasus*.

Blackburn Kangaroo

The Kangaroo was a landplane development of the Blackburn G.P. seaplane of 1916, and was designed for use as a bomber.

The wings could be folded and were almost identical to those of the seaplane, large extensions on the top wing being supported by king-posts above the outer interplane struts. The fuselage was unusually small in cross-section and its projection far in front of the wings was a distinguishing feature of the type. The undercarriage consisted of four wheels mounted in pairs on Vee-struts. Initially it was unsprung, but production Kangaroos incorporated an oleo shock-absorber in each front strut. The power plant consisted of two 250-hp Rolls-Royce Falcon engines.

Defensive armament comprised two Lewis machine-guns, in the front and rear cockpits, both on Scarff ring-mountings. A maximum bomb load of 920 lb could be carried, and usually consisted of four 230-lb bombs, carried internally and suspended by their noses. Four bomb racks were also installed under the fuselage.

Fifteen Kangaroos were built, of which eleven were delivered to the RAF in 1918. They were operated mainly by the anti-submarine squadron at Seaton Carew, from where 600 hours of patrol duty were flown. Twelve U-boats were sighted and eleven attacked, of which at least one was destroyed. This is a better record than that achieved by the more numerous Curtiss H.12 Large Americas on similar duties.

Blackburn Swift/Dart/Velos

The Blackburn Dart was a single-seat carrier-borne torpedo-carrier. It was developed from the Blackburn Swift, of which a prototype had been built in 1919, followed by small production quantities to fulfil overseas orders, although the Swift was not adopted by the FAA.

The Dart was a biplane with two-bay equal-span wings, and was powered by a 450-hp Napier Lion IIB or Lion V engine. Handley Page slots were fitted to the upper wings to contribute towards the good low-speed handling characteristics that are so essential for carrier-borne operations.

The fuselage was functional rather than aesthetic, and

BAT Bantam Mk I

Beardmore W.B. III

Blackburn Kangaroo

TYPE	DIMENSIONS span ft	span in	length ft	length in	height ft	height in	WEIGHT max t-o lb	PERFORMANCE max speed mph	at height ft	service ceiling ft	combat range miles	REMARKS
BAT Bantam Mk I	25	0	18	5	6	9	1,321	128	6,500	20,000	NA	Endurance 2¼ hours
Beardmore W.B. III	25	0	20	2	8	1	1,289	103	SL	12,400	NA	Endurance 2¾ hours
Kangaroo	74	10	46	0	16	10	8,017	100	SL	10,500	NA	Endurance 8 hours
Dart	45	6	35	6	12	3	6,400	110	SL	15,000	256	

Blackburn Dart

Blackburn Velos

Blackburn Ripon Mk IIA

Blackburn Iris Mk II

sloped sharply downward forward of the cockpit, to improve the pilot's view during the approach. The main undercarriage was built as two separate units, to permit the carriage of an 18-in torpedo beneath the fuselage. The Dart was one of the first aircraft to have this type of split undercarriage; some earlier types had to drop their wheels before releasing their torpedo.

The Dart's performance was not outstanding, but it was relatively easy to land on a carrier deck and was a useful machine for the FAA during its formative period, while the tactics of torpedo dropping were being developed. On 1 July 1926, a Dart, piloted by Flt Lt Boyce, made the first landing at night on board an aircraft carrier.

A twin-float training version of the Dart, known as the Velos, had a second cockpit and instruments for dual control, and was operated by one of the four RAF Reserve Training Schools of the period; a few were supplied to Greece and Spain.

A total of about 70 Darts had been built when production ceased in 1928; the type was finally declared obsolete in April 1935.

Blackburn Ripon

The Ripon was the FAA's standard carrier-borne torpedo-bomber in the early 1930s. It was a two-seat biplane, with equal-span single-bay staggered wings. These were slightly swept and could be folded to facilitate stowage.

Construction was conventional, consisting of a composite wood and metal airframe, fabric covered. Either the 570-hp Napier Lion XIA or 460-hp Bristol Jupiter VIII engine could be fitted.

Armament included one fixed Vickers machine-gun, synchronized to fire between the propeller blades, and a Lewis machine-gun mounted on a Fairey high-speed gun mounting or Scarff ring in the rear cockpit. As a torpedo-carrier, the Ripon could be fitted with either one 1,576-lb Mk VIII or one Mk X torpedo. Alternatively, a 1,100-lb smoke container could be carried, or a variety of bombs up to a maximum total of 1,650 lb.

The Ripon was fitted with spools for catapulting and was often used for long-range reconnaissance duties. For this rôle, the armament was removed and extra fuel tanks installed to give an endurance approaching 14 hours. At least two Ripons were fitted with twin floats.

The prototype appeared in 1928 and was designated Ripon Mk I. It was followed by a Mk II prototype, and production versions were designated Mk IIA. The Ripon Mk III was an all-metal version. A total of 92 Ripons were built; the type began to be superseded by Blackburn Baffins in 1934.

Blackburn Iris

Designed to Air Ministry Specification 14/24, the Iris was a large three-engined general reconnaissance and coastal patrol flying-boat. It was a biplane, with equal-span, two-bay wings outboard of a large-span centre-section assembly housing the engines. The hull, which included sleeping accommodation and cooking facilities for a crew of five, was of the two-step type, well flared to reduce spray.

The wooden-hulled prototype, designated Iris Mk I and powered by three 650-hp Rolls-Royce Condor IIIA engines, first flew in 1927. The engines were mounted above the lower centre-section on short tubular structures and drove tractor propellers. Fuel was carried in three separate slipper tanks, mounted one above each engine, under the top centre-section.

Armament consisted of three Lewis machine-guns, mounted in the bow, midship and tail cockpits. Maximum bomb load was 2,000 lb.

The wings and engines of the original prototype were later mounted on a new metal hull, the resulting flying-boat being designated Mk II.

Production 'boats, with all-metal wings and hull and Condor III B engines on redesigned mountings, were designated Iris Mk III. Four entered service with No. 209 Squadron in 1931; this was the only squadron to use the type. In its original form, the Mk III had a poor take-off performance and a tendency to porpoise. To improve the hydrodynamic qualities, the rear step was extended and a third step was fitted between the main and rear steps.

The Iris Mk IV was an experimental version fitted with three 700-hp Armstrong Siddeley Leopard air-cooled engines, the centre engine driving a pusher propeller.

The three Iris Mk Vs were conversions of the Mk III, powered by Rolls-Royce Buzzard IIMS engines in cleaned-up nacelles installed on improved mountings. One was again re-engined experimentally with 720-hp Napier Culverin diesel engines later.

The Iris remained in service until 1934, and is remembered mainly for having carried out a series of long-distance flights.

Blackburn Baffin

The Baffin succeeded the Ripon as the FAA's standard torpedo-bomber. Based closely upon its predecessor, it was a two-seat biplane with equal-span single-bay staggered wings, which could be folded to facilitate stowage. The major difference was the installation of a 565-hp Bristol Pegasus IM3 air-cooled radial engine in place of the Napier Lion water-cooled engine of the Ripon; but the improvement in performance was in fact only marginal.

Armament consisted of one fixed Vickers machine-gun synchronized to fire between the propeller blades, and one Lewis machine-gun on a Fairey high-speed mounting in the rear cockpit. As a torpedo-carrier, either one 1,576-lb Mk VIII or one Mk X torpedo could be carried. As a bomber, a mixed load of bombs could be carried up to a maximum of 1,730 lb, or a single 2,000-lb bomb.

The prototype Baffin, originally designated the B-5, had a cowled engine; production aircraft were uncowled. Fifteen were ordered and the Baffin went into service in 1934 with No. 82 Squadron. These production machines were followed by over 60 Ripons converted into Baffins. The type was declared obsolete in September 1937.

Blackburn Perth

This general-reconnaissance three-engined flying-boat was developed from, and superseded, the Iris. It was the biggest biplane flying-boat operated by the RAF.

The Perth had equal-span three-bay wings; the bottom centre-section rested on the hull and was braced to it by two pairs of parallel struts. Construction was metal, with fabric covering. Balanced ailerons were fitted to all wings.

Of the three 825-hp Rolls-Royce Buzzard II MS engines, the central one was mounted on a braced tubular structure on the lower centre-section, the outer engines being mounted directly on the splayed-out interplane struts. Each engine was normally supplied from its own aerofoil-shaped fuel tank, mounted underneath the top centre-section.

The Alclad-covered hull had two steps and provided sleeping and living accommodation for a crew of five. The pilots' cockpit was enclosed. Internal equipment included an auxiliary power unit for electrical services, an air compressor, a refuelling pump, sea anchors, fire extinguishers, life-belts, dinghy, canteen equipment,

Blackburn Iris Mk III

Blackburn Iris Mk IV

Blackburn Baffin

TYPE	DIMENSIONS span ft	span in	length ft	length in	height ft	height in	WEIGHT max t-o lb	PERFORMANCE max speed mph	at height ft	service ceiling ft	combat range miles	REMARKS
Ripon	44	10	36	9	12	10	7,405	126	SL	13,000	NA	
Iris Mk I	95	0	NA		NA		27,000	115	SL	NA	NA	
Iris Mk II	95	6	NA		NA		27,400	116	SL	NA	NA	
Iris Mk III	97	0	67	5	25	6	29,000	118	SL	10,000	470	
Iris Mk IV	97	0	NA		NA		NA	NA	NA	NA	NA	
Baffin	45	6	38	4	13	5	7,610	136	5,000	15,000	450	
Perth	97	0	70	0	26	5	32,500	132	SL	11,500	1300	

Blackburn Perth

Blackburn Lincock III for China

Blackburn Shark Mk I

Blackburn Shark Mk II floatplane, Portuguese Air Force

cooking stove, fresh water tanks and an ice chest, radio gear and sleeping berths.

Armament consisted of three machine-guns, mounted in bow, dorsal and tail positions, and one automatic 37-mm cannon also in the bow position. This gun fired 1½-lb shells at a rate of 100 rounds a minute, and was a unique weapon among the RAF aircraft of the day. The maximum bomb-load was 2,000 lb.

Only three Perths were built. These served with No. 209 Squadron until it was re-equipped with Singapores, after which they equipped No. 204 Squadron in 1936–7.

Blackburn Lincock

The Lincock was a private-venture single-seat fighter of unusually compact proportions, possessing notable performance and handling characteristics. A distinctive feature was the positioning of the fuselage midway between the wings, the lower wing being carried on N-struts below the fuselage, while the top wing was roughly in line with the pilot's eyes. Of wooden construction, and fabric-covered, the Lincock I was powered by an Armstrong Siddeley Lynx IV direct-drive engine and first flew in May 1928. It had a cross-axle undercarriage.

The Lincock II was redesigned with an all-metal structure and divided undercarriage, and with the fuselage faired into the lower wing. The engine was a geared Lynx driving a two-bladed Fairey propeller.

The Lincock III was a further development, with a cross-axle undercarriage and powered by either the Lynx IVC or Lynx Major engine. Two Lincock IIIs were supplied to China and two to Japan.

Blackburn Shark

The Shark was a two/three-seat torpedo-spotter-reconnaissance aircraft, designed to operate as either a landplane or a seaplane. It was developed from a private-venture prototype, the B-6, and embodied experience gained with the Dart, Ripon and Baffin. It first flew in 1934.

The Shark had unequal-span wings, features of which were a wide and shallow centre-section, to provide the crew with the best possible view, the distinctive N-type interplane bracing struts, rigidly braced by a compression strut on each side, and large ailerons on all wings which could be lowered as flaps. The folding wings had a metal structure, covered with fabric, and were secured by hydraulically-operated latch pins.

The fuselage was a semi-monocoque all-metal structure, the centre and rear portions forming watertight compartments. Either wheels or floats could be fitted, the wheel undercarriage being of the divided-axle type, with Blackburn oleo-pneumatic shock-absorbers.

Power was provided by a 700-hp Armstrong Siddeley Tiger VIc air-cooled radial engine.

Armament consisted of one fixed Vickers machine-gun, synchronized to fire between the propeller blades, and one Vickers-Berthier machine-gun in the rear cockpit.

The offensive load consisted of one 1,500-lb torpedo on crutches below the fuselage, or an equivalent weight of bombs carried on racks beneath the wings. The navigator, seated normally in the centre cockpit, acted as bomb-aimer, by taking up a prone position beneath the front cockpit and sighting the target through a bombing hatch. A camera could be fixed over the same aperture, which was covered by a water-tight door when not in use.

Shark Mk Is, of which 16 were built, went into service in 1935, with No. 820 Squadron. They were followed by 126 Shark Mk IIs which, in turn, were followed by 95 Shark Mk IIIs. A major improvement on the latter version was the introduction of a glazed canopy over the cockpits.

The Shark was superseded as a first-line aircraft by the Swordfish in 1938, but continued on training duties until the outbreak of war.

Blackburn Skua

Designed to Air Ministry Specification O.27/34, the Skua was the first British aircraft designed specially for dive-bombing and the first monoplane to go into service with the FAA. It was of all-metal construction, with folding wings to facilitate stowage on board carriers. The wing flaps were used not only for steepening the glide and reducing speed for carrier landings, but also to limit the speed in dive-bombing attacks, and were designed to be raised and lowered without appreciably changing the trim. The fuselage was a water-tight monocoque, capable of keeping the aircraft afloat, even with both cockpits flooded. It was stressed for catapulting and carried an arrester hook. The fin and rudder were set well forward of the tailplane.

Armament consisted of four Browning 0·303-in machine-guns in the wings and a Lewis machine-gun in the rear cockpit. The bomb-load normally comprised a single 500-lb bomb, carried on a special ejector gear which extracted it from the bomb-bay and flung it clear of the propeller in a steep dive.

Two prototypes were powered by Bristol Mercury poppet-valve engines, but production Skuas had a 905-hp Bristol Perseus XII sleeve-valve engine, with a long-chord cowling.

Skuas went into service in 1938 with No. 800 Squadron, on board the carrier HMS *Ark Royal*. When war started, Skuas had the distinction of being the first British aircraft to shoot down an enemy machine – a Dornier Do 18 flying-boat, off Norway – and followed this by dive-bombing and sinking the first large German cruiser lost in World War II, the *Königsberg*.

Skua production totalled 165 aircraft, and the type remained in first-line service until 1941, when it was superseded by the Fulmar and Sea Hurricane.

Blackburn Botha

The Botha was a general-reconnaissance aircraft and torpedo-bomber carrying a crew of four. Built to Air Ministry Specification M.15/35, it was of all-metal stressed-skin construction, and was powered by two 880-hp Bristol Perseus X or 930-hp Perseus XA engines.

Armament consisted of one fixed 0·303-in machine-gun, firing forward, and two 0.303-in machine-guns in a power-operated dorsal turret aft of the wings. The offensive load, consisting of either a torpedo, bombs or depth charges, was carried internally.

Botha Mk Is went into service in October 1939 with No. 608 Squadron and were used for patrols over the North Sea. They proved to be seriously under-powered and were not issued to other squadrons, being withdrawn from operational flying in April 1941. Bothas served subsequently with Air Navigation and Air Gunnery Schools until 1944.

Blackburn Roc

The Roc was a two-seat naval fighter which utilized the novel tactical feature of having no forward-firing guns, all the armament being concentrated in a powered turret.

This idea was first tried out on the Defiant, and the Roc was intended to be the Fleet Air Arm equivalent of the RAF type. Under combat conditions, however, the idea of a fighter bringing its guns to bear in broadside attacks on enemy aircraft proved to be quite unsound, once the element of surprise was lost, and, like the Defiant, the Roc saw only limited first-line service during World War II.

Developed from the Skua dive-bomber, the Roc was

Blackburn Skua

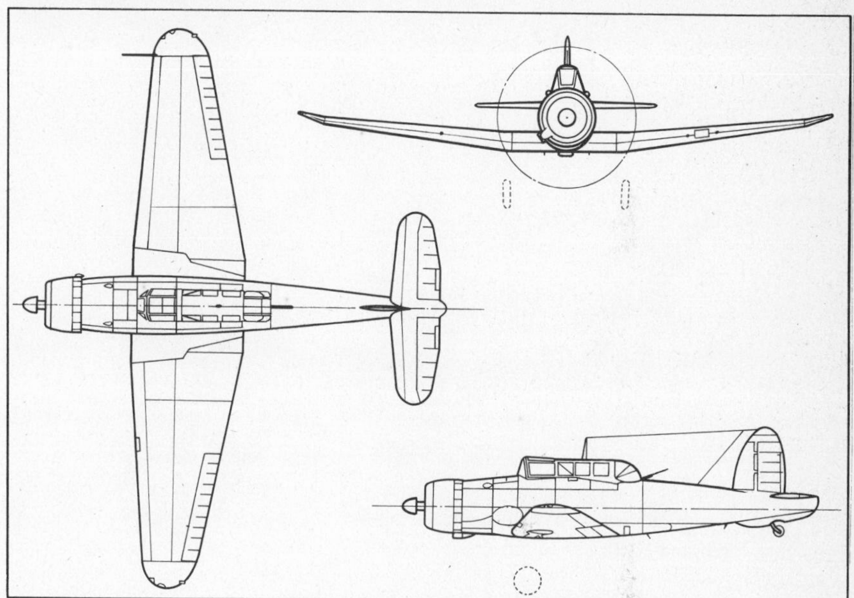

Blackburn Skua

Blackburn Botha

TYPE	DIMENSIONS						WEIGHT	PERFORMANCE				REMARKS
	span		*length*		*height*		*max t-o*	*max speed*	*at height*	*service ceiling*	*combat range*	
	ft	*in*	*ft*	*in*	*ft*	*in*	*lb*	*mph*	*ft*	*ft*	*miles*	
Lincock II	22	6	19	6	NA		NA	150	NA	NA	NA	
Shark Mk II	46	0	35	2	12	1	8,050	152	6,500	16,400	625	Max reconnaissance range 1,130 miles
Skua	46	2	35	7	12	6	8,228	225	6,500	20,200	760	
Botha	59	0	51	1	14	7	18,450	249	5,500	17,500	1,270	
Roc	46	0	35	7	12	1	8,800	194	NA	14,600	NA	Endurance 4½ hours

Blackburn Roc

Blackburn Firebrand F Mk I

Blackburn Firebrand TF Mk IV, No. 813 Squadron

of all-metal stressed-skin construction. The monocoque fuselage was wider than that of the Skua, to accommodate the turret, and increased dihedral was provided on the folding wings, which lacked the characteristic up-turned wing-tips of the dive-bomber. Water-tight compartments were provided in the wings and fuselage.

The Roc was powered by a 905-hp Bristol Perseus XII engine. Armament consisted of four 0·303-in Browning machine-guns in an electrically-operated Boulton Paul turret, and racks for light bombs were fitted beneath the wings. A total of 136 Rocs were built.

Blackburn Firebrand

Designed to Naval Specification N.11/40, as a single-seat short-range carrier-borne interceptor, the Firebrand ultimately went into service as a torpedo-strike fighter. It was a rugged aircraft which arrived just too late to see operational service in World War II.

The main reason for the change in rôle was that the superior performance of the contemporary Seafire naval fighter induced the Admiralty to concentrate on this type.

The prototype Firebrand, powered by a Napier Sabre III engine, first flew in February 1942 and was followed by nine production F Mk I machines. A feature of the neat engine installation was the mounting of the radiators in the wing-root leading-edges. Armament consisted of four 20-mm cannon in the wings.

The Mk II was essentially similar but had the centre-section widened by 18 in to accommodate a torpedo between the wheels. Designated TF Mk II, twelve production examples were built.

At about this time, the supply of Sabre engines was critical. It was decided to reserve them for the Hawker Typhoon and to fit the Bristol Centaurus in the Firebrand. The substitution of this comparatively big and clumsy radial engine involved a great deal of redesign and a big increase in weight. Under the designation TF Mk III, twenty-four Firebrands were built, powered by either the Centaurus VII or XI engine of 2,500-hp. These were operated from carriers, but experience showed that the vertical tail surfaces were too small, providing insufficient control during take-off.

Accordingly, the fin and rudder were enlarged on the Mk IV, which went into service with No. 813 Squadron in September 1945. Other changes introduced on this variant included wing dive-brakes and a two-position torpedo mounting. The dive-brakes comprised small flaps in the top and bottom of the wings near the leading-edge, and could be extended vertically by jacks. The special torpedo mounting was developed to allow the torpedo tail end to clear the ground without an excessively high undercarriage, and to enable it to be lowered to the correct angle for dropping in the air. Most Mk IIIs were converted into Mk IVs, and these were supplemented by 140 new production machines.

The last Firebrand variant was the TF Mk V, of which 105 were built, plus about 40 converted Mk IVs. Changes included the use of larger aileron tabs and horn-balanced elevators. The sub-variant VA had powered ailerons.

Boulton and Paul Sidestrand

The Sidestrand was a high-performance twin-engined day bomber. It was the RAF's first medium bomber.

It was a biplane with staggered equal-span square-tipped wings. Of metal construction and fabric-covered, these were made in three sections, comprising a centre-section and two outer panels. The centre-section was flat and extended to the engines, which were carried on hinged mountings, close to the upper surface of the bottom centre-section. The outer wings had dihedral and slight sweepback. Frise-type ailerons were fitted to both wings.

The fuselage, of rectangular section, with a domed top and bottom, was made up of a nose section, extending to the front spar, a centre section, to which the wings were attached, and the rear fuselage. A distinctive feature of the tail surfaces was the large servo-rudder. The undercarriage was of the divided type, mounted on two V-strut assemblies; the front members incorporated oleo units.

Armament consisted of three Lewis machine-guns, located in the nose and aft cockpits on Scarff ring-mountings, and in a ventral position.

Owing to the narrowness of the nose, the front gun could be fired almost vertically downward. The same feature also gave the pilot a good downward view.

Maximum bomb load was 1,050 lb. When aiming the bombs, the nose gunner lay flat along the floor, viewing through a transparent panel.

The prototype, designated Sidestrand Mk I and powered by two 425-hp Bristol Jupiter VI engines, appeared in 1926. During its flight trials, it proved remarkably manoeuvrable, and could be looped, rolled and spun. It could also maintain height on one engine – an uncommon ability in those days.

Mk Is entered service with No. 101 Squadron in April 1928, sufficient for only this one unit being ordered.

In service, the Sidestrand showed itself to be an excellent bombing platform and broke many existing RAF records for accuracy. During air exercises, pilots used the aircraft's manoeuvrability to good effect, often engaging fighters.

Several versions of the Sidestrand were produced, although production of the type totalled only 18 aircraft. The Sidestrand Mk II had ungeared Jupiter VI engines; the Mk III introduced structural refinements and 460-hp Jupiter VIIIF geared engines; and the Sidestrand IV had Jupiter XF supercharged engines and Townend ring cowlings. The type was declared obsolete in 1934.

Boulton Paul Overstrand

Developed from the Sidestrand, the Overstrand was a twin-engined medium bomber carrying a crew of five. Two 580-hp Bristol Pegasus IIM3 radial engines, compared with the 460-hp Jupiters of the earlier aircraft, gave the Overstrand a better performance and it could carry a heavier bomb-load. Its most interesting feature was the power-operated enclosed gun turret in the nose as it was the first RAF bomber so equipped.

The Overstrand was a biplane with equal-span three-bay staggered wings. As on the Sidestrand, the centre-section was flat and extended to the engines. The outer wings had dihedral and were slightly swept. The engines, fitted with Townend-style cowling rings, were mounted close to the top surface of the lower centre-section. Frise-type ailerons were fitted to the upper wings. The tail unit retained the servo-rudder of the Sidestrand.

The fuselage was of rectangular section, with a domed top and bottom, and incorporated several improvements over the Sidestrand, including an enclosed cockpit for the pilot, a protective windshield for the mid-upper gunner and cockpit heating for all crew members.

Armament consisted of three Lewis machine-guns, mounted in the nose and aft cockpits and in a ventral position. The maximum bomb-load was 1,600 lb.

Converted from a Sidestrand, the prototype Overstrand first flew in 1933 and was followed by three further conversions. Twenty-four production machines were produced to Air Ministry Specification 23/34. Initially these were designated Sidestrand Mk V; but in March 1934 the name was changed to Overstrand.

The type went into service in 1934 with No. 101 Squadron, replacing Sidestrands, and this Squadron was the only one equipped with the new bomber. In service the power-operated nose turret proved a great success. Gunners improved their air-to-air accuracy five-fold.

Overstrands remained in service as bombers until 1937. A few continued flying as gunnery trainers until 1941.

Boulton and Paul Sidestrand Mk II

Boulton and Paul Sidestrand Mk II

Boulton Paul Overstrand

TYPE	DIMENSIONS						WEIGHT	PERFORMANCE				REMARKS
	span ft	span in	length ft	length in	height ft	height in	max t-o lb	max speed mph	at height ft	service ceiling ft	combat range miles	
Firebrand Mk V	51	3	38	11	14	11	17,500	350	13,000	28,500	740	
Sidestrand Mk II	71	11	41	0	14	10	8,885	130	5,000	21,500	NA	
Sidestrand Mk III	71	11	46	0	14	9	10,200	140	10,000	24,000	500	
Overstrand	72	0	46	0	15	6	12,000	153	6,500	22,500	545	

Boulton Paul Defiant Mk I

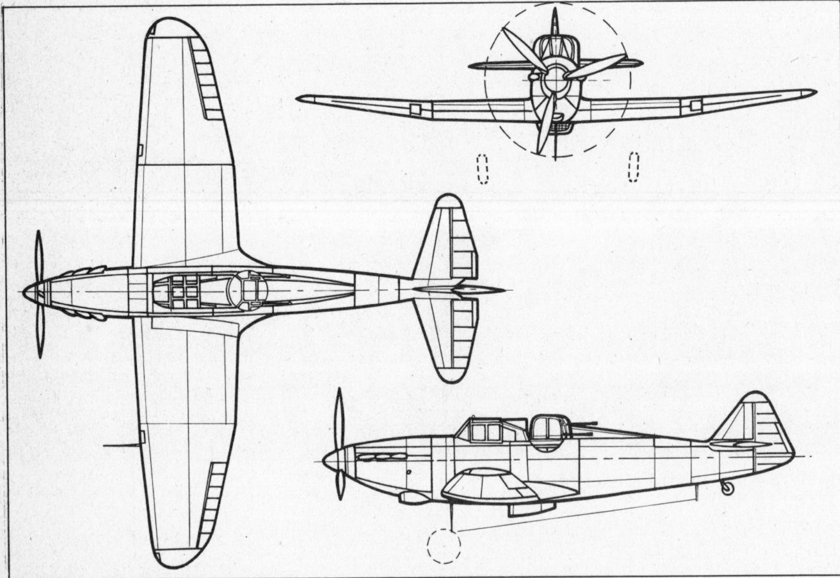
Boulton Paul Defiant Mk I

Boulton Paul Defiant Mk II

Bristol Scout C

Boulton Paul Defiant

The Defiant was a two-seat fighter which introduced the feature of having no forward-firing guns, all the armament being concentrated in a turret behind the pilot's cockpit.

Designed to Air Ministry Specification F.9/35, the prototype first flew in August 1937. It was a cantilever low-wing monoplane, of all-metal stressed-skin construction. The wing comprised a broad centre-section of almost constant chord and two tapering outer panels with rounded tips. Split flaps were fitted inboard of Frise-type ailerons. The monocoque fuselage was of elliptical section, flush riveted externally.

The undercarriage retracted inward into the centre-section. Armament consisted of four 0·303-in Browning machine-guns in a Boulton Paul power-operated turret.

Defiants were first used operationally in May 1940, and initially their unusual armament achieved its purpose. Some successes were due to enemy fighter pilots mistaking the Defiants for Hurricanes and diving on what they thought was a defenceless tail, only to find themselves facing the concentrated firepower of the four Brownings. In less than three weeks 65 enemy aircraft were shot down, 38 of them in one day.

However, this success was short-lived, as the enemy quickly altered his tactics and attacked from below, from directions not covered by the Defiant's gunner. The RAF squadrons began to suffer heavy losses and by August 1940 the Defiant had to be withdrawn from daylight operations.

It was then fitted with the highly secret airborne interception radar (AI Mk IV or VI) and used as a night fighter. It was most successful in this new rôle, and Defiants shot down more enemy aircraft than any other night fighter during the German blitz on London during the winter of 1940–41.

Defiant Mk Is were powered by a 1,030-hp Rolls-Royce Merlin III engine, and Mk IIs by a 1,260-hp Merlin XX. About 150 Defiant Mk IIIs, with the turret removed and winch gear installed, were used for target-towing, together with some Mk Is. A few Defiants were used also for air/sea rescue work and army co-operation duties. Altogether, 1,060 Defiants were built.

Bristol Scout

A small prototype single-seat biplane, known as the Bristol Scout A, appeared in 1914. For the time, its lines were clean and its 80-hp Gnome rotary engine gave it a creditable top speed of 97 mph. Two Scout Bs with minor detail improvements, were then produced and delivered to the RFC.

Production Scouts were known as Cs, and were powered by 80-hp Gnome, 80-hp Le Rhône, 80-hp Clerget or 110-hp Clerget engines. They were pleasant to fly and had excellent manoeuvrability, but their military usefulness was diminished by the lack of suitable armament. As they were intended for scouting duties, no regular armament was fitted, but pilots often carried a rifle, carbine or revolver. Some Scouts had Lewis guns, secured either to the fuselage and pointing sideways to clear the propeller, or to the top of the centre-section firing upward. Some enthusiasts used 0·45-in rifles firing incendiary-filled lead bullets and sporting types even tried duck guns firing chain shot. Anti-Zeppelin Scouts carried two containers, each housing 24 Ranken darts.

The second aerial Victoria Cross was gained in a Scout, when Captain L. G. Hawker, armed with a single-shot cavalry carbine mounted to fire at an outward angle brought down three enemy Albatros two-seaters armed with machine-guns.

Improvements resulted in the Scout D, the initial batches of which were powered by 80-hp Le Rhône engines and later machines by 100-hp Gnome Monosoupape engines. Some Ds had a Vickers machine-gun synchronized to fire through the propeller disc.

Bristol M.1C Monoplane

The Bristol M.1C was a single-seat monoplane scout with remarkably clean lines for its day and an impressive performance. Its production, in 1916, was a bold step in view of the War Office's pre-war "monoplane ban" which had created a lingering prejudice against aircraft of this type.

Construction was conventional, the basic fuselage structure consisting of a wooden, wire-braced box-girder. This was, however, faired by means of formers and stringers into a circular section and it was this classic streamline shape of the fuselage, completed by an enormous spinner almost covering the engine, which gave the Bristol monoplane an appearance far in advance of its time.

The prototype, designated M.1A, appeared in 1916. It quickly demonstrated its advanced qualities and clean aerodynamics, by reaching a maximum speed of 132 mph on the modest power provided by its 110-hp Clerget rotary engine.

Four more examples were ordered for service trials. Designated M.1B, these differed from the first prototype in having a redesigned cabane for the wing landing wires, and by having a Vickers machine-gun mounted on the port top longeron, synchronized to fire through the propeller disc.

These four M.1Bs provided further evidence of the monoplane's outstanding performance and manoeuvrability. The unrestricted view from the cockpit up and around – the area from which attacks usually came – represented a tremendous improvement over that from biplanes, and pilots liked the little monoplane's delightful handling qualities.

Production machines were designated M.1C, and were powered by the 110-hp Le Rhône engine. Other differences between these and the earlier models included repositioning of the machine-gun on top of the fuselage, and the provision of cut-outs in the root of each wing to enable the pilot to see downward.

Rumours of the M.1C's existence reached pilots of the RFC in France, who looked forward to receiving Britain's new "secret weapon" and using it to gain supremacy in the air. Unfortunately, they looked in vain, for no M.1Cs reached the Western Front.

The authorities had rejected the type for operational use in this vital area and further indicated their displeasure by ordering only 125. The effect, both material and psychological, which a new weapon, appreciably better than those of the enemy, can have is well known; the M.1C was such a weapon and there is little doubt that it would have established a brilliant combat reputation if it had been put to the test. The true reason for this incredible decision has never been revealed: the official view that the monoplane's landing speed of 49 mph was too high cannot really be accepted as constituting an adequate explanation.

In the event, the M.1C was used operationally only in the Middle East, where it engaged Turkish forces. On one occasion, two pilots put up such a frightening display of aerobatics that a Kurdish tribe, watching on the ground, deserted en masse and came over to the British side. Six M.1Cs served with the Chilean Air Force.

Bristol M.1C Monoplane

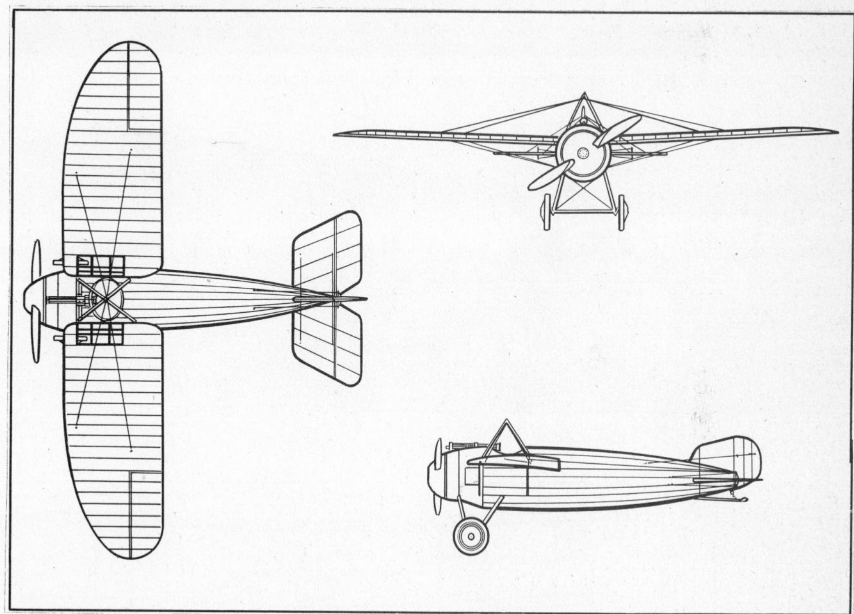

Bristol M.1C Monoplane

TYPE	DIMENSIONS span ft	in	length ft	in	height ft	in	WEIGHT max t-o lb	PERFORMANCE max speed mph	at height ft	service ceiling ft	combat range miles	REMARKS
Defiant Mk I	39	4	35	4	12	2	8,350	303	16,500	NA	NA	
Defiant Mk II	39	4	35	4	12	2	8,600	315	16,500	NA	NA	
Bristol Scout A	22	0	19	9	NA		957	97	NA	NA	NA	80 hp Gnome engine
Bristol Scout B	24	7	20	8	8	6	957	97	NA	NA	NA	80 hp Gnome engine
Bristol Scout C	24	7	20	8	8	6	1,415	109	3,000	14,000	NA	110 hp Clerget engine
Bristol Scout D	24	7	20	8	8	6	1,250	100	SL	NA	NA	80 hp Le Rhone engine
Bristol M.1A	30	9	20	3	NA		1,326	128	5,400	17,000	NA	110 hp Clerget
Bristol M.1B	30	9	20	8	7	7	1,370	115	6,500	15,000	NA	150 hp A.R.1
Bristol M.1C	30	9	20	5	7	9	1,348	130	SL	20,000	NA	Endurance 1¾ hours

Bristol Fighter (F.2A), Falcon engine

Bristol Fighter (F.2B), 275-hp Falcon III engine, No. 139 Squadron

Bristol Fighter (F.2B), 200-hp Arab engine

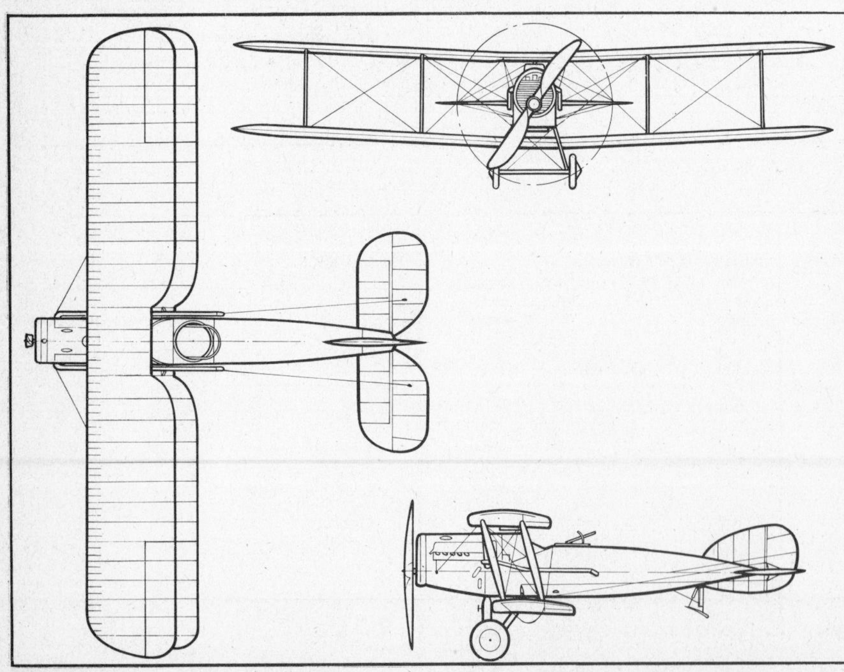

Bristol Fighter (F.2B), Falcon engine

Bristol Fighter

Known affectionately to its crews as the "Brisfit", the Bristol Fighter is generally regarded by air historians as the best general-purpose combat aircraft produced by any country during the 1914–18 War. It was structurally strong, had outstanding manoeuvrability and a reasonable top speed. The pilot and observer, seated back to back, operated almost as one man, enabling the aircraft to attack with the front gun, in the manner of contemporary single-seaters, but having the added advantage of a rearward-firing gun.

The "Brisfit" was intended as a replacement reconnaissance-fighter for the B.E.2 series designed by the Royal Aircraft Factory. The initial design study, known as the Bristol R.2A, was based on the 120-hp Beardmore engine, but as work progressed it became apparent that it would be underpowered. Accordingly, consideration was given to re-designing the aircraft around a Hispano-Suiza engine. Fortuitously, a new Rolls-Royce V-twelve engine, later known as the Falcon, became available at this moment.

With the Rolls-Royce engine, the new aircraft was designated the Bristol F.2A. Basically, it was a conventional biplane, but numerous detail features contributed to its overall combat efficiency. The fuselage was mounted mid-way between the wings, so that the pilot's eyes were in line with the top wing, giving him the widest possible field of view. The top of the rear fuselage had marked downsweep, allowing the observer, in the rear cockpit, a wide field of fire rearward. The mid position of the fuselage also allowed him to fire over the top wing with little elevation of his gun. The design obviously portrayed a fighting aircraft and Fighter it was named.

Two prototypes were built, one powered by a Rolls-Royce Falcon Mk I and the other by a 150-hp Hispano-Suiza. On these machines, the pilot's seat was protected by armour and an unusual feature was the large end-plates fitted to the inner end of each lower wing. They proved pleasant to fly; their high degree of manoeuvrability was evident and production began.

Differences on the production aircraft included removal of the seat armour and wing end-plates, and the adoption of squared tips to the wings in place of the pointed tips on the prototypes. Initial batches of production Fighters were powered by either the 190-hp Falcon I, the 220-hp Falcon II or the 275-hp Falcon III engines.

Armament consisted of a single fixed Vickers machine-gun mounted on top of the engine and synchronized by Constantinesco gear to fire between the propeller blades, plus either one or two Lewis machine-guns mounted on a Scarff ring in the rear cockpit. In addition, up to twelve 20-lb bombs could be a carried on racks under the bottom wing.

The first offensive patrol, by six F.2As of No. 48 Squadron was made on 5 April 1917 and was disastrous. The patrol was engaged by five Albatros D.IIIs led by the German ace Manfred von Richthofen, who promptly shot down two of the F.2As, thereby raising his total of victories to 36 while his pilots destroyed two more of the new British fighters. On landing, von Richthofen reported that he had sighted an unknown enemy aircraft, adding the comment: "The D.III Albatros was, both in speed and ability to climb, undoubtedly superior."

Von Richthofen was wrong; the fault lay in the way the Bristol Fighter had been used. Upon sighting von Richthofen, the British crews had fought as in previous two-seaters; the pilots tried to hold formation, while their observers returned the fire of the attacking Albatros. During later engagements, individual pilots tried using the F.2A as they would a single-seater – that is, using the forward-firing Vickers gun as the offensive weapon and leaving their observers to provide a "sting in their tail", a procedure which surprised more than one German pilot.

This change of tactics immediately revealed the "Brisfit's" superb manoeuvrability and endorsed its ruggedness, and crews flying F.2As began to build up an impressive score of victories. Capt McKeever, in particular, scored most of his 30 victories in an F.2A. After their initial disdain, German pilots began to respect the "Brisfit";

indeed, some enemy formations would not attack the British aircraft if more than three were flying together, however great their own numerical advantage.

Operational experience resulted in various alterations being made, including changes to the cowling in front of the pilot to improve his forward view, and filling in and completing as an aerofoil the centre-section of the bottom wing, which was formerly open. Aircraft embodying these modifications were designated F.2Bs.

The operational successes of the F.2As and F.2Bs led to increased production, which began to exceed the output of Rolls-Royce Falcon engines, and alternative power units had to be considered. Thus, a number of F.2Bs were fitted with the 200-hp Hispano-Suiza. The number so powered was kept as small as possible, partly because the lower horsepower resulted in a reduced performance, and partly because of unreliability of the French engine, due to the incorporation of a large number of incorrectly-treated gears and propeller shafts. The Hispano-Suiza-engined machines were reserved for squadrons engaged solely on reconnaissance work, leaving the Falcon-engined "Brisfits" for the fighter squadrons, where maximum performance was imperative.

Other production installations included the 200-hp Sunbeam Arab and the 230-hp Siddeley Puma, but the Falcon continued to power the majority of aircraft.

A number of Home Defence squadrons were equipped with the Bristol Fighter; but it was not ideal for these duties, as the water-cooled engine had a comparatively long warming-up period and the aircraft's long nose made landing on small aerodromes at night difficult.

Towards the end of 1917 plans were initiated to build 2,000 Bristol Fighters in the United States. These were intended to be fitted with the Liberty 12 engine in spite of warnings from the parent company that it was unsuitable. The first few machines produced in America confirmed the Bristol foreboding, by proving nose-heavy and difficult to fly. Only 27 were built before production was halted and the contract cancelled. Uncharitably, the US Army, who had pressed for use of the Liberty engine, condemned the airframe and declared the Fighter dangerous.

It certainly was – to the enemy – as is indicated by an action fought by two pilots of No. 22 Squadron on 7 May 1918. The two F.2Bs were patrolling over Arras when they attacked a superior force of seven Fokkers and shot down four of the enemy. The F.2Bs were themselves attacked by a new force of 15 enemy fighters, whereupon they promptly shot down four more Fokkers, and broke off the engagement only when their ammunition was exhausted.

Towards the end of the war other versions of the Fighter were produced in the United States, but were so heavily redesigned and modified that they were virtually a new type.

In Britain, production of the Fighter continued until 1926, by which time a grand total of 3,101 had been built, and "Brisfits" remained in service with the Royal Air Force until 1932. The post-war aircraft were progressively improved by the fitting of more efficient wings, better control surfaces, a balanced rudder, a long-travel undercarriage and, perhaps most important of all, Handley Page wing slots.

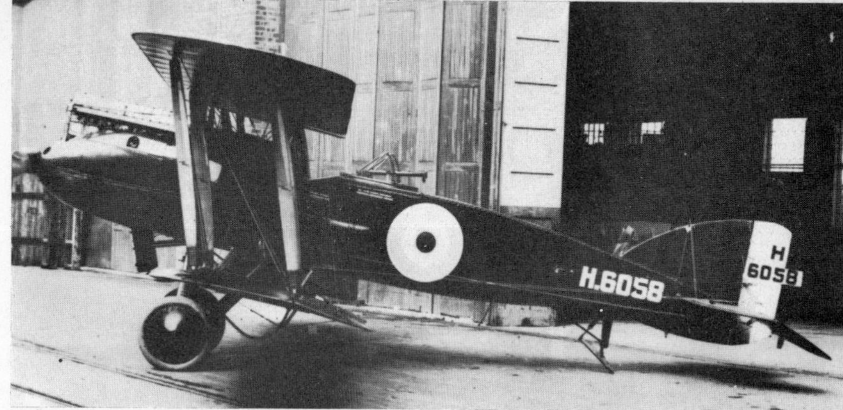

Bristol Fighter (F.2B), 230-hp Puma engine

Bristol Fighter (F.2B), Falcon III engine, Cambridge University Air Squadron

Bristol Fighter Mk III

TYPE	DIMENSIONS span ft	span in	length ft	length in	height ft	height in	WEIGHT max t-o lb	PERFORMANCE max speed mph	at height ft	service ceiling ft	combat range miles	REMARKS
Bristol F.2A	39	3	25	9	9	4	2,667	NA	NA	NA	NA	
Bristol F.2B	39	3	25	10	9	4	2,650	NA	NA	NA	NA	190 hp Falcon I
Bristol F.2B	39	3	25	10	9	9	2,860	111	10,000	20,000	NA	220 hp Falcon II
Bristol F.2B	39	3	25	10	9	9	2,848	123	4,000	19,500	NA	275 hp Falcon III
Bristol F.2B	39	3	24	8	9	6	2,630	105	10,000	19,000	NA	200 hp Hispano-Suiza
Bristol F.2B	39	3	24	10	9	5	2,804	104	10,000	17,000	NA	200 hp Arab
Bristol F.2B	39	3	26	0	9	5	2,810	104	10,000	20,000	NA	230 hp Puma

Bristol Bulldog II

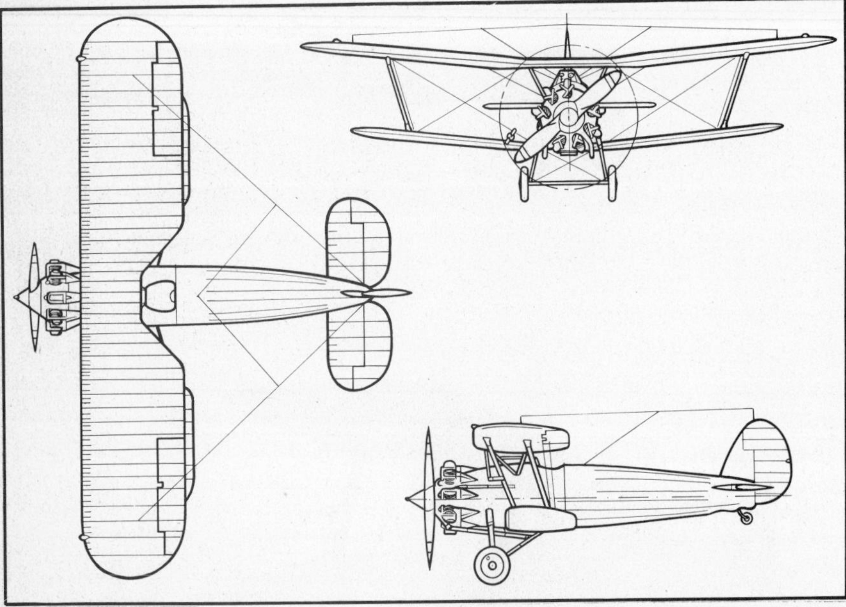
Bristol Bulldog IIA

Bristol Blenheim Mk I

Bristol Bulldog

Designed to Air Ministry Specification F.9/26, the Bulldog was a single-seat day and night fighter. It was adopted by the RAF to replace Siskins and Gamecocks after competitive trials against the Hawfinch, Partridge, S.S.16, A.W.16 and other types.

Of all-metal, fabric-covered construction, it was a biplane with unequal-span single-bay staggered wings, both of which had marked dihedral. Frise-type ailerons were fitted to the upper wing, which had a wide cut-out in the trailing-edge of the centre-section to improve the pilot's view forward and upward. The upper wing was attached to the fuselage by a pair of splayed-out N-struts and to the lower wing by a single pair of interplane struts each end. The box-girder fuselage was faired to an oval section by light steel frames and stringers. An adjustable tailplane was fitted. The undercarriage was of the cross-axle Vee-type, with a rubber-springing, oleo-damping unit in each telescopic front strut.

The Bulldog was powered by a 490-hp Bristol Jupiter VIIF or VIIFP air-cooled radial engine. Armament consisted of two fixed Vickers machine-guns, mounted one on each side of the cockpit and synchronized to fire between the propeller blades. Four 20-lb bombs could be carried under the wings. Equipment included oxygen apparatus and a short-wave radio transmitter and receiver.

The prototype, designated Mk I, first flew on 17 May 1927 and was followed by a second machine designated Mk II. Production Bulldog Mk IIs went into service in 1929 with No. 3 Squadron. By 1932, they equipped no fewer than nine squadrons, representing about 70 per cent of the United Kingdom fighter defence force, and they remained the most widely used RAF fighters until 1936.

After a batch of 46 Mk II aircraft had been produced, there followed the Bulldog Mk IIA, which had a strengthened structure, increased maximum weight, an improved oil system and a wider undercarriage with bigger wheels. Later Mk. IIAs also had a modified fin and a tailwheel instead of a tail skid. Aircraft with the tailwheel also had Bendix brakes. A total of 247 Mk IIA Bulldogs were built.

A further improved version, the Bulldog Mk IV, incorporated various aerodynamic refinements and was powered by the Bristol Mercury IVS2 geared engine fitted with a Townend cowling ring.

Fifty-five Bulldog Mk IIm two-seat, dual-control, advanced trainers were built for the RAF. These had a new rear fuselage to accommodate the second cockpit and redesigned tail surfaces, and were unarmed. They could be converted into the fighter version by changing the rear half of the fuselage and fitting machine-guns.

Bulldogs remained in front-line service until 1937.

Bristol Blenheim

When the Blenheim light bomber went into service with the RAF in 1937 it created headlines, not only by being nearly 100 mph faster than the Harts it superseded, but by outpacing the RAF's biplane fighters as well.

It was a military development of the six-passenger Bristol Type 142 built for Lord Rothermere for executive duties. When completed in 1935, this aircraft had created a sensation by achieving 280 mph in level flight while carrying its full design load. This was some 40 mph faster than the best fighters of the day, so Lord Rothermere named the aircraft *Britain First* and presented it to the nation as the forerunner of a high-speed medium bomber.

Designed to Air Ministry Specification B.28/35, the military prototype flew for the first time on 25 June 1936; but the potential of the type was so obvious that 150 production machines had already been ordered off the drawing board in August of the previous year.

Of all-metal stressed-skin construction, the wing was made in three sections, the outer portions tapering in chord and thickness. The mass-balanced Frise-type ailerons had a metal structure and were fabric-covered. Split trailing-edge flaps were fitted.

The fuselage was a light alloy monocoque structure, built up on frames and stringers. The main undercarriage legs retracted rearward hydraulically into the rear of the engine nacelles. The long single-tier bomb-bay was in the fuselage, under the wing, this shape being chosen to accommodate future developments in bomb design without extensive structural changes.

Armament consisted of one fixed 0·303-in Browning gun firing forward, and one Vickers K gun in a semi-rotatable dorsal turret. Maximum bomb-load was 1,000 lb.

Powered by two 840-hp Bristol Mercury VIII radial engines, Blenheim Mk Is went into service in 1937 with No. 114 Squadron. A total of 1,552 of this version were built, of which about 200 were converted into Mk IF night-fighters. These had their forward armament augmented by an under-fuselage gun-pack containing four 0·303-in Browning machine-guns. The IFs were employed during the German night air raids on London in 1940, when they pioneered use of the highly secret AI airborne interception radar, but were not quite fast enough to be really effective for night interception.

As soon as the Mk Is went into service, the customary demands for additional equipment led to the Blenheim Mk II. This was externally similar to the Mk I, but had an increased loaded weight and a strengthened undercarriage. No new production Mk IIs were built, Mk Is being modified to bring about the same result.

A requirement for longer range led to the Mk III which had additional fuel tanks in the wings and a lengthened nose to improve the accommodation of the navigator. Three development Mk IIIs were built, designated IIIA, IIIB and IIIC, in attempts to improve the pilot's view over the extended nose. The problem was solved by scalloping the navigator's roof on the port side. The modified IIIC was then sent to Canada as the prototype of the Bolingbroke, which was built in large numbers.

Having solved the problem of providing the pilot with an adequate view over the extended nose, the developed aircraft, powered by two 920-hp Bristol Mercury XV engines, was put into production as the Blenheim Mk IV, of which 1,930 were built.

During their period of service, various improvements were made to successive production batches. The first 80 Mk IVs had a slightly reduced range compared with the Mk I because of their more powerful engines; additional outboard wing tanks were installed from the 81st aircraft onward, these long-range machines being designated IVL. Armour plate was introduced, together with a rearward-firing 0·303-in machine-gun (in a blister under the nose and aimed by the navigator using a periscope) and a Bristol fully-rotatable turret mounting twin 0·303-in guns. Experimental installations included two 20-mm cannon and a 37-mm COW gun arranged to fire obliquely downward for ground strafing. Some Blenheim IVs operating with Coastal Command were fitted with a pack of four 0·303-in guns beneath the fuselage, as used on the night fighter Mk IFs.

In 1940, the Air Ministry issued Specification B.6/40. To meet this, the Blenheim was modified to have two 830-hp Bristol Mercury XXX engines, additional armour, a modified nose and a new oxygen system. Two prototypes were built, one as the Mk VA Type 160 (AD661) three-seat high-altitude day-bomber, with a semi-glazed nose, and the other as the Mk VB Type 160 (AD657) two-seat ground-strafing aircraft, with a four-gun battery in the nose. The idea was to fly along roads, raking them with machine-gun fire, and the name Bisley was allocated to

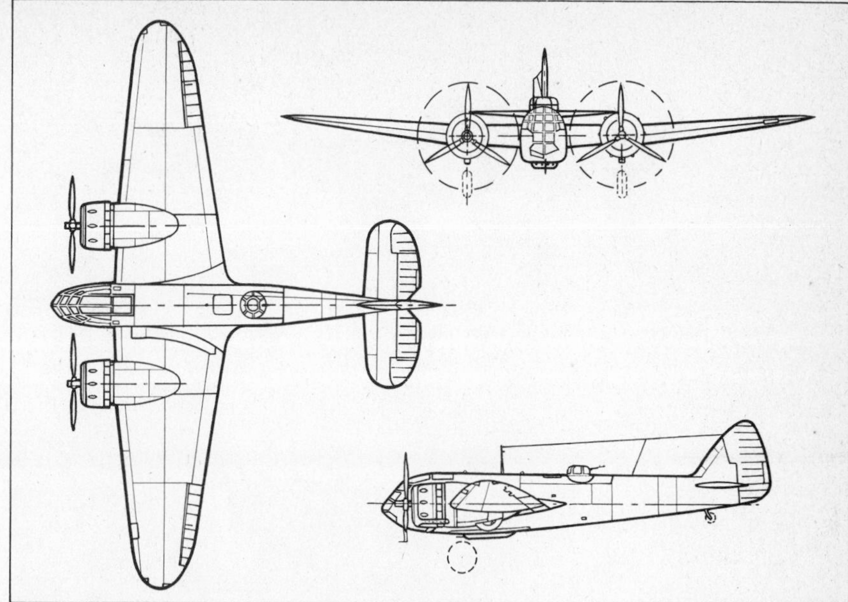

Bristol Blenheim Mk I

Bristol Blenheim Mk IV

Bristol Blenheim Mk V

TYPE	DIMENSIONS span ft	span in	length ft	length in	height ft	height in	WEIGHT max t-o lb	PERFORMANCE max speed mph	at height ft	service ceiling ft	combat range miles	REMARKS
Bulldog Mk II	33	11	25	0	9	10	NA	NA	NA	NA	NA	
Bulldog Mk IIA	33	11	25	0	9	10	NA	174	10,000	27,000	NA	
Bulldog Mk IV	33	11	NA		NA		NA	200	NA	NA	NA	
Blenheim Mk I	56	4	39	9	9	10	12,500	260	NA	27,280	1,125	
Blenheim Mk IVF	56	4	42	7	9	10	13,500	266	11,800	22,000	NA	
Blenheim Mk VD	56	4	44	0	9	10	17,000	240	NA	NA	1,000	

Bristol Bisley, prototype close-support aircraft

Bristol Bombay

Bristol Bombay

Bristol Beaufort Mk II

the projected production version, but development of this variant was dropped.

The variants ultimately put into production were the Type 160T Mk VC and the Type 160D Mk VD.

The Mk VC was a dual-control operational trainer, and the VD was essentially a tropicalized version of the VA prototype.

At an early stage the name Bisley was transferred from the projected ground-strafing Blenheim to the tropicalized Blenheim. References to this name, which was discarded ultimately in favour of the designation Blenheim VD, sometimes caused confusion.

A total of 940 Mk VDs were built. Each was armed with two rearward-firing 0·303-in machine-guns in a blister under the nose, and two 0·303-in guns in a dorsal turret, of the type used on later versions of the Mk IV.

The Mk V went into action in 1942 in North Africa, where it proved an inefficient combat aircraft and was not liked by its crews, who suffered heavy losses. During the Italian campaign, it was replaced by Baltimores and Venturas.

The Blenheim has the unique distinction of being the only type to have served in all wartime Commands of the RAF – Bomber, Fighter, Coastal, Army Co-operation and Training. Mk. Is were also supplied to Finland and Turkey. The Finnish machines had an enlarged bomb-bay to accommodate American and Swedish bombs, while the Turkish aircraft had a special high-gloss finish which made them slightly faster than their RAF counterparts.

Bristol Bombay

Designed to meet Air Ministry Specification C.26/31 for a troop-carrier and bomber-transport, the Bombay could carry either 24 fully-armed troops or a bomb-load of 2,000 lb. The aircraft's most interesting structural feature was its high wing, which was built upon seven spars of steel-strip construction, with light alloy ribs and a stressed-skin covering. Experiments with this type of multi-spar wing had been started in 1927. Hydraulically-operated split trailing-edge flaps were fitted.

The oval-section fuselage was of metal semi-monocoque construction, and was built in six sections. Instead of troops, the fuselage could accommodate either 10 stretcher cases, spare engines, or three water storage tanks. Defensive armament consisted of two Vickers K machine-guns, in manually-operated turrets at each end of the fuselage. When the Bombay operated as a bomber, a crew of four was carried; in a transport rôle, this was reduced to three.

The Bombay was powered by two 1,010-hp Bristol Pegasus XXII nine-cylinder radial engines, enclosed in long-chord cowlings. The undercarriage was fixed, and consisted of two long-stroke oleo legs, the upper ends of which were anchored to the engine mountings, while the lower ends were stabilized by Vee-struts attached to the bottom of the fuselage. The prototype had wheel spats, but these were eliminated on production machines.

The Bombay went into service in March 1939 and served with No. 117 and 267 (transport) Squadrons and No. 216 (night bombing and transport) Squadron. During the early months of World War II it was used mainly in the Middle East, where it replaced obsolete Valentia biplanes. About 50 Bombays were built.

Bristol Beaufort

The Beaufort was a reconnaissance-torpedo-bomber, produced to meet Air Ministry Specifications M.15/35 and G.24/35, which called for a twin Perseus-engined monoplane carrying an external torpedo, and a general reconnaissance bomber respectively. It was a cantilever mid-wing monoplane of all-metal stressed-skin construction.

The two-spar wing comprised a virtually untapered centre-section, passing through the fuselage, and two tapering outer panels. Hydraulically-operated split flaps were fitted between the ailerons and the oval-section, monocoque fuselage, which accommodated navigational, photographic and radio equipment.

The main undercarriage wheels were carried between pairs of oleo-pneumatic shock-absorbers and retracted hydraulically rearward into the engine nacelles. Standard armament consisted of two 0·303-in fixed forward-firing machine-guns in the nose, and two machine-guns in a Bristol power-operated dorsal turret. The maximum bomb-load was 1,500 lb, of which 1,000 lb was carried internally and 500 lb externally, or one 1,605-lb 18-in torpedo, semi-enclosed.

Powered by two 1,010-hp Bristol Taurus II fourteen-cylinder sleeve-valve engines, Beaufort Mk Is went into service in December 1939 with No. 22 Squadron, replacing Vildebeest biplanes. On later aircraft, 1,130-hp Taurus VI engines were installed and the defensive armament was increased, first by fitting beam machine-guns and then by adding a rearward-firing machine-gun in a blister under the nose. ASV (air-to-surface vessel) radar was installed in late production Mk Is.

Beaufort Mk IIs were powered by 1,200-hp Twin Wasp engines. Some Mk IIs were built as trainers and had the dorsal turret deleted.

Beauforts were Coastal Command's standard torpedo-bombers from 1940 to 1943, and acquitted themselves well in action over the North Sea, English Channel, the Atlantic, the Mediterranean and in the Western Desert. Production totalled 955 Mk Is and 166 Mk IIs plus 700 Twin Wasp-engined Mk VIIIs built in Australia.

Bristol Beaufighter

The Beaufighter was a two-seat twin-engined fighter, with heavy armament and high maximum speed which combined to make it one of the most formidable and versatile British combat aircraft of World War II. It was initiated as a private-venture long-range fighter in 1938, and consisted essentially of the wings, rear fuselage and tail unit of the Beaufort torpedo-bomber combined with a new front fuselage and more powerful engines. When the prototype was completed, the Air Ministry realized the potential of the design and issued Specification F.17/39 covering four prototypes.

Of all-metal stressed-skin construction, the two-spar wing was made in three portions: a nearly rectangular centre-section, passing through the fuselage, and two tapering outer wing panels. Hydraulically-operated split flaps were fitted between ailerons and fuselage.

The all-metal monocoque fuselage was made in three sections. The main undercarriage wheels were carried between two oleo-pneumatic shock-absorbers, and retracted rearward hydraulically into the engine nacelles.

Standard armament was four 20-mm cannon in the nose, firing forward, and six 0·303-in Browning machine-guns, two in the port wing and four in the starboard wing outboard of the oil-cooler ducts. This made the Beaufighter the most powerfully armed fighter in the world at the time it entered production.

Powered by two 1,590-hp Bristol Hercules XI air-cooled radial engines, Beaufighter Mk IFs went into service in September 1940, one aircraft being sent to No. 25 Squadron and one to No. 29. In service the heavy fire-power – one brief burst was sufficient to ensure almost certain destruction of any German fighter or bomber – and high maximum speed made the Beaufighter ideally suitable as a vehicle for AI (airborne interception radar). This had previously been tried out on Blenheim IFs, but these aircraft lacked the speed and fire-power to be really effective. Beaufighters, using AI Mk IV, were mainly responsible for causing the cessation of the German night blitz against London during the winter of 1940–41.

Bristol Beaufort Mk VIII, RAAF

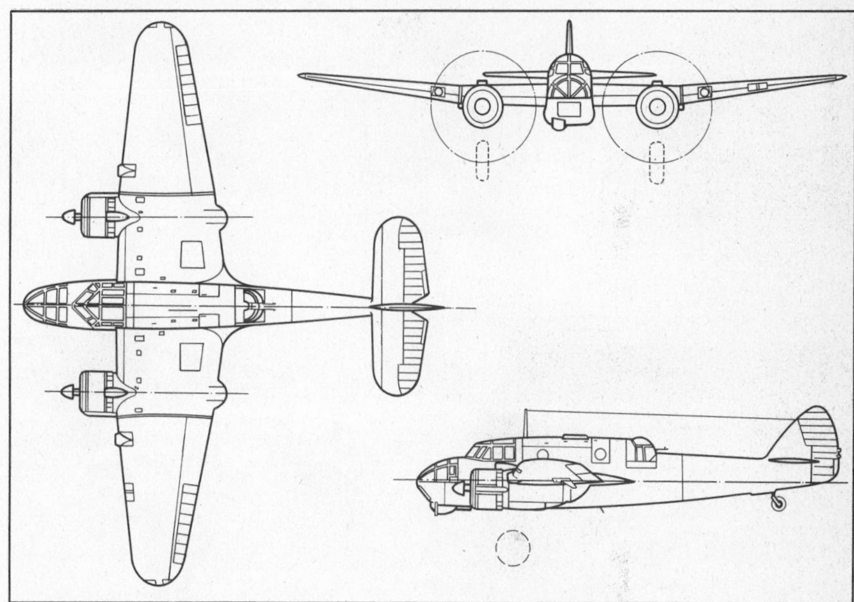

Bristol Beaufort Mk I

Bristol Beaufighter Mk VIC

TYPE	DIMENSIONS span ft	span in	length ft	length in	height ft	height in	WEIGHT max t-o lb	PERFORMANCE max speed mph	at height ft	service ceiling ft	combat range miles	REMARKS
Bombay	95	9	69	3	19	11	20,000	192	6,500	25,000	2,230	
Beaufort Mk I	57	10	44	7	12	5	21,228	265	6,000	NA	1,600	
Beaufort Mk II	57	10	44	7	NA		NA	NA	NA	NA	NA	

Bristol Beaufighter TF Mk X

Bristol Beaufighter TF Mk X

Bristol Beaufighter TF Mk X

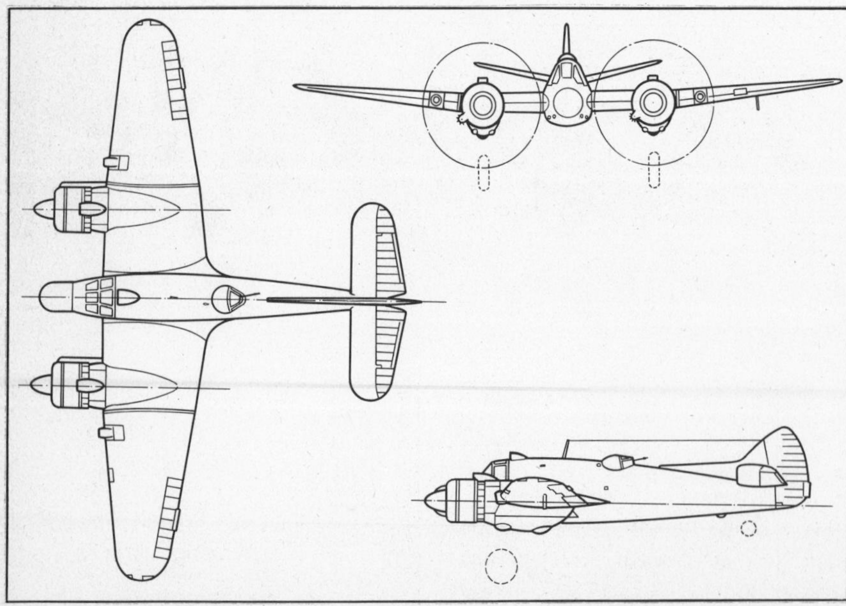
Bristol Beaufighter TF Mk X

Some Beaufighters were sent to the Middle East for long-range day-fighter duties in the Western Desert. These aircraft initially carried a 50-gallon fuel tank in the fuselage; later, the fuel was transferred to extra tanks in the wings in place of the machine-guns.

Beaufighter Mk IC was the designation given to the first Coastal Command version, which was fitted with additional radio and navigational equipment, including a folding chart table in the cockpit.

The next major production variant was the Mk IIF fighter, which had 1,280-hp Rolls-Royce Merlin XX engines owing to a shortage of Hercules engines. The neat Merlin installation reduced drag, resulting in a slight increase in maximum speed, but the reduced side area of the engines increased the Beaufighter's tendency to directional instability. To overcome this, the tail-plane was given 12° of dihedral, and this modification was adopted subsequently for all versions.

Mk III and IV were the designations allotted to two projected versions with a specially slim fuselage and powered by Hercules VI and Griffon engines respectively, but neither was built.

Two Mk V experimental aircraft were built, each armed with one 20-mm cannon in the fuselage, and with the wing armament supplemented by a Boulton Paul turret containing four 0·303-in Browning machine-guns, just aft of the pilot's cockpit. The drag of the turret reduced the speed by an unacceptable amount, and the experiment was abandoned.

The next major production variant was therefore the Mk VI, powered by two 1,670-hp Bristol Hercules VI or XVI radial engines. Like the Mk I, this was produced in both Fighter and Coastal Command versions, designated VIF and VIC respectively. This Mark introduced a rearward-firing Vickers K 0·303-in machine-gun in the aft cockpit, and two 250-lb bombs could be carried under the wings.

Experiments in 1941 had proved the Beaufighter suitable for torpedo dropping, and torpedo-carrying Mk VICs, unofficially known as "Torbeaus", revolutionized air-sea warfare and sank a great quantity of enemy shipping. To slow down these aircraft quickly from the fast approach speed to the slow dropping speed, special venturi-operated bellows-type airbrakes were fitted outboard of each engine. Mk VICs with eight rocket projectiles under the wing were also extremely effective anti-shipping weapons.

The Mk VIFs were the first version to be used by the RAF in the Far East against the Japanese, to whom the Beaufighter became known as the "Whispering Death".

Mk VII was the designation given to a proposed version with Hercules VIII turbo-supercharged engines driving four-bladed propellers, but which was abandoned.

Mk VIII and Mk IX were designations reserved for Australian-built Beaufighters, but never used.

The next production version was the Beaufighter TF Mk X, an anti-shipping strike fighter powered by 1,770-hp Hercules XVII engines. These were a development of the Hercules VI specially suited for low-level operations, and incorporated cropped impellers and fully automatic carburettors. To reduce the inherent tendency to swing at take-off, a dorsal fin extension was fitted to the Mk X. This version was equipped to carry a 1,650-lb or 2,127-lb torpedo, or eight rockets plus two 250-lb bombs under the wings, and often had ASV Mk VIII radar in a distinctive "thimble" nose radome. It proved formidably efficient, to the extent that two squadrons sank five U-boats in two days.

Before the Mk X went into service, sixty Mk VICs, powered by Hercules XVI engines and adapted to carry torpedoes, were delivered as Beaufighter Mk VIs (I.T.F.), the suffix standing for interim torpedo fighters. They were converted into Mk Xs when Hercules XVII engines became available.

Beaufighters were built under licence in Australia. Designated Mk 21, these aircraft were essentially similar to the TF Mk X, and were powered by Hercules XVIII engines, which were similar to the Hercules XVII but had both supercharger gears fully operational. On these aircraft, the six 0·303-in wing machine-guns were replaced by four 0·50-in guns. A distinguishing feature of the Australian machines was a bulge in the fuselage in front of the pilot; this accommodated a Sperry autopilot.

The Beaufighter Mk XIC, was, in spite of its late designation, an interim variant of the Mk VIC, and was produced to avoid interruption of production while torpedo kits were in short supply. It was essentially a Mk VIC powered by Hercules XVII engines, with the blowers cropped and locked in M ratio to give a low-altitude rating of 1,735 hp at 500 ft.

Beaufighters remained in first-line service until February 1950 and, following their withdrawal, many were converted for target-tug duties. Production totalled 5,926 aircraft, made up as follows:- Mk I, 914; Mk II, 450; Mk VI, 1,830; TF Mk X, 2,205; Mk XIC, 163; Mk 21 (Australian-built) 364.

Bristol Brigand

The Brigand was a light ground-attack bomber carrying a crew of three. It evolved from a design study for a torpedo-bomber intended to replace the Beaufighter in service with Coastal Command. At a late stage the need for such an aircraft disappeared and the Brigand was developed instead as a light bomber for service overseas.

Of all-metal stressed-skin construction, the Brigand utilized the wings, tail unit and twin Centaurus engines of the earlier Buckingham bomber/transport, but incorporated a new fuselage of smaller cross-section and dispensed with the former aircraft's power-operated turret.

The semi-monocoque fuselage was made in three sections, the front and centre portions being joined at the wing front spar, and the rear portion just forward of the tailplane. The wings carried bellows-operated dive-brakes controlled by a venturi in the leading-edge. Production aircraft were powered by two 2,470-hp Bristol Centaurus 57 engines.

In spite of the official change in rôle, the first 11 Brigands were completed as torpedo-bombers, with slinging gear below the fuselage for a 22-in torpedo. They served with Coastal Command from 1946 to 1947, and were then converted into the light attack bomber configuration, with the designation B Mk 1.

Armament consisted of four 20-mm cannon in the fuselage, with provision for up to 2,000 lb of bombs, or an equivalent load of rocket projectiles, under the wings.

Brigands went into service with the RAF in their new rôle in 1949, and production ceased in 1950 by which time 143 had been delivered. This total included 16 Met Mk 3 aircraft for meteorological reconnaissance and T Mk 4 and 5 radar-navigator trainers.

D.H.1.

Designed by the famous pioneer Geoffrey de Havilland for reconnaissance and interceptor duties, the D.H.1 was a pusher biplane with the crew of two accommodated in a short nacelle, at the rear end of which was mounted a 70-hp Renault engine. The pusher configuration was determined primarily by the lack of a suitable interrupter gear, to permit machine-gun fire through the propeller disc. The observer-gunner, located in the front cockpit, had an excellent field of fire for his Lewis gun, in all directions. The tail unit was carried by four booms which extended forward to the wings, enclosing the propeller disc.

Bristol Brigand TF Mk I

Bristol Brigand B Mk I

D.H. 1

TYPE	DIMENSIONS span ft	span in	length ft	length in	height ft	height in	WEIGHT max t-o lb	PERFORMANCE max speed mph	at height ft	service ceiling ft	combat range miles	REMARKS
Beaufighter Mk IF	57	10	41	4	15	10	20,800	323	15,000	28,900	NA	
Beaufighter Mk II	57	10			15	10	NA	330	NA	NA	NA	
Beaufighter Mk VIF	57	10	41	8	15	10	21,600	333	15,600	26,500	1,480	
Beaufighter TF Mk X	57	10	41	8	15	10	25,200	303	1,300	15,000	1,470	
Brigand	72	4	46	5	17	6	39,000	358	16,000	26,000	2,800	

D.H.2

D.H.2

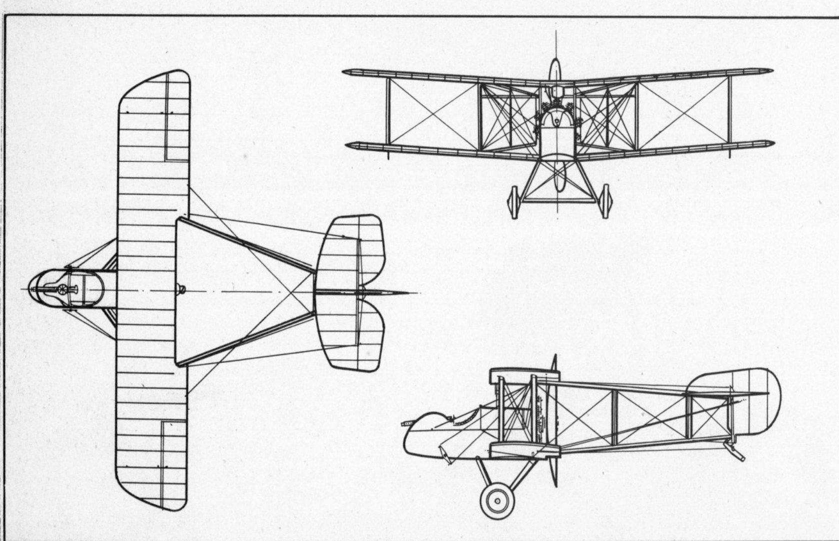
D.H.2

D.H.4, early production model, Eagle engine

Interesting features of the prototype, which appeared in 1915, were the coil springs and concealed oleo-struts of the undercarriage and the air-brakes. Resembling small wings, 3 ft long, the brakes projected on each side of the nacelle and could be rotated through 20° to present a flat surface to the airstream. They were not successful, however, and were soon removed. Production aircraft also changed to the then-conventional rubber cord for undercarriage shock absorption.

Later machines were fitted with the more powerful 120-hp Beardmore engine and were designated D.H.1As.

The D.H.1 was not, as the number implies, the first aircraft designed by de Havilland; it was the first designed by him for the Aircraft Manufacturing Company at which he was chief designer. De Havilland's outstanding qualities were already so well established that the "Airco" numerical designations were generally prefixed by his name and initials in preference to the Company name.

Only a few D.H.1s were built; they were used for Home Defence and training duties, and overseas in Palestine.

D.H.2.

Developed from the D.H.1, the D.H.2 was a single-seat scout powered by a 100-hp Gnome Monosoupape rotary engine. It retained the pusher configuration of its predecessor, made necessary by the continued lack of a suitable British interrupter gear permitting machine-gun fire through the propeller disc. Numerous detail refinements compared with the D.H.1 made it remarkably clean aerodynamically for a "pusher", and it was sturdy structurally.

Rather surprisingly, the prototype, which appeared in 1915, did not have a fixed machine-gun. Instead, a bracket was provided on each side of the windscreen, and the pilot had to mount and aim a Lewis gun from one or other of these while simultaneously flying the aircraft. On production machines, the gun movement was restricted to elevation only, but in combat most pilots treated it as a fixed weapon, aiming the complete machine instead of the gun.

The D.H.2 was sensitive on the controls and rather tricky to fly until pilots became used to its handling characteristics. During its early days, in fact, several pilots were killed through spinning, a phenomenon not then understood. During one such incident the aircraft caught fire and with grim humour pilots nicknamed it "The Spinning Incinerator." In combat, however, the light controls proved a decisive factor, and the type quickly established itself as a first-class fighting machine. All normal aerobatic manoeuvres could be executed and D.H.2 pilots were able to utilize the Immelmann turn as a precision military combat manoeuvre.

D.H.2s started entering service in useful numbers during the early part of 1916 when the Fokker monoplane, with its forward-firing synchronized machine-gun, was sweeping the Allied air forces from the skies. They quickly showed themselves superior to the Fokker in speed, manoeuvrability and rate-of-climb, and established a reputation of their own, and air supremacy for the RFC, particularly during the bitter and bloody first Battle of the Somme. On one occasion, four D.H.2s fought eleven enemy aircraft and destroyed three of them. A Victoria Cross was won in a D.H.2 in 1916, by Major L. W. B. Rees who, mistaking a formation of ten enemy bombers for British aircraft returning from a raid, joined them. Realizing his mistake, he attacked, forced two down and broke up the formation, causing the raid to be abandoned.

D.H.4

Designed in response to an official request for an aircraft for day bombing duties, the de Havilland D.H.4 was one of the great combat machines of the 1914–18 War. It was without doubt the best day bomber used by either the Allies or the Germans.

The main reason for the D.H.4's outstanding success was its excellent performance which, in later versions, was better even than that of the majority of the opposing German fighters then in service. It had a high ceiling which, together with a relatively high speed, enabled it to outdistance all but the fastest German scouts; this ability was naturally very popular with its crews.

The D.H.4 was a straightforward two-bay tractor biplane, constructed almost entirely of wood and fabric-covered. Unusual features of the fuselage were the covering of the front half with plywood, which improved the appearance and increased the strength considerably, and the fact that it was made in two portions, the fish-plated joint being just aft of the rear cockpit.

Also unusual was the distance between the two cockpits. The front cockpit was positioned as far forward as possible under the centre-section, to give the pilot the good forward and downward view required for bombing, while the rear cockpit was located half-way along the fuselage to give a good field of fire for the defensive Lewis machine-gun. Whilst succeeding in its primary purposes, this layout rendered normal communication between the crew difficult. On some machines, a crude speaking tube connected the cockpits, but this was not much good amid the noise of the engine and the slipstream.

Difficulty of communication reduced the combat efficiency of the aircraft once it was caught by enemy fighters, as the pilot and observer could not easily co-operate in positioning the aircraft to allow well-placed shots to be fired. This would have been serious but for the fact that, owing to its excellent performance, the D.H.4 seldom found itself in such a position.

The rear cockpit had full dual controls and, sometimes, duplicated flying instruments; the control column was detachable.

The tailplane was adjustable, for trimming, enabling the pilot to fly at any desired speed without effort.

The prototype D.H.4 was powered by a 230-hp Beardmore-Halford-Pullinger or B.H.P. engine, but early production machines had the 250-hp Rolls-Royce liquid-cooled V-twelve Eagle engine. As production progressed, D.H.4s were fitted with later marks of this superb engine, ending with the Eagle VIII, developing 375 hp. Other engines fitted in production D.H.4s included the 200-hp RAF 3a, the 260-hp Fiat and the 230-hp Siddeley Puma. The Fiat engines were purchased originally by Russia for use in 50 D.H.4s which that country had ordered from Britain. Twenty aircraft had been crated ready for despatch when, with the full agreement of the Russian government, they were diverted to the Western Front to help initiate a campaign of bombing raids on German towns, in retaliation for the Gotha raids against London which had begun in September 1917.

Several engines were fitted experimentally to D.H.4s during their career: American-built D.H.4s, for example, had Liberty 12 engines. Of interest is that of all the British aircraft selected for production in America only the D.H.4 was built in any number – nearly 5,000. It was also the only American-built British design actually to go into operational service in France; over 600 were at the Front at the time of the Armistice.

Maximum bomb-load of the D.H.4 was 460 lb, the

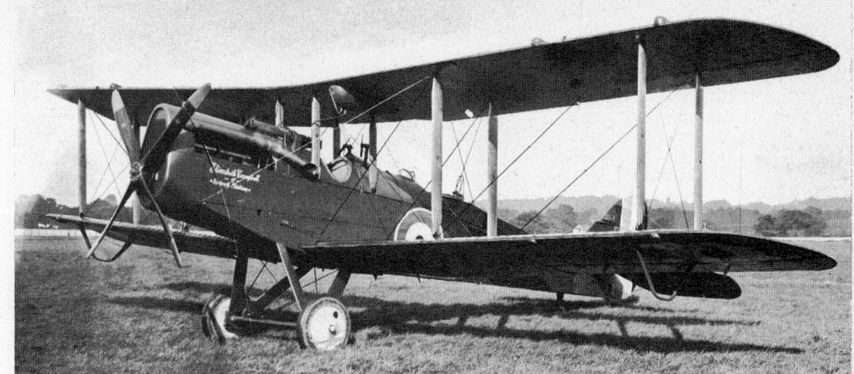

D.H.4, B.H.P. engine

D.H.4, with flotation bags and hydrofoil, RAF 3a engine

D.H.4 of No. 2 (Naval) Squadron, Eagle engine

TYPE	DIMENSIONS						WEIGHT	PERFORMANCE				REMARKS
	span ft	*span* in	*length* ft	*length* in	*height* ft	*height* in	*max t-o* lb	*max speed* mph	*at height* ft	*service ceiling* ft	*combat range* miles	
D.H.1	41	0	29	0	11	4	2,044	80	3,500	NA	NA	
D.H.1A	41	0	28	11	11	2	2,340	90	GL	13,500	NA	
D.H.2	28	3	25	2	9	6	1,441	93	GL	14,000	NA	100-hp Gnome
D.H.2	28	3	25	2	9	6	1,547	92	GL	NA	NA	110-hp Le Rhône
D.H.4	42	5	29	8	10	5	3,340	122	SL	17,500	NA	200-hp RAF 3a
D.H.4	42	5	30	8	10	1	3,344	106	6,500	17,400	NA	230-hp Puma
D.H.4	42	5	30	8	10	5	3,313	119	3,000	16,000	NA	250-hp Eagle
D.H.4	42	5	29	8	10	5	3,822	110	6,500	14,000	NA	260-hp Fiat
D.H.4	42	5	30	8	11	0	3,472	143	SL	22,000	NA	375-hp Eagle VIII
D.H.4	42	6	30	6	10	4	4,297	125	SL	19,500	NA	400-hp Liberty

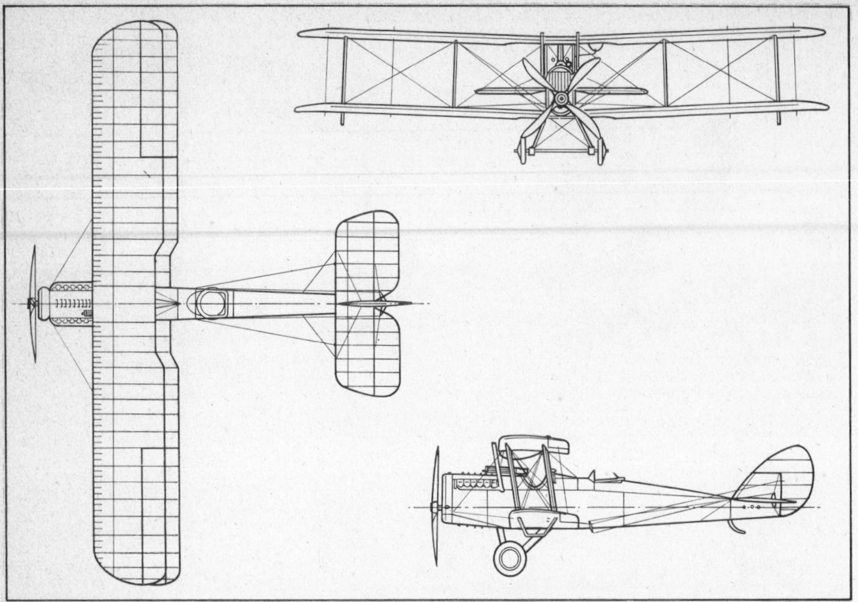

D.H.4

D.H.4B, American-built

D.H.5 prototype

D.H.5

bombs being carried on racks under the fuselage and each lower wing. If required, depth charges could be carried instead of the bombs. Defensive armament included either one or two Lewis machine-guns in the rear cockpit, and a fixed Vickers machine-gun mounted on top of the fuselage and synchronized by Constantinesco gear to fire through the propeller disc. RNAS D.H.4s, some of which were operated by the RFC, had twin Vickers machine-guns for the pilot. The American-built D.H.4s had two fixed Marlin machine-guns firing forward through the propeller disc and a pair of Lewis guns in the rear cockpit.

In service, the D.H.4, in addition to its primary rôle of day-bomber, was used also for fighter-reconnaissance, photographic, anti-submarine and anti-Zeppelin duties. Two RNAS D.H.4s were fitted with extra fuel tanks, giving them an endurance of about 14 hours, to enable a photographic reconnaissance sortie to be made over the Kiel Canal. The plan was not proceeded with and the aircraft were used instead for anti-Zeppelin patrols.

To improve their effectiveness against Zeppelins, two D.H.4s were specially modified to carry a Coventry Ordnance Works $1\frac{1}{2}$-pounder quick-firing gun, mounted with the muzzle pointing nearly vertically upward. The breech nearly touched the floor of the rear cockpit and the muzzle protruded through the top centre-section which was covered with sheet metal to protect it from blast. The pilot had a sight aligned parallel with the gun, which he aimed by manoeuvring the complete aircraft. When on target he signalled to the gunner to open fire.

The COW-armed D.H.4s were not used operationally as Germany ceased Zeppelin raids on Britain and the Armistice was signed before they could be used in France.

After the war, D.H.4s were used in Australia, Canada, Greece, Japan, New Guinea and Spain.

D.H.5.

The D.H.5 was a single-seat tractor biplane scout, designed in 1916. By then, the availability of machine-gun synchronizing gears, permitting fire between the propeller blades, enabled British fighter designers to depart from the less efficient "pusher" layout of the D.H.2 and F.E.8.

The intention behind the D.H.5 was to combine the superior performance of the tractor biplane with the uninterrupted forward and upward view obtained from the cockpit of "pushers". To this end, the wing arrangement was unusual in that it had pronounced back-stagger, the top wing being set back over two feet. The cockpit was located in line with the leading-edge of the top wing.

Construction of the fuselage was conventional, and consisted basically of a wire-braced plywood-reinforced box girder, covered with fabric. The line of the engine cowling was carried smoothly into the fuselage which, aft of the wing, was octagonal in section. The main undercarriage was a simple Vee-structure, with the wheels retained by rubber cord. Power was supplied by a 110-hp Le Rhône rotary engine.

The standard armament was one fixed forward-firing Vickers machine-gun, synchronized to fire between the propeller blades by the Constantinesco interrupter gear. Up to four 25-lb bombs could be carried on racks beneath the fuselage.

Production D.H.5s began to appear early in 1917, and were accompanied by the usual crop of rumours, accentuated in this case by the unusual configuration of the aircraft. The back-stagger, while succeeding in its primary object of providing the pilot with a first-class view forward and upward (although not rearward and upward, from which direction attacks against the D.H.5 were most often made), caused a considerable loss in aerodynamic efficiency due to increased turbulence between the wings. This made the stall characteristics more severe than on conventional biplanes, although not to the extent suggested by rumours of a stalling speed of 80 mph.

Overall, the D.H.5 was pleasant to fly, with sensitive aileron control. It was highly manoeuvrable and able to execute all normal aerobatics. However, it never became really popular, and is considered the least successful of Captain de Havilland's ten warplanes.

The D.H.5 went into service on the Western Front in

May 1917, but did not distinguish itself in aerial combat. Its performance was best low down, so it usually operated with Bristol Fighters and Sopwith Pups, these latter types looking after the higher airspace, while the D.H.5s patrolled the lower levels.

The excellent forward view from the cockpit made the D.H.5 particularly suitable for ground strafing and it was used extensively on this duty during the big infantry Battles of Ypres and Cambrai. This latter battle marked the end of the type's operational career, for all D.H.5 squadrons were re-equipped with S.E.5as by January 1918.

D.H.6

The D.H.6 was designed to meet a requirement for an easy-to-fly, easy-to-build, two-seat trainer and almost everything else was sacrificed to achieve structural simplicity. The fuselage was a wire-braced box structure of relatively narrow proportions, with a flat top decking. A simple Vee-undercarriage was fitted, with rubber cord shock-absorbers. The conventionally constructed, heavily cambered wings were distinguished by absolutely square tips, the stark simplicity of which gave rise to the legend that the wings were "made by the mile and bought by the yard."

Standard engine for the D.H.6 was the 90-hp RAF la, but when supplies ran short either the Curtiss OX-5 or the 80-hp Renault was substituted. As a trainer, the aircraft was easy to fly, with no vices; it was hard to stall and virtually unspinnable. For a time it was, together with the Armstrong Whitworth F.K.8, a standard British trainer, until the Avro 504K was generally adopted.

In January 1918, the U-boat menace was reaching its peak in coastal waters and to help control this a number of D.H.6s were diverted to anti-submarine patrol duties. They had not, of course, been designed for this work, and when carrying a single 100-lb bomb had to be flown as single-seaters as they could not lift a bomb and carry an observer at the same time.

However, despite their shortcomings the situation was so desperate that, as the Avro 504K came into widespread use, further D.H.6s were withdrawn from training units and another 200 were allocated to anti-submarine duties. Sorties were flown in all but the worst weather, their main operational value being that U-boat commanders rarely risked raising their periscopes in areas known to be patrolled by aircraft.

A total of 2,282 D.H.6s were built and the affection, or otherwise, that the type inspired in its crews is reflected in the unusually large crop of nicknames it received, including "The Clutching Hand", due to the heavy wing camber; "The Sky Hook", due to the tall exhaust stacks and its pronounced nose-up attitude in slow flight; "The Flying Coffin", due to the long cockpit; "The Dung Hunter" bestowed by Australians because of the cockpit's resemblance to a certain farm vehicle; and "The Crab".

D.H.9

In a single daylight raid on London in June 1917, German bombers caused more damage than in all the previous Zeppelin raids. This provided convincing proof of the value of aeroplanes as weapons of offence, and the Chief of the British Imperial General Staff requested that the

D.H.5

D.H.6 prototype RAF engine

D.H.6, Curtiss OX-5 engine

TYPE	DIMENSIONS span ft	in	length ft	in	height ft	in	WEIGHT max t-o lb	PERFORMANCE max speed mph	at height ft	service ceiling ft	combat range miles	REMARKS
D.H.5	25	8	22	0	9	1	1,492	102	10,000	16,000	NA	Endurance 2¾ hours
D.H.6	35	11	27	3	10	9	2,027	66	6,500	NA	NA	90-hp RAF 1a
D.H.6	35	11	27	3	10	9	1,926	75	2,000	6,100	NA	90-hp OX-5
D.H.6	35	11	27	3	10	9	2,011	72	2,000	5,400	NA	80-hp Renault
D.H.9	42	5	30	6	11	2	3,669	112	10,000	15,500	NA	230-hp BHP
D.H.9	42	5	30	6	11	2	3,325	111	6,500	15,500	NA	230-hp Puma

D.H.9, Fiat A-12 engine

D.H.9, BHP engine

D.H.9, Napier Lion engine

strength of the RFC be almost doubled, from 108 squadrons to 200, the majority of the new squadrons to be equipped with bombing aircraft.

To equip some of the new squadrons, 700 of the highly successful D.H.4s were ordered. In order to extend the area of operations, it was decided to produce also a development of this type, having a longer range. Plans for the improved aircraft were drawn up, but the modifications were so extensive that it soon came to be regarded as new type and was allocated the type number D.H.9. Despite the changes, introduction of the new type was considered unlikely to delay production by more than three weeks, and so the contracts for the D.H.4s were amended to specify D.H.9s. Calculations, assuming use of a 300-hp engine, indicated a promising performance.

Unfortunately, development troubles with the specified BHP engine caused it to be derated to 230 hp, and an engine of this power was installed in the prototype D.H.9 (a modified D.H.4) in July 1917. The loss of performance due to reduced engine power was soon evident and serious – the new machine was, in fact, inferior to the older Rolls-Royce-powered D.H.4, and could not maintain an altitude of 15,000 ft fully loaded.

Constructionally, the D.H.9 was very similar to the D.H.4; the wings and tail unit being identical. Changes to the fuselage were made. In particular, the pilot's cockpit was moved aft, so that he could communicate more readily with his observer, although this substantially reduced his view forward and downward. The engine installation differed from current British practice in that the radiator was under the fuselage instead of in front of the engine. The cowling thus curved towards the nose, giving the nose a "Hunnish" appearance. The cylinder block and oil tank, projecting upward, did nothing to enhance the installation. However, it was the bad engine which really spoiled an otherwise good aircraft.

At the time, the D.H.9 was described as "A D.H.4 which has been officially interfered with in order to be suitable for mass-production and the BHP motor". It certainly was suitable for mass-production: at one time D.H.9s were coming off the production lines at the rate of one every 40 minutes, a grand total of 3,204 being produced.

Armament consisted of one fixed forward-firing Vickers machine-gun, mounted on the top left of the fuselage and synchronized by Constantinesco gear to fire between the propeller blades, plus one or two Lewis machine-guns on a Scarff ring-mounting in the rear cockpit. A maximum bomb-load of 460 lb was specified, but 350 lb was the practical load.

The D.H.9 was thus expected to carry a greater bomb-load than the more powerful D.H.4, and it did so only at the expense of ceiling and performance. The lower ceiling was particularly serious and put the aircraft at a severe tactical disadvantage. It had to accept combat when and where the defending fighters chose, and losses were heavy. Matters were made worse by the unreliability of the engine, which was such that aircraft often had to return from raids, leaving the attacking squadrons under strength. On one occasion, out of 29 D.H.9s which started out to attack Aulnoye, no fewer than 15 had to turn back due to engine trouble.

In spite of its deficiency, the type was used vigorously, with individual pilots sometimes making as many as six sorties a day. Together with the Handley Page O/400, it served with the Independent Force and remained operational until the Armistice.

In the Middle East, against less well-equipped enemy forces, the D.H.9 tended to be more successful than it was on the Western Front.

Engines fitted to overcome the deficiencies of the BHP included the 250-hp Fiat A-12, and 430-hp Napier Lion which at last gave the D.H.9 a worthwhile performance; but the latter engine arrived too late to see service before the Armistice was signed.

Ambitious plans were made in America to produce no fewer than 14,000 D.H.9s, powered by the 400-hp Liberty 12A engine; but only a few were built before the end of the war, after which all contracts were cancelled.

Small numbers of D.H.9s served with the Belgian Flying Corps, the US Naval Northern Bombing Group in France, Denikin's White Army in Russia in 1919, where one was captured and used by the Red forces, and – in much modified form, powered by a Jupiter radial engine and known as the Mpala – with the South African Air Force up to 1937.

After the war, the D.H.9 was used for a variety of experimental purposes, involving revised armament, Handley Page slots and flight refuelling, and for pioneering work in the field of commercial aviation.

D.H.9A

In marked contrast with its predecessor, the D.H.9, for which the low power and unreliability of the BHP engine had gained an unenviable reputation, the D.H.9A was one of the RAF's outstanding aircraft, with a very long service record.

The urgent need for a replacement for the D.H.9 was soon obvious, but the shortage of suitable engines made a solution difficult. In August 1917, the United States announced its new Liberty engine, describing it as "the best aircraft engine produced in any country", although it had not flown at that time. An ambitious production programme was planned and Britain ordered 3,000 Liberties, for use in an improved two-seat day-bomber based on the D.H.9.

In the new aircraft, the radiator was repositioned immediately behind the propeller. Other changes included fitting new wings of increased span and chord; while the fuselage, instead of embodying a number of plywood bulkheads, was fully cross-braced by wires.

A standard D.H.9 was converted into the D.H.9A prototype which, owing to the late arrival of the Liberty engine, was fitted with a 375-hp Rolls-Royce Eagle VIII. Some production 9As also had an Eagle, but the standard engine fitted to the great majority was the 400-hp Liberty 12. Inevitably, this engine had its share of development problems, and over 1,000 modifications were made between September 1917 and February 1918. After a time, however, the Liberty proved as reliable as any engine of the period.

Armament of the D.H.9A consisted of one forward-firing fixed Vickers machine-gun, mounted in front of and to the left of the pilot, and synchronized by Constantinesco interrupter gear to fire between the propeller blades. The observer, in the rear cockpit, had either one or two Lewis machine-guns on a Scarff ring-mounting. A maximum bomb-load of 660 lb could be carried, the normal load consisting of two 230-lb bombs. This was about double the practical load of the D.H.9 and, more important, could be carried at 17,000 ft without loss of height.

The first squadron of D.H.9As, No. 110, was formed in June 1918, but did not arrive in France until 31 August 1918. The aircraft had been paid for by the Nizam of Hyderabad and, as each bore an inscription to this effect, the unit soon became known as the Hyderabad Squadron.

In service the aircraft, known as the "Nine-ack", proved reasonably effective, as its performance was good enough for it to be operated unescorted; but its contribution to the Independent Force's programme of strategic bombing of industrial targets was not great, as the Armistice limited its active service to about two months.

By the end of 1918 a total of 885 had been built by Westland, who were entrusted with development and manufacture of the type. Several hundred more were built

D.H.9A

D.H.9A. No. 30 Squadron

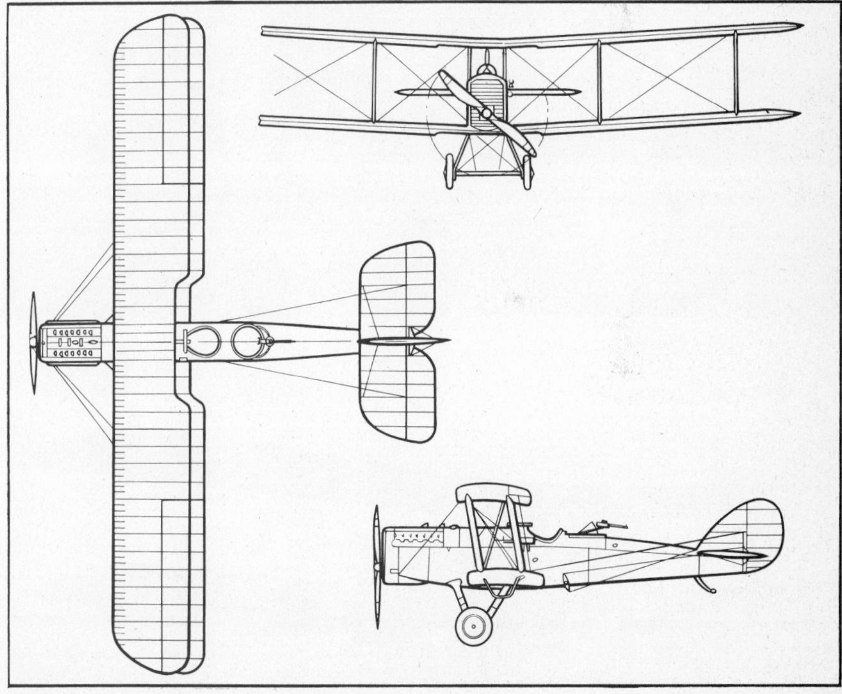

D.H.9A

TYPE	DIMENSIONS span ft	span in	length ft	length in	height ft	height in	WEIGHT max t-o lb	PERFORMANCE max speed mph	at height ft	service ceiling ft	combat range miles	REMARKS
D.H.9	42	5	30	6	11	2	3,600	118	10,000	17,500	NA	250-hp Fiat A-12
D.H.9	42	5	30	9	11	8	3,667	144	SL	23,000	NA	430-hp Lion
D.H.9	42	5	30	0	11	2	4,645	114	SL	NA	NA	400-hp Liberty 12-A
D.H.9A	45	11	30	3	11	4	4,815	110	10,000	14,000	NA	Eagle VIII
D.H.9A	45	11	30	3	11	4	4,645	114	10,000	16,750	NA	Liberty engine
D.H.9A	45	11	30	3	11	4	4,660	134	10,000	21,300	NA	Lion engine

D.H.9A, Westland-built, Napier Lion engine

D.H.10 Amiens Mk II

D.H.10 Amiens Mk III, No. 216 Squadron

de Havilland Mosquito NF Mk II

in post-war years in Britain. In addition, the type was put into production in Russia after the Revolution, with a local equivalent of the Liberty engine. In America, initial small batches of an order for 4,000 had been completed by the time of the Armistice, when the contract was cancelled. The standard US-built machines were designated USD-9A. A single variant, with wings of increased area and a 420-hp Liberty 12-A engine, was known as the USD-9B.

In the 1920s, the D.H.9A was used extensively for RAF policing duties in Iraq and along the North-West Frontier of India. Although air opposition during these operations was nil, engine failure and subsequent forced landing in desolate country usually ended in death through exposure, starvation or at the hands of warlike tribesmen.

In these duties the 9A demonstrated just how willing and sturdy a "work-horse" it was. In addition to carrying its crew, machine-guns and bombs, it often had a large tropical radiator, flare brackets and long-range fuel tanks stuck on the outside, together with a spare wheel, strapped in any convenient position, and emergency rations. The water ration, carried in an animal skin, was often hung from the gun ring over the side of the fuselage to keep it cool.

Some post-war 9As were fitted with a Napier Lion engine, and in 1926 the prototype of a version known as the D.H. Stag was built with a 465-hp Bristol Jupiter radial.

The D.H.9A remained in front-line service until 1931.

D.H.10 Amiens

Developed from the D.H.3 of 1916, the three-seat twin-engined D.H.10 was one of several promising new bombers for the RAF which just missed operational service in the 1914–18 War.

Distinctive features of the D.H.10 were its underslung fuselage, wide-track undercarriage and low-mounted engines. Fuselage construction was conventional, the front portion being a plywood-covered box and the rear portion a wire-braced box girder covered with fabric. The wings were of wood, braced internally by rods. The main undercarriage wheels were mounted directly beneath the engines, and two smaller wheels were mounted on each side of the nose of early models.

The first prototype, known officially as the Amiens Mk I and powered by two 230-hp BHP engines, first flew on 4 March 1918. On this aircraft the engines drove pusher propellers, but subsequent machines had a tractor layout. The second prototype, designated Amiens Mk II, was powered by two 360-hp Rolls-Royce Eagle VIII engines; the third, the Amiens Mk III, had two 400-hp Liberty 12s. Originally, the engines were mounted midway between the wings, but performance was improved by altering their position so that they were mounted directly on top of the lower wing. With the new engine installation the type was named Amiens Mk IIIA by the authorities and designated D.H.10A by the manufacturer.

Armament consisted of either one or two Lewis machine-guns mounted on a Scarff ring-mounting in each of the front and rear cockpits. The maximum bomb load was 900 lb, most of it carried internally in the fuselage.

A total of 1,295 D.H.10s were ordered, but only eight had been delivered by the time of the Armistice, of which two were in France with the Independent Force. Production ended after about 220 had been delivered. These aircraft were used by No. 120 Squadron on the air mail service between Hawkinge and Cologne in 1919, during which the first night mail operation was flown. Others were operated by No. 216 Squadron on the pioneer Cairo-Baghdad mail route.

de Havilland Mosquito

The D.H.98 Mosquito was one of the great British combat aircraft of World War II. Its versatility was outstanding: it remained the fastest type in Bomber Command for nearly ten years, until outpaced by the jet Canberra.

Operational flying soon demonstrated the validity of the original idea of a high-speed unarmed bomber. The Mosquito proved too fast to be intercepted, and towards the end of the war, flying at altitudes between 30,000 and 40,000 ft, it suffered a loss rate of only one per 2,000 sorties, the lowest by far of any type used by Bomber Command. It was particularly effective against pin-point targets. Thus, Mosquito bomber squadrons destroyed one V-1 flying bomb site for each 40 tons of bombs dropped, compared with 219 tons from Mitchells, 182 tons from Marauders and 165 tons from Fortresses. Mosquito fighters shot down 600 V-1 flying bombs in two months.

The Mosquito also established itself as a superb photo-reconnaissance aircraft, although details of the Marks used for such duties are outside the scope of this book.

The Mosquito was initiated as a private-venture light bomber in October 1938. Powered by two Rolls-Royce Merlins, it was conceived as an all-wooden aircraft, to conserve strategic materials, and carried no defensive armament, relying upon its speed to escape destruction. Officialdom showed little interest until 1940, when three prototypes were ordered.

The first of these, a bomber, flew on 25 November 1940, and early demonstrations quickly indicated that the Mosquito was no ordinary aeroplane. Its speed in level flight was nearly 400 mph and it displayed fighter-like manoeuvrability, performing with ease upward rolls with one engine stopped.

The second prototype was a fighter variant and incorporated a bullet-proof windscreen, reinforced wing spars and a modified nose to accommodate four 20-mm cannon and four 0·303-in machine-guns. It was designated Mk II.

The third prototype was a photo-reconnaissance variant.

In all its many forms, the Mosquito was a cantilever mid-wing monoplane, the one-piece wing being built up on two box-spars with spruce flanges and plywood webs. The skinning was plywood, that on the upper surface being double with the stringers sandwiched between the two skins. The plywood was covered with fabric. Hydraulically-operated slotted flaps were fitted between the ailerons and nacelles, and between nacelles and fuselage.

The oval-section monocoque fuselage was likewise an all-wood structure, the skin being a sandwich of balsa between two layers of plywood, and the bulkheads consisting of two plywood skins spaced by spruce blocks. It was built in two vertical halves, each being completely equipped with all wiring, pipe runs and controls before joining. A large cut-out in the underside of the fuselage received the wing, the lower portion of the cut-out being replaced after assembly.

The main undercarriage retracted rearward into the engine nacelles, each leg consisting of a pair of struts incorporating rubber springing and a large single wheel.

The engines were enclosed in special low-drag nacelles, and the radiators were buried in the leading-edge of the wing to minimize drag.

Ten Mk I's were equipped for photographic-reconnaissance duties. These were the first Mosquitoes to go into service and the first to make an operational sortie, this being a daylight flight over Paris on 20 September 1941.

Night fighter Mosquito NF Mk IIs went into service in May 1942, with No. 23 and No. 157 Squadrons. They were powered by 1,460-hp Merlin 21 or 23 engines and were fitted with AI Mk IV radar for intercepting bombers in the dark. Aircraft with this equipment can be identified by the characteristic "arrowhead" antenna; later, the improved AI Mk V radar was installed. Night fighters had a matt black finish, reducing their speed by 16 mph.

The Mosquito Mk IV was the first bomber version to go into service with the RAF, in No. 2 (Light Bomber) Group.

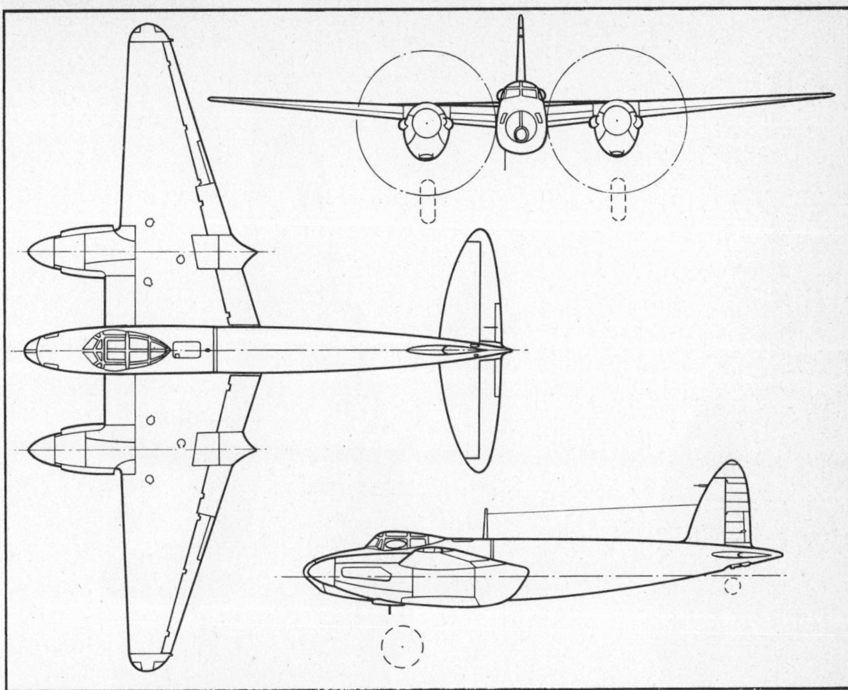

de Havilland Mosquito B Mk IV

de Havilland Mosquito FB Mk VI, armed with rockets

de Havilland Mosquito B Mk IX pathfinder with radar

TYPE	DIMENSIONS span ft	in	length ft	in	height ft	in	WEIGHT max t-o lb	PERFORMANCE max speed mph	at height ft	service ceiling ft	combat range miles	REMARKS
D.H.10 Amiens Mk I	62	9	38	10	14	6	6,950	100	10,000	15,000	NA	Bomber version
D.H.10 Amiens Mk I	62	9	38	10	14	6	5,814	NA	NA	18,000	NA	Home Defence version
D.H.10 Amiens Mk II	62	9	38	10	14	6	NA	117	SL	NA	NA	
D.H.10 Amiens Mk III	65	6	39	7	14	6	9,000	116	6,500	16,500	NA	Endurance 5¾ hours
D.H.10 Amiens Mk IIIA	65	6	39	7	14	6	9,000	126	6,500	17,500	NA	Endurance 5¾ hours

de Havilland Mosquito NF Mk XV

de Havilland Mosquito B Mk XVI

de Havilland Mosquito FB Mk XVIII

It was powered by two 1,250-hp Merlin XXI engines and could carry four 500-lb bombs. This was double the load envisaged in the original specification.

More than 50 Mk IVs were given bulged bomb-bays to accommodate the 4,000-lb "block-buster" bomb. The Mosquito was the only light bomber capable of carrying this weapon, hitherto carried only by the "heavies".

Other Mk IVs were converted for reconnaissance duties. The changes included lightening of the airframe by 1,850 lb to give them the maximum possible operational altitude.

Numerically, the major Mosquito variant was the FB Mk VI fighter-bomber, of which a total of 2,584 were built. Series I aircraft were powered by two 1,460-hp Merlin 21s or 23s and carried two 250-lb bombs in the rear half of the bomb-bay, the front half being occupied by the four cannon breeches. To extend the range, 50-gallon drop tanks could be fitted under the wings. Series 2 aircraft had 1,635-hp Merlin 25 engines and were able to carry an additional pair of 500-lb bombs in place of the wing drop tanks. Mosquito FB Mk VIs also went into service with Coastal Command, these aircraft usually carrying eight 60-lb rockets under the wings instead of bombs.

A great number of other Mosquito variants were produced, with Mark numbers which did not always appear in numerical sequence. To facilitate reference, these are arranged numerically below. The missing numbers are those allocated either to photo-reconnaissance and training aircraft, or to projected versions which were not built.

B Mk VII: This was the designation allotted to the first Canadian-built Mosquito.

BMk IX: This was an improved bomber variant powered by 1,680-hp Merlin 72 engines, superseding the Mk IV. The bomb-bay was bulged to accommodate a 4,000-lb "block-buster" bomb, this being double the original load of the Mk IV.

Some Mk IXs were used for pathfinding duties, and were equipped with the Oboe device which permitted accurate bombing through cloud.

NF Mk XII: This was a development of the NF Mk II, incorporating the new centimetric radar AI Mk VIII. Other changes included deletion of the four machine-guns. No new aircraft were built as Mk XIIs, all 97 of this variant being conversions of Mk IIs.

NF Mk XIII: This was the new production counterpart of the Mk XII conversion, 270 being built.

NF Mk XV: This was a high-altitude fighter variant, based on the modified prototype Mk XVI described below. Only five were built, as conversions of Mk IV bombers, with four 20-mm cannon in a blister housing and AI Mk VIII radar in the nose.

B Mk XVI: This was a bomber variant developed specially for "nuisance" raids, that is, raids where the psychological effect was greater than the material damage. A development of the Mk IX, it had a pressurized cabin and operated at an altitude of about 40,000 ft. It could carry the 4,000-lb "block-buster" bomb, together with two 50-gallon drop tanks under the wings. The Mk XVI was widely used, over 1,200 of the basic bomber being built.

The prototype Mk XVI bomber was fitted with four 20-mm cannon in September 1942, to combat high-flying Ju 86P reconnaissance aircraft. In addition, the wings were extended, and some armour and some fuel tanks were deleted to save weight, giving a ceiling of 43,000 ft.

NF Mk XVII was the designation allotted to 100 Mk XIII aircraft modified to take the American AI Mk X radar.

FB Mk XVIII: Initially named Tse-Tse, this was a version specially developed for Coastal Command, and was actually produced prior to the Mk VI. It was armed with a 57-mm six-pounder Molins gun and four 0·303-in machine-guns, plus two 500-lb bombs or eight rockets under the wings. Although effective against shipping and ground installations, only 27 of this version were built.

NF Mk XIX: This was the new production version of the Mk XVII equipped with American AI Mk X radar, and was powered by Merlin 25 engines. It had an increased loaded weight of 21,750 lb.

FB Mk 21 was the designation allotted to three Canadian-built Mosquitos powered by Packard Merlin 31s or 33s. They were used as prototypes for the FB Mk 26.

FB Mk 26 was one of the principal Canadian-built

Mosquitoes. It was basically similar to the UK-built FB Mk VI, but was powered by two Packard Merlin 225 engines.

The *NF Mk 30* was the last wartime night-fighter variant, and was introduced in 1944. Later models were powered by Merlin 76 engines, specially rated for high-altitude operations.

The *Sea Mosquito TR Mk 33* was a post-war carrier-borne torpedo-reconnaissance strike variant. It was developed from two converted FB Mk VI prototypes, the first of which, on 25 March 1944, had been the first British twin-engined aircraft to land on a carrier. The Mk 33 had folding wings and ASV radar, was powered by 1,640-hp Merlin 25s, and could carry an 18-in torpedo or a bomb-load of 2,000 lb. Up to eight 60-lb rocket projectiles could be carried under the wings, or two rockets and two 30-gallon drop tanks. A total of 50 Mk 33s were built.

The *B Mk 35*, first flown shortly before VE-day, was a developed version of the B XVI with Merlin 113-114 engines and a maximum speed of 422 mph. One hundred and twenty-two were built by Airspeed.

The *NF Mk 36* was a post-war development of the Mk 30, the major change being the installation of Merlin 113 engines.

The *Sea Mosquito TR Mk 37* was a development of the TR Mk 33, with British ASV radar and an enlarged nose to accommodate a bigger scanner. Six were delivered.

The *NF Mk 38* was essentially similar to the Mk 36, but was fitted with British AI Mk IX radar instead of American AI Mk X. To accommodate the British equipment, the cockpit was moved forward 5 in. The last of more than 80 of this variant was completed in November 1950, bringing Mosquito production in Britain to 6,439 aircraft. Total production, including those built in Canada and Australia, was 7,781 aircraft.

FB Mk 40 was the designation allotted to Australian-built Mosquitos. These were essentially similar to the FB Mk VI, the first 100 being powered by Packard Merlin 31s and the last 78 with Packard Merlin 33s.

The *FB Mk 42* was a variant of the FB Mk 40, powered by two-stage supercharged Merlin 69s. Only the prototype was built, becoming later the PR Mk 41 prototype.

de Havilland Vampire

The D.H.100 Vampire was the second jet fighter developed in Britain and appeared just too late to see service during World War II. It had a speed in excess of 500 mph over a wide operating altitude, possessed excellent manoeuvrability, was pleasant to fly and easy to handle. It was, in fact, an ideal aircraft with which to initiate pilots and air forces into the high-speed jet age, and was used for this purpose by more than 25 countries throughout the world.

Known initially as the Spider Crab, the Vampire was designed to Air Ministry Specification E.6/41. The prototype, powered by a 2,700-lb s t de Havilland Goblin centrifugal-flow turbojet, first flew in September 1943.

The outstanding feature of the aircraft was its twin-boom layout, which was chosen, after many other schemes had been investigated, to keep the jet pipe as short as

de Havilland Sea Mosquito TR Mk 33, wings folded

de Havilland Sea Mosquito TR Mk 37

de Havilland Vampire F Mk 1

TYPE	DIMENSIONS span ft	span in	length ft	length in	height ft	height in	WEIGHT max t-o lb	PERFORMANCE max speed mph	at height ft	service ceiling ft	combat range miles	REMARKS
Mosquito NF Mk II	54	2	40	11	15	3	20,000	370	14,000	34,500	1,860	
Mosquito B Mk IV	54	2	40	9	15	3	20,870	380	17,000	28,800	NA	
Mosquito FB Mk VI	54	2	40	6	15	3	22,300	380	13,000	36,000	1,705	
Mosquito NF Mk XII	54	2	40	11	15	3	20,000	370	14,000	34,500	1,860	
Mosquito NF Mk XIII	54	2	40	11	15	3	20,000	370	14,000	34,500	1,860	
Mosquito B Mk XVI	54	2	41	6	15	3	23,000	415	28,000	40,000	1,370	
Mosquito NF Mk XIX	54	2	40	11	15	3	21,750	372	13,000	34,500	1,830	
Mosquito NF Mk 30	54	2	41	9	15	3	21,600	407	28,000	39,000	1,770	
Mosquito TR Mk 33	54	2	42	3	13	6	22,500	385	13,500	30,000	1,260	

de Havilland Vampire FB Mk 6, Swiss-built for Swiss Air Force

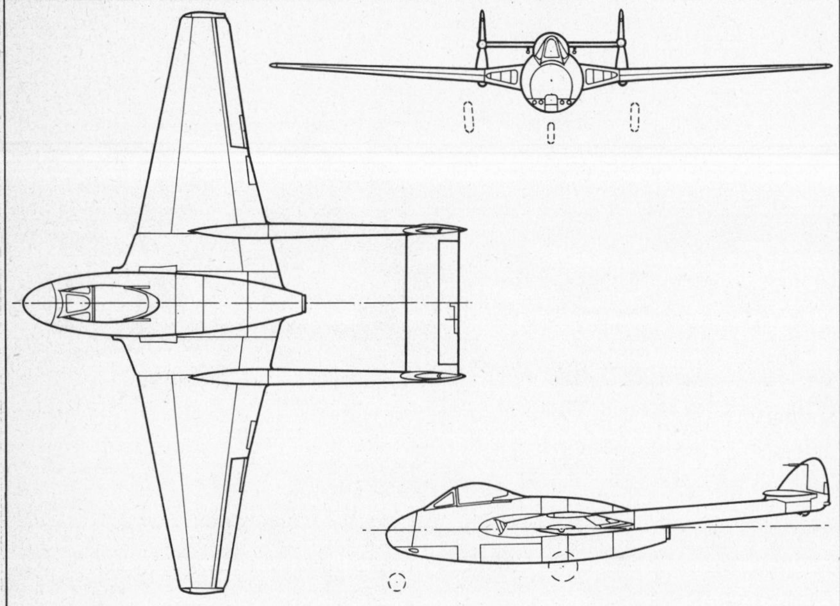
de Havilland Vampire FB Mk 5

de Havilland Vampire NF Mk 10

de Havilland Sea Vampire F Mk 20

possible and so minimise power losses. An additional advantage was that the pilot had an excellent field of view compared with that from twin-engined designs and those with fuselages embodying nose intakes.

The detail construction was conventional and straightforward. The entire aircraft was, in effect, built around the egg-shaped nacelle, which embodied the engine mounting, wing attachments and wing-root air intake system. The monocoque nacelle was of wood, consisting of balsa sandwiched between two thin plywood skins, and was made in two half-shells which were joined along the top and bottom.

The wing was of all-metal construction. Split flaps were fitted, outboard of which were air-brakes, each consisting of a single surface hinged centrally so that they were aerodynamically balanced when operated.

The main undercarriage, which could be made unusually short in the absence of a propeller, retracted outward into the wings; the nose leg retracted rearward into the nacelle.

Vampire F Mk Is went into service in 1946, with No. 247 Squadron. The first 40 machines were each powered by a 2,700-lb s t Goblin, as was the prototype; but subsequent aircraft had the 3,100-lb s t Goblin DGn2. The first 50 were unpressurized, but later aircraft had a pressurized cockpit. Still later models introduced a bubble canopy in place of the earlier three-piece type.

The F Mk I was superseded by the F Mk III, which had increased internal fuel capacity, provision for two 200-gallon drop tanks, and a redesigned tail assembly incorporating pointed fins, of the type fitted to the original prototype.

In 1949 the Mk III was supplemented by the FB Mk 5, a ground-attack fighter-bomber variant. This had a re-stressed wing of shorter span, with square tips, and a redesigned long-stroke undercarriage, and could carry on underwing racks up to 2,000 lb of bombs or rockets. The outstanding manoeuvrability of this variant was demonstrated publicly in Germany in 1950, when aircraft of No. 16 Squadron performed aerobatics while tied together.

The export version of the Vampire Mk 5 was designated FB Mk 52.

The last single-seat variant was the FB Mk 9. This was a refinement of the FB Mk 5, powered by a 3,350-lb s t Goblin DGn3, and had an air-conditioned cockpit, the refrigeration plant being housed in one wing which, consequently, had an enlarged fillet.

The NF Mk 10 night fighter was the first two-seat variant. Powered by a 3,350-lb s t Goblin 3, it used the wings and tail booms of the ordinary day fighter, but the nacelle was widened to accommodate a second seat for a radar navigator (the crew of two sitting side-by-side) and lengthened to carry AI Mk X interception radar.

Overall, the changes were sufficient for de Havilland to allot the new works designation DH 113 to the aircraft, which retained the armament of four 20-mm cannon fitted to earlier models.

The NF Mk 10 was initiated as a private venture for export, and was ordered by Egypt and India. When the sale of arms to Egypt was stopped, the RAF took over the aircraft which were to have been supplied to that country, to speed up re-equipment of its night fighter force, which still consisted mainly of ageing Mosquitos.

The Sea Vampire F 20 was a navalized version of the FB Mk 5, changes including a restressed airframe to cater for increased acceleration and landing loads. A Vee-type arrester hook was fitted, being stowed in a fairing above the jet outlet when not in use.

The prototype Sea Vampire, a converted Vampire I, gained the distinction of being the first jet aircraft in the world to land on and take off from a carrier, which it did on 3 December 1945, on board HMS *Ocean*.

An experimental version of the Sea Vampire, designated F 21, was used for an interesting series of deck landing trials in undercarriage-less form. For the trials, HMS *Warrior* was fitted with a rubberized deck and the aircraft had a specially-strengthened underside. Further trials were conducted ashore.

Vampire production totalled about 2,000 aircraft, including 800 T Mk 11 and T Mk 22 trainers.

de Havilland Hornet

The D.H.103 Hornet was initiated as a private-venture single-seat long-range fighter-bomber for use in the anticipated "island-hopping" campaign against the Japanese, but appeared too late to see service in World War II.

Official Specification F.12/43 was framed around the de Havilland proposals and it was to this that the prototype was actually built. It was exceptionally clean aerodynamically, particular care being paid to the cowling of the two 2,030-hp Rolls-Royce Merlin 130/131 engines, which drove high-efficiency de Havilland four-bladed propellers, rotating in opposite directions. The prototype first flew in July 1944, and reached the then-phenomenal top speed of 485 mph.

The slender fuselage, like that of the Mosquito, was an all-wood monocoque consisting essentially of a layer of balsa between two thin plywood skins. The wing, designed to higher strength factors, was a composite structure, with a double top skin of plywood and a lower skin of light alloy, and with composite wood and metal spars. This unique form of construction was made possible by the new technique of bonding metal to wood.

Armament consisted of four 20-mm cannon in the nose, with provision for two 1,000-lb bombs or eight 60-lb rockets beneath the wings.

Five Mk 2s were built for photo-reconnaissance duties, but this requirement ended with the war.

Hornet F Mk 1s went into service early in 1946, a total of 60 being delivered. They were superseded by F Mk 3s, incorporating a dorsal fillet on the fin and increased internal fuel tankage. These Hornets, of which over 200 were built, were the RAF's last piston-engined fighters.

The Sea Hornet F 20 was the Fleet Air Arm counterpart of the RAF's Mk 3, and was the first single-seat twin-engined fighter to operate from British carriers. Production models, of which 77 were built, had folding wings, arrester gear, tail-down accelerator gear and special naval radio equipment.

The Sea Hornet NF 21 was a two-seat development of the NF 20, produced primarily for night-fighting duties, and had an ASH scanner in the nose, flame-damping exhausts and a separate cockpit for a navigator/radar operator located just aft of the wing. A total of 78 NF 21s were delivered and were the FAA's standard carrier-borne night fighters from 1949 to 1954.

de Havilland Venom/Sea Venom

The D.H.112 Venom was a logical successor to the Vampire, and was produced in three main variants: a single-seat fighter-bomber, a two-seat night fighter and a two-seat carrier-borne all-weather fighter and strike fighter.

Although following the general configuration of the Vampire, the Venom was a completely new design, except for the fuselage. A major change was the installation of

de Havilland Hornet F Mk 3

de Havilland Sea Hornet NF 21

TYPE	DIMENSIONS span ft	span in	length ft	length in	height ft	height in	WEIGHT max t-o lb	PERFORMANCE max speed mph	at height ft	service ceiling ft	combat range miles	REMARKS
Vampire F Mk I	40	0	30	9	8	10	8,578	540	20,000	28,500	730	
Vampire F Mk III	40	0	30	9	8	10	11,970	540	20,000	28,500	1,390	With drop-tanks
Vampire FB Mk 5	38	0	30	9	NA		NA	NA	NA	NA	NA	
Vampire FB Mk 9	38	0	30	9	8	10	12,390	548	30,000	NA	1,220	
Vampire NF Mk 10	38	0	34	7	6	7	11,350	550	20,000	NA	1,220	
Sea Vampire F Mk 20	38	0	30	9	8	10	12,660	526	NA	NA	1,145	
Hornet F Mk I	45	0	36	8	14	2	17,700	472	22,000	35,000	15,000	
Hornet F Mk III	45	0	36	8	14	2	20,900	472	22,000	35,000	3,000	
Sea Hornet F Mk 20	45	0	36	8	14	2	18,250	467	22,000	35,000	1,500	With drop-tanks
Sea Hornet NF Mk 21	45	0	37	0	14	0	19,530	430	22,000	36,500	1,500	

de Havilland Venom FB 50 (Swiss-built Mk 1)

de Havilland Sea Venom F (AW) Mk 20

English Electric Canberra B Mk 2, bomb-bay doors open

English Electric Canberra B(I) Mk 6, No. 213 Squadron

a de Havilland Ghost engine in place of the lower-powered Goblin in the Vampire. The twin-boom arrangement was retained to keep duct losses to the minimum. To take full advantage of the increased thrust of the Ghost, new wings of reduced thickness-to-chord ratio and with a moderate sweep-back on the leading-edge were introduced. A further increase in aerodynamic efficiency was gained by mounting the long-range fuel tanks on the tips of the wings – on the Vampire they had been located at mid-span.

The Venom inherited the docile low-speed handling qualities and high-altitude manoeuvrability of the Vampire, but had a much better rate of climb and higher overall performance.

Venom FB Mk 1s went into service in 1952 with Nos. 11, 16 and 266 Squadrons. They were supplemented in 1955 by the FB Mk 4, which had power-operated ailerons, a redesigned tail unit and an ejection seat. These fighter-bomber variants were each powered by the 4,850-lb s t Ghost 103 engine, were armed with four 20-mm cannon in the nose, and could carry up to 2,000 lb of bombs or rockets. They were used operationally during the Suez Campaign in 1956. Production totalled over 350 Mk 1s and Mk 4s. In addition, an export version of the Mk 1, designated FB 50, was built under licence in Switzerland.

The Venom night fighter variants were designated NF Mk 2 and NF Mk 3. Essentially, these were Mk 1s fitted with a 4,950-lb s t Ghost 104, and with the fuselage widened to house a radar operator-navigator and lengthened to accommodate the airborne interception radar. Venom NF Mk 2s went into service in 1953, with No. 23 Squadron. They were superseded by the NF Mk 3, with an improved type of airborne interception radar, power-operated ailerons to improve manoeuvrability at high speeds, redesigned rudders and an improved clear-view hood.

A total of 60 NF Mk 2s were built and 129 NF Mk 3s.

The Sea Venom was developed from the RAF night fighter variants and was the Royal Navy's first all-weather jet fighter. Navalizing included the installation of a deck arrester hook, catapult spools and naval equipment. The wings folded to facilitate stowage.

Initial Sea Venoms, designated F(AW) Mk 20, were powered by Ghost 103 engines. They were followed by the Sea Venom F(AW) Mk 21 for the Fleet Air Arm and similar F(AW) Mk 53 for the Royal Australian Navy. These versions had an uprated Ghost 104 turbojet, power-operated ailerons, American AI radar and a clear-view canopy. An aerodynamic change was the deletion of the former tailplane extensions outboard of the booms. Late models also introduced improved Martin-Baker Mk 4 ejection seats.

The last Sea Venom variant was the F(AW) Mk 22, powered by a 5,300-lb s t Ghost 105.

All versions of the Sea Venom were armed with four 20-mm cannon in the fuselage and had provision for two 1,000-lb bombs or eight 60-lb rockets under the wings. The F(AW) 22 could carry two de Havilland Firestreak infra-red homing air-to-air missiles.

Altogether, 256 Sea Venoms were built.

English Electric Canberra

First jet bomber to serve with the RAF, the Canberra remained in production for ten years and was supplied also to numerous overseas air forces. It earned the distinction of being the only modern British aircraft to be built under licence in the United States, where it was manufactured by The Martin Company under the designation B-57.

Designed to Air Ministry Specification B.3/45, the prototype Canberra B Mk 1 flew on 13 May 1949. It was a cantilever mid-wing monoplane of all-metal stressed-skin construction. A low aspect ratio wing was chosen to ensure maximum fuel economy at the highest possible cruising altitude. Low wing loading helped to bestow upon the aircraft its fighter-like manoeuvrability.

The wing was a single-spar structure, utilizing a symmetrical high-speed aerofoil section. The ailerons were of the Irving-Westland type and incorporated spring-tabs. Wing air-brakes were fitted, consisting of drag-inducing channels which could be extended into the airflow from the top and bottom surfaces. The fuselage was a straightforward semi-monocoque structure, and the nosewheel undercarriage was also conventional, the nose unit retracting rearward into the fuselage and the main legs inward into the wing centre-section.

More than 20 different Mark numbers were allocated to British-built Canberras, some applicable to training and target towing variants and others, such as PR Mk 3, PR Mk 7 and PR Mk 9, to photo-reconnaissance aircraft. Details given below apply to bomber variants:

B Mk 1 was the designation given to the first four prototype Canberras. Designed as two-seat radar bombers, with a solid nose, three of these aircraft were powered by Rolls-Royce Avon turbojets, the other with Rolls-Royce Nenes.

The *B Mk 2* was the first production version, which entered service with No. 101 Squadron in 1951. Powered by two 6,500 lb s t Avon 101 engines, it carried a crew of three and had a transparent nose for visual bomb-aiming. Standard weapon load was 6,000 lb of bombs, including nuclear weapons, carried internally. No defensive armament was fitted, the bomber relying on its high speed to escape interception by fighters.

B Mk 6 was the next bomber variant, with 7,400-lb s t Avon 109 engines and increased fuel tankage for a longer range. This version was used against terrorists in Malaya, where it became the first RAF jet bomber to be used in action. It was also employed, with Mk 2 Canberras, during the Suez Campaign in 1956. A variant was the B(I) Mk 6, an interim intruder version, with a gun pack under the fuselage and underwing bombs, pending arrival of the B(I) Mk 8.

The *B(I) Mk 8* was a two-seat long-range night interdictor or high-altitude bomber and target marker, and was readily convertible from one rôle to the other. The usual large cockpit canopy was replaced by a fighter-type canopy, offset to port, for the pilot, and the navigator/bomb aimer was fully enclosed in the nose. In the interdictor rôle the armament consisted of underwing bombs and a detachable pack of four 20-mm Hispano cannon in the rear of the weapon-bay, plus three 1,000-lb bombs or 16 flares in the front of the bay. Export models were the B(I) Mk 12 for New Zealand and South Africa and the B(I) Mk 58 for India.

The *B Mk 15* was a conversion of the B Mk 6 bomber with two underwing attachments for 1,000-lb bombs, air-to-surface missiles or packs containing thirty-seven 2-in unguided rockets, in addition to full internal bomb-load. A camera was fitted in the nose and new radio equipment installed.

The *B Mk 16* was similar to the B Mk 15, but retained some of the radar equipment used in the Mk 6.

Altogether, 1,329 Canberras were built, including 48 B Mk 20s built in Australia and 403 Martin B-57s. Other overseas countries which purchased Canberras included Ecuador, France, Peru, Rhodesia, Sweden and Venezuela.

Fairey Hamble Baby

This aircraft represented an attempt by the Fairey Company at Hamble to improve on the Sopwith Baby seaplane of 1914. The Hamble Baby, although generally similar to the Sopwith, was virtually a new design.

English Electric Canberra B(I) Mk 8

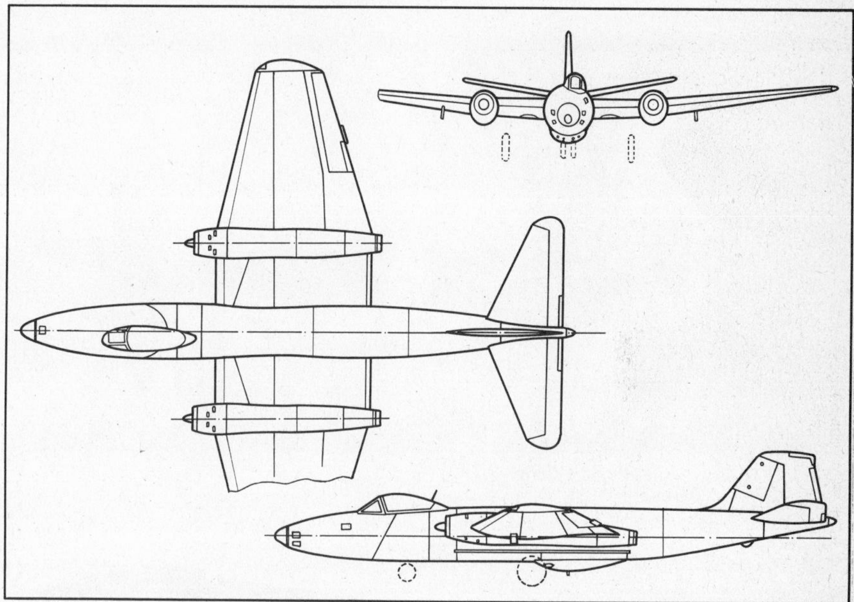

English Electric Canberra B(I) Mk 8

English Electric Canberra B Mk 16

TYPE	DIMENSIONS span ft	span in	length ft	length in	height ft	height in	WEIGHT max t-o lb	PERFORMANCE max speed mph	at height ft	service ceiling ft	combat range miles	REMARKS
Venom FB Mk 1	41	9	33	0	6	2	NA	640	NA	NA	NA	
Venom NF Mk 3	41	8	36	8	6	6	NA	630	NA	NA	1,000	
Sea Venom F(AW) Mk 21	42	10	36	7	8	6	NA	NA	NA	NA	NA	
Sea Venom F(AW) Mk 22	42	10	36	7			15,800	575	SL	NA	705	
Canberra B Mk 2	63	11	65	6	15	7	NA	NA	NA	NA	NA	
Canberra B Mk 6	63	11	65	6	15	7	55,000	541	40,000	48,000	3,400	With max load
Canberra B (I) Mk 8	63	11	65	6	15	7	56,250	541	40,000	48,000	3,630	

Fairey Hamble Baby

Fairey F.16 Campania, Eagle IV engine

Fairey F.22 Campania, 250-hp Maori engine

Fairey IIIA

Of greatest interest were the wings, which were completely redesigned and incorporated the Fairey Patent Camber Gear. This consisted of hinged trailing-edge flaps running the full length of each wing. In flight the flaps operated as ailerons in the normal manner, but they could also be lowered simultaneously as flaps to provide increased lift. This represented the first proper attempt to use flaps to increase lift, and the Camber Gear improved the Hamble Baby's load-carrying capacity.

The standard power plant consisted of a 110-hp or 130-hp Clerget engine. Armament was one Lewis machine-gun, fixed on top of the fuselage and synchronized to fire through the propeller disc. Two 65-lb bombs could be carried on racks under the fuselage.

In service with the RNAS, Hamble Babies were used for coastal patrols around Britain and for anti-submarine patrols in the Mediterranean and Aegean.

A number of Hamble Babies were produced as landplanes, with the wheels carried on the original float mounting struts, resulting in a very wide-track undercarriage. These landplanes were known as Hamble Baby Converts.

Fairey Campania

This two-seat reconnaissance seaplane was the first British aircraft developed specifically for operation from an aircraft carrier. Produced in 1916, it was designed to operate from the former Cunard passenger liner, the *Campania*, which had been converted into a carrier in 1915. Thus the Fairey Campania took its name from its intended mother ship.

Construction of the Campania was conventional, consisting of a wire-braced wooden structure, fabric-covered. The upper of the two-bay wings had a considerable extension, supported by a king-post above the outer interplane struts and braced by wires. To facilitate stowage on board ship, the wings could be folded. The long fuselage had a large tail float with a water rudder.

The first prototype was powered by a 250-hp Rolls-Royce Eagle IV engine; the second had the more powerful 275-hp Rolls-Royce Eagle V and embodied several other changes, including a more efficient wing aerofoil section. To improve the pilot's view upward, the trailing-edge of the centre-section of the top wing was cut away, and the wing-tip floats, formerly attached directly to the underside of the wings, were supported on short struts. A larger fin and rudder were fitted.

Armament consisted of one Lewis machine-gun on a Scarff ring-mounting in the rear cockpit, and a small bomb-load could be carried on racks beneath the fuselage.

The light construction of the floats made sea take-offs hazardous; so, to enable the seaplane to take off from the carrier a small wheeled trolley was developed, which fell away as the aircraft became airborne.

Owing to the heavy demand for Rolls-Royce Eagle engines, a number of Campanias were fitted with the 250-hp Sunbeam Maori II. Later still, some Campanias had the 345-hp Rolls-Royce Eagle VIII engine. The first machine to have the Sunbeam Maori carried the works number F.22, and Campanias with this engine are often referred to as F.22s. For similar reasons, Campanias with the Rolls-Royce Eagle V engine are known as F.17s.

In service Campanias had an undistinguished career, being used mainly for patrol duties in British home waters. In 1919, patrols were made from the seaplane carrier *Nairana*, at Archangel, against the Bolsheviks.

Fairey IIIA

The Fairey IIIA ship-borne two-seat biplane was intended as a replacement for the Sopwith 1½-Strutters which, by the end of 1917, were becoming obsolete.

The prototype was a landplane conversion of the experimental Fairey F.128 seaplane, officially known as "No. 10" because of its serial number, and was a relatively large aircraft. The conversion was effected mainly by replacing the floats with a simple Vee-undercarriage, and replacing the two original radiator blocks of the 260-hp Sunbeam Maori II engine, on each side of the cowling, by a single radiator behind the propeller.

Armament consisted of a single Lewis machine-gun in the rear cockpit, on a Scarff ring-mounting. Bombs could be carried on external racks.

The two-bay wings, which could be folded, were of equal span, and were fitted with Fairey Patent Camber Gear (trailing-edge flaps: see Hamble Baby entry).

Fifty IIIAs were built, and a few saw active service with the RAF; but the 1918 Armistice prevented their combat capabilities from being fully established. By 1919 the IIIA was officially considered obsolete.

Twenty-five Fairey IIIB bomber seaplanes were also built for the RNAS, with Maori engines. Although generally similar to the IIIA, they had extended upper wings spanning 62 ft 9 in.

Fairey IIIC

Last of the Fairey III series to be produced during the 1914–18 War, the type IIIC was a two-seat general duties seaplane. It was conventional in both general configuration and construction. The two-bay wings were of equal span, and the fuselage and float undercarriage were the same as on earlier aircraft in the series.

The major technical improvement offered by the IIIC over its predecessors was its 375-hp Rolls-Royce Eagle. This improved the power-to-weight ratio by over one-quarter, giving the IIIC its excellent performance.

Standard armament consisted of one fixed forward-firing Vickers machine-gun, synchronized to fire between the propeller blades, and one Lewis machine-gun on a Scarff ring-mounting in the rear cockpit. Small bombs could be carried on racks under the fuselage.

Thirty-five IIICs were built, but were too late to see service during the war. After the Armistice, they formed part of the equipment of the North Russian Expeditionary Force in 1919, when they operated from the aircraft carrier HMS *Pegasus*. In 1921 they were superseded by the more efficient and better known Fairey IIID.

Fairey IIID

Developed from the IIIC of 1918, the IIID was the first of the Fairey III series to enter service in large numbers. It was a three-seat reconnaissance aircraft which could be flown either as a landplane from carriers or shore stations, or as a seaplane catapulted from warships.

Externally the IIID was generally similar to its predecessor, being a conventional biplane with equal-span two-bay wings. The wings incorporated the Fairey Patent Camber Gear, originally developed for the Hamble Baby. This consisted of flaps running the full length of the trailing-edges. In flight the outer sections acted as ailerons in the normal manner, but for landing and take-off they could be lowered with the inner sections to increase lift. A minimum number of changes appear to have been made to accommodate the third cockpit for a second observer. Twin main floats were fitted on the seaplane version and, as on the IIIC, the tail float was mounted directly beneath the tail of the fuselage, with the wing-tip floats on short struts directly below the outer interplane struts.

Armament consisted of one forward-firing Vickers machine-gun, synchronized to fire between the propeller

Fairey IIIB

Fairey IIIC

Fairey IIID. No. 202 Squadron, Lion engine

TYPE	DIMENSIONS span ft	span in	length ft	length in	height ft	height in	WEIGHT max t-o lb	PERFORMANCE max speed mph	at height ft	service ceiling ft	combat range miles	REMARKS
Fairey Hamble Baby	27	9	23	4	9	6	1,946	90	2,000	7,600	NA	Endurance 6 hours
Campania	61	7	43	1	15	1	5,706	82	2,000	6,900	NA	275-hp Eagle V
Campania	61	7	43	1	15	1	5,329	85	SL	6,000	NA	250-hp Maori II
Campania	61	7	43	1	15	1	5,657	80	2,000	5,500	NA	345-hp Eagle VIII
Fairey IIIA	46	2	31	0	10	8	3,945	97	10,000	13,500	NA	
Fairey IIIC	46	1	36	0	12	2	4,800	110	2,000	15,000	NA	Endurance 5½ hours
Fairey IIID	46	1	37	0	11	4	4,918	106	NA	17,000	550	Eagle VIII

Fairey IIID, Lion V engine

Fairey Flycatcher

Fairey Flycatcher amphibian.

blades, and one Lewis machine-gun on a Scarff ring in the aft cockpit.

The IIID achieved a reputation for ruggedness, due to its sturdy construction, and of reliability due to the excellent performance of its 375-hp Rolls-Royce Eagle VIII or 450-hp Napier Lion IIB, V or VA engine, the Lion being the standard power plant.

The prototype first flew in August 1920, and the first service units, FAA Flights 441 and 444, were formed in 1924. The aircraft of No. 441 Flight were landplanes, with arrester hooks on their axles. They were operated from the carrier HMS *Argus*, which had fore-and-aft arrester wires; but several accidents occurred and the arrester hooks were removed in 1926. The aircraft of No. 444 Flight, based in HMS *Vindictive*, were seaplanes.

During the Chinese rebellion of 1927, Fairey IIIDs went to the aid of the Shanghai Defence Force.

A total of 207 Fairey IIIDs were built, the last being delivered to the FAA in 1926.

Fairey Flycatcher

Designed to meet Air Ministry Specification 6/22, the Flycatcher was a standard first-line single-seat carrier-borne fighter of the Fleet Air Arm throughout the period from 1923 to 1934.

It had a distinctive appearance, and incorporated a number of unconventional features. The equal-span single-bay wings were fitted with the Fairey Patent Camber Gear which had first been seen on the Hamble Baby of 1916. This consisted of flaps running along the entire trailing-edges of both wings. In flight the outer sections acted as ailerons in the normal manner, but for landing and take-off they could be lowered simultaneously with the inner sections. This materially shortened the take-off and landing runs, and steepened the glide path. The take-off run of the Flycatcher was in fact, short enough to enable the aircraft to operate from platforms mounted on the gun turrets of capital ships. It was the last FAA fighter to use this technique.

The fuselage, of composite wood and metal construction, covered with fabric, was likewise distinctive. An upsweep on the underside, combined with a low aspect ratio fin, gave it the impression of being "cocked-up" in flight. Completing the picture was an ungainly undercarriage, which could be interchanged with twin floats or combined wheels and floats for amphibious operations. On early aircraft, the wheel undercarriage spreader bar carried two steel jaws to engage the fore-and-aft arrester wires then in use. The Flycatcher was also the first FAA aircraft to have hydraulic wheel-brakes and with these the landing run was as short as 50 yards.

Unusually for a carrier type, the wings did not fold; but the whole airframe was built so that it could be dismantled quickly into sections not exceeding 13 ft 6 in in length to facilitate stowage.

Armament consisted of two fixed forward-firing Vickers machine-guns, synchronized to fire between the propeller blades. Four 20-lb bombs could be carried on racks beneath the wings.

The standard engine was a 400-hp Armstrong Siddeley Jaguar IV.

Production machines began to come off the assembly line in 1923 and entered service with No. 402 Flight in the same year. During the next decade they served in all the British carriers of the day and established a reputation the equal of many aircraft that were built in greater numbers or able to achieve fame in times of war.

Flycatchers were easy to fly, easy to land and yet highly manoeuvrable – so much so that pilots sometimes performed an exuberant slow roll immediately after take-off. Pilots and deck crews became so proficient in handling the aircraft that on one occasion six were landed and stowed below deck in 4 minutes 20 seconds. To speed up operations on board the carriers *Furious*, *Courageous* and *Glorious*, the aircraft could be flown straight out of the hangar deck and over the bows from a 60-ft tapered runway below the main deck. During this "slip-flight" operation, the Flycatchers usually dropped and almost touched the water before climbing away.

The aircraft's ruggedness and good diving qualities

enabled the FAA to develop a tactic known as converging bombing. In this, three Flycatchers attacked the same target simultaneously from different directions, diving almost vertically from an altitude of 2,000 ft. The technique became one of the most thrilling show-pieces of the great Hendon Air Displays in the 1920s.

Altogether, 192 Flycatchers were built; the type was declared obsolete in 1935.

Fairey Fawn

The Fawn was the first new light day-bomber to go into service with the RAF after the 1914–18 War. It was a two-seat landplane development of the experimental Pintail amphibian, and was designed originally for army reconnaissance duties. The prototype, designed to Specification 5/21, first flew in March 1923. Two subsequent prototypes had a longer fuselage to improve longitudinal stability; these, and the initial production machines, built to Specification 20/23, were designated Fawn IIs. Later aircraft were designated Fawn IIIs.

The Fawn was a biplane with two-bay equal-span wings. Construction was primarily of wood, fabric-covered. The engine was a 470-hp Napier Lion II. Armament consisted of one fixed forward-firing Vickers machine-gun, mounted on top of the fuselage and synchronized to fire between the propeller blades, and a single Lewis gun on a Scarff ring-mounting in the rear cockpit. Maximum bomb-load was 460 lb.

The Fawn went into service in 1923, and production ceased in 1926 after a total of 70 had been built.

Fairey Fox

The Fox was a two-seat day bomber, developed as a private venture. The prototype first flew on 3 January 1925 and attracted immediate attention by not only being some 50 mph faster than contemporary day bombers built to official Air Ministry Specifications, but by demonstrating its capability of outpacing the fighters of the day.

The reason for this impressive performance was the Fox's clean aerodynamic form. It was a single-bay biplane of conventional wood and fabric construction, but great care was taken during its design and manufacture to reduce drag to a minimum. All unnecessary projections and fittings were eliminated or carefully faired in. The observer's Lewis machine-gun, instead of being mounted on the conventional Scarff ring-mounting, was carried on a specially designed "high-speed" mounting. A single fixed Vickers gun was synchronized to fire between the propeller blades. Maximum bomb-load was 460 lb.

Main credit for the aircraft's low drag went to the American 480-hp Curtiss D.12 liquid-cooled engine. Of low frontal area, this was enclosed in a neat and closely-fitting cowling, carefully faired to match the fuselage contour. Its use reflected the forward thinking of Sir Richard Fairey who, during a visit to the USA in 1923, had seen the D.12 engine and immediately realized its great potential in an aircraft like the Fox.

In October 1925, the prototype was demonstrated before Air Chief Marshal Sir Hugh Trenchard, who instructed that a complete squadron be ordered at once. Production Foxes, built to Air Ministry Specification 21/25 and designated Mk Is, appeared in 1926 and were

Fairey Fawn II

Fairey Fox Mk I

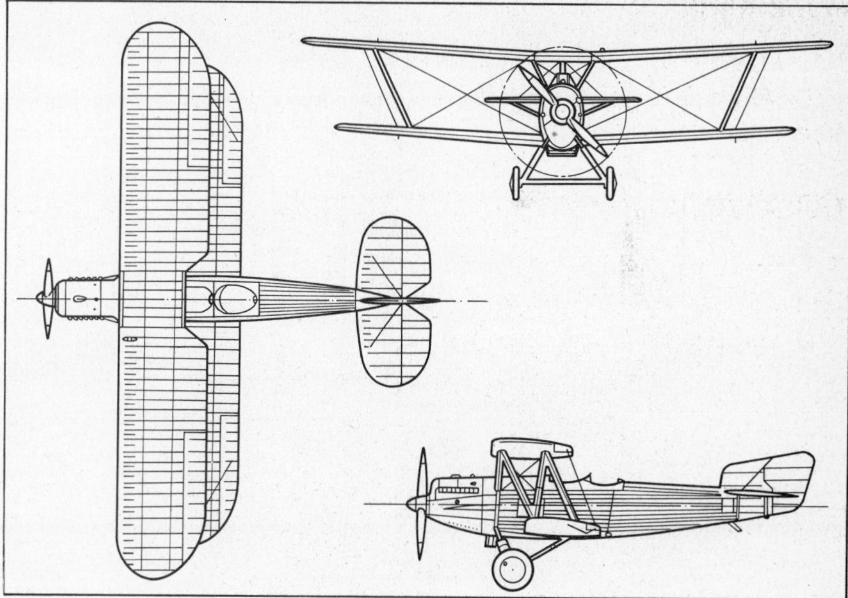
Fairey Fox Mk I

TYPE	DIMENSIONS span ft	span in	length ft	length in	height ft	height in	WEIGHT max t-o lb	PERFORMANCE max speed mph	at height ft	service ceiling ft	combat range miles	REMARKS
Flycatcher	29	0	23	0	12	0	2,979	133	5,000	19,000	311	Landplane
Flycatcher	29	0	29	0	13	4	3,579	126	5,000	14,000	311	Amphibian
Fawn II	49	11	32	1	11	11	5,834	114	NA	13,850	650	
Fawn III	49	11	32	1	11	11	NA	NA	NA	NA	NA	
Fox Mk I	38	0	31	2	10	8	4,117	156	SL	17,000	500	
Fox Mk IA	38	0	31	2	10	8	NA	NA	NA	NA	NA	

Fairey Fox Mk IA

Fairey IIIF Mk I

Fairey IIIF Mk III floatplane

Fairey IIIF Mk IV, all-metal version

issued to No. 12 Squadron at Andover, replacing the unit's Fawns. For the next five years, until it was re-equipped with Hawker Harts in 1931, No. 12 was the envy of all other squadrons. During exercises, its pilots proved the superiority of the Fox by consistently out-flying the opposing forces. In particular during the 1928 exercises, they succeeded in evading *all* the fighter defences. This unique period in the Squadron's history is commemorated by the emblem of a fox in its official badge.

It is remarkable that, in spite of such outstanding performance, only 28 Foxes were built for the RAF, owing to the stringent financial economies being practised by the British authorities during this period. Some were re-engined after a time, with Rolls-Royce Kestrels. Designated Fox Mk IA, they conformed with Air Ministry Specification 1/27. Many other Fairey Foxes were, however, built by Avions Fairey in Belgium (see page 48).

Fairey IIIF

Built to Air Ministry Specification 19/24, the prototype IIIF first flew on 19 March 1926. A total of 622 were built subsequently, of which more than 340 were delivered to the FAA as three-seat spotter-reconnaissance aircraft, making the IIIF the most widely-used type in that service between the wars. Versions delivered to the RAF were equipped as two-seat general-purpose biplanes to replace types such as the Bristol Fighter and D.H.9A.

The first production IIIF Mk I, powered by a 450-hp Napier Lion VA engine, flew in February 1927. This version entered service with the FAA in the following year, superseding the IIIDs of No. 440 Flight and forming the initial equipment of Nos. 445 and 446 Flights.

It was a conventional biplane, with wood and fabric equal-span two-bay wings of relatively high aspect ratio. The fuselage, comprising a braced all-metal structure with fabric covering, was of fine aerodynamic form, continuing the lines of the closely-cowled engine. Pilot, observer and wireless-telegraphist/gunner were accommodated in tandem in open cockpits.

Armament consisted of one fixed Vickers gun, synchronized to fire between the propeller blades, and one Lewis gun on a Scarff ring-mounting or Fairey high-speed mounting in the rear cockpit. Up to 500 lb of bombs could be carried on underwing racks.

The prototype IIIF Mk II, with the more powerful Lion XI engine, flew in August 1927 and was followed by 32 producton models for the FAA.

A further change of designation, to IIIF Mk III signified the transition from composite to all-metal construction. The wings of this version had corrugated drawn-tube spars with pressed ribs clipped on. The first Mk III flew for the first time on 26 March 1929, powered by a 570-hp Lion XIA engine, and this power plant remained standard on all subsequent IIIFs built for the FAA. The last batch of 10 Mk IIIs were fitted with dual controls for training duties.

Following the Mark III came the IIIB. Of all-metal construction, it had a specially strengthened fuselage to permit catapulting. The prototype flew on 6 June 1930 and a total of 166 were produced, the last of which was delivered in September 1932.

The naval IIIFs served all over the world and operated from every aircraft carrier of the Royal Navy. A twin-float seaplane version of Mk IIIB was used widely for reconnaissance duties on board battleships and cruisers being catapulted into action. Fairey IIIFs were also operated from catapults on aircraft carriers such as the *Hermes* and *Glorious*.

Landings on carriers were made without the assistance of arrester wires, as the IIIF served during the period when the original longitudinal wires had fallen out of favour and transverse wires had not yet been adopted. One IIIF was, however, used for early experiments with the rear-fuselage type of arrester hook which was to be standardized on carrier-borne biplanes in the 1930s.

Three IIIFs were used for early radio-controlled pilotless aircraft experiments. Known as Fairie Queens they had increased dihedral on their wings to improve stability. Other IIIFs, equipped with a windmill-driven winch, towed aerial targets for naval gunnery practice.

The IIIF was the last FAA aircraft designed specifically for reconnaissance duties and remained in service until January 1940.

IIIF Mk IVs for the RAF were produced in both composite and all-metal forms. Most were despatched to the Middle East for general-purpose duties, but one squadron was based at Northolt for communications work while two others formed part of the home day bomber force. Except for having only two seats, RAF aircraft were generally similar to their FAA counterparts.

Fairey Gordon

This two-seat day bomber and general-purpose aircraft was a development of the Fairey IIIF, and for a short time was known as the IIIF Mk V. It was a biplane, with equal-span two-bay wings of relatively high aspect ratio, and had the Fairey Patent Camber Gear fitted to the trailing-edge of both wings. The fuselage, comprising a braced all-metal structure with fabric covering, retained the fine lines of the IIIF. A neat V-strutted undercarriage was fitted.

The major change between the two types was the installation of a 525-hp Armstrong Siddeley Panther IIA air-cooled radial engine in place of the Napier Lion, which improved performance appreciably, particularly during take-off. The re-engining involved considerable design changes, including structural modifications to the front of the fuselage and redesigned fuel, oil and electrical systems. One unusual change involved mounting the Vickers machine-gun externally on the port side of the fuselage, instead of housing it within a blast trough.

Armament consisted of this Vickers gun, synchronized to fire between the propeller blades, and a Lewis machine-gun on a Scarff ring-mounting or Fairey high-speed mounting in the rear cockpit. The Gordon's maximum bomb load was 460 lb.

The prototype, a converted IIIF Mk IVB, first flew in 1930 and was followed by production aircraft built to Specification 18/30. These early models, designated Mk I, went into service in April 1931.

A later batch, to Specification 14/33, had a modified rear fuselage, Frise ailerons and a redesigned tail assembly, and were designated Mk II.

Production of the Gordon totalled 160 aircraft, plus about 30 IIIFs which were converted into Gordons.

Fairey Hendon

Known initially as the Fairey Night Bomber, the Hendon was a cantilever low-wing monoplane of rather advanced design for its time, with a crew of five.

The wing had a centre-section of uniform chord and thickness, built integrally with the fuselage. The outer wings tapered in chord and thickness. Construction was all-metal, internally braced by the Fairey pyramid principle and covered with fabric.

The deep fuselage was a metal structure, faired to an oval section and covered with fabric. The distinctive undercarriage consisted of two separate main units, carefully faired into the underside of the wing and braced by an inclined strut to the underside of the wing.

The prototype Hendon, which flew in November 1931, had two 460-hp Bristol Jupiter X radial engines, but was

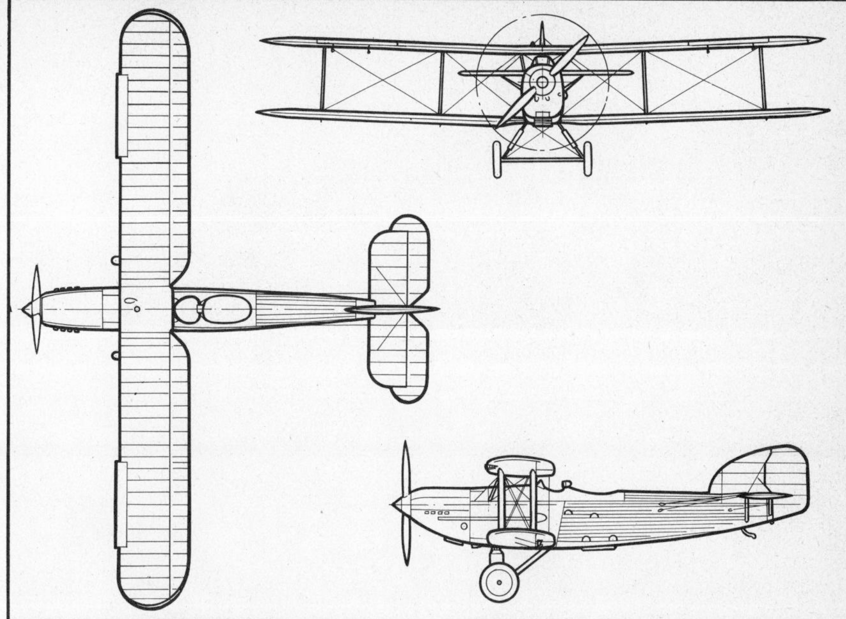

Fairey IIIF Mk IV

Fairey Gordon, No. 40 Squadron

Fairey Gordon, No. 6 Squadron

TYPE	DIMENSIONS span ft	span in	length ft	length in	height ft	height in	WEIGHT max t-o lb	PERFORMANCE max speed mph	at height ft	service ceiling ft	combat range miles	REMARKS
Fairey IIIF Mk I	45	9	34	4	14	3	NA	NA	NA	NA	NA	
Fairey IIIF Mk II	45	9	34	4	14	3	NA	NA	NA	NA	NA	
Fairey IIIF Mk III	45	9	34	4	14	3	NA	NA	NA	NA	NA	
Fairey IIIF Mk IIIB	45	9	34	4	14	3	6,301	120	10,000	20,000	NA	Endurance 4 hours
Fairey IIIF Mk IIIB	45	9	34	6	14	3	NA	NA	NA	NA	NA	Seaplane
Gordon Mk I	45	9	36	9	14	2	5,906	145	3,000	22,000	600	

Fairey Hendon prototype, Jupiter engines

Fairey Hendon Mk II

Fairey Swordfish Mk I

Fairey Swordfish Mk I floatplane

re-engined subsequently with two 480-hp Rolls-Royce Kestrel IIIS liquid-cooled Vee engines. The production version had 600-hp Kestrel VI engines, mounted on the centre-section and faired into the leading-edge. The radiators were mounted below the engine nacelles and in front of the main undercarriage units into which they were faired.

Armament consisted of a single Lewis machine-gun in a turret in the nose, one gun in a dorsal position halfway along the fuselage and another in the extreme tail, behind the twin-finned tail unit. A bomb-load of up to 1,660 lb was carried internally, within the deep centre-section.

Production Hendons were designated Mk II and went into service in 1936 with No. 38 Squadron, becoming the first low-wing cantilever monoplanes to serve with the RAF. No. 38 was the only squadron completely equipped with Hendons, of which 14 were built.

Fairey Swordfish

The Swordfish carrier-borne torpedo-spotter-reconnaissance biplane is one of the best remembered of all the British combat aircraft used in World War II. It was certainly the most famous type ever used by the FAA, and had the unique distinction of outlasting its "replacement", the Albacore, which was withdrawn from first-line service towards the end of 1943, whereas nine squadrons of Swordfish were still operational at the end of the war!

The story of this remarkable aircraft started in 1933, when the Fairey Company produced the TSR.I as a private venture. This was a biplane essentially similar to the Swordfish, and although the prototype was lost in an accident, its performance was sufficiently proved for it to be followed by a second, slightly larger, aircraft, the TSR.II. This flew for the first time in April 1934 and, following successful official tests, was adopted by the Air Ministry and named the Swordfish.

The Swordfish had single-bay biplane wings of almost-equal span. Of metal construction and fabric-covered, these comprised a wide centre-section and outer wings which could be folded aft to facilitate stowage. The upper centre-section was carried on a pyramid structure and incorporated a hoisting sling; the lower centre-section stubs were braced to the fuselage upper longerons by a pair of inverted V-struts. Ailerons were fitted to all four wings and the top wings had Handley Page slots.

The fuselage was a rectangular steel-tube structure, faired to an oval section and covered forward with quickly-detachable metal panels and aft with fabric. It was stressed for catapulting and was equipped with an arrester hook.

The undercarriage was of the divided-axle type. Each main unit consisted of an oleo shock-absorber leg, the top of which was anchored to the end of the lower centre-section front spar, while the lower end was hinged to the fuselage by the axle and forwardly-inclined radius rod. Medium-pressure types and pneumatic brakes were standard, but the wheel undercarriage was interchangeable with twin floats of special design.

Standard armament consisted of one fixed Vickers machine-gun, synchronized to fire between the propeller blades, and one Lewis or Vickers K machine-gun in the rear cockpit, on a Fairey high-speed gun mounting. The crutch between the undercarriage legs could carry either one 18-in, 1,610-lb torpedo or one 1,500-lb mine; alternatively, 1,500 lb of bombs could be carried, consisting either of two 500-lb and two 250-lb bombs, or three 500-lb bombs. Mk II Swordfish could carry eight 60-lb rockets, instead of the torpedo or bombs.

Pre-production Swordfish began to come off the assembly line in December 1935, and were delivered to the FAA in February 1936. Production aircraft, built to Air Ministry Specification S.38/34 and powered by a 690-hp Bristol Pegasus IIIM3 air-cooled radial engine, were designated Swordfish Mk I and went into service in July 1936, with No. 825 Squadron. By 1938 the Swordfish was the only torpedo-bomber in FAA service, and when war started in 1939 thirteen squadrons of Swordfish formed the spearhead of its offensive force.

During the war years a further thirteen first-line squadrons were equipped with this remarkable biplane.

In service, the quality of the Swordfish which earned it the affection of its pilots was its superb handling characteristics, particularly at low speeds, which made it particularly suitable for carrier-borne operations. This was also the main reason for its continued operational use when, by normal standards, it had long been obsolete. Only the Swordfish could land safely on a carrier deck pitching 20 to 30 ft up and down, in the dark. Only the Swordfish could have managed the feat of taking off from the torpedoed and sinking escort carrier *Nabob* when the stricken ship's deck was sloping *upward* towards the bows at about 20 degrees. All this and more the Swordfish did, in spite of its archaic appearance which earned it the nickname "Stringbag".

In the early months of the war, Swordfish were engaged on convoy and fleet protection duties. During the Norwegian campaign of 1940, they carried out the first co-ordinated torpedo attack ever launched from a carrier. Also during this campaign, Swordfish began minelaying, for which duty fuel tanks were fitted in the rear cockpit and the aircraft operated with a crew of two.

A few months later, other Swordfish carried out their epic attack on the Italian fleet at Taranto, which knocked out their three battleships, a cruiser, two destroyers and two auxiliary ships and altered the balance of naval power during a critical period of the war. During the same year, Malta-based Swordfish sank an average of 50,000 tons of enemy shipping a month for nine months.

In 1943 the Swordfish Mk II appeared. This had a strengthened lower wing for carrying and launching eight 60-lb rockets; previously, Swordfish Is had been used to test the suitability of this deadly new armament for FAA operations. Later batches of Mk II aircraft were fitted with the 750-hp Pegasus XXX engine.

The final production version was the Mk III. This had a radome below the fuselage housing an ASV Mk X radar scanner.

The Swordfish Mk IV was a conversion of earlier Marks for use in Canada and had an enclosed cockpit.

At the beginning of 1945, after nine years' service, nine first-line FAA squadrons were still equipped with Swordfish, and an aircraft of this type, serving with the RAF, attacked a midget submarine only 3½ hours before the German surrender. Less than a fortnight later, on 21 May 1945, the last FAA Swordfish squadron was disbanded.

A total of 2,391 Swordfish were built.

Fairey Battle

The Battle, a three-seat single-engined light bomber, was one of the key types selected for the RAF expansion programme in the mid-1930s. It was an all-metal cantilever low-wing monoplane, powered by a 1,030-hp Rolls-Royce Merlin I, II, III or V engine. The wings, tapered in chord and thickness, were built integrally with the fuselage. Each was built up on two spars, of girder-section at the root changing to a flanged-beam section at the tips. The metal ribs were pressed from sheet and incorporated flanged lightening holes and cut-outs for the Z-section skin stringers. Split trailing-edge flaps extended from the aileron to the fuselage on each side.

The oval fuselage was built in two sections. The front section, extending from the pilot's cockpit to the engine, was a bolted tubular structure covered with detachable metal panels. The rear section was a metal monocoque, stiffened with frames and stringers. The main undercarriage retracted rearward into the wing, leaving a

Fairey Swordfish Mk III

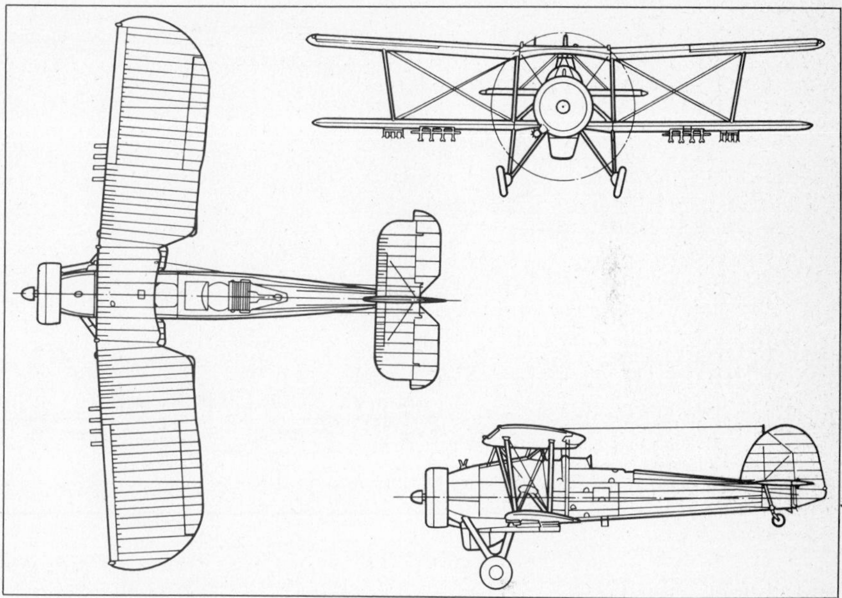

Fairey Swordfish Mk III

Fairey Battle, Belgian Air Force

TYPE	DIMENSIONS						WEIGHT	PERFORMANCE				REMARKS
	span		length		height		max t-o	max speed	at height	service ceiling	combat range	
	ft	in	ft	in	ft	in	lb	mph	ft	ft	miles	
Hendon Mk II	101	9	60	9	18	8	20,000	155	15,000	21,500	1,360	
Swordfish Mk I	45	6	36	4	12	10	9,250	139	4,750	10,700	1,030	For reconnaissance

Fairey Battle Mk I, Merlin III engine

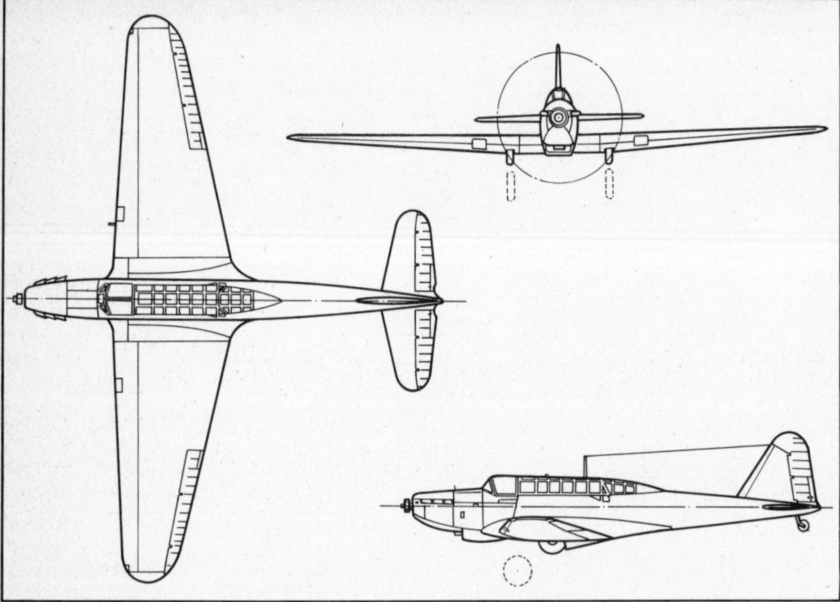
Fairey Battle Mk I

Fairey Albacore

Fairey Albacore

portion of each wheel protruding beneath the lower surface. The three cockpits were arranged in tandem and were covered with a continuous transparent fairing, with a sliding section over the pilot's cockpit and a hinged section over the rear cockpit giving free and sheltered use of the rear gun.

Armament consisted of one 0·303-in machine-gun in the starboard wing, and a Vickers K gun on a special mounting in the rear cockpit. Maximum bomb-load was 1,000 lb, stowed internally in four cells in the wings.

The Battle was designed to meet the requirements of Air Ministry Specification P.27/32, issued in 1933. The prototype first flew in March 1936 and production Battles went into service in 1937 with Nos. 52 and 63 Squadrons. By 1938, fifteen squadrons were equipped with the type. Production continued until 1941 and reached a total of 2,419 aircraft.

Although the Battle carried twice the weight of bombs twice as far as the biplane Harts and Hinds it replaced, it was already obsolescent when war started in 1939. However, it had to form the vanguard of the British Advanced Air Striking Force in France, and on 20 September 1939 a rear-gunner claimed the first German aircraft shot down during the war in the West. That the Battle was, however, outclassed was indicated on 30 September 1939, when four out of a flight of five were destroyed by Bf 109s.

During the German advance through the Low Countries, the RAF's first VCs were won – posthumously – with Battles during a heroic attack on 10 May 1940 against the bridges at Maastricht. Ten days later, during an all-out attack against German pontoon bridges at Sedan, 40 Battles were lost out of a striking force of 71.

After their withdrawal from bomber squadrons, Battles were diverted to training, large numbers being sent to Canada for use under the Commonwealth Air Training Plan. Some Battle Trainers had two separate cockpits. Other Battles became target tugs at Air Gunnery Schools.

Fairey Albacore

The Albacore was a carrier-borne torpedo-bomber, designed to Air Ministry Specification S.41/36 as a replacement for the Swordfish. It was a biplane, with equal-span single-bay wings of metal construction, with fabric covering. The wings folded rearward to facilitate stowage on board carriers. Hydraulically-operated flaps were fitted which could be used as air-brakes for dive-bombing.

Of most interest structurally was the fuselage which, being of all-metal monocoque construction, was unusual for a biplane. The crew of three sat in enclosed cockpits which could be electrically heated. An inflatable dinghy was carried and was ejected automatically if the aircraft ditched. The undercarriage was of the divided type, with faired legs.

Early Albacores were powered by a 1,065-hp Bristol Taurus II fourteen-cylinder sleeve-valve air-cooled engine, but later aircraft had the 1,130-hp Taurus XII.

Armament consisted of one fixed Vickers machine-gun in the starboard wing, firing forward, and two Vickers K machine-guns in the rear cockpit. One 18-in, 1,610-lb torpedo could be carried beneath the fuselage, or six 250-lb or four 500-lb bombs on racks under the wings.

Albacores went into service with the FAA in March 1940, with No. 826 Squadron, which was formed specially to operate the new aircraft. Compared with the Swordfish, it offered a distinct improvement in many respects. The crew compartment was much better, and the smooth-running sleeve-valve engine, with its variable-pitch propeller, provided both an excellent take-off performance and economical cruising. In spite of this, some pilots preferred the "Stringbag", and instead of replacing the Swordfish, the Albacore merely supplemented the older machine.

An unusual task for Albacores was the dropping of more than 12,000 flares during the two months prior to the battle of El Alamein, high-lighting the disposition of Rommel's troops. Albacore production ceased in 1943, by which time a total of 800 had been built. They served with distinction at the Battle of Matapan and in countless other actions at sea and ashore.

Fairey Fulmar

The Fulmar was a two-seat carrier-borne fighter designed to Air Ministry Specification O.8/38. It introduced into the FAA the same weight of fire-power – eight 0·303-in machine-guns – enjoyed by the RAF in the Hurricane and Spitfire. It did not, however have the performance of its land-based counterparts, owing to the additional weight of the navigator and equipment required to ensure the aircraft's safe rendezvous with its carrier after a mission. Most serious was the lack of speed, which meant that unless a pilot scored with his opening burst of fire, usually delivered during a diving attack from the rear, he rarely got a second chance.

The Fulmar was a cantilever monoplane, of all-metal stressed-skin construction, with folding wings to facilitate stowage on board carriers. The monocoque fuselage incorporated deck-arrester gear, catapult points and stowage for an inflatable dinghy. It was of fine aerodynamic form, with the navigator's cockpit separated from the pilot and enclosed by a transparent cover which followed the fuselage contour. The main undercarriage retracted inward into the wing roots.

Armament consisted of the eight fixed 0·303-in Browning machine-guns in the wings; in addition some aircraft had a single Vickers K gun in the rear cockpit.

Fulmar Mk Is, powered by a 1,080-hp Rolls-Royce Merlin VIII engine, went into service with the FAA in June 1940, with No. 808 Squadron. A total of 250 Mk Is were built, followed by 350 Mk IIs with 1,300-hp Merlin XXXs and tropical equipment.

Fairey Firefly

The Firefly was a two-seat carrier-borne fighter-reconnaissance aircraft. It had excellent all-round performance, the handling qualities at the lower end of the speed range being particularly good, and it was, perhaps, the best British specialized shipboard aeroplane produced during World War II.

Designed to meet the exacting Naval Specification N. 5/40, the Firefly was of all-metal stressed-skin construction, and was exceptionally clean aerodynamically. Of elliptical planform, the wings were fitted with Fairey-Youngman flaps. Essentially a secondary lifting aerofoil, these were normally housed flush with the wing contour, but could be extended beneath the trailing-edge in the line of flight to improve cruising speed and manoeuvrability. They could also be lowered at an angle to act as conventional flaps during take-off and landing. The wings folded.

The Firefly was armed with four fixed 20-mm cannon, this representing the heaviest concentration of fire-power provided up to that time for a carrier-borne fighter. Up to 2,000 lb of bombs or eight 60-lb rockets could be carried under the wings.

Initial production aircraft, powered by the 1,730-hp Rolls-Royce Griffon IIB engine, went into service with No. 1770 Squadron in October 1943, under the designation F Mk 1. Later machines had a redesigned pilot's canopy, giving more headroom, and fairings for the cannon barrels, which protruded from the wings. The 471st and subsequent aircraft were powered by the 1,990-hp Griffon XII.

The F 1 was superseded by the FR 1, a fighter-reconnaissance version incorporating ASH ship and submarine-detection radar, and was followed by the NF 2, a night-fighting variant with the secret AI Mk X

Fairey Fulmar Mk I

Fairey Fulmar Mk II

Fairey Firefly Mk I

TYPE	DIMENSIONS span ft	span in	length ft	length in	height ft	height in	WEIGHT max t-o lb	PERFORMANCE max speed mph	at height ft	service ceiling ft	combat range miles	REMARKS
Battle	54	0	52	2	15	6	10,792	241	13,000	23,500	1,050	
Albacore	50	0	39	9	15	3	12,600	161	4,000	15,000	710	
Fulmar Mk I	46	4	40	3	14	0	9,800	280	NA	26,000	800	

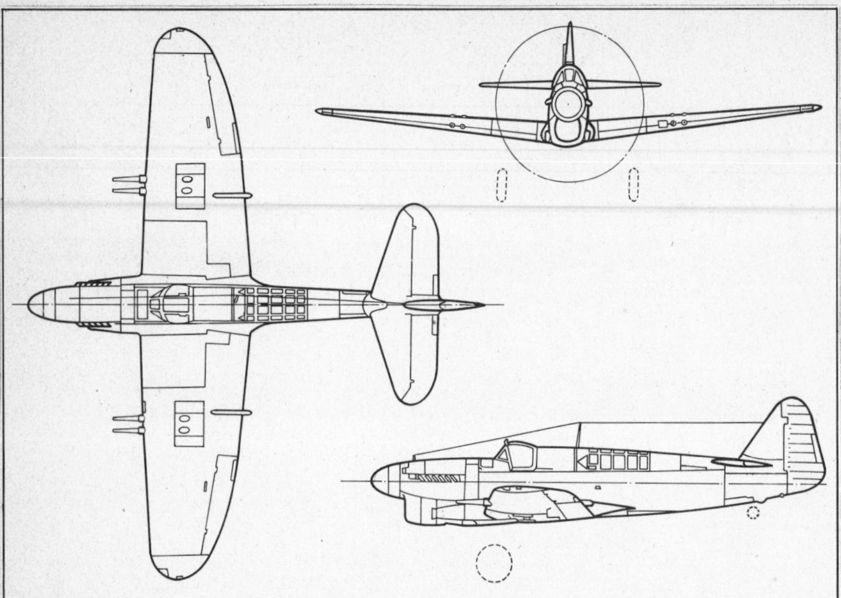
Fairey Firefly Mk 1

Fairey Firefly FR Mk 4

Fairey Firefly AS Mk 7

Fairey Barracuda Mk III

radar for the detection of enemy aircraft. The scanners for this equipment were mounted in two prominent radomes on the wing leading-edge, inboard of the cannon. To offset the CG changes caused by the heavy components of this early radar equipment, the fuselage was lengthened by 18 inches.

With the development of more compact radar, it was found possible to accommodate this in a container beneath the centre-section, permitting easy modification of F 1s for night fighter duties. Aircraft modified in this way were designated NF 1, and incorporated a radar pod beneath the fuselage, and shrouded exhausts. Final operational variant of the Mk 1 was the Firefly F 1A, which was the F 1 converted to FR 1 standard by the addition of ASH radar.

F Mk 3 was the designation given to a Firefly F 1 powered by a two-stage two-speed Griffon 61 engine. Trials proved the installation unsatisfactory, and it was decided to undertake an extensive redesign, the resulting aircraft being designated Mk 4.

When the fully-modified Mk 4 made its first appearance, it had notably different external characteristics. The radiators were housed in extensions of the centre-section leading-edges, the wing-tips were clipped, the leading-edge of the fin extended and two large fairings appeared beneath the wings, that on the port side housing auxiliary fuel, while a radar scanner was accommodated in the starboard fairing. Finally, a four-blade propeller replaced the earlier three-blade type.

The Mk 4s were followed on the production line by the Mk 5, with equipment for specialised rôles. It was delivered as the FR 5 day-fighter-reconnaissance aircraft, NF 5 night-fighter and AS 5 anti-submarine patrol aircraft. An important change introduced during production of the Mk 5s was that of power-folding wings.

In 1951 there appeared the first improved Firefly AS 6s, which became the leading type of anti-submarine aircraft with the FAA until the introduction of the Gannet.

Last Firefly variant to be built was the three-seat AS 7, an interim anti-submarine aircraft produced pending introduction of the Gannet AS 1. The many airframe changes included a return to the original full-span wing, a deep beard radiator and a revised tail unit.

A total of 1,638 Firefly aircraft were built (not including trainers and target drones), comprising 429 Mk 1s, 376 FR 1s, 37 NF 2s, 160 FR 4s (of which 40 went to the Netherlands), 352 Mk 5s, 133 AS 6s and 151 AS 7s.

Fairey Barracuda

The Barracuda was a three-seat carrier-borne torpedo-bomber and dive-bomber, and was intended to replace the Albacore.

It was an all-metal shoulder-wing monoplane, designed to meet the exacting demands of Air Ministry Specification S.24/37. This not only required a multi-purpose aircraft, but one able to operate from carriers, with all the attendant problems of folding wings and so on.

Distinctive features of the Barracuda were its high-mounted braced tailplane; its unusually shaped undercarriage, which retracted into each side of the fuselage and the underside of the wing; and the prominent Fairey-Youngman flaps beneath the wing trailing-edge.

Although the prototype first flew in December 1940, production was delayed nearly two years because of the priority awarded to other, more urgently-needed types.

The initial production batch of 25 aircraft, each powered by a 1,260-hp Rolls-Royce Merlin 30, were designated Mk I. They were followed by the Mk II, with a 1,640-hp Merlin 32, driving a four-bladed propeller.

The Mk III, generally similar to the Mk II, was produced specially for anti-submarine reconnaissance duties, and incorporated an ASV Mk X radar scanner in a radome under the fuselage.

All Marks were armed with a pair of manually-operated Vickers K guns in the rear cockpit. The Mk I could carry one 1,610-lb torpedo or one 1,500-lb mine below the fuselage, or 2,000 lb of bombs beneath the wings; the Mk II carried one 1,620-lb torpedo, four 450-lb depth charges or 1,500 lb of bombs; the Mk III carried one 1,572-lb torpedo or four 250-lb depth charges.

In service, the Barracuda proved an effective combat weapon, its exploits including a series of daring raids against the German battleship *Tirpitz*. In the course of its varying duties, it became festooned with equipment, including aerials, radomes, assisted take-off rockets, bombs, mines, lifeboats, and even containers under the wings for dropping secret agents in occupied France.

A total of 2,572 Mk I, II and III aircraft were built.

The Barracuda V was almost a completely new aircraft, the first production model of which flew in November 1945. Changes included the installation of a 2,020-hp Rolls-Royce Griffon 37 engine, re-stressing of the entire structure to improve the margin of safety in a dive, use of extended and redesigned wings, a new tail unit and repositioned radome, and deletion of the third crew position.

The Mk V carried no defensive armament. Maximum bomb-load was 2,000 lb, carried externally. It was intended as an interim type pending introduction of the Spearfish (later cancelled). About 30 were built: they did not enter first-line service, being used mainly for training.

Fairey Gannet

The Gannet was developed initially as a carrier-borne anti-submarine search and strike aircraft. An outstanding technological feature of the design was the Armstrong Siddeley Double Mamba power plant, which consisted of two Mamba turboprop engines placed side-by-side and each driving one of two co-axial, contra-rotating propellers. This arrangement had special advantages for Naval patrol duties, for each engine was controlled independently, so that one of them could be shut down and its propeller feathered, to give the economy of single-engined operation and so extend the patrol range. When extra power was required, for combat or take-off, both engines could be used.

A secondary advantage of the contra-rotating co-axial propellers was that, when using only one engine, there were no asymmetric problems of the kind encountered with conventional twin-engined aircraft. In addition, the Mamba engine could run on kerosene, wide-cut turbine fuel or Naval diesel fuel, which helped the Admiralty to eliminate petrol from carriers.

Structurally, the Gannet, which was built to the requirements of Specification GR.17/45, was of all-metal stressed-skin construction. The wings folded mechanically, the inner section folding up and the outer section downward simultaneously. Large flaps of the auxiliary aerofoil type were fitted.

The fuselage was a semi-monocoque structure, in which the crew of three each occupied a separate cockpit, with the pilot in the first, the observer-navigator in the second and the radio-radar operator in the third.

A feature of the fuselage was the exceptionally large weapons bay, permitting the carriage of all normal stores internally, including two homing torpedoes, or parachute mines or depth charges. Sixteen 60-lb rocket projectiles could be carried under the wings. Aft of the weapons bay was a retractable radar scanner.

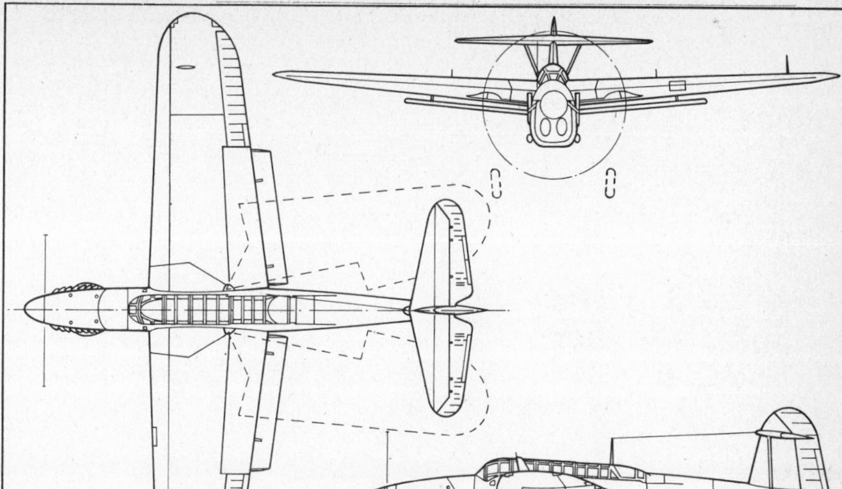

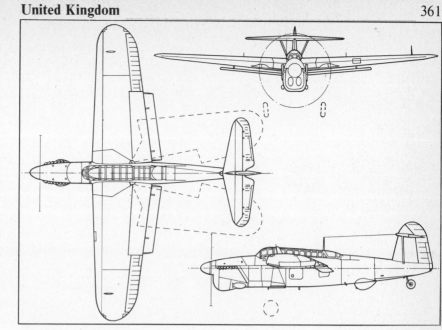

Fairey Barracuda Mk III

Fairey Barracuda Mk V

Fairey Gannet AS Mk 1

TYPE	DIMENSIONS span ft	span in	length ft	length in	height ft	height in	WEIGHT max t-o lb	PERFORMANCE max speed mph	at height ft	service ceiling ft	combat range miles	REMARKS
Firefly Mk I	44	6	37	7	13	7	14,020	316	14,000	28,000	1,070	
Firefly Mk IV	41	2	37	11	14	4	14,200	386	14,000	28,800	1,300	
Barracuda Mk I	49	2	39	9	15	1	13,500	235	11,000	18,400	524*	*With 2,000-lb bomb load
Barracuda Mk II	49	2	39	9	15	1	14,100	228	1,750	16,600	524*	*With 1,800-lb bomb load
Barracuda Mk III	49	2	39	9	15	1	14,100	239	1,750	20,000	684*	*With 1,572-lb torpedo
Barracuda Mk V	53	0	41	1	13	2	16,000	253	10,000	24,000	600*	*With 2,000-lb bomb load
Gannet AS Mk 1	54	4	43	0	13	8	NA	NA	NA	NA	NA	
Gannet AS Mk 4	54	4	43	0	13	8	22,506	300	NA	NA	NA	

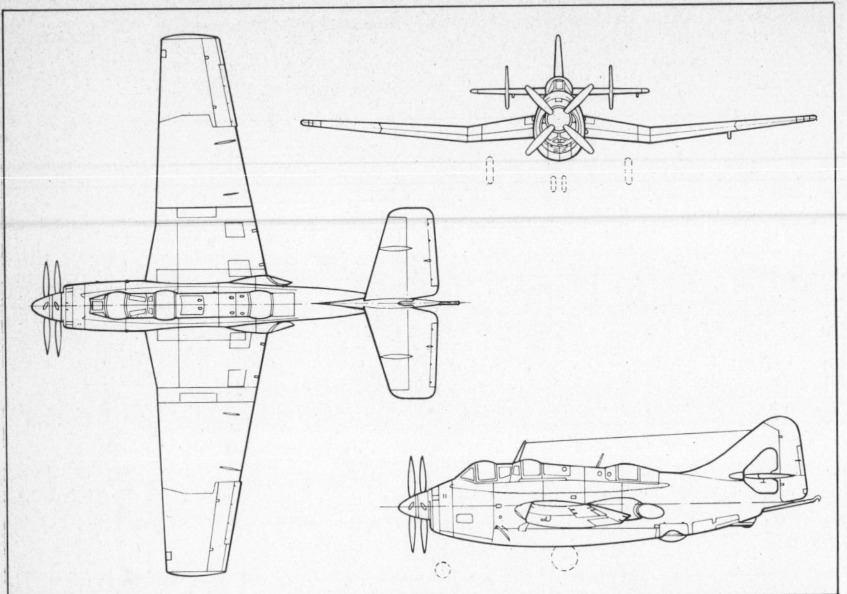
Fairey Gannet AS Mk 1

Fairey Gannet AEW Mk 3

Fairey Gannet AS Mk 4, Federal German Navy

Felixstowe F.2A

Gannet AS Mk 1s, powered by the 2,950-ehp Double Mamba 100, went into service in January 1955 with No. 826 Squadron. The T Mk 2 was a trainer variant of the Mk 1, with duplicated controls in the first and second cockpits; the radome was deleted.

The AEW Mk 3 was an early-warning variant, with more powerful engines and carrying a large radar scanner under the fuselage: the radar operators were accommodated inside the fuselage, the two normal rear cockpits being deleted.

The AS Mk 1 was superseded by the AS Mk 4, which was powered by the improved Double Mamba 101 ASMD 3 of 3,035 ehp. A trainer variant of the Gannet AS Mk 4 was built as the T Mk 5. AS Mk 6 and AS Mk 7 were designations applied to AS Mk 4 aircraft when fitted with specialized electronic equipment.

Gannets were supplied to Australia, Indonesia and West Germany.

Felixstowe F.2A

The Felixstowe F.2A was a British reconnaissance flying-boat based on the American Curtiss H.12. It was a brilliantly successful machine which established the flying-boat as a weapon of war—and the trend of British flying-boat design for over 20 years.

The F.2A was the brain child of Squadron Commander John C. Porte, who from 1914 had extolled the virtues of the flying-boat for military purposes. In September 1915 he assumed command of the RNAS Station at Felixstowe. Flying the H.4 Small Americas on operations, he became fully aware of their shortcomings, and set about the task of making them more seaworthy and thus of more value as combat aircraft.

Porte began by producing the Felixstowe F.1, which was the culmination of a series of experimental flying-boats, consisting essentially of the wings and tail units of Curtiss H.4s mounted on hulls of his own design. The first four hulls were variations on the Curtiss theme and were only partially successful but the fifth, a completely new design, proved to be markedly superior. A redesigned bow cut down the spray, and the hull form and step position resulted in excellent take-off and landing qualities. The new hull was named Porte 1, and the complete aircraft was designated the F.1. It was powered by two 150-hp Hispano-Suiza engines, which were installed in place of the two 100-hp Anzanis that had been standard on RNAS H.4s.

Following the success of the F.1, Porte began experimenting with the H.12 Large America, which was similar to, but bigger than the H.4 Small America. The superiority of his hull on the F.1 was clearly apparent; so Porte designed a new and bigger hull on similar lines, and mated it with the wings and tail unit of a Large America. Known as the F.2, this machine became the prototype of the aircraft which was to give outstanding service up to the end of the war and beyond.

Production machines began to come off the assembly lines in 1917. Designated F.2As, they were each powered by two 345-hp Rolls-Royce Eagle VIII engines. The Porte hull consisted basically of a cross-braced box girder, the prominent side fins being built on to the outside of the basic hull structure. The tail was relatively high, to keep the tailplane above the spray when taxying, and to give the waist gunners a good field of fire rearward. The hull was strong and seaworthy. Unfortunately, the effects of long exposure to the elements proved more severe than had been estimated and as operational experience was gained the hull had to be partially redesigned so as to withstand better the depredations of salt water.

The four-bay wings and tail surfaces, as might be expected, were similar to those of the Large America. The top wing extended considerably beyond the lower, being supported by king-posts above the outer interplane struts. The king-post structures were faired in with fabric to form two distinctive fin surfaces on top of the wing which, however, served no aerodynamic purpose.

Standard armament consisted of four Lewis machine-guns, one mounted in the nose, one in the upper rear cockpit just aft of the wings and the others in waist positions on each side of the hull. Two 230-lb bombs were carried on racks under the bottom wing. Variations of the defensive armament included a pair of Lewis guns in the nose and mid-upper positions, with, sometimes, an extra Lewis gun on top of the pilot's cockpit canopy. One of the F.2As at Felixstowe was modified to incorporate two "howdah" gun positions in the top wing. Located above the first pair of interplane struts, outboard of the engines, each position had a pair of Lewis guns mounted on a Scarff ring-mounting. The idea seems to have been to produce an escort fighter to protect other F.2As, but the installation was not a success.

In service, the F.2A operated from almost every flying-boat station of the RNAS, and bore the brunt of the long-range anti-submarine and anti-Zeppelin patrols over the North Sea. The big flying-boats fought numerous engagements with Brandenburg W.12 and W.29 seaplanes, their heavy defensive armament making up for slow speed and lack of manoeuvrability.

The F.2As also continued the famous "Spider's Web" patrol system initiated with the Curtiss H.12 Large Americas. Centred on the North Hinder Light Vessel, this consisted of an imaginary octagon, 60 miles across, with radial and inter-connecting circumferential lines, covering some 4,000 square miles of sea. By following a pre-arranged pattern, four flying-boats could search the whole area in three hours, giving the crews a good chance of spotting U-boats, which usually travelled on the surface here to conserve batteries.

On 4 June 1918, F.2As engaged in one of the greatest air battles of the entire war. Four F.2As and one Curtiss H.12 were patrolling the enemy coastline. One F.2A had been forced down by a fuel system failure and the Curtiss H.12 had set off in pursuit of some enemy aircraft which had attacked the disabled F.2A, when the remaining three F.2As were attacked by no fewer than 14 enemy seaplanes. In the ensuing running "dog-fight", the F.2As shot down six of the enemy without loss to themselves, and finally returned to their base at Great Yarmouth after having been airborne over six hours.

This action highlighted the dangers of being forced down in the sea and, afterwards, it was decided to paint the hulls of the F.2As in distinctive colours, to assist the identification of pilots in trouble. At some stations the design of the colour scheme was left to individual pilots, and some bizarre and gaudy schemes resulted. The "dazzle-painting" of one F.2A, consisting of diagonal yellow stripes on a bright red background, was described as so "terrible in appearance" that it was hoped it "would put the wind up the Hun." The colour scheme of each F.2A was charted, and details were held by all air and naval units in the area.

One F.2 was built with a lighter hull, incorporating redesigned steps and bow and with changes to the front gun position. Known as the F.2C, this version did not go into production, although the prototype was used operationally and played a leading part in the sinking by bombing of U-boat U.C.1. At one stage the F.2C was fitted with modified bomb-dropping mechanism, operated by compressed air instead of the normal cable, but this proved unreliable.

Felixstowe F.3

A development of the F.2A, the Felixstowe F.3 was a larger reconnaissance flying-boat, able to carry twice the bomb-load of the former aircraft over a longer range.

Externally the two types were almost identical, the slight increase in size not being readily apparent. The top wing extended considerably beyond the lower, and was supported by prominent king-posts on top of the outer interplane struts. As in the F.2A, the king-posts

Felixstowe F.2A

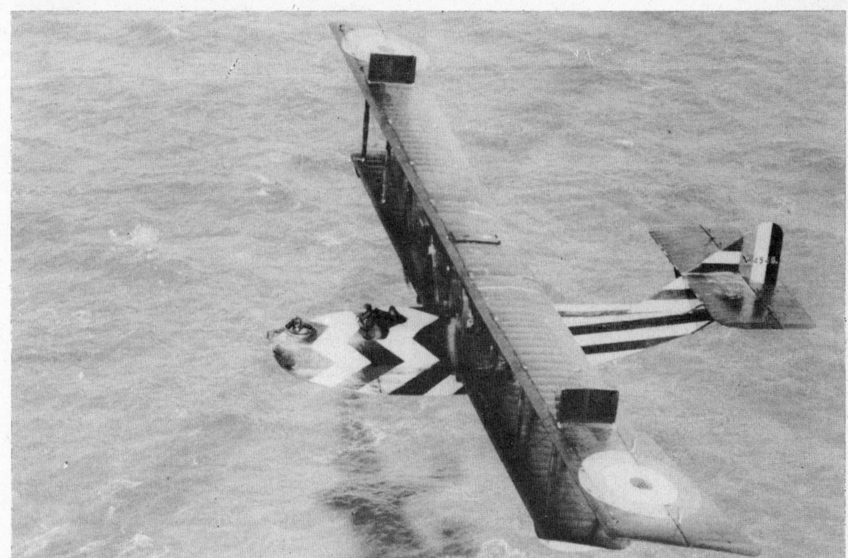

Felixstowe F.2A, dazzle-painted in accordance with RN practice, 1918

Felixstowe F.2A

TYPE	DIMENSIONS span ft	in	length ft	in	height ft	in	WEIGHT max t-o lb	PERFORMANCE max speed mph	at height ft	service ceiling ft	combat range miles	REMARKS
Felixstowe F.2A	95	7	46	3	17	6	10,978	95	2,000	9,600	NA	Endurance 6 hours
Felixstowe F.2C	95	0	46	0	17	6	10,240	98	2,000	10,300	NA	275-hp Rolls-Royce Mk II

Felixstowe F.3

Felixstowe F.3

Felixstowe F.5

Felixstowe F.5, Imperial Japanese Navy

were faired in with fabric to form fin surfaces on top of the wing; these served no aerodynamic purpose.

The hull was generally similar to that of the F.2A, but was three feet longer and had a different step arrangement; it was also constructed along different lines. Instead of being continuous athwartships, as on the F.2A, the cross-members were made in two halves and rebated into the keelson on either side. This proved unsatisfactory, as the hull planking tended to spring, with subsequent leakage; so additional members were introduced to strengthen the planking. The wing floats and tail surfaces were very similar to those of the F.2A.

Two 320-hp Sunbeam Cossack engines were installed in the prototype, but production F.3s had 345-hp Rolls-Royce Eagle VIIIs, driving opposite-rotating propellers.

The armament consisted of four Lewis machine-guns, one on a rotatable ring in the nose cockpit, one in the mid-upper cockpit just aft of the wings, and the others in waist positions on each side of the hull. A maximum of four 230-lb bombs could be carried on underwing racks.

Large numbers of F.3s were ordered, and production machines began coming off the assembly lines in 1917 at the same time as the F.2As. About 100 had been completed by the end of the war, when all contracts were either cancelled or severely curtailed.

Although able to carry a heavier warload farther than the F.2A, the F.3 was not so manoeuvrable and was thus less able to take on enemy seaplanes. Because of this, F.3s were generally sent to air stations engaged mainly on anti-submarine patrols that were out of range of enemy fighters. In addition to serving in British coastal waters, the F.3 was used extensively in the Mediterranean; some were built by local labour in Malta, so pressing was the demand for these aircraft.

One F.3 was fitted with a primitive form of automatic landing device similar to that used earlier on some Curtiss H.12 Large Americas. This consisted of an arm, interconnected to the control column and projecting slightly below the keel in flight. To alight, the pilot flew as slowly as he could, along a gently descending path. When the projecting stick struck the water it moved the control column backward, causing the flying-boat to settle smoothly. Several successful automatic landings were achieved with this device.

The F.3 remained operational until September 1921.

Felixstowe F.5

The Felixstowe F.5 was the standard general reconnaissance flying-boat in service with the RAF in the years following the 1914–18 War. It was the last of the famous series of boats designed by Lt-Cdr John Porte.

The prototype F.5, although closely resembling the earlier F.3, was a brand new design. The increased-span four-bay wings had a new aerofoil section, new ailerons and other detail improvements. The hull had open cockpits and, being deeper, was exceptionally seaworthy. During trials, the prototype proved to be some 10 mph faster than the F.3.

To facilitate production, however, the design was modified extensively to incorporate many F.3 components, as the jigs and tools for these were already available. The hull was planked overall and the wings were made identical with those of the F.3. The net result was that production aircraft were heavier than the prototype, and inferior in performance to the earlier F.3.

Powered by two 325-hp Rolls-Royce Eagle VII or 350-hp Eagle VIII engines, the production F.5s appeared too late to see service in the 1914–18 War.

Armament comprised one Lewis machine-gun on a rotatable mounting in the front cockpit, one Lewis gun in each waist position and one in the cockpit aft of the wings. Four 230-lb bombs could be carried on racks beneath the wings.

Fifteen F.5s served in the Imperial Japanese Naval Air Service in 1921. In 1922, a version of the F.5, powered by two 400-hp Liberty engines and known as the F.5L, was put into production in America to become the US Navy's standard flying-boat in the early 1920s. These US models could be armed with a 1½-pounder quick-firing gun and as many as 11 machine-guns.

Folland Gnat

The Gnat is a single-seat lightweight fighter or fighter-bomber. It represents an interesting effort to produce a relatively simple aircraft to halt the spiralling upward trend of increased weight and complexity in fighters.

The venture was seriously delayed in the early stages when development of the original engine around which the aircraft had been designed was abandoned. Two years passed before another suitable engine became available, and when the Gnat finally appeared its first-line combat effectiveness was questioned as it was not able to accommodate the extensive and bulky electronic equipment thought to be essential for the location and destruction of fast and high-flying targets.

However, the single-seat Gnat, which is one-third the size and about half the weight of a conventional jet fighter, serves usefully in the air forces of Finland and India, while the RAF is using a larger two-seat advanced trainer version.

Structurally, the Gnat is of conventional all-metal stressed-skin construction, and its design permits manufacture without the use of large and costly machine tools. The wing, made in one piece and built up on two spars with a thick skin, fits in a recess in the top of the fuselage where it is secured by bolts at four main points. The ailerons are powered and can be lowered to serve as flaps.

The Gnat fighter is powered by a 4,520-lb s t Bristol Siddeley Orpheus 701 turbojet engine, air being fed through two large intakes in the sides of the fuselage. In spite of the low power of this engine, the Gnat has a high subsonic speed in level flight, an exceptionally good rate of climb and a small turning radius.

Armament consists of two 30-mm Aden cannon mounted in the intake fairings, on each side of the fuselage, with provision for two 500-lb bombs or twelve 3-in rockets under the wings. Two of the Finnish machines have a modified nose housing cameras for reconnaissance missions.

Gloster Nightjar/Mars/Sparrowhawk

The Nightjar was one of a series of related designs produced by the Gloucestershire Aircraft Company, after it had taken over the Nieuport designs in 1920. Known as the Gloster Mars series, these aircraft were all based on the Nieuport Nighthawk and differed only in detail and power plant.

The Mars I, also known as the Gloster I and Bamel, was a racing biplane powered by a Napier Lion engine.

The Mars II was a single-seat fighter, 30 of which were built for the Japanese Navy in 1922, under the name Sparrowhawk I. It was powered by a 230-hp Bentley B.R.2 rotary engine.

The Mars III was a two-seat trainer version of the Sparrowhawk I. Ten were supplied to the Japanese Navy, which gave them the name Sparrowhawk II.

The Mars IV was a modified version of the Mars II, fitted with a hydrovane undercarriage and flotation gear to reduce the hazards of ditching.

The Mars VI was the Nighthawk as produced by the Gloucestershire Aircraft Company after it had taken over the Nieuport designs. Details are given under the Nighthawk entry.

The Mars X became the Nightjar. It was a single-seat carrier-borne fighter and was the Naval counterpart of the RAF Nighthawk, to which it was very similar. Many

Folland Gnat Mk 1, Finnish Air Force

Folland Gnat Mk 1, built by Hindustan Aeronautics for Indian Air Force

Gloster (Nieuport) Mars X (Nightjar)

Gloster (Nieuport) Mars X (Nightjar)

TYPE	DIMENSIONS span ft	span in	length ft	length in	height ft	height in	WEIGHT max t-o lb	PERFORMANCE max speed mph	at height ft	service ceiling ft	combat range miles	REMARKS
Felixstowe F.3	102	0	49	2	18	8	13,281	90	2,000	6,000	NA	Endurance 9½ hours
Felixstowe F.5	103	8	49	3	18	9	12,682	88	2,000	6,800	NA	Endurance 7 hours
F.5L	103	8	49	3	18	9	13,000	87	NA	NA	NA	Endurance 10 hours
Gnat	22	2	29	9	8	10	6,650*	0.98M		50,000	1,000	Interceptor version

Gloster Mars II (Sparrowhawk I), Imperial Japanese Navy

Gloster Grebe

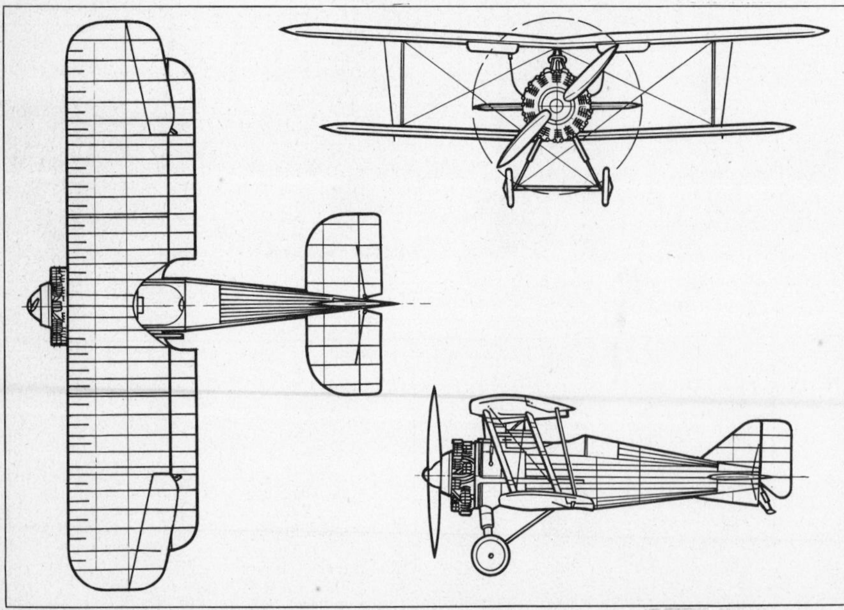
Gloster Grebe

Nightjars were, in fact, conversions of Nighthawk airframes which had been manufactured but not used, owing to the short-comings of the ABC Dragonfly engine, or of Nighthawk airframes which had been declared obsolete in 1923. The major difference in the Nightjar compared with its RAF predecessor was the engine, this being a 230-hp Bentley B.R.2. Other changes included a new undercarriage, with wider track and longer stroke, and with twin "jaws" on the axle fairing to engage fore-and-aft wires on the carrier decks.

Armament consisted of two fixed forward-firing Vickers machine-guns, mounted on each side of the fuselage, and synchronized to fire between the propeller blades.

Although the Nightjar was a standard Fleet Air Arm fighter, only about 12 were maintained in service, and the type was replaced in 1924 by the Parnall Plover and Fairey Flycatcher. Nightjars served with No. 203 Squadron during the Chanak crisis in Turkey in the early 1920s.

Gloster Grebe

Superseding the Sopwith Snipe, the Grebe single-seat fighter, together with its contemporary, the Armstrong Whitworth Siskin, was one of the first types selected for re-equipment of the RAF after the 1914–18 War.

It was produced by the Gloucestershire Aircraft Company, and was a single-bay biplane, with the upper wing slightly larger than the lower one. Aerodynamically, the upper wing had a high-lift aerofoil section and the lower wing had a medium-lift section. An unusual feature was that the ailerons of the upper wing were hinged parallel with the tapering trailing-edge of the outer ends of the wing, whereas the ailerons on the lower wing were hinged at right-angles to the airflow. During tests the aircraft developed wing flutter; to cure this, Vee-struts were introduced on some aircraft to brace the top wing extensions. The fuselage was a conventional braced box-girder structure, covered with fabric.

Three prototypes were built in 1923, at least one of which was fitted with a 325-hp Armstrong Siddeley Jaguar III engine. Production machines, known as Grebe IIs, had the more powerful 400-hp Armstrong Siddeley Jaguar IV engine, redesigned fuel tanks, an oleo undercarriage and other refinements. A total of 112 were built, including a number of two-seat dual-control training conversions.

Armament consisted of two Vickers machine-guns, mounted on top of the fuselage in front of the pilot, and synchronized to fire between the propeller blades.

The Grebe was popular in service, and was used for several experiments. It was the first British fighter to survive a terminal velocity dive of 240 mph. During another series of experiments, in 1926, two Grebes were launched successfully from the Airship R.33 while it was flying at a height of 2,000 ft.

The first squadron to be equipped fully with the Grebe was No. 25, which converted from its Snipes in 1924, and the type remained in first-line service until 1928 when it was replaced by the Armstrong Whitworth Siskin. Three Grebes from the Aeroplane and Armament Experimental Establishment, however, participated in the RAF Flying Display at Hendon in 1931.

Gloster Gamecock

Built to Air Ministry Specification 37/23, the Gamecock single-seat fighter was the last biplane of wooden construction to serve with the RAF. It was delightful to handle, had outstanding manoeuvrability, and was the first fighter that could do a 360° vertical roll and still be pushed over the top, hanging on its propeller.

A development of the Grebe, the prototype Gamecock first flew in February 1925. Major differences compared with its predecessor were that it had a 425-hp Bristol Jupiter engine, instead of the Armstrong Siddeley Jaguar; a rounded fuselage of improved aerodynamic form; modified armament, with the twin Vickers machine-guns mounted in troughs in each side of the fuselage; and improved ailerons. The second prototype had a Bristol Jupiter IV, like the first, but the third was fitted with a Jupiter VI, the standard engine on production aircraft.

The Gamecock was a single-bay biplane, with the upper wing slightly larger than the lower. The upper wing was made in two halves, and was supported at the centre on inverted Vee-struts from the fuselage and at each outer end by a single pair of interplane struts. The pilot sat close to the trailing-edge of the upper wing, which had a large cut-out to improve his view.

Production of Gamecock Mk Is began in 1926, to Specification 18/25, and the first squadron to receive the new fighter was No. 23 at Henlow. Some trouble was experienced with wing flutter, and later production aircraft had additional wing-to-fuselage struts as well as Vee-struts to brace the top wing extensions. The spinning qualities also were not so good as they might have been and pilots had standing orders not to attempt left-hand spins. During flight trials to investigate these foibles, a Gamecock was dived at 275 mph and completed 22 turns of a spin.

Gamecock Mk IIs differed from the Mk I principally in wing design. Instead of the wings meeting on the centre-line, a centre-section was inserted. Supported on struts, this had the effect of increasing the span of the top wing and improving the pilot's view. Minor changes included an improved windshield and fuel tanks; the latter, being broader but of similar capacity, projected below the wing less than formerly.

The Gamecock Mk III was a remodelled Mk I with a longer fuselage, different undercarriage and redesigned fin and rudder and was used for spinning experiments at the Royal Aircraft Establishment.

A number of Gamecock Mk IIs were supplied to the Finnish Air Force, and both Mk IIs and Mk IIIs were built under licence in Helsinki.

Gloster Gauntlet

The Gauntlet was the last open-cockpit single-seat fighter to serve with the RAF. At the time it was considered the world's finest day and night fighter.

Its outstanding performance was due to the care taken in the design of all detail fittings, to its finely streamlined fuselage, the thin wing sections used, the sinking within the wings of all bracing wire fittings, so that only the wires appeared through the fabric, the use of streamlined instead of oval wires, the streamlined undercarriage wheels, the deletion of all external control levers, the attention paid to reducing interference between the centre-section and the fuselage, and to the fairing of the lower wing into the fuselage.

It had equal-span metal wings, covered with fabric. Frise-type ailerons were fitted to all wings.

The fuselage was a braced rectangular metal structure, faired to an oval section and covered forward with metal panels and aft with fabric over a structure of hoops and stringers.

The undercarriage was of the cross-axle V-type, the front members incorporating Dowty oleo units. Wheel brakes were fitted, which could be operated differentially by pedals on the rudder bar, or simultaneously from the control column.

The power plant was a 645-hp Bristol Mercury VIS2 air-cooled radial engine.

Armament consisted of two fixed Vickers machine-guns, mounted in troughs on each side of the fuselage and synchronized to fire between the propeller blades. The guns were accessible from the cockpit.

Designated SS.19B, the prototype Gauntlet was developed from the experimental SS.18 and SS.19 six-gun fighters of 1932. During development the armament

Gloster Gamecock Mk II, Finnish Air Force

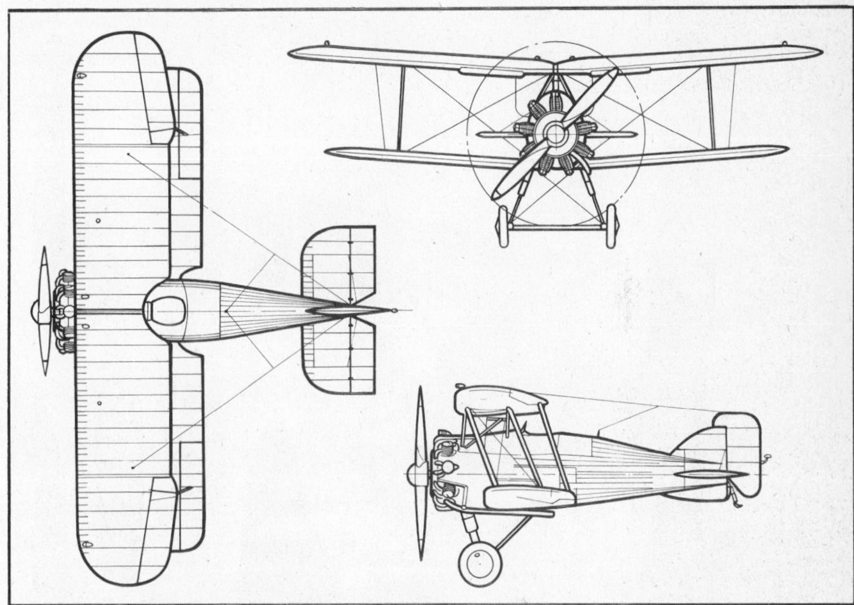
Gloster Gamecock I

Gloster Gauntlet, Royal Danish Air Force

TYPE	DIMENSIONS span ft	span in	length ft	length in	height ft	height in	WEIGHT max t-o lb	PERFORMANCE max speed mph	at height ft	service ceiling ft	combat range miles	REMARKS
Nightjar	28	0	19	2	9	7	2,165	108	6,500	15,000	NA	Endurance 2 hours
Grebe	29	4	20	3	9	3	2,614	152	SL	23,000	NA	Endurance 2¾ hours
Gamecock Mk I	29	9	19	8	9	8	2,863	155	5,000	22,000	NA	

Gloster Gladiator, No. 87 Squadron

Gloster Sea Gladiator; one of the machines used in defence of Malta

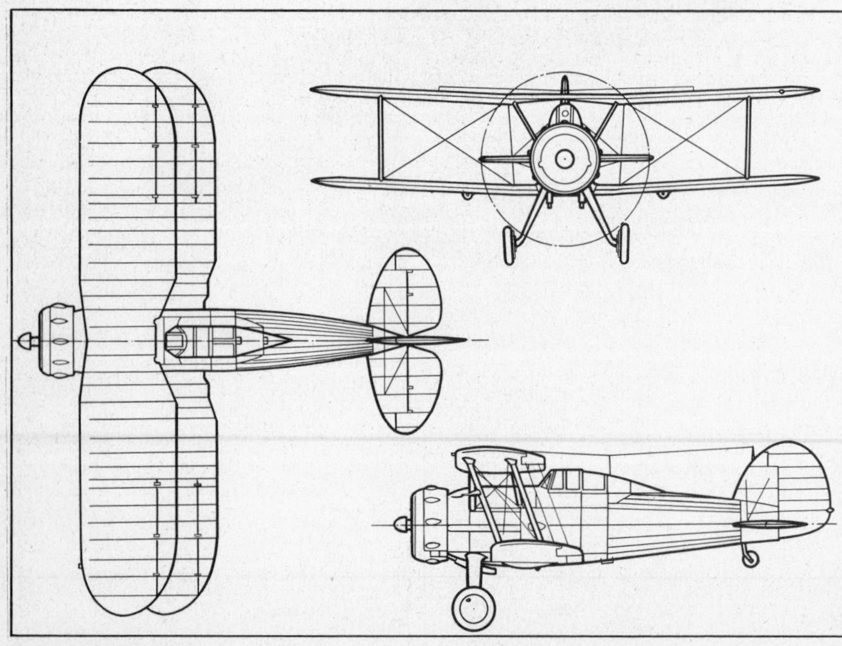
Gloster Gladiator

reverted to the more conventional two guns. The excellent performance of the new fighter was apparent as soon as the prototype flew and a development order was placed for 24 aircraft, designated Gauntlet Mk I, which went into service with No. 19 Squadron in May 1935.

These were followed by 204 of the Mk II version, which had a new type of wing and fuselage construction brought about by standardization of production methods subsequent to the merging of the Gloster Aircraft Co with the Hawker Siddeley organization. The performance of some aircraft was improved by fitting a three-blade fixed-pitch metal propeller, in place of the standard two-blade wooden type.

In service the Gauntlet proved popular and efficient. From 1935 to 1937 it was the fastest fighter in service with the RAF, and at the peak of its career, in 1937, it equipped no fewer than 14 squadrons of Fighter Command. It remained in service until 1939.

The Gauntlet was fitted with two-way radio equipment and an aircraft of No. 32 Squadron became the first RAF fighter to effect an interception while under the control of ground radar. This was in 1937, during early trials of the British invention, when the fighter was successfully homed on to an airliner flying over the Thames.

Gloster Gladiator

The Gladiator was the last biplane fighter operated by the RAF. Initiated as a private-venture development of the already highly-refined Gauntlet, it brought this class of aircraft to the peak of technical proficiency.

Of all-metal construction, with fabric covering, it had equal-span, single-bay wings, compared with the two-bay arrangement on the Gauntlet. An unusual feature was the fitting of small flaps to all wings; these served to increase drag rather than improve lift, the resultant steepened glide path facilitating landings at night. Ailerons were fitted to all four wings.

The fuselage was similar to that of the Gauntlet, and consisted of a braced rectangular metal girder structure, faired to an oval section and covered forward with metal panels and aft with fabric. An improved undercarriage was fitted, with two cantilever main legs mounting specially-designed, internally-sprung wheels.

Armament was four Browning 0·303-in machine-guns, of which two were mounted in troughs in the sides of the fuselage, accessible to the pilot, and two below the lower wings, firing outside the propeller disc.

The prototype Gladiator, designated SS.37 and fitted with a 645-hp Bristol Mercury VIS engine, first flew in September 1934. Initial Mk I production aircraft had the more powerful 840-hp Bristol Mercury IXS in a medium-chord cowling. Production machines also had an enclosed cockpit.

Gladiator Mk Is went into service in January 1937, with Nos. 3 and 72 Squadrons. They were followed by an improved Mk II version, powered by a Mercury VIIIA engine with an automatic-mixture-control carburettor and Hobson control box, and fitted with desert equipment, sand-excluders, a Vokes air cleaner and an accumulator which permitted electric starting from the cockpit.

When war began in 1939, the Gladiator had been largely superseded, but production continued until 1940. A Gladiator scored one of the RAF's first victories of the war when it shot down an He 111 over Scotland. During the Norwegian campaign in 1940, Gladiators operated from frozen lakes.

Gladiator Mk I and II production totalled 527 machines, 216 of which were exported as follows: Belgium (22), China (36), Greece (2), Finland (30), Iraq (15), Irish Free State (4), Latvia (26), Lithuania (14), Portugal (30), Norway (12) and Sweden (25).

Sixty Sea Gladiators were also built. These were essentially Mk IIs, powered by a Mercury VIIIA or IX engine, with an arrester hook, catapult points and a dinghy which was carried in a fairing under the fuselage.

Four Malta-based Sea Gladiators, three of them individually named *Faith*, *Hope* and *Charity*, won immortal fame by defending the island alone against Italy's Regia Aeronautica from 11 June to 28 June 1940.

Gloster/Armstrong Whitworth Meteor

The Meteor was the first jet aircraft to enter service with the RAF and the only Allied jet fighter to be used operationally during World War II. For so revolutionary a design, it proved exceptionally versatile, being developed, in addition to its primary single-seat fighter rôle, into a two-seat trainer and a two-seat all-weather night fighter, and being used for armed photo-reconnaissance and high-flying unarmed photo-reconnaissance, as well as for many second-line duties.

It was designed to Air Ministry Specification F. 9/40, the first issued in Britain for an operational jet aircraft and which called for a single-seat interceptor. A twin-engined layout was adopted; the types of turbojet available at the time developed insufficient thrust to produce the required performance with only one engine.

Twelve prototypes were ordered initially. This reflected both the growing complexity of fighters and an expectation that considerable development would be required to produce an efficient combat machine. In the event, only eight were completed, fitted with a variety of engines. The No. 5 airframe, powered by two 1,500-lb s t Halford (de Havilland) H 1 turbojets, was the first prototype to fly, on 5 March 1943.

Of all-metal stressed-skin construction, the Meteor was orthodox aerodynamically and structurally, except for its new type of power plant. Absence of propellers permitted an unusually short undercarriage, the main legs of which retracted into the centre-section, while the nose leg retracted rearward into a bay in front of and below the cockpit. The tailplane was mounted high up the fin, clear of the hot jet efflux.

The wing, of high-speed section, was of two-spar construction with a relatively thick skin. Conventional ailerons and split trailing-edge flaps were fitted, and air-brakes were housed in the top and bottom wing surfaces. The monocoque fuselage was built in three sections and incorporated four longerons and transverse frames. The cockpit was pressurized and located well forward, giving the pilot a good view, particularly forward and downward.

Of interest is that the name Thunderbolt was selected originally for the production aircraft; this was changed officially to Meteor in March 1942, because the former name had by then been given to the Republic P-47.

Twenty Mk Is were built, each powered by two 1,700-lb s t Rolls-Royce W.2B/23 Welland I centrifugal-compressor turbojets, and armed with four 20-mm cannon. The first of these was shipped to the USA in exchange for a Bell Airacomet, and three others were used for development purposes. The remaining 16 were delivered to the RAF, the first of them going into service with No. 616 Squadron in July 1944. On 4 August the new fighter claimed its first success when a pilot, whose guns had jammed, destroyed a V-1 flying bomb by flying alongside at 365 mph and tipping it over with his wing-tip. On the same day another Meteor destroyed a V-1 with its guns.

Mk II was the designation allotted to a variant powered by de Havilland Goblins of 2,700 lb s t; but only the prototype was built.

The Mk III was the first version to be manufactured in quantity. This was essentially similar to the Mk I, but introduced refinements such as a rearward-sliding cockpit hood and increased fuel tankage. Early Mk IIIs

Gloster Meteor Mk I

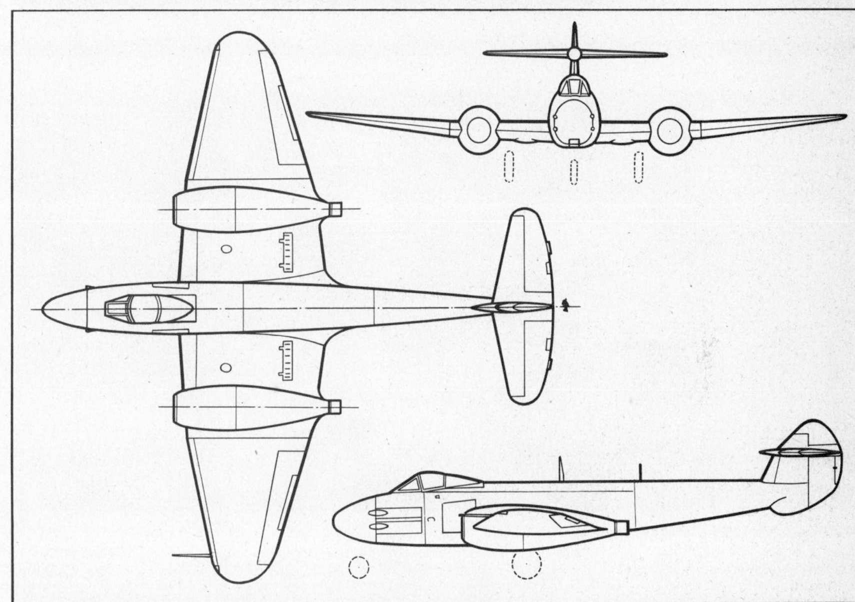

Gloster Meteor Mk III

Gloster Meteor F Mk 4

TYPE	DIMENSIONS span ft	span in	length ft	length in	height ft	height in	WEIGHT max t-o lb	PERFORMANCE max speed mph	at height ft	service ceiling ft	combat range miles	REMARKS
Gauntlet Mk I	32	9	26	2	10	4	3,950	228	15,800	35,500	460	
Gauntlet Mk II	32	9	26	2	10	4	3,970	230	15,500	33,500	460	
Gladiator Mk I	32	3	27	5	10	4	4,750	253	14,500	33,000	NA	
Gladiator Mk II	32	3	27	5	10	4	NA	NA	NA	NA	NA	
Sea Gladiator	32	3	27	5	10	4	5,420	245	15,000	32,000	425	

Gloster Meteor F Mk 8, Israeli Air Force

Gloster Meteor FR Mk 9

Gloster Meteor NF Mk 11, Royal Danish Air Force

Gloster Meteor NF Mk 14

were powered by Welland I engines, but from the 16th aircraft onwards Rolls-Royce W.2B/37 Derwent I engines of 2,000 lb s t were installed. The last 15 Mk IIIs had lengthened engine nacelles.

Two hundred and eighty Mk IIIs were built. A few were operational during the final advance into Germany.

In 1948, the Mk III was superseded by the Mk 4, of which 583 were built, powered by 3,500-lb s t Derwent 5 engines. Long before this, in September 1945, the Meteor Mk 4 *Britannia* had set up a new World Speed Record of 606 mph; in September 1946, this was raised to 616 mph by another Meteor. For the record attempts, the Meteor had its wings clipped to increase performance. The modification also improved the rate of roll and became standard on later Mk 4s.

The Meteor Mks 5, 6 and 7 were, respectively, photo-reconnaissance, experimental and training variants.

The next major combat variant was the Mk 8, which was the mainstay of Fighter Command from 1950 to 1955. Powered by two 3,600-lb s t Derwent 8 engines, this variant was extensively re-engineered, and had a completely redesigned tail unit, a lengthened fuselage and an improved cockpit canopy. Although intended basically for high-altitude interception, it could carry two 1,000-lb bombs on high-speed mountings beneath the wings, or up to 16 rocket projectiles for ground-attack duties. Meteor Mk 8s of the Royal Australian Air Force were the only British jet fighters to see action in Korea. This variant was also built under licence by Fokker in Holland and Avions Fairey in Belgium. Production totalled 1,090 in the UK and 480 on the Continent.

Mks 9 and 10 were photo-reconnaissance aircraft.

The NF 11 was a major variant produced to meet Specification F.24/48, which called for a jet night fighter. It was a development of the Mk 8 day fighter, with a lengthened nose to accommodate radar equipment, and an enlarged cockpit for the radar operator/navigator. Other changes included an increased wing span (back to that of the original Mk I) and transfer of the guns from the fuselage to the wings. The NF 12 had improved radar equipment, and the NF 13 was a tropicalized version of the NF 12, produced for operations in the Middle East. The last operational Meteor variant was the NF 14, of which 100 were built. This had an even-longer fuselage than the previous night fighters and an improved clear-vision cockpit canopy.

Design and manufacture of the two-seat night fighter Meteors were undertaken by the Armstrong Whitworth company. Subsequently, this company converted a number of NF 14s into NF(T) 14s for navigator training at RAF Air Navigation Schools. It also converted NF 11s into high-speed target towing aircraft, under the designation Meteor TT 20, with a windmill winch above the starboard wing, inboard of the engine nacelle.

Many Meteors were converted into radio-controlled targets by Flight Refuelling Ltd and Fairey Aviation Company of Australasia. The U Mk 15 (92 built) was a conversion of the F4. More than 100 F 8s were converted into U Mk 16s and U Mk 21s, for service at Llanbedr in Wales and Woomera respectively.

Gloster Javelin

Designed to Air Ministry Specification F.4/48, this two-seat all-weather fighter was the first twin-jet delta-wing aircraft to fly.

The inherently large area of the delta platform resulted in a low wing loading and good high-altitude performance. The wing's great internal volume, added to that of the wide fuselage, enabled the engines, undercarriage, a relatively large quantity of fuel and extensive equipment to be housed inside a well integrated, rigid and economical structure. A tailplane was fitted as this, in conjunction with wing flaps, facilitated night landings by permitting touch-downs to be made at near-normal angles of attack. Most deltas, lacking a tailplane, tend to land very nose-high.

The wing was a conventional all-metal two-spar stressed-skin structure, with compound sweep on all but the first prototypes. Power-boosted ailerons were fitted, inboard of which were hydraulically-operated slotted flaps. Slotted plate-type air-brakes were provided above and below each wing, near the trailing-edge.

The fuselage was of reasonably straightforward all-metal construction, with a massive main spar frame built into the central section. The nose was entirely filled by the massive airborne interception radar, and the crew of two, comprising a pilot and a radar-operator, were seated in tandem. The undercarriage was of the retractable tricycle type, and was actuated hydraulically.

After a somewhat lengthy development period, Javelin F (AW) Mk 1s went into service in 1956, with No. 46 Squadron. They were each powered by two 8,300-lb s t Bristol Siddeley Sapphire ASSa6 turbojets and were armed with four 30-mm Aden cannon in the wings. Forty were built.

The F (AW) Mk 2, of which 30 were built, was a development of the Mk 1, with different equipment, including American radar in a shorter nose.

The T Mk 3 was a dual-control trainer, the next combat variant being the F (AW) Mk 4 (50 built). This was similar to the Mk 1, but introduced an all-moving tailplane.

The F (AW) Mk 5 incorporated a new wing with increased internal fuel capacity, which increased considerably the already good endurance of the Javelin. Sixty-four were delivered.

The F (AW) Mk 6 was a developed version of the Mk 5 with American radar. The first of 33 built flew on 14 December 1956.

The F (AW) Mk 7 was powered by 11,000-lb s t Sapphire 203/204 turbojets and introduced a revised armament, consisting of two Aden cannon, mounted one in each wing, and four Firestreak air-to-air missiles carried under the wing. A sophisticated pylon design enabled the aircraft to fly almost as fast when carrying the four missiles as it did without them. Ninety-six Mk 7s were built.

The F (AW) Mk 8 (47 built) was essentially similar to the Mk 7, but was equipped with US radar and a Sperry autopilot. Other changes included the fitting of a drooped wing leading-edge and the installation of reheat for the engines which, with this in use, developed 12,300 lb s t.

The F (AW) Mk 9 was a Mk 7 modified to have reheat, and with provision for flight refuelling. The refuelling equipment comprised a long and ungainly probe mounted to the right side of the cockpit canopy and extending from just aft of the canopy to a point well in front of the nose of the aircraft.

Javelins remained in service with the RAF overseas until 1967.

Handley Page O/100 and O/400

First really practical heavy night bombers to go into service anywhere in the world, the Handley Page O/100 and O/400 were the biggest warplanes used by Britain in the 1914–18 War. The prototype O/100 was produced to meet an ambitious Admiralty Specification issued in December 1914, which called for an aircraft for oversea patrol duties carrying a heavy load of bombs. The Specification stipulated two engines, a crew of two, and the ability to carry six 112-lb bombs. A maximum speed of at least 72 mph was also required.

Gloster Javelin F(AW) Mk 1

Gloster Javelin F(AW) Mk 9, with flight refuelling probe

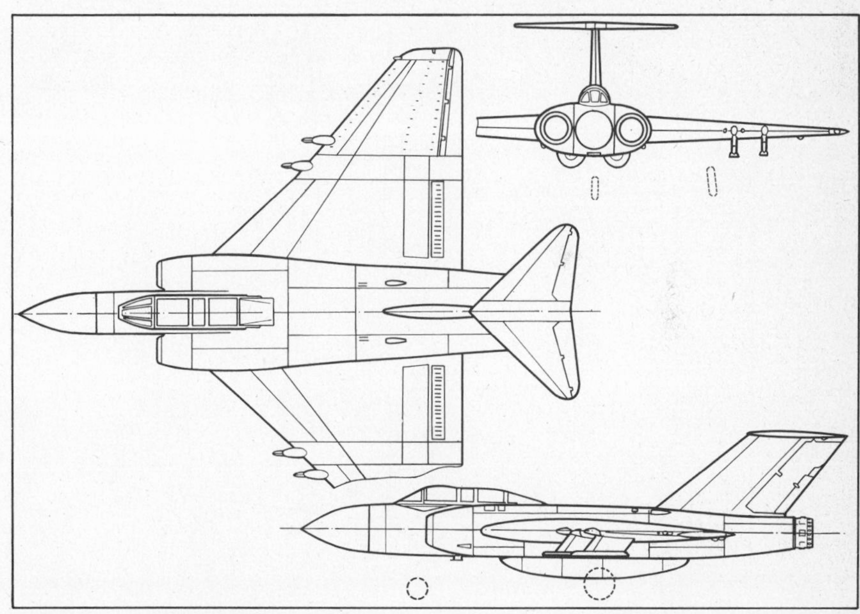

Gloster Javelin F(AW) Mk 9

TYPE	DIMENSIONS span ft	span in	length ft	length in	height ft	height in	WEIGHT max t-o lb	PERFORMANCE max speed mph	at height ft	service ceiling ft	combat range miles	REMARKS
Meteor Mk I	43	0	41	4	13	0	13,800	410	30,000	40,000	NA	
Meteor Mk III	43	0	41	4	13	0	8,810	493	30,000	44,000	1,340	
Meteor Mk 4	37	2	41	4	13	0	15,175	585	SL	50,000	NA	
Meteor Mk 8	37	2	44	7	13	10	19,100	590	SL	44,000	980	
Meteor NF Mk 11	43	0	48	6	13	10	22,000	579	9,840	43,000	920	
Javelin F(AW) Mk 1	52	0	57	0	16	3	NA	NA	NA	NA	NA	
Javelin F(AW) Mk 7	52	0	57	0	16	3	30,000	NA	NA	NA	NA	

Handley Page O/100 prototype

Handley Page O/100, Sunbeam Cossack engines

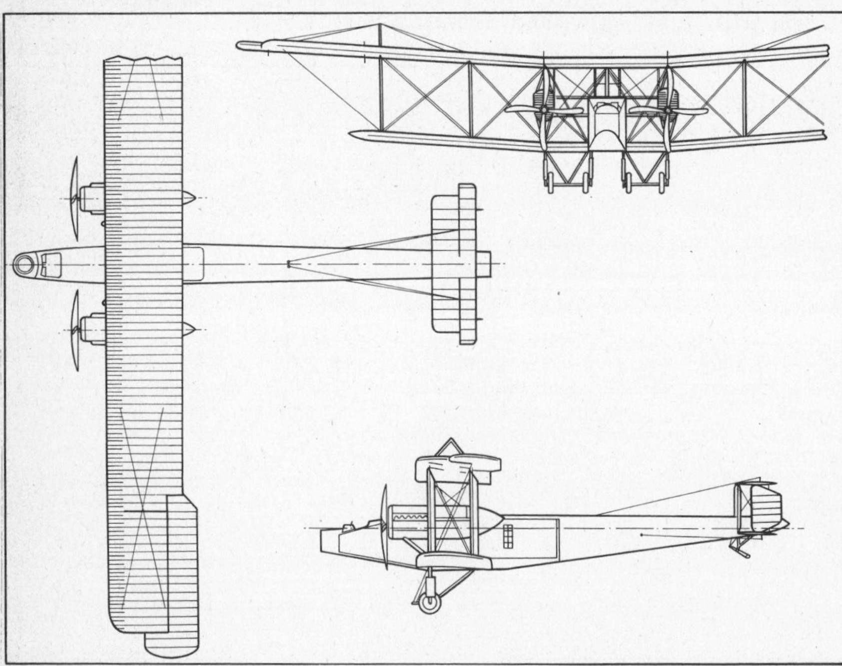
Handley Page O/100, Eagle engines

Handley Page O/400, Eagle engines

Such a challenge appealed to Sir Frederick Handley Page, who in 1909 had opened the first British factory built exclusively for the manufacture of aeroplanes. He accordingly set about designing a large bomber powered by two 120-hp Beardmore engines, to meet the specification. This project greatly impressed the authorities and Commodore (later Rear Admiral Sir Murray) Sueter, Director of the Air Department of the Admiralty, requested Handley Page to improve it and produce a "bloody paralyser" of an aeroplane. Accepting this as an official request, Handley Page dutifully enlarged his proposed bomber.

The result was the O/100, with a wing span exceeding 100 ft and powered by two 150-hp Sunbeam engines. Construction of such a machine posed many problems, as it was far bigger than any previously built in Britain. Taking no chances, Handley Page instituted a procedure whereby each main spar, rib, longeron, strut and fitting was structurally tested before acceptance. This foreshadowed the strict material and inspection standards which, today, are an integral part of aircraft development.

Concurrent with development of the airframe, Rolls-Royce were working on two new engines which became known eventually as the Eagle and Falcon. Test bench examples of the Eagle developed 300 hp at 2,000 rpm; but, to improve reliability, production engines were de-rated to 250 hp at 1,600 rpm and two of these power plants were installed in the prototype O/100. They were enclosed in armoured nacelles, each complete with its own armoured fuel tank.

Structurally, the O/100 prototype was conventional. The fuselage was a cross-braced box girder, which differed from contemporary aircraft only in its relative size. To assist production it was made in three sections: a front section, containing the front cockpits, a middle portion, containing the internal bomb-bay, and the tail section. The bombs were stowed vertically, nose upward, the bomb-bays being enclosed by small doors which were pushed open as the bombs fell. The crew sat in an enclosed cabin which was protected by bullet-proof glass and armour plate.

A massive undercarriage was fitted, consisting of two separate structures of steel tubes, supporting two pairs of big wheels, each wheel having its own shock absorber. A large sprung skid at the rear acted as an effective brake during landing.

Wing construction was also conventional, the wings being built in several sections, to facilitate production. Large extensions on the upper wing were supported by an A-shaped king-post above the outer interplane struts. Of particular interest is that the great wings were made to fold; this enabled the bombers to be stowed in the standard Bessonneau canvas field hangars of the time.

A biplane tail unit was fitted, embodying four horn-balanced elevators.

Production O/100s differed slightly from the prototype. The cockpit enclosure was removed, together with much of the armour plate. Flight trials showed pitch control to be unsatisfactory and to cure the trouble the "horns" were removed from the elevators. The tailplanes were unaltered, however, leaving the tail unit with the overhanging elevators which were a distinctive feature of the O/100.

Defensive armament comprised either a single Lewis gun or a pair on a Scarff ring-mounting in the nose cockpit, one or two Lewis guns in the upper rear cockpit, and a single Lewis gun mounted to fire rearward and downward through a hole in the floor of the fuselage, just aft of the wings. A few O/100s were fitted with two-pounder and six-pounder Davis guns, but these installations were not successful.

Maximum bomb-load was 2,000 lb. The loads consisted usually of eight 250-lb, sixteen 112-lb, three 520-lb or three 550-lb bombs, or a single 1,650-lb bomb.

The first O/100s went into service in November 1916. Unfortunately, the third machine to leave for France landed by accident behind the enemy lines, thus providing the Germans with an intact specimen of Britain's latest bomber. As can be imagined, it was inspected very thoroughly by German technicians and pilots.

The big bomber was used initially for daylight patrols but, following losses, was confined to night bombing, raids often being made by single machines.

Operations proved the O/100 to be a formidable warplane, by virtue of its big bomb-load. A single O/100 could carry three times the load of the contemporary Short Bomber, and six times the load of the D.H.4 day bomber. The saving in trained crews was also evident: six D.H.4s required 12 men, but the single O/100 was crewed by only three men.

A total of 46 O/100s were built and, during production, changes were made as a result of operational experience. The main change concerned the fuel system which was completely redesigned, the fuel tanks being removed from the engine nacelles and positioned above the bomb-bay, with two small gravity feed tanks installed in the upper wing. Following removal of the fuel tanks, the engine nacelles were shortened appreciably, and an ordinary interplane strut was fitted behind each nacelle. With other relatively minor changes, the improved version was designated O/400, and is the better known and more important of the two bombers.

Standard power plant of the O/400 was two Rolls-Royce Eagle Mk IV or Mk VIII engines, but a number had 320-hp Sunbeam Cossack, Sunbeam Maori or Fiat A.12*bis* engines.

As is usually the case with new weapons, the O/400 was at one stage very nearly abandoned. Britain's Air Board, convinced of the superiority of day bombing, suspended all orders for heavy night bombers. This decision was, however, short-lived and 100 O/400s were ordered. Following the first Gotha raids on England, the order was increased to 300 and then 700 aircraft.

In service, the improved bomber was used for several daring raids, including a low-level attack on a chemical works at Mannheim. As production got under way, substantial numbers of O/400s became operational, and on the night of 14/15 September 1918, 40 were despatched to bomb targets in the Saar area, the maximum force deployed at one time.

During September 1918, the O/400s began to deliver the big 1,650-lb bombs – the "block-busters" of the 1914–18 War. Out of the total of 700 O/400s ordered in Britain, about 400 were delivered before the Armistice.

About 100 more were built in America by the Standard Aircraft Corporation for the US Air Service. These American models were each powered by two 350-hp Liberty 12-N engines and had a maximum bomb-load of 3,000 lb. A few were sent to England, but the war ended before they could become operational.

Handley Page V/1500

Produced to carry a worthwhile bomb-load from bases in Britain to Berlin and other German industrial centres, the four-engined Handley Page V/1500 was the biggest aircraft built in Britain up to that time.

Orders for the experimental prototype were issued in July 1917. Built in great secrecy in Belfast, Ireland, and embodying all the experience gained during the development of the Handley Page O/100 and O/400 bombers, it flew for the first time in May 1918. Production models began to come off the lines in October 1918.

Despite its size, the V/1500 was reasonably conventional. To assist production, the top wing was made in five sections and the lower in six; although they spanned 126 ft, the wings could be folded.

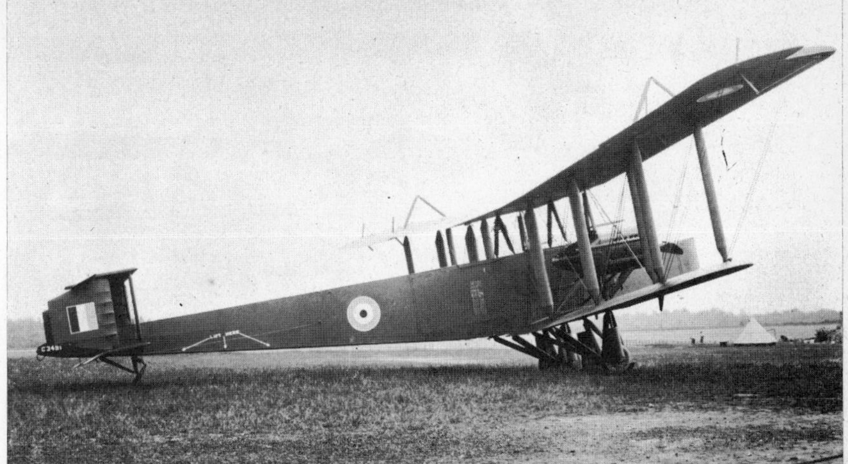

Handley Page O/400, Eagle engines

Handley Page O/400, Eagle engines, wings folded

Handley Page O/400 (H.M. Air Liner *Silver Star*), RAF Communication Wing

TYPE	DIMENSIONS span ft	span in	length ft	length in	height ft	height in	WEIGHT max t-o lb	PERFORMANCE max speed mph	at height ft	service ceiling ft	combat range miles	REMARKS
Handley Page O/400	100	0	62	10	22	0	NA	87	6,500	9,000	NA	Fiat engines
Handley Page O/400	100	0	62	10	22	0	11,670	78	6,500	5,500	NA	Maori engines
Handley Page O/400	100	0	62	10	22	0	13,360	97	SL	8,500	NA	Eagle VIII engines
Handley Page O/400	100	0	62	10	22	0	14,300	92	SL	10,000	NA	Liberty engines

Handley Page V/1500

Handley Page V/1500 prototype

Handley Page Hyderabad

Handley Page Hinaidi, No. 99 Squadron

To power the bomber, Rolls-Royce started work on an enlarged version of the Eagle, to be known as the Condor, developing 600 hp. This was not available in time, and four 375-hp Rolls-Royce Eagle VIII engines were fitted instead. These were mounted midway between the wings, in two tandem pairs. Unusually, the front engines each drove a two-bladed propeller, while the rear engines drove a smaller four-bladed propeller. On the prototype, the engines were at one time enclosed in bulky nacelles, but these were discarded on production machines, saving 500 lb of weight with little loss in performance.

The cross-braced box-girder fuselage was made in three sections. The first section contained the front gunner and pilot and the centre portion housed the bomb-bay. The rear section embodied a cat-walk giving access to the rear gun position at the extreme tail. Four 5-ft diameter wheels were fitted, each carried by a massive V-structure, the front members of which incorporated an oleo shock-absorber.

Defensive armament consisted of either a single Lewis machine-gun or pair of guns on a Scarff ring-mounting in the nose cockpit, one Lewis gun on a central socket-and-pillar mounting or two Lewis guns mounted to fire through a dorsal trap door in the fuselage aft of the wings, and a single Lewis gun on a Scarff ring-mounting in the tail.

The maximum bomb-load was 7,500 lb, and normally consisted of thirty 250-lb bombs. By the end of 1918, a 3,300-lb bomb had been developed for delivery by this aircraft.

A total of 255 V/1500s were ordered, but only six had been delivered by the time the Armistice was signed, and none of these was used operationally. The big bomber's capabilities thus remained untested; but it is interesting as a triumph of British aeronautical engineering, for pioneering the tail defensive gun position, and for inaugurating the policy of long-range strategic bombing. This remained RAF policy between the wars and culminated in the mighty Bomber Command striking force of World War II.

In December 1918, a V/1500 made the first through flight from Britain to India. Later, this aircraft took part in the Afghan War of 1920, when it made a single raid on Kabul—the V/1500's sole operational sortie.

Handley Page Hyderabad

This twin-engined heavy night bomber was developed from the Handley Page W.8 airliner to meet Air Ministry Specification 31/22. It was the last RAF night bomber of wooden construction, except for the smaller de Havilland Mosquito of World War II.

The prototype Hyderabad, known by the manufacturer as the HP24 (W.8D), flew for the first time in October 1923. In general appearance it did not seem much of an improvement over its twin-engined predecessors of 1914–18 vintage, and neither did its performance. It was a biplane with equal-span wings, the lower wing only having slight dihedral. The top wing incorporated the patented Handley Page slots, which gave it a high degree of lateral stability.

The power plant consisted of two 450-hp Napier Lion engines, mounted midway between the wings. Two fuel tanks, beneath the upper wing, provided a gravity feed to each engine.

The fuselage had a distinctive step-down from the pilot's cockpit to the nose-gunner's cockpit, and an equally distinctive angular fin and rudder. A four-wheeled undercarriage was fitted, and was constructed as two separate assemblies of two wheels.

Defensive armament consisted of three Lewis machine-guns, mounted in the nose and dorsal cockpits and in a ventral position aft of the wings, firing downward and to the rear. Maximum bomb load was 1,100 lb.

The Hyderabad went into service with No. 99 Squadron in April 1926; the second squadron, No. 10, was not formed until January 1928. The type was withdrawn from first-line service at the end of 1930, but remained in use by squadrons of the Auxiliary Air Force until 1933. A total of 45 Hyderabads were built.

Handley Page Hinaidi

The Hinaidi was a heavy night bomber developed from the Hyderabad.

It was a twin-engined biplane with slightly swept, equal-span, two-bay wings and carried a crew of four. The main differences compared with the Hyderabad were the fitting of 440-hp Bristol Jupiter VIII radial engines instead of the Napier Lions and, in the production version, use of an all-metal structure instead of wood. The net result was that the Hinaidi had a slightly better performance and carried a heavier war-load than the earlier bomber.

The prototype, a converted Hyderabad, first flew in March 1927. Production models, built to Air Ministry Specification 13/29 and designated Mk II, entered service with No. 99 Squadron in 1929.

Armament consisted of three Lewis machine-guns, in the nose and dorsal cockpits and in a ventral position just aft of the wings. The maximum bomb-load was 1,448 lb.

A troop-carrying version of the Hinaidi, known as the Clive, could carry 23 troops.

A total of 33 Hinaidis were built and six Hyderabads were converted into Hinaidis. They began to be replaced by Heyfords in 1933.

Handley Page Heyford

The outstanding feature of the Heyford twin-engined heavy night bomber was the attachment of the fuselage to the upper wing, instead of to the lower wing, as was conventional. The reason for this was to facilitate rapid re-arming, the bombs being stowed internally in the lower centre-section, which was specially thickened for the purpose.

The wings, of metal construction with fabric covering, were of equal span, with blunt tips. Ailerons were fitted to each wing, and the upper wing incorporated Handley Page slots.

The front of the rectangular-section fuselage was a metal-covered braced structure; the rear portion was a wire-braced steel-tube structure, with fabric covering.

The main undercarriage consisted of two separate units, mounted close to and just forward of the lower centre-section. From the undercarriage, struts extended to the engine nacelles, which were mounted directly to the underside of the upper centre-section. Equipment included an automatic pilot, radio and cameras.

Armament consisted of three Lewis machine-guns, mounted in the nose and dorsal cockpits, on screenable rotating mountings, and in a retractable "dustbin" ventral turret aft of the wing. The normal bomb-load was 2,800 lb, but a maximum of 3,500 lb could be carried over short ranges.

The prototype Heyford, designated H.P. 38, first flew in June 1930. Mk 1 models (H.P. 50), produced to Air Ministry Specification 23/32, went into service in 1933, with No. 99 Squadron. They were each powered by two 525-hp Rolls-Royce Kestrel IIIS engines, and were followed by a small batch of Mk IAs. These, in turn, were followed by Mk IIs and Mk IIIs, powered by 640-hp Kestrel VI engines, until a total of 122 Heyfords had been produced.

Heyfords remained in first-line service until replaced by Wellingtons in 1939, but some continued to be used for various ancillary duties during the early years of World War II.

Handley Page Heyford, ventral turret extended

Handley Page Heyford Mk IA

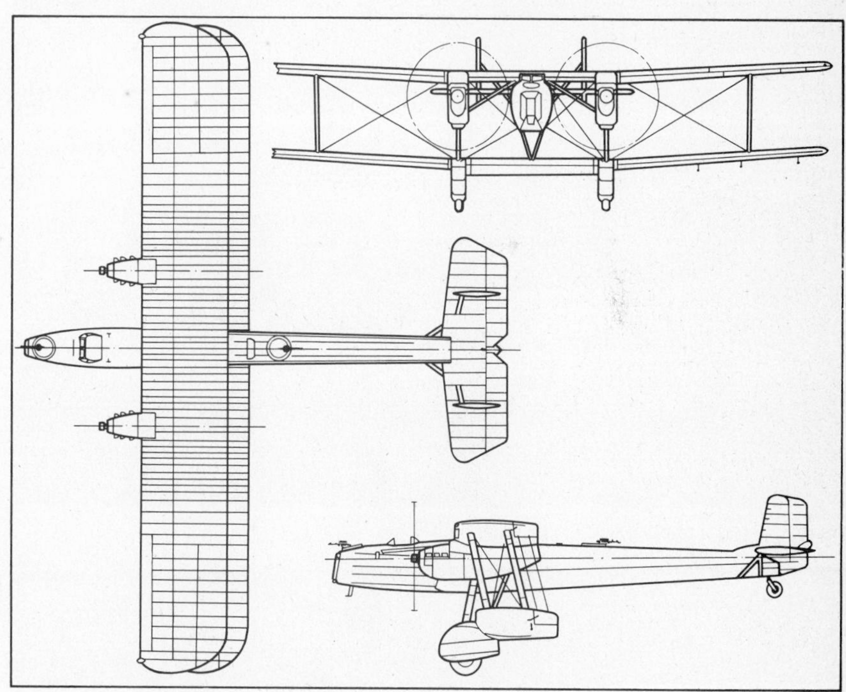
Handley Page Heyford

TYPE	DIMENSIONS						WEIGHT	PERFORMANCE				REMARKS
	span		length		height		max t-o	max speed	at height	service ceiling	combat range	
	ft	in	ft	in	ft	in	lb	mph	ft	ft	miles	
Handley Page V/1500	126	0	62	0	23	0	24,700	97	8,750	10,000	1,200	
Hyderabad	75	0	59	2	16	9	13,590	109	SL	14,000	NA	
Hinaidi Mk II	75	0	59	2	17	0	14,500	122	SL	14,500	850	
Heyford	75	0	58	0	17	6	16,900	142	13,000	21,000	920	

Handley Page Harrow Mk I

Handley Page Harrow Mk I

Handley Page Hampden Mk I, Canadian-built

Handley Page Hampden Mk I

Handley Page Harrow

A heavy bomber with a crew of five, the Harrow was one of the first monoplane bombers to be used by the RAF. It was adapted from the earlier HP.51 troop transport, to meet an urgent requirement for a bomber during the RAF expansion programme of the mid-1930s.

The cantilever wing was built in three sections and was tapered in chord and thickness. Its structure was metal, and the section forward of the single main spar was metal covered; aft of the spar, the wing was covered with fabric. Handley Page automatic slots were fitted to the leading-edge of the outer wings, and slotted ailerons and hydraulically-operated slotted flaps were carried on the trailing-edge.

The fuselage was constructed in three sections. The nose section consisted of a metal-covered duralumin framework, while the centre and aft sections were fabric covered, over a light tubular structure.

The undercarriage was of the divided type and was fixed. Because of the high position of the wing, the main legs were long and were a distinctive feature of the aircraft. The wheels were covered with large streamlined fairings.

Armament consisted of four 0·303-in Browning machine-guns, mounted in nose, dorsal and tail power-operated turrets, two guns being located in the tail turret. The maximum bomb-load was 3,000 lb and was stowed internally in the fuselage, below the floor of the centre-section.

Production Harrows, designated Mk I and powered by two 830-hp Pegasus X engines, went into service in April 1937, with No. 214 Squadron. Mk II Harrows were fitted with two 925-hp Pegasus XX engines. Thirty-nine Mk Is were built, followed by 61 Mk IIs.

When war started in 1939, Harrows had been superseded in bomber squadrons by Wellingtons; but during the war the survivors were used for transport duties, casualty evacuation, and for mine-laying – "Operation Mutton."

The transport Harrows each carried 20 passengers and were unarmed, streamlined fairings replacing the gun-turrets. They were sometimes known as Sparrows.

Handley Page Hampden and Hereford

The four-seat Hampden was the last of the twin-engined medium bombers to go into service during the expansion of Bomber Command in the late 1930s.

Of all-metal construction, with a flush-riveted stressed skin, the wings tapered in chord and thickness, the trailing-edges sweeping forward sharply. Wing-tip slots were fitted, together with hydraulically-operated trailing-edge flaps, giving the low landing speed of 73 mph.

The fuselage was an all-metal monocoque. It had a distinctive deep fore-body, housing the crew, and a relatively slender tail-boom, carrying the tailplane and twin fins and rudders – a configuration which led to the nicknames "Flying Panhandle" and "Flying Suitcase". The fuselage was built in three portions: the nose, centre-section and tail boom, the two latter being built in halves, split longitudinally, to facilitate production. The undercarriage retracted rearward into the engine nacelles. Maximum bomb-load was 4,000 lb, stowed internally in the fuselage beneath the wings.

The prototype was powered by two Bristol Pegasus PE.55a engines, but production Hampdens had two 1,000-hp Pegasus XVIIIs. They went into service in August 1938, with No. 49 Squadron, and when war broke out in the following year equipped eight squadrons.

During operations, the Hampden proved to have serious deficiencies, particularly in its defensive armament, which consisted of four 0·303-in machine-guns. The fixed forward-firing gun proved almost useless, and the single guns in the nose, dorsal and ventral positions had limited traverse, leaving a number of blind spots. In addition, the cramped quarters led to crew fatigue on long flights and it was almost impossible for crew members to gain access to each other's cockpits in an emergency. Losses during early daylight raids were very heavy and the type was virtually grounded.

To improve the defensive armament, the dorsal and ventral positions were each fitted with twin Vickers K machine-guns. In addition, armour plate was installed and flame-damping exhaust pipes were fitted for night flying. Thus modified, the Hampden did useful work in Bomber Command's night offensive from 1940 to 1942, taking part in the RAF's first raid on Berlin and in the famous 1,000-bomber raid on Cologne.

Hampdens were withdrawn from bombing duties in September 1942, but continued on operations with Coastal Command as torpedo-bombers. A single Mk II version was tested with Wright Cyclone engines.

A variant of the Hampden was the Hereford, powered by two 1,000-hp 16-cylinder H-type Napier Dagger engines. It went into service in 1940 with one flight of No. 185 Squadron, but after a short period was relegated to bomber crew training duties.

A total of 1,270 Hampdens were built in Britain; in addition, a small number were built in Canada. Only 100 Herefords were ordered.

Handley Page Halifax

The Halifax was a four-engined heavy bomber which, together with the Lancaster, formed the backbone of Bomber Command's offensive against Germany between 1941 and 1945, dropping a total of 255,000 short tons of bombs in 75,532 sorties.

It was produced to meet Air Ministry Specification P.13/36, issued in 1936, which called for an all-metal mid-wing medium-heavy bomber, to be powered by two Rolls-Royce Vulture 24-cylinder X-type engines. In the early stages, the aircraft was planned to have these engines, but a shortage of Vultures was anticipated and the design was altered to take four Rolls-Royce Merlins instead. This was fortunate, as the Vulture, used on the ill-fated Avro Manchester, entered service insufficiently developed, so that it proved unreliable.

Of all-metal stressed-skin construction, the Halifax was specially designed for quantity production. Each major component was made up of transportable sections, the sections themselves being sub-divided to prevent congestion of labour and so facilitate manufacture. The two-spar wing was in five main sections – the centre-section, carrying the inboard engines, two intermediate sections and two outer wing extensions, carrying the outer engines at their roots. Detachable trailing-edge sections were fitted to the rear spars; the leading-edge of the outer section was armoured and incorporated balloon cable cutters. Handley Page slotted trailing-edge flaps were fitted between the ailerons and the fuselage.

Of oval section, the monocoque fuselage was made in four main sections.

A crew of seven was normally carried, comprising two pilots, navigator, radio operator and three gunners; all crew positions were armoured.

Halifax Mk Is went into service in November 1940, with No. 35 Squadron. Each was powered by four 1,280-hp Rolls-Royce Merlin X engines, and was armed with two 0·303-in Browning machine-guns in a nose turret, and four Brownings in a Boulton Paul hydraulically-operated turret in the extreme tail, plus manually-operated beam guns on some machines. The maximum bomb-load was 13,000 lb, carried in the fuselage and in the centre-section on each side of the fuselage. Mk I sub-variants were the Series II aircraft, stressed for a loaded weight of 60,000 lb, and the Series III, with increased fuel tankage.

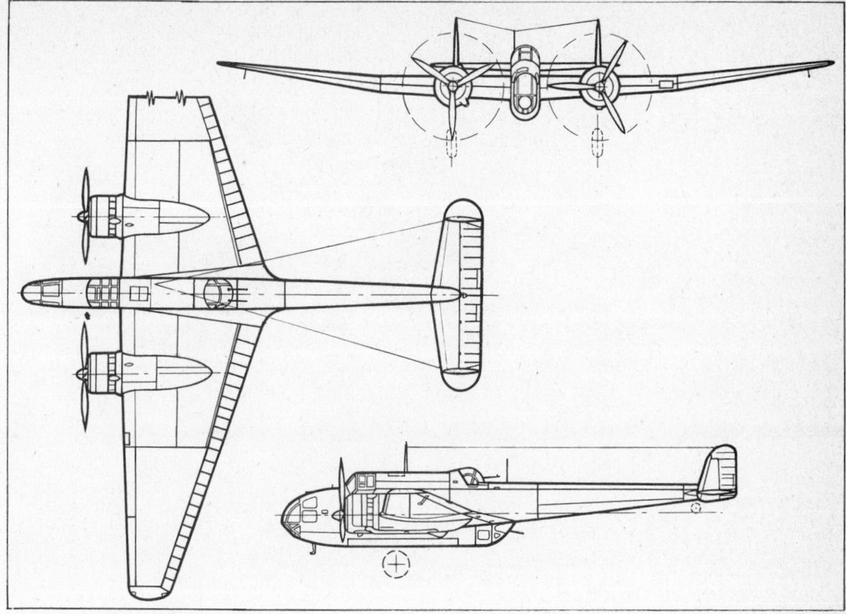

Handley Page Hampden Mk I

Handley Page Hereford

Handley Page Halifax Mk II Series I

TYPE	DIMENSIONS span ft	span in	length ft	length in	height ft	height in	WEIGHT max t-o lb	PERFORMANCE max speed mph	at height ft	service ceiling ft	combat range miles	REMARKS
Harrow Mk I	88	5	82	2	19	5	23,000	190	10,000	NA	1,250	
Harrow Mk II	88	5	82	2	19	5	23,000	200	10,000	22,800	1,250	
Hampden	69	2	53	7	14	11	18,756	254	13,800	19,000	1,200	

Handley Page Halifax B Mk III

Handley Page Halifax B Mk VI

Handley Page Halifax GR Mk VI, No. 224 Squadron

The Halifax Mk I was followed by the Mk II, with four 1,390-hp Merlin XX engines, which was also produced in a number of sub-variants. The Mk II Series I had flame-damping exhaust muffs and mounted a Boulton Paul two-gun dorsal turret amidships, but had the beam armament deleted. It was developed into the Series I (Special), on which the drag-producing flame-damping muffs were removed, together with the dorsal turret. In addition, the two-gun nose turret, which experience had shown was seldom used, was replaced by a streamlined fairing.

In turn, this variant was further developed into the Series IA. This was powered by four 1,390-hp Merlin XXII engines, in improved cowlings, had a lengthened streamlined transparent nose and re-introduced a low-drag dorsal twin-gun turret. A 20-mph increase in speed resulted from these aerodynamic refinements.

Late Series IA aircraft introduced the large rectangular tail fins which became standard; these dampened yaw effects and improved bombing accuracy. A Halifax was, incidentally, the first RAF aircraft to use the secret H2S blind bombing radar device.

Some Halifax Mk IIs served with Coastal Command. Designated GR II Series IA, these machines had an 0·50-in machine-gun in the nose.

The Halifax Mk III was the first variant not to have Merlin engines, being powered by four 1,615-hp Bristol Hercules XVIs and having a retractable tailwheel and an H2S scanner or ventral gun. Late Halifax Mk IIIs had extended wings.

Halifax Mk IV was the designation allotted to a projected improved version of the Mk II which was not produced.

The Halifax Mk V was similar to the Mk II, but with Dowty undercarriage and hydraulic equipment instead of Messier equipment.

The Halifax Mk VI was powered by four 1,800-hp Bristol Hercules 100 engines, with special carburettor filters for use in the tropics. It also had an improved fuel system, arranged so that each engine was fed independently from its own group of tanks.

Halifax Mks III, V and VII were used extensively for paratroop and glider-tug duties, and were the only aircraft able to tow the big Hamilcar glider. "Halibags", as they were nicknamed, were also used for parachuting arms and agents into occupied Europe, and for radio countermeasures duties.

The Halifax Mk VII, the final bomber version, was similar to the Mk VI, but was powered by Hercules XVI engines, owing to a shortage of Hercules 100s.

The Halifax made its last combat sortie on 25 April 1945, against gun batteries on the Frisian Islands, and was withdrawn from Bomber Command immediately after the war. It was then used by Coastal Command, and for training parachutists and for supply dropping, and special variants were produced for these duties.

Halifax production totalled 6,176 aircraft.

Handley Page Victor

The Victor was the third and last of the V-class four-jet long-range medium bombers to go into service with the RAF.

It is of all-metal stressed-skin construction, the outstanding feature of the design being the unique crescent-shaped wing. On this, the angle of sweepback decreases progressively from root to tip, in three distinct stages, with the outer sections being only slightly swept. In addition, the thickness-to-chord ratio is graduated along the span, to give a constant critical Mach number over the whole wing. Thus, the Victor wing combines the advantages of a low aspect ratio wing with pronounced sweepback, as required for high speed, with those of a high aspect ratio wing of moderate sweepback, for good control during approach and landing. The lift capability of the wing is further increased by flaps on the leading-edge and Fowler-type flaps on the inboard section of the trailing-edge.

The fuselage, accommodating a crew of five, is a semi-monocoque structure with a large dielectric panel under the nose, which is of a distinctive bulged shape.

The doors of the capacious bomb-bay retract inward to open. The tailplane, incorporating two degrees of sweep-back on the leading-edge, is mounted on top of the fin.

Victor B Mk 1s went into service in 1958, with No. 10 Squadron. The efficiency of the crescent wing was soon indicated by the high praise of pilots for the docile handling qualities of the aircraft during landing, and by the fact that the Victor had been flown faster than sound in a shallow dive. These early machines were powered by four 11,000-lb s t Bristol Siddeley Sapphire ASSa7 turbojets. Victor B Mk 1As differed from Mk Is in having sophisticated electronic countermeasures equipment in the rear fuselage.

Victor B Mk 2s are of improved design with four 17,250-lb s t Rolls-Royce Conway turbojets and the ability to carry the nuclear-armed Blue Steel stand-off bomb, which can be programmed to make either high- or low-altitude run-ins to the target.

To extend the period of the aircraft's effectiveness as a deterrent weapon in the face of the growing efficiency of anti-aircraft missile systems, Victors have been modified so that penetration to the target can be made at a low level, below radar screens. When so adapted, the aircraft is camouflaged on the upper surface and carries specialized equipment permitting accurate navigation at low altitudes.

Many Mk 1 Victors have been modified into flight refuelling tankers (BK Mk 1/1A), able to service three aircraft at once. Also in service is the B(SR) Mk 2, a strategic reconnaissance version of the Mk 2 able to utilize both photographic and radar-mapping techniques.

Hawker Woodcock

The Woodcock was the first aircraft produced in series by the H.G. Hawker Engineering Company, which had been formed in 1920 as the successor to the war-famous firm of Sopwith. It was a single-seat fighter, and in the ensuing years the company was to become renowned throughout the world as a specialist in this category.

Two prototypes were built. The first had two-bay wings and was powered by an Armstrong Siddeley Jaguar radial engine. The second prototype had single-bay wings and a 420-hp Bristol Jupiter radial engine, an interesting feature of which was the metal "helmets" fitted over each cylinder head to reduce drag.

The second prototype was designated Mk II, and was the version eventually ordered for the RAF. It was a biplane, of conventional wooden construction, with fabric covering. A popular feature with pilots was the unusually wide undercarriage.

Armament consisted of two fixed forward-firing Vickers machine-guns, unusually mounted on the outside of the fuselage in line with the cockpit and synchronized to fire between the propeller blades.

The Woodcock went into service with No. 3 Squadron in May 1925, replacing the veteran Sopwith Snipes of 1918 vintage, and remained operational until 1928. A total of 62 Woodcocks were built and were intended for use as both day and night fighters.

Handley Page Victor B Mk 1, No. 15 Squadron

Handley Page Victor B Mk 2, with Blue Steel missile

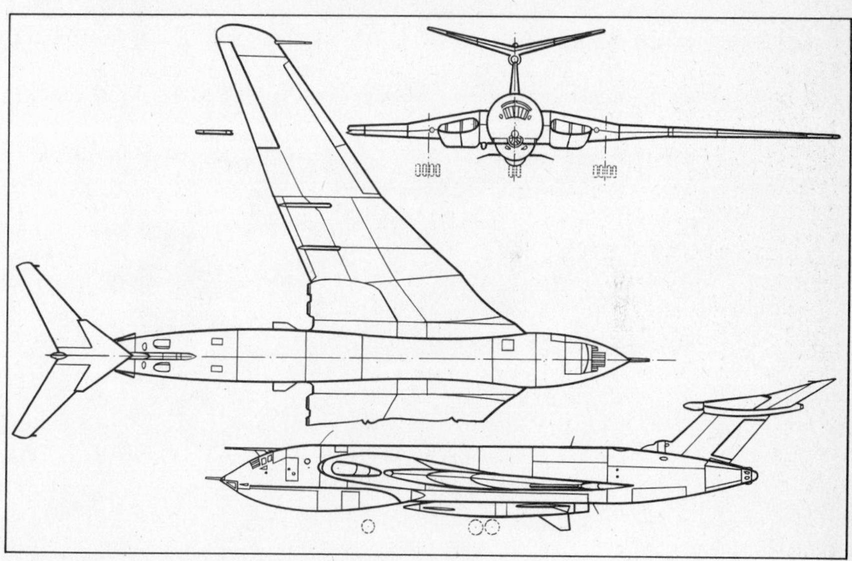
Handley Page Victor B Mk 2, with Blue Steel missile

TYPE	DIMENSIONS span ft	span in	length ft	length in	height ft	height in	WEIGHT max t-o lb	PERFORMANCE max speed mph	at height ft	service ceiling ft	combat range miles	REMARKS
Halifax Mk I	98	10	70	1	20	0	60,000	265	17,500	22,800	1,860	With 5,800-lb bomb load
Halifax Mk II	98	10	71	7	NA		60,000	285	17,500	NA	NA	
Halifax Mk III	104	2	71	7	NA		65,000	NA	NA	NA	NA	
Halifax Mk V	104	2	71	7	NA		60,000	NA	NA	NA	NA	
Halifax Mk VI	104	2	71	7	NA		68,000	312	22,000	24,000	2,400	With reduced bomb load
Halifax Mk VII	104	2	71	7	NA		65,000	NA	NA	NA	NA	
Victor B Mk 1	110	0	114	11	28	1	NA	NA	NA	NA	NA	
Victor B Mk 2	120	0	114	11	30	1	NA	NA	NA	NA	NA	
Woodcock Mk II	32	6	23	3	10	3	3,040	138	NA	20,000	NA	Endurance 3½ hours

Hawker Woodcock Mk II

Hawker Horsley Mk II torpedo-bomber

Hawker Dantorp

Hawker Dantorp floatplane

A variant was the Danecock (Dankok), developed for the Danish Naval Air Service. This had lower wings of reduced span, raked interplane struts and a slightly smaller fuselage. Three were built by Hawkers, and 12 more were built under licence in Denmark.

Hawker Horsley

Designed to Air Ministry Specification 26/23, the Horsley was adopted as the standard day bomber of the RAF after exhaustive competitive tests with the Bristol Berkeley, Handley Page Handcross and Westland Yeovil.

It was a two-seat biplane with unequal-span wings, utilizing a special high-lift, relatively thick, aerofoil section. The upper wing had an appreciably bigger chord than the lower wing and was of fabric-covered wooden construction, in three sections. The top centre-section was supported above the fuselage by an A-strut assembly, and from the lower wing by two N-type interplane struts. The outer wings were supported near their tips by a pair of splayed-out interplane struts.

The fuselage was built in two sections, the front portion being of steel and the rear of wooden construction, all fabric-covered. A prone bombing position was provided under and forward of the pilot's cockpit, with a sliding panel for aiming. A wide-track undercarriage of the divided axle type was fitted.

Power was provided by a 670-hp Rolls-Royce Condor IIIA geared and water-cooled engine.

Armament consisted of one fixed forward-firing Vickers machine-gun, synchronized to fire between the propeller blades, and a Lewis machine-gun on a Scarff ring-mounting in the rear cockpit. A maximum bomb-load of 600 lb could be carried on racks under the fuselage and wings. Alternatively, a single 2,150-lb torpedo could be carried; this was the heaviest weapon of its type carried by any landplane up to that time.

The torpedo-carrying Horsley was identical to the bomber version, except for the massive torpedo-carrying crutch and internal equipment. In spite of its size, the Horsley was remarkably manoeuvrable, with almost the controllability of a fighter.

Production machines went into service in 1927, replacing Fairey Fawns in Nos. 11 and 100 (Bomber) Squadrons. The first torpedo-carrying versions went to the Scottish-based No. 36 Squadron in June 1928.

Early production models were designated Mk IIs; Mk IIIs were later aircraft of all-metal construction.

Horsleys were used for a number of long-distance flights, the most notable being an attempt on the World's Long Distance record, then standing at 3,350 miles, to be accomplished by flying non-stop from Britain to India. The Horsley was forced down in the Persian Gulf after flying 3,420 miles in 34½ hours. This unofficial record was held for only two hours, being beaten by Lindbergh's New York-Paris flight.

A total of 119 Horsleys were built, production ceasing in 1932. The bomber version remained in service until 1934 and the torpedo-bomber until 1935. A small number served with the Greek Air Force.

Hawker Dantorp

The Dantorp was an export version of the Horsley torpedo-bomber, of which two were delivered to Denmark in 1933. It differed from the British version in having an 805-hp Armstrong Siddeley Leopard IIIA engine in place of the usual Rolls-Royce Condor, and in the installation of an 80-gallon auxiliary fuel tank.

The Dantorps were flown extensively, on both wheel and float undercarriages; but no further production was undertaken, although the Danish Government had licence rights. One British-built machine made the first non-stop flight from Copenhagen to the Faroes.

Hawker Hart

The Hart was a two-seat biplane bomber. Designed to Air Ministry Specification 12/26, it was adopted as the RAF's new standard light day bomber after competitive trials with the Fairey Fox II and Avro Antelope.

Of all-metal construction, with fabric covering, the Hart had unequal-span, single-bay, staggered wings. The upper centre-section had a deep cut-out in the trailing-edge to improve the pilot's view, and was carried above the fuselage on four splayed-out struts. The outer wings were supported near each tip by a single pair of splayed-out N-type interplane struts. Ailerons were fitted only to the upper wing, which also embodied Handley Page slots. A distinctive feature was the marked sweepback of the top wing, which contrasted with the straight lower wing.

The fuselage was a braced metal box-girder, faired to an oval section and covered with fabric. Construction was of duralumin, with the more highly stressed parts in steel. The undercarriage was of the cross-axle Vee type, the front legs incorporating oleo struts.

Armament consisted of a single fixed Vickers machine-gun, mounted in a trough to one side of the engine and synchronized to fire between the propeller blades, and a Lewis machine-gun on a Hawker gun ring in the rear cockpit. The gunner acted also as bomb-aimer and sighted through an aperture in the cockpit floor. Maximum bomb-load was 500 lb.

The standard engine was the 525-hp Rolls-Royce Kestrel 1B, but some machines were fitted with the 510-hp Kestrel X (DR) and there were literally dozens of experimental engine installations.

The prototype Hart first flew in June 1928, and was followed by a batch of 15 development aircraft, built to Specification 9/29. These were issued to No. 33 Squadron in 1930, and quickly demonstrated their excellent performance, which was better than that of most contemporary single-seat fighters.

The Hart proved to be one of the most adaptable types ever used by the RAF and many variants appeared during the long production run, which totalled 983 machines.

Major sub-variants included the Hart C for communication duties, the Hart India, the Hart Special, developed for use in the tropics, and the Hart Trainer. The Hart Special was fitted with a de-rated Kestrel X engine and tropical radiator, and a redesigned undercarriage with heavy-duty tyres and wheel brakes, and carried comprehensive desert equipment.

On the Hart Trainers, the rear cockpit was modified for dual controls and blind flying equipment.

Harts were supplied to numerous countries, including Estonia, South Africa, Southern Rhodesia, Sweden and Yugoslavia. The Swedish machines had 580-hp Bristol Pegasus radials, four British-built aircraft being supplemented by 42 built under licence.

On the North West Frontier of India, the Hart served until 1939, when it was replaced by the Blenheim.

Hawker Fury I

The Fury single-seat interceptor fighter was the first RAF aircraft to enter squadron service with a speed better than 200 mph. It was the finest biplane fighter of its day, with sensitive controls, a high rate of climb and outstanding manoeuvrability.

Developed from the Hawker F.20/27 and the Hornet prototype, the Fury met a new service requirement which called for a higher rate of climb and a higher maximum speed than contemporary fighters, at the expense of endurance. It was adopted as the RAF's standard interceptor after exhaustive competitive trials with the Fairey Firefly IIM.

Hawker Hart, No. 6 Squadron

Hawker Hart, Pegasus engine, Swedish version

Hawker Fury Mk I, No. 1 Squadron

TYPE	DIMENSIONS span ft	span in	length ft	length in	height ft	height in	WEIGHT max t-o lb	PERFORMANCE max speed mph	at height ft	service ceiling ft	combat range miles	REMARKS
Horsley Mk II	56	9	38	3	13	8	7,800	126	NA	14,000	NA	Day-bomber
Horsley Mk II	56	9	38	3	NA		9,271	NA	NA	NA	NA	Torpedo-bomber
Dantorp	56	9	NA		13	8	9,950	125	NA	14,000	NA	
Hart	37	3	29	4	10	5	4,554	184	NA	21,000	470	Bomber version

Hawker Fury Series I, Hornet engine, Persian Air Force

Hawker Fury Series II, Mercury engine, Persian Air Force

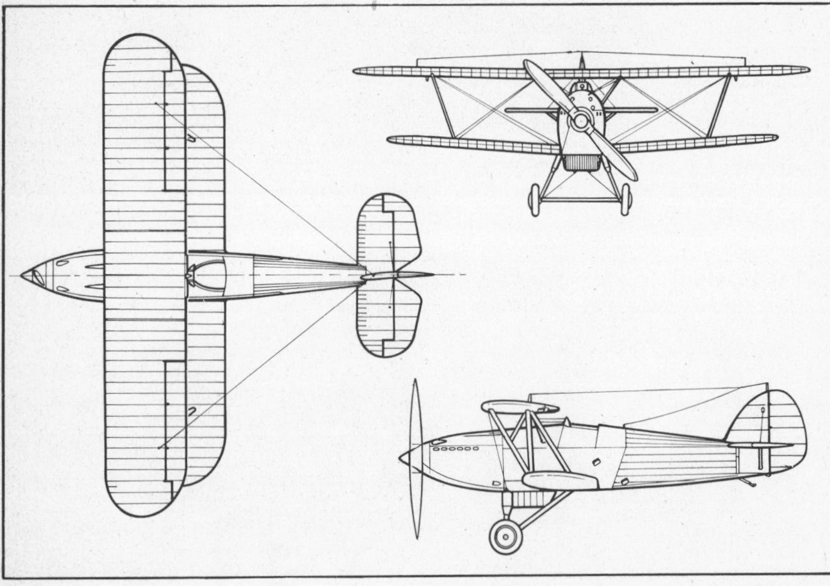
Hawker Fury Mk I

Hawker Turret Demon

The Fury had unequal-span, single-bay, staggered wings, with metal spars, wooden ribs and fabric covering. The centre-section of the upper wing was supported above the fuselage by a pair of splayed-out N-struts, and the outer wings were supported near each tip by a single pair of splayed-out N-type interplane struts. Ailerons were fitted to the top wing only.

Basically a braced metal box-girder, the fuselage was faired to an oval section, the nose being covered with quickly-detachable metal cowling panels and the rear part with fabric. The undercarriage was of the cross-axle Vee type, the front legs incorporating oleo-cum-rubber shock-absorbers.

Standard engine was a closely-cowled 525-hp Rolls-Royce Kestrel IIS, but a large number of experimental engine installations were flight tested.

Armament consisted of two fixed Vickers machine-guns, mounted above the engine and synchronized to fire between the propeller blades.

Built to Air Ministry Specification 13/30, production aircraft, designated Fury Mk I, went into service with No. 43 Squadron in 1931. They proved popular with their pilots, who were delighted with the 30-mph superiority they had over contemporary fighters and with the Fury's excellent rate of climb and manoeuvrability. A total of 146 Fury Is were built and the type remained in first-line service until 1939.

Fury Is served also with the air forces of Norway (1), Yugoslavia (6), Portugal (3) and Persia (now Iran) (20), the Persian machines having Pratt & Whitney Hornet or Bristol Mercury radials. The later Fury Mk II is described separately.

Hawker Demon

Developed from the Hart bomber, the Demon was a two-seat fighter and its adoption by the RAF re-introduced this class of aircraft which it had not used since the 1914–18 War.

Built to Air Ministry Specification 15/30, the prototype Demon was a converted Hart. Major changes included the fitting of a 560-hp fully-supercharged Rolls-Royce Kestrel V(DR) engine, the installation of two-way radio equipment and a redesigned rear cockpit. The coaming of the latter was altered to slope downward and forward, and it was fitted with a tilted gun-ring, to improve the arc of fire.

The Demon was of all-metal construction and fabric-covered, with unequal-span single-bay staggered wings. The trailing-edge of the upper centre-section had a deep cut-out to improve the pilot's view, and was supported above the fuselage on a pair of splayed-out struts. The outer wings were supported near each tip by a pair of splayed-out N-type interplane struts.

The fuselage was a braced metal box-girder, faired to an oval section and covered with fabric. The undercarriage was of the cross-axle Vee type, the front legs embodying oleo struts.

Armament consisted of two fixed Vickers machine-guns, mounted in troughs on each side of the engine and synchronized to fire between the propeller blades and a Lewis machine-gun mounted on the tilted gun ring in the rear cockpit. Some Demons were fitted with an additional Vickers gun on the starboard side of the fuselage. Light bombs could be carried on racks beneath the wings.

An initial batch of Demons, known at the time as Hart Fighters, was issued to a flight of No. 23 Squadron in May 1931. Production Demons were built to Air Ministry Specification 6/32. Early machines were fitted with the 485-hp Rolls-Royce Kestrel IIS engine, but later the derated 580-hp Kestrel V or 640-hp Kestrel V was installed.

As might be expected, it was not easy for the rear gunner to operate efficiently in a 200-mph slipstream; to ease the problem a special hydraulically-operated "lobster-back" shield was developed by Frazer Nash to protect the gunner. Normally closed, this opened up in proportion to the movement of the gunner. The shield was fitted to all later Demons, which were consequently known as Turret Demons.

Sixty-four Demons were supplied to the Australian Government for general-purpose duties. These had more comprehensive equipment than the standard RAF version, including a message pick-up hook, and a tailwheel replaced the normal tail skid.

A total of 308 Demons were built, and the type remained in service with the RAF until 1939.

Hawker Nimrod

The Nimrod was a single-seat carrier-borne version of the Fury interceptor. Although externally similar to its RAF counterpart, it was a distinct type in its own right and differed considerably both structurally and in equipment.

The Nimrod was a biplane with unequal-span, single-bay, staggered wings, of greater span than those of the Fury. The centre-section of the upper wing was supported above the fuselage by a pair of splayed-out N-struts, and the outer wings were supported near each tip by a single pair of splayed-out N-type interplane struts. Ailerons were fitted to the top wing only.

The fuselage was a braced metal box-girder, faired to an oval section. The nose was covered with quickly-detachable metal cowling panels, and the rear with fabric. Compared with the Fury, the fuselage was strengthened to permit catapulting, and was fitted with a deck arrester hook and a larger fuel tank. Additional equipment included more comprehensive radio gear, oxygen, hoisting gear and cockpit lighting and heating. The undercarriage was of the cross-axle Vee type, the front legs incorporating oleo-cum-rubber shock-absorbers. Flotation bags, fitted in the rear fuselage, and flotation boxes in the top wing were designed to keep the aircraft afloat should it come down in the sea.

Armament consisted of two fixed Vickers machine-guns, mounted above the engine and synchronized to fire between the propeller blades. Light bombs could be carried on racks under the starboard wing.

In the early design stages, the Nimrod was known as the Norn, and was developed from the N.21/26 private-venture prototype, itself a development of the Hoopoe. The prototype Nimrod, powered by a 480-hp Rolls-Royce Kestrel IS engine, first flew in 1930. Later, a 525-hp Kestrel IIMS was installed. The second Nimrod prototype was fitted with twin floats.

Initial production models were designated Nimrod Mk I and 42 of these were built. They went into service in 1932, replacing the long-serving Fairey Flycatchers of Nos. 402, 408 and 409 Fleet Fighter Flights.

An improved version, fitted with an up-rated 650-hp Rolls-Royce Kestrel V and introducing modified wings and tail unit, was designated Nimrod Mk II. A total of 36 of this variant were built, and those operated by No. 802 Squadron, on board the carrier *Glorious*, were still in service in May 1939. The Nimrod was superseded by the Sea Gladiator and Skua.

Hawker Osprey

The Osprey was a two-seat carrier-borne fighter-reconnaissance aircraft. It was the naval version of the Hart day-bomber, and pioneered the introduction of this class of aircraft on board carriers.

It was a biplane with unequal-span, single-bay, staggered wings, which could be folded to facilitate stowage. Wing construction was of stainless steel and

Hawker Demon, RAAF

Hawker Nimrod Mk I

Hawker Nimrod Mk I floatplane

TYPE	DIMENSIONS span ft	span in	length ft	length in	height ft	height in	WEIGHT max t-o lb	PERFORMANCE max speed mph	at height ft	service ceiling ft	combat range miles	REMARKS
Fury I	30	0	26	8	10	2	3,490	207	14,000	28,000	305	
Demon	37	3	29	7	10	5	4,668	182	16,400	27,500	NA	
Nimrod Mk I	33	6	27	0	9	9	4,258	181	13,120	26,000	NA	Endurance 1.65 hours
Nimrod Mk II	33	6	27	0	9	9	4,258	195	14,000	26,000	NA	

Hawker Osprey Mk I

Hawker Osprey Mk III floatplane

Hawker Hardy, Kestrel IB engine, No. 6 Squadron

Hawker Hartbees

duralumin, fabric-covered. The top centre-section was of short chord, to improve the pilot's view, and was supported above the fuselage on four splayed-out struts. The outer wings were supported near each tip by a single pair of splayed-out interplane struts. Ailerons were fitted only to the top wing, which also embodied Handley Page slots. The Osprey retained the distinctive Hart feature of having a swept top wing and straight lower wings.

The fuselage was a braced stainless steel box-girder, faired to an oval section and covered with fabric. Compared with the Hart, it was strengthened to permit catapulting, and housed flotation bags.

Either a wheel or twin-float undercarriage could be fitted. With wheels, the main units were of the cross-axle Vee type, the front legs incorporating oleo struts.

Armament consisted of one fixed Vickers machine-gun, synchronized to fire between the propeller blades, and a Lewis machine-gun on a movable mounting in the rear cockpit.

The prototype Osprey was actually the Hart prototype, modified to meet the requirements of Air Ministry Specification O.22/26, and first flew in 1930.

An initial production batch of 28 aircraft followed. Designated Osprey Mk I, the first of these went into service in November 1932, with Flights No. 404 and 409 of the Fleet Air Arm, replacing Fairey Flycatchers.

The next batch of 16 aircraft were designated Osprey Mk II, and the third batch were Osprey Mk IIIs. These were each powered by a 525-hp Rolls-Royce Kestrel IIMS engine, but the next and final batch of 27 Ospreys, designated Mk IV, had the uprated 640-hp Kestrel V.

Hawker Hardy

This two-seat general-purpose biplane was a development of the Hart and Audax, adapted to carry the more comprehensive equipment required for general duties.

Of all-metal construction, with fabric covering, it had unequal-span, single-bay, staggered wings. The upper centre-section had a deep cut-out in the trailing-edge to improve the pilot's view, and was carried above the fuselage on four splayed-out struts. The outer wings were supported near each tip by a single pair of splayed-out N-type interplane struts. Ailerons were fitted only to the upper wing, which also embodied Handley Page slots.

The fuselage was a braced metal box-girder, faired to an oval section and covered with fabric. The undercarriage was of the cross-axle Vee type, the front legs incorporating oleo struts.

Armament consisted of a single fixed Vickers machine-gun, mounted on the port side of the nose and synchronized to fire between the propeller blades, and a Lewis machine-gun on a mounting in the rear cockpit. Four 20-lb bombs could be carried on racks under the lower wings. The Hardy was powered by either a 530-hp Rolls-Royce Kestrel IB or a 580-hp Kestrel X.

Specialized equipment weighed nearly 200 lb, and included a tropical survival kit, water containers, message pick-up hook, a tropical radiator and racks for supply containers under the lower wings. In service, some machines were fitted with large-section, low-pressure tyres to facilitate operation from rough landing strips in the desert.

The Hardy, 47 of which were built, went into service in 1935 with No. 30 Squadron at Mosul in Iraq, where it superseded the Wapiti. The type survived to see service in 1940 against the Italian forces in East Africa and one aircraft at least was still flying on communications duties in June 1941.

Hawker Hartbees

This two-seat ground support aircraft was yet another member of the versatile Hart family, developed via the Audax army co-operation biplane. Produced to meet the specific requirements of the South African Air Force, it resembled the original version of the Demon in construction and appearance; but it had only a single forward-firing Vickers gun, plus the observer's Lewis gun and light bombs, and was specially equipped for service duties in tropical climates.

The first of four Hawker-built Hartbees flew on 28 June 1935. Two of these aircraft were standard "light-weight" models, the others had additional cockpit armour. They were followed by 65 similar aircraft built under licence at the Roberts Heights factory, Pretoria. Standard power plant for the Hartbees was the 608-hp Rolls-Royce Kestrel VFP.

Most notable exploit of the SAAF Hartbees was a mass raid, in company with ex-RAF Harts, against Italian positions on the Kenya-Ethiopia border on 11 June 1940. Surviving aircraft served as trainers until 1946.

Hawker Hind

The Hind two-seat light bomber was produced to meet Air Ministry Specification G.7/34 for an interim replacement for the Hart. The idea was to enable extra squadrons to be formed rapidly, as part of the RAF expansion of the mid-1930s, without waiting for the more advanced Blenheims and Battles, the introduction into service of which was several years away. Thus, the Hind became the last biplane light bomber of the RAF.

It was based on the Hart, but differed in having the more powerful supercharged 640-hp Rolls-Royce Kestrel V engine and improvements in the prone bomb-aiming position and in the rear cockpit, which was cut down in a way similar to that of the Demon to improve the field of fire for the gunner. Minor refinements included a tail-wheel, in place of a skid, and "ram-horn" exhaust manifolds.

Armament consisted of one Vickers Mk III or V machine-gun, mounted on the port side of the nose and synchronized to fire between the propeller blades, and one Lewis machine-gun on a ring in the rear cockpit. Maximum bomb-load was 510 lb, made up of 230-lb, 112-lb, 25-lb and 20-lb bombs.

The prototype Hind first flew on 12 September 1934, and production aircraft began leaving the lines a year later. Machines of the first batch were used to equip one flight of each of Nos. 18, 21 and 34 Squadrons. Production mounted rapidly, and by April 1937 no fewer than 338 Hinds were in service with the RAF, equipping 20 bomber squadrons. A further 114 were serving with seven squadrons of the Auxiliary Air Force.

When, at the end of 1937, Bomber Command began to receive Battles and Blenheims, large numbers of the superseded Hinds were converted into dual-control trainers, to equip the proposed Volunteer Reserve Flying Training Schools. During the conversion, the rear gun was removed and the rear cockpit redesigned to accommodate the instructor's duplicated controls and instruments. The forward-firing Vickers gun was also removed from some trainers.

A total of 527 Hinds were supplied to the RAF, and the type was exported to numerous overseas countries, including Afghanistan (20), Ireland (6), Kenya (6), Latvia (3), New Zealand (30), Persia (35), South Africa (22), Switzerland (1) and Yugoslavia (3). The Swiss and Afghan bombers, like the RAF machines, were powered by the Kestrel V; the Yugoslav Hinds had the Kestrel XVI and Gnome-Rhône K-9 Mistral; Persian aircraft had the Bristol Mercury VIII and Latvian machines the Mercury IX. Some of the Persian and Afghan Hinds were in service until the late 1940s.

Hawker Hind

Hawker Hind, Mercury IX engine, Latvian Air Force

Hawker Hind, Gnome-Rhône K-9 Mistral engine, Yugoslav Air Force

TYPE	DIMENSIONS						WEIGHT	PERFORMANCE				REMARKS
	span ft	span in	length ft	length in	height ft	height in	max t-o lb	max speed mph	at height ft	service ceiling ft	combat range miles	
Osprey Mk IV	37	0	29	4	10	5	NA	176	13,120	22,000	NA	Landplane
Osprey Mk IV	37	0	31	10	12	5	NA	169	NA	22,000	NA	Seaplane
Hardy	37	3	29	7	10	7	5,005	161	SL	17,000	NA	
Hartbees	37	3	29	7	10	5	4,787	176	6,000	22,000	NA	
Hind	37	3	29	7	10	7	5,298	186	16,400	26,400	430	

Hawker Fury Mk II, No. 25 Squadron

Hawker Spanish Fury, Spanish Air Force

Hawker Yugoslav Fury Series II, Yugoslav Air Force

Hawker Hurricane prototype

Hawker Fury Mk II

Developed from the Fury Mk I, this single-seat fighter was produced to meet a requirement for six squadrons of an interim replacement until the monoplane Hurricane became available.

In general configuration it closely resembled the Mk I, having unequal-span, single-bay, staggered wings, with metal spars, wooden ribs and fabric covering. The centre-section of the upper wing was supported above the fuselage by a pair of splayed-out N-struts; the outer wings were supported near each tip by a pair of splayed-out N-type interplane struts. Ailerons were fitted to the top wing only.

The fuselage was a braced rectangular box section, built on the Warren-girder principle, faired to an oval section by stringers and covered with fabric. The undercarriage was of the cross-axle Vee type, with oleo-rubber shock-absorbers. The wheels were spatted.

Armament consisted of two fixed Vickers machine-guns, mounted in the top decking above the engine and synchronized to fire between the propeller blades.

The Fury Mk II was powered by a 640-hp Rolls-Royce Kestrel VI engine. This 20 per cent increase in power raised the top speed by about 8 per cent compared with the Mk I, and improved the rate of climb by 34 per cent. To offset the higher fuel consumption of the new engine, an additional tank was added in front of the cockpit; the weight of this extra fuel reduced the top speed slightly below what otherwise would have been obtained.

Fury Mk IIs went into service in 1937 with No. 25 Squadron and the type remained operational until 1938. Ninety-nine were built for the RAF; in addition Fury Mk IIs were supplied to Yugoslavia (10), Spain (3) and South Africa (6). The Yugoslav machines were powered by 745-hp Rolls-Royce Kestrels with low-drag radiators, and had a cantilever undercarriage and provision for four guns. The Spanish Furies each had a 700-hp Hispano-Suiza 12X Brs engine and a cantilever undercarriage.

The Fury Mk II should not be confused with the Intermediate Fury or the High Speed Fury – sometimes referred to, incorrectly, as the Super Fury. These two versions were private-venture prototypes, produced to investigate contemporary problems in fighter technology. During trials they were fitted with a variety of engines, including the 700-hp Rolls-Royce steam-cooled Goshawk and the 1,000-hp Rolls-Royce PV-12, which later became famous as the Merlin.

Hawker Hurricane

The Hurricane was one of the great fighters of World War II. It will be remembered forever for the part it played during the Battle of Britain in 1940 when, together with the Spitfire, it withstood and overcame the numerically superior Luftwaffe, then master of conquered Continental Europe. During this vital aerial battle, Hurricanes shot down more enemy aircraft than did all the other defences, air and ground, combined.

The development of the Hurricane started in 1933 when Hawkers began the design of a Fury Monoplane, to be powered by a Rolls-Royce Goshawk engine and with a fixed, spatted undercarriage. Early in 1934 the design was modified to accommodate the new Rolls-Royce PV-12 engine, later to become famous as the Merlin; at the same time the undercarriage was altered to retract inward and an enclosed cockpit was introduced.

So promising was the project that the Air Ministry drafted Specification F.36/34 around the design as it stood, and then immediately accepted the aircraft as conforming to the Specification!

The prototype, powered by a Merlin C engine, driving a two-bladed fixed-pitch wooden propeller, first flew on 6 November 1935. Brief handling trials confirmed the estimated performance, and in June 1936 an order for 600 production models was placed. Powered by the improved 1,030-hp Merlin II engine, Hurricane Mk Is entered service in 1937 with a flight of No. 111 Squadron.

The speed with which the Hurricane went into service reflected the fact that its construction differed little from that of the Fury. The low cantilever wings comprised a centre-section of parallel chord and two tapering outer wings, of two-spar construction with a metal leading-edge and, on early Mk Is, fabric covering elsewhere. All-metal split flaps extended from the ailerons to beneath the fuselage.

The fuselage was a tubular-metal, cross-braced, rectangular Warren-girder structure, covered at the front with large detachable metal panels and aft with fabric over light wooden formers. The undercarriage shock-absorber struts were hinged at the end of the centre-section and retracted inward hydraulically. This arrangement gave the Hurricane a relatively wide track, making it stable and easy to handle on the ground.

The unprecedented armament consisted of eight 0.303-in Browning machine-guns, arranged in groups of four in each wing and firing outside the propeller disc.

As production of the Mk I built up, various improvements were made, including the introduction of metal-skinned wings, two-pitch three-bladed propellers, and Merlin III engines with triple ejector exhaust manifolds.

When war started in 1939, Hurricanes equipped 19 squadrons of Fighter Command, and on the eve of the Battle of Britain 26 squadrons were so equipped. During the Battle, the one and only Victoria Cross to be awarded to Fighter Command was gained by a Hurricane pilot. Flight Lieutenant Nicholson was attacked and his aircraft seriously damaged and set alight by a Messerschmitt Bf 110 over Southampton. Nicholson, wounded and badly burnt, was about to bale out when he noticed that the enemy fighter had overshot and was ahead of him. He stayed long enough to bring his sights to bear and shoot down the Bf 110. Then, his Hurricane enveloped in flame, Nicholson baled out.

Successor to the Mk I in production was the Mk II, fitted with the more powerful Merlin XX. This engine, which developed 1,185 hp initially, and later 1,280 hp, was specially designed for easy production.

The early Mk IIs were pure interceptor fighters and had a top speed of 342 mph. Later machines had a slightly lengthened nose and provision for a modified wing, housing heavier armament; they were designated Mk IIA Series 2, and saw limited use in the night defence of London during the "Blitz" in the winter of 1940–41.

The heavier armament consisted of an additional four Browning machine-guns, and aircraft so armed were designated Mk IIB.

During 1941, many Hurricanes were used for fighter-bomber duties, carrying either two 250-lb bombs or two 500-lb bombs. Other changes introduced during this period included self-sealing fuel tanks, a large Vokes filter below the nose for desert operations, and provision for carrying either two 45-gallon or two 90-gallon underwing fuel tanks.

In the quest for ever-heavier armament, the possibility of fitting 20-mm cannon had been under consideration since 1936, and in 1939 a trial installation of two Oerlikon guns of this calibre was made on a Hurricane I. New trials with four Oerlikons were carried out in June 1940, and production models of this heavily-armed version were designated Mk IIC. On early aircraft, utilizing converted wings, the cannon had the Chatellerault feed mechanism, but true IICs had drum-fed guns.

By 1942 the Hurricane was becoming outclassed as an interceptor. From then on it was used increasingly for ground attack purposes, its effectiveness for this duty being increased greatly by further armament developments.

First was the installation of rocket projectiles, which gave the Hurricane a fire-power equal to a broadside from a destroyer. This was followed by the installation of two 40-mm cannon under the wings, aircraft so armed being designated Mk IID. With these heavy cannon, the

Hawker Hurricane Mk I, No. 111 Squadron

Hawker Hurricane Mk IIC

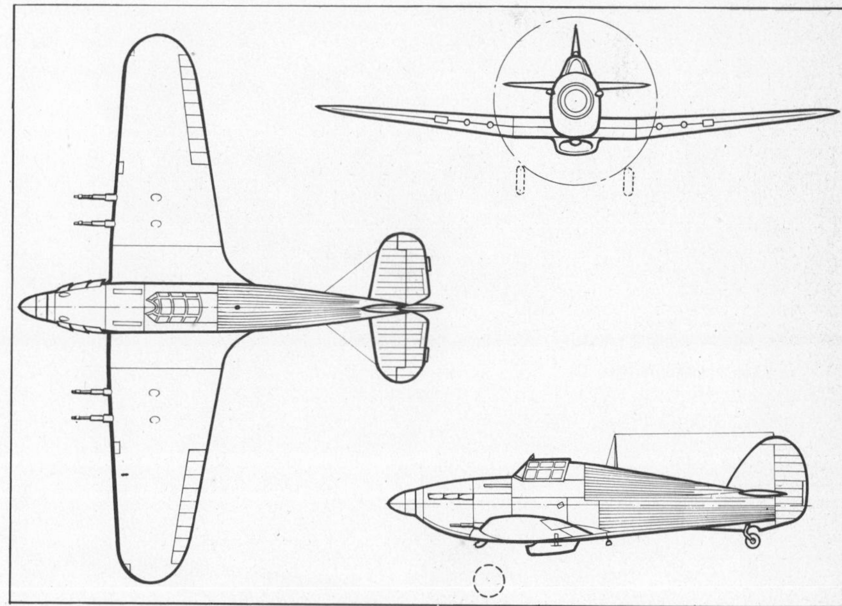
Hawker Hurricane Mk IIC

TYPE	DIMENSIONS span ft	span in	length ft	length in	height ft	height in	WEIGHT max t-o lb	PERFORMANCE max speed mph	at height ft	service ceiling ft	combat range miles	REMARKS
Fury II	30	0	26	9	10	2	3,609	223	16,400	29,500	260	

Hawker Hurricane Mk IIC

Hawker Hurricane Mk IID, with two 40-mm cannon

Hawker Sea Hurricane Mk IA

Hawker Sea Hurricane Mk IB

Hurricane's top speed was reduced to 286 mph; but IIDs proved a most effective anti-tank weapon in North Africa against Rommel's armour and in Burma against the Japanese. The IIDs retained a pair of Browning machine-guns, firing tracer ammunition for sighting.

The last major production version of the Hurricane was the Mk IV. The Mk III was a projected variant with the US Packard-built Merlin, but none was built and only two Mk Vs were completed. This last-named variant was an experimental development of the Mk IV, with a Merlin 32 boosted for low-level operation, and a four-blade propeller.

The Mk IV was essentially a ground-attack fighter, powered by a 1,620-hp Merlin 24 or 27 engine and with a "universal armament" wing. This housed a fixed armament of two Browning machine-guns for sighting purposes, and could, in addition, carry either two 40-mm cannon or long-range fuel tanks; eight rocket projectiles with 60-lb warheads; small bomb carriers (SBC); smoke curtain installations (SCI); or two 250-lb or 500-lb GP, HE, AP or incendiary bombs. For protection against ground fire, the Mk IV had an additional 350 lb of armour plate, the angular armour around the radiator being a distinctive recognition feature.

Another important variant of the Hurricane served with the Merchant Ship Fighter Units. Known as a Sea Hurricane, it was usually a converted Mk IA, modified for catapulting from the decks of merchant ships. Details are given under the Sea Hurricane entry.

Experimental Hurricanes included the Hillson Slip Wing Hurricane of 1940, with a jettisonable top wing to provide extra lift for take-off. The additional wing was supported on two N-shaped strut assemblies mounted on the centre-section and braced to each side of the fuselage.

Proposals included a scheme for mounting Hurricanes on top of Liberator bombers, to provide fighter protection during Atlantic patrols; to a similar end, experiments were made in towing a Hurricane behind a Wellington. Almost unknown is the experimental installation of an upward-firing rocket-tube behind the pilot. Code-named "Sunflower Seed", the intention was to fit such rockets to US bombers, to counter enemy bombing attacks on their massed daylight formations.

In addition to the Hurricanes built in Britain, many were produced by the Canadian Car and Foundry Company. These Canadian-built models, except for an initial batch of standard Mk Is, had Packard Merlin engines and were designated Mks X, XI, XII and XIIA. The Mk X had a Packard Merlin 28, without propeller spinner, and corresponded to the 12-gun Mk IIB. Few were delivered to the RAF, as many were lost at sea and others were retained by the RCAF. The similar Mk XI was built to RCAF specification and was used mainly for training. Main Canadian version was the Mk XII, with Packard Merlin 29 and, successively, 12-gun, four-cannon and "universal" wings. Many were delivered to the Russian and Indian Air Forces. The Mk XIIA and Sea Hurricane XIIA differed in having eight-gun wings.

Hurricane production in Britain totalled 12,780 aircraft, and in Canada, 1,451 aircraft. Hurricanes were supplied to numerous air forces, including those of Belgium (20), Canada (868), Egypt (20), Finland (12), India (300), Ireland (12), Persia (now Iran) (29), Poland (1), Portugal (40), Rumania (12), South Africa (50), Turkey (29), and Yugoslavia (24). In addition, no fewer than 2,952 Hurricanes were despatched to Russia, although the number actually received was considerably less owing to heavy losses to North Cape convoys.

Hawker Sea Hurricane

The Sea Hurricane was the ship-borne version of the RAF Hurricane, and was the first single-seat monoplane fighter to be used on board carriers of the Royal Navy. It closely resembled the RAF model, the major difference being the fitting of catapult spools and a deck arrester hook. Most Sea Hurricanes, in fact, were conversions, only a few airframes being manufactured as Sea Hurricanes.

The first 50 aircraft, designated Sea Hurricane Mk IA, did not have hooks. Nicknamed "Hurricats", these were hurriedly produced for use from catapult-equipped merchant ships, known as CAM-ships, which were introduced to combat the menace of the long-range Focke-Wulf Fw 200 Condor bomber. The Sea Hurricanes were launched when a Condor was located and, often being out of range of land, had to "ditch" after the engagement. The pilot, with luck, was then picked up by one of the ships of the convoy he was trying to protect.

The next batch of conversions, from Hurricane Mk IIAs Series 2, had hooks, and were known either as Sea Hurricane Mk IBs, or Hooked Hurricane IIs. They were followed by Mk ICs, armed with four 20-mm cannon.

The next variant, the Sea Hurricane Mk IIC, had an arrester hook but no catapult spools, and was fitted with the more powerful 1,460-hp Rolls-Royce Merlin XX engine. It had full Fleet Air Arm radio equipment and carried a signal pistol and cartridges.

Final variant was the Sea Hurricane Mk XIIA, a conversion of the Canadian-built Hurricane, powered by a Packard Merlin 29 engine.

The Sea Hurricane's greatest action took place when a vital convoy sailed for Malta in August 1942. For three days, 70 Hurricanes helped to ward off continuous attacks by as many as 500 German and Italian bombers, torpedo-bombers and escorting fighters. Thirty-nine of the enemy were destroyed, for the loss of eight convoy aircraft.

Sea Hurricane new production aircraft and conversions totalled about 800.

Hawker Typhoon

The Typhoon single-seat fighter was designed to Air Ministry Specification F.18/37 as a successor to the Hurricane. Owing to the demands of war, it was put into service before it had been fully developed, leaving squadron pilots with the unwelcome and dangerous task of discovering the aircraft's shortcomings. At one time these proved so serious that it was officially suggested that the Typhoon should be withdrawn from service.

Much of the trouble was attributable to the aircraft's unreliable 2,100-hp Napier Sabre I 24-cylinder H-type engine which was pressed into service still suffering from teething troubles. The Sabre I was soon replaced by the more reliable 2,180-hp Sabre IIA, this in turn being superseded by the 2,200-hp Sabre IIB and 2,260-hp Sabre IIC, the latter sometimes driving a four-bladed propeller.

The Typhoon combined the traditional Hawker box-girder fuselage with stressed-skin construction. The front portion of the fuselage, including the cockpit, was a braced tubular structure; but aft of this the fuselage was a monocoque shell attached to the front portion at four points. Early machines had a framed cockpit hood and a car-type door, but these were replaced after a short time by a one-piece transparent sliding canopy. Each wing was made in one piece, except for a detachable tip, the root end being attached directly to the fuselage. The undercarriage had an exceptionally wide track and retracted inward into the anhedral section of the wing.

The specification had called for an armament of twelve 0·303-in machine-guns, and a few aircraft, designated Mk IA, had these; but the majority of Typhoons were Mk IBs with four 20-mm Hispano cannon.

In service, in addition to engine and structural

Hawker Typhoon IA

Hawker Typhoon IB

Hawker Typhoon IB night fighter

TYPE	DIMENSIONS span ft	span in	length ft	length in	height ft	height in	WEIGHT max t-o lb	PERFORMANCE max speed mph	at height ft	service ceiling ft	combat range miles	REMARKS
Hurricane Mk I	40	0	31	5	13	1	6,600	324	17,500	34,200	900	Range with two combat-stressed 44-gal drop-tanks (Mk I–Mk IV)
Hurricane Mk IIA	40	0	32	0	13	1	8,050	342	NA	36,300	950	
Hurricane Mk IIB	40	0	32	0	13	1	8,250	340	NA	36,000	940	
Hurricane Mk IIC	40	0	32	0	13	1	8,100	336	22,000	35,600	920	
Hurricane Mk IID	40	0	32	0	13	1	7,850	286	NA	32,100	900	
Hurricane Mk IV	40	0	32	0	13	1	8,450	330	NA	32,600	910	
Sea Hurricane Mk IIC	40	0	32	3	13	3	8,100	342	22,000	35,600	970*	*With auxiliary tanks

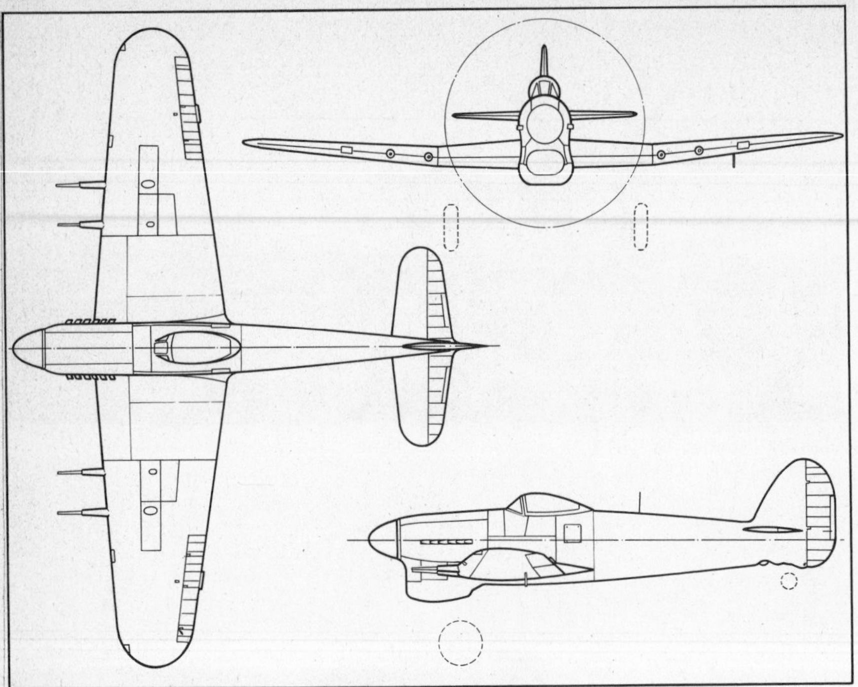

Hawker Typhoon Mk IB

Hawker Tempest Mk V Series 1

Hawker Tempest Mk V Series 2

troubles, the fighter proved to have a disappointing performance, its rate of climb being low and speed falling off alarmingly with altitude. However, it was fast low down and was the only aircraft which could intercept the new German Focke-Wulf Fw 190s which had begun to make low-altitude raids over Britain.

The Typhoon really excelled as a close-support ground-attack fighter, and for this purpose was progressively modified to carry first two 250-lb bombs, then two 500-lb and finally two 1,000-lb bombs. It was the only single-engined, single-seat fighter-bomber capable of carrying such a load and, during the height of the Typhoons' cross-Channel sweeps, they were destroying 150 locomotives a month with bombs and rockets.

It was the installation of eight 3-in rocket projectiles, with 60-lb warheads, which enabled the Typhoons to establish their reputation among the great fighters of World War II. Armed with these weapons, they were outstandingly effective during the bitter ground battles at Caen and Falaise in 1944, when they devastated the German *Panzer* divisions, destroying no fewer than 137 tanks in one attack and so opening the way for the Allied armies to advance into France and Belgium. Other successes included spectacular attacks on German Army headquarters – that against the Fifteenth Army HQ at Dordrecht killing two generals and more than 70 other staff officers.

A few Typhoons used for fighter-reconnaissance duties were equipped with cameras and designated FR Mk 1B.

One Typhoon NF Mk IB was fitted experimentally with AI Mk IV airborne interception radar, but was not a success owing to the difficulty of flying it at night.

Typhoon production totalled 3,330 aircraft.

Hawker Tempest

Experience had shown that although the Typhoon was stable at all level speeds, buffeting and aileron reversal occurred when it was dived at speeds of around 500 mph, preventing the accurate aiming of the guns. To overcome this problem, plans were made to fit a new thin-section laminar-flow wing. The revised aircraft was known originally as the Typhoon II, but complementary changes made it so different that the new name Tempest was allocated.

The Tempest's fuselage was basically similar to that of the Typhoon, consisting of a braced tubular front portion and a monocoque rear portion; but it was lengthened to house an additional fuel tank to offset the loss of fuel previously accommodated in the Typhoon's thick wings. The new wing, of semi-elliptical planform, was about five inches thinner at the root, with a thickness-to-chord ratio of 14.5 per cent at the root, decreasing to 10 per cent at the tip.

Armament consisted of four 20-mm cannon in the wings, and up to 2,000-lb of bombs or eight 60-lb rocket projectiles carried beneath the wings.

Tempest Mk I was the designation allotted to a prototype, actually the second, powered by a Napier Sabre IV engine. The engine was closely cowled and the oil cooler and radiators were sunk unobtrusively in the wing leading-edges. During its flight trials, this aircraft achieved 466 mph at 24,500 ft, but production plans were abandoned owing to difficulties with the engine.

The Mk II was powered by the 2,520-hp Bristol Centaurus V or VI 18-cylinder air-cooled radial engine, and came after the Tempest V (*see below*) which was given production priority. Intended for use against the Japanese in the Far East, the Mk II went into service in November 1945 and was thus too late for operational use. It was the most powerful single-engined fighter of its day and was the RAF's last single-seat piston-engined fighter-bomber. A total of 450 were built.

The designations Mk III and Mk IV were allotted to prototypes which were to be powered by Rolls-Royce Griffon engines; but were not, in fact, built.

The Mk V preceded the Mk II and was the only variant to be used operationally. It had the by-now well-proved Napier Sabre II 24-cylinder H-type engine and inherited the distinctive chin radiator of the Typhoon. After some initial propeller overspeeding problems had been solved, the Tempest V established itself as one of the most effective fighters of the war. It achieved successes against the Messerschmitt Me 262 jet fighter and claimed 638 of the 1,771 V-1 flying bombs destroyed by the RAF, thus contributing the major share towards the defeat of this German secret weapon. The first 100 Mk Vs, with the cannon barrels projecting ahead of the wing, were designated Series 1. The following 705 aircraft, with short-barrelled Hispano Mk V cannon enclosed completely within the wing, detachable rear fuselages and other improvements, were known as Series 2. Early Mk Vs were powered by 2,180-hp Sabre IIAs; later aircraft had the 2,200-hp Sabre IIB and 2,260-hp Sabre IIC.

The last Tempest variant was the Mk VI, powered by the 2,340-hp Sabre V engine. The bigger radiator required by this engine necessitated moving the oil cooler from the chin position to the leading-edge of the starboard wing. Like the Mk II, the Mk VI was too late to see operational service. A total of 142 were built.

Eighty-nine ex-RAF Tempest IIs were supplied to India after the war, and 24 were built for Pakistan. Many Mk V and VI fighters were converted into target tugs; designated TT 5 and TT 6, they served at the RAF Armament Training Station on Sylt, Germany, for several years.

Hawker Fury/Sea Fury

The Fury monoplane was a single-seat fighter-bomber, which was developed originally for the RAF but was built only in small numbers for export. The Sea Fury was its carrier-borne counterpart, and was the FAA's principal single-seat fighter from 1947 to 1953. It proved to be the last piston-engined fighter to serve in first-line squadrons of the Royal Navy.

The basic design evolved from studies undertaken in 1942 to examine the practicability of developing a lighter version of the Tempest, by eliminating the centre-section and joining the two outer wing sections together. The resulting design was tailored to meet Specification F.6/42, the preparation of which had been influenced by the landing, intact, in England of one of the latest Focke-Wulf Fw 190 fighters, the pilot having lost his way. The Hawker project was known at that stage as the "Tempest Light Fighter (Centaurus)."

From this evolved the Fury, intended as a replacement for the Tempest, and the Sea Fury, produced to meet Specification N.7/43 (subsequently N.22/43) for a naval interceptor fighter.

Six prototypes of the Fury were ordered, to the new Specification F.2/43, and the first of these, powered by a Centaurus XII radial engine, flew on 1 September 1944. It was followed by a prototype with a Rolls-Royce Griffon 85 engine; but the Centaurus was specified for production aircraft and the second prototype was used as an engine test-bed. Re-engined with a Sabre VII, and fitted with wing radiators, it became the fastest of the Hawker piston-engined fighters, with a top speed of 485 mph.

With the end of the war in Europe, RAF orders for the Fury were cancelled, although 60 aircraft were completed for Iraq, and development was concentrated on the naval version.

Of all-metal stressed-skin construction, the wings of the Sea Fury were basically Tempest wings joined together on the centre-line as envisaged in the original

Hawker Tempest Mk II

Hawker Fury prototype, Sabre VII engine

Hawker Fury prototype, Griffon 85 engine

TYPE	DIMENSIONS						WEIGHT	PERFORMANCE				REMARKS
	span		length		height		max t-o	max speed	at height	service ceiling	combat range	
	ft	in	ft	in	ft	in	lb	mph	ft	ft	miles	
Typhoon Mk IB	41	7	31	11	15	4	13,250	412	19,000	35,200	980*	*With drop-tanks
Tempest Mk II	41	0	34	5	15	10	11,400	440	15,000	37,000	1,640*	*With drop-tanks
Tempest Mk V	41	0	33	8	16	1	11,500	427	18,500	36,000	1,530*	*With drop-tanks
Tempest Mk VI	41	0	33	10	16	1	11,700	438	17,800	38,000	750	
Sea Fury F Mk X	38	5	34	3	15	10	NA	NA	NA	NA	NA	
Sea Fury FB Mk XI	38	5	34	8	15	10	12,500	460	18,000	35,800	1,040*	*With drop-tanks

Hawker Sea Fury FB Mk 11

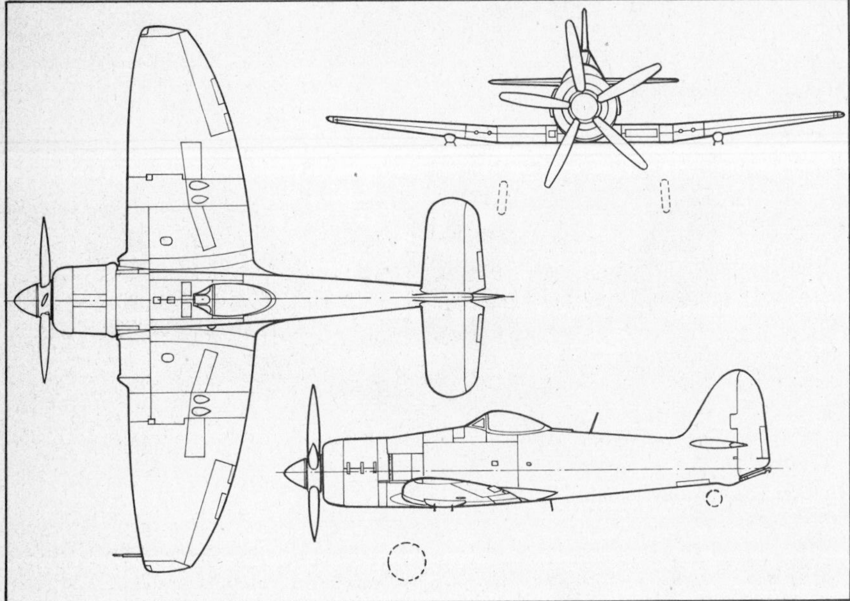
Hawker Sea Fury FB Mk 11

Hawker/Armstrong Whitworth Sea Hawk FGA Mk 6

Hawker/Armstrong Whitworth Sea Hawk Mk 100, Federal German Navy

project study, and with a hinge outboard of the cannon to permit them to fold. The fuselage was of monocoque construction throughout, and embodied a distinctive slope forward of the cockpit, to give the pilot the required view over the nose during deck landings. The power plant was a 2,480-hp Bristol Centaurus XVIII radial engine.

The first 50 production machines were designated F Mk 10 and went into service in 1947. This variant was armed with four 20-mm Hispano Mk V cannon, and was superseded by the FB Mk 11 which, in addition to wing cannon, had provision for a variety of under-wing stores, including two 1,000-lb bombs or twelve 60-lb rocket projectiles. Other changes included a longer arrester hook and the installation of rocket-assisted take-off gear (RATOG).

A total of 615 FB Mk 11s were delivered to the Royal Navy.

Sea Furies were used throughout the Korean War, where they often had to engage Russian-built MiG-15 jet fighters, and succeeded in destroying several of their much faster opponents.

Sea Furies also served with the Royal Australian and Canadian Navies, and were supplied to Burma, Cuba, Egypt, the Netherlands, Pakistan and West Germany.

A total of 65 Furies and 860 Sea Furies were built, the latter figure including a number of tandem two-seat trainers.

Hawker/Armstrong Whitworth Sea Hawk

The Sea Hawk was a single-seat carrier-borne interceptor fighter. Designed to Specification N.7/46, it was developed from the Hawker P.1040 experimental jet fighter, which itself evolved from a proposal to install a turbojet engine in the fuselage of a Fury piston-engined aircraft.

In its final form, the Sea Hawk was a mid-wing monoplane of conventional all-metal stressed-skin construction, the outstanding technical feature being its unique power plant installation. The engine was mounted amidships, the air entering through intakes in the wing leading-edge roots and leaving via bifurcated jet-pipes exhausting on each side of the fuselage just aft of the wing.

When this unorthodox arrangement was proposed, the authorities took many months to accept it. Eventually, they realized that the compact low-drag layout made best use of the limited engine power then available. It also helped to give the aircraft excellent manoeuvrability and handling characteristics, although the maximum speed of 630 mph was a little on the low side.

By dispensing with the usual nose intake and long jet-pipe, this engine installation permitted all the internal fuel to be accommodated in the fuselage, sufficient being carried for a duration of well over two hours. It also enabled the pilot to be positioned at the extreme nose, giving an unusually fine field of view. The wing stubs were built integrally with the centre fuselage and the outer wings folded to facilitate stowage.

Powered by a 5,000-lb s t Rolls-Royce Nene RN 4 (Mk 101) engine, Sea Hawk F Mk 1s began to enter service in March 1953, with No. 806 Squadron of the Fleet Air Arm. Armament of this variant was four 20-mm Hispano cannon mounted in the bottom of the fuselage.

After completion by Hawkers of the first 35, responsibility for production and further development of the Sea Hawk was transferred to the Armstrong Whitworth company, leaving the parent company free to concentrate on the Hunter.

Sea Hawk F Mk 2s introduced power-assisted ailerons to improve stability and control. They were followed by the FB Mk 3 fighter-bomber, with a strengthened wing and underwing attachments for carrying drop tanks or two 500-lb bombs, 3-in or 5-in rockets, mines or sonobuoys.

This version was superseded by the F Mk 4, which had additional wing strong-points for carrying up to twenty 3-in rockets with 60-lb warheads. The FGA Mk 4 could carry four 500-lb bombs.

To improve performance, and particularly speed, up-rated Nene Mk 103 engines, developing 5,200 lb s t, were installed in a number of Mk 3s and Mk 4s, the re-engined aircraft being designated Mk 5 and Mk 6 respectively. About 50 of each Mark were so modified and a total of 86 new Mk 6s were built.

Sea Hawks were used operationally during the Suez Campaign in 1956. Over 550 were built for the FAA and for service with the navies of Australia, Germany (64), India (25) and the Netherlands (32). The first 32 German aircraft were Sea Hawk Mk 100 day fighters; the remainder were Mk 101 all-weather fighters with a large radar pod under the starboard wing. Some of the Dutch Mk 50 aircraft were equipped to carry a Sidewinder air-to-air missile under each wing.

Hawker Hunter

The Hunter is a single-seat day fighter which, although not supersonic in level flight, has such excellent handling qualities at all speeds that it remains in first-line service with foreign air forces 20 years after its design was started. It epitomizes, in its class, peak development of the subsonic jet.

The Hunter evolved from studies initiated by Hawkers in 1946 for an interceptor using the new Rolls-Royce AJ65 engine, later to be known as the Avon. The project, designated P.1067, incorporated swept wings, a high-mounted tailplane, a nose intake and armament of two 30-mm Aden cannon.

Early in 1948, Specification F.3/48 was issued; the P.1067 matched this closely, and detail design work started. During development, the tailplane was moved lower down the fin and the engine intake ducts were transferred to the wing roots.

At the same time, armament was increased to four Aden cannon. To facilitate rearming, the guns were mounted in a detachable pack containing the gun-bodies and magazines. After a sortie, this could be removed and replaced by a loaded pack in a few minutes.

Structurally, the Hunter is of all-metal stressed-skin construction. The wing has 40 degrees of sweep-back. The fuselage is made in three sections: the nose, including cockpit, armament pack and nose-wheel; the centre-section, with integral wing roots, intake ducts and engine mounting; and the detachable rear fuselage, with integral fin base. An air-brake, consisting of a curved flap conforming to the fuselage contour, is fitted to the underside of the rear fuselage. This brake can be operated at all speeds and altitudes without upsetting the aircraft's stability. All flying controls are power-operated.

The undercarriage is of the retractable nose-wheel type, with the main legs retracting hydraulically into the wing roots and the nose unit forward into the fuselage nose.

Hunter F Mk 1s, powered by a 7,500-lb s t Rolls-Royce Avon RA 7, went into service in July 1954, with No. 43 Squadron. Trouble was experienced with these early Hunters when the guns were fired at high altitudes, causing engine surging, and an altitude restriction had to be imposed to prevent the risk of the engine "flaming out" and stopping.

The F Mk 2 introduced the 8,000-lb s t Armstrong Siddeley Sapphire Mk 101. It had no gun-firing restrictions, but only a few were built.

The Mk 3 was an experimental aircraft powered by the new Rolls-Royce Avon RA 7R, developing 9,600-lb s t with reheat. On 7 September 1953, this machine flew at 727·6 mph, to set up a new World's Absolute Speed Record, and a few days later established a 100-kilometre closed-circuit record of 709 mph.

The Mk 4 was a much-improved variant of the Mk 1,

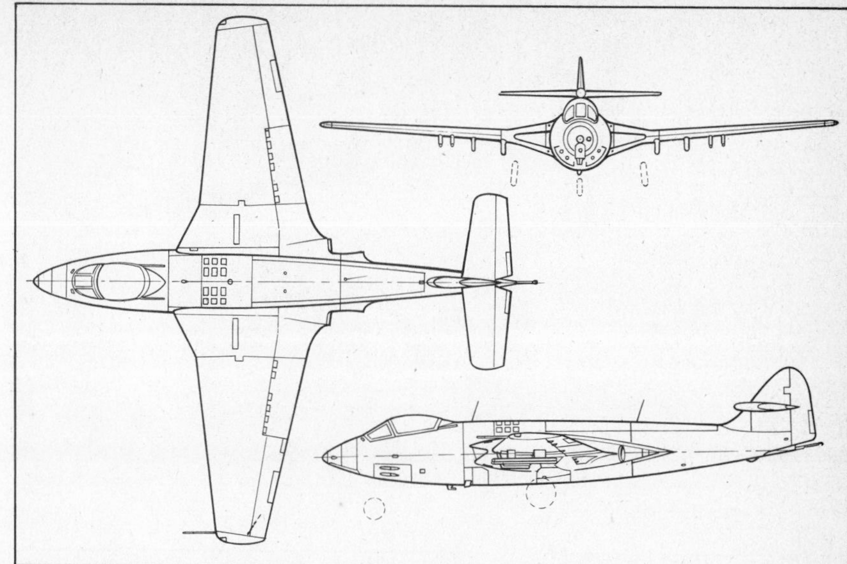

Hawker/Armstrong Whitworth Sea Hawk FGA Mk 6

Hawker Hunter Mk 50, with Sidewinders, Swedish Air Force

Hawker Hunter F(GA) Mk 9, No. 20 Squadron

TYPE	DIMENSIONS span ft	in	length ft	in	height ft	in	WEIGHT max t-o lb	PERFORMANCE max speed mph	at height ft	service ceiling ft	combat range miles	REMARKS
Sea Hawk F Mk 1	39	0	39	8	8	8	NA	NA	NA	NA	NA	
Sea Hawk FB Mk 4	39	0	39	8	8	8	NA	NA	NA	NA	NA	
Sea Hawk F(GA) Mk 6	39	0	39	8	8	8	16,200	0.84M	36,000	44,500	1,400*	*With drop-tanks

Hawker Hunter FR Mk 10

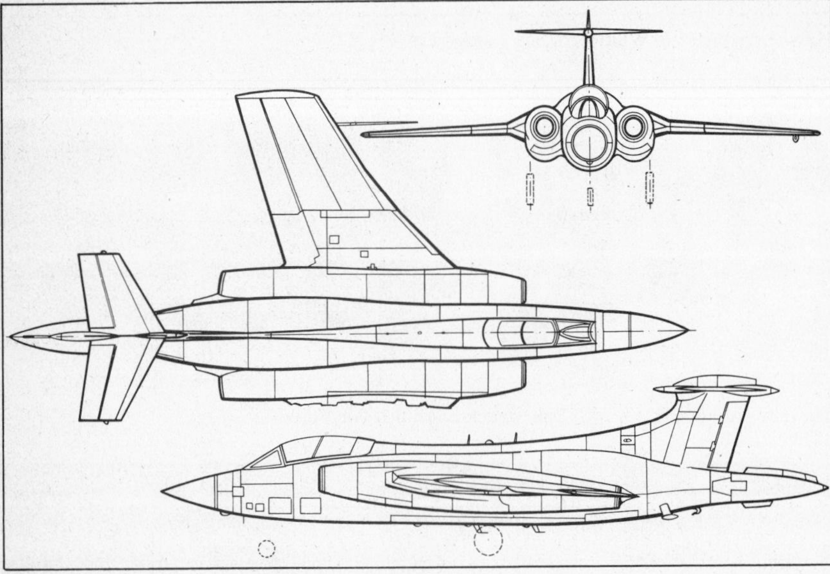
Hawker Siddeley (Blackburn) Buccaneer S Mk1

Hawker Siddeley (Blackburn) Buccaneer S Mk 2, air-brakes extended

with increased internal fuel stowage and four underwing strong-points for carrying a variety of stores. The inner points could carry two 1,000-lb bombs, 2-in multiple rocket batteries or 100-gallon Napalm bombs; the outer points could carry drop tanks or rocket projectiles. This version could also be adapted to carry two Sidewinder air-to-air missiles. Its Avon engine embodied modifications to alleviate the problem of surging during gun-firing which had been experienced with the Mk 1.

The Hunter F Mk 5 was a development of the F Mk 2, incorporating the increased internal fuel stowage and wing strong-points introduced on the Mk 4.

The F Mk 6 was a development of the Mk 4, powered by the new 10,000-lb s t Rolls-Royce Avon Mk 320 engine and fitted with improved controls. These developments considerably increased the Hunter's performance and gave it a new lease of life. To reduce the pitch-up tendency at high speeds and altitudes, under high loading, later aircraft were fitted with an extended, or dog-tooth, wing leading-edge; some Mk 4s were similarly modified.

The T Mk 7 was a two-seat trainer variant, with wider forward fuselage for side-by-side seating of the instructor and pupil.

The T Mk 8 was a Naval version of the T Mk 7, which it resembled closely, except for the addition of airfield arrester gear under the rear fuselage, for training purposes.

The F(GA) Mk 9 was a developed version of the F Mk 6, with the slightly more powerful Avon Mk 207, and specially equipped for ground-attack duties. To permit the aircraft to land on small airfields, a tail parachute was fitted and two 230-gallon drop tanks could be carried in addition to the normal underwing stores.

The FR Mk 10 was a fighter-reconnaissance version of the F Mk 6, carrying one forward-facing and two oblique cameras, while retaining the standard armament of four Aden guns. It was powered by the Avon Mk 207 engine and was equipped with a tail parachute similar to that of the F(GA) Mk 9.

Final production version for British forces was the GA Mk 11, a conversion of the Mk 4, for use by the Royal Navy as a single-seat advanced ground-attack trainer. Changes included removal of the Aden guns and fitting of an arrester hook and TACAN navigational system.

A total of 1,985 Hunters were built, including 460 manufactured by Fokker and Aviolanda in Holland and by Avions Fairey and SABCA in Belgium, and 102 two-seat aircraft. Export Hunters, allotted 50 series Mark numbers, were supplied to Denmark (32), India (182), Iraq (35), Jordan (2), Kuwait (6), Lebanon (13), Peru (17), Rhodesia (12), Sweden (120), Switzerland (100), and Saudi Arabia (6). Some of these were refurbished aircraft, from British, Dutch or Belgian production.

Hawker Siddeley (Blackburn) Buccaneer

The Buccaneer is a two-seat twin-engined carrier-borne strike aircraft, designed for sustained flight at near-sonic speed at sea level. It is a cantilever mid-wing monoplane. The wing incorporates graded sweepback on the leading-edge, and is of all-metal multi-spar design with integrally-stiffened thick skins machined from the solid. A "super-circulation" boundary layer control system is embodied, with air outlets near the leading-edges and forward of the drooping ailerons and plain flaps.

The fuselage is a semi-monocoque structure, bulged at the rear end in conformity with the "area-rule"; the distinctive tail-cone is made up of two sideways-opening air-brakes. Carrier stowage is facilitated by folding the wings upward, hinging the fuselage nose-cone sideways and opening the air-brakes. The fuselage houses a large internal bomb-bay, with a rotating door capable of accommodating a wide variety of stores, including nuclear weapons or a camera pack. Four underwing pylons carry additional stores, such as Bullpup air-to-ground missiles, or packs of 2-in or 3-in rockets.

The all-moving horizontal tail surface is attached to the tip of the fin, which is pivoted to move with it. A "super-circulation" boundary layer control system is incorporated in the tailplane, the air outlet slots being in the underskin.

Advanced radar navigation and weapon-delivery electronic systems are carried, the two being integrated to provide a weapon system for attack.

Buccaneer S Mk 1s went into service in July 1962, with No. 801 Squadron. These early production machines were each powered by two 7,100-lb s t Bristol Siddeley Gyron Junior Mk 101 turbojet engines, and were superseded by the S Mk 2, powered by two 11,255-lb s t Rolls-Royce RB 168 Spey turbofan engines. The increased power and lower fuel consumption of these fan engines appreciably improved the take-off, climb, high-speed and range performance, making the S Mk 2s much more formidable combat weapons.

Sixteen Buccaneer S Mk 50s, supplied to South Africa, are similar to the S Mk 2 but have a Bristol Siddeley BS 605 twin-chamber retractable rocket engine of 8,000 lb s t in the rear fuselage to boost take-off performance.

Hawker Siddeley (de Havilland) Sea Vixen

The Sea Vixen two-seat carrier-borne interceptor fighter is a development of the D.H.110, which was initiated as a potential all-weather fighter for the RAF. When the Javelin was selected for Fighter Command, the D.H.110 was extensively re-engineered to make it suitable for carrier operations and the first fully-developed Sea Vixen flew on 20 March 1957.

Of all-metal stressed-skin construction, the Sea Vixen is a cantilever mid-wing monoplane with a twin-boom layout. The wings, which fold upward hydraulically, are three-spar structures with integrally-machined skins. Large Fowler-type flaps are fitted to the trailing-edge on each side of the tail-booms; as the flaps extend, the rear portion of the tailplane moves upward to cancel resulting trim changes.

The fuselage comprises a monocoque nacelle, housing the pilot in an offset cockpit and a radar operator internally. The pointed nose of the nacelle encloses GEC airborne interception radar, and the entire nose hinges sideways to facilitate maintenance and stowage.

Twin booms support the tailplane and the twin fins and rudders. The Sea Vixen probably represents the peak development of such a configuration, as a twin-boom layout is not ideal for supersonic flight.

Power is provided by two 11,250-lb s t Rolls-Royce Avon Mk 208 turbojets, mounted side-by-side in the rear of the nacelle.

Sea Vixen F(AW) Mk 1s went into service in July 1959, with No. 892 Squadron. Standard armament of this variant was two retractable packs totalling twenty-eight 2-in rockets, plus a wide variety of underwing stores, such as: four Firestreak infra-red homing air-to-air missiles; four 500-lb bombs; two Firestreaks and forty-eight 2-in rockets or two 500-lb bombs; eighteen 3-in air-to-surface rockets. Two external fuel tanks could be carried with any of the above loads and the tanks could be interchanged with Bullpup air-to-surface missiles.

Hawker Siddeley (Blackburn) Buccaneer S Mk 50, with auxiliary rocket, SAAF

Hawker Siddeley (de Havilland) Sea Vixen F(AW) Mk 1

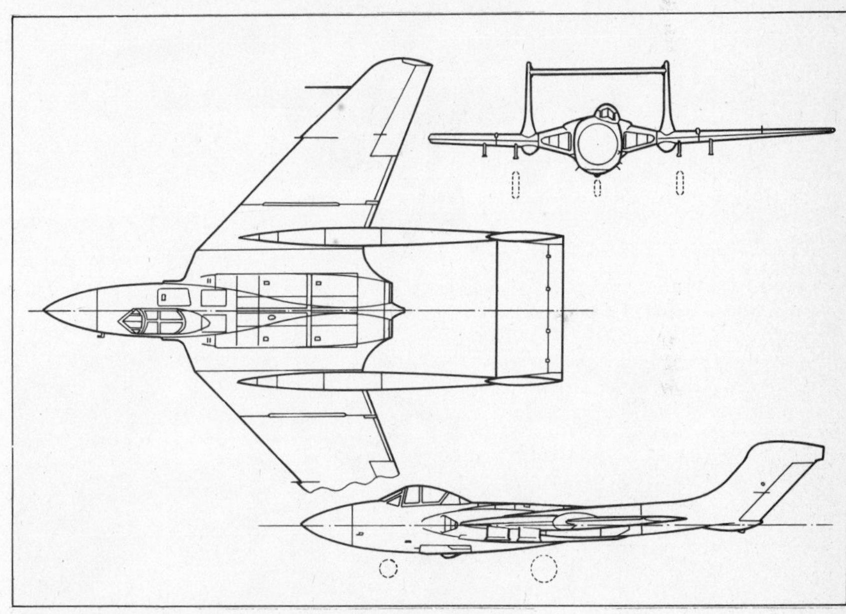

Hawker Siddeley (de Havilland) Sea Vixen F(AW) Mk 1

TYPE	DIMENSIONS						WEIGHT	PERFORMANCE				REMARKS
	span ft	span in	length ft	length in	height ft	height in	max t-o lb	max speed mph	at height ft	service ceiling ft	combat range miles	
Hunter F Mk 1	33	8	45	10	13	2	16,200*	NA	NA	48,800	NA	*Clean
Hunter F Mk 2	33	8	45	10	13	2	16,200*	NA	NA	50,000	NA	*Clean
Hunter F Mk 4	33	8	45	10	13	2	17,100*	NA	NA	NA	NA	*Clean
Hunter F Mk 5	33	8	45	10	13	2	17,100*	NA	NA	50,000		*Clean
Hunter F Mk 6	33	8	45	10	13	2	24,000	715	36,000	55,000	1,840	*With 1,052 Imp.gal. and no reserves
Hunter FGA Mk 9	33	8	45	10	13	2	18,000	715	36,000	55,000	1,840	*With 1,052 Imp.gal. and no reserves
Buccaneer S Mk 1	42	4	63	5	16	6	NA	NA	NA	NA	NA	
Sea Vixen F(AW) Mk 1	50	0	53	6	11	0	NA	720	NA	48,000	NA	
Sea Vixen F(AW) Mk 2	50	0	53	6	11	0	NA	720	NA	48,000	NA	

Hawker Siddeley (de Havilland) Sea Vixen F(AW) Mk 2 No. 766 Squadron

Hawker Siddeley P.1127 prototype

Hawker Siddeley P.1127 Kestrel, Anglo-American-German Squadron

Hawker Siddeley Harrier FGA Mk 1

The Mk 1 was superseded by the F(AW) Mk 2. This is essentially similar to the Mk 1, but can carry the more advanced Red Top air-to-air missile, the additional fire control equipment for which is housed, with extra fuel, in forward extensions of the tail-booms. Many Mk 1 Sea Vixens have been converted to Mk 2 standard.

Hawker Siddeley P.1127 Kestrel/Harrier

The P.1127 is the first combat design to combine transonic speed with the ability to take off and land vertically. By doing so, it makes front-line fighter squadrons independent of vulnerable fixed bases, being able to operate from jungle clearings, beaches, roads or the decks of ships at sea.

Its design was started by the late Sir Sydney Camm in 1958, in collaboration with Bristol Siddeley Engines, makers of the aircraft's Pegasus vectored-thrust turbofan. This engine is fitted with four rotating exhaust nozzles. By diverting the exhaust downward, these enable the P.1127 to take off vertically by the jet-lift technique. At a safe height, the pilot rotates the nozzles slowly, to obtain forward thrust as well as lift. When the aircraft is flying fast enough for the wings to provide sufficient lift to support it, the nozzles are rotated fully rearward, so that all engine thrust is used for propulsion. Landing is the reverse of take-off.

When there is sufficient space for a forward run, the P.1127 can operate as a STOL (short take-off and landing) aircraft, with the nozzles in an intermediate position, enabling it to carry an increased load of weapons or fuel.

The first of six prototypes of the P.1127 made its first tethered hovering flight on 21 October 1960. The first full transitions from vertical to horizontal flight and vice versa were made on 12 September 1961, afterwards becoming routine. Nine pre-production P.1127s were ordered next, with the name Kestrel F(GA)Mk 1, for evaluation by a joint Anglo-American-German squadron. These were each powered by a 15,200-lb s t Pegasus 5 turbofan. The production P.1127, ordered for the RAF with the name Harrier, has a 19,000-lb s t Pegasus 6 and several detail changes. In particular, the streamlined fairings housing the balancer wheels of its undercarriage are inset from the wingtips and the sweepback is increased to 40°. A production order for the RAF (six development aircraft, possibly followed by 60 operational aircraft and 10 two-seat conversion trainers) was announced early in 1965. All six development machines had flown by mid-1967, and deliveries of operational Harriers are due to begin in 1969.

The Harrier is a single-seater of orthodox all-metal construction. The small wings are made in one piece and are so light that they can be lifted off quickly when the engine has to be removed for overhaul. The undercarriage is of the "zero-track" type, with a nose-wheel and twin-wheel main unit in tandem under the fuselage, plus the wingtip balancers. Stability in hovering and low-speed flight is maintained by a system of "puffer-jets", in which compressed air is ejected through nozzles at the nose, tail and wingtips. Operation of the "puffer-jets" is automatic, via the normal stick and rudder controls. Only additional control in the cockpit is a lever by which the engine nozzles are rotated. As a result, the Harrier is so simple to control that experienced pilots have learned to fly it in under one hour.

As well as rockets, bombs, fuel tanks and other stores carried under the wings, the Harrier can carry cameras in an under-belly pack for reconnaissance duties.

Hunting Provost

Designed to Air Ministry Specification T.16/48, the prototype Provost flew on 24 February 1950, powered by an Armstrong Siddeley Cheetah 18 engine. After competitive trials against the Handley Page HPR-2, the Provost was ordered into production in February 1951 as the standard basic trainer of the RAF, with an Alvis Leonides engine, as fitted to the third prototype. Deliveries began in 1953 and small quantities of an armed version were also supplied to foreign air forces.

The Provost was a cantilever low-wing monoplane, of conventional all-metal stressed-skin construction. The fuselage was a monocoque structure, with the crew of two sitting side-by-side in an enclosed cockpit. Each main leg of the fixed undercarriage was a cantilever unit containing a British Messier oleo-pneumatic shock-absorber strut. Standard power plant was a 550-hp Leonides 25 nine-cylinder air-cooled, geared and supercharged engine.

The Provost had good handling characteristics and was fully aerobatic. For a trainer, its manoeuvrability was exceptionally good, with a rate of roll exceeding 90 degrees a second.

The armed version was developed for light "policing" duties in smaller countries. It could carry either two 0·303-in machine-guns, or a camera gun and two 250-lb bombs, or eight 25-lb bombs and four or six 60-lb rocket projectiles.

Standard T Mk 51 export Provosts were delivered to the Irish Air Corps and Royal Malaysian Air Force. T Mk 52 armed Provosts were supplied to the Royal Rhodesian Air Force; others, designated T Mk 53, went to Burma, Iraq, Muscat and the Sudan. A total of 461 of all versions were built.

Hunting Jet Provost and BAC 167

When Hunting developed the Jet Provost as the RAF's first jet primary and basic trainer, they retained the overall geometry of the Leonides-engined Provost wherever possible in order to reproduce the fine handling characteristics of the earlier aircraft. The prototype flew for the first time on 26 June 1954 and the much-refined Jet Provost T Mk 3 was adopted eventually by the RAF as the first jet trainer ordered by any air force for use by pupils without any previous piston-engined instruction.

It was soon evident that the aircraft's relatively high performance, combined with docile handling qualities, made it suitable for light ground-attack duties and weapon training. As a result, Hunting developed an armed export version of the T Mk 3, designated the T Mk 51.

Differing from the trainer only in the addition of armament, the T Mk51 is a cantilever low-wing monoplane of all-metal stressed-skin construction. The crew of two sit side-by-side on Martin-Baker ejection seats and have an excellent all-round view. Power plant is a 1,750-lb s t Bristol Siddeley Viper 102 turbojet.

The T Mk 51 is armed with two 0·303-in machine-guns, mounted in the walls of the air intakes, and has underwing attachments for a variety of stores, such as eight 25-lb bombs and four 60-lb rockets, or two 250-lb bombs.

Twelve Jet Provost T Mk 51s were supplied to Ceylon, six to Kuwait and four to the Sudan. They were followed by the T Mk 52, an armed version of the RAF's Jet Provost T Mk 4 trainer, with a 2,500-lb s t Viper 202 turbojet. This version was sold to the air forces of Sudan (4), Venezuela (15) and Iraq (20).

Latest developments of the Jet Provost series are the pressurized T Mk 5 trainer for the RAF and the BAC 167, which is generally similar but has a 3,410-lb s t Viper Srs 20 turbojet and six underwing attachments for up to 3,000 lb of weapons. First order for the BAC 167 was placed by Saudi Arabia in 1966.

Mann, Egerton Type B

Designed for reconnaissance and bombing duties, the Mann, Egerton Type B was a two-seat biplane seaplane, distinguished by the enormous extensions of the top wing. These were supported by tall king-posts above the outer interplane struts and were extensively braced from below. The wings could be folded.

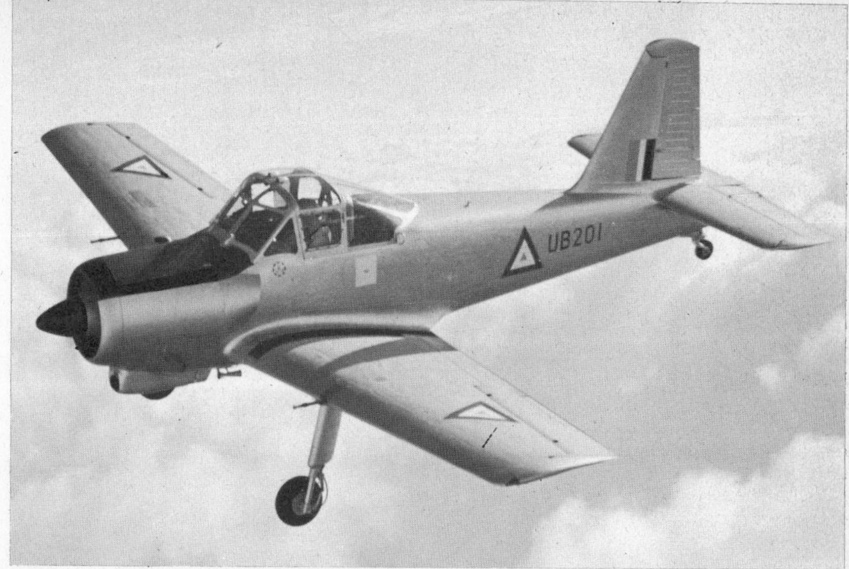

Hunting Provost T Mk 53, Burmese Air Force

Hunting Jet Provost, T Mk 51, Royal Ceylon Air Force

Mann, Egerton Type B

TYPE	DIMENSIONS span ft	span in	length ft	length in	height ft	height in	WEIGHT max t-o lb	PERFORMANCE max speed mph	at height ft	service ceiling ft	combat range miles	REMARKS
Hawker Siddeley Harrier GR Mk 1	25	0	46	0	11	0	22,000	680	SL	NA	1,200	
Provost	35	2	29	0	12	2	4,400	195	SL	22,500	650	
Jet Provost T Mk 52	36	11	32	5	10	2	7,400	410	20,000	31,000	700	

Martinsyde S.1, early version

Martinsyde S.1, later version

Martinsyde G.100

Martinsyde G.100, No. 27 Squadron

Powered by a 225-hp Sunbeam engine, the Type B was intended to be an improvement over the Short 184. Mann, Egerton and Company had built several of the Short seaplanes for the Admiralty, and gave these machines, produced under sub-contract, their own designation, Type A. The Type B was very similar to the Short 184, and incorporated a large number of common components, particularly in the fuselage, tail unit and float support structure.

Ten Type Bs were delivered, in 1916, and were used by the RNAS for patrol duties.

Martinsyde S.1

Known also as the Martinsyde Scout, the S.1, produced by Martin and Handasyde, was a small single-seat biplane, powered by a closely-cowled 80-hp Gnome engine.

Fuselage construction was conventional and ailerons were fitted to each of the equal-span single-bay wings. A refinement was the fitting of small wheels at the forward ends of the skids, which made the undercarriage look out of proportion to the rather pleasing lines of the rest of the aircraft.

On later S.1s this four-wheel undercarriage was replaced by a plain two-wheel Vee undercarriage.

Small numbers of S.1s went into service with RFC squadrons in France towards the end of 1914, their relatively poor performance being somewhat offset by the upward- and forward-firing Lewis machine-gun which was mounted on the top wing.

An S.1 was concerned in one of the most incredible escapes which occurred during the war. Its pilot, Captain L. A. Strange, had emptied a drum of ammunition while attacking an enemy aircraft and, when trying to fit a new drum, found that it had jammed. To help free the drum, Strange stood up, holding the control stick between his knees. He lost his grip on the stick and the S.1 pulled up in a steep climb, flicked over and went into an inverted spin. Strange was thrown right out of the cockpit but managed to retain his hold on the jammed ammunition drum – which, fortunately, did not come off! After dropping more than 5,000 ft, Captain Strange managed to right the aircraft and climb back into the cockpit.

Martinsyde G.100 and G.102 Elephant

The Martinsyde G.100 of 1915 was a single-seat long-range fighting scout, powered by a 120-hp Beardmore engine. The prototype had a three-bladed propeller, but production models switched to a two-blader and had a different engine cowling that was much improved aerodynamically. In fact, the generally clean lines of the G. 100 gave it a tendency to float before touch-down, when landing, and this surprised pilots who were accustomed to aircraft with so much drag that they landed immediately the throttle was closed!

Armament consisted of one Lewis machine-gun mounted above the centre-section, firing forward and upward, and, strangely, a second Lewis, firing aft, on a mounting behind the cockpit on the port side of the fuselage. Various bomb-loads could be carried, varying from a single 230-lb bomb to four 65-lb bombs – the heavier weapons being attached to racks under the wings.

An improved version, with the more powerful 160-hp Beardmore engine, appeared after a time and was designated G.102. Designed to have an endurance of $5\frac{1}{2}$ hours, it was a relatively large aeroplane, which explains why it was usually known as the Elephant.

Elephants were rather heavy on the controls and so tended to be used more for reconnaissance duties, photography and bombing than for fighting. It is, in fact, as a bomber, with a particular aptitude for low-level attacks, that the type is best remembered.

A total of about 300 Martinsyde G.100s and G.102s were built.

Martinsyde F.3

The F.3 single-seat fighter was the third of the Martinsyde "F" series of military biplanes. The first, the F.1, was a large two-seat fighter. For some reason known only to the designer, the observer on this aircraft was located in the front cockpit, directly under the relatively low top wing, where his view was at a minimum and his field of fire almost non-existent. Development of the type was not proceeded with.

The F.2 was also a two-seat fighter and, although a distinct improvement over the F.1, was nowhere near as efficient as its contemporaries, such as the Bristol Fighter. In particular, the pilot's view on this aircraft was almost as poor as was the observer's on the F.1.

The F.3 was the first single-seater of the "F" series. Much smaller than its predecessors, it was a relatively straightforward single-bay biplane. To avoid recurrence of the strong adverse criticism of the view from the F.1 and F.2, the fuselage of the F.3 was made relatively deep, so that the pilot, seated high, aft of the upper wing, had his head almost in line with the trailing-edge. Close attention was paid to detail design and to achieving a high standard of workmanship, in order to reduce drag to a minimum. This factor helped to give the little aircraft an excellent performance.

Armament consisted of two forward-firing Vickers machine-guns, synchronized to fire between the propeller blades. Initially, the prototype was powered by an experimental version of the Rolls-Royce Falcon engine, developing 285 hp; later, a standard 275-hp engine was fitted. At that time, however, the Rolls-Royce engines were needed urgently for other types, and plans were made to fit the 300-hp Hispano-Suiza engine in production machines. Instead, further modifications were made, until the aircraft had changed to such an extent that it was redesignated the F.4.

Only six F.3s were built, four of which were used at Home Defence stations.

Martinsyde F.4 Buzzard

Conceived ahead of its time, the Martinsyde F.4 was more akin to post-war single-seat fighters than to its predecessors, which were mere fighting scouts. It was bigger and more substantial than the scouts, and although it could match their aerobatic capability, it used up more airspace in doing so.

The F.4 was a conventional biplane, with the top surface of the single-bay wings positioned low down, near the top of the relatively deep fuselage. The pilot, seated behind the wing, had his eyes level with the trailing-edge and thus had a good view forward and upward; his view rearward and upward was, of course, unrestricted.

A simple Vee-undercarriage was fitted. Power was provided by a 300-hp Hispano-Suiza engine, which gave the F.4 an excellent performance. Its top speed of 145 mph is sometimes claimed to be the highest of all World War I aeroplanes: it was certainly the fastest British type.

Armament consisted of two fixed forward-firing Vickers machine-guns, mounted above the engine and synchronized to fire between the propeller blades. The guns were neatly enclosed by the upper cowling. Racks were provided for a small load of bombs for ground-attack duties.

Officially named the Buzzard Mk I, the F.4 was ordered in large numbers, but only about 65 had been built by the time the Armistice was signed, and none had entered service with the RAF. During the Peace Conference in

Martinsyde F.3, 275-hp Falcon engine

Martinsyde F.4 Buzzard

Martinsyde F.4 Buzzard

TYPE	DIMENSIONS span ft	span in	length ft	length in	height ft	height in	WEIGHT max t-o lb	PERFORMANCE max speed mph	at height ft	service ceiling ft	combat range miles	REMARKS
Martinsyde S.1	27	8	21	0	NA		NA	87	SL	NA	NA	
Martinsyde G.100	38	0	26	6	9	8	2,424	95	6,500	14,000	NA	
Martinsyde F.3	32	10	25	6	8	8	2,446	130	10,000	21,500	NA	Endurance $2\frac{1}{4}$ hours
Martinsyde Elephant G.102	38	0	27	0	9	8	2,458	104	2,000	16,000	NA	
Martinsyde F.4	32	9	25	6	10	4	2,398	145	15,000	24,000	NA	

Nieuport Nighthawk

Nieuport Nighthawk

Nieuport (Gloster Mars VI) Nighthawk, Jaguar III engine

Nieuport (Gloster Mars VI) Nighthawk, Jaguar III engine

1919, two F.4s were used by the RAF Communications Wing to carry important despatches between London and Paris, the 215-mile journey once being covered in the creditable time of 1 hour 15 minutes.

Subsequently, the F.4 was used for a variety of purposes, including civil racing, and experimental floatplane and two-seat reconnaissance versions were built.

Nieuport Nighthawk

The Nighthawk was a single-seat fighter, which was produced by the Nieuport and General Aircraft Company, to meet the RAF Specification for the Type I S.S. Fighter, issued in 1918.

It was a conventional biplane, with equal-span two-bay wings. To facilitate production, it utilized many parts of the S.E.5a, such as fuselage fittings, control column and rudder bar, undercarriage axle and wheels.

The power plant was a 320-hp ABC Dragonfly I nine-cylinder radial engine which, because of its remarkable power-to-weight ratio – it weighed about 600 lb – had been chosen for large-scale production. Over 11,000, in fact, were ordered and the new engine was specified for most of the generation of British military aircraft under development at the time of the Armistice.

Armament consisted of two fixed forward-firing Vickers machine-guns, mounted on top of the fuselage in front of the pilot and synchronized to fire between the propeller blades.

The Nighthawk had an excellent performance, its rate of climb, maximum speed and manoeuvrability being outstanding. Unfortunately, after the Dragonfly had entered production it proved to have serious deficiencies. It was heavier than anticipated, developed less power and, worst of all, vibrated so badly that it failed mechanically after only a few hours. Had the war continued this would have had an extremely serious effect on British military airpower, in view of the extent to which the industry was committed to the engine. At one stage, when the Dragonfly had been developed to the state that it would run reliably for 2½ hours, it was suggested seriously that the solution to the problem might be to replace the engine of each aircraft after each patrol!

In 1920 the Nieuport design was taken over by the Gloucestershire Aircraft Company (Gloster), whereupon the Nighthawk became the Mars VI in that company's Mars series of Nieuport developments. Mars VI Nighthawks were fitted with either a 385-hp Bristol Jupiter IV or 325-hp Armstrong Siddeley Jaguar III engine. Their performance was excellent, the maximum speed with either engine being about 150 mph, but only small quantities were built for the RAF. These aircraft saw limited service in Britain, and overseas in India and Mesopotamia.

In addition to these RAF machines, 25 Mars VI Nighthawks with Jaguar engines were delivered to the Greek Air Force.

Norman Thompson N.T.4.

Designed by the Norman Thompson Flight Company (formerly White and Thompson), the N.T.4 was a twin-engined flying-boat of the same general configuration as the Curtiss H.4. It went into service with the RNAS in 1915 and was known as an America, although it was a quite different aeroplane, not connected with the Curtiss flying-boat.

Early N.T.4s were powered by two 150-hp Hispano-Suiza engines, driving two-bladed pusher propellers. The engines, completely uncowled, were mounted towards the top of the interplane struts. The finely-shaped single-step hull was constructed on boat-like lines, with an enclosed cockpit. This increased crew comfort, but restricted the view so essential in a reconnaissance aircraft.

Later machines were each powered by two 200-hp Hispano-Suizas, and were designated N.T.4a. On these, the area of cockpit glazing was substantially increased to improve the view; on some the cockpit top was glazed. N.T.4as were used by the RNAS for patrols in home waters and for training.

No regular armament was carried, but some N.T.4s had a Lewis gun mounted on a bracket above the cockpit, and bombs were carried on wing racks.

The prototype machine was used to try out a formidable two-pounder Davis gun installation. This was mounted above the cockpit, firing forward, but it did not prove successful.

A total of about 50 N.T.4s and N.T.4as are believed to have been built.

Parnall Plover

Produced to meet an Air Ministry specification for a deck landing fighter to supersede the Nieuport Nightjar, the Plover was a single-seat carrier-borne aircraft which could be operated as either a landplane or an amphibian.

It was a conventional biplane, with equal-span single-bay wings. The wheel undercarriage could be interchanged with twin floats incorporating wheels. Armament consisted of two fixed forward-firing Vickers machine-guns which were synchronized to fire between the propeller blades.

The specification required the Plover to utilize either the Bristol Jupiter or Armstrong Siddeley Jaguar radial engine, and three prototypes were built. The first two were fitted with the 436-hp Jupiter engine and the third with a 385-hp Jaguar.

A small quantity of production aircraft, with the Jupiter engine, were built in 1923, and the type entered service with FAA Flights No. 403 and 404, alongside Nieuport Nightjars and Fairey Flycatchers. In service, the Flycatcher soon proved its superiority, the Plover having a tendency toward structural weakness; and after a short period the Parnall fighter passed into obscurity.

Pemberton-Billing P.B.25

A development of the prototype P.B.23, which appeared in 1915, the P.B.25 was a single-seat pusher scout of distinctive appearance. The reason for this was that the fuselage nacelle, of finely streamlined shape, was mounted midway between the biplane wings.

The prototype was the twenty-third design for an aeroplane by pioneer Pemberton-Billing, hence its designation. It had straight wings, and the nacelle was covered with aluminium alloy sheet metal, a bold departure from the fabric in general use at the time. The bullet-like nacelle gained the aircraft the nickname "Push-Prodge", short for pusher projectile.

Production machines had a more powerful engine and sweptback wings; in addition the nacelle, now fitted with a head fairing, was covered with fabric. These and other modifications led to a change of designation, to P.B.25, although the Admiralty, who ordered 20 of the type, referred to the aircraft officially as the Pemberton-Billing Scout.

Standard power unit was the 100-hp Gnome Monosoupape, but at least one aircraft was fitted with a 110-hp Clerget engine. The tailplane and rudders were supported by four tail-booms, remarkably free from interconnecting struts and bracing wires.

Armament consisted of one Lewis machine-gun, mounted on the nacelle in front of the pilot.

The P.B.25 does not appear to have been used operationally.

Norman Thompson N.T.4a

Parnall Plover

Pemberton-Billing P.B.25

TYPE	DIMENSIONS span ft	in	length ft	in	height ft	in	WEIGHT max t-o lb	PERFORMANCE max speed mph	at height ft	service ceiling ft	combat range miles	REMARKS
Nighthawk	28	0	18	6	9	6	2,218	151	SL	24,500	NA	Dragonfly engine
Nighthawk	28	0	18	6	9	6	2,270	150	SL	NA	NA	Jupiter engine
Norman Thompson N.T.4	78	7	41	6	14	10	6,469	95	2,000	11,700	NA	
Plover	29	0	23	0	12	0	2,984	142	SL	23,000	NA	
P.B.25	33	0	24	1	10	5	1,576	99	NA	15,300	NA	Endurance 3 hours

B.E.2c

B.E.2c

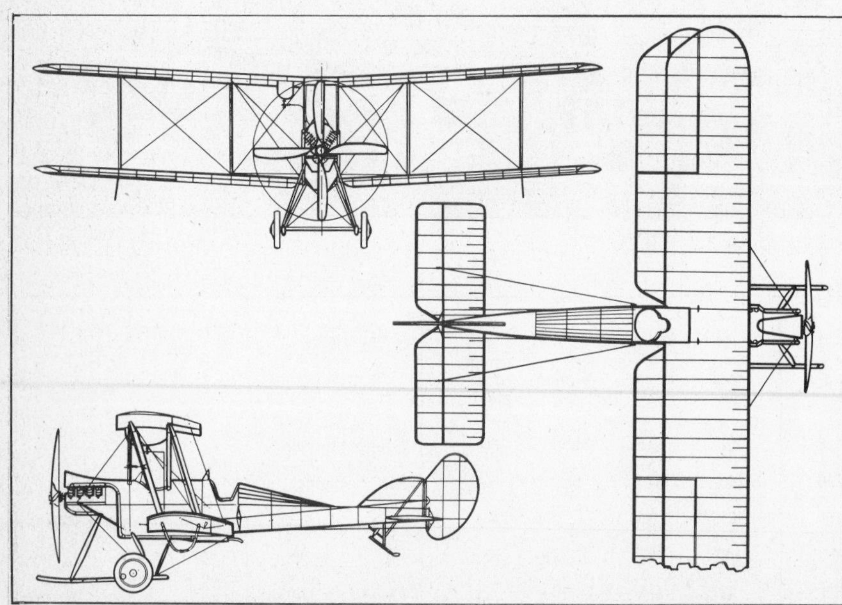

B.E.2c

Note: Royal Aircraft Factory designs are listed on the next six pages under their designations. The name of the Factory is not used as part of the aircraft designation.

B.E.2c

A product of the Royal Aircraft Factory, the B.E.2c was designed as an inherently stable aircraft, following a series of experiments with the earlier B.E.2a.

The prototype appeared in 1914 and was of rather spidery design, with a conventional wire-braced box-girder fuselage, and wings with wooden spars and ribs. Steel tubing was used for the structure of the fin and rudder. Covering was fabric, apart from the metal engine cowling and plywood used for the decking around the cockpits.

Early trials quickly demonstrated the B.E.2c's easy "hands off" flying qualities, resulting from its in-built stability.

This very feature, initially thought to be so desirable, meant that the aircraft was at a serious disadvantage during aerial combat. It proved to be virtually defenceless and, being almost incapable of aerobatics, was readily out-manoeuvred by opposing enemy scouts – particularly the Fokker monoplanes with machine-guns firing through the propeller disc, which shot down the B.E.s in great numbers. The B.E.2c is in fact, credited with being responsible for more casualties in a given period than any other RFC type.

It is on record that the frustrated pilots of one squadron removed the Lewis gun, since the observer in the front cockpit, hedged in by wings, struts and wires, had an extremely limited field of fire and found it virtually impossible to bring the gun to bear on an enemy. They considered the resultant slight increase in speed of greater benefit than the gun. Other pilots tried to attack enemy aircraft by means of a lead weight, winched down from the cockpit, which they attempted to entangle in the propeller of the enemy machines.

Early B.E.2cs were powered by a 70-hp RAF 1a engine. Initially, much of this was exposed, but later a cowling was fitted over the sump. The standard engine, however, was the 90-hp RAF 1a, which was accompanied by a strange variety of exhaust stacks. The general arrangement had twin vertical stacks leading up to and above the top wing, but others were of different shapes and length. Some of the B.E.2cs, built for the RNAS, had extra-long stacks, running down each side of the fuselage and ending just aft of the rear cockpit.

Other engines fitted to B.E.2cs included the 105-hp RAF 1b, 105-hp RAF 1d, 90-hp Curtiss OX-5 and 150-hp Hispano-Suiza.

The armament varied considerably and was never really efficient, with the observer occupying the front seat. Normally, it consisted of a single Lewis gun, but up to four were fitted to some B.E.2cs, plus the usual crew-carried assortment of rifles and carbines. Some Home Defence B.E.2cs carried 24 Ranken darts, plus two 20-lb high-explosive bombs and two 16-lb incendiary bombs for use against Zeppelins. Ten Le Prieur rockets could also be carried. An assortment of bombs could be fitted, up to a maximum load of 224 lb, when the aircraft was flown without the observer.

One B.E.2c was used to test the Constantinesco synchronizing gear for machine-guns, which represented a great improvement over earlier devices. Some B.E.2cs were fitted with armour; the great weight of this – about a quarter of a ton – detracted still further from the aircraft's poor performance, but it was effective – one aircraft survived long enough to get through 80 new wings in three months!

In spite of their poor combat record, large numbers of B.E.2cs were produced, and they were, on official orders, still in service in 1918, long after they had become obsolete.

B.E.8

Designed by the Royal Aircraft Factory, the B.E.8 was a two-seat scout biplane powered by an 80-hp Gnome. On the first few machines which appeared in 1912, the crew sat in a large single cockpit, the fuselage had no fin and the engine drove a two-bladed propeller. The engine was largely enclosed in a distinctive bulbous cowling, which earned the aircraft the nickname of "The Bloater."

Production models, built by the British and Colonial Aeroplane Co, had a short top-decking fitted between the seats to form separate cockpits, a fin and a four-bladed propeller. Lateral control was by wing warping.

There was no standard armament, but the pilots and observers had the usual rifles, carbines, revolvers or hand grenades. A single 100-lb bomb could be carried.

A few B.E.8s saw service in France during the early months of the war. They were used for reconnaissance duties and, in addition, carried out one or two bombing raids.

A development was the B.E.8a, with improved wings incorporating ailerons, and a redesigned tail unit. One B.E.8a was fitted with the experimental 120-hp RAF 2 nine-cylinder radial engine which was designed at Farnborough in 1913.

R.E.7

The R.E.7 was a big two-bay biplane, with long strut-braced extensions on the top wing. Wing construction was conventional, as was the rear of the fuselage, but the front of the fuselage was built up on a steel-tube box-girder. The undercarriage incorporated oleo-units and had a characteristic small nose-wheel projecting ahead of the propeller. An unusual feature, in view of the generally unclean lines, was the air-brakes fitted to some R.E.7s. Consisting of flat plates, these were hinged at their forward edge to each side of the fuselage, in line with the forward centre-section struts.

Various engines were fitted, including the 120-hp Beardmore, 160-hp Beardmore, 150-hp RAF 4a, 190-hp Rolls-Royce Falcon, 250-hp Rolls-Royce Mk III, 200-hp RAF 3a and 225-hp Sunbeam. Some of these were only experimental installations.

No regular defensive armament was fitted, the crew taking along rifles, revolvers or a Lewis gun. In any case, the observer-gunner, in the front cockpit, had a limited field of view and action. A small number of R.E.7s were converted into three-seaters, the third cockpit, aft of the pilot, being fitted with a rotating gun-mounting carrying a Lewis gun.

The main characteristic of the R.E.7 was its relatively great weight-lifting capacity, for it could carry the big 336-lb bomb which had been developed by the Royal Aircraft Factory.

The R.E.7 went into service early in 1916, when the Fokker monoplane menace was approaching its climax, and was used initially for escort duties. Inadequate armament prevented its being effective for this work, and it achieved more success as a bomber during its brief operational career.

F.E.2b

This product of the Royal Aircraft Factory was a pusher biplane developed from the earlier F.E.2a, which had been designed from the start as a combat aircraft. Both fighter and bomber versions were produced. The pusher configuration was a direct consequence of the lack of a suitable interrupter gear that would permit machine-gun fire between the propeller blades.

The first few F.E.2as were powered by a 100-hp Green

B.E.8, Central Flying School, Upavon

B.E.8a

R.E.7

TYPE	DIMENSIONS						WEIGHT	PERFORMANCE				REMARKS
	span		length		height		max t-o	max speed	at height	service ceiling	combat range	
	ft	in	ft	in	ft	in	lb	mph	ft	ft	miles	
B.E. 2c	37	0	27	3	11	1	2,142	72	6,500	10,000	NA	RAF la engine
B.E. 8	39	6	27	3	NA		NA	70	SL	NA	NA	
B.E. 8a	37	8	27	3	NA		NA	NA	NA	NA	NA	
R.E.7	57	0	31	10	12	7	3,449*	85	SL	6,500	NA	*With 336-lb bomb and with RAF 4A engine

F.E.2b. No. 22 Squadron

F.E.2b

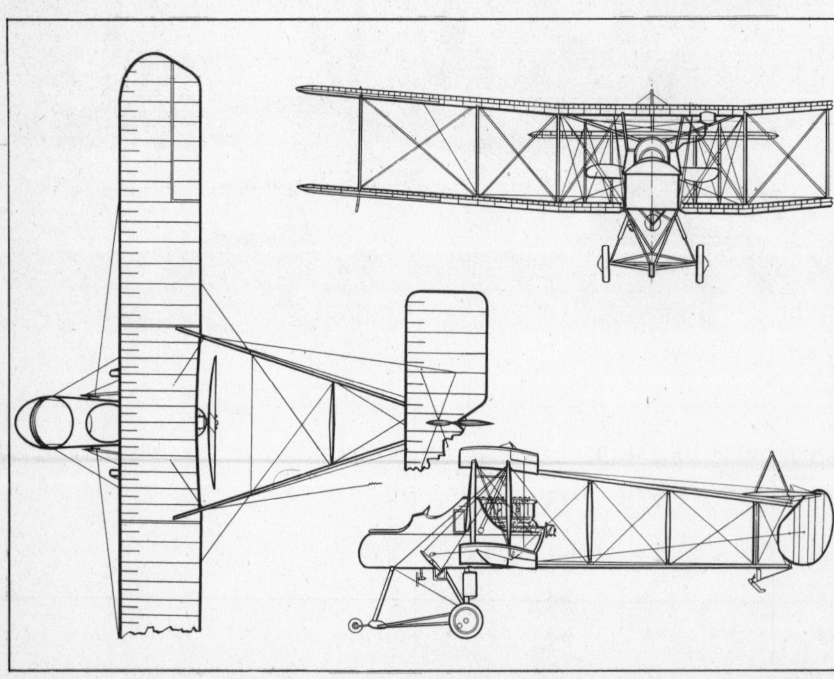
F.E.2b

engine, but this proved unsatisfactory. Accordingly, the 120-hp six-cylinder in-line Beardmore engine was substituted, and the re-engined machines were redesignated F.E.2b.

They had three-bay wings, and the undercarriage incorporated oleo-units and a small nose-wheel, carried well forward, to reduce the risk of overturning when landing. Later F.E.2bs were fitted with 160-hp Beardmores, and many aircraft with this engine had the nose-wheel removed from the undercarriage to give a further slight improvement in performance.

The observer occupied the front seat, and had an excellent view and field of fire. The Beardmore engine, mounted at the rear of the stubby nacelle, was completely uncowled.

A great variety of armament was fitted during the operational life of the F.E.2b, as individual squadrons evolved installations to suit their particular tactics. Initially a single Lewis gun was mounted on a bracket on the nose of the nacelle; later, a second Lewis gun was fitted on a telescopic mounting between the cockpits, for defence against attacks from the rear. The firing of this second gun entailed the observer standing up on his seat (when he had one) and facing backward – not easy in an 80-mph slipstream and with no parachute!

A few F.E.2bs were fitted with Vickers one-pounder quick-firing pom-pom guns and these proved excellent weapons for attacks against trains. Others, in Home Defence squadrons, were armed with 0·45-in Maxim guns; single-seat versions had one or two Lewis guns fixed to fire forward. Fighter-reconnaissance versions carried up to eight 20-lb bombs and the night bomber version could carry a wide variety of bomb loads, up to a maximum of three 112-lb bombs.

Of particular interest was the installation of a small searchlight on the nose of one F.E.2b, with a Lewis gun secured to each side of it, so that the searchlight illuminated the target for the guns.

Small numbers of F.E.2bs went into service on the Western Front in 1915, just as the Fokker monoplane, with its deadly synchronized forward-firing machine-gun, was beginning to scourge the skies of Allied aircraft. It soon established itself as a first-class combat machine, mainly because of the unobstructed forward field of fire. Useful numbers of F.E.2bs arrived in 1916 and, in co-operation with the D.H.2, began to check the Fokkers' activities. A notable success was the shooting down of the German Fokker ace, Max Immelmann, on 18 June 1916, by Second Lieut. G. R. McCubbin and his gunner, Corporal J. H. Walker.

The days of the "pusher" were, however, numbered. The introduction by Germany of the new Albatros and Halberstadt scouts towards the end of 1916 saw both the F.E.2b and D.H.2 outclassed. The F.E.2b continued on night bombing missions and, as it was found to be peculiarly suitable for night flying, was also adopted by the Home Defence force to counter Zeppelin and Gotha attacks by night.

A total of 1,939 F.E.2bs were built.

B.E.12

The B.E.12 represented an attempt by the Royal Aircraft Factory to produce quickly an aircraft to combat the growing menace of the Fokker monoplane. To reduce development time, it was decided to "improve" a standard B.E.2c biplane. The original 90-hp RAF 1a engine was removed and the fuselage was modified slightly to accept the more powerful 150-hp RAF 4a. The aircraft was then converted into a single-seater by the simple process of fairing-in the observer's cockpit. The result was the prototype B.E.12. Production models were essentially similar, except that improvements were made to the fuel system, exhaust system and tail surfaces.

Introduced into service in 1916, the B.E.12 proved a poor combat aircraft. What the authorities seem to have overlooked was the fact that the B.E.2c was inherently stable and that the mere fact of installing a more powerful engine did not alter its basic aerodynamics. The B.E.12, therefore, was so stable that it could not be manoeuvred easily. Nor was its efficiency improved by its armament, which consisted initially of one or two Lewis guns, mounted on brackets outside the cockpit, and splayed outward to clear the propeller disc. To use the guns, the aircraft had to be flown crabwise. Later, the availability of a crude form of Vickers interrupter gear enabled a Vickers machine-gun, firing straight forward, to be installed. Even then, the lack of manoeuvrability still prevented the B.E.12 from being effective.

Its performance was so poor that General Trenchard took the drastic step of requesting that no more of the type should be sent out from Britain, even though he was desperately short of aircraft, and that those already in France should be recalled and employed for Home Defence.

A development of the B.E.12, with new B.E.2e-type wings and tailplane, was known as the B.E.12a. Powered by the 200-hp Hispano-Suiza engine, the B.E.12b was specially developed for Home Defence duties. A total of 468 B.E.12s and 12as were delivered to RFC and RAF Squadrons, followed by more than 100 B.E.12bs.

F.E.8

This single-seat pusher biplane scout was a product of the Royal Aircraft Factory. It bore a close resemblance to the D.H.2, but this configuration was almost forced on the designer of the F.E.8 owing to the continued absence of a suitable British interrupter gear permitting machine-gun fire through the propeller disc.

The prototype, powered by a 100-hp Gnome Monosoupape, appeared in 1915 and was quite clean for a "pusher". Unusual features were the large spinner fitted behind the four-bladed propeller and the position of the single Lewis machine-gun; this was mounted low in the nose, with only a short length of the barrel protruding.

On production machines, the spinner was removed and the Lewis gun was repositioned on top of the fuselage, where reloading was facilitated and stoppages could be investigated.

The 100-hp Gnome Monosoupape remained the standard engine, but some F.E.8s were powered by a 110-hp Le Rhône or 110-hp Clerget.

As with some other aircraft of the time, the F.E.8 was disliked initially by pilots and considered fatal in a spin. This rumour was laid by a test pilot who deliberately put his aircraft into a series of spins, in each direction, regaining full control each time.

The F.E.8 went into service with the RFC on the Western Front in August 1916, and for a few weeks it had reasonable success. However, although pleasant to fly, it proved to be less manoeuvrable than its contemporary, the D.H.2 – and the opposing German types. It was, in fact, obsolete. This fact was dramatically underlined when nine F.E.8s of No. 40 Squadron were attacked by a formation led by the German ace Manfred von Richthofen. In a classic "dog-fight" lasting over half-an-hour, four F.E.8s were shot down in flames; four others were damaged and force-landed. The pilot of the surviving F.E.8 was wounded and he too had to force-land.

The F.E.8 was the last pusher fighter used by the RFC, which accepted a total of 182 into service.

B.E.12

B.E.12a

F.E.8, 100-hp Monosoupape engine

TYPE	DIMENSIONS span ft	in	length ft	in	height ft	in	WEIGHT max t-o lb	PERFORMANCE max speed mph	at height ft	service ceiling ft	combat range miles	REMARKS
F.E.2b	47	9	32	3	12	7	2,967	80	SL	19,000	NA	120-hp Beardmore
F.E.2b	47	9	32	3	12	7	3,037	91	SL	11,000	NA	160-hp Beardmore
B.E.12	37	0	27	3	11	1	2,352	102	SL	12,500	NA	
B.E.12a	40	9	27	3	12	0	2,327	NA	NA	NA	NA	
B.E.12b	37	0	NA		NA		NA	NA	NA	NA	NA	
F.E.8	31	6	23	8	9	2	1,346	94	SL	14,500	NA	100-hp Monosoupape
F.E.8	31	6	23	8	9	2	1,470	94	SL	NA	NA	110-hp Le Rhône
F.E.8	31	6	23	8	9	2	1,390	97	SL	NA	NA	110-hp Clerget

S.E.5, Capt Albert Ball VC in cockpit

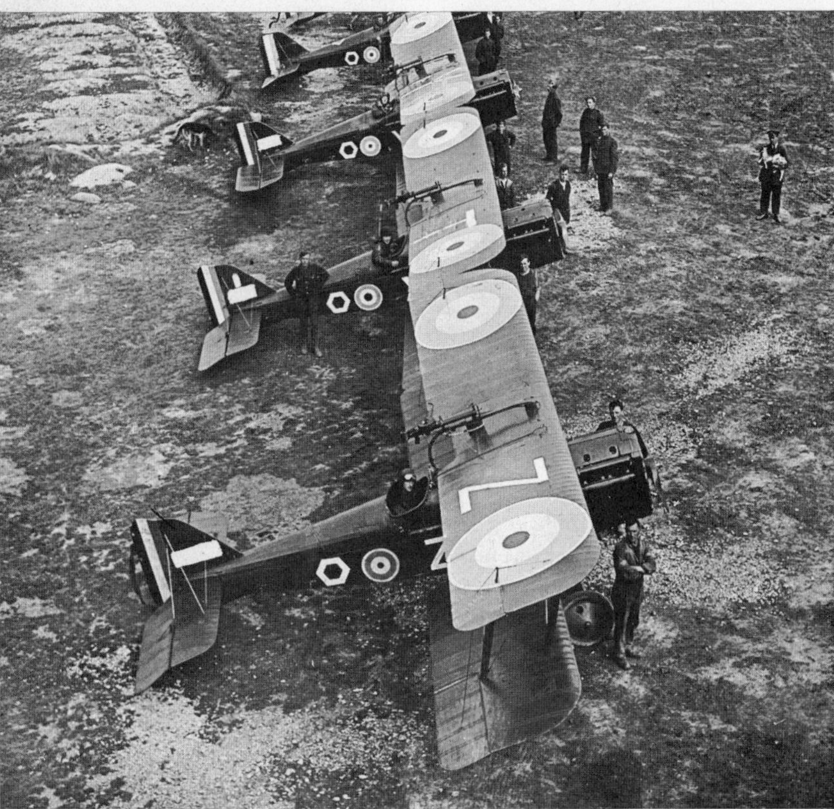
S.E.5a, No. 85 Squadron

S.E.5a, No. 61 (Home Defence) Squadron

S.E.5a

The S.E.5a single-seat fighter scout was the best aircraft produced by the Royal Aircraft Factory, and its fame is only slightly less than that of the Sopwith Camel. The Camel shot down more enemy aircraft than did the S.E.5a, but it is significant that many of the Allies' great aces, such as Bishop, Beauchamp-Proctor, Mannock, McElroy and McCudden, won the majority of their victories while flying S.E.5s and S.E.5as.

When designing the S.E.5, the Farnborough intention – mindful of the short and all-too-inadequate training of the period – was to produce an aircraft that would be relatively easy to fly.

They achieved this aim brilliantly, although the degree of inherent stability was not so marked as it was on the ill-fated B.E.2 series, where its excessiveness destroyed the machine's combat ability.

The S.E.5 was not as manoeuvrable as the Camel; it was not so compact and its engine was a stationary type. Most Camel pilots, used to the help they could obtain from their aircraft's rotary engine, did not like the S.E.5. Nevertheless, it had remarkable diving and zooming qualities and its stability made it a steady gun platform, enabling pilots to open fire from a greater range than was possible on other, less stable, types.

Structurally, the S.E.5 was conventional and robust. The fuselage was a wire-braced box-girder and the wings, with wooden spars and ribs, were braced internally. The fuselage was slightly narrower than usual, giving the pilot a good view downward; a small headrest was fitted behind the cockpit. The sides of the nose portion were of plywood, and the fuel tank, mounted on the upper longerons, was shaped to form the top of the fuselage. The tailplane was adjustable in flight, and the elevator control lines were run internally, which contributed to the general neatness of the tail unit.

The landing wheels were supported on steel Vee-struts, with rubber cord shock-absorbers.

Production S.E.5s began to come off the assembly lines in March 1917, and were powered by the 150-hp eight-cylinder, water-cooled Hispano-Suiza, a French engine of advanced design.

Further development of this engine resulted in a 200-hp version and this was fitted to later aircraft, which were designated S.E.5a.

High hopes were held for this engine, as is indicated by the order for 8,000 placed by Britain with the Mayen company in France; but its introduction was accompanied by serious technical troubles. Engines produced under licence in England proved equally unreliable; one got through four crankshafts in only sixteen hours' running. The condition of engines delivered from a second French supplier was such that, on arrival, they had to be sent away to be overhauled. At one time, hundreds of new S.E.5as were in store, awaiting engines. By October 1917, the situation had become so serious that faulty engines were actually fitted into aircraft and sent into action. This tragic decision, obviously not made by pilots, was defended on the grounds that it was better to have defective engines than no engines at all!

Similar technical troubles were experienced with the armament. Normally two guns were fitted – a Lewis machine-gun mounted on the top centre-section, and a Vickers machine-gun, mounted on the port side of the fuselage in front of the cockpit and synchronized to fire between the propeller blades. The Lewis gun was carried on a Foster mounting and its fire converged with that of the Vickers gun at a range of 50 yd. The mounting was curved at the rear, allowing the gun to be slid rearward until it was nearly vertical. This feature was adopted as the first British ace, Captain Ball, had achieved considerable success with a vertically-mounted gun on his Nieuport Scout; it also facilitated re-loading.

The Vickers gun was synchronized by the Constantinesco hydraulically-operated gear, which gave a great deal of trouble. Often the gun would not fire and when it did there was a good chance of its shooting off the propeller – after which the engine fell off.

However, when all went well, the S.E.5a proved a redoubtable combat aircraft, respected by the enemy. Its great strength enabled pilots to dive at high speeds and to take violent evasive action when necessary, without fear of the wings' breaking off. Its climbing qualities also were unsurpassed.

The aircraft's strength was amply demonstrated on 28 April 1917, when Lt G. C. Maxwell's S.E.5, damaged by anti-aircraft fire and virtually out of control, hit the ground at 140 mph, shed the engine, skidded a hundred yards, and only then fell to bits, allowing the pilot to walk away unhurt.

Another pilot flew through the side of a house and emerged unhurt.

Major E. Mannock, VC, DSO, MC, the leading British fighter ace of the 1914–18 War, scored 50 of his 73 victories in an S.E.5.

In service, the S.E.5 was frequently modified to suit the wisnes of individual pilots. Most common change was removal of the headrest to improve the view rearward. Some pilots reduced the dihedral to increase manoeuvrability. McCudden got an extra 3 mph out of his S.E.5a by fitting a spinner, a trophy from an LVG C.V. that he had shot down. By carefully tuning his engine, he also increased the aircraft's service ceiling to 20,000 ft, compared with the normal 17,000 ft.

As production of the S.E.5a continued, more powerful versions of the Hispano-Suiza engine, first of 220 hp and then 240 hp, were developed and installed. In December 1917, a Wolseley Viper – a high-compression development of the Hispano-Suiza – was fitted to an S.E.5, and this became the standard engine for the last production machines.

In the closing stages of the war, S.E.5s and 5as were used extensively for ground-attack duties, in support of Allied infantry. For this work they carried four 25-lb bombs on racks under the fuselage.

In addition to serving on the Western Front, S.E.5s and 5as equipped four Home Defence squadrons. However, the relatively long warming-up period of their water-cooled engines meant that they were not suited for these duties, which required rapid take-offs as soon as the approaching enemy had been detected.

S.E.5s were used by the American Expeditionary Force, and plans were under way for 1,000 of them to be built in America, by the Curtiss Company, when the contract was cancelled following the signing of the Armistice.

Saro London

The London was a general reconnaissance biplane flying-boat, with a crew of six. The top wing was made in three sections and was of considerably larger span and chord than the lower wings, each of which was made in two sections. The outer sections of the lower wings, most susceptible to damage, were replaceable without extensive re-rigging. The structure was of stainless steel, with fabric covering, except for the upper surface of the lower wings, near the fuselage, which was metal covered. Ailerons were fitted to the upper wing only.

The hull embodied two steps and was "planked" distinctively with straight strips of Alclad, the absence of double-curvature skinning simplifying production and repairs. The cockpit was enclosed.

S.E.5a, Wolseley Viper engine

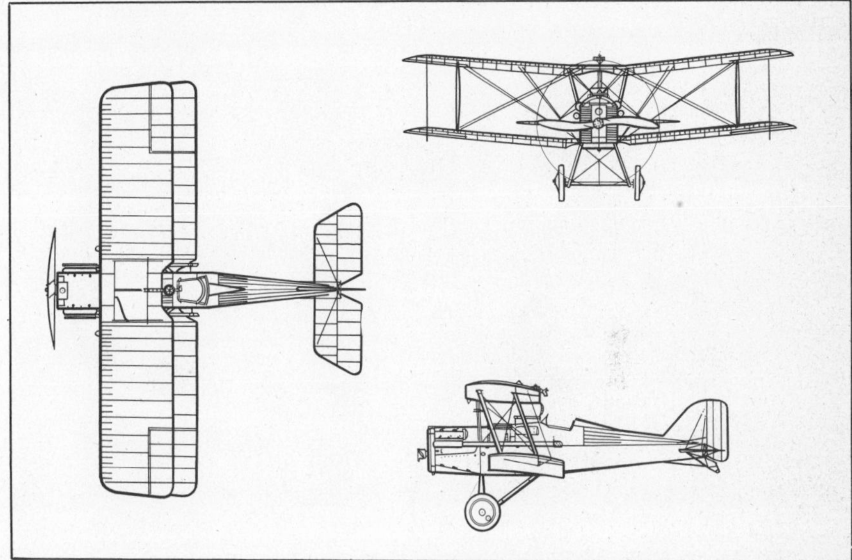
S.E.5a, Wolseley Viper engine

Saro London prototype

TYPE	DIMENSIONS span ft	in	length ft	in	height ft	in	WEIGHT max t-o lb	PERFORMANCE max speed mph	at height ft	service ceiling ft	combat range miles	REMARKS
S.E.5	26	7	21	4	9	5	1,930	119	6,500	17,000	NA	150-hp Hispano-Suiza
S.E.5	26	7	21	4	9	5	1,976	125	1,000	18,000	NA	200-hp Viper
S.E.5a	26	7	20	11	9	6	1,953	121	15,000	22,000	NA	200-hp Hispano-Suiza
S.E.5a	26	7	20	11	9	6	NA	135	SL	NA	NA	240-hp Hispano-Suiza
S.E.5a	26	7	20	11	9	6	1,940	137	SL	NA	NA	200-hp Viper
London Mk II	80	0	56	9	18	9	18,400	155	6,250	19,900	1,740	

Saro London Mk II

Saro Lerwick

Short Folder

Short Folder, modified with three-bay wings

The two engines were mounted on the top wing, outboard of the centre-section, and were supported by massive interplane struts.

Armament consisted of three Lewis machine-guns, mounted in bow, midship and tail positions. The maximum bomb load was 2,000 lb.

Powered by Bristol Pegasus III engines in polygonal cowlings, the first ten production Londons were designated Mk I and went into service in 1936 with No. 204 Squadron. Mk II 'boats were fitted with 1,000-hp Bristol Pegasus Xs, in circular cowlings, and drove four-bladed propellers. A total of 37 Mk IIs were built.

Two Londons were on patrol over the North Sea when war started in 1939, and the type remained in service at Gibraltar until late 1941, when it was superseded by the Catalina.

Saro Lerwick

The Lerwick was a twin-engined general reconnaissance flying-boat, carrying a crew of six.

Designed to Air Ministry Specification R.1/36, it was a high-wing monoplane, of all-metal stressed-skin construction. A minor innovation was the cantilever mounting of the stabilizing floats under the outer ends of the wings.

The power plant comprised two 1,375-hp Bristol Hercules II sleeve-valve radial engines.

Armament consisted of one Vickers machine-gun in a turret in the nose, two 0·303-in Browning machine-guns in a dorsal turret, and four more Brownings in a tail turret, all turrets being power-operated. Maximum bomb load was 2,000 lb: four 500-lb or eight 250-lb bombs.

The Lerwick went into service in 1940, with No. 209 Squadron, its portly hull quickly gaining it the nickname of "Flying Pig". Its operational record is obscure and after about a year it was abruptly withdrawn from service.

About 26 Lerwicks were built, and the type was officially declared obsolete in 1942.

Short Folder

Produced in 1913, this was the first British aircraft to have folding wings. The first two examples (serial numbers 81 and 82) bore a strong resemblance to the earlier Short Type 41 seaplanes and, in consequence, were often referred to by this designation. Generally, however, the Folder is considered a distinct type in its own right.

The two-seat rectangular fuselage was of conventional wire-braced wood construction. Extensions to the upper wings were braced by long sloping struts, secured to the lower wings. The aircraft was powered by a 160-hp Gnome two-row 14-cylinder rotary engine, a distinctive feature of the installation being the funnel-like exhaust stack projecting from the cowling.

The prototype Folder, fitted with an early type of wireless transmitter, was used during the Royal Navy manoeuvres of 1913, when it was carried on board the seaplane carrier *Hermes*. The folding wings facilitated stowage and confirmed that this feature would be useful on future shipborne aircraft.

Succeeding Folders differed from the first two. The wing area was increased by lengthening the extensions of the upper wing; the float strut system was simplified and, on some machines, the wings could be folded from the cockpit. A bomb-load of up to 80 lb could be carried on external racks.

Round about this time, early experiments were being made with torpedo-carrying aircraft and Mr Winston Churchill, then First Lord of the Admiralty, urged that British experiments should be accelerated. Accordingly, a Folder was modified to take the necessary attachments and the first successful drop, with a 14-in 810-lb torpedo, took place on 28 July 1914. The experiments continued up to the outbreak of war and in the succeeding weeks.

Two Folders took part in a seven-plane attack on Cuxhaven on 25 December 1914. Three others were despatched to South Africa in 1915 to help locate the German light cruiser *Königsberg*, hidden up the Rufiji river delta; but they proved unsuitable for the task, owing to the high temperature and humidity of the area.

Short Seaplane, Admiralty Types 827 and 830

These were single-engined two-seat seaplanes, designed for reconnaissance and bombing duties. The designations were derived from the Admiralty's curious system of allocating Type Numbers according to the serial numbers of the first examples built.

The initial order for 12 machines was placed in 1914; the 827s being powered by a 150-hp Sunbeam Nubian water-cooled V-eight engine, and the 830s by the 135-hp Salmson (Canton-Unné) radial engine. As production got under way, the Sunbeam engine became standard, and eventually at least 107 Short 827s and 19 Short 830s were completed.

Armament included an occasional Lewis gun for the observer and small bombs carried beneath the fuselage.

In home waters the aircraft were used for patrol duties in the English Channel and North Sea. Some were operated from seaplane carriers. In 1916, a small number of 827s were despatched to Zanzibar, where they were used successfully during the East African campaign. Other 827s, equipped with wireless transmitters, operated in Mesopotamia; and two, converted into landplanes, were used to bomb Turkish forces advancing towards Kut al Imara.

Short Seaplane, Admiralty Type 184

Produced in 1915, the Short Seaplane, Admiralty Type 184, was a two-seat torpedo-bomber reconnaissance seaplane, with folding wings to facilitate stowage on board warships. The designation 184 resulted from the Admiralty's habit of referring to aircraft by the serial number allocated to the first machine. However, as early versions were powered by a 225-hp Sunbeam engine, they were generally known as "225s", and this reference continued even when more powerful engines were subsequently fitted. These included the 260-hp Sunbeam, 275-hp Sunbeam Maori III, 250-hp Rolls-Royce Eagle and 240-hp Renault.

Some 184s were converted into single-seat bombers, these being known as Short Type Ds.

For defence, the observer, in the rear cockpit, was provided with a Lewis gun on a movable mounting. The bomb-load arrangements varied considerably. The standard two-seater could carry one 14-in torpedo between the floats, or one 520-lb bomb, one 500-lb bomb, four 100-lb or four 112-lb bombs, three 65-lb bombs together with several smaller bombs, or one 264-lb and one 100-lb bomb. The single-seat version carried nine 65-lb bombs, stowed vertically within the fuselage in front of the pilot.

The 184 established the Short Brothers' reputation as designers of first-class seaplanes and was used extensively during the war. One took part in the Battle of Jutland; another made history during the Dardanelles campaign when it became the first aircraft in the world

Short Seaplane, Admiralty Type 830

Short Seaplane, Admiralty Type 184, 260-hp Sunbeam engine

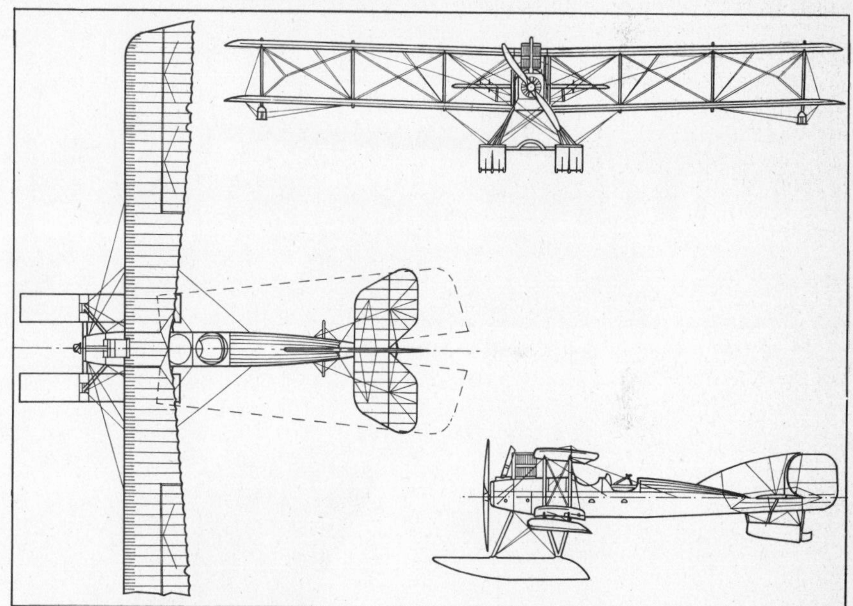

Short Seaplane, Admiralty Type 184

TYPE	DIMENSIONS span ft	span in	length ft	length in	height ft	height in	WEIGHT max t-o lb	PERFORMANCE max speed mph	at height ft	service ceiling ft	combat range miles	REMARKS
Lerwick	80	10	63	7	20	0	28,400	213	NA	NA	NA	
Short Folder	67	0	39	0	NA		3,040	78	NA	NA	400	Original aircraft had 2-bay 56-ft span wings
Short 827	53	11	35	3	13	6	3,400	61	2,000	NA	NA	
Short 830	53	11	35	3	13	6	3,324	70	2,000	NA	NA	
Short 184	63	6	40	7	13	6	5,100	75	2,000	NA	NA	225-hp Sunbeam
Short 184	63	6	40	7	13	6	5,560	80	2,000	5,700	NA	240 hp Renault
Short 184 (Sage built)	63	6	40	7	13	6	5,190	85	2,000	5,000	NA	240-hp Renault
Short 184 (Phoenix built)	63	6	40	7	13	6	5,244	76	2,000	5,500	NA	240-hp Renault
Short 184	63	6	40	7	13	6	5,363	88	2,000	9,000	NA	260-hp Sunbeam
Short 184 (Robey built)	63	6	40	7	13	6	5,287	82	6,500	6,900	NA	260-hp Sunbeam

Short Bomber prototype, 225-hp Sunbeam engine

Short Bomber, 250-hp Rolls-Royce engine

Short Bomber, 250-hp Rolls-Royce engine, wings folded

Short 320

to sink an enemy ship at sea by means of a torpedo.

A small number of 184s were delivered after the war to Estonia, Greece and Japan. Altogether, more than 650 were built.

Short Bomber

The outstanding characteristic of this two-seat bomber was its huge high aspect ratio wings. A landplane development of the Short 184 seaplane, the Bomber was produced to meet the requirements of an Admiralty competition held in 1915 for an aircraft capable of carrying a heavy load of bombs a long distance. The prototype had two-bay wings and a short fuselage, but production machines had enlarged three-bay wings, with long extensions on the upper wing, supported by king-posts. On some later aircraft the fuselage also was lengthened. A sturdy but cumbersome four-wheel undercarriage was fitted.

Most Short Bombers were powered by the 250-hp Rolls-Royce Eagle engine, but those built under sub-contract by the Sunbeam Company had a 225-hp Sunbeam engine. Maximum bomb-load was 920 lb and consisted of either four 230-lb bombs or eight 112-lb bombs. On the prototype, defence was provided by a single Lewis machine-gun mounted on top of the centre-section. An indication of the lack of appreciation of combat conditions by designers of the installation is that the observer, in order to reach and fire the gun, was expected to climb out of his cockpit and stand up on the decking between the two cockpits. On later machines, the gun was located in the cockpit on a ring-mounting.

In service with the RNAS, the Short Bomber was used to bomb Ostend and Zeebrugge. It carried twice the bomb-load of accompanying Caudrons, but was not an outstanding success operationally. Its main achievement was that its range and load-carrying capacity helped to initiate the concept of bombing "strategic" targets such as industrial centres and munition works far behind the front line.

In 1916, plans were made to create an RNAS unit for strategic bombing, the Wing to consist of 15 Short Bombers and 20 Sopwith 1½-Strutters. Activation of the unit was seriously retarded by transfer of the 1½-Strutters to the RFC, which needed additional aircraft urgently for the Somme offensive; but the Wing is considered as constituting the beginning of the Independent Force operated by the RAF in 1918.

Short 320

The Short 320 of 1916 was designed to meet an official requirement for a long-range seaplane capable of carrying the new Mark IX torpedo. This weapon weighed 1,000 lb and contained a 170-lb TNT warhead.

As might be expected, the 320 turned out to be relatively large, and early versions were powered by the 310-hp Sunbeam Cossack water-cooled V-twelve engine. Most production machines, however, had a Sunbeam Cossack of 320 hp, and it was the numerical value of the horsepower of this engine which was adopted, rather curiously, as the official designation for the type. A feature of the engine installation was the bulky box-like radiator mounted on top of the engine – right in front of the pilot.

The construction of the wings, fuselage and tail unit was conventional; the float undercarriage, however, was specially designed to cater for carrying and dropping a torpedo. The weapon was carried beneath the fuselage, well above the upper surface of the floats, and the rear float attachment points were supported by Vee-struts to the bottom wings.

Some 320s were reserved for long-range reconnaissance and anti-submarine duties, and on these the torpedo crutch was replaced by racks for two 230-lb bombs.

Defensive armament consisted of a Lewis machine-gun on a Scarff ring-mounting, above the front cockpit, in line with and attached to the top wing. This position gave a good field of fire, the only drawback being that the observer, in order to man the gun, had to clamber out of his cockpit and stand on the decking!

The Short 320 went into service with the RNAS and

was based at various seaplane stations around Britain and in the Mediterranean. In September 1917, an attack by six Italian-based 320s was planned against submarines laying off Cattaro. The seaplanes, carrying their torpedoes, were towed on special rafts to within 50 miles of the target, as the heavily-laden machines could not carry sufficient fuel for a longer return flight. Unfortunately, a gale sprang up and the attack had to be abandoned. Rather surprisingly, no further attacks of this kind were made.

Four 320s were used at Calshot in February 1918 for a series of experiments to provide information on the behaviour of air-dropped torpedoes. The tests were very successful, but official preference for landplane torpedo-carriers resulted in the rapid disappearance of the 320 from the operational scene.

One 320 served in the Imperial Japanese Navy. A total of 137 appear to have been built.

Short Rangoon

This general reconnaissance flying-boat was a military development of the Short Calcutta 15-passenger three-engined 'boats operated by Imperial Airways.

It had unequal-span wings, with an all-metal structure and fabric covering. The upper and lower centre-sections were interconnected by a system of struts which also supported the three engines midway between the wings. The three 540-hp Bristol Jupiter XIF engines were installed as complete power plants, with their oil tanks and oil coolers. Fuel was carried in tanks built into the top centre-section, which was thickened locally.

The hull, of all-metal stressed-skin construction, had two steps and a concave Vee bottom. The Rangoon was destined for service in the Near East, and the spacious hull contained sleeping bunks, cooking facilities and fresh water stowage for the crew of five. The pilots were accommodated in an enclosed cockpit.

Armament consisted of three Lewis machine-guns, mounted in the bow cockpit, on a Scarff ring-mounting, and in two staggered cockpits aft of the wing, one on each side of the centre-line. The maximum bomb-load was 1,000 lb.

The Rangoon went into service in 1931, with No. 203 Squadron. This unit was stationed at Basrah, in Iraq, and the Rangoon's all-metal hull resisted well the effects of long exposure at moorings. Also advantageous was the flying-boat's ability to take off and fly on only two of its three engines.

Six Rangoons were built, and they remained in service until 1935.

Short Singapore III

The Singapore III general reconnaissance flying-boat was the final service version of a series which originated with the Singapore I in 1926.

It was a biplane with unequal span single-bay wings, outboard of a large centre-section assembly. The centre-section planes were separated by four massive interplane struts, which also formed the engine mountings. Four 560-hp Rolls-Royce Kestrels were mounted in tandem pairs midway up the struts, one engine of each pair (Kestrel IIIMs) driving a tractor propeller and the other (Kestrel IIMs) a pusher propeller.

The hull was of all-metal construction, with two steps, and the underwater planing surface was specially designed

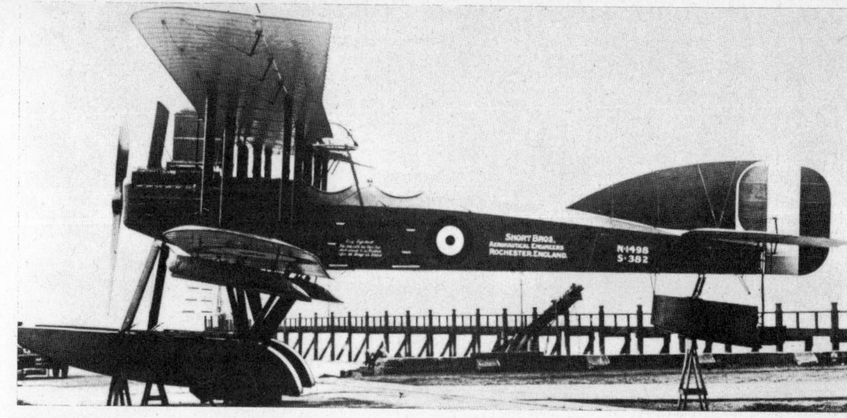

Short 320

Short Rangoon

Short Singapore III

TYPE	DIMENSIONS span ft	in	length ft	in	height ft	in	WEIGHT max t-o lb	PERFORMANCE max speed mph	at height ft	service ceiling ft	combat range miles	REMARKS
Short Bomber	85	0	45	0	15	0	6,800	77	6,500	9,500	NA	Endurance 6 hours
Short 320	75	0	45	9	17	6	7,013	77	2,000	3,500	NA	310-hp Sunbeam
Short 320	75	0	45	9	17	6	7,014	72	1,200	3,000	NA	320-hp Sunbeam
Rangoon	93	0	66	9	23	9	22,500	115	NA	12,000	650	

Short Singapore III

Short Sunderland Mk II

Short Sunderland Mk III

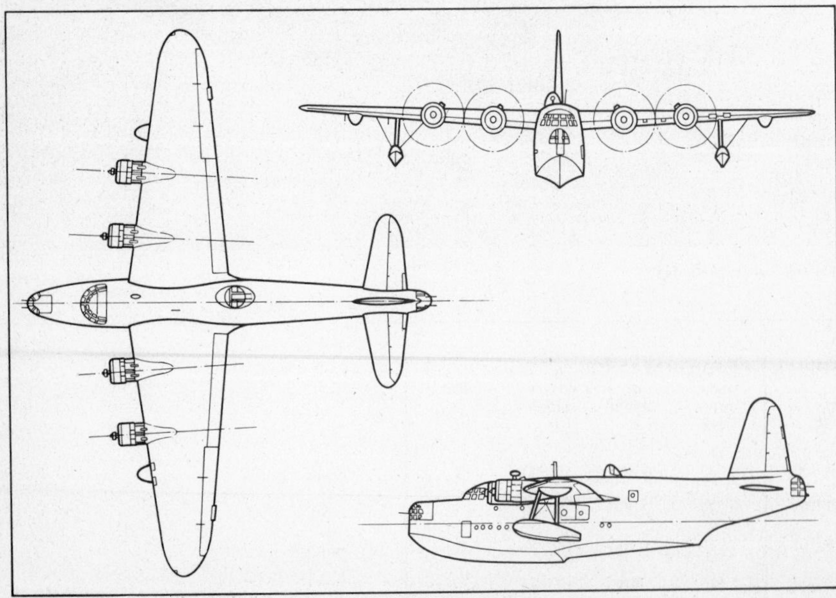
Short Sunderland Mk III

to eliminate any tendency to porpoise. Heavy spar frames were located in line with the wings and triple-finned tail unit.

Accommodation was provided within the hull for a crew of six. The bomb-aimer's position was in the extreme bow, together with the stowage for mooring gear. Immediately aft was the enclosed pilot's cockpit, with side-by-side seats and full dual controls. Aft again was the officers' quarters, containing the navigational charts and equipment and two bunks. Between the spars was accommodation for an engineer and wireless operator, and aft of the rear spars was the crew's quarters, with three bunks. Equipment included cooking gear, a work-bench with a vice, drogues, a dinghy and engineers' ladders and slinging gear to enable engines to be changed while afloat.

Armament consisted of three Lewis machine-guns, in the bow position on a Scarff ring-mounting, in the midship position aft of the wings, and in a cockpit in the extreme tail. The midship gun was on a sliding mounting so that it could fire vertically downward on each side of the hull. Maximum bomb-load was 2,000 lb.

The first Singapore III flew in July 1934, and was followed by a total of 37 production models for the RAF. The type went into service in 1935, with No. 230 Squadron. During the Spanish Civil War, Singapore IIIs based in Africa carried out special anti-piracy patrols to protect British shipping in the Mediterranean. Some remained in service for a short period after the outbreak of war in 1939.

Short Sunderland

This long-range general reconnaissance and anti-submarine flying-boat was a military development of the famous "C" Class Empire 'boats. Its success in the military rôle is indicated by the fact that it remained operational with the Royal Air Force until May 1959 – 21 years after it first went into service. No other RAF combat type can equal this record of longevity.

Produced to meet the requirements of Air Ministry Specification R.2/33, calling for a four-engined monoplane flying-boat to replace the biplanes then in service, the Sunderland was of all-metal, stressed-skin construction.

The wing was built up around a main spar, consisting of four extruded T-section members forming the corners of a strong torsion-box girder, to which the leading- and trailing-edge assemblies were attached.

The two-step two-deck hull consisted of channel-section frames, interconnected by Z-section stiffeners and with a metal skin. At the front of the upper deck was the flight compartment, accommodating the two pilots, radio operator, navigator and engineer. Aft was stowage for the reconnaissance flares and maintenance cradles. In the bows were the bomb-aimer's position and gun turret. On the lower deck were the mooring compartments, with stairs to the upper deck, a lavatory, officers' wardroom, galley, bomb compartment, crew quarters and beam gun positions. The rear of the hull contained a work bench, collapsible dinghy, flares and sea markers.

The Sunderland Mk I was powered by four 1,065-hp Bristol Pegasus XVIII nine-cylinder radial engines.

Armament consisted of no fewer than ten 0·303-in machine-guns. Four were housed in a Frazer-Nash power-operated gun-turret in the bow, and four in a similar turret in the extreme tail. Two manually-operated Vickers guns, on pillar mountings, provided the midship armament. Maximum bomb-load was 2,000 lb, carried internally, the bombs being run out through the side of the hull on rails under the wings for dropping.

Sunderland Mk Is went into service in the middle of 1938, with Nos. 210 and 230 Squadrons, superseding Singapore IIIs.

During the war the heavy defensive armament proved highly effective. One Sunderland, attacked by six Junkers Ju 88s, shot down one in flames, forced another to land and drove the remaining four away. On another occasion a Sunderland shot down three out of eight attacking Ju 88s. Such feats gained it the nickname of "Flying Porcupine" from the Germans.

Introducing various refinements, Sunderland Mk IIs followed the Mk Is into service, and later models incorporated a power-operated dorsal turret in place of the manually-operated beam guns.

The Mk III retained the improved armament and, in addition, introduced an improved planning bottom to the hull, the forward step being considerably shallower.

The next Sunderland variant was the Mk V, the Mk IV being renamed the Seaford. (Most of the small number of Seafords built were converted for civil use).

The Mk V appeared in 1943 and introduced a change of power plant, being fitted with four 1,200-hp Pratt & Whitney Twin Wasp R-1830 engines. This version also introduced heavier nose armament, in the form of four additional fixed machine-guns in the bows, firing forward. These guns were needed to counter the 20- and 37-mm guns being mounted on the conning towers of U-boats in 1943, and their effectiveness was demonstrated on 8 January 1944 when a Sunderland, attacking a U-boat, opened fire at a range of over 1,000 yards, knocked out all the U-boat's guns, and then sank it with depth charges.

After World War II, Sunderlands were used throughout the Korean War, in Malaysia, where they each carried 200 fragmentation bombs, and, in more peaceful vein, in the British North Greenland Expedition of 1951–4.

A total of 721 Sunderlands of all Marks were built. Some were used after the war by the French Navy; ten were supplied to the Royal New Zealand Air Force, with which they remained in first-line service until 1966.

Short Stirling

The Stirling was the first of the three heavy strategic bombers initiated by the British Air Staff in 1936 and which during World War II formed the backbone of Bomber Command's offensive against Germany.

Designed to Air Ministry Specification B.12/36, it was a four-engined monoplane of all-metal stressed-skin construction. The specification placed a limit on wing span, so that the bomber could be housed in standard RAF hangars; this resulted in a wing of comparatively low aspect ratio, as the designers increased the chord to obtain the necessary wing area. In turn, this low aspect ratio resulted in a relatively low ceiling, which proved a serious handicap in action. The wing construction was generally similar to that of the Sunderland, consisting of a main spar torsion-box, to which the leading- and trailing-edge assemblies were attached. Gouge-type flaps were fitted inboard of the ailerons.

The fuselage was a slab-sided monocoque structure, with the bomb-bay occupying almost all of the interior below the wing. The bay held a maximum load of 14,000 lb, which could be carried 590 miles. With the load reduced to 3,500 lb, the range was increased to 2,010 miles. The bay was, however, divided into sections, which meant that the heaviest bomb which could be accommodated was a 4,000-pounder. This limited the usefulness of the Stirling as a warplane.

The shoulder position of the wing resulted in a tall and very complicated main undercarriage, and a correspondingly complicated retraction sequence, into the nacelles of the inboard engines.

Defensive armament consisted of two 0.303-in Browning machine-guns in each of the nose and dorsal power-operated turrets, and four guns in a power-operated tail turret.

Short Sunderland GR Mk V

Short Stirling Mk II (converted Mk I)

Short Stirling Mk III

TYPE	DIMENSIONS						WEIGHT	PERFORMANCE				REMARKS
	span		length		height		max t-o	max speed	at height	service ceiling	combat range	
	ft	in	ft	in	ft	in	lb	mph	ft	ft	miles	
Singapore III	90	0	76	0	23	7	27,500	145	2,000	15,000	1,000	
Sunderland Mk I	112	10	85	4	NA		50,100	210	NA	NA	NA	
Sunderland Mk II	112	10	85	4	NA		58,000	205	NA	NA	NA	
Sunderland Mk III	112	10	85	4	NA		58,000	212	NA	NA	NA	
Sunderland Mk V	112	10	85	4	32	10	60,000	213	5,000	17,900	2,980	

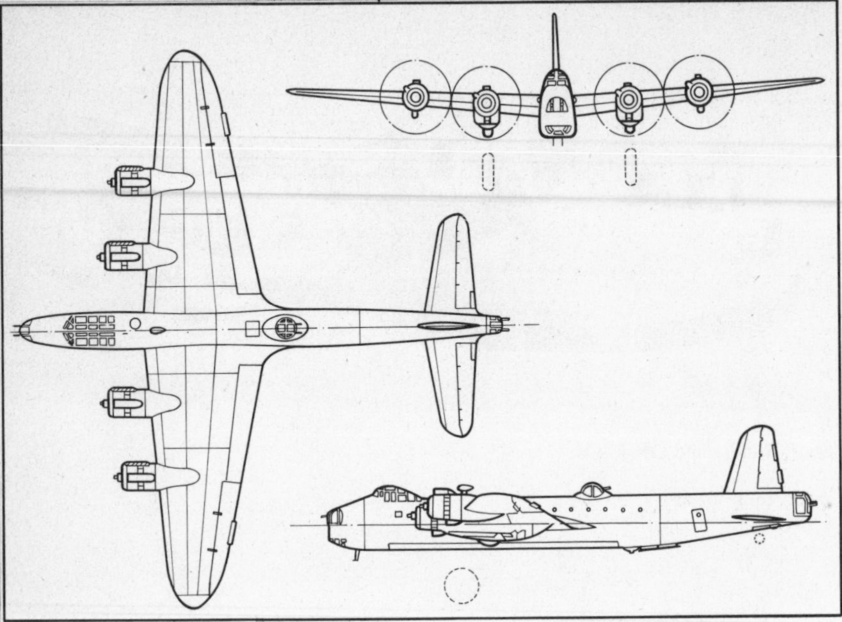
Short Stirling Mk III

Sopwith Tabloid

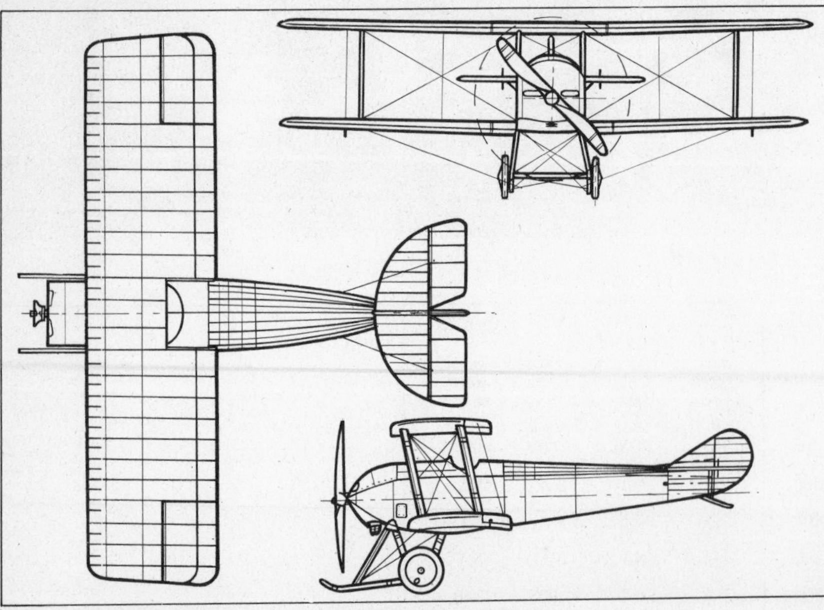
Sopwith Tabloid

The two prototype Stirlings were each powered by four 1,375-hp Bristol Hercules II engines, but production Mk I aircraft had 1,595-hp Hercules XI engines. They went into service in August 1940, with No. 7 Squadron, constituting the first four-engined RAF bomber squadron of the war. Their initial sortie was made on 10 February 1941, when three Stirlings dropped fifty-six 500-lb bombs on oil storage tanks at Rotterdam. In that same year, Stirlings pioneered the use of an early form of Oboe blind bombing device, during attacks on German warships at Brest.

The Stirling Mk II was a version powered by Wright Cyclone engines; not many of this type were built.

The Mk III was a major improvement, powered by 1,650-hp Bristol Hercules XVI engines, and incorporated a new type of dorsal gun turret. This was the standard version in Bomber Command during 1943 and 1944.

The Stirling Mk IV was a version adapted for glider towing and transport duties, retaining only the dorsal gun-turret, and the Mk V was a special unarmed transport capable of carrying 40 troops.

Production of Stirling bombers exceeded 1,630 aircraft, made up of 756 Mk Is and more than 875 Mk IIIs.

Sopwith Tabloid

When it appeared in 1913 the Tabloid astonished the aviation world. Carrying a pilot, passenger and fuel for 2½ hours, it could climb to 1,200 ft in one minute and travel at 92 mph in level flight – figures never attained previously by any biplane, British or foreign. With the B.E.2 and Avro 500, and following a series of accidents to monoplanes, the Tabloid reversed the growing preference for monoplanes, which was not to return for 20 years.

Designed in secret by T. O. M. Sopwith and F. Sigrist, the Tabloid was intended originally for demonstration flying and racing. The fuselage was a simple box structure, wire-braced and fabric-covered. Two persons were accommodated side-by-side in a large single cockpit. The clean lines of the fuselage were enhanced by an unusual aluminium cowling, which enclosed almost entirely the 80-hp Gnome rotary engine, except for two small inlet slits and an exhaust outlet at the bottom. The wings had a single pair of interplane struts each side. On the prototype, lateral control was by wing warping, but the production machines were fitted with ailerons.

Although the Tabloid was developed as a civil aircraft, its military potential was obvious, and single-seat production versions were ordered for both the RFC and the RNAS.

An early success was the attack by two RNAS Tabloids on the airship sheds at Cologne and Düsseldorf, the first-ever air raid on Germany. The Cologne attack was not successful, but at Düsseldorf the new Zeppelin Z-IX was destroyed by fire, complete with the shed in which it was housed.

Tabloids of the RFC were used for scouting duties. No regular armament was carried, although pilots tried rifles, carbines, revolvers and flechettes (steel darts). Some aircraft were also fitted with a machine-gun mounted at an angle to fire clear of the propeller disc. With such an arrangement, it was necessary to fly the aircraft crabwise while carrying out an attack.

One RNAS Tabloid was fitted experimentally with a Lewis gun firing forward through the propeller disc, the blades being fitted with steel deflector plates to prevent them being damaged by bullets. First utilized by the French pilot, Roland Garros, the idea was improved on by Anthony Fokker, who designed propeller interrupter gear which "timed" the bullets to pass between the blades.

Sopwith Schneider and Baby

Developed from the Schneider Trophy-winning Tabloid of 1914, which itself was a variant of the racing Tabloid of 1913, the Sopwith Schneider was a high-performance single-seat seaplane.

The early days of the war had demonstrated the need

for fast seaplanes, and the Schneider was put into production in 1914. It closely resembled its forebears, differences including a strengthened undercarriage, an enlarged fin, and a small aperture in the centre of the top wing to permit the installation of a Lewis gun. The 100-hp Gnome Monosoupape engine and its distinctive cowling were retained. Lateral control on early machines was by wing warping, but later Schneiders had conventional ailerons.

By 1915 Zeppelin operations over the North Sea, and German U-boat operations under it, began to embarrass British Naval patrols. Deployed to protect this area, the Schneiders carried a single 60-lb bomb for attacking U-boats and incendiary ammunition for anti-Zeppelin patrols.

The Schneiders soon began to accumulate additional equipment, starting a trend which is continued by Naval aircraft today. To carry home messages, a pigeon or two were stowed on board. Engine failures were not uncommon, and to help pilots who made forced landings to survive, an emergency ration pack became standard equipment. To enable the pilot to stay put on water, a sea anchor became a necessity. Inevitably, performance began to deteriorate; so the more powerful 110-hp Clerget engine was installed, enclosed by a horseshoe shaped cowling.

Schneiders with the Clerget engine were officially designated Sopwith Baby; but many authorities continued to use the original name, while others started calling the Schneiders Babies.

An improved Baby, embodying a lift-increasing camber device, was produced by the Fairey Company at Hamble; this development was called the Fairey Hamble Baby.

Other Babies, with improved wings, were built by the Blackburn Company. Later Blackburn Babies were powered by the 130-hp Clerget engine. Of interest is that the first 40 of these were armed only with containers of Ranken darts.

A small number of Blackburn Babies served with the Royal Norwegian Naval Air Service.

Sopwith Seaplane, Admiralty Type 860

The Sopwith Seaplane, Admiralty Type 860, was a two-seat biplane designed to carry a torpedo. The type number resulted from the Admiralty's habit of allotting the serial number of the first aircraft of a series as the official type number.

Large three-bay wings were fitted, and these could be folded to facilitate stowage on board ship. The strutage of the pontoon-like floats incorporated a springing device to cushion the shock of alighting on water; the 810-lb, 14-in torpedo was supported by crutches fitted at the centre of each of the two interfloat struts.

Power was supplied by a 225-hp Sunbeam engine, a distinctive feature of the installation being the massive central exhaust stack.

Only small numbers of the 860 were built, owing to the decision to standardize on the Short Seaplane, Admiralty Type 184.

They were used by the RNAS for patrol duties in home waters during 1915 and 1916.

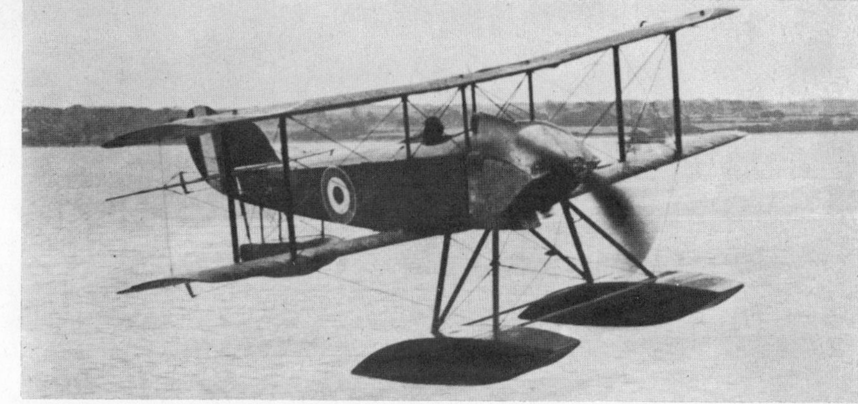

Sopwith Schneider, late model with ailerons

Sopwith Baby, Blackburn-built, 130-hp Clerget engine

Sopwith Seaplane, Admiralty Type 860

TYPE	DIMENSIONS span ft	span in	length ft	length in	height ft	height in	WEIGHT max t-o lb	PERFORMANCE max speed mph	at height ft	service ceiling ft	combat range miles	REMARKS
Stirling Mk I	99	1	87	3	22	9	59,400	260	NA	NA	2,330	
Stirling Mk II	99	1	87	3	22	9	59,400	NA	NA	NA	NA	
Stirling Mk III	99	1	87	3	22	·9	70,000	270	14,500	17,000	590*	*With max bomb load
Sopwith Tabloid	25	6	20	4	8	5	1,120	92	NA	NA	315	
Sopwith Schneider	25	8	22	10	10	0	1,580	92	SL	NA	NA	110-hp Clerget
Sopwith Baby	25	8	23	0	10	0	1,715	100	SL	NA	NA	130-hp Clerget

Sopwith 1½-Strutter, Westland-built, 130-hp Clerget engine

Sopwith 1½-Strutter, single-seat bomber version

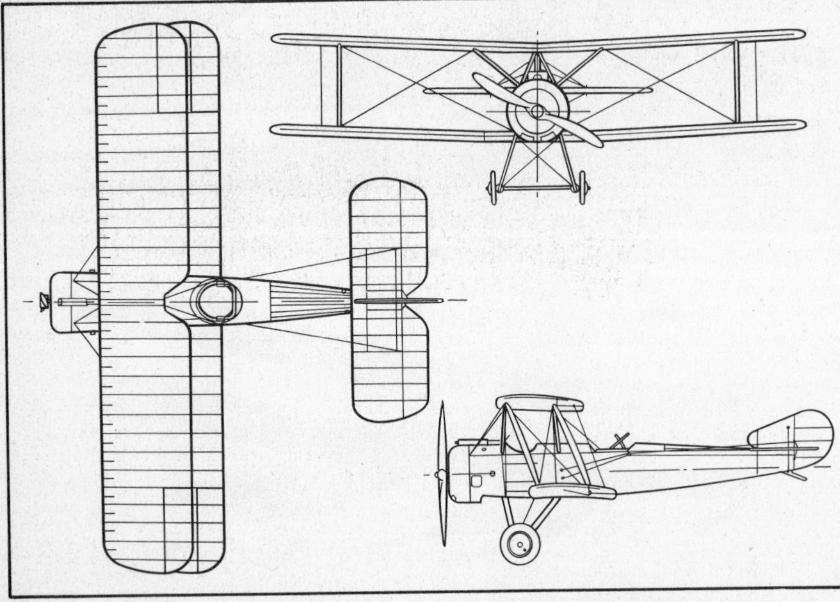

Sopwith 1½-Strutter

Sopwith Pup, 80-hp Gnome engine

Sopwith 1½-Strutter

Known officially by the Admiralty as the Sopwith Type 9700, and designated Sopwith Two-Seater by the RFC, the 1½-Strutter was a two-seat tractor reconnaissance/fighter biplane. The nickname by which it is best remembered was due to the W-arrangement of the struts supporting the centre-section of the top wing. The outer ones were about half the length of the outer interplane struts – hence the "1½ struts."

Structurally, the 1½-Strutter was conventional, and it was fabric-covered except for some plywood decking around the cockpits. Unusual details included an adjustable tailplane, operated by a control-wheel in the pilot's cockpit, and air-brakes fitted to the lower centre-section. The air-brakes consisted of two square surfaces, hinged so that when fully open they projected above and below the wing. The fin was of the shape which was to become a characteristic "trademark" of later Sopwith designs. A Vee undercarriage was fitted, each wheel being mounted on a half-axle, with the inner end pivoting at the centre of the spreader bar. Shock absorption was by the then-conventional rubber cord, binding the outer end of each half-axle to the apex of the Vee struts.

The prototype, which appeared in 1915, was powered by a 110-hp Clerget rotary engine enclosed by an open-fronted cowling. This was the standard power unit, but some later machines had a 130-hp Clerget or 110-hp Le Rhône engine.

Standard armament included one fixed Vickers machine-gun, firing forward, and one free Lewis machine-gun in the rear cockpit. The Vickers machine-gun was mounted on top of the fuselage in front of the pilot, and was synchronized to fire between the propeller blades by either Vickers, Sopwith-Kauper, Scarff-Dibovski or Ross synchronizing gear.

Historically, the 1½-Strutter is important as being the first British aircraft to go into service with an interrupter gear permitting a fixed machine-gun to fire through the propeller disc. The free Lewis machine-gun was supported on a variety of mountings, including Nieuport and Scarff rings.

A bomb-load of up to 130 lb could be carried by the standard two-seat models; a single-seat bomber version could carry up to 224 lb of bombs.

The 1½-Strutter went into service early in 1916 with both the RNAS and RFC. On the Western Front, it immediately proved an effective combat type, due largely to the increased effectiveness of its armament compared with that of the older "pusher" types which it began to supersede. There is no doubt that many enemy pilots attacking 1½-Strutters were surprised by its armament, for at that time it was rare to encounter a tractor two-seater with a forward-firing gun.

Within a few months, however, the introduction of new German Albatros and Halberstadt scouts saw the 1½-Strutters of the RFC beginning to be outclassed.

The RNAS 1½-Strutters had a longer operational life and it was this service that initiated the single-seat version for long-range bombing. On this, the bombs were carried internally in a 12-cell compartment immediately aft of the cockpit.

Towards the end of the war, 1½-Strutters began to serve as shipborne aircraft with both wheel and skid undercarriages. The first take-off by a two-seat aircraft from a British warship was made by a 1½-Strutter, this feat being achieved by the aircraft running along a short platform mounted on top of a gun turret.

1½-Strutters served with the air forces of Russia, France, Belgium, Rumania, Japan and Latvia and with the American Expeditionary Force. At least 1,513 were built in Britain; many more than this were produced abroad, in France and Russia.

Sopwith Pup

The Sopwith Pup is universally acclaimed as the aircraft with the most delightful flying qualities of any produced during the 1914–18 War. Indeed, some pilots who have flown later, more sophisticated types, consider the Pu the most perfect flying machine ever made. As a combat type, although somewhat underpowered, it remained sensitive on control and fully aerobatic up to 15,000 ft, and could hold its height better than any other aircraft, Allied or German, of the period.

As with many aircraft of the 1914–18 War, the origin of the Pup's name is not the least interesting thing about it. Legend has it that pilots who first flew the new scout looked upon it as a small 1½-Strutter – an offspring of the 1½-Strutter – that is, its "Pup." The nickname was completely unofficial; the authorities tried hard to prevent it from getting into general use, and to persuade everyone to use Sopwith Type 9901, this being the official Admiralty designation, based upon a serial number of an early production machine. The harder they tried, the more the pilots used the nickname, and today the little biplane is never known as anything but Pup.

In general construction and configuration, the Pup was a classic of simplicity. The wings, each with ailerons, were of equal span and had raked tips. There was a large cut-out in the trailing-edge of the centre-section of the top wing, under which the pilot sat. The standard power unit was the 80-hp Le Rhône rotary engine, and a tribute to the general design of the Pup is that its excellent performance was achieved on such relatively low horsepower.

Standard armament was a single Vickers machine-gun, mounted on top of the fuselage directly in front of the pilot and synchronized to fire between the propeller blades by the Sopwith-Kauper mechanical interrupter gear. However, some Pups were armed with a single Lewis machine-gun, firing forward and upward through a cut-out in the centre-section. For anti-Zeppelin duties, some Pups were fitted with Le Prieur rockets, four being attached to each pair of interplane struts; on these aircraft, this complement of rockets sometimes comprised the total armament.

The Pup went into service with the RNAS and RFC in 1916 and quickly established a reputation for itself, as a result of its excellent manoeuvrability and ability to hold its height in combat. By the end of the year, the pilots of one squadron (No. 8 Naval) had scored 20 victories.

Manfred von Richthofen, the German fighter ace, after encountering a Pup, wrote: "We saw immediately that the enemy aircraft was superior to ours."

During the great infantry battles of Ypres, Messines and Cambrai, the Pup was used with great success, being one of the few British types with a performance equal to that of the contemporary German Albatros. In combat against this latter aircraft, pilots found they could turn twice to the German machine's once.

RNAS Pups were used for a series of pioneering experiments in the operation of landplanes from ships. Of historic interest was the landing, on 2 August 1917, by Squadron Commander E. H. Dunning, on the flight deck of the aircraft carrier *Furious* – the first ever made on a ship under way in the open sea. During subsequent experiments, a variety of skid undercarriages were tried in attempts to shorten the landing run and to eliminate the danger of tyres bursting, and crude forms of arrester gear were developed.

Sopwith Pup, skid landing gear

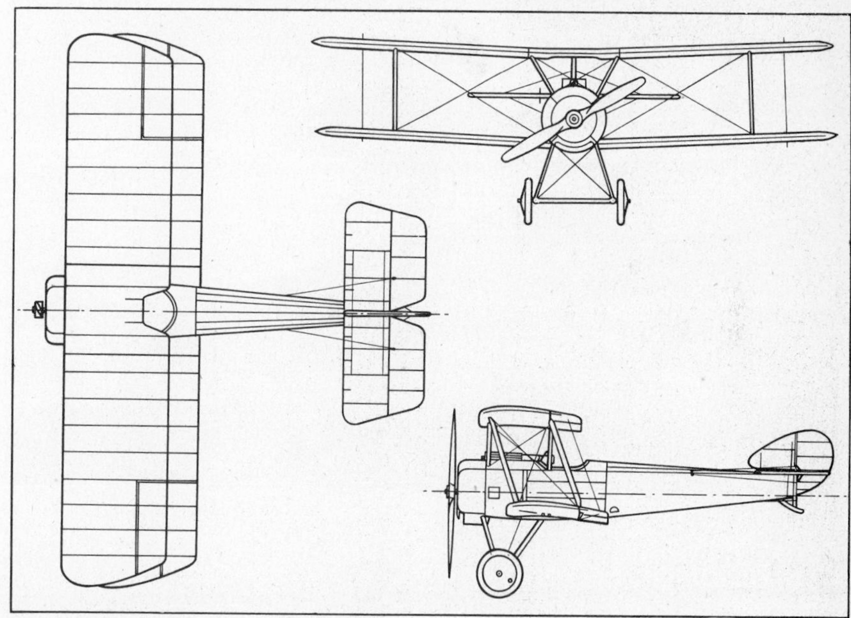
Sopwith Pup

TYPE	DIMENSIONS span ft	in	length ft	in	height ft	in	WEIGHT max t-o lb	PERFORMANCE max speed mph	at height ft	service ceiling ft	combat range miles	REMARKS
1½-Strutter (2-seat)	33	6	25	3	10	3	2,149	106	SL	–	NA	110-hp Clerget
1½-Strutter (2-seat)	33	6	25	3	10	3	2,150	100	6,500	15,500	NA	130-hp Clerget
1½-Strutter (2-seat)	33	6	25	3	10	3	2,205	103	10,000	16,000	NA	110-hp Le Rhône
1½-Strutter (single-seat)	33	6	25	3	10	3	2,362	94	10,000	12,500	NA	110-hp Clerget
1½-Strutter (single-seat)	33	6	25	3	10	3	2,342	98	10,000	13,000	NA	130-hp Clerget
Pup	26	6	19	4	9	5	1,225	111	SL	17,500	NA	80-hp Le Rhône
Pup	26	6	19	4	9	5	1,297	110	SL	18,500	NA	100-hp Monosoupape

Sopwith Triplane prototype

Sopwith Triplane

Sopwith Triplane, Hispano-Suiza engine

Pups were used also for home defence duties, many of these being fitted with the more powerful 100-hp Gnome Monosoupape engine, which further improved the aircraft's combat efficiency.

Sopwith Triplane

Intended to provide the pilot with the best possible field of view and a high degree of manoeuvrability, the Sopwith Triplane was one of the most unusual combat aircraft of the 1914–18 War. By using three wings instead of two, their chord could be reduced. The centre wing was level with the pilot's head and therefore cut off little of his view, while the narrow top and bottom wings obscured less sky and ground than did the relatively broad-chord wings of a biplane.

The short span conferred a high rate of roll, although not quite so good as that of the best biplanes, such as the Sopwith Pup, which the Triplane followed. Perhaps most important of all, the large total area of the three wings gave an excellent rate of climb. The Sopwith Triplane, in fact, could outclimb all its German contemporaries – an advantage which was used to the full when it went into action.

Apart from having three wings, the Triplane was conventional structurally. A feature of the wings was the single, broad, interplane strut on each side; this was continuous from the top wing to the bottom, passing through a slot in the centre wing. A minimum of bracing wires gave the Triplane a clean appearance in spite of its multiplicity of wings.

The prototype, which appeared on 28 May 1916, was powered by a 110-hp Clerget engine. This remained the standard power plant, although the performance of some later Triplanes was improved by fitting the more powerful 130-hp Clerget. The date on which the prototype appeared dispels the popular fallacy that the triplane idea was initiated by the Germans. The reverse is the case, for the Sopwith Triplane provoked an almost endless succession of triplanes from German designers as they endeavoured to produce something its equal in performance. Although it cannot be said that Anthony Fokker copied the Sopwith type when he designed his famous Dr 1, he is known to have studied carefully the remains of one which had been shot down.

Standard armament was a single fixed Vickers machine gun, mounted on top of the fuselage and synchronized to fire between the propeller blades, although a few aircraft had twin guns.

The Triplane was ordered initially for the RFC; bu before production machines could be delivered th Navy received urgent requests – owing to the intensit of the fighting on the Western Front after the Battl of the Somme – to divert aircraft to that area. Th Admiralty immediately handed over to the RFC a batc of Spad VIIs – in return for a promise of the Triplane when these were built. Because of the unusual exchange the Triplanes were used operationally only by the RNAS

In service, the Triplanes quickly made their mark On one occasion, 13 of them engaged 15 enemy aircra and destroyed five without loss. Episodes such as thi gave the Sopwith type a reputation a little better tha it probably deserved. The mere sight of a "Tripehound unnerved some enemy pilots, and its performance, par ticularly its rate of climb, distressed the rest.

The famous B Flight of No. 10 Naval Squadron fle Triplanes. This unit, manned entirely by Canadian achieved renown as the "Black Flight". Its five aircraf painted all black except for squadron and rudder mark ings, were individually named the *Black Maria* (th Commander's), *Black Death, Black Roger, Black Prin* and *Black Sheep*. In the three months from May to Jul 1917, the Black Flight destroyed no fewer than 87 enem aircraft. Towards the end of 1917, progress had ove taken the Triplane, and it was replaced by the Came

The two experimental Hispano-Suiza-engined Tr planes produced by Sopwiths towards the end of 191 are often described wrongly as variants of the Clerg Triplane. In fact, they were a completely different typ and were more a development of the 1½ Strutter than the Pup, as was the Clerget Triplane.

Sopwith Camel

The Sopwith Camel destroyed 1,294 enemy aircraft, and thus holds the unique distinction of having achieved more victories in combat than any other single type during the 1914–18 War. It is certainly the most famous aircraft of that war.

Known initially as the Sopwith Biplane F.1, the Camel was a single-seat tractor fighter, developed from the Sopwith Pup. Structurally it was conventional, the wings and fuselage being wire-braced wooden structures, with fabric covering. Standard power plant was the 130-hp Clerget rotary engine, but a number of Camels were powered by the 110-hp Le Rhône.

Characteristic features of the F.1 were its short nose and the pronounced dihedral on the bottom wing, which contrasted noticeably with the flat top wing. The twin Vickers machine-guns comprising the armament were mounted on top of the fuselage, in front of the pilot. The breeches of the guns were enclosed by a distinctive "humped" cover, and it was this from which the aircraft obtained its nickname "Camel", and which was finally adopted as the official name.

The best-known feature of the Camel's performance was its outstanding manoeuvrability. This was due partly o the concentration of all the heavy items – the engine, uel, pilot and armament – into a compact space, and partly to the torque produced by the big rotary engine. The Camel was, in fact, probably the most manoeuvrable aircraft ever built. It spun quickly and had an extremely sensitive elevator. It could execute right-hand turns with incredible swiftness, due to the great gyroscopic orce of the engine and the short fuselage. Some pilots, when wishing to turn 90 degrees to the left, preferred o turn 270 degrees to the right, as it seemed to be quicker!

Not surprisingly, this made the Camel a tricky aircraft o master, and several pupils were killed during their first olo flights. Those who survived became devotees to the Camel, and would not exchange their mount for any other.

Another reason for the Camel's efficiency as a combat aircraft was its armament. It was not the first two-gun ighter by any means; but its closely-mounted Vickers nachine-guns gave the Camel a higher rate of fire than ts predecessors. Also, the Vickers guns, being belt-fed, lid not require the frequent reloading of magazine-fed guns.

Four 25-lb bombs could be carried on racks under the uselage.

Camels began to enter service with both the RFC and RNAS in the middle of 1917. On the Western Front, hey performed a variety of duties, being used extensively or ground strafing in support of infantry in the trenches. But it was in "dog-fighting" that the Camel excelled, nd its exploits are numerous and almost legendary. On ne occasion, 24 Camels encountered and engaged three eparate German formations in the course of a single atrol, destroying a total of six of the enemy.

Captain J. L. Trollope of No. 43 Squadron created record by shooting down six enemy machines in one ay – made up of two D.F.W. two-seaters and an Albatros cout before dinner, and three two-seaters before tea. o prove that this was no fluke, Captain H. W. Woollett f No. 209 Squadron equalled the feat a few days later y destroying a Pfalz, a Fokker and four unidentified ircraft within 24 hours. By January 1918, air superiority ver the Western Front had passed to the Allies.

On 21 April 1918, the Camel gained its greatest, nd yet in some ways its saddest, victory. Eight Camels f No. 209 Squadron, led by a Canadian pilot, Captain . R. Brown, were making a routine patrol near the

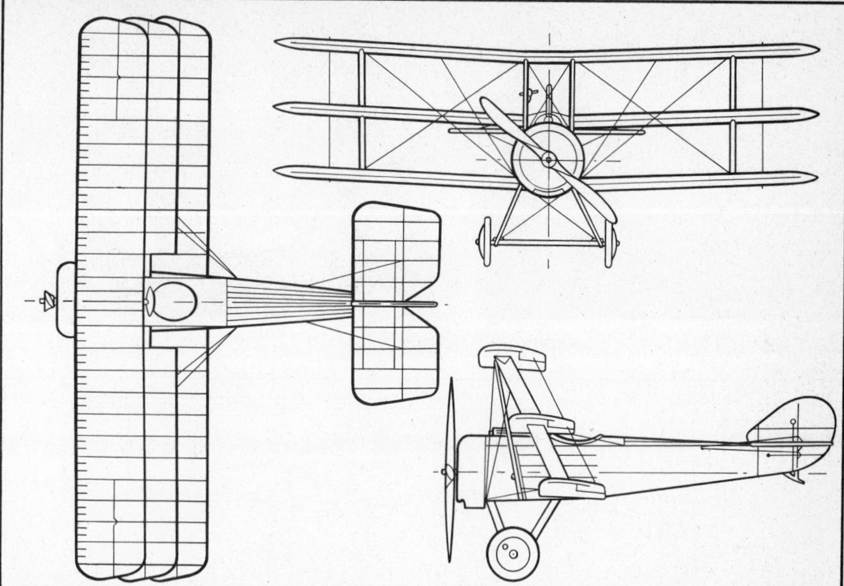

Sopwith Triplane

Sopwith F.1 Camel, 130-hp Clerget engine

Sopwith Camel flown by Major W.G. Barker VC

TYPE	DIMENSIONS						WEIGHT	PERFORMANCE				REMARKS
	span		*length*		*height*		*max t-o*	*max speed*	*at height*	*service ceiling*	*combat range*	
	ft	*in*	*ft*	*in*	*ft*	*in*	*lb*	*mph*	*ft*	*ft*	*miles*	
Sopwith Triplane	26	6	18	10	10	6	1,541	117	5,000	20,500	NA	130-hp Clerget

Sopwith F.1 Camel, dark finish for night fighting

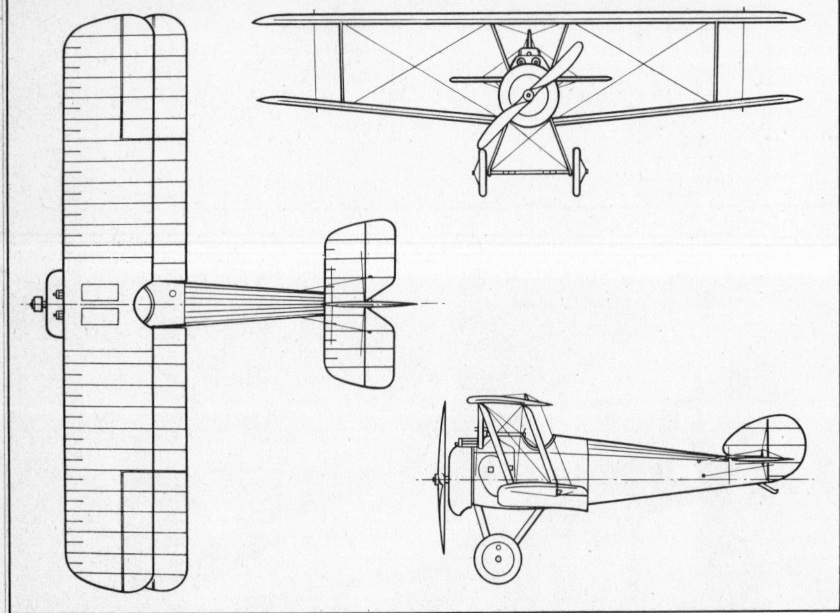
Sopwith F.1 Camel

Sopwith 2F.1 Camel

Sopwith 2F.1 Camel, Estonian Air Force

Somme. The Camels joined in a dog-fight between two Fokker Dr. Is and two R.E.8s, and in turn were engaged by a mixed flight of 15 Fokker Dr. Is and Albatros D.Vs which had been watching the whole incident. A Fokker dived at Brown's companion, and Brown in turn dived after the Fokker. He fired one quick burst from his guns and the all-red triplane fell away and crashed. So died Baron Manfred von Richthofen, the leading German ace, with 80 victories to his credit.

RNAS Camels were substantially similar to those supplied to the RFC, although the more powerful 150-hp Bentley B.R.1 rotary engine eventually became the standard power plant for the naval machines. Many RNAS Camel Squadrons were seconded to the Army and served alongside those of the RFC, their combat exploits rivalling those of their RFC counterparts. No. 209 Squadron, whose leader shot down Richthofen, was, in fact, a former Naval squadron (No. 9).

Some Camels were allocated to Home Defence duties, where they were used for anti-Zeppelin and anti-Gotha patrols. On 25 January 1918, two Camels took off at night, attacked a Gotha over east London and shot it down. This was the first victory achieved at night in combat between aeroplanes, and was an astonishing feat bearing in mind that no navigational or combat aids were available at the time.

The Vickers machine-guns on standard Camels were very close to the pilot, who was blinded by their flash when they were fired at night. To overcome this, the night-fighting Camels were modified to take two Lewis machine-guns mounted on the centre-section. To enable the guns to be fired upward and to facilitate reloading, the cockpit was moved rearward to position the pilot behind the wing. Most night fighter Camels had Le Rhône engines.

A major variant of the Camel was the 2F.1, developed specially as a shipboard fighter. An important difference was that the fuselage was made in two halves, so that the rear half and tail unit could be detached to facilitate stowage on board ship. A minor modification was the substitution of steel tubes instead of wooden struts to support the centre-section; being much thinner than wooden struts, they provided an easy method of distinguishing between the two versions. The armament was also changed, one of the Vickers guns being removed in favour of a Lewis gun above the top wing.

The 2F.1 Camels were operated mainly in the North Sea area, where they were used to intercept Zeppelins. To this end, they were carried on numerous warships, from which they took off along short platforms mounted on top of the gun turrets, after the manner of the earlier Pups which they superseded. 2F.1 Camels were also flown from aircraft carriers, and from specially designed lighters towed behind destroyers.

On 10 August 1918, Lt S. D. Culley took off from a lighter to attack the Zeppelin L.53, flying at a height of 19,000 ft. This was above the Camel's ceiling; but Culley managed to get under his quarry, pull back the control column, and fire into the airship, which burst into flames. This was the last Zeppelin to be shot down during the war.

Camels were used for a wide variety of experimental purposes including the first dive-bombing tests. One, designated F.1/1, was built with special tapered wings; another, the Trench Fighter T.F.1, was armour-plated and had two Lewis machine-guns firing downward through the floor of the cockpit. An F.1 Camel was fitted with an experimental 150-hp Gnome Monosoupape engine, the power output of which was varied by cutting out certain cylinders; another F.1 was fitted with the 180-hp Le Rhône rotary engine. Tests were made with jettisonable undercarriages, to facilitate ditching in the sea, which was inherent in lighter-borne operations, and with a variety of deck arrester gear.

Most interesting of all, perhaps, were experiments conducted in an attempt to develop a means of protecting British airships against enemy interceptors. The idea was for the airship to carry a small fighter, which could be released if the airship were attacked.

Airship R.23 was used for the experiments, and on the underside of this a special flat surface was suspended

The top wing of the Camel fitted against this surface, being held in position at the centre by a quick-release hook. A successful drop was made, the pilot starting his engine after release and landing safely, but the signing of the Armistice made continuance of the experiments unnecessary.

A total of 5,490 Camels were built, serving also in the air forces of Canada, Belgium and Greece, with the American Expeditionary Force and with Slavo-British forces fighting the Bolsheviks in Russia.

Sopwith B.1

The Sopwith B.1 was a single-seat tractor biplane bomber, the development of which was partly inspired by the success of the single-seat version of the 1½-Strutter.

Powered by a 200-hp Hispano-Suiza engine, the prototype appeared in 1917 and was an orthodox two-bay biplane. The wings were of equal span, with ailerons top and bottom.

The bomb-load totalled 560 lb and was accommodated internally, the bombs being stowed vertically in a compartment aft of the cockpit.

Initial performance trials were promising, the bomb-load detracting little from the aircraft's top speed and climbing capabilities. Operational trials were conducted by the RNAS Fifth Wing at Dunkirk, from where a B.1 made several bombing raids. During these, it had a single Lewis machine-gun mounted on top of the engine cowling and synchronized to fire between the propeller blades.

Location of the bomb-load some distance from the centre of gravity seems to have made the B.1 a tiring machine to fly, as it was tail-heavy when loaded and nose-heavy when light. Its overall qualities were such that the RNAS decided not to adopt the type and the B.1 was not produced in quantity.

Sopwith T.1 Cuckoo

On 9 October 1916, Commodore (later Rear-Admiral Sir) Murray Sueter, Director of the Air Department of the Admiralty, issued a Most Secret Memorandum. It requested Sopwith to investigate the possibility of building a torpedo-carrying aircraft capable of carrying either one or two 1,000-lb torpedoes, with fuel sufficient for sorties of up to four hours' endurance. Remarkably, the memorandum suggested the possibility of using catapults to help launch the aircraft – in spite of the fact that no such catapult existed at the time.

The requirement was not easy to fulfil, but eventually Sopwith presented plans of a single-engined single-seat biplane, capable of carrying one torpedo. This project, designated T.1, was the first landplane designed specifically to operate from ships as a torpedo-carrier.

The prototype emerged in June 1917, and was a conventional three-bay biplane. The relatively large wings folded to facilitate stowage on board carriers. Construction was orthodox, the fuselage being a wire-braced box-girder, fabric-covered. The tail surfaces were of characteristic Sopwith shape. A sturdy wide-track divided undercarriage was fitted, to facilitate dropping of the 18-in Mk IX 1,000-lb torpedo, which was carried externally under the fuselage.

Sopwith B.1

Sopwith T.1 Cuckoo prototype, 200-hp Hispano engine, wings folded

Sopwith T.1 Cuckoo, Blackburn-built, 200-hp Sunbeam Arab engine

TYPE	DIMENSIONS						WEIGHT	PERFORMANCE				REMARKS
	span		*length*		*height*		*max t-o*	*max speed*	*at height*	*service ceiling*	*combat range*	
	ft	*in*	*ft*	*in*	*ft*	*in*	*lb*	*mph*	*ft*	*ft*	*miles*	
Camel F.1	28	0	18	9	8	6	1,453	115	6,500	19,000	NA	130-hp Clerget
Camel F.1	28	0	18	8	8	6	1,422	122	SL	24,000	NA	110-hp Le Rhône
Camel F.1	28	0	18	6	8	6	1,470	117	10,000	21,000	NA	150-hp B.R.1
Camel F.1	28	0	19	0	8	9	1,387	110	10,000	18,500	NA	100-hp Monosoupape
Camel 2F.1	26	11	18	6	9	1	1,523	114	10,000	19,000	NA	130-hp Clerget
Camel 2F.1	26	11	18	8	9	1	1,530	124	6,500	17,300	NA	150-hp B.R.1
Sopwith B.1	38	6	27	0	9	6	3,035	NA	NA	17,000*	NA	*With 560 lb bomb load

Sopwith T.1 Cuckoo, Blackburn-built, 200-hp Sunbeam Arab engine

Sopwith 5F.1 Dolphin

Sopwith 5F.1 Dolphin, night-flying version with overturn hoops above wings

Sopwith 7F.1 Snipe

The prototype was powered by a 200-hp Hispano-Suiza engine and 100 production models were ordered on completion of the official trials at the Isle of Grain in July 1917; later, the orders were increased to a total of 350 aircraft. During tests, the aircraft, now known as the Cuckoo, behaved well. It was pleasant to fly, and ditched relatively easily – a popular feature in view of the unreliable engines of that time.

Owing to the heavy demand for Hispano-Suiza engines for S.E.5as, production Cuckoos were powered by 200-hp Sunbeam Arabs. Another change was lengthening of the tail-skid to give adequate ground clearance for the tail of the torpedo. Operations in cold weather indicated a need to warm the torpedoes, and this was accomplished on some aircraft by fitting long exhaust pipes which sloped downward toward the torpedo.

Other engines installed in the Cuckoo included the 275-hp Rolls-Royce Falcon III and 200-hp Wolseley W.4A Viper, machines with the Viper being designated Cuckoo Mk IIs. A total of 90 Cuckoos had been delivered when the Armistice was signed and production then ceased. During its short operational life the type had little opportunity to make a name for itself by demonstrating its ability to "lay its eggs in other people's nests", like its counterpart in nature. However, it pointed the way to the torpedo-carriers of the Fleet Air Arm which achieved so much in World War II. Equally significant is that six Cuckoo Mk IIs were taken to Japan by a British Air Mission in 1922, giving the Imperial Japanese Navy its first experience of a combat technique which it learned all too well.

Sopwith 5F.1 Dolphin

Fighter pilots who spot an enemy aircraft first have an immediate advantage, and the unusual configuration of the Sopwith Dolphin resulted from an attempt to give the pilot the best view possible.

The fuselage was deeper than normal, and the top wing was set low, so that the pilot sat with his head protruding through the wing. This arrangement gave him a completely unobstructed view upward and all around, although the less important downward view was necessarily restricted.

With the position of the top wing dictated by the cockpit, the lower wing had to be positioned ahead of it, in order to obtain the correct aerodynamic relationship. The resultant back-stagger completed the unusual appearance of the Dolphin.

Structurally, the airframe was conventional, the fuselage being essentially a wire-braced box-girder. The top decking, which gave the fuselage its deep shape, was built up on top of this basic structure, and the sides of the fuselage were covered with plywood, as was the decking around the cockpit. A small, simple, Vee-undercarriage was fitted.

Wing construction was of wood, with fabric covering and external bracing by Rafwires.

Powered by a 200-hp Hispano-Suiza engine, with a car-type radiator, the prototype appeared in May 1917. Production models switched to side radiators, which permitted a much cleaner nose shape.

The Dolphin was the first British multi-gun fighter. Standard armament consisted of two Vickers machine-guns, mounted above the engine and synchronized by Constantinesco gear to fire between the propeller blades, and two free Lewis machine-guns mounted on the front of the centre-section, firing forward and upward. In service, however, many pilots preferred to dispense with the Lewis guns, or mount them elsewhere. Four 25-lb bombs could be carried for ground-attack duties.

The Dolphin was quite pleasant to fly and had a good performance at height; but the unusual stall characteristics resulting from the back-stagger caused a high accident rate initially. Owing to the exposed position of the pilot, a nose-over after a bad landing was usually fatal and resulted in the nickname "Blockbuster" being applied to the aircraft. To safeguard the pilot, some Dolphins, especially those in training squadrons, were fitted with a crash pylon on each side of the cockpit.

In service, the Dolphin was handicapped (like the

early S.E.5a) by chronic unreliability of the French-built geared Hispano-Suiza engine. This prevented its inherent operational capabilities from being fully demonstrated.

A Mark II version, powered by a new 300-hp Hispano-Suiza engine, had a better performance than any of its contemporaries; but only small numbers had been built before the war ended. To overcome the troubles experienced with the geared 200-hp Hispano-Suiza engines, a number of Dolphins, designated Mk. IIIs, were fitted with the direct-drive version of this engine.

Over 1,500 Dolphins were built, of which only some 600 were issued to training and operational squadrons, the bulk of the others being in store when the war ended.

Sopwith 7F.1 Snipe

Intended to succeed the Camel, the Snipe was designed around the 230-hp Bentley Rotary B.R.2 engine. This developed an extra 80 hp compared with the B.R.1, which had been fitted to a number of Camels, for a weight increase of less than 100 lb. With this new engine the Snipe was, perhaps, the best fighter scout produced by any nation during the 1914–18 War, and it represented the ultimate development of the small rotary-powered aircraft peculiar to that war.

The first prototype, completed before a B.R.2 engine was available and so powered by a B.R.1, was a single-bay biplane, bearing a strong resemblance to the Camel. A major difference was the marked dihedral of the top wing which being equal to that of the lower wing, brought the centre-section almost to the level of the pilot's eyes. His view was further improved by a large cut-out in the centre-section. A simple Vee-undercarriage was fitted, shock-absorption being by rubber cord.

A second prototype was built with a B.R.2 engine, which gave it a first-class performance, particularly in rate of climb. However, it was considered that the single-bay wings were not sufficiently strong and the third prototype was built with two-bay wings. The drag of the extra struts and bracing reduced the maximum speed considerably, but the rate of climb remained excellent, being superior to that of the Camel and Dolphin.

The Snipe was highly manoeuvrable, retaining the tight turning characteristic of the Camel and other rotary-engined types; but it did not have the extreme sensitiveness and viciousness of the Camel which made the latter so dangerous in inexperienced hands. The sixth prototype was fitted with the experimental 320-hp ABC Dragonfly radial engine, with which it achieved the remarkable speed of 156 mph; but production machines retained the B.R.2.

The standard armament was a pair of forward-firing Vickers machine-guns, mounted on top of the fuselage in front of the pilot and synchronized to fire between the propeller blades. The guns were enclosed in the same kind of distinctive hump-like fairing which had given the Camel its name, although the fairing was of better form and enclosed more of the guns. Four 25-lb bombs could be carried on racks under the fuselage.

Production aircraft were officially designated Snipe Mk I, and deliveries began in the summer of 1918. About 200 had been built by the time of the Armistice, of which

Sopwith 7F.1 Snipe

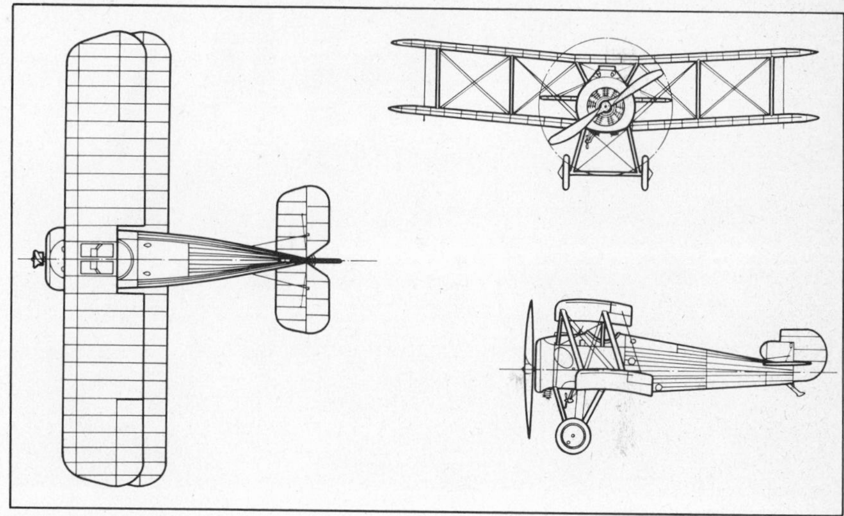
Sopwith 7F.1 Snipe

TYPE	DIMENSIONS span ft	in	length ft	in	height ft	in	WEIGHT max t-o lb	PERFORMANCE max speed mph	at height ft	service ceiling ft	combat range miles	REMARKS
Cuckoo	46	9	28	6	11	0	3,572	103	6,500	15,600	NA	200-hp Hispano-Suiza
Cuckoo	46	9	28	6	10	8	3,883	103	2,000	12,100	NA	200-hp Arab
Cuckoo	46	9	28	5	11	3	3,875	92	6,500	13,700	NA	200-hp Viper
Cuckoo Mk II	46	9	28	6	11	0	4,350	101	6,500	13,400	NA	275-hp Falcon III
Dolphin Mk I	32	6	22	3	8	6	1,959	121	10,000	20,000	NA	With crash pylons and one Lewis gun.
Dolphin Mk II	32	6	22	3	8	6	2,358	140	10,000	24,600	NA	
Dolphin Mk III	32	6	22	3	8	6	2,000	117	10,000	19,000	NA	

Sopwith TF.2 Salamander

Sopwith TF.2 Salamander

Sopwith Dragon

fewer than 100 had reached France. Nevertheless during its brief operational career, the Snipe established itself as the best Allied fighter, its ability to make tighter turns more than compensating for the slightly higher maximum speed of the Fokker D.VII, its chief adversary. It was in a Snipe that Major W. G. Barker of No. 201 Squadron fought his outstanding single-handed engagement against 15 Fokker D.VIIs on 27 October 1918, for which action he was awarded the Victoria Cross.

After the war, the Snipe was adopted as the RAF's standard fighter. Production continued into 1919, until a total of 497 had been built. Owing to financial economies, the Snipe remained in squadron service until 1926, by which time it had, as a typical 1914–18 War type, become distinctly dated. About 40 were converted into two-seaters for dual-control training duties.

Sopwith T.F.2 Salamander

The Salamander was developed from the Snipe specifically for ground-attack duties, in an attempt to overcome the stalemate in the trench warfare of the period.

Known originally as the Sopwith T.F.2, it was an equal-span two-bay biplane, closely resembling the Snipe and powered by the same 230-hp B.R.2 engine. To protect the pilot and fuel tanks against ground fire, the entire forward portion of the fuselage was constructed of armour plate, which weighed 650 lb. The longerons of the rear fuselage extended aft from this immensely-strong box-like container. Fairings shaped the sides of armour into the contour of the circular engine cowling.

Normal armament consisted of two fixed Vickers machine-guns, mounted on top of the fuselage in front of the pilot and synchronized to fire between the propeller blades. Each gun was provided with 2,000 rounds of ammunition. To increase the effectiveness of the aircraft still further, experimental multiple-gun installations were made, and one Salamander was fitted with a battery of no fewer than eight machine-guns, firing forward and downward through the bottom of the fuselage.

Only a few Salamanders had reached France by the time of the Armistice and none of these saw operational service. Production continued into 1919, until a total of 82 had been built; but the Salamander was not given a place in the peacetime RAF.

Sopwith Dragon

Another development of the Snipe, the Dragon was powered by a 360-hp A.B.C. Dragonfly IA engine, of which an experimental installation in the Snipe, in April 1918, had proved so promising.

The prototype Dragon, a modified Snipe, appeared in 1919 and was a conventional equal-span two-bay biplane. The plain ailerons of the prototype were replaced on production models with horn-balanced ailerons on the upper wings.

Armament was two fixed forward-firing Vickers machine-guns, mounted on top of the fuselage in front of the pilot and synchronized to fire between the propeller blades.

A total of 76 Dragons were built, of which one was sent to America for test purposes. However, they achieved no marked success, owing to the unreliability and excessive vibration of the A.B.C. engine.

Supermarine Southampton

The Southampton was the first new flying-boat to enter service after the 1914–18 War, and superseded the famous but ageing Felixstowe F.5s of 1918 vintage. A development of the civil Swan, the prototype was built to Air Ministry Specification R.18/24, for coastal defence and to accompany the Fleet to sea.

It was a large biplane and the wings, of fabric-covered wooden construction, were built in three sections. The centre-section extended to the inner pair of interplane struts and was braced by four sets of struts arranged in the form of a W. The outer wing sections, of equal span, were braced by a single pair of interplane struts.

The Southampton was powered by two 470-hp Napier Lion V engines, mounted mid-way between the top and bottom centre-sections on removable mountings. Each engine was self-contained with its radiator, oil tank, oil cooler and all instruments, and could be removed without disturbing the main wing structure. The fuel was carried in two prominent tanks mounted beneath the upper wing near the end of the centre-section, providing gravity feed to each engine.

Armament consisted of three Lewis machine-guns, one in the bow cockpit and two amidships, each on a Scarff ring-mounting. Normal bomb-load was 1,100 lb, but two 18-in torpedoes could be carried, one on each side of the hull.

Early production boats, like the prototype, had a wooden hull. Internally, this was free of obstruction and could be equipped with hammocks and cooking facilities, enabling the crew of five to sleep on board and to remain afloat for long periods. The two pilot's cockpits were arranged in tandem, the rear cockpit containing the navigational equipment.

The wooden hull was not entirely satisfactory, particularly during operations away from Britain where shore facilities were scanty or non-existent, and a duralumin hull was developed. This reduced the structural weight by 540 lb, and lightened the aircraft by a further 400 lb by eliminating water soakage. Aircraft with the new hull were designated Mk IIs, and made up the majority of the total of 78 Southamptons built. Metal wings were also developed. These were approximately 200 lb lighter than the wooden wings and were interchangeable with them.

Southamptons entered service with No. 480 (Coastal Reconnaissance) Flight in September 1925, and the subsequent introduction of the metal-hulled machines heralded an era of great flights by RAF flying-boats. These included a 9,000-mile Baltic cruise, a 19,500-mile return flight from Singapore to Nicobar and the Andaman Islands, and, most famous of all, a 27,000-miles cruise by the "Far East Flight" in 1927. The Flight, consisting of four Southamptons, left Felixstowe on 14 October 1927 and flew to Singapore, via the Mediterranean and India, round Australia and back to Singapore, on to Hong Kong and then back once more to Singapore. This was the finest piece of organized formation flying the world had seen up to that time.

Eight Southamptons, re-engined with 450-hp Lorraine water-cooled engines, were supplied to the Argentine Navy; other Southamptons were used by the RAAF and the Imperial Japanese Navy. The Southampton IV, fitted with two 525-hp Rolls-Royce Kestrel III engines became the prototype Scapa. The Southampton X, fitted with three 460-hp Armstrong Siddeley Panther radials, had an experimental steel hull and redesigned wings.

Supermarine Scapa

This general reconnaissance flying-boat was a radically improved, re-engined and re-engineered version of the Southampton; initially, in fact, it was known as the Southampton Mk IV.

It had equal-span single-bay wings of metal con-

Supermarine Southampton Mk I

Supermarine Southampton, Kestrel engines

Supermarine Southampton, Imperial Japanese Navy

TYPE	DIMENSIONS span ft	span in	length ft	length in	height ft	height in	WEIGHT max t-o lb	PERFORMANCE max speed mph	at height ft	service ceiling ft	combat range miles	REMARKS
Snipe 7F.1	31	1	19	10	9	6	2,020	121	10,000	19,500	NA	Endurance 3 hours
Snipe 7F.1a	31	1	19	10	9	6	2,271	114	10,000	15,000	NA	Long range version
Salamander	31	3	19	6	9	4	2,512	125	500	13,000	NA	Endurance 1¼ hours
Dragon	31	1	21	9	9	6	2,132	150	NA	25,000	NA	
Southampton Mk I	75	0	51	1	22	4	14,300	108	NA	NA	600	
Southampton Mk II	75	0	51	1	22	4	15,200	108	SL	14,000	930	
Southampton MK III	75	0	51	1	22	4	13,994	109	NA	NA	NA	

Supermarine Scapa

Supermarine Stranraer

Supermarine Spitfire prototype

Supermarine Spitfire Mk I, Merlin II engine

struction, with fabric covering, and was powered by two 525-hp Rolls-Royce Kestrel IIIMS engines. These were neatly faired into the underside of the top centre-section, the installation contrasting with the complicated array of bracing struts and wires of the between-wing arrangement on the Southampton.

The hull was redesigned with straighter sides to give more internal capacity, the pilots being seated side-by-side in an enclosed cockpit. Twin fins and rudders replaced the triple surfaces of the Southampton.

Armament consisted of three Lewis machine-guns mounted in the bow cockpit and in two staggered dorsal cockpits aft of the wings. The Scarff ring-mounting of the bow cockpit could be slid back for mooring operations. Maximum bomb-load was 1,000 lb.

Internal equipment included radio gear, a collapsible dinghy, engine-ladder, maintenance platform, spare propeller, sea drogues, a cooking stove, an ice-chest and water storage tanks.

Fifteen Scapas were built and entered service in 1934 with No. 202 Squadron. The Scapa was withdrawn from first-line service in 1938.

Supermarine Stranraer

The Stranraer was a twin-engined general reconnaissance flying-boat with a crew of six. Known originally as the Southampton Mk V, it was officially renamed in 1935.

It was a biplane with fabric-covered unequal-span two-bay metal wings. The centre-section of the upper wing was carried above the hull by splayed-out struts, which also supported the engine nacelles, mounted close to the underside of the wing. Narrow-chord ailerons were fitted to all wings.

The all-metal hull had two steps and consisted of a structure of transverse frames and longitudinal stringers, the whole covered with smooth Alclad plating.

Production Stranraers were powered by two 875-hp Bristol Pegasus X air-cooled radial engines, fitted with Townend cowling rings. Two fuel tanks were installed in the upper centre-section, and two oil tanks formed its leading-edge. Provision could be made for the carriage of a spare engine, or a torpedo, on the lower centre-section.

Armament consisted of three Lewis machine-guns, mounted in bow, dorsal and tail positions. The maximum bomb-load was 1,000 lb.

Stranraers went into service in 1936, with No. 228 Squadron, with which they served until 1939. After the outbreak of war some continued to operate with Nos. 201 and 209 Squadrons from bases in Scotland until withdrawn in 1940.

Twenty-three Stranraers were built, and the type was also built under licence in Canada for the RCAF.

Supermarine Spitfire

The Spitfire was one of the greatest, if not the very greatest, combat aircraft ever built. It was certainly the most famous fighter of World War II, when its distinctive pointed wing-tips enabled ordinary people in their millions to distinguish it from its contemporaries. Together with the Hurricane, it withstood and overcame the German Luftwaffe during the vital Battle of Britain in 1940, and afterwards was used in combat all over the world. Its development potential led to a succession of variants probably unequalled by any other type, and it had the distinction of being the only Allied fighter to remain in continuous production throughout the war.

The grandfather of the Spitfire was the Supermarine S6B racing seaplane which won the Schneider Trophy outright for Britain in 1931. From this evolved the Supermarine F.7/30 single-seat fighter, which had an open cockpit, fixed undercarriage and inverted-gull wing, and was powered by a Rolls-Royce Goshawk engine. This met the requirements of the Air Ministry Specification, but was not advanced enough for its designer, R. J. Mitchell who set about designing an improved machine.

While he was so engaged, Air Ministry Specification F.5/34 was issued, specifying eight instead of four machine-guns; simultaneously Rolls-Royce announced their new PV.12 engine. Mitchell accommodated the revised armament and the PV.12 in the smallest practicable airframe and refined the aerodynamics to a high degree. In a moment of inspiration, the new aircraft was given its name – the Spitfire. At about the same time, Rolls-Royce named their PV.12 engine the Merlin.

The prototype Spitfire, built to Specification F.37/34, and powered by a Merlin C engine, first flew on 5 March 1936. Only a few test flights were required to demonstrate the aircraft's excellent all-round performance and it was apparent that Mitchell had produced a fighter second-to-none in the world. In June 1936, the Air Ministry ordered 450, a large number for that time.

Few changes were made, or were needed, on the production models. Modifications included deletion of the semi-circular wheel fairings attached to the bottom of the leg fairings, fitting of a tailwheel instead of a tail-skid, and introduction of a bulged canopy and a bullet-proof windscreen.

Structurally, the new fighter was as advanced as its aerodynamics. It was the first all-metal fighter produced in Britain. Each wing was built up on two spars, although so high a proportion of the loads was taken by the front spar that it was virtually a single-spar structure. This front spar, together with the leading-edge skin, formed a box of great torsional strength. The construction of its booms was unusual, consisting of a series of tubes, each of push fit inside the other, the number being progressively reduced from the root to the tip; at the tip the remaining tubes were cut away to form first a channel and then a simple angle section. The main undercarriage pivoted on the front spar and retracted outward and slightly rearward into the wing. This gave the Spitfire a relatively narrow track and was, perhaps, the one feature its pilots would have wished to see improved.

The fuselage comprised three separate sections: the engine mounting, centre fuselage and rear fuselage. The engine mounting was a tubular structure, strengthened by a large horseshoe-shaped frame forming a cross-member. At the preliminary design stage, the oil coolers were mounted under the engine; later, they were transferred to the underside of the port wing to reduce drag, but the fuselage nose lines were unaltered; this explains the full-breasted profile of the Spitfire.

The centre fuselage was of semi-monocoque construction, being built up on four longerons and 15 frames, and extended to a point just forward of the fin. The rear fuselage and fin were designed as an integral assembly, with the fuselage frames extending upward to form the fin spars – an advanced feature for its time.

Spitfire Mk Is, powered by Merlin IIs and armed with four 0·303-in machine-guns in the wings, went into service in June 1938, with No. 19 Squadron.

When war started in September 1939, Spitfires equipped nine full squadrons, and partly equipped two other units. On 16 October of that year Spitfires shot down two

Supermarine Spitfire Mk IA, Merlin III engine, No. 65 Squadron

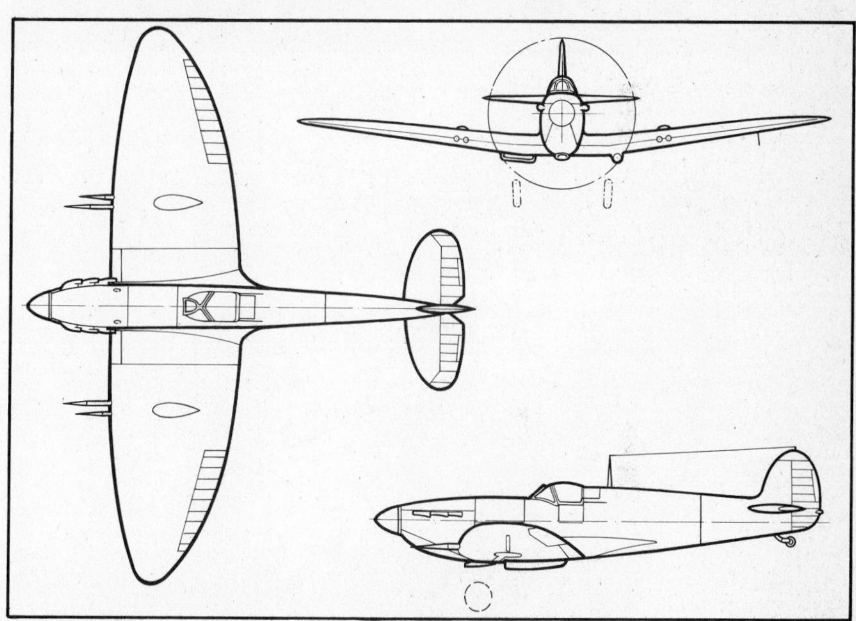

Supermarine Spitfire Mk VC

TYPE	DIMENSIONS						WEIGHT	PERFORMANCE				REMARKS
	span		*length*		*height*		*max t-o*	*max speed*	*at height*	*service ceiling*	*combat range*	
	ft	*in*	*ft*	*in*	*ft*	*in*	*lb*	*mph*	*ft*	*ft*	*miles*	
Scapa	75	0	53	0	21	0	16,040	142	3,280	15,480	1,100	
Stranraer	85	0	54	10	21	9	19,000	165	6,000	18,500	1,000	
Spitfire Mk I	36	10	29	11	11	5	5,784	355	19,000	34,000	NA	
Spitfire Mk II	36	10	29	11	11	5	6,527	357	17,000	37,200	500	
Spitfire Mk III	36	10	29	11	11	5	NA	NA	NA	NA	NA	Experimental
Spitfire Mk IV	36	10	29	11	11	5	7,178	372	NA	39,600	NA	Unarmed reconnaissance version
Spitfire Mk VA	36 32	10 2	29	11	11	5	6,417	374 357	13,000 6,000	37,000 36,500	1,135	
Spitfire Mk VB	36 32	10 2	29	11	NA		6,650	374 357	13,000 6,000	37,000 36,500	1,135	
Spitfire Mk VC	36 32	10 2	29	11	NA		6,785	374 357	13,000 6,000	37,000 36,500	1,135	
Spitfire Mk VI	40	2	29	11	NA		6,797	364	NA	NA	NA	Special high-altitude version

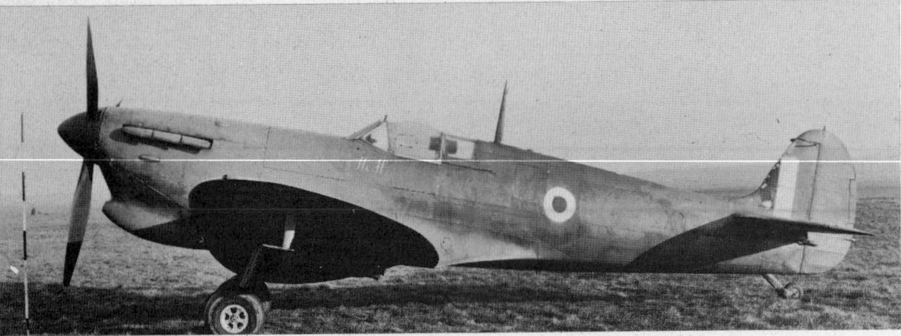

Supermarine Spitfire Mk VA, tropical version

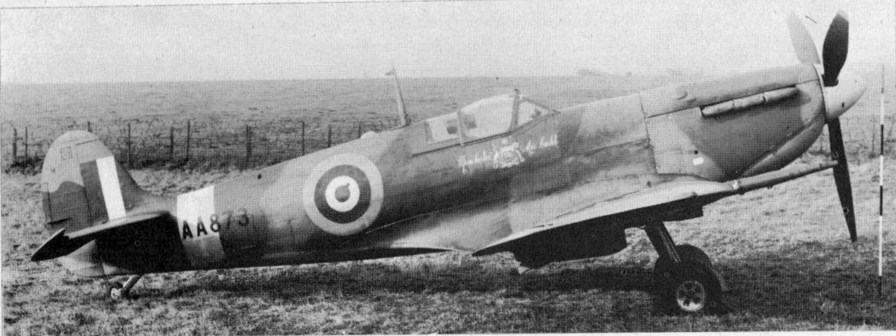

Supermarine Spitfire Mk VB

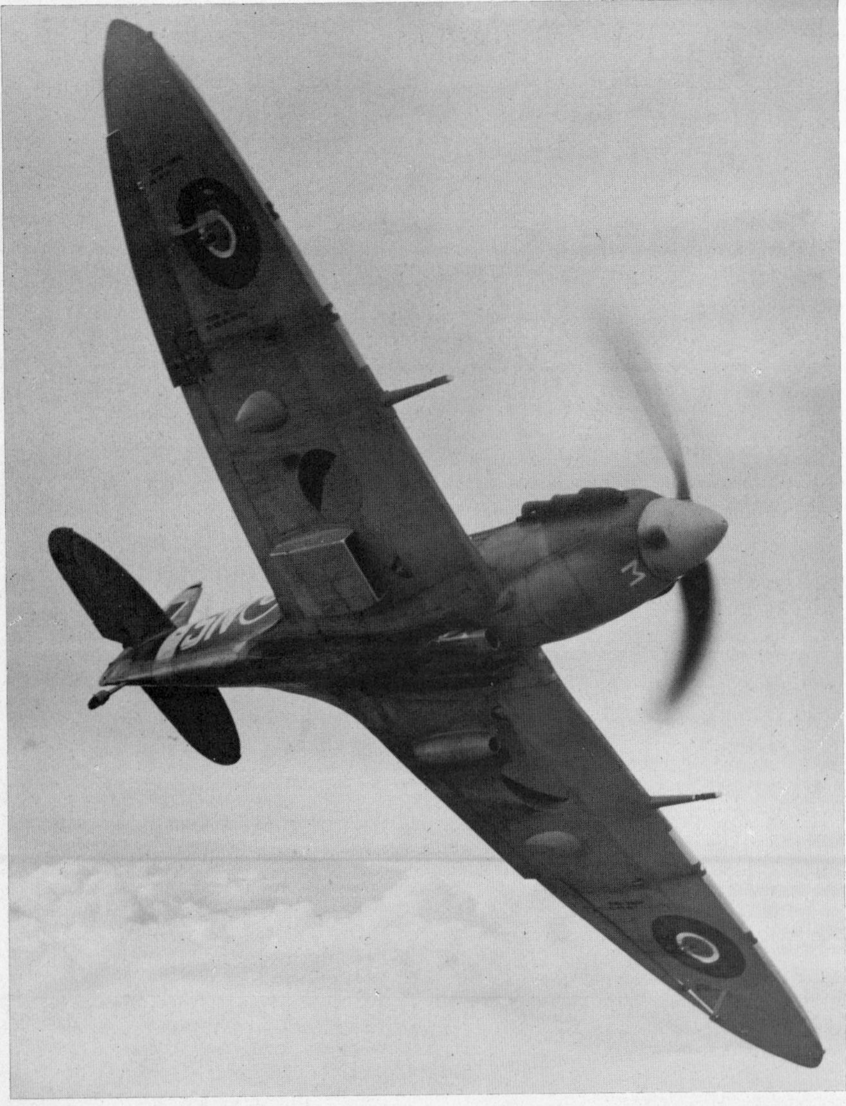

Supermarine Spitfire Mk VB

Heinkel He 111 bombers over the Firth of Forth; these were the first enemy aircraft shot down over Great Britain since 1918.

Early models had two-bladed fixed-pitch propellers, but three-blade variable pitch and three-blade constant-speed propellers were fitted later, with a significant increase in rate of climb and ceiling. Later Mk Is were also armed with eight machine-guns and were designated Mk IA. Another version, the Mk IB, had two 20-mm cannon and four machine-guns, this combination being particularly effective against the armoured aircraft introduced by the Germans during the latter stages of the Battle of Britain.

Spitfire Mk IIs were powered by the 1,175-hp Merlin XII engine, in place of the Merlin II or III. Mk IIAs were armed with eight 0.303-in machine-guns, and Mk IIBs with two 20-mm cannon and four 0·303-in machine-guns. Mk IIs initiated Fighter Command's offensive sweeps over Occupied Europe, these sorties being known as "Rhubarbs". A number of Mk IIs, designated IICs, were equipped to carry dinghies and food for Air-Sea Rescue duties.

Powered by a 1,260-hp Merlin XX, the Spitfire Mk III was a "private-venture" model used for general development work. It was a converted MK 1.

To meet the need for a fast reconnaissance aircraft, the PR IV was developed. This version, powered by a 1,100-hp Merlin 45, 46, 50, 55 or 56, carried one F.52 vertical camera with 36-in lens, one 14-in F.24 or two 20-in F.8 cameras, and was unarmed. Initially, the photographic Spitfires had been designated A, B, C, D, E and F, the G being the version finally put into production as the Mk IV.

The Mk V was powered by the 1,440-hp Merlin 45 and introduced a number of refinements, including a clearer internal bullet-proof windscreen; tropical machines had a Vokes filter in a large fairing under the nose. Three sub-variants were produced: the VA, armed with eight 0·303-in machine-guns, the VB, with two 20-mm cannon and four machine-guns, and the VC with "universal" wings capable of taking either armament plus two 250-lb bombs. Alternatively, a single 500-lb bomb could be carried beneath the fuselage, and both the VB and VC could carry long-range belly fuel tanks.

The Mk V was the mainstay of Fighter Command during 1941 and 1942, and often more than 500 of them would be engaged in a single Rhubarb sweep. Spitfire Mk VBs were also the first to serve overseas, 15 being despatched to Malta in March 1942. From 1943, most Spitfire Mk Vs had the tips of their wings clipped.

To combat the very high-flying reconnaissance Ju 86Ps used by the Germans in the Middle East, a high-altitude development of the Mk V was produced. Designated Mk VI, this had an increased wing span and a cockpit pressurized on the "constant-leak" principle by means of a blower incorporated in the high-altitude-rated Merlin 47 engine. The cockpit cover was placed over the pilot before take-off and locked by him by four clamp levers. Once locked it could not be opened, although it could be jettisoned.

The Mk VII was another high-altitude variant, and was the first Spitfire to have the new 1,660-hp Merlin 61 with a two-speed two-stage supercharger. Like the Mk VI, it had extended wing-tips, to maintain performance at altitude, plus a retractable tailwheel and, on later models, large-chord pointed rudder. A few Mk VIIs were fitted with cameras for reconnaissance duties.

The Mk VIII was virtually an unpressurized Mk VII the need for high-altitude fighters having decreased with the lack of success of the Ju 86P. Chronologically the Mk VIII came after the Mk IX, this numerical inconsistency being due to production arrangements and priorities.

The Mk VIII, with a Merlin 61 engine, was developed to meet the challenge of Germany's new Focke-Wulf Fw 190 fighter, which was proving superior to the Spitfire Mk V. So serious did the Fw 190 menace become that the Mk IX also was hurriedly produced as a stop-gap measure. This was basically a Mk VC adapted to take the 1,660-hp Merlin 61; many in fact were conversions. The new engine resulted in a lengthening of the fuselage and an additional radiator was mounted under the port wing; this ended the asymmetry which had caused so much comment on the original prototype.

With the new engine, the Spitfire's performance matched that of the Fw 190 and in some aspects was superior, and the Mk IX became the most widely used of all variants. Like the Mk VIII, it was built in low-altitude, medium-altitude and high-altitude versions – with clipped, standard and extended wings respectively – and one variant, the IXE, had two 0·50 machine-guns in place of the four 0·303-in guns normally used with the two 20-mm cannon.

The Mk X was a long-range photographic reconnaissance version and was essentially a combination of the PR VII and the Mk IX. The cockpit was pressurized and the whole of the wing leading-edge was used as a fuel tank.

The Mk XI was also a long-range photographic reconnaissance version and replaced the earlier PR IVs. An adaptation of the Mk IX, it was similar to the Spitfire X, except that it was tropicalized and did not have a pressurized cockpit. For ultra-long-range missions a belly fuel tank could be fitted, increasing the range to 2,000 miles. To the same end, particular attention was paid to the surface finish.

The PR XI was the mainstay of the Photographic Reconnaissance Unit of Coastal Command for the latter part of the war, and remained in service for several years after the war. On 9 July 1945, a Spitfire PR XI, taking part in "Operation Eclipse", climbed to 34,000 ft, taking the highest pictures of an eclipse of the sun then on record.

The superiority of the Mk IX over the Fw 190 was such that the Germans quickly took steps to derate the latter from a high-altitude fighter to a formidable low-level fighter-bomber. To counter such tactics, Rolls-Royce and Vickers collaborated in installing the Griffon III or IV engine, rated to deliver its maximum power of 1,735 hp at 1,000 ft, in specially-strengthened Mk VC airframes. Known as Mk XIIs, the new Spitfires proved eminently suitable for this rôle.

Installation of the Griffon necessitated a completely new engine mounting. The tubular structure used for the Merlins was replaced by two box-section bearers. There was no cross-bracing between the bearers, other than that provided by the engine itself; this contributed to the small frontal area of the installation.

Experience had shown that in photographic reconnaissance work it was often necessary to fly very low to obtain close-ups of particular targets, and the Mk XIII was produced especially for this duty. The production models, powered by specially-derated 1,620-hp Merlin 32s, were converted from PR VIIs. The cannon armament was removed, but the four outer machine-guns were retained to enable pilots to keep down the heads of enemy anti-aircraft gunners while over the target.

The next major Spitfire variant was the Mk XIV. Like the Mk XII, this was powered by a Griffon engine; but, whereas the Mk XII was a low-altitude fighter, the XIV

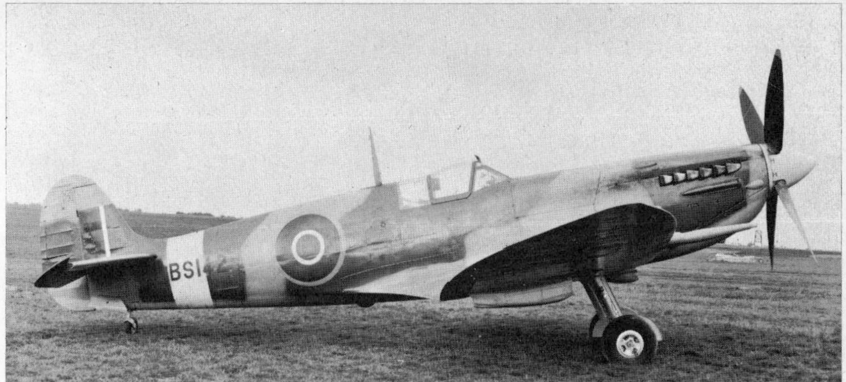

Supermarine Spitfire Mk VII

Supermarine Spitfire Mk IXE, Royal Danish Air Force

Supermarine Spitfire LF Mk IX, Turkish Air Force

TYPE	DIMENSIONS span ft	span in	length ft	length in	height ft in	WEIGHT max t-o lb	PERFORMANCE max speed mph	at height ft	service ceiling ft	combat range miles	REMARKS
Spitfire Mk VII	40	2	31	4	NA	7,875	408	25,000	43,000	1,180	Special high-altitude version
Spitfire Mk F VIII	32	2	30	4	NA	7,767	408	25,000	43,000	NA	
Spitfire Mk LF VIII	36	10	30	4	NA	7,767	404	21,000	41,500	NA	
Spitfire Mk HF VIII	40	2	30	4	NA	7,767	416	27,500	44,000	1,180	
Spitfire Mk HF IX	36	10	31	4	NA	7,500	416	27,500	45,000	980	
Spitfire Mk LF IX	32	2	30	6	NA	7,500	404	21,000	42,500	980	
Spitfire Mk X	NA		NA		NA	8,159	416	NA	NA	900	Unarmed reconnaissance version
Spitfire Mk XI	36	10	31	4	NA	7,900	422	NA	NA	2,000	Unarmed reconnaissance version
Spitfire Mk XII	32	8	31	10	NA	7,400	393	18,000	40,000	493	Special low-altitude version
Spitfire Mk XIII	NA		NA		NA	NA	400	NA	NA	700	Armed reconnaissance version

Supermarine Spitfire PR Mk XI

Supermarine Spitfire Mk XIV

Supermarine Spitfire FR Mk XVIII

Supermarine Spitfire PR Mk XIX

was designed for maximum performance at high altitude. Based upon the Mk VIII airframe, it was an interim type pending the introduction of the fully re-designed Mk XVIII.

The Mk XIV was powered by a 2,050-hp Griffon 65 engine, driving a five-bladed propeller and specially designed to deliver its maximum thrust above 30,000 ft. The engine had a two-stage two-speed supercharger and an inter-cooler. It lengthened the nose and, to offset this, the fin area was increased; another aerodynamic change was a moving inboard of the ailerons to improve lateral control. In sum, the changes were almost sufficient to warrant a new name for the aircraft.

Later XIVs had sliding rear-view bubble hoods, requiring further extensive structural modifications. The extensive changes, plus the fact that the Griffon propeller rotated in the opposite direction to those driven by Merlins, made the new Mark feel quite different to the previous "Spits" which so many thousands of pilots had grown to love, although it was undoubtedly a formidable high-altitude combat machine. A Mk XIV was the first Allied aircraft to shoot down one of Germany's new Messerschmitt Me 262 jet fighters. It was also used extensively to intercept the flying bombs launched against England during the closing stages of the war, destroying more than 300 of them.

Aircraft with blister hoods were designated Mk XIVE, and had a "universal" armament, consisting of two 20-mm cannon and two 0·50 in. machine-guns. A fighter-reconnaissance version, carrying a camera, was designated FR Mk XIVE; this retained the wing armament.

There was no Mk XV or XVII, these numbers being reserved for possible developments which never materialized

The Mk XVI was the last major variant to use the Merlin engine. Externally similar to the Mk IX, it was powered by the Packard-built Merlin 266 (equivalent to the British Merlin 66) developing 1,705 hp.

The Mk XVIII was the full production version of the interim Mk XIV, with strengthened wings and landing gear, and increased internal fuel tankage. Two versions were built, the standard fighter version being designated F XVIII, while the fighter-reconnaissance version was known as the FR XVIII, mounting two oblique and one vertical F. 24 cameras, or one vertical F.52 camera. Some of the FR machines had pressurized cockpits, were tropicalized and had further increased fuel tankage.

The Mk XIX was an unarmed photographic-reconnaissance version, produced to replace the ageing Spitfire Mk XI. Fitted with a universal camera installation, it was essentially a Mk XIV airframe with modified Mk VC wings. The first 20 production models, powered by Griffon 65 engines, were unpressurized; but subsequent aircraft, with Griffon 66 engines, were pressurized and had increased fuel tankage in the wings.

Mk XX was the designation given unofficially to the Mk III used for the prototype Griffon IIB engine installation in 1941.

The next production Spitfire variant, the F Mk 21, involved major structural changes, including a completely redesigned wing of increased area and new planform, embodying strengthened spar booms. With the new wings, the Spitfire lost its distinctive elliptical wing shape which had helped to make it so well-known.

The F Mk 21 was in production at the end of hostilities; it was this mark which gained the Spitfire the distinction of being the only Allied fighter in continuous production throughout the war, but it appeared too late to see operational service.

The Mk 21 was followed by the Mk 22; this differed by having a sliding rear-view bubble hood and redesigned rear fuselage, and by having a 24-volt, instead of a 12-volt, electrical system. Some 21s and 22s were fitted with the 2,375-hp Griffon 65 engine, driving contra-rotating propellers, and later models had a completely-redesigned tail unit. Spitfire 22s formed the backbone of the Royal Auxiliary Air Force from 1946 to 1951 and also served with the Middle East Air Force.

The designation Mk 23 was allotted to aircraft intended to have a different electrical system, but was not used.

The final production version of the Spitfire was the

Mk 24. This was essentially similar to the Mk 22, with the redesigned tail unit, and was armed with zero-length rocket launchers and four short-barrel 20-mm Hispano cannon.

The last Spitfire 24 was rolled out in October 1947, ten years after the first Spitfire Mk Is had emerged. During this decade the Spitfire's power had more than doubled, its maximum speed increased by 35 per cent, its weight by 40 per cent and its rate of climb by 80 per cent. At the end of its long career it could still hold its own with other, much later, piston-engined fighters.

A grand total of 20,334 Spitfires was produced, including the following quantities of individual variants:

Mk I	1,566
Mk IIA	750
Mk IIB	170
Mk IV	229
Mk VA	94
Mk VB	3,923
Mk VC	2,447
Mk VPRC	15
Mk VI	100
Mk VII	140
Mk VIII	1,658
Mk IX	5,665
Mk X	16
Mk XI	471
Mk XII	100
Mk XIV	957
Mk XVI	1,054
Mk XVIII	300
Mk XIX	225
Mk 21	122
Mk 22	278
Mk 24	54

Supermarine Seafire

The Seafire was the carrier-borne version of the RAF Spitfire landbased fighter. Prior to the manufacture of Seafires as such, RAF Mk VBs were "navalized" merely by the installation of a retractable deck arrester hook under the rear fuselage and slinging points, with which they were re-designated Seafire Mk IB. In common with the RAF VBs, some of the Seafire conversions had clipped wings and a deep tropical filter under the nose. They were powered by Rolls-Royce Merlin 45, 46, 50, 50A, 55 or 56 engines, according to the individual Spitfire converted, and were armed with two 20-mm cannon and four 0.303-in machine-guns.

The second Seafire variant was the Mk IIC. Built from the start as a Seafire, it was generally similar to the Seafire Mk IB except that it had catapult-spools, a strengthened undercarriage and the Spitfire C-type "universal" armament wing, capable of mounting four 20-mm cannon or any earlier gun combinations. Three sub-variants were produced. The standard model was the F Mk IIC. The LF Mk IIC was powered by a low-rated 1,645-hp Merlin engine driving a four-bladed propeller and was produced

Supermarine Spitfire F Mk 24

Supermarine Spitfire, experimental floatplane version

Supermarine Seafire Mk IB

TYPE	DIMENSIONS span ft	span in	length ft	length in	height ft	height in	WEIGHT max t-o lb	PERFORMANCE max speed mph	at height ft	service ceiling ft	combat range miles	REMARKS
Spitfire Mk XIV	36	10	32	8	12	8	8,375	448	26,000	44,500	850	High altitude version
Spitfire Mk XVI	32	8	31	4	12	7¾	7,500	405	22,000	40,500	980	Packard-Merlin version
Spitfire Mk XVIII	36	10	33	4	NA		9,320	442	26,000	41,000	NA	High altitude version
Spitfire Mk XIX	36	10	32	8	12	8	9,000	446	26,000	43,000	1,550	Unarmed reconnaissance version
Spitfire Mk XX	36	10	30	6	NA		NA	NA	NA	NA	NA	Prototype Griffon engine installation
Spitfire Mk 21	36	11	32	8	NA		9,900	454	26,000	43,500	880	
Spitfire Mk 22	36	11	32	11	NA		9,900	454	26,000	43,500	880	
Spitfire Mk 24	36	11	32	11	NA		9,900	454	26,000	NA	NA	
Seafire Mk IB	36	8	30	0	11	2	6,700	365	16,000	36,400	770*	*With auxiliary tank
Seafire L Mk IIC	36	8	30	0	11	2	7,000	333	5,000	32,000	755*	*With auxiliary tank

Supermarine Seafire F Mk XV

Supermarine Seafire F Mk 46

Supermarine Seafire F Mk 47

Supermarine Attacker F Mk 1

specially for low-altitude operations. PR Mk IICs carried cameras for photographic reconnaissance duties.

The Seafire Mk III, generally powered by the 1,585-hp Merlin 55M engine, introduced a manually-operated double-folding wing, which increased its flexibility for carrier operations as hangar lifts could be utilized. It could be fitted with RATOG (rocket-assisted take-off gear) and later models could carry a 30-gallon drop tank below the fuselage to increase their range.

The Mk III was the major Merlin-engined version, and was produced in several sub-variants. The LF Mk III was the low-altitude version and the FR Mk III, fitted with two F.24 cameras, the fighter-reconnaissance version. Seafire Mk IIIs had both clipped and full-span wings, and could carry either two 250-lb bombs under the wings or a single 500-lb bomb under the fuselage.

Mks IV to XIV were reserved for possible Merlin-engined Seafire developments, but were not allocated.

The next variant was thus the Seafire Mk XV, the first Griffon-engined version. Designed to Specification N.4/43, it was powered by the 1,850-hp Griffon VI, driving a four-bladed propeller. It was essentially a Seafire Mk III, with the broad-chord rudder of the Spitfire XII and increased internal wing fuel capacity. The first 50 production models had a mid-fuselage Vee type arrester hook; but from the 51st airframe this was superseded by a sting-type hook, mounted in the extreme tail, the bottom of the rudder being cut away to accommodate the hook. Armament consisted of two 20-mm cannon and four 0·303-in machine-guns. Four Squadrons – Nos. 802, 803, 805 and 806 – of Seafire Mk XVs were in process of being formed in May 1945, when the war in Europe ended.

The Mk XVs were supplemented in September 1945 by Seafire Mk XVIIs. A refinement of the earlier version, these had a clear-view cockpit hood, cut-away rear fuselage and increased fuel capacity in the fuselage. They were produced in two sub-variants, the F Mk XVII being the standard fighter and the FR Mk XVII being equipped for fighter-reconnaissance duties; on the latter variant the additional fuselage fuel tank was replaced by two F.24 cameras.

The Seafire Mk 45 was the navalized version of the RAF's Spitfire Mk 21, and was powered by the Griffon series 61/85 engine, driving either a five-bladed propeller or six-bladed contra-rotating propellers. It had naval radio equipment, modified undercarriage leg fairings and a tailwheel guard to facilitate the use of arrester wires, and was armed with four 20-mm cannon. The wings did not fold.

The Seafire Mk 46 was generally similar to the Mk 45, but had a clear-view cockpit hood and cut-away rear fuselage. Later models also had the redesigned and enlarged fin and rudder of the Spitfire 24. A few aircraft, fitted with a single oblique F.24 camera behind the pilot, were given the designation Seafire FR Mk 46.

The final Seafire variant was the Mk 47. This was the FAA version of the Spitfire Mk 24, and was fully navalized. The wings folded upward, a single hinge-line being positioned just outboard of the undercarriage wheel bays; the tips did not fold down like those of earlier Seafires. The carburettor intake was repositioned just behind the propeller and short-barrel Hispano 20-mm cannon were fitted. An additional 33-gallon fuel tank was fitted in the fuselage and could be augmented by a 90-gallon drop tank plus two underwing 23-gallon tanks.

Seafire Mk 47s served in the Korean War, No. 800 Squadron flying 360 offensive patrols. The last Seafire was retired in November 1954.

Merlin-engined Seafire production totalled around 1,770 aircraft, and Griffon-engined versions about 780 aircraft.

Supermarine Attacker

This single-seat fighter was the first carrier-borne jet aircraft to be standardized in FAA first-line squadrons. It evolved from a project originated as a land-based fighter for the RAF. The first prototype, an RAF model, flew on 27 July 1946; the second prototype, produced to Specification E.1/45 for the Navy, with a longer-stroke undercarriage, lift spoilers and a deck arrester hook, first flew on 17 June 1947.

Of all-metal stressed-skin construction, the Attacker utilized the laminar-flow wing developed for the Spiteful – a successor to the Spitfire which did not go into service. The fuselage was exceptionally clean aerodynamically – perhaps of better form than any previous body – the lines being broken only by the cockpit canopy and the engine air intakes flanking the cockpit. The fine lines could, however, be spoilt by the attachment of an enormous 250-gallon belly fuel tank for maximum-range missions.

The main undercarriage, inherited from the Seafang, the Naval version of the Spiteful, was longer than it need have been on a propeller-less aircraft; but, in combination with the retractable tailwheel, set the wing at nearly the optimum angle for maximum lift at take-off.

The Attacker was powered by the 5,100-lb s t Rolls-Royce Nene 3 engine, and was the first type to use this powerful new turbojet.

Attacker F 1s went into service in August 1951, with No. 800 Squadron. They were armed with four 20-mm Hispano Mk V cannon and were superseded by the FB 1 with provision for carrying, in addition, eight 60-lb rocket projectiles or two 1,000-lb bombs below the wings. In turn, these models were superseded by the FB 2, powered by the Nene 102 engine and fitted with improved ailerons and a redesigned cockpit canopy. Later FB 2s introduced a dorsal fin extension.

A total of 145 Attackers were built for the FAA, made up of 61 F 1s and FB 1s and 84 FB 2s. In addition, 36 land-based Attackers were supplied to Pakistan.

Supermarine Swift

The Swift was designed as a single-seat high-altitude interceptor. F Mk 1 aircraft, armed with two 30-mm Aden cannon, and F Mk 2 aircraft, with increased armament of four cannon, went into service in February 1954, with No. 56 Squadron. In so doing, the Swift became the first British sweptwing jet fighter to go into service; but it encountered severe aerodynamic problems and was withdrawn from Fighter Command in May 1955.

Structurally, it was a cantilever low-wing monoplane of all-metal stressed-skin construction, powered by a 7,500-lb s t Rolls-Royce Avon RA 7 turbojet engine. The undercarriage was of the nose-wheel type, with hydraulic retraction. The ailerons were power-operated.

Twenty Mk 1s and 16 Mk 2s were built. In addition to increased armament, the latter introduced a cranked leading-edge to the wing.

The F Mk 3, with an Avon 108 and reheat, and the F Mk 4, with reheat and a variable-incidence tailplane, never became operational.

After its withdrawal from interception duties, the rôle of the Swift was changed to that of fighter-reconnaissance, and the FR Mk 5 was produced. Powered by a 7,175-lb s t Avon 114 (9,450 lb with reheat), this had a lengthened nose accommodating three cameras, a new

Supermarine Attacker, Pakistani Air Force

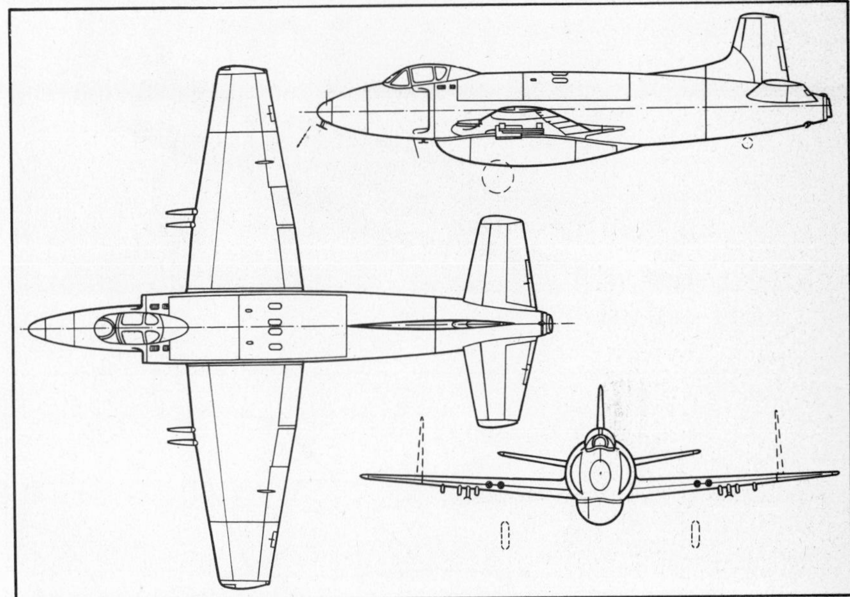
Supermarine Attacker FB Mk 2

Supermarine Swift F Mk 3

TYPE	DIMENSIONS span ft	span in	length ft	length in	height ft	height in	WEIGHT max t-o lb	PERFORMANCE max speed mph	at height ft	service ceiling ft	combat range miles	REMARKS
Seafire F Mk III	36	8	30	0	11	2	7,100	352	12,250	33,800	725*	*With auxiliary tank
Seafire FR Mk III	36	8	30	0	11	2	7,200	341	6,000	31,500	771*	*With auxiliary tank
Seafire Mk XV	36	10	32	3	10	8	8,000	383	13,500	35,500	640*	*With auxiliary tank
Seafire Mk XVII	36	10	32	3	10	8	8,000	387	13,500	35,200	860*	*With auxiliary tank
Seafire Mk 45	36	11	33	7	12	9	9,400	438	25,000	41,000	740*	*With auxiliary tank
Seafire Mk 46	36	11	33	7	12	9	9,730	NA	NA	NA	NA	
Seafire Mk 47	36	11	34	4	12	9	11,615	452	20,500	43,100	940*	*With drop-tanks
Attacker F Mk 1	36	11	37	6	9	11	11,500	590	SL	45,000	1,190	With ventral tank
Swift F Mk 1	32	4	41	5	12	6	NA	NA	NA	NA	NA	
Swift FR Mk 5	32	4	42	3	12	6	21,400	685	SL	NA	480	

Supermarine Swift FR Mk 5, No. 2 Squadron

Supermarine Scimitar F Mk 1

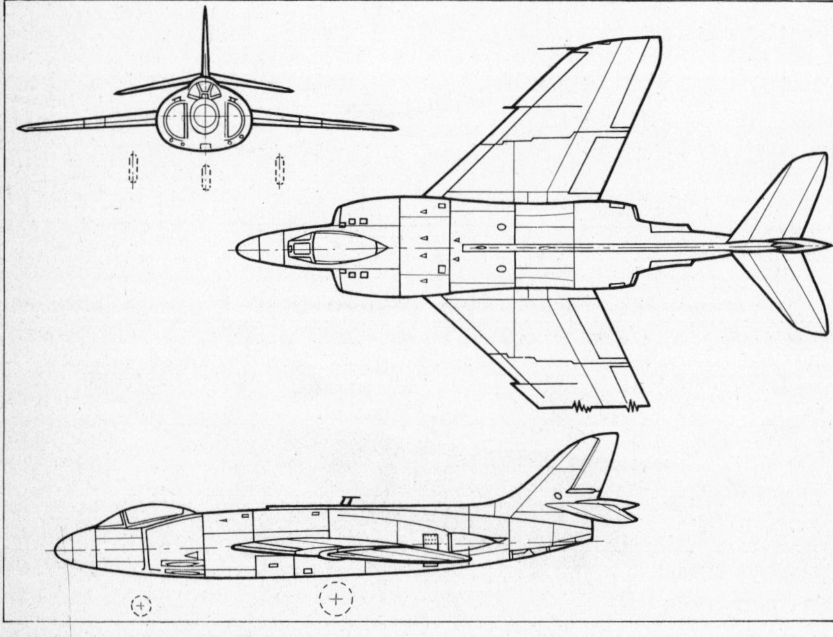

Supermarine Scimitar F Mk 1

Vickers F.B.5, early model

wing of increased chord at the tips, resulting in a distinctive "saw-tooth" leading-edge, a clear-view cockpit canopy and a ventral drop tank. It was armed with two 30-mm cannon and had provision for eight air-to-ground rockets under the wing.

A total of 62 FR Mk 5s were built. They served with two RAF squadrons in Germany from 1956 to 1961, and won the 1957 and 1959 reconnaissance competitions organized by NATO.

Supermarine Scimitar

The Scimitar, a single-seat carrier-borne interceptor and strike fighter, was the first sweptwing aircraft to be produced for the FAA. It was supersonic in a dive, and was capable of low-level attacks with tactical nuclear weapons, high-level interception with air-to-air guided missiles, or fighter-reconnaissance duties over extreme ranges.

Designed to Naval Specification N.113D, it was of all-metal stressed-skin construction. The "saw-tooth" sweptback wing was a three-spar structure, fitted with trailing-edge flaps of the "blown" type. These were fed by high-pressure air taken from each engine compressor to the top surface of each flap, the effect being to delay the onset of turbulence over the wing at high angles of attack and low speed, during landing, and also to lower the speed required for catapult-assisted take-offs. The wing folded to facilitate stowage.

The fuselage was a semi-monocoque structure, and the entire nose forward of the pressurized and air-conditioned cockpit hinged to one side to provide access to the radar equipment and to reduce the overall length. The tricycle undercarriage and tail bumper retracted hydraulically.

Power was provided by two 11,250-lb s t Rolls-Royce Avon Mk 202 turbojets, mounted closely side-by-side within the centre of the fuselage.

Fixed armament consisted of four 30-mm Aden cannon, mounted in the bottom of the fuselage. For interception duties, these could be supplemented by 96 unguided air-to-air rockets, or four Sidewinder infra-red homing missiles carried under the wings. In the strike rôle, the Scimitar could carry a tactical nuclear bomb, together with the equipment needed for its accurate delivery, or non-nuclear weapons such as Bullpup air-to-ground guided missiles, bombs or rockets. For reconnaissance duties, oblique cameras could be installed in an interchangeable nose fairing or in a small pod under the front fuselage.

For extreme ranges, two 100-gallon or 250-gallon fuel tanks could be carried under the wing; the aircraft could also act as a "buddy" tanker, carrying the FR Mk 20 refuelling pack, with retractable drogue, on the starboard inner pylon.

Scimitar F Mk 1s went into service in June 1958 and remained in first-line service until 1965. Seventy-six were built.

Vickers F.B.5

Known originally as the Vickers Fighting Biplane No. 5, the F.B.5 was the first real combat aircraft of the British air forces. Produced prior to the outbreak of the 1914–18 War, its configuration resulted entirely from the desire to produce a machine suitable for aerial fighting. The 100-hp Gnome Monosoupape engine was installed to "push" the aircraft, despite the inherently lower performance, because nobody had yet conceived a technique that would enable a machine-gun to be fired through the propeller disc of a tractor design.

The observer, located in the front of the nacelle, had a superb field of view. On early F.B.5s, he manned a belt-fed Maxim or Vickers gun, on a ball and socket mounting. With this arrangement, however, it was difficult to aim the gun and its field of fire was limited. Stowage of the ammunition belt also presented difficulties. Later F.B.5s, therefore, carried a Lewis drum-fed machine-gun on a spigot. This provided the gunner with a much more flexible weapon.

As with many aircraft of that time, slight variations

were made as production proceeded. Various nacelle and wing shapes were incorporated, and a few machines employed wing warping instead of ailerons.

When it first appeared, the F.B.5 was the only machine then in service with proper provision for mounting a machine-gun; this, and its sturdy construction, led to its familiar nickname of "Gunbus". In service, the F.B.5 was used for escort duties, long-range reconnaissance, photography and artillery observation.

One F.B.5 was fitted with a pair of Lewis guns and another, powered by a 110-hp Clerget engine, was fitted with armour to protect it from ground fire.

Vickers F.B.14

Fourteenth "Fighting Biplane" designed by Vickers, the F.B.14 was a two-seat reconnaissance aircraft. It was designed originally around the 230-hp B.H.P. engine, but development troubles with this unit resulted in the aircraft being fitted first with a 160-hp Beardmore engine and then – when this also gave trouble – with the 120-hp Beardmore, the expected performance dropping sharply with each engine change.

A distinctive feature of these installations was the ugly exhaust manifold, culminating in a vertical "funnel".

Structurally, the F.B.14 was unusual for its time, in that the fuselage was of steel tubing. The upper wing was appreciably larger than the lower, and the single pair of interplane struts on each side was raked sharply outward. Transparent panels in the centre of the upper wing, and in the roots of the lower wings, slightly improved the view for the pilot, who was located directly under the top wing. A simple Vee undercarriage was fitted.

Armament consisted of one fixed Vickers machine-gun, mounted above the engine and sychronized to fire between the propeller blades, and one free Lewis machine-gun on a Scarff ring-mounting in the rear cockpit.

Owing to the poor performance with the Beardmore, alternative engines were tried, including the 150-hp Lorraine-Dietrich, with which unit the type was designated F.B.14A.

Later aircraft were fitted with wings of increased span and a 250-hp Rolls-Royce Eagle IV engine; these were designated F.B.14D.

The final variant was the F.B.14F, powered by the air-cooled V-twelve 150-hp RAF 4a engine. This version of the aircraft proved almost impossible to spin.

About 50 F.B.14s were built, of which six were issued to Home Defence units in 1917. Their only recorded "combat" was an uneventful chase by a single F.B.14D of some Gothas returning from a daylight raid on London.

Vickers F.B.19

The Vickers Fighting Biplane No. 19 was single-seat fighter, powered by a 100-hp Gnome Monosoupape engine and characterized by a relatively short, dumpy, fuselage. The wings were unstaggered, a large cut-out being provided in the top wing to give the pilot a reasonable view upward.

Armament consisted of one Vickers machine-gun, synchronized to fire between the propeller blades by the Vickers-Challenger interrupter gear. Mounted on the port side of the fuselage, the gun lay in a trough so that it

Vickers F.B.5, enlarged rudder

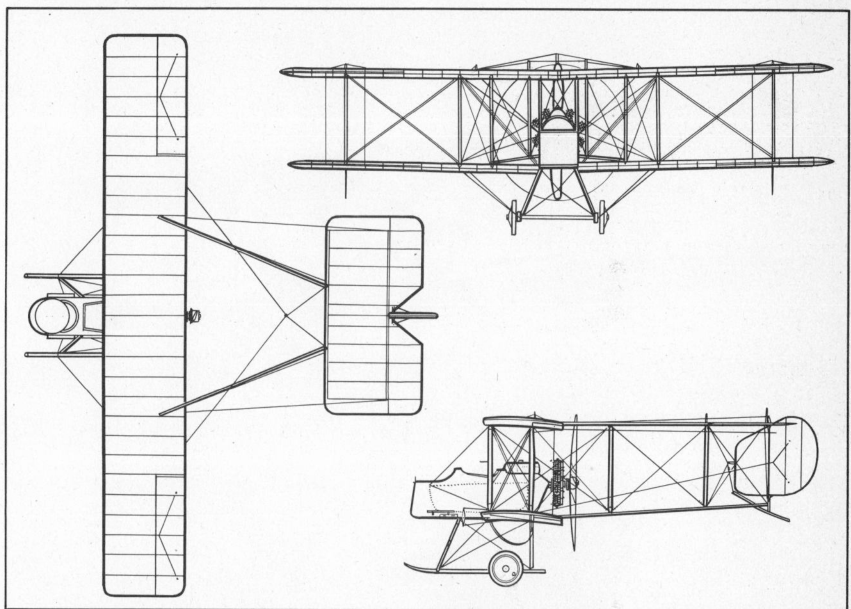

Vickers F.B.5

Vickers F.B.14, 160-hp Beardmore engine

TYPE	DIMENSIONS span ft	span in	length ft	length in	height ft	height in	WEIGHT max t-o lb	PERFORMANCE max speed mph	at height ft	service ceiling ft	combat range miles	REMARKS
Scimitar F Mk 1	37	2	55	4	15	3	NA	NA	NA	NA	NA	
Vickers F.B.5	36	6	27	2	7	0	2,050	70	5,000	9,000	360	
Vickers F.B.14	39	6	28	5	10	0	2,603	100	SL	10,000	NA	160 hp Beardmore
Vickers F.B.14A	39	6	26	6	10	0	2,620	101	5,000	11,500	NA	Endurance 3 hours
Vickers F.B.14D	42	0	30	8	10	3	3,308	111	6,500	15,500	NA	Endurance 3½ hours
Vickers F.B.14F	39	6	27	0	10	6	2,587	97	6,500	14,000	NA	Endurance 2½ hours

Vickers F.B.19 Mk II

Vickers F.B.27 Vimy Mk IV, No. 216 Squadron

Vickers Virginia IX

Vickers Virginia VII, No. 7 Squadron

was partially enclosed; its line of fire ran inside the engine cowling, a small hole in the latter permitting the passage of bullets. In this initial form, the type was known as the F.B.19 Mk I.

Later machines had pronounced stagger on the wings and, powered by either a 110-hp Clerget or 110-hp Le Rhône, were known as F.B.19 Mk IIs.

Both versions served briefly in France, where the RFC nicknamed the type the Vickers Bullet. It did not distinguish itself. In Britain, a few were used on Home Defence duties. Some F.B.19s were supplied to Russia, where it is thought that they saw service on the Eastern Front.

Vickers F.B.27 Vimy

Like the Handley Page V/1500 and D.H.10 Amiens, the Vimy was a heavy bomber initiated in 1917 to put into effect Britain's plan for the strategic bombing of industrial targets in Germany. By the time of the Armistice, however, only one example had reached France and this arrived too late to see operational service.

Carrying the Vickers type number F.B.27, the Vimy was the biggest aircraft built by the company up to that time; the prototype, powered by two 200-hp Hispano-Suiza engines, flew for the first time on 30 November 1917. It was a conventional three-bay biplane, with the engines mounted midway between the wings. The wing centre-sections extended to the engines and only the outer wings had dihedral, the tail unit was a biplane structure with twin balanced rudders; there were no fixed fins.

Armament consisted of a single Lewis machine-gun in the nose cockpit and another in a cockpit aft of the wings, both carried on Scarff ring-mountings. The maximum bomb-load was 2,476 lb, made up normally of eighteen 112-lb bombs and two 230-lb bombs carried on racks under the fuselage and lower centre-section.

As well as having revised wings and ailerons, the second prototype was powered by two 260-hp Sunbeam Maori engines; the third, virtually a production machine, had two 260-hp Fiat A-12 engines.

Initial production aircraft had Fiat engines, but the majority had 360-hp Rolls-Royce Eagle VIIIs, with which they were designated Vimy Mk IV. With these engines, the Vimy could carry its bomb-load for 900 miles at 98 mph, at a height of 5,000 ft. About 300 Eagle-engined Vimys were built.

After the war, the Vimy achieved immortality with a series of long-distance flights, including the first non-stop crossing of the Atlantic by Captain John Alcock and Arthur Whitten Brown, on 14/15 June 1919, and the first flight from Britain to Australia. Leaving Britain on 12 November 1919, the "Australian" Vimy completed its 11,000-mile journey 29 days later, after an incredible series of adventures and mishaps.

The Vimy was superseded by Virginias in first-line squadrons in 1924 and 1925, but remained in service on bomber duties in Northern Ireland until January 1929. About 80 Vimys were re-engined with Jupiter or Jaguar radials for use by Flying Training Schools and for parachute training duties. A passenger-carrying version, known as the Vimy Commercial, was used on a small scale.

Vickers Virginia

Developed to Air Ministry Specification 1/21, as a replacement for the Vimy, the Virginia was the backbone of the RAF heavy night bomber force from 1924 to 1937. It was a large twin-engined biplane and, because of its multitude of struts and bracing wires, was not particularly clean looking.

The prototype, built in 1922, was powered by two Napier Lion engines, mounted on the lower wings and enclosed within rectangular nacelles. On production aircraft these were replaced by oval nacelles of improved streamline form. Construction was conventional, consisting of a braced wooden framework, covered with fabric.

Armament consisted of a single Lewis machine-gun in the nose and a pair of Lewis guns in the gunner's cockpit, initially aft of the wings but later in the extreme tail. The maximum bomb-load carried was 3,000 lb. One Virginia, the Mk VIII, was fitted experimentally with twin nacelles for gunners in the upper wing.

The Virginia went into service in 1924, with Nos. 7 and 58 Squadrons, those of No. 7 Squadron being the first RAF bombers fitted with automatic pilots.

During its long service career, the Virginia was developed through several versions.

Early production machines, designated Mk Is, were similar to the prototype, with straight wings and dihedral on the lower wings only. Later versions had dihedral on all surfaces.

Major changes were made on the Virginia Mk VII. The nose of the fuselage was lengthened and redesigned, and the outer panels of the wings were slightly swept, outboard of the centre-section.

The Virginia IX retained the wooden construction of the earlier versions, but introduced the gunner's cockpit in the extreme tail.

On the last version, the Mk X, the structure became all-metal, with fabric covering. This version also had Handley Page slots on the outer sections of the upper wing. On the last few a tailwheel replaced the tail-skid.

A total of 126 Virginias were built, of which 53 were of the Mk X version. After their withdrawal from first-line squadrons, a few Virginias were used for parachute training from the Home Aircraft Depot at Henlow.

Vickers Wibault Scout

The Wibault Scout, Vickers Type 121, was a single-seat monoplane fighter built specially for the Chilean Air Force. It was designed to the Vickers-Wibault patent system of all-metal construction, the main feature of which was the metal skin. This acted as a covering only and was not stressed. Powered by a 450-hp Bristol Jupiter VI engine, the Scout was of parasol configuration, each wing being braced by two sloping struts from under the fuselage to its mid-span.

Twenty-six were built and were delivered to Chile during 1926 and 1927.

Vickers Type 143 Scout

The Type 143 Scout was a single-seat biplane fighter, built specially for the Bolivian Air Force. It was powered by a 500-hp Bristol Jupiter VIA engine and was distinctive in having the fuselage positioned midway between the upper and lower wings, after the fashion of the Bristol Fighter of the 1914–18 War. This arrangement gave the maximum possible effective wing area and contributed towards the good performance that was so essential at the high-altitude landing grounds of Bolivia.

Six Scouts were delivered in 1930 and saw service during the Gran Chaco War with Paraguay in 1932.

Vickers Vildebeest

The Vildebeest was a two-seat torpedo-bomber, designed to replace the Hawker Horsley. It had equal-span single-bay square-tipped wings, with a metal structure and

Vickers Wibault Scout

Vickers Type 143 Scout

TYPE	DIMENSIONS span ft	span in	length ft	length in	height ft	height in	WEIGHT max t-o lb	PERFORMANCE max speed mph	at height ft	service ceiling ft	combat range miles	REMARKS
Vickers F.B.19 Mk I	24	0	18	2	8	3	1,485	102	10,000	17,500	NA	
Vickers F.B.19 Mk II	24	0	18	2	8	3	1,475	98	10,000	16,500	NA	110-hp Clerget
Vickers F.B.19 Mk II	24	0	18	2	8	3	1,478	98	10,000	15,000	NA	110-hp Le Rhône
Vimy Mk III	67	2	43	6	15	3	10,808	98	SL	6,500	900	Fiat A-12
Vimy Mk IV	67	2	43	6	15	3	12,500	103	SL	7,000	900	Eagle VIII
Virginia Mk X	87	8	62	3	18	2	17,600	108	5,000	15,530	985	
Vickers Wibault	36	1	23	8	9	6	2,078	141	15,700	23,000	NA	
Vickers 143	33	6	26	3	11	0	2,246	150	11,500	20,000	NA	

Vickers Vildebeest Mk II

Vickers Vildebeest, Spanish-built (CASA), Hispano-Suiza engine

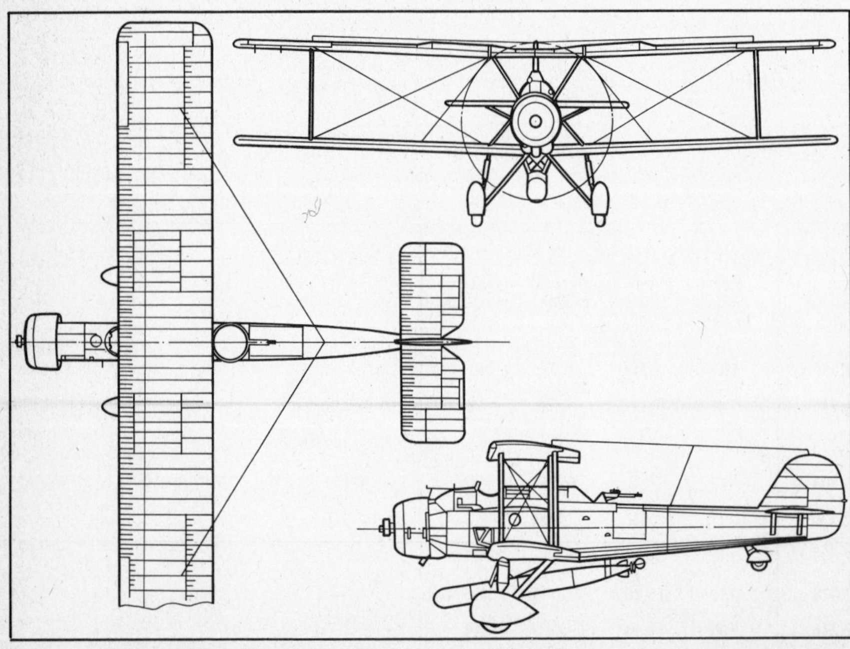
Vickers Vildebeest Mk IV

fabric covering. The centre-section of the top wing was supported above the fuselage on two pairs of splayed-out struts; the outer wings were supported by a single pair of interplane struts each side. Ailerons were fitted to all wings and in the top wing were incorporated Handley Page slots.

The fuselage was basically a wire-braced duralumin box-girder, fabric-covered. The undercarriage was of the divided-axle Vee-type, so that the torpedo could be carried under the centre of the fuselage; each front leg consisted of a Vickers oleo-compression unit. The standard wheeled undercarriage could be replaced with twin floats.

Armament consisted of one Vickers machine-gun, mounted on the port side of the fuselage in front of the pilot and synchronized to fire between the propeller blades, and one Lewis machine-gun on a Scarff ring-mounting in the rear cockpit. Either one 18-in torpedo or 1,000 lb of bombs could be carried.

Initial production Vildebeests, designated Mk I, went into service in 1933 with No. 100 Squadron. They were followed by the Mk II, powered by a 660-hp Bristol Pegasus IIM3 engine, and the Mk III which had a redesigned rear cockpit. A total of 152 Mk Is, IIs and IIIs were built, and were followed by a final batch of 57 of the Mk IV. This last version was fitted with the 825-hp Bristol Perseus VIII sleeve-valve engine, in a special low-drag long-chord cowling and driving a three-blade Rotol propeller.

Owing to delays in the introduction of its successor, the Beaufort, the Vildebeest – by then a 10-year-old design – was still in service in 1939 when war broke out. It was, in fact, the only torpedo-bomber available to Coastal Command at that time. Outclassed, two Vildebeest Squadrons suffered heavy losses against the Japanese during the invasion of Singapore in 1941. The last two survivors were lost in Sumatra in the following year.

Vickers Vincent

Produced to supersede the RAF's Wapitis and Fairey IIIFs, the Vincent was a three-seat general-purpose biplane developed from the Vildebeest torpedo-bomber. It was basically similar to the latter, but was adapted to carry a long-range fuel tank under the fuselage in the position occupied by the torpedo on the Vildebeest, increasing its range to 1,250 miles. In addition, a message pick-up hook was fitted for army co-operation duties, together with a considerable amount of special equipment needed for operations in the Middle East. It retained the 660-hp Bristol Pegasus IIM3 engine of its predecessor.

Like the Vildebeest, the Vincent had equal-span single-bay square-tipped wings, with a metal structure and fabric-covering. The centre-section was supported above the fuselage on a pair of splayed-out struts, the outer wings being supported by a single pair of interplane struts each side.

Ailerons were fitted to all four wings and the top wing incorporated Handley Page slots.

The fuselage was basically a wire-braced duralumin box-girder, fabric-covered. The divided undercarriage of the Vildebeest was retained.

Armament consisted of one fixed Vickers machine-gun, mounted on the port upper longeron and synchronized to fire between the propeller blades, and one Lewis machine-gun in the rear cockpit. The maximum bomb-load was 1,000 lb.

The first "production" Vincent was actually a converted Vildebeest Mk II, as were some later aircraft, and the type went into service in 1934, with No. 8 Squadron. A total of 197 Vincents were built, including Vildebeest conversions. A small number were still in service at the outbreak of war in 1939, and Vincents were still being used operationally in Iraq in 1941.

Vickers Wellesley

The Wellesley was a two-seat single-engined general-purpose bomber. It was begun as a private-venture design, in an attempt to meet Air Ministry Specification G.4/31.

Features of the aircraft were its unique geodetic construction and the unusual method of accommodating the bomb-load. The structure comprised an ingenious "criss-cross" lattice which was light and yet stiff torsionally. It was designed on the principle that if a rectangular panel, cross-braced by two curved stiffeners crossing at their mid-points, is subjected to shear loads, the tendency of the stiffener to bow in compression is counteracted by the tendency of the other stiffeners to straighten.

Geodetic construction was used for both the wings and the fuselage. The wing was built around two duralumin-tube spars, the geodetic lattice forming the profile. Of the fuselage, the front portion was a metal monocoque, the rear portion being a geodetic structure with tubular longerons and a profile structure of intersecting duralumin members. The undercarriage comprised two cantilever legs, incorporating oleo-pneumatic shock-absorbers, and retracted inward hydraulically, into the underside of the wings.

The Wellesley was powered by a 925-hp Bristol Pegasus XX nine-cylinder air-cooled radial engine. Armament consisted of one fixed machine-gun, mounted in the wing and firing forward, and a Vickers K machine-gun in the rear cockpit, on a movable mounting. Maximum bomb-load was 2,000 lb, carried in two containers under the wing.

Wellesley Mk Is went into service in 1937 with No. 76 Squadron, and the aircraft was used operationally during the early years of World War II. It is, however, best remembered for its achievement in gaining the World's Long Distance Record in 1938, when two RAF Wellesleys (a third aircraft started, but landed early) flew from Ismailia, Egypt, to Darwin, Australia – a distance of 7,162 miles – being airborne nearly 48 hours.

Later Wellesleys had a continuous canopy covering the two cockpits and were designated Mk II. Production of Mk Is and IIs totalled 176 aircraft.

Vickers Wellington

Designed to meet the requirements of Air Ministry Specification B.9/32, issued in 1932, the Wellington twin-engined long-range bomber formed the backbone of Bomber Command's offensive against Germany during the early years of World War II.

It was a cantilever mid-wing monoplane, utilizing the ingenious geodetic form of lattice-work construction first employed on the Wellesley. The result was a structure which was light and yet stiff torsionally, and one which could withstand extensive damage without failure.

The wing was constructed in three sections, the main spar of the centre-section passing through the fuselage. The outer wing panels were built around a single main spar and two auxiliary spars, close to the leading and trailing-edges. To these spars were attached a series of geodetic panels, conforming to the wing aerofoil contour and covered with fabric.

Of oval cross-section, the fuselage consisted basically of six main frames connected by a series of longitudinal geodetic skin panels built up on longerons. After the panels were secured in position, the whole fuselage was covered with fabric.

Wellington Mk Is were powered by two 1,000-hp Bristol Pegasus XVIII air-cooled radial engines, except for the first production machine, which had Pegasus Xs.

Vickers Vincent

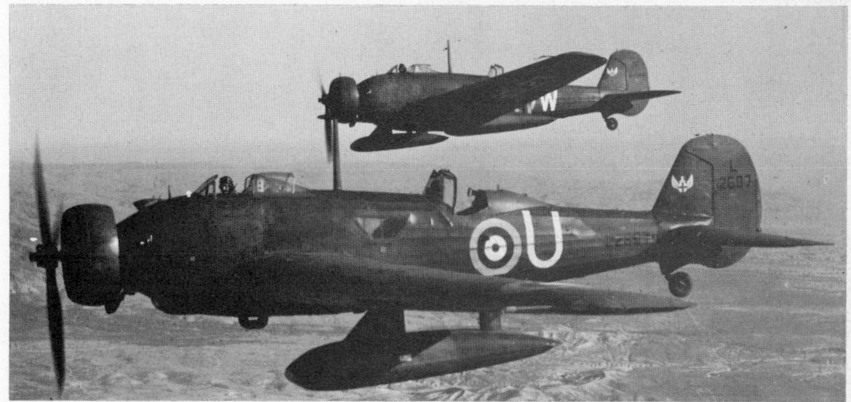

Vickers Wellesley Mk I, No. 14 Squadron

Vickers Wellington Mk II

TYPE	DIMENSIONS span ft	span in	length ft	length in	height ft	height in	WEIGHT max t-o lb	PERFORMANCE max speed mph	at height ft	service ceiling ft	combat range miles	REMARKS
Vildebeest Mk IV	49	0	37	8	NA		8,500	156	17,000	NA	630	
Vincent	49	0	36	8	17	9	8,100	142	4,920	17,000	1,250	
Wellesley Mk I	74	7	39	3	12	4	11,100	228	19,680	33,000	1,110	
Wellington Mk IC	86	2	64	7	17	0	25,800	235	15,500	19,000	2,550	
Wellington Mk II	86	2	64	7	17	0	27,600	247	NA	23,500	2,220	
Wellington Mk III	86	2	60	10	17	0	29,500	255	12,500	22,000	2,085	
Wellington Mk IV	86	2	NA		NA		31,600	229	NA	21,250	2,180	
Wellington Mk V	98	2	NA		NA		32,000	292	NA	36,800	2,250	

Vickers Wellington DWI, with degaussing ring

Vickers Wellington Mk III

Vickers Wellington Mk VI, pressurized version

Vickers Wellington GR Mk VIII

The maximum bomb-load was 4,500 lb, housed in a long compartment in the lower half of the fuselage. Defensive armament consisted of two 0·303-in machine-guns in a Vickers nose turret and two more in a tail turret, with a single gun in a Nash and Thompson retractable ventral "dustbin". On the Mk IA, the two Vickers turrets were replaced by Nash and Thompson turrets; and on the Mk IC the ventral turret was replaced by two 0·303-in guns in beam positions.

This defensive armament was heavy for the time and it was hoped that Wellingtons flying in formation would, by their combined turret fire-power, be able to ward off fighters and so permit daylight operations. Operational experience during the war proved this theory to be mistaken; out of 24 Wellingtons that took part in an armed reconnaissance of Wilhelmshaven on 18 December 1939, ten were shot down and three badly damaged by Messerschmitt Bf 109 and Bf 110 fighters which attacked broadside on. After this, Wellingtons were generally used only for night operations, on which they built up a great reputation for reliability and ruggedness. In April 1941, they were first to drop the deadly 4,000-lb "block-buster" bomb, during a raid on Emden, and helped to initiate the Pathfinder target-indicating tactics. In service, the Wellington was known as "The Wimpey", after J. Wellington Wimpey, Popeye's friend.

An interesting early duty for Wellingtons was exploding magnetic mines, Germany's first "secret weapons." For this task, a huge 48-ft diameter light alloy hoop was fitted to the aircraft and was used to radiate a magnetic field to trigger the mines. Known as the DW I, this version was highly successful.

The Mk II was powered by two 1,145-hp Rolls-Royce Merlin X engines, and the Mk III, which was the main early bomber version (1,519 being built), by two 1,375-hp Bristol Hercules III engines. The Wellington Mk IV had two Pratt & Whitney Twin Wasps.

Only three Mk Vs were built. Specially designed for high-altitude operations, they were powered by Hercules engines and had a completely redesigned nose incorporating a pressurized cabin. With 12-ft extensions on the wings, they reached 40,000 ft.

The Mk VI, powered by two 1,600-hp Rolls-Royce Merlin 60 R6SM engines, was also a high-altitude version and went into service with No. 109 Squadron in 1941.

Mk VII was the designation of an experimental model, powered by Merlin engines and carrying a 40-mm cannon in a large dorsal turret, incorporating a predictor sight and an offset cupola. This machine was tested originally with a standard tail unit, but was fitted later with twin fins and rudders.

The Mk VIII was the first of a long line of general reconnaissance versions, upon which development was concentrated after the withdrawal of Wellingtons from first-line bombing duties over Germany.

Powered by Pegasus XVIII engines, the GR VIIIs carried ASV Mk II radar, involving a distinctive row of masts along the top of the fuselage. Some also had a Leigh Light airborne searchlight.

The Mk IX was a Mk IC converted for special troop-carrying duties.

The Mk X, of which 3,804 were built, was the last bomber variant. It was essentially an improved Mk III, powered by two Hercules XVIII engines.

The Mk XI, powered by either Hercules VI or XVI engines, had ASV Mk III radar in a distinctive chin radome under the nose; this installation did not have the fuselage masts. To accommodate the radome, the nose turret was deleted. A retractable Leigh Light was fitted, and two 18-in. torpedoes could be carried.

The Mk XII was similarly powered, and carried a retractable Leigh Light in the rear of the bomb-bay.

The Mk XIII, with Hercules XVII engines, had ASV Mk II radar, with its array of fuselage aerials. A nose gun-turret was fitted to this version.

The Mk XIV was the last general reconnaissance version. It was similar to the Mk XII, but was powered by two Hercules XVII engines.

Wellingtons were also used as radar "flying class-rooms", crew trainers and for transport duties. Production totalled 11,461 aircraft.

Vickers Warwick

The Warwick was a twin-engined bomber produced to Air Ministry Specification B. 1/35 and intended to be a replacement for the Wellington.

Although the first prototype flew in August 1939, troubles with its Rolls-Royce Vulture engines resulted in a subsequent prototype being re-engined with Bristol Centaurus engines. Shortages of the Centaurus, in turn, resulted in the substitution of 1,850-hp Pratt and Whitney Double Wasp engines, delaying the appearance of production aircraft until July 1942, by which time the type was already obsolescent.

Of geodetic construction, with fabric covering, the Warwick was armed with eight 0·303-in Browning machine-guns, two each in nose and dorsal turrets, with four in a tail turret. The bomb-load was 2,000 lb.

Apart from a small initial batch of bombers, most of the 399 Warwick Mk Is were used for Air/Sea Rescue duties, for which they carried an airborne lifeboat.

When Centaurus engines became available, these were installed. Aircraft so powered were designated GR II, and 139 were built. The twin nose-turret guns were replaced by a manually operated 0·50-in machine-gun.

The Mk III was a long-range transport variant, capable of carrying 24 troops more than 2,000 miles.

The last Warwick version to enter service was the Mk V, of which 210 were built. Intended for general reconnaissance duties, this had a modified nose housing a radar scanner, and carried a Leigh Light.

Vickers Valiant

The Valiant was a long-range medium bomber, designed to Air Ministry Specification B.9/48, and was the first of Britain's "Vee" class of four-jet bombers to enter squadron service.

Of all-metal stressed-skin construction, it was a cantilever shoulder-wing monoplane with compound sweepback on the leading-edge. The wing was a conventional two-spar structure, with double-slotted flaps, powered ailerons and air-brakes. The fuselage was a semi-monocoque structure and incorporated a large dielectric panel under the nose. Airflow spoilers extended forward of the bomb-bay and a section of the fuselage aft of the bomb-bay hinged upward, to deflect the air-flow when the bomb doors were open. The undercarriage was of the retractable tricycle type, and was electrically operated.

Early Valiants were powered by four 9,500-lb s t Rolls-Royce Avon 201 turbojets; later machines had the 10,000-lb s t Avon 204 or 205. Take-off power could be supplemented by two de Havilland Super Sprite rocket engines, giving 8,400 lb of additional thrust. The rockets were pack-mounted under the wings and could be jettisoned after take-off. No defensive armament was fitted, and the maximum bomb-load was 10,000 lb.

Valiant B Mk 1s went into service in 1955, superseding the long-serving Lincolns, and were used in action during the Suez Campaign in the following year. To extend their

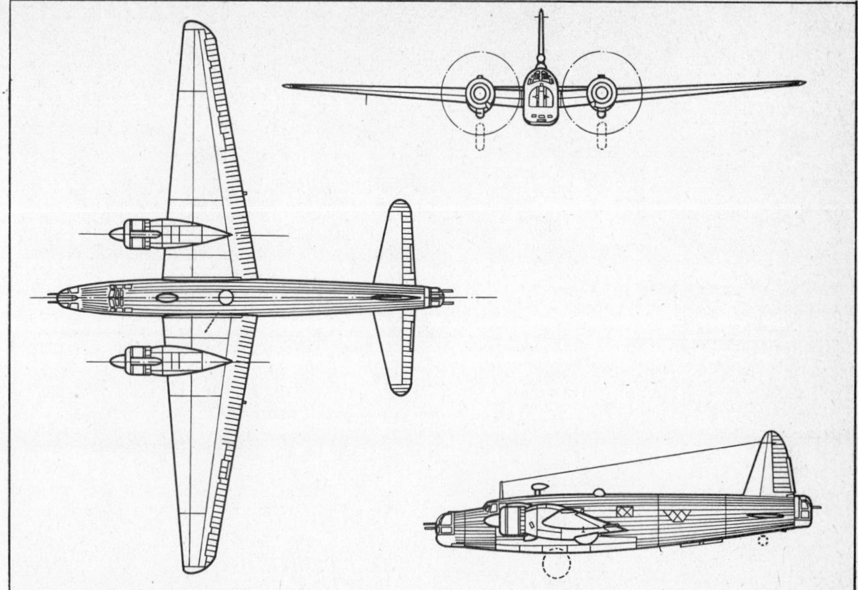

Vickers Wellington Mk X

Vickers Warwick GR Mk V

Vickers Valiant B(PR)K Mk 1

TYPE	DIMENSIONS span ft	span in	length ft	length in	height ft	height in	WEIGHT max t-o lb	PERFORMANCE max speed mph	at height ft	service ceiling ft	combat range miles	REMARKS
Wellington Mk VI	86	2	NA		NA		31,600	300	NA	38,500	2,180	
Wellington Mk VIII	86	2	NA		NA		25,800	235	NA	19,000	2,550	
Wellington Mk X	86	2	NA		NA		29,500	255	NA	22,000	2,085	
Wellington Mk XI	86	2	60	10	17	0	29,500	255	NA	19,000	2,020	
Wellington Mk XII	86	2	NA		NA		36,500	256	NA	18,500	1,810	
Wellington Mk XIII	86	2	NA		NA		31,000	250	NA	16,000	1,760	
Wellington Mk XIV	86	2	NA		NA		31,000	250	NA	16,000	1,760	
Warwick Mk I	96	8	72	3	18	6	45,000	224	NA	NA	NA	
Valiant B Mk 1	114	4	108	3	32	2	175,000	0.84M	30,000	54,000	4,500	

Vickers Valiant B(K) Mk 1

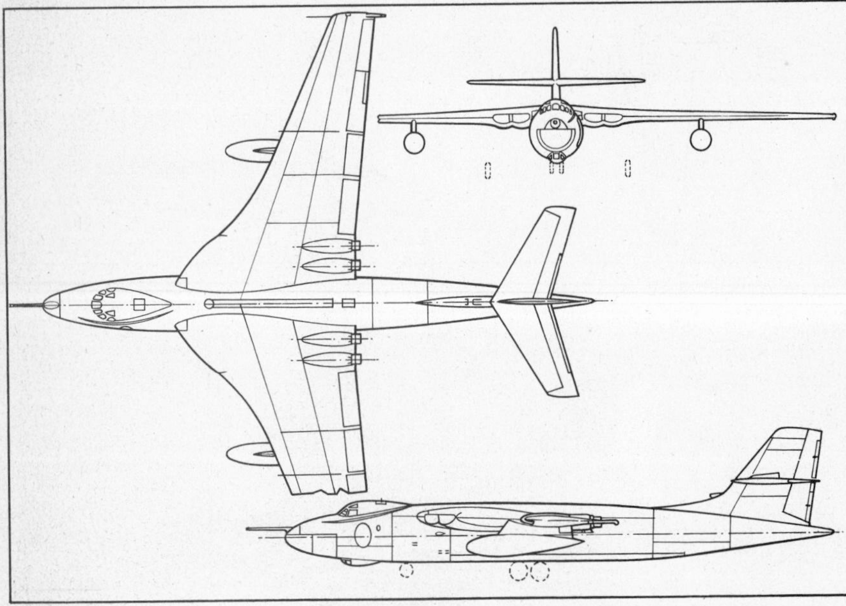

Vickers Valiant B(K) Mk 1

Westland Wapiti Mk I, Jupiter VI engine

Westland Wapiti Mk IIA, No. 30 Squadron

range, auxiliary tanks could be mounted under the wings.

Eleven B(PR)1 long-range strategic reconnaissance models were delivered, followed by 14 multi-rôle B(PR)K Mk 1s, suitable for bomber, photo-reconnaissance and flight refuelling tanker-receiver duties. The last variant, of which 48 were built, was the B(K) Mk 1, capable of carrying 5,000 gallons of transferable fuel as a tanker.

Valiants were used to drop the first British atomic and hydrogen bombs during development tests in the Pacific in 1956–57. A total of 111 were built, including a single B Mk 2 Pathfinder prototype, with lengthened nose and a landing gear similar to that of the Tupolev Tu-16, with main gear bogies which retracted into fairings on the wing trailing-edges.

Fatigue failures in the main wing structure led to the grounding of all Valiants in October 1964 and their subsequent scrapping.

Westland Wapiti

This two-seat general-purpose biplane was designed to replace the D.H.9A, which was still in service in large numbers in 1926 in spite of its 1914–18 parentage.

The official specification called for an aircraft with increased load-carrying and stowage capacity, but which was to incorporate as many D.H.9A parts as possible.

Accordingly, the prototype Wapiti, fitted with a 420-hp Bristol Jupiter VI engine, had a new fuselage 5½ in wider and 12 in deeper than that of the D.H.9A, but utilized the wings, ailerons, interplane struts and tail surfaces of the de Havilland type. A new undercarriage was fitted, the rear struts of which embodied Westland patent oleo-pneumatic shock-absorber units. During the first flight, early in 1927, it was discovered that the changes to the fuselage lines had adversely affected the effectiveness of the rudder, and a greatly enlarged and distinctive fin and rudder were substituted.

An initial production batch of 25 aircraft, designated Wapiti Mk Is, was ordered for service trials with No. 84 Squadron in Iraq. Like the prototype, these machines were powered by the ungeared Jupiter VI engine.

The initial contract was followed by a larger order for an improved version, to Air Ministry Specification 16/31 and powered by the 460-hp Jupiter VI engine. Early Wapitis had had a wire-braced wooden fuselage and wooden wings, but the new Mk IIs had an all-metal structure, including the wings and interplane struts. Handley Page slots were fitted to the outer sections of the top wing.

Although the Wapiti was designed primarily as a general-purpose type, a large number of special versions appeared during its long career. These included the army cooperation Wapiti, with lengthened fuselage and message hook, brakes and tailwheel; the seaplane Wapiti, with twin floats; the Arctic Wapiti, with a ski undercarriage; the Long-Range Wapiti, for desert patrol; the target-towing Wapiti; and the Wapiti Mk VI trainer, with dual controls. To enable it to perform its varied duties, the Wapiti could carry such additional equipment as an auxiliary fuel tank, oxygen, radio, photographic equipment, spare wheel and tail-skid, fitter's tool box, engine spares, normal and emergency rations, water, bedding and its crew's personal gear.

The various versions were powered by a variety of Bristol Jupiter engines, such as the 550-hp Jupiter VII, VIIIF, IXF and XFa, and a range of Armstrong Siddeley engines, including the Jaguar S and Panther.

Standard armament consisted of one fixed Vickers machine-gun, mounted on the port side of the fuselage and synchronized to fire between the propeller blades, and a Lewis machine-gun on a Scarff ring-mounting in the rear cockpit. In addition, a variety of bombs could be carried up to a total load of 580 lb.

Production of the Wapiti ended in 1932, by which time 512 had been built for the RAF and total production neared the 1,000 mark. The type was retired from the Auxiliary Air Force at home in 1937, but Wapitis were still in service in India in 1939.

Overseas, the Wapiti was used by the RAAF and SAAF, and by the Governments of Hedjaz and China. It was built under licence in South Africa.

Westland Wallace

After producing more than 500 Wapitis, Westland Aircraft was encouraged to embody the accumulated experience in a private-venture design. Referred to initially as the Wapiti VII, the new aircraft had a lengthened fuselage and a spatted undercarriage with wheel brakes. After a successful tour of South America, further refinements were made to the prototype, including the fitting of a divided-axle undercarriage and the installation of a Bristol Pegasus engine with a Townend cowling ring. By this time, the performance and appearance of the aircraft differed so much from that of a standard Wapiti that it was given the designation P.V.6.

Following Air Ministry acceptance trials as a general-purpose machine, an order was placed for twelve Wapitis to be converted to the "private-venture" standard. These conversions, built to Air Ministry Specification 19/32 and powered by 570-hp Bristol Pegasus IIM3 engines, were given the name Wallace Mk I.

Like the Wapiti, the Wallace had equal-span two-bay staggered wings. Ailerons were fitted to all wings and the top wing incorporated Handley Page slots.

The lengthened fuselage retained the metal-box girder structure, was faired to an oval section and covered with fabric.

The standard armament consisted of one fixed Vickers machine-gun, mounted on the port side of the fuselage and synchronized to fire between the propeller blades, and a Lewis machine-gun mounted on the decking behind the rear cockpit. A maximum bomb-load of 580 lb could be carried.

Wallace Mk Is went into service in 1933, with No. 501 Squadron. Production of this version totalled 55 aircraft, all converted Wapitis, and they were followed by an improved version. Designated Wallace Mk II, this had the more powerful 680-hp Pegasus IV and a canopy enclosing both cockpits. It was the first RAF machine to be so equipped and, apart from the greatly increased comfort, it enabled the rear gunner, whose canopy enveloped him "lobster-back" fashion, to use his gun with increased accuracy.

The original private-venture prototype, was converted for service with the Houston Mount Everest Expedition of 1933, when, in company with another Westland prototype, it became one of the first aeroplanes to fly over the highest mountain on earth.

A total of 104 Wallace Mk IIs were built. Some of them, converted for target-towing duties, were still in use in 1943.

Westland Lysander

The Lysander was a two-seat army co-operation aeroplane, but its wartime duties qualified it for inclusion as a combat type.

The single-spar wings were of all-metal construction, with metal skinning from the leading-edge to the spar, and fabric covering aft. Slotted flaps were fitted, these being arranged to lower automatically when the inboard slats opened; together they produced a stalling speed of only 65 mph. The fuselage was essentially a metal box-girder structure, the faired oval section being obtained by the use of detachable panels, consisting of wooden formers and stringers with fabric covering.

The legs of the fixed undercarriage were formed from a single light alloy extrusion of box form.

Westland Wallace Mk I

Westland Wallace Mk II

Westland Lysander Mk I

TYPE	DIMENSIONS span ft	span in	length ft	length in	height ft	height in	WEIGHT max t-o lb	PERFORMANCE max speed mph	at height ft	service ceiling ft	combat range miles	REMARKS
Wapiti Mk IIA	46	5	32	6	11	10	5,400	140	5,000	20,600	360	Jupiter VIII
Wapiti Seaplane	46	5	33	11	NA		5,400	134	5,000	18,100	610	Jupiter VIII F
Wallace Mk I	46	5	34	2	11	6	NA	158	15,000	24,100	NA	
Wallace Mk II	46	5	34	2	11	6	5,750	180	15,000	30,000	470	

Westland Whirlwind Mk I, No. 263 Squadron

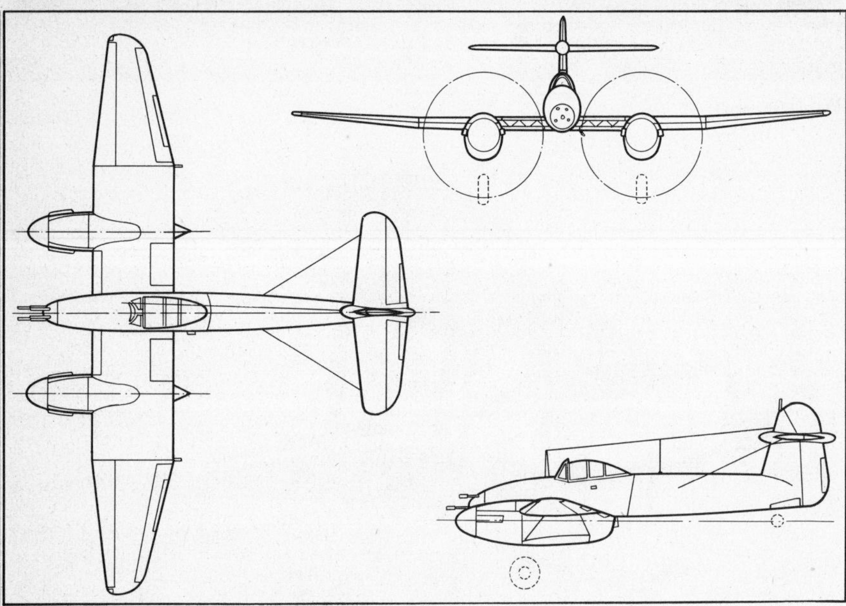

Westland Whirlwind Mk I

Westland Wyvern TF Mk 2

Westland Wyvern S Mk 4

Armament consisted of one 0·303-in Browning machine-gun, operated by the pilot, in each wheel spat, firing outside the propeller disc, and a free Browning in the rear cockpit. Twelve small anti-personnel bombs could be carried under small stub-wings fitted to the spats.

Lysander Mk Is, powered by an 890-hp Bristol Mercury XII nine-cylinder radial engine, first went into service in 1938, with No. 16 Squadron. In World War II they were affectionately known as "Lizzies" and their distinctive appearance caused some people to divide aircraft into two classes – aeroplanes and Lysanders! During the war they were used for night fighting, ground attack, target towing, glider towing and air-sea rescue, their ability to fly slowly under complete control proving invaluable for the latter duty.

Mk II Lysanders had a 905-hp Bristol Perseus XII engine, and the Mk III an 870-hp Mercury XX or XXX. Some Mk IIIs were fitted with twin machine-guns in the rear cockpit, these being designated Mk IIIA. Mk IIISAS's, fitted with a long-range fuel tank and a side ladder, were used to transport Allied agents into enemy occupied territory and to pick up VIP "evacuees".

Westland Whirlwind

Designed to Air Ministry Specification F.37/35, this long-range fighter was the first single-seat twin-engined aircraft to go into first-line service.

The basic feature of the Whirlwind was its concentration of fire-power, four 20-mm Hispano cannon being closely grouped in the nose of the fuselage.

Of all-metal stressed-skin construction, the wing consisted of a single-spar wide-span centre-section, of constant chord, and two tapering outer wing panels. High-lift Fowler-type flaps extended from aileron to aileron.

The monocoque fuselage was extremely slim, its frontal area being less than that of the engine nacelles. The cockpit was enclosed by a transparent canopy, giving the pilot an excellent all-round view. The main undercarriage retracted rearward into the engine nacelles, and the tail-wheel was also fully retractable.

The Whirlwind was powered by two 885-hp Rolls-Royce Peregrine liquid-cooled engines. A feature of the installation was the position of the coolant radiators, which were fitted inside the centre-section, receiving air through leading-edge ducts between the fuselage and engine nacelles.

The Whirlwind went into service in June 1940, with No. 263 Squadron. It was pleasant to fly and highly manoeuvrable. Low down its performance was equal to, if not better than, that of contemporary single-engined fighters. Unfortunately, its service career was marred by troubles experienced with the Peregrine engines, and restricted by the relatively high landing speed of 80 mph, which limited the number of airfields from which it could operate.

In 1942, Whirlwinds were fitted with racks for two 250-lb bombs, or one 500-lb bomb, and were used for low-level cross-Channel ground strafing sorties. A total of 112 were built.

Westland Wyvern

The Wyvern was a single-seat carrier-borne strike aircraft, designed originally to Specification N.11/44, which envisaged the use of a turboprop engine. As such a power plant was not available at the time, the first six prototypes and the ten Wyvern TF Mk 1 pre-production machines were each powered by a 2,690-hp Rolls-Royce Eagle 22 piston-engine. The first prototype flew on 12 December 1946.

They were followed by three TF Mk 2 prototypes, of which one had a 4,030-hp Rolls-Royce Clyde turboprop and the others a 4,110-hp Armstrong Siddeley Python 3 turboprop. The Python was chosen for the production version, of which 20 were ordered; but only 13 of these were completed as TF Mk 2s. The others were built as TFMk 4s, with a cut-back engine cowling to permit cartridge starting, a strengthened cockpit canopy and small auxiliary tail-fins on a dihedral tailplane. A further 87 TF 4s were built from scratch and four TF 2s were converted to TF 4 standard.

The Wyvern TF Mk 4 (the designation was changed to S Mk 4 in 1953) was a conventional all-metal stressed-skin monoplane with a retractable tailwheel undercarriage. Its Python 3 turboprop drove two large four-bladed contra-rotating propellers which produced particularly difficult problems of control, solved eventually by the installation of a Rotol inertia controller.

Standard armament was four 20-mm cannon in the wings, supplemented by a 20-in torpedo, bombs or mines, or by a combination of depth charges under the fuselage and sixteen 60-lb rockets under the wings.

After a lengthy development period, the Wyvern S 4 went into service with No. 813 Squadron of the FAA in May 1953. It eventually equipped four first-line squadrons, two of which took part at Suez in 1956.

A single Wyvern T Mk 3 was built as a tandem two-seat dual-control training version of the TF Mk 2, with a Python engine.

Westland Whirlwind HAS Mk 7

The Whirlwind HAS Mk 7 was one of many military developments of the Westland-built Sikorsky S-55 civil helicopter, and was the first helicopter built in Britain specifically for anti-submarine duties.

It was of the single main rotor and anti-torque tail rotor configuration, the all-metal rotor blades having extruded spars and light alloy-skinned trailing-edges.

The undercarriage was of the four-wheel type, the forward pair of wheels castoring. Power was provided by a 750-hp de-rated Alvis Leonides Major 755 air-cooled engine.

The fuselage was a rectangular light-alloy semi-monocoque structure, with a metal boom carrying the tail rotor. Compared with other Whirlwind variants, the floor was raised to enable a homing torpedo to be carried in a special open bay under the cabin, the fuel tanks being repositioned on each side of the bay. Specialized equipment included radar and dipping sonar for the detection and location of submarines. A hook could be fitted to the rear of the cabin for towing mine-sweeping gear.

Whirlwind HAS Mk 7s went into service with the Royal Navy in May 1957, replacing fixed-wing Gannets on aircraft carriers. Many were converted to turbine-powered HAR Mk 9 standard in the mid-1960s.

Westland Wessex

The Wessex is a turbine-engined development of the American Sikorsky S-58 helicopter, and was put into production initially for anti-submarine duties with the Royal Navy. It is of conventional all-metal semi-monocoque construction, with four-blade all-metal main and tail rotors. It has an aeroplane-type non-retractable tailwheel undercarriage, folding main rotor and a folding rear fuselage to reduce its overall length for stowage.

Powered by a 1,450-hp Napier Gazelle Mk 161 shaft-turbine engine, the Wessex HAS Mk 1 anti-submarine helicopter entered first-line service with No. 815 Squadron of the Royal Navy on 4 July 1961. It carries a crew of four and very extensive operational equipment, including an autopilot, autostabilization gear, Doppler radar and dipping sonar search equipment. Normal anti-submarine weapons comprise one or two homing torpedoes, carried

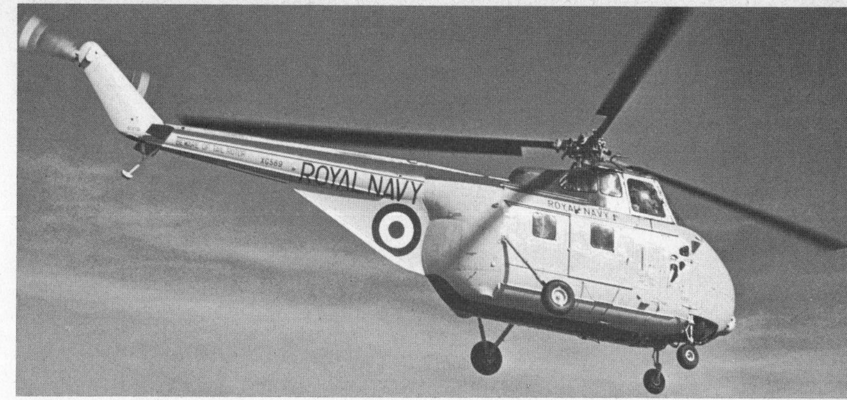

Westland Whirlwind HAS Mk 7

Westland Wessex HAS Mk 3, No. 706 Squadron

Westland Wessex HU Mk 5

TYPE	DIMENSIONS span ft	span in	length ft	length in	height ft	height in	WEIGHT max t-o lb	PERFORMANCE max speed mph	at height ft	service ceiling ft	combat range miles	REMARKS
Lysander Mk I	50	0	30	6	11	6	5,920	237	10,000	26,000	600	
Lysander Mk III SAS	50	0	30	6	11	6	10,000	NA	NA	NA	NA	Endurance 8 hours
Whirlwind	45	0	32	9	11	7	10,270	360	15,000	30,000	NA	
Wyvern S 3	44	0	42	3	15	9	24,500	383	Sea level	28,000	904	
Whirlwind HAS Mk 7	53	0	41	8	15	4	8,000	106	Sea level	13,000	335	

Westland Wasp HAS Mk 1

Wight Seaplane, Admiralty Type 840, Beardmore-built

Bell P-39D Airacobra

Bell P-39K Airacobra

on the sides of the fuselage, but these can be replaced or supplemented by four Nord AS.11 wire-guided missiles, machine-guns or rocket launchers.

Like other versions of the Wessex, the Mk 1 is used also as a combat transport, carrying up to 16 fully-equipped Marine Commandos, eight stretchers or internal or external freight.

The Wessex HAS Mk 3, which began to enter service in 1967, is similar to the Mk 1 but has a 1,600-hp Gazelle Mk 165 and new search radar in a "hump-back" radome.

Twenty-seven HAS Mk 31s, delivered to the Royal Australian Navy, differ from the Mk 1 mainly in having a more powerful 1,540-hp Gazelle Mk 162 engine.

Westland Wasp HAS Mk 1

Powered by a 710-shp Bristol Siddeley Nimbus 103 or 104 shaft-turbine, the Wasp HAS Mk 1 was designed for anti-submarine duties, operating from small platforms on naval frigates. First flown on 28 October 1962, it is standard equipment in the Royal Navy and has been sold also to South Africa (10), Brazil (3), New Zealand (2) and the Netherlands (12). Normal payload comprises a crew of two and two homing torpedoes. Three passengers or two stretchers can be carried in the rear of the cabin.

Wight Seaplane, Admiralty Type 840

The Wight Seaplane, Admiralty Type 840, was a large two-seat torpedo-carrying biplane, designed to the same requirements as the Short Type 184.

A distinctive feature of the 840 was its undercarriage, the main floats being so long that no tail float was needed. The folding wings were four-bay structures, and large extensions to the upper surface were braced by king-posts mounted above the outermost interplane struts. Small stabilizing floats were fitted under the tips of the lower wings. The fuselage was long and slender. The tailplane was braced by struts attached to the fin and top of the fuselage and to a small king-post projecting down from the fuselage. Power plant was a single 225-hp Sunbeam.

The 840 carried a 14-in 810-lb torpedo or an equivalent weight of bombs. No defensive armament was fitted.

Owing to production difficulties at the parent factory, construction of the Wight seaplane was extensively sub-contracted. A total of 67 machines were delivered and these served with the RNAS on anti-submarine patrols between 1915 and 1917. One operated from Gibraltar.

U.S.A.

Bell P-39 Airacobra

Among United States fighters of the World War II era, the P-39 was unique, having its engine – a turbo-supercharged Allison V-1710 in the prototype – buried in the centre-fuselage. From the engine, a 10-ft extension shaft ran forward under the cockpit floor to drive the propeller. This arrangement was adopted primarily to permit installation of a heavy-calibre gun in the nose. As originally designed, the P-39 (Bell Model 12) had a 37-mm T-9 cannon firing through the propeller hub and two 0·50-in machine-guns in the upper front fuselage firing through the propeller disc.

Apart from the radical engine position, the Bell design was conventional in appearance, although it was the first single-engined fighter with a tricycle undercarriage ever ordered by the United States Army Air Corps, which contracted for one prototype on 7 October 1937. This was first flown, as the XP-39, in April 1939, and after undergoing a short series of trials it was modified into the XP-39B, with revised radiator and with the turbo-supercharger deleted. First flown on 25 November 1939, the XP-39B established the design standard for the 13 pre-production YP-39s ordered in April 1939, the first of which appeared in September 1940.

Initial production models of the Bell fighter were designated P-39C (after a brief period as P-45s). Only 20 appeared before they were superseded by the P-39D, with leak-proof fuel tanks and four 0·30-in machine-guns in the wings as well as the three nose guns. A bomb or a fuel tank could be carried under the fuselage. The United States Army Air Corps purchased 404 P-39Ds for its own use and 494 P-39D-1s and P-39D-2s for lend-lease in 1941.

First overseas interest in the Bell design came from Britain, which placed an order for 675 on 13 April 1940; export versions were the Bell Model 14 and had a 20-mm nose gun in place of the 37-mm weapon. Comparatively few Airacobras reached Britain, where they equipped one RAF fighter squadron; more than 200 were passed on to the Soviet Air Force and as many again were retained by the USAAF under the designation P-400 after the war with Japan began.

From April 1942, P-39s of the USAAF were in action from bases in Hawaii, Panama, Alaska and New Guinea against Japanese attackers; and from July 1942 against German targets in Europe. The January 1940 decision to delete the turbo-supercharger was soon found to have restricted the P-39's usefulness as a fighter; but late in 1942 the type began operating in a ground-attack rôle in North Africa with considerable success. Despite early operational difficulties with the P-39, production continued at high pressure, for an eventual total of 9,558. Of these, 4,773 went to the Russian Air Force under lend-lease arrangements, and a small quantity found their way to the Portuguese Air Force after forced landings in Portugal. Late in the war, the Free French forces received 165 P-39s.

Production variants accounted for a number of different designations with few major changes in design. The P-39F had an Aeroproducts, in place of Curtiss, propeller; the P-39J had a V-1710-59 rather than -35 engine; the P-39K had a V-1710-63 engine and Aeroproducts propeller; the P-39L was similar with a Curtiss propeller; the P-39M had a V-1710-83 engine; the P-39N had a V-1710-85 and was lighter than preceding versions; and the P-39Q introduced two 0·50-in wing guns in external fairings, replacing the four 0·30-in guns.

A version of the Bell Airacobra was designed for the United States Navy as the XFL-1 Airabonita. It had a tail-wheel landing gear and an arrester hook. First flown on 13 May 1940, it was not put into production.

Bell P-59 Airacomet

Only one type of jet-propelled fighter was delivered to the USAAF in quantity during World War II. Designed to gain experience with the new type of prime mover invented in Britain by Frank Whittle, this was the Bell P-59, developed at high speed and put into production with remarkably little trouble.

The choice of the Bell company for the important task of designing the country's first jet was influenced by the closeness of its plant to the General Electric factory at Schenectady, where its Whittle-type engines were to be built. Work on the engine was initiated on 4 September 1941; design and construction of three prototypes of a fighter to be powered by it began on 5 September 1941.

Bell P-39L Airacobra

Bell P-39Q Airacobra

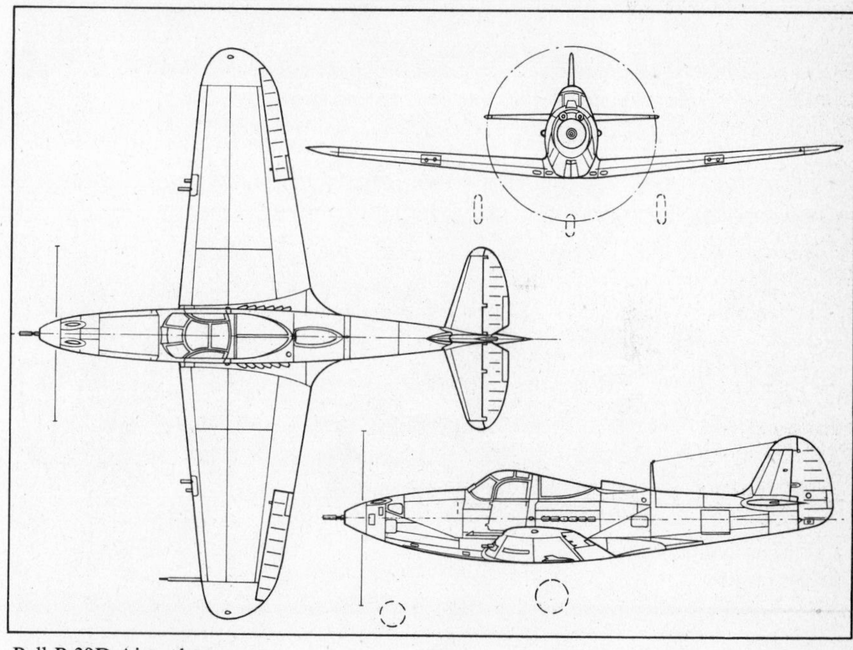

Bell P-39D Airacobra

TYPE	DIMENSIONS span ft	in	length ft	in	height ft	in	WEIGHT max t-o lb	PERFORMANCE max speed mph	at height ft	service ceiling ft	combat range miles	REMARKS
Wessex HAS Mk 1	56	0	65	9	15	10	12,600	132	SL	14,200	600*	*With auxiliary tanks
Wasp HAS Mk 1	32	3	30	4	8	11	5,500	120	SL	12,200	270	
Wight Admiralty Type 840	61	0	41	0	NA		4,453	81	NA	NA	NA	Endurance 7 hours
Bell P-39C	34	0	30	2	11	10	7,075	368	13,600	33,300	600	First operational version
Bell P-39K	34	0	30	2	11	10	8,400	368	13,800	32,000	750	V-1710-63 engine
Bell P-39N	34	0	30	2	12	5	8,200	399	9,700	38,500	750	
Bell YP-59A	45	6	38	2	12	0	12,562	409	35,000	43,200	NA	Service trials
Bell P-59B	45	6	38	10	12	4	13,700	413	30,000	46,200	375	

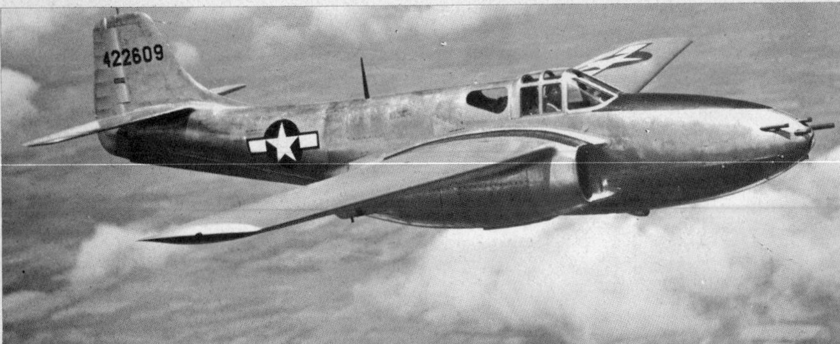

Bell P-59A Airacomet

Bell YP-59A Airacomet drone director, with open cockpit forward of pilot

Bell P-63A Kingcobra

Bell P-63A Kingcobra

In an effort to preserve secrecy, the three prototypes were designated XP-59A, the XP-59 being a Bell design for a piston-engined twin-boom fighter. Secrecy also influenced the choice of the dry lake bed at Muroc in the Californian desert as the site for the jet's first flight.

Because the engines were so revolutionary, Bell designers chose to eschew innovations in airframe design and the P-59 turned out to be a conventional mid-wing monoplane with a straight-tapered wing and a short tricycle undercarriage. The two General Electric I-A engines fitted snugly at the wing/fuselage junction, and the two 37-mm cannon were mounted in the nose.

First taxi runs and short hops were made by the prototype XP-59A at Muroc on 1 October 1942, only one year after work began, and the first official flight was made on 2 October 1942. Following the three XP-59As were 13 YP-59As, with I-16 engines and – in the final four – revised armament of one 37-mm gun and three 0·50-in guns. Two YP-59As were evaluated by the US Navy and one was exchanged for a British Gloster Meteor.

A production order for 100 Airacomets was placed, but later reduced to 50 when it was found that the aircraft was insufficiently stable for use as a fighter. The first 20 production models were P-59As with J31-GE-3 engines, and the other 30 were P-59Bs with J31-GE-5s, more internal fuel and small changes.

For operational evaluation the P-59s were issued to the 412th Fighter Group, but the Airacomet did not become operational, being used instead for research, engine development and as a drone director.

Bell P-63 Kingcobra

Early in the design life of the Bell P-39, work began on a completely new wing, with a suitable aerofoil section to achieve laminar flow. Prototypes were ordered in April 1941 as XP-39Es, followed in June 1941 by a contract for two prototypes of a new design using a similar wing section. Known as the P-63, this proved to be the only American fighter produced in major quantities which was begun after the USA entered the war and was flying before its end.

In general layout the P-63 was similar to the P-39, with more emphasis on features required for ground-attack work. The first XP-63 flew on 7 December 1942, two months after the initial production order had been placed. The engine in the P-63A – deliveries of which began in October 1943 – was a V-1710-95 and armament comprised one 37-mm and two 0·50-in calibre guns in the nose. Later aircraft had two more 0·50-in guns, in underwing fairings, and the armour protection was progressively increased together with the underwing load.

After producing 1,725 P-63As, Bell went on to build 1,227 P-63Cs with V-1710-117 engines and greater fuel capacity. Final production total for all P-63s was 3,303, including experimental versions. No fewer than 2,421 of these were allocated to the Soviet Air Force under lend-lease and in Russia the Kingcobra performed extremely well in the ground-attack rôle. The Free French forces received 300 P-63s and the production total included more than 300 P-63G armoured target aircraft. Very few P-63 fighters saw service of any kind with the USAAF; none appears to have reached operational status.

Bellanca 28-110

Although the Bellanca company was responsible for a long and successful line of light planes and transport aircraft in the two inter-war decades, it never succeeded in selling an operational aircraft to the US armed forces. Some foreign interest was aroused in 1937, however, with a militarized version of the Bellanca Model 28.

The Model 28 had originated in 1936 as the 28-70, designed for a speed dash across the Atlantic. Powered by a 700-hp Pratt & Whitney Wasp engine, the 28-70 was a stubby low-wing monoplane with two seats in tandem beneath a long cockpit enclosure. The undercarriage was retractable and the wings were eventually wire-braced, above and below. Construction was basically metal, with fabric covering.

A version of the same design, with a 900-hp Wasp engine, was ordered in 1937 for use in France on mail-carrying flights. The entire batch of 20 of these, known as Model 28-90s, was acquired before delivery for use in Spain, where the Civil War was being fought. In keeping with American neutrality towards the two factions in Spain, delivery of the Bellanca aircraft was therefore barred by the government.

In 1938, the Chinese government ordered a quantity of Bellanca 28-110 fighters and although these were powered by the 1,000-hp Wasp R-1830 engine, it appeared probable that the Chinese machines incorporated at least portions of the earlier Model 28-90s. Little was heard of the 28-110s after delivery. For their day, they were comparatively heavily-armed, with five machine-guns and 1,600 lb of bombs.

Bellanca 77-140

In the early 1930s the Bellanca company produced a number of designs for transport aircraft featuring a lifting strut to brace the high wing. In combination with the stub wing carrying the undercarriage, the strut almost gave the Bellanca Airbus and other members of the family a biplane or sesquiplane appearance.

Several examples of the Bellanca transport were purchased by the US Army, but variants of the design intended for more warlike operation aroused little interest. The only exception was the Bellanca 77-140, a private-venture adaptation of the lift-strut design theme, of which a few were exported to Colombia. No records of their subsequent use appear to exist.

Powered by two Wright R-1820 Cyclones on the top wing, the 77-140 carried an armament of five guns and 2,300 lb of bombs. It could operate on floats or wheels.

Berliner-Joyce P-16/PB-1

Early in 1929, some four years after the last two-seat fighter had been built for US Army Air Corps use, a new design competition for such an aircraft was initiated. Design proposals by Boeing, Curtiss and Berliner-Joyce were evaluated and in June 1929 the last-mentioned company was awarded a contract for a prototype of its design.

Designated XP-16, the fighter had a supercharged Curtiss V-1570-25 in-line engine and was delivered for flight testing in October 1929. The most interesting feature of the design was the manner in which the single-bay, unequal-span wings were arranged to fair into the fuselage, giving the top wing a "gull" effect.

Following tests with the prototype, the Army Air Corps placed a contract for 25 YP-16s, sufficient for a full-scale service evaluation. This was conducted by the 1st Fighter Group, starting in 1932. During their period in service, these aircraft were re-designated PB-1, as the first types ever designated in the "Pursuit, Biplane," category.

The gull-wing arrangement on the PB-1 was also employed by Berliner-Joyce for its XFJ-1 and XF2J-1 fighter prototypes for the Navy, but neither these nor the elegant XF3J-1 found favour and the company went out of business in 1934.

Boeing (Engineering Division) GA-1

Experience of the American Expeditionary Force in France in 1918 inevitably influenced the development of military aircraft in the United States in ensuing years. A

Bellanca 28–90B

Bellanca 77–140

Berliner-Joyce P-16/PB-1

TYPE	DIMENSIONS span ft	span in	length ft	length in	height ft	height in	WEIGHT max t-o lb	PERFORMANCE max speed mph	at height ft	service ceiling ft	combat range miles	REMARKS
Bell P-63A	38	4	32	8	12	7	10,500	408	24,450	43,000	390	
Bell P-63C	38	4	32	8	12	7	10,700	410	25,000	38,600	320	
Bellanca 28–90	46	2	26	6	7	0	7,849	280	6,500	30,500	800	
Bellanca 77–140	76	0	40	0	14	0	16,333	190	7,000	23,500	710	
Berliner-Joyce PB-1 (YP-16)	34	0	28	2	9	0	3,996	175	SL	21,600	650	

Boeing GAX

Boeing FB-1

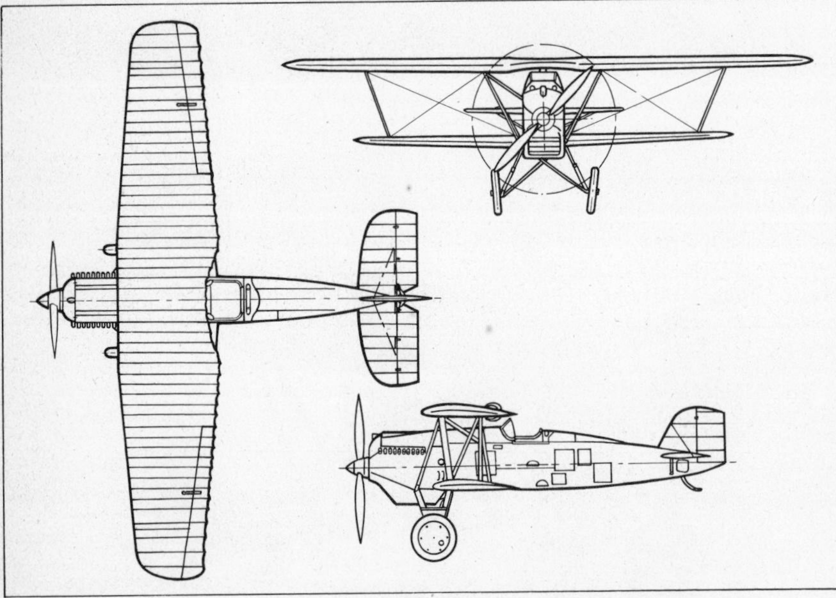
Boeing PW-9C

Boeing PW-9D

specific example of this is provided by the GAX/GA-1 triplanes. The GAX, or Ground Attack Experimental, was designed and built at McCook Field in 1920 to investigate the value of heavily-armoured aircraft which could fly slowly above ground troops and bring to bear a heavy weight of gunfire. Its designer was I. M. Laddon.

The GAX was of all-wood construction and was powered by two 435-hp Liberty engines, mounted as pushers. It carried a ton of armour plating, $\frac{1}{4}$-inch thick, to protect the engines and the crew, consisting of a pilot and four gunners. The nose gunner had a 37-mm cannon and another gun pointing aft above the wings. The rear gunner looked after another upper gun and two downward guns in the rear fuselage, firing through slits in the armour. Two more gunners were located at the front of the engine nacelles, ahead of the engines, each with two 0·30-in guns.

Boeing won a production contract for 20 examples of the design, designated GA-1, but service trials in Mexico were unsatisfactory and the contract was halved.

Boeing PW-9/FB-1

In the years following the 1914–18 War, the US aircraft industry, like that of other nations, devoted much effort to attempting to forecast probable military requirements and to designing aircraft for such requirements. One likely market in the early 1920s was in the production of single-seat fighters for the US Army Air Service and Boeing was among the companies which began private-venture development of a suitable aircraft – identified as Model 15.

Frank Tyndall flew the prototype Model 15 on 29 April 1923, and after the Army had tested it at McCook Field, Boeing received a contract, on 9 September 1923, for this machine and two other prototypes to be designated XPW-9. Structurally, the Boeing fighter was in vogue, with a steel-tube, fabric-covered fuselage and tail unit, and a wooden wing, also fabric-covered. The wings were tapered in planform and the engine was a 435-hp Curtiss D-12. Armament comprised one 0·30-in and one 0·50-in machine-gun under the cowling, firing through the propeller disc.

Boeing's initiative in developing the Model 15 was rewarded on 19 September 1924 with an order for 12 production model PW-9s, increased to 30 in the following December. The PW-9s differed in minor detail from the prototypes, and had split-axle in place of straight-axle landing gear.

Deliveries began in October 1925 and a follow-on order was placed in the same month for 25 slightly modified versions called PW-9As. Two 1926 contracts resulted in production of 39 PW-9Cs, in which further small refinements were introduced. The final contract, in August 1927, covered 16 PW-9Ds, after a prototype had been built and tested. Changes included addition of balance area to the top of the rudder, a redesigned radiator, wheel brakes and smaller items.

All the production models of the PW-9 series had the 440-hp Curtiss D-12-D engine, but one PW-9D was temporarily re-engined with a 600-hp Curtiss V-1570 and was re-designated XP-7. An earlier PW-9 was flown experimentally with a special set of Thomas-Morse metal wings, with corrugated aluminium covering.

In addition to the production of PW-9s for the Army Air Corps, Boeing built a further quantity for the US Navy which in December 1924 ordered 14 examples of the Boeing Model 15 as FB-1s. These were similar in all major respects to the PW-9, but some became FB-2s when fitted with arrester gear for operation on board the USS *Langley*. Experimental Navy models were two FB-3s with Packard 1A-1500 engines (also flown as floatplanes) and the FB-4 with a Wright P-1 radial engine. The 27 production model FB-5s for the Navy had 525-hp Packard 2A-1500 engines and a single FB-6 had a 400-hp Wasp R-1340.

Boeing PB

Following the end of the 1914–18 War, while the US Army expended considerable effort to completing transcontinental flights with various of its new aircraft, the Navy concentrated its attention on long overwater flights

Especially, the crossing from the United States west coast to Hawaii represented a yardstick for non-stop performance to be sought after in new designs.

The Boeing PB-1 (Model 50) of 1925, built for a trans-Pacific flight by the Navy, was the company's first post-war flying-boat, and the first design by a private company purchased by the Navy after the war. It was of conventional design, its most unusual feature being the mounting of two engines (800-hp Packard 2A-2540 in-lines) back-to-back on the centre-line between the wings. Provision was made for 2,000 lb of bombs.

After serving with the Navy for two years, the sole PB-1 was re-engined with two Pratt & Whitney R-1690 Hornet radials, fore and aft in the central nacelle. In this form the boat was re-designated XPB-2.

Boeing PB-1

Boeing TB-1

Although the Boeing company was a major supplier of fighters and trainers to the US Navy in the inter-wars period, it achieved little success in marketing other types for Naval use. Only a single flying-boat (the PB-1) was delivered in the period, and little more success attended the sole Boeing attempt to produce a torpedo-bomber. This was the Model 63, designated TB-1 and built to US Navy specifications. Three examples were ordered in May 1925 and were operated for several years, but no further production took place.

The TB-1, delivered in April 1926, was a large single-bay biplane with a 770-hp Packard 1A-2500 in-line engine. Two open cockpits were provided – one for pilot and torpedo-man side-by-side forward of the wing and another further aft for the gunner, with two machine-guns.

The TB-1 could operate on floats or with a land undercarriage. Whichever was fitted, the space under the fuselage and between the legs was uninterrupted and accommodated a 1,740-lb torpedo. The wings could be folded for carrier stowage.

Boeing TB-1 (XTB-1)

Boeing F2B, F3B

As a direct result of selling the FB series of fighters (based on the PW-9) to the US Navy, Boeing developed in 1926 a new fighter especially for carrier-based operation. It differed from the FB series in having a balanced rudder and by using a Pratt & Whitney R-1340B Wasp radial engine. The latter installation was virtually identical with that used in the experimental FB-6.

After testing an XF2B-1 prototype (Boeing Model 69) in 1926, the Navy placed a production order for 32. Two additional examples were built in 1927–8 as Model 69Bs, for export to Japan and Brazil respectively.

A further refinement of the same design appeared as Model 74 and was tested by the Navy under the designation XF3B-1. It had the same wings as the F2B-1, but a more powerful engine and other refinements. As a result of flight trials with the XF3B-1, new, larger wings were designed to improve the high-altitude performance and the type then went into production. Boeing built 73 F3B-1s for the Navy.

Both the F2B and F3B operated as fighter-bombers, with provision beneath the wings for 125 lb of bombs. Two forward-firing machine-guns were fitted.

Boeing F3B-1

TYPE	DIMENSIONS span ft	span in	length ft	length in	height ft	height in	WEIGHT max t-o lb	PERFORMANCE max speed mph	at height ft	service ceiling ft	combat range miles	REMARKS
Boeing GA-1	65	6	33	7	14	3	9,740	105	SL	11,500	160	
Boeing PW-9	32	1	22	10	8	8	3,030	165	SL	20,175	NA	Endurance 2 hr 35 min
Boeing PW-9D	32	0	24	2	8	8	3,234	155	SL	18,230	NA	Endurance 2.87 hr
Boeing FB-1	32	0	23	6	8	9	2,944	167	SL	21,200	509	Navy version of PW-9
Boeing PB-1	87	6	59	5	22	2	26,822	125	SL	3,300	2,230	
Boeing TB-1	55	0	42	7	15	1	10,703	106	SL	2,600	850	
Boeing F2B-1	30	1	22	11	10	1	3,204	158	SL	21,500	372	
Boeing F3B-1	33	0	24	10	10	1	3,340	156	SL	20,900	NA	

Boeing P-12B

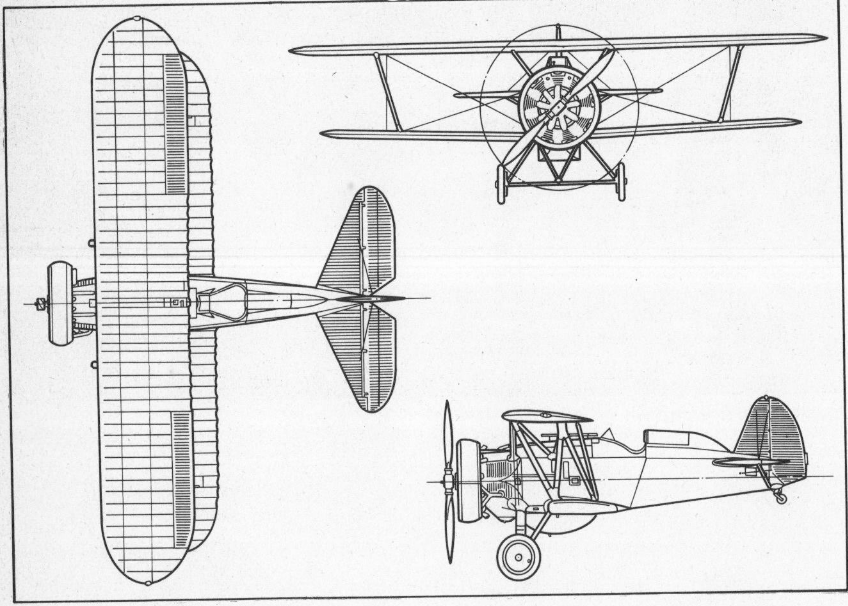
Boeing P-12E

Boeing F4B-3

Boeing Y1B-9A

Boeing P-12, F4B, Model 100

Attempts to achieve commonality between Air Force and Navy requirements have not always been successful, and in the case of the latest TFX (F-111) programme it resulted in one of the most controversial decisions ever taken by a US Defense Secretary. The requirements for land-based and carrier-based operations were not always so disparate, however, and the Boeing F4B/P-12 series provides an outstanding example of a single design effectively serving in two rôles.

Between 1928 and 1933, Boeing built 586 aircraft in this design series, setting a record for production of a basic US military aircraft that was not eclipsed until 1940. Progenitors of the series were two aircraft built as a private venture by Boeing and known as Model 83 and Model 89. The two types were similar, with wooden wings, aluminium-tube fuselage structure and open cockpit. The engine was a 400-hp R-1340C Wasp radial, and the Model 83 first flew on 25 June 1928.

Both prototypes were tested by the US Navy under the designation XF4B-1, starting August 1928. A production order for 27 F4B-1s (Model 99) followed the evaluation, and so enthusiastic was the official report that the Army Air Corps took the unusual step of placing a production order without conducting an independent assessment. The initial Army order was for nine P-12s (Model 102) and a single XP-12A (Model 101), the latter having a long-chord NACA engine cowl, Frise ailerons and a shorter undercarriage. First flight dates were 6 May 1929 for the F4B-1; 11 April 1929 for the P-12 and 10 May 1929 for the P-12A.

The Army purchased 90 P-12Bs (Model 102B) with Frise ailerons and short undercarriage, then 96 P-12Cs with a ring cowling round the engine and a further modified undercarriage. The 35 P-12Ds had the 525-hp R-1340-17 engine, not the R-1340-9 of the earlier models. The Navy purchased 46 F4B-2s with Frise ailerons, ring cowl and split-axle undercarriage.

While production of these aircraft proceeded, Boeing developed a semi-monocoque duralumin fuselage and demonstrated the new feature in a version of the same design called Model 218. After this prototype had been evaluated by both the Navy and the Army it was exported to China, where it went into action against Japanese aggressors and was eventually shot down.

The all-metal fuselage was specified for the next production batches of the Boeing fighter, comprising 110 P-12Es (Model 234) and 25 P-12Fs (Model 251) for the Army and 21 F4B-3s and 74 F4B-4s (Model 235) for the Navy. The F4B-4 model introduced a broad-chord vertical tail and larger headrest behind the open cockpit. Differences between the P-12E and P-12F were limited to the engine, respectively the R-1340-17 and R-1340-19.

Fourteen F4B-4s were exported to Brazil, followed by nine Model 267s, combining features of the P-12E and F4B-3. Included in the total production of this classic biplane fighter were two Model 100Es for Spain and a single Model 100F used by Pratt & Whitney for engine development.

Boeing B-9

Although not built in large numbers, and operated only on a service trial basis by the US Army Air Corps, the B-9 was a significant aircraft in the history of bomber design. Incorporating such advanced features – for 1931 – as a retractable landing gear and all-metal construction, it put US bomber performance into the same bracket as that of contemporary fighters for the first time.

Like many technological advances, the B-9 was the result of private-venture initiative by Boeing rather than an officially-sponsored requirement. Pursuing an aggressive design policy, Boeing had produced its Model 200 Monomail, a low-wing, all-metal commercial mail and freight carrier with internal bracing for the wing and a retractable undercarriage. Having proved the load-carrying ability and overall performance of the Monomail, the company then put in hand the construction of two prototypes of a twin-engined bomber with the same design features.

Following normal inter-war practice, the Air Corps undertook to test the prototype Boeing bomber, Model 215, at Wright Field and it was given the experimental designation XB-901. The first flight was made on 29 April 1931, and the bomber was flown across country in June at an average speed of 158 mph. The Air Corps liked what it saw of the XB-901 and gave Boeing a contract to buy it and six others.

As tested, the prototype had unsupercharged R-1860-13 Hornet engines. When these were changed for supercharged R-1860-11s, the top speed went up to 188 mph and the designation became YB-9. Five production aircraft, delivered in 1932 and 1933 as Model 246, and designated Y1B-9A, were similar. Final aircraft on the contract was the second prototype, already started by Boeing. This was completed as Model 214 (Y1B-9) with Curtiss V-1570-29 in-line engines.

The B-9 carried a crew of five in open cockpits and had an armament of 2,200 lb of bombs and two 0·30-in machine-guns.

Boeing P-26

When the Boeing company flew its Model 200 Monomail commercial mail carrier in May 1930, it established new design and engineering features which were quickly applied to both bomber and fighter designs. The first Boeing fighter to take advantage of the all-metal, cantilever low-wing philosophy was the Model 248, three prototypes of which were laid down at the company's own expense in 1931. The US Army Air Corps collaborated in the design and provided military equipment for the prototypes, the first of which flew on 30 March 1932.

For official trials, the three Boeing fighters were designated XP-936; purchased subsequently by the Army Air Corps, they became XP-26, Y1P-26 and P-26 respectively. When the Army ordered a production quantity of a slightly refined version of the Model 248 in January 1933, they became its first monoplane fighters and its first all-metal production fighters. The contract covered production of 111 Boeing Model 266s and these were built as P-26As. Deliveries began in December 1933 and the P-26As became standard equipment for Air Corps pursuit groups in Hawaii and the Panama Canal Zone. All were modified after delivery to have wing flaps.

The first two of a second contract for 25 of the Boeing fighters were delivered as P-26Bs, with R-1340-33 fuel-injection engines, and the other 23 as P-26Cs with R-1340-27 engines (as fitted in the P-26As) and minor control changes. They were all eventually modified to P-26B standard.

One export model of the design was sold to Spain as Model 281 and 11 more went to China, where they were used in combat against Japanese invaders in 1937. Boeing P-26As turned over to the Philippine Army in 1941 were in action on the day of the Pearl Harbor attack.

Boeing P-26A

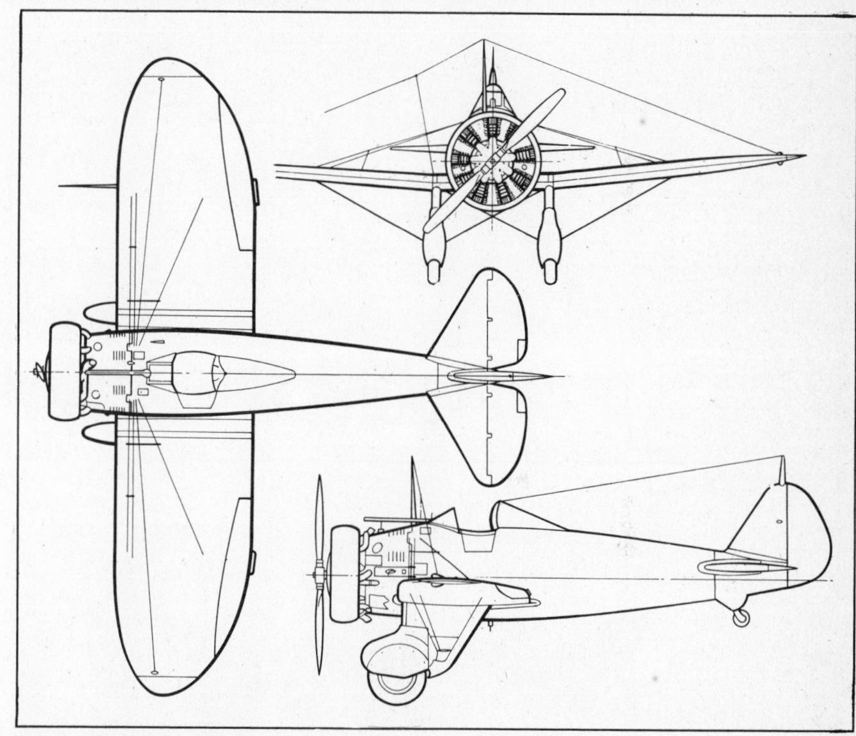

Boeing P-26A

TYPE	DIMENSIONS						WEIGHT	PERFORMANCE				REMARKS
	span ft	*span* in	*length* ft	*length* in	*height* ft	*height* in	*max t-o* lb	*max speed* mph	*at height* ft	*service ceiling* ft	*combat range* miles	
Boeing P-12	30	0	20	1	9	7	2,536	171	5,000	28,200	NA	
Boeing P-12B	30	0	20	3	8	10	2,638	166·5	5,000	27,450	540	
Boeing P-12D	30	0	20	1	8	8	2,648	188	7,000	25,400	475	
Boeing P-12E	30	0	20	3	9	0	2,690	189	7,000	26,300	NA	
Boeing P-12F	30	0	20	3	9	0	2,726	194·5	10,000	31,400	NA	
Boeing F4B-1	30	0	20	1	9	4	3,169	176	6,000	27,700	371	
Boeing F4B-2	30	0	20	1	9	1	3,260	186	6,000	26,900	403	
Boeing F4B-4	30	0	20	5	9	9	3,611	187	6,000	27,500	401	
Boeing Y1B-9A	76	10	52	0	12	0	14,320	188	6,000	20,750	540	
Boeing P-26A	27	11½	23	10	10	5	3,012	234	7,500	27,400	360	
Boeing 281	27	11½	23	7¼	7	10½	3,390	235	6,000	28,200	386	

Boeing Y1B-17 Flying Fortress

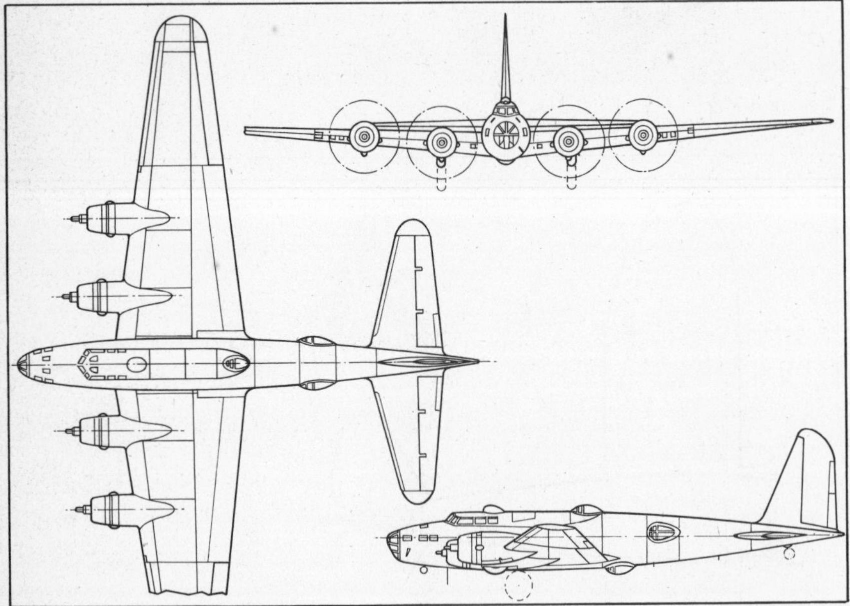

Boeing B-17B Flying Fortress

Boeing B-17C Flying Fortress, RAF

Boeing B-17F Flying Fortress

Boeing B-17/PB-1 Flying Fortress

Destined to become the spearhead of the United States Army Air Force's attacks on Occupied Europe during World War II, the B-17 began life as a purely defensive weapon. When Boeing started work on its Model 299 bomber in 1934, the offensive rôle of air power was still ill-defined and only dimly recognized. Even the adoption of the four-engined Model 299 in the strictly circumscribed rôle of off-shore anti-shipping defence brought strong opposition from the US Navy.

The Air Corps outlined a new requirement for a multi-engined bomber early in 1934 and announced in August of the same year that a prototype competition would be held in 1935. Hitherto, the term "multi-engined" had usually meant twin-engined, but Boeing decided to adopt a four-engined layout in order to obtain a big performance advance on the Martin B-10.

The Boeing 299 was conceived as a clean, low-wing monoplane with internal bomb stowage and five enclosed gun stations for defence. Construction of a prototype was rushed, at Boeing's expense, to achieve a first flight on 28 July 1935. When it was delivered to Wright Field for tests one month later, it flew across the continent at an average speed of 252 mph – an unprecedented performance for a bomber.

Air Corps acceptance of the B-17, as the Model 299 was designated, was enthusiastic but funds were short. By August 1939, on the eve of the outbreak of war in Europe, a total of 90 B-17s had been ordered but fewer than 30 had been delivered. Under a March 1940 agreement, 20 B-17Cs already in production were released for use by the Royal Air Force, in return for information on operational experience in Europe. This feed-back of information, following marginally successful high-altitude daylight missions over Germany in 1941, led to development of the B-17D and B-17E. The former introduced self-sealing tanks and small refinements, while the latter was an extensive re-design to increase armour and armament.

While the original Model 299 had been powered by Pratt & Whitney Hornet R-1690E engines of 750 hp each, all subsequent production models had versions of the Wright Cyclone R-1820. The first production version was the Y1B-17 (later B-17), which differed from the prototype in only minor detail and in its engines. Twelve of these were followed by 39 B-17Bs which made use of turbo-supercharged engines after trial in a single Y1B-17A. In the B-17Cs, of which 38 were procured, the two side gun blisters were removed and the ventral blister was replaced by a larger, flatter fairing. Only minor changes distinguished the 42 B-17Ds.

In the B-17E, a determined effort was made to make the Flying Fortress more battleworthy. Important innovations were a tail turret, a ventral "ball" turret, a power-operated front upper turret, use of 0·50-in machine-guns throughout, and enlarged tail surfaces.

Boeing built 512 B-17Es and 45 of these went to the RAF on lend-lease. Operating both in Europe and the Pacific, the B-17E was the first variant really to live up to the name of "Flying Fortress". This and the slightly different B-17F became widely used; the latter was also the subject of a massive manufacturing programme in which Douglas and Lockheed-Vega participated with the Boeing factory at Seattle. In all, 3,400 B-17Fs were built, 19 going to the RAF.

A further modification, to improve the ability of the B-17 to repel attacking fighters, produced the B-17G, with a two-gun "chin" turret. Production totalled 4,035 by Boeing, 2,395 by Douglas and 2,250 by Lockheed; at the peak, Boeing's Seattle plant alone was turning out 16 B-17Gs every 24 hours. The RAF received 85 B-17Gs.

Apart from the straightforward bomber variants of the B-17, several other versions appeared. These included about 25 aircraft converted into BQ-7 radio-controlled bombers and some F-9 long-range reconnaissance versions. In addition, a heavily-armed version of the design was produced as the B-40, in an unsuccessful attempt to provide an escort fighter for the B-17 formations. One prototype and 20 production conversions were made, some B-40s carrying up to 30 machine-guns and cannon.

Forty B-17s were transferred to the USN for anti-submarine and early-warning duties as PB-1Ws. These carried a massive radome under the fuselage.

Boeing B-29 Superfortress

If for no other reason, the B-29 is sure of its place in history as the aircraft used for the only two atomic bomb attacks of World War II, over Hiroshima on 6 August 1945 and Nagasaki on 14 August 1945. In fact, the B-29 has other claims to fame. In conventional operations against Japan in 1944 and 1945, it gave convincing demonstrations of strategic bombing; it became the first bomber to equip the newly-formed USAF Strategic Air Command in 1946, and it was one of the first types to see action in the Korean War in June 1950.

The Superfortress, as the B-29 was named, was produced to meet an official requirement for a "Hemisphere Defense Weapon", issued to industry in February 1940. Boeing designers had prepared a series of project studies for bombers with very-long-range characteristics as developments of the XB-15 and B-17 designs, and these studies were taken a stage further in Model 345, submitted in response to the USAF. request. Model 345 featured a streamlined, circular-section fuselage with pressurized accommodation for the crew, a mid-wing of high aspect ratio and four Wright R-3350 radial engines in low-drag nacelles. Armament was concentrated in remotely controlled turrets, two above and two below the fuselage, each containing two 0·50-in machine-guns, with three more guns in a tail mounting.

The Boeing 345 was adjudged best of four design proposals considered by the USAAF and two prototypes were ordered as XB-29s on 24 August 1940. These two aircraft first flew on 21 September 1942 and 28 December 1942 respectively. By this time more than 1,500 B-29s had been ordered and production was being established at two Boeing plants, in Wichita and Renton, and at Bell's Marietta plant and Martin's Omaha factory.

First of the pre-production Superfortresses flew on 26 June 1943, and deliveries to the first unit were made in July. Operations of the B-29 were concentrated against Japanese targets, initially from bases in India and China, starting on 5 June 1944. Providing and provisioning bases for the B-29 was itself a major problem in logistics; during 1944, five bases were built in the Mariana Islands, each large enough for 180 B-29s, and from these bases devastating attacks against the Japanese mainland began.

Production of the B-29 totalled 1,644 from Wichita, 668 from Marietta and 536 from Omaha. Renton produced 1,122 B-29As, with increased span and other small changes, and Bell also produced 311 B-29Bs at Marietta, with all but the tail armament deleted to increase the payload. Contracts for more than 5,000 more B-29s were cancelled after Japan's surrender in August 1945, but development proceeded on an improved version which became the B-50 (see page 456). Many special B-29 variants appeared, for photo and weather reconnaissance, as flight refuelling tankers and for air/sea rescue. These were all conversions of the original bombers.

Four B-29s were obtained by the US Navy and modified

Boeing B-17G Flying Fortress

Boeing F-13A, photo-reconnaissance version of B-29A Superfortress

Boeing Washington B Mk 1, RAF

TYPE	DIMENSIONS span ft	span in	length ft	length in	height ft	height in	WEIGHT max t-o lb	PERFORMANCE max speed mph	at height ft	service ceiling ft	combat range miles	REMARKS
Boeing YB-17	103	9	68	4	18	4	42,600	256	14,000	30,600	1,377	
Boeing B-17B	103	9	67	11	15	5	46,650	291.5	25,000	36,000	2,400	
Boeing B-17C	103	9	67	11	15	5	49,650	323	25,000	37,000	2,000	
Boeing B-17E	103	9	73	10	19	2	53,000	317	25,000	36,600	2,000	
Boeing B-17F	103	9	74	9	19	1	55,000	299	25,000	37,500	1,300	
Boeing B-17G	103	9	74	4	19	1	65,500	287	25,000	35,600	2,000	
Boeing B-29	141	3	99	0	29	7	124,000	358	25,000	31,850	3,250	
Boeing B-29A	141	3	99	0	29	7	141,100	358	25,000	31,850	4,100	

Boeing B-50D Superfortress

Boeing YDB-47E Stratojet, with GAM-63 Rascal missile

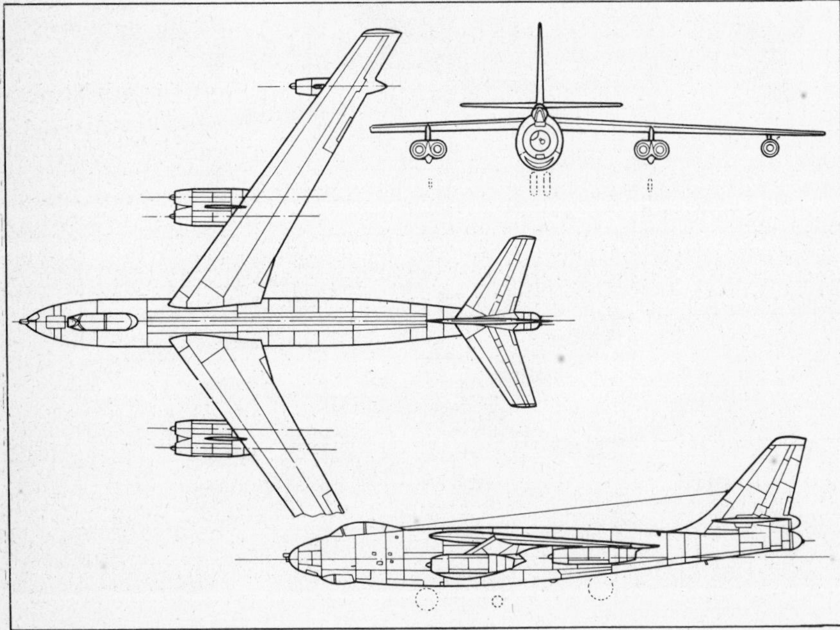
Boeing B-47E Stratojet

Boeing RB-47E Stratojet

for service in the airborne early-warning role as P2B-1Ss.

In 1950, 70 B-29s and B-29As were taken out of storage and supplied to the RAF under the American military aid programme. They were named Washington B Mk 1s and served with Bomber Command for four years.

Boeing B-50 Superfortress

Phase II of Superfortress development (see above) began in 1944 with the conversion of a B-29 to have Pratt & Whitney R-4360 Wasp Major engines. This prototype was re-designated XB-44 and a new production version with the same engines and other improvements became the B-50. Work began on the B-50s at Renton in 1945 and the first of 79 B-50As flew on 25 June 1947. Changes apart from the engines included a taller fin and rudder, a lighter but stronger wing structure, higher operating weights, stronger undercarriage, hydraulic rudder boost and other improvements. A further increase in maximum weight, from 140,000 lb to 170,000 lb was made in the B-50B, of which 45 were built in 1949.

To extend the aircraft's range, two 700 US-gallon external fuel tanks were designed for underwing installation on the B-50D. Production of the Superfortress concluded with 222 of this model. All B-50s were delivered to Strategic Air Command, and starting in 1947 many of the earlier versions were converted to serve with strategic reconnaissance squadrons, carrying cameras and electronic search equipment.

Other conversion programmes produced TB-50 trainers, WB-50s for weather reconnaissance and finally 126 KB-50 jet-boosted flight-refuelling tankers.

Boeing B-47 Stratojet

During 1944, with the first jet fighters already n production, plans were made by the USAAF to initiate development of jet bombers. So that a start could be made, the requirements were kept as simple as possible – a 2,000-mile range and a speed of 500 mph at 40,000 ft. By the end of 1944, four designs had been submitted and all were ordered for prototype trials. Only two achieved quantity production, and of these the Boeing bomber was built in the greater numbers.

Influenced by the results of German aerodynamic research, which began to become available during 1945, Boeing revised their submission towards the end of that year. As a result, the Boeing XB-47 was the only one of the quartet of prototypes to have a swept-back wing, and was also the last to fly, on 17 December 1947. With its slender, streamlined fuselage, bicycle landing gear, high aspect ratio laminar-flow wing and six podded engines, the XB-47 was a big step forward aerodynamically, structurally and operationally. It was the first aeroplane developed as a complete weapon system and the first jet bomber to serve in quantity with Strategic Air Command.

Production of the Stratojet began with an order for ten B-47As, which had J47 turbojets replacing the prototype's J35s. The first of these flew on 25 June 1950, at about the same time that the Korean War brought a sudden increase in the demand for weapons of all kinds – including the B-47. New production lines were established by Lockheed at Marietta and Douglas at Tulsa to supplement the Boeing output from Wichita. These three lines together built 380 B-47Bs, which could carry 1,500-gallon underwing fuel tanks and had provision for in-flight refuelling. Many were later converted for reconnaissance or training as RB-47Bs and TB-47Bs, or to B-47B-II standard with later engines, revised tail armament and ejection seats.

The B-47E followed the B-47B into production at all three factories in 1952, the first flight being made on 30 January 1953. This version differed from the B-47B in having J47-GE-25 engines instead of -11 or -23 models; two 20-mm cannon in the radar-controlled tail turret instead of 12·7-mm guns; a jettisonable JATO pack in place of a fixed installation; a 16-ft drag parachute to shorten the landing run; and ejection seats for the crew of three who sat in tandem under the large canopy.

Production of the B-47E included 1,359 bombers and

255 RB-47E reconnaissance versions with cameras in the bomb-bay, with all three production lines contributing to the total. At Wichita, Boeing also built 35 RB-47Hs, a version specially equipped for electronic reconnaissance around the Russian borders. This Stratojet model carried a pod in the bomb-bay containing electronic recording gear and three operators. Several other variants were introduced, by modification of the B-47, for weather reconnaissance (RB-47K and WB-47), missile launching (YDB-47B) and target drones (QB-47).

At peak deployment of the B-47, in 1957, Strategic Air Command had 1,800 in service. This total then declined, but the B-47 remained an important component in the USAF's armoury until 1966, when it was transferred to reserve status.

Boeing B-52 Stratofortress

Although the B-52 appeared in 1952 as the "big brother" of the B-47 Stratojet and became the most significant strategic bomber operated by the USAF in its deterrent rôle, the aircraft began life in a very different guise. Official interest in a very long-range turbine-engined bomber dates back to April 1945. The relative merits of turboprop and turbojet engines at that time were such that it appeared necessary to use the turboprop to obtain the appropriate range.

Boeing won a design contest in June 1946, but further study showed that the required range, even using turboprops, could be obtained only by use of flight refuelling. By 1948, the turbojet was becoming more attractive and the whole design was changed to introduce the new engines and a swept-back wing – this despite the fact that a prototype contract for two XB-52s had already been placed with the company.

The first of the two B-52 prototypes flew on 15 April 1952, and its design was revealed to be similar in general principles to that of the B-47. One significant change made in the B-52A production models, the first of which flew on 5 August 1954, was in flight deck layout, with two pilots side-by-side instead of in tandem. Provision was also made for in-flight refuelling, under-wing tanks, cross-wind landing gear and later engines. Three B-52As were followed by 47 B-52Bs and RB-52Bs (the latter carrying a camera/electronics reconnaissance pack in the bomb-bay with a two-man operating crew).

Strategic Air Command received its first B-52B in June 1955 and deliveries of the B-52 continued from then until October 1962. In all, the Boeing factories at Seattle and Wichita built a total of 744 B-52s and a substantial number of these remained in service in 1968 as SAC's primary manned bomber, capable of delivering a nuclear weapon to any target in the world at short notice. A proportion of the B-52 force was constantly airborne, with weapons in the bomb-bay and target maps on the flight deck, to provide the USA with the shortest possible "reaction" time in the event of a surprise attack.

Versions of the Stratofortress, designated B-52C, B-52D, B-52E and B-52F, were built at both Seattle and Wichita and differed from each other primarily in the engine model and operational equipment fitted. In the B-52G, exclusively a Wichita version and first

Boeing ERB-47H Stratojet

Boeing B-52D Stratofortress

Boeing B-52G Stratofortress, with AGM-28 Hound Dog missiles

TYPE	DIMENSIONS span ft	in	length ft	in	height ft	in	WEIGHT max t-o lb	PERFORMANCE max speed mph	at height ft	service ceiling ft	combat range miles	REMARKS
Boeing B-50A	141	3	99	0	32	8	168,480	385	25,000	37,000	4,650	
Boeing B-50D	141	3	99	0	32	8	173,000	380	25,000	36,700	4,900	
Boeing B-47B	116	0	107	2	27	11	185,000	630+	SL	45,000	3,870	
Boeing B-47E	116	0	109	10	27	11	206,700	606	16,300	40,500	4,000	
Boeing B-52B	185	0	157	7	48	3	400,000	NA	NA	NA	NA	
Boeing B-52G	185	0	157	7	40	8	480,000	660	20,000	55,000	10,000	
Boeing B-52H	185	0	157	7	40	8	490,000	630	40,000	55,000	12,000	

Boeing B-52H Stratofortress, with Skybolt test vehicles

Brewster XSBA-1

Brewster B-339D Buffalo, Netherlands East Indies Air Force

Brewster F2A-1 Buffalo, Finnish Air Force

flown on 26 October 1958, integral fuel tankage was provided in the wing, provision was made for the North American AGM-28 Hound Dog missile to be carried under each wing and a remotely-controlled tail turret was introduced. Production of this version totalled 193.

Final production version of the Stratofortress was the B-52H, with TF33 turbofan engines. The lower fuel consumption of these engines gave a significant increase in range, as demonstrated in January 1962 when a B-52H flew 12,519 miles non-stop from Okinawa to Madrid. The B-52H had also been designed to carry four GAM-77 Skybolt air-to-surface missiles, but development of this weapon was cancelled in 1962. The first B-52H was flown on 6 March 1961, and the last of 102 built was completed in March 1962.

Brewster SBA/SBN

When the US Navy launched its two big new aircraft carriers in 1936 – the USS *Enterprise* and *Yorktown* – the way was opened for procurement of additional aircraft to equip these ships. Particular interest centred on the two-seat scout-bomber at that time, and four new prototypes appeared in 1936 in the "SB" (scout-bomber) category, as well as a couple of new torpedo bombers.

One of the 1936-model SBs was the first product of the Brewster company. A clean mid-wing monoplane with a Wright R-1820-4 radial engine, this was the XSBA-1. The crew of two sat in tandem beneath a long "glasshouse" canopy and the design featured the inward-retracting undercarriage, with wheel stowage in the fuselage, which was to become a characteristic of later Brewster designs. Bomb stowage was internal.

The XSBA-1 began its tests in April 1936 and was fitted later with a 950-hp XR-1820-22 engine, in which form it achieved a top speed of 263 mph.

Because the Brewster company did not at the time have adequate capacity, quantity production of the type was entrusted to the Naval Aircraft Factory, which turned out 30, as SBN-1s. Production deliveries were extended over the period from November 1940 to March 1942, by which time the design had been overtaken by newer types. A few equipped VT-8 squadron for training before this unit went on board the USS *Hornet*.

Brewster F2A Buffalo

When deliveries of the Brewster F2A began in June 1939, it was the first monoplane fighter to go into service with the US Navy. Like many other aeroplanes which established new standards, the F2As achieved little operational success but they served their purpose in setting the scene for those which followed. Before ordering the Brewster fighter, the Navy had tested prototypes of the Curtiss Hawk 75 and a variant of the Seversky P-35. These trials indicated that carrier operations would need a specially-developed fighter, and the Brewster Model 139 resulted from this specific Navy requirement.

Ordered in June 1936, the prototype XF2A-1 was first flown in January 1938. Powered by a Wright XR-1820-22 radial engine, it was an all-metal mid-wing monoplane with split flaps to hold down the landing speed and a characteristic Brewster landing gear. Armament comprised one 0·30-in and one 0·50-in machine-gun. A production order was placed in June 1938 for 54 F2A-1s (Model B-239) with R-1820-34 engines. Only eleven of these were delivered to the US Navy, serving on board the USS *Saratoga*; the remainder were released for export, with one other example, to Finland via Sweden in 1939.

For export, these aircraft had R-1820-G5 engines and four 0·5-in Colt-Browning machine-guns. They were in service with the Finnish Air Force by February 1940 and served with conspicuous success for five years.

Meanwhile, flight testing of the original Brewster prototype, re-engined with an R-1820-40 as the XF2A-2, had begun in July 1939 and a production batch of 43 F2A-2s was ordered to replace those released for Finland. During production of the F2A-2, the armament was increased to four 0·5-in guns and provision was made for two 100-lb bombs under each wing.

In an effort to make the Brewster fighter more combat-worthy, increased armour protection for the pilot and fuel tank, and an armoured windscreen, were introduced in the F2A-3. The USN ordered 108 in January 1941 and 21 of these, operated by the Marine Corps in the Battle of Midway, were the only examples to see combat in US service. The single XF2A-4 had a pressurized cabin.

Export orders for land-based versions of the design were obtained from Belgian and British Purchasing Commissions in 1939 and 1940. Belgium ordered 40 (Model B-339) but most were diverted to Britain after Belgium fell in 1940. Another 170 (Model B-339E) were ordered for the RAF for service in the Far East, but proved no match for Japanese attackers and were soon withdrawn from front-line service.

The Netherlands East Indies air force purchased 72 export models, designated B-339D, and these saw service from January 1942 in the Pacific area. Another 20 B-439s were ordered for the Netherlands East Indies but there is no evidence that these were delivered.

A total of 507 of all versions were built.

Brewster SB2A Buccaneer

While the Naval Aircraft Factory was getting the first Brewster design (the SBA-1, see page 458) into production, work went ahead on a larger development of the same aircraft. Ordered by the US Navy in April 1939, this XSB2A-1 had a similar configuration but provision was made for a power-operated turret at the rear of the cabin enclosure, and the main wheels retracted into the wing rather than the fuselage. Internal stowage was provided for a 1,000-lb bomb.

The XSB2A-1 was first flown on 17 June 1941, and production deliveries began in July 1942 of 450 ordered by the RAF. Named Bermuda, these did not have the prototype's dorsal turret, and never saw front-line service. Many were adapted as target tugs after delivery to Britain.

Another export contract was negotiated with the Netherlands East Indies, for 160 aircraft, but these were commandeered by the US Navy in March 1943, before delivery. Designated SB2A-4s, they were allocated to the Marines for use as trainers.

The US Navy gave the Brewster dive-bomber the name Buccaneer and ordered 140. The first 80 were SB2A-2s, armed with four 0·30-in and two 0·50-in guns. The final 60 were SB2A-3s, with folding wings and arrester gear for carrier operations. These aircraft never reached operational squadrons, being relegated to training and other second-line duties.

Consolidated P2Y

Consolidated Aircraft Company, in Buffalo, New York, obtained its first contract to build a flying-boat for the US Navy on 28 February 1928. The aircraft, designated XPY-1, had been designed by Navy engineers, as part of a continuing effort to produce a patrol flying-boat with sufficient range to fly between oversea bases in Hawaii, the Philippines, Alaska and the Canal Zone.

The XPY-1 was a parasol monoplane with a 100-ft span, fabric-covered wing, a single-step hull and three engines – two between the wing and fuselage and one above the wing. A small production batch of virtually the same design was built by Glenn L. Martin, while Consolidated won a contract on 26 May 1931 for a new prototype, the XP2Y-1.

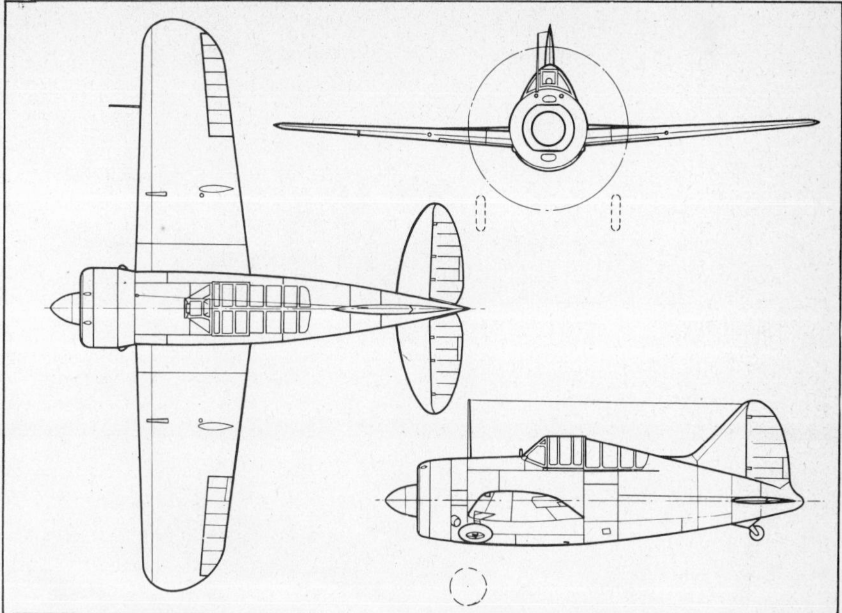

Brewster F2A-2 Buffalo

Brewster SB2A-2 Buccaneer

Brewster Bermuda Mk I, RAF

TYPE	DIMENSIONS span ft	span in	length ft	length in	height ft	height in	WEIGHT max t-o lb	PERFORMANCE max speed mph	at height ft	service ceiling ft	combat range miles	REMARKS
Brewster SBN-1	39	0	27	8	12	5	6,759	254	15,200	28,300	1,015	
Brewster F2A-1	35	0	26	0	11	8	5,370	301	17,000	32,500	1,095	
Brewster F2A-3	35	0	26	4	12	0	7,159	321	16,500	33,200	965	
Brewster SB2A-2	47	0	39	2	15	5	14,289	274	12,000	24,900	720	
Brewster SB2A-4	47	0	39	2	15	5	13,811	275	12,000	25,400	750	

Consolidated P2Y-2

Consolidated A-11

Consolidated PB-2A

Consolidated PBY-5A Catalina

The XP2Y-1, delivered on 18 April 1932, added small-span lower wings and stabilizing floats in place of the pontoons used on the XPY-1. The engines were three 575-hp Wright Cyclones in ring cowls, but the top engine was removed during May and the 46 production models were delivered as twin-engined sesquiplanes.

The first 23 production aircraft were P2Y-1s, and six of these 'boats from Navy Squadron VP-10F flew in formation non-stop from San Francisco to Hawaii in January 1934. After one P2Y-1 had been modified to XP2Y-2 standard, with R-1820-88 engines in nacelles on, instead of under, the wing, another 23 similar aircraft were built as P2Y-3s, the engines being R-1820-90s. Consolidated also built six of these flying-boats for Argentina and sold one each to Japan and Colombia. They remained in service for training with the USN until after the end of 1941.

Consolidated P-30/PB-2/A-11

Prior to the outbreak of World War II, only one two-seat monoplane fighter entered service with the USAAC. This was the Consolidated PB-2, the outcome of a somewhat protracted development programme which began in 1931 at the Lockheed plant in Detroit. Lockheed, then a subsidiary of Detroit Aircraft, projected a two-seat monoplane fighter variant of its commercial Altair. This was studied as the XP-900, and the USAAC then purchased the prototype as the YP-24 and ordered eight more examples – four Y1P-24s and four Y1A-9s in the attack category.

Detroit Aircraft failed to honour this contract, but Lockheed engineers responsible for design of the YP-24 joined Consolidated and in March 1932 the latter company obtained contracts for two examples of a similar aircraft, one designated Y1P-25 and the other XA-11. Of all-metal construction, these two prototypes had the Curtiss V-1570-27 engine, the pursuit with a turbo-supercharger and the attack aircraft without. Like the original Altair, they had tandem cockpits under a long canopy, and inward-retracting landing gear.

Both the Y1P-25 and the XA-11 suffered mishaps during flight tests, but not before they had demonstrated a sufficiently promising performance for additional examples to be ordered, comprising four P-30s and four A-11s. The P-30s had 675-hp V-1570-57 engines and other changes. They were followed, after trials in August 1934 at Wright Field, by 50 P-30As ordered in December 1934. Soon after delivery, these aircraft were redesignated PB-2A, and two surviving P-30s became PB-2s.

The PB-2A carried an armament of two fixed forward-firing guns and a single 0·30-in gun on a flexible mount in the rear cockpit. Experience showed that at the speeds made possible by the comparatively advanced shape of the PB-2A, the rear gunner had little hope of aiming accurately and the two-seat pursuit category was dropped.

Consolidated PBY Catalina

On 28 October 1933, the US Navy signed a contract with Consolidated for the construction of a prototype flying-boat of new design, in competition with a Douglas design, the XP3D. These prototypes were the first Navy patrol boats to have cantilever wings, dispensing with the liberal strutting which previously had been necessary. Both were twin-engined and the Consolidated prototype, designated XP3Y-1 and designed by Isaac M. Laddon, had unique retractable floats beneath the wings, which formed the wingtips when retracted. The wing was carried parasol fashion by a large pylon above the fuselage. The engines were 825-hp Pratt & Whitney R-1830-54 Wasps.

Construction of the XP3Y-1 was all-metal. It carried four 0·30-in guns, including one in a manual turret in the nose, and could carry up to two tons of bombs. Delivered from the Consolidated factory at Buffalo on 28 March 1935, the XP3Y-1 showed a promising performance including a high speed of 184 mph. In May 1936, it was redesignated XPBY-1 and the 60 production models ordered by the US Navy one year earlier took the PBY-1 designation. Navy Squadron VP11F took delivery of the XPBY-1 in October 1936 and the first production PBY-1s followed a little later. These aircraft had R-1830-64 engines, as did the 50 PBY-2s ordered in July 1936. Sixty-six PBY-3s ordered in November 1936 had R-1830-66 engines and 33 PBY-4s ordered in December 1937 had 1,050-hp R-1830-72s. All but the first PBY-4 had large transparent blisters over the waist gun positions, in place of sliding hatches, and these blisters became a characteristic feature of late aircraft in the series.

Permission for the new flying-boat to be exported was granted to Consolidated in 1938, and three were immediately ordered by the U.S.S.R. where the type subsequently went into production as the GST. Re-engined with M-62 radials, the GST was built in large numbers in the Soviet Union and served as standard equipment throughout the war. A single example of the PBY was also purchased by the Royal Air Force and was delivered in July 1939 for evaluation.

The RAF gave the Consolidated 'boat the name Catalina, and this same name was adopted by the US Navy on 1 October 1941. An initial RAF contract for 50 was doubled during 1940, and other export contracts were placed by France for 30, by Canada for 50, by Australia for 18 and by the Netherlands East Indies for 36.

While work progressed on these contracts, the PBY-5 was put into production for the US Navy. This variant had 1,200-hp R-1830-82 or -92 engines and redesigned vertical tail surfaces, as well as many detail improvements. The British Catalina Is were similar, with export R-1830-S1C3G engines and revised armament. The first 14 for Canada were designated Catalina Ia (the name Canso being adopted later) while another 36, later transferred to the RAF, were Catalina IIAs.

Two hundred PBY-5s were ordered by the US Navy in December 1939, but in November the XPBY-5A had appeared as a rebuild of the first PBY-4, with amphibian capability. These aircraft differed primarily in having a retractable tricycle undercarriage in the hull. The Navy ordered the final 33 aircraft on its PBY-5 contract to be completed to this standard and another 134 PBY-5As were ordered in November 1940. Twelve went to the RAF as Catalina IIIs and another 12 were included in the Netherlands East Indies contract.

Additional contracts from the US Navy brought production of the PBY-5 for that service to a total of 753, while PBY-5A production came to a final total of 794. The RAF received 225 PBY-5Bs under lend-lease and designated them Catalina Ia; another 97, with anti-submarine and anti-shipping radar, were used by Coastal Command as Catalina IVAs. The USAAF received 56 of the amphibians on transfer from the Navy as OA-10s.

Production of the PBY series ended at the Convair plant in San Diego in March 1944, but four other production lines had been established, apart from that in Russia. First had been the Naval Aircraft Factory, awarded a contract in July 1941 for 156 aircraft. Designated PBN-1 Nomad, these began to appear in February 1943, and featured a taller vertical tail and detail improvements; 137 of this batch went to Russia. A similar model went into production at a new Consolidated factory in New Orleans in July 1943, and 235 were built as PBY-6A amphibians. The Navy transferred 75 to the Army as

Consolidated Catalina GR Mk IIA, RAF

Consolidated OA-10A

TYPE	DIMENSIONS						WEIGHT	PERFORMANCE				REMARKS
	span		*length*		*height*		*max t-o*	*max speed*	*at height*	*service ceiling*	*combat range*	
	ft	*in*	*ft*	*in*	*ft*	*in*	*lb*	*mph*	*ft*	*ft*	*miles*	
Consolidated P2Y-1	100	0	61	9	16	8	21,547	126	SL	11,000	1,768	
Consolidated P2Y-3	100	0	61	9	19	1	25,266	139	4,000	16,100	1,180	
Consolidated P-30	43	11	29	4	8	4	5,092	239	15,000	NA	495	
Consolidated PB-2A	43	11	30	0	8	3	5,643	2,745	25,000	28,000	508	
Consolidated PBY-1	104	0	65	2	18	6	28,500	177	8,000	20,900	1,210	
Consolidated PBY-4	104	0	65	2	18	6	32,011	197	12,000	24,100	1,285	
Consolidated PBY-5	104	0	63	10	18	11	34,000	195	7,000	17,700	2,370	
Consolidated PBY-5A	104	0	63	10	20	2	35,300	179	7,000	14,700	1,660	

Consolidated PB2Y-2 Coronado

Consolidated Coronado Mk I (PB2Y-3), RAF

Consolidated LB-30A Liberator, RAF

Consolidated B-24D Liberator, 98th Bombardment Group

OA-10Bs and another 48 went to the Soviet Union.

Two more production lines were established in Canada, by Boeing at Vancouver and Canadian Vickers at Montreal. The latter built 230 PBV-1A amphibians, all of which were transferred to the Army as OA-10As, and another 149 Cansos for the RCAF. Boeing built 240 PB2B-1s, similar to the PBY-5, almost all of which went to the Royal Air Force as Catalina IVBs. The 50 PB2B-2s had the tall fin of the PBN-1 and these, too, were allocated to the RAF in the closing stages of the war, with the designation Catalina VI. Boeing also produced 17 Catalinas and 55 Canso amphibians for the RCAF.

Including Russian production of the GST, the grand total of Catalina variants built approached 4,000 – believed to be the largest total for any flying-boat design in the world. Catalinas served with distinction in most operational theatres and continued in service for several years after the war. Surplus aircraft were also obtained by numerous overseas air forces for overwater patrol duties, and later standards of radar and other specialized equipment were added in post-war modifications.

Consolidated PB2Y Coronado

With the Consolidated PBY established in production and service, the US Navy drew up a specification in 1936 for a flying-boat with a better performance and greater load-carrying ability. Prototypes of four-engined 'boats of advanced design were built by Sikorsky (XPBS-1) and Consolidated to meet this requirement. The Consolidated 'boat, ordered in July 1936 and first flown on 17 December 1937 as the XPB2Y-1, had some features of the PBY, including the retractable wing-tip floats and all-metal construction. The large hull accommodated a crew of ten and a 12,000-lb bomb-load, together with two 0·30-in and two 0·50-in guns. The engines were R-1830-72s.

In the course of a lengthy period of development, the XPB2Y-1 twice underwent modifications of the tail unit and rear hull shape. Further changes were made in the hull design of the PB2Y-2, six examples of which were ordered in March 1939. Armament was increased in this version to six 0·50s and the type name Coronado was adopted when the PB2Y-2 went into service in 1941. One of the six aircraft was converted into the XPB2Y-2B with R-1830-88 engines, self-sealing fuel tanks, 2,000 lb of armour protection and eight 0·50-in guns. This was the standard for 210 production model PB2Y-3s delivered between June 1942 and the end of 1943. Ten were supplied to the RAF and were used as transports, as were 31 converted to PB2Y-3R for the USN, with turrets and other military equipment deleted and provision for 44 passengers.

The PB2Y-3Rs were re-engined with R-1830-92s for improved performance low down, and a similar programme was completed to convert PB2Y-3s into PB2Y-5s, with increased fuel capacity and extra equipment. Several PB2Y-5H models served as ambulances in the Pacific area, with accommodation for 25 stretchers.

Consolidated B-24/PB4Y Liberator

Design work on the aircraft which became the B-24 Liberator began early in 1939, with the object of producing a bomber with better performance than that of the Boeing B-17 (page 454). Although the B-24's operational performance never proved to be an exceptional advance on that of the B-17, the Consolidated bomber served with great distinction during World War II in many different rôles.

The Consolidated Model 32 was designed to take advantage of the research into wings of high aspect ratio undertaken in the United States by an engineer named Davis. This type of wing was first flown by Consolidated on its Model 31 flying-boat, from which the Model 32 also inherited huge twin fins and rudders. The high-lift characteristics of the Davis wing made it possible to adopt a smaller angle of attack, with consequently lower drag and better range. Long range – at least 3,000 miles – was a basic requirement in the United States Army Air Corps specification for the new bomber.

Another important characteristic of the B-24 was its deep, capacious fuselage, which not only permitted internal stowage of a variety of offensive weapons but also made possible adaptation of the design for transport duties. The wing was mounted high on the fuselage to avoid restricting the internal stowage. A tricycle undercarriage was used, for the first time on a large aircraft, although Douglas had also chosen this type for the even larger XB-19, which flew 18 months after the first B-24.

Armament of the Consolidated bomber was, initially, modest: a single gun in the large, completely transparent nose and others, hand-held, at the fuselage waist, dorsal and ventral positions and in the tail.

A contract for a single XB-24 prototype was received by Consolidated on 30 March 1939, with a first flight target nine months later. Consolidated bettered the target by one day and flew the XB-24 on 29 December 1939. By this date, the USAAC had ordered 43 more B-24s, including seven YB-24s for service trials, and the French government had ordered 120. The latter order was added subsequently to a British order for 164 of the new bombers, placed in 1940.

The YB-24s were delivered in 1940 and were followed by the first of the French Liberators which were diverted to Britain. The type name was allotted originally by the RAF and later adopted for the US versions as well. Because of their very long range, these aircraft were of particular value for the Trans-Atlantic Return Ferry Service, an organization which flew ferry pilots back to North America after they had made delivery flights to the United Kingdom. Consequently the first Liberators, called LB-30s, were used in this transport rôle. They were followed, later in 1941, by 20 Liberator Is which went into service with RAF Coastal Command to close the "Atlantic Gap" – that portion of the Atlantic which previously was out of patrol range of land-based bombers in the United Kingdom and United States. These Liberator Is carried an early type of ASV (air-surface vessel) radar and a pack of four 20-mm cannon under the forward fuselage, plus five guns in the fuselage.

Deliveries of the B-24A to the USAAF began in June 1941. Nine were built with six 0·50-in and two 0·30-in guns, and these were used as transports by the Ferry Command. They were followed by nine B-24Cs, which were the first to have the characteristic elliptical cowling, resulting from the use of turbo-superchargers and consequent re-location of the oil coolers on each side of the R-1830-41 engines. The B-24C had a Martin dorsal turret and a Consolidated tail turret, with two guns apiece.

Boulton Paul dorsal and tail turrets were fitted in the 139 Liberator IIs supplied to Britain, with the mechanically-supercharged R-1830-33 engines.

Generally similar to the B-24C, but with R-1830-43 engines and a higher gross weight, the B-24D was the first variant used operationally by USAAF bomber units, in the spring of 1942. Production totalled 2,738, of which 303 were built at a new Consolidated factory at Fort Worth, 2,425 at the original San Diego plant and 10 by Douglas at Tulsa. Armament of the B-24D varied according to the production standard, the later aircraft having ten 0·50-in Brownings and a bomb-load of 12,800 lb. Some B-24Ds also had a Briggs-Sperry two-gun ball turret aft of the bomb-bay, and others had provision to carry two 4,000-lb bombs externally under each wing.

Under lend-lease, the RAF received 260 Liberator IIIs, equivalent to the B-24D but with Boulton Paul turrets, and 122 B-24Ds. These became Liberator IIIAs and Liberator Vs respectively, the latter going to Coastal Command to replace the Liberator II.

Consolidated B-24H Liberator

Consolidated Liberator GR Mk VI (B-24J), RAF

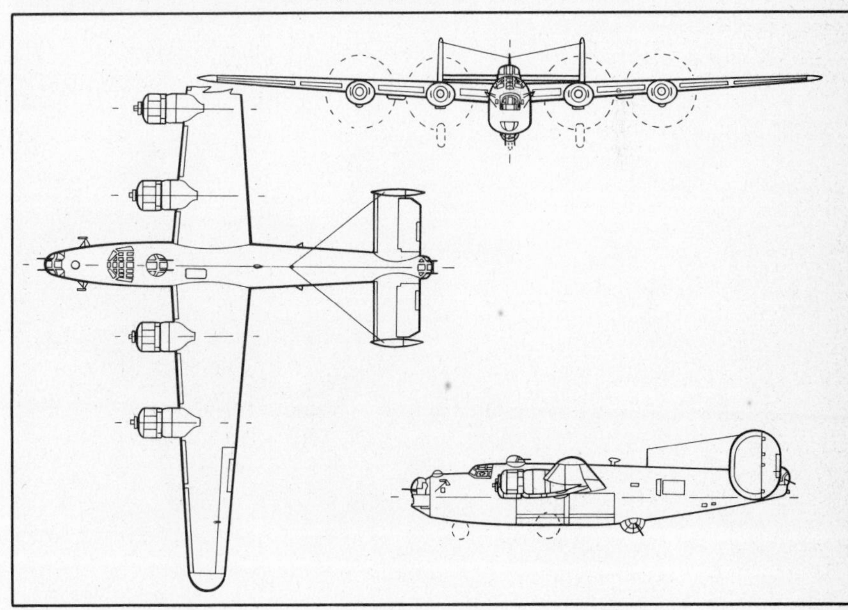

Consolidated B-24J Liberator

TYPE	DIMENSIONS span ft	in	length ft	in	height ft	in	WEIGHT max t-o lb	PERFORMANCE max speed mph	at height ft	service ceiling ft	combat range miles	REMARKS
Consolidated PB2Y-3	115	0	79	3	27	6	68,000	224	19,500	20,900	2,310	

Consolidated B-24J Liberator

Consolidated Liberator (A72), RAAF

Consolidated PB4Y-2 Privateer

Consolidated B-32

Production for the USAAF continued with the B-24E, built at three factories: 144 by Convair at Fort Worth, 167 by Douglas and 480 by the Ford Motor Co at a new plant at Willow Run. Modified propellers were the principal distinguishing feature of the "E" model. Another Liberator production line, operated by North American at Dallas, built 430 B-24Gs, which were similar to the "D" but in some cases had a nose turret, by Emerson or Consolidated.

With this nose turret, R-1830-65 engines and other minor changes, the B-24H was built at Fort Worth (738), at Willow Run (1,780) and at Tulsa (582). Again only minor changes distinguished the B-24J, of which the five factories built a total of 6,678, with a Motor Products nose turret and a Briggs ball turret. The RAF received 1,278 examples of the B-24J, which it used as Liberator VI and VII in Bomber and Coastal Command versions. The US Navy received 977 aircraft, mostly similar to the B-24J, which it designated PB4Y-1 and used for overwater patrols. In most cases, radar replaced the ball turret, and an Erco nose turret replaced the Consolidated turret. First PB4Y-1s were B-24Ds transferred by the Air Force under an agreement of June 1942.

With the tail turret removed and a two-gun manual station instead, the B-24L was built by Consolidated at San Diego (417) and Ford at Willow Run (1,250). These two factories concluded production with, respectively, 916 and 1,677 examples of the B-24M with a Motor Products tail turret.

Although Liberators served with distinction alongside B-17s in Europe, their biggest contribution to the USAAF effort was in the Pacific theatre, where long range was of particular value. Besides being used as bombers and patrol aircraft, the Liberators proved valuable as transports, designated C-87 by the USAAF and RY by the USN. About 100 B-24s were converted for photographic reconnaissance as F-7s, with extra fuel and cameras in the bomb-bay.

By the time the war ended in 1945, the USAAF had decided that future versions of the B-24 should have a single fin and rudder for better stability and control. Following trials with the single-fin XB-24K in 1943, Ford's Willow Run plant was chosen to build the similar B-24N. Only seven YB-24Ns had been built when contracts for another 5,168 were cancelled in May 1945. A transport version, projected as the C-87C, was not built but the USN received 46 similar single-finned RY-3s.

Also for the Navy, Consolidated developed a version of the Liberator with an almost completely new fuselage and a single fin and rudder. This was the PB4Y-2 Privateer, the three prototypes for which were produced by modifying B-24Ds in 1943. Major differences were a 7-ft lengthening of the front fuselage, and the addition of a second dorsal turret and two blister-type waist gun positions to increase the total armament to twelve 0·50-in guns. Deliveries of the PB4Y-2 began in July 1944 and 739 were built, including the three XPB4Y-2s. Some were equipped to carry ASM-N-2 Bat air-to-surface missiles and were designated PB4Y-2B; others, with special gear for anti-submarine duty, were designated PB4Y-2s. The designation was changed to P4Y in the Patrol category in 1951, and some P4Y-2Gs were used by the US Coast Guard for rescue and weather reconnaissance. Some P4Y-2s were used by the French Navy and by the Chinese Nationalist Air Force.

Consolidated B-32 Dominator

Consolidated was one of four companies which submitted designs for a "Hemisphere Defense Weapon" requested by the USAAF in 1940. While Boeing's design (which became the B-29 Superfortress) was judged the best, Consolidated's was sufficiently promising for three prototypes to be ordered in September 1940.

Development of the Consolidated design, based on experience with the B-24, proceeded in parallel with the B-29 and the first XB-32 flew on 7 September 1942. It was smaller than the Boeing bomber and carried its high aspect ratio wing high on the fuselage. The first prototype had a rounded nose and twin fins and rudders; the second, flown on 2 July 1943, had a stepped windscreen; the third, flown on 9 November 1943, switched to a single fin and rudder, which was adopted on the production models. As well as a maximum bomb load of 20,000 lb, the XB-32 was to have two 20-mm and fourteen 0·50-in guns in remotely-controlled turrets.

Production was initiated at Consolidated's Fort Worth and San Diego plants, but pressurization and remote turret controls were deleted to suit the B-32 to a lower-altitude rôle in the Pacific. Deliveries began in November 1944, by which time the B-29 was in action. Only 115 B-32s were built (including a single example from the San Diego line) and 1,588 were cancelled.

Of the B-32s completed, 40 were TB-32s used for crew training. In the closing days of the war, 15 B-32s became operational in the Western Pacific, but the type was quickly retired after the war.

Convair B-36

German domination of almost the whole of Europe – except Britain – in 1941 led the USAAF to face the possibility that it would be necessary to attack European targets from North American bases. An aircraft to meet this need, the USAAF concluded, would have to be able to fly 5,000 miles with a 10,000-lb bomb-load and then return to its base, cruising at 240-300 mph at 35,000 ft. A maximum bomb-load of 72,000 lb was to be carried over shorter ranges.

Convair won the 1941 design competition for such an aircraft with its Model 37 (officially designated B-36), a 278,000-lb six-engined bomber with a 230-ft span. Construction of the two prototypes was slow, as the project enjoyed lower priority than the development and production of the B-24 and B-32; but interest quickened in 1943 when the B-36 was seen to have potential value in the war against Japan, and a production contract for 100 was placed. Nevertheless, the war was over before the first XB-36 flew on 8 August 1946.

Largest aircraft ordered by the USAAF up to that time, the XB-36 was powered by six Pratt & Whitney R-4360 engines buried in the 6-ft thick wing and driving pusher propellers. Forward and rear crew compartments were connected by a pressurized tunnel, 80 ft long, through which crewmen moved on a wheeled trolley.

Deliveries to Strategic Air Command of the first production version, the B-36A, began in August 1947; unarmed, it was used for crew familiarization while the B-36B was being built. The "B" itself was fully operational, with sixteen 20-mm cannon disposed in six retractable, remotely-controlled turrets and on nose and tail mountings. The 22 B-36As and 73 B-36Bs introduced four-wheel bogie main undercarriage units and had a gross weight of 328,000 lb.

To boost the speed to a possible maximum of 435 mph, and the operating ceiling to 45,000 ft or more, Convair added four J47 turbojets in paired pods, one under each outer wing. This produced the B-36D, with a gross weight of 358,000 lb and the ability to carry two 42,000-lb "Grand Slam" bombs; 64 B-36Bs were converted to this standard and 22 more aircraft were built as B-36Ds. Another seven B-36Bs became RB-36Ds, with 14 cameras replacing two of the four bomb-bays and the crew increased to 22; Convair also built 17 RB-36Ds from scratch.

Small changes distinguished the RB-36E, of which 22

Consolidated B-32

Convair B-36H

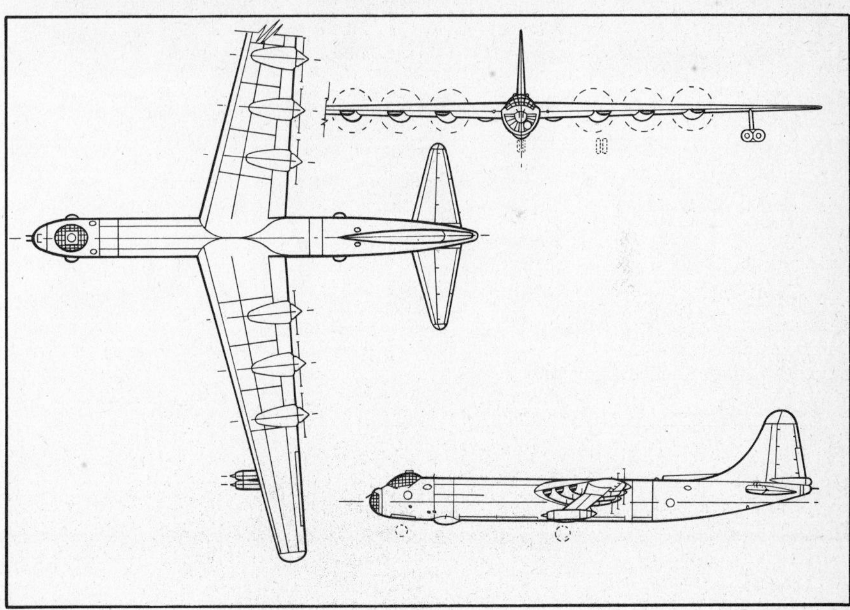
Convair B-36J

TYPE	DIMENSIONS span ft	span in	length ft	length in	height ft	height in	WEIGHT max t-o lb	PERFORMANCE max speed mph	at height ft	service ceiling ft	combat range miles	REMARKS
Consolidated B-24C	110	0	66	4	18	0	53,700	313	25,000	34,000	2,100	
Consolidated B-24D	110	0	66	4	17	11	60,000	303	25,000	32,000	2,850	
Consolidated B-24J	110	0	67	2	18	0	65,000	290	25,000	28,000	2,100	
Consolidated B-24M	110	0	67	2	18	0	64,500	300	30,000	28,000	2,100	
Consolidated P4Y-2	110	0	74	7	29	2	64,000	247	14,000	19,500	2,630	
Consolidated B-32	135	0	82	1	33	0	111,500	357	30,000	30,700	2,500	

Convair GRB-36D, modified to carry parasite fighter

Convair F-102A Delta Dagger

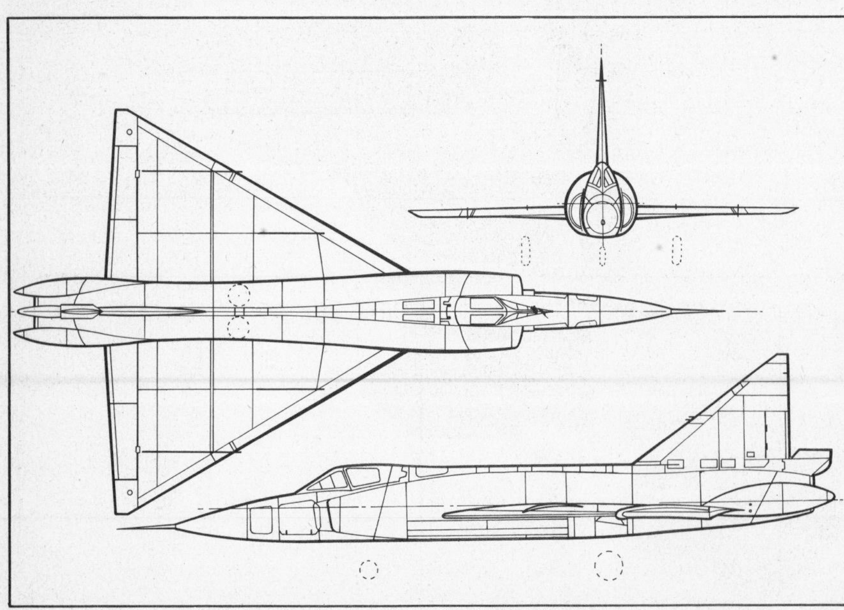

Convair F-102A Delta Dagger

were produced by converting B-36As and the second prototype B-36, and the 28 B-36Fs and 24 RB-36Fs built by Convair. In service with SAC, these aircraft gave many convincing demonstrations of their effectiveness and formed a major part of the US deterrent force during the 1950s. Unrefuelled flights of 24 hours' duration were possible with a considerable bomb-load; with bomb-bay fuel tanks endurance was over 50 hours.

During 1952–3, the B-36 became the subject of experiments recalling those two decades before with the Curtiss F9C Sparrowhawk (page 475). Since no escort fighter could match the endurance of the B-36, a parasite fighter was proposed, to be carried by the bomber itself. The intention was to use the specially-developed McDonnell XF-85, but early trials were not successful. The same idea was then adapted to provide reconnaissance versions of the B-36 with even greater effective range by adding under the fuselage a Republic RF-84F which could make the final penetration to the target while the carrier-aircraft stood off, awaiting its return. Trials were completed successfully and one squadron of modified GRF-84Fs was formed, about a dozen GRB-36Ds being modified as carriers.

Rounding off B-36 production were 81 B-36Hs, 73 RB-36Hs and 33 B-36Js. The final version carried extra fuel and operated at a maximum weight of 410,000 lb. A few were specially modified for clandestine reconnaissance missions, with most of the armament removed and other weight-saving changes to permit very high-altitude operation. The last B-36J was retired from service with SAC in February 1959.

Convair F-102 Delta Dagger

Use of a delta wing to achieve high speeds was the subject of extensive research in Germany before and during World War II by Dr Alexander Lippisch. In 1948, Convair made use of this research, in consultation with Dr Lippisch, to design a Mach 1·5 fighter for the USAF. Theories were put to the test in the XF-92A, the first true delta-wing powered aircraft to fly; this was a scale model of the proposed fighter, but development of the F-92 itself was dropped. Instead, in 1950, a new specification was drawn up for an all-weather interceptor and Convair met the requirement by scaling up the XF-92A design in the ratio 1·22 to 1.

Prototypes of the new design, the YF-102, were first flown on 24 October 1953 and 11 January 1954, and were found to have serious deficiencies in performance. A major re-work of the design introduced an area-ruled fuselage – the first application of the Whitcomb theories to reduce drag. First flown on 20 December 1954, the new YF-102A achieved supersonic flight satisfactorily and full production proceeded, to provide the USAF with its first operational delta, as well as its first fighter to dispense with gun armament completely, in favour of guided missiles and unguided rockets.

The first of the 975 F-102As that were built were in service by 1956 with squadrons of Air Defense Command and the type later served in both Greenland and Europe. The USAF also purchased 111 examples of the TF-102A, which was similar to the F-102A, but with a widened front fuselage seating two, for use as a combat trainer. Both versions of the Delta Dagger carried an armament of six Hughes Falcon missiles internally plus 24 unguided air rockets in the missile-bay doors.

Convair B-58 Hustler

Convair's early experience in delta-wing design, with the XF-92A and F-102 led to adoption of this configuration for a supersonic bomber study which began in 1949 under USAF contract. By 1952 detailed design of prototypes could begin, and on 13 October 1954 the USAF placed its first contract for construction of a supersonic strategic bomber.

The Convair Model 4, or B-58 Hustler, had many unusual features, most radical of which was the use of a disposable "weapon pod" containing a nuclear bomb and the fuel to be consumed on the outward journey to the target. Later, this idea was modified with the

introduction of a two-component pod, the larger, lower pod containing fuel and the other carrying both fuel and a bomb, reconnaissance pack or electronic equipment.

The B-58's J79 turbojet engines were pod-mounted beneath the delta wing. Armament comprised a single 20-mm Vulcan multi-barrel radar-aimed gun in the tail, and the crew of three sat in tandem.

Thirteen B-58As were ordered on the first contract, for development trials, and the first of these flew on 11 November 1956. Another 17 were ordered subsequently, also for the flight development programme. The majority of these early aircraft were re-worked subsequently, to bring them up to final production standard, and eight were converted to TB-58As with dual controls in the front two cockpits.

Three production contracts placed in 1959–61 covered a total of 86 B-58As and the first of these flew in September 1959. The first B-58A operational unit, Strategic Air Command's 43rd Bomb Wing at Carswell AFB, was activated on 15 March 1960 and a second wing was formed at Bunker Hill at a later date.

Capable of in-flight refuelling, the B-58A has demonstrated its ability to fly at speeds greater than Mach 2 for over an hour at a time, and non-stop missions of more than 18 hours have been flown, with two refuellings.

Convair F-106 Delta Dart

Experience with the F-102 led to development of an extensively modified and improved version of the same design during 1955. Initially designated F-102B, this later became the F-106. The J57 engine was replaced by a Pratt & Whitney J75 turbojet and the engine intakes were moved aft, to be as close as possible to the engine. Other changes included installation of the Hughes MA-1 electronic guidance and fire-control system.

First flight of the developed delta was made on 26 December 1956, and deliveries to the USAF began in mid-1959. Like the F-102, the F-106 was developed in single- and two-seat versions, the latter being the F-106B. This was a combat trainer with tandem seats, compared with the side-by-side layout used in the two-seat TF-102A.

The first F-106B flew at Edwards Air Force Base in April 1958. All F-106As and F-106Bs were earmarked for Air Defense Command, and served at home bases and overseas. Operated in conjunction with the SAGE (Semi-Automatic Ground Environment) air defence system, the Delta Dart carried an armament of two MB-1 Genie unguided air rockets with nuclear warheads, plus up to four Hughes Falcons.

Curtiss H-4

When it offered a £10,000 prize in 1913 for the first direct crossing of the Atlantic by air, the *Daily Mail* was indirectly responsible for initiating development of a famous line of Curtiss flying-boats. To compete for the prize, Rodman Wanamaker commissioned the Curtiss Airplane Co to build a flying-boat, and this appeared in 1914 as the *America* with two 90-hp Curtiss engines and a 72-ft span. The *America* carried a crew of two, one of whom was to be, on the record attempt, John Porte, an English pilot and engineer who had just joined Curtiss.

Plans for the flight were interrupted by the outbreak

Convair B-58A Hustler, carrying single-component pod; two-component pod to right

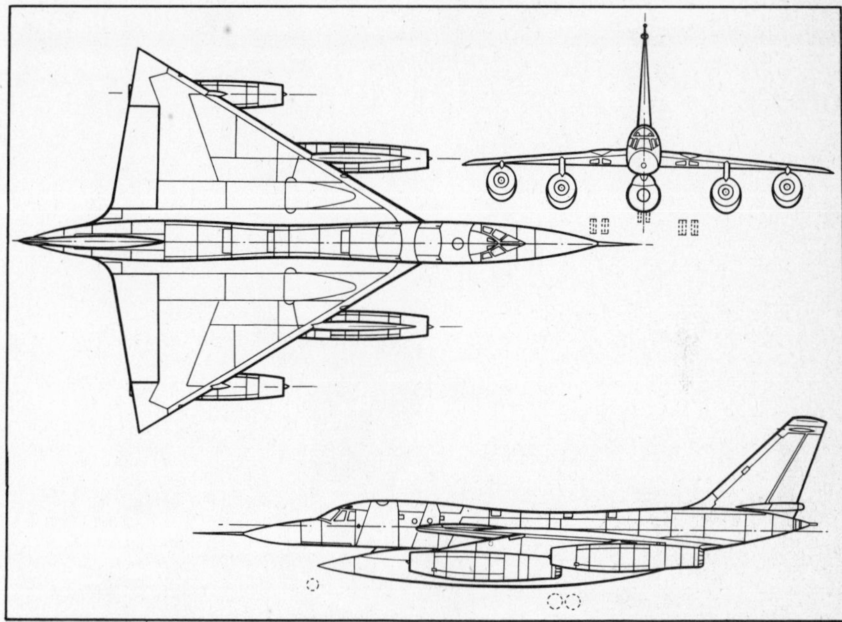
Convair B-58A Hustler

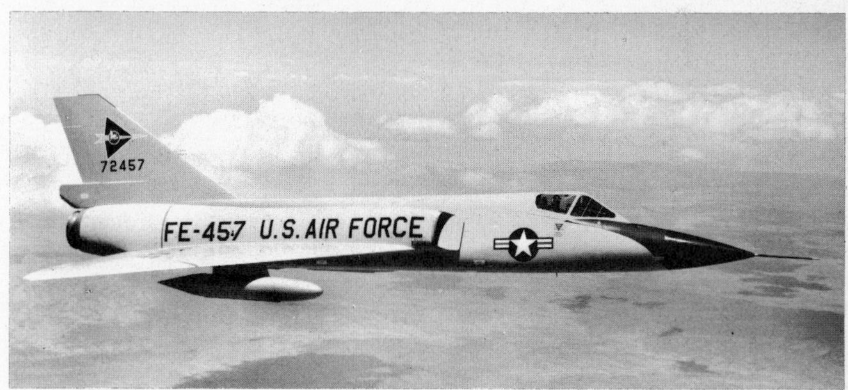

Convair F-106A Delta Dart

TYPE	DIMENSIONS span ft	span in	length ft	length in	height ft	height in	WEIGHT max t-o lb	PERFORMANCE max speed mph	at height ft	service ceiling ft	combat range miles	REMARKS
Convair B-36B	230	0	162	1	46	8	328,000	381	34,500	42,500	8,175	
Convair B-36D	230	0	162	1	46	8	357,500	439	32,120	45,200	7,500	
Convair B-36J	230	0	162	1	46	8	410,000	411	36,400	39,900	6,800	
Convair F-102	38	1½	68	4½	21	2½	31,500	825	40,000	54,000	1,000	
Convair B-58A	56	10	96	9	31	5	160,000	1,385	40,000	60,000	2,400	
Convair F-106A	38	3½	70	8¾	20	3½	38,250	1,525	40,000	57,000	1,150	

Curtiss H-4, RNAS

Curtiss H-12, modified by RNAS

Curtiss HS-1

of war, which also led John Porte to rejoin the Royal Naval Air Service as a Squadron Commander. He caused an order to be placed for two Curtiss flying-boats similar to the *America*. These were delivered in November 1914. Four more followed in 1915, plus eight built under licence by the Aircraft Manufacturing Co in Britain. Most of these had 90-hp Curtiss OX-5 engines, but a switch was made to 100-hp Anzani engines in a batch of 50 ordered in 1915. These were designated Curtiss H-4s and were usually called "Small Americas" to distinguish them from the H-8/H-12 "Large Americas".

The H-4s were of wooden construction, and a distinctive feature was the flare-out of the hull at the bows, to deflect spray from the cockpit and engines. Armament comprised a single machine-gun in the bows and bombs beneath the wings. The H-4s were used for some operational patrols, and also provided a basis for experiments by John Porte and his design team at Felixstowe. The results of these experiments proved of value both to Curtiss and to Porte in the evolution of later flying-boats.

Curtiss H-12

RNAS experience with the Curtiss H-4 "Small America" flying-boats showed that they were underpowered. An effort to correct this failing was made in the larger H-8, one example of which was delivered in July 1916. With two 160-hp Curtiss engines, the H-8 still suffered from low performance, so two 275-hp Rolls-Royce Eagles were substituted in the similar H-12.

The RNAS ordered 50 examples of the H-12 without waiting for prototype trials. Deliveries began in 1917. Similar in appearance to the H-4, the "Large America" had a crew of four, armament of three Lewis guns and provision for two 236-lb bombs under the wings. On 14 May 1917, an H-12 became the first American-built aeroplane to destroy an enemy aircraft in the 1914–18 War, shooting down a Zeppelin. Later that month, an H-12 scored the first aerial victory against a submarine.

A second batch of H-12s was ordered for British service, but only 21 were built before the Armistice. Of the total of 71 built, 20 were made available to the US Navy, which retained one with Curtiss engines and re-engined the others with Liberty 12s.

Curtiss HS

Between America's entry into the 1914–18 War in 1917 and the signing of the Armistice in 1918, the number of flying-boats in service with the US Navy increased from six to 1,172. The greater proportion of these were single-engined Curtiss 'boats designated HS-2.

This design originated as the HS-1, first flown on 21 October 1917. It combined Curtiss experience in hull design on the *America* series with the wings of the R-type seaplane. A single 360-hp Liberty engine drove a pusher propeller. The HS-1 carried a single gun in the bows and two 230-lb bombs or a 500-lb torpedo. The HS-1's first flight is also believed to have been the first time the famous Liberty engine was flown.

The HS-2 production models had larger wings, the total area being increased from 653 sq ft to 803 sq ft. Curtiss built 673 and production was initiated by five other manufacturers to meet the enormous USN demand. Thus, LWF built 250, Standard 80, Gallaudet 60, Boeing 25 and Loughead 2. In addition, several HS-2s were constructed locally at Service stations from spares.

Small modifications were introduced in the HS-3, of which Curtiss built four and the Naval Aircraft Factory two. The HS-2s were used for patrols, principally over the Atlantic from US bases; but some were assigned to Europe, the first eight reaching Pavillac, France, in May 1918 and flying there in June. Forty were still in service in 1925.

Curtiss H-16

As a further development of the H-4/H-8/H-12 series Curtiss developed the H-16 for use by the Royal Naval Air Service. Whereas the earlier types had a single-step hull, the H-16 introduced a double-step type, as well as a balanced rudder and improved rear armament, comprising two guns in the rear cockpit and one each side in beam positions. The bomb-load was increased to four 230-lb bombs or a 600-lb torpedo.

An initial order for 15 H-16s from the Admiralty was followed by another for 110 of these big 'boats. Fifty of the final batch were cancelled, leaving 75 delivered; all had 345-hp Rolls-Royce Eagle engines.

Curtiss also built 74 H-16s for the US Navy. These had 400-hp Liberty engines and deliveries began in February 1918, to the Naval unit at Hampton Roads. The same engines powered a second batch of 150 H-16s ordered from the Naval Aircraft Factory in November 1917. The first H-16 on this contract, which was also the first aircraft built by the NAF, flew on 27 March 1918. Delivery of the 'boats was completed between March and October 1918; 33 were still serving in 1925.

Curtiss NC-4

The earliest patrol flying-boats of the US Navy were derived from the privately-financed *America* (see under Curtiss H-4, page 467) which had been designed for an attempted Atlantic crossing. Although this flight was never made, transatlantic capability was written into a Navy specification for a new large flying-boat, which was drawn up soon after America's entry into the 1914–18 War. This capability was needed to permit delivery of the boats to Europe by air.

Curtiss and Navy engineers collaborated closely in the design of the new flying-boat, which was designated NC (Navy Curtiss). The layout was a break with Curtiss tradition, for the NC had a short hull (45 ft) and a structure of spruce outriggers from the hull and wings to carry the biplane tail unit. Three 400-hp Liberty engines were mounted on struts between the wings, which were of unequal span; a fourth Liberty, with pusher propeller, was added later.

Four NCs were built by Curtiss, the first flying on October 1918. Too late for the war, they were chosen for an attempt on the transatlantic crossing, which had still not been made by an aeroplane. The aircraft were numbered NC-1, NC-2, NC-3 and NC-4, and the Navy appointed a team under Commander John H. Towers to make the flight in the first, third and fourth aircraft. They left Newfoundland on 16 May 1919, and NC-4, commanded by Lt-Cmdr Albert C. Read, reached the Azores next day. Ten days later it flew on to Lisbon, Portugal and then to Plymouth, England, to complete the first Atlantic crossing by air.

Six more NCs were built by the Naval Aircraft Factory at Philadelphia in 1919–20. Numbered NC-5 to NC-10 inclusive, they originally had three Liberty engines apiece; two were lost before a conversion programme to add the fourth Liberty could be implemented. These NC 'boats served with the Navy's East Coast Squadron from 1920 to 1922, visiting Cuba and Panama during this period. The older Curtiss H-16 and HS-2 flying-boats outlived the NCs by a number of years.

Curtiss/Orenco Model D

Although the United States was a combatant power in the 1914–18 War for a total of 19 months, no aircraft of American design reached the European front, nor indeed

Curtiss H-16

Curtiss NC-4

Curtiss NC-4

TYPE	DIMENSIONS						WEIGHT	PERFORMANCE				REMARKS
	span ft	span in	length ft	length in	height ft	height in	max t-o lb	max speed mph	at height ft	service ceiling ft	combat range miles	
Curtiss H-4	72	0	36	0	16	0	4,983	NA	NA	NA	NA	
Curtiss H-12	92	8	46	0	16	9	7,989	85	2,000	NA	NA	
Curtiss HS-2	74	0	38	6	14	7	6,432	82.5	SL	5,200	517	
Curtiss H-16	95	1	46	2	17	9	10,900	95	2,000	9,950	378	
Curtiss NC-4	126	0	68	3	24	6	28,000	90	SL	4,500	1,470	

Curtiss/Orenco Model D, experimental version with turbosupercharger

Curtiss TS-1

Curtiss/Martin SC-1 floatplane

did a fighter or bomber of US design get into production before the war ended. Plans were made to produce fighting aircraft on a grandiose scale, but time was wasted in trying to adapt existing European types for production in the USA, with modifications. Meanwhile, squadrons of the American Expeditionary Force flew "borrowed" French and British types.

The first single-seat fighter of US design appeared in January 1919. Designed by the Army Engineering Division, it was built by the Ordnance Engineering Company (Orenco) of Baldwin, Long Island. Basis of the design was the 300-hp Wright-Hispano H engine, which was specified officially; in layout, the Orenco D was conventional but its performance was reasonably promising. The Army tested four prototypes built by Orenco, and decided to purchase a production batch of 50 more. The contract was put out to tender and Curtiss was low-bidder. Its version of the Orenco D had a 330-hp Wright-Hispano engine and higher weights than the prototypes, with consequently lower performance.

Curtiss had already become involved in fighter production when it was chosen to tool-up to build 1,000 British S.E.5As. Only one of these was completed – with a 180-hp Wright-Hispano E engine – but Curtiss assembled 56 others from British-built parts.

Experience with the S.E.5A and the Orenco D was an inauspicious beginning in fighter production for Curtiss. But the company went on to produce some of the most famous of all American fighters, the Hawk series, as described later.

Curtiss TS, FC, F2C, F3C and F4C

A date of unusual significance for the US Navy was 20 March 1922, for on that day its first aircraft carrier was commissioned. Converted from the collier *Jupiter*, it was renamed USS *Langley*.

The development of specialized aircraft to serve on board the *Langley* and other carriers thus became a priority issue in 1922. When *Langley* was commissioned, the Navy had no single-seat fighters in service; not until May 1922 did the first specially-designed fighter appear. Designed at the NAF, it was built as the Curtiss TS-1 and was a small biplane with a 200-hp Wright J-1 air-cooled radial. An unusual feature was the location of the fuel tank in the centre-section of the lower wing, under the fuselage, from where it could be jettisoned in an emergency. Armament was one 0·30-in machine-gun.

Production of the TS-1 by Curtiss totalled 34. In addition, the Naval Aircraft Factory built five TS-1s, two TS-2s with 240-hp Aeromarine water-cooled engines and one TS-3 with a 220-hp Wright E-2, also water-cooled. The first operational TS-1s were delivered in December 1922, for service on board the *Langley*.

After the Navy's system of aircraft designation had been modified in March 1923, the Curtiss fighters were re-designated FC-1, F2C-1 and F3C-1. Curtiss also built two F4C-1s of similar design, with fabric-covered metal construction and Wright J-3 radial engines.

Curtiss CS/SC

Although the US Navy lagged somewhat in the early development of specialized fighters, it showed greater initiative in respect of the torpedo-bomber. By 1922, when the first Navy fighter appeared, several types of patrol bomber had already been put into production.

The first Curtiss design in this class was the CS-1, which appeared in late 1923. Powered by a 525-hp Wright T-2 in-line engine, the CS-1 was unusual among biplanes in that the upper wing had a smaller span than the lower. Wheels or floats were interchangeable and a 1,618-lb torpedo could be slung beneath the fuselage.

Curtiss delivered six CS-1s and two CS-2s with the 585-hp Wright T-3 engine and increased fuel capacity. In the early months of 1924 the USN decided to adopt the Curtiss bomber as a replacement for its Douglas DT-2s and, following the practice of the day, bids for the production contract were invited from the industry.

The Martin company was low bidder, at about two-thirds the Curtiss price, and contracts were placed for

35 aircraft designated SC-1 (T-2 engines) and 40 SC-2s or T2M-1s (T-3 engines). Deliveries were completed by 9 January 1926. Subsequent modification programmes produced two SC-6s and a single SC-7.

Curtiss PW-8

On 23 June 1924 Lt Russell Maughan of the United States Army Air Service succeeded in flying across the USA, coast-to-coast, within the hours of daylight. This first dawn-to-dusk trans-continental flight was made in a Curtiss PW-8, the first of the Curtiss single-seat fighters and progenitor of the famous line of Hawks.

The PW-8 was designed around a 435-hp Curtiss D-12 in-line engine, with a conventional welded steel-tube fuselage. The two-bay wings were of all-wood construction and the tail unit was a fabric-covered metal structure. Armament comprised one 0·30-in and one 0·50-in machine-gun under the engine cowl, firing through the propeller disc.

Several changes were made on the second prototype XPW-8, which differed from the first in having a divided, instead of split-axle, landing gear; a smooth top cowling line, instead of indented; strut-connected ailerons and unbalanced elevators. These modifications were adopted as standard on the 25 production PW-8s which were ordered in September 1923 and delivered between June and August 1924.

The PW-8s had surface radiators in the wings, but these were eliminated from the third of the original test aircraft which was modified to have a centre-section radiator and single-bay wings. In this guise it became the XPW-8A. Later, a tunnel-type radiator was substituted under the nose. When another new set of wings, of tapered planform and Clark Y section, was introduced, the same aeroplane became the XPW-8B.

Curtiss P-1/F6C Hawk

In March 1925, the Curtiss company was awarded a contract to produce 15 fighters similar to the XPW-8B (see above). These received the designation P-1, as the first aircraft in the new USAAC category for fighters, and the first was tested at McCook Field on 17 August 1925. The engine was the 435-hp Curtiss V-1150-1(D-12) and the first ten aircraft were identical with the XPW-8B in all but minor detail. In the final five, the 500-hp Curtiss V-1400 engine was used and these aircraft were designated P-2.

Nine examples of the Curtiss Hawk were also ordered by the US Navy in March 1925. Seven were delivered as F6C-1s and two as F6C-2s, powered by 400-hp Curtiss D-12 engines and with provision for wheels or floats.

Further production contracts for the Hawk were placed by the Army Air Corps in 1925 and 1926, with 25 ordered in each year. The first of these two batches were designated P-1A, with a 3-in longer fuselage and extra service equipment; these were the first of the series to serve in pursuit squadrons in quantity. Further small changes were made in the 1926 batch of P-1Bs, delivery of which began in October; in particular, they had the 435-hp Curtiss V-1150-3 engine.

Final Army contract for P-1s was placed in October 1928, when 33 P-1Cs were ordered. These had the V-1150-3

Curtiss PW-8

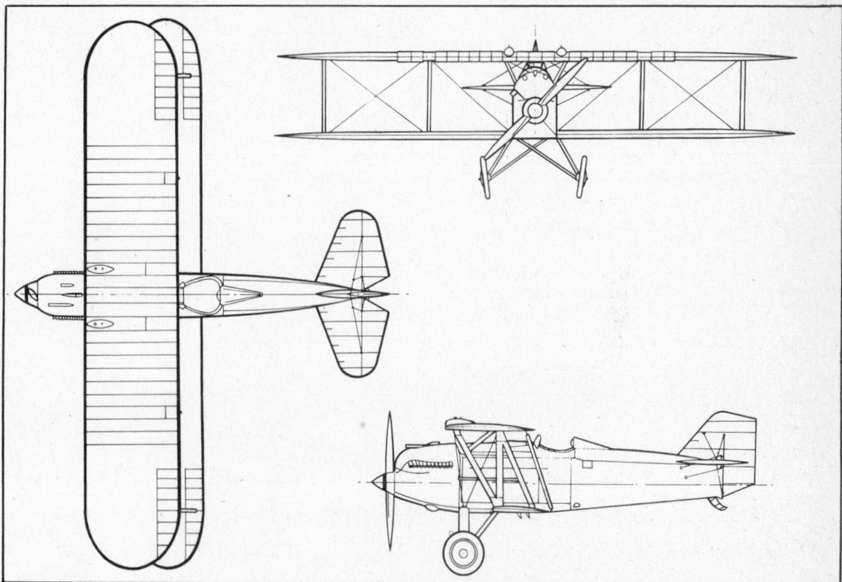

Curtiss PW-8

Curtiss P-1B Hawk

TYPE	DIMENSIONS span ft	span in	length ft	length in	height ft	height in	WEIGHT max t-o lb	PERFORMANCE max speed mph	at height ft	service ceiling ft	combat range miles	REMARKS
Curtiss Orenco D	33	0	21	5½	8	4	2,820	139.5	SL	18,450	NA	
Curtiss TS-1	25	0	22	1	9	0	1,920	125	SL	16,250	482	Data for landplane
Curtiss CS-1	56	6	40	3	16	0	8,670	100	SL	6,900	430	Data for seaplane
Curtiss SC-1	56	6	38	5	15	3	8,310	100	SL	7,950	403	Landplane by Martin
Curtiss SC-2	56	6	41	9	16	0	9,323	101	SL	5,430	335	Seaplane by Martin
Curtiss PW-8	32	0	22	6	8	10	3,150	165	SL	21,700	440	

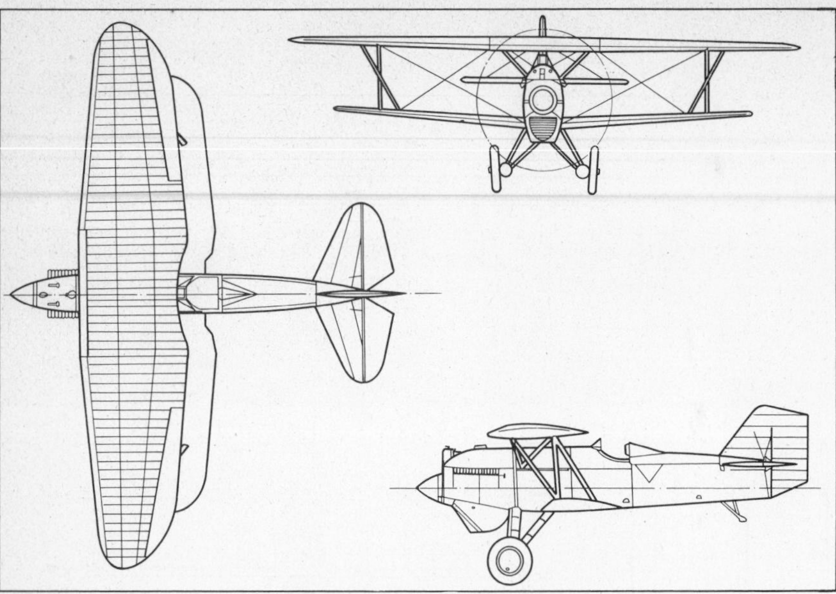
Curtiss P-1 Hawk

Curtiss A-3

Curtiss F7C-1

engine, wheel brakes and further changes in equipment, increasing the weight and decreasing performance. The Navy's 35 F6C-3s were similar, with arrester gear added.

After the P-1Cs had been delivered, in April 1929, the Army initiated conversion programmes to acquire a further 71 Hawks. These had been ordered and built in 1926 and 1927 as advanced trainers, differing from the P-1 primarily in power plant. The aircraft involved were 35 AT-4s with 180-hp Wright V-720 engines; five AT-5s with 220-hp Wright R-790-1 air-cooled radials and 31 similar AT-5As. All these were re-engined with the 435-hp Curtiss V-1150-3 and redesignated P-1D, P-1E and P-1F respectively. One P-1A was sold to Japan; Chile bought eight P-1As and eight P-1Bs.

Air-cooled radial engines found little favour for fighters in the Army Air Corps at this time, but a few Hawks were so engined. One P-1A was converted to XP-3A standard, with a Pratt & Whitney R-1340-9 and five more P-3As were built with R-1340-3s.

The USN, conversely, found the air-cooled engine particularly suited to carrier operations and in 1926 successfully tested a Curtiss XF6C-4 with the R-1340. Subsequently, 31 similarly-powered F6C-4s were put into service. Some Curtiss Hawks with the Pratt & Whitney engine were exported to Cuba.

In an effort to improve the performance of the Hawk at high altitudes, a turbo-supercharged V-1150-3 engine was used in the five P-5s. These aircraft had an inferior performance at low altitude, but had a service ceiling of 30,500 ft and a good speed at high altitude. Problems with the turbo-supercharger, developed from the original work of Dr Sanford Moss at General Electric, prevented further exploitation of the P-5.

All production models of the P-1 series were armed with two 0·30-in guns in the cowl, firing forward through the propeller. The Curtiss Hawks, with their distinctive tapered wings, shared with the Boeing biplane fighters the task of equipping front-line Army Air Corps squadrons for much of the inter-war period.

Curtiss A-3

Out of its experience with light bombers during the 1914–18 War, when the D.H.4 and Breguet 14 were used by squadrons of the American Expeditionary Force in support of infantry, the Army Air Service drew up a new requirement in 1926 for a ground-attack aircraft. Between 1918 and 1922, considerable efforts had been expended to develop a heavily-armed and armoured trench straffer, but with little success. The 1926 requirement, therefore, placed greater emphasis upon quality of design than upon novelty.

Developments of already-well-proven aircraft types were looked upon with interest, and both Douglas and Curtiss offered to arm their existing two-seat observation aircraft, the O-2 and O-1. After comparison of the two, the Army picked the Curtiss proposal, which was then designated A-3 in the newly-created category for attack aircraft. The Curtiss design was already in production as the Falcon, and the A-3 retained most characteristics of its forebear.

A contract for A-3s was placed by the Army in February 1927 and subsequent re-orders brought the total built to 76. Deliveries began towards the end of 1927, with the A-3 replacing D.H.4s which were still in front-line service after ten years. A further production batch, ordered in 1929 and 1930, was identified as A-3B, the differences being those developed for the O-1E model of the observation Falcon – Frise ailerons, horn-balanced elevators, improved cowling lines and a tail-wheel. Production of the A-3B totalled 78. Both versions of the Curtiss attack bomber were powered by the 435-hp Curtiss V-1150 engine.

Curtiss F7C

Satisfied with its experience of Curtiss Hawks, the US Navy awarded Curtiss a contract in June 1927 for a new fighter designed from the outset for carrier-based operation. The prototype was developed by Curtiss as a private venture and was first flown on 28 February1927. It was a conventional single-seat fighter with a 450-hp Pratt & Whitney R-1340-B Wasp engine, split-axle undercarriage and – in typical Curtiss manner – a straight lower wing and swept-back top wing.

Only the prototype XF7C-1 was fitted with arrester gear for carrier operation. This aircraft was also tested as a floatplane. A production batch of 17 F7C-1s, delivery of which began in December 1928, achieved little success and most were transferred to the US Marine Corps, to serve with VF-5M and VF-9M Squadrons. One was used for a series of experiments on cowlings, spinners and propellers.

Curtiss P-6 Hawk

During the late 1920s, both the US Army and Navy participated in the annual National Air Races, and the intense rivalry of these events served to quicken the pace of aircraft development. A case in point was the modification, in 1927, of two Curtiss Hawks to be powered by the then-new Curtiss Conqueror V-1570 engine. These were a P-2 and a P-1A fuselage with XPW-8A wings and wing radiators. Redesignated XP-6 and XP-6A, they took second and first place respectively, at 189 mph and 201 mph.

Performance of this order could not be overlooked, and the Army ordered a service test batch of nine YP-6s in October 1928. They had the standard Curtiss Hawk wings but a considerably-altered fuselage outline through better streamlining. Delivery was made to the Army between October 1929 and December 1930, and during 1932 those still in service were modified into P-6Ds with turbosuperchargers. Nine P-6As, ordered at the same time as the YP-6s, were similar but had Prestone cooling; this was the trade name for a system using ethylene glycol in place of water in the radiators. These also were converted to P-6Ds in 1932.

Development work on two prototype Hawks, designated YP-20 and XP-22, led to important improvements in the next production series, the P-6E. The fuselage contours were changed to get rid of the deep chest of the earlier P-6s, a single-strut undercarriage with wheel spats was introduced, as well as a tail-wheel, and the engine was the 700-hp V-1570-23 with Prestone cooling. An order for 46 was placed in July 1931 and delivery was made in 1932.

The final aircraft on the P-6E contract was completed as the XP-23, with a new metal fuselage and V-1570-23 engine. The XP-23, which achieved 220 mph at 15,000 ft, was not only the last of the biplane Hawks – it was also the last biplane fighter procured by the US Army Air Corps.

In addition to the Army P-6s, Curtiss built eight for the Netherlands East Indies, and sold a single example to Mitsubishi in Japan in 1930.

Curtiss P-6D Hawk

Curtiss P-6E Hawk

TYPE	DIMENSIONS span ft	span in	length ft	length in	height ft	height in	WEIGHT max t-o lb	PERFORMANCE max speed mph	at height ft	service ceiling ft	combat range miles	REMARKS
Curtiss P-1	31	7	22	10	8	7	3,238	163	SL	22,500	325	
Curtiss P-1B	31	7	22	8	8	11	3,562	160	SL	21,400	NA	
Curtiss P-1C	31	6	23	3	8	6	2,973	154	SL	20,800	600	
Curtiss F6C-2	31	6	22	8	10	0	2,838	159	SL	22,700	330	
Curtiss F6C-4	31	6	22	6	10	11	3,171	155	SL	22,900	361	
Curtiss P-5	31	6	23	8	9	3	3,350	1[illegible]6	SL	31,900	NA	
Curtiss A-3	38	0	28	4	10	1	4,378	141	NA	15,600	630	V-1150-3 engine
Curtiss A-3B	38	0	27	2	10	6	4,476	139	SL	14,100	628	V-1150-5 engine
Curtiss F7C-1	32	8	22	2	10	4	3219	151	SL	23,350	330	
Curtiss P-6A	31	6	23	7	8	7	3172	178	SL	27,200	NA	
Curtiss P-6D	31	6	23	7	8	7	3,483	197	13,000	32,000	NA	
Curtiss P-6E	31	6	23	2	8	10	3,392	198	SL	24,700	285	

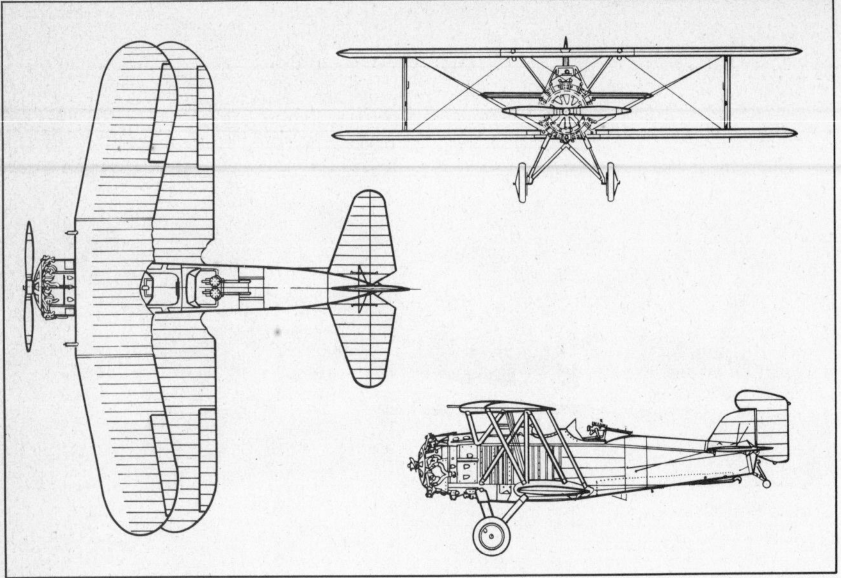
Curtiss F8C-4

Curtiss F8C-5/O2C-1

Curtiss B-2

Curtiss B-2

Curtiss F8C

When the US Marine Corps sought, in 1927, a light attack aircraft to replace its DH-4Bs of 1914–18 War vintage, it was logical to turn to types already developed for the Army Air Corps for the same purpose. The requirement was for a two-seat fighter capable of use in the observation and light bombing rôle, particularly in support of Marine operations such as those conducted in the Caribbean in the early 1920s. To meet the need, a version of the Curtiss O-1 and A-3 Falcon was selected, the principal new feature for the Marines being the use of a Pratt & Whitney R-1340 Wasp air-cooled radial engine in place of the Army's Curtiss D-12 installation.

Two prototypes, designated XF8C-1, were purchased on an order dated 30 June 1927, with delivery early in 1928. These were followed by 4 F8C-1s and 21 similar F8C-3s; all were delivered to the Marine Corps, which later redesignated them OC-1 and OC-2 respectively. The second XF8C-1 became the XOC-3 when fitted with a Curtiss H-1640 engine. The OCs were the first Curtiss types to carry the name Helldiver which was retained for all subsequent Curtiss dive bombers; they carried an armament of two 0·30-in guns in the lower wings, two more in the rear cockpit and ten 17-lb bombs under the wings.

A heavier bomb-load, comprising two 116-lb bombs under each wing or a single 500-lb bomb under the fuselage, was carried by the XF8C-2, which also had two 0·30-in guns in the upper wings. This version was followed by the similar F8C-4, which appeared in May 1930 with an R-1340-88 engine. Twenty-seven F8C-4s were built, and were transferred to Reserve Squadrons after brief service with Marine and Navy units.

The Pratt & Whitney R-1340C engine was used in the F8C-5, of which 61 examples were delivered in 1930–31. These were redesignated O2C-1s and, with another 30 built as such, served with Marine and Navy squadrons.

Two XF8C-6s were modified F8C-5s with supercharged engines and wing slots. The single XF8C-7 was delivered as a command transport in November 1930, for the use of the Assistant Secretary of the Navy for Aeronautics. It had a Wright R-1820-64 engine, wheel fairings and an enclosed cockpit. The designation later became XO2C-2 for a short period, and the Navy also purchased three O2C-2s – heavier and more powerful variants of the Helldiver design which also carried the designations XF10C-1 and XS3C-1 for a time.

Curtiss B-2

The Curtiss company entered the large bomber field with production of 50 Martin NBS-1s. The experience gained was put to good use, first in the design and construction of two XNBS-4s, based on the Martin designs, and then in the development of the Curtiss XB-2 Condor. The XB-2 also could be considered as a derivative of the NBS-1, from which it differed in having a steel-tube fuselage, Curtiss Conqueror engines and a new Curtiss-developed aerofoil section.

The XB-2 was tested in September 1927, with 600-hp Curtiss V-1570 engines. With a gross weight of 16,344 lb, it achieved a top speed of 130 mph and could carry bomb-loads of up to 4,000 lb. An unusual – but not unique – feature of the XB-2 was the location of gunners in the rear of each engine nacelle, where they enjoyed a comparatively good field of fire to the rear. Each gunner had two Lewis guns, and two more were mounted in the nose.

Early in 1928, the XB-2 was one of five bomber types competing for new Army orders. Three of the competitors were quickly eliminated, leaving the XB-2 and the Keystone XLB-6. The Curtiss aircraft had the better performance but Keystone offered the lowest price – partly because it had already built 35 LB-5s, from which the XLB-6 was directly developed. There also was some resistance to the XB-2 because it was "too big for existing hangars", but its excellent performance could not be completely overlooked and twelve examples were ordered under the designation B-2. Deliveries began in May 1929.

Curtiss F9C Sparrowhawk

The eight Curtiss F9Cs built for the United States Navy in 1931–2 served as "parasite" fighters with the airships USS *Akron* and *Macon*. Consequently they occupy a unique place in the annals of the United States Navy, since no other aircraft were produced for this comparatively short-lived project.

The *Akron* and *Macon*, designed in 1929, were intended to be the first units of a marine fleet of lighter-than-air craft serving the USN in the early-warning rôle. Each was 785 ft long, and was powered by eight 580-hp Maybach engines. In keeping with their primary reconnaissance mission, these two airships were each provided with a "spy basket" by means of which an observer could be lowered 4,000 ft below the airship, which could thus remain in cloud cover while a crewman spied out the land – or the ocean – beneath.

It was partly as an extension of this idea that the parasite fighter was conceived, although the need to defend the airship from attack was apparent. The Curtiss XF9C-1 was ordered on 30 June 1930, together with similar prototypes from Fokker and Berliner-Joyce, for evaluation in a United States Navy design competition. Official records suggest that the requirement at this stage was for a new carrier-based fighter and that provision for airship operation was not written into the specification. However, the aircraft's small size and light weight made the XF9C-1 of particular value in the latter rôle. The XF9C-1 first flew on 12 February 1931, and was evaluated at NAS Anacostia. Most of the improvements recommended following these tests were incorporated in a second prototype, first flown as a Curtiss demonstrator and eventually purchased by the Navy as XF9C-2. Six production model F9C-2's were ordered in 1931 and delivered in 1932 specifically for airship operation.

The engine was a Wright R-975 close-cowled radial and the main wheels were provided with pants. Armament comprised two forward-firing guns.

Six F9C-2's and the XF9C-1 were allocated to the "*Akron* unit" in 1932, and the first hook-on test was made on 16 June. This was followed by a whole series of trials with 104 successful contacts by 11 July when the evaluation ended. The Sparrowhawks remained with the *Akron* until the airship crashed on 4 April 1933. Thereafter the six F9C-2's and the XF9C-*2* were attached to the *Macon* unit (the XF9C-1 being withdrawn), and operated for two years without a single serious accident or incident. However, the *Macon* was lost on 12 February 1935, with four of the F9C-2's on board. This ended the airship parasite fighter experiment and the surviving Sparrowhawks continued to fly only as run-abouts.

Curtiss F11C Goshawk

Space restrictions on board aircraft carriers have always led navies to seek multi-purpose capability in their aircraft. This can be seen particularly clearly in the types developed for use by the US Navy in the 1930s, with such new categories as scout-bombers, scout-fighters and bomber-fighters appearing. The bomber-fighter, of which the Curtiss Goshawk was a prime example, was no more than a single-seat fighter with the ability to carry small bombs under the wings.

Two prototypes of the Curtiss design were ordered by the USN on 16 April 1932, with the designations XF11C-1 and XF11C-2. These were conventional biplanes, developed from the F6C (page 471) and the Army's P-6E Hawk fighters, with respectively, a Wright

Curtiss XF9C-1 Sparrowhawk

Curtiss F9C-2 Sparrowhawk, with airship attachment hook

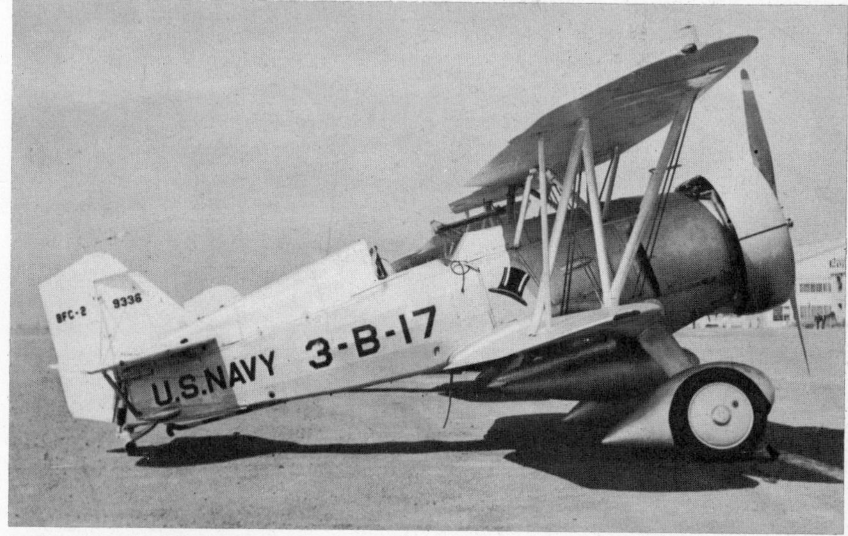

Curtiss F11C-2/BFC-2 Goshawk

TYPE	DIMENSIONS span ft	span in	length ft	length in	height ft	height in	WEIGHT max t-o lb	PERFORMANCE max speed mph	at height ft	service ceiling ft	combat range miles	REMARKS
Curtiss F8C-4	32	1	25	11	10	6	4,367	137.5	SL	17,300	378	
Curtiss B-2	90	0	47	6	16	3	16,516	132	SL	17,000	780	
Curtiss F9C-2	25	6	20	1	7	1	2,888	176.5	SL	19,200	366	

Curtiss F11C-3/BF2C-1 Goshawk

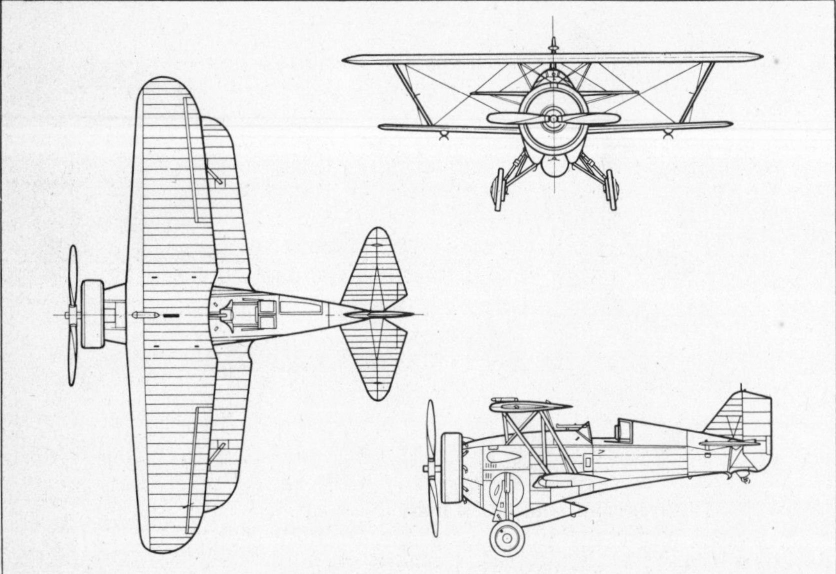

Curtiss F11C-3/BF2C-1 Goshawk

Curtiss A-8 Shrike

Curtiss A-12 Shrike

R-1510-98 twin-row Whirlwind and a Wright SR-1820-7 single-row Cyclone for power. First to fly was th XF11C-2, on 25 March 1932.

Naval evaluation led to a contract for 28 F11C-2s i October 1932. Deliveries to VF-1B squadron began i April 1933 and the final aircraft, completed in May, wa extensively modified as the XF11C-3. This -3 versio of the Goshawk was the Curtiss reply to the Grumma FF (page 499) and had a similar arrangement fo the undercarriage to retract into the deepened forwar fuselage. This feature improved the top speed by 25 mph despite a big increase in weight, and Curtiss won a pro duction contract for 27 F11C-3s in February 1934. A of these Goshawks carried two 0·30-in guns and ha provision for four 116-lb bombs under the wings an one 474-lb bomb under the fuselage.

In March 1934, the Navy changed the Goshaw designation to indicate the bombing capability. Th F11C-2s already in service became BFC-2s and th F11C-3s were renumbered BF2C-1s. The latter wer the last Curtiss biplanes to serve with the US Navy.

A total of 251 Goshawks was exported by Curtiss in four versions, known as Hawks. The Hawk I an Hawk II were similar to the BFC-2, with 710-h R-1820F-3 Cyclone engines and, respectively, 50-ga and 94-gal internal fuel capacity. The Hawk III and I had the BF2C's retractable undercarriage and the 750-h R-1820F-53 engine. China purchased more than 10 Hawk IIs and IIIs, in addition to a licence to build th type. Other countries which bought Hawks include Turkey (24 Hawk IIs) and Germany (2 Hawk IIs) Bolivia, Colombia, Cuba, Argentina and Spain.

Curtiss A-8, A-10, A-12 Shrike

To obtain an attack aeroplane of higher performanc than the A-3 series, the United States Army Air Corp indicated in 1929 that it would be interested in a suitably armed monoplane. Prototypes were built by the Atlantic Fokker Company (XA-7) and by Curtiss (XA-8), bot being low-wing monoplanes with Curtiss V-1570 Con queror in-line engines and heavily spatted undercarriages

Testing of the Fokker design began in January 193 and of the Curtiss machine later the same year. In con sequence, Curtiss received a contract on 29 Septembe 1931 for a service test batch of 13 YA-8s. They wer all-metal machines, with the pilot and gunner in enclose cockpits, several feet apart, and were the first America combat aircraft to have wing slots and flaps.

Service trials with the YA-8s began in June 193 Armament comprised four 0·30-in machine-guns in th wings with two more, forward firing, in the whee fairings and another for the rear gunner. Four 100-l bombs could be carried. A production order for 46 ai craft, to be designated A-8B, was placed in February 193

One of the service test batch aircraft was flown wit a 675-hp geared Conqueror engine as the Y1A-8. Anothe YA-8 was rebuilt in 1933 with a 625-hp Pratt & Whitne R-1620-9 Hornet radial engine and re-designated YA-1 This was in line with Army Air Corps policy, whic favoured the radial engine because of its better econom and decreased vulnerability compared with the liqui cooled in-line. A radial engine – the 690-hp Wrigh Cyclone – was also chosen for the production mode of the Shrike, which then were redesignated A-1

Curtiss BT-32

Most combat aircraft built in the USA originated to home requirement and were ordered first by one of th American armed forces. Among the few exception built specially for export, was the Curtiss BT-32 – bomber version of the Condor transport, which itse enjoyed considerable success in the commercial fiel and remained in production for a number of years i different versions.

The Condor was a big biplane with the fuselage an two engine nacelles mounted on the lower wing, and th upper wing clear of the top of the fuselage. One of it less-usual features was a retractable undercarriage.

From the Condor, Curtiss developed the BT-32 f

China. The principal design changes were stowage for a bomb-load of 3,968 lb and the addition of five gun positions, each with a single 0·30-in gun; these were in the nose, at two points on top of the fuselage and in side and bottom panels in the fuselage. Wright R-1820F-2 Cyclone engines gave the BT-32 a top speed of 180 mph at 7,000 ft.

The BT-32 was the last large biplane built in America, in 1934. It was supplied to the Chiang Kai-Shek forces but nothing is known of its operational use. The availability of more modern bomber monoplanes ended export of the BT-32.

Curtiss SBC Helldiver, Cleveland

Biplanes built by the Curtiss company for the US Army Air Corps and Navy have several claims to fame. Among them, the Hawk (page 473) was the Army's last biplane fighter, while the SBC Helldiver was the last combat biplane produced in the United States. Paradoxically, the SBC began life as a monoplane.

In 1932, the USN had ordered a single prototype of a new Curtiss two-seat fighter, the XF12C-1. Its features included a parasol wing, an enclosed cockpit for the two crewmen in tandem, and an undercarriage which retracted into the fuselage. The XF12C-1 flew in 1933 and was re-designated XS4C-1 at the end of the year, as a scout. The rôle was changed again in January 1934 when the aircraft became the XSBC-1 as a scout bomber; but the parasol wing was not strong enough for dive-bombing and the prototype crashed in September 1934.

A complete re-design was put in hand and the prototype was rebuilt during 1935, making its second "first flight" on 9 December as the XSBC-2. The fuselage design was similar to that of the original, but the canopy now faired back into the fin; the wings were completely new as the aircraft was now a biplane. In March 1936, the engine was changed from a 700-hp Wright R-1510-12 to an 825-hp Pratt & Whitney R-1535-82 and the designation changed to XSBC-3.

On 29 August 1936, the USN awarded Curtiss a production contract for 83 SBC-3s, similar to the prototype, with R-1535-94 engines. Armament comprised a single ·30-in gun in the cowling and another in the rear cockpit. A single 500-lb bomb could be carried under the fuselage, and was usually delivered in a dive-bombing attack. Deliveries to the Navy began on 17 July 1937, to equip VS-5 Squadron.

The last aircraft of the production batch was re-engined with the larger-diameter, single-row Wright R-1820-22 and was redesignated XSBC-4. With a -34 engine and the ability to carry a 1,000-lb bomb, production model SBC-4s were ordered in January 1938. Deliveries began in March 1939; production of this final variant totalled 174.

Fifty SBC-4s were released by the USN for sale to France in 1940, but were too late for combat. Five of this batch went to the RAF, which called them Clevelands but found no operational rôle for them.

Curtiss BT-32

Curtiss BT-32 floatplane

Curtiss SBC-3 Helldiver

TYPE	DIMENSIONS span ft	span in	length ft	length in	height ft	height in	WEIGHT max t-o lb	PERFORMANCE max speed mph	at height ft	service ceiling ft	combat range miles	REMARKS
Curtiss F11C-2	31	6	25	0	10	7	4,638	205	SL	24,300	560	
Curtiss BF2C-1	31	6	23	0	10	10	5,086	225	8,000	27,000	797	
Curtiss Hawk III	31	6	23	6	9	11	4,317	240	SL	25,800	575	
Curtiss Hawk IV	31	6	23	6	10	10	4,598	248	12,500	29,700	577	
Curtiss YA-8	44	3	32	10	9	0	5,706	183	SL	18,100	425	
Curtiss A-12	44	0	32	3	9	4	5,900	177	SL	15,150	510	
Curtiss BT-32	82	0	49	6	16	4	17,500	180	4,100	22,000	840	
Curtiss SBC-3	34	0	28	1	13	2	6,904	220	9,500	23,800	635	
Curtiss SBC-4	34	0	27	6	13	2	7,141	237	15,200	27,300	555	

Curtiss Y1A-18 Shrike

Curtiss P-36A, camouflaged for war games

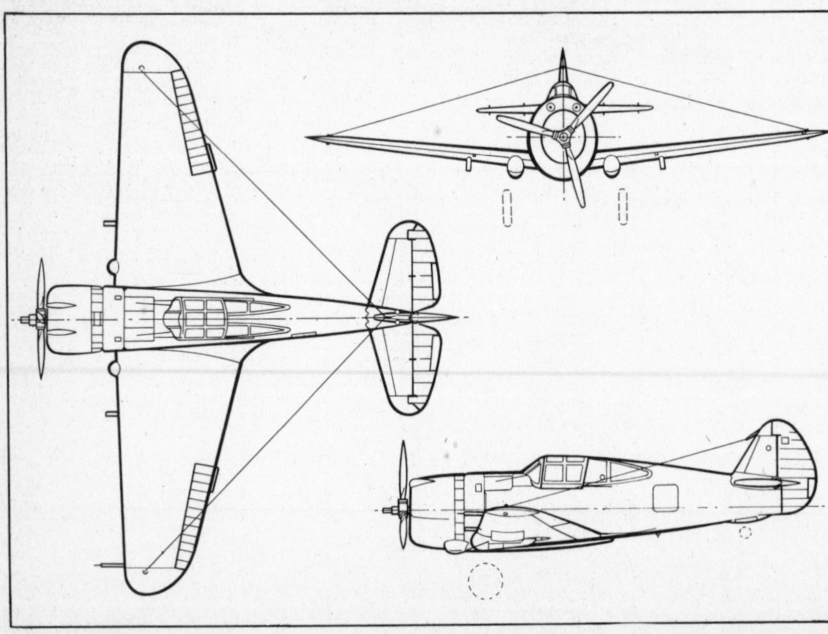

Curtiss P-36

Curtiss A-18 Shrike

Although the A-18 shared the name Shrike with the A-8/A-10/A-12 series, it was a completely different design, originating in 1934 as the Curtiss Model 76. The earlier single-engined Shrikes had set the pattern for Army attack aircraft for nearly a decade from 1931 onwards, but the search for higher performance led inexorably towards a twin-engined layout. A prototype of the Curtiss 76 was built with company funds for Army evaluation at Wright Field, and was powered by experimental Curtiss XR-1510 two-row radial engines. After tests, it was purchased by the Army, designated XA-14 and re-engined with 735-hp Wright R-1670-5 engines.

The XA-14 was an elegant, well-streamlined aircraft of all-metal construction, seating its two crew members under a long cockpit enclosure. Costs, inevitably, were higher than for a single-engined type and only a service test quantity of 13 was ordered, in July 1936.

The production model was identified as the Y1A-18 and was almost identical with the XA-14 apart from installation of 600-hp Wright R-1820-47 engines. Armament comprised four forward-firing guns and a fifth for rear defence, and the bomb-load was 654 lb.

Curtiss P-36

With its famous series of Hawk biplane fighters clearly coming to the end of their useful life, the Curtiss Airplane Division of Curtiss-Wright Corporation initiated development of a monoplane fighter towards the end of 1934. A prototype was built with company funds and was ready by May 1935 to be submitted in a USAAC design competition at Wright Field. Powered by an experimental 900-hp Wright R-1670 two-row radial engine, the Model 75, as the new fighter was designated, was a sturdy low-wing monoplane, with an enclosed cockpit for the pilot and a retractable undercarriage so arranged that the main wheels turned through 90° to lie flush in the wings.

After modification to Hawk 75-B configuration, with a Wright XR-1820-39 single-row radial engine and revised cockpit and tail unit, the prototype was again tested by the Air Corps in April 1936. These trials led to a contract for three examples, designated Y1P-36, which were delivered in February 1937 with 1,050-hp Pratt & Whitney R-1830-13 engines. The Y1P-36s demonstrated that the design performance could be achieved, with a top speed of 294·5 mph at 10,000 ft; this, plus the favourable reports of test pilots on the control characteristics, resulted in a production contract for 210 aircraft.

Delivery began in April 1938, the total being made up of 177 P-36As and 31 P-36Cs, plus single prototypes of the XP-40 and XP-42. The P-36A had an R-1830-13 Twin Wasp engine and achieved 313 mph at 10,000 ft. Its armament comprised one 0·30-in and one 0·50-in machine-gun in the engine cowling. Two more 0·30-in guns in the wings distinguished the P-36C, which also had an R-1830-17 engine.

By February 1941, P-36s were operational with USAAC pursuit squadrons outside the USA and at least four P-36As went into action successfully against the Japanese at Pearl Harbor in December 1941. More operational use was made of the export versions of the Hawk 75, described separately.

One export order, for 30 Hawk 75A-8s for Norway, was unfulfilled because of the occupation of that country. The aircraft went instead to Canada, and then to the USAAF with the designation P-36G. They were later presented to Peru. The P-36 also served as the basic airframe for a number of power plant, propeller and armament experiments.

Curtiss Hawk 75 (Export)

In 1937, the Curtiss Airplane Division began development of a version of the Hawk 75 (P-36) design particularly for export. Emphasis was placed upon simplicity and low cost, so this model had a fixed, faired undercarriage and a lower-powered engine – the 875-hp Wright GR-1820-G3. Armament was to P-36A standard, con prising one 0·50-in and one 0·30-in gun, plus wing racks for 300 lb of bombs.

The prototype of the export Hawk 75 was presented to the Chinese government – a gesture which earned Curtiss a contract for 112 similar aircraft designated Hawk 75M and delivered in 1938.

A similar model, designated Hawk 75M, was produced for the Royal Siamese Air Force in 1939–40. This had two additional wing guns, as on the P-36C, and 25 were built. They saw action when Thailand invaded Indo-China in January 1941, and later that year against Japanese forces.

The Argentine purchased 30 Hawk 750s, another similar variant, and also acquired a licence to build this type. Subsequently, the government factory at Cordoba manufactured 200 for the Argentine Air Force.

Versions of the P-36 proved even more successful for export, starting in May 1939 when a French purchasing commission ordered 100 Hawk 75A-1 fighters with Pratt & Whitney R-1830-SC3-G engines. A distinguishing feature of the French version was the use of four 7·5-mm guns and several items of French-built equipment. Delivery began at the end of 1938, all but the first few examples arriving unassembled, to be put together by SNCAC at Bourges.

Further French orders were placed for 100 Hawk 75A-2s (six guns), 135 Hawk 75A-3s (six guns and R-1830-SC3-G engine) and 395 Hawk 75A-4s (Wright GR-1820-G205A Cyclone engine). All the Hawk 75A-1s and -2s were delivered, but only 91 assorted -3s and -4s arrived before France fell.

Of the Hawk 75As laid down for France but not delivered, 227 were supplied to the Royal Air Force, which named them Mohawk III (Hawk 75A-3) and Mohawk IV (Hawk 75A-4). Some of the earlier French Hawk 75s taken over in the field were designated Mohawk I and II. After being fitted with six machine-guns and British equipment, many went to India, where they remained operational on the Burma front until the end of 1943. Other Mohawks were shipped to South Africa and Portugal.

Norway contracted for 12 Hawk 75A-6s (R-1830-SC3-G engine) in 1939 and subsequently doubled this order. About half reached Norway, but were not assembled by the time the country was overrun; the remainder went to "Little Norway" in Canada for training, together with 30 Hawk 75A-8s (GR-1820-G205A engine) which Norway had also ordered.

Eight of the Norwegian aircraft were found by German troops when Norway was occupied, and these were eventually sold by Germany to Finland, together with 36 Hawk 75A-1s, -2s and -3s captured in France.

A licence to build the Hawk 75A was obtained by Hindustan Aircraft Ltd in India in 1941 and five examples were built before policy changed and the plan was abandoned. Another export order came from Iran in 1941, for ten Hawk 75A-9s (Cyclone engine). These were discovered by British forces in August 1941 and eventually equipped an RAF squadron in the Far East.

The Netherlands government ordered 35 Hawk 75A-7s (Cyclone 9), but these could not be delivered because Holland had been occupied. Instead, 24 went to the Netherlands East Indies, where they became operational against invading Japanese forces.

Curtiss Hawk 75 (Export)

Curtiss Hawk 75A, Armée de l'Air

Curtiss Mohawk IV, RAF

TYPE	DIMENSIONS span ft	span in	length ft	length in	height ft	height in	WEIGHT max t-o lb	PERFORMANCE max speed mph	at height ft	service ceiling ft	combat range miles	REMARKS
Curtiss Y1A-18	59	6	42	4	15	0	13,170	238·5	3,500	28,650	1,443	
Curtiss P-36A	37	4	28	6	12	2	6,010	313	10,000	33,000	825	
Curtiss P-36C	37	4	28	6	12	2	6,150	311	10,000	33,700	820	
Curtiss Hawk 75	37	4	28	7	9	4	6,418	280	10,700	31,800	547	
Curtiss Hawk 75A-1	37	4	28	7	9	4	5,692	303	19,000	32,800	677	
Curtiss Hawk 75A-4	37	4	28	10	9	6	5,750	323	15,100	32,700	1,000	

Curtiss-Wright CW-21

Curtiss-Wright CW-21B

Curtiss SB2C-4 Helldiver

Curtiss A-25A Helldiver

Curtiss-Wright CW-21

Most aircraft bearing the Curtiss name were products of the Curtiss Airplane Division of Curtiss-Wright Corporation. A few, however, were products of the St-Louis Division of the parent company, one such being the Curtiss-Wright CW-21 Demon. The philosophy of this design was to produce a lightweight interceptor, taking as a basis the two-seat CW-19R.

Like other successful Curtiss designs, the CW-21 was intended particularly for export. The first flight was made in January 1939 and in the same year China ordered 35 examples, of which 32 were to be supplied as components for assembly in China. Powered by a 1,000-hp Wright Cyclone R-1820-G5, the CW-21 was armed with two machine-guns, one each of 0·30-in and 0·50-in calibre, firing through the propeller disc. The main legs of the undercarriage retracted backward, to lie in fairings under the wings.

Twenty-four examples of an improved model, the CW-21B, were ordered by the Netherlands East Indies in 1940 and delivery began in the same year. Armament was increased to four guns and the undercarriage retracted inward, for the wheels to lie in a fairing under the fuselage. A few CW-21Bs saw brief and unsuccessful service against Japanese forces in 1942.

Finally, three CW-21Bs were sent to China for use by the American Volunteer Group in 1941. All were lost in poor visibility on their delivery flight from Rangoon to Kunming.

Curtiss SB2C/A-25 Helldiver

Production of 7,200 examples of the monoplane Helldiver made this the most successful of all USN dive-bombers and the second most-produced of all Curtiss-designed aeroplanes. It had its origin in a US Navy requirement for a sturdy, high-performance dive-bomber and inherited its name from the earlier Curtiss biplane, the SBC, which served the Navy in a similar rôle (page 477). Ordered on 15 May 1939, the prototype XSB2C-1, as the new type was designated, first flew on 18 December 1940 but crashed early in 1941. Powered by a 1,700-hp Wright R-2600-8 radial engine, the XSB2C-1 was similar in configuration to the Brewster SB2A (page 459) with which it was in direct competition.

An initial production order for SB2C-1s was placed in November 1940, before the prototype flew, and the latter's crash did not lessen the Navy's faith in the aircraft. Several factors combined to delay deliveries, however, including a long list modifications and establishment of a new factory in which to produce the Helldiver. The first SB2C-1 rolled from this line, at Columbus, Ohio, in June 1942, with an armament of six machine-guns and a 1,000-lb bomb-load; later, two 20-mm cannon replaced the four wing guns.

Production of the SB2C-1 totalled 978. Subsequent orders kept the Helldiver in production until 1945, with several variants introduced successively. The SB2C-3 (1,112 built) used the 1,900-hp R-2600-20 engine and a four-blade propeller, while the SB2C-4 (2,045 built) had provision for eight 5-in rockets or 1,000 lb of bombs beneath the wings. This version was also the first to carry radar search equipment, in underwing radome. An increase in fuel capacity was the principal new feature of the SB2C-5, of which 970 were built.

During 1941, the USAAC found an urgent need for a dive-bomber of this type, and contracts were placed with Douglas (page 486) and with Curtiss. The 900 Helldivers bought by the Air Corps, under the designation A-25A, were without the usual naval equipment and wing-folding gear, but most were transferred to the US Marine Corps as SB2C-1As after delivery.

Additional production lines for the Helldiver were laid down by Fairchild in Canada and by Canadian Car and Foundry. Fairchild flew its first Helldiver, an SBF-1 on 28 August 1943, and built a total of 300, including SBF-3 and SBF-4 versions. CCF built 894 in SBW-1, -3, -4 and -5 versions, flying the first on 29 July 1943. Twenty-six SBW-1Bs were supplied to Britain, but were not used operationally.

Helldivers remained in service with the USN until 1949, and some were supplied to foreign air forces, including those of Italy, Greece and France, the latter for use in the war in Indo-China.

Curtiss P-40 Warhawk, Tomahawk, Kittyhawk

Between 1938 and 1944, a grand total of 13,738 examples of the Curtiss P-40 was built. The last of the Hawks, the P-40 served with the United States Army Air Force in all operational areas during World War II and with the air forces of several other nations. Never outstanding as a fighting machine, it nevertheless proved to be rugged and capable of adaptation to suit the needs of the day.

The P-40 design originated in July 1937 as a variant of the P-36 (page 478) modified to have the then-new Allison V-1710-19 liquid-cooled in-line engine, supercharged for combat at medium altitudes. Since the airframe was already developed, the P-40 was quickly available (first flight was made in October 1938). So, although its performance fell short of that specified by the USAAC in a specification issued on 25 January 1939, the P-40 was ordered into large-scale production on the same day (27 April 1939) that contracts were awarded for the first development batches of Lockheed P-38 Lightnings and Bell P-39 Airacobras. This April order was for 524 P-40s, reduced later to 200 to allow Curtiss to concentrate on 140 similar Hawk 81A-1s for France.

Delivery of the French Hawks would have begun after France had been occupied; the aircraft were, consequently, transferred to the Royal Air Force, which bestowed on them the name Tomahawk I. With only two forward-firing guns and a modest performance, the Tomahawk Is were poorly suited to European combat conditions and most of them served with Army Co-operation units or were transferred to the Middle East. Some improvement was offered in the Tomahawk IIA, of which Britain received 110. These had two wing guns in addition to those in the fuselage, and such essential features as self-sealing fuel tanks and additional armour. A similar model for the USAAF was designated P-40B, of which 131 were built.

The addition of two more wing guns and other changes produced the P-40C, of which 193 went to the USAAF and 930 to Britain as Tomahawk IIBs. At least 13 RAF squadrons flew the Tomahawk II, as well as units of the RAAF and SAAF. One hundred IIBs were transferred to China, where they equipped the "Flying Tiger" units; 195 others went to the U.S.S.R. becoming the first US fighters to see action on the Soviet front. Other P-40s were supplied to the Turkish Air Force.

A major re-design produced the P-40D in 1941. This variant had the Allison V-1710-39 engine, which allowed the fuselage to be shortened by 6 in; the nose radiator was deepened and the nose guns removed. Four 0·50-in wing guns were fitted, and provision was made for a 500-lb bomb under the fuselage and smaller bombs on wing racks. Britain had ordered 560 of these new Hawks in May 1940 and put them into service as Kittyhawk Is, some with wing armament increased to six guns. Only 22 of the four-gun variant went to the USAAF, as P-40Ds, followed by 820 six-gun P-40Es. Another 1,500 P-40Es were for lend-lease delivery to Britain, as Kittyhawk IAs, twelve

Curtiss P-40

Curtiss Kittyhawk I, RAF

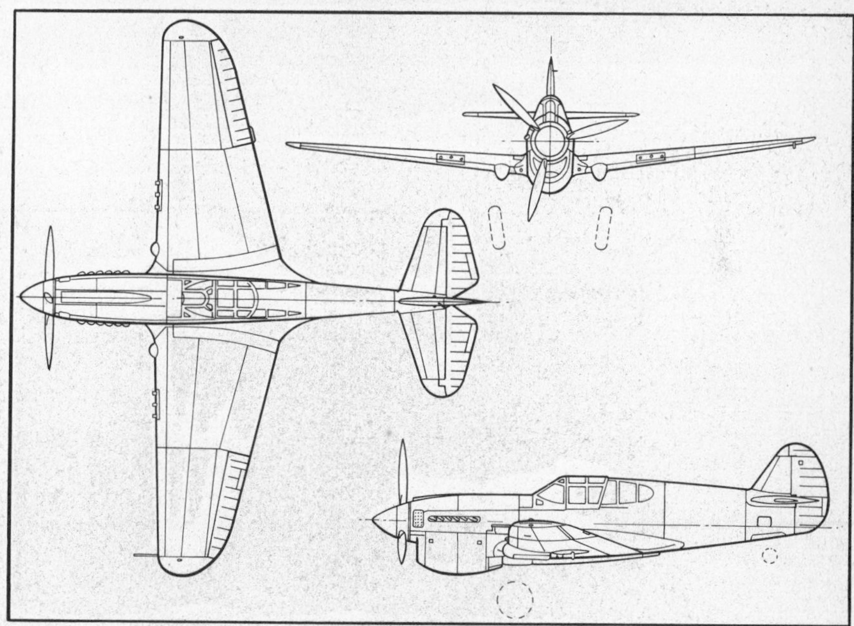
Curtiss P-40E

TYPE	DIMENSIONS span ft	span in	length ft	length in	height ft	height in	WEIGHT max t-o lb	PERFORMANCE max speed mph	at height ft	service ceiling ft	combat range miles	REMARKS
Curtiss CW-21	35	0	26	6	8	8	4,250	304	NA	35,000	NA	
Curtiss CW-21B	35	0	27	2	8	11	4,500	314	12,200	34,300	630	
Curtiss SB2C-1	49	9	36	8	13	2	16,607	281	12,400	24,700	1,110	
Curtiss SB2C-3	49	9	36	8	13	2	16,471	294	16,700	29,300	1,165	
Curtiss SB2C-5	49	9	36	8	13	2	16,287	290	16,500	27,600	1,324	
Curtiss A-25A	49	9	36	8	14	6	16,000	275	15,000	26,800	700	Army SB2C

Curtiss P-40F Warhawk

Curtiss P-40N Warhawk

de Havilland/Boeing D.H.4

de Havilland/Boeing DH-4M

went to the RCAF in March 1942 and others to the RAAF.

An important development in 1941 was the modification of a P-40D to have a Rolls-Royce Merlin 28 engine, as the XP-40F. This had a considerably improved performance, especially at higher altitudes, and the P-40F was put into production with the Packard-built Merlin, designated V-1650-1. Production totalled 1,311, including 250 allotted to the RAF as Kittyhawk IIs but not delivered; 100 were supplied to the Soviet Air Force and others to the Free French Forces. Most P-40Fs had a modification to lengthen the fuselage by 26 in for improved directional stability. The P-40K had the V-1710-73 engine and a dorsal fin; 1,300 were built, and many were supplied to the RCAF, as well as 21 to the RAF.

Similar to the P-40F, the P-40L was lightened by removing two wing guns and other equipment; 700 were built before a shortage of Merlins led to re-introduction of the Allison engine for subsequent variants.

Three hundred P-40Fs and P-40Ls were re-engined with the Allison V-1710-81 engine in 1944 and redesignated P-40R-1 and P-40R-2. The -40M was similarly engined, and 600 were built for the RAF as Kittyhawk IIIs. The P-40N was again similar, but with the weight-reducing modifications of the P-40L. This proved to be the most-produced of all P-40 variants, with 4,219 built in several distinct versions. Later P-40Ns had the wing armament restored to six guns, provision for 1,500-lb of bombs under the wings and V-1710-99 or V-1710-115 engines. Under lend-lease arrangements, 586 P-40Ns were supplied to the RAF, RAAF and RNZAF, for use in the Far Eastern theatre as Kittyhawk IVs.

Production of the P-40 ended in December 1944, but the type continued in service until the closing stages of the war.

de Havilland D.H.4/Boeing O2B

Only one type of aircraft built in the United States reached the stage of operational service against the enemy during the 1914–18 War. This was the D.H. 4, a two-seat scout and light bomber designed in England (see page 336) and produced by Aircraft Manufacturing Co.

Shortly after America entered the war in 1917, a large-scale technical mission was despatched to Europe, under Major Raynal C. Bolling, to examine French and British military aircraft production. Among the recommendations of this Commission were that the United States should purchase fighters in Europe, and should embark upon the production of selected European designs under licence. The D.H.4 was chosen for immediate large-scale production, and by the time of the Armistice just over 10,000 had been ordered from US sources.

The choice of the D.H.4 by the Army was influenced by its ability to mount the US-developed Liberty engine, a 400-hp Vee in-line unit which was one of America's most important contributions to the 1914–18 War. A sample British-built D.H.4 was shipped to the United States in the summer of 1917 and was assigned to the Dayton-Wright Airplane Company at Dayton, Ohio, where it arrived on 15 August. There, an early example of the Liberty 12 was installed, and flight trials began on 29 October. Dayton-Wright became the principal contractor for D.H.4 production, contracts eventually totalling 5,006 aircraft, (of which 1,902 were cancelled after the Armistice). Additional sources of D.H.4s were provided by the Fisher Body Company, whose contracts totalled 4,000 (2,400 cancelled), and Standard Aircraft Corporation, with 1,000 ordered but only 140 built before the Armistice ended production.

The first Dayton-built D.H.4 despatched to the American Expeditionary Force in France left New Jersey on 15 March 1918, but was lost at sea *en route*. Consequently, the AEF did not receive its first American-built warplane until 17 May. On 2 August, the first sortie over enemy territory was made by the type, and squadron re-equipment proceeded apace. Production also built up rapidly, from 15 in April to 1,097 in October 1918. By 11 November, when the Armistice was signed, the three companies had produced 3,431 D.H.4s, and another 1,415 were built before production ended in 1919. Of these some 1,200 had reached France by the war's end. Equipping five bombing and seven observation squadrons of the AEF, there were 196 at the front, and a total of 325 in the Zone of Advance on 11 November 1918.

Produced in greater quantity than any other 1914–18 War aircraft in the United States, except the Curtiss "Jenny", the D.H.4 became the subject of extensive development and modification. The first variants were the work of the Engineering Division of the Bureau of Aircraft Production and were intended to overcome one of the weak points of the original design – the location of the fuel tank in the fuselage between the two cockpits. A single D.H.4A (not to be confused with the British variant of the same designation) with a revised fuel system, in July 1918, was followed by a D.H.4B in which the main fuel tank and the front cockpit were reversed, bringing the pilot and observer closer together. Fuel capacity was increased to 88 gallons and, with a 416-hp Liberty 12A engine, the gross weight went up from 4,300 lb to 4,595 lb. Tested in October 1918, the D.H.4B was a success, and the Army arranged for the conversion to this standard of most surviving D.H.4s between 1919 and 1923. Some of these conversions were handled at Air Depots, but most (totalling 1,538) were contracted out to ten different companies, including Thomas Morse, Gallaudet, Aeromarine and LWF. Sub-variants of this type included the B-1, with a 110-US gallon tank; the B-2 with a 76-gallon leak-proof tank; and the B-3 with a 135-gallon tank. Besides these basic post-war models, more than 60 other specialized variants were produced.

There were, for example, the D.H.4 Amb 1 and D.H.4 Amb 2 ambulances, with accommodation for one and two stretchers respectively; the DH-4B-4 and XDH-4B-5, two airways versions by Engineering Division; the DH-4BK equipped for night flying; the DH-4BM single-seater for communications and the DH-4BM-1 with dual controls; the DH-4BT, a dual-control trainer and the XDH-4BP and DH-4BP-1 photographic survey versions. Among re-engined variants were the DH-4BW with a 300-hp Wright H, the DH-4C with a 350-hp Packard 1A-1237 and the XDH-4B5 with a supercharged Liberty. The XDH-4L had a 185-gallon tank, giving an endurance of 9 hours.

In 1923, the DH-4 design was modernized as the DH-4M, with a steel-tube fuselage, Liberty 12A engine, new equipment and gross weight of 4,510 lb. In this form it was put back into production, Boeing obtaining an Army contract for 150, of which 53 appeared as DH-4Ms and the remainder as DH-4M-1s, differing in the extent of new parts used. Boeing also built 30 for the US Marine Corps as O2B-1s and sold six to Cuba.

In 1924, Atlantic was awarded a contract for 135 more of the new type, designated DH-4M-2s. All utilized wings already manufactured for DH-4Bs.

DH-4 components also were used in other post-war products of several manufacturers to meet Army requirements. Both Boeing and Atlantic made use of their DH-4M production experience in 1924 Corps Observation prototypes. The Boeing XCO-7 had a revised, thick wing section but was otherwise a DH-4M, as also was the XCO-7A with a wide-track undercarriage. The XCO-7B was similar with a Liberty V-1410 inverted engine. Atlantic's XCO-8 was a DH-4M-2 with COA-1 wings.

de Havilland/Boeing DH-4M-1

de Havilland/Boeing O2B-1

de Havilland/Boeing D.H.4 Ambulance

TYPE	DIMENSIONS span ft	span in	length ft	length in	height ft	height in	WEIGHT max t-o lb	PERFORMANCE max speed mph	at height ft	service ceiling ft	combat range miles	REMARKS
Curtiss P-40	37	4	31	9	12	4	7,215	357	15,000	32,750	350	
Curtiss P-40C	37	4	31	9	12	4	8,058	345	15,000	29,500	NA	
Curtiss P-40E	37	4	31	9	12	4	9,200	354	15,000	29,000	NA	
Curtiss P-40F	37	4	33	4	12	4	9,350	364	20,000	34,400	375	
Curtiss P-40M	37	4	33	4	12	4	91,000	360	20,000	30,000	350	
Curtiss P-40N	37	4	33	4	12	4	11,400	350	16,400	31,000	340	
D.H.4	45	5½	29	11	9	8	3,582	124	SL	19,600	270	
D.H.4B	42	5	29	11	9	8	4,595	118	SL	12,800	550	

Douglas DT-1

Douglas T2D-1

Douglas P2D-1

Douglas Y1B-7, camouflaged for war games

The DH-4Bs and -4Ms remained in large-scale service until 1928 for observation and attack duties, and, as indicated above, served in a number of pioneering rôles. In the latter respect, mention should be made of the flight refuelling trials made in 1923 with a DH-4 receiver, carrying an extra fuel tank, with a large filling point in the rear fuselage; and the DH-4B-1 tanker which trailed a 50-ft length of hose with a quick-acting shut-off valve. The first successful contacts were made on 27 June 1923, and on 27/28 August the receiver remained airborne for 37 hours 15 minutes in the first conclusive demonstration of flight refuelling.

Douglas DT

First military aircraft to carry the famous Douglas name – now among the most distinguished in world aviation – was a torpedo-bomber ordered by the US Navy for a 1922 competition. Three examples were ordered from Douglas in 1921 with the designation DT-1, and trials with the first indicated that the type was superior to four other designs evaluated by the Navy.

The DT-1 was based on the Douglas Cloudster, and was a squat biplane with a crew of two, folding wings and an interchangeable wheel/float undercarriage. A 1,835-lb torpedo could be carried under the fuselage. The engine was a 400-hp Liberty.

Douglas received contracts for 38 DT-2s, which had nose radiators in place of the fuselage side radiators of the DT-1; the second and third DT-1s were also completed to this standard. Additional contracts were placed with LWF for 20 DT-2s, 11 of which were converted by Dayton Wright to SDW-1s. Douglas also built a number of DT-2Bs, with Wright T-3 engines, for the Norwegian and Peruvian Navies in 1924–5. Four Douglas World Cruiser aircraft, similar to the DT-2, were used by the US Army for the first round-the-world flight in 1924.

Five DT-4s and a DT-5 built by the Naval Aircraft Factory in 1923 had Wright T-2 engines, geared in the the DT-5. Another variation was a 450-hp Wright Cyclone in the DT-6. DT-2s remained in service until 1926.

Douglas T2D/P2D

The US Navy's first twin-engined torpedo-bombers were designed in 1925 to a BuAer specification. A single prototype (XTN-1) was ordered from the Naval Aircraft Factory, while Douglas received a contract in July 1925 for three examples of the almost-identical XT2D-1 design. Completed during 1926, the T2D was a 10,000-lb equal-span biplane, powered by two 525-hp Wright R-1750 uncowled radials. Nine more T2D-1s ordered in 1927 served briefly with front-line units in 1928.

During 1927, one XT2D-1 was assigned to Squadron VT-2B and is reported to have operated off the carrier USS *Langley*. This appears to be the first operation of a twin-engined aircraft from an aircraft carrier. Most T2D-1s were operated as floatplanes by VJ-1B, attached to the seaplane tender USS *Aroostook*.

With the decision to use the T2D-1s from shore bases, another 18 ordered in June 1930 were redesignated P2D-1s, with 575-hp R-1820 engines. They served with Patrol Squadron VP-3 until replaced by PBY-1s early in 1937.

Douglas B-7

First monoplane in the US Army "Bomber" category, the Douglas B-7 was a by-product of a programme which was started to meet a need for a fast twin-engined observation aircraft. Both Douglas and the United States Fokker company obtained Army contracts to build prototypes, and it was decided that second prototypes of each design could conveniently be completed as bombers.

The Douglas XB-7 was a gull-wing monoplane with two 600-hp Curtiss V-1570-25 engines carried on struts beneath the wing. The main wheels retracted backward, and the crew of four had open cockpits.

After testing of the XB-7 in 1930, Douglas was awarded a service test contract for seven YB-7s, with 675-hp V-1570-27 engines and minor changes compared with the prototype. They proved to be some 60 mph faster than the

Keystone bomber biplanes then in service, but the pace of aeronautical development was so rapid at that time that the YB-7s were themselves overtaken by the new all-metal low-wing monoplanes in 1931.

Douglas B-18

To meet a 1934 US Army requirement for a bomber to replace the Martin B-10 (page 527), Douglas designed a new fuselage which could be used with the wings and tail unit of the DC-2 transport, then in production. The resulting DB-1 (Douglas Bomber 1), powered by two 930-hp Wright R-1820-45 Cyclone engines, was in competition with a Martin prototype and the Boeing B-17.

Trials at Wright Field, in August 1935, resulted in an immediate contract for 133 aircraft, designated B-18; another 217 followed as B-18As with R-1820-53 engines, higher weight and revised nose contours. These went into service with many bomber units in 1940, but were soon replaced by B-17s after the war began for America in 1941. A total of 122 were converted into B-18Bs for anti-submarine duties in the Caribbean, with a radome replacing the observer's position in the nose and magnetic anomaly detection (MAD) equipment in a rear fairing.

Twenty B-18As were used, also for maritime duties, by the Royal Canadian Air Force, which gave them the type name Digby Mk I.

The B-18 was operated by a crew of six, including three gunners, each with a 0.30-in machine-gun – one in the nose, one in a dorsal turret and one in a ventral turret. One B-18 was completed with a power-operated nose turret and was known as the DB-2.

Douglas TBD Devastator

Contracts placed by the US Navy on 30 June 1934 led to development of the first carrier-based monoplanes to be put into production for that Service. The contracts went to Douglas and Great Lakes, and were for prototypes of torpedo-bombers suitable for operation from a new generation of carriers, of which the USS *Ranger* (commissioned in 1934) was the first. Douglas's XTBD-1 proved to be a monoplane, while Great Lakes produced, in the XTBG-1, the last of the biplane torpedo-bombers.

The Douglas XTBD-1, delivered to the US Navy on 24 April 1935, set a fashion for torpedo-bombers which was to survive for more than a decade, with its low wing, long cockpit for tandem seating of the crew of three, and backward-retracting main wheels which, when up, protruded from the wings to give partial protection in a crash-landing. The wings folded upward for stowage on board carriers and – a new feature – folding was power-actuated rather than manual. Powered by an 800-hp Pratt & Whitney XR-1830-60 engine, the XTBD-1 could carry a 1,000-lb bomb or a 15-ft torpedo beneath the fuselage, and was armed with two 0·30-in guns.

After successful prototype trials, the Douglas torpedo-bomber was ordered into production on 3 February 1936. Deliveries began on 25 June 1937, to give the US Navy, temporarily, one of the best carrier-based attack aeroplanes in the world. Production models, of which 129 were built, had an 850-hp R-1830-64 engine, revised cowling and raised canopy over the pilot's cockpit.

Douglas B-18

Douglas B-18A

Douglas B-18B

TYPE	DIMENSIONS						WEIGHT	PERFORMANCE				REMARKS
	span ft	span in	length ft	length in	height ft	height in	max t-o lb	max speed mph	at height ft	service ceiling ft	combat range miles	
Douglas DT-2	50	0	37	8	15	1	7,293	99	SL	7,400	274	Seaplane model
Douglas DT-4	50	0	34	5	13	5	6,989	108	SL	11,075	240	Landplane model
Douglas T2D-1	57	0	44	4	16	11	11,357	124	SL	11,400	384	Landplane model
Douglas P2D-1	57	0	43	11	17	6	12,791	138	SL	11,700	1,010	Landplane model
Douglas YB-7	65	3	46	7	12	1	11,177	182	SL	20,400	411	
Douglas B-18	89	6	56	8	15	2	27,087	217	10,000	24,200	1,200	
Douglas B-18A	89	6	57	10	15	2	27,673	215	10,000	23,900	NA	

Douglas TBD-1 Devastator

Douglas SBD-1 Dauntless

Douglas A-24B Dauntless

Douglas Dauntless DB Mk 1 (SBD-5), RN

The 100 or so TBDs still in service when Japan attacked American bases at the end of 1941 were named Devastators and were in action as early as February 1942 in strikes against Japanese forces in the Marshall and Gilbert Islands. Meeting little opposition, the TBDs inflicted considerable damage and claimed a Japanese cruiser sunk as well as other shipping destroyed. A few months later, however, the US Navy lost 35 Devastators on a single day during the Battle of Midway, when they were trapped between flak from the ships and waiting Zeros.

On this inauspicious note, the operational career of the TBD ended; but newer types cast in the same mould were already in production and eventually fulfilled the promise which was inherent in the Devastator's design.

Douglas SBD Dauntless

The history of America's most successful dive-bomber of World War II began in 1934 when the Northrop Aircraft Co obtained a US Navy contract to build the prototype of an advanced new machine to replace the biplanes then in service. The Northrop company had been set up two years previously by a former Douglas engineer who wanted to specialize in the then-new techniques of all-metal stressed-skin construction. Douglas retained financial and technical links with the Northrop company, which was destined to become the El Segundo division of Douglas in 1938. The Northrop dive-bomber of 1934 thus became the Douglas SBD of World War II.

In general configuration and structural design, the Northrop XBT-1 was similar to the A-17 produced for the Army Air Corps. It featured a low wing, tandem seating for the crew of two in a single cockpit, and backward-retracting main wheels. Principal armament was the 1,000-lb bomb carried under the fuselage on a crutch, which swung down before release of the bomb to prevent the weapon from hitting the propeller when released. Perforated split flaps at the wing trailing-edge were used for stability and control during the dive, and to overcome some buffet encountered on initial tests.

When first delivered for Navy trials, the XBT-1 had a 700-hp R-1535-66 engine; this was replaced later by the R-1535-94, which was the power plant for the 54 production model BT-1s ordered in September 1936.

One of these aircraft was delivered as the BT-1S with an experimental tricycle undercarriage, the nose-wheel being fixed. The last aircraft on the contract was completed, during 1938, as the XBT-2, with a series of aerodynamic refinements, a 1,000-hp Wright XR-1820-32 engine and inward-retracting main wheels.

When a production contract was placed for this variant, in April 1939, the designation was changed to reflect the Douglas ownership of the design, the new cipher being SBD. Starting in May 1940, Douglas El Segundo delivered 57 SBD-1s, similar to the XBT-2 but with a taller fin and rudder. These were followed by 87 SBD-2s with increased fuel capacity. These versions had two 0·30-in guns in the engine cowling and a third for the observer.

Increased armament – 0·50s in the cowling and two 0·30s for rear defence – distinguished the SBD-3, which appeared in March 1941. Other improvements were self-sealing fuel tanks, protective armour and a 1,000-hp R-1820-52 engine. Initially, the US Navy ordered 174 of this version, but the total increased to 584 after the Japanese attack on Pearl Harbor. A further 168 were built (as SBD-3As) for the US Army, which became interested in dive-bombers after their short-term successes with the Luftwaffe in Europe. These aircraft were virtually identical with their Navy counterparts, apart from deletion of the deck hook and use of a pneumatic rather than solid rubber tail-wheel.

SBDs were in operational use with the US Navy from December 1941; those of the Army, designated A-24, were first operational early in 1942 in the Netherlands East Indies, with inconspicuous results. Production continued at a high level at El Segundo, however, with 780 SBD-4s and 170 SBD-4As, the latter for the Army as A-24As. Distinguishing feature of this version was the use of a 24-volt electrical system.

A second production line, established by Douglas at Tulsa, produced 3,024 SBD-5s, with the 1,200-hp

R-1820-60 engine. Of this quantity, 615 were allocated to the Army as A-24Bs; a few others were supplied to the Royal Air Force and to Mexico. Final production version was the SBD-6, with a 1,350-hp R-1820-66 engine. Douglas built 451, to bring the grand total of Dauntless production to 5,936. These aircraft inflicted crippling damage on the Japanese fleet, in actions such as the Battle of the Coral Sea, Midway and the Solomons campaign.

Douglas DB-7, A-20 Havoc, and Boston (Bombers)

One of the most-produced and most widely-operated light bombers of World War II, the Douglas DB-7 owed its inception to a US Army Air Corps design competition initiated in 1938. The specification represented a big advance on the attack types then in service, such as the Northrop/Douglas A-17. By the time details had been communicated to the manufacturing industry, the Douglas design team led by Jack Northrop, with E. H. "Ed" Heinemann as his chief lieutenant, had already prepared designs for a twin-engined attack bomber, designated the Douglas Model 7A.

Details of this design were submitted to the Army Air Corps in July 1938, and Douglas was among the companies invited to build prototypes and to submit bids for production quantities by March 1939. During the detail design and prototype construction phase, the design was modified into the Model 7B, with more advanced characteristics and better performance. When the DB-7B prototype appeared, it was seen to be a shoulder-wing monoplane with two 1,100-hp Pratt & Whitney Twin Wasp R-1830 radial engines and – for the first time on a US warplane – a nose-wheel undercarriage. Retractable dorsal and ventral turrets were supplemented by four 0·30-in guns in two blisters, one on each side of the nose. For ground-attack duties, provision was made for four more guns in the nose itself, the whole nose section being interchangeable with one incorporating a bomb-aiming panel and navigation station.

This prototype was first flown in December 1938. Its development had by this time attracted the attention of the French Purchasing Commission which, as a matter of urgency, was seeking US warplanes to re-equip the French Air Force. In January 1939, with a member of the French Commission on board, the Model 7B was lost when it went out of control after an engine failure.

Despite this setback, France ordered 100 of the Douglas bombers in February 1939, specifying a number of design changes which were to produce an aeroplane of considerably different appearance. The fuselage was deepened, with the result that the wing became mid- rather than shoulder-mounted; the nose lines became more streamlined; the nacelles were moved down below the wings; and, most important, the fuselage was narrowed, making it impossible to accommodate crew members side-by-side.

The new design was designated DB-7 (for Douglas Bomber) and the production prototype flew at El Segundo on 17 August 1939. Powered by 1,050-hp R-1830-SC3G engines, it bore French markings and carried an armament of four forward-firing 7·5-mm French guns, plus two more for rear defence, one above and one below the fuselage. The bomb-load was 1,764 lb.

French orders for the DB-7 were increased to 270, the

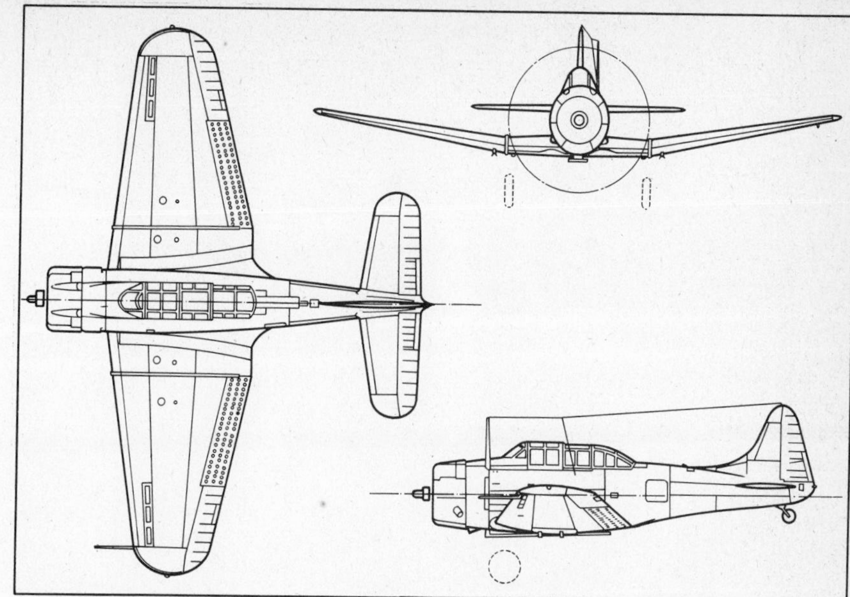

Douglas A-24B Dauntless

Douglas A-20A Havoc

Douglas Boston Mk III, RAF

TYPE	DIMENSIONS span ft	span in	length ft	length in	height ft	height in	WEIGHT max t-o lb	PERFORMANCE max speed mph	at height ft	service ceiling ft	combat range miles	REMARKS
Douglas TBD-1	50	0	35	0	15	1	10,194	206	8,000	19,700	435	
Douglas BT-1	41	6	31	8	9	11	7,197	222	9,500	25,300	550	Northrop production
Douglas SBD-1	41	6	32	2	13	7	9,790	253	16,000	29,600	860	BT-2 production by Douglas
Douglas SBD-3	41	6	32	8	13	7	10,400	250	16,000	27,100	1,345	A-24 similar
Douglas SBD-5	41	6	33	0	12	11	10,700	252	13,800	24,300	1,115	A-24B similar
Douglas SBD-6	41	6	33	0	12	11	10,882	262	15,600	28,600	1,230	

Douglas Boston (A28), RAAF

Douglas Boston Mk III, RAF; trials with dorsal turret

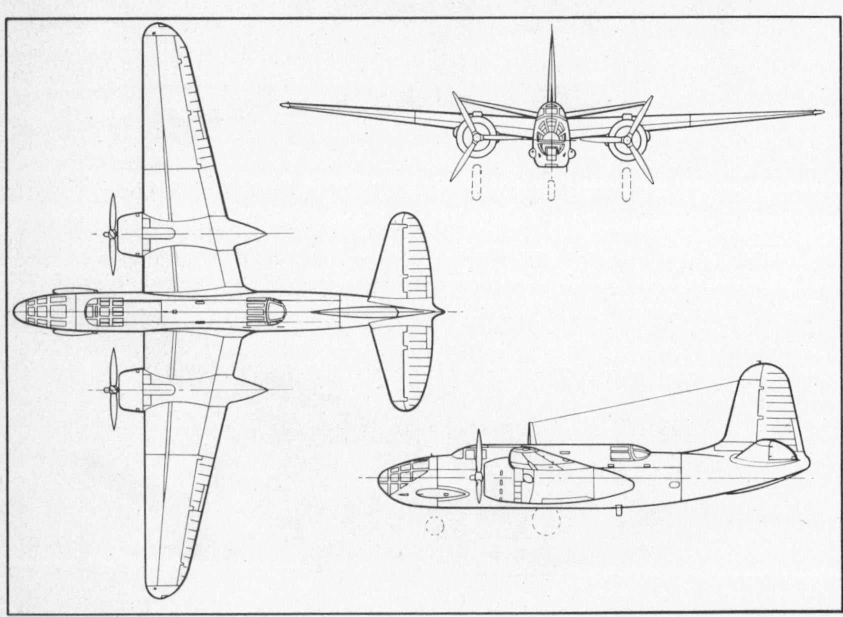
Douglas A-20C Boston

Douglas Boston Mk IV (A-20C), RAF

second batch to have 1,200-hp R-1830-S3C-4G engines. Of this total, only 85 of the first batch and 23 of the second were delivered, the remainder being transferred to Britain after the fall of France. The aircraft which did reach France, via Casablanca, were first in action on 31 May 1940. Others saw service in North Africa, first in the hands of the French Air Force, and, later, the Vichy Air Force.

France had also ordered 100 of a new version with 1,600-hp Wright R-2600-A5B engines. Designated DB-7A, this version had longer nacelles and a broader fin and rudder, adopted after one of the earlier French machines had been flown experimentally with twin fins and rudders. This entire order was transferred to Britain.

The British Purchasing Commission had itself selected the DB-7 as one of the types to be procured for the Royal Air Force. Orders were placed in 1940 for the DB-7B version, similar to the R-2600-engined version ordered by France, but armed with seven 0·303-in guns. The RAF obtained 781, including 240 built by Boeing. Designated Boston III, they were in service from February 1942 onward against targets in occupied Europe.

The remaining 15 aircraft from France's original 100-plane contract went to Britain as Boston Is and were used primarily as trainers for nose-wheel landing gear experience. The French-contracted aircraft with R-1830-S3C4G engines were designated Boston II and were mostly converted to Havoc I fighters (see separate entry); while the 100 French machines with R-2600 engines (less one which crashed) became Havoc II fighters.

Additional Bostons which were acquired by the RAF at Abadan in 1942 were destined for Russia but were "exchanged" for 50 Spitfires. Later variants of the Boston were lend-lease versions of USAAF A-20s, as described below. Deliveries of the latter had begun in 1940, but when America was drawn into the war, 213 DB-7Bs from the British contracts were transferred to the USAAF, which operated them under the Douglas designation.

The USAAC had placed its first production contracts for the DB-7 on 20 May 1939, three months after France first ordered the type. The initial contracts were for 123 A-20As, with R-2600-3 engines, and 63 A-20s with turbosupercharged R-2600-7 engines. Three of the A-20s were eventually converted to F-3s for photo reconnaissance, and the remainder became P-70s (see separate entry for DB-7 fighter variants). Delivery of the A-20As began in December 1940 and this type was serving overseas by 1941, one squadron being caught on the ground in the attack on Pearl Harbor. The total produced eventually rose to 143, of which 17 were modified to have R-2600-11 engines. One A-20A was purchased by the US Navy and designated BD-1.

Late in 1940, plans were completed for a major expansion of A-20 production, with orders for 999 A-20Bs and 775 of a reconnaissance version, the O-53 (subsequently cancelled). Built at a new Douglas plant at Long Beach, the A-20B had R-2600-11 engines, two 0·50-in guns in the nose, one in the dorsal position and one 0·30-in gun, remotely controlled, in each of the nacelles, firing aft. Provision was also made for greater fuel capacity. Of the A-20Bs built for the USAAC, 665 went to Russia on lend-lease; the USN acquired eight as BD-2s.

Features of the DB-7B produced for the RAF were incorporated in the A-20C, of which 808 were built by Douglas at Santa Monica. These had R-2600-23 engines, seven 0·30-in guns, more armour protection and higher gross weight. The RAF was allocated 202, including 140 built by Boeing, and these were designated Boston IIIAs, to distinguish them from the direct-purchase Boston IIIs.

The A-20C was the first version of the Douglas bomber flown in combat by US Army squadrons. The 15th Bombardment Squadron, operating from English bases in July 1942, was soon followed by other units in the UK and North Africa, and the type then remained in combat use up to the end of the war. Operations in the New Guinea area began in August 1942 and, as already noted, deliveries to the Soviet Union began in March 1942. Included in more than 3,000 supplied to the U.S.S.R. were 48 DB-7Cs ordered in 1940 by the Dutch Government.

The next operational version after the A-20C was the A-20G, production of which totalled 2,850. This type reverted to the "solid" nose of the fighter versions, but retained the bomb-bay and later had its bomb-load increased to 4,000 lb, by the addition of underwing racks. Various A-20G sub-variants had different nose armament, such as four 20-mm and two 0·50-in guns, or six 0·50-in guns; and one series had a wider rear fuselage to accommodate a Martin dorsal turret with two 0·50-in guns. With an external ventral fuel tank, the maximum endurance was increased to 10½ hours. Similar to the A-20G, but with 1,700-hp R-2600-29 engines, the A-20H was a little faster; 412 were built.

Versions similar to both the A-20G and A-20H, but with a new type of frameless, transparent nose, were designated A-20J and A-20K, and were the final production versions. Douglas built 450 A-20Js and 413 A-20Ks. The RAF received 169 of the "J" model as Boston IVs and 90 of the "K" model as Boston Vs.

When production ended in September 1944, the final tally was 7,385, including those exported. Under lend-lease the U.S.S.R. had been allocated 3,125. In addition to deliveries to France and Britain already mentioned, Brazil received 31, and the RCAF took a small number on charge from the RAF.

Operationally, the A-20 served successfully in a wide varity of rôles, which included torpedo-dropping and smoke-screen laying as well as attack bombing and fighting. It was very much a "pilot's aeroplane", a virtue not unconnected with the Douglas name it bore.

Douglas DB-7, Havoc, P-70 (Fighters)

Although the DB-7 had been designed as an attack bomber (see previous entry), one of its earliest operational rôles was as a fighter, in the hands of the Royal Air Force. The first aircraft of the DB-7 family to reach Britain were not those ordered by the British Purchasing Commission in 1940, but a quantity built on French contracts and diverted to Britain after the fall of France.

Among these aircraft were 147 DB-7s, with R-1830-S3C4G engines, which were designated Boston II upon arrival in Britain. Almost all were converted subsequently to Havoc I fighters (the name Ranger was bestowed temporarily but discarded). The first Havocs retained four 0·303-in guns in a shallow fairing under the nose, as specified by the French, and carried up to 2,400 lb of bombs internally. So armed, they operated as fighter intruders by night over the continent of Europe from the end of 1940 onwards. Known at one time as Havoc IVs, these versions later became Havoc I (Intruder).

The basic Havoc I was a night fighter with a "solid" nose fairing containing four guns, in addition to the four under the nose. The early AI Mk VI radar, with "arrowhead" aerial, was also carried. An alternative night fighting scheme was to use "hunter-killer" teams of radar- and searchlight-equipped search aircraft and a single-seat fighter. For this rôle, some 31 Havocs were fitted with the 2,700-million-candlepower Helmore Turbinlite, plus AI Mk VI and special formation lights above the wings to allow Hurricanes to remain in contact. The idea was for the Havoc to track its target by radar and illuminate it at the critical moment, so that the Hurricane could press

Douglas DB-7A special, one of three twin-rudder machines

Douglas Havoc II night fighter, 12-gun nose, RAF

Douglas Turbinlite Havoc I, RAF

TYPE	DIMENSIONS span ft	span in	length ft	length in	height ft	height in	WEIGHT max t-o lb	PERFORMANCE max speed mph	at height ft	service ceiling ft	combat range miles	REMARKS
Douglas DB-7	61	4	45	11	15	10	16,000	314	15,000	28,570	630	
Douglas DB-7A	61	4	48	0	15	10	16,700	323	12,800	27,680	490	
Douglas DB-7B	61	4	47	3	18	1	19,750	321	12,800	25,170	525	
Douglas A-20A	61	4	47	7	17	7	20,711	347	12,400	28,175	675	
Douglas A-20B	61	4	48	0	18	1	23,800	350	12,000	28,600	825	
Douglas A-20C	61	4	47	3	17	7	24,500	342	13,000	25,320	745	
Douglas A-20G	61	4	48	0	17	7	27,200	339	12,400	25,800	1,090	A-20H similar
Douglas A-20J	61	4	48	4	17	7	27,000	317	10,700	23,100	1,000	A-20K similar
Douglas P-70	61	4	47	7	17	7	21,264	329	14,000	28,250	1,060	

Douglas A-20G Havoc

Douglas A-20G Havoc

Douglas B-23 Dragon

Douglas BTD-1 Destroyer

home a surprise attack. At least ten RAF squadrons operated these Turbinlite Havocs, with little success.

Another night fighting scheme produced the Havoc III variant, later redesignated Havoc I (Pandora). This involved trailing an explosive charge 2,000 ft beneath the aircraft, in the path of the enemy. The device was known as the LAM, or Long Aerial Mine, and was used by only one squadron, for a short period.

Heaviest armament carried by any RAF version of the Douglas aircraft was twelve 0·303-in guns concentrated in the nose of the Havoc II. An entire French contract for 100 DB-7As with R-2600 engines (less one which crashed in the US) was taken over by the RAF and these became Havoc IIs. The new nose was designed by Martin-Baker.

Developments which in some ways paralleled this British work began in America in September 1941, when the Massachusetts Institute of Technology had prepared its first airborne radar set. This was fitted in the nose of an A-20 which was then redesignated XP-70. The armament comprised four 20-mm cannon in a tray below the bomb-bay.

A further 59 A-20s were similarly converted into P-70s during 1942, to provide the USAAF with urgently-needed night fighters. These were used operationally in the Pacific area but suffered from a restricted service ceiling.

To provide operational trainers for units working-up prior to re-equipment with the P-61 Black Widow, later A-20 versions were also converted into night fighters with six 0·50-in nose guns: 39 A-20Cs and 65 A-20Gs became P-70As, and 105 A-20Gs became P-70Bs.

Douglas B-23 Dragon

To improve the B-18 (page 485), Douglas proposed in 1938 a version with R-2600-1 engines. This was given the designation B-22 by the USAAC, but production plans were dropped in favour of the B-23, a further development of the same design.

The principal difference between the B-18 and the B-23 lay in the fuselage design. Of smaller cross-section and with better streamlining, the B-23's fuselage incorporated the first tail gun position in a USAAC bomber, with a single 0·50-in gun. Three 0·30-in guns were carried in nose, dorsal and ventral positions.

Douglas flew the first B-23 on 27 July 1939. No prototype had been ordered, a single contract for 38 figuring in the FY1939 (1939 fiscal year) purchases of the USAAC. The Dragons saw brief service in the early days of the war, before being withdrawn from patrol duties and used for training. Twelve were converted for transport and glider-towing duties, as UC-67s, in 1942.

Douglas BTD Destroyer

Most of the US Navy's outstanding success in its air attack against Japanese targets at sea was achieved with two classes of aircraft: the three-seat torpedo-bomber (of which the Douglas TBD-1 Devastator was the first practical example) and the two-seat dive-bomber (of which the Douglas SBD Dauntless was the outstanding example). Operational experience with these two types during the early war years, coupled with the development of new high-powered engines, led the Navy to initiate work on a new category of aircraft combining both functions and flown by a one-man crew.

First of several carrier-borne types developed by Douglas in this period was the XSB2D-1 Destroyer, two prototypes of which were ordered in June 1941. It was a two-seat dive-bomber, incorporating new features such as an internal bomb-bay and a tricycle undercarriage – the first designed for use on an aircraft carrier. The XSB2D-1 did not achieve production but formed the basis of the Douglas BTD-1 when the Navy first raised the requirement for a single-seat torpedo/dive-bomber.

Principal changes between the two types were deletion of the second crewman and the dorsal and ventral turrets he controlled, enlargement of the fuselage bomb-bay to accommodate a torpedo or 3,200 lb of bombs, and the addition of two wing-mounted 20-mm guns.

The BTD-1 was powered by a 2,300-hp Wright R-3350-14 engine, and had air-brakes in the fuselage sides. Production contracts were placed in April 1942 and were increased in August 1943 to a total of 358 aircraft. Deliveries began in June 1944, but contracts were cancelled after 28 had been built, and the Destroyer's chief claim to fame remains the fact that it was the forerunner of the Skyraider.

Douglas A-26 (B-26) Invader

One of the few types of aircraft which passed through all the stages from initial conception to operational service wholly within the period of World War II, the Douglas A-26 Invader was designed along similar lines to the A-20 Havoc (see page 487), which it was intended to succeed. It proved to be the last multi-engined attack bomber produced for the USAF, but its operational usefulness outlived expectations and the Invader not only served throughout the Korean War but found a new lease of life for COIN duties in the Congo and Vietnam.

Three prototypes were ordered from Douglas in June 1941. The formula followed that of the A-20 quite closely, with a shoulder-wing, three-man crew, large underslung nacelles for the 2,000-hp R-2800-27 engines, and interchangeable nose armament. Remotely-controlled dorsal and ventral turrets each housed two 0·50-in guns in the first prototype, the XA-26, which had a transparent bombardier's nose and two more guns in the nose. The internal bomb-bay had a capacity of 3,000 lb. The XA-26 made its first flight on 10 July 1942.

Alternative armament was installed on the other two prototypes. The XA-26A appeared as a night fighter with AI radar in the nose, four 20-mm guns in a ventral tray and four 0·50-in guns in the top turret. The XA-26B had a single 75-mm cannon in the nose.

The Invader was first ordered in the attack version as the A-26B, but with the nose armament changed to six (or, later, eight) 0·50-in guns. The bomb-load was increased to 4,000 lb, and R-2800-27 or -71 engines were fitted. An early development was the addition of underwing gun packs, with a total of eight more guns. To increase still further the forward firepower for ground-attack duties, the top turret could be locked forward and controlled by the pilot. External pick-up points on the wings could carry 2,000 lb of bombs, 16 rockets or extra fuel.

Production lines for the A-26B were established at Long Beach and Tulsa, and these factories built 1,150 and 205 respectively. Operational use of the A-26B began in the European theatre on 19 November 1944, and in the Pacific area later.

A bombardier nose was featured in the A-26C model, which appeared in 1945 and saw limited service in the closing stages of the war. Two 0·50-in guns were carried in the nose, other armament remaining as in the A-26B. Production totalled 1,091, all but five of which were built at Tulsa. A few were converted for reconnaissance, as FA-26Cs, and others carried radar bomb-sights under the front fuselage.

Large numbers of Invaders were cancelled at the end of the war, including new models under development; but those already delivered became the major equipment of Tactical Air Command upon its formation in 1946. The designations changed to B-26B and B-26C after the Martin Marauder passed out of service in 1948, with an unarmed day and night reconnaissance version designated RB-26C.

Operating in support of US forces in action in Korea, B-26s flew their first sortie on 27 June 1950, and the last bombs of that war were dropped by B-26s on 27 July

Douglas A-26B (B-26B) Invader

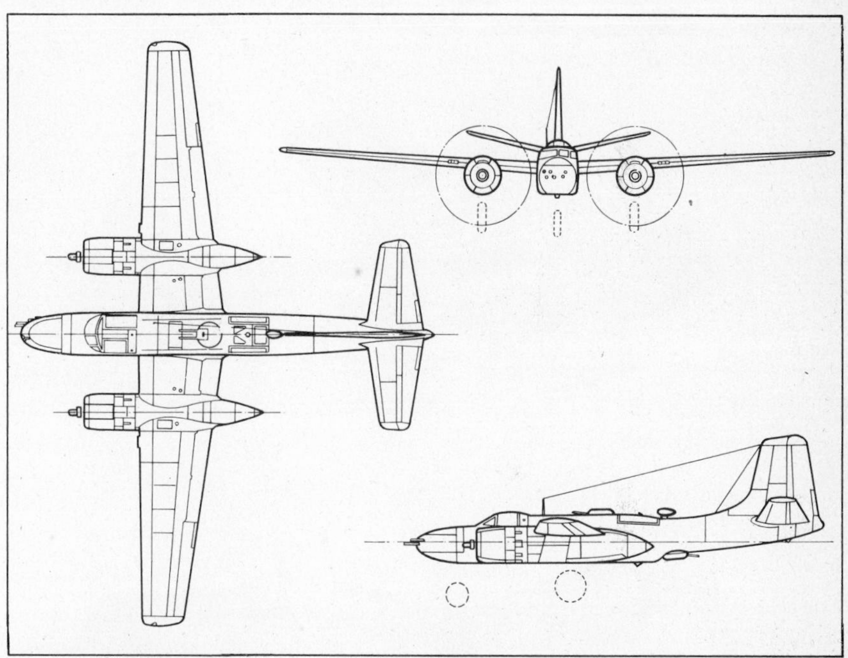
Douglas A-26B (B-26B) Invader

Douglas A-26C (B-26C) Invader, with radome, turrets deleted

TYPE	DIMENSIONS span ft	in	length ft	in	height ft	in	WEIGHT max t-o lb	PERFORMANCE max speed mph	at height ft	service ceiling ft	combat range miles	REMARKS
Douglas B-23	92	0	58	4	18	6	30,477	282	12,000	31,600	1,455	
Douglas BTD-1	45	0	38	7	13	7	19,000	344	16,100	23,600	1,480	

Douglas A-26C (B-26C) Invader

Douglas (On Mark) B-26K Counter Invader

Douglas AD-1 Skyraider

Douglas Skyraider AEW Mk I (AD-4W), RN

Douglas AD-5 (A-1E) Skyraider

1953 – 30 minutes before the cease-fire took effect. Korean operations brought a number of modifications, including higher operating weights and increased armament. Some B-26Bs flew with eight guns in the nose, three in each wing and four in the turrets; supplemented by 4,000 lb of bombs and fourteen 5-in rockets under the wings. Also in Korea, B-26Cs used H2S radar in the fuselage for night bombing.

Invaders were similarly deployed in actions against the Viet Cong in South Vietnam until 1963, when several accidents drew attention to the reduced safety of these ageing aircraft. However, the On Mark Engineering Company was able to remedy this situation by developing a special counter-insurgency version under USAF contract, as the YB-26K. First flown early in 1963, the YB-26K had a completely remanufactured airframe, embodying many of the improvements developed by On Mark for their commercial conversions of the B-26 for the executive market. Engines were 2,500-hp R-2800-103W radials; other new features included permanent wing-tip tanks, greater internal fuel capacity and further increased armament. Up to 8,000 lb of stores could be carried externally, and a reconnaissance camera was included as standard.

After evaluation of the prototype, the USAF ordered conversion of 40 Invaders to B-26K standard and On Mark flew the first of these on 25 May 1964.

Douglas A-1 Skyraider

One of the most successful of all Douglas aircraft produced for the US Navy, the Skyraider was too late for operational use in World War II – during which the design originated – but played a major rôle in operations in Korea and Vietnam. The requirement, drawn up in 1944, was for an aircraft capable of fulfilling two distinct missions, dive-bombing and torpedo attack. Unlike the types already serving the US Navy in these rôles, the new type was to be a single-seater and prototypes were ordered from four companies.

Douglas received a contract for 25 pre-production models of its new design in July 1944. The type was known initially as the Destroyer II (Destroyer I having been the limited-production BTD-1) and was designated XBT2D-1. Unlike some of the other attack aircraft being developed concurrently for the US Navy, it was a conventional low-wing monoplane, powered by a 2,500-hp Wright R-3350-24W engine. Its design gross weight of 17,500 lb was later to rise to 25,000 lb and among its outstanding characteristics was its ability to carry an enormous range of external stores from as many as 15 points under the wings and fuselage.

The first XBT2D-1 flew for the first time on 18 March 1945. A production order was placed for 548 similar aircraft, to be designated AD-1 Skyraider, but this particular contract was reduced after the war against Japan had ended. While the first AD-1s were being built, plans were made to adapt the design for new missions. One XBT2D-1P appeared in 1946 with cameras for reconnaissance duties. More radical modifications produced two XBT2D-1Ns and a single XBT2D-1Q in 1947. The -1Ns had radar and a searchlight under the wings and carried two radar operators in the capacious fuselage to guide aircraft in night attacks, while the -1Q was an ECM (electronic countermeasures) version with an operator in the fuselage behind the pilot for the special equipment.

On the initial production contract, 242 AD-1s were eventually built, plus 35 AD-1Qs similar to the prototype described above. One XAD-1W, converted from an XBT2D-1, was modified as an airborne early warning aircraft, with a large "inverted mushroom" radome under the fuselage, and the success of this trial installation led to production orders in due course.

One final conversion of an XBT2D-1 produced the XAD-2, in which the inner wing structure was strengthened, operating weights were increased, fuel capacity was raised and a 2,700-hp R-3350-26W engine was introduced. After this prototype was lost during trials in 1948, an AD-1 was converted to similar standard in 1949, and Douglas then built 156 AD-2s and 21 AD-2Qs for ECM duties, plus a single AD-2U with equipment for target-towing. Two AD-2Ds were produced by conversion for drone control duties.

Production orders for the Skyraider figured annually in US Navy procurement plans from 1948. The type had entered service in 1947 with VA-19A in the Pacific and was deployed on board the USS *Midway* in the same year. Progressive development of the airframe led to many additional versions before production ended in February 1957, after 3,180 Skyraiders had been built.

The AD-3, appearing in 1948, featured further structural changes and improvements in the landing gear, plus a redesigned cockpit cover. Production of this version totalled 125, with another 69 for specific roles – 15 AD-3Ns equipped for night attack, 23 AD-3Qs with ECM equipment and 31 AD-3Ws with airborne early warning radar. Two of the -3Ws were converted into AD-3Es with special anti-submarine detection gear, and two AD-3Ns became AD-3Ss with complementary submarine strike equipment.

During 1949, the AD-4 replaced the AD-3 in production, bringing a further series of improvements and introduction of APS-19A radar in place of APS-4. Production of the basic model totalled 372 (with another 85 cancelled); of these, 25 were converted to AD-4B standard, with provision for carrying tactical nuclear weapons, and 63 were "winterized" as AD-4Ls. Douglas built another 165 AD-4Bs as new aircraft.

The 307 AD-4Ns had equipment for night operation, but 100 were later stripped for day attack duties as AD-4NAs, while another 37 were winterized as AD-4NLs. There were also 39 AD-4Qs with ECM equipment and 168 AD-4Ws with AEW radar, 50 of the latter being supplied to the Royal Navy in 1953 to serve with No. 849 Squadron for airborne early warning duties on board aircraft carriers at sea, and designated Skyraider AEW Mk 1.

After being withdrawn from US Navy units, 84 AD-4s were supplied to France, to equip light ground-attack squadrons of the Armée de l'Air.

Five years' operational experience with the Skyraider was distilled by Douglas to produce the AD-5 (first flown on 17 August 1951) which set unprecedented standards for versatility in a military aircraft. Important design changes included widening the fuselage for side-by-side seating, lengthening it by 2 ft, and increasing the vertical tail area. The basic airframe could be converted rapidly, by using specially-produced kits, to operate in any one of several forms, including a 12-seat transport, a 2,000-lb freight carrier, an ambulance to carry four stretchers or a target tug. These conversions could be carried out on any of the production variants, which comprised 212 AD-5s, 239 AD-5Ns, 218 AD-5Ws and one AD-5S. Also, 54 AD-5Qs were converted from AD-5Ns.

During 1962, the Skyraider was redesignated A-1 in the new Department of Defense tri-Service scheme. The AD-5, -5W, -5Q and -5N thus became, respectively, A-1E, EA-1E, EA-1F and A-1G. In addition to serving with the US Navy, the A-1E was adopted by the USAF's Tactical Air Command, which obtained 50 from Navy surplus to equip the 1st Air Commando Group engaged in COIN

Douglas AD-6 (A-1H) Skyraider, wings folded

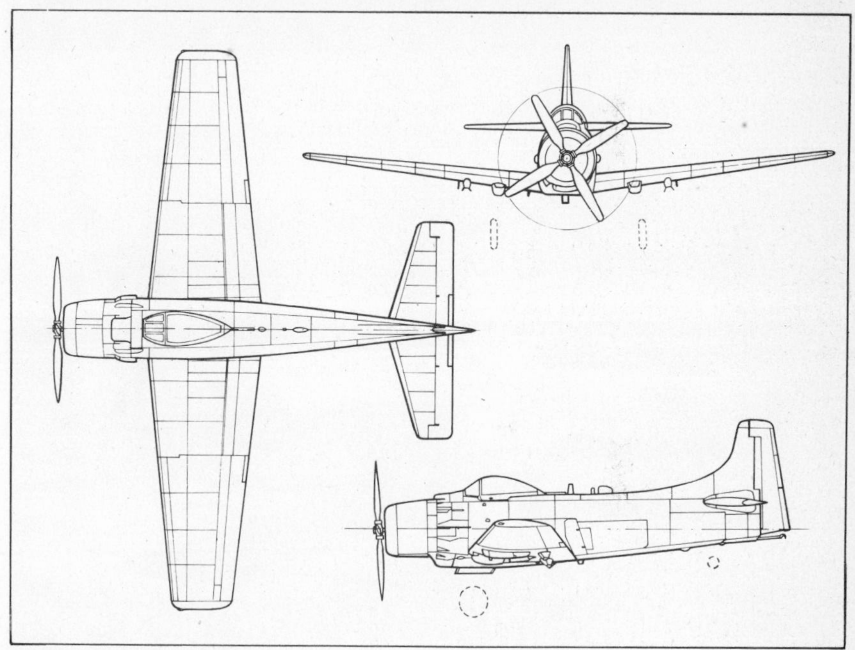
Douglas AD-6 (A-1H) Skyraider

TYPE	DIMENSIONS span ft	span in	length ft	length in	height ft	height in	WEIGHT max t-o lb	PERFORMANCE max speed mph	at height ft	service ceiling ft	combat range miles	REMARKS
Douglas A-26B	70	0	50	0	18	6	35,000	355	15,000	22,100	1,400	Later B-26B
Douglas A-26C	70	0	51	3	18	3	35,000	373	10,000	22,100	1,400	Later B-26C
Douglas B-26K	71	6	50	0	18	6	43,370	397	SL	30,000	1,150	Conversions by On Mark
Douglas AD-1	50	0	39	5	9	0	18,030	366	13,500	33,000	1,935	
Douglas AD-2	50	0	38	2	15	5	18,263	321	18,300	32,700	915	
Douglas AD-3	50	0	38	2	15	5	18.575	321	18,300	32,300	900	
Douglas AD-4	50	0	38	2	15	5	18,861	321	18,300	32,200	900	Also Skyraider AEW.1
Douglas AD-5	50	0	40	1	15	10	18,799	345	15,000	NA	2,500	
Douglas AD-7	50	9	38	10	15	8¼	25,000	318	18,500	32,000	900	Re-designated A-1J

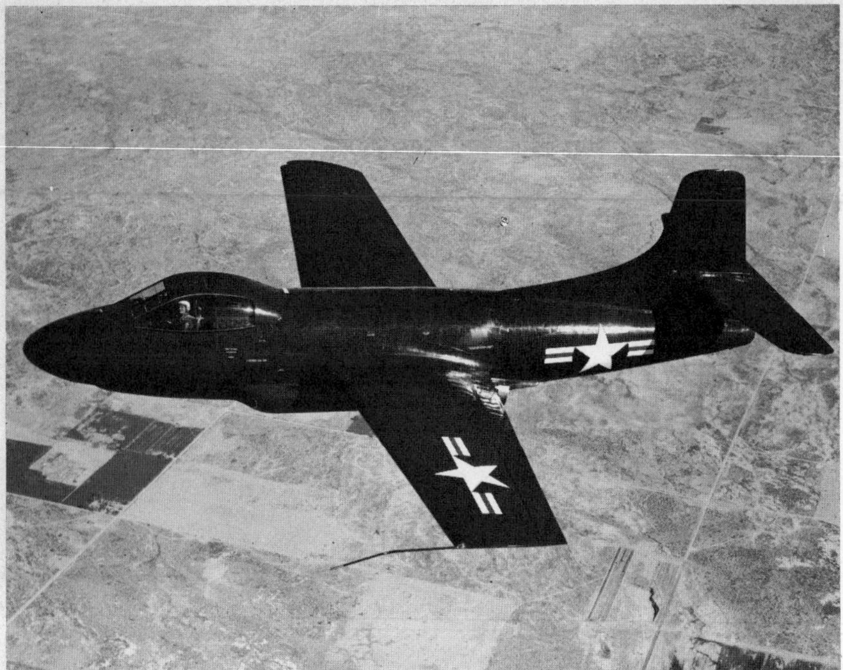

Douglas F3D-2T2 Skynight

Douglas F4D-1 Skyray, Squadron VF-213

operations in support of the South Vietnam forces. A number of A-1Es also were supplied to the Vietnam Air Force.

Derived from the AD-4, the AD-6 (later A-1H) differed primarily in being equipped for low-level attack bombing. It was a single-seater, like all Skyraiders other than the AD-5 series, and 713 were built. Of these, 30 went to the Vietnam Air Force, the rest serving with the US Navy.

Final production version of the Skyraider was the AD-7 (later A-1J), which differed from the AD-6 in having an R-3350-26WE engine and structural strengthening of the wings for the low-level tactical rôle. Production totalled 72 and this version was in service with the US Navy until early in 1968.

Douglas F3D Skynight

Development of the Skynight was originated to meet a US Navy requirement for a radar-equipped two-seat night fighter – a somewhat specialized type which was quickly passed over in favour of the more versatile all-weather single-seater. Designed in the immediate post-war period, the Skynight followed contemporary design practice, with an unswept wing and the engines side-by-side in the lower fuselage. Pilot and observer sat side-by-side and, to assist high-speed bale-out, a tunnel ran from the cockpit through the bottom of the fuselage.

The first of three prototype XF3D-1s flew on 23 March 1948, with two 3,000-lb s t Westinghouse J34-WE-22 turbojets. The initial production batch for the US Navy totalled 28; these were F3D-1s, with J34-WE-32 engines, and the first flew on 13 February 1950. Some were later converted into F3D-1M missile carriers.

Designed to utilize the 4,600-lb s t J46-WE-3 turbojet the F3D-2 suffered from the cancellation of this engine. The 3,400-lb s t J34-WE-36 was substituted and the first of 237 F3D-2s flew on 14 February 1951; these aircraft served only with US Marine squadrons, including one operating in Korea, where the Skynight destroyed more enemy aircraft than any other Navy or Marine type.

Operational for only a short period, the F3D-2s later gave valuable service for research and development tasks. Sixteen became F3D-2M missile carriers and 30 were converted into F3D-2Q countermeasures aircraft. For special training duties, the F3D-2T and F3D-2T2 carried appropriate equipment. The final conversion, in 1958, produced the F3D-2B with special armament.

In 1962 the F3D series was redesignated as follows: F-10A (F3D-1), F-10B (F3D-2), EF-10B (F3D-2Q), MF-10B (F3D-2M) and TF-10B (F3D-2T2).

Douglas F4D Skyray

Designed to a US Navy requirement which originated in 1948, the distinctive little Skyray demonstrated its high performance by setting a World Air Speed Record in 1953. Its operational service was curtailed, however, by the advent of larger and heavier single-seat fighters, which were needed to carry the full range of weapons and electronic gear specified by the Navy. The Skyray also suffered from delays in jet-engine development which led to a change of power plant at a late stage.

Two prototypes of the Skyray were ordered on 16 December 1948. The aircraft had been designed at the Douglas El Segundo plant, under the guidance of Ed Heinemann, and one of its most noticeable features was the delta wing with rounded tips. Because of the high angle of attack on landing approach (a characteristic of delta-winged aircraft) the Skyray had a small tail-wheel built into a ventral fairing, although the undercarriage was of the nose-wheel type.

The first XF4D-1 flew on 23 January 1951, powered temporarily by a 5,000-lb s t Allison J35-A-17 turbojet. It had been designed around the Westinghouse J40, and the prototype was re-engined successively with a 7,000-lb s t XJ40-WE-6 and an 11,600-lb s t (with afterburning) XJ40-WE-8. With the latter engine, a World Air Speed Record of 752·9 mph was established, but plans to use the J40-WE-10 in production aircraft had to be abandoned when the Westinghouse engine project was cancelled after prolonged delays. The Pratt & Whitney J57-P-2, rated at

14,500 lb s t with afterburning was substituted, this in turn being superseded by the 16,000 lb s t J57-P-8 in later production aircraft.

First flight of the first Pratt & Whitney-engined F4D-1 was made on 5 June 1954, and the first delivery to a Navy unit took place on 16 April 1956. Production totalled 419, all in the F4D-1 version, and these served with US Navy and US Marine squadrons for a number of years. The last production aircraft came off the El Segundo line in December 1958.

The Skyray carried four 20-mm guns in the wing and had six wing strong-points for external stores, which could include two 300-US gallon tanks, two 2,000-lb bombs or a wide range of missiles, rockets and other stores. Among international records set by Skyrays were some for rate of climb and time to height, including a climb to 50,000 ft in 2·6 minutes from a standing start.

A direct, enlarged development of the Skyray, at first designated F4D-2, became the F5D-1 Skylancer. Powered by a J57-P-12, the first Skylancer flew in April 1956. Production plans were dropped after four had been built, and 57 more then on order were cancelled.

Douglas A-3 Skywarrior

First all-jet attack aircraft designed for the US Navy, the Skywarrior was evolved to take advantage of the super-carriers projected in 1949. Preliminary US Navy requirements for a carrier-based strategic nuclear bomber were outlined to the Douglas company in 1947 and project design was completed in the following two years. To meet the requirements, a high wing position was inevitable, the centre-section passing through the fuselage above the internal weapons bay. Two engines were hung in pods from the wings and the three units of the undercarriage all retracted into the fuselage.

Provision was made for a crew of three, with a radar bombing system in the nose and a Westinghouse remotely-controlled gun barbette in the tail. Two prototypes were ordered in March 1949, and both were powered by 7,000-lb s t Westinghouse XJ40-WE-3 engines. Designated XA3D-1, the first Skywarrior flew on 28 October 1952, by which time production orders had been placed. Plans to use the 7,500-lb s t J40-WE-12 were abandoned, however, because of development problems with this engine, and the Pratt & Whitney J57 was substituted. The first YA3D-1 with this power plant flew on 16 September 1953, and production A3D-1s began to reach the Fleet in 1956, VAH-1 (Heavy Attack Squadron One) being the first unit equipped.

Douglas built 50 A3D-1s, these later being redesignated A-3A and relegated to conversion training. One of these aircraft was converted to the YA3D-1P (YRA-3A) with photo-reconnaissance equipment. Five others became YA3D-1Qs and A3D-1Qs (YEA-3A, EA-3A) with ECM equipment in the rear fuselage replacing the tail barbette. Others later became TA-3As with dual controls.

Initially designated A3D-1B, the A3D-2 (A-3B) had equipment for all-weather operation, 10,500 lb s t J57-P-10 engines and higher weights, up to 82,000 lb. Improvements were made in the weapon-carrying and weapon-launching capability. The A-3B entered USN squadron service in 1957. Douglas built 164 of this variant.

First flown on 22 July 1958, the A3D-2P (RA-3B) had a redesigned fuselage carrying two operators for its photo-reconnaissance equipment, in addition to the flight crew of three. Production totalled 30, to equip two squadrons

Douglas F4D-1 Skyray

Douglas A3D-2 (A-3B) Skywarrior, Squadron VAH-1

Douglas A3D-2 (A-3B) Skywarrior, with late-model nose and tail, Squadron VAH-4

TYPE	DIMENSIONS						WEIGHT	PERFORMANCE				REMARKS
	span		*length*		*height*		*max t-o*	*max speed*	*at height*	*service ceiling*	*combat range*	
	ft	*in*	*ft*	*in*	*ft*	*in*	*lb*	*mph*	*ft*	*ft*	*miles*	
Douglas F3D-1	50	0	45	5	16	1	21,500	543	11,000	42,800	717	Data for prototype
Douglas F3D-2	50	0	45	5	16	1	27,000	600	20,000	NA	1,200	
Douglas F4D-1	33	6	45	8	13	0	27,000	695	36,000	48,000	950	
Douglas A-3B	72	6	76	4	22	9	82,000	610	10,000	41,000	2,000	Originally A3D-2

Douglas A3D-2Q (EA-3B) Skywarrior

Douglas A4D-5 (A-4E) Skyhawk

Douglas A4D-5 (A-4E) Skyhawk, Squadron VA-55

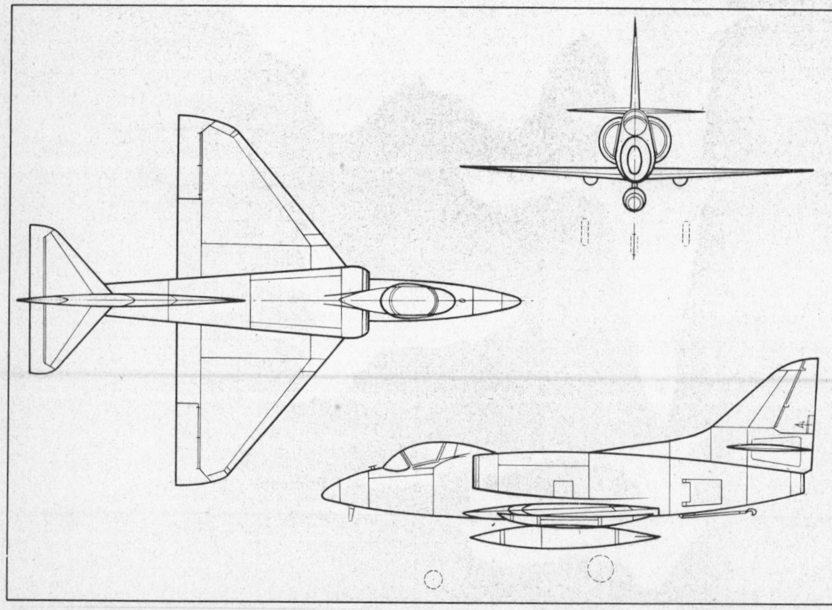
Douglas A4D-2N (A-4C) Skyhawk

which provided detached flights to operate in conjunction with the US Navy's Carrier Air Wings.

Another redesign of the fuselage produced the A3D-2Q (EA-3B) radar countermeasures version, first flown on 10 December 1958. This carried four electronics operators to look after the forward- and side-looking radar and other special equipment. Twenty-four were built.

Final Skywarrior production version, of which 12 were built, was the A3D-2T (TA-3B) with a pressurized fuselage accommodating pilot, instructor and six radar/navigator pupils. The first A3D-2T flew on 29 August 1959.

Douglas A-4 Skyhawk

First flown at El Segundo, California, on 22 June 1954, the prototype Skyhawk quickly attracted the appellation "Heinemann's Hot Rod", for it was an exercise in miniaturization by Ed Heinemann, then a senior Douglas designer. By going back to first principles in structural design and exercising a rigid control over equipment weight, Heinemann's team, long versed in US Navy specifications, produced an aeroplane which met official requirements at only half the permitted gross weight.

After inspection of a mock-up in 1952, the US Navy ordered prototypes and pre-production models in June of that year, with the first production orders following before the first flight. The two prototypes were designated YA4D-1 and were followed by 165 production model A4D-1s, these designations later changing to YA-4A and A-4A when the entire Skyhawk series was redesignated in 1962. The prototypes had a 7,200-lb s t J65-W-2 engine, whereas the J65-W-4 of 7,800-lb s t was used in the production model. Three external pick-up points were provided, one for a maximum of 3,000 lb under the fuselage, and one to carry up to 1,000 lb under each wing. These pick-ups could carry a large variety of stores including fuel tanks, bombs, rockets, gun pods or guided missiles.

The first pre-production A4D-1 flew on 14 August 1954, and the formal entry of the Skyhawk into US Navy service took place on 26 October 1956. Flight development and design evolution had already produced a new version, the A4D-2 (A-4B), which first flew on 26 March 1956. This was powered by a 7,700-lb s t J65-W-16A engine and had a hydraulically-powered rudder and an improved and better-equipped cockpit. A flight refuelling probe subsequently became standard on the A4D-2, production of which totalled 542. It remained in service with attack squadrons of the US Navy and Marine Corps from 1957 to 1965.

Fifty were subsequently reconditioned for the Argentine Air Force.

To permit night and limited all-weather operations, the A4D-2N (A-4C) was fitted with terrain-avoidance radar, an autopilot and a low-level ejection seat. Production totalled 638, making this the most-produced Skyhawk variant.

The A4D-3 designation was allotted to a 1958 proposal to install a Pratt & Whitney J52 engine in the Skyhawk. Four prototypes were ordered but cancelled before completion. Also unbuilt was the A4D-4 project. A more complete re-design of the Skyhawk, coupled with use of the J52-P-6A engine of 8,500-lb s t, produced the A4D-5 (A-4E), first flown on 12 July 1961.

Apart from the engine change, this version had two additional wing pylons and a maximum external load of 8,200 lb. The maximum gross weight increased to 24,500 lb, compared with the prototype's 15,000 lb, and this called for strengthening of the undercarriage and catapult gear.

A two-seat training version of the Skyhawk was first flown on 30 June 1965 as the TA-4E, later being redesignated TA-4F, and delivery of 139 for the USN began in 1966. The A-4E was followed into production by the A-4F which, like the TA-4F, had the 9,300 lb s t J52-P-8A engine and a number of other detail improvements. The Royal Australian Navy ordered eight A-4Gs and two TA-4Gs for 1967 delivery. Douglas delivered the 2,000th Skyhawk in July 1967.

Douglas B-66 Destroyer

America's involvement in the Korean War had a considerable influence on the pattern of military aircraft development in the United States in the early 1950s. One result was renewed interest in the light attack bomber, and to obtain suitable aircraft quickly the USAF reviewed all existing types to assess their potential in the ground-support rôle. This led, in March 1951, to the decision to produce the English Electric Canberra in the U.S.A. as the Martin B-57 (page 532), followed in February 1952 by the decision to adopt a version of the US Navy's A3D Skywarrior (page 495).

No prototypes were ordered, as the Skywarrior was already a proven type, but the USAF version, first flown on 25 June 1954 as the RB-66A, proved to be extensively redesigned. Only five RB-66As were completed; intended for all-weather night photographic reconnaissance, they were used primarily for service introduction.

The RB-66B, first flown on 28 June 1954, was the principal production version, intended for the same rôle as the RB-66A. In all, 145 of this model were built, and they equipped tactical reconnaissance squadrons of the USAFE from 1957 onwards, conducting photographic reconnaissance along the borders of Communist Europe.

With the reconnaissance capability deleted, the B-66B served with TAC as a light bomber carrying conventional or nuclear weapons. The 72 aircraft of this type were the only bomber versions of the Destroyer built, although RB-66Bs could be converted for use as bombers. A more specialized reconnaissance version, the RB-66C, first flew on 29 October 1955. It had a pressurized four-man electronic counter-measures compartment between the front and rear fuselage tanks, in the space usually occupied by the bomb-bay. Wing-tip radomes and other indications of the specialized rôle were features of the RB-66C; 36 examples were built.

Destroyer production ended with 36 WB-66Ds, designed for weather reconnaissance under operational conditions. Electronic equipment and two observers were carried in the fuselage, and the tail armament of two 20-mm guns in a radar-controlled turret was retained.

General Dynamics F-111

Outcome of a 1960 requirement for a tactical fighter (the TFX specification), the F-111 marked two milestones in US military aircraft history. It was the first tactical fighter designed from the start to meet the requirements of two of the major fighting services – the USAF and the USN; and it was the world's first combat aircraft to incorporate variable sweep-back on the wings. Of several companies originally competing for the TFX contract, General Dynamics (in association with Grumman) and Boeing were named "semi-finalists", and after more than a year of intensive detail design and wind tunnel development of the two designs – both with variable sweep – the General Dynamics Fort Worth Division project was announced as the winner on 24 November 1962.

In basic layout, the F-111 is a high-wing monoplane with a crew of two seated side-by-side in a McDonnell escape capsule, and two Pratt & Whitney JTF10A-20 (TF30) turbofans side-by-side in the rear fuselage, with lateral intakes beneath the fixed portion of the wing. The outer wing panels have a minimum sweep-back angle of 16°, and are infinitely variable up to the

Douglas B-66B Destroyer

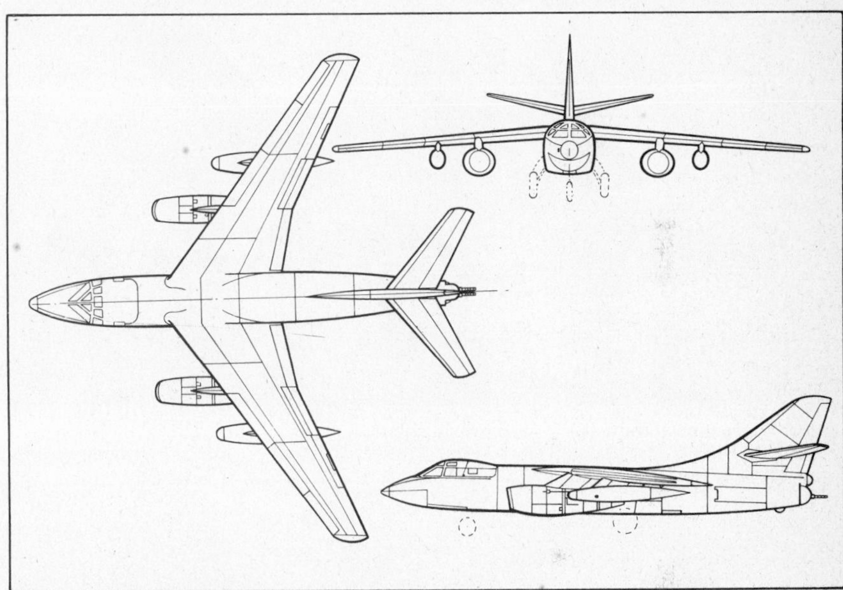

Douglas B-66B Destroyer

Douglas RB-66C Destroyer

TYPE	DIMENSIONS span ft	in	length ft	in	height ft	in	WEIGHT max t-o lb	PERFORMANCE max speed mph	at height ft	service ceiling ft	combat range miles	REMARKS
Douglas A-4A	27	6	39	1	15	2	15,000	NA	NA	NA	NA	Originally A4D-1
Douglas A-4B	27	6	39	6	15	2	15,000	676	SL	NA	1,150	Originally A4D-2
Douglas A-4E	27	6	42	10¾	15	2	24,500	685	SL	49,000	920	Originally A4D-5
Douglas RB-66B	72	6	75	2	23	7	83,000	620	10,000	45,000	1,650	
Douglas RB-66C	72	6	75	2	23	7	79,000	620	10,000	45,000	1,900	

General Dynamics F-111A, wings swept

General Dynamics/Grumman F-111B, wings extended

General Dynamics FB-111A

Great Lakes BG-1

maximum of 72·5°. At the latter angle, the wing trailing-edge almost coincides with the leading-edge of the tail-plane, thus turning the aircraft effectively into a delta-winged type.

Design armament of the F-111 varies according to rôle, but includes up to eight wing pylons, four of these being on the hinged wing panels and arranged to rotate as the wing moves, to keep the weapons they carry normal to the line of flight at all times. New air-to-air and air-to-ground missiles were developed in parallel with the F-111, to succeed the Sidewinder and Bullpup.

Initial contract for the General Dynamics fighter covered a development batch of 23 aircraft, eighteen being F-111As in USAF configuration, and the other five F-111Bs for the US Navy. The latter version has a number of differences for its specific Navy rôle, including a shorter nose radome, greater wing span, different armament and specialised avionic equipment.

Roll-out of the first F-111A was made 23 months after the contract was signed, on 15 October 1964, and the first flight was made on 21 December 1964 with the wings at 26 degrees sweepback. During the second flight, on 6 January 1965, the wings were operated through the full range of sweep angles. Additional aircraft joined the flight test programme early in 1965, and supersonic speed was first reached on March 5.

The first F-111B, assembled by Grumman, flew on 18 May and the long-span 'B' wing was also fitted to the fourth F-111A for preliminary tests carrying four simulated Hughes AIM-54A Phoenix missiles.

When the TFX programme started, eventual procurement for the two services was projected as high as 2,000 aircraft, but this estimate was later scaled down and in 1966, the USAF's Tactical Air Command was planning to buy a total of about 1,350, while the US Navy had yet to be convinced that such a heavy machine was a practical proposition for operation from aircraft carriers.

In April 1965, a letter contract was awarded to General Dynamics for 407 F-111As and 24 F-111Bs, this covering deliveries up to mid-1968. Other orders include 24 F-111Cs ordered for the RAAF in October 1963, for delivery in 1968 as Canberra replacements, but 50 F-111Ks to be operated by the Royal Air Force were cancelled in 1968.

Under development for the USAF is a reconnaissance variant designated RF-111A, and 210 FB-111 bombers have been ordered to replace the B-58A Hustler and B-52C to F versions of the Stratofortress in service with Strategic Air Command.

Great Lakes BG-1

In October 1928, the Great Lakes Aircraft Corporation purchased the Glenn L. Martin factory at Cleveland, after Martin had moved to Baltimore. Together with the factory, Great Lakes was given the opportunity to continue production of the Martin T4M-1 torpedo-bomber and the company's first products for the US Navy were developments of the Martin design, designated TG-2 (see page 526).

Features of the TG-2 were retained in the next Great Lakes prototype, the XBG-1 dive-bomber ordered in June 1932. The requirement was for a two-seat aircraft which could carry a 1,000-lb bomb under its fuselage. The XBG-1 was in competition with the Consolidated XB2Y-1.

Completed in June 1933, it was powered by a Pratt & Whitney R-1535-64 Wasp radial engine and carried two 0·30-in guns, one forward-firing and one mounted in the rear cockpit.

The Great Lakes design was chosen for service, and contracts in November 1933, January 1934 and February 1935 brought total production of the type to 60. Deliveries to Navy Squadron VB-3B began on 24 October 1934, with nearly half of the production batch going subsequently to the Marines for Squadrons VB-4M and VP-6M. Later production aircraft had R-1535-82 engines.

The BG-1 was the only combat aircraft of original design produced in quantity by Great Lakes; but three other prototypes, the XB2G-1, the XSG-1 and the XTBG-1, were built before the company went out of business in 1936.

Grumman FF-1

Grumman Aircraft Engineering Corporation, one of the foremost producers of combat aircraft for the US Navy for 30 years, began to build carrier-based fighters in 1931. It had established contact with the US Navy in the first year of its life, by designing floats to convert seaplanes to amphibians. Out of this contact grew a Navy contract for a prototype of the first Grumman aeroplane, a two-seat fighter biplane.

The contract was placed on 2 April 1931, for one aircraft, designated XFF-1. Powered by a 575-hp Wright R-1820E engine, it was the first Navy fighter to have a retractable undercarriage, the main wheels being stowed flush in the lower fuselage sides, ahead of the lower wing leading-edge. The two tandem cockpits were covered by a single canopy.

Flown late in 1931, the XFF-1 achieved 195 mph, a higher speed than could be boasted by any single-seater then in service. Re-engined later with a 750-hp R-1820F, it reached 201 mph. With equipment changes for scouting duties, a second prototype of the basic design was designated XSF-1.

The US Navy placed contracts for 27 Grumman FF-1 fighters, with R-1820-78 engines. When dual controls had been fitted, to permit the aircraft to be used as fighter-trainers, they became FF-2s. In addition, the Navy bought 34 SF-1s, with R-1820-84 engines. The single XSF-2 had a Pratt & Whitney Wasp engine.

A licence to build the type in Canada was sold to Canadian Car & Foundry Co Ltd, who produced a total of 57. Fifteen of these served with the RCAF with the name Goblin I; one went to Nicaragua and one to Japan, the remainder being sold to Turkey, which passed them on to the Spanish Republican air force.

Grumman F2F and F3F

Pursuing the theme of the two-seat FF-1 and SF-1, Grumman next produced for the Navy a single-seat fighter biplane, the XF2F-1. Ordered in November 1932, it made its first flight on 18 October 1933, powered by a 625-hp Pratt & Whitney XR-1535-44 engine. The formula was the same as for the earlier design, with retractable main wheels and an enclosed cockpit. The considerable depth of the fuselage behind the engine, required to accommodate the wheel wells, gave the Grumman design a characteristic stubby appearance that was enhanced by the narrow gap between the wings.

The F2F-1 carried two 0.30-in guns and two 116-lb bombs. Production models differed little from the prototype, but use of the 650-hp R-1535-72 engine gave a small increase in performance, to a maximum speed of 231 mph. Fifty-five were purchased by the Navy, with deliveries starting in 1935 to squadrons attached to the carriers USS *Lexington* and *Ranger*. They ended their useful life in 1941 as gunnery trainers.

Progressive development of the F2F-1 design led to the XF3F-1, ordered as a prototype in October 1934. Particular attention was given to improving the manoeuvrability, by lengthening the fuselage and increasing the wing span. The engine was an R-1535-72. The prototype crashed in March 1935 and was replaced by a second

Grumman FF-1

Grumman Goblin Mk I, RCAF

Grumman F3F-1

TYPE	DIMENSIONS span ft	span in	length ft	length in	height ft	height in	WEIGHT max t-o lb	PERFORMANCE max speed mph	at height ft	service ceiling ft	combat range miles	REMARKS
General Dynamics F-111A	63	0	73	6	17	1½	70,000	1,650	40,000	NA	3,800	
General Dynamics F-111B	70	0	66	9	16	8	68,000	1,650	40,000	NA	3,800	
Great Lakes BG-1	36	0	28	9	11	0	6,347	188	8,900	20,100	550	
Grumman FF-2	34	6	24	6	11	1	4,828	207	4,000	21,100	921	
Grumman F2F-1	28	6	21	5	9	1	3,847	231	7,500	27,100	985	
Grumman F3F-1	32	0	23	3	9	4	4,403	231	7,500	28,500	882	
Grumman F3F-3	32	0	23	3	9	4	4,403	264	15,200	33,200	980	

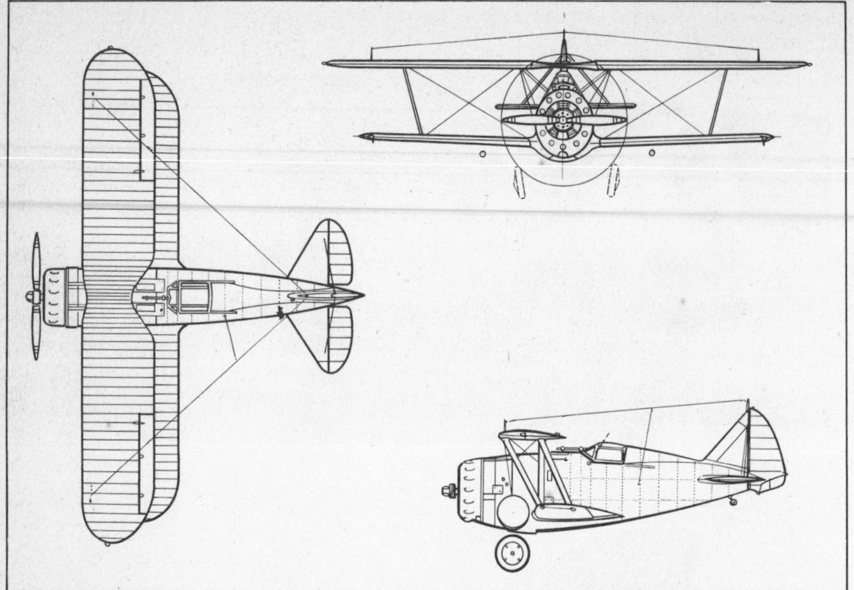

Grumman F3F-1

Grumman F3F-2

Grumman G-36A Wildcat, built for the Aéronavale

Grumman G-36B Martlet II (Wildcat II), RN

airframe with the same serial number. Somewhat heavier than the F2F-1, the XF3F-1 was also a little slower, at 226 mph; but this was restored to 231 mph in the 54 production model F3F-1s, with R-1535-84 engines, ordered in August 1935 and delivered in 1936.

An engine change, from the two-row Wasp to the single-row Cyclone XR-1820-22, produced the prototype XF3F-2. The Navy bought 81 F3F-2s with this engine in 1937 and another 27 similar F3F-3s, delivered in 1938–9. By the time war broke out in Europe, the Grumman single-seaters were equipping all fighter squadrons of the US Navy and Marines, and they remained in service as front-line aircraft until the spring of 1941.

Grumman F4F Wildcat

When, late in 1935, the US Navy announced a design competition for a new high-performance carrier-based fighter, Grumman submitted a design which continued the series of biplanes initiated with the FF-1. Known as the Grumman Model 16, it was smaller than the F3F-1 then in production and, powered by an 800-hp Wright R-1670 engine, had an estimated top speed of 264 mph.

Grumman won a Navy contract to build a prototype, designated XF4F-1, but while detail design was in progress, performance of the F3F series was brought into the same bracket by installation of the R-1820 engine. This, coupled with a Navy contract awarded to Brewster for a monoplane fighter (XF2A-1), led Grumman to drop the original XF4F-1 in favour of a monoplane. On 28 July 1936, the US Navy formalized the change with a contract for the XF4F-2 monoplane.

The XF4F-2 retained many characteristics of the earlier Grumman biplanes, including the method of retracting the wheels into the forward fuselage. A mid-wing position was adopted, provision being made for two wing-mounted guns or two 100-lb bombs; these were in addition to two fuselage-mounted guns firing through the propeller disc. The engine was a 1,050-hp Twin Wasp R-1830-66.

Following the first flight on 2 September 1937, the XF4F-2 underwent a full evaluation by the Navy in 1938, leading to selection of the competitive Brewster design. While the latter went into production, Grumman was given a contract for a new prototype, designated XF4F-3, to be powered by a later-model engine with a two-stage supercharger. This aircraft flew on 12 February 1939, with a 1,200-hp XR-1830-76 engine, rated at 1,050 hp at 11,000 ft and 1,000 hp at 19,000 ft. In August 1939 the first production contract was placed, for 54 F4F-3s.

The first production F4F-3 flew in February 1940. A new feature of the production model was that the tail-plane was raised to a position on the fin instead of being low on the fuselage; and all but the first two F4F-3s had four wing-mounted 0·50-in guns but none in the fuselage.

Almost simultaneously with the initial US Navy order, Grumman had concluded a contract with France to supply 100 G-36A fighters. These were essentially F4F-3s with the 1,200-hp Wright R-1820-G205A engine. Flight trials with the new engine began in the spring of 1940, and the entire French contract (reduced to 81 aircraft) was transferred to Britain in June. Named Martlet I, these aircraft began to reach the Fleet Air Arm at the end of July 1940.

A trial installation of the Wright engine in the second and third production F4F-3s, in the summer of 1940, produced the two XF4F-5s. This version was not produced for the US Navy, but continuing problems with the two-stage supercharger in the F4F-3 led to another test aircraft, the XF4F-6, flown late in 1940 with a two-speed, single-stage supercharger on its R-1830-90 engine. During 1941, 65 similarly-engined F4F-3As were produced under Navy contract.

This same engine was chosen for a version of the design ordered in 1940 by Britain as the G-36B Martlet II, the most important feature of this variant being its folding wings. One hundred were ordered, but delays in developing the wing-folding mechanism led to the first ten being delivered to F4F-3A standard. These were similar to the Martlet III, the designation of 30 G-36As ordered by Greece at the end of 1940 but delivered to Britain after the fall of Greece.

Folding wings had first been tried out on the experimental XF4F-4, flown in April 1941 with a hydraulic wing-folding mechanism. This was abandoned in favour of a manual folding system in the production version, delivery of which to both the US Navy and the British Fleet Air Arm began towards the end of 1941. Martlet IIs were in service on board British carriers by September 1941; thereafter Grumman "cats" were a mainstay of British carrier-borne fighter forces in World War II.

Production models with folding wings for the US Navy were designated F4F-4. They followed a total of 285 "dash 3" models and the 65 F4F-3As. The first F4F-3s had reached operational units of the US Navy at the end of 1940 and the squadron strength steadily increased throughout 1941. The Grumman fighter was first in combat on 9 December, operated by VMF-211 from Wake Island. After this first encounter, when a raiding Japanese bomber was destroyed, the Wildcat, as the US Navy had named the F4F, was frequently in action.

Production of the F4F-4 by Grumman totalled 1,169, plus 220 for Britain as Martlet IVs. In addition, Eastern Aircraft (a group of factories previously building GM automobiles) was established as a second source. A contract for 1,800 aircraft was placed on 18 April 1942; these were to be similar to the F4F-4 and were designated FM-1. Eastern flew its first FM-1 on 31 August 1942, eventually delivering 839 to the USN and 311 to Britain as Martlet Vs (later re-named Wildcat Vs).

To maintain the performance of the Wildcat despite increasing weights, which were associated inevitably with the introduction of new equipment, Grumman produced the XF4F-6. This was powered by the Wright R-1820-56 engine, which was considerably lighter than the R-1830 but gave 150 hp more for take-off. After successful trials with two prototypes, this version went into production as the FM-2 at the Eastern Aircraft plant. Production totalled 4,437, plus 340 Wildcat VIs for Britain. The FM-2 was, incidentally, the first of the series since the F4F-3 to have a significant change of outline, as the fin and rudder were heightened.

In addition to the fighter versions and prototypes mentioned above, Grumman evolved a photo-reconnaissance version, the F4F-7. This had a fixed wing, with additional fuel, giving an endurance of more than 24 hours and bringing the gross weight to 10,328 lb, compared with 7,952 lb for the heaviest of the fighter versions, the F4F-4. Of 100 ordered, only 21 were built.

One Wildcat was flown as a floatplane. Another wartime experiment involved towing F4Fs behind larger aircraft to investigate means of increasing the range of fighters for escort and ferry flights. Single F4Fs were towed, with engine stopped and propeller feathered, by a Douglas BD-1; on one occasion, two F4Fs were towed simultaneously by a B-17 for eight hours.

Production of the Wildcat, as the FM-2, continued until August 1945; and although later fighters became available, the wartime record of the type was outstanding. Especially in the Pacific in 1942 and 1943, and in the Atlantic with the FAA, the Wildcat marked a turning point in naval air warfare.

Grumman TBF/TBM Avenger

Destined to become the US Navy's standard torpedo-bomber of World War II and to remain in operational

Grumman Wildcat V (F4F-4), RN

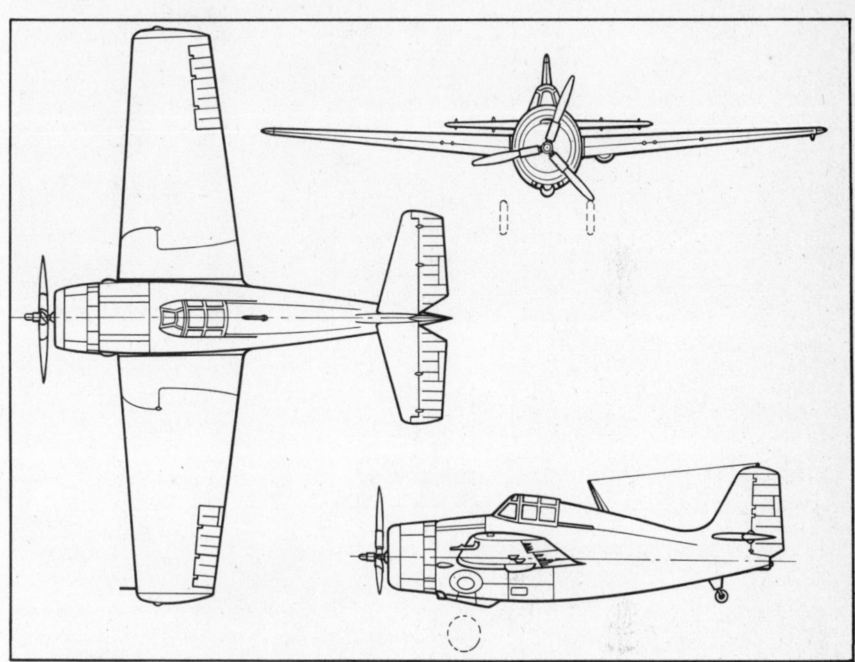

Grumman F4F-4 Wildcat

Grumman TBF-1 Avenger

TYPE	DIMENSIONS						WEIGHT	PERFORMANCE				REMARKS
	span		*length*		*height*		*max t-o*	*max speed*	*at height*	*service ceiling*	*combat range*	
	ft	*in*	*ft*	*in*	*ft*	*in*	*lb*	*mph*	*ft*	*ft*	*miles*	
Grumman F4F-3	38	0	28	9	11	10	8,152	330	21,100	37,500	845	
Grumman F4F-4	38	0	28	9	11	10	7,952	318	19,400	34,900	770	
Grumman FM-2	38	0	28	11	11	5	8,271	332	28,800	34,700	900	
Grumman G-36A	38	0	28	9	11	10	5,876	325	15,500	28,000	1,150	

Grumman Avenger I (TBF-1), RN

Grumman TBM-3E Avenger, RCN

Grumman TBM-3W Avenger, RCN

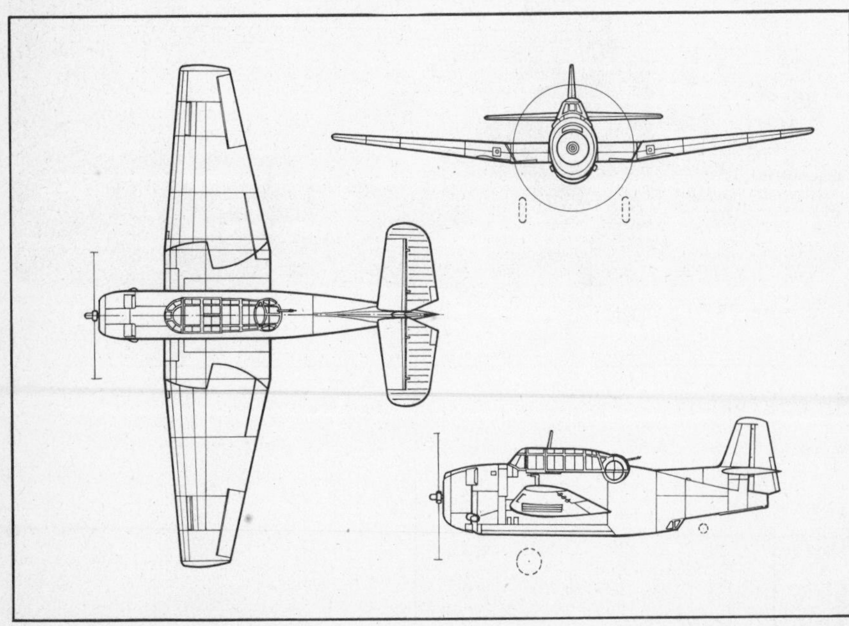
Grumman TBF-1 Avenger

service for some 15 years, the Grumman TBF was not ordered until 8 April 1940, when the Navy placed a contract for two XTBF-1 prototypes. Grumman had no previous experience of torpedo-carrying aircraft, but had been specializing for several years in the design and production of fighters for the US Navy. The TBF, although larger, retained typical Grumman lines, with a squat fuselage and angular wings and tail unit. The wing was mid-mounted on the fuselage, above the bomb-bay, which could accommodate a torpedo or a 2,000-lb bomb. The armament included a 0·50-in machine-gun in a power-operated dorsal turret, a ventral 0·30-in machine-gun and another of the same calibre in the engine cowling.

A crew of three was carried – pilot, dorsal gunner and a bombardier who could also reach the ventral gun. Power was provided by a 1,700-hp Wright R-2600-8.

Eight months after the prototypes were ordered, the US Navy placed an initial production contract for 286 TBF-1s. The prototype flew on 1 August 1941, and deliveries to the US Navy began on 30 January 1942, to Squadron VT-8. This same unit, flying from land bases, took the TBF-1 into action for the first time on 4 June 1942, during the Battle of Midway.

Grumman built a total of 2,293 Avengers between 1942 and December 1943. All were basically TBF-1s or TBF-1Cs, the latter having two 0·50-in machine-guns in the wings and provision for drop tanks. Included in the Grumman total were the XTBF-1 prototypes, a single XTBF-2 with an XR-2600-10 engine and the XTBF-3 with an R-2600-20. The Royal Navy received 402 of these aircraft, the majority being designated TBF-1B for lease-lend purposes, and the first squadron (No. 832) was operating by the spring of 1943 – initially from the USS *Saratoga*, from which the unit was first in action on 27 June during the landings in the Middle Solomons. The RNZAF received 63 TBF-1s.

The Eastern Aircraft Division of General Motors, already involved in Wildcat production, was chosen as a second source of Avenger production and built 2,882 TBM-1s and TBM-1Cs, equivalent to the TBF-1 and -1C, between September 1942 and April 1944. The Royal Navy received 334 TBM-1s which it designated Avenger II.

Following Grumman's XTBF-3, Eastern Aircraft produced a similar XTBM-3, with R-2600-20 engine and a strengthened wing to carry rocket projectiles, fuel tanks or radar pod. Delivery of the TBM-3 began in April 1944. Eastern built 4,664, including 222 for the Royal Navy as Avenger IIIs.

The ending of production was far from being the end of the Avenger's useful life, and many special-purpose variants appeared between 1945 and 1954, when the US Navy retired the type from front-line service. Addition of special anti-submarine gear produced the TBM-3E, which became the principal post-war operational version. Besides serving with the US Navy, this variant operated with the Royal Navy as the Avenger AS Mk 4, after 100 had been supplied during 1953; with the Royal Canadian Navy, which received about 115; and with the French Aéronavale.

When fitted with APS-20 search radar, with a large radome under the fuselage, the Avenger became the TBM-3W, and a further revision of the electronic equipment produced the TBM-3W-2; these variants, which had the rear turret deleted, served with the Aéronavale, the Japanese Maritime Self-Defence Force and the Royal Netherlands Navy. With equipment intended specifically for anti-submarine strike duties, the TBM-3S and TBM-3S-2 were also used by Japan and the Netherlands. A target-towing version was designated TBM-3U, and one of the final variants was the TBM-3R, a seven-seat Avenger used for "Carrier-On board Delivery" of vital supplies and priority personnel.

Grumman F6F Hellcat

With the F4F established in production and beginning to reach operational status, the US Navy awarded Grumman a contract, on 30 June 1941, to build prototypes of a new fighter designated F6F. Although larger and more powerful than the Wildcat, the F6F bore a strong family resemblance to the earlier type, and the similarities between the two designs made it possible to develop and put the F6F into production in a very short time. The first operational sortie was flown only 14 months after the prototype first flew.

The original intention was to build four prototypes. The first, designated XF6F-1, was to have a 1,700-hp Wright R-2600-10 engine with two-stage supercharger. The second, designated XF6F-3, was to have a 2,000-hp Pratt & Whitney R-2800-10 with two-stage supercharger; the XF6F-2 was to have a Wright R-2600-16 with turbo-supercharger, and the XF6F-4 was to have a Pratt & Whitney R-2800-27 with two-speed supercharger.

The XF6F-1 flew for the first time on 26 June 1942. With the realization that the most powerful engine available would be needed to combat the Japanese, and the need for haste, this prototype was re-engined with an R-2800-10 and it made its second "first flight" as the XF6F-3 on 30 July 1942. F6F-3 production aircraft, the first of which flew on 4 October 1942, were virtually identical.

The Hellcat, as the type was named, carried an armament of six 0·50-in guns in the wings and, unlike its Grumman predecessors, its main wheels twisted through 90° during retraction backward into the wings.

The first production order for Hellcats had been placed a month before the first prototype flew, and contracts accumulated quickly. By mid-1944, when later models of the Hellcat became available, Grumman had built 4,423 F6F-3s, plus 205 F6F-3Ns and 18 F6F-3Es. The "N" model was a night fighter carrying APS-6 radar in a pod under the starboard wing; the "E" had a similar installation of APS-4 radar.

Equipping squadron VF-5 on board the USS *Yorktown*, F6F-3s were first in action against Japanese targets on 31 August 1943. Squadron VF-9, on board the USS Essex, had been the first to equip with the Hellcat at the beginning of the year. Replacing the Wildcat, the F6F became the principal carrier-borne fighter with the US fleet in 1944 and maintained a performance advantage over Japanese types right up to the end of the war. Hellcats also operated with the Fleet Air Arm, which received the first of 252 lend-lease F6F-3s in July 1943.

The airframe intended originally as the XF6F-2 (the engine was changed to a Pratt & Whitney R-2800-16 with turbosupercharger) and the airframe intended originally as the XF6F-4 were both delivered as standard production F6F-5s, the special power plant installations being cancelled. Two XF6F-6s (first flown on 6 July 1944) had 2,100-hp R-2800-18W engines and four-blade propellers, but this version was not put into production.

The R-2800-10W was retained in F6F-5s which began to appear in mid-1944. Changes included modifications to the cowling and windshield, more armour protection and provision for 2,000 lb of bombs under the centre-section and six rocket projectiles under the wings. Two 20-mm cannon could replace the inner machine-guns in the wings.

Grumman built 6,436 F6F-5s and approximately 1,190 F6F-5Ns, the latter with APS-6 in a starboard wing pod, for night fighting. The Royal Navy received 930 "dash 5" Hellcats, inluding about 70 night fighters. These it designated Hellcat F Mk II and NF Mk II respectively.

Official statistics show that carrier-based Hellcats in service with the US Navy destroyed 4,947 enemy aircraft

Grumman F6F-3 Hellcat

Grumman F6F-5 Hellcat

Grumman Hellcat F Mk I (F6F-3), RN

TYPE	DIMENSIONS span ft	in	length ft	in	height ft	in	WEIGHT max t-o lb	PERFORMANCE max speed mph	at height ft	service ceiling ft	combat range miles	REMARKS
Grumman TBF-1	54	2	40	0	16	5	15,905	271	12,000	22,400	1,215	
Grumman TBM-3	54	2	40	0	16	5	18,250	267	15,000	23,400	1,130	
Grumman TBM-3E	54	2	40	11½	NA		17,895	276	16,500	30,100	1,010	
Grumman F6F-3	42	10	33	7	13	1	15,487	375	17,300	37,300	1,090	
Grumman F6F-5N	42	10	33	7	13	1	14,250	366	23,200	36,700	880	

Grumman F7F-3 Tigercat

Grumman F7F-3N Tigercat

Grumman F8F-1 Bearcat

Grumman F8F-2 Bearcat

in air-to-air combat by the end of the war, with another 209 claimed by land-based squadrons. After 1945, Hellcats were exported for use by other nations, particularly in South America, while the US Navy converted a number to F6F-5K configuration as target drones for missile tests, and to F6F-5P for photographic reconnaissance.

Grumman F7F Tigercat

Ordered on 30 June 1941 – simultaneously with the F6F Hellcat – the F7F was as radical as the F6F was conventional. It was the first twin-engined fighter to enter production for service on board aircraft carriers and the first Navy fighter to have a nose-wheel undercarriage. The single-seat twin-engined configuration was chosen to achieve a high performance and the heaviest armament attempted in a Navy fighter.

Grumman had previous twin-engine experience with the Model G-34 XF5F-1, which was undergoing flight tests at the time design work on the F7F began. For the latter aircraft, named eventually the Tigercat, Grumman chose a shoulder-wing layout, with a slender fuselage and two 2,100-hp R-2800-22W engines in large underslung nacelles. The armament comprised four 0·50-in guns in the nose and four 20-mm cannon in the wings, plus provision for two 1,000-lb bombs, six rockets or a standard Navy torpedo.

The first of two XF7F-1 prototypes flew in December 1943, by which time Grumman had an order for 500 Tigercats for US Marine squadrons.

Thirty-four F7F-1 single-seaters (equipped with radar) were delivered; one was modified and redesignated XF7F-2N to serve as a prototype for 66 F7F-2Ns. These were two-seat night fighters; the observer sat behind the pilot, more advanced radar was installed and the nose guns were removed. The size of the F7F made it particularly suitable as a night fighter.

The F7F-2Ns were followed by 250 F7F-3s, -3Ns and -3Ps, starting in March 1945. These were powered by R-2800-34W engines and had larger tail surfaces. The -3s were single-seat day fighters with all guns installed and an extra fuel tank in place of the radar operator; they were convertible to and from -3Ns, which were two-seaters equipped similarly to the -2Ns. The -3s were single-seat photo-reconnaissance aircraft, with cameras installed aft in the fuselage; the wing guns were removed and they carried a radio direction finder antenna on the fuselage turtleback. The F7F-4Ns, of which 12 were delivered in late 1946, were similar to the -3Ns, with advanced radar, modified landing gear and structural strengthening of the wings. The -4Ns were the only F7Fs for which deck-landings were permitted.

Tigercats reached Marine squadrons too late for operational service; two F7F-2Ns supplied to the RN for evaluation were the only examples in foreign service.

Grumman F8F Bearcat

To develop still further the Wildcat/Hellcat line, the US Navy ordered prototypes of a new piston-engined carrier-borne fighter on 27 November 1943. Powered by a 2,100-hp R-2800-22W radial engine, the XF8F-1 had the same low-wing layout and stubby appearance of the earlier Grumman fighters. The designers successfully reversed the trend towards larger and heavier aircraft, by rigorously limiting the overall size to the smallest airframe which would contain the big Double Wasp engine and the specified armament and fuel. This produced an aircraft smaller than the F6F Hellcat, but capable of carrying two 1,000-lb bombs or drop tanks or four rockets in addition to four wing-mounted 0·50-in machine-guns.

The first of two XF8F-1 prototypes flew on 21 August 1944, only ten months after the contract had been placed, and the first production F8F-1 flew five months later. Grumman received a contract for 2,023 Bearcats on 6 October 1944, and General Motors was selected as a second source, with a contract for 1,876. These were to have been designated F3M-1 and would have succeeded the FM-2 at the Eastern Aircraft factory; the entire contract was cancelled at the end of the war.

Production F8F-1s were powered by the 2,100-hp R-2800-34W engine and differed from the prototype in having a small dorsal fin and increased fuel capacity. Deliveries to the Navy began on 1 December 1944, and the first squadron, VP-19 (PAC), was working up when the war ended. Bearcat production continued at Grumman, with 208 delivered by the end of 1945, and a total of 765 F8F-1s was completed.

New contracts were placed subsequently for later versions of the Bearcat. These included 100 F8F-1Bs, with four 20-mm cannon in the wings in place of the machine-guns, and 36 F8F-1N night fighters. The F8F-2 had a revised engine cowling, taller fin and rudder and cannon armament; Grumman built 293 of the basic model, plus 12 F8F-N2 night fighters and 60 camera-equipped F8F-2Ps with only two wing cannon. These variants were delivered between 1946 and 1949, and equipped a number of US Navy squadrons.

Surplus Bearcats, with modified fuel system and designated F8F-1D, were supplied to France to be used by the Armée de l'Air in the war in Indo-China, and a number of these were transferred later to the Vietnam Air Force. In addition, the Thai Air Force received 100 F8F-1Ds and 29 F8F-1Bs.

Grumman F8F-1 Bearcat

Grumman AF Guardian

As a development of the F7F Tigercat, Grumman designed a larger multi-seat torpedo-bomber powered by two R-2800-22 Wasp radial engines. Envisaged as a replacement for the TBF Avenger, it was designated XTB2F-1 in 1944 but was cancelled in January 1945. Its place was taken by the Grumman G-70, which had been designed late in 1944 and was ordered in February 1945, when construction began on two prototypes designated XTB3F-1.

The G-70 reverted to the highly-successful Avenger formula of a single-engined mid-wing design, but dispensed with defensive armament. Reliance was placed, instead, on speed, the 2,300-hp R-2800-46 Double Wasp being supplemented by a 1,600-lb s t Westinghouse 19XB turbojet in the tail.

A top speed of 356 mph was estimated; but the idea of jet augmentation was abandoned soon after the XTB3F-1 made its first flight on 19 December 1945, and the Westinghouse J30 engine was used only in the prototype.

The increasing importance of anti-submarine warfare led to the Grumman design being revised, as the XTB3F-1S, with a large search radar in the bomb-bay. Rapid development of anti-submarine weapons and detection equipment outstripped airframe development at this particular stage, immediately after the war, and two versions of the Guardian were evolved to operate in "hunter-killer" teams. These were the AF-2S and AF-2W, of which the US Navy obtained a total of 386.

Retaining the overall characteristics of the original prototype, the AF-2 had a 2,400-hp R-2800-48W engine and additional fin area, in the form of small surfaces on each tailplane. The AF-2W, with a crew of four, including two radar specialists in the deep fuselage, carried the large radome in the bomb-bay and operated as the

Grumman AF-2S Guardian

Grumman AF-2W Guardian

TYPE	DIMENSIONS						WEIGHT	PERFORMANCE				REMARKS
	span ft	*span* in	*length* ft	*length* in	*height* ft	*height* in	*max t-o* lb	*max speed* mph	*at height* ft	*service ceiling* ft	*combat range* miles	
Grumman F7F-1	51	6	45	4½	15	2	22,560	427	19,200	36,200	1,170	
Grumman F7F-2N	51	6	45	4½	15	2	26,194	421	20,600	39,800	960	
Grumman F7F-3	51	6	45	4	16	7	25,720	435	22,200	40,700	1,200	
Grumman F7F-4N	51	6	46	10	16	7	26,167	430	21,900	40,450	810	
Grumman F8F-1	35	10	28	3	13	10	12,947	421	19,700	38,700	1,105	
Grumman F8F-2	35	6	27	8	12	2	13,494	447	28,000	40,700	865	
Grumman AF-2S	60	8	43	4	16	2	25,500	317	16,000	32,500	1,500	
Grumman AF-2W	60	8	43	4	16	2	22,500	318	16,000	32,200	1,500	

Grumman F9F-4 Panther

Grumman F9F-5P Panther

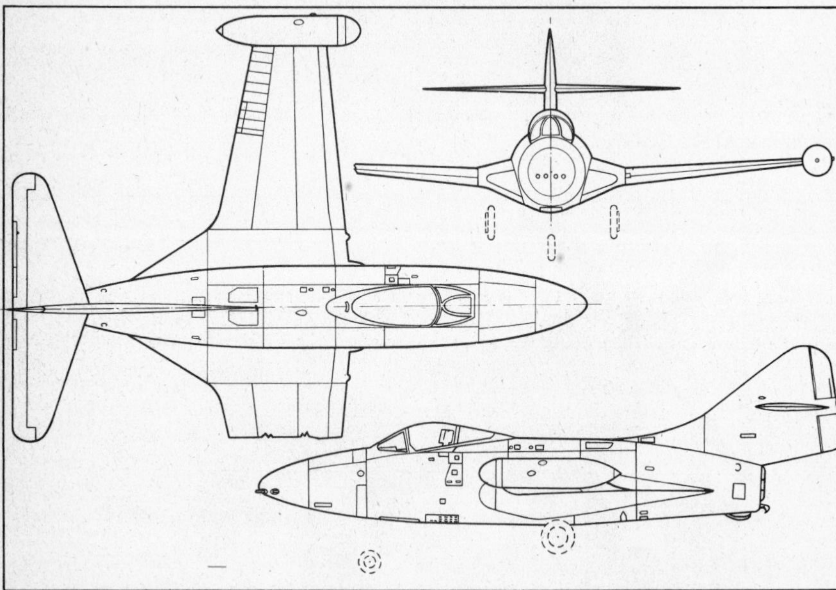
Grumman F9F-2 Panther

Grumman F9F-8 Cougar

"hunter", searching at low altitude for submarine periscopes. When a target was located, the AF-2S partner pin-pointed it with the help of APS-30 radar under the starboard wing, and was intended to attack it with depth charges or homing torpedoes dropped from the internal weapons-bay. The first AF-2 flew on 18 November 1948, and Squadron VS-25 was the first to equip in October 1950. Changes in equipment resulted in the designations AF-3W and AF-3S being used for the final batches.

Production of the AF-2W totalled 156, and of the AF-2S, 190. The 16 AF-3W and 25 AF-3S Guardians with which production ended brought the total built to 387 plus prototypes.

Grumman F9F Panther

Grumman's first jet fighter for the US Navy was designed in the closing days of World War II, with four Westinghouse J30 turbojets grouped in the wing. Intended to serve as a night fighter, it was ordered on 22 April 1946 as the XF9F-1, but was cancelled a few months later and succeeded by the XF9F-2, powered more conventionally by a single turbojet in the centre-fuselage. The two prototypes, with the Grumman model number G-79, used imported Rolls-Royce Nenes of 5,000 lb s t, and flew first on 4 November 1947.

The G-79 featured wing-root intakes and a single tailpipe under the rudder. The tailplane was mounted well up the fin and the pilot was ahead of the wing to ensure good visibility. Armament comprised four 20-mm guns, and six underwing rockets or 1,000-lb of bombs. Wing-tip tanks were a permanent installation.

Production model F9F-2s had the Pratt & Whitney-built Nene in the J42-P-6 or P-8 versions; the first flew on 24 November 1947 and Squadron VF-51 began to equip in May 1949. Production totalled 567, plus 54 more converted from F9F-3s. The latter had 4,600-lb s t Allison J33-A-8 engines, the original installation of which, in the XF9F-3, had been an insurance against failure of the Nene programme and was first flown on 16 August 1948.

A later version with Allison J33-A-C6 was designated F9F-4, but the 109 aircraft of this type that were ordered became part of a total contract for 761 F9F-5s with 6,250-lb s t J48-P-2 engine, lengthened fuselage and taller fin. The F9F-5 first flew on 21 December 1949, later aircraft having -4 or -6A engines. Production was completed at the end of 1952, some of the final aircraft being fitted with cameras in the nose for reconnaissance, as F9F-5Ps.

The Panther equipped a number of Navy and Marine fighter squadrons, and was the first Naval jet fighter to see combat, when F9F-2s went into action on 6 August 1950, after being launched from the USS *Philippine Sea*.

Grumman F9F Cougar

Although not the first swept-wing fighter designed for the US Navy, the Cougar was the first to see active service on board an aircraft carrier. By taking the fuselage and power plant of the F9F Panther, already in production, and adding new sweptback wings and tail unit, Grumman reduced development time on the Cougar, which first flew on 20 September 1951, less than a year after design began. The F9F designation was continued for the new design, but the popular name was changed.

The F9F-6 was ordered on 2 March 1951, and was powered by a J48-P-8 engine. Armament was the same as the Panther's – four 20-mm wing-mounted guns – and two 1,000-lb bombs could be carried. Delivery to Squadron VF-32 began in December 1951.

In addition to the F9F-6 fighter, Grumman produced the camera-equipped F9F-6P for reconnaissance. The F9F-7 had a J33-A-16 engine but was externally identical with the F9F-6. External changes on the F9F-8, first flown on 18 December 1953, included a longer fuselage, an increase in fuel capacity, cambered wing leading-edges and a small radome under the nose. The engine was the 7,200-lb s t J48-P-8. Final production version of the Cougar was the F9F-8T, a two-seat trainer with tandem seating and a 34-in longer fuselage, which was first flown on 4 April 1956.

Production was completed at the end of 1959, with 1,985 Cougars delivered. In addition to serving as front-line equipment with Navy and Marine squadrons, Cougars were used for a number of research and development programmes. These produced new variants designated F9F-6D (drone control), F9F-6K and -6K2 (target drones) and F9F-8B (with revised armament). In 1962, Cougars still in service were redesignated as follows: F9F-6 to F-9F; F9F-6D to DF-9F; F9F-6K to QF-9F; F9F-6K2 to QF-9G; F9F-7 to F-9H; F9F-8 to F-9J; F9F-8B to AF-9J; F9F-8P to RF-9J and F9F-8T to TF-9J.

Grumman S-2 Tracker

Grumman designed its G-89 to meet a US Navy requirement for an aircraft combining search and attack capability in the anti-submarine rôle. Previously, separate versions of the Grumman AF-2 had been produced to operate in "hunter-killer" pairs. Since the aircraft was intended only for operations against submarines, high speeds were not needed, the primary requirement being good load-carrying and long range, coupled with a reasonable cruising performance.

To meet the requirement, Grumman designed a twin-engined high-wing monoplane, with 1,525-hp Wright R-1820-82WA piston-engines, an internal weapons-bay and additional stowage space in the ends of the nacelles. A retractable APS-38 search radar was located in the rear fuselage and, for night searches, a 70-million-candlepower searchlight was mounted under the starboard wing. To fix a submarine's position, after its initial detection by means of sono-buoys, an ASQ-10 magnetic anomaly detector was fitted in a retractable fairing in the rear of the fuselage, above the arrester hook for carrier operations.

The US Navy gave Grumman a contract for one prototype G-89 on 30 June 1950, and this aircraft, designated XS2F-1, made its first flight on 4 December 1952. Production versions were designated originally in the S2F, TF and WF series, and were subsequently re-designated in the S-2, C-1 and E-1 series respectively.

Approximately 500 S-2A Trackers were built under US Navy contracts, the first of these entering service with Anti-Submarine Squadron VS-26 in February 1954; many other units were equipped subsequently. Under MAP and other arrangements, the US Navy supplied 24 S-2As to the Royal Netherlands Navy, 48 to the Italian Air Force, 60 to the Japanese Maritime Self-Defence Force and 6 to the Argentine Naval Aviation. In addition, de Havilland Canada built 100 under licence as CS2F-1s for the Royal Canadian Navy. Some of these later became CS2F-2s and -3s with modified equipment; 13 were supplied to Brazil for service aboard the *Minas Gerais* and 17 went to the Royal Netherlands Navy.

US Navy Trackers, modified to carry AQA-3 Jezebel passive long-range acoustic search equipment, were designated S-2B; a number modified for use by training squadrons became TS-2As. A production batch of 60 S-2Cs had enlarged bomb-bay (with an offset extension to port) to carry new weapons, and enlarged tail surfaces. Most of these were modified to US-2C utility transports or RS-2C reconnaissance aircraft.

The second major production version of the Tracker

Grumman F9F-8P Cougar

Grumman S2F-1 (S-2A) Tracker

Grumman S2F-3 (S-2D) Tracker

TYPE	DIMENSIONS span ft	in	length ft	in	height ft	in	WEIGHT max t-o lb	PERFORMANCE max speed mph	at height ft	service ceiling ft	combat range miles	REMARKS
Grumman F9F-2	38	0	37	3	11	4	19,494	526	22,000	44,600	1,353	
Grumman F9F-5	38	0	38	10	12	3	18,721	579	5,000	42,800	1,300	
Grumman F9F-8	36	5	42	7	15	0	20,000	690	40,000	50,000	1,000	Re-designated F-9J
Grumman S-2A	69	8	42	0	16	3½	26,300	287	SL	23,000	900	
Grumman S-2D	72	7	43	6	17	6	26,147	280	SL	22,000	1,352	

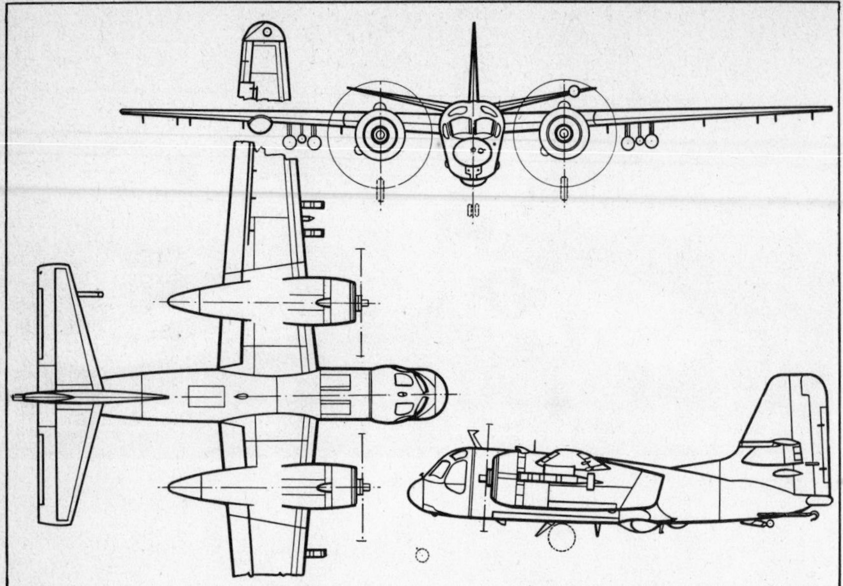
Grumman S2F-3 (S-2D) Tracker

Grumman F11F-1 Tiger

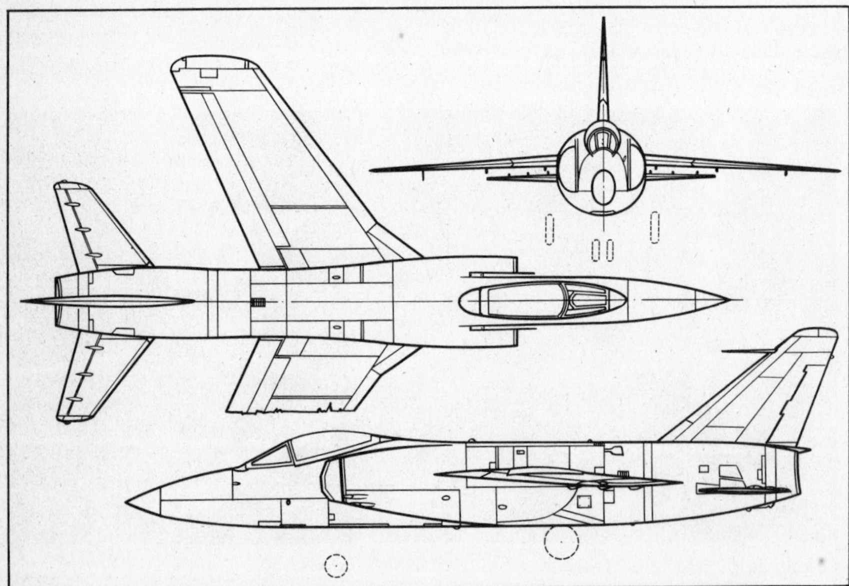
Grumman F11F-1 Tiger

Grumman A-6A Intruder

was the S-2D (originally S2F-3), first flown on 21 May 1959. This had a longer and wider front fuselage, increased wing span and larger tail surfaces, increased fuel capacity and enlarged nacelles to carry 16 sonobuoys each side. At least 15 USN squadrons operated the S-2D, starting in May 1961. Three more flew the S-2E, which differed only in having AQA-3 Jezebel equipment.

Non-combatant versions of the Tracker were produced for the US Navy as the C-1A Trader, with a nine-seat fuselage, and the E-1B Tracer with airborne early warning radar in a massive radome over the fuselage and triple fins and rudders.

Grumman F11F Tiger

On 27 April 1953, the US Navy placed contracts with Grumman for a further development of the original F9F. Almost a complete redesign of the Tiger/Cougar fighters, the Grumman G-98 was at first designated F9F-9, but became F11F-1 after the first three aircraft had been delivered and was again changed, to F-11, in 1962.

The F-11 was the first carrier-borne single-seat fighter with supersonic capability. It had a modest degree of area-ruling on the fuselage and was powered by a Wright J65-W-4 turbojet, rated at 7,800-lb s t. The prototype, which had a -6 engine, made its first flight on 30 July 1954. Armament comprised four 20-mm cannon and two or four Sidewinder air-to-air missiles under the wings.

Production F-11As entered service with Squadron VA-156 in March 1957; this unit combined fighter and attack rôles. Deliveries ended in December 1958 with 201 built, including two F11F-1Fs with 15,000-lb s t J79-GE-3A engines and a Mach 2 performance.

Grumman A-6 Intruder

A US Navy requirement was drawn up in 1956 for a high-performance carrier-borne strike aircraft in which emphasis was to be placed upon all-weather operational capability, long range with suitable navaids, and the ability to carry a wide range of tactical weapons. The specification was born of the Navy's experience in the Korean War and was intended to produce an aircraft suitable for use in limited warfare, with the emphasis upon tactical sorties. The aircraft was also required to have a high subsonic speed at low altitude for "under the radar" penetration; in this respect it was the US Navy's nearest equivalent to the Royal Navy's Buccaneer.

Eight US airframe manufacturers submitted designs in May 1957, and the Grumman proposal was accepted in December. Contracts were placed for a batch of eight aircraft, designated A2F-1 and named Intruder, to be used for development and evaluation. The designation was subsequently changed to A-6A. The first of the trials aircraft flew on 19 April 1960, and delivery of the first of an initial batch of 67 production A-6As began three years later. The original design featured tilting tailpipes on the two Pratt & Whitney J52-P-6s, intended to improve take-off by vectoring the thrust downward 23°. This feature was abandoned for production and the jet-pipes were given a 7° fixed downward tilt.

Other features of the A-6A include full-span leading and trailing-edge flaps, with inset spoilers serving as ailerons; a fixed flight refuelling probe ahead of the cockpit, which seats two side-by-side; and DIANE, the Digital Integrated Attack and Navigation system which can fly the aircraft through a complete mission (except take-off and landing) including all manoeuvres necessary for weapons delivery.

The A-6A went into operational service with Squadron VA-75 in March 1965, on board the USS *Independence*. The US Navy also ordered 12 EA-6As, which carry electronic countermeasures equipment and can be recognized externally by additional antennae and radomes, including one at the top of the redesigned fin. The first EA-6A flew in 1965. A more fully-equipped ECM version, designated EA-6B, entered production in 1966. This has a new front fuselage to accommodate a crew of four, including two electronics operators. Standard power plant on all later Intruders comprises two 9,300-lb s t J52-P-8A turbojets.

Hall PH

The pattern for US Navy patrol flying-boats in the inter-war years was set by the Naval Aircraft Factory, with a series of prototypes built between 1923 and 1932. The first of these were based on the hull designs of the Felixstowe F-5 (see page 364); all were of similar layout, with biplane wings above the hull, open cockpits and two engines in nacelles carried on interplane struts.

From 1927 onward, production contracts were placed with established aircraft manufacturers for batches of flying-boats based on these NAF prototypes. One went to Hall Aluminium Company for a development of the PN-11 with improved hull and other changes. Designated XPH-1, the prototype was ordered in December 1927 and appeared two years later, with GR-1750 engines.

A production contract for nine PH-1s was placed in June 1930 and deliveries began in June 1932, to Navy Squadron VP-8, the only unit to operate the type. The PH-1s had R-1820-86 engines, and enclosed cockpits for the pilots. Armament remained four 0·30-in guns, two each in forward and rear cockpits on Lewis rings. These aircraft were operational until 1937.

Five PH-2s were ordered from Hall in June 1936, with R-1820-F51 Cyclone engines, to provide the US Coast Guard with a patrol and rescue 'boat. Seven PH-3s, with detail refinements, also went to the Coast Guard, and some of these remained in service for anti-submarine patrols in the early stages of World War II.

Keystone/Huff-Daland Bombers

Until 1925, US Army bombers were traditionally twin-engined biplanes in the mould of the Martin MB-2 and its derivatives. The Huff-Daland XLB-1 broke with this convention by having a single 750-hp Packard 1A-2540 engine in the nose, and the bomb-aiming panel in the fuselage behind the wings. Designated in the new Light Bomber category, the XLB-1 was designed to have a better range than its predecessors and it could carry its 1,500-lb bomb-load nearly 1,000 miles at 114 mph. The crew of three included a gunner in the rear fuselage, with two upward-firing guns and a third in the floor. Two more guns were fixed in the lower wing.

A service trials batch of ten LB-1s was ordered in November 1925, these being similar to the prototype apart from installation of the 787-hp 2A-2540 engine. Delivery began in July 1927, by which time the Army had decided not to continue with single-engined bombers, the twin-engined type being preferred on grounds of safety and to permit a nose-gunner to be carried. During 1926, Huff-Daland proposed a twin-engined version of the LB-1 and a prototype was ordered as the XLB-3; this was to have air-cooled Liberty engines, one on each lower wing, but the engine did not materialize and the project was revised as the XLB-3A, with two 410-hp Pratt & Whitney R-1340-1 engines. It appeared eventually in 1928, by which time it had additional fins and rudders on each tailplane.

Following the XLB-3 contract, Huff-Daland was given an order for an XLB-5, which was again based on the LB-1 airframe and was powered by two Liberty V-1650-3 engines of 400 hp. It was followed in 1928 by ten LB-5s with 420-hp V-1650-3 engines, a small increase in wing span,

Grumman EA-6A Intruder

Hall PH-3

Huff-Daland LB-1

TYPE	DIMENSIONS span ft	span in	length ft	length in	height ft	height in	WEIGHT max t-o lb	PERFORMANCE max speed mph	at height ft	service ceiling ft	combat range miles	REMARKS
Grumman F-11A	31	7½	44	11	13	3	24,078	890	40,000	50,500	700	Originally F11F-1
Grumman A-6A	53	0	54	7	15	10	54,000	685	SL	NA	1,250	
Hall PH-1	72	10	51	10	17	6	16,379	134	SL	11,200	1,580	
Hall PH-3	72	10	51	0	19	10	17,679	159	3,200	21,350	1,937	
Keystone/Huff Daland LB-1	66	6	46	2	14	11	12,415	120	SL	11,150	430	
Keystone LB-5	67	0	44	8	16	10	12,155	107	SL	8,000	435	

Keystone B-4A

Keystone LB-5A

Keystone PK-1

Lockheed Hudson Mk VI, RAF

higher weights and a triple tail unit. A change to a twin tail unit distinguished the LB-5A, of which the Army received 25 in 1928.

During 1927, Huff-Daland re-organized as the Keystone Aircraft Corporation. Thus, the LB-5As were delivered as Keystone aircraft, as were all subsequent developments of the type.

The last of the LB-5s was completed as the XLB-6, which had a completely new set of parallel-chord wings, with 525-hp Wright R-1750-1 Cyclone radials suspended between the wings instead of being mounted on the lower wing. The production models had a longer fuselage and comprised 17 LB-6s with R-1750 engines and 18 LB-7s with Pratt & Whitney R-1690-3 Hornet radials. Various trial engine installations in LB-6s and LB-7s accounted for the LB-8, LB-9, LB-10, LB-11 and LB-12, single examples of which were produced.

After these trials had been analysed, Keystone received a contract for 63 LB-10As, the largest bomber order in a decade. The LB-10A was the first of a new series featuring a minor change in wing-tip profile, a single fin and rudder and other detail refinements. Before deliveries began, the LB category had been abandoned and the B (for Bombardment) series begun. Consequently, the first 36 Keystones on this contract appeared as B-3As, with 525-hp R-1690-3 engines, and the other 27 as B-5As with 525-hp R-1750-3s.

The Army had also ordered, in 1930, seven LB-13s and three LB-14s. Five of the former were built as Y1B-4s with 575-hp R-1860-7s, the other two LB-13s becoming (with three converted B-3As) Y1B-6s powered by 575-hp Wright R-1820-1 Cyclones. The LB-14s were redesignated Y1B-5s but appear to have been cancelled before completion.

Final production contracts for the Keystone bombers were placed in 1931 and were for 25 B-4As (R-1860-7 engines) and 39 B-6As (R-1820-1 engines). The long series of bombers from the original single-engined Huff-Daland design to the last B-6A provided the US Army Air Corps with the bulk of its bomber force until the coming of the all-metal monoplanes in the middle 1930s.

Keystone PK-1

Keystone Aircraft Corporation was among the manufacturers which succeeded in obtaining contracts to produce in quantity variants of the flying-boat designs evolved at the Naval Aircraft Factory in the late 1920s. On 30 November 1929, Keystone received an order for 18 'boats, designated PK-1.

Following the formula established by the NAF for biplane flying-boats, with two radial engines on struts between the wings and open cockpits for the pilots and gunners, the PK-1s were powered by Wright R-1820-64 Cyclones. They incorporated some features of the XP4N-1 (itself a development of the PN-12 with geared R-1820-64 engines) including twin fins and rudders. Ring cowls on the PK-1's engines improved performance.

Deliveries of the PK-1s were begun in mid-1931, to Navy patrol Squadron VP-1F, with which unit they served at Pearl Harbor until the end of 1938.

Lockheed A-28, A-29 Hudson

One of the most important US aircraft purchased by Britain for use in World War II, the Lockheed Hudson was designed at short notice specifically to meet British requirements. During 1938, the British Purchasing Commission in America was seeking an aircraft for coastal reconnaissance, and Lockheed rapidly produced a mock-up based on the Model 14 civil transport.

The British team accepted the Lockheed proposal and placed an order for 250 of the Model 214s, as the military version was known, in June 1938, while the type was still on the drawing board. Apart from internal equipment, the military type differed from the Model 14 primarily in having a large two-gun turret in the rear fuselage. Many Hudsons, as the RAF named the type, flew without this turret; when fitted it was a power-operated Boulton Paul model with 0·303-in guns. Two more guns were mounted in the nose.

The first Hudson flew on 10 December 1938, and deliveries to Britain began in February 1939, so that the first squadrons (Nos. 224 and 223) were operational by the time the war started. Patrols around the British coast began immediately, and on 8 October 1939, a Hudson from No. 224 Squadron became the first RAF aircraft to destroy a German aircraft in World War II. As early as January 1940, a few Hudsons were operating with Coastal Command, carrying the early form of ASV.

As the Hudson settled down in service, further orders were placed with Lockheed. Production of the initial Hudson I totalled 350; these had 1,000-hp Wright R-1820-G102A engines and two-position propellers. The 20 Hudson IIs differed only in having fully-variable Hydromatic propellers and a five-man crew. A change of power plant, to 1,200-hp GR-1820-G205As, distinguished the Hudson III, of which 428 were purchased: this version also had two additional beam gun positions and, after the first 150, additional fuel tankage.

Another engine change, to 1,050-hp Pratt & Whitney R-1830-SC3Gs, produced the Australian Hudson I (LAC Model 314), of which 100 went to the RAAF. The 309 Hudson Vs had 1,200-hp S3C4-G engines.

During 1941, further Hudsons were purchased for Britain under lend-lease arrangements, and for the first time the type received a US Army designation – A-28 with Twin Wasps and A-29 with Cyclones. The 82 A-28s went to the RAF as Hudson IVs; 450 A-28As, equipped for target-towing as well as bombing, became Hudson VIs. Contracts for the RA-29, RA-29A and C-63, the latter for trooping, totalled 800, of which 382 went to the RAF as Hudson IIIs. The rest, and some other Hudsons, were repossessed by the USAAC and pressed into service.

Twenty Hudson IIIs, with R-1820 engines, were requisitioned by the US Navy in October 1941 and went into service as PBO-1s with VP-82 squadron at Argentia, Newfoundland. Equipped to carry four 325-lb depth charges, aircraft from this squadron claimed the first US success against German U-boats on 1 March 1942. With the RAF, Hudsons operated on offensive patrols well into 1943 – in some cases with rocket armament – and thereafter many were modified to serve as transports.

Lockheed P-38 Lightning

Operating out of a US base in Iceland, a Lockheed P-38 was the first US Army Air Force fighter to shoot down a German aircraft – a Focke-Wulf Fw 200 – in World War II. From then until the war's end, the P-38 was continuously in action on all combat fronts. Its long range and twin-engined reliability made it especially valuable as an escort fighter for the deep-penetration daylight raids by USAAF B-17s and B-24s over Europe and for fighter-strike missions in the Southwest Pacific.

Lockheed began design studies for a high-performance fighter during 1937. The Army Air Corps had announced a design competition in February of that year, for an

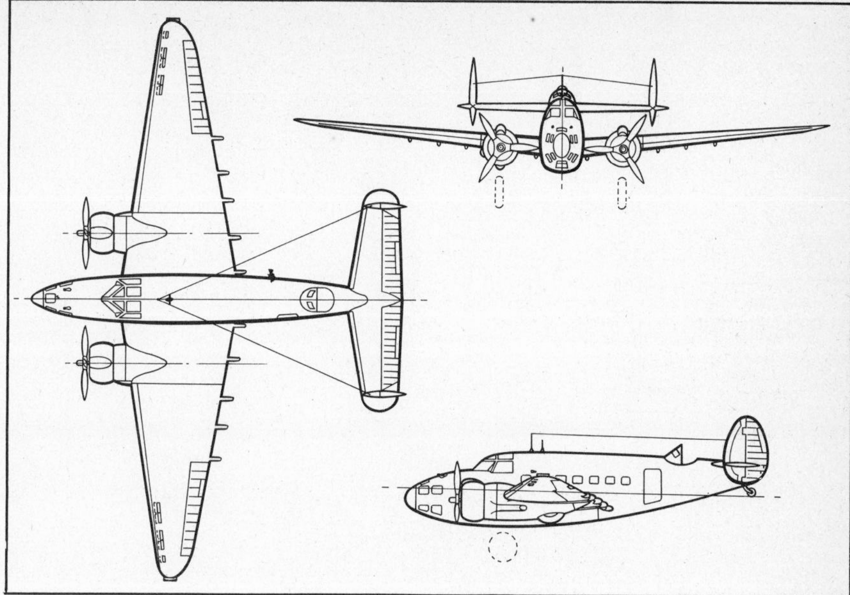

Lockheed A-28

Lockheed A-29A

Lockheed P-38H Lightning

TYPE	DIMENSIONS						WEIGHT	PERFORMANCE				REMARKS
	span ft	span in	length ft	length in	height ft	height in	max t-o lb	max speed mph	at height ft	service ceiling ft	combat range miles	
Keystone LB-6	75	0	43	5	18	1	13,440	114	SL	11,650	632	
Keystone LB-7	75	0	43	5	18	1	12,903	114	SL	13,325	432	
Keystone B-3A	74	8	48	10	15	9	12,952	114	SL	12,700	860	
Keystone B-4A	74	8	48	10	15	9	13,209	121	SL	14,000	855	
Keystone B-5A	74	8	48	10	15	9	12,952	111	SL	10,600	815	
Keystone B-6A	74	9	48	10	17	2	13,374	121	SL	14,100	363	
Keystone PK-1	72	0	48	11	16	9	17,074	120	SL	9,700	1,250	
Hudson I	65	6	44	4	11	10	17,500	246	NA	2,500	1,960	
Hudson III	65	6	44	4	11	10	20,000	255	NA	24,500	2,160	
Hudson VI	65	6	44	4	11	10	22,360	261	NA	27,000	2,160	
Lockheed A-29	65	6	44	4	11	11	21,000	253	15,000	26,500	1,550	

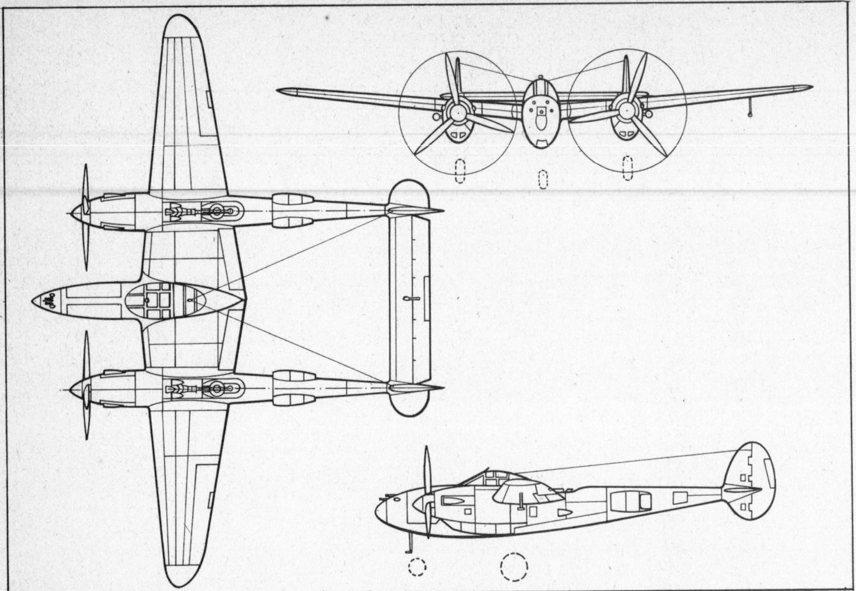
Lockheed P-38E Lightning

Lockheed P-38J Lightning

Lockheed P-38L Lightning, Droop-Snoot conversion

Lockheed P-38J Lightning, Pathfinder conversion

experimental pursuit having the tactical mission of interception and attack of hostile aircraft at high altitude. A top speed of 360 mph was specified, with a 6-minute climb to 20,000 ft. This performance could be achieved only by using two engines and a variety of possible layouts were studied: conventional wing-mounted engines, both tractor and pusher; buried fuselage engines with transmission to wing-mounted propellers; a twin-fuselage with pilot's cockpit offset on one side; and twin-booms with a central fuselage containing push-and-pull engines.

The twin-boom arrangement was eventually adopted for the Lockheed submission. Other features of the final design were a tricycle undercarriage, engine turbosuperchargers, heavy nose-mounted armament and a high wing loading, characteristic of Lockheed designs. With this Model 22 proposal, Lockheed won the design competition and a contract for one prototype, designated XP-38, was awarded on 23 June 1937. Detailed design and mock-up evaluation took a year; construction started in July 1938, and the first flight was made from March Field, California, on 27 January 1939. Two weeks later, the XP-38 leapt into prominence with a 7-hour dash across the continent, terminating in a disastrous but non-fatal undershoot at Mitchell Field on Long Island, New York.

A service test batch of 13 YP-38s had already been ordered and the first of these flew on 16 September 1940. It had 1,150-hp Allison V-1710-27/29 (handed) engines in place of the XP-38's 960-hp V-1710-11/15s, and the armament comprised a 37-mm cannon, two 0.50-in machine-guns and two 0·30-in guns in the nose. The first production contract had been placed, meanwhile, in September 1939, and Lockheed began delivery of 29 P-38s and one P-38A in mid-1941. These were similar to the YP-38s, but had four 0·50-in guns in the nose, as had the original XP-38. They were followed by 36 P-38Ds, which had self-sealing fuel tanks, revised tailplane incidence angle to overcome a buffeting problem and other small modifications.

Delivered in the second half of 1941, the P-38D was the first USAAC version to carry the name Lightning, which had been adopted for the version of the Lockheed fighter ordered by the Royal Air Force in 1940. Deliveries to Britain of the Lightning I began in December 1941, this version having low-powered and unhanded V-1710-15 engines without superchargers; production totalled 143, but performance was unsatisfactory and only three reached Britain. The majority were repossessed by the USAAC when America entered the war, to be used as trainers or for modification into P-38Fs. Similarly, 524 Lightning IIs on British contract, with more powerful supercharged engines, were absorbed by the USAAC prior to delivery, some being modified into P-38Gs.

While building the RAF's Lightnings, Lockheed began work on the next USAAF variant, the P-38E. This had a 20-mm cannon, instead of the usual 37-mm weapon in the nose, following a British decision to use the smaller gun with its higher rate of fire; and the quantity of ammunition carried in the nose was doubled. Production totalled 210 before a switch to 1,325-hp V-1710-49/53 engines early in 1942 introduced the P-38F. This was the first Lightning to have racks for external stores beneath the inner wings – bombs, torpedoes, smoke curtain canisters or drop tanks up to 2,000 lb in weight – and the "manoeuvring flap" which could be extended 8° at combat speeds to increase manoeuvrability by increasing wing lift and reducing the risk of stalling. Lockheed built 527 P-38Fs and 1,082 P-38Gs, the latter having V-1710-51/55 engines and equipment changes.

Deliveries of these versions of the Lightning to overseas theatres began in 1942 and the first combat operation was flown from UK bases on 1 September. By November, Lightnings were operating from bases in North Africa and also in the Southwest Pacific. In the spring of 1943, the P-38H appeared in service, with 1,425-hp V-1710-89/91 engines and external racks for a total load of 3,200 lb; 601 were built. Cooling problems with these high-powered engines led to a redesign of the cowling to incorporate a chin intake beneath the spinner, to provide air for the oil radiator and intercooler. This modification in turn made room in the wing leading-edge for additional fuel, which could be supplemented by underwing tanks to obtain a maximum endurance of 12 hours. First model to have these changes was the P-38J, with the same engines and equipment as the P-38H; production totalled 2,970. Then came the most-produced variant of all, the P-38L, with 1,600-hp V-1710-111/113 engines and provision for tiers of rocket projectiles beneath the outer wing panels. Lockheed built 3,810 and a further 113 were built by Vultee before a contract for 2,000 was cancelled on VJ-day.

To suit changing conditions in Europe, the Droop-Snoot and Pathfinder P-38s were produced as field modifications. The former had a lengthened nose incorporating a complete bomb-aiming station, and was used as a lead ship for formations of P-38s operating as fighter-bombers. The Pathfinder carried a radar bomb-sight in a large nose radome. Another post-production conversion produced 75 P-38Ms for use in the Pacific as night fighters. These had an observer's position behind and above the pilot, and radar in a small fairing under the nose.

Throughout the Lightning's career as a fighter, equivalent versions were produced for armed or unarmed photographic reconnaissance. These were designated F-4 and F-5, 500 being built between 1942 and 1945. Others were produced by conversion of P-38 fighters.

Lockheed B-34, B-37, PV-1, Ventura

Encouraged by the early success of the Hudson programme, the British Purchasing Commission gave Lockheed approval to develop a similar military derivative of the larger commercial Model 18. Closely resembling the Model 14 Hudson in general appearance, the Ventura, as the new type was named, had 2,000-hp Pratt & Whitney GR-2800-S1A4Gs, a 2,500-lb bomb-load and eight 0·30-in guns – two in a dorsal turret, two in a "stepped" ventral position and four in the nose. The RAF ordered 875 in 1940 and the first flight was made on 31 July 1941.

Deliveries to the RAF began during 1942 and the first operation was made on 3 November in that year by aircraft of No. 21 Squadron, Bomber Command. After 188 Ventura Is had been delivered, production switched to the Ventura II with R-2800-31 engines, a 3,000-lb bomb-load and two more guns on flexible mounts in the fuselage. Orders were increased by 200 with a lend-lease contract for Ventura IIAs, but total deliveries of this version were restricted to about 300 when the type was found of limited value in daylight raids over Europe.

Meanwhile, the USAAF had given the Ventura the designation B-34 for lend-lease purposes, and retained a quantity of Ventura IIAs under this designation. More than 300 Venturas from the earlier British contract were also absorbed by the Army Air Force as R-37s (the company Model number), B-34As or, when modified as navigation trainers, B-34Bs.

A version with Wright R-2600-13 engines and revised equipment was projected as Ventura III, and a contract for 550 was placed. The designation was changed to B-37, and the entire programme cancelled after 18 deliveries, to give priority to USN requirements for the type.

The Navy had requisitioned 27 aircraft from the British

Lockheed P-38M Lightning

Lockheed PV-1 Ventura

Lockheed Ventura Mk I, RAF

TYPE	DIMENSIONS span ft	span in	length ft	length in	height ft	height in	WEIGHT max t-o lb	PERFORMANCE max. speed mph	at height ft	service ceiling ft	combat range miles	REMARKS
Lockheed P-38	52	0	37	10	9	10	14,348	405	20,000	38,000	650	
Lockheed P-38D	52	0	37	10	9	10	15,500	390	25,000	39,000	400	
Lockheed P-322	52	0	37	10	9	10	14,467	357	NA	40,000	NA	
Lockheed P-38E	52	0	37	10	9	10	15,482	395	NA	39,000	500	
Lockheed P-38F	52	0	37	10	9	10	18,000	395	25,000	39,000	425	
Lockheed P-38G	52	0	37	10	9	10	19,800	400	25,000	39,000	350	
Lockheed P-38H	52	0	37	10	9	10	20,300	402	25,000	NA	300	
Lockheed P-38J	52	0	37	10	9	10	21,600	414	25,000	44,000	450	
Lockheed P-38L	52	0	37	10	9	10	21,600	414	25,000	44,000	450	

Lockheed PV-2 Harpoon

Lockheed P-80A Shooting Star

Lockheed FP-80A Shooting Star, with cameras in nose

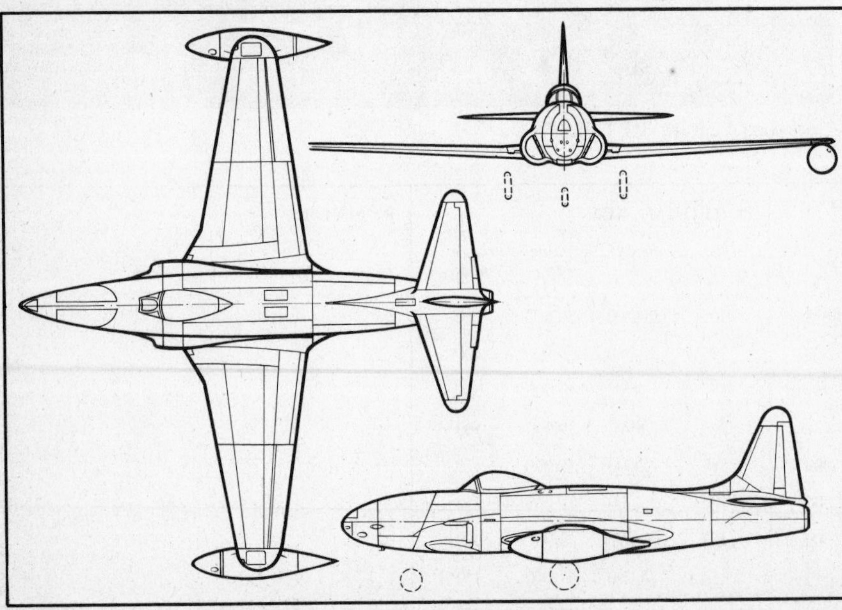

Lockheed P-80C (F-80C) Shooting Star

contract for Ventura IIs in September 1942, pending initial deliveries from a contract placed on 24 July the same year. The Navy production version was designated PV-1, as a Vega-built patrol bomber, while the requisitioned British aircraft were called PV-3s. The PV-1 had two 0·50-in guns in the nose and the top turret, two ventral 0·30s, bomb-bay fittings for six depth charges or 500-lb bombs or a torpedo, and underwing points for two drop tanks. The engines were R-2800-31s. Some modified PV-1s had Mk IV radar in the nose and six 0·50-in guns.

Delivery of the PV-1s began in December 1942, the first aircraft following the PBO-1 Hudsons into service with Squadron VP-82. From that time onward, the US Navy had exclusive rights to PV-1 production. The 1,600 built included 388 supplied to the RAF under lend-lease as Ventura GR Mk Vs and flown by Coastal Command.

A further development of the same design for the US Navy appeared in 1944 as the PV-2 Harpoon. The span was increased, larger fins and rudders fitted, and the internal arrangements improved. The armament included five forward-firing 0·50-in guns in the nose and a two-gun turret, plus underwing points for bombs and rockets, and the internal weapons-bay.

A contract for 500 PV-2s was placed on 30 June 1943, and deliveries began in March 1944, all to the US Navy, followed by 35 of a 100-plane contract for PV-2Ds, this version having eight nose guns. Some Harpoons were delivered as PV-2Cs without the outer wing fuel tanks, and were used for training and test flying only.

Eleven USN Reserve Wings operated PV-2s after they were withdrawn from front-line operational service soon after the war's end. Many were also supplied to other countries for maritime reconnaissance as they became surplus to US requirements, the recipients comprising France, Italy, Japan, Portugal and Peru.

Lockheed P-80 Shooting Star

Soon after America's first jet-propelled aircraft, the Bell XP-59, had made its first flight, in September 1942, the USAAF began making plans for the development of fighters utilizing this new mode of propulsion. The first of the new types to fly, and the first jet to become operational with the USAAF, was the Lockheed P-80 Shooting Star. Its development began on 23 June 1943, when the company received formal notification to build a single-seat aircraft with fighter potential, powered by a British de Havilland H-1 turbojet (forerunner of the Goblin).

The Lockheed design team was led by Clarence L. Johnson, who was to achieve fame subsequently for his development of the F-104, U-2 and A-11. In keeping with Lockheed tradition, an extremely rapid schedule was drawn up, with a target of 180 days to first flight. This was exceeded handsomely, the prototype XP-80 flying for the first time on 8 January 1944. It was a small low-wing monoplane with a thin, laminar-flow wing section and an air-intake on each side of the fuselage ahead of the wing leading-edge. Armament comprised five 0·50-in guns in the nose. A top speed of just over 600 mph was demonstrated by the XP-80, but plans to build the H-1 in America as the Allis-Chalmers J36 ran into difficulties and the next two prototypes of the Lockheed aircraft were completed as XP-80As, powered by the 3,750-lb s General Electric I-40. The first XP-80A flew on 10 Jun 1944, and was a little larger than the XP-80, as well as heavier. Thirteen YP-80As for service trials had earl production model J33 engines, six nose guns and several weight-saving features. First delivered in October 1944 the YP-80As were too late to see combat in World War II.

Massive production plans, involving 5,000 aircraft to be built by Lockheed and North American, wer curtailed drastically after VJ-Day; but the P-80 was nevertheless, chosen to re-equip front-line pursuit groups of the USAAF and Lockheed began delivery of 67 P-80As in December 1945. These had the Allison J33-A-9 engine, wing-tip tanks and provision for underwing bombs, rocket launchers or fuel tanks. A thinner wing section, provision for JATO, a 4,600-lb s t J33-A-2 engine with water-alcohol injection, and improved gun distinguished the P-80B; the final 240 aircraft on the original Lockheed contract were completed to the standard and many P-80As were subsequently modified.

Further contracts were placed in 1948 and 1949 for a total of 798 P-80Cs, with J33-A-23 engine and additional provision for underwing loads. This version was stationed in the Far East in 1950 when the Korean War started and became operational early in that conflict. Over 15,000 sorties were flown by F-80s (the designation changed from "P" to "F" in 1948) in the first four months of the Korean War, and on 8 November 1950, an F-80 and a MiG-15 engaged in what was probably the first combat between two jet fighters, the MiG being destroyed.

After several years of front-line service, many F-80s were allocated to Air National Guard units and to a variety of experimental duties. A considerable number were converted for reconnaissance duties as RF-80s. The Shooting Star also gave birth to the T-33A "T-Bird" trainer, basically an F-80 with lengthened fuselage for pupil and instructor in tandem seats. Production of the T-33A totalled 5,819 for the USAAF and export.

Lockheed P-2 Neptune

Production of the PV-1 version of the Ventura (see page 513) for the US Navy brought the Lockheed company into close contact with the problems of over-water patrol operations against ships and submarines. Out of this early experience developed one of the most significant of post-war maritime reconnaissance aircraft, the Neptune. Prototypes were ordered by the US Navy on 4 April 1944, coincident with a contract for the first 15 production aircraft, although the project studies had begun as early as 1941.

Designated P2V, in continuation of the series begun with the PV-1, the Lockheed Model 26 was not strictly a Vega design as suggested by the "V" symbol, but was a product of the company's Burbank division. It was the first land-based aircraft designed from the outset to operate in the maritime reconnaissance rôle and was destined to remain in production for two decades and to serve with a dozen nations. In broad terms, the P2V continued the design trend set by the Ventura, with two large piston-engines on a mid-mounted wing which passed through the fuselage above the weapons bay. Like the PV-1 and PV-2, the P2V had a dorsal turret and nose-mounted guns for defence, and provision for underwing stores. Unlike the earlier designs, converted from commercial transports, the P2V had a fuselage arranged for maximum crew efficiency under combat conditions, and capacious enough to accommodate various electronic aids to target detection and destruction.

First flown on 17 May 1945, the first XP2V-1 was powered by two 2,300-hp Wright R-3350-8 Cyclone engines and had an armament of six 0·50-in guns, including two in a tail turret. Two 2,000-lb torpedoes or twelve 325-lb depth charges could be carried internally. A second XP2V-1 was followed by 15 P2V-1s which were similarly powered and could carry up to 16 rockets under the wings. Deliveries to US Navy squadron VP-ML-2 began in March 1947. Prior to this event, one of the P2V-1s had been modified for long-range flights and in September 1946, this aircraft, named the *Truculent Turtle*, set a world distance record of 11,236 miles.

Features of the *Truculent Turtle*, including a lengthened

Lockheed RT-33A Shooting Star, reconnaissance conversion of T-33A

Lockheed P2V-2 Neptune

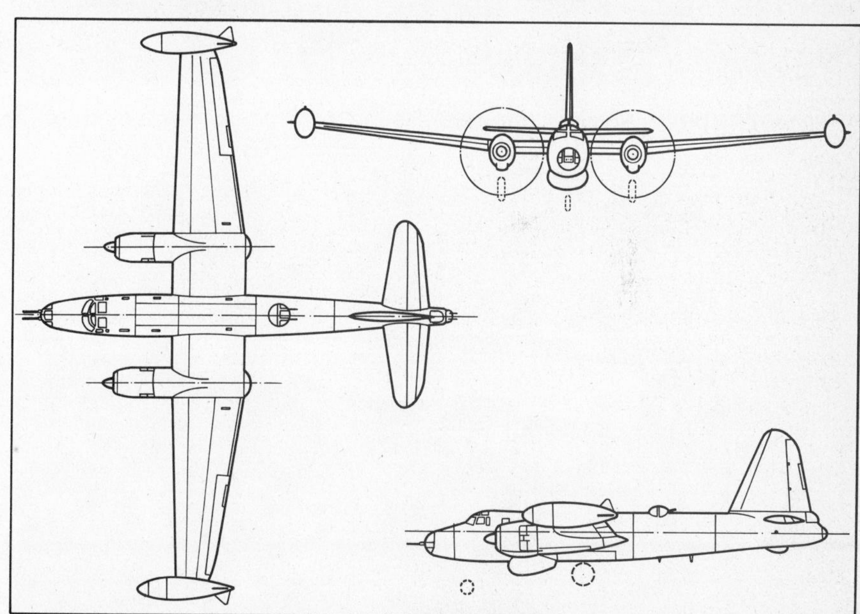

Lockheed P-2E (P2V-5) Neptune

TYPE	DIMENSIONS span ft	span in	length ft	length in	height ft	height in	WEIGHT max t-o lb	PERFORMANCE max speed mph	at height ft	service ceiling ft	combat range miles	REMARKS
Lockheed Ventura I	65	6	51	5	11	11	26,000	312	NA	25,200	1,000	
Lockheed Ventura II	65	6	51	5	11	11	27,750	315	15,500	24,000	950	B-34A similar
Lockheed PV-1	65	6	51	9	13	2	31,077	312	13,800	26,300	1,660	US Navy Ventura II
Lockheed PV-2	75	0	52	1	13	3	36,000	282	13,700	23,900	1,790	
Lockheed XP-80A	39	0	34	6	11	4	13,750	553	5,700	48,500	560	
Lockheed P-80A	39	11	34	6	11	4	14,500	558	SL	45,000	540	
Lockheed P-80C	39	11	34	6	11	4	16,856	580	7,000	42,750	1,380	

Lockheed P-2D (P2V-4) Neptune

Lockheed P-2E (P2V-5) Neptune

Lockheed P-2H (P2V-7) Neptune

Lockheed Neptune, ski landing gear

nose, were incorporated in the P2V-2, together with 2,800-hp R-3350-24Ws. The nose armament was increased to six guns, and all but the first few aircraft had 20-mm cannon in the rear turret. Of the 81 P2V-2s built between June 1947 and July 1948, two later became P2V-2Ms with ski equipment for Antarctic operations and another was the P2V-2S with a prototype search radar installation.

Only a change of power plant, to the 3,080-hp R-3350-26W, distinguished the first 40 P2V-3s from the P2V-2; these were delivered to the US Navy between August 1948 and January 1950. Eleven P2V-3Cs had equipment for carrier operation, following trials with a modified P2V-2 on board the USS *Coral Sea* during 1948, and on 7 March 1949, a P2V-3C took off from the *Coral Sea* at a record weight for carrier decks of 74,000 lb. Two other aircraft in the series were P2V-3Zs, equipped as VIP transports for front-line operation. Finally, Lockheed delivered 30 P2V-3Ws, the first Neptunes to carry APS-20 search radar, with a large radome under the forward fuselage and two operators in the crew.

Equipped, like the P2V-3W, for anti-submarine duties with APS-20 radar, the P2V-4 had new electronic equipment, and greater range as a result of the addition of wing-tip tanks which became a feature of all subsequent variants of the Neptune. All 52 P2V-4s were built for the US Navy, some being powered by 3,250-hp R-3350-30W Turbo-Compound engines. This was the first version of the Neptune to be redesignated in the unified tri-service scheme in 1962, when it became the P-2D.

A major change of nose contours, to introduce an Emerson twin 20-mm ball turret, marked the P2V-5, which first flew on 29 December 1950. The wing-tip tanks were enlarged and a searchlight, linked to illuminate the target on which the nose guns were trained, was installed in the nose of the starboard tank. Orders for the P2V-5 increased rapidly to meet US commitments in the Korean War, the total built being 424. This figure included the first Neptunes exported: 12 to the RAAF and 36 to the RAF, the latter being an MDAP deal. After four years' service with four squadrons of RAF Coastal Command, these P2V-5s were returned to US Government jurisdiction, whereupon 12 were allocated to the Royal Netherlands Navy (going subsequently to the Portuguese Air Force); six were supplied to the Argentine Navy and 14 to the Brazilian Air Force.

Post-delivery modifications considerably altered the appearance of P2V-5s serving with the US Navy. The Emerson turret was replaced by a glazed nose with an observation position, MAD (magnetic anomaly detection) gear was installed in the rear fuselage, ventral armament was deleted, and two 3,400-lb s t Westinghouse J34-WE-34 turbojets were pod-mounted under the wings to boost the take-off and over-target performance. So modified, the aircraft became P2V-5F (later P-2E). Another modification programme introduced Julie active explosive echo-sounding and Jezebel passive detector systems in the P2V-5FS (later SP-2E), and aircraft of these two types were still with front-line US Navy squadrons in 1966, as well as USN Air Reserve Training Units.

Equipped for mine-laying, in addition to other duties such as night torpedo attack, bombing and reconnaissance, the P2V-6 (later P-2F) first flew on 16 October 1952 and followed the P2V-5 into production. The 83 built included a quantity for MDAP, these going to France's Aéronavale. US Navy versions included the TP-2F (P2V-6T) trainer and MP-2F (P2V-6M) carrying a Fairchild Petrel air-to-surface missile under each wing. Retrospectively fitted with J34 jet-pods, aircraft of this type became P-2Gs (originally P2V-6F).

The original trial installation of jet-pods on a P2V-5 had been intended to prove the value of the scheme for later production variants. The boosted production version, which was also the last Neptune type built, was the P2V-7 (P-2H). The YP-2H prototype first flew on 26 April 1954 and had a number of refinements apart from the auxiliary jets. The engines were 3,700-hp R-3350-32W Turbo-Compounds and the crew accommodation was revised to improve comfort on very long missions. Some P-2Hs had 20-mm in place of 0·50-in guns in the dorsal turret, but the latter was eventually removed completely. As well as the basic P-2H, the US Navy received a number of aircraft equipped for Antarctic operation as LP-2Js (P2V-7LP) and the final production Neptunes, which were modified to have Julie and Jezebel equipment, became SP-2Hs (P2V-7S).

Production of the P-2H by Lockheed ended in September 1962. Apart from the US Navy, recipients of this version included the RAAF, which purchased 12; the RCAF with 25; France, with enough for four Aéronavale *flottilles*; and the Royal Netherlands Navy, which received the final 15 and modified them to carry Nord AS12 air-to-surface missiles under the wings.

During 1959, Kawasaki in Japan began building a version of the Neptune basically similar to the P-2H, following delivery of 16 by Lockheed to the JMSDF. Contracts placed with Kawasaki totalled 48, and these aircraft are being followed by quantities of a turboprop-powered development of the Neptune (see page 242).

Lockheed F-94 Starfire

Following development of the two-seat T-33 from the original P-80 Shooting Star, Lockheed began development of a similar two-seat night and all-weather fighter in 1949. The first prototype of the new design, designated YF-94, had begun life as an F-80 and subsequently became the prototype T-33. As the YF-94, it had a 6,000-lb thrust J33-A-33 engine with afterburner, a radar operator in the rear cockpit and a redesigned front end, with air search radar above four 0·50-in guns. Production of 110 similar F-94As began in 1949, deliveries starting in June 1950 to equip all-weather fighter squadrons with jet aircraft for the first time.

Small improvements distinguished the F-94B, 357 examples of which were built; most noticeable was the raising of the tip-tanks to the centre-line of the wings, instead of just beneath. Much more radical changes were made in the F-94C (which was initially designated F-97A). This had a thinner wing (10 per cent instead of 13 per cent thickness/chord ratio), an 8,750-lb s t Pratt & Whitney J48-P-5 engine, and a new nose design with the radome centred and surrounded by a ring of twenty-four 2·75-in Mighty Mouse air-to-air rockets faired by a retractable shield. Pods carrying 12 more of these rockets could be mounted on the leading-edge of each wing, and the tailplane was swept back to allow the critical Mach number to rise from 0·80 to 0·85.

Production of the F-94C totalled 387, and these aircraft followed the earlier version in service with fighter-interceptor and fighter-all-weather wings in the USA and Far East. After retiring from front-line service, many F-94s were issued to Air National Guard squadrons.

Lockheed F-104 Starfighter

Destined to become one of the most widely-operated fighters of the 1960s, the Lockheed F-104 was built in only limited numbers for the USAF. Its success lay in its widespread adoption for manufacture under licence, in Japan, Canada, Germany, Holland, Italy and Belgium.

The design, Lockheed Model 83, originated in November 1952 as Weapons System WS-303A for a

Lockheed F-94A Starfire

Lockheed F-94C Starfire

Lockheed F-94C Starfire

TYPE	DIMENSIONS span ft	span in	length ft	length in	height ft	height in	WEIGHT max t-o lb	PERFORMANCE max speed mph	at height ft	service ceiling ft	combat range miles	REMARKS
Lockheed P2V-1	100	0	75	4	28	6	61,153	303	15,300	27,000	4,130	
Lockheed P2V-2	100	0	77	10	28	1	63,078	320	13,500	26,000	3,985	
Lockheed P2V-3	100	0	77	10	28	1	64,100	338	13,000	28,000	3,935	
Lockheed P-2D (P2V-4)	100	0	77	10	28	1	74,129	352	9,500	31,000	4,200	
Lockheed P-2E (P2V-5)	102	0	81	7	28	1	76,152	341	NA	29,000	4,750	
Lockheed P-2H (P2V-7)	103	10	91	4	29	4	75,500	356	10,000	22,000	2,200	
Lockheed F-94A	38	11	40	1	12	8	15,330	606	SL	49,750	1,079	
Lockheed F-94C	42	5	44	6	14	11	24,200	585	30,000	51,400	1,200	

Lockheed F-104A Starfighter, Sidewinder missiles on wing tips

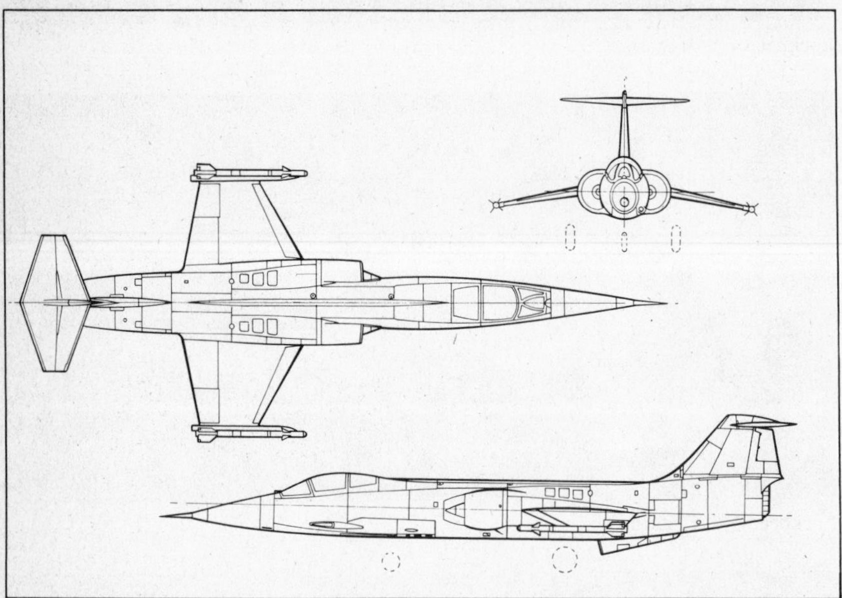

Lockheed F-104C Starfighter

Lockheed RF-104G Starfighter, Royal Netherlands Air Force

Lockheed F-104G Starfighter, Fokker-built, Luftwaffe

tactical day fighter in which high performance was the foremost requirement.

Two prototypes of the Lockheed design were ordered in March 1953 as XF-104s and the first flight was made on 7 February 1954. Both prototypes had a 10,000-lb s t Wright XJ65-W-6 engine, based on the British Sapphire design, but this was changed for a General Electric J79 with afterburner in subsequent aircraft. The 15 YF-104As for service trials had the J79-GE-3 engine and shock-control centre-bodies in the air-intakes. The YF-104As were the first to carry the designed armament, comprising a 20-mm M-61 multi-barrel gun in the fuselage and a Sidewinder air-to-air missile at each wing-tip, as an alternative to fuel tanks.

Production of the Starfighter began in 1955 and the first of 155 F-104As flew for the first time on 17 February 1956. Operational equipment of the production version included a downward-firing ejection seat and the AN/ASG-14T1 radar fire-control system. Allocated for service with Air Defense Command, the F-104As began to reach squadrons in January 1958, but persistent difficulties caused the type to be grounded three months later. Before returning to service they were fitted with the J 79-GE-3B engine and a ventral fin was added. After about 18 months' service, the F-104As were withdrawn from Air Defense Command; 25 went to the Chinese Nationalist Air Force and 12 to the Pakistan Air Force, while others equipped two ANG squadrons.

Adapted to operate with Tactical Air Command, the F-104C was a multi-mission version, powered by a 15,800-lb s t (with afterburning) J79-GE-7 and with in-flight refuelling provision, blown flaps and underwing pylons to carry two 1,000-lb bombs, two Sidewinders (in addition to those at the wing-tips) or two rocket pods. The F-104C could carry an additional bomb under the fuselage centre-line, and was fitted with the ASG-14 fire-control system. The 77 machines of this type built equipped one division of TAC from 1959 to 1965. Two-seat operational trainer versions of both the F-104A and C were also produced, as the F-104B and D respectively.

Based on experience with the F-104C, and aimed primarily at a German requirement for a close-support strike-fighter, the F-104G was developed as a Lockheed-financed project in 1958. Whilst retaining the overall configuration of the earlier Starfighters, the F-104G was extensively redesigned internally to ensure the required airframe strength, and NASARR radar was specified for target detection and tracking. Increased vertical tail area was provided and blown flaps were introduced as well as "manoeuvring flaps" at the trailing-edge. Many changes were made to the aircraft's sytems.

Germany signed a contract with Lockheed on 18 March 1959 for development of the F-104G and its subsequent production under licence in Germany. The original plans were modified in 1960/61 when the F-104G was chosen also to equip the air forces of the Netherlands, Belgium and Italy, each country to participate in its production. Four production groups were established, one comprising a consortium of four West German companies, the second made up of three other German factories and two Dutch, the others being Belgian and Italian groups respectively. Orders for F-104Gs built in Europe totalled 604 for the Luftwaffe, 120 for the Netherlands, 99 for Belgium and 124 for Italy; in addition, Germany ordered 96 from Lockheed, and Belgium and Italy ordered one each. The Netherlands purchase includes a small number of RF-104Gs with a camera pack in place of the Vulcan gun.

Lockheed flew the first F-104G at Burbank on 5 October 1960, and began delivery to Germany in May 1961. The first European-built Starfighter followed in August, from the German group.

A further batch of 140 F-104Gs were ordered from Canadair by the US Department of Defense, these aircraft being allocated through the Military Assistance Programme to Denmark (25), Norway (16), Greece (36) and Turkey (38). The first of these flew at Montreal on 30 July 1963, and followed production of 200 CF-104s by Canadair for the RCAF.

The Starfighter had been chosen by Canada in July 1959 as a Sabre replacement for the No. 1 Air Division in Europe; The CF-104 (RCAF designation, after a brief period as CF-111) was basically an F-104G, powered by the Orenda-built J79-OEL-7 engine, but minus the Vulcan cannon and its associated sighting computer, and with the NASARR optimized for the air-to-ground mode. The CF-104 was thus intended primarily for close-support, and provision was made for a Vicom reconnaissance pod carrying four Vinten cameras, and increased internal fuel. Designated CL-90 by Canadair, the first CF-104 flew at Palmdale on 26 May 1961, and all 200 had been built by September 1963.

Japan concluded an agreement to build the Starfighter on 29 January 1960, and Mitsubishi established a production line of F-104Js during 1963. The "J" is basically a "G" but equipped primarily as an interceptor. The initial Japanese programme involved three F-104Js built by Lockheed and 177 assembled or built in Japan.

A two-seat version of the F-104G was developed by Lockheed as the TF-104G, to provide advanced pilot training in an airframe retaining limited operational capability. The M-61 cannon and autopilot were deleted to make space for the second cockpit, but the store-carrying capability of the wings was retained. The Luftwaffe ordered a total of 167 TF-104Gs from Lockheed, including 30 used for Luftwaffe pilot training in the USA. Ten were purchased by the Netherlands, 12 by Italy and 3 by Belgium, and 28 were ordered for distribution under the MAP to countries including Denmark.

Japan purchased 20 two-seat F-104DJs from Lockheed, for assembly in Japan. These were similar to the F-104D, with Japanese equipment. The Canadian two-seater was designated CF-104D, a total of 38 being built by Canadair between 1961 and 1964.

Latest version of the Starfighter is the F-104S, with a 17,900 lb s t J79-GE-JIF turbojet and provision for Sparrow air-to-air missiles; 145 were ordered by the Italian Air Force in 1967, for production in Italy.

Lockheed P-3 Orion

Ten years after the Lockheed Neptune entered service with the US Navy, the Chief of Naval Operations issued Type Specification No.146 for a new land-based anti-submarine aircraft. Dated August 1957, this requirement set limits on cost and delivery times that dictated the choice of an existing airframe modified for ASW work, rather than a completely new type.

In the competition which followed, Lockheed successfully submitted plans for a variant of the Electra commercial transport.

Changes from the original design to produce the ASW Orion included deleting a 7-ft section of fuselage ahead of the wing, completely redesigning the cabin interior, introducing a bomb-bay forward of the wing and adding electronic search equipment in a nose radome and an MAD tail fairing. Military versions of the Electra engine, designated Allison T56-A-10W, were introduced with water-alcohol power augmentation. Driving Hamilton Standard four-blade propellers, these engines are rated at 4,500 eshp.

Structurally, the Orion resembles the Electra, with a semi-monocoque fuselage made up of rings, stringers and fatigue-resistant skins. The basic wing structure comprises a single-cell torsion box with integrally-machined skins, making up the fuel tank. Fuel is also carried in the wing centre-section and in a flexible tank in the fuselage.

Control system of the Orion is conventional, with one-piece ailerons, rudder and elevator, a variable-incidence tailplane and Fowler-type flaps. All flying controls are hydraulically-boosted.

Lockheed F-104S Starfighter, Italian-built, with Sparrow missiles

Lockheed P-3A Orion

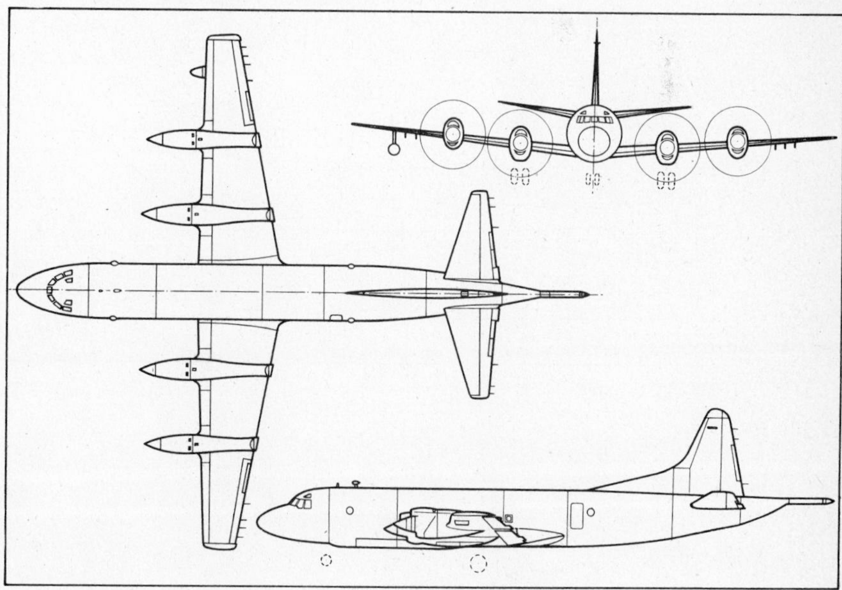
Lockheed P-3A Orion

TYPE	DIMENSIONS span ft	span in	length ft	length in	height ft	height in	WEIGHT max t-o lb	PERFORMANCE max speed mph	at height ft	service ceiling ft	combat range miles	REMARKS
Lockheed F-104C	21	11	54	9	13	6	23,590	1,450	40,000	55,000+	1,000+	
Lockheed F-104G	21	11	54	9	13	6	25,027	1,550	40,000	55,000	1,380	

Lockheed P-3B Orion, Squadron VP-49

LTV F-8A(F8U-1) Crusader, Squadron VF-32

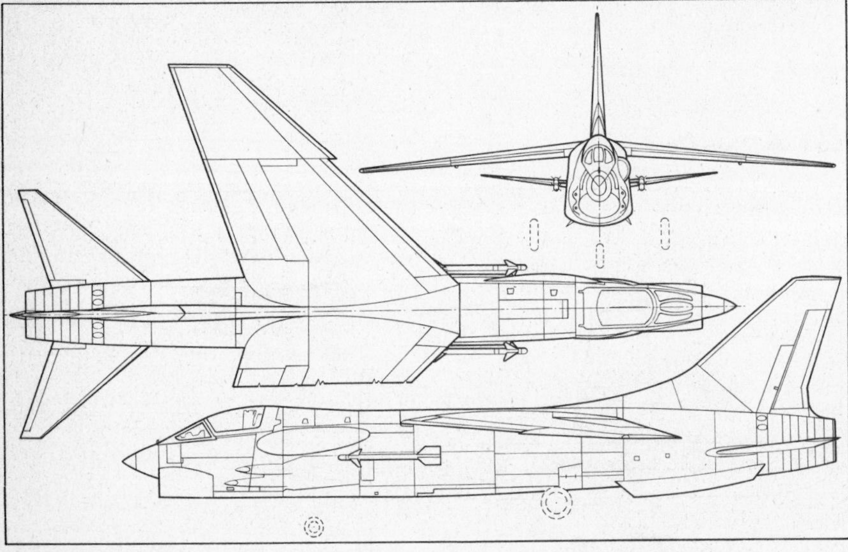
LTV F-8C (F8U-2) Crusader

LTV F-8E (F8U-2NE) Crusader

To test some of the new aerodynamic features of the Orion design, including the MAD tail fairing, Lockheed modified an Electra prototype. This made its first flight on 19 August 1958, and was followed on 25 November 1959 by the first genuine Orion, an operational prototype designated YP3V-1. The "P3V" designation was later changed to P-3, and the first flight of a production P-3A Orion was made on 31 March 1961.

US Navy squadrons VP-8 and VP-44 were the first to operate the Orion, and its introduction into service was marked by formal ceremonies at Patuxent River NAS on 13 August 1962. The 100th Orion was delivered in November 1964. A change of power plant to the 4,910-eshp T56-A-14 brought a change of designation to P-3B for aircraft produced in 1966–8, including five for the RNZAF and 10 for the RAAF.

With the same engines, but the A-NEW range of equipment to improve submarine detection capability, the P-3C followed the P-3B into production in 1968.

The Orion is designed to carry a wide variety of anti-submarine weapons internally and under the wings. A powerful searchlight is located under the starboard wing on production aircraft. To extend endurance in the search area the Orion can be flown on two engines at low altitude, at speeds as low as 170 mph. To reach the search area, speeds above 400 mph can be attained; in 1963 a standard Orion without extra tankage flew 6,220 miles in 14¼ hours at an average of 436 mph.

LTV F-8 Crusader

After producing the unusual F6U and highly unorthodox F7U, the Chance Vought company reverted to a more conventional layout for its next US Navy fighter, the design of which began in 1952 to meet an official requirement for a supersonic air-superiority fighter. In competition with seven other designs, the Chance Vought proposal was selected for development, and a contract awarded on 29 June 1953 covered the construction of two prototypes, designated XF8U-1.

The design placed the pilot far forward in the nose, above the chin intake for the Pratt & Whitney J57 turbojet, and to ensure an adequate forward view combined with a reasonably low landing speed, the XF8U-1 made use of a unique variable-incidence wing. Raising the wing leading-edge through seven degrees of arc enhanced the angle of attack for landing without tilting the fuselage nose into the air; simultaneously, the ailerons, a portion of the trailing-edge flaps and the entire leading-edge flap were drooped automatically to increase the wing lift.

The XF8U-1, with a J57-P-11 engine, first flew on 25 March 1955, and was followed by the second prototype on 30 September 1955. Production aircraft, designated F8U-1 and F8U-2, were later redesignated in the F-8 series as described below, while the manufacturers became part of Ling-Temco-Vought Inc. Deliveries of the F-8A to the US Navy's VF-32, the first operational Crusader squadron, began on 25 March 1957. This version had a J57-P-12 or P-4A engine and an armament of four 20-mm cannon, plus a rocket pack in the fuselage with 32 HVARs (on early aircraft only) and, after later modification, two fuselage-mounted Sidewinder air-to-air missiles. Production of the F-8A totalled 318; another 130 fitted with a small interception radar in the nose cone were designated F-8B (orginally F8U-1E). First flown on 17 December 1956, the RF-8A (F8U-1P) carried five cameras in place of the internal armament; 144 of these were produced, of which 53 were modernized as RF-8Gs in 1965–6.

The feasibility of producing a two-seat combat training version of the F-8 was studied with the YTF-8A, an F-8A conversion, first flown on 6 February 1962 and powered by a de-rated J57-P-20 engine. Other early Crusaders were later converted for drone and drone control duties as DF-8A (F8U-1D) and QF-8A (F8U-1KD).

Succeeding the F-8A as a day air-superiority fighter, the F-8C (F8U-2) was powered by a J57-P-16 offering a 700-lb increase in afterburning thrust. Two YF-8C trials aircraft were followed by the first of 187 production aircraft on 20 August 1958, these eventually serving with five Navy and four Marine squadrons. Better all-weather capability, achieved through a Vought push-button autopilot and extra electronic equipment, accounted for a change in designation to F-8D (F8U-2N) for the next production version, which was powered by a J57-P-20. The extra power permitted the F-8D to operate at higher weights and to carry four Sidewinders on the fuselage. The first production F-8D flew on 16 February 1960; 152 were built.

The addition of underwing strong-points for a maximum of 5,000 lb of weapons distinguished the F-8E (F8U-2NE), the prototype of which (YF-8E) first flew on 30 June 1961. Delivery of the F-8E began late in 1961 and continued until mid-1964, a total of 286 being built.

By the end of 1964, the F-8 was serving as the standard fleet fighter of the US Navy, although deliveries of the F-4 were beginning to supplement and even replace it in some units. Two *flottilles* of the French Aéronavale were equipped with the F-8E (FN) during 1965; 42 of these were ordered in 1963, and the first production example flew on 26 June 1964. The F-8E (FN) incorporated a number of modifications, including blown flaps to reduce landing speed, for operation from smaller carriers.

During 1966, LTV initiated a modernization programme for F-8D and F-8E Crusaders, which were redesignated F-8H and F-8J after modification.

LTV A-7A Corsair II

A design contest initiated by the US Navy on 17 May 1963 for a single-seat lightweight attack aircraft (VAL) to replace the Douglas A-4 Skyhawk, brought a response from four companies, with Ling-Temco-Vought being named winner of the contest on 11 February 1964. The LTV design proposal was based on the F-8 Crusader, with modifications to match the subsonic requirements of the VAL specification, which required an aircraft able to carry more than 10,000 lb of stores externally.

Compared with the F-8, the A-7, as the LTV design was designated, has slightly reduced wing sweepback, a shorter fuselage, non-afterburning engine, fixed-incidence wing and outboard ailerons. The wings have a total of six strong-points, four with a 3,500-lb capacity each and two with a 2,500-lb capacity. The A-7 has a 500-lb station on each side of the fuselage, like the F-8, and a built-in armament of two 20-mm cannon. The engine is an 11,350-lb s t Pratt & Whitney TF30-P-6 turbofan.

The initial contract awarded to LTV on 19 March 1964 was for seven A-7As for flight development and further orders brought the total of this version to 199.

First of the A-7A trials aircraft made its first flight on 27 September 1965 and deliveries to the US Navy began in the autumn of 1966. The A-7A was to be followed by the A-7B with TF30-P-8 engine and other changes, the two-seat A-7C and the A-7E with improved avionics. In 1966 the USAF ordered a version of the Corsair II as the A-7D, to be powered by the Rolls-Royce Spey engine built by Allison as the TF41.

McDonnell FH-1 Phantom

The US Navy's first pure-jet fighter began to take shape in 1943 after a letter of intent had been given to the McDonnell Aircraft Corporation. Choice of McDonnell,

LTV RF-8G Crusader

LTV A-7A Corsair II, Squadron VA-174

LTV A-7A Corsair II, Squadron VA-147

TYPE	DIMENSIONS						WEIGHT	PERFORMANCE				REMARKS
	span ft	span in	length ft	length in	height ft	height in	max t-o lb	max speed mph	at height ft	service ceiling ft	combat range miles	
Lockheed P-3A	99	8	116	10	33	8	130,000	460	24,000	30,000	5,000	Originally P3V-1
LTV F-8A	35	8	54	3	15	9	27,000	1,100	40,000	60,000	1,200	
LTV F-8D	35	8	54	3	15	9	34,000	1,100	40,000	60,000	1,200	
LTV F-8E	35	2	54	6	15	9	34,000	1,100	40,000	59,000	1,200	
LTV A-7A	38	9	46	1	16	3	32,500	685	NA	NA	1,400	

McDonnell FH-1 Phantom

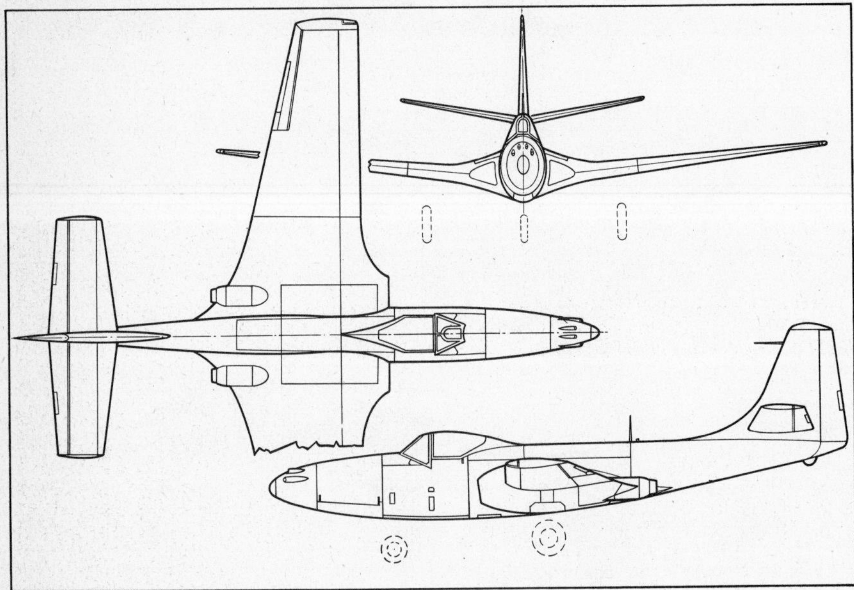
McDonnell FH-1 Phantom

McDonnell F2H-2 Banshee

McDonnell F2H-3 Banshee, RCN

at that time a young and comparatively inexperienced company, was influenced by the fact that all the major aircraft manufacturers were heavily committed to large-scale production of established aircraft. The novelty of jet propulsion, in any case, tended to favour an uninhibited approach to the design problems.

McDonnell proposed a number of alternative designs, based on engines of various sizes which were being projected by Westinghouse, ranging from one version with eight 9·5-in-diameter turbojets through six- and four-engined versions to the twin-engined design with 1,165 lb s t Westinghouse 19XB-2B engines which became the subject of a prototype contract on 30 August 1943.

Apart from the engines buried in the thickened wing roots, the McDonnell fighter was of conventional straight-wing design. Armament comprised four 0·50-in guns in the nose. The prototype, designated XFD-1, first flew on 26 January 1945 and a production contract for 100 FD-1s was placed on 7 March 1945. The designation was changed later to FH-1 to avoid confusion with Navy-designated Douglas aircraft. Only 60 FH-1s were delivered, starting on 23 July 1947 and ending on 27 May 1948. The service designation of the engines was J30-WE-20, rated at 1,600 lb s t each.

The prototype XFD-1 became the first US jet to operate from an aircraft carrier on 21 July 1946, when Lt-Cdr James Davidson made a series of landings and take-offs on board the USS *Franklin D. Roosevelt*. The production FH-1s served with Navy and Marine units.

McDonnell F2H Banshee

A March 1945 contract, placed by the US Navy with McDonnell Aircraft Corporation, covered the design and construction of two prototypes of a new fighter for the US Navy based on the FH-1. Initially designated F2D-1, these prototypes were soon re-designated XF2H-1. In appearance they closely resembled the FH-1s but were somewhat larger, with two 3,000-lb s t Westinghouse J34-WE-22 engines. The first flight was made on 11 January 1947, and delivery of an initial batch of 56 F2H-1s began in March 1949, to Navy Squadron VF-171. Armament comprised four 20-mm cannon in the nose.

The F2H-2, which appeared in 1949, had a longer fuselage to accommodate more fuel, and fixed wing-tip tanks. Production totalled 334 under two contracts, between August 1949 and September 1952, making this the most-produced of all Banshee variants. Power was provided by J34-WE-34 turbojets rated at 3,150-lb s t, and all the aircraft of this model were later modified for probe-and-drogue flight refuelling. The US Navy also took delivery of 14 F2H-2N night fighters with radar in the nose, and 58 F2H-2Ps with lengthened noses carrying cameras.

To achieve a further increase in range, the Banshee's fuselage was again lengthened in the F2H-3, by 2 ft 7 in, with two new fuel tanks installed in the extra fuselage bay. Search radar was fitted in the nose and the four cannon were re-located further aft in the fuselage sides—features retained in the final production version, the F2H-4, which had 3,600-lb s t J34-WE-38 engines.

When the Korean War broke out, the Banshee was in operational service with the US Navy and the F2H-2 was soon in combat, particularly as a fighter-bomber. After passing out of first-line service, 39 F2H-3s were sold to the Royal Canadian Navy in 1955–6 and were used to equip two fighter squadrons to serve on board HMCS *Bonaventure*. The F2H-3s and F2H-4s still in USN service in 1962 became F-2Cs and F-2Ds respectively.

McDonnell F3H Demon

Third in the series of US Navy fighters by McDonnell, the Demon was the least satisfactory of the family, being dogged by misfortune in the early stages of development. It was the aircraft most directly affected by the failure of the Westinghouse J40 programme, and as much as $200 million is reported to have been spent in unsuccessful efforts to put the initial version into service. Nevertheless, the basic design proved eventually to be satisfactory and, after an alternative engine had been installed, some 500 were built for US Navy squadrons.

The US Navy requirement when the two prototype XF3H-1s were ordered, on 30 September 1949, was for a high-performance interceptor able to match the land-based contemporaries. Breaking with their early Navy fighter configurations, McDonnell adopted a single-engined layout with lateral intakes and a short jet-pipe exhausting under the tail. The wings and tail unit were swept-back, and the engine was a 7,200-lb s t XJ40-WE-6.

The first XF3H-1 flew on 7 August 1951, but was destroyed soon after in the first of 11 accidents which cost the lives of four test pilots during the flight trials. Before the prototype flew, production of 150 F3H-1Ns had been ordered, these being intended to have all-weather capability and more fuel than the prototypes. Consequently, the gross weight increased to 29,000 lb from 22,000 lb, and the more powerful J40-WE-24 was specified.

After production contracts had been increased to a total of 528 aircraft and plans for a second production line (by Temco) had been made, it became clear that the J40 could not be developed to the required power and the J40-WE-22 of 7,200 lb s t was used only in the first 56 production aircraft. These proved so under-powered that 21 were permanently grounded and 29 were converted to F3H-2s, the others being lost in accidents. In the F3H-2, first flown in June 1955, a 9,700-lb s t (14,250 lb with afterburner) Allison J71-A-2 engine was used, and the wing area was increased by extending the roots forward.

The F3H-2 appeared in three variants, with different external armament. The F3H-2 carried varied loads for operation as a strike fighter; the F3H-2M (79 built) was modified to carry four AIM-7C Sparrow III missiles and the F3H-2N (146 built) had limited all-weather capability, carrying four AIM–9C Sidewinders. These three versions were redesignated respectively, F-3B, MF-3B and F-3C in 1962. When production ended in November 1959, a grand total of 519 Demons had been built.

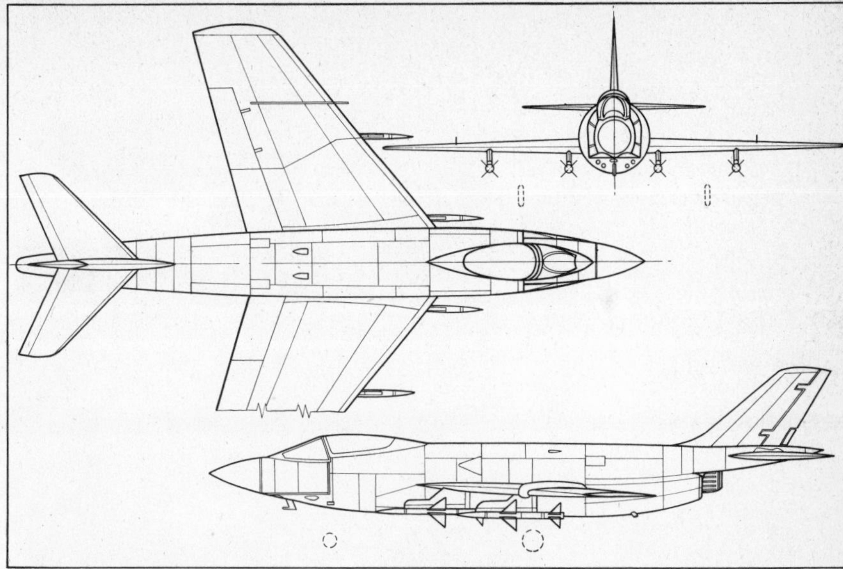
McDonnell F3H-2M Demon

McDonnell F3H-2N Demon

McDonnell F-101 Voodoo

Second of the USAF's Century-series fighters, the F-101 Voodoo appeared in 1954, having been designed as a penetration and long-range escort fighter to serve with Strategic Air Command. The design was based on an earlier McDonnell prototype, the XF-88, and no prototype of the F-101 was built as such. The first aircraft, an F-101A, flew on 29 September 1954, an initial production contract having been placed two years before, for 29 trials aircraft.

Powered by two afterburning J57-P-13 turbojets, the F-101A had a notably long range, with three external tanks to supplement internal fuel tankage. Alternatively, air-to-air missiles or bombs could be carried on the external load-points, supplementing the fixed armament of four 20-mm guns. In service, one of these guns was usually removed to make room for installation of TACAN equipment.

Before the F-101A flew, SAC cancelled its requirement, but production of 50 continued for Tactical Air Command, which eventually equipped the three squadrons of the 81st Tactical Fighter Wing with F-101As. To suit the Voodoo more specifically to TAC operations, including low-level fighter-bomber missions, the F-101C had a stronger wing and provision for a tactical nuclear weapon to be carried. The 47 F-101Cs built were also issued to the 81st TF Wing, starting in the spring of 1957. Both the "A" and "C" models had reconnaissance equivalents,

McDonnell CF-101B Voodoo, RCAF

TYPE	DIMENSIONS span ft	span in	length ft	length in	height ft	height in	WEIGHT max t-o lb	PERFORMANCE max speed mph	at height ft	service ceiling ft	combat range miles	REMARKS
McDonnell FH-1	40	9	38	9	14	2	12,035	479	SL	41,100	695	
McDonnell F2H-1	41	6	39	0	14	5	18,940	587	SL	48,500	1,278	
McDonnell F2H-2	44	10	40	2	14	6	22,312	532	10,000	44,800	1,475	
McDonnell F2H-4	44	11	47	6	14	5	19,000	610	NA	56,000	2,000	
McDonnell F3H-2M	35	4	58	11	14	7	33,900	647	30,000	42,650	1,370	Became MF-3B

McDonnell RF-101C Voodoo

McDonnell F-4B Phantom II

McDonnell RF-4C Phantom II

McDonnell F-4E Phantom II

designated RF-101A and RF-101C. These had four cameras in a lengthened nose and two more in the fuselage; they also served with TAC, which received 35 RF-101As and 166 RF-101Cs. Twenty-five of the latter were supplied subsequently to the Chinese Nationalist Air Force.

To serve Air Defense Command as a long-range interceptor, the F-101B was developed. Similar to the F-101C, it had J57-P-55 turbojets and a lengthened cockpit with two seats in tandem, an observer being carried behind the pilot. Armament comprised three Hughes Falcon air-to-air missiles, plus two Douglas Genie unguided rockets with nuclear warheads. The first F-101B flew on 27 March 1957, and this version served with at least nine USAF squadrons. Production of the Voodoo ended in March 1961 after 478 F-101Bs had been built. In service with ADC, some were equipped with full dual control and were designated TF-101B.

After passing out of first-line service with ADC, 66 F-101Bs were transferred to the RCAF, including ten with dual control, these being re-designated after modification to Canadian requirements as F-101F and TF-101F respectively. The RCAF designations were CF-101B and CF-101F.

McDonnell F-4 Phantom II

One of the most significant combat aircraft of the 1960s, the McDonnell F-4 originated to a US Navy requirement and was subsequently adopted by the USAF and by the RAF and Royal Navy. In appearance, the Phantom II is the antithesis of clean aerodynamic design, but this belies its outstanding performance.

The original US Navy specification called for a single-seat twin-engined attack fighter for carrier operation, and a letter of intent to order the McDonnell design to this specification was placed on 18 October 1954. At this time the new aircraft was designated AH-1; the designation was changed to F4H-1 by US Navy directive on 26 May 1955, and the rôle was altered to that of missile-armed fighter. This called for considerable re-design, to accommodate higher performance AI radar, a second crew-man, six missiles in a semi-submerged installation and other changes. The original contract for two YAH-1s was changed to one for a total of 23 F4H-1 test aircraft, the first of which flew on 27 May 1958. The original power plant comprised two General Electric J79-GE-3A engines loaned by the Air Force; the production power plant for the first batch of Phantom IIs was the 16,150-lb s t (with afterburning) J79-GE-2 or -2A.

Basic armament comprised four Sparrow III air-to-air missiles in recesses under the fuselage and wing centre-section. To these were added, during the initial development stages, two more Sparrows on underwing pylons which, alternatively, could carry two Sidewinders. In the course of test flying with the trials aircraft, a number of changes were introduced, including anhedral on the tailplane, a larger nose radome and flap blowing for boundary-layer control. Trials were made with one aircraft in the ground-attack rôle, designated F4H-1F and equipped to carry a large external load.

After competitive evaluation against the Chance Vought F8U-3 Crusader III, the F4H-1 was selected as standard Navy and Marine equipment in December 1958 and plans were made for large-scale production and service. Deliveries to a special USN unit, VF-101, for transition training, began at the end of December 1960.

Another competitive evaluation of the Phantom II, during 1961, led to its selection by the USAF for service with Tactical Air Command as an air-superiority fighter and close-support aircraft. When orders were placed, in March 1962, the Phantom II became the first Navy fighter ever adopted by the USAF for a major service rôle. For a short time, the USAF versions were designated F-110A and RF-110A (the latter being for reconnaissance) but all Phantom IIs were then re-designated F-4 in a unified inter-Service system. The test and early production aircraft for the USN and USMC became F-4As. The later production models, with J79-GE-8 engine, became the F-4B and RF-4B, while the USAF versions became the F-4C and RF-4C.

Pending production of the F-4C, the USAF operated a number of F-4Bs for training and familiarization. The production F-4C, first flown on 27 May 1963, has J79-GE-15 engines with cartridge starters, provision for flying-boom in place of probe-and-drogue flight refuelling, and other changes. The first of two YRF-4Cs flew on 20 August 1963 and the first RF-4C on 18 May 1964. The Navy's first RF-4B flew on 12 March 1965, by which time F-4Bs were serving with at least 12 USN and six USMC squadrons.

New versions of the Phantom II developed for all three US Services include the F-4D (first flight 8 December 1965) and F-4E (first flight of production aircraft on 30 June 1967) for the USAF, incorporating new equipment to improve the air-to-air and air-to-ground attack capability. For the US Navy, the F-4G has new communications equipment and the F-4J (first flight 27 May 1966) introduced a Doppler fire-control radar system.

During 1964, the British Government decided to adopt the Phantom II to equip Royal Navy fighter squadrons, instead of proceeding with development of the Hawker Siddeley P.1154 VTOL fighter in the Naval rôle. A year later, the P.1154 was cancelled completely and an additional quantity of Phantoms was ordered for the RAF. The British version has two Rolls-Royce Spey-25R turbofans and other changes, suiting it for operation from British aircraft carriers. The RN and RAF versions are identified, respectively, as the F-4K (first flight 27 June 1966) and F-4M (first flight 17 February 1967).

Martin MB-2/Curtiss NBS-1

Glenn L. Martin, one of America's air pioneers, re-established his own company late in 1917 after several years of partnership with Wright, and quickly obtained a contract (on 17 January 1918) to build ten twin-engined bombers, under the designation MB-1. The project was intended to better the performance of the Handley Page O/400, which was being built in the USA. Its rôle was to include corps reconnaissance as well as bombing.

The layout followed contemporary practice, with a crew of four and two 400-hp Liberty 12 A engines mounted between the wings. Gun positions were located in the nose, behind the pilots, and under the fuselage aft of the wings. The first MB-1 (or GMB) flew in August 1918. It was comparatively small and had a top speed of 120 mph. Four of the initial batch were equipped for reconnaissance, four as bombers, one for long-range flights and one as a transport, designated T-1 (or GMT). Four more MB-1s were built later, three as bombers and one as a transport, plus six for the Government Postal Service. The US Navy bought two for evaluation and then ordered ten similar aircraft, designated TM-1 (Martin MTB), with folding wings and provision for a 1,620-lb torpedo beneath the fuselage.

Developed from the MB-1, the MB-2 had larger span wings, which could be folded aft alongside the fuselage, and 420-hp Liberty engines mounted on the lower wings. Twenty were ordered from Martin in 1920; 15 of these had the new "night bomber, short-range" designation NBS-1.

Further contracts for the Martin bomber were put out to competitive tender, with the result that Lowe, Willard and Fowler (LWF) won a contract for 35 NBS-1s, and Curtiss gained a contract for 50, of which 20 had turbo-supercharged engines. A final order for 25 went to

McDonnell F-4K Phantom II, RN

Martin MB-2

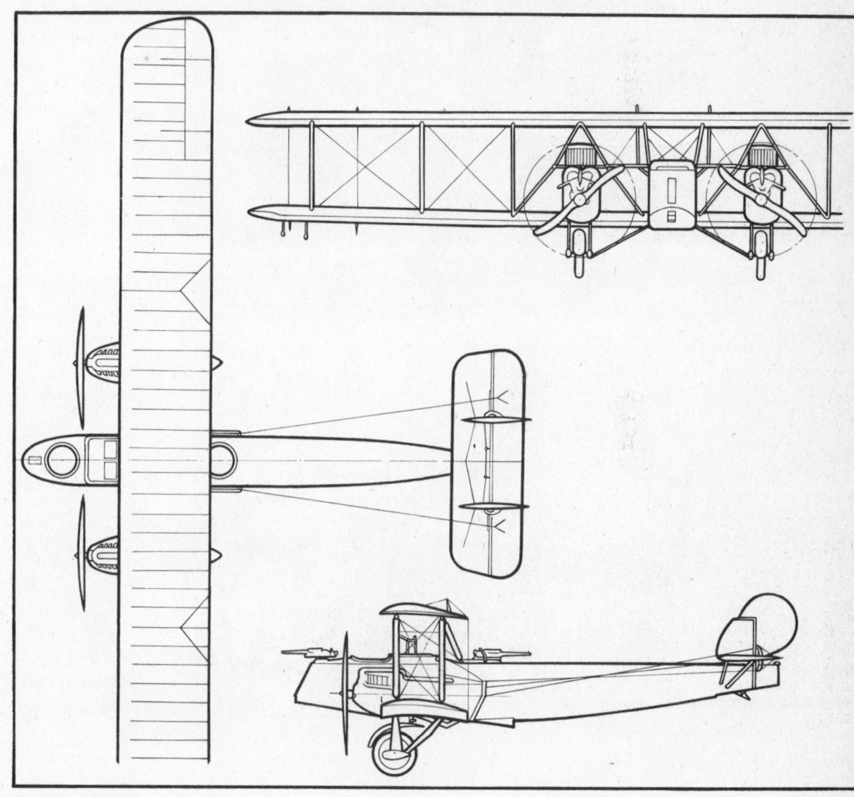
Martin MB-2

TYPE	DIMENSIONS span ft	span in	length ft	length in	height ft	height in	WEIGHT max t-o lb	PERFORMANCE max speed mph	at height ft	service ceiling ft	combat range miles	REMARKS
McDonnell F-101A	39	8	67	$4\frac{3}{4}$	18	0	NA	1,100	42,000	48,000	1,700	
McDonnell F-101B	39	8	67	$4\frac{3}{4}$	18	0	46,500	1,220	40,000	51,000	1,550	
McDonnell F-101C	39	8	67	$4\frac{3}{4}$	18	0	47,000	1,120	40,000	52,000	1,700	
McDonnell F-4B	38	$4\frac{3}{4}$	58	$3\frac{1}{4}$	16	3	54,600	1,584	48,000	62,000	800	
Martin MTB(TM-1)	71	5	46	6	15	0	12,078	105	SL	8,500	490	
Martin MB-2 (NBS-1)	74	2	42	8	14	8	12,119	99	SL	8,500	558	Data for NBS-1

Martin TM-1 (MTB)

Martin T3M-1

Martin T4M

Martin P3M-1

Aeromarine in 1922. These aircraft formed the bulk of the Army bomber force until deliveries of the Huff-Daland/Keystone biplanes began. In July 1925, 90 NBS-1s were still on strength.

Martin T3M/T4M/TG

Taking advantage of experience gained in production of Curtiss-designed SC-1 and SC-2 torpedo-bombers for the US Navy, the Glenn L. Martin Company developed an improved version which the Navy ordered in 1925. Designated T3M-1, it used the same wings as the SC-2 but had a new welded-steel fuselage structure. The location of the pilot and torpedoman was moved forward, ahead of the wing, leaving the gunner in the rear.

Like most of its contemporaries, the T3M-1 could operate on floats or wheels and was designed for carrier-borne use. The 24 T3M-1s, delivery of which began late in 1926, had 575-hp Wright T3B engines. They were followed by 100 T3M-2s with 710-hp Packard 3A-2500 engines, delivered in 1927 and thus available in time to equip the first torpedo-bomber squadron to embark in the USS *Lexington* in December of that year. A noticeable difference in the later model was that the span of the lower wing was reduced to match that of the upper.

One T3M-2 became the prototype XT3M-3, with a Pratt & Whitney Hornet air-cooled radial engine, and this power plant was also used in the new XT4M-1, which appeared in April 1927. Apart from the change of power plant the newer model (Martin 74) differed from the T3M-2 primarily in having shorter wings and a revised rudder. The final T3M-2 became the XT3M-4 prototype, with a Wright R-1750 air-cooled radial engine.

The US Navy bought 102 production model T4M-1s from Martin, these being powered by the R-1690-24 engine. Further developments of the same design appeared as Great Lakes aircraft after the Cleveland plant of Glenn L. Martin had been sold to the former Corporation in October 1928. Production based on the T4M comprised 18 TG-1s, with R-1690-28 engine and revised landing gear, and 32 TG-2s with the R-1820-56 Cyclone.

The series of Martin and Great Lakes torpedo-bombers remained in service for many years, until replaced by the new generation of monoplanes. Great Lakes, in the interim, sought vainly to prolong the useful life of the biplane with the XTBG-1 prototype of August 1935 – the last torpedo-biplane built for the US Navy.

Martin P3M

The 2,350-mile stretch of water between the Californian coast and Hawaii challenged the ingenuity of US naval aircraft designers throughout the 1920s. The NAF PN-9 came close to bridging the gap (see page 533) and this range requirement figured prominently in the design of a large monoplane flying-boat prepared by the Bureau of Aeronautics. It had a metal hull and fabric-covered metal wing structure, twin fins and rudders, four open cockpits and three 450-hp Pratt & Whitney R-1340-38 radial engines, one on each side under the wing and one on the centre-line above the wing.

A prototype of this design, with 100-ft wing span, was ordered on 28 February 1928 from Consolidated Aircraft and was delivered in the late summer of 1929. The top engine was later deleted and a production order was put out to tender. Low bidder was Glenn L. Martin, who built nine P3Ms under a June 1929 contract. These included P3M-1s with 450-hp Pratt & Whitney R-1340s, and P3M-2s with 525-hp R-1690-32s.

Martin BM/T5M

Closely related to the classic biplane torpedo-bombers of the 1930s were the large dive-bombers which the US Navy purchased at the same time. The technique of dive-bombing having been demonstrated successfully with the two-seat Curtiss F8C fighter in 1928, its application to larger aircraft followed naturally.

The two prototype dive-bombers ordered in June 1928 were both to be based on BuAer design No. 77. Hence, when they appeared, these aircraft were almost identical, although they had been ordered from and were built in two different factories – Martin (the XT5M-1) and Naval Aircraft Factory (XT2N-1). The former had a 525-hp Pratt & Whitney R-1690-22 engine, while the latter was powered by a 525-hp Wright R-1750. Both were two-seat single-bay biplanes, with one forward and one rear-defence 0·30-in gun and provision for a 1,000-lb bomb under the fuselage.

The XT5M-1 was redesignated BM-1 for production, using the US Navy's new B-for-Bomber prefix for the first time, and Martin won a contract for 12 aircraft in April 1931. The BM-1s had R-1690-44 engines, ring cowlings and spatted main wheels. First flight was made in September 1931 and deliveries began in 1932, the BM-1s being followed by 21 BM-2s. The first BM-1 reached the USS *Lexington* on 1 July 1932.

Martin B-10, B-12, B-14.

Having been responsible for much of the US Army's bomber force in the 1920s, the Martin company was in the forefront of development of monoplane bombers in the 1930s. Its Model 123 was built in a company-funded programme and, when tested in 1932, proved faster than the fighters then in service with the Army. The aircraft was of all-metal construction, its features including internal bomb stowage, a retractable undercarriage and close-cowled 600-hp Wright SR-1820-E Cyclones.

In its original form, the Martin bomber was delivered for official trials on 20 March 1932, and was given the experimental designation XB-907. Subsequently, it was modified to have 675-hp R-1820-F Cyclones in long-chord cowlings, the span was increased and a rotating nose turret was fitted, mounting a 0·303-in gun. In this form the prototype, re-designated XB-907A, achieved 207 mph. Too good to be ignored, the Martin design was ordered into production on 17 January 1933, and the prototype was purchased, becoming the XB-10.

The production model (Martin 139) had two separate cockpit enclosures, one over the pilot and one over the radio operator and rear gunner, the latter having both ventral and dorsal 0·303-in guns. The bomb-load was 2,260 lb. Deliveries began in June 1934, the first 14 aircraft being YB-10s with 775-hp R-1820-25 engines. Seven YB-12s had 775-hp R-1690-11 Hornet engines and a top speed of 212 mph; and the final batch covered by the original 1933 contract comprised 25 similar B-12As, with increased fuel capacity. A number of these aircraft were modified, after going into service with the Army Air Corps, for coastal defence duties, operating as floatplanes. Some also became B-10M and B-12AM target tugs. Two experimental models were the YB-10A, with R-1830-31 Cyclones, and the XB-14 with YR-1830-9 Twin Wasps.

New Army contracts in 1934 and 1935 kept the Martin bomber in production through 1936. These orders covered 103 B-10Bs with 775-hp R-1820-33 radials and small refinements. Delivered during 1935 and 1936, they served with Army bomber squadrons for several years.

Martin BM-1

Martin B-12A

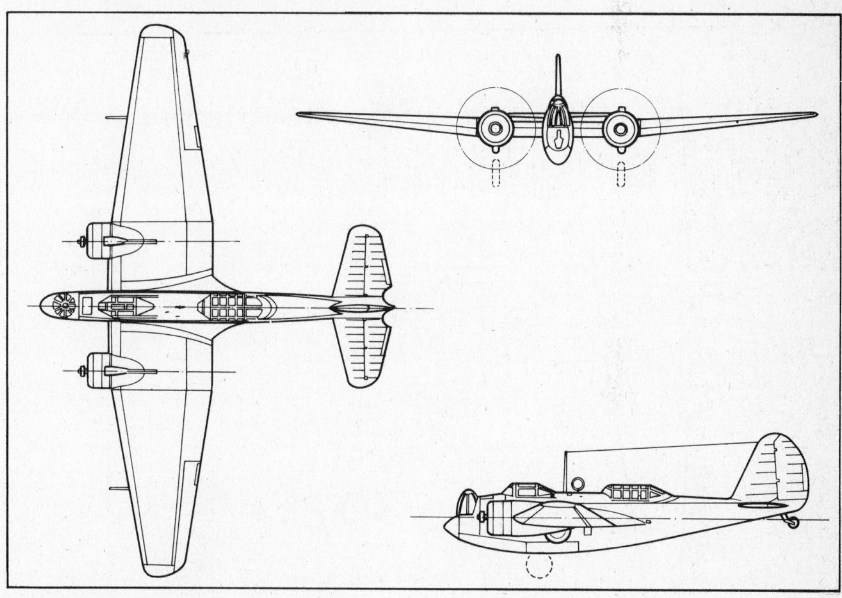

Martin B-10B

TYPE	DIMENSIONS span ft	span in	length ft	length in	height ft	height in	WEIGHT max t-o lb	PERFORMANCE max speed mph	at height ft	service ceiling ft	combat range miles	REMARKS
Martin T3M-1	56	7	41	9	15	1	8,979	109	SL	5,700	525	
Martin T3M-2	56	7	41	4	15	1	9,503	109	SL	7,900	634	
Martin T4M-1	53	0	35	7	14	9	8,071	114	SL	10,150	363	
Martin TG-2	53	0	34	8	14	10	7,236	127	SL	11,500	330	
Martin P3M-2	100	0	61	9	16	8	17,977	115	SL	11,900	1,010	
Martin BM-1	41	0	28	9	12	4	6,259	145	SL	16,400	409	
Martin XB-10	70	7	45	0	10	4	12,560	207	6,000	21,000	600	
Martin B-12A	70	6	45	3	11	0	14,200	212	6,500	24,600	1,360	
Martin B-10B	70	6	44	9	15	5	14,600	213	10,000	24,200	1,240	
Martin 166	70	10	44	2	11	7	15,624	260	NA	25,200	2,080	

Martin 166

Martin PBM-1 Mariner

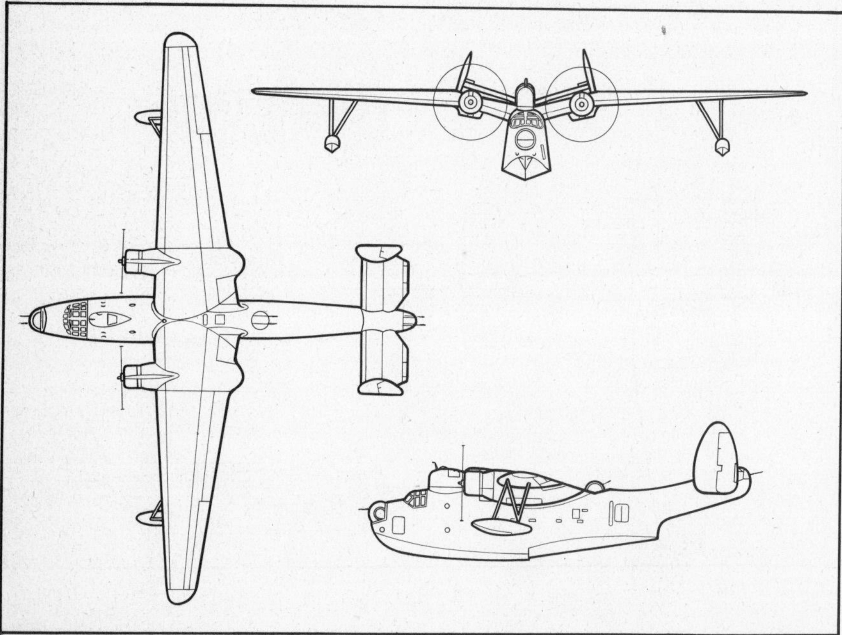

Martin PBM-3D Mariner

Martin PBM-5 Mariner

A further 189 examples of the Martin bomber were built up to 1939, for export. Largest overseas contract came from the Netherlands East Indies, whose government ordered 120 Martin 139Ws, with 850-hp R-1820-G Cyclones; these were amongst the first US-built bombers to operate in World War II. Later aircraft in the contract were delivered as Martin 166s, with a continuous transparent canopy over the cockpits.

Twenty-five Martin 139s were purchased by Argentina, 20 by Turkey, 9 by China and 6 by Siam. One was sold to Russia.

Martin PBM Mariner

Although built in smaller numbers than the Consolidated PBY Catalina, the Martin Mariner played a major rôle in World War II operations by the US Navy and, being of somewhat later design, showed a marked superiority over the Catalina in performance and battle-worthiness. The design of this twin-engined flying-boat (Martin Model 162) began during 1937 and a $\frac{1}{4}$-scale single-seat "model" was completed to investigate the handling qualities in the air and on the sea. The US Navy awarded a prototype contract for a single XPBM-1 on 3 June 1937, and this flew for the first time on 18 February 1939. Like the $\frac{1}{4}$-scale Model 162A, it had a flat tailplane, but the Mariner's characteristic dihedral tail appeared on the 20 production PBM-1s, ordered in December 1937 and delivered in 1940–41.

The PBM-1 had two 1,600-hp Wright R-2600-6 Cyclone engines and weapon-bays in each nacelle to carry a total of 2,000 lb of bombs or depth charges. Nose and dorsal turrets, and waist and tail positions, mounted five 0·50-in and one 0·30-in gun. A single XPBM-2 had increased fuel capacity.

Shortly after delivery of the PBM-1s began, in September 1940, large production contracts were placed with Martin, leading to new versions which appeared in 1942, powered by 1,700-hp R-2600-12 engines. The small retractable wing floats of the PBM-1 gave way, on these subsequent versions, to larger strut-braced floats.

Fifty PBM-3Rs were delivered for transport duties, with all armament deleted and special facilities for loading and stowing freight; they went into service with the US Naval Air Transport Service, primarily in the Pacific area. For combat use, the PBM-3C had improved internal armour protection, nose and dorsal twin-gun turrets and sea-search radar, carried in a large radome above and behind the cockpit. After delivering 272 PBM-3Cs, Martin built 201 PBM-3Ds with 1,900-hp R-2600-22 engines and increased armour and armament. Thirty-two PBM-3Bs were built for lend-lease to the Royal Air Force, serving briefly with No. 523 Squadron in 1943–4, before several were returned to the US Navy during 1944.

As the character of the war at sea changed, the need grew for aircraft better able to deal with submarines, and the PBM-3S appeared in 1944 specifically for this rôle. It had R-2600-12 engines, greater fuel capacity, reduced armour and no power turrets, the defensive armament comprising only four hand-held guns. Martin built 156 of this version.

The PBM-5 version, prototypes of which appeared in May 1943, had 2,100-hp Pratt & Whitney R-2800-34 engines, eight 0·50-in guns, including two each in nose and dorsal turrets, and APS-15 radar in a small streamlined radome pylon-mounted above the fuselage. Production totalled 589 (plus two prototypes); 460 more were cancelled after VJ-Day. Post-war, some Mariners had new search equipment added, becoming PBM-5Es.

Final version of the Mariner was the amphibious PBM-5A, with R-2800-34 engines and a retractable tricycle undercarriage. Thirty-six were built, the last being delivered in April 1949; they served in the anti-submarine rôle and with the US Coast Guard for air-sea rescue.

Martin 167 Maryland

Drawing on their experience with the series of monoplane bombers built for the US Army and foreign nations since 1932, the Glenn L. Martin Co designed a light bomber in

1938 to participate in the Army's design competition for a new twin-engined attack aircraft. This was required to carry a 1,200-lb bomb-load for 1,200 miles at not less than 200 mph, and led to development of the Douglas DB-7 (see page 487).

Martin's entry was the Model 167, which was delivered to Wright Field on 14 March 1939 for evaluation as the XA-22. It was a slender mid-wing monoplane with 1,200-hp R-1830-37 Wasp radials. Armament comprised four wing guns, one ventral gun and one dorsal gun in a retractable turret, all of 0·30-in calibre, and 1,800 lb of bombs.

No Army contract followed these trials but already, on 26 January 1939, Martin had received a contract from France for 115 similar 167Fs, the first of which flew in August 1939. The initial contract was increased subsequently, but the final 50 were diverted to Britain after the fall of France, entering service as Maryland Is. Approximately 30 more were absorbed into the RAF direct from French service use, and 75 more Maryland Is to the same standard, with R-1830-SC3G engines, were purchased by Britain.

A change of engine to the two-stage R-1830-S3C4-G Wasp produced the Maryland II, 150 of which were purchased from Martin by Britain.

Marylands served primarily in the Middle East in 1940–41, operating as light bombers and on reconnaissance duties. Later many were transferred to the South African Air Force, while a few went to the Fleet Air Arm for target-towing duties.

Martin B-26 Marauder

The Glenn L. Martin company, having produced two of the most-used US Army bombers in the period 1919–39, was well placed to compete in a new design competition for medium bombers which the USAAC announced on 25 January 1939. The Martin B-10/B-12 series had then been in service for some five years, and had already become the first bombers of original US design to see operations. Martin's Model 179, submitted in July, was rated high in the official evaluation and a production order for 201 was placed in August – an unprecedented step, which sought to speed deliveries by omitting the prototype testing stage.

The Martin design, designated B-26 by the USAAC and subsequently named Marauder, had a nicely streamlined, if somewhat portly fuselage, with nose and tail guns in hand-operated mounts and a twin-gun dorsal turret; another gun fired rearward and downward from an aperture in the floor behind the bomb-bay. The B-26 was designed to derive its high-speed performance from optimizing the wing loading for the cruise condition rather than for landing. Even in its original form it had a higher wing loading than any previous Army aircraft; the inevitable weight growth in subsequent versions pushed the figure higher still and led to a crop of difficulties associated with the undercarriage and an alarmingly high accident rate during landings. To limit the increase in wing loading, a new wing was introduced in later B-26s, with the span increased by 6 ft and area by 57 sq ft.

The first B-26 flew on 25 November 1940, and production of the original version totalled 201, with R-2800-5 engines. Deliveries began in 1941, and during the same year the B-26A appeared, with shackles for a torpedo under the fuselage, 0·50-in guns in the nose and tail, optional fuel tanks in the bomb-bay and higher gross weight. B-26As were deployed overseas, to Australia, on 8 December 1941, and were in operation from April

Martin PBM-5A Mariner amphibian

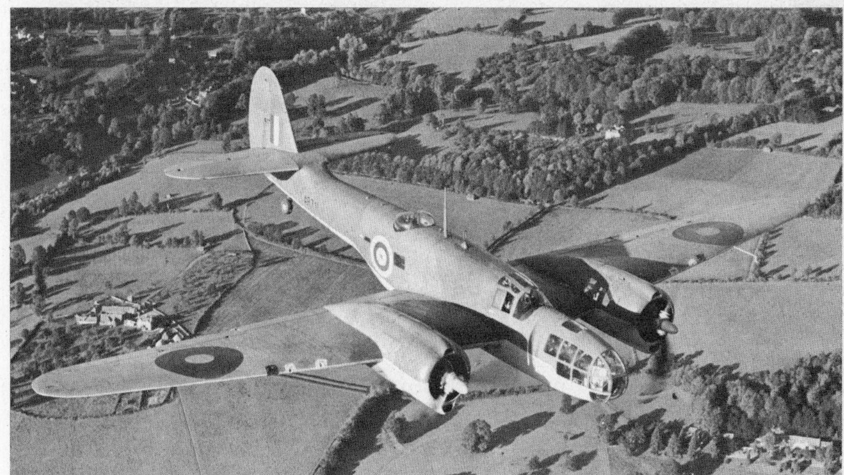

Martin Maryland Mk I, RAF

Martin B-26B Marauder, with package guns

TYPE	DIMENSIONS span ft	span in	length ft	length in	height ft	height in	WEIGHT max t-o lb	PERFORMANCE max speed mph	at height ft	service ceiling ft	combat range miles	REMARKS
Martin PBM-1	118	0	77	2	24	6	41,139	214	12,000	22,400	3,450	
Martin PBM-3C	118	0	80	0	27	6	58,000	198	13,000	16,900	2,137	
Martin PBM-5	118	0	79	10	27	6	60,000	215	19,200	20,200	2,700	
Martin 167F	61	4	46	8	10	0	17,000	280	5,000	20,000	750	

Martin B-26G Marauder

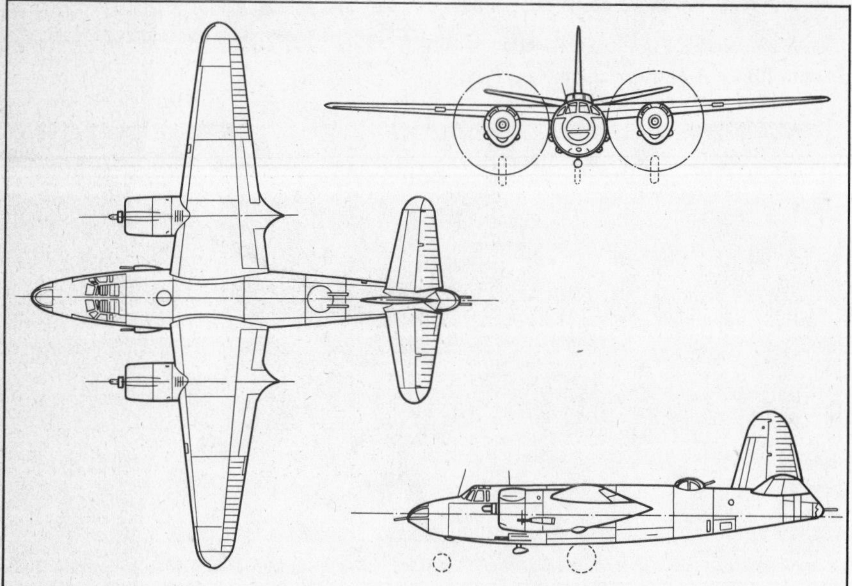
Martin B-26G Marauder

Martin Baltimore Mk I, RAF

Martin Baltimore Mk V, RAF

1942 onward against targets in New Guinea, using the bomb-bay fuel tanks and, consequently, carrying only a 2,000-lb bomb-load. Other actions in the Pacific area followed, including torpedo attacks against Japanese shipping in the Battle of Midway. Also during 1942, the B-26s were in action from bases in Alaska and, starting in November, from North Africa.

After building 139 B-26As, Martin produced the B-26B, with a number of important modifications, introduced in stages. These included better crew protection, twin tail guns, a new ventral gun position or twin beam guns, R-2800-41 or -43 engines, and a longer nose-wheel unit. After 641 B-26Bs had been completed, the new wing was introduced, together with a taller fin and rudder and further increases in the armament, which put up the gross weight still further. In this later form, Martin built 1,242 B-26Bs at its Baltimore factory, and 1,235 similar B-26Cs, at a new production line established in Omaha.

The B-26B entered service in Europe on 14 May 1943, when a small force from the US Eighth Air Force attacked Ijmuiden and suffered total destruction This inauspicious start was attributable to faulty use of the Marauder's capabilities rather than to any shortcoming in the aircraft itself. Subsequently, units of the Ninth Air Force achieved conspicuous success in the tactical rôle, supporting the attack on Europe mounted from the UK.

Further refinements in the Marauder design, to improve take-off performance, included an increase of 3·5° in wing incidence on the B-26F. Martin built 300, of which 200 went to the RAF under lend-lease arrangements as Marauder IIs (previously, Britain had received 52 B-26As for service as Marauder Is in the Middle East). Final production version was the B-26G, differing only in detail from the B-26F; the 950 built included 150 for the RAF, as Marauder IIIs, and 57 TB-26Gs stripped of armament and operational equipment for use as trainers.

Martin delivered the last B-26G in March 1945 and the USAAF declared the type obsolete in 1948, by which time few remained in service. Some B-26s served in 1944–5 with French Air Force units and remained in service in France for several years.

Martin A-30 Baltimore

To improve the operational effectiveness of the Maryland, Martin designed the Model 187 during 1940, based particularly on British requirements. Whilst retaining the same overall configuration as the Maryland, the new type had several important changes, including a deepened fuselage permitting direct intercommunication between the four crew members, self-sealing fuel tanks, 211 lb of armour protection and 1,600-hp Wright R-2600-A5Bs.

First flown on 14 June 1941, the Martin 187 was named Baltimore by the RAF, which had ordered 400 in May 1940. Further contracts were placed under lend-lease arrangements, for which purpose the type was given the USAAF designation A-30, although it never served with the American forces.

The original 400 aircraft were delivered in three versions. The Baltimore I (50) and II (150) differed only in dorsal armament, the Mk I having a single hand-operated Vickers K gun and the Mk II a twin-Vickers installation; both had four fixed wing guns, four fixed downward-firing guns and one ventral gun. The Baltimore III (150 supplied) had a Boulton Paul dorsal turret, with four 0·303-in guns.

Lend-lease purchases comprised 281 Baltimore IIIAs (same as the Mk III), 294 Baltimore IVs with a Martin dorsal turret mounting two 0·50-in guns, and 600 Baltimore Vs (A-30A) with 1,700-hp R-2600-29 engines.

Like the Maryland, the Baltimore served exclusively in the Middle East, where it equipped at least seven RAF and two SAAF squadrons from March 1942 onwards. It remained in active service up to the end of the war, and was used also in small numbers by British naval units for target towing and other duties.

Martin AM-1 Mauler

One of the lessons to come out of World War II was that defensive armament was of dubious advantage and that the higher performance which could be achieved without the weight of gunners and gun turrets was often a greater asset. The US Navy, with three years' experience of intensive carrier-based attack operations, began development in 1944 of four new single-seat torpedo-bombers, all of them large single-engined monoplanes with offensive loads as great as those carried by contemporary twin-engined bombers.

The Martin aircraft in this category (Model 210) was one of the two types to achieve production status from the original quartet of prototypes (see also Douglas AD-1, page 492). Designated XBTM-1 in the "BT" category, combining the former TB (torpedo-bomber) and SB (dive-bomber) groups, the prototypes were ordered in January 1944 and the first flight was made on 26 August 1944. Each was powered by a 3,000-hp Pratt & Whitney XR-4360-4 air-cooled radial, armed with four 20-mm cannon and had strong-points beneath the fuselage and wings to carry three torpedoes, twelve bombs, or rockets.

A production order for 750 BTM-1s was placed on 15 January 1945, and the first production aircraft made its first flight on 16 December 1946, by which time the designation had been amended to AM-1 in the new attack category. Test aircraft were delivered during 1947, with the first production models going to an operational unit, VA-17A, on 1 March 1948. The AM-1 showed a remarkable load-carrying ability, lifting, on one occasion, 10,689 lb of armament and 3,940 lb of fuel at a gross weight of 29,332 lb for take-off.

Production of the AM-1 was curtailed when 152 had been built, including the prototypes, and all had been delivered by October 1949. Several operational attack squadrons flew the Mauler briefly, but all were assigned to Reserve units in 1950. Addition of special electronic gear later produced the AM-1Q for radar counter-measures.

Martin P4M Mercator

The idea of boosting the performance of overwater patrol aircraft by adding jet power to piston-engines, as exemplified by the later Lockheed Neptunes (see page 515), was first proposed by Glenn L. Martin. As early as 1944, this company had completed designs for a patrol bomber in a similar category to the Neptune, but incorporating a 4,000-lb s t J33-A-4 engine in the nacelle of each of the 2,975-hp R-4360-4 Wasp Major radials.

Apart from the unorthodox power plant, the Martin design (Model 219) was notable for its armament. This included a ball turret in the nose and a dorsal turret, each with two 0·50-in guns, a 0·50-in gun on each side of the fuselage and two 20-mm cannon in the tail.

The Navy ordered two XP4M-1 prototypes on 6 July 1944 and the first of these flew on 20 September 1946. After a somewhat protracted period of development, a production batch of 19 P4M-1 Mercators was built, similar to the prototypes, but with 20-mm nose guns and 4,600-lb s t J33-A-23 turbojets, which increased the cruising speed by at least 100 mph. The first P4M-1 was delivered to VP-21 Squadron on 28 June 1950, and the Mercators served with this unit for a number of years.

Martin AM-1 Mauler

Martin AM-1 Mauler

Martin P4M-1 Mercator

TYPE	DIMENSIONS span ft	span in	length ft	length in	height ft	height in	WEIGHT max t-o lb	PERFORMANCE max speed mph	at height ft	service ceiling ft	combat range miles	REMARKS
Martin B-26	65	0	56	0	19	10	32,000	315	15,000	25,000	1,000	
Martin B-26A	65	0	58	3	19	10	33,022	313	NA	23,500	1,000	
Martin B-26B	65	0	58	3	19	10	34,000	317	14,500	23,500	1,150	
Martin B-26F	71	0	56	1	20	4	38,000	277	10,000	20,000	1,300	
Martin B-26G	71	0	56	1	20	4	38,200	283	5,000	19,800	1,100	
Martin Baltimore I	61	4	48	6	11	3	22,958	308	13,000	22,300	1,082	
Martin Baltimore V	61	4	48	6	14	2	27,850	320	15,000	25,000	980	
Martin AM-1	50	0	41	2	16	10	23,000	367	16,000	26,800	1,200	
Martin P4M-1	114	0	84	0	26	1	88,378	415	20,100	34,600	2,840	

Martin P-5A (P5M-1) Marlin

Martin P-5B (P5M-2) Marlin, Aéronavale

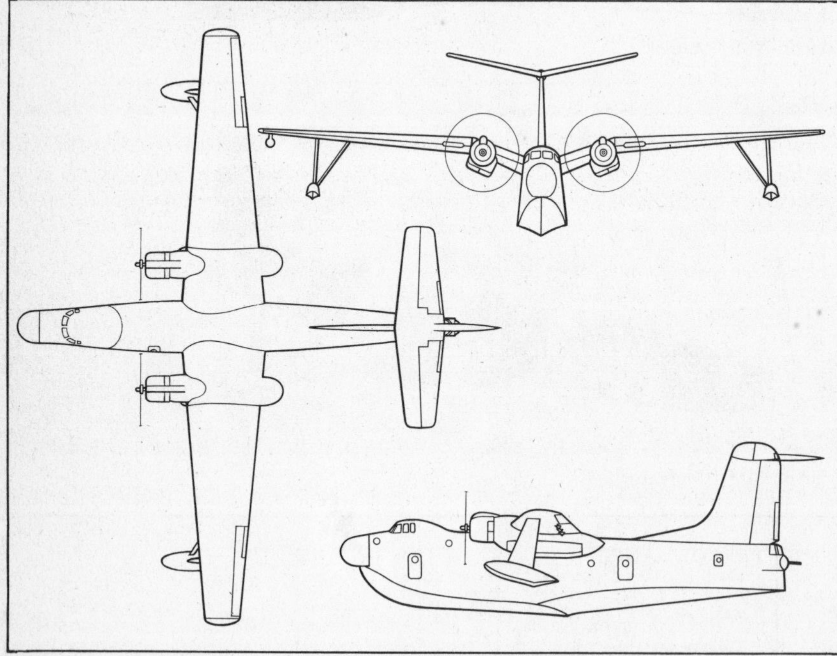
Martin P-5B (P5M-2) Marlin

Martin B-57B

Martin P-5 Marlin

Destined to become the last manned aircraft of Martin design for many years, the Marlin was designed in 1946 to replace the wartime PBM Mariner, one of the US Navy's most widely-used patrol flying-boats. The new design differed primarily in hull design, hydrodynamic research having led to a new and more efficient shape of finer length-to-beam ratio. Designated XP5M-1, a prototype was ordered by the US Navy on 26 June 1946, and flew for the first time on 30 April 1948. It used the wing and upper hull of the Mariner but had remotely-controlled nose and tail turrets, and a power-operated dorsal turret.

Production P5M-1s incorporated many changes from the prototype. A large radome for the APS-80 radar scanner replaced the nose turret; a pylon replaced struts to carry the wing-tip floats; the flight deck layout was improved; the dorsal turret was abandoned and weapons bays were introduced in the nacelles of the R-3350-30WA engines. Between 1951 and 1954, the US Navy received 114 P5M-1s, the first operational unit taking delivery of its first Marlin on 23 April 1952. Subsequent modification of the equipment to include magnetic anomaly detectors and Julie and Jezebel underwater detection equipment led to the designation P5M-1S, the two versions being redesignated P-5A and SP-5A respectively in 1962. Some Marlins, equipped for training, were designated P5M-1T (later TP-5A), and the US Coast Guard received a few P5M-1Gs for air-sea rescue duties.

A number of changes were introduced on the P5M-2, first flown in August 1953. Noticeably, the tail unit was re-designed with a "T" configuration, the bow chine-line was lowered and R-3350-32WA engines were installed. MAD equipment was carried in a radome at the fin-tailplane intersection. Approximately 100 P5M-2s were delivered to the US Navy between 1954 and 1960, these later being redesignated P-5B and SP-5B, the latter with up-dated equipment. Several squadrons of Marlins were still on active duty at the beginning of 1966. In addition, ten supplied to France in 1958-9 were serving with the Aéronavale.

One Marlin was fitted, during 1964, with a jet unit in the tail in order to evaluate this means of boosting the performance.

Martin B-57 Canberra

Adoption of the English Electric Canberra (see page 348) by the USAF in 1951 marked the first occasion since World War II that a foreign-designed combat aircraft had been chosen for use by an American Service. To meet the USAF need for a tactical high-performance bomber, Glenn L. Martin was given a contract to produce the Canberra under licence, following close evaluation of the British design, two examples of which were flown across the Atlantic to the Martin Baltimore factory.

The first Martin-built Canberra flew on 20 July 1953, this being a B-57A retaining most features of the British Canberra B Mk 2, but having Wright J65-W-1 (licence-built Sapphire) engines. Eight B-57As were followed by 67 RB-57As with cameras in the rear bomb-bay for dual-rôle operation. While these aircraft were being built and put into service in 1953-4, the design was developed to produce a variant more specifically able to meet USAF requirements. This led to the B-57B, which had a new front fuselage with tandem in place of side-by-side seating for a two-man crew, fixed wing armament of four 20-mm cannon or eight 0·50-in guns, wing hard-points for bombs or rockets and a rotary bomb-door. The first B-57B flew on 28 June 1954, and deliveries to Tactical Air Command began in January 1955, production totalling 202. In addition, TAC received 38 B-57Cs, similar to the "B" model but with dual controls. Also similar was the B-57E, used primarily as a target tug.

The excellent high-flying performance of the Canberra led to the development of special reconnaissance versions. The first of these was the RB-57D, 20 examples of which were built by Martin for strategic reconnaissance with cameras or electronic gear. The RB-57D had J57-P-5 engines, a new long-span wing and other changes; the first 14 were single-seaters, of which 7 had provision for air-to-air refuelling, while the final 6 were two seaters.

During 1953, the RB-57F was developed by General Dynamics at Fort Worth as a new reconnaissance and very high-altitude research aircraft. This was a B-57B conversion with TF33-P-11 turbofan engines plus J60-P-9 turbojets in underwing pods, a new wing with a span of 122 ft and a longer nose. The two-seat RB-57F had an endurance of more than 10 hours on internal tankage and was reported to cruise at altitudes above 90,000 feet. At least 12 were converted under contracts placed during 1964.

Naval Aircraft Factory PT

The PT-1 and PT-2 torpedo biplanes built for the US Navy by the Naval Aircraft Factory at Philadelphia were undistinguished designs based on original Curtiss types, their principal claim to fame being that they were built in greater quantity than any previous torpedo-carrier.

The Navy had become acutely conscious of the value of torpedo-carrying attack aircraft after British and German types achieved success (albeit limited) during the 1914–18 War. A number of existing aircraft types were examined, and a few Curtiss R-6s were tested as torpedo-carriers. They were found to be too frail for the task, but sufficiently promising for further development, which was put in hand at the Naval Aircraft Factory in 1921. The outcome of this work was the PT-1, which comprised the R-6 fuselage married to Curtiss HS wings, the whole powered by a 400-hp Liberty engine.

A total of 33 of these biplanes reached the Navy, made up of 13 PT-1s and 18 slightly modified PT-2s. Deliveries began on 30 August 1921, and the first operational unit to fly the PT-1, Navy Squadron VT-1, received its first aircraft on 4 October 1921.

Naval Aircraft Factory PN, PM, PH, PD and PK

Development of flying-boats for the US Navy was a major preoccupation at the Philadelphia plant of the Naval Aircraft Factory throughout the 1920s. The aircraft which resulted conformed to a pattern established during the 1914–18 War, with biplane wings mounted above the hull and two engines carried on struts between the wings. This had been the configuration of the British-designed, American-engined F.5L (see page 364) which was among the most successful of 1914–18 'boats.

Improved versions of the F5L were evolved at the Naval Aircraft Factory, among them the F7L. This was re-designated PN-7 as the first aircraft in the new "patrol" category. NAF built 13 'boats designated from PN-7 to PN-12 and P4N in the same series, primarily as prototypes, although some reached squadrons for operational use. The PN-7 was based on a modified F-5 hull to which were attached new wings, and was powered by two 525-hp Wright T-2 in-line engines, the radiators for which were located between the engines and the top wing. The PN-7 had a crew of five, all in open cockpits in the hull, with an armament of Lewis guns fore and aft and a 1,000-lb bomb-load. Two were built.

With Wright T-3 engines, the PN-8 was similar in appearance but had a metal hull, the wooden hull of

General Dynamics/Martin RB-57F

Naval Aircraft Factory PT-2

Naval Aircraft Factory PN-9

TYPE	DIMENSIONS span ft	in	length ft	in	height ft	in	WEIGHT max t-o lb	PERFORMANCE max speed mph	at height ft	service ceiling ft	combat range miles	REMARKS
Martin P-5A(P5M-1)	118	0	90	8	37	3	72,837	262	NA	22,400	3,600	
Martin SP-5B(P5M-2)	118	2	101	1	32	8	85,000	250	SL	24,000	2,050	
Martin B-57A	64	0	65	6	15	7	51,000	582	40,000	48,000	2,300	
Martin B-57B	64	0	65	6	15	7	55,000	582	40,000	48,000	2,300	
Martin RB-57D	106	0	65	6	14	10	NA	632	40,000	70,000	NA	
Martin RB-57F	122	0	63	10	NA		NA	NA	NA	95,000	NA	
NAF PT-1	74	0	34	5	16	7	6,798	96	SL	8,800	NA	

Naval Aircraft Factory (Martin) PM-2

Naval Aircraft Factory (Douglas) PD-1

North American NA-50

North American P-64

the PN-7 and earlier 'boats having proved troublesome through water soakage. The PN-9 had 480-hp Packard 1A-1500 engines and increased fuel capacity – sufficient for an attempt to be made in 1925 on the first non-stop flight from San Francisco to Hawaii. The flight ended after 28¼ hours, some 250 miles short of Hawaii, but the excellent seaworthiness of the metal hull was demonstrated when the aircraft was "sailed" the remaining distance in 10 days.

The two PN-10s had Packard 2A-1500 engines, and metal in place of wooden wing structure. Air-cooled radial engines were adopted in the final PN 'boats – 525-hp Pratt & Whitney R-1690s in two twin-tailed PN-11s and 525-hp Wright R-1750Ds in two PN-12s (which were ordered as PN-10s). The single XP4N-1 was basically a PN-12 with geared engines and twin-tail design, and the two XP4N- 2s, also powered by R-1820-64 radials, had more fuel.

By the late 1920s, the replacement of 1914–18 War aircraft still serving with US Navy units had become a matter of urgency, and steps were taken to have the basic NAF designs built in quantity by other manufacturers.

On 29 December 1927, Douglas received a contract to build 25 'boats similar to the PN-12, and these were delivered between 6 June 1929 and 3 June 1930, as PD-1s.

On the same day that the PD-1s were ordered, the Hall Aluminium Co was awarded a contract for a single XPH-1, which had an improved hull, a balanced rudder and geared 537-hp Wright GR-1750 engines. The prototype was tested at the end of 1929, and formed the basis for a series of Hall flying-boats which continued in service until the beginning of World War II.

The Martin company received a contract on 31 May 1929 to build 25 PM-1 'boats (plus five more ordered later). These were based, like the PD-1, on the PN-12 and had uncowled R-1820-64 Cyclone engines and balanced rudders. The twin tail unit of the XP4N-1 was adopted on the 25 Martin PM-2s, ordered in June 1930, and these aircraft had ring cowls on their engines, as used on the Hall PH-1s. Virtually identical with the PM-2s were the 18 Keystone PK-1s ordered on 30 November 1929 and delivered between April and December 1931.

In all, 121 of the big biplane 'boats were built at five different factories between 1923 and 1931. They served around the US coastline and at overseas bases, particularly in Hawaii, well into the 1930s, until replaced by the new breed of monoplanes.

North American NA-44, NA-50, NA-69, A-27, P-64

North American's famous NA-16 design, which formed the basis of the AT-6 Texan and Harvard advanced trainers used throughout World War II, also gave rise to a number of combat versions. Most of the trainer variants of the NA-16 could, in fact, carry armament, including a fixed forward gun, a flexibly-mounted gun in the rear cockpit and underwing bombs.

A more specifically combat variant was the NA-44, produced in 1938 as a light attack bomber. Powered by a 775-hp Wright Cyclone, it had provision for four forward-firing guns and one aft, and 400 lb of bombs. After demonstrations by the prototype in South America, Brazil ordered 31, which were delivered in 1940, and Siam ordered 10 similar NA-69s. Delivery of the latter was being made in October 1941, but they were sequestered by the US Army in the Philippines while *en route*, in order that they should not fall into Japanese hands, and were pressed into service with the USAAC under the designation A-27.

Another derivative of the NA-16, with basically the same wing, retractable undercarriage and rear fuselage, was the single-seat NA-50, built in 1939. The engine was a Cyclone R-1820-77 and the NA-50 was armed with two 0·30-in guns in the cowling, with provision for two 20-mm wing guns and 550 lb of bombs under the wings. Seven were sold to Peru in 1939–40.

Six similar single-seaters, designated NA-68, were built in 1940 for Siam but, like the NA-69s mentioned above, these were seized by the US Army Air Corps, which designated them P-64 and put them into service as advanced trainers.

North American B-25 Mitchell

One of the most outstanding medium bombers of World War II, the Mitchell originated as one of two designs ordered into production by the USAAC in August 1939 without the formality of prototype testing. The competition had been announced on 25 January 1939, and the successful designs were the North American NA-62 and Martin 179, the latter becoming the B-26 Marauder.

One year and one week after receiving a contract to build 184 of its new aircraft, with the designation B-25, North American flew the first of them, on 19 August 1940. It had 1,350-hp R-2600-9 engines in big underslung nacelles on the shoulder wing, twin fins with a tail gun position between, and a nose-wheel undercarriage – the same layout as had been used in the North American NA-40 prototype entered a year earlier in an Army competition for a new attack bomber but lost in a crash at Wright Field. Armament comprised a total of four guns in the fuselage, with proposed installation of three more in the wings; the bomb-bay could hold 3,000 lb of bombs.

By the end of 1940, 24 B-25s had been delivered. The first nine had constant dihedral, but thereafter dihedral on the outer panels was eliminated, giving the B-25 its gull-winged appearance. In the early months of 1941, 40 B-25As were built, with armour protection and self-sealing fuel tanks, followed by 119 B-25Bs, in which a Bendix power-operated turret and a two-gun retractable ventral turret replaced the prone gunner's position in the tail.

Large-scale production of the Mitchell got under way in 1940 after the USAAF ordered the B-25C from North American at Inglewood (Los Angeles) and the similar B-25D from the company's new plant at Kansas City. Both models were similar to the B-25B, but had R-2600-13 engines, increased fuel capacity and extra operational equipment. Production of the C and D totalled 1,619 and 2,290 respectively, deliveries beginning in January 1942. By this time, the earlier models were already in service, for overwater patrols around the US coastline and in the Southwest Pacific. Destruction of a Japanese submarine on 24 December 1941 was the first operational success by a Mitchell, in this case a B-25A. In April 1942, 16 B-25Bs made one of World War II's most epic raids, operating off the USS *Hornet* on a near-suicidal 800-mile mission to Tokyo in a raid of great psychological but little military value.

A number of early production Mitchells were diverted for lend-lease delivery to America's allies. The Soviet Union began to receive B-25Bs in March 1942 and was eventually to receive 870 Mitchells of all types. The RAF received 23 B-26Bs as Mitchell Is, which were used for training in preparation for the delivery of 167 B-25Cs and 371 B-25Ds which were operated as Mitchell IIs. Other wartime deliveries of B-25s included 249 to the Netherlands, 131 to China and 29 to Brazil.

North American B-25C Mitchell

North American B-25H Mitchell

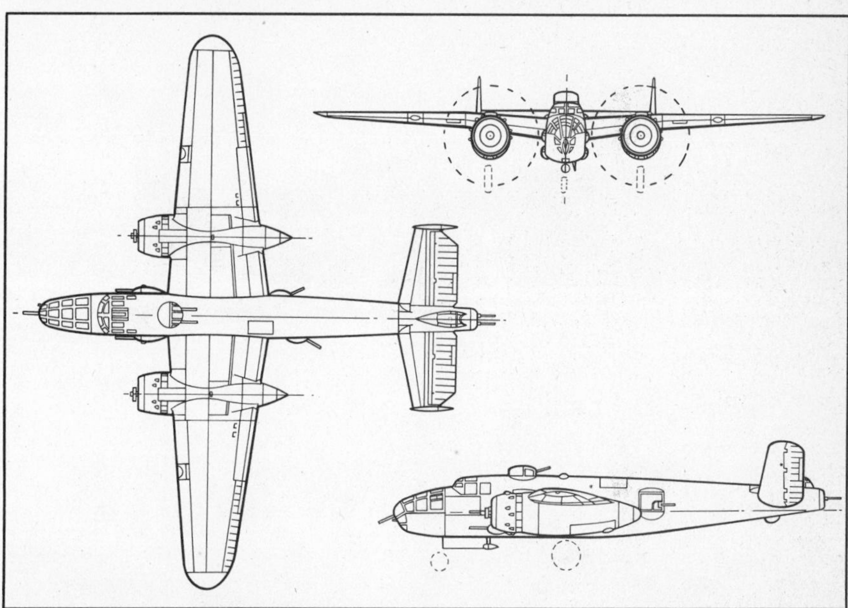

North American B-25J Mitchell

TYPE	DIMENSIONS						WEIGHT	PERFORMANCE				REMARKS
	span		length		height		max t-o	max speed	at height	service ceiling	combat range	
	ft	in	ft	in	ft	in	lb	mph	ft	ft	miles	
NAF PN-7	72	10	49	1	15	4	14,203	105	SL	9,200	655	
NAF PN-9	72	10	49	2	16	6	19,610	115	SL	3,080	2,550	
NAF PN-10	72	10	49	2	16	9	19,029	114	SL	4,500	1,508	
NAF PN-12	72	10	49	2	16	9	14,122	114	SL	10,900	1,309	
NAF PD-1	72	10	49	2	16	0	14,988	121	SL	11,600	1,465	
NAF PH-1	72	10	51	10	17	6	16,379	135	SL	11,200	1,580	
NAF PH-3	72	10	51	0	19	10	17,679	159	3,200	21,350	1,937	
NAF PM-1	72	10	49	2	16	4	16,117	119	SL	8,500	1,305	
NAF PM-2	72	0	49	0	16	9	19,062	119	SL	9,500	1,347	
NAF PK-1	72	0	48	11	16	9	17,074	120	SL	9,700	1,250	
North American NA-69(A-27)	42	0	29	0	12	2	6,700	250	11,500	28,000	575	
North American NA-68(P-64)	37	3	27	0	9	0	6,800	270	8,700	27,500	630	

North American B-25J Mitchell, eight-gun nose version

North American Mitchell (A47), RAAF

North American Mustang I, RAF

North American P-51 Mustang

North American Mustang III, RAF, with rockets

Field modification of 175 Mitchells in the Southwest Pacific produced a version with ten 0·50-in guns – four in a "solid" nose and four in blisters alongside the nose, plus two in the dorsal turret. Another armament modification produced the XB-25G, with a standard Army 75-mm gun in the nose. Firing 15-lb shells and aimed with the help of two 0·50-in guns alongside it, the 75-mm gun was a highly destructive weapon for use against shipping and 405 B-25Gs were built with this armament. The same 75-mm gun, plus fourteen 0·50-in machine-guns, was carried by the B-25H, of which North American built 1,000, exclusively for the Pacific area of operations, where they served from February 1944.

In the B-25H, the dorsal turret was moved forward, close behind the cockpit; and this arrangement was retained on the B-25J, which reverted, however, to a bombardier nose with three 0·50-in guns. The bomb load remained 3,000 lb. Production totalled 4,318 at Kansas City, in several distinct sub-versions, one of which had a "solid" nose containing eight guns to add to ten carried elsewhere, and underwing rockets. In January 1943, the USAAF assigned 500 of its Mitchells to the US Navy, which received 248 B-25Hs and 252 B-25Js as PBJ-1H and PBJ-1J respectively, plus 206 more PBJ-1Js later. These served primarily as medium bombers with Marine Corps units.

Post-war, the B-25 soldiered on in the USAF for several years, serving briefly with Strategic Air Command and for longer with Tactical Air Command before passing into use as a trainer and staff transport, operational until 1960. Many B-25s served with other air forces – notably those of the Netherlands, Canada, China and various South American countries – for varying periods, and some were still in service in 1968.

North American P-51 Mustang

Still in service as a fighter with South American air forces in 1968, the Mustang was one of World War II's finest fighters, and one of the few aircraft conceived after the start of that conflict to see large-scale service before its termination. Utilizing a laminar-flow wing section, the Mustang was the first American fighter to incorporate the lessons of air combat in Europe, and owed its existence to the insistence of a British Purchasing Commission that these lessons should be heeded.

The general requirement for a fighter of more advanced design and with better operational performance than any then available in the United States was put to North American Aviation early in 1940 by the British Commission. To match British practice, the aircraft was required to have an in-line engine and an armament of eight machine-guns. A prototype was to be completed within 120 days of go-ahead. North American bettered the target by three days when the prototype of their NA-73 was rolled out in the late summer of 1940, but delays in delivery of the 1,100-hp Allison V-1710-F3R engine kept the aircraft on the ground for another six weeks. Striking features of the NA-73 were seen to include its angular lines – simplifying production – and its wide-track inward-retracting landing gear.

British contracts established the Mustang (the name bestowed by the RAF) in production at the North American plant in Los Angeles, the US Army Air Corps sanctioning export of the new type in return for an opportunity to evaluate two early production models, which were designated XP-51 for this purpose. The first order was for 320 Mustang Is, two later contracts increasing the total to 620; the first of these arrived in Britain in November 1941. They were armed with four 0·50-in and four 0·30-in machine-guns and were faster than any fighter then in service with the RAF. However, their low-altitude engines limited their operational effectiveness, and most were modified for Army Co-operation duties, with an oblique camera behind the cockpit. Of the total of Mustang Is ordered, 20 were lost at sea, 10 were re-shipped to Russia and a number were used for armament and power plant experiments in the UK. In the latter category were four fitted by Rolls-Royce with high-altitude Merlin 60-series engines, leading to a major re-design of the Mustang by North American late in 1942, to take advantage of the performance gain offered by the Merlin.

Meanwhile, the USAAF had placed its first production contract for the type, using lend-lease funds to order 150 P-51s in September 1940. These had four 20-mm cannon in the wings but were otherwise similar to the Mustang Is. All were intended for the RAF, which called them Mustang IAs, but the USAAF re-possessed 55 for modification to F-6As, with two oblique cameras for tactical reconnaissance duties. Two others were used for prototype installation, in August 1942, of Packard Merlin V-1650-3s, after the Rolls-Royce work noted above. Known briefly as XP-78s, they were redesignated XP-51Bs.

Before production of the Merlin-engined versions began, the USAAF acquired 500 A-36As and 310 P-51As. The former were dive-bombers with six 0·50-in guns, underwing bombs and speed brakes above and below the wing. The P-51As also had bomb racks; distinguishing features were the 1,200-hp V-1710-81 engine, provision for drop tanks, and an armament of only four 0·50-in guns. Fifty went to the RAF on lend-lease as Mustang IIs and 35 were converted into F-6Bs with cameras. While these versions were being delivered, the XP-51Bs were demonstrating a top speed of 441 mph at 30,000 ft, and a major production effort began.

For production, the P-51B had increased fuel, four 0·50-in guns in the wings, and wing racks for two 1,000-lb bombs or 150-US gallon drop tanks. At Los Angeles, North American built 1,988, while a new factory at Dallas turned out 1,750 similar P-51Cs. The RAF received 274 Bs and 636 P-51Cs, designating them Mustang III and fitting a new cockpit canopy with bulged sides. The USAAF converted 91 assorted B and C models into F-6C reconnaissance fighters.

Starting in December 1943, the P-51B was in operation with the US Eighth Air Force, escorting bomber formations; and its combination of speed, manoeuvrability and range made it not only the most popular but also the most effective fighter operational over Europe in the last two years of the war. For the loss of 2,520 P-51s in combat in Europe, the USAAF claimed the destruction, by this type, of 4,950 enemy aircraft in the air and 4,131 on the ground – a better ratio than any other US fighter.

A redesigned rear fuselage, with a new "tear drop" canopy providing all-round vision, distinguished the P-51D, which occupied the production lines in 1944. Totals were 6,502 at Los Angeles, and 1,454 at Dallas, plus 1,337 similar aircraft built at Dallas with an Aeroproducts propeller and designated P-51K. The RAF received 281 P-51Ds and 595 P-51Ks under lend-lease and designated them Mustang IV, while the USAAF increased its reconnaissance force with 136 F-6Ds and 163 F-6Ks converted from the fighters. The RAF's Mustang IIIs and IVs, operational from early in 1944, flew bomber escort duties from the UK, and fighter-bomber sorties with 2nd TAF from France and with the Desert Air Force. They also scored notable successes against German V-1 flying-bombs over Southern England.

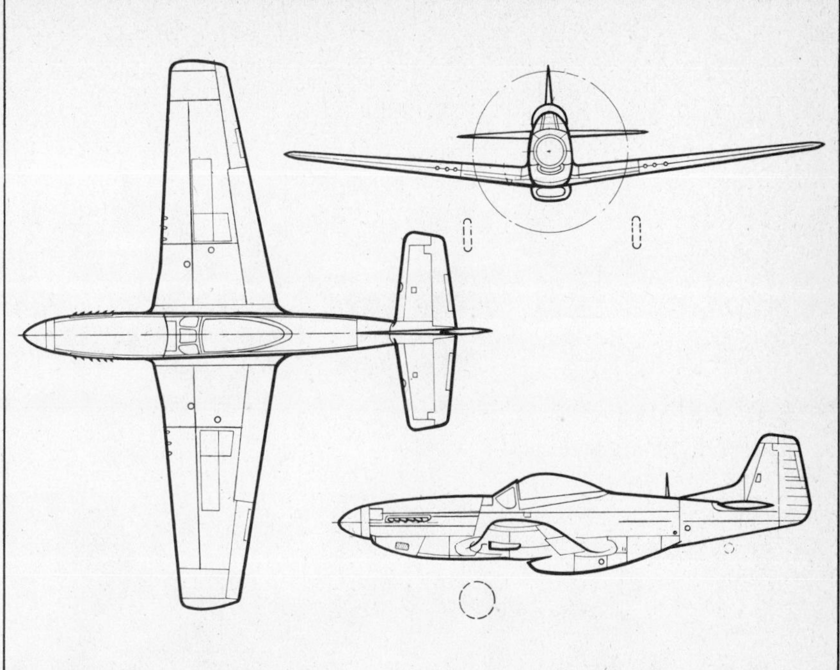

North American P-51D Mustang

North American P-51D Mustang

TYPE	DIMENSIONS span ft	in	length ft	in	height ft	in	WEIGHT max t-o lb	PERFORMANCE max speed mph	at height ft	service ceiling ft	combat range miles	REMARKS
North American B-25	67	6	54	1	14	10	27,310	322	15,000	30,000	2,000	
North American B-25A	67	7	54	1	15	9	27,100	315	15,000	27,000	1,350	
North American B-25B	67	7	52	11	15	9	28,460	300	15,000	23,500	1,300	
North American B-25C	67	7	52	11	15	10	34,000	284	15,000	21,200	1,500	
North American B-25G	67	7	51	0	15	9	35,000	281	15,000	24,300	1,560	
North American B-25H	67	7	51	0	15	9	36,047	275	13,000	23,800	1,350	
North American B-25J	67	7	52	11	16	4	35,000	272	13,000	24,200	1,350	
North American PBJ-1J	67	7	53	7½	16	4	34,846	278	12,700	24,300	2,010	
North American P-51	37	0	32	3	12	2	8,400	382	13,000	30,800	625	
North American P-51A	37	0	32	3	12	2	9,000	390	20,000	31,350	450	
North American A-36A	37	0	32	3	12	2	10,000	310	5,000	25,100	550	
North American P-51C	37	0	32	3	13	8	11,800	439	25,000	41,900	400	

North American XP-51F Mustang

North American P-51K Mustang

Cavalier F-51D Mustang

North American XP-82 Twin Mustang

Further development of the Mustang design led to several experimental versions during 1944; the outcome of these was the P-51H, which appeared in February 1945. Production totalled 555 at the Inglewood plant in Los Angeles before the end of the war brought wholesale cancellation of outstanding contracts for over 3,000.

The P-51 remained with the USAF until beyond 1950, and was the only World War II piston-engined fighter to survive so long with that Service – long enough to see operational service in the Korean War. Post-war, the Mustang was built under licence in Australia by Commonwealth Aircraft Company, which supplied 60 to the RAAF; while large numbers of surplus USAF machines – mostly P-51Ds – passed into service with many other nations, including Canada, Sweden, Switzerland, China and most of the South American and Asian countries within the US sphere of influence.

In a surprise move in 1967, the USAF ordered the F-51D back into production for counter-insurgency duties. Assembled by Cavalier Aircraft Corporation from component parts (some newly manufactured, others from war surplus stocks), these Cavalier F-51Ds have two seats in tandem, updated systems and electronics, reinforced wing spars, a taller tail-fin and improved armament. Six 0·50-in machine-guns are supplemented by six underwing attachments, each capable of carrying up to 750 lb of stores.

North American P-82 Twin Mustang

In the search for an aircraft with sufficient range to escort bombers, including the B-29 Superfortress, on operations in the Pacific area in the latter stages of World War II, the USAF sponsored prototypes of the Twin Mustang in 1944. The idea of using components of a well-proven airframe in this way was not unique, the Heinkel He 111Z-1 being another well-known example; but the Twin Mustang was to prove the most successful of such aircraft, as well as the only American example. The requirement, to obtain the necessary range, included two engines for reliability, two pilots to avoid excessive fatigue and adequate fuel.

The North American solution was to take two entirely standard P-51 Mustang fuselages, complete with power plant, plus one starboard and one port wing panel, and to join these with a new centre-wing panel and tailplane. The two prototypes, designated XP-82, had "handed" propellers to avoid excessive torque on take-off, driven by V-1650-23/25 engines. A third prototype, the XP-82A, had two V-1710-119 engines with common propeller rotation, but the production aircraft reverted to the handed arrangement. First flight of the XP-82A was made on 15 April 1945. Armament comprised six 0·50-in guns in the wing centre-section and there were five underwing pick-ups, two each side and one under the centre-section, capable of carrying bombs or drop tanks.

Of 500 P-82Bs ordered in 1944, only 20 were completed before VJ-Day cancellation of the contract. Two of these were modified in 1946, as prototype night fighters, the major innovation being the AI radar in a fairing under and ahead of the centre-section. With SCR-720 radar, the prototype was designated P-82C, and with APS-4, P-82D. The starboard crewman became the observer/radar operator instead of a second pilot.

A batch of 250 Twin Mustangs was ordered in 1946, comprising 100 P-82E dual-control escort fighters, 100 P-82F night fighters with APS-4 radar, and 50 P-82Gs with SCR-720 radar. All had handed Allison V-1710-143/145 engines, and were redesignated F-82 in 1948. They replaced P-61 Black Widows in service with Air Defense Command in 1948 and several squadrons had been deployed to Japan by 1950, these being on hand to participate in the Korean War. An F-82 of the 68th Fighter (All-Weather) Squadron, 8th F-B Wing, is credited with destroying the first enemy aircraft in that conflict.

After retiring from service in the Far East, some F-82s were assigned to Alaska, where 14 F-82Fs and Gs were winterized and redesignated F-82H.

North American FJ-1 Fury

Progenitor of North American's highly successful line of Sabre and Super Sabre fighters, the Fury originated in

1944 as a design study for a US Navy fighter. The NA-134 design was a straight-wing monoplane with a 4,000-lb s t Allison J35-A-5 turbojet in the fuselage and "straight-through" ducting. Location of the cockpit above the intake duct gave the design a somewhat portly appearance, but the promised performance was good and the US Navy ordered three prototypes on New Year's Day, 1945. Soon after, the USAF ordered prototypes of a similar design, the NA-140; but after a mock-up review in June 1945, the latter design was changed to incorporate swept wings and appeared eventually as the F-86 Sabre.

The first XFJ-1, as the Navy's new fighter had been designated, made its first flight on 1946. Already, on 18 May 1945, a contract had been placed for 100 production model FJ-1s, but this was cut later to 30. Deliveries began in November 1947 to Navy Squadron VF-5A, and service on board the USS *Boxer* began in March of the following year.

The single-seat FJ-1 was armed with six 0·50-in machine-guns in the side walls of the air intake, and was the last US Navy fighter to have this armament, the 20-mm cannon then becoming standard. The later series of Furies, FJ-2 to FJ-4, are described later under their revised F-1 designation.

North American B-45 Tornado

The application of early turbojet engines to bombers posed many difficulties which had not been encountered – or proved less troublesome – in the design of the first jet fighters. Consequently, a number of prototypes were built in the period around the end of World War II with quite different configurations but all designed to do essentially the same job. The USAF, in particular, backed the construction of five diverse jet bombers in 1944–5, in a programme which was to produce both the first operational aircraft in this class, the North American B-45, and the more advanced and strategically more significant Boeing B-47 Stratojet.

Three prototypes of the North American NA-130 design were ordered in December 1944 after the USAF had invited design tenders to an April specification for a bomber able to fly at 500 mph, with an operational ceiling of 40,000 ft, and an operating radius of 1,000 miles with an 8,000-lb bomb-load. The aircraft was required to carry a maximum load of 22,000 lb, and was to have defensive armament only in the tail, its speed being expected to offer sufficient defence against head-on attack.

The North American design was in most respects conventional, with a straight wing, single tail unit, and crew of four, including two pilots in tandem. Engines were 4,000-lb s t Allison J35-A-11s, paired in close-fitting nacelles under the shoulder-mounted wings. By the time the first XB-45 flew on 17 March 1947, the USAF had placed its first jet bomber order with North American, for 96 B-45As. The first few of these flew originally with J35 engines, but the production power plant comprised four 4,000-lb s t J47-GE-3s or -9s. Named Tornado, the B-45A entered service with the 47th Bombardment Group in November 1948 and remained in active service for ten years, for much of that time in Europe. Fourteen were modified later into TB-45A target tugs.

Ten B-45Cs, the first of which flew on 3 May 1949, had

North American P-82F (F-82F) Twin Mustang

North American FJ-1 Fury

North American B-45A Tornado

TYPE	DIMENSIONS span ft	span in	length ft	length in	height ft	height in	WEIGHT max t-o lb	PERFORMANCE max speed mph	at height ft	service ceiling ft	combat range miles	REMARKS
North American P-51D	37	0	32	3	13	8	11,600	437	25,000	41,900	950	
North American P-51H	37	0	33	4	13	8	11,054	487	25,000	41,600	940	
North American P-82E	51	3	39	1	13	10	24,864	465	21,000	40,000	2,504	
North American P-82F	51	3	42	2	13	10	26,208	460	21,000	38,500	2,200	
North American FJ-1	38	2	34	5	14	10	15,600	547	9,000	32,000	1,500	
North American B-45A	89	0	75	4	25	2	95,558	580	SL	46,250	1,000	
North American B-45C	96	0	75	4	25	2	112,952	579	SL	43,200	1,910	Span over tip-tanks

North American RB-45C Tornado

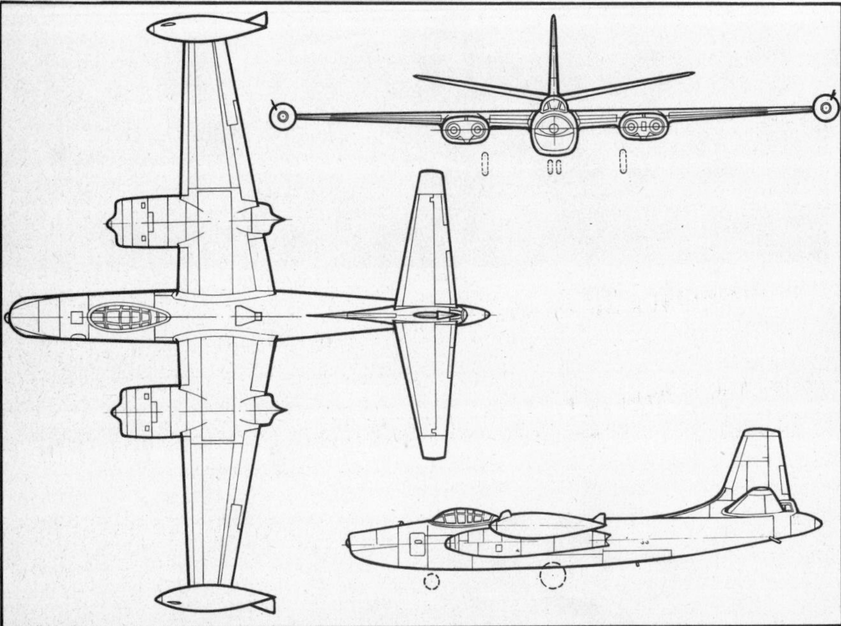
North American RB-45C Tornado

North American F-86D Sabre

5,200-lb s t J47-GE-13/15 engines, strengthened airframes, higher gross weight and 1,200-US gallon tanks at the wing-tips. They were followed by 33 RB-45Cs with added cameras and reconnaissance equipment in a re-designed nose, provision for flight refuelling and increased internal fuel capacity. The RB-45Cs served with USAF units in Europe and in the Far East, the latter including operational sorties over Korea.

North American F-86 Sabre

Destined to become one of the truly great combat aircraft of all time, the North American Sabre represented a somewhat hesitant step into the unknowns of swept-wing aerodynamics when it was conceived in 1945. Indeed, the earliest design study for a new USAF high-performance jet fighter, under the company designation NA-140, featured a straight wing with tip-tanks, and in this form it received a USAF contract for three prototypes in May 1945. Subsequently, an analysis of German test results by North American engineers led to the conclusion that a swept-back wing would bestow major performance gains, provided the problem of low-speed stability could be overcome. In November 1945, the USAF approved a proposal to redesign the XP-86 (NA-140) to have swept wings, the planform adopted being that studied in Germany for the Me 262 (but not adopted). Use of automatic slots on the wing leading-edge proved to be the key to low-speed stability.

The first of the three XP-86s appeared in August 1947, powered by a 4,000-lb s t J35-C-3 engine, and was first flown on 1 October of that year. As well as the swept-back wing, it had swept tail surfaces; the engine air-flow was of the "straight-through" type, with a nose intake and tailpipe extending to the end of the fuselage. Planned armament was six 0·50-in guns in the front fuselage. The prototype exceeded Mach 1 (in a shallow dive) on 26 April 1948, being the second US aircraft to do so.

Production of the Sabre was ordered by the USAF in December 1946, with a contract for 33 F-86As (until June 1948, the designation was P-86); 521 more were added later. Deliveries began in February and March 1949 to the First Fighter Group, following extensive development trials. The F-86A differed from the prototypes in having a J47-GE-1, -7 or -13 engine, and an operational armament which could include bombs or rockets under the wings as well as the six machine-guns. Five USAF Groups were equipped eventually with the F-86A and one of these, the 4th Fighter-Interceptor Wing, became the first to operate Sabres in the Korean War, on 17 December 1950. There followed many actions between Sabres and MiG-15s – the first conflict between swept-wing jet fighters – in which the Sabres displayed a marked superiority, preventing the MiGs from achieving all-important air control.

The F-86A was succeeded in the day interceptor rôle by the F-86E, first flown on 23 September 1950 and differing from the "A" primarily in having an all-flying tail. Production by North American totalled 336, and 60 more of similar standard were built for the USAF by Canadair (see page 50).

Powered by a 5,910-lb s t J47-GE-27 engine, the F-86F first flew on 19 March 1952 and became the major production day fighter version of the Sabre. Apart from the more powerful engine, which improved performance, the F-86F introduced a series of equipment changes in stages related primarily to the underwing loads which could be carried. In the course of production of the F-86F, the so-called "6-3" wing was introduced, with increased chord on the leading-edge instead of slots. Initial production, at North American factories in Los Angeles and Columbus, totalled 1,079, primarily for USAF units. Beginning in 1954, Sabres of this model began to reach other nations, under the auspices of MDAP, going in large quantity to Nationalist China (327) and Spain (244), and in lesser quantities to Norway (90), South Korea (122), Portugal (50), Philippines (40), Thailand (40), Argentina (28), Venezuela (22) and Peru (14).

To fulfil the MDAP commitments, met initially from surplus USAF stock, North American built a further 280 F-86Fs, and then 180 more for Japan, which als acquired a production licence under which Mitsubishi assembled 300 aircraft from imported components. From the final North American production batch, 120 F-86Fs were supplied to the Pakistan Air Force.

Although both the F-86E and F-86F carried underwing stores and operated in the ground-support rôle when required, the full fighter-bomber potential of the Sabre was realized only with the development of the F-86H, which was first flown on 30 April 1953. This had four underwing strong-points, a clamshell type cockpit canopy and a deepened fuselage accommodating more fuel and a J79-GE-3 engine. Production totalled 475, all but the first 113 carrying an armament of four 20-mm cannon.

Development of an all-weather variant of the Sabre had begun at North American in March 1949 and USAF interest was shown immediately, leading by October 1949 to a contract for two YF-86Ds and 122 F-86Ds.

These proved to be the first of many, for production of the F-86D eventually totalled 2,504, more than any other single Sabre version. First flown on 22 December 1949, the YF-86D had only some 25 per cent of its components in common with the day fighter; the wings and landing gear were substantially unchanged, but the fuselage was almost wholly new in detail. The engine was a J47-GE-17 or -33 with afterburner, and installation of radar in a fairing in the nose produced the most obvious difference in the F-86D profile. In place of the cannon armament, a retractable pack of twenty-four 2·75-in Mighty Mouse unguided air-to-air rockets was fitted in the under-fuselage. Later F-86Ds were built with a drag-chute installation and most of the earlier models were modified eventually in this respect.

At the peak of its deployment, the F-86D equipped 20 Air Defense Command Wings in the USA, Europe and Far East. When released from the USAF, the type was supplied under MDAP and other arrangements, the recipients including Japan (106), Denmark (38), Philippines (18), Greece (50), Turkey (50), Yugoslavia (130), Nationalist China and South Korea. A total of 981 F-86Ds were modernized in 1956–7, undergoing modifications to permit their operation with the Semi-Automatic Ground Environment (SAGE) equipment. These went back to the USAF as F-86Ls, with equipment changes and modified wing-tips and leading-edges.

Another version of the "Sabre Dog" was developed by North American specifically for NATO nations, the first of two prototypes flying as the YF-86K on 15 July 1954. The primary difference was in armament, the F-86K having four 20-mm guns in place of the ventral rocket pack. In addition to 120 built by North American, 221 F-86Ks were assembled by Fiat, which supplied 63 to the Italian Air Force, 60 to France, 88 to the Luftwaffe, 6 to the Netherlands and 4 to Norway. The two YF-86Ks went to the Italian Air Force also, while other NAA-built aircraft went to the Royal Netherlands Air Force (59) and Norway (60). The Dutch F-86Ks were transferred later to the Turkish Air Force, and Thailand received a few F-86Ls.

Including Canadian and Australian production versions, described separately, the Sabre proved to be one of the most widely-used jet fighters of the 1950s, as well as one of the most-produced.

The Sabre's attributes of good all-round performance, comparative ease of handling and combat-worthiness placed it far ahead of most of its contemporaries and it remained in front-line service well into the 1960s.

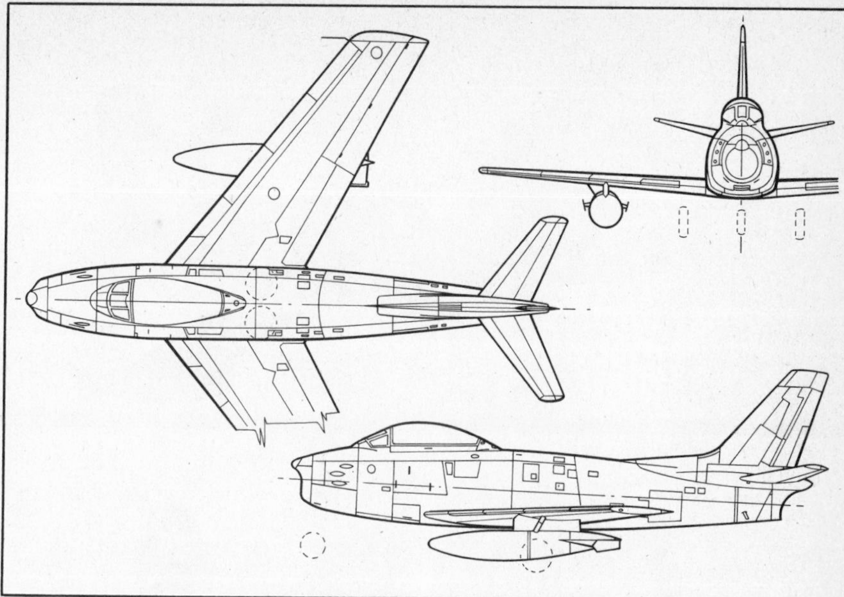

North American F-86E Sabre

North American RF-86F Sabre, Japanese-built, with reconnaissance cameras

North American F-86H Sabre

TYPE	DIMENSIONS span ft	span in	length ft	length in	height ft	height in	WEIGHT max t-o lb	PERFORMANCE max speed mph	at height ft	service ceiling ft	combat range miles	REMARKS
North American F-86A	37	1	37	6	14	8	16,357	675	2,500	48,300	1,270	
North American F-86E	37	1	37	6	14	8	16,500	679	SL	47,200	650	
North American F-86F	37	1	37	6	14	8	17,000	610	35,000	50,000	785	
North American F-86H	37	1	38	8	15	0	24,296	617	35,000	50,800	850	
North American F-86D	37	1	40	4	15	0	18,483	625	35,000	54,600	836	

North American AJ-1 Savage

North American AJ-2P Savage

North American AJ-2 tanker, Squadron VAH-11

North American FJ-2 Fury

North American AJ-1 Savage

To take advantage of the increasing size of aircraft carriers, and to acquire a strategic nuclear strike capability, the US Navy initiated development of a new attack-bomber of advanced design on 24 June 1946. At the time it was conceived, the North American XAJ-1, as the type was designated, was the largest aircraft designed for carrier operations. It was designed as a conventional twin-piston-engined aircraft, but added a 4,000-lb Allison J33-A-19 in the rear fuselage to obtain the required high speed over the target without the penalty of jet-engine fuel consumption in the cruise. Normal deck-landing features, including arrester gear and folding wings, were incorporated.

The prototype XAJ-1 first flew on 3 July 1948, and a production batch of 43 AJ-1s was ordered from North American in Los Angeles. With 2,400-hp R-2800-44W piston-engines and a 4,600-lb s t J33-A-10 turbojet, the first AJ-1 flew in May 1949. The AJ-1 was unarmed and had a crew of three; the production models introduced wing-tip fuel tanks. Deliveries began in September 1949, to VC-5 Squadron, but the type encountered several difficulties and the period of operational service was limited.

Despite the difficulties with the AJ-1s, a further batch of 100 aircraft was ordered from North American's Columbus factory and these appeared in two models, the AJ-2 and AJ-2P. The AJ-2P, first flown on 6 March 1952, had a taller fin and rudder, increased fuel capacity, a tailplane without dihedral, a re-designed nose and five cameras, plus equipment for day or night photography. The AJ-2, first flown on 19 February 1953, was similar apart from the reconnaissance gear, and both the -2 models had R-2800-48 piston-engines plus a single J33-A-10.

Many AJ-1s and, later, AJ-2s, were modified to serve the US Navy as flight refuelling tankers. For this rôle, the jet-engine was removed; a hose-and-reel unit was installed in its place, and extra fuel tanks were fitted in the bomb-bay. A few AJ-1s still serving in 1962 were redesignated A-2A and AJ-2s became A-2Bs.

North American F-1 Fury

Appearance of sweptwing Soviet fighters over Korea in 1950 quickly forced the US Navy to seek higher-performance fighters than those already in service, leading to a rare case of an existing land-based fighter being adapted successfully for carrier-borne operation. On 8 March 1951, the US Navy ordered a prototype of the USAF's F-86 Sabre, with the minimum necessary modification for naval use. The type was designated XFJ-2 although it differed substantially from the FJ-1 Fury, with its sweptback wings and tail unit, and the first flight was made on 27 December 1951. This aircraft was essentially an F-86E with arrester gear; it was followed by the XFJ-2B, which was the first to have the Navy-specified armament of four 20-mm cannon. Production FJ-2s, with 6,100-lb s t J47-GE-27 engines and folding wings, were built at Columbus and began to reach Marine Squadron VMF-122 in January 1954.

A change of engine, to the 7,200-lb s t Wright J65-W-2, characterized the FJ-3, first flown on 3 July 1953. Production deliveries began in December 1953 and this type became the first aircraft to operate on board the USS *Forrestal* in 1956. A number of FJ-3s were modified later for flight development of Navy air-to-air and air-to-ground missiles, as FJ-3D and FJ-3D2 directors and FJ-3M missile-carriers with six Sidewinder missiles. These were redesignated DF-1C, DF-1D and MF-1C respectively in 1962, when the FJ-3 itself became the F-1C.

A larger wing and re-designed fuselage, plus a taller fin and longer-stroke undercarriage, gave the next variant, the FJ-4, a distinctive appearance. This was first flown on 28 October 1954, and production deliveries began in March 1955. The power plant was a 7,800-lb s t J65-W-4. Production totalled 152 and these were redesignated F-1E in 1962.

Final Fury variant was the FJ-4B, which had a J65-W-16A turbojet and equipment to operate as a close-support fighter. The number of underwing pick-ups was increased to carry six Sidewinder or five Bullpup missiles, bombs or rockets or four external tanks, and LABS equipment was installed. The first FJ-4B flew on 3 December 1956; 222 were built, later becoming AF-1Es.

North American F-100 Super Sabre

By coincidence, the first group of USAF fighters with a true supersonic performance were also the first with "F" designations in the hundreds – a fact which quickly earned these designs the collective title of the "Century" fighters. The original trio comprised the North American F-100, the McDonnell F-101 and the Convair F-102; later, the Lockheed F-104, Republic F-105 and Convair F-106 also came into the Century series.

The first of the Century fighters, North American's Super Sabre, began as a company-funded design study based on the F-86 Sabre and known as the Sabre 45, because the wing sweepback was increased to 45 degrees. Official support for the project came in January 1951. By the time contracts were placed, on 1 November 1951, for two prototypes and 110 production models, little of the original Sabre was recognizable. The new aircraft had a low-mounted slab tailplane and a Pratt & Whitney J57 turbojet fed via an oval intake in the nose. The two YF-100A prototypes flew on 25 May and 14 October 1953 respectively. Production F-100As followed from October 1953 onward, powered by the 9,700-lb s t J57-P-7 and armed with four 20-mm cannon plus an assortment of underwing stores on six strong-points.

Operational deployment of the F-100A as a tactical day fighter began at the end of 1953, but full service use was delayed by control difficulties which sprang basically from the unknowns of supersonic flight and led to a series of accidents, a period of grounding and modifications to the airframe. Production of the F-100A totalled 203, the final 36 having J57-P-39 engines.

For use as a fighter-bomber, the F-100C appeared in 1955, with a stiffened wing and a total of eight strong-points. Production totalled 451 from the Los Angeles factory and 25 from a second source established at Columbus. The maximum underwing load was 6,000 lb, but this figure increased to 7,500 lb in the F-100D, which followed the "C" into production at Los Angeles and Columbus in January and June 1956 respectively. Other changes included an enlarged fin and rudder, a Minneapolis-Honeywell supersonic auto-pilot and new landing flaps on the inboard trailing-edges. The two factories built 940 and 334 F-100 Ds respectively.

All the single-seat Super Sabres, the successive models of which served with Tactical Air Command of the USAF until 1965, had an internal armament of four 20-mm M-39 cannon. This was reduced to only two guns in the F-100F, the final production version, which had a 3-ft longer fuselage and a second seat in tandem, in order to combine the operational rôles with combat proficiency training. Between March 1957 and October 1959, 339 F-100Fs were built.

Subsequent to delivery, many F-100Ds were modified to carry AIM-9B Sidewinder or AGM-12A Bullpup missiles beneath the wings, for air-to-air and air-to-ground use respectively. As the later Super Sabres became

North American FJ-3M (MF-1C) Fury, with Sidewinder missiles

North American FJ-4B (AF-1E) Fury, with Bullpup missiles

North American F-100C Super Sabre

TYPE	DIMENSIONS span ft	in	length ft	in	height ft	in	WEIGHT max t-o lb	PERFORMANCE max speed mph	at height ft	service ceiling ft	combat range miles	REMARKS
North American AJ-1	75	0	65	0	NA		55,000	420	NA	NA	NA	Span over tip-tanks
North American AJ-2	71	5	65	0	21	5	55,000	425	NA	NA	2,200	Without tip-tanks
North American FJ-2	37	1	37	6	14	8	18,000	690	SL	50,000	785	
North American FJ-3(F-1C)	37	1	37	7	13	8	21,876	681	SL	49,000	990	
North American FJ-4(F-1E)	39	1	36	4	13	11	23,700	680	SL	46,800	2,020	
North American FJ-4B(AF-1E)	39	1	36	6	13	11	26,000	715	SL	45,000	2,700	
North American F-100A	36	7	46	2	13	4	28,000	770	SL	NA	NA	
North American F-100D	38	9	47	0	15	0	34,832	864	35,000	44,900	1,200	

North American F-100D Super Sabre, Royal Danish Air Force

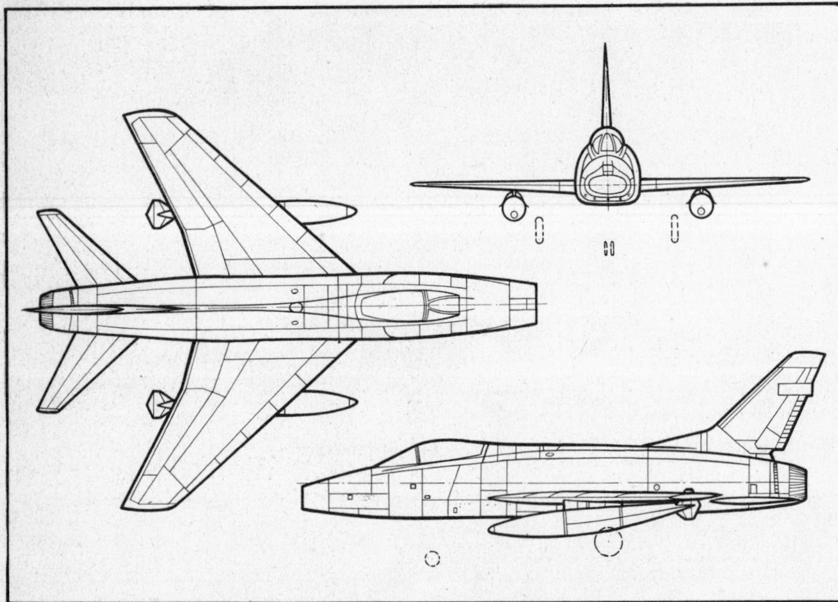
North American F-100D Super Sabre

North American (Sud-Aviation) T-28A Fennec, Armée de l'Air

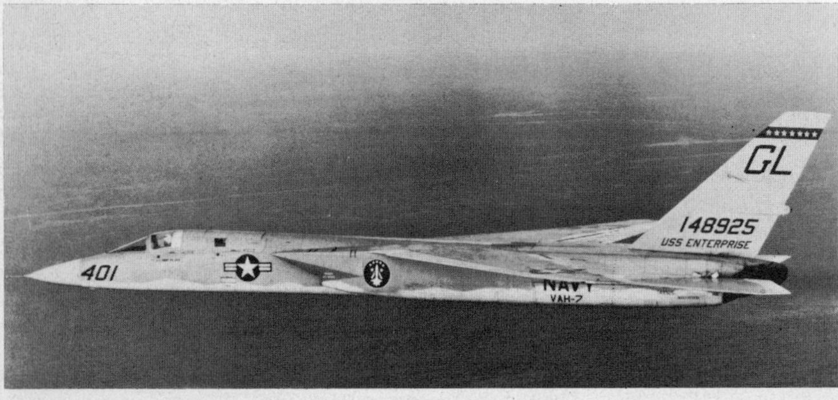

North American A-5A Vigilante

available, the USAF released earlier models to its allies. In 1960, Nationalist China received 60 F-100As, while 260 F-100Cs – more than half of the total built – went to the Turkish Air Force. Production of the F-100D included a quantity for the Mutual Assistance Programme, these going to the Armée de l'Air in France and to the Royal Danish Air Force. Both of these Services and the Turkish Air Force also received a number of F-100Fs.

North American T-28D

Although designed as a trainer, the North American T-28 has achieved considerable success in an operational, offensive rôle, as a light armed attack aircraft. The scheme to convert surplus USAF and USN T-28 trainers for this rôle was developed by North American primarily to meet the need for an inexpensive and versatile counter-insurgency aircraft for operations in South-East Asia.

Modifications for the armed T-28D version consist of installing a 1,425-hp Wright R-1820-56S engine and strengthening the wing to carry various types of armament on a total of six strong-points. Possible loads are pods containing the General Electric multi-barrel Minigun, 500-lb bombs, napalm, rockets or fuel tanks.

For operational use, the T-28D is flown normally as a single-seater, from the front cockpit; but the second seat is retained and can be used by an observer. Up to mid-1965, North American had converted well over 200 of the basic trainers to T-28Ds.

Prior to the USAF's decision to use the T-28D, North American had proposed civil and military versions of the T-28A with the name Nomad, and PacAero Engineering Corporation was licensed to market this conversion. After evaluation by the French Air Force, the military version of the Nomad was ordered and, under a sub-licence from PacAero, Sud-Aviation undertook the conversion of 135 T-28As. In French service these conversions were named Fennec; like the later T-28D they were fitted with R-1820 engines and underwing pylons to carry four bombs, or two gun pods each mounting two 12·5-mm machine-guns.

A large number of Fennecs saw operational service in Algeria from mid-1960 until the end of hostilities.

North American A-5 Vigilante

Largest attack bomber ever built for operations on board US Navy aircraft carriers, the A-5 had a somewhat unsatisfactory career in the primary attack rôle, but was developed into a highly-effective reconnaissance strike aircraft. The original requirement was announced by the US Navy in 1955, and called for an aircraft with all-weather capability and a higher performance than any previous attack bomber; the North American entry in this design competition was awarded a letter contract on 29 June 1956. Two prototypes were ordered in August, with the original designation of YA3J-1, and the first of these flew for the first time on 31 August 1958.

Key features of the A3J design were the high wing of typically North American sweptback configuration, and the two side-by-side General Electric YJ79-GE-2 engines, each rated at 16,150-lb s t with afterburning. The engines were fed via variable-geometry intakes, used for the first time in a production aircraft; another first was the so-called "linear" bomb-bay, which ran the length of the aircraft between the engines and was designed to eject the bombs rearward. Primary armament was to be a free-falling nuclear weapon, to which two fuel tanks were attached in the bomb-bay; fuel from these tanks was used first and they were then ejected with the weapon to act as aerodynamic stabilizers.

Deliveries of production A-5As (originally A3J-1s) began in 1960 and the first Navy unit to receive the type was VAH-7, in June 1961. Production A-5As had J79-GE-2, -4 or -8 engines, the REINS bombing-navigation system and provision for tanks, bombs or rockets on two underwing pylons.

The A-5A was followed into production by the A-5B, which had extra fuel in a hump-backed fuselage, larger flaps, improved boundary-layer control by blowing air over the entire wing surface, and four instead of two underwing pylons. First flight of an A-5B was made on 29 April 1962, but production plans were amended when it was decided to abandon the primary attack rôle.

In place of the attack rôle, the Navy substituted reconnaissance as the primary mission, and A-5Bs still in production were converted before delivery to RA-5C configuration. The latter has electronic equipment and fuel in the bomb-bay; an advanced sideways-looking radar in a long ventral fairing and a large variety of photographic and electronic reconnaissance equipment. The first RA-5C flew on 30 June 1962 and RVAH-5 had aircraft of this type in operation by June 1964. During 1964, North American began converting A-5As (55 of which were built) to RA-5C standard, and squadrons RVAH-1, -7, -9 and -11 were detailed to operate with the Vigilante in the reconnaissance rôle.

Northrop A-17/A-33

Having established its Gamma and Delta monoplanes in commercial service, the Northrop Corporation produced a private-venture military derivative of the same design in the autumn of 1933, called the Model 2-C. Initial flight trials showed promising performance and the US Army purchased this aircraft in June 1934 for evaluation under the designation YA-13. An all-metal low-wing monoplane, powered by a 712-hp Wright R-1820-37 radial engine, the YA-13 was a typical product of its age, distinguished by large "trousers" which faired the main undercarriage into the wings. Armament comprised four 0·30-in guns in the wings and a fifth in the rear cockpit for tail defence, and 600-lb of bombs.

While the YA-13 was being evaluated by the US Army, Northrop developed the improved Model 2E, with a 750-hp R-1820-F53, a semi-retractable bomb-aiming panel under the rear cockpit, an 1,100-lb bomb-load and only two wing guns. A single example of the 2E was purchased by the Royal Air Force in 1934 for comparative evaluation against British types, and Northrop built about 150 of a similar model for China in 1935.

At the end of 1934, the US Army placed an order with Northrop for 110 light attack-bombers based on the YA-13, but with 800-hp Pratt & Whitney R-1830 Wasp engines. A trial installation of this power plant in the prototype produced the Model 2F (XA-16) but a major redesign of the tail proved to be necessary to match the higher power, and to avoid this complication the Army specified the 750-hp R-1535-11 Wasp Junior in production model A-17s, delivery of which began in August 1935. Other changes from the prototype included open-sided wheel fairings, perforated flaps and internal stowage for twenty 30-lb bombs.

A-17s became standard equipment with several Army attack groups, being joined in 1936 by the first of 100 A-17As ordered in December 1935, with retractable main gear and 825-hp R-1535-13 engine. Additional orders brought the total of A-17As built to 129, plus two three-seat command transports designated A-17AS, with 600-hp R-1340-45 Wasp engines.

Development of high-performance light bombers such as the Douglas DB-7 curtailed the useful life of the A-17, and in June 1940 a total of 93 A-17As were released by the Army for Douglas to sell abroad, in exchange for an additional 20 A-20s added to the production line at Douglas's expense. Of this total, 61 were sold to the RAF, which designated them Nomad; the majority of these were passed on to the South African Air Force for use as target tugs. France acquired 32, but these got no further than Martinique, and saw no active service.

North American RA-5C Vigilante

Northrop A-17

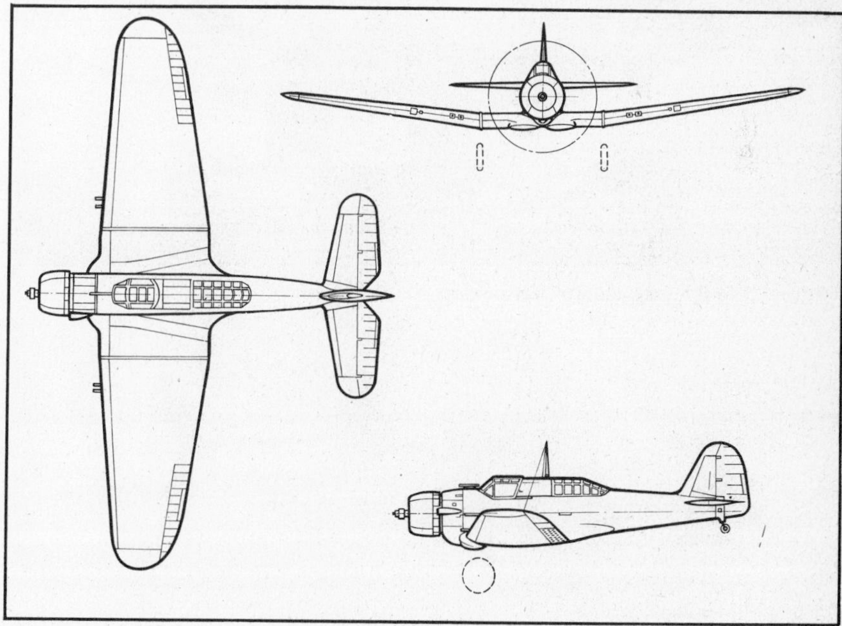

Northrop A-17A

TYPE	DIMENSIONS span ft	span in	length ft	length in	height ft	height in	WEIGHT max t-o lb	PERFORMANCE max speed mph	at height ft	service ceiling ft	combat range miles	REMARKS
North American T-28D	40	7	32	9	12	7	8,250	352	18,000	37,000	1,200	
North American A-5A	53	0	73	2½	19	4¾	62,000	1,385	40,000	67,000	2,000	
North American RA-5C	53	0	73	2½	19	4¾	70,000	1,385	40,000	67,000	2,400	

Northrop A-17A

Northrop B5 (A-17), Swedish-built

Northrop N-3PB floatplane, Royal Norwegian Naval Air Force

Northrop P-61B Black Widow

Northrop P-61C Black Widow

Considerable success was enjoyed by versions of the A-17 designed for export, these being produced initially by Northrop Corporation and then by Douglas Aircraft Co after the latter acquired Northrop in August 1937, as its El Segundo Division. Sweden purchased a prototype, designated Northrop 8A-1, and a production licence in 1937, this model being in effect the A-17 with a Bristol Hercules XXIV engine. Known as the B5B and B5C in the Swedish Air Force, the type was produced by the ASJA at Linköping, which built 64 and 39, respectively, of the two versions. Powered by the 840-hp R-1820G-3 Cyclone engine, the 30 Northrop 8A-2s purchased by the Argentine Air Force were also similar to the A-17.

Peru ordered a special high-altitude version of the design from Douglas in 1938, the distinguishing feature being the 1,000-hp GR-1820G-103 engine. Ten were built, designated DB-8A-3P and having the retractable main gear of the A-17A. Eighteen examples of a similar version, designated DB-8A-3N, were ordered by the Netherlands, with the 1,050-hp Pratt & Whitney R-1830-SC3G; these saw brief service in 1940 against the Luftwaffe. Also in 1940, Iraq purchased 15 DB-8A-4s, identical in most respects with the Peruvian model.

Most powerful of all the Northrop/Douglas attack-bombers was the DB-8A-5, with the 1,200-hp Wright R-1820-87 Cyclone. Thirty-six ordered by Norway were diverted to Canada, to be used as trainers by Norwegian forces which had escaped the German invasion of their homeland. Armament was increased to two 0·50-in and three 0·30-in guns, plus 1,800 lb of bombs. Peru ordered 34 of the same version, but 31 of these were requisitioned by the US Army in 1942 before delivery and designated A-33; these, too, served primarily as trainers.

Northrop N-3PB

Many features of the Northrop Model 2 and 8A low-wing monoplanes were incorporated in the N-3PB patrol bomber seaplane which was developed largely to meet Norwegian requirements in 1939. The design was the first undertaken by the newly-established Northrop Aircraft Inc, following purchase of the original Northrop Corp by Douglas Aircraft. The Norwegian purchasing commission in the USA ordered 24 of the new seaplanes early in 1940, specifying use of the Wright R-1820-G205A Cyclone, which was also to be used in Norwegian 8A-5s.

The N-3PB was an all-metal low-wing monoplane, with a crew of three in tandem under a long cockpit canopy and provision for a 2,000-lb torpedo under the fuselage between the large twin floats. Armament comprised four 0·50-in guns fixed in the wings and two 0·30s, flexibly mounted in the rear fuselage for dorsal and ventral use.

The first N-3PB flew in 1940, but despite rapid production of the entire batch of 24, none could be delivered before Norway fell to the German invasion. Consequently, the floatplanes were used to equip a Norwegian-manned unit, No. 330 Squadron, under RAF control in Iceland. Escort and anti-submarine patrols were flown for a year or so until the N-3PBs were relegated to training duties.

Northrop P-61 Black Widow

Development, early in World War II, of effective airborne radar for air interception led to a requirement for a new type of specialized night fighter capable of carrying such equipment, an operator, and comprehensive armament. In several cases, the requirement was met by adapting existing twin-engined fighters and light bombers, including the Beaufighter, Mosquito, A-20 Havoc, Ju 88 and Bf 110. But early operational reports from Europe of encounters between the RAF's radar-equipped fighters and German bombers led the US Army to issue a general requirement for a specialized radar-equipped night fighter. The Northrop response to this was a large twin-engined, twin-boom aircraft with a crew of three. Leaving the nose free for the disc antenna of the AI radar, the design had the armament located in a remotely-controlled top turret and in the belly, mounting, respectively, four 0.50-in guns and four 20-mm cannons.

The Army Air Corps ordered two prototypes of

11 January 1941, giving them the designation XP-61. While work proceeded on these, production orders reached Northrop in a steady procession – for 13 YP-61 service test models in March 1941, 150 P-61s in September 1941 and 410 more in February 1941. First flight of an XP-61 was made on 21 May 1942, and the second XP-61 and all 13 YP-61s followed within five months. Production models, incorporating the results of experience with the test aircraft, began to appear a year later, their all-black finish leading to the appropriate popular name of Black Widow, after the venomous North American spider.

Northrop built 200 of the first production model, the P-61A, but the top turret caused severe buffeting and was deleted after the first 37 aircraft. Operational service began in the South Pacific area with the 18th Fighter Group, in the early summer of 1944, and the first operational success was recorded on 7 July. Between then and the end of 1944, P-61s were issued to most USAAF night fighter squadrons in the Pacific and European areas. The P-61A was followed by 450 P-61Bs, which were given added light attack or intruder capability by underwing strong-points for four 1,600-lb bombs or 300-gallon tanks; the final 250 also had the original dorsal turret restored. Finally, Northrop built 41 P-61Cs, with 2,800-hp R-2800-73 engines in place of the 2,000-hp R-2800-10 or -65s of the earlier models. A photographic reconnaissance version designated F-15A (later RF-61C) was built in 1946 and named Reporter; the 35 examples of this type finally passed out of service in 1952.

Northrop F-89 Scorpion

Experience gained by Northrop in development of the P-61 Black Widow led the company to propose, in December 1945, a jet fighter with all-weather capability to replace the P-61. Acceptance of the proposal by the USAF brought a contract for two prototypes in December 1946, and the first of these flew on 16 August 1948.

The Northrop design was typical of the state of the art for 1945, with a straight tapered mid-wing and a pair of J35-A-9 engines side-by-side in the lower fuselage beneath the cockpit floor. Pilot and observer were seated in tandem beneath a long cockpit enclosure, and the four cannon were grouped in the nose, around the AI radar installation. A novelty was the use of decelerons – ailerons which could also be split open to act as airbrakes. The second prototype, designated XF-89A, had J35-A-21 engines with afterburners, and dispensed with the XF-89's all-black external finish.

Production orders, which eventually totalled 1,050, were first placed in July 1949 and deliveries of the F-89A Scorpion began a year later. The F-89A was generally similar to the XF-89A, but had six nose guns and underwing strong-points which could carry up to 3,200 lb of bombs and 32 rocket projectiles. Only 18 were delivered before the addition of several new items of equipment led to a change of designation to F-89B, 30 examples of which were built. These models began to reach all-weather

Northrop F-89A Scorpion

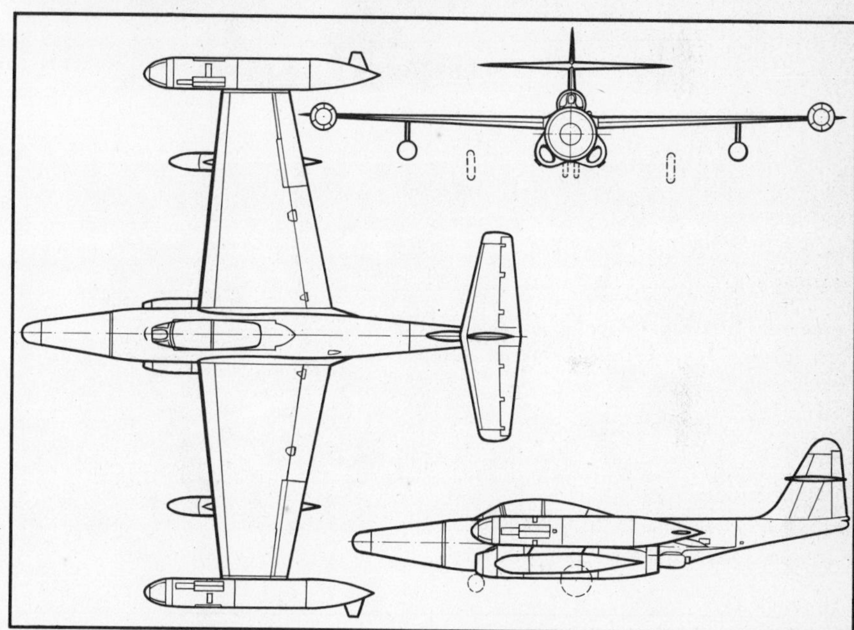

Northrop F-89H Scorpion

TYPE	DIMENSIONS span ft	span in	length ft	length in	height ft	height in	WEIGHT max t-o lb	PERFORMANCE max speed mph	at height ft	service ceiling ft	combat range miles	REMARKS
Northrop A-17	47	9	32	0	12	0	7,337	206	SL	20,700	650	
Northrop A-17A	47	9	31	8	12	0	7,550	220	2,500	19,400	732	
Northrop 8A-1(B5)	47	9	31	9	12	11	7,500	219	6,250	22,500	1,380	
Northrop DB-8A-3N	47	9	32	5	9	9	8,948	260	NA	29,600	910	
Northrop DB-8A-5	47	9	32	6	9	4	9,200	248	15,700	29,000	NA	
Northrop 2E	48	0	28	10	9	1	7,600	210	11,500	23,600	NA	
Northrop N-3PB	48	11	38	0	12	0	10,600	257	16,400	28,800	1,400	
Northrop P-61A	66	0	48	11	14	8	32,400	369	20,000	33,100	NA	
Northrop P-61B	66	0	49	7	14	8	38,000	366	20,000	33,100	NA	
Northrop P-61C	66	0	49	7	14	8	40,300	430	30,000	41,000	415	

Northrop F-89D Scorpion

Northrop F-89J Scorpion

Northrop F-5A, Royal Norwegian Air Force

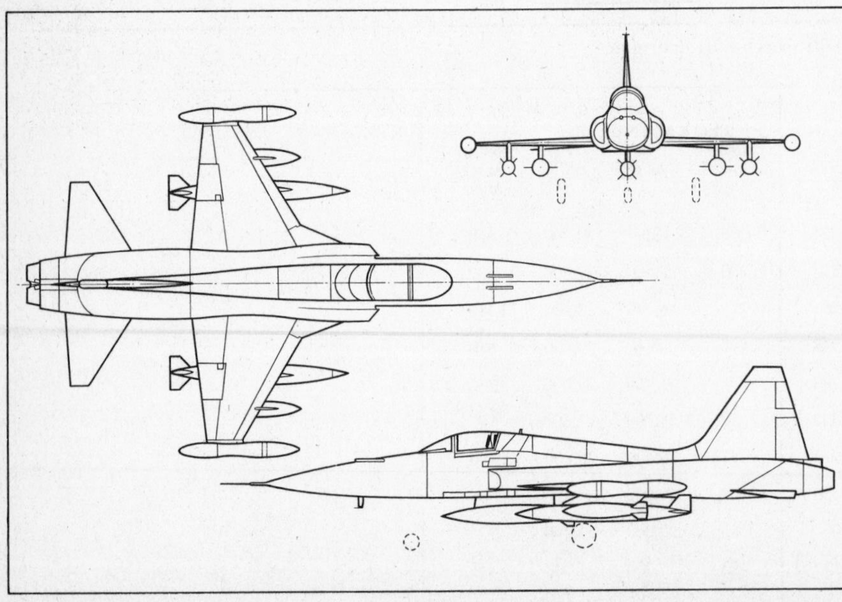
Northrop F-5A

squadrons of Air Defense Command in the middle of 1951, being the first multi-seat jet all-weather fighters to equip USAF units.

A further series of internal equipment changes, plus a redesigned elevator with internal mass-balance, distinguished the F-89C, which had J35-A-21, -21A, -33 or -33A engines. Production totalled 164. All the early Scorpion models had fixed tanks at the wing-tips, but these were replaced on the F-89D by pods containing fifty-two 2·75-in rockets as well as fuel. This was the most-produced Scorpion, with 682 examples built.

Further refinement of the weapon pods produced an installation which combined 21 rockets with three retractable Hughes GAR-1, -2, -3 or -4 Falcon missiles. At the same time, the Scorpion wing was adapted to carry up to six more Falcons, thus increasing the fire-power of the F-89H version very considerably. Delivery of 156 began in 1956, but front-line service with ADC units, in the USA and Alaska, was somewhat short-term as the higher-performing F-102s became available in 1957. A programme to up-date F-89Ds to F-89J standard began in 1956, the major change being to permit installation of a Douglas MB-1 Genie nuclear-tipped unguided rocket on each of two underwing pylons, plus four Falcons under the wings and two rocket pods at the wing-tips. A new fire-control system and more powerful engines were fitted in the 350 F-89Js converted. Together with F-89Ds and F-89Hs, many of the "J" model passed into service with Reserve and National Guard units in the late 1950s.

Northrop F-5

Characterized by its compactness and outstanding cost-effectiveness, the Northrop F-5 represented a "middle-of-the-road" philosophy when its design was initiated in the mid-1950s. Believing that the ultra-large Mach 2 fighters then in vogue were too sophisticated and too expensive for many nations, whilst the lightweight fighters lacked combat effectiveness, Northrop designers set out to produce a fighter which was the best possible compromise between performance, versatility, supportability and cost.

In parallel with the fighter design, Northrop evolved a closely similar two-seat trainer, and this gained official USAF support as the T-38A Talon in 1957. Subsequently, Northrop laid down three prototypes of the fighter as a private venture and the first of these flew on 30 July 1959. Following successful flight demonstrations with two prototypes, designated N-156F Freedom Fighters, the US Government announced on 25 April 1962 that it was ordering the type into quantity production as the standard new all-purpose fighter to be supplied overseas through the MAP. The third prototype was then completed, flying in July 1963 as the production prototype with a strengthened wing, greater external load-carrying ability and 3,050-lb s t General Electric J85-GE-13 engines in place of the YJ85-GE-1s and J85-GE-5s flown in the earlier prototypes. The first F-5As off the production line flew in 1963 and the first of a tandem two-seat version, the F-5B, in February 1964.

Initial MAP orders were for about 170 aircraft (including some 18 F-5Bs), to be supplied to several allied nations, including Iran, South Korea and Greece. Subsequently, Norway ordered 64 and Spain ordered 70 of the Northrop fighters, and other nations receiving F-5s from the US Government included Nationalist China, South Vietnam and Thailand.

A batch of early production aircraft was retained by the USAF to equip a training unit for overseas personnel. The USAF also acquired a squadron of F-5As in 1965 to conduct a full-scale operational evaluation in Vietnam.

Also in 1965, Canada selected the F-5 as its new standard fighter, with an order for 125. These aircraft, CF-5A single-seaters and CF-5D two-seaters, were built by Canadair, with J85-GE-15 turbojets produced by Orenda Engines in Canada. In 1966, the Netherlands ordered 105 NF-5s, including some two-seaters, from the Canadian production line.

The F-5 in its single-seat version carries a built-in armament of two 20-mm Colt-Browning M-39 cannon;

these are omitted from the two-seaters, but both types carry an extensive range of external stores, up to 6,200 lb in weight, on seven stations – one under the fuselage, two under each wing and one on each wing-tip.

Packard - Le Pere LUSAC - 11

Although no warplane of US design saw active service in the 1914–18 War, two examples of one design did, in fact, reach France before the Armistice.

The aircraft in question was the LUSAC-11 two-seat fighter, a biplane in the classic tradition of French and Italian designers of the period. The obvious European inspiration for the lines of this good-looking two-bay biplane was not difficult to explain, since its designer was Capt Le Pere, a member of the French aviation mission to the US government.

The LUSAC-11 was designed around a 400-hp Liberty engine and utilized a plywood fuselage and "box" interplane struts, which made it possible to dispense with incidence rigging wires. An unusual feature was a tilting radiator in the upper wing centre-section. Two 0·30-in guns were fixed to fire forward, with two more on a Scarff ring in the rear cockpit.

Production of the LUSAC-11 was handled by Packard Motor Car Co, which built two prototypes and a production batch of 25; further large contracts were cancelled when the war ended.

Republic P-43 Lancer

After trials with the final Seversky P-35, fitted with supercharger and designated XP-41, Seversky engineers produced an alternative development of the AP-35 airframe with a turbosupercharger in the fuselage behind the cockpit. The private-venture prototype, designated AP-4, differed further from the P-35 in having an inward-retracting undercarriage.

In March 1939, the USAAC ordered 13 examples of the AP-4 for service trials, under the designation YP-43. Powered by the 1,200-hp R-1830-55 engine, these differed from the AP-4 in several details, to improve performance, and the armament was increased to two 0·50-in and two 0·30-in guns.

Production orders for the Lancer, as the type was named, were placed in 1940, largely as an expedient to keep the production line open while the company (which had been re-organized as Republic Aviation Corporation in 1939) completed designs and production plans for the P-47 Thunderbolt. The production orders were for 54 P-43s and 80 P-43As, with R-1830-35 and R-1830-39 engines respectively. A further stop-gap order, in 1941, was for 125 P-43A-1s, of which 108 were destined for China under lend-lease. These had R-1830-57 engines, four 0·50-in guns and other improvements; they saw limited active service against Japanese forces.

The earlier Lancers were not issued to USAAF fighting units, but were modified to reconnaissance configuration – 150 as P-43Bs and two as P-43Cs with different camera installations. The 17 P-43A-1s which did not go to China were supplied to the RAAF, after conversion for the reconnaissance rôle.

Northrop F-5B

Packard-Le Pere LUSAC-11

Republic P-43 Lancer

TYPE	DIMENSIONS span ft	span in	length ft	length in	height ft	height in	WEIGHT max t-o lb	PERFORMANCE max speed mph	at height ft	service ceiling ft	combat range miles	REMARKS
Northrop F-89A	56	0	53	6	17	8	42,000	570	35,000	40,000	1,300	
Northrop F-89D	59	8	53	10	17	6	41,000	610	NA	52,000	875	
Northrop F-89H	59	8	53	10	17	7	46,000	595	36,000	40,000	1,100	
Northrop F-89J	59	8	53	10	17	7	42,590	595	36,000	NA	NA	
Northrop F-5A	25	3	47	2	13	2	19,756	945	36,860	50,000	600	
Packard-Le Pere-LUSAC 11	41	7	25	3	10	7	3,746	133	SL	20,200	320	
Republic P-43	36	0	28	6	14	0	7,935	349	25,000	38,000	800	
Republic P-43A	36	0	28	6	14	0	8,480	356	20,000	36,000	650	

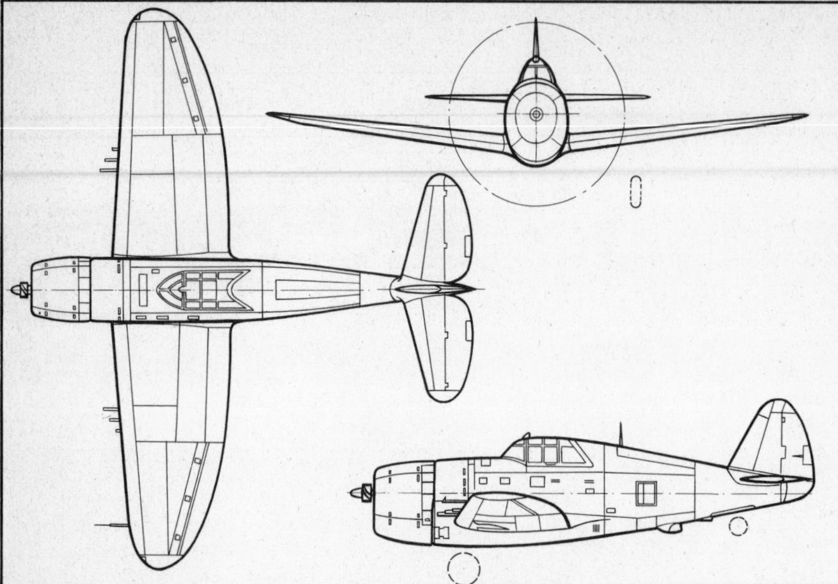

Republic P-47C Thunderbolt

Republic P-47D Thunderbolt

Republic P-47D Thunderbolt

Republic P-47M Thunderbolt, with rocket tubes

Republic P-47 Thunderbolt

Continuing the line of fighters begun in 1935 with the Seversky P-35, Alexander Kartveli and his design team were working on two new projects at the start of 1939. One was a straight development of the P-43 (see page 549) with a Pratt & Whitney R-2180 or R-2800 engine; the other was an attempt to meet official requirements with a much smaller and lighter aircraft, powered by an Allison V-1710-39 liquid-cooled in-line engine. Both these projects received official support, with a production contract for the former as the P-44 and prototype contracts for the latter as the XP-47 and XP-47A. In the event, neither type was destined to be built in the form envisaged in September 1939, for the air fighting over Europe in the early months of World War II forced a revision of USAAC views on fighter design. So when, in June 1940, Kartveli offered a major redesign of the XP-47 at almost twice the gross weight, with an eight-gun armament and a turbo-supercharged XR-2800 Double Wasp engine, both the P-44 and the XP-47 contracts were cancelled.

In their place, Republic received contracts during September 1940 for one XP-47B and 773 production P-47Bs and Cs. The new aircraft was the largest single-engined fighter then designed, with a 2,000-hp R-2800-21 radial and eight 0.50-in machine-guns in the wings, which had a semi-elliptical planform of the type favoured by Kartveli. First flown on 6 May 1941, the XP-47B had a top speed of 412 mph and, despite some doubts about the aircraft's handling qualities, particularly at low altitudes, the Thunderbolt became top priority for USAAF re-equipment.

By the end of 1942, two fighter groups were equipped with the P-47B. Moving to Europe early in 1943, they joined the Eighth Air Force in its assault on Occupied Europe, going into action on 8 April 1943. Early operations naturally revealed drawbacks as well as advantages: in particular, the range was inadequate for bomber escort duties, and manoeuvrability was poor. But the P-47C was already rolling off the Republic line at Long Island, with provision for external tanks under the belly and a lengthened fuselage to improve manoeuvrability. This model was operating in Europe by mid-1943, and in the Mediterranean theatre in November. Thunderbolts became operational in the Southwest Pacific in June 1943 and in China in April 1944.

Powered by an R-2800-21 or -59 engine, the latter rated at 2,300-hp, early model P-47Ds were similar to the P-47C in most respects. Strengthening of the wing permitted the carriage of fuel tanks or bombs (up to 2,500 lb on wing and fuselage shackles) and the P-47D began to demonstrate its outstanding characteristics as a fighter-bomber as well as a bomber escort towards the end of 1943.

Additional production lines for the Thunderbolt were laid down by Republic at Evansville and by Curtiss at Buffalo; production of versions up to the P-47D-22 totalled 3,962 at Farmingdale, Long Island, and 1,461 at Evansville, while Curtiss built 354 similar P-47Gs. Production then switched to the P-47D-25 and later versions, with a bubble canopy and cut-down rear fuselage for all-round vision, and more internal fuel. Farmingdale built 2,547 and Evansville 4,632.

The Royal Air Force received 240 early P-47Ds and 590 of the later series, designating them Thunderbolt I and II respectively, and using them in Southeast Asia. Another 203 went to Russia on lend-lease and 88 to Brazil.

Among a number of Thunderbolt variants which remained purely experimental was the XP-47J, which was powered by a 2,800-hp R-2800-57 with fan-assisted cooling and had a lightweight wing and reduced armament. It achieved 504 mph on official tests – the highest speed ever reached by a piston-engined aircraft in level flight. The same engine with a conventional cooling arrangement was used in a standard P-47D airframe to produce the P-47M; 130 were built, primarily for European operations to combat the V-1 flying-bomb.

Whereas the P-47M was lightened by removal of the underwing racks, the near-contemporary P-47N was the heaviest of all the Thunderbolts, at 20,450 lb. It had the

R-2800-57 engine and a larger, stronger wing which could carry four drop tanks. Added to the internal fuel tanks, these gave an endurance of more than nine hours. The 1,000-mile radius of action was intended for bomber-escort duties in the Pacific, and 1,667 were delivered from Farmingdale plus 149 from Evansville.

The grand total of 15,660 was the largest number of any single fighter type ever acquired by the USAAF. Approximately two-thirds of these found their way into action with that Air Force, and 5,222 were lost. The combat loss rate of less then 0·7 per cent was exceptionally low, reflecting the Thunderbolt's rugged construction, which allowed it to survive battle damage, and its high performance.

Following the replacement of the Thunderbolts by jet-fighters, many were made available to other nations and served for several years with the air forces of France, Italy, Turkey, Iran, Nationalist China, Yugoslavia and, in the Americas, Bolivia, Brazil, Chile, Colombia, Dominica, Ecuador, Guatemala, Honduras, Mexico, Nicaragua and Peru. The P-47D was in operation as late as 1953 in the Guatemalan revolution, and a few were still in use in South America in 1966.

Republic P-84 Thunderjet

Republic's mighty Thunderbolt was the last radial-engined fighter to serve in quantity with the USAF. Its jet successor, the Thunderjet, proved in turn to be the last straight-winged subsonic fighter used operationally by that Service. Although a completely new design, it retained a number of the Thunderbolt's attributes, including a good ground-attack capability. It also had the ability to deliver tactical nuclear weapons.

Development of the Thunderjet began in 1944 and the design was laid out round a single General Electric J35-GE-7 turbojet, with straight-through airflow, and a low, straight-tapered wing. USAF backing came early in 1945, with an order for three prototypes and 400 production models, and the first XP-84 flew on 28 February 1946. The first 15 production aircraft were YP-84As, with J35-A-15 engines, provision for tip-tanks and six 0·50-in machine-guns. Provision for eight underwing rockets, and an ejection seat, were added on the 224 P-84Bs, which had the 4,000-lb s t J35-A-15C. The 191 P-84Cs were almost identical. Designations were changed to F-84B and F-84C in June 1948.

Operational experience with the early Thunderjets was reflected in the F-84D with its thicker wing skin, new fuel system and improved undercarriage. A 5,000-lb s t J35-A-17D engine was fitted in the 154 F-84Ds and in the 843 F-84Es which had a 12-in longer fuselage to improve comfort in the cockpit, a radar gun-sight, new wing-tip tanks and shackles for two underwing tanks. Both the F-84D and F-84E were operating in Korea by early 1951, at first as bomber escorts and later in the primary design rôle as tactical fighter-bombers.

With provision for 4,000 lb of external weapons, including a nuclear bomb, the F-84G was powered by a 5,600-lb s t J35-A-29, and had a receptacle in the port wing

Republic P-47N Thunderbolt

Republic P-84E (F-84E) Thunderjet

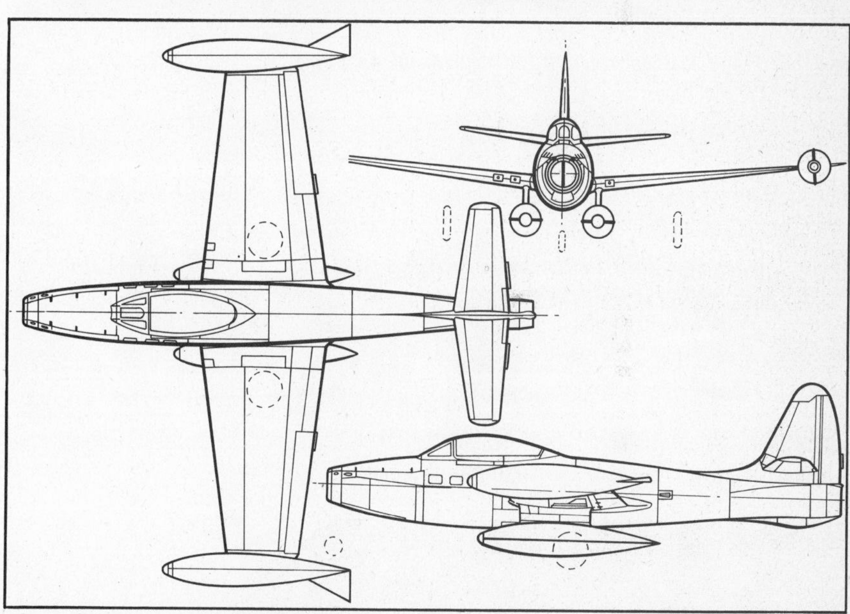
Republic P-84E (F-84E) Thunderjet

TYPE	DIMENSIONS span ft	span in	length ft	length in	height ft	height in	WEIGHT max t-o lb	PERFORMANCE max speed mph	at height ft	service ceiling ft	combat range miles	REMARKS
Republic P-47B	40	9	35	0	12	8	12,700	412	25,800	38,000	575	
Republic P-47C	40	9	36	1	14	2	14,925	433	30,000	42,000	NA	
Republic P-47D	40	9	36	1	14	2	19,400	428	30,000	42,000	475	
Republic P-47N	42	7	36	1	14	8	20,450	467	32,500	43,000	800	
Republic P-84B	36	5	37	5	12	10	19,689	587	4,000	40,750	1,282	
Republic P-84C	36	5	37	5	12	10	19,798	587	4,000	40,600	1,274	
Republic P-84D	36	5	37	5	12	10	20,076	587	4,000	39,300	1,198	
Republic P-84E	36	5	38	6	12	10	22,463	613	SL	43,220	1,485	
Republic P-84G	36	5	38	1	12	7	23,525	622	SL	40,500	2,000	

Republic F-84G Thunderjet, Royal Danish Air Force

Republic F-84F Thunderstreak, Royal Netherlands Air Force

Republic RF-84F Thunderflash, Royal Danish Air Force

Republic YF-84F Thunderflash, FICON aircraft

for the boom of the Boeing flight refuelling system. Coupled with the use of an auto-pilot, flight refuelling capability allowed the F-84G to operate with Strategic Air Command in Fighter Escort Wings from 1952 to 1956. Tactical Air Command kept the type in service somewhat longer.

Production of the F-84G totalled 3,025; of these, 1,936 were purchased with MAP funds, together with 100 of the F-84Es, for delivery to NATO air forces and other countries receiving US military aid. In the former category were France, Belgium, Denmark, Greece, Italy, the Netherlands, Norway, Portugal and Turkey; other countries which received the F-84s were Nationalist China, Iran, Thailand and Yugoslavia.

Republic F-84F Thunderstreak

To offer a fighter of higher performance at the lowest possible cost, Republic put forward, during 1949, a proposal to combine the standard F-84E fuselage with a sweptback wing. Limited USAF support allowed design work to proceed and a prototype (a converted F-84 airframe) flew on 3 June 1950, as the YF-96A. Powered by a 5,200-lb s t Allison XJ35-A-25, the XF-96A had a new sweptback tail unit as well as the sweptback wing, but its performance remained subsonic.

When the outbreak of the Korean War freed more funds for fighter procurement, the USAF proposed a further redesign of the XF-96A, which was redesignated YF-84F in September 1950, and a second prototype, with a Wright YJ65-W-1 (licence-built Sapphire), flew on 14 February 1951. In this form, and re-named Thunderstreak, the Republic fighter went into production for both Tactical Air Command and Strategic Air Command, as a fighter-bomber and bomber escort respectively.

Production deliveries of the F-84F to USAF units began in 1954, and Republic built 2,474; a further 237 were built by General Motors during the production effort mounted at the time of the Korean War. Included in the total were 1,301 aircraft earmarked for NATO air forces, the Thunderstreak becoming one of the major types supplied by the US under its MAP programme and remaining in service, in some cases, until the late 1960s. Some 450 F-84Fs went to Germany for the Luftwaffe; about 200 were supplied to Italy, 197 to Belgium, 150 to France, 175 to Norway and about 75 to the Netherlands. A smaller number of F-84Fs supplied to Greece and Turkey were supplemented in the mid-1960s by additional aircraft released from the Luftwaffe as the F-104G came into service.

Development of an armed photo-reconnaissance version of the F-84F began in 1952 and resulted in production of the RF-84F Thunderflash. In order to accommodate a camera-bay in the nose of the fuselage, with provision for up to six cameras, the RF-84F was redesigned to have wing-root intakes for the 7,800-lb s t Wright J65-W-7 engine. The first YRF-84F flew in February 1952 and delivery of production aircraft to SAC began in March 1954. Of 715 built, 386 were for NATO air forces, going to the Luftwaffe, the Armée de l'Air, and to the Belgian, Danish, Italian, Dutch, Norwegian, Greek and Turkish air forces. The Chinese Nationalist Air Force also received enough for one squadron.

The Thunderflash was the subject of an unusual experiment in 1953, when the FICON (fighter in Convair) project was initiated as a means of extending the range of the reconnaissance aircraft. With a retractable hook in the nose, the FICON aircraft were carried on a trapeze beneath a Convair B-36, being capable of air-launch and recovery. To clear the B-36's bomb-bay, the tailplane was given marked dihedral. Following prototype trials, 25 aircraft were converted to RF-84K configuration, but the development of in-flight refuelling and changed operational requirements led to their early retirement.

Republic F-105 Thunderchief

In continuous production of fighters for the US Air Forces for more than two decades, Republic Aviation achieved its ultimate success with the F-105 Thunderchief, the company's final product before it became part of the

Fairchild Hiller organization. Like the Super Sabre, the Thunderchief began as a private-venture study for an aircraft to follow one already in production – Republic's F-84F Thunderstreak. The new design took shape around the powerful Pratt & Whitney J75 engine, as a massive, highly sophisticated tactical fighter-bomber, with a secondary interceptor rôle. Official backing came in 1954 with contracts for a trial batch of 15 F-105s.

The first two, designated YF-105A, flew with the J57-P-25 engine, as the J75 was not available in time; the first flight took place on 22 October 1955. Considerable airframe redesign for higher performance accompanied introduction of the J75-P-3 in the third aircraft, designated F-105B. Flown on 26 May 1956, it had an area-ruled fuselage and the unique swept-forward intakes in the wing-roots which became a distinctive feature of all Thunderchiefs. The initial batch of trials aircraft included nine more F-105Bs and these were followed by 65 true production models, entering service with the 4th Tactical Fighter Wing in 1958.

The F-105B was the heaviest single-seater to enter service with the USAF, grossing over 40,000 lb and capable of carrying 8,000 lb of bombs internally and 4,000 lb externally – as much as the B-17 of World War II. Full foul-weather capability was achieved only with the addition of the General Electric FC-5 integrated automatic flight and fire-control system which distinguished the F-105D, the principal production version of the Thunderchief.

Powered by the 26,500-lb s t J75-P-19W engine, the F-105D was armed, like the F-105B, with a single M-61 Vulcan 20-mm gun and 1,029 rounds of ammunition which could be expended in a single 15-second burst. External weapon capability was increased on the F-105D, which could carry its total 12,000-lb ordnance load externally if required. Four AIM-9 Sidewinder or AGM-12 Bullpup missiles could be carried.

The F-105D was first issued to Tactical Air Force units in 1961, initially in the United States and shortly after in Germany. In 1965, F-105Ds went into action in Vietnam in the tactical ground-attack rôle.

On 11 June 1963, Republic flew the first F-105F, a two-seat trainer which retained the full combat capability of the single-seater. The fuselage was lengthened to accommodate a second seat and the maximum weight went up to 54,000 lb. A small number of F-105Fs was included with the final production run of the F-105D; production of the latter ended in 1964, after several hundred had been built.

Ryan FR-1 Fireball

The special requirements of carrier-deck operations led the US Navy, at the end of 1942, to draw up an outline specification for a new fighter with a composite power plant – a piston-engine plus a turbojet. Such a combination seemed to be the best way, at that time, to take advantage of the newly-developed jet-engine for high combat speeds without hopelessly compromising take-off and landing performance. From nine companies invited to investigate the proposal, Ryan Aeronautical Corporation was selected in January 1943, and in the following month a contract was placed covering three prototypes of the Ryan Model 28 (designated XFR-1). Subsequently named Fireball, the Ryan fighter progressed rapidly, and a production contract was awarded on 7 December 1943, six months before the first flight.

Republic F-105D Thunderchief

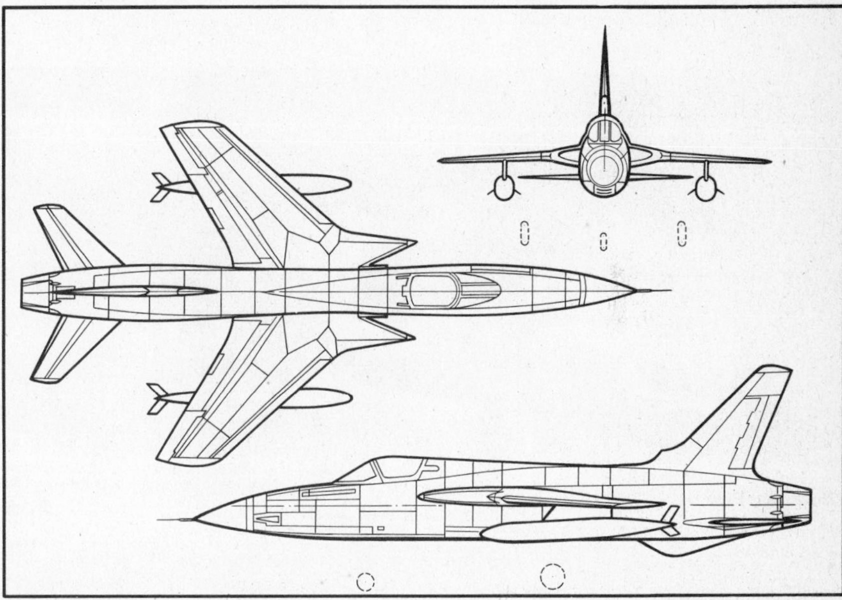
Republic F-105D Thunderchief

Republic F-105F Thunderchief

TYPE	DIMENSIONS span ft	span in	length ft	length in	height ft	height in	WEIGHT max t-o lb	PERFORMANCE max speed mph	at height ft	service ceiling ft	combat range miles	REMARKS
Republic F-84F	33	7	43	5	14	5	28,000	658	20,000	46,000	1,650	
Republic RF-84F	33	7	47	8	15	0	28,000	720	SL	NA	2,200	
Republic F-105B	34	11	63	1	19	8	40,000	1,254	40,000	50,000	2,000	
Republic F-105D	34	11	67	0	19	8	52,546	1,390	36,000	NA	1,840	

Ryan FR-1 Fireball, propeller feathered

Seversky P-35

Seversky 2PA-L

Sikorsky SH-3D Sea King, Spanish Navy

The Fireball was in many ways typical of contemporary practice, being a low-wing monoplane with radial piston engine (a 1,350-hp R-1820-72W Cyclone) in the nose, and a tricycle undercarriage. Use of a laminar-flow aerofoil was an advanced feature for its time; the Fireball was also the first US Navy fighter to have a completely flush-riveted exterior and metal-covered control surfaces. Armament comprised four 0·50-in machine-guns in the wings, with provision for two 1,000-lb bombs. The jet-engine, a 1,600-lb s t General Electric I-16 (later J31) was installed in the fuselage behind the cockpit and was fed by way of air-intakes in the wing-root leading-edges.

First flight of the XFR-1 was made on 25 June 1944, but the jet engine was not installed until the following month. The second prototype flew on 20 September 1944, and production deliveries began in March 1945, to Navy Squadron VF-66, this unit becoming responsible for much of the testing of the type. Production contracts by this time totalled 1,300 FR-1s, but the end of the war against Japan brought cancellation of 634 of the first series of 700, and all 600 on a second contract. All 66 FR-1s built were delivered during 1945, many of them going direct to test centres and the remainder to VF-66. This unit's aircraft and personnel were transferred later to VF-41, which in turn was re-designated VF-1E in 1946.

The only unit to fly the Fireball operationally, VF-1E conducted a number of successful operations on board aircraft carriers and on 6 November 1945 one FR-1 was landed on the USS *Wake Island* on the jet unit alone, after the Cyclone had failed. This was the first "all-jet" landing on an aircraft carrier, albeit in a composite aircraft.

Seversky P-35 and EP-1

A series of design competitions held by the US Army Air Corps in 1935 and 1936 produced a new breed of all-metal low-wing monoplanes with enclosed cockpits and retractable undercarriages. Typical of the new designs was the Seversky SEV-1XP, the second version of a design by Alexander Kartveli and the beginning of a line which produced the Thunderbolt to serve in World War II. The Kartveli design began as a tandem two-seater (the SEV-2XP) but the prototype was rebuilt in single-seat guise for evaluation at Wright Field in August 1935. First powered by an 850-hp Wright R-1820-G5, the SEV-1 was later re-engined with a 950-hp Pratt & Whitney R-1830-9, being re-designated SEV-7.

With the Twin Wasp engine, the Seversky fighter was ordered by the USAAC, which placed a production contract for 77, designated P-35. All but the first aircraft had open wheel fairings and dihedral on the wing; the last of the batch was fitted with a supercharged R-1830-19 engine and redesignated XP-41.

An export model of the design (the EP-1), with an R-1830-45 engine and heavier armament, was ordered by Sweden, three contracts placed in 1939 and 1940 totalling 120 aircraft. Designated J9 by the Swedish Air Force, 60 of these had been delivered by June 1940. The other 60 were requisitioned by the US Government and supplied to the USAAF as P-35As; 48 of them were shipped to the Philippines during 1941, but only eight remained serviceable two days after the Japanese attacks began. The remaining 12 were supplied to Ecuador.

During 1937, Seversky also succeeded in exporting examples of the two-seat version of the design, which had a 1,000-hp R-1820 Cyclone and was designated 2PA-L. Two were sold to the U.S.S.R., with manufacturing rights, and 20 went to Japan in 1938, receiving the Japanese designation A8V1.

Sikorsky SH-3 Sea King

As early as 1945, the US Navy began investigating the possibility of using helicopters in the anti-submarine rôle. The ability to hover motionless over the sea opened up a number of new methods of submarine detection, and in June 1952 orders were placed for a version of the Sikorsky S-55 for operational service with anti-submarine squadrons. Designated HSS-1 and known as "The Hiss", the type was named Seabat and began to reach US Navy units in August 1955. Although it could carry weapons externally, the "Hiss" normally operated only as a search aircraft, using dipping sonar.

To add the full killer capability to that of the hunter in a single helicopter, the US Navy drew up a new weapon system requirement in 1957 which led to design of the Sikorsky S-61. Although deriving much useful experience from the HSS-1, Sikorsky designed a completely new aircraft around two 1,050-shp General Electric T58 shaft-turbine engines – a fact which was not obvious from the original HSS-2 designation but became clear when the first S-61 appeared on 11 March 1959.

Following service trials, the Fleet Introduction Programme began in May 1960 and the first US Navy Squadron, VHS-10, was equipped in September 1961. The designation was changed to SH-3A in June 1962, and a new production version, the SH-3D, began to appear in 1965 with 1,400-shp T58-GE-10 engines replacing the earlier 1,250-shp -8Bs.

Eight helicopters similar to the SH-3A were ordered by the Royal Canadian Navy, designated CHSS-2 and delivered in 1963–4. Eleven SH-3As were ordered by the Japanese Maritime Self-Defence Force in 1962, plus a licence for Mitsubishi to assemble or produce the type. The Italian Navy adopted the SH-3D in 1965 and the Royal Navy ordered a similar version in 1966, to be built under licence by Westland. A distinctive feature of the British machines is a new search radar installation.

Spartan Zeus

The protracted battle of General Chiang Kai-Shek's forces in China, which began long before World War II, led to a steady demand for warplanes and brought a number of companies into the military aircraft field. A typical example was the Spartan company, which had produced a five-seat low-wing monoplane for the US domestic light aircraft market in 1935. Known as the Executive, this was powered by a 400-hp Pratt & Whitney R-985 Wasp radial engine and provided the basis for a hasty conversion, in 1938, to a light-bomber configuration for China.

Three of the cabin seats were removed and replaced by a flexibly-mounted machine-gun in a hatch; two more guns were mounted to fire forward, and a rack for 300 lb of bombs was fitted under the fuselage.

Heartened by their success in selling the Executive to China, Spartan produced, later in 1938, the Zeus, another light bomber with somewhat higher performance. Based on the Executive, the Zeus had the crew of two in tandem beneath a long canopy, and a 500-hp R-1340 Wasp engine. Armament comprised two machine-guns and a 250-lb bomb-load. A small number of Zeus were delivered to Mexico.

Thomas Morse MB-3

Although no fighters of original US design became operational during the 1914–18 War, the official policy of using proven foreign designs to equip the Army Air Corps was reversed in the spring of 1918. One of the companies then invited to design a single-seat fighter which would outperform the French SPADs serving with the Army was the Thomas Morse Aircraft Corporation.

Spartan Zeus

Thomas Morse MB-3A

Thomas Morse MB-3A, General W. B. Mitchell's aircraft

TYPE	DIMENSIONS						WEIGHT	PERFORMANCE				REMARKS
	span ft	span in	length ft	length in	height ft	height in	max t-o lb	max speed mph	at height ft	service ceiling ft	combat range miles	
Ryan FR-1	40	0	32	4	13	11	11,652	404	17,800	43,100	1,620	
Seversky P-35	36	0	25	2	9	1	6,295	282	10,000	30,600	1,150	
Seversky P-35A(EP-1)	36	0	26	10	9	9	6,723	290	12,000	31,400	600	
Seversky 2PA-L	36	0	25	5	9	6	5,952	290	16,500	30,000	NA	
Sikorsky SH-3A	62	0	72	5	16	8	17,768	159	SL	12,800	540	
Spartan Zeus	39	0	27	3	8	6	4,953	234	5,000	29,400	760	

Thomas Morse MB-3A, Boeing revised tail unit

Vought VE-7

Vought FU-1 floatplane

Vought V-80 Corsair

Four prototypes of its MB-3 design were ordered and the first of these flew on 21 February 1919. It was a small and conventional biplane, powered by a 300-hp Wright "H" engine based on the French Hispano-Suiza.

Fifty production MB-3As ordered from Thomas Morse were delivered in 1922 and incorporated numerous refinements and modifications. In particular, the radiator was split in two and mounted on each side of the fuselage, rather than in the top wing, and the two fuselage-mounted 0·30-in guns were faired in.

The MB-3A was accepted as the standard single-seat pursuit for the Army Air Corps in the early 1920s and a further batch of 200 was produced. Under the competitive bidding system then extant, six companies sought the contract, which was awarded to Boeing as the lowest bidder. Valued at nearly $1·5 million, this contract for 200 MB-3As, placed in February 1922, was to prove the largest single purchase of pursuit fighters until 1937.

The Boeing MB-3As were similar in almost all respects to the Thomas Morse machines, but the final 50 had revised tail units with the fin area more than doubled. After some five years of front-line service, in the USA and overseas, a number of MB-3As were assigned to training duties as MB-3Ms.

Vought VE-7SF

The Lewis and Vought VE-7, designed in 1917, was intended as an advanced trainer, but planned large-scale production was terminated in favour of the Curtiss "Jenny" in its JN-4H version. Nevertheless, between 1920 and 1924, the US Navy received 129 VE-7s in several versions, primarily for training duties. With a single machine-gun mounted on the fuselage ahead of the cockpit, the VE-7SF served as a single-seat fighter, some 51 of the total on Navy strength being of this type, including 11 built by the Naval Aircraft Factory. Two squadrons operated the VE-7SF, including Fighter Plane Squadron One, and on 17 October 1922 the first ever take-off from an aircraft carrier in the US Navy – the USS *Langley* – was made by a VE-7SF flown by Lt V. C. Griffin.

Vought FU-1

First procured by the US Navy in 1922, the Vought VO-1 biplane became the standard observation aircraft on board the battleships and cruisers of the fleet for nearly a decade, some 150 being built. In January 1927, a single-seat version appeared as the FU-1 training fighter.

Ordered originally as the VO-3, the FU-1 was an equal-span biplane powered by a 200-hp Wright R-1790. It was operated frequently with a single float (plus wing-tip stabilizers) from catapults on battleships, but was also operable with a conventional wheel chassis.

Twenty FU-1s were built and were used to equip Squadron VF-2B aboard the USS *Langley* in 1927-8. Late in 1928, the 18 surviving FU-1s were converted to two-seat FU-2 trainers and the majority continued in service for utility purposes. While the observation designs were continued by Vought from the VO-1, the FU-1 was a dead-end as a fighter and it was to be another decade before this company produced another.

Vought V-80 Corsair

In its more than two decades of producing fighters and bombers for the US Navy, the Vought company had little success in the export field. An exception was the V-80, a conventional biplane in the Corsair series, sold to Argentina in 1933. Designed as a single-seat naval fighter, it had an enclosed cockpit and interchangeable wheels and floats. It was powered by a 675-hp Pratt & Whitney R-1690 engine and carried an armament of four guns and four 116-lb bombs.

Vought SBU, V-142

Whilst continuing to provide the major part of the US Navy's force of observation and scouting aircraft in the inter-war period, the Vought company was less successful in its efforts to produce a naval fighter. The FU-1 in fact served as little more than a fighter-trainer, and the XF2U-1, related to the Corsair observation biplane, was unsuccessful. The next Vought fighter, the XF3U-1, was ordered in 1932 as a two-seat fighter, potentially a replacement for the famed Curtiss Helldiver.

Armed with one fixed forward-firing and one flexible dorsal gun, and carrying a 500-lb bomb-load, the Vought fighter was redesignated, before service, in a new "SB" Scout-Bomber category, as the XSBU-1. It was powered by a 700-hp R-1535-80 engine, in a long-chord NACA cowl, and a long canopy covered the tandem cockpits. First flight of the XF3U-1 was made on 22 June 1933, and it was later rebuilt, with modifications, as the XSBU-1.

The Navy ordered 84 SBU-1s in January 1935, with R-1535-82 engines, and deliveries began in November of the same year to VS-3B; VS-1 and VS-2 were later re-equipped, and the SBU-1s were still in use in 1940, operating with the Neutrality Patrol. A second batch of 40 aircraft had R-1535-98 engines and were designated SBU-2, for use by Naval Reserve units in 1937–8.

An export version of the Vought fighter-bomber, known as the V-142, went to Argentina.

Vought SB2U, V-156

A further development of the Vought SBU, ordered on 7 February 1935, was virtually the same design with backward-retracting main wheels. Known as the XSB3U-1, it was evaluated at the US Naval Air Station, Anacostia, in the spring of 1936, alongside another new Vought scout bomber, the XSB2U-1. This had been ordered on 11 October 1934, and was the first monoplane scout bomber for the Navy.

A low-wing monoplane of all-metal construction, the XSB2U-1 had upward-folding wings for carrier stowage and followed the pattern of earlier scout bombers in having a pilot and observer in tandem beneath a single long canopy. Another feature typical of the era was the backward-retracting undercarriage, the wheels of which turned through 90° to lie flat in the wing. Armament comprised one fixed and one flexible 0·30-in gun and up to 1,000 lb of bombs. First flight of the prototype was made on 4 January 1936.

On 26 October 1936, the US Navy ordered 54 SB2U-1s with R-1535-96 engines, and these were followed by 58 SB2U-2s. Deliveries began on 20 December 1937, to VB-3, the same unit that had first received the Vought SBU-1s. The R-1535-02 engine was used in the final production batch of 57 SB2U-3s, which were ordered in September 1939, with extra fuel and 0·50-in guns.

Vought secured an export contract for 20 V-156s (similar to the SB2U-2) from France in 1939, and Britain subsequently ordered 50 which went to the Royal Navy with the name Chesapeake. These had four forward-firing guns and British equipment, but proved unsuitable for operation from British carriers.

Vought F4U Corsair

Perhaps the best of all the US fighters used in World War II, and certainly the best naval fighter used in combat, the Vought Corsair had other claims to fame. It remained

Vought SBU-1

Vought SB2U-1 Vindicator

Vought Chesapeake (V-156B-1), RN

TYPE	DIMENSIONS span ft	span in	length ft	length in	height ft	height in	WEIGHT max t-o lb	PERFORMANCE max speed mph	at height ft	service ceiling ft	combat range miles	REMARKS
Thomas Morse MB-3A	26	0	20	0	8	7	2,540	141	SL	19,500	NA	Endurance 2hr 15min
Vought VE-7SF	NA		NA		NA		NA	117	SL	15,000	291	
Vought FU-1	34	4	24	5	8	10	2,409	147	13,000	27,300	430	
Vought V-80	36	0	27	7	10	5	4,597	197	6,000	27,800	760	
Vought SBU-1	33	3	27	9	12	0	5,618	205	8,900	24,400	548	
Vought SB2U-1	42	0	34	0	10	3	7,278	250	9,500	27,400	635	
Vought SB2U-3	42	0	34	0	10	3	9,421	243	9,500	23,600	1,120	

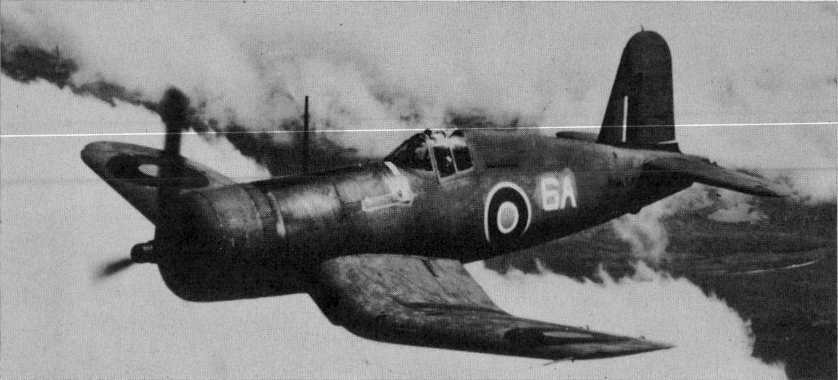

Vought Corsair Mk I (F4U-1), RN

Vought F4U-1A Corsair, with blown canopy and centre-line bomb

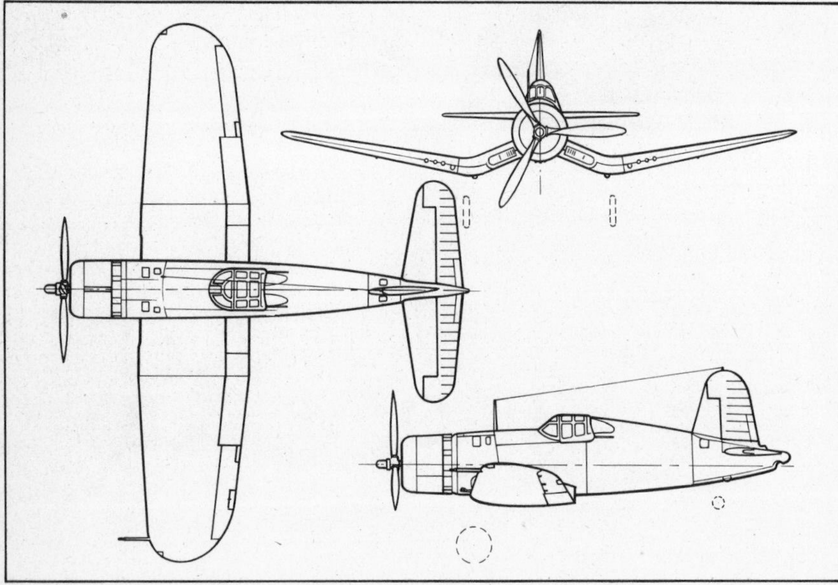
Vought F4U-1 Corsair

Vought F4U-5NL Corsair

in production for a longer period than any other American fighter – 11 years – and it was the last piston-engined fighter in production for the US forces. Official figures credit the Corsair with an 11:1 ratio of kills to losses in combat with Japanese aircraft inWorld War II.

A prototype of the Vought V-166B was ordered on 30 June 1938, after it had been entered for a Navy design contest for a new carrier-based fighter with performance as good as contemporary land-based fighters. The engine was the Pratt & Whitney XR-2800 Double Wasp, rated at 2,000 hp, and armament comprised two 0·50-in guns in the nose and two more in the wings.

Designated XF4U-1, the Vought prototype first flew on 29 May 1940, and five months later achieved 404 mph during a test flight – the first US aircraft to exceed 400 mph in level flight. Production of 584 F4U-1s was authorized on 30 June 1941, but reports of air combat in Europe indicated the need for certain changes in the production model, including heavier armament, self-sealing fuel tanks and armour protection. Fuel tanks, displaced from the wings to accommodate extra guns, were located in the fuselage, this in turn causing the cockpit to be re-located three feet further aft, with adverse effect on the pilot's visibility. The fuselage guns were removed and an R-2800-8 engine replaced the XR-2800-4 that had powered the prototype.

Production deliveries began on 3 October 1942, the first F4U-1 having flown on 2 June. First unit equipped was VF-12; but carrier tests on board the USS *Saratoga* in September 1942 had shown up the aircraft's poor forward visibility and high landing speed, and the Corsair was consequently earmarked for land-based squadrons, primarily those of the Marines. The first such unit, VMF-124, was also the first to take the Corsair into combat at Bougainville on 13 February 1943. Eight Marine squadrons were flying F4U-1s in the Pacific by August 1943, and were joined a month later by land-based Navy squadrons.

The initial Corsair production order was soon increased, to meet the rapidly-expanding requirements of America's war effort, and the VGB programme was initiated, comprising the Vought, Goodyear and Brewster companies as a Corsair manufacturing unit. All three built near-identical models, the Brewster version of the F4U-1 being the F3A-1 and the Goodyear version, with fixed wings, being the FG-1. Seeking to improve forward visibility, Vought fitted a new raised cockpit hood on the 689th F4U-1 and this was also introduced on the Brewster and Goodyear lines. After 1,550 F4U-1s had been built, the R-2800-8W engine with water injection was introduced, together with fittings for a 160-gallon drop tank and two 1,000-lb bombs or eight 5-in rockets under the wings, in a version designated F4U-1D and FG-1D. Another Vought-built variant, the F4U-1C, had four 20-mm cannon in place of the six wing guns.

By late summer 1944, Vought had built 4,102 F4U-1s, Brewster had built 735 F3A-1s and then closed its Johnsonville plant, and Goodyear had built 3,808 FG-1s and -1Ds. Included in these totals were 95 F4U-1s, 510 F4U-1Ds, 430 F3A-1s and 977 FG-1Ds for Britain under lend-lease arrangements,these being designated Corsair I, II, III and IV respectively. A further 370 Corsairs went to the RNZAF. British Corsairs were modified to serve on board British carriers, with 16 in clipped from the wing-tips for below-decks stowage; and Corsair IIs from No. 1834 Squadron, on board HMS *Victorious* became operational in April 1944, nine months before the first US Navy unit to serve at sea.

During 1943, twelve Corsairs were modified as F4U-2s with a small AI radar in a wing-tip radome, and one of these achieved the first radar-guided interception recorded by the US Navy in October 1943. Another modification of rôle produced the camera-carrying F4U-1P in the Pacific area.

Late in 1944, Chance Vought (as the former Vought Sikorsky Division of United Aircraft had been re-named after re-organization) and Goodyear switched to production of a new version of the Corsair, with a 2,100-hp R-2800-18W engine, six 0·50-in guns and numerous detail refinements. Prototypes first flew in April and July; the first production model, an F4U-4, flew on 7 October, and deliveries began on 31 October; the equivalent Goodyear model was the FG-4.

By VJ-Day, with consequent cancellation of outstanding orders, Vought had built, or was building, 2,356 of the -4 series, including 300 F4U-4Cs and a number of radar-equipped versions, including the F4U-4E with APS-4 and F4U-4N with APS-6. Some F4U-4P reconnaissance versions were converted after delivery. Goodyear built 200 FG-4s and five each of the F2G-1 and F2G-2 developed under a March 1944 contract, with the 3,000-hp Pratt & Whitney R-4360-4 engine.

Final wartime development of the Corsair, during 1945, was the XF4U-5 with a 2,450-hp R-2800-32(E) engine, an all-metal wing skin (all the wartime combat versions of the Corsair had fabric-covered main planes) and other improvements which boosted the speed to 462 mph at 31,400 ft. First flight of the XF4U-5 was made on 21 December 1945.

The Corsair production line was re-established, first at Connecticut and then at Dallas, to build 223 F4U-5s, 315 F4U-5Ns and 30 F4U-5Ps. They were followed by 110 AU-1s (originally F4U-6) built for the US Marines for ground-support duties in Korea. Powered by the R-2800-83W engine, rated for low-altitude operation, the AU-1 could carry up to 4,000 lb of bombs or ten rockets. Finally, Chance Vought built 90 F4U-7s for France's Aéronavale; these had R-2800-18W engines for all-altitude operation but were otherwise similar to the AU-1s. Production ended in December 1952 with 12,571 examples of the fighter built.

Corsairs continued in second-line service with the US Navy until the mid-1950s and with the French Navy until the early 1960s. Some surplus F4U-5s passed into service with South American countries in small numbers.

Vought TBU (TBY) Sea Wolf

In an attempt to develop a second torpedo-bomber in the new monoplane category exemplified by the TBF Avenger, the US Navy contracted with Chance Vought on 22 April 1940 for a single prototype designated XTBU-1. Vought had long experience of building scout bombers and observation aircraft for the Navy, and in the XTBU-1 the company ably met the specific requirements for a carrier-based monoplane, with internal stowage for the torpedo and a good performance.

The prototype flew on 22 December 1941, and was a mid-wing monoplane with a long cockpit canopy over the three crew positions – pilot, radio operator and gunner in a dorsal turret with a single 0·50-in gun. Another 0·50-in gun was mounted in the cowling of the 2,000-hp Pratt & Whitney R-2800-20 engine, and there was an 0·30-in gun in a ventral position behind the weapon-bay.

The XTBU-1 demonstrated a top speed of 311 mph, representing a substantial advance on the TBF's performance, and the USN decided to buy the type in quantity. With Chance Vought fully committed to production of the F4U Corsair, arrangements were made with Convair to tackle the production of 1,100 Sea Wolfs, under a contract placed on 6 September 1943, at a new factory in Allentown, Pennsylvania.

Vought F4U-7 Corsair, Aéronavale

Vought AU-1 Corsair

Vought XTBU-1 Sea Wolf

TYPE	DIMENSIONS						WEIGHT	PERFORMANCE				REMARKS
	span ft	span in	length ft	length in	height ft	height in	max t-o lb	max speed mph	at height ft	service ceiling ft	combat range miles	
Vought F4U-1	41	0	33	4	16	1	14,000	417	19,900	36,900	1,015	
Vought F4U-2	41	0	33	4	16	1	13,112	381	23,500	33,900	955	
Vought F4U-4	41	0	33	8	14	9	14,670	446	26,200	41,500	1,005	
Vought F4U-5	41	0	33	6	14	9	15,079	462	31,400	44,100	1,036	
Vought F4U-5N	41	0	34	6	14	9	14,106	470	26,800	41,400	1,120	
Vought AU-1	41	0	34	1	14	9	19,398	238	9,500	19,500	484	
Vought F4U-7	41	0	34	6½	14	9	13,426	450	26,000	NA	NA	
Vought TBY-2(TBU-1)	56	11	39	2½	15	6	18,488	306	13,000	27,200	1,505	

Chance Vought F6U-1 Pirate

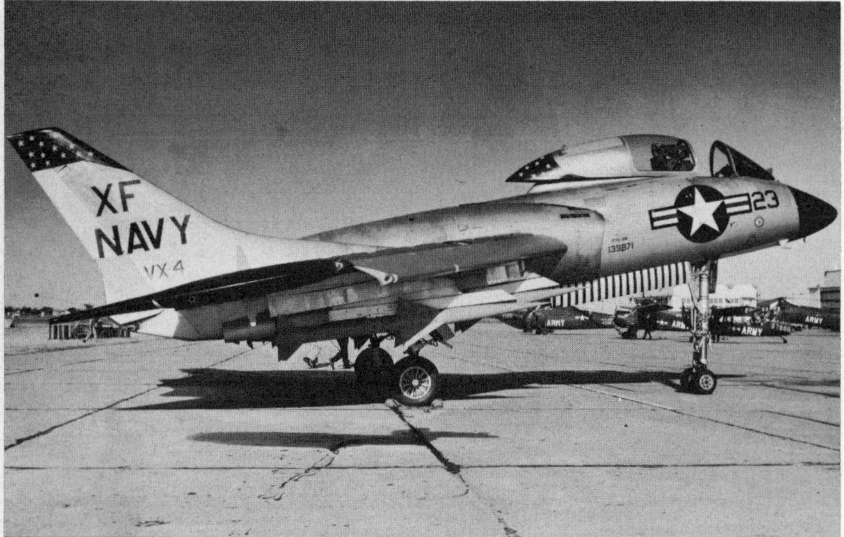

Chance Vought F7U-3M Cutlass, with Sparrow missiles

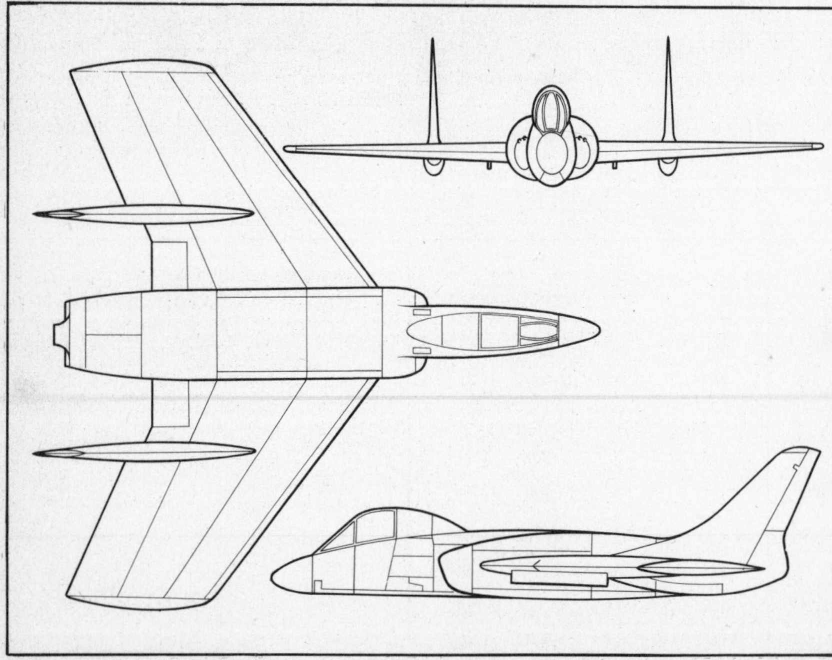

Chance Vought F7U-3 Cutlass

First of the Convair TBY-2s, as the production aircraft were designated, was delivered in November 1944 and the 180th and last in September 1945, when the contract was cancelled. The TBY-2 had three fixed 0·50-in guns, plus the dorsal and ventral armament, and added a radome on the starboard wing. None ever reached an operational unit.

Chance Vought F6U-1 Pirate

Having established an outstanding reputation with its F4U Corsair series of Navy fighters, the Chance Vought Division of United Aircraft turned its attention to a jet-propelled successor in 1944, gaining a USN contract on 29 December for three prototypes of the XF6U-1. The design was unexceptional, making use of a straight wing with root intakes to feed the single Westinghouse J34-WE-22 engine in the comparatively deep fuselage. Tricycle landing gear, drop tanks at the wing-tips and four 20-mm cannon grouped in the nose were all features typical of the state of the designer's art in 1944, but an innovation was the use of Metalite skins, comprising a balsa wood core between thin aluminium sheets.

First flight of the XF6U-1 was made on 2 October 1946, and flight development led to a decision to use an afterburner in the production aircraft – the first USN fighter to have this feature. In April 1948, one of the prototypes was re-engined with a J34-WE-30A engine,with Solar afterburner, and the first production model with the same power plant flew in July 1949.

Thirty F6U-1s were acquired by the USN, the first being delivered in December 1949 to Squadron VX-3, and delivery of the whole batch was completed in three months. Compared with the prototypes, the F6U-1s had longer rear fuselages and more wing area with bigger root fillets. A large dorsal fin was added and small fins were fitted near the tips of the tailplane.

Chance Vought F7U Cutlass

Taking advantage of data on German aeronautical research which became available during 1945, the Chance Vought company laid out designs for a highly unconventional tailless fighter. The wing, of almost parallel chord, had a sweepback of 38 degrees and incorporated elevons and inset fins and rudders. Like a delta-winged design, the Vought design needed an unusually long nose-wheel to achieve the necessary angle of attack for take-off. Power was provided by two Westinghouse J34-WE-32s with afterburners, side-by-side in the rear fuselage. The pilot had a pressurized cockpit and an ejection seat.

Three prototypes of the design were ordered on 25 June 1946, with the designation XF7U-1, and flight testing began on 29 September 1948. Performance included a top speed of 672 mph and was sufficiently promising for production orders to be placed by the US Navy; the first production F7U-1 flew in March 1950. Only 14 were built, these being assigned to the Advanced Training Command at NAS Corpus Christi in January 1952.

Difficulties with the J34 engine and other problems led to an extensive redesign of the Cutlass as the F7U-3, around two 4,600 lb s t J46-WE-8As, and the first of these new models (powered temporarily by J35-A-21A engines) flew on 20 December 1951. The J46 did not become available until 1953, and deliveries of the production-standard F7U-3 began in December 1954. It was assigned to four squadrons–VF-81 and VF-83 in the east, VF-122 and VF-124 in the western US.

The F7U-3 was armed with four 20-mm cannon in the intake fairings, and carried a radar-ranging gunsight. Later, provision was made for four Sparrow I air-to-air missiles on the F7U-3M and a reconnaissance version, the F7U-3P, also went into service. Production of the F7U-3 variants totalled 288, with the final delivery in December 1955. The Cutlass served until the end of 1958.

Vultee V-11, V-12, A-19

One of the few successful American combat aircraft developed for the export market without the prior backing of the US Services, the Vultee V-11 was closely related to the V-1A transport, a 1934 design which served with some airlines until single-engined equipment was banned for commercial use. Exploiting the basic design with a three-seat version, armed with six machine-guns and up to 3,000 lb of bombs, some accommodated internally, Vultee quickly found a market for their light bomber. First deliveries were part of a batch of 30 for China; Turkey ordered 40 and Brazil 26. The U.S.S.R. also purchased examples, and subsequently built versions of the V-11 in Russia. All export models of the V-11 were powered by a Wright Cyclone engine, the actual model and power varying between contracts.

In June 1938, after most of the export orders had been filled, the US Army Air Corps ordered seven examples of the design for service trials, at a time when twin-engined attack bombers were beginning to appear. These V-11s were designated YA-19 and had 1,200-hp Pratt & Whitney Wasp R-1830-17 engines. They achieved no notable success, but were precursors of the Army's Vultee Vengeance dive-bombers which marked the end of a generation of aircraft of this type.

Before the Vengeance appeared, Vultee improved the V-11 by refining the fuselage lines and installing a 900-hp R-1820-G105A. The calibre of two of the four wing guns was increased from 0·30-in to 0·50-in. China ordered 26 of these V-12Cs, and 52 V-12Ds, which had R-2600-A5B engines. Single examples of each were tested in 1940, the rest going to China unassembled.

Vultee P-66 Vanguard

Having succeeded in producing a light bomber for export, the Vultee company turned its attention in 1939 to the single-seat fighter market. The private-venture prototype, known as the Vultee Model 48 Vanguard, flew in September and was notable, in its initial form, for the low-drag cowling around its 1,200-hp Pratt & Whitney R-1830-S4C4-G engine, which was almost completely enclosed and provided with retractable cooling ducts. This produced cooling problems, as well as excessive weight, and the prototype was re-worked eventually to have a more conventional cowling for its radial engine. Armament was intended to comprise ten 0·30-in guns, of which two would be rearward-firing and aimed by mirrors; this idea also was abandoned later.

In February 1940, Vultee won a Swedish contract for 144 Vanguards, but eight months later the US State Department barred export of warplanes to Sweden. Consequently, the Vanguards were assigned to Britain and the first few appeared in RAF markings. Plans to use the aircraft as advanced trainers in Canada were dropped, however, and they were re-assigned to China as part of the lend-lease programme. The USAAF designation P-66 was allocated for lend-lease purposes and a few examples went, apparently, to the USAAF. Total deliveries to China were reported to be 129.

Vultee A-31, A-35 Vengeance

Continuing the line of single-engined light attack-bombers which began with the V-11 and V-12 (see above), Vultee designed the V-72 with the special requirements of dive-bombing in mind. European interest in the true dive-

Chance Vought F7U-3P Cutlass

Vultee V-11

Vultee P-66 Vanguard

TYPE	DIMENSIONS span ft	span in	length ft	length in	height ft	height in	WEIGHT max t-o lb	PERFORMANCE max speed mph	at height ft	service ceiling ft	combat range miles	REMARKS
Vought F6U-1	32	10	35	8	12	11	12,571	600	SL	49,000	730	
Vought F7U-1	38	8	39	7	9	10	16,840	672	20,000	41,400	1,170	
Vought F7U-3	38	8	44	3	14	7	31,642	610	36,000	40,000	660	
Vultee V-11	50	0	37	6	10	0	11,437	229	5,800	23,000	1,225	
Vultee V-12C	50	0	38	2	12	11	12,078	254	18,000	25,200	NA	
Vultee V-12D	50	0	38	2	12	11	12,853	281	11,000	28,000	NA	
Vultee P-66	36	0	28	5	9	5	7,384	340	15,100	28,200	850	

Vultee V-72 Vengeance

Vultee Vengeance IV, RAAF

Anatra VI

bomber preceded by several years official US recognition that such a type could serve a useful purpose, and it was the Royal Air Force that adopted the Vultee design for production in 1940. Named the Vengeance, the V-72 was an angular mid-wing monoplane with internal stowage for 2,000 lb of bombs, and large air-brakes on the wings for control in the dive. The engine was a 1,600-hp Wright R-2600-19.

The initial RAF order for 700 led Vultee to arrange a second production line at the new Northrop factory, where 200 aircraft were to be built. After signing of the Lend-Lease Bill in March 1941, the Army Air Force ordered another 300 for the RAF (200 to be built by Northrop) and the type was then designated A-31. The first 500 Vultee-built V-72s were designated Vengeance II, while those by Northrop were Vengeance I and IA (the latter being lend-lease); the 100 Vultee-built lend-lease models were Vengeance IIIs. All were similar except in small details. At least 243 of the aircraft ordered by Britain went to the USAAF after Pearl Harbor, retaining their V-72 designation; a few A-31s also went to the Army for trial purposes.

With modifications to match USAAF standard requirements, the Vengeance was redesignated A-35A, this version having four 0·50-in guns in the wings and a fifth in the rear cockpit. Vultee built 100, plus 831 A-35Bs with six wing guns and a 1,700-hp R-2600-13 engine. Of this total, 562 were allocated to the RAF and RAAF as Vengeance IVs and 29 went to Brazil.

Little operational use was made of the A-31 and A-35 by the USAAF. Many of the earlier Vengeances were modified by the RAF as target tugs, but the Vengeance IV saw considerable active service in Burma. Its operational career was, however, undistinguished.

U.S.S.R.

Anatra VI

The Zavod A.A. Anatra (A.A. Anatra Works), one of the five largest aircraft firms in Russia during the 1914–18 War, had factories at Odessa and Simferopol in the Ukraine. By 1917, its total monthly production was 80 aircraft, of Nieuport, Voisin and Anatra designs.

The Anatra VI was probably the most unpopular aircraft used by Russian airmen during the 1914–18 War.

It was designed by Lieutenant V. Ivanov in 1915 and was basically a modified Voisin Type 5 two-seat reconnaissance biplane – one of the French designs built by the Anatra Company (also by Duks, Shchetinin and Lebedev) and used widely by the Imperial air force. The designation "VI" indicated Voisin Ivanov.

Ivanov tried to improve the Voisin's maximum speed and rate of climb. In fact, the VI, which was powered by a 150-hp Salmson Canton-Unné, achieved a maximum speed 13 mph higher than that of the French Voisin, and climbed to 2,000 m (6,560 ft) in 5 minutes less. But in getting this improvement, Ivanov had sacrificed lateral stability and the controls were less effective. This was particularly evident when the aircraft was flying slowly.

In appearance, the VI differed from the Voisin only in detail. The fuselage nacelle was deeper; the lower part of the rudder of the cruciform tail unit was shortened; and the aileron area was reduced by having ailerons on the upper wing only. The undercarriage structure does not appear to have been altered, even though the VI was at least 100 lb heavier. As a result, it gave way frequently on landing.

The Anatra company received a contract for 139 VIs, to be delivered between March 1915 and March 1916; but the work was not in fact completed until the middle of 1918.

As a result of his visits to units which had experienced fatal accidents with the VI, Lieutenant Colonel V. M. Tkachev, in his capacity as Inspector of Army Aviation on the South West Front, reported to the Commander-in-

Chief that pilots were suspicious of the VI because lateral stability and control generally were worse than on normal Voisins. He requested that the VI be withdrawn.

Ivanov enlarged the ailerons and strengthened the aircraft, and tested the new VI personally in March 1917. On two test flights, the modified machine reached its ceiling of 2,900 m (9,515 ft) in 38½ minutes; take-off run was 150 yd and landing run 190 yd. Nevertheless, the Commission which had ordered the tests reported that aileron response was poor and that the aircraft "demanded great care and attention from the pilot".

The old prejudices remained and in April 1917, after ten crashes in the 5th Siberian Corps Air Detachment, another Commission stated that construction work by the factory was very careless, poor-quality materials had been used, and some detail points of design, particularly of the undercarriage, had been miscalculated.

In defence of Anatra, it has been claimed that it was the only large Russian aircraft company which did not have its headquarters in St Petersburg or Moscow and, from the point of view of technical advice and standard of personnel, etc, this was regarded as being a handicap.

Owing to shortages of alternative equipment, the VI had to be used in spite of its inadequacies and unpopularity – an unpopularity which spread to the company's other aircraft, particularly the Anatra D. Its armament consisted of a single machine-gun, operated by the observer.

Anatra D

The Anatra D or Anade, like the Lebed' 12, was a two-seat reconnaissance two-bay biplane derived from the German Albatros, but was smaller than the Lebed. The designation Anatra D indicates that the designer was Dekar – and the aircraft was, in fact, sometimes known as Anatra Dekar. The first Anades were powered by the 100-hp Gnome Monosoupape which gave a maximum speed of only 78 mph, but manoeuvrability and climb were said to be good, the time taken to climb to 2,000 m (6,560 ft) being 16½ minutes. On 26 April 1916, after being approved by the Central Military Technical Board, 80 production models were ordered.

When the Anade went into service with Corps Squadrons in the summer of 1916, it inherited the unfortunate reputation of the Anatra VI, and airmen were quick to criticize it for its sensitive controls and tendency to nose-dive when gliding. One of the steps taken by the firm to overcome these faults was to fit a more powerful engine and, powered by a 130-hp Clerget rotary, the new version became known as the Anatra Cler.

As a result of a conference on defence in October 1916, the Anatra company received an order for 400 Anatra Ds, of which 250 were to be built at Odessa and 150 at Simferopol, at a price of 12,000 roubles (£1,333) each. The Simferopol factory, which itself had just been completed, was to have produced 25 Anatra Ds per month between January and June 1917, but deliveries did not, in fact, start until the middle of 1917, at a rate of 15-20 aircraft per month. A further contract for 300 aircraft was awarded to the firm during the latter part of 1917, but in spite of these large orders it is thought that only about 200 Anatra Ds were completed.

In June 1917, six Anatra Ds newly delivered to the 4th Artillery Air Detachment crashed. To overcome

Anatra D

TYPE	DIMENSIONS						WEIGHT	PERFORMANCE				REMARKS
	span		length		height		max t-o	max speed	at height	service ceiling	combat range	
	ft	in	ft	in	ft	in	lb	mph	ft	ft	miles	
Vultee A-31 (Vengeance I)	48	0	39	9	15	4	14,300	275	11,000	22,500	700	
Vultee A-35	48	0	39	9	15	4	15,600	273	11,000	21,500	600	
Vultee A-35B	48	0	39	9	15	4	17,100	279	13,500	22,300	550	
Anatra VI	48	2¾	31	2	NA		2,646	77·7	NA	11,482	3½ hr	Development of Voisin. About 150 built
Anatra D	37	8¾	25	3	NA		1,907	82	NA	13,123	3½ hr	205 completed

Anatra DS

Anatra DS

Anatra DS

Archangelskii Ar-2

opposition to the aircraft resulting from accidents of this sort, the commander of the 11th Army Air Detachment, Staff Captain Makarov, on 31 May 1917, publicly carried out aerobatics, including two consecutive loops, on a 100-hp Gnome-engined Anade which had flown 60 hours on operations. Twenty-two pilots, observers and mechanics signed a statement in support of the achievement. And from the South West Front, Colonel V. M. Tkachev reported to his headquarters that the Anade was, in the opinion of squadron commanders, quite satisfactory although power was lost through poor engine cooling. The moral seemed to be that provided the Anade was handled with respect it would not give trouble.

In the meantime, however, supplies of raw materials had become scarce and the air force agreed to an Anatra request to make the wing spars in two halves, glued together over a 12-in joint which was wrapped with glued linen. One result of this was the fatal accident of the French Anatra works pilot Lieutenant Robinet and his mechanic Omelin. On 17 July 1917, they took off in a Clerget-engined Anade and performed aerobatics over Odessa; during a loop, the port lower wing broke and the aircraft went into a spin and crashed.

Armament of the Anade was a single 7·62-mm machine-gun, on the observer's ring mounting.

Anatra DS

The final version of the Anatra D was the Anatra DS, or Anasal, powered by a 150-hp Salmson-Canton-Unné nine-cylinder water-cooled radial engine. Even this increase in power did not make the Anasal faultless – possibly due to the close-fitting cowling, the engine often overheated and caught fire. Nevertheless, about 80 aircraft of this type were completed by the Anatra factories.

During the Revolution and Civil War a number of Anasals, along with other types, flown by pilots of Czechoslovak origin, joined the Czechoslovak legions which, after fighting for a time on the side of the White Russians, battled their way past the Reds, across Siberia to freedom. In this way, several Anasals eventually reached Czechoslovakia where, fitted with dual controls, they were used as trainers. Three served the West Bohemian Aero Club at Plzen in this capacity for some years during the 1920s, and one survivor found its way into the National Technical Museum at Prague.

The Anasal was a two-bay braced biplane of wooden construction. The slightly sweptback (4·5°) wings had two main spars and were fabric-covered. Ailerons were fitted to the upper wings only. Some Anasals had unstaggered wings; most, however, had 4 inches of back stagger. Wing area was 398·3 sq ft – an increase of 21·5 sq ft over the Anade.

The fuselage, which was of wooden construction, was covered with aluminium from the engine cowling to the front undercarriage strut; the rest was fabric-covered. The radiators were attached to the front struts of the cabane and were also of aluminium. The undercarriage was made from steel tube, with shock-absorption by rubber cord.

The tail unit consisted of a fabric-covered steel-tube frame. The fin leading-edge was usually slightly rounded, but some early Anasals had straight fins.

Armament comprised one fixed, synchronized 7·62-mm Vickers machine-gun mounted on the fuselage and firing through the propeller disc, and a 7·62-mm Lewis machine-gun on a ring mounting.

Archangelskii Ar-2(SB-RK)

Known originally as the SB-RK, this development of the SB-2*bis* was redesignated Ar-2 under the new Soviet designation system introduced in 1940. The "Ar" stood for the first syllable of the name of its designer, A. A. Archangelskii, whose team finished the design in 1938-9.

Two M-105R engines, fitted with two-stage compressors, provided 1,100 hp each for take-off, as against the 960 hp provided by the M-103 engines of the SB-2*bis*. The wing area of the Ar-2 was 86 sq ft less than that of its predecessor. Two fence-type air-brakes were fitted under the wings to equip the Ar-2 for dive-bombing.

The nose gunner's position was extensively modified as compared with the SB-2 series. In place of twin 7·62-mm ShKAS machine-guns capable of only limited movement in the horizontal plane, the Ar-2 had one 7·62-mm machine-gun with an improved field of fire, installed in a redesigned, extensively-glazed nose. In addition, single 7·62-mm ShKAS weapons were flexibly mounted in dorsal and ventral positions. The bomb-bay could accommodate six 220-lb bombs or two 551-lb bombs or a single 1,102-lb bomb. There was also provision for up to 1,102-lb of bombs on underwing racks.

Tunnel-type radiators for the Ar-2's M-105R engines were enclosed within the wing profile, with air inlets in the leading-edges of the wings and outlets on the upper surface just behind the rear spar. This feature of the Ar-2 resulted in a considerable reduction in drag.

Ar-2s saw action in some numbers following the German invasion of the Soviet Union in 1941.

Archangelskii Ar-2

Beriev MBR-2

In the decade before World War II, G. M. Beriev proved himself a successful designer of naval aircraft. The MBR-2 was built under his direction in 1931. It was powered initially by a water-cooled 550-hp M-17, which was replaced in the later MBR-2*bis* by the 750-hp M-34.

The MBR-2 was a high-wing monoplane with a single fin and rudder. The pusher engine was raised above the hull on a pair of "N" struts. The pilot was accommodated in an enclosed cabin and there were open gunners' cockpits in bow and dorsal positions. Armament comprised three movable 7·62-mm machine-guns. Late production machines had a manually-operated gun turret in place of the open dorsal cockpit. A 660-lb load of bombs, mines or depth charges could be carried on underwing racks.

The wings of the MBR-2 were of all-metal construction. The hull, which had a double step, was of wood. The ability with which the aircraft performed a multitude of tasks was increased by the ease with which it could be converted to operate on skis or a wheel undercarriage.

The good stability, and outstanding visibility enjoyed by the crew, made the MBR-2 popular with naval pilots. Its range with 1,190 lb of fuel was 596 miles; with 1,852 lb of fuel this could be increased to 932 miles.

A civil version, designated MP-2, carried eight passengers and was also built in numbers for service on Soviet air routes.

More than 1,300 aircraft of the MBR-2 and MBR-2*bis* series were built over a long period, stretching right into the early stages of World War II. They saw widespread service in every theatre of Soviet naval operations throughout the war, as bombers, reconnaissance machines and on convoy escort duties.

Beriev MBR-2

Beriev MBR-2

Beriev KOR-1

A programme for the reorganization and modernization of the Soviet Navy was laid down during the Soviet First Five-Year Plan. Naval units of pre-Revolution vintage were overhauled and refitted, and their combat potential was improved. This modernization included the installation of catapults on battleships and cruisers, for reconnaissance seaplanes which were intended to reconnoitre the area around the ship, to direct long-range

TYPE	DIMENSIONS span ft	span in	length ft	length in	height ft	height in	WEIGHT max t-o lb	PERFORMANCE max speed mph	at height ft	service ceiling ft	combat range miles	REMARKS
Anatra DS	40	7	26	6¾	10	5½	2,566	89·5	SL	14,107	3½ hr	About 100 built
Archangelskii Ar-2	59	0⅝	40	8¼	NA		14,660 15,873	295·1 284·6[3]	16,404 13,779[3]	32,808	932[1] 1,305[2] 621[3]	[1] At 199 mph [2] At 193 mph [3] With 2204 lb bomb load
Beriev MBR-2	62	4	44	3⅜	NA		9,220	121·1	NA	NA	NA	With M-17 engine
Beriev MBR-2*bis*	62	4	44	3⅜	NA		NA	136·7	NA	16,404	596-932	With M-34 engine

Beriev KOR-1

Beriev Be-6

Beriev Be-10

gunfire and to perform light bombing and liaison missions. On completion of their tasks the seaplanes were hoisted back on board their parent ship by means of a crane.

The preoccupation of Soviet design bureaux with work on basic aircraft types precluded them from producing the required catapult seaplanes within the time stipulated by the Naval authorities. The German Heinkel HD 55 single-engined catapult flying-boat accordingly entered Soviet naval service, with the designation KR-1.

Not until 1934–5 was it possible for G. M. Beriev's team to design aircraft of the kind required. They then produced a single-bay single-float biplane with I-struts. Its metal airframe was covered with fabric, except for the forepart of the fuselage which was skinned with duralumin. The floats were also of duralumin. Power was provided by a 750-hp nine-cylinder M-25 radial engine, driving a three-bladed constant-speed propeller.

The floatplane was designated KOR-1 and was armed with two 7·62-mm ShKAS machine-guns, positioned in projecting fairings on top of the centre-section of the upper wing. Another 7·62-mm ShKAS gun was carried on a flexible mounting in the rear cockpit, for use by the observer.

KOR-1s entered service in 1938 and, apart from catapult operations, were utilized for coastal reconnaissance and as air observation posts for coastal artillery. When Hitler attacked the Soviet Union, the type was already obsolete and scheduled for replacement by the single-engined KOR-2(Be-2) monoplane flying-boat. However, in the period of the initial onslaught, Soviet naval aviation suffered from a grave shortage of combat landplanes. In this emergency, all airworthy KOR-1s were put on wheel undercarriages and were used for ground attack, mainly against the Rumanian Army on the Black Sea Front. According to Soviet naval pilots, the landplane version was one of the ugliest machines of all times. In fact, the story goes that its appearance was so freakish that Rumanian fighter pilots neglected to open fire, just staring in amazement!

Beriev Be-6

Designed by Georgi Mikhailovich Beriev, the Be-6 (NATO code-name "Madge") is a twin-engined reconnaissance and anti-submarine flying-boat, powered by two ASh-73 radial engines of 2,000 hp each, and carrying a crew of eight. It joined A-VMF (Naval Air Squadrons) in the early 1950s. It is employed mainly on local reconnaissance and patrol work in the Black Sea, Baltic Sea and Pacific and Arctic Oceans. Original mine-laying duties have probably been taken over by the newer M-12 (Be-12).

Under combat conditions the Be-6 is likely to be highly vulnerable, but to help offset this, defensive armament comprises 20-mm cannon in nose and dorsal positions and a remotely-controlled tail gun turret. A load of about 2–3 tons of bombs, mines, depth charges, torpedoes, and other stores can be carried on racks beneath the wings, immediately outboard of the engines.

There is a retractable radome under the rear of the hull and MAD (magnetic anomaly detectors) are fitted on some aircraft to aid submarine detection.

Beriev Be-10

Similar in hull shape to the US Marlin, the Be-10 (NATO code-name "Mallow") was designed by G.M. Beriev's bureau. It is a long-range maritime reconnaissance aircraft, and, being the only turbojet-driven flying-boat in service in the world, was one of the biggest surprises of the 1961 Soviet Aviation Day display at Tushino.

It is powered by two Type AL-7PB turbojets of 14,330-lb s t each, and a spray fence is mounted each side of the nose to prevent water entering the engine intakes. Armament comprises twin 23-mm cannon in a radar-directed but manned tail turret. None of the Be-10s has been seen carrying visible attack weapons. This may imply a rotating weapon-door in the bottom of the hull, but it seems logical to expect such an aircraft to carry anti-shipping missiles, homing torpedoes, depth charges, mines or rockets on underwing pylons.

A fighter-type canopy covers the flight deck and there is an observation position in the extreme nose. High-set "gull" wings have a short centre-section with dihedral, and sharply-sweptback outer panels, each with two boundary-layer fences. Marked anhedral on the outer wings permits the non-retractable stabilizing floats to be mounted on the wing-tips on shallow fairings. The large single-step hull provides ample space for fuel and crew comfort on long flights.

Several records have been established by the Be-10. On 7 August 1961, pilot Nikolai Andrievsky, with navigator and radio operator, set up an international speed record for seaplanes by averaging 566·69 mph (912 kmh) over a 15/25-km course. On 3 September 1961, a Be-10 covered a 1,000-km closed circuit at 544·56 mph with a payload of 11,023 lb. It set up records also in the no-payload, 1,000-kg and 2,000-kg categories. In the same month it lifted an 11,023-lb payload to a record height of 46,135 ft, qualifying also for international records with 1,000-kg and 2,000-kg payloads; a 22,046-lb payload to 41,775 ft; 33,069-lb payload to 39,360 ft and a maximum of 33,523 lb to 6,562 ft. Finally, it set up a seaplane altitude record (without payload) of 49,088 ft. All of the last 11 records were set up by Georgi Buryanov and a crew of two.

Beriev Be-12 Chaika (Seagull)

Successor to the Be-6, this amphibious anti-submarine patrol aircraft (NATO code-name "Mail") has two AI-20 turboprop engines of 4,000 shp each, mounted in nacelles on the high-set "gull" wings and driving four-bladed propellers. Stabilizing floats are mounted near the wing-tips. The undercarriage is of the tail-wheel type, the main gear retracting through 180° into the sides of the fuselage, while the tail-wheel retracts upwards into the stern. MAD (magnetic anomaly detector) equipment is housed in the tail "sting".

Under the service designation M-12, an amphibian of this type was used to establish six officially-recognized international height records in Class C.3 Group II, for turboprop-powered amphibians, during the period 23–7 October 1964. These were for an altitude of 39,977 ft without payload, altitude of 37,290 ft with payload of 1,000 kg and 2,000 kg, altitude of 35,055 ft with 5,000-kg payload, altitude of 30,682 ft with 10,000-kg payload, and maximum payload of 22,266 lb lifted to a height of 6,560 ft. In each case, the crew consisted of M. Mikhailov, I. Kouprianov and L. Kuznetsov.

Chetverikov MDR-6

In 1936, the poor performance of the MDR-4 then in naval service led to several teams being allocated the urgent task of designing a new fast long-range reconnaissance flying-boat. The MDR-6 prototype was built in TsAGI to the design of J. V. Chetverikov. It first flew in 1938 and series production began in the following year.

The MDR-6 was an all-metal monoplane, with gull wings and a single fin and rudder. Nacelles for the two M-63 engines were set above the leading-edges of the wings at a sharp angle of attack. They gave the aircraft an exceptional performance, which included a maximum speed of 223.1 mph. Loaded weight was 14,990 lb and ceiling 28,525 ft. A considerable improvement on these figures was achieved by the MDR-6A, a modified version

Beriev Be-10

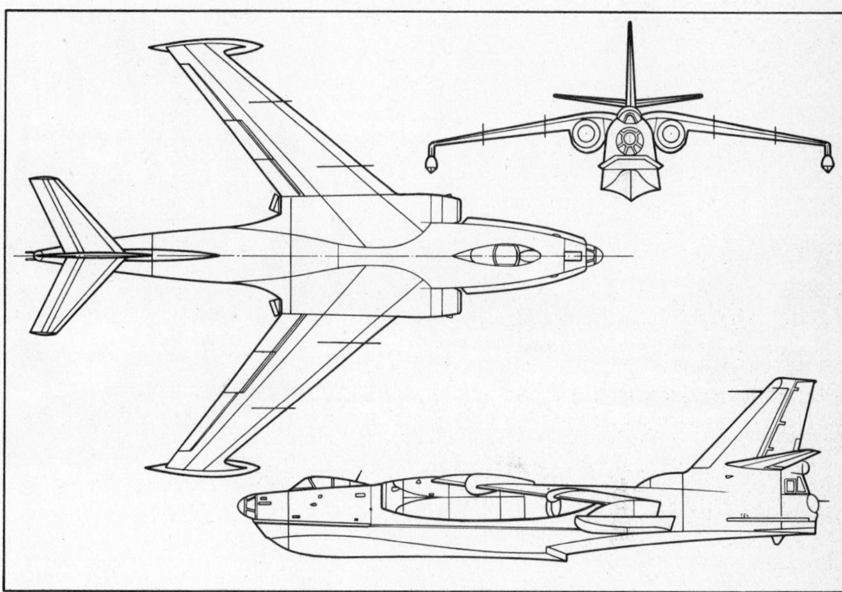

Beriev Be-10

Beriev Be-12 Chaika

TYPE	DIMENSIONS span ft	span in	length ft	length in	height ft in	WEIGHT max t-o lb	PERFORMANCE max speed mph	at height ft	service ceiling ft	combat range miles	REMARKS
Beriev KOR-1	36	1⅛	29	0⅜	NA	5,030	147·9	7,217	24,113	385	Standard catapult float biplane
Beriev Be-6	108	3¼	84	0 (approx)	NA	51,588	258	7,875	NA	3,045	Minimum flying speed 96 mph
Beriev Be-10	98	0 (approx)	132	0 (approx)	NA	100,000 (approx)	470	25,000 (approx)	45,000	1,000 (radius)	
Beriev Be-12	108	3¼	NA		NA	NA	NA	NA	NA	NA	Amphibian. AI-20 turboprops

Chetverikov MDR-6

de Havilland R-1

with VK-105 in-line engines, each developing 1,050 hp. The prototype was produced in 1941, with a revised tail unit incorporating twin fins and rudders; but this version was built only in small numbers as the VK-105 engines were needed to power single-seat fighters. An alternative designation for the MDR-6A was MDR-8.

The MDR-6B, a simplified MDR-6A, was built in considerable numbers from 1944, when the volume of VK-105 engine production was sufficient to allow larger allocations to flying-boat production. The retractable wing-tip floats which had been a feature of MDR-6A were abandoned and the MDR-6B reverted to the fixed, strutted floats which had characterized the first production machines.

Defensive armament comprised four 7·62-mm machine-guns. There were manually-operated nose and dorsal gun turrets. Underwing racks could carry bombs, depth charges, mines or torpedoes in various weight combinations up to a total of 1,320 lb.

In its several versions, the MDR-6 served with naval aviation detachments in every sphere of activity from 1939 right through World War II and on into the mid-1950s.

de Havilland R-1

From 1922 onward, the USSR made every effort to replace the obsolete 1914–18 War aircraft then in service with new machines, preferably of Russian manufacture. Nevertheless, the government was forced to purchase some 300 foreign reconnaissance biplanes, including Fokkers from Holland and Ansaldos from Italy. At the same time, N. N. Polikarpov directed work on a Soviet version of the D.H.9A and two production prototypes were ready by the autumn of 1923.

This two-seat two-bay biplane, with the new military designation R-1, went into immediate series production and output rose steadily during the winter of 1923–4. A variety of foreign engines were utilized for these early models, but the standard power plant in later years was the Soviet-built version of the Liberty engine, the M-5.

Several outstanding long-distance flights were accomplished on R-1s, including a mass flight from Moscow to Pekin, which ended on 17 July 1925. Mikhail Gromov, who had participated in the flight, then flew on to Tokyo in his R-1 by three long stages. In 1926, the R-1 took part in other long-distance and mass flights to Turkey and Persia. A. P. Mezhraup covered a distance of 1,205 miles in a flying time of 11 hours 16 minutes during a long-distance flight from Moscow to Ankara, via Sevastopol and Kharkov.

The R-1 closely resembled the D.H.9A externally, but had an improved payload/weight ratio of 35 per cent, as against 33.5 per cent for the original D.H.9A. Over 2,800 were produced by Soviet factories and remained standard Soviet Air Force equipment for many years, surviving well into the 1930s. Armament comprised a single forward-firing synchronized PV-1 machine-gun and two DA-2 guns of the same calibre on the rear cockpit mounting. Light bombs were carried on racks beneath the wings.

Grigorovich I-2

D.P. Grigorovich began design work on the I-2 single-seat fighter biplane in the summer of 1924. In September of that year, A.I. Zhukov flew the prototype for the first time.

The I-2 was of composite construction, with a 400-hp M-5 water-cooled engine. It was a single-bay biplane with "I"-type interplane struts, braced with streamline wires. The monocoque fuselage was of plywood.

A number of defects were soon apparent. The cockpit was cramped and the armament badly laid out. The pilot had only limited visibility and had great difficulty in pulling out of a flat spin. Testing by pilots Zhukov, M.M. Gromov and A.F. Anisimov continued and, as a result, the 1-2 was substantially modified. The new version, known as the I-2*bis*, had considerably improved aerodynamic qualities. The tail surfaces were revised to achieve better handling characteristics, taking on a more angular aspect. The pilot's cockpit was enlarged and he had the benefit of much improved visibility.

The I-2 and I-2*bis* were produced in quantity for Soviet fighter units, a total of 200 being built. Two fixed forward-firing synchronized 7·62-mm machine-guns were standard armament.

Production of the I-2 and I-2*bis* lasted from 1925 until 1928 and they had the distinction of being the first Soviet-designed single-seat fighters to leave the State factories in large numbers. The organization of series production of these domestic designs was regarded as a major achievement on the part of the infant aviation industry, inasmuch as it reduced the degree of dependence on foreign machines.

On 1 April 1925, M.V. Frunze was able to sign an order, under the authority of the Revolutionary Council of the Republic, removing all obsolete and foreign fighters from first-line service status.

Grigorovich TSh-2 (TsKB-21)

The Soviet ground-attack aircraft which gained world-wide fame during World War II were preceded by a number of pioneer projects and prototypes dating back to the early 1930s.

Only one of these, the TSh-2 of 1931, achieved sufficient success to warrant limited production. A batch of ten was produced.

As early as 1924, the Technical Research Committee of the VVS (Soviet Air Force) had prepared a technical and tactical specification for a ground-attack aircraft, but the lack of a sufficiently powerful engine prevented practical development at that time.

In 1930, the Tsentralnoye Konstruktorskoye Byuro (TsKB) set about designing two-seat ground-attack aircraft based on the R-5 and powered by an M-17 engine. Four experimental aircraft were built in the TsKB under the supervision of D.P. Grigorovich. The first of these was started as the LSh (meaning light ground-attack) or TsKB-5, which was to have had its BMW VI engine totally enclosed in armour. The two cockpits were to be covered by an armoured canopy, with observation louvres and a periscope.

In the event, the excessive weight of the armour led to conversion of the uncompleted LSh as the first prototype of the TsKB-6 or TSh-1 ("TSh" for heavy ground attack), which made its initial flights on a ski undercarriage in February 1931, piloted by Piontkowski and Bucholz. The armour was simpler than on the LSh and the cockpits were open. Armament comprised eight PV-1 7·62-mm machine-guns, four under each lower wing, in detachable gun packs. Three prototypes were built to test different methods of constructing the armour – by welding, bolting and riveting – and different methods of engine cooling – by water or ethyl-glycol.

The final version of TSh-1 had a bolted armour "box" and a water-cooled M-17 engine.

At the end of 1931, the production version of the TsKB-6, designated TSh-2 or TsKB-21, was developed. Even at that early stage in assault-plane development, the designers had attempted to incorporate the armour into the structure of the aircraft, thus reducing the

Grigorovich I-2

Grigorovich I-2*bis*

Grigorovich TSh-1

TYPE	DIMENSIONS						WEIGHT	PERFORMANCE				REMARKS
	span		length		height		max t-o	max speed	at height	service ceiling	combat range	
	ft	in	ft	in	ft	in	lb	mph	ft	ft	miles	
Chetverikov MDR-6	64	11½	48	2¾	NA		14,990	223·7	NA	28,527	NA	With M-63 engines
Chetverikov MDR-6A	64	11½	48	2¾	NA		16,540	267·1	NA	39,370	NA	With VK-105 engines
Chetverikov MDR-6B	64	11½	48	2¾	NA		26,500	236·1	NA	39,370	NA	With VK-105 engines
de Havilland R-1	45	8⅜	30	0⅝	NA		2,290	110	NA	13,123	NA	
Grigorovich I-2*bis*	35	5¼	24	0⅛	9	10⅛	3,421	150·3 134·2	SL 16,404	20,341 NA	NA NA	160 mph attained in factory testing with different propeller
Grigorovich TSh-2	50	10½	NA		NA		NA	133·6	NA	NA	NA	Design bureau TsKB-21

Grigorovich TSh-1, ski landing gear

Grigorovich PI-1

Ilyushin DB-3, captured aircraft, Finnish markings

"dead weight" of the armour. The TSh-2 differed from its predecessor in housing the machine-guns in the specially thickened lower wings instead of in gun packs. The upper wings of the TSh-2 were identical with those of the R-5, but the lower wings were of slightly larger span.

Further ground-attack machines were developed. The ShON of 1931 was an unarmoured aircraft with folding wings, enabling it to be transported by train to the intended scene of operations, in the troubled area of Turkestan. But the revolt by tribesmen in that area petered out before the ShON was ready for use. The TShB differed from all the other designs in that it carried bombs, but this feature, in particular, contributed to its poor performance.

The TSh-3 was a single-engined low-wing monoplane with a fixed, trousered undercarriage. None of these later types passed the prototype stage; so, only the TSh-2 registered a limited success in the *Shturmovik* field, a decade before its renowned descendant of World War II, the Ilyushin Il-2.

Grigorovich PI-1 (DG-52)

In the early 1930s, availability of a large-bore recoilless cannon of Soviet design led to the development of specialized fighters capable of utilizing this new weapon. After several years of experiment, with a number of prototypes, the PI-1 (Bureau number DG-52) of D.P. Grigorovich was the only design to enter limited production, attaining service status in 1934.

Early tests in 1931 were carried out with a modified Tupolev I-4 and the TsKB-7, both armed with a 67-mm recoilless cannon, which ejected the spent cartridges to the rear. At a meeting held on 19 December 1931, it was decided to continue cannon fighter development along two lines: light fighters to carry two 67/75-mm guns, and heavier types armed with two 100/150-mm cannon. Three new prototypes flew in 1934–5; these were the ANT-23 (I-12), a twin-boom heavy fighter with two engines in tandem; the two-seat twin-engined ANT-29 (DIP); and the single-seat PI-1, which was armed with two 75-mm APK cannon, fitted beneath the wings, and a single synchronized ShKAS machine-gun. This latter machine was a low-wing monoplane with retractable undercarriage, powered by an M-25 radial engine. Maximum speed in level flight was 255 mph (410 kmh), which was attained at 6,850 ft (3,000 m).

The APK cannon installation proved unreliable and unsafe. Furthermore, its low rate of fire and small supply of heavy shells was inadequate to sustain an effective burst of fire under combat conditions. Since this offered little chance of hitting the target, use of the APK cannon was abandoned.

The PI-1 had its heavy guns replaced by two 20-mm ShVAK cannon in 1936. This weapon had a high rate of fire and a large reserve of ammunition, but the PI-1 thus equipped was inferior in performance to the identically-armed I-16, then being produced in series. The Grigorovich fighter was, accordingly, taken off the assembly lines.

An experimental development of the basic design was flown under the designation PI-4.

Ilyushin DB-3 (TsKB-30)

Late in 1933, two Soviet design teams began work to meet an official requirement for a long-range twin-engined bomber. P.O. Sukhoi headed a group from A.N. Tupolev's design bureau and S.V. Ilyushin led TsKB team No. 3.

Sukhoi's team set out to produce a twin-engined machine which, aerodynamically, would follow their earlier single-engined record-breaking ANT-25. The resulting ANT-37 (military designation DB-2) appeared in 1935 and reached a top speed of only 186 mph at sea level and 211 mph at its service ceiling. The elongated high aspect wings of the DB-2 helped to reduce the so-called "induced drag", but when the aircraft was flown at a higher speed another kind of drag, known as "profile drag", increased.

At its maximum speed, the DB-2 vibrated violently at certain altitudes, and this shortcoming led to the crash of the first prototype in June 1935, during its official trials. Modifications to the second prototype reduced tail surface vibration and it was able to accomplish a non-stop flight from Moscow to Omsk and back, covering 3,078 miles in 23 hours 20 minutes. Cruising speed, however, was only 132·5 mph and the DB-2 did not go into production. Nevertheless, in September 1938, a crew of three Soviet airwomen used the prototype, then named *Rodina*, to set up an officially recognized international distance record of 3,695 miles which remained unbeaten for 15 years.

Trials of the TsKB-26, created by S. V. Ilyushin and his team, began in 1935. With the same range as the DB-2, it achieved a much higher speed. The DB-3, to give its military designation, had a higher wing loading than its rival and its wings had a much lower aspect ratio. It could cruise at 199 mph at 15,000 ft, and its range with a 1,100-lb bomb-load was 2,485 miles.

Although quite a heavy aircraft, the DB-3 was highly manoeuvrable and one example was looped at a Tushino Air Display by test pilot V. K. Kokkinaki. Following successful trials, the second variant of the DB-3, bearing the design bureau designation TsKB-30, was accepted by the Soviet Air Force. The first production DB-3s were delivered in 1937 and output rose steadily from then onward.

The DB-3 was a cantilever low-wing monoplane of all-metal construction, with the exception of fabric covering on the tail control surfaces.

The crew numbered three; defensive armament comprised three movable 7·62-mm ShKAS machine-guns, one each in manually-operated nose and dorsal turrets and a third in a ventral position, firing through a trap in the fuselage floor.

The main undercarriage units retracted backward into the engine nacelles, leaving the wheels partially exposed. Up to 4,850 lb of bombs could be carried. The bomb-bay could accommodate three 1,100-lb or two 2,200-lb bombs, with additional bombs attached to external racks when shorter-range missions were to be flown.

The DB-3 was the mainstay of the Soviet long-range bomber force for a number of years. As part of a continuous programme of development, the 765-hp M-85 radial engines which powered the prototypes and early production machines were replaced after a time by M-86 engines of 960 hp each.

The DB-3 saw active service during World War II against Finland and, in the early period of the war, against Germany.

Ilyushin Il-2

Russia's immense efforts to develop an effective low-level ground-attack aircraft were concentrated eventually on a design by the Ilyushin team. In 1938, the two-seat prototype TsKB-55 or BSh-2 ("BSh" = *Bronirovannii Shturmovik* or Armoured Attacker) appeared, powered by an AM-35 liquid-cooled engine. The most striking

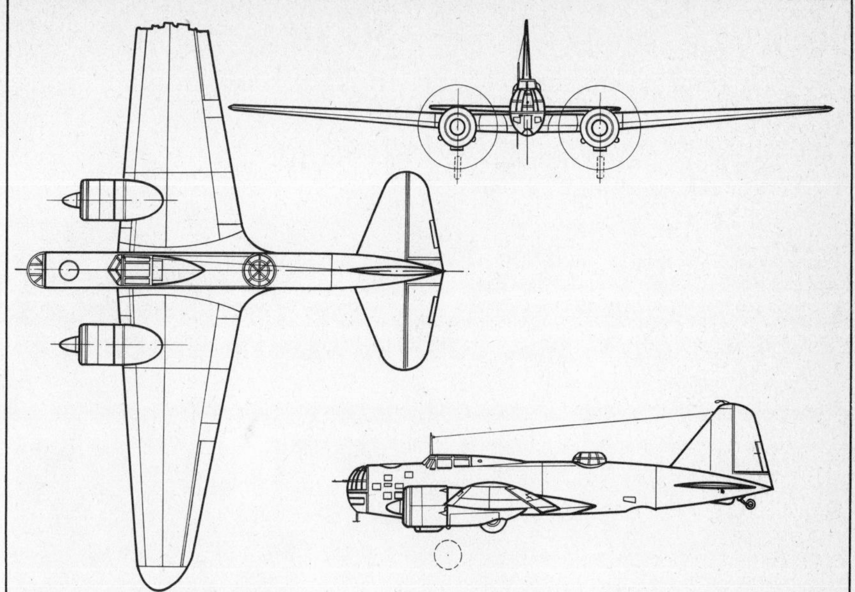

Ilyushin DB-3

Ilyushin Il-2, single-seat version

TYPE	DIMENSIONS span ft in	length ft in	height ft in	WEIGHT max t-o lb	PERFORMANCE max speed mph	at height ft	service ceiling ft	combat range miles	REMARKS
Grigorovich PI-1	NA	NA	NA	NA	270	NA	NA	NA	
Ilyushin DB-3	70 2½	46 11	NA	20,626	242·3	15,091	27,558	2,485[1]	[1] With 1,102-lb bomb load, cruising at 198·8 mph at 4,600 ft
				16,755[2]	253·3	13,779			[2] With 2,204-lb bomb load and 1,918-lb fuel
				20,833[3]				807[4]	[3] With 5,511-lb bomb load and 2,888-lb fuel
									[4] Cruising at 217 mph
				19,841[5]				1,864[6]	[5] With 1,102-lb bomb load and 6,305-lb fuel
									[6] Cruising at 186 mph
				21,384[7]					[7] With 1,102-lb bomb load and 7,848-lb fuel
				14,550			23,950[8]		[8] At 14,550-lb loaded weight

Ilyushin Il-2, single-seat version

Ilyushin Il-2, two-seat version

Ilyushin Il-2, two-seat version

feature of the aircraft was the strong armour protection provided for its vital areas. A uniform armour shell enclosed the engine, radiator and oil cooler, fuel tanks and crew. The weight of this armour exceeded 1,540 lb and represented about 15 per cent of the total loaded weight. Its shell form, as opposed to the use of separate steel plates, permitted embodiment of the armour into the stressed structure of the aircraft.

The BSh-2 was of mixed construction. The rear fuselage was a wooden monocoque, while the wings and tail surfaces were of duralumin. Test pilot V. K. Kokkinaki took the prototype into the air for the first time on 30 December 1939. Development was rather prolonged and a second prototype was built for official trials. These were held during the summer of 1940 and demonstrated that, in spite of obvious advantages, the BSh-2 was underpowered and suffered from poor longitudinal stability. To overcome the problems, Ilyushin's team produced a modified prototype, the TsKB-57, powered by the new AM-38 engine which achieved its maximum efficiency at a lower altitude, with a nominal output at sea level 370 hp greater than the AM-35 and with 23 per cent more power at take-off than its predecessor.

Since ground-attack aircraft, intended for low-level missions, do not require good high-altitude performance, the altitude at which TsKB-57 reached its top speed was reduced from 13,000 ft to 9,850 ft. The space previously allotted to the rear gunner's position was filled by an extra fuel tank, making the TsKB-57 a single-seater with a fuel capacity 50 per cent greater than that of the TsKB-55. Four fixed 7·62-mm ShKAS machine-guns had been fitted in the TsKB-55. Two of these were replaced by two 20-mm ShVAK cannon in the TsKB-57, so as to provide effective offensive power against armoured ground vehicles. In addition, eight 82-mm rocket missiles could be carried under the wings, together with four 220-lb bombs. Better stability was achieved by repositioning the centre of gravity and increasing the area of the tail surfaces.

The TsKB-57 flew on 12 October 1940, with Kokkinaki at the controls. In March 1941, its official trials successfully concluded, the machine entered production as the Il-2. Top speed was 292 mph and landing speed 87 mph. A bomb-load of 1,100–1,325 lb was carried.

In July-August 1941, a number of Il-2s participated in fighting on the Central Front. General A. I. Yeremiyenko reported on 24 August: "In spite of only being recently introduced, the new aircraft acquitted themselves very well."

From the start of the German invasion, there was a steady increase in the numbers of Il-2s and AM-38 engines produced. More and more new ground-attack regiments and divisions were formed. In a telegram to the aircraft factory workers on 24 December 1941, Stalin said that the Il-2 was "as essential to the Red Army as air and bread." Every effort was made to boost Il-2 output and in a single 12-month period in 1942–3 a reduction of 37·9 per cent was made in the number of man-hours required to turn out each machine. Between July 1942 and July 1943, the number of operational Il-2s increased fourfold.

In 1942, a conference of ground-attack pilots, test pilots and designers had made important decisions regarding future development of the Il-2. Three major requirements were listed: (1) Rear defence against fighter attacks, (2) Better offensive anti-tank armament, and (3) Greater manoeuvrability and a shorter take-off run to cut down risks involved in operations from front-line airfields.

As a result, the Il-2 was fitted with 20-mm VYa cannon, which had a higher muzzle velocity and shells of greater explosive power than the ShVAK cannon of the same calibre which they replaced. The power of the AM-38 was boosted and the compression ratio was reduced from 6·8 to 6·0, allowing the use of lower grade fuel. Low-level operations being the rule, the maximum-efficiency altitude was reduced from 5,400 ft to 2,450 ft. These modifications to the single-seater were soon made. In July 1942 the Il-2 with the AM-38F engine (1,750 hp at take-off) and VYa cannon completed its official trials, and it began to reach operational units of the Soviet Air Force that autumn.

Extensive experiments were conducted to improve the Il-2's aerodynamic qualities. Inclusion of the oil cooler in the same duct as the engine radiator made it less vulnerable and increased the top speed by 6–7 mph. The general cockpit shape was improved, tail-wheel fairings were introduced and the rear armour and firewall were sealed more effectively. With these and other minor improvements, an experimental Il-2 soon showed a top speed 22 mph higher than that of standard production machines.

Meanwhile, evaluation of two-seat versions of both the Il-2 and the Sukhoi-6, which provided the required movable gun for rear defence, had led to adoption of the Ilyushin design for quantity production. The armoured gunner's position was equipped with a 12·7-mm UBT machine-gun, with 150 rounds, and was situated behind the fuel tank.

On 30 October 1942, Il-2 two-seaters first joined in operations on the Central Front and were an immediate success. Operational tests took place on the Stalingrad Front in January and February 1943. In the space of a few days the new Il-2s shot down ten Bf 109 fighters. The ensuing trials report stated: "The Il-2 with a rear gunner's position for a UBT gun can be introduced with advantage into ground-attack units. It is capable of carrying out missions without fighter escort." Subsequently, all production Il-2s had defensive armament of this type.

Operational pilots were enthusiastic about the Il-2's qualities. The newspaper *Krasnyi Flot* (Red Fleet) commented "The Il-2's firepower, invulnerability and manoeuvrability have been proved many times. In arduous combat conditions our best assault pilots have frequently been on the winning side in duels with German aircraft."

The advantage enjoyed by the I1-2 over some German aircraft permitted its use to maintain the blockade of encircled enemy troops. Il-2s were used in this manner at Stalingrad, in the Korsun-Shevchenko area and elsewhere.

On occasion, Il-2s are known to have dispersed and shot down Ju 87 dive-bombers before proceeding to attack the German troops.

In the summer of 1943, the German Command flung the new Tiger and Panther tanks into the battle for the Kursk salient. Their thicker armour was almost immune to attack by the original Il-2, but a new prototype with an AM-38F engine and two 37-mm cannon in place of 20-mm weapons had been built in the previous spring. The new Il-2's bomb-load could include 200 PTAB-2·5-1·5 special cumulative-action anti-tank bombs. By June, Il-2s with the new weapons were destroying many of the latest German tanks in the Kursk salient. They frequently sought out opposing armour in its concentration areas and, by knocking out large numbers of tanks at that stage, prevented the enemy from mounting intended attacks.

The Il-2 was one of the Soviet Union's most effective weapons in the war with Germany. No other country

Ilyushin I1-2, two-seat version, Polish Air Force

TYPE	DIMENSIONS						WEIGHT	PERFORMANCE				REMARKS
	span ft	span in	length ft	length in	height ft	height in	max t-o lb	max speed mph	at height ft	service ceiling ft	combat range miles	
Ilyushin Il-2	47	10⅞	38	2¾	NA		11,683	262·8[1]	SL	24,606[2]	372[3]	[1] With 882-lb bomb load
								257·8[1]	8,202			[2] Max ceiling
								253·5[1]	16,404			[3] At 186 mph
								270·3[4]	SL			[4] Performance without bombs
								280·2[4]	8,202			
								268·4[4]	16,404			
							12,125[5]				466[6]	[5] With 1,323-lb bomb load [6] At 174 mph
Ilyushin Il-2 M3	47	10⅞	39	4½	11	1⅞	12,947	231·1[7]	SL	NA	475[8]	With AM-38F engine
								251 264[9]	4,921	21,325	372	[7] With engine working at normal revs [8] At 174 mph [9] Maximum

Ilyushin Il-4 (DB-3F)

Ilyushin Il-4 (DB-3F)

Ilyushin Il-4 (DB-3F), captured aircraft, Finnish markings

possessed a comparable ground-attack aircraft during World War II, and Russian sources go so far as to claim that no other design played such a decisive rôle. Be that as it may, the Il-2s occupy a unique position in the history of ground-attack aircraft development. About 35,000 were produced and they fought with considerable success on every front where Soviet military forces were engaged.

Ilyushin Il-4 (DB-3F)

In 1938, radical modifications were made to the DB-3 all-metal long-range bomber. These included complete revision of the forepart of the fuselage. The nose section accommodating the navigator/bomb-aimer was elongated. The manually-operated nose turret, which gave a characteristically bluff outline to the DB-3, was deleted and replaced by a simple universal joint mounting, similar to that employed on the German Heinkel He 111H bomber.

In place of the original M-86 engines, more efficient M-87A radials were installed. These developed 950 hp at 15,500 ft and drove the new VISh-23 propellers. The modified aircraft, initially designated DB-3F, became the Il-4 under the new designation system introduced in 1940, the "Il" standing for the first syllable of the name of its designer, S. V. Ilyushin.

Official trials ended in June 1939, and the DB-3F was placed in series production for the VVS. By the following year, large numbers of this bomber, which proved itself an outstanding and reliable machine, had been delivered. Unfortunately, during the early months of the war with Germany, evacuation of factories building the M-87A engine and an acute shortage of metal alloys led to a disastrous fall in output. Ilyushin's team began an urgent redesign of the structure, as a consequence of which the navigator/bomb-aimer's cockpit, the tail fairing and the floor of the main cabin were all able to be manufactured of wood. By the summer of 1942 the outer wing panels were also of wood, and at this period the M-88B radial engine was introduced as a standard power plant. With engine production now firmly re-established, production figures for the Il-4 increased steadily year by year, until the last of these bombers came off the assembly lines in 1944.

Introduction of wooden components had led to increased loaded weight; but the Il-4 retained its high performance, the maximum speed of the version with wooden outer wing sections being only 4 mph less than that of the all-metal version. Maximum range of this variant was 2,647 miles at 163·5 mph, and 2,228 miles at 213 mph.

Equipment included high-powered two-way radio, the Chaika radio compass and the APG-1 automatic pilot. The Il-4 also had a liquid de-icing system for the propellers and the pilot's cockpit hood. Its long range was explained by its great fuel capacity. Fuel comprised 27·4 per cent of the Il-4's loaded weight as against 23 per cent for the Heinkel He 111H and 16·8 per cent for the Junkers Ju 88A.

Defensive armament consisted of three movable 7·62-mm ShKAS machine-guns, one mounted in front on the universal join, one in a manually-operated dorsal turret and the third in a ventral position, on a retractable cradle which allowed the periscopically-sighted machine-gun to be extended below the fuselage when in the firing position. Under the general policy of improving defensive armament on Soviet bombers, the 7·62-mm ShKAS machine-guns were replaced later by 12·7-mm BS weapons.

The bomb-load of the Il-4 varied, according to operational requirements, from 2,205 lb to 5,510 lb. Typical bomb-loads for normal missions were either ten 220-lb bombs, suspended from a pair of DER-21 racks in the bomb-bay, or three 1,100-lb bombs, carried externally on racks under the fuselage. A single 2,205-lb bomb could be carried externally as an alternative load. In overload condition, for short-range attacks, the 2,205-lb internal bomb-load could be supplemented by up to 3,305 lb of bombs carried externally.

The version of the Il-4 that was widely adopted for naval operations could carry a 2,072-lb torpedo slung externally beneath the fuselage. It remained in service for a number of years after World War II.

The Il-4 was one of the hardest-worked bombers in Soviet service. It was first utilized in combat during the "Winter War" with Finland in 1939–40 and then flew on every front on which Russian forces were engaged against the Germans and their allies between 1941 and 1945. It was continually in operation against military and industrial targets inside Germany and at shorter distances behind the enemy lines. The first Soviet air raid on Berlin was made by a group of Il-4 bombers of the Naval Air Force, led by Colonel Preobrazhensky, on the night of 8 August 1941.

The bombers are said to have been guided to the city by its bright lights, thereafter dimmed until the end of the war.

Ilyushin Il-10

In 1943, new types of two-seat ground-attack aircraft designed by the bureaux of P. O. Sukhoi and S. V. Ilyushin were ready for their test flights. The Ilyushin prototype was an all-metal low-wing monoplane with a new AM-42 engine. The design team had thoroughly studied reports on the operational use of the Il-2, as well as numerous suggestions by ground-attack crews. As a result, as many ideas from the front-line as possible were incorporated in the new machine.

Great attention was paid to aerodynamic refinement of the Il-10, as the new type was designated. An improved layout was devised for the radiator and oil cooler. The undercarriage system was altered, the main wheels turning through 90 degrees as they retracted backward to lie flat in the wings. This enabled the undercarriage fairings to be reduced in size. The tailwheel was also made retractable. Overall drag was reduced by 50 per cent compared with the Il-2.

The AM-42 engine delivered 2,000 hp at take-off, against the 1,750 hp of the AM-38F in the Il-2. A dorsal turret with a 20-mm cannon replaced the former UBT 12·7-mm gun. The Il-10 was heavily armoured and, unlike the Il-2, its rear gunner's position was integral with the rest of the armour shell.

Offensive armament consisted of two 20-mm VYa cannon in the wings. These were later supplanted by more effective NS 23 cannon.

In June 1944, the Il-10 successfully completed its official trials and, by decision of the State Committee of Defence, was preferred to the Sukhoi Su-6 and put into series production. From October of that year it began entering service with ground-attack units of the Soviet Air Force.

The Il-10 participated in its first operations during February 1945, when battles were already being fought on German territory.

At the conclusion of operational testing, it was reported that the Il-10 had the following advantages over the Il-2: (1) a wider speed range and greater manœuvrability facilitated the task of escorting fighters and permitted the active participation of the Il-10 in air combat, (2) the crew had full armour protection, and (3) easy handling characteristics and the comparatively simple

Ilyushin Il-10

Ilyushin Il-10

Ilyushin Il-10

TYPE	DIMENSIONS						WEIGHT	PERFORMANCE				REMARKS
	span		length		height		max t-o	max speed	at height	service ceiling	combat range	
	ft	in	ft	in	ft	in	lb	mph	ft	ft	miles	
Ilyushin Il-4(DB-3F)	70	$4\frac{1}{8}$	48	$6\frac{3}{4}$		NA	22,167	276·5	20,997	29,527	2,174[1]	M-87A engines [1] Maximum
							18,485–22,167	254·7	21,325	32,808	2,361	M-88B engines & partly wooden constr.
							16,975[2] 22,046[3]				1,615[4]	[2] With 2204-lb bomb-load and 1,918-lb fuel [3] With 2204-lb bomb-load and 6,979-lb fuel
Ilyushin Il-10	45	$7\frac{1}{8}$	40	$0\frac{1}{4}$	11	$5\frac{3}{4}$	13,968	311·3	9,186	NA	403	[4] At 199 mph

Ilyushin Il-10

Ilyushin Il-28

Ilyushin Il-28, Hungarian Air Force

Ilyushin Il-28, Finnish Air Force

conversion training of crews and ground personnel permitted the re-equipment of ground-attack units within the shortest possible time.

Ilyushin's Il-10 soldiered on into the 1950s with the air forces of the Soviet Union and many of that nation's allies and friends. It saw combat service for the last time with the Communist Northern Forces during the Korean War.

Ilyushin Il-28

The Il-28, NATO code-name "Beagle", is a light tactical bomber and reconnaissance aircraft designed by Sergi Vladimirovich Ilyushin. It is estimated that no fewer than 10,000 of these aeroplanes have been produced since the prototype – thought to have been powered by two RD-10 turbojets – made its first flight in 1947.

Production aircraft, powered by two VK-1 turbojets rated at 5,950 lb s t each, entered service late in 1949 and early 1950, equipping first Air Regiments based in Siberia and East Germany. By mid-1950 the Soviet Air Force had a front-line strength of about 2,500 Il-28s, and in 1951 some 700 were added to the strength of the A-VMF (Naval Air Squadrons).

An estimated 800 have been supplied to air forces outside the Soviet Union. About 500 went to China, but a considerable number of these have probably been cannibalized to maintain a reasonable rate of serviceability, due to recent difficulties in obtaining spares from Russia. The Il-28 serves also with the air forces of Czechoslovakia (under the designation B-228), Poland, East Germany, Hungary, Indonesia, Finland, North Korea, Rumania, the United Arab Republic, Federal Nigeria and Afghanistan. Russia supplied 33 to Fidel Castro, but after American protests these were shipped out of Cuba in December 1962.

Defensive armament of the Il-28 comprises two 23-mm cannon mounted in the nose, and two 20-mm cannon in a manned rear turret, but the latter has no gun-laying radar or tail-warning equipment. Bomb-load consists of either four 1,000-lb or twelve 550-lb bombs, and a crew of three are accommodated.

Recent developments include a version with a second radome on the undersurface, presumably housing radar countermeasures equipment. Il-28s serving currently with the A-VMF have a single, but larger, radome and are probably engaged on anti-submarine duties in the Baltic and Black Seas. There is also a trainer version with the designation Il-28U and the Finnish Air Force uses one of its aircraft for target-towing. A de-militarized variant, for freight and mail duties, known as the Il-20, served with Aeroflot.

Junkers H-21

Following signature of the Versailles Treaty, aircraft building in Germany was limited to machines with a ceiling of not more than 13,125 ft (4,000 m) or capable of carrying a load of not more than 1,325 lb (600 kg). Inevitably, German manufacturers looked abroad for opportunities to develop their more ambitious projects. The Treaty of Rapallo, in 1922, laid the basis for Russo-German co-operation; soon afterwards the Junkers company made an agreement with the Soviet government which led to the establishment of an aircraft factory and the construction of Junkers designs in the Soviet Union.

The factory was built at Fili, near Moscow; but its existence as a branch of the Junkers concern was short, lasting only until 1924. Professor Junkers blamed Russian red tape for the failure, whereas the Soviet authorities claimed that the Germans were not interested in helping the embryo Soviet aircraft industry, but were concerned solely with turning out excessively-priced and outdated aircraft.

The Junkers H-21, of which at least 100 were produced during the short life of the Russian Junkers factory, was a two-seat reconnaissance-fighter. It was a parasol monoplane, powered by a 185-hp BMW III water-cooled engine, and followed closely the outline of the earlier Junkers T-19, T-23 and T-26 sporting aircraft from which it had been developed. Of typical Junkers all-metal construction, covered with corrugated metal sheeting, the H-21 carried a rather poor payload which limited its range of action. Supplementary fuel tanks were fitted to the sides of the fuselage.

One or two synchronized machine-guns fired forward, operated by the pilot. Movement of the observer's single ring-mounted machine-gun was facilitated by the building up of the rear cockpit level with the surrounding upper fuselage decking.

Junkers H-21s entered service with the Soviet air arm in 1924–5 and saw some action against counter-revolutionary forces in the Turkestan area. A single-seat version was designated H-22.

Junkers R-42

The R-42 was a military development of the well-known G.24 commercial transport and corresponded to the Swedish-built K-30L. Like its predecessor, the R-42 was an all-metal cantilever monoplane. In common with other Junkers-designed aircraft of the period, it had a multi-spar wing structure and an outer covering of corrugated metal sheeting.

Power was provided by three Junkers L-5 engines, each developing 300 hp. A bomb-load of 2,205-2,645 lb was carried.

Defensive armament comprised five machine-guns and special care was taken to achieve the maximum field of fire. There were two ring mountings, each with twin guns, one behind the other on top of the fuselage. A fully-retractable "dustbin", housing the fifth machine-gun, was located in a ventral position.

R-42 bombers entered Soviet service in the winter of 1925–6, receiving the alternative designation Ju.G-1. They formed the second heavy bomber *escadrilya* and soon replaced also the obsolete and rather unpopular Farman bombers which had equipped the first unit of heavy bombers to be organized after the Revolution. The two *escadrilyas* formed a brigade and the latter was the nucleus of the Soviet heavy bomber force of the period.

The R-42 could easily be converted into a floatplane and a number of such conversions, designated R-42W (equivalent to the German-Swedish K-30W), served with the Soviet Naval Air Force and on Russia's civil air routes.

In the spring of 1931, some of these Junkers bombers were converted for passenger carrying and remained in service on secondary routes for a considerable period of time.

Kamov Ka-15

Designed by Nikolai I. Kamov and developed via the earlier single-seat Ka-10 and Ka-10M, the Ka-15 is a two-seat light utility helicopter. It was first identified in 1956 and serves with the A-VMF (Soviet Naval Squadrons) from cruisers, for patrol and reconnaissance, and land-based for air/sea rescue, anti-submarine and patrol/reconnaissance duties. Ka-15s are used also for ice patrols from Soviet Navy arctic bases.

Like most Kamov designs, the Ka-15 has two contra-rotating fully-articulated three-blade rotors of wood construction, plywood-covered and filled with foam plastic. Power plant is a 275-hp AI-14V nine-cylinder radial air-cooled engine.

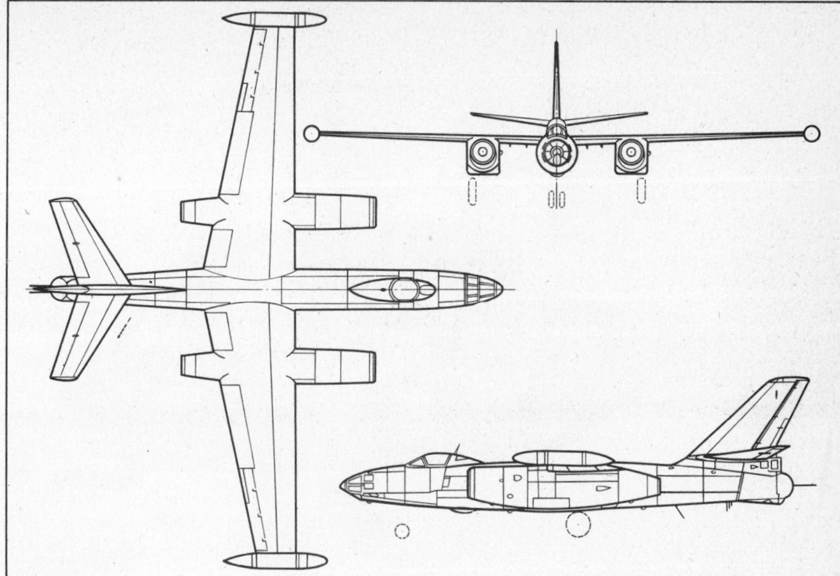

Ilyushin Il-28

Junkers H-21

Kamov Ka-15

TYPE	DIMENSIONS						WEIGHT	PERFORMANCE				REMARKS
	span ft	*span* in	*length* ft	*length* in	*height* ft	*height* in	*max t-o* lb	*max speed* mph	*at height* ft	*service ceiling* ft	*combat range* miles	
Ilyushin Il-28	64		58		22		43,000	580	19,680	41,000	685/850 (radius)	
Junkers H-21												No data available
Junkers R-42												No data available
Kamov Ka-15	32	8½	19	6	10	10		93		9,840		Max endurance 4hr Hovering out of ground effect = 2,230 ft

Kamov Ka-20

Kocherghin DI-6

Kocherghin DI-6

A Ka-15 set up an officially-recognized International record on 6 May 1959, by averaging 105·91 mph over a 500-km circuit (Class E-1-c). On this occasion it had a take-off weight of 2,976 lb. NATO code-name is "Hen".

Kamov Ka-20

First seen in the 1961 Soviet Aviation Day display, the Ka-20 is apparently designed as a specialized anti-submarine helicopter, for both the hunter and killer rôles, with a crew of three or four. It serves on ships of the Soviet navy.

A search radar installation is fitted in the large radome under the nose; other equipment, covered by a blister fairing, is mounted under the tail-boom. Main armament comprises two air-to-surface missiles carried on outriggers on either side of the cabin. Power is provided by two small shaft-turbine engines mounted side-by-side above the cabin and rated at around 900 shp each. They drive two three-bladed co-axial contra-rotating rotors. NATO code-name is "Harp".

Kocherghin DI-6

In the mid-1930s, Soviet fighter tactics were wedded to the principle of close co-operation between groups of fast monoplanes and groups of manoeuvrable biplanes. In an attempt to devise an aircraft capable of engaging both classes of fighter with equal success, a team led by S. A. Kocherghin turned to the two-seat biplane layout. Working under the general supervision of V. P. Yatsenko, they produced the DI-6 (bureau designation TsKB-11) in 1934. Test flights began in the same year.

The DI-6 had an inward-retracting undercarriage and was powered by a "high-altitude" air-cooled engine, the Wright Cyclone SGR-1820-F-3. This power plant was superseded on production machines by the Soviet-built M-25 radial. The wings were braced with wide "I" struts and the upper wing was attached to the fuselage by conventional "N"-type centre-section struts. The pilot's cockpit was open, but the rear cockpit was enclosed by a glazed canopy. Armament consisted of four fixed forward-firing 7·62-mm ShKAS machine-guns and one movable gun of the same type manned by the gunner.

The wings spanned only 10 inches more than those of the I-15, and the DI-6 was only 2 ft 11·4 in longer than the single-seater. Maximum speed was 239 mph, against the 223·5 mph of the I-15. At a height of 3,300 ft the DI-6 could make a 180 degree turn in eleven seconds, compared with eight seconds taken by the I-15.

It was envisaged that in combat the dorsal gunner's fire would be invaluable during tight turns and when dealing with attacks by faster monoplanes from the rear. The gunner had an excellent field of fire, enhanced by the fact that the horizontal tail surfaces were set high on the fin and rudder.

On conclusion of official trials in December 1935, the new fighter entered series production. One unconfirmed Soviet source claimed that the DI-6 was successfully employed in air battles with the Japanese over the Khalkin-Gol in Mongolia during May and August 1939. However, the DI-6 formula was considered to offer no prospect for further development and design work on two-seat fighter biplanes was subsequently suspended.

Lavochkin LaGG-3

The prototype of the I-22 fighter, later designated LaGG-1, was conceived and built in 1938–9 by a team under the joint leadership of S. A. Lavochkin, V. P. Gorbunov and M. I. Gudkov. It flew for the first time on 30 March 1939, piloted by P. N. Nikotchin.

In appearance the I-22 was a conventional low-wing monoplane. The main undercarriage units retracted inward and the pilot's cockpit was fitted with a sliding canopy. The airframe, however, represented a departure from conventionality, since it was constructed from plastic-bonded wood. The fuselage was built up on birch frames with plywood facing on both sides. The wooden longerons were of continuous triangular cross-section with the base towards the skin, which was made up of diagonal strips of plywood. A plastic bonding was utilized as an adhesive and the same phenol-formaldehyde resin was used to impregnate the wood of the structure. A conventional centre-section and two outer panels formed the wings, which comprised a plywood skin bonded to wooden structure.

The weight of the aircraft was increased considerably by this method of construction and, despite careful streamlining and a good overall finish, performance inevitably suffered.

After successfully completing its flight trials, the LaGG-1 was put into quantity production. It was armed with a 20-mm or 23-mm cannon, firing through the hollow propeller shaft, and two 12·7-mm machine-guns.

While assembly was getting under way the weight of the structure was reduced by careful re-design. In addition, the more powerful M-105PF in-line engine, driving a three-bladed VISh-61P propeller, replaced the M-105P previously installed. These modifications were incorporated in the course of production and the fighter was given the new designation LaGG-3. Its wings were fitted with leading-edge slots. The rudder mass-balances were of the external type on early production machines, but of the internal type on later models. On some versions the tailwheel was fixed, while on others it was fully retractable.

Some aspects of the LaGG-3's combat characteristics – particularly a tendency to go into a spin when coming out of a tight turn – gave cause for concern. Lt-Col Gruzdev of the NII-VVS test centre carried out a great deal of practical research to counteract the shortcomings, and his findings were incorporated in instructions issued to squadrons that were operating the LaGG-3, with good effect.

Armament combinations for the production LaGG-3 normally included one 20-mm ShVAK or 23-mm VIa cannon with either (a) a single 12·7-mm BS machine-gun; or (b) a single BS machine-gun and a single 7·62-mm ShKAS machine-gun; or (c) one BS and two ShKAS machine-guns. Loads carried on underwing racks included six RS-82 rocket missiles or two 220-lb and two 22-lb bombs; or two 110-lb and four 55-lb bombs.

LaGG-3s which performed escort duties for assault groups of Ilyushin Il-2s had an armament of three 12·7-mm BS machine-guns and two 7·62-mm ShKAS machine-guns. The underwing offensive load was replaced by two 22-gallon auxiliary fuel tanks.

The LaGG-3 was produced in series and employed extensively in combat during the early stages of the war with Germany. It attracted particular notice on the Finnish Front, giving a fair account of itself under difficult operational conditions.

In general, the LaGG-3's performance and tactical qualities were comparable with those of the 1941-vintage Messerschmitt Bf 109. However, it had a poorer rate of climb and a lower service ceiling than the contemporary Yakovlev Yak-1.

Lavochkin La-5

Of the three single-seat fighters designed in 1939–40 and introduced into Soviet fighter elements in the earliest stages of the war with Germany, the LaGG-3

Lavochkin LaGG-3, captured aircraft, Finnish markings

Lavochkin LaGG-3

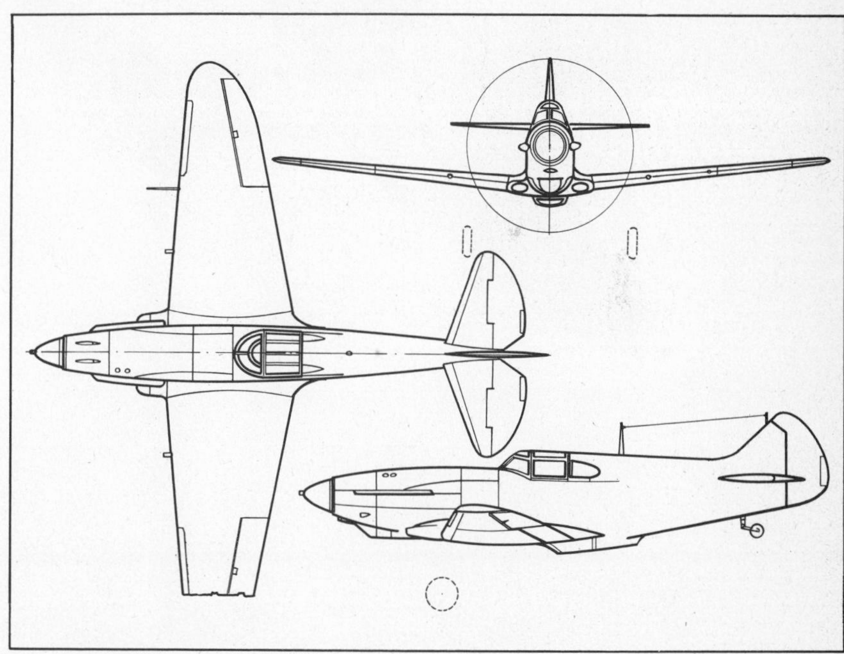

Lavochkin LaGG-3

TYPE	DIMENSIONS						WEIGHT	PERFORMANCE				REMARKS
	span		length		height		max t-o	max speed	at height	service ceiling	combat range	
	ft	in	ft	in	ft	in	lb	mph	ft	ft	miles	
Kamov Ka-20	51 (rotor dia)	8	32	4	17	7½	16,000*	140*	SL	11,500	NA	*Estimated
Kocherghin DI-6	35	5½	25	7	NA		4,288	239·2		27,886	528	Design bureau TsKB-11
Lavochkin LaGG-1	32	1⅞	29	1¼	NA		6,543	375·9 320	6,240 SL	31,496	 403	
Lavochkin LaGG-3	32	1⅞	29	1¼	NA		6,316 7,032– 7,230	352·9 347·9 308·8	12,795 16,404 SL	33,464 29,527	NA 403	

Lavochkin La-5FN

Lavochkin La-5FN

Lavochkin La-7

had the poorest performance. In 1941, in fact, Lavochkin's team had already set to work to improve the basic design, with the aim of achieving a considerable increase in speed and better combat capability. At the end of that year a LaGG-3 airframe was fitted with an M-82 radial engine, giving more power at high altitudes than the M-105PF. But the increased frontal area of the radial power plant prevented more than a modest speed increase. With the M-82, top speed was 373 mph at 21,200 ft, as compared with 353 mph at 12,800 ft attained by the standard LaGG-3. The time taken to reach 16,400 ft (5,000 m) was reduced by only 18 seconds.

The designers realized that further steps had to be taken to find a suitable replacement for the LaGG-3. So, while small numbers of the M-82-engined fighter were being built as the LaG-5, another version was under test with the 1,330-hp M-82F engine. Structurally very similar to the LaGG-3, the new machine, designated La-5, had an all-round-vision canopy for the pilot, a retractable tailwheel, and two synchronized 20-mm ShVAK cannon in the forward fuselage above the engine.

Factory and official trials were concluded by June 1942 and the type was immediately put into production. On entering combat in the autumn of 1942, it proved to be almost 28 mph faster than the German Bf 109G-2 at altitudes up to 20,000 ft. The Messerschmitt fighter, however, had a better rate of climb, and during the winter of 1942–3 Lavochkin's team tackled the task of improving the La-5 in this respect. Weight was reduced by cutting down fuel capacity and introducing metal wing spars in place of wooden spars. The total weight saving was in the order of 379 lb. The ASh-82FN engine, with direct fuel injection, was installed in the revised airframe. Take-off power of this engine was 1,700 hp, with a nominal power at sea level of 1,510 hp – 180 hp more than the standard La-5 power plant.

The reduced-weight fighter with the ASh-82FN engine was designated La-5FN. It could climb to 16,400 ft (5,000 m) in 4·7 minutes. In the summer of 1943, large numbers of La-5FNs took part in air battles over the Kursk-Orlov salient, where they played a vital rôle. The German Command had pinned its hopes on the Luftwaffe's Fw 190A-4 fighters, many of which were sent into action. Up to 22,300 ft (6,800 m) the La-5FN had a speed advantage over the Bf 109G-2; but at heights above 23,600 ft (7,200 m) it was slower than the German fighter. The Soviet fighter surpassed the German type in rate of climb, time taken to complete a 180-degree turn, and vertical manoeuvre.

During the war, the La-5FN gained well-deserved popularity with Russian pilots because of its exceptional manoeuvrability. It remained steady during very tight turns and produced a very positive response to the ailerons. The aileron area of the La-5FN was greater in proportion to wing area than on any other production fighter in the world at that time, the ailerons representing 8·02 per cent of the wing area, as against 7·7 per cent for the Yak-1 and 6·3 per cent for the Bf 109. Such qualities were the outcome of close collaboration between Lavochkin's team and TsAGI, in devising a control system which made the La-5FN easy to handle in the air – a true pilot's aeroplane.

Externally, the La-5FN differed from the La-5 in detail only. One visible difference was in the air intake, which extended over the whole length of the top of the engine cowling on the La-5, whereas on the La-5FN it was set further back along the cowling.

A number of leading Soviet pilots achieved their early successes on the La-5 and La-5FN, including I. N. Kojedub, who first made his mark during the Kursk salient fighting.

The two-seat fighter-trainer version of the La-5, with M-82F engine, was designated La-5UTI and also went into quantity production.

Lavochkin La-7

In 1943, continuing its improvement of the La-5, the Lavochkin design team brought out a modified version under the designation La-7. The new fighter was able to offer an improved performance, although powered by exactly the same engine as the La-5FN – the ASh-82FN radial. The designers had concentrated their efforts on refining the shape of the aircraft and, in particular, the engine cowling. The intake over the cowling was deleted and the oil coolant radiator under the engine was moved back to a position under the fuselage, just below the trailing-edge of the wings. The general impression that this created was of a beautifully-streamlined engine cowling and a sleek fuselage profile.

The basic structure of the La-5FN was retained and, despite increased armament, the total weight increased by only 214 lb, thanks to a reduction in the weight of fuel carried to 750 lb. Range fell, in consequence, from the 475 miles of the La-5FN to 394 miles, and the La-7's endurance was limited to one hour.

The general combat qualities and performance of the La-7 were considerably higher than those of La-5FN. Top speed was 422·5 mph, compared with 402·5 mph for its predecessor. Climb to 16,400 ft took 4 minutes 27 seconds, about 15 seconds less than the La-5FN.

Three 20-mm ShVAK cannon were installed in the front upper fuselage decking, above the engine, with two cannon offset to port and one to starboard. They delivered a total weight of 7½ lb of shells per second, as against 4 lb per second delivered by the La-5FN.

During 1944, attempts to improve performance for brief periods in combat led to the installation of a liquid-fuel rocket motor in the tail of the La-7. The fuel supply was sufficient for 3 to 3½ minutes of flight with the rocket in operation. Two prototypes, designated La-7R, were tested between October 1944 and February 1945, by G. M. Shiyanov and A. V. Davidov. A top speed of 461 mph at 9,840 ft (3,000 m) was reached, representing an increase of 53 mph from a total rocket thrust of 661 lb. In the course of testing, however, it was discovered that acid vapours were weakening the fuselage structure.

Meanwhile, the production La-7 had begun to enter service in the second half of 1944. At the same time, the Germans were introducing the reduced-weight Fw 190 A-8 fighter with BMW 80Q engine, which had an emergency power boost of five minutes duration. Combat experience indicated that the La-7 was able to fight on level terms with both the Focke-Wulf fighter and the Messerschmitt Bf 109 G-6.

A number of Soviet aces flew the Lavochkin La-7. The machine in which Ivan Kojedub secured many of his 62 victories is exhibited at the Central Soviet Air Force Museum in Moscow.

Lavochkin La-9 and La-11

The Lavochkin La-9 was a low-wing monoplane powered by an 1,850 hp Ash-82 FNV engine. Its design was a direct result of development work carried out on the preceding La-7 single-seat fighter.

With factory and official trials satisfactorily completed, the new fighter went into large-scale production and began to enter service with the Soviet Air Force in 1944. Although too late for use in World War II, the La-9 proved a very effective fighter, with a maximum speed of 429 mph at 20,500 ft and good all-round flying qualities. It differed from the La-7 in having a redesigned cockpit and more pointed fin and rudder. The horizontal tail surfaces and wing-tips were square-cut. Duralumin was utilized to a large extent in its construction.

Lavochkin La-7, Czechoslovak Air Force

Lavochkin La-9

Lavochkin La-9

TYPE	DIMENSIONS						WEIGHT	PERFORMANCE				REMARKS
	span		*length*		*height*		*max t-o*	*max speed*	*at height*	*service ceiling*	*combat range*	
	ft	*in*	*ft*	*in*	*ft*	*in*	*lb*	*mph*	*ft*	*ft*	*miles*	
Lavochkin LaG-5	32	1⅞	27	10¾	9	3	NA	372·8 385·2	21,161 20,341	NA	NA	M-82 engine
Lavochkin La-5	32	1⅞	27	10¾	9	3	NA	389	19,685	NA	NA	
Lavochkin La-5FN	32	1⅞	27	10⅝	9	3	7,407	386·5 402·6	16,404 20,997	32,808	 475	
Lavochkin La-7	32	1⅞	27	10⅝	9	3	7,495	424·4 422·5	18,372 20,997	 34,448	394	

Lavochkin La-11

Lavochkin La-11

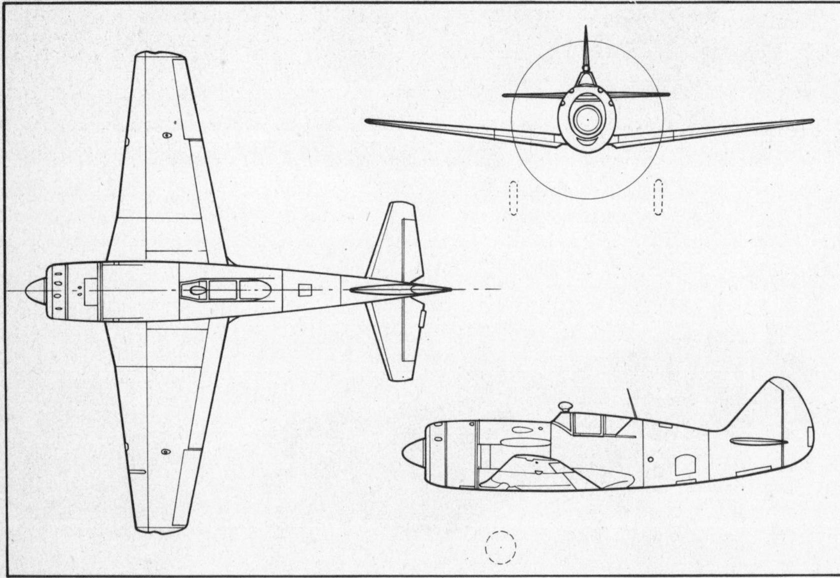
Lavochkin La-11

Lavochkin La-15UTI

During the immediate post-war period, the La-9 flew with first-line Soviet fighter units, and within a few years of the end of the war had been exported to a number of Russia's allies, including China, for use in interceptor and escort fighter rôles. A number of experiments with auxiliary jet and rocket units were carried out with the type, and at the Tushino Air Display on 18 August 1946, a formation of La-9s appeared equipped with underwing impulse ducts similar to those fitted to the German Fieseler Fi 103 flying bomb (V-1).

An La-9 was also test-flown with a rocket unit in the extreme rear of the fuselage.

With a view to improving the effectiveness of the La-9 as an escort fighter, an official requirement was issued by the Soviet authorities for a single-seater of greater range. To meet it, Lavochkin's team produced the La-11, of all-metal stressed-skin construction. This was built in large numbers from 1945 onward, just too late to engage in World War II combat operations. The fuel capacity was increased from 181 gallons to 242 gallons, at the cost of a slightly increased loaded weight and reduced armament. The La-9 had carried four NS 23 cannon of 23-mm calibre in the upper decking of the forward fuselage, over the engine. In the La-11, only three of these cannon were fitted, two to port and one to starboard.

Externally, the La-11 differed from the La-9 in having a small air intake under the engine cowling. The oil coolant radiator fitted under the fuselage of the La-7 and La-9, near the wing trailing-edge, was deleted on the La-11. The wing area was slightly reduced by comparison with the La-9.

The La-11 was Sergei Lavochkin's last piston-engined fighter design.

Aircraft of this type helped to equip the Communist Northern Air Force during the Korean War.

Lavochkin La-15

Developed in parallel with the MiG-15, the La-15 was the first of Semyon A. Lavochkin's jet fighters to go into service. The prototype, the La-174, was evolved from the experimental La-168 and production was started in the summer of 1948. Power plant was an RD-500 turbojet, rated at 3,500 lb s t. Armament consisted of two 23-mm cannon mounted under the nose. Rockets or bombs could be carried under the wings. An unusual feature of the La-15 was its shoulder-mounted wing, swept at 37 degrees 20 minutes. The type was employed in limited numbers as a ground-attack fighter. A two-seat trainer version, the La-15UTI, had the design bureau designation La-180. At least one La-15 survives in the Soviet Union, at Monino, near Moscow. NATO code-name of the single-seat version was "Fantail".

Lebed' 12

The Aktionernoe Obitsestvo Vozdukhoplavaniya V. A. Lebedev (V. A. Lebedev Aeronautics Co Ltd), was established at Petrograd Novaya Derevnya in 1912 as Petersburg Aviation Ltd (PTA). It was one of the five largest aircraft companies in Imperial Russia and, in 1917, set up a new factory at Taganrog; another was being built at the same time at Penze. During the 1914–18 War, these factories produced Farman, Nieuport, Morane, Deperdussin, Voisin, Sopwith and Lebed' aircraft at a rate of 30 per month in 1916 and 75 a month in 1917.

In 1915, a captured Albatros – probably a B.II – was evaluated by the company and this, together with the Lebed' VII, formed the basis for the Lebed' 12 two-seat reconnaissance aircraft.

The first of the new machines was completed at the end of 1915 and was tested by Lieut Sleptsov on 28 December. His report was favourable: he considered it generally superior to the Albatros, with less engine vibration, but added that it was inclined to bounce on landing.

On 19 April 1916, the company received a contract from the Central Military Technical Board for 225 Lebed'

12s (value 13,000 roubles: £1,500 each) and spares. The first of these was tested by Military Aviator Michaelov at the Komandantskii Aerodrome, Petrograd, on 4 August 1916. With a load of 275–350 kg (606–772 lb) the aircraft climbed to 1,640 ft in 6 minutes; 3,280 ft in 13 minutes and 6,560 ft in 28 minutes; its ceiling was 9,740 ft; maximum speed 84 mph; and take-off run about 110 yards at 47–50 mph. The 150-hp Salmson 9-cylinder water-cooled engine "... worked well, giving an average of 1,325 rpm." As a result of these tests the Lebed' 12 was pronounced "fit for work at the front".

About ten were delivered to the War Department, and the aircraft entered service at the front in October 1916. There were, however, criticisms from pilots who flew the Lebed' 12: it went easily into a dive, from which it was difficult to recover, this resulting in a number of fatal accidents; the engine exhaust was too close to the cockpit, which was unpleasant for the crew; and the observer's Shkulnik gun mounting was badly designed. It was replaced later by a Kolpakov mounting.

A slightly more powerful engine – the 160-hp Salmson – was fitted to later aircraft, and by June 1917 about 80 Lebed' 12s had been delivered to the War Department. At about this time the aircraft was modified and re-named Lebed' 13; under a new contract, 200 were ordered, some of which were supplied on floats or skis for the Navy. By 1 March 1919, 216 Lebed' 12s and 171 sets of spares had been built by the Lebedev factories. There were plans for the Slessarenko Company to build the type, but a number of difficulties arose and, in fact, this company did not complete any.

The Lebed' 12 was a two-bay wire-braced biplane. The fuselage was constructed from wood, including spruce longerons; the forward part was planked with 3-mm, and the rear fuselage with 2-mm plywood. The engine mounting consisted of a frame made from four steel tubes bolted to the front bulkhead. A metal cowling enclosed the engine, except for the tops of the cylinder heads. The undercarriage legs were of elliptical-section welded steel-tube packed with wood, carrying two 760 × 100-mm wheels on a steel axle. (Some wheels had exposed steel spokes, while others had aluminium discs fitted over them).

The wings were mostly constructed from pine, with two box spars; wing area was 452 sq ft. The tailplane, which could be folded forward along the fuselage sides to facilitate transport, was also made from wood, but the fin and rudder were of steel-tube construction. All flying surfaces were fabric-covered.

The petrol tanks were constructed from copper or brass, covered with rubber, and their total capacity was 57 Imperial gallons, with a 5-Imperial gallon emergency tank. Capacity of the Lebed' 12's oil tank was 5·3 Imperial gallons.

The observer was seated normally behind the pilot, but when the aircraft was used for pilot training the pupil sat in the front seat.

Armament comprised one 7·62-mm Colt machine-gun on a Shkulnik movable gun mounting for the observer, and four Shkulnik bomb-racks. Not only the gun mounting, but also the racks had to be replaced after a time by Kolpakov equipment.

Mikoyan-Gurevich MiG-3

Among the high-altitude fighter designs produced in the Soviet Union during the 1939–40 period, the most

Lavochkin La-15

Lebed' 12

Lebed' 12

TYPE	DIMENSIONS					WEIGHT	PERFORMANCE				REMARKS
	span		length		height		max	at	service	combat	
	ft	in	ft	in	ft in	max t-o lb	speed mph	height ft	ceiling ft	range miles	
Lavochkin La-9	34	9⅜	29	6⅜	NA	NA	428·7	20,505	NA	1,078	
Lavochkin La-11	32	7⅜	28	3½	NA		459	NA	35,433	466	
Lavochkin La-15	29	0	34	5	NA	8,490	637	16,000	42,900	735	
Lebed' 12	43	1¾	26	1¼	NA	1,672	82·6	NA	11,482	3hr	Developed from Albatros. 216 built

Mikoyan-Gurevich MiG-1, non-standard cockpit canopy fitted

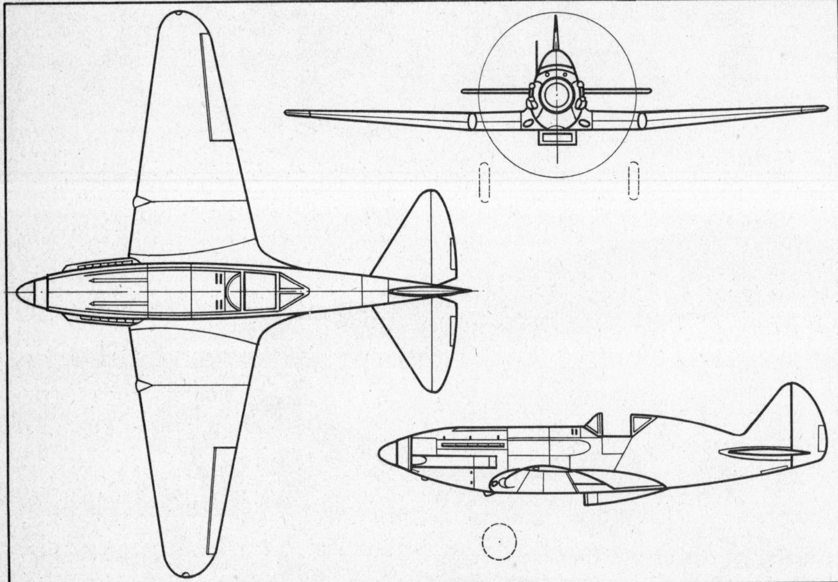

Mikoyan-Gurevich MiG-1

Mikoyan-Gurevich MiG-3

Mikoyan-Gurevich MiG-3

successful was the I-61, submitted by a team under the leadership of A. I. Mikoyan and M. I. Gurevich. Work on the project had begun towards the end of 1939. An official requirement that the new fighter should be capable of operating at altitudes above 19,685 ft (6,000 m) predetermined the choice of the AM-35A engine, which developed its maximum of 1,200 hp at an altitude of 23,600 ft.

Features of the AM-35A in turn dictated some of the I-61's characteristics. Its heaviness increased the loaded weight of the fighter, and one result was that the armament was restricted to one 12·7-mm machine-gun and two 7·62-mm guns.

Wood was the principal material used in the rear fuselage and fin structure, and for the outer wing panels. The forepart of the fuselage was of welded steel tubes, and the central section of the wings was of all-metal construction with a duralumin sheet covering.

The I-61 prototype was designed and built in only four months and was flown by test pilot A. N. Yekatov for the first time on 5 April 1940. Official trials were completed by the following August and the MiG-1, as it was then designated, was ordered into production immediately.

Early MiG-1s had a maximum speed of 390 mph at 23,000 ft – 3 mph slower than the prototype had flown at a similar height. The reason was that it had not been found possible to retain the high-quality finish of the prototype in the production models. Nevertheless, Soviet sources claim that the Mikoyan-Gurevich MiG-1 was the fastest production military aircraft in the world during the period 1940–41.

At the end of 1940, the MiG-1 was modified in order to increase its range, reduce vulnerability and improve handling characteristics at high angles of incidence. The revised design became the MiG-3 and won a 1941 Stalin Prize for its designer. It retained the low-wing configuration and general outline of its predecessor, with main wheels retracting inward into the wings and a fully retractable tailwheel, but differed in a number of respects. The open cockpit of the MiG-1 was replaced by a sliding, glazed canopy. Behind the canopy, the upper fuselage had glazed panels in order to improve vision to the rear. The dihedral on the outer wing panels was increased. An additional 52-gallon fuel tank was located beneath the pilot's seat, and the VISh-22 propeller of the MiG-1 was replaced by a VISh-61Sh three-bladed propeller. The ventral radiator was increased in size and located further forward.

The MiG-3 was built in large numbers, output (including MiG-1s) totalling 2,100, and it formed the backbone of the Russian high-altitude fighter force. Early wartime experience showed that it was outstanding at altitudes above 16,400 ft (5,000 m), as at this height it achieved a higher performance and showed better tactical characteristics than any fighters the German Luftwaffe had available before 1942.

Below this altitude, however, speed and climb were inferior and, as a result, the MiG-3 had little value as a front-line fighter.

From the earliest days of the war, it was clear that the armament of one heavy and two light machine-guns was inadequate for the MiG-3. Two additional 12·7-mm BS machine-guns were accordingly installed under the wings. This modification, and increased armour protection introduced at the same time, were installed in the aircraft at their operational airfields.

Production of the MiG-3 lasted only until the autumn of 1941, when manufacture of the AM-35A was halted to clear the way for ever-increasing output of AM-38 engines for the more urgently needed Ilyushin Il-2 ground-attack aircraft.

Mikoyan-Gurevich MiG-9

A specification was issued by the Soviet authorities in February 1945, calling for a single-seat jet-propelled fighter. The design team headed by Mikoyan and Gurevich was one of several which produced prototypes in answer to the official requirement. Their project was designated I-300 and was an all-metal mid-wing monoplane powered by two 1,760-lb s t RD-20 turbojets developed from captured German BMW 003 units. The turbojets were mounted side-by-side, with the intakes set in the nose of the aircraft, separated by a bulkhead. A 37-mm Nudelmann cannon projected from this bulkhead and two 23-mm Nudelmann-Suranov cannon were mounted in the lower part of the nose. The turbojets exhausted under the rear fuselage, with the outlets situated at points just beneath the trailing-edges of the wings. Pneumatic systems were utilized to operate the undercarriage, brakes and flaps and to charge the cannon. A tricycle undercarriage was fitted.

The first flight of the I-300 took place on 24 April 1946–the same day as that of the Yak-15, evolved by the Yakovlev team to the same specification. The I-300, however, was superior to the Yak-15, being an entirely new design whereas the Yakovlev machine was an adaptation of a standard Yak-3 airframe to accommodate a single RD-20 turbojet.

During test flights, the I-300 recorded a maximum speed of 566 mph, which was 53 mph faster than the best performance achieved by its rival.

Engineer test pilot A. N. Grinchik, who made the initial flight, contributed a great deal towards development of the design, and his unexplained death in an accident, on 11 July 1946, may have been connected with the I-300, or MiG-9 as it was by then designated.

Mikoyan and his colleagues had faced many problems new to them during the course of design and development. To avoid loss of stability caused by the compressibility problem at high speeds, it was found essential to utilize a wing of thin section. This, in turn, set problems concerning accommodation of the large amount of fuel required and housing of the undercarriage in the narrow wing. Finally, the wing was almost completely filled with flexible tanks which contained a fuel load of 351 gallons. In order to reduce the size of the main undercarriage units, levered suspension and smaller shock-absorbers of new design were adopted.

Danger of the ailerons tearing away from the wings at high speeds became apparent during test flying, and split-type ailerons were introduced to counteract this tendency.

As a result of the time, effort and skill expended on overcoming all the aerodynamic and structural problems, the MiG-9 emerged as a fighter bearing comparison with any foreign type of the period. It was among the first jet types to equip Soviet single-seat fighter squadrons, serving in some numbers with the VVS until the advent of the "second generation" of Russian jet fighters, and was given the NATO code-name "Fargo".

Mikoyan-Gurevich MiG-15

Of Korean War fame, the MiG-15 (NATO code-name "Fagot"), was in production from 1948 until the mid-1950s, during which period many thousands were built and served with the air arms of the Soviet Union, China, Algeria, Albania, Bulgaria, Czechoslovakia, East Germany, Hungary, North Korea, Poland, the United Arab Republic and Rumania.

The type has been licence-built in large numbers in Czechoslovakia and Poland. Over 1,000 were supplied to China alone.

The prototype MiG-15 made its first flight on 30 December 1947, powered by a Rolls-Royce Nene turbojet engine, which the British government had released for export. After the initial flight a number of modifications were made to the machine, but it crashed after a time,

Mikoyan-Gurevich MiG-9

Mikoyan-Gurevich MiG-9

Mikoyan-Gurevich MiG-9

TYPE	DIMENSIONS						WEIGHT	PERFORMANCE				REMARKS
	span		length		height		max t-o	max speed	at height	service ceiling	combat range	
	ft	in	ft	in	ft	in	lb	mph	ft	ft	miles	
Mikoyan-Gurevich MiG-1	33	9⅝	26	8⅞	NA		6,770	390·2	22,965	39,369	453	AM-35A engine. Prototype reached 402·9 mph at 22,638 ft
Mikoyan-Gurevich MiG-3	33	9⅝	26	8⅞	NA		7,390	397·6	25,590	39,369	776	
Mikoyan-Gurevich MiG-9	32	9¾	NA		NA		11,177	559·2	16,404	42,651	NA	

Mikoyan-Gurevich MiG-15

Mikoyan-Gurevich MiG-15, Czechoslovak Air Force

Mikoyan-Gurevich MiG-15, ground-attack version

killing the test pilot. The second prototype was modified extensively. The wing structure was strengthened and a few degrees of anhedral replaced the dihedral of the first prototype. Leading-edge slots were introduced experimentally to improve low-speed characteristics, but were replaced later by boundary-layer fences on the inboard panels. Further flight testing resulted in cutting back the jet pipe under the tail surfaces, and lowering the tailplane from the tip of the fin to approximately one-third down.

Substantial numbers of MiG-15s were in service with Soviet forces by the end of 1948, joining the A-VMF (Naval Air Squadrons) in 1951 and satellite air forces by early 1952. They were armed with one 23-mm cannon under the port side of the nose, and one 37-mm cannon under the starboard side. This proved inadequate and trials were carried out with one 37-mm cannon and two 12·7-mm machine-guns (port), an all-machine-gun installation and a single 45-mm cannon. Finally, the standard armament became one 37-mm N cannon below the starboard side, and two 23-mm NS cannon below the port side of the nose. The guns were mounted in a carriage which could be lowered for easy maintenance when a panel was removed. An underwing load of rockets or two 1,000-lb bombs could be carried. Ejector seats were not fitted initially, although these later became standard.

Power plant of the production series was initially the RD-45 turbojet – virtually a copy of the Nene – rated at 5,450 lb s t. As production continued, the slightly improved RD-45A and RD-45FA, later re-designated VK-1, became standard. Licence-built MiG-15s were designated LIM-1 (Polish) and S-102 (Czechoslovak), with production beginning in 1952–3.

Towards the end of the Korean War, the improved MiG-15*bis* replaced the earlier model. It was almost identical, but had revised air-brakes and perforated flaps. Power plant was initially a centrifugal-flow VK-1 turbojet rated at 5,950 lb s t and 6,750 lb s t with water injection. The final production series had a VK-1A turbojet, rated at 6,990 lb s t with water injection. MiG-15*bis* armament comprised one 37-mm N cannon with 40 rounds, mounted under the starboard side of the nose, and two 23-mm NS cannon, each with 80 rounds, mounted under the port side of the nose. External attachments for stores of up to 1,100 lb could be carried.

In Poland the MiG-15*bis* was built at Mielec as the LIM-2, and in Czechoslovakia as the S-103. The type was phased out of production in the U.S.S.R. during 1953–4, but was manufactured under licence until about 1955.

Well-tried under combat conditions in Korea, the MiG-15 series compared favourably with the American F-86 Sabre and, in fact, with any jet fighter in service anywhere in the world at that time. It had a better rate of climb than the F-86, a tighter turning circle and far better service ceiling. Above 35,000 ft it was also faster than the Sabre. However, a really tight turn was liable to result in a snap roll and an uncontrollable spin. Fore and aft stability left something to be desired and directional snaking occurred at high speeds. This, and the fact that no radar gunsight was fitted, made it an inferior gun platform.

A version designated MiG-15F was reported, with an F-86D-type nose radome. It was probably intended to offset some of the combat disadvantages of the earlier model. It did not enter service in any numbers.

In Korea, Chinese MiG-15s enjoyed adequate and consistent early-warning of the approach of UN bombers and fighters due to the availability of this type of radar unit. This enabled the MiG-15s to be airborne in time to gain a height advantage over their opponents, upon whom they would dive from out of the sun. The relative lack of Chinese success in these interceptions was due to inferior pilot training standards.

In addition to the basic fighter version, the tandem two-seat MiG-15UTI (NATO code-name "Midget") operational trainer has been built in quantity, with an RD-45 turbojet. The MiG-15*bis* and MiG-15UTI continue in service in Russia, Albania, Bulgaria, China, Cuba, Czechoslovakia, Egypt, East Germany, Hungary, Iraq, North Korea, Poland, Rumania, North Vietnam and the Yemen.

Mikoyan-Gurevich MiG-17

Designed to remedy defects in the MiG-15 revealed in combat over Korea, Russian sources claimed that the MiG-17 is not merely an improved version of the earlier machine but an entirely new aircraft. This seems extremely unlikely and Western experts consider it to be basically an aerodynamically refined MiG-15. It has been built under licence in China, Czechoslovakia and Poland and serves 21 air forces including those of Albania, Afghanistan, Bulgaria, East Germany, Guinea, Hungary, Indonesia, Iraq, North Korea, North Vietnam, Morocco, Rumania and the United Arab Republic.

By 1953–4 the MiG-17 was replacing the MiG-15 in Soviet Air and Naval Service. The initial production model, code-named by NATO "Fresco-A," was powered by a VK-1 centrifugal-flow turbojet rated at 5,950 lb s t. Although it retained the two 23-mm (lower port nose) and one 37-mm (lower starboard nose) cannon armament of the MiG-15, fire rate and ammunition capacity were improved.

The MiG-17 "Fresco-A" can be distinguished from later MiG-17 day fighters by its elongated air-brakes and slightly longer fuselage. The "Fresco-B" day-fighters were generally similar to the -A, but had rectangular air-brakes repositioned from the rear fuselage to aft of the wing trailing-edge. This model retained the VK-1 turbojet and the same armament but did not enter service in any large numbers.

Operational since the mid-1950s, the most widely-used variant of the day-fighter is the "Fresco-C," powered by a VK-1A turbojet, rated at 5,950 lb s t dry or 6,990 lb s t with afterburner. Air-brakes of rectangular form have been returned to the rear fuselage position, and the "Fresco-C" is generally similar to the "Fresco-A" but has the tail cone cut back around the afterburning nozzle. Armament consists of one 37-mm NS-2 cannon under the lower starboard nose and two 23-mm NR VYa cannon. A supplementary 23-mm gun package is sometimes installed at the wing tank position. Four underwing packs of eight 55-mm air-to-air rockets, or a total of 1,100 lb of bombs can be carried. Normally two external tanks of 88 Imp gallons each are fitted.

This variant has been built under licence in China, at Mukden, and began to equip Chinese squadrons in 1955. In Poland it was built under the designation LIM-5 and in Czechoslovakia as the S-104. The version designated MiG-17PF and code-named "Fresco-D" is the standard all-weather version of this single-seat interceptor. Armament is revised to three 23-mm cannon and 32 55-mm rockets in external pods below wings. Reports indicate that 210-mm air-to-surface weapons can be carried. Power plant is an afterburning VK-1A.

SCAN ODD interception radar is installed in the air intake cone and upper lip.

"Fresco-E" was not used in any great numbers and was basically a MiG-17PF minus afterburner. MiG-17s remaining in Soviet service are of the MiG-17PF type but with four underwing beam-riding missiles in lieu of the usual cannon armament. In Poland a specially modified LIM-5 has been developed. This is a re-worked "Fresco-C" type airframe and is intended for rough field operation.

Mkoyan-Gurevich MiG-17

Mikoyan-Gurevich MiG-17

Mikoyan-Gurevich MiG-17PF

TYPE	DIMENSIONS span ft	span in	length ft	length in	height ft	height in	WEIGHT max t-o lb	PERFORMANCE max speed mph	at height ft	service ceiling ft	combat range miles	REMARKS
Mikoyan-Gurevich MiG-15	33	1	36	3¼	11	1¾	11,270	668 656	SL 10,000	51,000	560	
Mikoyan-Gurevich MiG-15*bis*	33	1	36	3¼	11	1¾	11,085	684/746		51,000	560	NATO: "Fagot-B". Initial climb-10,400 ft/min
Mikoyan-Gurevich MiG-17	31	0	36	3	11	0	14,750	645 725	50,000 low altitude	57,500	255-350 (radius)	NATO: "Fresco-C". Landing speed 127mph
Mikoyan-Gurevich MiG-17PF	31	0	36	3	11	0	14,750	656 630	35,000 50,000	58,000	300 (radius)	NATO: "Fresco-D"

Mikoyan-Gurevich MiG-19PD, with "Alkali" missiles

Mikoyan-Gurevich MiG-19, Czechoslovak Air Force

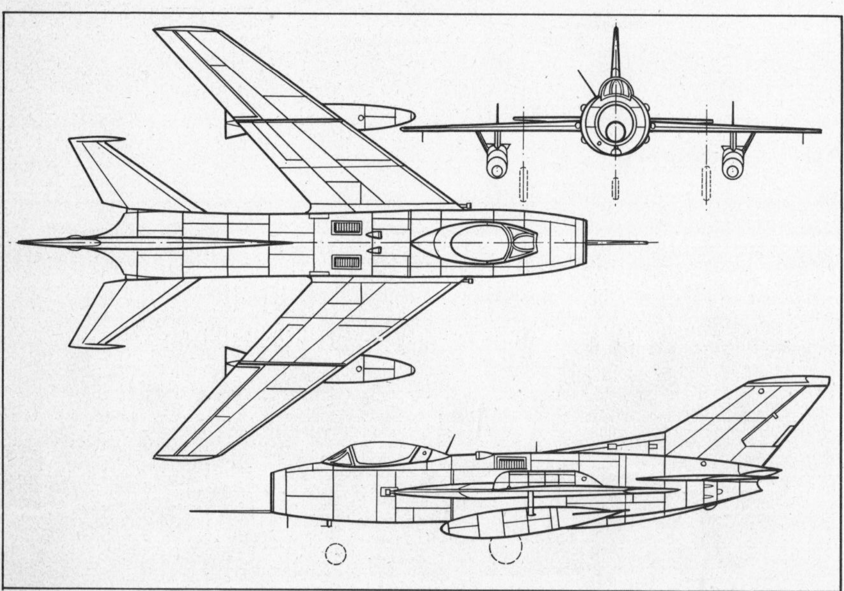
Mikoyan-Gurevich MiG-19

Mikoyan-Gurevich MiG-21F, Indian Air Force

Twin main wheels are fitted and, in order to accommodate these when retracted, the undersurface of the inboard wing has been lowered, providing almost twice the original depth. Armament is the standard "Fresco-C" type or three 23-mm NR-23 cannon. The VK-1A turbojet is retained. Maximum take-off weight is approximately 14,500 lb. Take-off run is 700 yds and landing run 620 yds. Service ceiling is 50,000 ft. Low-level radius of action at Mach 0·75 is approximately 140 miles. Many thousands of MiG-17s have been built and the type is likely to remain in service outside the U.S.S.R. for some years ahead.

Mikoyan-Gurevich MiG-19

First flown in 1953, the MiG-19 marked another success for the design team of Artem Ivanovich Mikoyan and Mikhail Iossipovich Gurevich. It was originally tested under the designation TsAGI-418, but entered service with the Soviet Air Force as the MiG-19 in 1955 and became the first Soviet production interceptor fighter capable of speeds in excess of Mach 1·0. The initial production version first appeared in public at the 1955 Soviet Air Display and is code-named "Farmer-A" by NATO. The "Farmer-A" is armed with one 37-mm N cannon (fire rate 500 rpm) mounted below the starboard side of the nose, and two 23-mm NR cannon (fire rate 800 rpm each) mounted at the wing-roots. This type still remains in front-line service in China today. Power plant is two AM-5 axial-flow turbojets rated, with afterburner, at 6,700 lb s t each. Zero-length rocket launch take-off was tried experimentally on a "Farmer-A" airframe, but was not adopted for general use.

A few "Farmer-As" had a revised armament of two 30-mm wing-root cannon. In 1958 a night-fighter variant, designated MiG-19D, appeared and was code-named "Farmer-B". This model was armed with two 23-mm cannon mounted at the wing roots and eight 55-mm unguided air-to-air rockets carried in two pods below the wings.

The night-fighter is 1·8 ft longer than day-fighter variants, and has SCAN ODD interception radar equipment in the upper intake lip and in a "bullet" fairing mounted on the air intake splitter.

Powered by two AM-9b axial-flow turbojets, rated at 5,500 lb s t (7,150 lb s t with afterburner), the standard MiG-19 day-fighter is "Farmer-C". This has three 30-mm cannon in place of the earlier forms of armament and has additional ventral air-brakes. "Farmer-C" has been built in Poland as the LIM-7 and in Czechoslovakia. Two RD-9F axial-flow turbojets provide 5,500 lb s t and 7,200 lb s t with afterburner.

Current night-fighter version is the MiG-19PD, coded "Farmer-D". This has no guns but carries four beam-riding missiles slung from pylons under the wing leading-edges. Turbojets are of the RD-9F type and SCAN ODD radar equipment is installed. Recent photographs depict the MiG-19PD with a modified cockpit canopy, having only forward and side vision. In addition to the nations already mentioned, this single-seat interceptor fighter is operated by the air forces of Cuba, East Germany, Iraq, Indonesia, North Korea, Syria, the United Arab Republic, Pakistan and Yugoslavia.

Mikoyan-Gurevich MiG-21

This short-range single-seat delta-wing fighter was seen for the first time in prototype form at the 1956 Soviet Aviation Day display over Moscow. It was at first thought to be a Sukhoi design, but was identified subsequently as the MiG-21. It is now standard equipment in the air forces of the Soviet Union, its allies and friends, including Cuba, Czechoslovakia, Egypt, Finland, East Germany, Hungary, India, Indonesia, Iraq, Poland, Rumania, Syria, North Vietnam and Yugoslavia.

The MiG-21 is being built in Czechoslovakia and under licence in India.

The standard MiG-21F (NATO code-name "Fishbed-C") is a short-range clear-weather fighter with a cantilever mid-set monoplane wing of delta planform. Sweepback is approximately 60° and there is slight anhedral. The circular-section all-metal fuselage has a small air intake centre-body. The tail unit is a cantilever all-metal structure with all surfaces sharply swept. All units of the tricycle landing gear retract into the fuselage. A brake-parachute, housed originally a small door on the port underside of the rear fuselage, has since been transferred to an acorn housing at the base of the rudder. Power plant consists of one TDR Mk R37F turbojet, rated at 9,500 lb s t dry and at 12,500 lb s t with afterburner.

Armament comprises two 30-mm cannon in long fairings on the fuselage undersurface (though many "Fishbed-Cs" now carry only one cannon, the port fairing being blanked off). Two "Atoll" air-to-air infra-red homing missiles, similar to the American Sidewinder, are carried on underwing attachments. There is also a central underfuselage attachment for external stores.

In parallel service in Russia and Czechoslovakia are a tandem two-seat trainer version (NATO code-name "Mongol") and the "Fishbed-D", which incorporates a number of changes to improve operational capability and performance. In particular, it has a new forward fuselage of lengthened and less-tapering form, with a larger intake centre-body, presumably housing improved radar to enhance all-weather capability. Identified officially as the MiG-21PF (F = boosted), this aircraft has an uprated turbojet, under-fuselage air-brakes and wider-chord fin and rudder.

Experimental versions of the MiG-21 include a STOL prototype, demonstrated at the Domodedovo air display in July 1967.

This STOL aircraft had an extra section, some 4 ft long, inserted in its fuselage aft of the cockpit, to house a vertically-mounted lift-jet engine.

Mikoyan MiG-23

The Mikoyan MiG-23 multi-purpose fighter was entering service with the Soviet Air Force in summer 1967. It is a twin-jet single-seater, with high-mounted cropped delta wings and a unique twin-finned tail unit. The box-like air-intake ducts, with wedge-shaped inlets, are similar to those of the North American Vigilante. Its low aspect ratio wings, low-set tailplane, and large ventral fins should help to ensure stability during low-level flying at supersonic speed, and it has set officially-recognized speed records at up to 1,852 mph.

Soviet sources have described this aircraft as an all-weather interceptor, but it looks as if it would also make a formidable low-level strike aircraft. Its NATO code-name is "Foxbat".

Mosca MB*bis*

The Moskovskiy Aviatsionni Zavod Mosca (Mosca Moscow Aviation Works) was set up by the Savoia designer, F. E. Mosca, who had been persuaded to go to Moscow by the Russian pilots Lerkhe and Yankovsky while they were visiting Italy. By the end of 1916, the factory was producing about five Nieuport and Morane J scouts per month. By 1917, production of all aircraft had increased to 15 per month.

The Mosca MB, which made its first flight in July 1915, was a single-seat high-wing monoplane fighter based on the

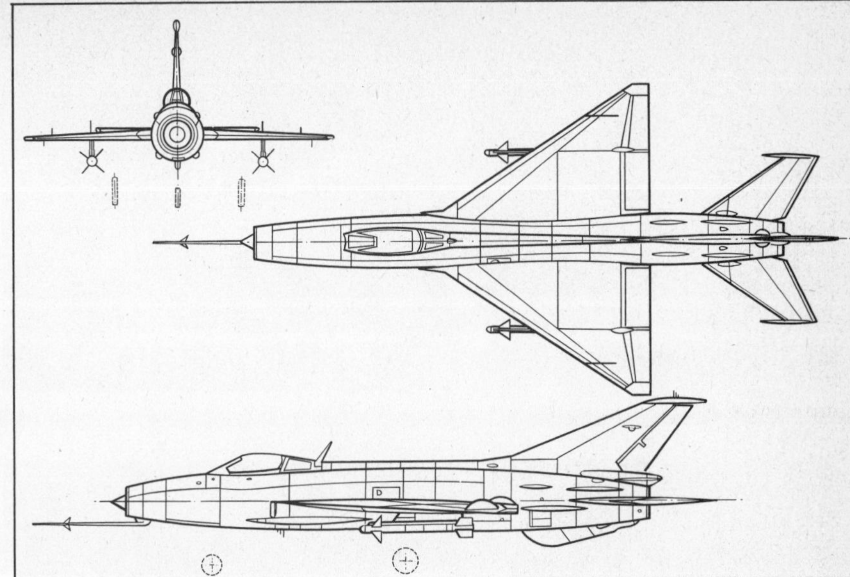

Mikoyan-Gurevich MiG-21F

Mikoyan-Gurevich MiG-21PF, with JATO

Mikoyan MiG-23

TYPE	DIMENSIONS span ft	in	length ft	in	height ft	in	WEIGHT max t-o lb	PERFORMANCE max speed mph	at height ft	service ceiling ft	combat range miles	REMARKS
Mikoyan-Gurevich MiG-19	32	0	37	6	NA		19,840	Mach 1·3 860 740	20,000 36,000 50,000	55,000	600/850 (radius)	NATO: "Farmer-C"
Mikoyan-Gurevich MiG-19PD	32	0	37	6	NA		22,500	Mach 1·3	20,000	58,000	600/850 (radius)	NATO: "Farmer-D"
Mikoyan-Gurevich MiG-21	25	0	55	0	NA		18,800	1,320	36,000	NA	375 (radius)	NATO: "Fishbed-C"
Mikoyan-Gurevich MiG-21 PF	25	0	57	0	NA		20,500	1,520	36,000	NA	400 (radius)	NATO: "Fishbed-D"
Mikoyan MiG-23	40	0	69	0	NA		NA	1,850	40,000	75,000		NATO: "Foxbat"

Mosca MB*bis*

Myasishchev Mya-4

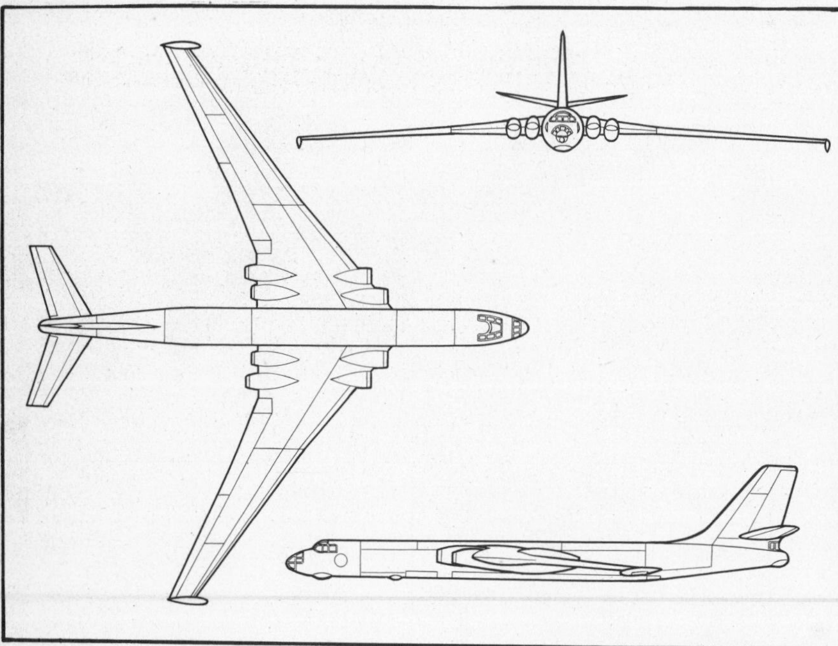
Myasishchev Mya-4

Morane J. It was smaller, however, with a wing area of 129·2 sq ft, and later versions had ailerons instead of wing warping control. The Morane J's slab-sided fuselage was retained, but the MB had a new, smaller rounded tail unit with a small under-fin between the fuselage and tailskid; the wings and tail unit folded up alongside the fuselage to facilitate transportation. Construction was entirely of wood, with fabric covering. The MB was powered by an 80-hp Le Rhône rotary engine, which gave a maximum speed of 81 mph; time taken to climb to 6,560 ft was 8·5 minutes. Manoeuvrability was considered quite good.

The MB's original armament was awkward, to say the least: a fixed machine-gun was mounted in front of the pilot, at an angle of about 40° to the aircraft's centre line. While ensuring that the gun fired outside the propeller disc, such an arrangement must have made it extremely difficult to manoeuvre into a firing position. Later, on the MB*bis* production version, a synchronized machine-gun was fitted.

In October 1916, the Mosca factory received large orders from the State Defence Conference, for 225 MB*bis* with 80-hp or 110-hp Le Rhône or 110-hp Clerget engines, and 100 Nieuport 11s; 225 aircraft were to be handed over to the Administration of the Military Air Fleet by 1 July 1917. By the end of May, however, only about 25 MB*bis* scouts had been delivered, and the delivery date was deferred until April 1918.

Myasishchev Mya-4

Designed by a team headed by V. M. Myasishchev, this four-jet long-range heavy bomber was reported initially during the summer of 1953, when it was tested under the designation TsAGI-428. Code-named "Bison" by NATO, its first public appearance was made over Moscow in May 1954, and it joined Soviet Air Force DA (Dalnaya Aviatsiya) units during 1955/6.

Introduction of the Mya-4 gave the Soviet Air Force the capacity to deliver atomic or thermo-nuclear bombs over intercontinental ranges, with the help of flight refuelling in extreme cases.

In much the same class as the B-52, the Mya-4 shares the US bomber's undercarriage configuration, with tandem main wheel bogies under its fuselage, fore and aft of the bomb-bay, and outboard balancer wheels which, in the case of the "Bison", retract into wing-tip fairings. Power plants are four Mikulin AM-3D axial-flow turbojets of 19,180 lb s t each. A crew of eight or more is carried.

Later production aircraft lacked the glazed nose panelling of the earlier machines and were fitted with a flight refuelling probe. Some Soviet Naval units were re-equipped with "Bisons" early in 1960, and these now operate the 201-M version, with radar built into a more pointed nose and 28,660-lb s t D-15 engines.

Defensive armament comprises twin 23-mm cannon in radar-controlled barbettes forward of the wing on top of the fuselage, and forward of the bomb-bay below, plus twin 23-mm cannon in the manually-directed tail turret. A fixed 23-mm cannon is mounted in the starboard side of the nose.

A bomb-load of 10,000 lb can be carried for 7,000 miles at 520 mph without flight refuelling.

Nyeman R-10 (KhAI-5)

During World War II it was widely believed in aviation circles in the U.S.A. and Great Britain that R-10 was the Soviet designation for a Russian licence-built version of the American Vultee V-11. In fact, 36 V-11GBs were built in the U.S.S.R. under licence during 1937-8 under the designation BSL-1. They were soon turned over to Aeroflot for use as high-speed postal aircraft and were then redesignated PS-43.

Subsequently, when the R-10 was acknowledged as a Soviet design, it was credited erroneously to the designer N. N. Polikarpov. It is now known that R-10 was the military designation of the KhAI-5, a product of the design team of the Kharkov Aeronautical Institute headed by I. G. Nyeman and a logical development of the KhAI-l which had been built in 1932. The test flights of this low-wing single-engined civil monoplane were conducted by B. N. Kudrin. During official trials he flew with six passengers on board at a maximum speed of 201 mph. Since this exceeded the top speed achieved by the Polikarpov-Grigorovich I-5, at that time the principal Soviet interceptor fighter, it is hardly surprising that this passenger transport with its retractable undercarriage should have attracted the attention of the Soviet Air Force.

About 40 KhAI-1 transports were built between 1934 and 1937 for service on Soviet internal air routes. The military development of the KhAI-1 was designed and tested in 1935–6.

As the Nyeman R-10 it entered series production in 1937 and was built in quantity, approximately 500 machines being completed.

Power was provided by an M-25V radial engine of 750 hp driving a two-bladed VISh-6 propeller. The main undercarriage legs retracted inward into wells in the wings, but the tailwheel did not retract. The wings were of distinctive form, with a tapering leading-edge and a straight trailing-edge. The pilot was protected by an enclosed, sliding canopy and the observer-gunner had a partially-retractable turret housing a single 7·62-mm ShKAS machine-gun. Armour plate was fitted as a protection for the crew.

There were two fixed 7·62-mm ShKAS machine-guns in the wings. Range with an 882-lb load of bombs was 745 miles.

Unfortunately for its crews, the R-10 was already outmoded when it entered service with the Soviet Air Force. Reports indicate that it saw limited operational service in Mongolia during the 1938–9 clashes with the Japanese. R-10s were also stationed in squadron strength at airfields in the Soviet sector after the partition of Poland between Germany and Russia in September 1939. They were seen and occasionally shot down by the Luftwaffe during the initial onslaught on the Soviet Union in June 1941.

Petlyakov Pe-8 (Tupolev ANT-42)

The task of developing, to a 1934 specification, a fast long-range bomber capable of carrying a heavy bomb-load over long distances fell almost inevitably to A. N. Tupolev's design team. The new type was designated ANT-42, or TB-7. It differed appreciably from its predecessors in having a high wing loading and engines capable of high-altitude performance. Its maximum speed was intended to be attained at 26,250 ft (8,000 m), as against 13,125 ft (4,000 m) for the TB-3; and the appreciably higher acceptable wing loading meant that wing area could be reduced by 505 sq ft. During the development period of 1934–7, no production engines were available which could maintain their efficiency at altitudes over 14,750 ft. The designers solved the problem by installing an M-100 engine in the fuselage solely to drive a central ACN-2 supercharger for four AM-34FRN engines.

The TB-7 flew for the first time on 27 December 1936. This and subsequent test flights between January and March 1937, were made without the ACN-2 supercharging system in operation. The first flight with the system switched on was not made until 10 August 1937, when the aircraft's high speed and ceiling were at once apparent. At 26,250-29,500 ft, the top speed exceeded that of German Bf 109B and He 112 fighters. The report at the conclusion of the official trials stated: "With such handling and tactical characteristics, the TB-7 represents a wholly

Myasishchev Mya-4 (201-M)

Nyeman R-10 (KhAI-5)

Petlyakov Pe-8 (Tupolev ANT-42)

Petlyakov Pe-8

TYPE	DIMENSIONS						WEIGHT	PERFORMANCE				REMARKS
	span		*length*		*height*		*max t-o*	*max speed*	*at height*	*service ceiling*	*combat range*	
	ft	*in*	*ft*	*in*	*ft*	*in*	*lb*	*mph*	*ft*	*ft*	*miles*	
Mosca MB*bis*	20	4	17	0¾	NA		1,168	81	SL	13,779	2hr 20min	Developed from French Morane J
Myasishchev Mya-4	170	7	162	5	50	0	352,750	620	10,000	40,000	3,000	
Nyeman R-10	47	2⅞	32	9¾	NA		NA	223·7	9,842	NA	745	

Petlyakov Pe-8

Petlyakov Pe-2

Petlyakov Pe-2

Petlyakov Pe-2

modern aircraft. Its speed of 250 mph at 26,250 ft (8,000 m) makes it, at that height, a very difficult target for contemporary fighters."

During 1938–9, V. M. Petlyakov directed development work to prepare the TB-7 for series production. AM-35A engines, which did not require the rather cumbersome ACN-2 supercharging system, were installed in 1939. With the TB-7's flight trials completed successfully, production got under way at the end of that year. Redesignated Pe-8 at the end of 1940, the heavy bomber was further developed by Petlyakov and his colleagues.

Armament of the Pe-8 consisted of two 7·62-mm ShKAS machine-guns in a manually-operated nose turret, one movable 12·7-mm Beresin machine-gun in the rear of each inboard engine nacelle, a 20-mm ShVAK cannon in a dorsal turret and a similar weapon in an electrically-operated tail turret.

A formation of Pe-8s with AM-35A engines made a successful attack on Berlin in the summer of 1941. Many more raids deep behind the German lines, were made subsequently by Pe-8s, with both AM-35As and M-30B diesel engines, but the type was never available in large numbers.

Pe-8 No. 66, powered by AM-35A engines, achieved fame by making two outstanding long-distance flights over enemy territory to Scotland and the United States in 1942. During the second of these flights, over the route Moscow-Dundee-Iceland-Canada-Washington-Newfoundland-Greenland-Iceland-Scotland-Moscow, a distance of 11,060 miles was covered at an average altitude of 26,250 ft.

The M-30B diesel engines, designed by A. D. Charomsky, which were installed in early 1941, were intended to achieve better fuel economy. With this power plant, the Pe-8 had a range of 4,860 miles with 4,400 lb of bombs. Its loaded weight was 68,355 lb. The diesels, however, had a number of shortcomings which outweighed their obvious advantages, while the AM-35A engines were taken out of production to make way for AM-38s for ground-attack aircraft. The M-82 radial engine was tried out on the Pe-8, but with disappointing results, the aircraft's top speed being only 252 mph.

When Petlyakov was killed in a flying accident in the autumn of 1942, he was succeeded by I. F. Nyezval, who continued development of the Pe-8 by improving the general aerodynamic form and introducing M-82FN engines with direct fuel injection. The gun positions at the rear of the inboard engine nacelles were deleted on this version, which went into production in 1943. Top speed was 280 mph and range 3,730 miles. This final development of the type was taken out of production in 1944.

At no time did the Pe-8 displace the Il-4 as the backbone of the Soviet long-range bombing force. The comparatively small numbers that were produced are explained partly by the many design changes which were thrust upon it and partly by the fact that the Soviet Command was satisfied with the performance of the large numbers of twin-engined Il-4s and smaller numbers of Yer-2 long-range bombers at its disposal.

Petlyakov Pe-2

In 1938–9 a team headed by V. M. Petlyakov produced a design for a fast twin-engined fighter with a pressurized cockpit, under the provisional designation VI-100 (VI = *Vysotnii Istrebityel* = high-altitude fighter). Great care was taken to achieve the best aerodynamic form and the overall dimensions of the aircraft were reduced to the utmost. The radiators were located in the wings. The fuselage had the smallest possible cross-section and its interior was designed so as to utilize every available inch of space for useful load. Power was provided by two liquid-cooled M-105 engines with TK-3 superchargers, which maintained their efficiency at heights over 16,000 ft.

It was apparent as the project progressed that it would be comparatively simple to change the rôle to that of a high-altitude bomber and tests of this version, still known as the VI-100, began in 1939. High level bombing soon proved inaccurate and from then on the function was changed to dive-bombing. Dive-brakes were fitted under the wings, and the aircraft was re-designated PB-100. Official trials were completed in 1940 and production of the Pe-2, as it was by then known, began in that June.

The Pe-2, with its high top speed of 335·5 mph, replaced the obsolescent SB-2*bis* and Ar-2, with maximum speeds of 263 and 284.5 mph respectively.

Initially, defensive armament comprised four 7·62-mm ShKAS machine-guns, one flexibly mounted in the rear cockpit and two firing forward from the upper fuselage decking. The fourth weapon was on a ventral mounting which was retractable and was operated by means of a periscopic sight. Normal offensive load was 1,325 lb of bombs, with a maximum of 2,205 lb. Up to 441 lb of bombs could be accommodated in the fuselage bomb-bay and 220 lb in the rear of the engine nacelles. The internal load could be supplemented by four 220-lb bombs on external racks which could, alternatively, carry the entire load of either four 550-lb or two 1,100-lb bombs.

In 1941, when 458 Pe-2 bombers were manufactured, V. M. Petlyakov's team produced an extensively modified version for interceptor duties, designated Pe-3*bis*. Offensive armament was strengthened by the addition of a 20-mm ShVAK cannon and a 12·7-mm machine-gun. The dive-brakes were deleted and special underwing flaps were introduced to improve manoeuvrability. The Pe-3*bis* interceptor fighter entered series production in 1941 and was also employed on high-speed reconnaissance duties.

At first, when few Pe-2s were available, they were used very effectively for raids on heavily defended areas. The standard German fighter at that time, the Messerschmitt Bf 109E, was not fast enough to intercept the attacking Pe-2s. The Soviet State Defence Committee took extraordinary measures to ensure maximum production of the type and, despite the evacuation of factories to eastern areas, output was maintained.

Pe-2 development kept pace with improvements in the performance of German fighters. Operational bomber crews during 1942 requested increased defensive armament to combat the new Bf 109 F, which was faster than the Pe-2 at altitudes up to 13,000 ft. A new turret, housing a 12·7-mm UBT gun, was quickly developed to replace the observer's 7·62-mm weapon on a flexible mounting. The turret was designated FT (*Frontovoye Trebovanye* = Frontal Demand) and, from July 1942, mobile factory teams installed the FT turret on all operational Pe-2s at their front-line airfields. At the same time, extra armour for the pilot and gunner-radio operator was fitted. Two additional 7·62-mm beam guns were fitted on some machines, and the ventral 7·62-mm gun was supplanted by a weapon of 12·7-mm calibre.

Later in 1942, the faster Bf 109G-2 made its appearance. Accordingly, more powerful M-105PF engines were installed on production Pe-2s from February 1943.

Petlyakov Pe-2

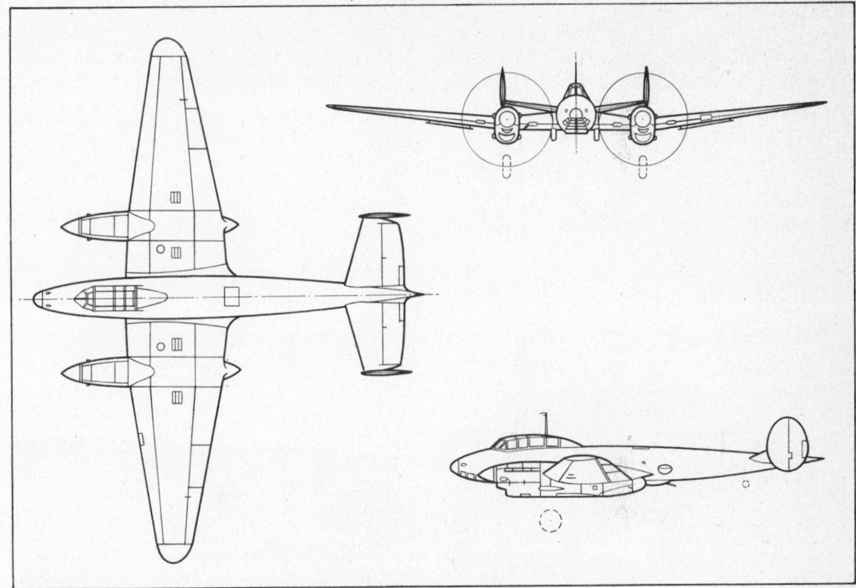

Petlyakov Pe-2

TYPE	DIMENSIONS						WEIGHT	PERFORMANCE				REMARKS
	span		length		height		max-t-o	max speed	at height	service ceiling	combat range	
	ft	in	ft	in	ft	in	lb	mph	ft	ft	miles	
												Version with AM-35A engines
Petlyakov Pe-8 (TB-7)	131	0⅜	73	8⅝	20	0⅛	63,052[1]	234·8	SL	32,972[2]	2,038[1]	[1] With 4,408-lb bomb load
											2,361[3]	[2] After dropping bomb load
								275·9	20,997			[3] Max range at 175 mph at 20,000 ft
							68,255[5]	234·8	SL	32,972[2]	2,321[4]	[4] Max range at 178 mph at 20,000 ft
								265·9	15,091			[5] With 8,816-lb bomb load
								274	20,997			
							73,468[6]	234·2	SL	22,965	2,982[7]	[6] With 4,408-lb bomb load and max fuel
								265·3	15,091	(loaded)		[7] At 228 mph at 20,000 ft.
								272·1	24,934	31,988[2]	3,382[8]	[8] Max range at 184 mph at 20,000 ft
												Version with M-82 engines
							65,918[9]	223·7	17,388	29,035	2,501[10]	[9] Normal
							68,519[11]	240·5	19,865		1,242[12]	[10] With 11,600-lb bomb load and max fuel
												[11] Maximum
								234·9	19,865			[12] With 8,816-lb bomb load
												Version with Diesel engines
Petlyakov Pe-2	56	3½	41	4⅛	NA		16,540–18,780	335·5	16,404	28,871	745	With M-105R engines
	56	3½	41	4⅛			16,540–18,780	335·5	16,404	28,871		With M-105RA engines
							16,980	361			720	With VK-105PF engines
Petlyakov Pe-2 I	56	3½	41	4⅛	NA		NA	408·2	18,701	NA	NA	With VK-107A engines

Petlyakov Pe-2

Petlyakov Pe-2, captured aircraft, Finnish markings

Polikarpov I-1

As well as higher maximum speed, the new engines provided a shorter take-off run – an important asset when flying from small front-line airfields. Many aerodynamic improvements were also made as a result of intensive collaboration, begun in 1942, between a group of scientists and the factory staff. The wing profile was slightly modified, the wing surface finish was improved, the oil-cooler intakes were re-shaped and as many sources of drag as possible throughout the structure were eliminated or considerably reduced. Finally, the wing bomb-racks were enclosed in fairings. With the new power units, and as a result of all the intensive refinement, the Pe-2's top speed rose by 25·5 mph.

To ensure greater safety for the crew, the fuel tanks were covered with a protective layer of self-sealing rubber. Also, from July 1943, empty spaces in the wing fuel tanks – as the fuel was consumed – were filled with a neutral gas produced from cooled exhaust gases, thus considerably reducing the danger of fire during combat.

Variants of the Pe-2 included a trainer, the Pe-2 UT, with dual controls; the Pe-2 R reconnaissance version, with greater range; and a fast interceptor, the Pe-2 I. This last model went into series production in 1944 and was powered by two VK-107As, each giving 1,650 hp at take-off. Maximum speed was 408 mph at 18,700 ft. A bomber version of the Pe-2 I could carry 4,400 lb of bombs internally, and had a maximum bomb-load of up to 6,615 lb.

The Pe-2 was an outstanding aircraft in every respect. From 1942 onward, it formed the mainstay of Soviet tactical bombing units and, together with the Ilyushin Il-2, it accounted for the bulk of Russian bomber production in World War II. It participated in operations against the Germans and their allies from the Arctic to the Black Sea. It was code-named "Buck" by NATO.

Polikarpov I-1 M-5 (IL-400)

The first Soviet-designed fighter to enter production was the I-1, a cantilever low-wing monoplane with a water-cooled M-5 engine, developing 400 hp and driving a two-bladed wooden propeller. The prototype had been designated IL-400 (L-400 standing for the 400-hp Liberty engine from which the Soviet M-5 was developed) and was a product of the design team led by Nikolai N. Polikarpov. Armament comprised two 7·62-mm machine-guns.

The prototype first flew on 23 August 1923. During the take-off run, the aircraft left the ground prematurely and went into a steep climb, despite the fact that the pilot, Artzeulov, had the control column well forward. At a height of between 30 and 60 ft, with its nose still high, the aircraft stalled and crashed.

When test flying was resumed, it was soon clear that the fighter was very unstable. Detailed wind tunnel tests with a model of the I-1 traced the cause of the disaster to the prototype to incorrect position of the centre of gravity. It was found that even a slight departure from the optimum position had an adverse effect on the aircraft's longitudinal stability. A revised engine mounting on the production I-1 moved the centre of gravity further forward and cured the trouble.

Flight testing by A. I. Zhukov, as well as service squadron experience, showed that the aircraft still stalled when the control stick was pulled back sharply during tight turns and when going into or coming out of steep climbs. Considerable difficulty was also experienced in pulling out of a flat spin.

The I-1's handling difficulties called for great skill from its pilots and limited its suitability for the tight manoeuvring that was so essential to successful air combat at that time. No real answer was found to the problems and the I-1 was regarded as a failure. Nevertheless, in attempting various solutions a basis was found for further development of the single-seat low-wing monoplane fighter formula.

Polikarpov I-3

The I-3 single-seat biplane fighter was a 1927 design by a team which was led by N. N. Polikarpov and formed part of the Landplane Department of Aviatrust (OSS-TsKB).

It represented a development of an earlier design, the 2I-N1 – the first Soviet two-seat fighter – which was powered by a 400-hp Napier engine and attained 166·5 mph. The 2I-N1 itself had not been taken beyond the prototype stage.

The I-3 was quite a fast aircraft, with a maximum speed of over 186 mph; but it suffered from poor manoeuvrability due to the weight of its 600/650-hp M-17 in-line engine. In spite of this shortcoming, its high speed kept it in production until 1934. A total of approximately 400 were built and were widely used by Soviet Air Force fighter units.

Construction of the I-3 was mainly of wood, with monocoque fuselage of oval cross-section. The upper wing was of greater span than the lower one. The wings had a positive stagger and were also of wood, covered with fabric and braced with "N" struts and streamline wires. The metal undercarriage was fitted with rubber shock-absorbers. Armament comprised two synchronized 7·62-mm machine-guns.

In the spring of 1929, the I-3 prototype was modified into a two-seat fighter and redesignated DI-2. The wing span was slightly increased and the fuselage was lengthened to accommodate a rear cockpit with twin machine-guns. The DI-2 did not go into quantity production.

Polikarpov R-5

The design team led by Nikolai N. Polikarpov produced the prototype of the R-5 in 1928. With the successful conclusion of its official trials, in 1930, the new light bomber was claimed to be superior to its known contemporaries, including the redoubtable Fokker C-V. That same year, the R-5 secured first place in the international competition for reconnaissance bombers held in Teheran, Persia, where it had been opposed by British, Dutch and French aircraft in the same category. It proved a first-class machine, with a good performance for its time, being simple to handle and capable of undertaking a wide range of tasks.

In the early 1930s, the R-5 became one of the most widely used types in the Soviet Air Force. From 1931 to 1937, more than 6,000 of all versions were built, as compared with the 100 Tupolev R-3s which had been constructed between 1926 and 1929.

The R-5 was a two-seat biplane of mixed construction, the main material being wood. The wings, of unequal span, were braced by "N"-type interplane struts, with ailerons on the upper wings only. The undercarriage was of conventional type, with a tail-skid, but, as with most Soviet types, the wheels could easily be replaced by skis. Armament included a single 7·62-mm PV-1 machine-gun, fixed on the port side of the upper fuselage decking and synchronized to fire between the blades of the two-bladed wooden propeller. The observer was provided with a movable 7·62-mm DA-1 machine-gun mounted on the rear cockpit. Normal bomb-load was 550 lb.

Basically a reconnaissance-bomber, the R-5 was built in many modified versions to fulfil a wide variety of rôles. The R-5a or MR-5 (TsKB-10), a naval floatplane version, first appeared in 1931; while the R-5T single-seat torpedo-bomber was produced in 1932. The R-5Sh two-seat assault aircraft was armed with five fixed forward-firing 7·62-mm PV-1 machine-guns, two movable 7·62-mm DP guns on a dorsal mounting and a 1,102-lb bomb-load.

The P-5 and P-5a were civil variants, with enclosed pilot's cockpits and the rear military cockpit replaced by a small cabin, with an access door for passengers on the port side of the fuselage. They served for many years with Aeroflot. Other versions of the R-5 were employed

Polikarpov I-3

Polikarpov R-5

Polikarpov R-5, ski landing gear

TYPE	DIMENSIONS						WEIGHT	PERFORMANCE				REMARKS
	span		*length*		*height*		*max t-o*	*max speed*	*at height*	*service ceiling*	*combat range*	
	ft	*in*	*ft*	*in*	*ft*	*in*	*lb*	*mph*	*ft*	*ft*	*miles*	
Polikarpov I-1M-5	34	5⅜	NA		NA		3,370	164	SL	NA	NA	
Polikarpov I-3	36	5	26	6⅛	11	0¼	4,107	186	SL	23,621	NA	

Polikarpov R-5SSS

Polikarpov-Grigorovich I-5

Polikarpov-Grigorovich I-5

as ambulance machines and also as advanced trainers.

In 1934, an improved model of the bomber- reconnaissance R-5 appeared. It was fitted with the M-17F engine – a version of the M-17 boosted to give 650 hp – and was given the designation R-5SSS. To improve its aerodynamic characteristics, the main undercarriage wheels were enclosed in spats. A single flexible ShKAS machine-gun was provided for the observer and a number of other small refinements were incorporated in the design. Top speed was increased to 153 mph. The R-5SSS was produced in some numbers and entered squadron service.

The R-5 took part in the fighting against the Japanese in Mongolia during 1938–9 and in the Finnish War during the winter of 1939–40. It flew with the Government forces during the early stages of the Spanish Civil War, when it was nicknamed "Natasha".

During World War II, some R-5s had their bomb racks modified to carry containers for medical or other supplies. An ambulance version carried two wounded patients, in containers under each lower wing. A civil version of the R-5SSS, with an enclosed passenger cabin aft of the pilot's cockpit, survived into the post-war period as a feeder-line aircraft with Aeroflot.

Polikarpov-Grigorovich I-5

On 10 August 1927, N. N. Polikarpov presented his report on *The Manoeuvrability of the High-Powered Fighter* to a joint meeting of the Technical Council of Aviatrust (TsKB) and representatives of TsAGI and the VVS. He pointed out the necessity of reducing the weight of fighters in order to improve manoeuvrability. More power meant, inevitably, a heavier engine and this led in turn to higher wing loading and reduced powers of manoeuvre. It was in this same report that Polikarpov drew attention to the higher efficiency of contemporary air-cooled radials by comparison with in-line engines. He proposed a new fighter, based on the in-line-engined I-3 but powered by a radial engine of between 420 and 480 hp.

In the following month, the decision was taken to authorize design and construction of the I-5, an M-22-powered prototype embodying Polikarpov's ideas. The design team, placed under the leadership of Polikarpov and D. P. Grigorovich, paid special attention to reducing the weight of the airframe and keeping the overall size of the I-5 to the minimum.

Early experimental I-5s had individual helmeted fairings for the engine cylinders, but production fighters were the first Soviet aircraft to employ Townend rings in order to reduce engine drag still further.

The armament of twin synchronized 7·62-mm PV-1 machine-guns, standard for that time, was increased to four guns on late production machines. Russian sources claim that the I-5 thus became, simultaneously, the most heavily-armed and the lightest of all production fighters of the period.

The I-5 took off for the first time on 29 April 1930, piloted by B. L. Bucholtz and in the presence of the Soviet Commander-in-Chief, K. E. Voroshilov. The second prototype, named *Klim Voroshilov*, flew on 22 May of that same year. Early factory tests revealed its exceptional performance. In particular, the I-5's outstanding rate of climb and excellent handling characteristics placed it high among the single-seat fighters of 1930–31 vintage.

The I-5 was of mixed construction, with fabric covering. It was a biplane of unequal span and chord, braced by "N" struts. Ailerons were fitted on the upper wings only.

It was while flying an I-5 that V. A. Stepanchonok became the first pilot to execute an inverted spin and survive to perfect the manoeuvre.

Quantity production lasted for several years and approximately 800 I-5s were built. They were the forerunners of a long line of manoeuvrable radial-engined fighter biplanes which were designed in the U.S.S.R. during the 1930s.

The I-5 served in Russian fighter squadrons for many years from 1931 onward, and German troops who overran Soviet aerodromes in the initial onslaught on the USSR came across many I-5s which had still been in use as fighter-trainers.

Polikarpov I-15 (TsKB-3)

When the I-15 single-seat fighter entered squadron service, the Soviet Air Force of the mid-1930s could boast a highly-manoeuvrable operational aircraft with a top speed of 224 mph.

The I-15 was one result of a Soviet design policy which, for seven years from 1932, developed biplane and monoplane single-seat fighters in parallel. With the engines of limited power that were then available, the monoplane, although faster in level flight, could not match the rate of climb of the biplane. Thus, the tactics of the Soviet fighter force were based on close co-operation between formations of monoplanes and biplanes. The faster monoplanes were intended to intercept the enemy and engage him in combat, giving the biplanes an opportunity to catch up and finish off the enemy by out-manoeuvring him. In practice, it proved almost impossible to achieve the degree of co-ordination required between the two groups in the fast-changing situations of aerial combat, at a time when pilots were still without radio contact. This became evident in the air battles over Spain and Mongolia (Khalkin Gol), when effective co-operation could not be achieved between groups of I-15s and monoplane I-16s.

Polikarpov's Aviatrust (TsKB) team began work on the I-15 (then known as TsKB-3) in 1932, as a logical development of the successful I-5. The prototype was fitted with a Wright Cyclone SGR-1820-F-3 radial, but production aircraft had the Soviet version of the Cyclone, the M-25 of 715 hp. The I-15 was a single-bay sesquiplane of mixed construction, with fabric covering. The wings were of unequal chord with single "I"-shaped interplane struts. Ailerons were fitted only to the upper wing, which was gull-shaped and faired into the fuselage, giving the pilot an excellent view forward. The main undercarriage units were of the single-strut cantilever type. Basic armament was two 7·62-mm machine-guns, mounted on the forward fuselage decking, but this could be supplemented by two further weapons of the same calibre.

With its wing loading reduced to 11·9 lb per sq ft, the I-15 was even more manoeuvrable than the I-5. Speed in level flight was much increased and the time taken to carry out a 180-degree turn was reduced. Prototype test flights of the I-15 began in October 1933, with V. P. Chkalov at the controls.

The production I-15 began to equip Soviet fighter formations from 1934 onward. It had a higher rate of climb and better manoeuvrability than contemporaries such as the Boeing P-26A and Fiat C.R.32, although its top speed was slightly lower.

On 21 November 1935, V. K. Kokkinaki reached an altitude of 47,818 ft in a reduced-weight version of the I-15. This was 433 ft above the then-official record set up by Donati on a specially-built Caproni Ca.114a.

The I-15 fought in the Sino-Japanese conflict and played a prominent part on the side of the Republican Forces in the Spanish Civil War, the first 25 machines (of a total of over 500 I-15s and I-15*bis* sent) reaching Spain in November 1936.

Polikarpov I-15 (TsKB-3), Spanish Air Force

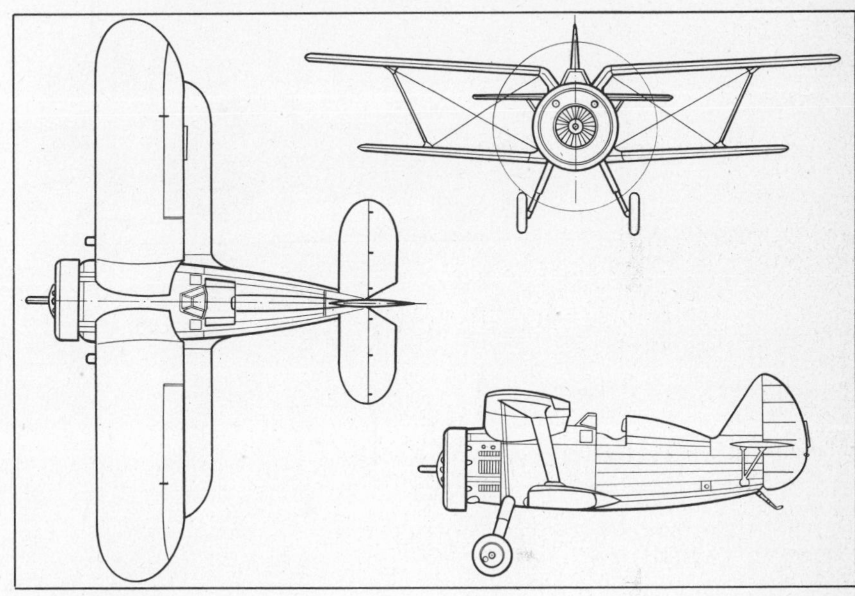

Polikarpov I-15

Polikarpov I-16 (TsKB-12)

Groups of I-16 fighters appeared in the wake of TB-3 bombers over Red Square, Moscow, on May Day 1935, and so provided evidence that the Soviet Union possessed

TYPE	DIMENSIONS span ft	span in	length ft	length in	height ft	height in	WEIGHT max t-o lb	PERFORMANCE max speed mph	at height ft	service ceiling ft	combat range miles	REMARKS
Polikarpov R-5	50	10¼	34	5⅜	11	9¾	6,515–7,380	142·9	SL	20,997	683	With M-17 engine
Polikarpov R-5SSS								152·8				With M-17F engine
Polikarpov-Grigorovitch I-5	31	7⅞	19	8⅝	NA		2,987	177·7	SL	26,575	NA	
Polikarpov I-15	31	11⅞	20	7½	9	7	3,027	223·7	NA	29,527	450	

Polikarpov I-16, first production version, 450-hp M-22 engine

Polikarpov I-16, M-25 engine

Polikarpov I-16, Type 24

Polikarpov I-16, captured aircraft, Finnish markings

the first low-wing single-seat fighter monoplane with a retractable undercarriage to achieve service status. Its general layout set the fashion for world fighter design, until the advent of the first jet-propelled combat types towards the close of World War II.

In 1932, two Soviet design teams had begun the design of low-wing fighter monoplanes with retractable undercarriages. Tupolev and his colleagues in TsAGI contributed the all-metal ANT-31 (military designation I-14), test-flying of which began in May 1933. It had two synchronized PV-1 machine-guns, two 20-mm wing cannon and four underwing bomb racks, and introduced a number of refinements new to Soviet aircraft. A flush-riveted smooth metal skin and an enclosed cockpit reduced drag to the minimum. Oleo-pneumatic shock-absorbers and wheel brakes were fitted. Top speed with a 570-hp Bristol Mercury exceeded that of the I-15 at 16,400 ft by 25 mph; at 10,000 ft the I-15 was marginally faster.

Polikarpov and his TsKB design team developed the I-16, or TsKB-12, single-seat fighter which first took the air on 31 December 1933, with V. P. Chkalov at the controls. Its 450-hp M-22 engine gave the prototype a speed of 234 mph. The two wing-mounted 7·62-mm ShKAS machine-guns had a rate of fire of 1,800 rpm – over one-and-a-half times faster than the PV-1 machine-gun then in use. Designated I-16 Type 1, the aircraft completed factory and official trials and entered squadron service during the second half of 1934.

The more powerful M-25 engine was fitted in the second prototypes of both the I-14 and I-16. The M-25-powered I-14*bis* flew on 12 February 1934, and tests revealed control weaknesses which required extensive modifications. Series production had been planned, but there were successive postponements until all further work on the I-14 was abandoned in 1936.

The M-25-powered I-16 (TsKB-12*bis*) registered a top speed of 282 mph during its first flight on 18 February 1934, but despite its high performance it did not go into production until 18 months later. Soviet fighter airfields of that time could not accommodate a machine with a take-off run of 755 ft and a landing run of 985 ft. In July 1935, however, a decision was taken to extend the runways at airfields where the I-16 and other advanced aircraft could be based. Immediately after this, the I-16 Type 4 with M-25 engine went into production, followed by the Type 6 with the 725-hp M-25A radial.

The I-16 had a lower power loading than its contemporaries and surpassed them in speed and rate of climb, but its poor stability in most flight conditions, and particularly its instability in turning and climbing, caused problems for all but the most experienced pilots. Priority was, accordingly, given to producing a two-seat training version, the UTI-4, which left the factories from 1935 onward in the ratio of one for every four I-16s

I-16 development was continuous. The Type 10, powered by the 750-hp M-25V engine, had two synchronized and two wing-mounted ShKAS machine-guns and dispensed with the enclosed cockpit of the earlier versions. The Type 17 had the usual wing machine-guns replaced by 20-mm cannon. These versions were produced in quantity. The TsKB-18, tested for ground attack with six PV-1 machine-guns, remained a prototype.

Improved firepower and equipment led to the penalties of increased overall weight and power loading. This, in turn, led to a poorer climb rate and higher landing and take-off speeds. The maximum speed of all the M-25-powered versions varied between 280 mph and 283 mph.

The I-16 Type 10 succeeded earlier versions in the fighting over Mongolia and in Spain, where it met the Messerschmitt Bf 109B of the Condor Legion. It surpassed the German machine in all-round performance, except in the execution of a 180-degree turn, where its opponent had a slight edge. The German fighter, however, was soon developed into the Bf 109E as a result of combat experience, and this model inevitably outclassed the I-16 – a 1932–3 design reaching the end of its potential.

Improved performance was essential, and in 1937 the I-16 was tested with an M-62 radial engine with two-speed supercharger, offering 850 hp at 5,000 ft. Top speed increased to 288 mph at 15,750 ft. Principal production models with the M-62 engine were the Types 18 and 24.

With the still more powerful M-63 engine, improved aerodynamic qualities and an enclosed cockpit, the fighter reached 326 mph at 15,750 ft.

I-16s with M-62 and M-63 engines saw years of operational service against the Germans in World War II. The first unit to be honoured with the name "Guards Fighter Regiment" flew this type.

During the Mongolian "Incident" against the Japanese in 1939, five I-16s had been combat-tested with rockets. In 1941–2, rocket-carrying I-16s operated against aircraft and against ground targets with outstanding success. Final production I-16s had the two wing guns deleted and a large-bore machine-gun fitted under the forward part of the fuselage. Subsequently, a number of I-16s already in service were modified to this standard.

When the last I-16s were taken off front-line duties in the spring of 1943, this distinctive rotund monoplane had been the mainstay of the Soviet Air Force for close on ten years, taking the full brunt of the initial German onslaught in 1941 and 1942.

Polikarpov I-17 (TsKB-15)

The first prototype of the I-17 was designed and built by N. N. Polikarpov's team under the designation TsKB-15, and flew for the first time on 1 September 1934. It was a low-wing monoplane of mixed construction, with an inward-retracting undercarriage, and was armed with two cannon and two wing-mounted machine-guns. Power was provided by an 860-hp M-100 in-line engine, driving a two-bladed metal propeller. As with the earlier versions of I-16, the windscreen and canopy were built in one piece and slid forward to provide access to the cockpit.

A modified and improved version, designated TsKB-19, was displayed at the Paris Salon in 1936. Top speed was 311 mph and underwing racks could carry a total of 220 lb of bombs. The TsKb-19 had four machine-guns in the wings and a cannon firing through the hollow propeller shaft. Ceiling was 23,000 ft and range 497 miles. In this form, the fighter was built in limited numbers, with the military designation I-17-2.

In 1935, there appeared an experimental reduced-weight version, the I-17-3, or TsKB-33, with a top speed of 332 mph and armament of three machine-guns.

The I-17 Z of 1936 was a parasite fighter for the defence of heavy bombers and was intended to be carried by TB-3 bombers and launched while in the air. It differed from the standard version in having a smaller wing area, a retracting hook and no undercarriage.

Polikarpov R-Z

In 1935 there appeared the final development in the R-5 series of two-seat light bomber-reconnaissance biplanes. Major changes included the provision of a glazed canopy for the crew and the installation of a new power plant – the AM-34RN engine incorporating reduction gear and

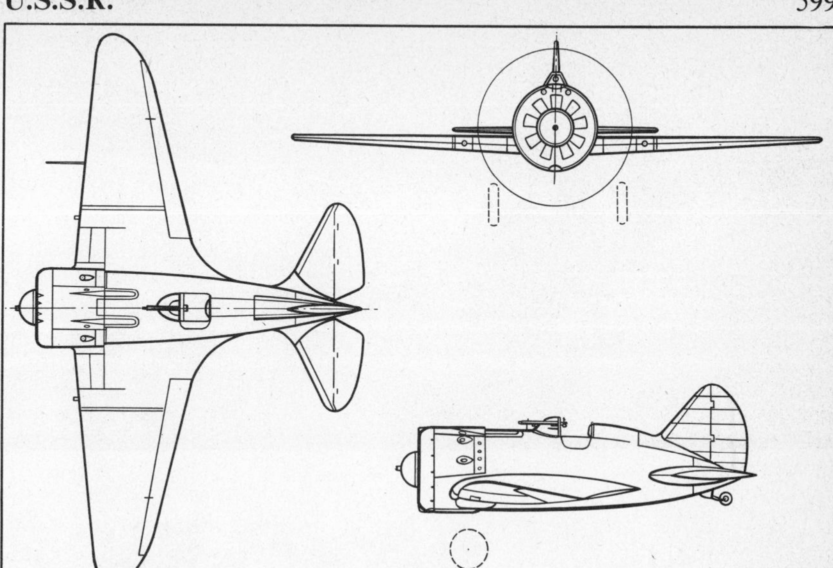

Polikarpov I-16

Polikarpov I-17-2 (TsKB-19)

TYPE	DIMENSIONS span ft	span in	length ft	length in	height ft	height in	WEIGHT max t-o lb	PERFORMANCE max speed mph	at height ft	service ceiling ft	combat range miles	REMARKS
Polikarpov I-16. Type 1	29	6⅜	19	11	NA		2,961	223·7	SL			Year 1934. M-22 engine
Type 4	29	6⅜	19	11	NA		3,135	282·1		30,446	509	Year 1935. M-25 engine
Type 6	29	6⅜	19	11	8	1¼	3,659	282·7		29,527	403	Year 1936. M-25A engine
Type 10	29	6⅜	19	11	8	1¼	3,782	279·6 approx		26,246	497	Year 1937. M-25V engine Year 1938. M-25V engine
Type 17	29	6⅜	19	11	NA		3,990	279·6 approx				Year 1939. M-62 engine
Type 18	29	6⅜	20	1¼	8	5	4,034	288·3	15,748			Year 1939. M-62 engine Max wt 4,520 lb
Type 24	29	6⅜	20	1¼	8	5	4,215	326·2	SL	29,530	250 435 (with aux tanks)	
Polikarpov I-17-2	33	1⅝	24	3⅜	8	5	4,222	304·4	NA		497	
Polikarpov I-17-3								332·4				

Polikarpov R-Z

Polikarpov I-15*bis*

Polikarpov I-15bis, Finnish Air Force

driving a two-bladed metal propeller. The tailplane was re-designed, and the fin and rudder acquired a more pointed contour. The R-5's fixed undercarriage and single-bay wing layout with "N"-type interplane struts were retained.

The new light bomber was designated R-Z and, following successful tests, was placed in quantity production. Over 1,000 R-Zs were built, largely for use in the ground-attack rôle.

The pilot operated a fixed PV-1 machine-gun and the observer was provided with a movable 7·62-mm ShKAS machine-gun. A bomb-load of up to 1,100 lb could be carried on underwing racks.

Fuel for the AM-34RN engine was contained in two fuselage tanks and in two smaller tanks in the centre-section of the upper wing. Total capacity was 155 gallons.

Limited numbers of R-Zs were despatched to Spain by the Soviet Government in support of the Republican forces during the Civil War, and some of the type were still serving with the Soviet Air Force during the early stages of the German attack on the USSR in 1941.

Polikarpov I-15*bis* (TsKB-3*bis*)

The success of the I-15 biplane against Japanese Navy Mitsubishi A5M monoplanes, during the China conflict, encouraged the Soviet authorities to increase the production of biplane single-seat fighters and so reverse the trend which had led to I-15 deliveries equalling only 1·4 per cent of I-16 monoplane production during 1936. The I-15, with Soviet "volunteer" pilots, was inflicting heavy losses on Japanese units with such exotic names as "The Flying Samurai" and "The Four Lords of the Winds". Simultaneously, the I-16 was failing to provide the answer to the agile Italian and German fighter biplanes in Spain. Everything seemed to point to the need for an improved biplane fighter.

Polikarpov's design team began work immediately and the new I-15*bis* was built and tested within a year. Official trials were completed successfully in early 1937, and the I-15*bis* was placed in immediate quantity production, although it subsequently underwent many modifications and improvements. Several hundred were despatched to Spain in time to enter combat before the end of 1937. Soon afterwards, the fighter appeared in the Far East in air battles against the Japanese.

During the heavy fighting in Mongolia in May 1939, there were reports that the entire Soviet fighter force, having sustained heavy losses, had been withdrawn from action. Poor tactics had prevented the I-16 from using its speed to full advantage, and the manoeuvrable I-15*bis*, no match in speed for the opposing Nakajima Ki-27 fighters, suffered heavily as a result.

The I-15*bis* represented an extensive modification of the I-15. The distinctive "gull"-shaped upper wing of the earlier type was replaced by a wing supported above the fuselage on a pair of "N" centre-section struts. Its M-25V engine, delivering 750 hp at 9,500 ft, was enclosed in a long-chord cowling. The cantilever single-strut undercarriage of the I-15 was retained and some machines had wheel spats fitted. Standard armament was four 7·62-mm ShKAS synchronized machine-guns. A pair of auxiliary fuel tanks could be carried under the lower wings as an alternative to a bomb-load of up to 331 lb.

The I-15*bis* fought in the 1939–40 war with Finland and was still serving in some numbers, largely in the dive-bomber rôle, when the Germans launched their attack on the Soviet Union on 22 June 1941.

Polikarpov I-153

In a report presented to the Soviet authorities in November 1937, Nikolai N. Polikarpov stressed how the call for greater speed confronted fighter designers with complex problems. More power meant heavier engines and greater fuel consumption, with consequent requirements for greater fuel tank capacity. In 1920, the weight of fuel carried by a single-seat fighter had equalled only 6 per cent of its loaded weight, but the percentage had risen to 13–14 by 1935. Increased overall weight led to higher wing loading and, inevitably, manoeuvrability suffered.

Two distinctly separate lines of action were followed in an endeavour to overcome the difficulties outlined by Polikarpov. The I-153 and IS-1 (the latter an experimental biplane-monoplane combination) represented an attempt to combine manoeuvrability and high speed in a single aircraft, while powerfully-engined low-wing monoplanes with retractable undercarriages were developed by the school which placed reliance mainly on speed and firepower.

The first I-153 prototype appeared in 1938. Its original power plant, the M-25V radial, was soon replaced by an M-62 engine, with which it reached 275 mph at 15,000 ft during trials. Later production machines were powered by the M-63 radial.

Four synchronized 7·62-mm ShKAS machine-guns in the forward fuselage formed an effective armament and provision was made for six RS-80 rocket missiles or two 165-lb bombs on underwing racks. Alternatively, these could be replaced by two 22-gallon auxiliary fuel tanks. The main fuel tank, with a capacity of 68 gallons, was housed in the fuselage between the engine and the cockpit. The back of the pilot's seat was protected by 9-mm armour plate.

The I-153 reverted to the gull-shaped upper wing configuration of the I-15 and was appropriately nicknamed the "Chaika" (Gull). The wings were constructed of wood, with two spars, and were fabric-covered. The fuselage had a welded tubular-steel main structure, surrounded by light wooden formers and stringers which gave the machine its rotund, streamlined shape. The fuselage covering was of fabric, except for the engine cowling and one or two of the foremost bays which had detachable light metal skin panels. The cowling fitted closely over the whole engine and was flat at the front, air being admitted individually to each cylinder through comparatively small openings in the cowling.

The undercarriage consisted of two semi-cantilever shock-struts which retracted rearward, turning through 90 degrees to lie flush in recesses in the bottom of the fuselage and lower wing-roots.

When fighting broke out again in Mongolia in the summer of 1939, the increased support needed urgently by Red Army units fighting the Japanese led to air battles more massive than any which had occurred in Spain or China. The extremely manoeuvrable Nakajima Ki-27 fighter of the Japanese Army proved superior to the Soviet I-15*bis* and could easily evade the faster but less agile I-16. The Japanese soon established complete air supremacy; so the Soviet High Command decided to send the newly-produced I-153 straight into action. Stalin attached great importance to the new fighter and is reported to have interrupted the briefing of pilots due to leave for Mongolia in order to find out how much progress had been made in perfecting a variable-pitch propeller for it.

In the event, the propeller was not ready in time and the I-153 first went into action fitted with a fixed-pitch propeller.

Initially, complete surprise was achieved by the I-153s, which the Japanese mistook for the slow I-15*bis*. Russian pilots are supposed to have adopted the ruse of approaching the combat area with their wheels down, giving the I-153 the appearance of the I-15*bis*, and then retracting the undercarriage when confronted by the Japanese. There is little evidence to support this attractive story; in fact, technical difficulties would have been encountered in climbing to operational height with the fighter's undercarriage still lowered and in operating the retracting mechanism during comparatively high-

Polikarpov I-153

Polikarpov I-153, captured aircraft, Finnish markings

Polikarpov I-153, ski landing gear

TYPE	DIMENSIONS						WEIGHT	PERFORMANCE				REMARKS
	span		*length*		*height*		*max t-o*	*max speed*	*at height*	*service ceiling*	*combat range*	
	ft	*in*	*ft*	*in*	*ft*	*in*	*lb*	*mph*	*ft*	*ft*	*miles*	
Polikarpov R-Z	50	10¼	31	9⅞	NA		7,715	180·2	11,480	26,247	621	
Polikarpov I-15*bis*	33	6	20	9¼	9	10	3,827	229·9	NA	26,245	497	Max loaded weight 4,189 lb
Polikarpov I-153	32	9¾	20	2⅞	9	3	4,431 (max)	267·2[1] 248·5[2]	16,404	35,105	298	[1] M-63 engine and normal loaded weight (4,100 lb) [2] With M-62R engine

Polikarpov Po-2

Polikarpov Po-2 (U-2VS)

Polikarpov Po-2

speed flight. One pilot who served in this theatre of war is reported as saying: "Who in his right mind would go into action with the wheels down? When you are fighting, there is no time for funny tricks!"

The I-153 soon displayed its marked superiority over the Ki-27 and, consequently, production was stepped up considerably. It fought on an extensive scale in Finland during both the "Winter War" and the "Continuation War". Large numbers were in service when the Germans launched their attack on the USSR in June 1941. Their excellent manoeuvrability compensated to some degree for their slowness compared with the opposing Messerschmitt fighters, and they acquitted themselves reasonably well in action.

Soviet sources indicate that, concurrently with quantity production of the I-153, a further development, designated the I-190, was being studied by N. N. Polikarpov's design team. No details of the I-190 are available, other than that it was a more streamlined and more powerfully-engined biplane.

Polikarpov Po-2

In 1943 designer Nikolai N. Polikarpov joked that the Germans had come to believe that his U-2 biplane, having shed its peaceful guise, was able to fly up to a window and look over the sill to see if the enemy was inside! To the tired German front-line troops, however, the U-2 was no subject for humour.

Although it was designed in 1927 as a primary trainer, 13,500 of all versions of the U-2 had been built by June 1941, for service at military and civil training schools, as transports or ambulances, and for agricultural and forestry work. When war came, the U-2 was found to be ideally suited to a more aggressive rôle as a nuisance raider, its objective being to wear down enemy troops and to lower morale by attacking front-line positions during the hours of darkness. The version developed for this task was designated U-2VS, "VS" denoting *Voyskovaya Serya* or Military Series. Underwing racks were fitted, capable of carrying up to 550 lb of bombs, and a single 7·62-mm ShKAS machine-gun was mounted in the observer's cockpit.

Dozens of night bomber regiments were formed with U-2VS aircraft, which used to cross the enemy's lines at low altitude, at night, their engines at low revs, drop bombs on the trenches, attack transport columns, ammunition and fuel dumps with incendiaries, and make good their escape under cover of darkness, evading anti-aircraft defences and enemy fighters without great difficulty.

At Stalingrad, hundreds of U-2s bombed German positions in non-stop night and dawn attacks. During the great Russian counter-offensives, the U-2VS gave good account of itself in street battles and in fighting over difficult terrain. In 1945, many were used by night and day in a similar manner in the battle for Berlin, operating right up to the last hours of the war in Europe. On some machines, rocket missiles replaced bombs as the offensive load.

The U-2VS proved itself an important operational military aircraft, and during the course of the war a number of units equipped with the type won the distinction of being named as "Guards Regiments".

Other wartime functions of the U-2 were reconnaissance, liaison, and dropping supplies to partisans. New ambulance versions, including one which carried a patient on each lower wing in a kind of "pannier nacelle", and a night artillery observation post (U-2NAK) made their appearance. A new headquarters and liaison version, the U-2ShS, had a cabin for up to four passengers.

The U-2 was easy to handle, safe to fly, had a low landing speed and could operate from small unprepared strips. Both the airframe and the 110-hp M-11 uncowled radial engine were simple to service and maintain. All these characteristics, which had made the U-2 so popular in pre-war years, were even more valuable when it came to perform its wartime duties.

There were whole transport regiments of U-2s, as well as similarly-equipped ambulance and liaison regiments. In this category, a Soviet regiment comprised 42 aircraft.

Immediately after Polikarpov's death in 1944, the Soviet Government ordered the U-2 to be re-designated Po-2 in memory and honour of its designer. In Polikarpov's obituary, *Pravda* for 31 July 1944 affirmed: "His U-2, outstanding and popular not only among Soviet pilots, but also among all the men of the Soviet Army and members of guerilla units, renders invaluable services to our country in its fight against the aggressors."

Even had Polikarpov not been such a prolific designer, the Po-2 would have guaranteed him a place in Soviet military annals. The career of this nimble little biplane spanned more than a quarter of a century: it appears to have remained in production longer than any other known aircraft. In the U.S.S.R., it was manufactured from 1928 up to 1952, about 20,000 in all being constructed. The CSS-13, a Polish licence-built version, was produced from 1948 to 1954. The history of Polikarpov's diminutive trainer-turned-bomber provides an outstanding example of the Russian aptitude for ingenious adaptation carried to a fine art.

Shchetinin M-5

Dmitrii Petrovich Grigorovich's M-5, known also as the Shchetinin 5, ShM-5 or Sh-5, was a 2/3-seat trainer and reconnaissance flying-boat designed in 1915 and developed from a pre-war series of flying-boats, the first of which, the M-1, was designed in 1913. The designation "M" denoted *morskoi* (= naval).

The Pervoe Rossiskoe Tovarishchestvo Vozdukhoplana Vaniya S. S. Shchetinin (the First Russian Aeronautics Company S. S. Shchetinin) was established in St Petersburg in 1909, and D. P. Grigorovich joined the company about 1912 or 1913. Between 1915–17, about 300 M-5s were produced for the Imperial Navy, twelve Navy squadrons being equipped with M-5s and M-9s.

The M-5 was a two-bay braced biplane flying-boat of all wooden construction; the hull was planked with 3-ply and the wings and tail surfaces were fabric-covered. The general design of the hull was followed in nearly all of Grigorovich's wartime flying-boats: high bow, flared at the water line to the single step, the aft section being unusually slender, little more than a boom, to support the distinctive Grigorovich tail unit. The unusual feature of the latter was the fin with sharply tapered leading-edge from above and below the high-mounted tailplane, so that the whole structure appeared to be mounted on the rudder post. It was, however, braced by a system of struts and wires.

The wings were of normal two-spar construction, with scalloped trailing-edge, ailerons on upper surfaces only, and a total wing area of 409 sq ft. The engine mounting struts supported a 100-hp Gnome Monosoupape engine, which drove a two-blade pusher propeller. One of the claims made for the M-5 was that it could ride out 5-ft waves successfully; it was also able to take off from light snow. When used as a reconnaissance aircraft, a single 7·62-mm Vickers machine-gun was carried on a ring mounting in the bows.

Parts from an M-5 were used to form the basis of a two-seat flying-boat designed by Lieut N. A. Olechnovich during 1916–17, to test his theories on a "shock-absorbing hull".

The results of these experiments were taken to England by Lieut Olechnovich in 1917, and were made available to the Supermarine Aviation Company.

Shchetinin M-9

The M-9, larger and more powerful than the M-5 from which it was developed, was built in even greater numbers,

Shchetinin M-5

Shchetinin M-5

Shchetinin M-5

TYPE	DIMENSIONS						WEIGHT	PERFORMANCE				REMARKS
	span		length		height		max t-o	max speed	at height	service ceiling	combat range	
	ft	in	ft	in	ft	in	lb	mph	ft	ft	miles	
Polikarpov Po-2 (U-2)	37	4⅞	26	8⅞	9	10⅞	2,167	90·7	328	13,123	267	
Shchetinin M-5	45	3⅛	29	2¼	NA		2,116	65	NA	11,482	4 hr	About 300 built. Shipboard & land-based

Shchetinin M-9

Shchetinin M-9, Finnish Air Force

Shchetinin M-9

Sikorsky Il'ya Muromets

about 500 being produced. Though designed as a reconnaissance bomber, accommodating a crew of two, it appears to have been quite capable of defending itself against enemy floatplanes and scouts.

Design of the prototype was completed in December 1915; it was tested in January 1916 and put into production immediately. It was of all-wood construction, and was generally similar in appearance to the M-5. The rudder was enlarged and its outline changed slightly, as was the tailplane to match; all had "extended tips" to give increased area. Wing area was increased to 589·86 sq ft.

The M-9 was powered by a Salmson Canton Unné engine, nominally of 150 hp, though, in practice, it was often less. Radiators were mounted on either side of the engine. Later versions had the 220-hp Renault liquid-cooled Vee engine as an alternative to the Salmson Canton Unné.

The observer normally sat beside the pilot, and gained access to the front cockpit, to operate the movable Lewis gun, via a gangway inside the nose.

In the summer of 1916 some M-9s were armed with a 37-mm quick-firing semi-automatic cannon. Normal bomb-load was only about 143 lb, but bombs and ammunition totalling 196 kg could be carried.

The Imperial Navy used M-9s extensively in the Baltic and Black Seas. One squadron (six aircraft) was carried by the converted transport *Orlitsa* (*Eaglet*). M-9s were also carried by the *Imperator Nikolai I* (*Emperor Nicholas I*) and *Imperator Aleksandr I* (*Emperor Alexander I*), and were stationed at shore bases such as Kielkond (now Kihelkonna) on Oesel Island (now Saaremaa), and Reval (now Tallinn).

It was at Kielkond that the Russian pioneer of Polar aviation, Jan Jozefovich Nagorski, (or Nagurskii), was stationed in June 1916 when he led a formation of nine M-9s in a bombing raid on the German air station at Angern. The Russian formation was attacked by German fighters and, in taking evasive action, Nagurskii looped the loop. On 17 September 1916, he did two successive loops, deliberately and with full load, over his base, and this was witnessed by his colleagues. These were the first occasions on which such a manoeuvre had been successfully carried out by a flying-boat – and the first time that a Russian had looped a Russian-designed and built aircraft.

Shchetinin M-15

The Shchetinin works put at least four of Grigorovich's other wartime designs into production, among which were the M-11 fighter, and M-20 and M-15 reconnaissance flying-boats. Few details of the first two are available, but the M-15 was a two-seater first built in 1916, the result of continuous development of the M-5 design.

Considerably smaller than the M-9 – wing area was 482·2 sq ft, gross weight 2,910 lb – it was also faster, its 140-hp Hispano-Suiza liquid-cooled Vee engine providing a maximum speed of 78 mph. The radiator was mounted directly in front of the engine.

The M-15 retained the same general outline as its predecessors. However, the engine mounting struts were far more prominent, since there were twelve of them. The shape of the fin and rudder was changed again, the under part of the rudder becoming rounded; and the two-bay wings were slightly swept back.

Armament was a single Lewis gun mounted in the front cockpit.

Sikorsky Il'ya Muromets

The great Russo-Baltic Wagon Works (RBVZ) was only partly concerned with aircraft production but, in 1917, it was producing 30 aircraft per month, including three or four four-engined heavy bombers.

Igor Ivanovich Sikorsky's *Russkii Vitiaz* (Russian Knight) of May 1913 was the first four-engined aircraft in the world. The *Il'ya Muromets* (named after a 10th century legendary hero) which followed it in December, was developed in 1914 into the first multi-engined heavy bomber to go into service with any air force in the world. The name "Il'ya Muromets" became a class name, and the different wartime types which were produced by the RBVZ were known as IM-B, -V, -G, -D and -Ye, with sub-types such as IM-E2. They are believed to fit into the Sikorsky type number system S-23–S-27.

The second *Il'ya Muromets* was completed in the spring of 1914 and, on 18 June 1914, established a world endurance record when carrying six passengers. Between 29 June and 11 July, piloted by Igor Sikorsky and Captain Prussis, it flew from St Petersburg to Kiev and back, taking but 10½ hours for the return journey which was completed with only one intermediate stop. The success of this flight gained the RBVZ an order for ten military IMs. They were intended initially for long-range reconnaissance, but the load-carrying potential and consequent utility of this type as a bomber soon became apparent. As early as February 1914, the first *Il'ya Muromets* had, by lifting 16 passengers, set up a world record for passenger carrying. In July, this same aircraft was tested for the Russian Navy on floats; in practice, however, IMs seem only to have had either wheel or ski undercarriage.

Initially, the performance of the IM bombers did not come up to expectations and military commanders expressed opposition to the heavy aircraft. It was at this point that, in December 1914, the Eskadra Vozduchnykh Korablei (Squadron of Flying Ships – EVK) was established.

The first bomber pilots and crews were recruited from among the company's test pilots and engineers – the RBVZ Chairman was made a General and took command of the special unit. The aircraft's designer was a frequent visitor to the EVK at the Front.

The second IM–which had made the flight to Kiev–was christened *Kievskii* and was then commanded by Captain G.G. Gorshkov. The *Kievskii* was powered by two 125-hp and two 140-hp Argus in-line engines, had a wing span of 101 ft 7 in and a gross weight of 10,250 lb.

The IM-B was the first true military Il'ya Muromets. Apart from the power plant – and the redesigned nose of the Type B Improved – it was very similar to the pre-war machine, which was a four-bay braced biplane of wooden construction with fabric covering. Wings were of unequal span, with ailerons on the upper surfaces only. The nose of the 62 ft 4 in fuselage was very short. Partly as a result of this, the centre of gravity was farther back than normal – which meant that considerable piloting skill was needed to land the aircraft. The tail unit was subject to many changes, and the IM-B had a large central rudder, with two small rudders on top of the tailplane.

Initially, the IM-B was unarmed, but at the instigation of EVK crews all later IMs were armed – with more and more weapons progressively, until the final versions were veritable "flying porcupines". The IM-B was armed in the field during the winter of 1914–15 with three machine-guns mounted in the fuselage sides for shooting at ground targets. It carried a total load (i.e. crew of four, fuel and bombs) of 2,645 lb and was powered by two 135-hp and two 200-hp Salmson radial engines.

The IM-V, which was designed as a bomber in 1914 and was delivered to the squadron early in 1915, was smaller; the wing span was decreased by 3 ft 10 in, the wing area by 270 sq ft, and the fuselage length by 6 ft 2½ in. Structure weight was also reduced, but the useful load was increased by 550–650 lb. Production Type Vs were powered by four 150-hp Sunbeam 8-cylinder liquid-cooled Vee engines; forty of these were bought from England, and the rest were built under licence in Russia.

The IM-Gl, which followed in 1915, carried 110 lb

Sikorsky Il'ya Muromets

Sikorsky Il'ya Muromets

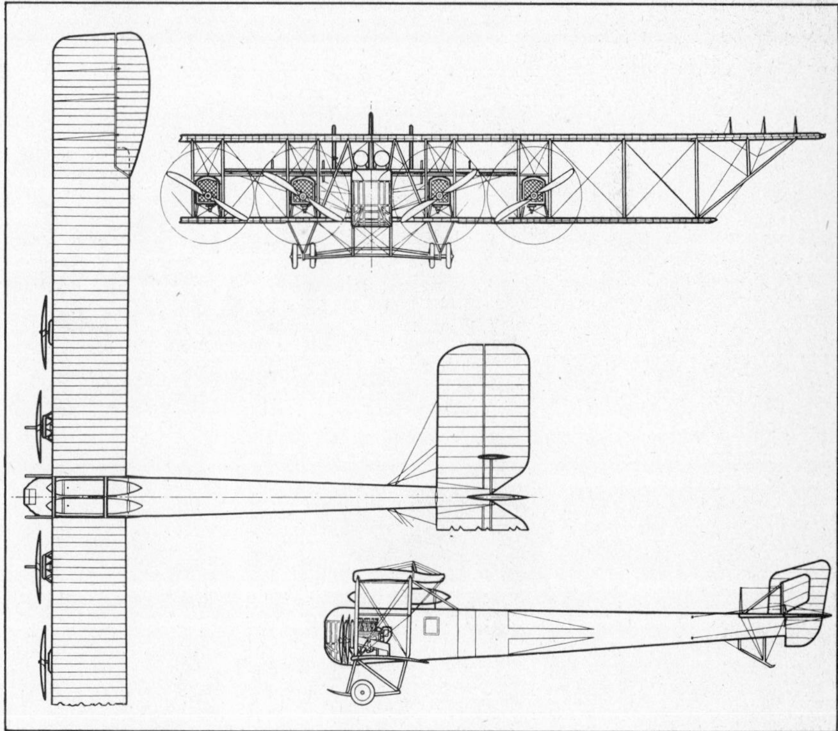

Sikorsky Il'ya Muromets

TYPE	DIMENSIONS						WEIGHT	PERFORMANCE				REMARKS
	span ft	*span* in	*length* ft	*length* in	*height* ft	*height* in	*max t-o* lb	*max speed* mph	*at height* ft	*service ceiling* ft	*combat range* miles	
Shchetinin M-9	52	1⅞	29	6¼	NA		3,395	68	NA	9,842	3½ hr	
Shchetinin M-15	39	0⅜	27	7⅞	NA		2,910	78	NA	11,482	5½ hr	

Sikorsky Il'ya Muromets IM-V

Sikorsky Il'ya Muromets

Sikorsky Il'ya Muromets, ski landing gear; close-up of tail gun turret

Sikorsky Il'ya Muromets

more useful load, including a heavier defensive armament. The wing chord was greatly increased, wing area went up from 1,345·5 sq ft to 1,717·9 sq ft and the wings were slightly back-staggered. The IM-Gl was powered at first with Argus engines (totalling 500–560 hp) – others had Sunbeam engines.

Armament included machine-guns firing from positions cut in the upper wing centre-section, and a platform ("crow's nest") under the fuselage, as well as through doors and windows.

The IM-G2, of which about twenty were built, had a strengthened wing and the area was again increased slightly. Defensive armament of the -G2 included machine-gun positions in the nose and the tail. This latter position necessitated revision of the tail unit: the centre rudder was removed and the outer rudders extended below the tailplane. In some cases, the centre fin was retained at the back of the gunner.

Four RBZ-6 (or MRB) six-cylinder liquid-cooled in-line engines gave the IM-G2 a total of 600 hp. This engine, sometimes known as the "Russobalt", had been designed and built by the RBVZ under the direction of Engineer Kireev, because of a general shortage of suitable engines, and became available towards the end of 1916.

The IM-G3 did not differ greatly from the -G2, apart from its engines and armament. Mixed power plants were employed – two 150-hp RBZ-6 and two 220-hp Renault engines – and the -G3 was sometimes called the "Renault-balt". With the increased power, load was again increased, to 3,527 lb. The rear gunner's cockpit was enlarged and another machine-gun was fired through trap doors in the fuselage floor and above the fuselage. Bomb storage was modified so that the weapons could be dropped either horizontally or vertically, about 2,000 lb of bombs being carried.

Breakages of early IMs during the winter of 1916–17 were responsible for further strengthening of the structure, and these modifications were incorporated in the -G4.

The IM-D, which did not go into production, was built in 1916 and was powered by four Sunbeam engines mounted in tandem pairs.

The largest Il'ya Muromets was the IM-Ye2 which had a wing span of 113 ft 2¼ in, and gross weight of 15,432 lb. In 1917, this version was armed with a 50-mm cannon and eight machine-guns; however, the cannon installation was not very successful owing to a slow rate of fire. Four 220-hp Renault 12-cylinder liquid-cooled Vee engines gave this giant a maximum speed of 81 mph, but the IM-Ye2 did not go into production. Six IM-Yel bombers (slightly smaller) were completed in 1916, powered by 220-hp Renault engines; armed with seven machine-guns, the total useful load was 4,850 lb.

The IM-Ye was the first IM since the Type V to have a new fuselage length, although there had been several modifications to the nose. The Type B Improved had a knife-edge nose, whereas other IMs had a flat glass panel, hinged at the sides, to permit a machine-gun to be fired through the opening. As mentioned above, the tail unit was modified to allow installation of a rear gunner's cockpit, although some early IMs had a single large fin and rudder.

Construction of this huge aeroplane was largely of wood with fabric covering, although some metal was employed. Tests were carried out with 10-mm armour plate, made from pressed metal shavings, used to protect the lower part of the pilots' cabin and the back of the seats. Self-sealing fuel tanks were specially designed for the Il'ya Muromets, and these were normally mounted above the fuselage underneath the upper wing centre-section.

One IM-V was used for tests with a 920-lb bomb.

About eighty IMs were built, about half of which were used at the front – the remainder being used for training. They were by no means easy to fly and a considerable amount of training was necessary not only for pilots, but for all members of the crew, which numbered from four to seven.

IMs were used by both sides during the Civil War, and

in January 1920, the Il'ya Muromets initiated passenger services on two routes: Sarapyl-Ekaterinburg and Moscow-Kharkov.

Sikorsky S-16

The Sikorsky S-16 was one of the first production aircraft to be armed with a synchronized machine-gun firing through the propeller disc.

Designed by Igor Ivanovich Sikorsky and constructed by the Russo-Baltiiskiy Vagonnyi Zavod (RBVZ, or Russo-Baltic Wagon Works) at St Petersburg, a total of about 20 were built. Most of these appear to have been delivered to the EVK (Squadron of Flying Ships, see page 605) for reconnaissance and escort duties. The first S-16 was completed on 6 February 1915; two more were delivered to the EVK in March; and in September a contract for 18 was signed with the War Department. The first production S-16 was completed on 17 December 1915.

Seven were delivered to the Squadron at the beginning of 1916, but by this time the S-16 was out-dated and outclassed by its German counterparts. The price agreed between the War Department and the Russo-Baltic Wagon Works was 9,500 roubles (£1,056) for each machine.

It had been intended originally to power the S-16 with a 90/110-hp Le Rhône engine, but this was not available and the 80-hp Gnome 7-cylinder rotary – with which it was seriously underpowered – had to be used instead. A NYeZh propeller, designed by Professor N. Ye. Zhukovsky, was fitted. The S-16z, first tested in September 1916, was powered by a 100-hp engine – probably the Gnome Monosoupape. An experimental S-16 was fitted with the 60-hp Russian Kalep engine – this particular aircraft had the wing area increased from 272·9 sq ft to 294·36 sq ft.

Construction was of wood with fabric covering. Although designed as a two-seater, the S-16 was often flown as a single-seater. Some had ailerons on both upper and lower wings, and this version had a straight fin leading-edge; others had ailerons on the upper wings only and a curved fin. The four-wheel undercarriage was derived from that fitted to the S-6, S-10 and other pre-war Sikorsky designs, and was doubtless intended for taxiing over rough ground; alternatively, floats or skis could be fitted.

A synchronizing gear had been developed by Lieutenant Lavrov, but difficulties were experienced with it, and in September 1916 these were summed up in a report as being due to "careless construction" resulting in frequent repairs having to be made both on the ground and in the air. It was perhaps because of this that a second gun was mounted above the wing, firing outside the propeller disc.

Although seriously underpowered, the S-16 was both pleasant and easy to fly; it was a very stable machine and control was described by one pilot as delicate and sensitive.

From the S-16 was developed the S-17 (an experimental armoured version with a 150-hp Sunbeam engine) and the S-20. It was armed with one synchronized 7·62-mm Maxim or Vickers machine-gun on the port upper side of the cowling and/or a Lewis gun above the centre-section.

Sikorsky S-16, ski landing gear

Sikorsky S-16

TYPE	DIMENSIONS span ft	span in	length ft	length in	height ft	height in	WEIGHT max t-o lb	PERFORMANCE max speed mph	at height ft	service ceiling ft	combat range miles	REMARKS
Sikorsky IM-B	101	6½	62	4	NA		10,572	60	NA	6,560	4 hr	First military Ilya Muromets. About 4 built
Sikorsky IM-V	97	9⅛	56	1	NA		10,130	75	NA	9,840	5 hr	30 built, plus 3 more powered by Argus engines
Sikorsky IM-G2	100	2¾	56	1	NA		11,684	71·5	NA	9,840	6 hr	About 20 built, plus 15 G-3 model
Sikorsky IM-Ye1	102	10⅛	59	8⅛	NA		15,432	85	NA	10,500	4 hr	6 completed
Sikorsky S.16	27	6	20	4	9	1½	1,490	73	SL	11,482	NA	About 20 built

Sikorsky S-20

Sukhoi Su-2

Sukhoi Su-2

Sukhoi Su-6

Sikorsky S-20

The S-20, which was designed at the end of 1916, was developed from both the S-16 and the Nieuport 17 – the latter was licence-built by the RBVZ.

Powered by an 80-hp or 110-hp Le Rhône, the S-20 was, like the S-16, underpowered and only a few were built for delivery to the EVK. A maximum speed of 118 mph was claimed for the 110-hp Le Rhône-engined S-20, together with a climb to 6,540 ft in 6 minutes 20 seconds; so it is interesting to speculate what the performance of this aircraft would have been with a 150-hp or 200-hp engine, such as was available to the British, French and German designers at that time.

Russian pilots who had the opportunity to fly all three types of aircraft said that the S-20 was faster than the Nieuport 17 and the equal of the Vickers F.B.19.

Though the upper wing shape was very similar to the Nieuport's, the lower wing was only slightly smaller in area. The fin and rudder showed S-16 influence. The fuselage narrowed sharply behind the closely cowled engine; while the undercarriage was much cleaner than that of the S-16. Armament probably consisted of a single 7·62-mm Vickers machine-gun mounted on top of the engine cowling.

Sukhoi Su-2

The Su-2 began as a 1936 light bomber project, conceived hurriedly as a replacement for the disappointing R-10. Test flights of the prototype, designated ANT-51, in August 1937, indicated a top speed of 250 mph, with an 820-hp M-62 engine. It was a low-wing monoplane, with an inward-retracting main undercarriage and retractable tailwheel. The production version had a normal bomb-load of 882 lb, carried partly in a small ventral bomb-bay and partly on underwing racks, as against the 440 lb carried by the prototype. Maximum permissible bomb-load for short-range operations was 1,325 lb. Provision was made for fitting launching rails for ten RS-82 rocket missiles. Extra crew armour was also introduced: 9-mm armour protected the back of the pilot's seat and similar protection was afforded the cockpit sides and the floor around the rear-gunner's turret.

Power plant was an M-88B twin-row radial of 950 hp, driving a three-bladed VISh-23 propeller. Fuel capacity totalled 153 gallons. There were four forward-firing ShKAS 7·62-mm wing-mounted machine-guns, with a similar weapon for the observer mounted in a manually-operated dorsal turret at the rear of the raised crew canopy.

This aircraft was placed in series production in 1940 under the functional designation BB-1. Early in 1941 it was redesignated Su-2 and saw service in some numbers during the early stages of the German attack on the Soviet Union.

Some reports referred to a single-seat version also being in action.

Late production Su-2s were fitted with the more powerful 1,000-hp M-82 engine. With this power plant, the top speed rose to 302 mph at 19,000 ft, compared with 283 mph at 14,500 ft for the M-88B-powered model.

An Su-2 with M-82 engine was tested with a 7·62-mm ShKAS machine-gun on a flexible, retractable ventral mounting.

The experimental M-90 engine made its appearance in 1941 and was tested in an Su-2 airframe. This prototype was designated Su-4.

Difficulties encountered in meeting a specification for a multi-purpose machine to combine the rôles of light bombing, reconnaissance and ground-attack had an adverse effect on the performance of the Su-2. It suffered heavily in action and was withdrawn from front-line service during 1942.

Sukhoi Su-6

The Su-6 was an outstanding aircraft, but had the misfortune to appear in competition with the Ilyushin Il-2 at each stage of its development. P. O. Sukhoi's team encountered some delays with their design, and the Su-6 was still at the assembly stage when the Il-2 went into production immediately after completing its official trials in March 1941.

The first model of the Su-6 was a single-seat ground-attack monoplane of all-metal construction, powered by the 2,000-hp ASh-71 12-cylinder engine and armed with two 23-mm cannon and two 7·62-mm machine-guns in the wings. A total of 880 lb of bombs was carried, partly in the bomb-bay and partly on underwing racks. Alternatively, the aircraft could carry ten RS-82 rocket missiles.

In addition to its heavier armament, the Su-6 was found in many respects to have a performance superior to that of its rival; but the Il-2 was already in production and difficulties with the ASh-71 engine finally sealed the fate of the single-seat Su-6, which was not accepted by the Soviet Air Force.

At the beginning of 1942, extensive redesign of the Il-2 was requested, including its conversion to two-seat configuration with rear defence. A two-seat Su-6 was tested at the same time as the Il-2 Type 3. The revised Su-6 had a 2,200-hp ASh-71 radial engine and was armed with two 37-mm anti-tank cannon and two fixed 7·62-mm ShKAS machine-guns. In addition the rear gunner was provided with a movable UBT 12·7-mm machine-gun. The urgent need for large numbers of assault aircraft led to acceptance of the Il-2 Type 3, which could be turned out on production lines already in existence, but a small series of the Su-6 entered service in the Far East.

The third version of Su-6 appeared in 1943, in competition with the new Il-10. Power for both prototypes was the 12-cylinder AM-42 engine, developing 2,000 hp, which in the case of Su-6 drove a four-bladed propeller. Armament remained similar to that of the 1942 version, but the main wheels were modified to retract rearward, lying flush in the wings covered by two square doors.

This final version also appeared in only limited quantities and the Su-6 was fated never to meet the enemy in combat.

Sukhoi Su-7

Allocated the NATO code-name "Fitter", the Su-7 is a close-support and ground-attack fighter designed by Pavel Osipovich Sukhoi. It was the first of his designs to enter quantity production after re-establishment of his design bureau in 1953.

The prototype was seen for the first time at Tushino, in the 1956 Soviet Air Display, and was then powered by an unspecified single-shaft turbojet providing 14,500 lb s t, or 19,840 lb s t with afterburner.

The wing of the Su-7 has 62° sweep at the leading-edge, and features large area-increasing flaps which, however, limit the number of underwing weapon pylons that can be fitted. Internal fuel tankage can be supplemented by twin drop tanks mounted beneath the fuselage, and there is provision for flight refuelling.

Armament comprises two 30-mm cannon mounted in the wing roots; ventral pylons can accommodate two 1,000-lb bombs, and the underwing pylons can carry a single bomb of up to 550 lb or a pod housing 19 unguided rockets of 55-mm calibre.

The latest Su-7Bs are reported to be powered by an uprated engine developing 22,050 lb s t with afterburner, and other modifications include movement of the pitot

Sukhoi Su-6, second type, with two 37-mm anti-tank cannon

Sukhoi Su-6, second type

Sukhoi Su-7B, with JATO

TYPE	DIMENSIONS span ft	span in	length ft	length in	height ft in	WEIGHT max t-o lb	PERFORMANCE max speed mph	at height ft	service ceiling ft	combat range miles	REMARKS
Sikorsky S-20	26	10½	21	4	NA	1,654	118	SL	20,470	NA	As with S-16 used by EVK
Sukhoi Su-2	46	11	33	7⅝	NA	8,994	282·7 302	14,435 19,192	28,871	745	With M-88B engine With M-82 engine
Sukhoi Su-6	44	3½	30	3¾	NA	11,576	327·4 297	8,202 SL	26,246	279	ASh-71 engine
	44	3½	31	2	NA	13,670	323·1 301·3	8,202 SL	26,246	497	AM-42 engine

Sukhoi Su-7B

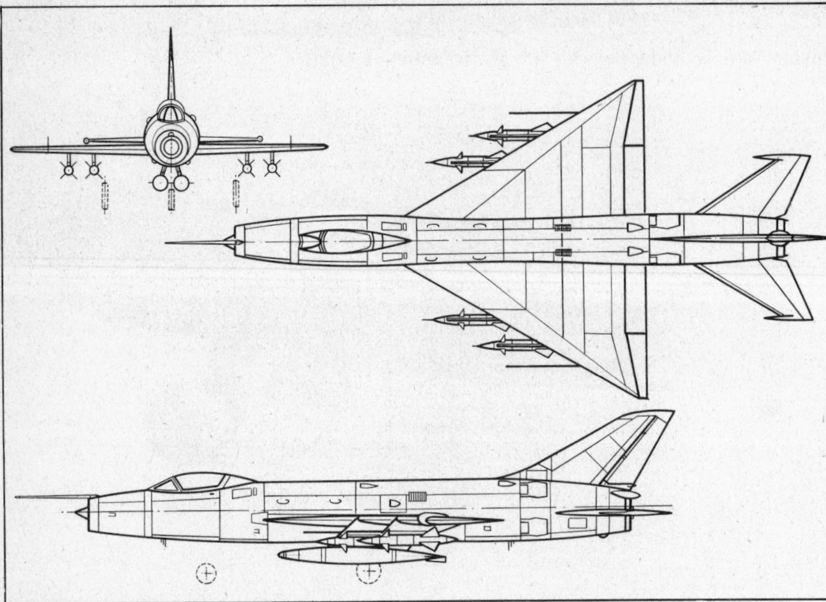

Sukhoi Su-9, early production version

Sukhoi Su-9, late production version

Sukhoi "Flagon-A"

boom, from a position centrally above the air intake to an offset point on the starboard, and provision of an acorn fairing, housing twin brake-chutes, at the base of the rudder. Two assisted take-off rockets can be attached under the fuselage.

Serving currently with the Soviet Air Force, the Su-7 has also been supplied to other countries, including Czechoslovakia, Poland and the United Arab Republic.

An Su-7 was modified into Russia's first experimental "swing-wing" aircraft, by pivoting the outer 13 ft of each wing and fitting a large fence between each fixed and movable panel.

Sukhoi Su-9

When first seen at Tushino during the 1956 Soviet Aviation Day display, this single-seat all-weather fighter had a small conical radome above its air intake; this version was given the NATO code-name "Fishpot-A". Later aircraft had a more orthodox circular air intake with a central cone for the radar; aircraft of this configuration were allocated the code-name "Fishpot-B". This version was selected for production, and examples began to enter service in 1959.

Evolved in parallel with the Su-7, the Su-9 is similar in general layout to its Mikoyan contemporary, the MiG-21, although a larger and heavier aircraft with more powerful engine, rated at 14,500 lb s t dry and 20,046 lb s t with reheat.

No fixed armament is carried, but four of the Soviet Air Force's standard radar-homing air-to-air missiles (NATO code-name "Alkali") on underwing attachments provide offensive armament, and two under-fuselage side-by-side fuel tanks supplement wing tankage.

More recent production Su-9s have slightly larger air intakes which could denote an uprated engine, and feature four petal-type air-brakes, in pairs on each side of the rear fuselage. Their armament consists of two "Anab" missiles.

Sukhoi "Flagon-A"

A new single-seat twin-jet Sukhoi all-weather interceptor entered service with the Soviet Air Force in 1967, presumably as a replacement for the Su-9. Its wings and tail unit bear an obvious family likeness to its predecessor; but side-mounted air intakes take the place of the Su-9's nose intake. This has enabled Sukhoi to fit a large search radar, inside a conical nose-cone. The air intakes embody "splitter" plates, like those of the McDonnell Phantom II, to prevent boundary-layer air from entering the intakes.

The mid-set delta wings and swept tail are similar in size to those of the Su-9. Armament is also the same, comprising two "Anab" air-to-air missiles, with alternative infra-red and radar homing heads, on underwing pylons. The cleaner design and increased power of two afterburning engines should give a maximum speed of around Mach 2·5. The NATO code-name is "Flagon-A".

A STOL version ("Flagon-B"), with three lift-jets installed vertically in the centre-fuselage, was demonstrated at the Domodedovo air display in July 1967. Apart from having slightly extended wingtips, with compound leading-edge sweep, the STOL machine appeared to be almost identical with the standard fighter. The added versatility offered by its STOL capability might well justify production for the Soviet Air Force.

Tupolev R-3 (ANT-3)

While output of the R-1, the Soviet Union's first mass-produced aircraft, was gathering momentum, work was in hand at TsAGI to meet a specification laid down by the Soviet Air Force for an all-metal light bomber-reconnaissance aircraft. In 1924, the team led by A. N. Tupolev completed design of the ANT-3, which was designated R-3 in its military guise. It was a two-seat biplane built of Kolchug aluminium, a Soviet alloy claimed to be stronger than normal duralumin and named after the Russian town where it was first produced.

It was the first all-metal Soviet-designed aircraft built in quantity. With the exception of the engine cowling, the entire fuselage was covered with corrugated Kolchug aluminium sheeting. The distinctive triangular section of the fuselage permitted excellent downward visibility. Unequal-span wings were braced with Y-shaped struts. The upper wing had no dihedral, but there was considerable dihedral on the lower wing.

Various power plants were installed in the prototype and early production models including the 400-hp Liberty and 450-hp Lorraine-Dietrich and Napier engines. In later aircraft, these were replaced by the Soviet-built M-5.

Factory test flights by V. N. Phillipov were made in September and October 1925. V. M. Gromov then piloted the R-3 on its official trials. These were concluded successfully in May 1926, whereupon the R-3 went into quantity production. It could be adapted easily for ground-attack or light bombing duties. In addition, during the late 1920s and early 1930s, some ANT-3s were flown on Soviet air mail routes.

Standard armament of the military version comprised one fixed forward-firing Vickers machine-gun, operated by the pilot, and another 7·62-mm gun mounted over the rear cockpit. Maximum bomb-load, carried on racks under the wing, was 440 lb. Some R-3s were fitted with four forward-firing machine-guns for the assault rôle. In 1929, a version of the R-3 powered by an M-17 engine was produced in prototype form as the R-4.

In performance, the R-3 was the equal of its foreign contemporaries. Proof of this was given by a number of successful long-distance flights. M. M. Gromov in *Proletariat*, an ANT-3 registered RR-SOV, visited five European capitals during a period of three days in 1926. In the following year, Shestakov flew an R-3 13,675 miles, from Moscow to Tokyo, in 153 hours of flying time.

Tupolev TB-1 (ANT-4)

Design of the TB-1, bureau designation ANT-4, was initiated in 1924 by a TsAGI team under A. N. Tupolev. The first prototype was completed in 1925. Test pilot Tomashevsky began trials in November of that year.

The TB-1 was a cantilever low-wing monoplane, and the basic material used in its construction was Soviet-produced Kolchugaluminium, a duralumin-type alloy, in the form of tubes and sheets.

The thick cantilever five-spar wing was designed by V. M. Petlyakov. It was built in three sections – a large central section integral with the centre part of the fuselage and two smaller outer panels. The metal fuselage was covered with a corrugated metal skin and also consisted of three parts, one of which was embodied in the wing centre-section. The tail surfaces were all-metal with a corrugated skin.

The low-wing monoplane layout was still in the early stages of development and a number of problems connected with the construction of an all-metal thick-profile cantilever wing had to be solved. Within a comparatively short time, the scientists and designers connected with TsAGI had worked out a reliable method of calculating stresses for such a wing. V. M. Petlyakov played a leading rôle in this work and was, in fact, responsible for the wing design of all TsAGI-ANT aircraft from the ANT-1 to the huge ANT-20.

A large machine for its time, the TB-1 set the pattern for Soviet bomber development during the next ten to twelve years. Power was provided by two M-17 engines and the large fuel tanks essential for the required range

Tupolev R-3 (ANT-3)

Tupolev TB-1 (ANT-4)

Tupolev TB-1, carrying two I-4 fighters above wings

TYPE	DIMENSIONS span ft	in	length ft	in	height ft	in	WEIGHT max t-o lb	PERFORMANCE max speed mph	at height ft	service ceiling ft	combat range miles	REMARKS
Sukhoi Su-7	30	0*	56	0*	NA		30,000	1,056	36,000	NA	NA	*Estimated. Initial climb: 30,000 ft/min.
Sukhoi Su-9	26	0*	56	0*	NA		29,000	Mach 1·6	29,000	55,000	NA	Initial climb: 27,0000 ft/min.
Sukhoi "Flagon-A"	30	0*	68	0*	NA		NA	Mach 2·5	40,000	NA	NA	
Tupolev R-3 (ANT-3)	43	3¾	32	5¾	12	9½	4,596	128·6	SL	13,123	434	
Tupolev TB-1 (ANT-4)	89	11¼	59	0½	19	11¾	15,038	123	SL	15,419	621	Max loaded weight: 17,144 lb. Record machine, span 94 ft 2¼ in.

Tupolev MTB-1 floatplane

Tupolev I-4 (ANT-5)

Tupolev Kr-6

Tupolev Kr-6

of action were accommodated in the thick wing. In performance the TB-1 compared favourably with contemporary foreign bombers. Its range/load figures varied from an endurance of 9 hours with 2,205 lb of bombs to 2½ hours with 6,615 lb.

Flight characteristics were generally good, although the thickness of the wings caused a shifting of the centre of gravity when the speed was increased. As a result, considerable forces were exerted on the control column. The crews of later bombers, including the TB-3 and the experimental six-engined TB-4, suffered similar discomforts.

TB-1s established a number of payload and distance records, including the well-known flight from Moscow to New York in 1929 by the pilot Schestakov. A torpedo floatplane version, designated MTB-1, was used by Soviet naval squadrons, and the transport variant of the TB-1 had a long and active life on the internal routes of the Civil Aviation and Northern Sea Routes Authorities. In March 1937, it was an ANT-4 piloted by Lyapedevsky which made the first landing on drifting ice in the vicinity of the trapped Soviet ice-breaker *Chelyuskin*.

The TB-1 had a crew of six. Six 7·62-mm DA-2 machine-guns were carried on flexible mountings, with defensive positions in the nose and amidships. The engine instrument panel was located behind the pilots' cockpits, and passages in the wings provided access to the fuel tanks and engines.

Quantity production continued until 1932, a total of 200 TB-1s being built. Apart from its own achievements the TB-1's significance lay in the basis it provided for further development. This followed two distinct lines. The first saw the evolution of the ANT-4 into the smaller and aerodynamically more refined ANT-7 for multi-seat fighter duties. The second led to a new four-engined design of far greater dimensions, the ANT-6, which was later to achieve world renown as the TB-3.

Tupolev I-4 (ANT-5)

The ANT-5, or I-4 to give it its military designation, was an all-metal single-seat fighter with characteristically angular wings and tailplane. It was powered by an uncowled 420-hp M-22 engine. The layout was that of a sesquiplane, with the upper wing considerably larger than the "stub" type lower wings, to which it was attached by a pair of "Y"-shaped struts. Armament was two 7·62-mm synchronized PV-1 machine-guns.

P. O. Sukhoi headed the team which began work on the project in the spring of 1926. The team was located in TsAGI and was under the general supervision of the redoubtable A. N. Tupolev. The new fighter was ready for testing by mid-1927 and was flown by leading test pilots M. M. Gromov, A. F. Anisimov and A. B. Yumashev in July and August of that year. The tests took place at the NII-VVS (Air Force Testing Institute) and those who piloted the machine recorded unanimously that it had excellent manoeuvrability and was easy to fly.

The I-4 attained a top speed of 160 mph at sea level and could climb to 16,400 ft (5,000 m) in 10·9 minutes. A 180-degree turn was performed in 11·5 seconds and ceiling was 25,100 ft.

Series production began in 1928 and the I-4 was soon in squadron service. Its strong, reliable and durable structure ensured its continued use and, in fact, quantity production was spread over a period of some six years, about 370 of the type being manufactured. During that time, the I-4 was frequently modified and took part in a great deal of experimental work. This included adaptation as a parasite fighter, a pair of I-4s being carried into the air attached to the upper wing surfaces of TB-1 bombers and then air-launched. Other I-4s were employed as test-beds for the new heavy recoilless cannon which appeared in Russia in the early 1930s.

Tupolev Kr-6 (ANT-7 or R-6)

The ANT-7 took off for the first time on 11 September 1929, with Mikhail M. Gromov as pilot. P. M. Stefanovsky flew the aircraft on its official service trials, which began in March of the following year. Soon afterwards, two versions were put into production – the Kr-6 multi-seat fighter (Kr = Cruiser) and the R-6 long-range reconnaissance machine (R = Reconnaissance). A seaplane version was built for the Soviet Navy and, at a later stage, passenger-carrying adaptations went into service as the P-6 (landplane) and MP-6 (floatplane).

A three-seat low-wing monoplane, the ANT-7 was a development of the ANT-4 (TB-1) and had the same power plant, comprising two M-17 in-line engines. Nevertheless, its top speed was 26 mph higher than that of the earlier type. The greatly enhanced performance was due to reduced overall dimensions, careful streamlining and elimination of potential sources of drag. Although differing in a number of important details, not least in size, the ANT-7 was frequently identified incorrectly as the ANT-4 during its subsequent service career.

The Kr-6 escort fighter was armed with four movable DA machine-guns mounted in nose, dorsal and ventral positions. With a top speed of 150 mph at sea level, it was only slightly slower than contemporary single-seat fighters. Its French equivalent, the Blériot 127, forerunner of that country's *Multiplace de combat* category, was 28 mph slower than the Kr-6. Furthermore, while the Blériot 127 was built in sufficient numbers to equip only a single *escadrille* on an experimental basis, a grand total of 400 of the various versions of the ANT-7 was delivered.

R-6 reconnaissance aircraft and Kr-6 multi-seat fighters were both in squadron service for a number of years from 1931 onwards. A civil ANT-7 achieved renown by making a preliminary reconnaissance over the North Pole, prior to the landing there of three heavily-laden ANT-6s, with members of the 1937 Soviet Arctic Expedition. The Red Air Force still used the type for second-line duties in 1941 and a number were discovered on Soviet aerodromes by the advancing German forces. A few ANT-7s were still being flown by Aeroflot on transport duties during the immediate post-war period.

Tupolev TB-3 (ANT-6)

The history of this heavy bomber dates back to early December 1925, when TsAGI and Ostechbyuro (the Special Technical Bureau) agreed to the building of an aircraft capable of carrying a 2,200/4,850-lb payload and to be powered by engines developing a total of 2,000 hp.

The TB-3 (design bureau designation ANT-6) was an all-metal low-wing monoplane with a rigid corrugated metal skin. It was developed by A. N. Tupolev and his colleagues from the earlier TB-1 and followed the earlier design very closely in structural detail.

The original prototype was built in 1929–30, and its first flight, on 22 December 1930, almost ended in disaster. At take-off, pilot Mikhail Gromov pushed the throttle levers right forward, applying full power. When the machine was airborne and the speed increasing, the forces exerted on the control column began to build up and Gromov was forced to use both hands to hold it in the correct position. While he was fully occupied in this way, the two starboard engine throttle levers began to creep back to the "low revs" position. The TB-3 went into a steep turn, with the starboard wing dipping dangerously low over the aerodrome hangars. It was only prompt action by other members of the crew that saved the day. The throttle levers were quickly pushed back to the correct position and were held there for the rest of the flight. A throttle locking device was subsequently installed in record time!

The TB-3's loaded weight of 16-19 tons was greater

Tupolev TB-3 (ANT-6)

Tupolev TB-3

TYPE	DIMENSIONS span ft	span in	length ft	length in	height ft	height in	WEIGHT max t-o lb	PERFORMANCE max speed mph	at height ft	service ceiling ft	combat range miles	REMARKS
Tupolev I-4 (ANT-5)	37	4¾	23	10⅝	9	2¼	3,007	159·7	SL	25,098	NA	
Tupolev Kr-6 (ANT-7)	76	1⅜	48	4⅝	NA		11,554	150	SL	19,849	NA	Recce. version = R-6.

Tupolev TB-3, dropping parachutists

Tupolev TB-3

than that of any contemporary landplane and it achieved the very high payload coefficient of 0·46. Normal loaded weight was 35,280 lb, but overloading up to 42,335 lb and even 54,020 lb was permissible on later versions. The TB-3 was designed to withstand stresses 20 per cent higher than normal and this allowed modification without considerable increase in structure weight which might otherwise have ensued. Utilization in a greater variety of rôles was thus possible.

The American 600-hp Curtiss Conqueror engines which had powered the prototype on its initial flights were replaced in February 1931 by Soviet-built M-17s, each developing a maximum 730 hp and with a nominal rating of 500 hp. On successful completion of official trials, the TB-3 was accepted by the VVS as equipment for the heavy bomber squadrons, in the knowledge that M-34 engines of greater power would shortly be available for installation in improved versions of the aircraft.

An important part in the task of placing this large aircraft in quantity production was played by A. N. Tupolev's assistant, V. M. Petlyakov. The team of factory and official test pilots also had a major rôle in eliminating the aircraft's numerous shortcomings and simplifying the handling of the aircraft until it could be entrusted to pilots with no more than average qualifications.

Nine TB-3s were ready in time to fly over Red Square on May Day 1932. Production soon gathered momentum, and on May Day 1933 fifty TB-3s were seen over Moscow. In the 1934 parade, more than 250 of the 500 or so aircraft which flew over Moscow were TB-3s. This vast output of the only four-engined machines to constitute an effective heavy bombing force in the world in the 1930s was tangible evidence of the industrialization then taking place in the Soviet Union.

Early M-17-powered TB-3s were protected by no fewer than ten machine-guns disposed in five mountings, each for twin 7·62-mm DA.2 weapons. One position was in the nose of the aircraft and there were two dorsal posts. The latter were situated one behind the other and could be offset together either to port or to starboard of the wide fuselage. These different locations were intended presumably to improve the field of fire when the bombers flew in formation. The remaining twin-gun mountings were in two underwing turrets. Bomb-load varied between 2,200 lb and 4,850 lb, according to the mission to be performed and the weight of fuel to be carried.

A prototype TB-3 with M-34 engines was completed in March 1933 and passed its official trials in the autumn of that year. This model introduced wheel brakes and dispensed with the underwing turrets and separate wireless compartment of the M-17-powered version. The modified bomber displayed only a marginally-better rate of climb than its predecessor and top speed was actually lower. The power plant was subsequently revised, and in September and October 1933 the TB-3 carried out factory test flights with M-34R engines ("R" = *Reductornyi*, i.e. fitted with reduction gear). A new defensive position, replacing the deleted underwing turrets, was installed in the extreme rear fuselage, which was extended aft of the fin and rudder. Performance was much improved, despite the increased weight, and this version entered quantity production as the TB-3 Model 1934.

In the course of official flying trials in August 1934, one TB-3 with M-34R engines, carrying a 4,410-lb bomb-load, covered 1,535 miles before landing, in a flight of 13 hours' duration. Weight unladen was 25,800 lb and on this occasion the aircraft's loaded weight was 46,300 lb.

In the same year, the TB-3 was fitted with M-34RN engines, with reduction gear and supercharger. The installation of this new power plant achieved an appreciable increase in speed and ceiling, and was accompanied by other measures designed to improve performance through aerodynamic refinement of the aircraft. The corrugated skin of the wing and tail areas was covered with fabric and this raised the top speed by between 12 and 15 mph. The introduction of a fairing between the wing and the fuselage further increased the speed by 5–6 mph and the ceiling by 650–980 ft. The changes also rendered the controls of the aircraft more effective.

The total speed increase of this model was 9 mph at sea level and between 42 and 45 mph at higher ltitudes.

The production TB-3 incorporating all these modifications was claimed to have a higher performance and to carry a greater bomb-load than any other heavy bomber being manufactured in quantity at that time.

German test reports on the late production TB-3 with AM-34RN engines indicated a normal bomb-load of 4,410 lb, with a maximum permitted load of 12,800 lb for short-range attacks. A variety of bombs could be carried, disposed on 26 racks in the fuselage bomb-bay and 12 racks under the wings and fuselage. The normal internal load was twenty-six 220-lb bombs, but reduction to eighteen allowed additional external loads of twelve 550-lb, or eight 1,100-lb or three 2,205-lb bombs.

The introduction of more powerful M-34RNF engines from 1935 onward still further improved the performance of production TB-3s. In 1937, a smooth skin covering was adopted in place of corrugated surfaces and the two tandem-wheel main undercarriage assemblies were replaced by large single wheels with improved low-pressure tyres. Re-design eliminated all remaining structural protrusions.

Throughout the TB-3's development, some saving in weight was achieved by reducing the number of crew members and the defensive armament. The introduction of quick-firing ShKAS machine-guns and improved layout of the armament, including the tail gunner's post, permitted the number of machine-guns to be reduced to three without any consequent decrease in firepower. The crew was reduced from ten to six. In final production models of the TB-3, the nose and dorsal gunners' positions were fitted with manually-operated turrets.

Many outstanding flights were accomplished by TB-3s, particularly in support of Soviet Arctic expeditions. Transport versions in widespread use by the Civil Air Fleet and Sevmorput (Northern Sea Routes Authority) prior to World War II were designated G-2. The TB-3 was used widely for carrying paratroops and also took part in a number of experiments with parasite fighters. Some were adapted to carry armoured cars or light tanks between the main undercarriage legs.

Eight hundred of all versions of the TB-3 were built. Its activities included operations against the Japanese in the Lake Hasan area in July and August 1938; actions near the River Khalkin-Gol from May to September 1939 against the same enemy; participation in the occupation of Eastern Poland in September 1939; and service in the Winter War against Finland between November 1939 and March 1940. The TB-3 was still in service as a night bomber in 1941 and served on a major scale as a transport aircraft throughout the war.

Tupolev MDR-2 (ANT-8)

The TsAGI design team gained experience of water-borne aircraft when a floatplane version of the TB-1 was produced in some numbers under the designation MTB-1. Following this, a naval reconnaissance-bomber flying boat was projected, utilizing the wings and power plant of the ANT-7. Experiments were carried a stage further with a specially-built hull, the bottom of which was made adjustable so that the optimum angle for the "step" could be ascertained.

Design of the MDR-2, or ANT-8, was begun in 1930 and the prototype appeared in the following year. It was a shoulder-wing monoplane flying-boat, intended for long-range reconnaissance, with bombing as a secondary

Tupolev TB-3

Tupolev TB-3, carrying armoured vehicle

Tupolev MDR-2 (ANT-8)

TYPE	DIMENSIONS						WEIGHT	PERFORMANCE				REMARKS
	span		*length*		*height*		*max t-o*	*max speed*	*at height*	*service ceiling*	*combat range*	
	ft	*in*	*ft*	*in*	*ft*	*in*	*lb*	*mph*	*ft*	*ft*	*miles*	
Tupolev TB-3 Type 1932	132	10⅜	81	0	NA		38,360	133·6 103·4	SL 9,842	12,467	1,367	M-17 engines
Tupolev TB-3 Type 1934	132	10⅜	82	8¼	NA		41,021	143·5 131·1	SL 9,842	15,091	1,553	M-34R engines
Tupolev TB-3 Type 1936	137	1½	82	8¼	NA		41,226	152·2 179	SL 9,842	25,393	1,553	M-34RN engines
Tupolev MDR-2 (ANT-8)	76	1⅜	60	8½	24	7½	15,432	135	NA	16,404	932	

Tupolev MDR-2 (ANT-8)

Tupolev RD-DB-1 (ANT-25)

Tupolev MDR-4 (ANT-27)

Tupolev MDR-4 (ANT-27)

rôle. Power was provided by two M-17 engines, which were placed above the wings, each on a pair of supporting "N" struts. The engines drove pusher propellers.

Of all-metal construction, the MDR-2 could carry a useful payload and showed good stability on the water. Kolchug aluminium was the main material employed, but the bottom of the hull and a limited number of other parts were of steel.

The useful load of 5,900 lb included bombs, three machine-guns of 7·62-mm calibre in dorsal and bow positions, and a crew of five.

Tupolev RD-DB-1 (ANT-25)

The remarkable success of the ANT-25 on its long-distance record flights led to development of a military version, the RD-DB-1, in 1933–4. This was produced only in limited numbers.

The story of the ANT-25 dated from early 1932, when P. O. Sukhoi's team, working under the supervision of A. N. Tupolev, started work on a project for a long-distance machine which had been outlined by a special Government Commission in 1931. Construction began in June 1932, and the first flight was made by M. M. Gromov on 22 June 1933.

The ANT-25 was an all-metal cantilever low-wing monoplane with an 860-hp M-34 engine and a semi-retractable undercarriage. The wing had the unusually high aspect ratio of 13:1 and an area of 947 sq ft, the aim being to reduce the induced drag at cruising speeds. The stresses on a wing of such elongated form were relieved by the weight of the fuel tanks which were built into the wings along almost the whole span. In flight, the fuel in the central tanks was used up first, followed by the outer tanks, working outward progressively and simultaneously on both sides. This method of stress reduction resulted in a lighter wing structure and permitted the maximum possible loaded weight to be combined with the minimum possible empty weight.

Tests showed that, at a loaded weight of 15,100 lb, the aircraft became airborne at a speed of 97 mph, after a 46·5-second take-off run over a distance of 3,250 ft. However, the loaded weight for the record flight would have to be 25,350 lb and, to permit take-off at such a weight, a long, wide concrete runway with a ramp at the end was built specially for the ANT-25 near the town of Schelkovo.

After two abortive attempts, the ANT-25 made a non-stop flight of 7,711 miles over a triangular route (Schelkovo, Moscow-Tula-Ryazan) in 1934; but since the Soviet Union was not then an FAI member state the record was not recognized internationally. Other famous flights by ANT-25s included two to the U.S.A. in 1937, the first by Chkalov covering 5,301 miles non-stop and the second by Gromov covering 6,305 miles.

The military version was slow and suffered from poor defensive armament and low operational ceiling. Experience with the RD-DB-1 led, in fact, to suspension of the ANT-36 (RB-BB) bomber project. Nevertheless, later Soviet military designs benefited from the practical and theoretical research carried out with the ANT-25.

Tupolev MDR-4 (ANT-27)

The ANT-27 (military designation MDR-4) was produced by a TsAGI team in 1933, together with a number of other designs for Soviet Naval Aviation, as part of the Second Five Year Plan. The first prototype was lost in a crash in April 1934. A second prototype was completed by the autumn of the same year, but met a similar fate to the first, crashing during official trials in September 1935.

After that, it was only the acute need for a flying-boat in the long-range reconnaissance-bomber category that compelled the authorities to order into production this unproven aircraft with a rather poor performance.

The MDR-4 was a shoulder-wing monoplane with an enclosed pilot's cabin. The wings were built in three sections, with considerable dihedral on the two outer panels. The centre-section supported three M-34R engines, which were carried above the wings on "N" struts. The outer engines had tractor propellers, and the central one was of the pusher type. The hull had a double step. Underwing floats were fitted. Strut-braced horizontal tail surfaces were carried high on the single angular fin.

Machine-guns were mounted in turrets in the nose, amidships and in the tail.

Top speed at sea level was 145 mph and ceiling was 17,900 ft. A small series of fifteen MDR-4s entered service with Naval long-range bombing and reconnaissance units in April 1936. The tactical characteristics were no better than had been anticipated, and this gave a spur to efforts then being made to produce more efficient long-range flying-boats.

Tupolev SB-2 (ANT-40)

In 1933–4, a team headed by A. N. Tupolev designed a high-speed bomber with the bureau number ANT-40 and the military designation SB. The aircraft was developed from two previous experimental twin-engined fighters, the MI-3 and DIP, which had the bureau numbers ANT-21 and ANT-29 respectively.

The SB was a twin-engined cantilever mid-wing monoplane. The main undercarriage units retracted rearward into the engine nacelles, leaving the wheels partially exposed. Great care was taken to streamline the fuselage and to ensure the smooth fairing of the wings into the body of the aircraft. The result was a fast bomber with outstanding aerodynamic qualities.

It was intended to meet an official requirement issued in the summer of 1933 for a three-seat bomber capable of a top speed of 205 mph – half as fast again as the TB-3 and R-5 then in service – and with a ceiling of 26,250 ft (8,000 m). By contrast, the specified range of 435 miles was short and the bomb load of 1,110 lb small.

The specification was entirely new in concept and set the designers the difficult task of producing a fast tactical bomber capable of close co-operation with either Army or Navy units. The landing speed was not to exceed 70 mph, to enable the aircraft to operate successfully from small unprepared airfields. For the same reason, strict limitations were imposed on the length of take-off and landing runs.

The SB's airframe differed considerably from those of previous TsAGI-designed aircraft. A smooth duralumin covering for the wings and fuselage was employed for the first time, and a monocoque fuselage structure was adopted in place of the old system, built up on frames. As a result, the usable interior capacity of the bomber was greatly increased.

To determine whether M-25 radial engines or M-100 in-line engines were more suitable, two prototypes were constructed simultaneously, the first with 700-hp M-25s and the second with 750-hp liquid-cooled M-100s with distinctive radiators. Both types of engine were fitted with superchargers.

On the basis of very thorough calculations and detailed estimates of high performance, the decision was taken in April 1934 to place the SB in series production. At that time the first prototype was still uncompleted.

The prototype with M-25 radials, designated SB-1, was the first to fly, on 7 October 1934. Subsequent test flights indicated a performance adequate to meet the official specifications. However, the M-100-powered prototype, which flew less than three months later, on 30 December, exceeded the official requirements in every respect. This machine, by then designated SB-2, incorporated a number of features that were thought necessary by A. N. Tupolev for the accomplishment of a wider range of operational duties. Its M-100 in-line engines each

Tupolev SB-2 (ANT-40)

Tupolev SB-2*bis*

Tupolev SB-2*bis*, captured aircraft, Finnish markings

TYPE	DIMENSIONS						WEIGHT	PERFORMANCE				REMARKS
	span		length		height		max t-o	max speed	at height	service ceiling	combat range	
	ft	in	ft	in	ft	in	lb	mph	ft	ft	miles	
Tupolev RD-DB-1 (ANT-25)	111	6⅝	43	11⅝	NA		24,807	130·5	NA	22,965	6,835	
Tupolev MDR-4 (ANT-27)	NA		NA		NA		32,320	145	SL	17,900	1,242	

Tupolev SB-2*bis*

Tupolev Tu-2

developed 184 hp more at altitude than the M-25s on the SB-1 and, having only half the frontal area of the radials, caused less drag and contributed considerably towards the SB-2's better performance. Another advantage of the second prototype was its greater fuel tank capacity, which enabled it to be re-classified as a medium-range bomber. Its speed made it a difficult target for anti-aircraft fire and it was faster than contemporary single-seat fighters such as the Fiat C.R.32, which also appeared in 1934.

The clear superiority of the SB-2 during factory trials led to the decision at that stage to choose it as the production prototype. By the time official trials were completed in July 1935, preparations for quantity production were already under way, and by early 1936 delivery of the SB-2 to VVS units had begun. Production lines had been laid down at a number of factories and peak output amounted to 13 machines per day.

At altitudes over 16,400 ft (5,000 m) the production SB-2 was faster than the latest German fighter of 1937, the Messerschmitt Bf 109B. Rate of climb was better at all altitudes than the Boeing P-26A then in service with US Army Air Corps pursuit squadrons and was superior to that of the Fiat C.R.32 at heights over 21,300 ft (6,500 m). The maximum speed of the SB-2 comfortably exceeded that of the best production bombers of other countries.

A continuing programme of modification and improvement was carried out by the design team from 1934 to 1940. In 1936 the installation of M-100A engines led to an increase of 3–4 mph in top speed and enabled the bomb-load to be raised to 1,325 lb. The bomber thus modified took a minute less to reach 16,400 ft (5,000 m).

With availability of the M-103 engine in 1938, a revised version, the SB-2*bis*, made its appearance, utilizing the new power plant. The M-103 engines were housed in smooth cowlings and drove VISh-22 variable-pitch propellers. They were mainly responsible, with their greater horsepower and more efficient radiators, for an increased maximum speed of 280 mph at 13,500 ft. Overload weight rose to 17,200 lb and range to 1,430 miles carrying an 1,100-lb bomb-load.

The SB-2 series relied on a defensive armament of four 7·62-mm ShKAS machine-guns. Two movable guns were located in the nose, firing through slots which had good vertical but poor lateral traverse. A single gun on a dorsal mounting was operated by the gunner/radio operator. The fourth weapon was operated from a ventral position. Some variants of both the SB-2 and SB-2*bis* had a glazed dorsal turret in place of the original sliding hood.

An offensive load of six 220-lb bombs could be accommodated in the bomb-bay. Alternative loads were two 550-lb bombs or a single 1,100-lb bomb.

Civil transport versions of the SB-2, known as PS-40s, had served on a number of Aeroflot routes from 1938 onwards. In due course, a civil conversion of the SB-2*bis* also appeared and was known as the PS-41.

Considerable numbers of the original SB-2 were despatched to China when that country was attacked by the Japanese. Others served the Republican cause in the Spanish Civil War between 1936 and 1939. The type operated with Soviet bomber units against the Japanese during the series of Mongolian border incidents in 1938 and 1939. It was still in service in some quantity during the attack on Finland in the winter of 1939–40 and in the early stages of the war with Germany, by which time it had been relegated exclusively to the night bombing rôle. The SB-2*bis* joined the SB-2 in the Finnish campaign and bore a heavy burden as the principal medium-range bomber during the early stages of the German invasion.

Both the SB-2 and SB-2*bis* were produced in very large quantities and played a major rôle in the modernization of the Soviet bomber force during the late 1930s. It was their misfortune to be still in service, despite their obsolescence, when Russia became involved in World War II.

Tupolev Tu-2

A 1938 Soviet specification called for a bombing aircraft with a considerable range of action and a maximum speed close to that of a single-seat fighter. The entire bomb-load was to be accommodated internally and structural design and equipment were to allow for use of the machine in the dive-bombing rôle.

"Aircraft 103" was a project of the Tupolev design team in answer to these requirements. The prototype, bearing the bureau number ANT-58, had the new experimental AM-37 engines and flew for the first time in October 1940. During its subsequent flying trials, the ANT-58 demonstrated outstanding performance. So, when all the essential stages of the trials had been concluded successfully, preparations were made for series production of the new bomber, now powered by M-82 radial engines and designated Tu-2. The plans did not come to fruition until the beginning of the war with Germany.

The Tu-2, the second major Soviet tactical bomber to be mass-produced during World War II, was placed in production early in 1942. In September of that year the first three production models flew on operational trials with an Air Army on the Kalininsk sector of the front.

The new aircraft were greeted with great enthusiasm by their crews, whose report had this to say:

"The Tu-2 with M-82 engines provides the right answer to tactical demands made on the modern bomber. Good features include (1) A large bomb-load with adequate range, (2) Radial air-cooled engines which reduce vulnerability as compared with liquid-cooled power plant, (3) A good defensive armament layout, (4) Flight can be maintained on one engine, (5) Conversion crew training can be accomplished easily, and (6) A crew of four is suited to operational conditions."

Powered by two 1,850-hp ASh-82FN radial engines, the Tu-2 had a maximum speed of 342 mph. Normal bomb-load was 2,200 lb, with a maximum of 6,600 lb. Single 12·7-mm Beresin machine-guns were mounted in dorsal and ventral positions. A further weapon of the same type was operated from the rear of the cockpit canopy, and a 20-mm or 23-mm cannon, intended largely for ground-attack purposes, was mounted in the leading-edge of each wing.

The Tu-2 was an all-metal mid-wing monoplane with a fuselage of semi-monocoque construction. The main undercarriage units retracted fully into the engine nacelles. The tailwheel was also fully retractable.

Despite the fact that it was capable of carrying a considerably greater bomb-load over longer distances than the Petlyakov Pe-2, the Tupolev bomber was produced during the war in the ratio of one for every ten Pe-2s. This was mainly because it became available later, after massive production of the Pe-2 had been started. Production of the Tu-2 continued, however, after the war, finally ceasing in 1948. It served into the 1950s with the Soviet, Polish and Chinese Air Forces and was in action during the Korean War.

Post-war models of the Tu-2, which received the NATO code-name "Bat", included a close-support version with a 37-mm cannon installed on the port side of an unglazed nose.

In 1946, the high-altitude Tu-6 appeared, with wings of greater span than the standard Tu-2. Other points of difference were revised engine nacelles, a lengthened nose section and enlarged tail unit.

Tupolev Tu-2

Tupolev Tu-2

TYPE	DIMENSIONS						WEIGHT	PERFORMANCE				REMARKS
	span		length		height		max t-o	max speed	at height	service ceiling	combat range	
	ft	in	ft	in	ft	in	lb	mph	ft	ft	miles	
Tupolev SB-2 (ANT-40)	66	8½	40	3⅛	10	8	11,023[1] 13,443[2] 12,637[3]	253[1] 254·7[2] 263·5[3]	 13,123[3]	30,840+ 27,887[2] 31,354[3 4] 34,448[5]	 745[2]	[1] Prototype [2] Production model [3] Model with M-100A engines: [4] with a constant-speed propeller [5] with VISh-22 variable-pitch propeller A.A.Archangelskii had major role in design
Tupolev SB-2*bis* (ANT-41)	66	8½	40	3⅛	10	8	21,164	279·6	16,404	NA	994*	*At 186·4 mph
Tupolev Tu-2	61	10½	45	3⅝	13	9⅜	28,219	341·7	17,716	31,167	1,553	With ASh-82FN engines With 3,306-lb bomb-load

Tupolev Tu-4

Tupolev Tu-12

Tupolev Tu-14

Tupolev Tu-14

Tupolev Tu-4

According to Soviet sources, the Tu-4 has a rather unusual history, beginning with the circumstances in which the decision about its construction was taken, and ending with the fact that its manufacture started not with one or two prototypes but with a whole series.

The Soviet Tu-4, code-named "Bull" by NATO, is basically a Tupolev-constructed Boeing B-29. Except for a whip radio aerial below the rear fuselage, the Tu-4 is externally indistinguishable from the B-29. During World War II both Stalin and Golovanov had tried, without success, to get a quantity of B-29s under Lend-Lease arrangements. Consequently, 31 July 1944 was a fortunate day for the Kremlin, for on that day a USAF B-29, engaged on an operation over Japanese targets, was forced to divert to Russia through fuel shortage. This machine landed on a grass airfield at Vladivostok Bay. Also in 1944, the Soviet Union acquired two other complete B-29s which landed short of fuel in Soviet Far East territory. All three machines were detained, and another crashed in Russia after its crew had baled out.

Construction of an initial batch of 20 "Chinese copies" was begun in 1945 and in 1946 Russia tried, again unsuccessfully, to buy B-29 undercarriage assemblies, wheels and tyres in the United States. The first three Tu-4s appeared in the 1947 Soviet Aviation Day Display at Tushino aerodrome. For the Russians this was an advanced aircraft, and gave the Soviet aircraft industry an opportunity of getting acquainted in a short period of time with new kinds of instruments, mechanisms and whole systems. As Russia had also acquired the Western secrets of the atomic bomb at about the same time as its first B-29, the Tu-4 represented a formidable weapon.

By the end of 1946, series production was in progress at factories in or near Moscow, Kazan, Tashkent and Novosibirsk. By 1950, several hundred machines had been delivered to the Soviet Strategic Air Command, DA (Dalnaya Aviatsiya), and in 1953 three Air Regiments – about 1,000 aircraft – were in service. However, at night or in bad weather the Tu-4 crews still lacked radar bomb-sights and long-range navigation aids and the Korean War was an indication of the kind of difficult operating conditions which the Tu-4 might encounter in daylight operation against Western pilots.

The Tu-4 is powered by four ASh-73TK radials of 2,000 hp each (copies of the Wright R-3350s), the less-powerful engines being compensated by the reduced weight of the Tu-4 by comparison with the American version. The radial engines have Soviet-designed four-bladed propellers. Armament consists of 12·7-mm guns.

At the end of the Korean War, the Chinese Air Force received between 50 and 100 Tu-4s, these being delivered to an air base near Peking. It is doubtful if any remain serviceable today. Soviet DA units began to re-equip with jet-engined aircraft in 1955–6 and by 1959–60 all front-line Tu-4s had been replaced. In the early 1960s they were relegated to tanker-refuelling duties and to long-range radar navigational training. Some Tu-4s were also used by the A-VDV (Transport Command) for use as paratroop transports, with fore and aft under-fuselage exit bays.

During the Korean War, a variant was reported in use as a "ferry-ship" for MiG-15s, the fighters being carried below the outboard wing sections. Developments include the Tu-70 (NATO code-name "Cart") transport with redesigned fuselage. This made its first flight in 1946 but less than 12 are believed to have been built. They were evaluated by the A-VDV and by Aeroflot as freighters. The Tu-75 (NATO, "Barge") was, in turn, developed via the Tu-70 but this bomber, circa 1950, proved unsuccessful.

Tupolev Tu-12

Only sketchy details are available of the Tu-12 – the first Soviet-designed jet bomber. It is believed to have gone into production on a very limited scale.

First seen at the 1947 Soviet Aviation Day flying display, the Tu-12 was, like the Yak-15, the result of a hasty marriage of a piston-engined airframe (in this case that of the Tu-2) to a jet engine. Two 4,400-lb s t RD-500 gas turbines provided the power for the production Tu-12. The prototype was probably powered by the 1,980-lb s t RD-10 (Junkers Jumo 004B) since the Russian copy of the Rolls-Royce Derwent V (RD-500) could not have been available until about 1948. Apart from this the only other major difference between the Tu-2 and Tu-12 was the redesigned nose and the resultant increased fuselage length.

It seems likely that the Tu-12 was produced to provide Soviet bomber crews with jet experience during the period when the more radical new jet bombers, such as the Il-28, were being developed.

The Tupolev design bureau designation was Tu-77.

Tupolev Tu-14

Towards the end of the 1940s, when the MiG-15 and other modern Soviet fighters were being developed, the S. V. Ilyushin and A. N. Tupolev teams designed three jet-engined light bombers. These were the Il-28, which made its first flight in 1947 and had straight wings and all-swept tail; the Tu-82 (Tupolev design bureau designation) which made its first flight in February 1949 and had all-swept flying surfaces; and the Tu-14, which had only a swept tailplane. The Il-28 and Tu-14 were the only two to go into production and, in the case of the latter, this was only small-scale production for the A-VMF.

The cumbersome tail gun position and tail fin and rudder were slightly remiscent of the Tu-4 heavy bomber, but in other respects the Tu-14 had more in common with the Il-28 than with its predecessor the Tu-12. Like the Il-28, the Tu-14 was powered by two 6,000-lb s t VK-1 engines, developed from the Rolls-Royce Nene engines imported in 1948. It is believed to have carried a crew of five.

The NATO code-name "Bosun" was allocated when the production Tu-14 entered service, probably in 1950. Later models had a dorsal fin added, and a ventral radome. Armament was two 23-mm cannon in the nose and two more in a manned tail position. Two 1,850-lb torpedoes or an equivalent weight of bombs could be carried.

Tupolev Tu-16

The Tu-16's first public appearance was in 1954, when nine took part in the annual May Day flypast; from it was derived the Tu-104 airliner which made its first flight on 17 June 1955. On Soviet Aviation Day 1955, fifty-four Tu-16s flew over Tushino, and the type is assumed to have been in squadron service since that date. It is used as a medium and reconnaissance bomber by Dalnaya Aviatsiya (long-range aviation) and as a maritime reconnaissance aircraft by the A-VMF (Naval air fleet): about 24 were delivered to the Egyptian Air Force, and 12 were sent to Indonesia in 1961, the first two being handed over on 2 July.

The Tu-16, developed from the Tu-14 and Tu-82, was the first Tupolev jet-engined bomber to go into really large-scale production, the first Soviet swept-wing bomber in production and the first Soviet aircraft to have its engines buried in the wing-roots. Probably the most heavily-armed jet bomber ever built, its otherwise clean lines are spoiled by gun positions and observation blisters – reminiscent of the Tu-4.

The all-swept flying surfaces are common to the civil Tu-104 – only the fuselage is completely different. It is a cantilever high mid-wing monoplane with slight anhedral and with 35° of sweep. There are two wing fences

Tupolev Tu-16, escorted by two USN F-48s

Tupolev Tu-16, Indonesian Air Force, with "Kennel" missiles

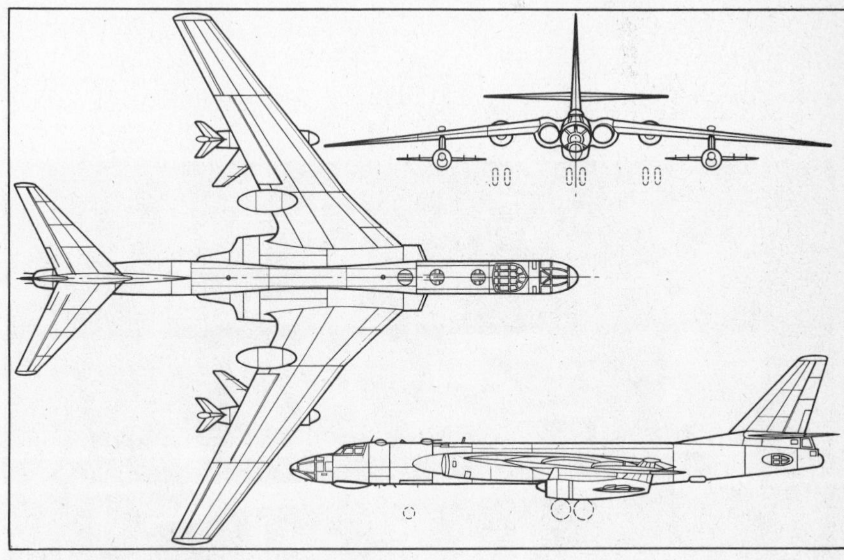
Tupolev Tu-16, with "Kennel" missiles

TYPE	DIMENSIONS						WEIGHT	PERFORMANCE				REMARKS
	span		*length*		*height*		*max t-o*	*max speed*	*at height*	*service ceiling*	*combat range*	
	ft	*in*	*ft*	*in*	*ft*	*in*	*lb*	*mph*	*ft*	*ft*	*miles*	
Tupolev Tu-4	141	3	99	0	27	9	104,940	NA	NA	36,745	1,500-2,000	Soviet version of B-29
Tupolev Tu-12	62*		48*		NA		NA	NA	NA	NA	NA	*Estimated
Tupolev Tu-14	70*		65*		NA		55,000*	560*	NA	NA	NA	*Estimated

Tupolev Tu-16, with "Kipper" missile

Tupolev Tu-20, with "Kangaroo" missile

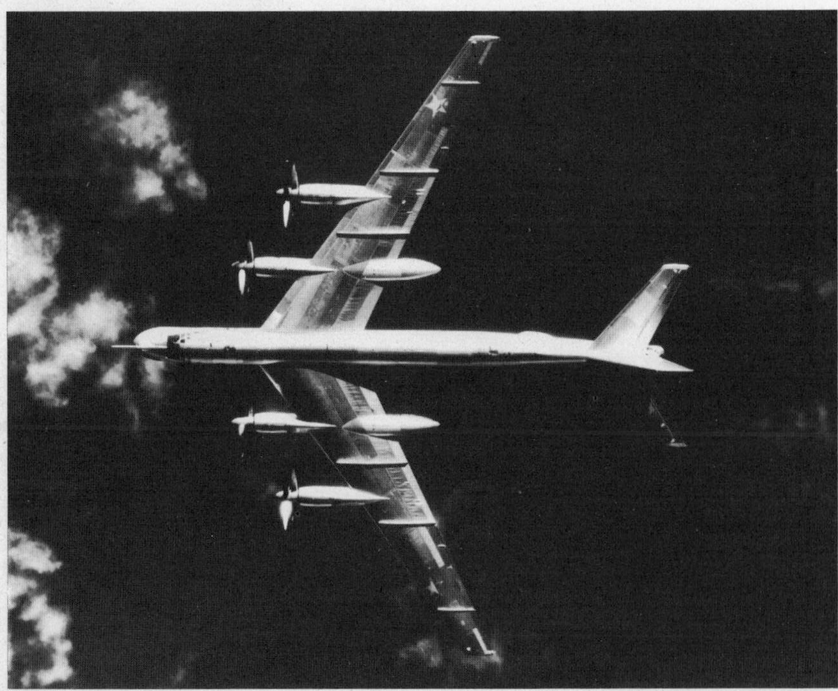

Tupolev Tu-20 ("Bear-B")

outboard of the nacelles which project beyond the wing trailing-edge and house the four-wheel bogies of the main undercarriage units.

Early production Tu-16s are thought to have been powered by two 18,080-lb s t AM-3 jet engines; later versions have two Mikulin AM-3M turbojet engines each rated at about 20,950 lb s t at sea level. There is provision for flight refuelling and a crew of about seven is carried.

The Tu-16 has the NATO code-name "Badger". At least three versions have been identified by Western observers:

"Badger-A" the 1954 Tu-16, produced in large numbers for Dalnaya Aviatsiya and A-VMF, is the basic bomber with glazed nose and internally-stowed free-fall bombs. The chin-mounted navigational radar and navaid aerials on the starboard tail and forward fuselage are supplemented in late production aircraft by a strake aerial on the port forward fuselage. VMF "Badger-As" have two electronic intelligence pods mounted on underwing pylons and additional ventral radar blisters. The wing fences were also extended to the wing leading-edge on later A types.

"Badger-B" the missile-carrying Tu-16 first seen in numbers at the 1961 Tushino display. Two underwing pylons to carry swept-wing anti-shipping missiles (NATO code-name "Kennel") are a distinguishing feature of this version – they are shorter and broader than the radar pylons of the Type A. One published photograph also shows three more ventral camera windows in the mid fuselage section. Most, if not all, of the Indonesian Tu-16s are of the B type.

"Badger-C" missile-carrier first seen at 1961 Soviet Aviation Day display, and assumed to have been in service since 1959. Fuselage length is increased by a large, squat search radar, which replaces the familiar glazed nose. A large stand-off bomb (NATO code-name "Kipper") is carried under the fuselage and is stated to be for anti-shipping use.

Armament consists of twin 23-mm cannon in remote-controlled barbettes in forward, dorsal and rear ventral positions; twin 23-mm cannon in a tail position controlled by automatic gun-ranging radar; and one fixed 23-mm cannon on the starboard side of the nose. A bomb load up to 19,800 lb (9,000 kg) is carried by "Badger-A"; "Kennel" missiles are carried by "Badger-B"; and "Kipper" missiles by "Badger-C".

Tupolev Tu-20

The Tu-20 was first seen in public during the 1955 Soviet Aviation Day fly-past, when an idea of this heavy bomber's vast size was given by seven attendant MiG-17s. Since that date, the Tu-20 has been in squadron service with the VVS-DA and A-VMF. The Tu-114 civil transport adaptation, which made its debut in 1957, has also given good service with Aeroflot. It has a fuselage of larger diameter than that of the Tu-20, but seems to have been preceded by the Tu-114D (D indicating *Dal'-niyi* – long-range), a civil transport which retained the long slender fuselage of the Tu-20. In the spring of 1958, the Tu-114D made a 5,280-mile non-stop flight (Moscow-Irkutsk-Moscow) at an average speed of 497 mph.

The Tu-20 was developed alongside the Tu-16 from the Tu-4 (from which it inherited its very heavy defensive armament) and from the piston-engined Tu-85 (code-name "Barge") of 1949. It has almost exactly the same nose and tail form as the Tu-16, even to the rear observation blisters. The wing shape also is generally similar, although the Tu-20 has 37 degrees of sweepback compared with the Tu-16's 35 degrees. The four Kuznetsov NK-12M turboprop engines, driving contra-rotating propellers, make the Tu-20 the fastest propeller-driven aircraft in the world. Each gave 12,000 hp originally, but the current NK-12M is rated at 15,000 hp. The four-wheel bogies of the main undercarriage units retract into fairings extending from the inner engine nacelles.

The Tupolev design bureau designation is reported to be Tu-95 and the USAF and NATO code-names are "Type 40" and "Bear" respectively.

There are three main versions as follows:

"Bear-A" was the first service version, with large fuselage bomb-bays and chin radome.

"*Bear-B*" was first seen in the 1961 Tushino fly-past, when 15 took part, each carrying a large air-surface missile (NATO code-name "Kangaroo") partly enclosed in the bomb-bay and with a large nose radome like that of "Badger-C". "Bear-B" has a small blister on the starboard side of the rear fuselage, just forward of the glazed observation blister. The version used by the A-VMF for maritime reconnaissance has a nose probe for in-flight refuelling.

"*Bear-C*" differs from "Bear-B" in having a small blister on each side of the rear fuselage.

Armament comprises twin 23-mm cannon in a manned tail turret, and in remote-controlled turrets in ventral rear and dorsal forward positions.

About 20,000 lb of bombs or one "Kangaroo" missile can be carried.

Tupolev Tu-22

The Tu-22 was one of the advanced types displayed in the 1961 Soviet Aviation Day fly-past and is the Soviet equivalent of the B-58 Hustler. It is a two/three-seat reconnaissance bomber which has probably augmented the Tu-16 rather than replaced it entirely.

The position of the two engines above the rear fuselage, at the base of the fin and rudder, is quite new, and has resulted in the tailplane being mounted on the lower part of the rear fuselage, directly behind the wings. Beneath the twin-jet efflux is a radar-directed rear gun. As yet there is no confirmation of the engine type, but the most likely choice would seem to be the 28,660-lb D-15 which, it is estimated, gives the aircraft a maximum speed of Mach 1·3-1·5. A possible alternative would be the older but well-tested 20,950-lb AM-3M.

Two versions of the Tu-22 (NATO code-name "Blinder") have been observed, of which the missile-carrying model has a stand-off bomb partially enclosed in the weapons bay and a broader nose than the reconnaissance type (of which nine flew over Tushino), which has camera windows under the fuselage nose. Both have large pointed nose radomes and the bomber has what appears to be a nose flight refuelling probe.

Like the Tu-16 and -20, "Blinder's" bogie undercarriage retracts into nacelles extending beyond the wing trailing-edge. The wings themselves have 45–50 degrees of sweepback (70 degrees at the wing-roots), with compound taper and short wing fences beyond the undercarriage fairings.

The Tu-22 is in squadron service and is regarded as the flagship of Russia's strategic bomber force. The missile carried by the bomber version has the NATO code-name "Kitchen".

Tupolev "Fiddler"

First seen at the 1961 Soviet Aviation Day display, this formidable-looking long-range interceptor was allocated the NATO code-name "Fiddler", and for a considerable time was thought to be the product of one of the Yakovlev design bureaux. It is now known to emanate from the design team headed by Andrei Tupolev.

"Fiddler's" rôle is that of a highly-sophisticated long-range interceptor, with the secondary rôle of tactical strike fighter. It has been developed from "Backfin" – first reported late in 1957 – which was generally similar in

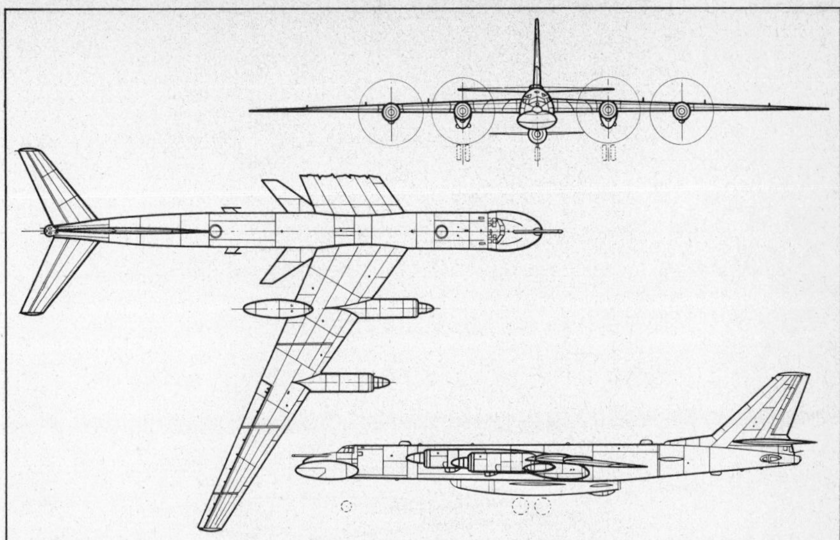

Tupolev Tu-20, with "Kangaroo" missile

Tupolev Tu-22

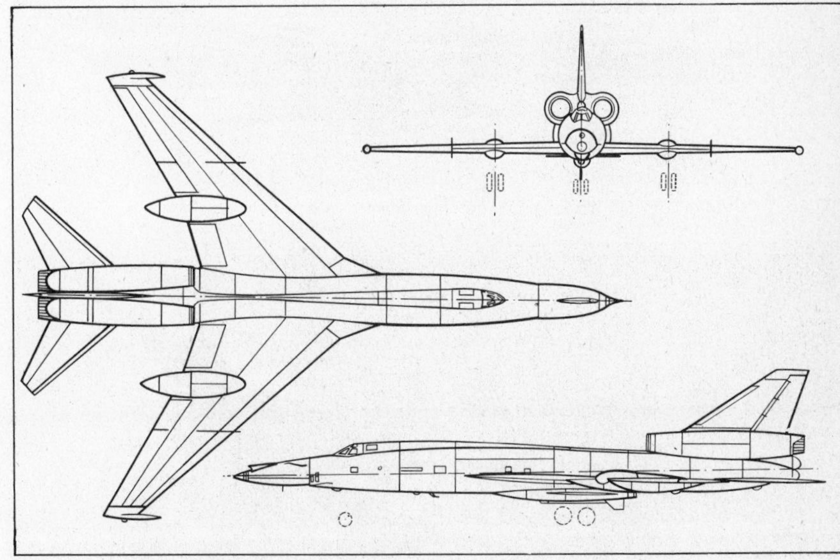

Tupolev Tu-22, with "Kitchen" missile

TYPE	DIMENSIONS						WEIGHT	PERFORMANCE				REMARKS
	span		*length*		*height*		*max t-o*	*max speed*	*at height*	*service ceiling*	*combat range*	
	ft	*in*	*ft*	*in*	*ft*	*in*	*lb*	*mph*	*ft*	*ft*	*miles*	
Tupolev Tu-16	110	0*	120	0*	35	6*	175,000*	587	35,000*	42,650	3,975	"Badger-B" *Estimated. Type C had length increased by about 5 ft
Tupolev Tu-20	163	0*	150	0*	NA		340,000*	560*	41,000*		7,800*	"Bear-A" *Estimated
Tupolev Tu-22	80	0*	130	0*	NA		NA	Mach 1·5	40,000		NA	"Blinder"

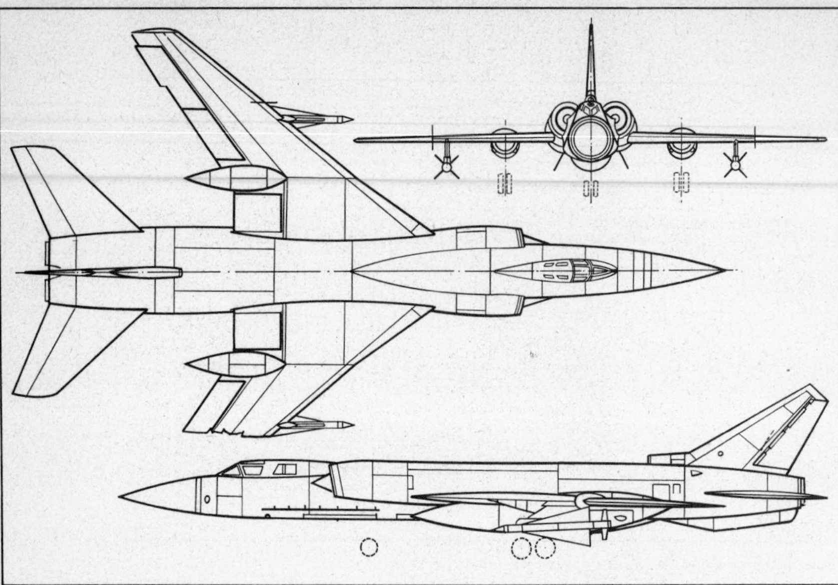

Tupolev "Fiddler" in original form with belly fairing

Tupolev "Fiddler" armed with four "Ash" missiles

Tupolev "Fiddler" armed with four "Ash" missiles

appearance but which did not itself go into production.

The mid-set wings, with slight anhedral, are sharply swept – the inner panels being similar to "Firebar's", but the outer panels are more tapered; aileron trim-tabs are fitted. The wide-track main undercarriage units comprise four-wheel bogies, which should enable the aircraft to operate from unprepared surfaces; they retract into nacelles extending beyond the wing trailing-edges. The tail unit is also sharply swept.

The fuselage is area-ruled, being waisted at the middle of the wing centre-section. The shoulder-mounted air intakes have half-cone shock bodies, and it is estimated that the two afterburning turbojet engines each give about 22,000 lb s t with reheat. The dielectric nose-cone probably houses AI radar. That it is supplemented by more radar is suggested by aerials on the sides of the fuselage.

The crew of two sit in tandem behind a Vee-shaped windscreen under a mostly-metal cockpit hood. The slab-sided fin and rudder have a small air intake in the base for cooling the engine bay. Maximum speed has been estimated at about Mach 1·75, with a loaded weight somewhere between 70,000 and 100,000 lb. "Fiddler" is reported to have been in service with VVS squadrons since the winter of 1961–2. Armament comprises four "Ash" air-to-air missiles, mounted on pylons beneath the wings.

When the "Fiddler" was first seen, a large under-fuselage fairing was fitted, possibly as an external fuel tank: but this was not on the machines seen at the 1967 Soviet air display.

Yakovlev Yak-1

The I-26 was the most outstanding of a number of new Soviet single-seat fighter prototypes which appeared in 1939 and 1940, in response to an official requirement issued in 1938. The Ya-26, as it was also called, was the work of a team led by A. S. Yakovlev – one of several new designing groups set up in 1938 to prepare projects to meet the new fighter specification. Yakovlev's fighter represented a radical departure from previous Russian design practice. It was notable for its refined, graceful lines and for the lightness of its structure. The wooden wing was built in one piece. The fuselage structure was of welded steel tubes, with a plywood covering faced with fabric. Power was provided by an M-105P twelve-cylinder in-line engine with a two-speed supercharger. The main undercarriage units and the tailwheel were fully retractable.

Test flights were carried out in the spring of 1939 by Yu. I. Pyontkovsky, and excellent manoeuvrability and speed were soon demonstrated. The impression created in government circles is evidenced by the award of the Order of Lenin to Yakovlev in April 1939.

After the completion of a full programme of flight testing, series production was initiated. Early I-26s participated in the traditional Red Square fly-past on May Day 1940, and were seen to differ from the prototype in several respects. The oil cooler intake was moved from just forward of the wing leading-edge, on the underside of the fuselage, to just below the nose of the aircraft. The ventral radiator was reduced in size and the air intake for the carburettor was moved from beneath the nose to the wing-roots.

As with the prototype, the main undercarriage legs retracted inward to lie flush in the wings, but the tailwheel was now of the fixed type.

About sixty I-26s were completed in 1940; in the main they equipped squadrons which had been given the special task of testing the fighter intensively under rigorous service conditions. The Yak-1, as it was by then known, had not yet reached front-line fighter units when the Germans launched their attack in June 1941. Immediately after the invasion began, the factories manufacturing the fighter were transferred hundreds of miles to the east, away from the potential battle areas. Yet within one month of arrival at the new sites, Yak-1s were again leaving the production lines.

The engine design group of V. Ya. Klimov developed

a more powerful version of the M-105 engine in 1940. The new M-105PF, driving a VISh-105 propeller, provided 1,240 hp against the 1,050 hp of the M-105P, with VISh-61 propeller, installed in early production Yak-1s. The new engine was introduced in production Yak-1s and these improved machines also had a deeper ventral radiator bath, located further forward. The initial production version of the Yak-1 had been armed with a 20-mm ShVAK cannon, firing through the hollow propeller hub, and two wing-mounted 7·62-mm machine-guns. In later production models, the two 7·62-mm weapons were replaced by a single 12·7-mm UBS machine-gun.

The Yak-1 was the first of a long line of successful and renowned "Yak" fighters, which were produced to a total of about 37,000 during World War II. The Yak-1 and its family rank in fame with the great Spitfire, Mustang, Zero and Messerschmitt Bf 109, and were undoubtedly the most effective front-line fighters in Soviet service during the first two years of the war against Germany and its allies.

Yakovlev Yak-3

To overcome German fighter superiority at heights above 16,400 ft (5,000 m), considerable Soviet design effort was directed at improving the performance of the Yak-1 and Yak-9. In the main, the designers concentrated on improving the aerodynamic qualities of the aircraft and boosting the power of the M-105PF engine.

Increased speed was achieved by reducing drag and by modifications which included reducing the wing area, better streamlining of the fuselage and a modified radiator installation. Improved rate of climb was obtained by cutting down the airframe weight, and reducing the fuel capacity and weight of armament. These modifications were embodied in the Yak-1M, built in 1942, and development of this prototype resulted in the Yak-3 fighter.

Compared with the production Yak-1, the Yak-3 had a lower loaded weight and smaller wing area, while the oil cooler was re-sited and positioned in the wing, with an air outlet under the wing. The outline of the cockpit canopy was improved, giving better visibility, and a modified radiator helped to reduce drag.

The improved aerodynamic shape and reduced weight of the Yak-3 permitted an increase in speed of 31 mph with the same engine as on the production Yak-9. The Yak-3 also had a better climb rate, acceleration and turning circle than its principal opponent, the Messerschmitt Bf 109G-2, and was considerably faster at altitudes up to 20,000 ft.

Soviet squadrons flying the Yak-3 inflicted heavy losses on the Luftwaffe. On 14 July 1944, eight Yak-3 fighters attacked 60 enemy aircraft and shot down three Ju 88 bombers and four Bf 109 fighters without loss to themselves. In another engagement on the same day, 18 Yak-3s fought 30 enemy fighters and claimed 15 shot down for the loss of a single Yak-3. The German Commanding General was forced to issue an instruction to his pilots, advising them to avoid combat "with those Yakovlev fighters which have no oil cooler on the nose and have an inclined aerial mast".

The first Yak-3 fighters with M-105PF engines had entered operational service prior to the Kursk battle and by early 1944 a number of fighter regiments were fully equipped with the type. At this time, the new VK-107A engine was installed in a Yak-3, and with this power plant a maximum speed of 447 mph was attained

Yakovlev Yak-1

Yakovlev Yak-3

Yakovlev Yak-3, Normandie-Niemen Fighter Regiment

TYPE	DIMENSIONS span ft	in	length ft	in	height ft	in	WEIGHT max t-o lb	PERFORMANCE max speed mph	at height ft	service ceiling ft	combat range miles	REMARKS
Tupolev "Fiddler"	65	0*	95	0*	NA		NA	1,150*	36,000	NA	NA	*Estimated
Yakovlev Yak-1	32	9¾	27	9¾	8	0	6,217	363·5 372·5	16,404 11,541	32,808	528	M-105PF engine

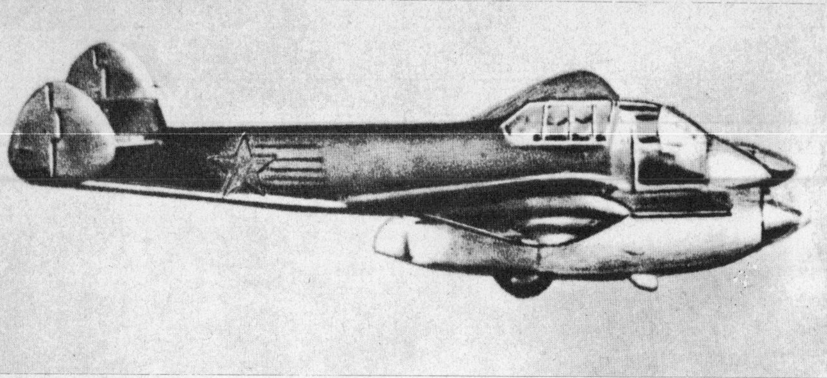
Yakovlev Yak-4

Yakovlev Yak-4

Yakovlev Yak-7

at 19,000 ft during official trials. In this form, the Yak-3 had a 62/74-mph advantage in speed over the German Bf 109G-2 and Fw 190A-4 fighters.

The report issued at the conclusion of the trials maintained that: "The Yak-3 fitted with the VK-107A engine, in terms of basic performance and combat qualities – maximum horizontal speed, climb rate and climbing speed, at altitudes from sea level to the aircraft's practical ceiling of 38,700 ft (11,800 m) – represents the best fighter aircraft among known Soviet and foreign types."

The Yak-3 with VK-107A engine was built in series, but did not go into action due to the ending of the war in Europe. It was the finest piston-engined fighter to serve in the Soviet Air Force, with manoeuvrability and climb comparable with the best of its foreign contemporaries.

Although, as with all Soviet wartime fighters, the Yak-3's cockpit equipment was austere by Western standards, it soon acquired a reputation as a fighter fast and simple to handle. The respect enjoyed by the Yak-3 in the Soviet Union is evidenced by the decision of the French pilots of the Normandie-Niemen Fighter Regiment, organized and operating in Russia, to choose it as their equipment from the very wide selection of types offered them by the Soviet authorities.

The Yak-3(ZhRD) was an experimental prototype, completed in early 1945, with a VK-105PF engine augmented by a liquid-fuel rocket engine in the tail. It reached a top speed of 485 mph during its flight tests.

Yakovlev Yak-4

The BB-22 twin-engined high-speed bomber was conceived in 1938 by a design team led by A. S. Yakovlev. Power was provided by two liquid-cooled in-line M-103 engines, giving 960 hp each at 13,125 ft and driving VISh-22 three-bladed propellers. Flight-tested in 1939, the new bomber attained a top speed of 335·5 mph and a range of 497 miles. Quantity production was initiated in 1940, and shortly afterwards the BB-22 became the Yak-2 under the new designation system which was then adopted.

The Yak-2 was intended for long-range reconnaissance, in addition to light bombing at short range and ground-attack missions, and was introduced alongside the Sukhoi Su-2 to replace the obsolete R-5, R-Z, and R-10 reconnaissance bombers. It was a low-wing monoplane with twin fins and rudders, and had sleek attractive lines. It was of mixed metal and wood construction, all control surfaces being fabric-covered. The crew of two were accommodated under a fully-glazed, raised canopy. The tail-wheel was retractable and the main undercarriage legs retracted rearward into the engine nacelles, leaving part of the wheels exposed. For winter operations, semi-retractable skis could be fitted.

The load of 440 lb of bombs, carried internally in a ventral bomb-bay, could be supplemented by an additional offensive load on under-wing racks, bringing the normal bomb-load to 880 lb and the maximum load to 1,325 lb. A fixed 7·62-mm ShKAS machine-gun was provided for the pilot, while the observer operated a similar weapon on a flexible mounting.

The Yak-2 was soon developed into the Yak-4 and surviving Yak-2s were converted for high-speed transport and liaison duties, the rear part of the glazed crew canopy being deleted and the top fuselage line altered so as to remain unbroken from aft of the pilot's cockpit to the tailplane.

The Yak-4 had two VK-105 R in-line engines, each delivering 1,100 hp for take-off. Dive-brakes were fitted under the wings and the aircraft structure was strengthened. The original single-wheel main undercarriage units were each replaced by a side-by-side twin-wheel assembly. A further forward-firing 7·62-mm ShKAS machine-gun was installed and the pilot was provided with additional 9-mm armour protection.

Operational experience against the invading Germans soon showed that the attempt to create an all-purpose aircraft had led to a dangerous increase in vulnerability, particularly when ground-attack work required formations of Yak-4s to fly low over enemy troop concentrations.

Similar duties performed by Ilyushin Il-2s resulted in a much lower rate of loss. Partly as a result of this combat experience, and partly to reduce the number of different types currently in production to fulfil the same rôle, the Yak-4 was taken out of production in 1942. The majority of Yak-4s remaining in service were assigned to high-altitude reconnaissance duties for the remainder of their service life.

Yakovlev Yak-7

Simultaneously with development of the Yak-1 fighter, Yakovlev's design team produced a two-seat fighter-trainer variant, the UTI-26, which completed its flight tests in early 1941. Placed in production as a standard Soviet training machine later in 1941, it was then designated Yak-7V.

From the trainer was developed the Yak-7A single-seat fighter, which incorporated a number of detailed improvements, including a better control system, but was very similar to the Yak-1 externally. A slightly different upper fuselage line aft of the cockpit was the only means of identification. The original armament of one 20-mm cannon and one 12·7-mm machine-gun was retained.

The Yak-7B made its appearance at the end of 1941. It featured a smaller ventral radiator, located in the same position as on early production Yak-1s. An all-round-vision canopy was fitted for the first time and became standard on the Yak-7's successor, the Yak-9. Power was still provided by the M-105PF engine, but as a result of concentrated efforts to seal the fuselage more effectively and to ensure that the air circulation in the radiators was more efficient, top speed rose to 381 mph.

The Yak-7VRD was flown experimentally with two ramjet engines under the wings. These increased the speed for limited combat periods by between 37 and 55 mph; but in normal flight with ramjets switched off performance was much reduced as compared with the standard Yak-7, because of the additional drag.

It is worthy of note that the wartime development of Yakovlev fighters followed two distinct lines. A development programme which stemmed directly from the Yak-1 resulted in the Yak-3, the fastest and most manoeuvrable Soviet fighter of its day, while the Yak-7 was modified progressively into the Yak-9, which in its numerous variants became the mainstay of the Russian fighter force from the autumn of 1942.

Yakovlev Yak-9 (1st generation)

In 1942 the Yak-7 design was modified. The wing spars were now of a light alloy, although the wooden ribs and plywood covering were retained. The metal spars were smaller, due to their higher proportional strength, and so the wing was much lighter and provided extra space for fuel. The payload was increased by 324 lb while the empty weight of the aircraft increased by only 110 lb.

The machine which incorporated these changes was referred to originally as the Yak-7 DI (*Dalnyi Istrebityel* = Long-range fighter), but on entering series production was redesignated Yak-9. It began rolling out of the assembly shops in the second half of 1942 and by the autumn was being used in the Stalingrad battles. It was then that the first air combat took place between Yak-9s

Yakovlev Yak-7

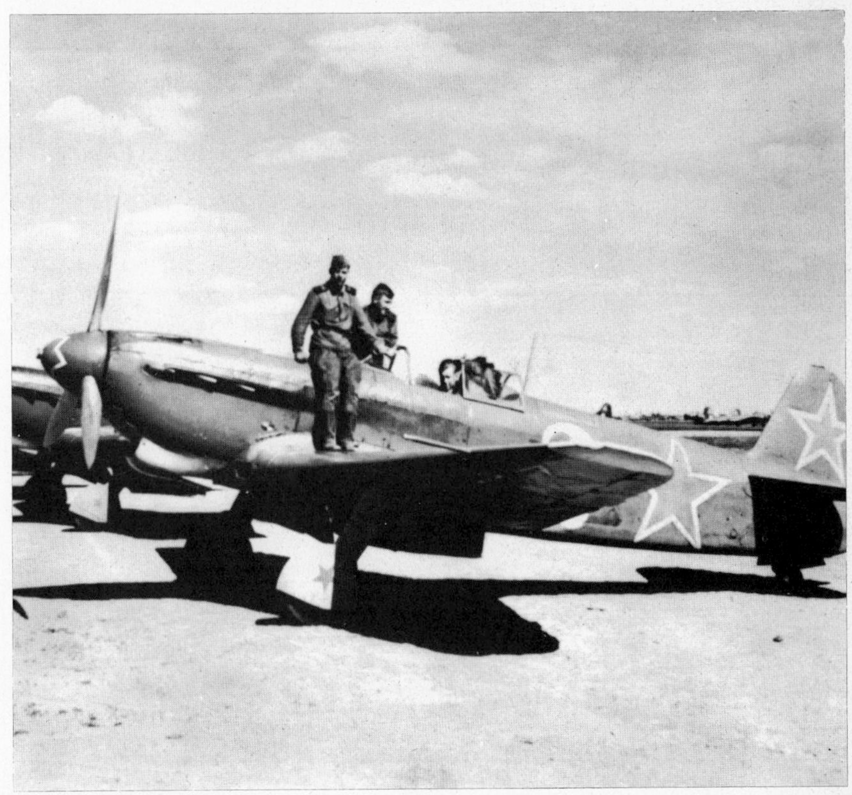

Yakovlev Yak-9DD

TYPE	DIMENSIONS						WEIGHT	PERFORMANCE				REMARKS
	span		*length*		*height*		*max t-o*	*max speed*	*at height*	*service ceiling*	*combat range*	
	ft	*in*	*ft*	*in*	*ft*	*in*	*lb*	*mph*	*ft*	*ft*	*miles*	
Yakovlev Yak-3	30	$2\frac{1}{4}$	27	$10\frac{5}{8}$	8	0	5,864	398·9 447·3	16,404 18,864	35,432	506	With VK-105PF engine With VK-107A engine
Yakovlev Yak-2	45	$11\frac{1}{8}$	33	$4\frac{1}{2}$	NA		11,464	335·5	16,404	29,527	497	M-103 engines
Yakovlev Yak-4	45	$11\frac{1}{8}$	33	$4\frac{1}{4}$	NA		NA	352·3	15,740	39,041	994*	VK-105R engines *Without bombs
Yakovlev Yak-7B	32	$9\frac{3}{4}$	27	$9\frac{3}{4}$	8	0	6,636	380·9	10,498	NA	515	M-105PF engine
Yakovlev Yak-9	32	$9\frac{3}{4}$	28	$0\frac{5}{8}$	8	0	6,746	366·6 374	16,404 10,498	NA	 565	 Yak-9T range: 515 miles

Yakovlev Yak-9D

Yakovlev Yak-9T, Polish Air Force

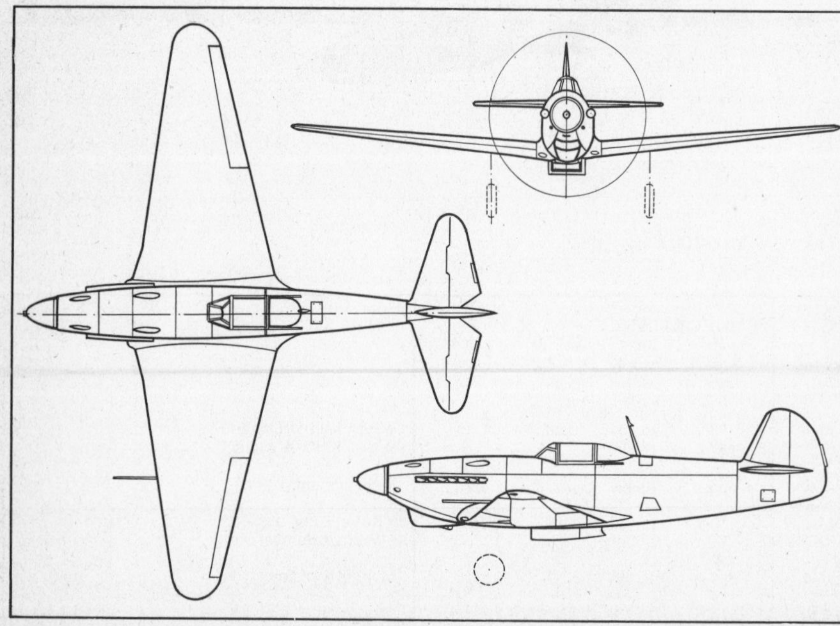
Yakovlev Yak-9D

and the newly-introduced Messerschmitt Bf 109G-2s. The Yak-9 had a slight edge in top speed (6–18 mph) at altitudes up to 15,700 ft, whereas between 19,700 ft and 23,000 ft the Bf 109G-2 was 25–37 mph faster. Consequently the Yak-9 groups endeavoured to engage their opponents at heights between 6,500 and 13,000 ft, where they held the advantage in performance. The Yak-9 could climb to 16,400 ft (5,000 m) in 4 minutes 54 seconds, which was 24 seconds less than the time needed by the Bf 109 G-2.

The year 1943 saw the initiation of work to instal the 37-mm 11-P-37 cannon, which was intended to deal with the latest German tanks. To accommodate this weapon, the pilot's cockpit was moved back 15·7 inches. Thus modified, the machine was known as the Yak-9T. Subsequently, some Yak-9Ts were fitted with 12·7-mm, 20-mm, or 23-mm weapons in place of the 37-mm cannon.

The Yak-9K appeared in 1944, with a 45-mm cannon firing through the propeller shaft. Yak-9T and Yak-9K fighters were frequently employed on ground-attack duties against tanks, armoured transporters, self-propelled guns and other heavily-armoured ground vehicles.

Another version was the Yak-9B which had a bomb-bay large enough to accommodate an 882-lb bomb-load in its centre fuselage.

When the Soviet Army embarked on large-scale offensive operations, effective fighter cover was required by mechanized and tank units which had broken through gaps in the German defences. Yakovlev's team accordingly produced a long-range variant of the Yak-9 called the Yak-9D (*Dalnyi* = Long-range) early in 1943. The Yak-9DD followed in 1944, possessing an even greater range. Its introduction permitted fighter cover for Allied and Soviet bombers to be extended up to 500–600 miles behind the enemy lines. In 1944, a group of these fighters flew from Russian territory to Southern Italy. From the aerodrome at Bari they operated in support of Tito's partisan forces in Yugoslavia.

The Yak-9 family was the most numerous among Soviet fighters from 1942 until the end of the war. As well as equipping many Russian fighter regiments, they were flown by both Polish and French units serving on the Russo-German front. Pilots of the French Normandie-Niemen Group personally testified to the Yak-9's good low-altitude performance, to its lightness on the controls and to its ability to out-turn its opponents.

Yakovlev Yak-9 (2nd generation)

When the new VK-107A in-line engine became available in 1942, it was fitted to a production Yak-9T in place of the VK-105PF. Apart from the engine change, the new aircraft, designated Yak-9U, was improved aerodynamically and had increased armament. The prototype was completed in December 1943. During test flights in January 1944, a maximum speed 62 mph greater than that of the production Yak-9 was achieved.

Yak-9U fighters began entering operational service early in the second half of 1944 and showed overwhelming superiority in all-round performance and combat qualities, at every altitude between sea level and their practical ceiling, over all types of German operational fighters on the Eastern front.

The Yak-9U attained 434 mph at 18,000 ft and, with its improved powers of climb, a height of 16,400 ft (5,000 m) was reached in 4 minutes 54 seconds.

A greater amount of metal was introduced into the structure of the Yak-9U. Its oil coolant radiator was moved to the port wing-root leading-edge, while the carburettor air intake was moved to a similar position on the starboard side of the aircraft. This type was retained in the immediate post-war years as a first-line fighter, and the First Polish Fighter Regiment flew Yak-9Us until the arrival of the Yak-23 in 1949.

The Yak-9P ("P" for *Pyerethvatchik* = Interceptor) was the culmination of Yakovlev's long line of piston-engined fighters. It was built in 1945 and was initially designated Yak-11, although this designation was subsequently given to the new Soviet advanced trainer.

The wings and fuselage were of all-metal construction.

The fuselage was covered mainly by detachable metal panels, which continued to just behind the pilot's cockpit. Every effort had been made to achieve maximum refinement of the aircraft's lines. The result was an attractive design with a very smooth profile.

The Yak-9P was armed with a 20-mm ShVAK cannon, firing through the propeller shaft, and two 12·7-mm BS machine-guns, mounted over the engine. Two 220-lb bombs could be carried under the wings. A radio-compass was situated behind the cockpit and was covered by a transparent screen. Maximum speed was 415 mph and range 890 miles.

Several Soviet satellite air arms flew the Yak-9P during the post-war years. A North Korean Yak-9P captured by United Nations forces was found to have been manufactured at State Factory No. 286 at Kamensk-Uralsk. This aircraft is currently on display at the USAF Museum at Wright-Patterson Air Force Base.

Yakovlev Yak-15

When World War II ended the U.S.S.R., alone among the major combatants, had not produced a jet-engined combat aircraft. In December 1945, A. S. Yakovlev was summoned to the Kremlin to discuss the idea of producing the German Me 262 in the U.S.S.R. but, by then, the Yak-15 was in an advanced state of development. The Yak-3 airframe had already been adapted for the installation of a liquid rocket engine, but this experimental aircraft crashed.

The Yak-15 jet-engined fighter was a direct development of the Yak-3 and the prototype retained the mid-mounted wings, cockpit, tailplane and even the tailwheel undercarriage of this latter type. Major alterations were confined to the forward fuselage which now housed a 1,980-lb s t German Junkers Jumo 004B (Soviet designation RD-10) turbojet. The jet efflux was below the pilot's cockpit and the underside of the fuselage had to be sheathed in metal. In production machines heat-resistant stainless steel was used and the tailwheel also was all-metal.

The Yak-15 made its first flight on 24 April 1946, in the hands of test pilot M. I. Ivanhov, and made its first public appearance at the Soviet Aviation Day display on 18 August 1946. Between August and November the factory tooled up and completed a dozen of the type for participation in the October Revolution Day fly-past over Red Square, but bad weather kept the aircraft grounded. In 1947, A. S. Yakovlev was awarded a Stalin prize for his work on the Yak-15, and the four test pilots were all made Heroes of the Soviet Union.

In spite of its obvious limitations, the Yak-15 went into immediate production and became the first Soviet jet fighter to enter squadron service. Armament comprised two 23-mm NS-23 cannon mounted above the nose.

Yakovlev Yak-17

The Yak-17 first appeared in about 1947 and was an improved version of the Yak-15 which it eventually superseded on the production lines. The tail-wheel

Yakovlev Yak-9P, captured aircraft, US markings

Yakovlev Yak-15

Yakovlev Yak-17

TYPE	DIMENSIONS						WEIGHT	PERFORMANCE				REMARKS
	span		*length*		*height*		*max t-o*	*max speed*	*at height*	*service ceiling*	*combat range*	
	ft	*in*	*ft*	*in*	*ft*	*in*	*lb*	*mph*	*ft*	*ft*	*miles*	
Yakovlev Yak-9D	32	$9\frac{3}{4}$	28	$0\frac{5}{8}$	8	0	6,834	310 332 359	SL 7,720 16,404	32,300	870	
Yakovlev Yak-9DD	32	$9\frac{3}{4}$	28	$0\frac{5}{8}$	8	0	7,275	NA	NA	NA	1,242-1,367	
Yakovlev Yak-9U	32	$9\frac{3}{4}$	28	$6\frac{1}{2}$	NA		NA	433·7	18,044	NA		VK-107 engine
Yakovlev Yak-9P	32	0	26	3	NA		7,000	415	14,993	NA	574-901	
Yakovlev Yak-15	30	$2\frac{1}{4}$	27	$10\frac{1}{2}$	7	$2\frac{3}{4}$	7,054 (approx)	503	NA	41,010	370	Polish source
Yakovlev Yak-17	31	$5\frac{1}{2}$	27	$2\frac{1}{4}$	6	10	7,054	515	9,840	42,650	460	Polish source

Yakovlev Yak-23

Yakovlev Yak-23, Polish Air Force

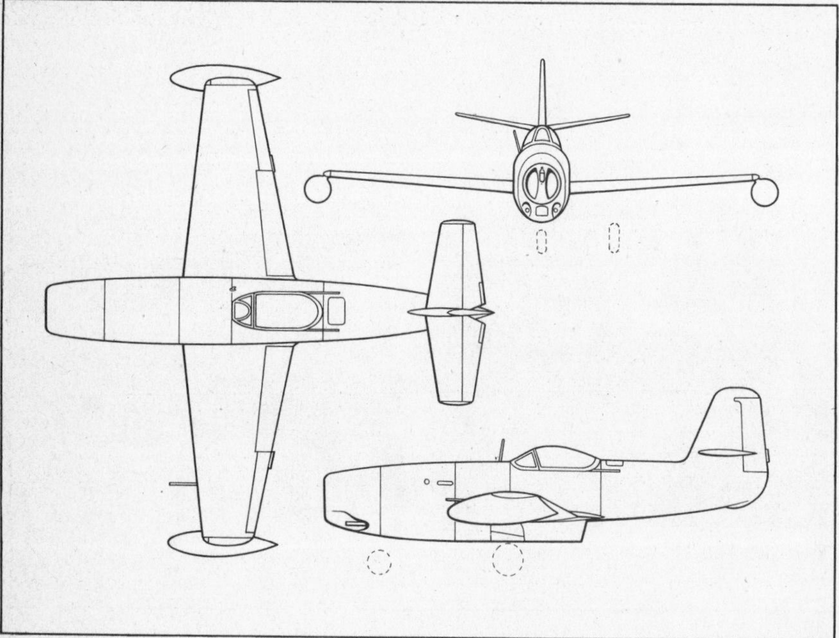
Yakovlev Yak-23

Yakovlev Yak-25

undercarriage of the latter had not been entirely satisfactory and the Yak-17 had a tricycle undercarriage, the nosewheel of which retracted partially into a blister fairing below the jet intake. The fin and rudder were entirely re-designed and enlarged after it had been found that the Yak-3-type fin and rudder were inadequate for the increased side area of the jet engine pod. The later RD-10A turbojet with which the Yak-17 was powered developed 2,200-lb s t. Armament was unchanged, comprising two 23-mm NS-23 cannon. The Yak-17 was used also in Czechoslovakia and Poland and received the NATO code-name "Feather".

The Yak-17UTI was the first Soviet jet trainer and, like the wartime Yak-7V (see page 627), was a tandem two-seat adaptation of a front-line fighter. Apart from the lengthened cockpit enclosure and fuselage, it did not differ very much from the ordinary Yak-17. It was not normally armed, but occasionally a single 12·7-mm Beresina machine-gun was fitted. The Yak-17UTI was code-named "Magnet" by NATO. Quite a number appear to have been produced and, in addition to VVS service, they were used in Czechoslovakia and Poland.

Yakovlev Yak-23

First produced in 1947, the Yak-23 was an all-metal development of the Yak-15 and -17. It had altogether cleaner lines and looked less of a jet adaption of a piston-engined fighter. Improvements included a completely-retractable tricycle undercarriage, redesigned wing, tailplane mounted on the fin (instead of on the fuselage), and a bifurcated air intake for its more powerful engine – the 3,527-lb s t RD-500, Soviet copy of the Rolls-Royce Derwent.

The Yak-23, which was in the light fighter class, was the first Soviet fighter to be equipped with an ejector seat, and was also used for early trials with afterburners.

Only a comparatively small number were built, as the MiG-15 was perfected shortly afterwards and became the second standard fighter of VVS squadrons. Nevertheless, the Yak-23 equipped several satellite air forces, including those of Poland, Czechoslovakia and Bulgaria, before the MiG-15 was made available to them. One example (coded HX-57) is on exhibition outside the National Technical Museum in Prague, Czechoslovakia.

NATO code-name for the Yak-23 was "Flora". Its armament consisted of two 25-mm cannon mounted above the nose.

Yakovlev Yak-25

The Yak-25 was the first Soviet two-seat twin-jet all-weather fighter, and it made its first public appearance at the 1955 Soviet Aviation Day fly-past at Tushino. Gradual development of this aircraft led to the "Firebar" and "Brewer" of 1961. The Yak-25's own NATO code-name is "Flashlight-A."

"*Flashlight-A*", powered by two 5,500-lb (approx) RD-9 engines, featured all-swept flying surfaces, high-mounted tailplane, mid-wing with slight anhedral, underslung engine nacelles, and a form of bicycle undercarriage known as "zero-track", i.e., two main wheels mounted side by side and a nosewheel, with wing-tip outriggers. The crew of two (pilot and radar operator) were seated in tandem. Design features included a small under-fuselage fin, air-brakes and two full-chord fences on the parallel-chord wings. The radar scanner was housed in a very blunt nose-cone reminiscent of British installations at the end of World War II.

Although not an outstanding type for its time, the Yak-25 fulfilled a requirement which had long been neglected by Soviet designers, and therefore it should not be compared too critically with its Western counterparts. It gave Soviet airmen the opportunity to develop interception techniques hitherto almost unknown to them. Armament comprised two 37-mm N cannon mounted under the nose, and a ventral pack of 55-mm unguided air-to-air rockets.

"*Flashlight-B*", first seen at the 1956 Tushino display, was a tactical strike and reconnaissance version with pointed glazed nose and shortened canopy – the observer was moved from behind the pilot to the forward fuselage. Other external differences were: extended engine nacelles (possibly for reheat); extended leading-edge at wing roots; ventral radome and strakes indicating an internal bomb-bay.

"Flashlight-C" was an improvement of the all-weather fighter "Flashlight-A" and looked like a solid-nose "Flashlight-B" with the observer again seated behind the pilot. Later the wing span was slightly increased beyond the outrigger housings, the leading-edges of the outer wing panels were extended and "drooped", and the wing fences were omitted altogether.

"Flashlight-D" entered service in 1959, and was the reconnaissance version of "Flashlight-C" with the new modified wing. "Brewer" was a direct development of the D type, which was armed with one 30-mm cannon under the nose.

It is believed that neither "Flashlight-B" nor "C" went into squadron service with the VVS. "Flashlight-A" and "D", on the other hand, were used in fairly large numbers.

Yakovlev Yak-28

Continued development of the later "Flashlight" aircraft led to a new series of two-seat fighters and reconnaissance bombers, first seen in some numbers and variety at the 1961 Tushino display. NATO observers were somewhat confused by the appearance of three almost identical derivations of "Flashlight", which differed only slightly from each other. The aircraft were originally code-named as follows:

"Firebar-A": two of the three glazed-nose aircraft, one of which had no ventral radome and, apparently, no weapons bay.

"Firebar-B": the solid-nosed version.

"Firebar-C": the third glazed-nose aircraft, with ventral radome and stakes which indicated a weapons bay.

"Firebar-A", it now appears, was only a prototype or development aircraft. And once it was realized that "Firebar-C" was a tactical light bomber it was given the new code-name "Brewer".

The development of "Firebar" and "Brewer" is obviously traced from "Flashlight-D". The principal differences between the latter and "Brewer" are: the wings have been moved from the mid-wing to shoulder-wing position and have increased anhedral. The inner wing panels are further extended at the leading- and trailing-edges – the planform otherwise remains the same. The engine nacelles are larger in diameter to accommodate the more powerful engines – thought to be the same as fitted to contemporary MiG fighters and giving about 12,500 lb s t with reheat. The air intakes have centre-body shock cones.

The fuselage shape is only slightly changed, as are the area and sweep of the tail unit. The aft unit of the bicycle undercarriage retracts into the rear fuselage and the nose unit retracts forward – this change leaves the centre part of the fuselage belly clear for radome and weapons or bomb-bay.

It is estimated that the new aircraft weighs about 35,000 lb and that maximum speed is about Mach 1·1. It is thought to have been in service since 1961–2.

"Firebar-B" differs from "Brewer" by having a "solid" nose, housing radar; the crew of two sit in tandem under an extended hood. "Firebar" has no weapon-bay strakes nor ventral radome.

"Firebar-B" appears to be fitted with no conventional weapons, but carries two air-to-air missiles on underwing

Yakovlev Yak-25

Yakovlev Yak-28 ("Firebar")

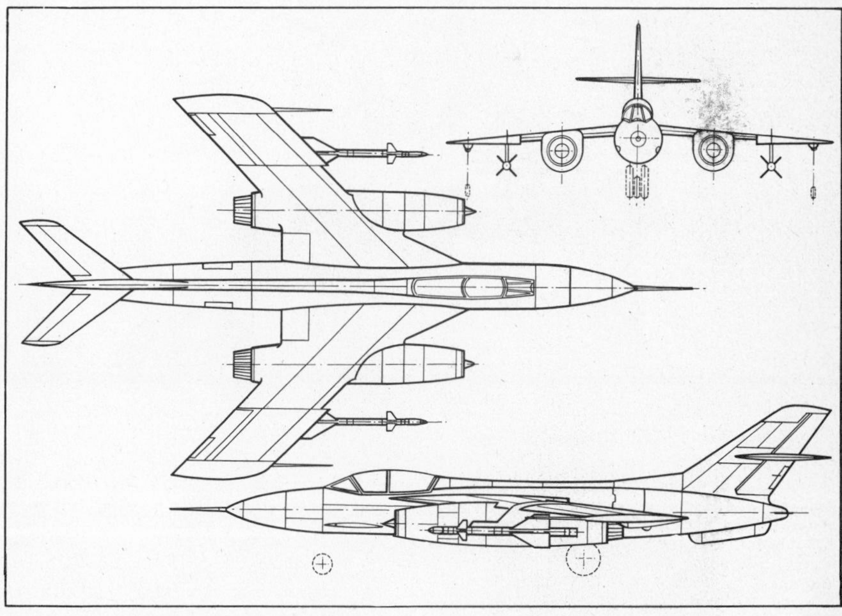

Yakovlev Yak-28, with "Anab" missiles

TYPE	DIMENSIONS span ft	span in	length ft	length in	height ft	height in	WEIGHT max t-o lb	PERFORMANCE max speed mph	at height ft	service ceiling ft	combat range miles	REMARKS
Yakovlev Yak-23	28	6	26	9¼	9	10	10,990	549		48,555	2 hr	Polish source
Yakovlev Yak-25	36	0*	50	0*	NA		25,000*	Mach 0.9	SL	50,000*	2,000*	*Estimated.
Yakovlev Yak-28	38	6*	59	0*	NA		35,000*	735	36,000	NA	1,150	*Estimated. "Brewer"

Yakovlev "Brewer"

Yermolayev Yer-2, ACh-30 diesel engines

Yermolayev Yer-2

pylons; "Brewer" has a single cannon, which is mounted on the starboard side of the fuselage nose.

Yermolayev Yer-2

Designed before the German attack on the USSR, and intended as a replacement for the Ilyushin DB-3, the prototype of this all-metal long-range bomber was designated DB-240. It represented a well-streamlined development of the experimental Stal-7 passenger machine, which had displayed considerable long-distance capabilities.

The DB-240, a low-wing monoplane with inverted gull wings, was powered by two M-105 engines. Test flying began in June 1940, and in October of the same year it entered series production as the Yer-2. The initial service model had the cockpit offset to port, the pilot and co-pilot being seated in tandem. Loaded weight was 24,910 lb and top speed 311 mph at 19,750 ft. Range with a 2,200-lb bomb-load was 2,545 miles.

Towards the end of 1940, one of the Yer-2 prototypes was fitted with ACh-30 diesel engines, designed by A. D. Charomsky, to achieve maximum fuel economy. With the diesels, range with a bomb-load of 2,200 lb rose to 3,107 miles. Early in 1941, a long-range non-stop flight from Moscow to Omsk and back was made by a Yer-2 with ACh-30 engines. During the flight, a full bomb-load was dropped after completing half the total distance. The diesels each provided 1,250 hp at 19,700 ft and official trials of the Yer-2 with this power plant were completed satisfactorily in December 1943. Normal loaded weight of this version was 32,740 lb and the maximum overloaded weight 40,960 lb.

The diesel-engined Yer-2 retained the twin fins and rudders of the earlier version, but differed in having wing and tail surfaces of increased area, a strengthened undercarriage and a new cockpit layout. The cabin was now situated symmetrically and accommodated the pilot and co-pilot side-by-side. Top speed was 261 mph at 19,700 ft. Normal bomb-load was 2,200 lb, and with this load a range of 3,107 miles was attained at a cruising speed of 199 mph, with a ceiling of 13,125 ft. A maximum of 11,025 lb of bombs could be carried. Defensive armament was one 20-mm cannon and two 12·7-mm machine-guns.

Both versions of the Yer-2 served with Soviet long-range bombing squadrons engaged on attacking the German hinterland, although in far smaller numbers than the Ilyushin Il-4.

Yugoslavia

Ikarus IK-2

Although its fighter squadrons were then equipped predominantly with aircraft purchased or built under licence from Czechoslovakia, France and the United Kingdom, the Royal Yugoslav Air Force decided in 1934 to give a chance to budding designers in its own country. It therefore placed a prototype order with the Ikarus company for the IK-1, an all-metal monoplane with a high braced wing, which had been designed by the young engineers Sivčev and Ilic.

The IK-1 had broad wings with a large Vee cut-out in the trailing-edge and a rather heavy-looking faired undercarriage, braced to the wing supports. Its enclosed cockpit was set well back beyond the wing cut-out, which must have hampered the pilot's oblique forward view. Power was supplied by an 860-hp Hispano-Suiza 12Ycrs liquid-cooled engine – the *moteur-canon* engine, with a built-in 20-mm Hispano-Suiza HS-404 cannon firing through the propeller hub – and a radiator protruded prominently beneath the fuselage, between the main wheel supports. Two 7·92-mm Darne machine-guns were installed ahead of the cockpit as additional armament.

The IK-1 prototype, which first flew in April 1935, crashed on its second flight when it failed to pull out of a dive. The career of the type might have ended there, but subsequent investigation proved that the fault lay not in the basic design but in the construction of the actual machine. A second, slightly-modified aircraft, designated IK-2, vindicated its predecessor when put through a full test programme, and a production order was placed with Ikarus for 12 IK-2s. These were delivered before the end of 1937; eight were still in service when Yugoslavia was invaded by the Germans in April 1941. A proposed reconnaissance development, the IK-4, was abandoned in favour of the Henschel Hs 126.

Rogožarski IK-3

In 1936, in collaboration with another Yugoslav aircraft designer, Zrnić, the two engineers responsible for the IK-1 and IK-2 produced a much more modern proposal for a single-seat fighter, the IK-3. Rather reminiscent of the French M-S 406 in general configuration, the IK-3 was a low-wing monoplane of wood and metal construction and featured a tailwheel undercarriage of which all three units were retractable. The Prva Srpska Fabrika Aeroplana Zivojin Rogožarski of Belgrade was entrusted with manufacture of the prototype, which made its first flight in the early months of 1938, powered by an 890-hp Hispano-Suiza 12Y-29 liquid-cooled engine. The installed armament consisted of the engine-mounted HS-404 20-mm cannon, firing through the propeller hub, and twin 7·92-mm FN-Browning guns in the upper engine decking.

By a strange coincidence, the IK-3 prototype was lost a year later in circumstances rather similar to those which attended the loss of the IK-1; again the fault was revealed to lie elsewhere than in the design of the aircraft and an initial series of 12 production models was ordered for the Air Force. Apart from a change to the 920-hp Hispano 12Ycrs engine (supplied by the Avia factory in Czechoslovakia), the production IK-3 differed little from the prototype. When delivered to a squadron for evaluation in mid-1940, the IK-3 proved instantly popular, having an excellent performance, easy handling qualities and first-class manoeuvrability. A second line of 25 IK-3s had just been laid down when the Germans invaded Yugoslavia in April 1941.

A developed version with a 1,100-hp Hispano-Suiza 12Y-51 had been proposed, but this project was negated by the German occupation. One IK-3 was fitted experimentally with an engine of comparable power – the 1,103-hp Rolls-Royce Merlin III – but was deliberately sabotaged before it had flown to prevent it falling into enemy hands. Another project upon which work had begun was the IK-5, a heavily-armed long-range fighter with twin 12Y engines.

S.49A and S.49C

For a number of years after Yugoslavia's liberation from the German occupation of World War II, the air force was strengthened and re-equipped entirely with combat aircraft supplied by, or built under licence from the Soviet Union. When Yugoslavia made its break with the Cominform in 1948, it began to make plans to re-institute its own industry.

The first fighter aircraft to make its appearance under the new constitution was the S.49A, a low-wing wood and metal monoplane which was, to all intents and purposes,

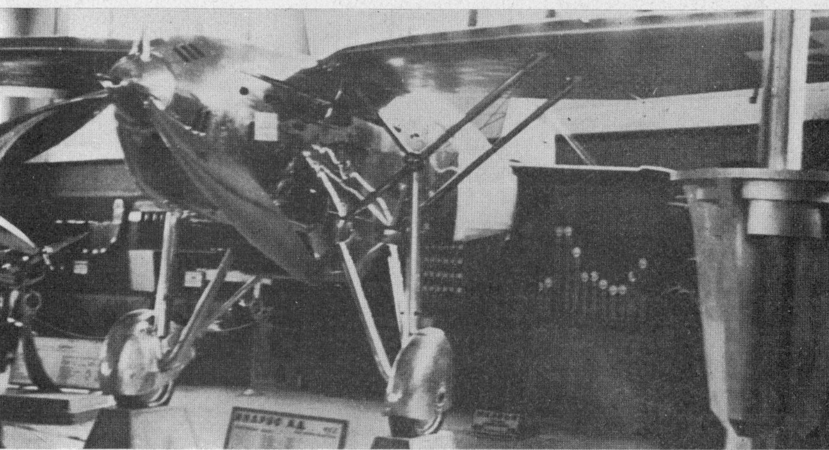

Ikarus IK-2

Rogožarski IK-3

S.49A

TYPE	DIMENSIONS span ft	span in	length ft	length in	height ft	height in	WEIGHT max t-o lb	PERFORMANCE max speed mph	at height ft	service ceiling ft	combat range miles	REMARKS
Yermolayev Yer-2	67	7	NA		NA		24,912	310·7	19,685	NA	2,548	M-105 engines
							32,739–40,962	261	19,685	NA	3,107	ACh-30 engines
Ikarus IK-2	37	4¾	25	10⅓	12	7⅓	4,255	266	16,400	34,450 max	248	
Rogožarski IK-3	33	9½	27	4¾	10	8	5,291	327	17,715	26,250	310	

S.49C

S.49C

SIM-XIV-H, Series 0

SIM-XIV-H, Series 1

a modified version of the Russian Yak-9P. Redesigned by the triumvirate of Popvic, Sivčev and Zrnić, the S.49A in fact appeared identical to the Yak-9 from an external viewpoint, except for a new fin and rudder outline. Powered by a 1,210-hp Klimov VK-105PF 12-cylinder Vee engine (a copy of the Hispano-Suiza 12Y), it was armed with a single 20-mm cannon, firing through the propeller hub, and four 12·7-mm machine-guns installed in the upper engine cowling. It was placed in production in 1950, at the former Ikarus plant at Zemun, and first deliveries to Yugoslav Air Force squadrons were made towards the end of May 1951.

Later, with the acquisition of 80 Hispano-Suiza 12Z-11y engines of 1,500 hp, from France, under the European off-shore procurement programme, the Yugoslav government was able to put into production the S.49C. This version, further modified and of all-metal construction, had only the nose cannon and two machine-guns, but made provision to carry four small bombs or 82-mm or 12·7-mm rockets beneath the wings. It superseded the S.49A in the middle 1950s, but by the end of that decade both types had become relegated to conversion training and miscellaneous minor duties.

SIM-XIV-H

Although designed primarily for reconnaissance, the SIM-XIV-H was also employed on anti-shipping duties after the outbreak of World War II, and a small number were still engaged on such missions against Axis shipping two or three years later.

The SIM-XIV-H was a three-seat twin-float seaplane, designed by Sima Milutinovic, and made its maiden flight on 8 February 1938, powered by two 240-hp Argus As 10c eight-cylinder inverted Vee engines. There followed six pre-production Series 0 aircraft, retaining the same power plant but having modified wings and tailplane and dispensing with the movable nose gun-turret; and six production Series 1 machines, with further wing modifications and the substitution of 270-hp Argus As 10e engines.

All 12 aircraft went into service with the Royal Yugoslav Navy. They carried a pair of 7·5-mm FN-Browning guns for defensive purposes, and could be equipped for minelaying or to carry a dozen 27½-lb bombs or one 220-lb and two 110-lb bombs. A further 12 machines on the assembly line were not completed owing to the German invasion of Yugoslavia.

TYPE	DIMENSIONS						WEIGHT	PERFORMANCE				REMARKS
	span		length		height		max t-o	max speed	at height	service ceiling	combat range	
	ft	in	ft	in	ft	in	lb	mph	ft	ft	miles	
S.49C	33	9½	29	9	9	6	7,645	391	5,000	32,800	480	
SIM-XIV-H	49	10½	36	8⅞	14	8⅓	7,386	151	SL	14,240	522	Data for Series 1

Addenda

CANADA – Canadair CL-41G

The CL-41G is a light tactical trainer and close-support development of the Canadair CL-41A jet trainer used by the RCAF (as the CT-114 Tutor), and was first flown in June 1964. Compared with the Tutor, the CL-41G has a more powerful General Electric J85-J4 turbojet engine of 2,950 lb s t, armour protection for the crew, and six underwing attachment points on which weapons up to a total weight of 3,500 lb can be mounted. These stores include gun or rocket pods, bombs, napalm tanks, Sidewinder air-to-air missiles or auxiliary fuel tanks. Twenty CL-41G aircraft were ordered by the Royal Malaysian Air Force, and delivery of these began in 1967.

Span 36 ft 6 in; *length* 32 ft 0 in; *height* 9 ft $3\frac{3}{4}$ in; *max take-off weight* 11,288 lb; *max speed* 480 mph at 28,500 ft; *service ceiling* 42,200 ft; *max range* 1,430 miles. (Performance figures are without external stores.)

Canadair CL-41G, Royal Malaysian Air Force

CZECHOSLOVAKIA
L-29 Delfin (Dolphin)

In the early 1960s, following the first flight of the prototype on 5 April 1959, the Delfin (NATO code-name "Maya") was selected as a standard basic and advanced jet trainer for the air forces of the Warsaw Treaty nations. Over 1,500 have since been built and are in service with the air forces of Czechoslovakia, the U.S.S.R., Bulgaria, Egypt, the German Democratic Republic, Hungary, Indonesia, Rumania, Syria and Uganda. An armed version, the L-29R, is in service with the Nigerian air force. This has nose-mounted cameras and underwing points for two 220-lb bombs, eight air-to-surface rockets, two 7.62-mm machine-gun pods or two auxiliary fuel tanks. Both models have the domestic M-701 turbojet of 1,962 lb s t.

Span 33 ft 9 in; *length* 35 ft $5\frac{1}{2}$ in; *height* 10 ft 3 in; *max take-off weight* 7,906 lb; *max speed* 376 mph at 16,400 ft; *service ceiling* 36,100 ft; *max range* 540 miles.

L-29R Delfin, Nigerian Air Force

FRANCE – Dassault Mirage F

Although it utilizes the same basic fuselage as the Mirage III (see page 83), the Mirage F is virtually a new design, having high-mounted sweptback wings instead of the low-mounted delta wings of the original Mirage. First version to fly, on 12 June 1966, was the two-seat Mirage F2 attack fighter, powered initially by a Pratt & Whitney TF30 turbofan engine and later by a 20,500 lb s t (with afterburning) SNECMA TF-306 turbofan. The all-weather Mirage F1 interceptor, which first flew on 23 December 1966, is much smaller, with scaled-down F2 wings and a 15,400 lb s t (with afterburning) Atar 9K turbojet engine. Three further F1s and a static test airframe were ordered in 1967, and quantity production of the F1 is expected once these have completed their test programme.

Data for F1: *span* 27 ft $10\frac{1}{2}$ in; *length* 49 ft $2\frac{1}{2}$ in; *height* 14 ft 9 in; *max take-off weight* 24,470 lb; *max speed* 1,450 mph above 40,000 ft; *service ceiling* 65,600 ft; *max range* 2,050 miles.

Dassault Mirage F1, single-seat interceptor

FRANCE
Sud-Aviation S.A.321 Super Frelon

The Super Frelon anti-submarine helicopter in service with the Aéronavale was developed, with assistance from Sikorsky, from the S.A.3200 Frelon (Hornet) prototype which flew for the first time on 10 June 1959. A prototype of the ASW version of the Super Frelon flew on 28 May 1963, and production aircraft entered squadron service early in 1966. Power plant of the Super Frelon is three 1,500 shp Turbomeca Turmo III C 3 shaft-turbines, mounted above the main cabin. Specialized equipment includes four homing torpedoes, and minesweeping, minelaying or ship-towing gear. The tail section and main rotor blades can be folded to reduce stowage space on

Sud-Aviation S.A. 321 Super Frelon

Sepecat (Breguet/BAC) Jaguar, first (two-seat) prototype

Shin Meiwa PX-S

Hawker Siddeley Nimrod MR Mk 1

board an aircraft carrier. Assault transport versions of the Super Frelon also serve with the French forces, and have been supplied to the air forces of Israel (5) and South Africa (16).

Rotor diameter 62 ft 0 in; *length* 65 ft 10¾ in; *height* 16 ft 2½ in; *max take-off weight* 26,455 lb; *max speed* 158 mph at SL; *service ceiling* 10,800 ft; *range* 572 miles.

FRANCE/UNITED KINGDOM
Sepecat (Breguet/BAC) Jaguar

The French and British governments have each ordered an initial 200 examples of the Jaguar, of which the first (two-seat) prototype flew on 8 September 1968. The Jaguar's design has been evolved jointly by the British and French industries, including the power plant which consists of two Rolls-Royce/Turbomeca Adour turbofans, each developing 6,950 lb s t with afterburning. Seven prototypes will precede the main programme, with production aircraft entering service in 1971. Jaguars will be built for both countries in single-seat tactical support form (including a carrier version for the French Navy) and as two-seat combat trainers. The strike versions will be armed with two 30-mm DEFA or Aden cannon and carry up to 10,000 lb of weapons on five pylons.

Span 27 ft 10¼ in; *length* 50 ft 11 in; *height* 14 ft 8⅜ in; *max take-off weight* 29,800 lb; *max speed* 1,120 mph at 36,000 ft; *service ceiling* 46,000 ft; *ferry range* 2,858 miles.

JAPAN – Shin Meiwa PX-S

Shin Meiwa (formerly Kawanishi) was awarded a contract in January 1966 to develop a new anti-submarine flying-boat for the Japanese Maritime Self-Defence Force, following aerodynamic tests carried out some two to three years previously with a specially-modified Grumman UF-1 Albatross designated UF-XS. A prototype of the full-sized flying-boat, the PX-S, flew for the first time on 6 October 1967. It was handed over in 1968 to the JMSDF, for whom an initial batch of 14 is to be built, with delivery to begin in 1971. A further quantity may be ordered later. Features of the PX-S are a first-class STOL performance and the ability to operate in very rough weather, including 30-mph winds and seas with a 10-ft wave height. It carries a crew of 10 men, and a comprehensive range of ASW equipment that includes a search radar in the nose, MAD "sting" in an extended tail-cone, and internally-stowed sonar, Jezebel sonobuoy and Julie echo-ranging equipment, and anti-submarine bombs. In addition, four homing torpedoes and six 5-in air-to-surface rockets can be carried under the wings.

Span 107 ft 7⅜ in; *length* 109 ft 10⅞ in; *height* 31 ft 9⅞ in; *max take-off weight* 86,862 lb; *max speed* 340 mph at 5,000 ft; *service ceiling* 29,500 ft; *max range* 2,948 miles.

UNITED KINGDOM
Hawker Siddeley Nimrod

The Nimrod maritime patrol aircraft is derived from the Hawker Siddeley (de Havilland) Comet 4C jet transport, with 11,500 lb s t Rolls-Royce Spey Mk 250 turbofan engines and a 6 ft 6 in shorter modified fuselage, accommodating a weapons bay and navigation, search and other operational equipment. An electronics pod is mounted above the fin and the tail-cone is extended to house an MAD "sting". The first of two modified Comet 4C prototypes was flown on 23 May 1967, and 38 production Nimrods are being built for the RAF. The Nimrod carries a crew of 11 and a wide range of internal weapons that includes homing torpedoes and depth charges; air-to-surface missiles can be carried on underwing pylons.

Span 114 ft 10 in; *length* 127 ft 0 in; *height* 30 ft 0 in; *max take-off weight* approx 170,000 lb; *max speed* approx 500 mph at 30,000 ft; *endurance* over 12 hr.

U.S.A. – Bell AH-1 HueyCobra

After the US Army had initiated development of the AAFSS armed helicopter for support and escort tasks in Vietnam, it accepted Bell's proposals for the production of an "interim AAFSS" based upon the highly successful UH-1 Iroquois series of general-purpose helicopters. Using its experience of armed helicopters, gained through operations with specially-modified UH-1s in Vietnam, Bell developed a new low-profile fuselage to be used with the H-1's engine and rotor system. A private-venture prototype was built as the Bell 209 HueyCobra and flew for the first time on 7 September 1965, this being followed by an Army order for two pre-production aircraft and a production batch under the designation AH-1G. Seating pilot and gunner in tandem, the HueyCobra has an Emerson nose turret with one or two 7.62-mm Miniguns or a pair of 40-mm grenade launchers, and carries bombs, rockets or gun pods on four hardpoints under the stub wings. Production orders totalled 838 by mid-1968, at which time the AH-1G was in service in Vietnam. A twin-engined version for the US Marine Corps has been ordered as the AH-1J.

Rotor diameter 44 ft 0 in; *length* 44 ft 5 in; *height* 13 ft 5½ in; *max take-off weight* 8,625 lb; *max speed* 196 mph; *range* 425 miles.

U.S.A. – Cessna A-37

Operations by the USAF in Vietnam in the mid-1960s led to the development of a number of aircraft for specialized operational rôles which, in order to meet the very tight time-scales involved, were based upon existing designs. Typical of these aircraft were the Cessna A-37 light attack monoplanes derived from the T-37 jet trainer. The idea of a heavily-armed and higher-powered version of the T-37 was investigated initially with two YAT-37D prototypes, the first of which flew on 22 October 1963. These had General Electric J85-GE-5 turbojets and six wing hardpoints. No production orders were placed, but in August 1966 the USAF called for urgent delivery of 39 A-37As, these being airframes already in production as T-37Bs, but completed with J85-GE-17A engines and eight wing strong-points. Twenty-five A-37As equipped a squadron which became operational in Vietnam in the autumn of 1967 in the ground support rôle, carrying a variety of bombs, rockets and other ordnance.

In May 1968, Cessna began delivery of 177 A-37Bs with higher-rated engines, together with provision for in-flight refuelling, increased fuel capacity and strengthened airframes.

Data for A-37B: *span* 35 ft 9½ in; *length* 29 ft 3 in; *height* 9 ft 2 in; *max take-off weight* 12,000 lb; *max speed* 476 mph; *ferry range* 1,200 miles.

U.S.A.
Gunships (AC-47, AC-119, AC-130)

Among the more bizarre developments which owed their origin to the unprecedented combat situations arising in Vietnam was the appearance there in November 1965 of a squadron of armed Douglas AC-47 gunships. Versions of the venerable C-47 "Gooney Bird" or Dakota, these gunships each carried three General Electric 7.62-mm Miniguns which have a rate of fire of 6,000 rpm; the AC-47s carried enough ammunition for three minutes' firing by each gun.

The initial programme covered conversion of 25 aircraft but the considerable tactical success enjoyed by these AC-47s, known in the field as "Puff the Magic Dragon" or "Spooky", led to further modifications and the development of new gunships. The first to appear was an AC-130 (Gunship 2), this being a Lockheed Hercules carrying four 20-mm Vulcan multi-barrel cannon and four 7.62-mm Miniguns in the lower fuselage sides. This prototype was tested in Vietnam during 1967 and six more were then ordered, together with four AC-130s differently equipped as Hunter 1s.

During 1968, Fairchild Hiller was under contract to produce the AC-119 Gunship 3 with two 20-mm and four 7.62-mm guns. Initial contracts covered 26 each of AC-119Gs and AC-119Ks, the latter having underwing jet boost engines. A programme to acquire an additional 176 AC-119s and 32 AC-130s was under consideration in the spring of 1968.

Bell AH-1G HueyCobra

Cessna A-37A

Douglas AC-47

Lockheed AH-56A Cheyenne

Soko Jastreb-1

Soko P-2 Kraguj

U.S.A. – Lockheed AH-56 Cheyenne

Operational experience in Vietnam showed the value of armed helicopters in support of ground and airborne operations. Troop-carrying and casualty-evacuation helicopters operating over a hostile environment, within range of concentrated small-arms fire from the ground, proved excessively vulnerable and this led quickly to the development of armed support helicopters which could accompany the unarmed types through all phases of an operation and could make the enemy "keep his head down". Whilst the initial demand was met by adapting the Bell UH-1 Iroquois, a design requirement was drawn up by the US Army in 1965 for an Advanced Aerial Fire Support System (AAFSS). From competing proposals made by Lockheed and Sikorsky, the Army chose the Lockheed design for prototype construction and the first flight of this type, the AH-56A Cheyenne, was made on 21 September 1967. Making use of the Lockheed rigid-rotor principle, which bestows remarkable manoeuvrability, the AH-56A has a 3,435-shp General Electric T64-GE-16 turboshaft engine and two tail rotors – one anti-torque and one to provide thrust. The armament includes a 7.62-mm multi-barrel Minigun or a 40-mm grenade launcher in an Emerson turret in the nose, a 30-mm cannon in a ventral turret and six hard points under the fuselage and wings for a variety of stores. An initial order for 375 was placed in January 1968.

Rotor diameter 50 ft 4$\frac{3}{4}$ in; *length* 54 ft 8 in; *height* 13 ft 8$\frac{1}{2}$ in; *max take-off weight* 28,000 lb; *max speed* 253 mph at sea level; *service ceiling* 26,000 ft; *normal range* 875 miles.

YUGOSLAVIA – Soko Jastreb (Hawk)

The Jastreb, which is in production for the Yugoslav Air Force, is a single-seat strike (Jastreb-1) and armed reconnaissance (Jastreb-2) development of the G2-A Galeb jet trainer, retaining the front cockpit of the latter and having a more powerful Rolls-Royce Bristol Viper 531 turbojet of 3,000 lb s t. The Jastreb has three nose-mounted 0.50-in Colt-Browning machine-guns and underwing attachment points for two 550-lb bombs or two 55-lb bombs and four 145-lb air-to-surface rockets. Additional rockets (or additional cameras in the case of the Jastreb-2) can be fitted in place of the wingtip fuel tanks, and there is provision in both versions for assisted take-off by means of two 992-lb s t booster rockets.

Data for Jastreb-1: *span* 38 ft 4 in (including tip-tanks); *length* 35 ft 1$\frac{1}{2}$ in; *height* 11 ft 11$\frac{1}{2}$ in; *max take-off weight* 10,010 lb; *max speed* 510 mph at 19,680 ft; *service ceiling* 39,375 ft; *max range* 945 miles.

YUGOSLAVIA – Soko P-2 Kraguj

The Kraguj is a simple, lightweight close-support aircraft, with a 340-hp Lycoming GSO-480-B1A6 six-cylinder air-cooled piston-engine, of which the prototype was first flown in 1966. It is in production and in service with the Yugoslav Air Force and is an easily-deployed aircraft that can operate from unprepared forward strips in a tactical or light transport rôle. Two 7.7-mm machine-guns are mounted in the wings, and the Kraguj has underwing attachment points for a total weapons load of some 1,100 lb, which may include two 220-lb bombs, two 330-gallon napalm tanks, two launchers each with 12 air-to-surface rockets, or two 57-mm or 127-mm air-to-surface rockets.

Span 34 ft 10$\frac{7}{8}$ in; *length* 26 ft 0$\frac{1}{4}$ in; *height* 9 ft 10 in; *max take-off weight* 3,580 lb; *max speed* 183 mph at 5,000 ft; *max range* 500 miles.

Acknowledgments

The publisher is indebted to the undermentioned individuals, journals, air forces and other bodies for providing the pictures listed below, and to all others who kindly supplied photographs; all line drawings are by John W. Wood. Cardinal numbers refer to pages, ordinals in brackets refer to position on the page.

The Aeroplane
36(3rd,4th); 80(2nd); 106(2nd); 149 (2nd); 325(1st); 380(3rd);382(2nd); 386 (1st, 3rd); 387(2nd); 428(3rd); 440(1st); 462(3rd); 529(2nd); 581(1st)

Air Review (Tokyo)
496(1st); 497(2nd); 541(2nd)

Associated Press
602(2nd); 610(1st)

Aviation Week
624(2nd)

Fred E. Bamberger
498(4th)

BIIL
287(2nd)

Warren M. Bodie
256(2nd); 489(1st); 491(2nd); 531 (2nd); 539(1st)

Peter M. Bowers
446(4th); 447(2nd); 448(2nd,3rd); 449(3rd); 455(2nd); 460(2nd,3rd); 464(4th); 473(1st); 474(3rd); 481(1st); 485(3rd); 514(4th); 534(4th); 535(2nd); 536(1st); 546(5th); 549(3rd)

Charles E. Brown
48(4th); 315(3rd); 322(4th); 323(1st, 2nd); 325(3rd); 329(2nd,3rd); 330(3rd); 343(2nd); 344(2nd); 346(4th); 347(1st); 348(2nd); 352(2nd); 356(2nd,4th); 359(3rd); 360(4th); 368(1st); 369(2nd); 375(1st,2nd); 376(3rd); 378(3rd); 381 (1st); 382(4th); 384(2nd); 388(1st,3rd); 407(3rd); 411(3rd); 432 (4th); 439(2nd, 3rd); 443(3rd); 444(4th); 454(3rd); 455 (1st); 502(1st); 503(3rd); 513(3rd)

Camera Press
576(2nd)

Canadian Armed Forces
52(1st); 53(1st); 316(4th); 502(2nd, 3rd); 522(4th)

Crown Copyright
34(1st); 51(1st); 343(3rd); 344(3rd); 346(3rd); 347(2nd); 357(1st); 360(3rd); 361(2nd); 369(1st); 377(3rd); 378(1st); 389(1st); 390(2nd); 393(3rd); 430(3rd, 4th); 432(1st); 492(4th); 536(5th)

J. G. Davison
550(4th)

Etablissement Cinématographique des Armées
Jacket, rear (*bottom*); 68(3rd); 90(1st); 109(2nd); 119(3rd); 120(1st, 4th); 124(3rd)

Finnish Air Force
55(1st); 65(1st,2nd); 66(1st); 80(1st); 93(1st); 112(1st); 174(3rd); 277(2nd); 280(3rd); 367(1st); 458(4th); 570(3rd); 574(3rd); 576(4th); 579(1st); 598(4th); 600(3rd); 601(2nd); 604(2nd); 617(3rd)

Flight International
Jacket, front (*centre left*); 39(1st); 315(1st); 316(2nd); 321(3rd); 334(2nd); 335(1st,3rd); 338(4th); 354(1st,3rd); 355(2nd); 356(3rd); 380(2nd); 381(2nd, 3rd); 382(1st); 383(1st,2nd); 385(1st); 387(1st); 402(1st); 426(1st); 433(1st)

Geoffrey R. Hunter
82(2nd)

Imperial War Museum
12(1st,2nd); 21; 25(2nd); 26(1st,2nd); 27(1st); 28; 30(1st,2nd); 32(1st); 33(1st,3rd); 34(2nd); 37(2nd); 67(2nd); 94(2nd); 95(1st); 101(4th); 104(3rd); 109(1st); 112(4th); 113(1st); 116(1st); 121(1st); 127(2nd); 128(1st); 129(1st); 130(3rd); 132(2nd); 134(3rd); 135(1st, 2nd,3rd); 136(1st,2nd,3rd,4th); 138 (1st); 139(3rd); 140(3rd); 141(1st,3rd); 142(1st); 146(2nd); 151(3rd); 153(1st); 154(2nd); 155(1st); 156(1st,4th); 157 (1st); 158(4th); 159(3rd); 160(1st,4th); 161(1st,2nd); 162(4th); 164(1st); 166 (4th); 170(1st); 171(1st); 172(4th); 173(1st,2nd,3rd); 174(1st); 176(3rd); 178(4th); 179(1st); 181(3rd); 182(1st); 183(2nd); 185(1st); 187(2nd); 188(3rd, 4th); 189(1st,3rd); 190(2nd,3rd); 191 (1st,3rd); 192(1st,2nd,3rd,4th); 193 (1st,2nd,3rd); 194(1st); 196(3rd); 198 (1st,2nd); 200(2nd); 202(1st); 207(3rd); 213(2nd); 217(3rd); 221(3rd); 222(1st); 223(1st); 232(3rd); 238(1st); 267(3rd); 272(1st); 306(2nd,3rd); 307(1st,2nd, 3rd); 308(1st,2nd,3rd,4th); 313(1st); 314(1st); 319(1st,2nd); 326(4th); 328 (1st,2nd); 329(1st); 332(3rd); 336(1st); 337(1st); 339(1st,3rd); 350(3rd,4th); 351(2nd); 359(4th); 363(2nd,3rd); 364(1st,2nd,3rd); 365(3rd,4th); 368 (2nd); 372(2nd); 374(1st); 388(4th); 398(1st,2nd,3rd,4th); 399(1st,2nd); 400(1st,2nd); 401(1st); 403(1st,2nd); 404(1st); 405(1st,2nd,3rd); 406(1st); 407(1st); 408(4th); 411(1st); 415(1st); 416(4th); 419(3rd); 420(3rd); 422(2nd); 424(1st); 444(1st); 463(2nd); 469(1st); 564(2nd); 574(2nd); 592(3rd,4th); 598 (2nd,3rd); 614(1st); 618(1st); 627(2nd)

Indian Air Force
196(1st); 588(4th)

Indonesian Air Force
621(2nd)

International News Photos
586(1st)

Italian Air Force
Jacket, rear (*top right*); 10(2nd); 196(2nd); 197(1st,2nd); 198(3rd); 199(1st,2nd); 200(3rd); 202(4th); 203(1st); 204(2nd,4th); 205(1st,2nd); 207(2nd); 208(2nd,3rd,4th); 210(2nd, 3rd); 211(2nd); 212(3rd); 214(2nd, 4th); 218(3rd); 220(1st); 224(2nd); 225(1st); 226(1st,2nd); 227(3rd)

Bryan H. Jackson
394(3rd)

Karel Kliment
575(2nd); 586(3rd); 593(1st); 619(2nd)

Koku Fan
239(2nd)

Art Krieger
555(1st)

William T. Larkins
461(2nd); 475(3rd); 546(4th)

Letectvi Kosmonautika
589(2nd); 631(2nd); 632(1st)

Howard Levy
235(3rd); 447(1st); 462(4th); 464(1st); 482(2nd); 486(3rd); 511(2nd); 529 (3rd); 535(1st); 550(2nd); 558(4th)

R. Lopacki
282(4th)

Peter R. March
396(1st); 445(2nd)

Harold G. Martin
449(1st); 504(1st,2nd); 505(3rd); 506 (2nd); 551(1st)

R. R. Martin
484(4th)

T. Matsuzaki
533(1st)

Ministère des Armées "AIR"
82(1st); 125(2nd)

Ministry of Defence
Jacket, front (*centre right, bottom*); 14(2nd); 18; 39(2nd); 126(3rd); 310 (4th); 311(3rd); 312(3rd); 313(3rd); 314(3rd); 317(2nd); 318(3rd); 320(3rd); 321(2nd); 326(1st,3rd); 327(1st); 331 (3rd); 332(2nd,4th); 333(3rd); 334 (1st); 336(4th); 337(2nd,3rd); 340 (2nd); 341(2nd); 342(1st,3rd,4th); 345(2nd); 348(4th); 349(1st); 350(3rd); 352(3rd); 353(2nd); 354(4th); 355(3rd); 358(3rd); 359(2nd); 360(2nd); 363(1st); 366(2nd); 371(2nd); 373(1st,3rd); 377 (2nd); 379(2nd); 383(3rd); 400(3rd); 406(3rd); 409(2nd); 412(1st,2nd,3rd); 413(3rd); 418(2nd); 421(3rd); 423(1st); 425(1st); 426(3rd); 428(1st,2nd); 429 (1st); 430(1st); 431(3rd); 434(4th); 436(2nd,3rd,4th); 438(1st); 439(1st); 440(2nd, 3rd); 442(3rd,4th); 455(3rd); 468(1st); 479(3rd); 481(2nd); 488(2nd); 489(2nd,3rd); 516(2nd); 590(2nd); 591(1st)

Musée de l'Air
66(4th); 73(1st); 86(3rd,4th); 90(2nd); 92(2nd,4th); 93(2nd); 94(3rd); 102(1st); 113(3rd); 115(2nd); 117(3rd); 132(4th); 133(3rd)

Norad
523(3rd)

Novosti
41(1st); 588(1st); 589(2nd); 591(1st); 609(3rd); 610(3rd); 623(2nd); 624(3rd)

Cyril Peckham
417(1st)

Stephen P. Peltz
50(2nd); 51(3rd); 80(3rd); 125(1st); 126(1st); 220(3rd); 318(2nd); 349(3rd); 394(1st); 446(1st); 524(3rd); 545(1st); 635(2nd)

Planet News
613(1st)

B. C. Reed
485(1st); 490(3rd)

Repules
576(3rd); 583(1st)

Royal Aeronautical Society
8; 9(1st,2nd); 446(2nd)

Royal Aircraft Establishment
340(1st)

Royal Australian Air Force
42(4th); 44(1st,2nd,3rd); 45(1st); 358 (1st); 465(2nd); 488(1st); 536(2nd); 562(2nd)

Royal Danish Air Force
64(1st); 380(4th); 429(2nd); 544(1st); 552(1st,3rd)

Royal Naval Air Station, Brawdy
362(2nd).

Royal Netherlands Air Force
273(2nd,3rd); 274(3rd); 275(1st,2nd); 276(1st); 278(1st,2nd,3rd); 281(1st); 515(1st); 518(3rd); 552(2nd)

Royal Norwegian Air Force
206(4th); 274(1st); 281(3rd)

A. U. Schmidt
477(4th); 510(1st); 539(3rd); 540(1st)

B. M. Service
78(1st); 520(1st)

Smithsonian Institution
14(1st)

Spanish Air Force
597(1st)

Swedish Air Force
47(1st); 294(1st); 300(2nd); 393(2nd); 546(2nd)

Swiss Air Force
86(2nd); 87(1st); 111(2nd); 120(3rd); 183(1st); 274(2nd); 304(1st,2nd,3rd); 305(1st,3rd); 306(1st)

Index to Aircraft

Page numbers in italics refer to illustrations and/or text in the Historical Introduction; other page numbers refer to articles in the main text. Entries are arranged so that numbers precede letters, Roman numerals being listed before Arabic numerals.